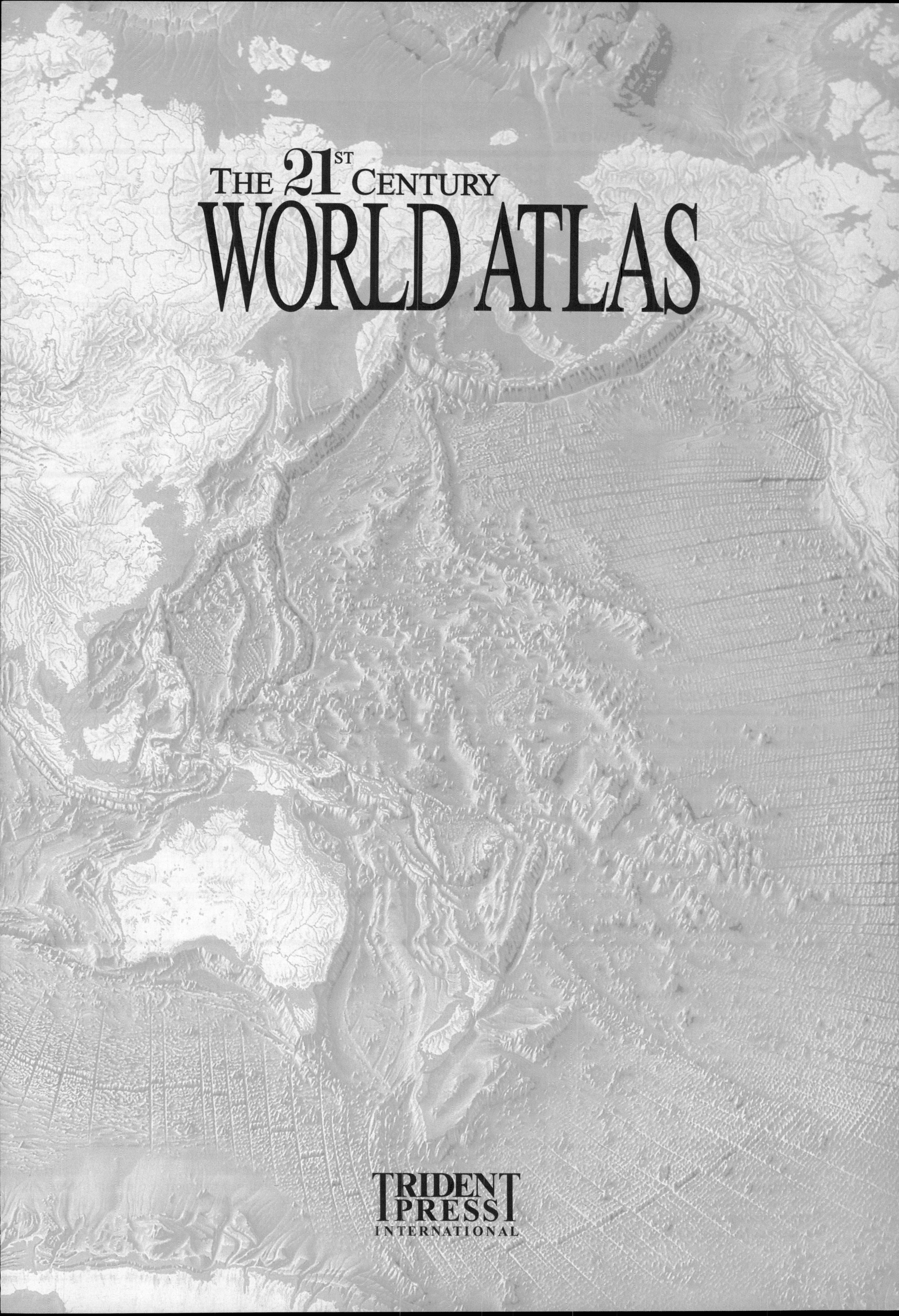

THE 21ST CENTURY WORLD ATLAS

TRIDENT PRESS INTERNATIONAL

GEOPOLITICAL FRAMEWORK

The Earth

Satellite image in color, analysis of temperatures and presence o

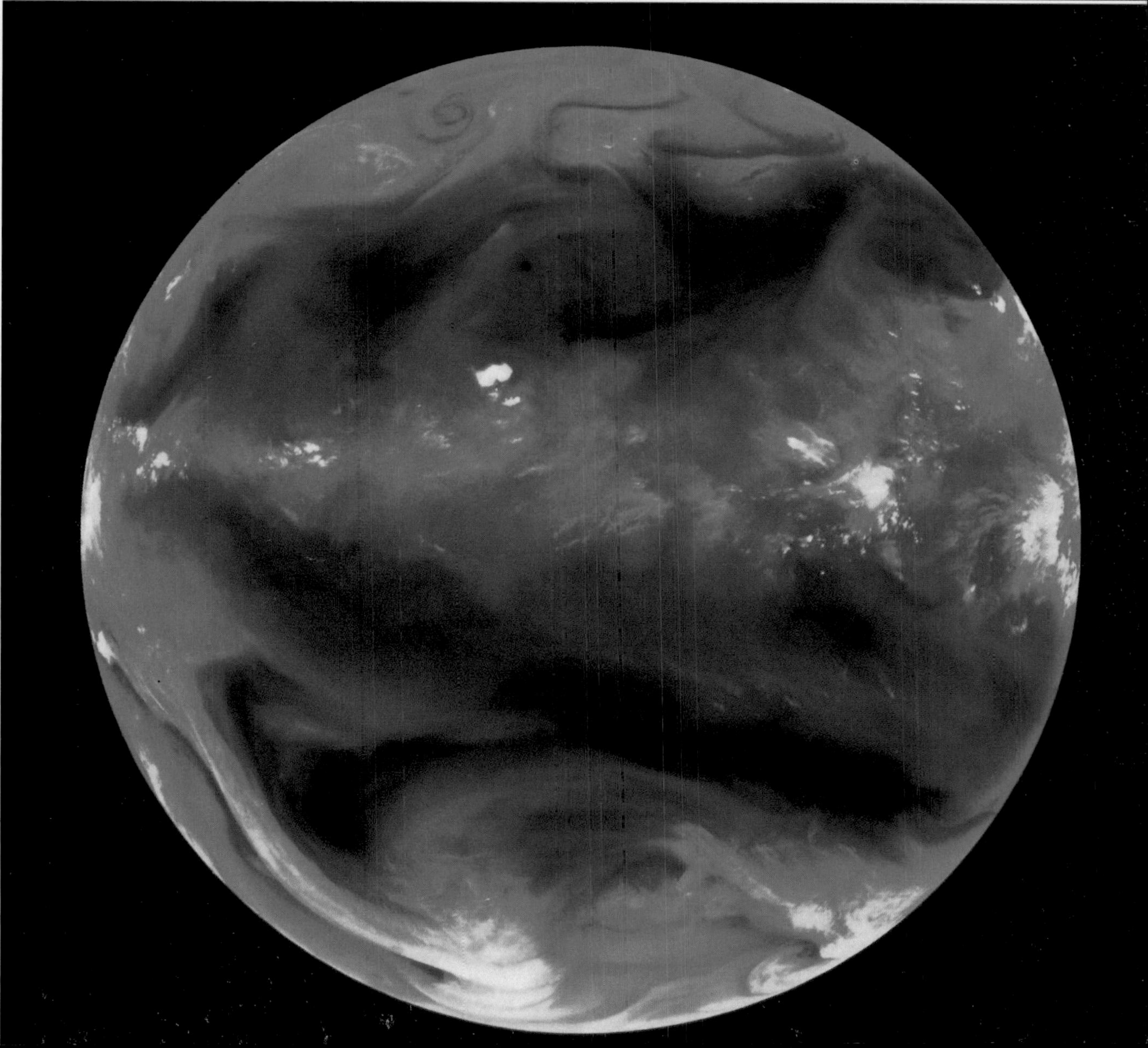

Earth digital elevation model
Globe view over Europe, Asia and Oceania

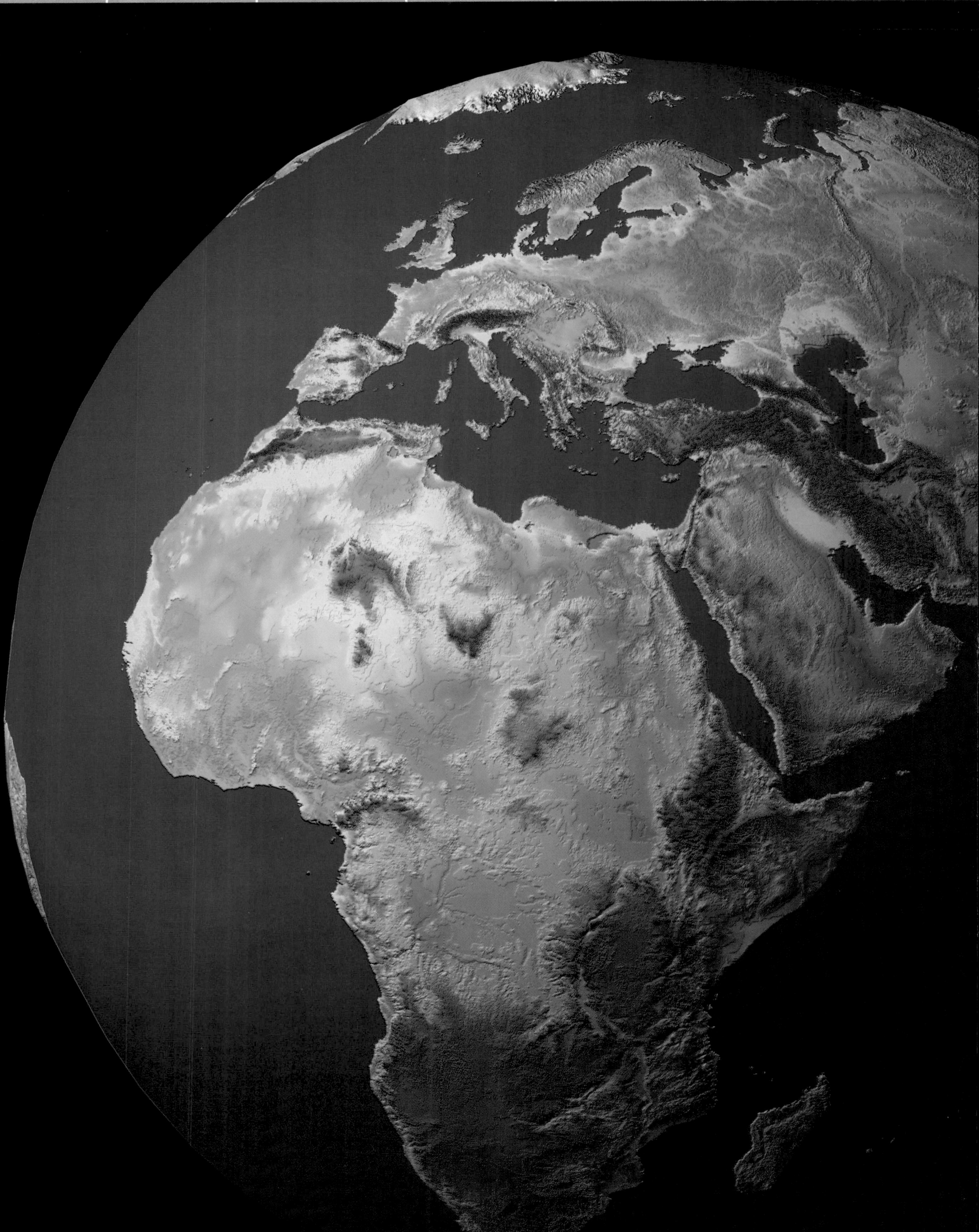

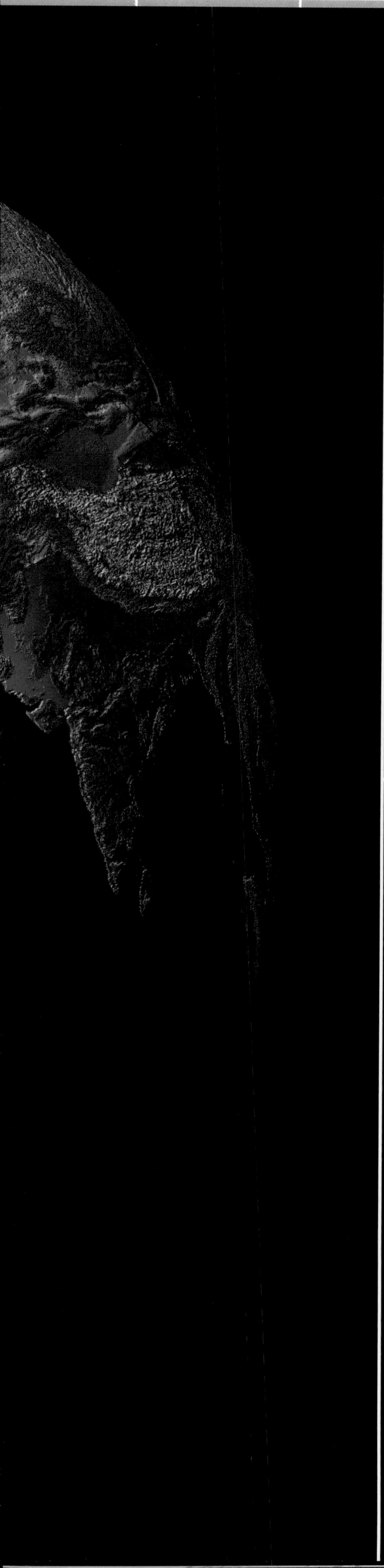

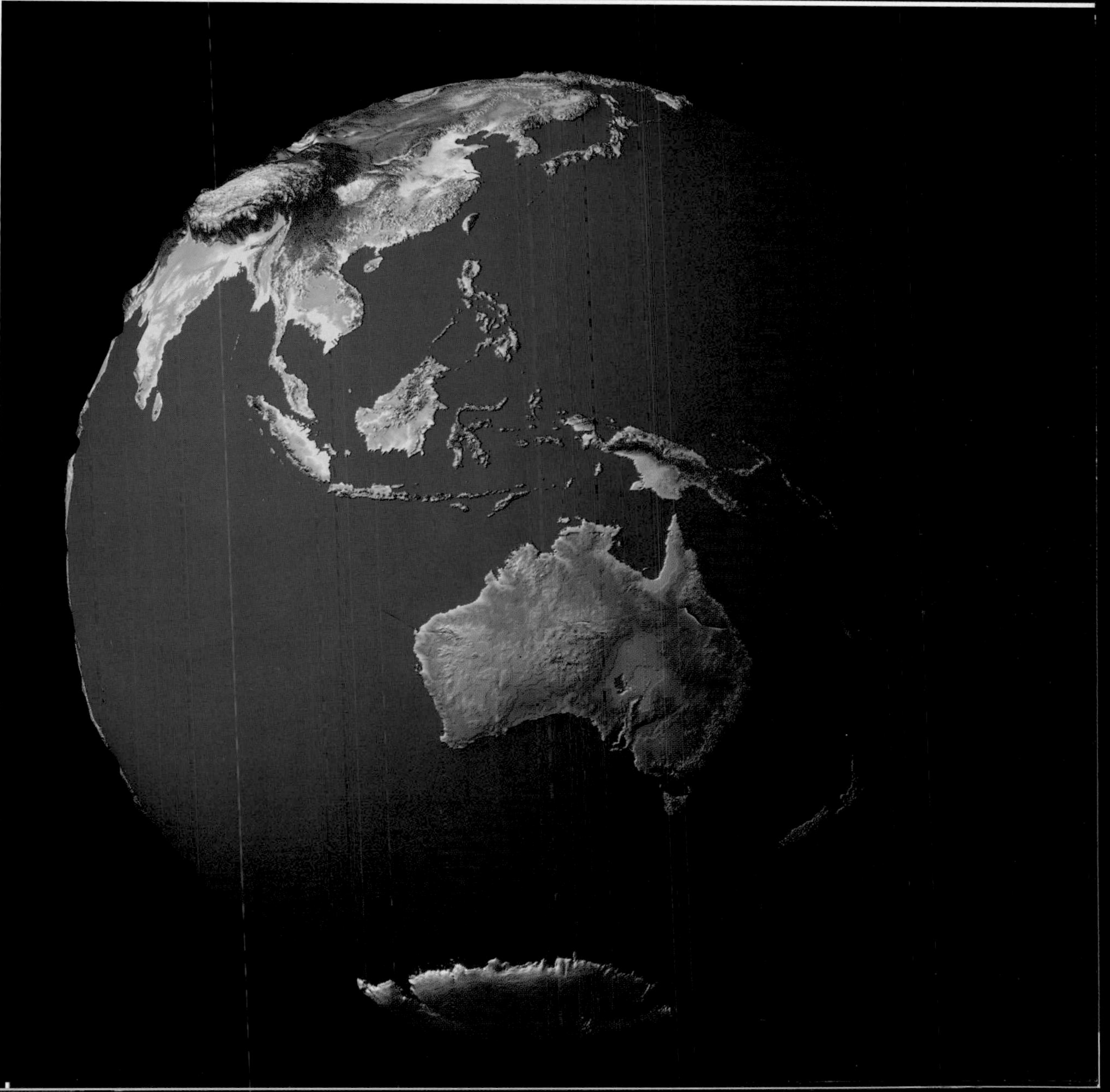

North Pole
Digital elevation model

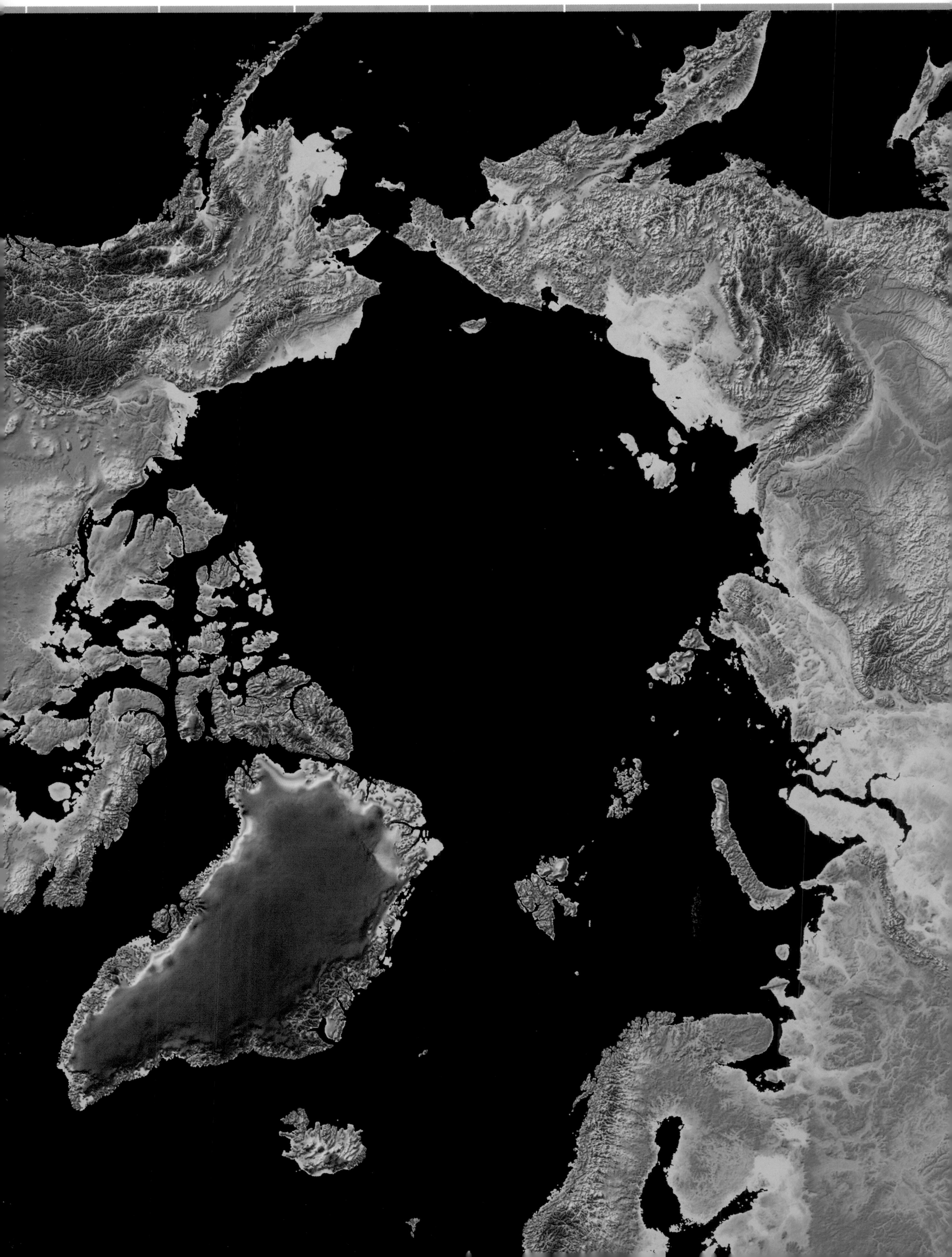

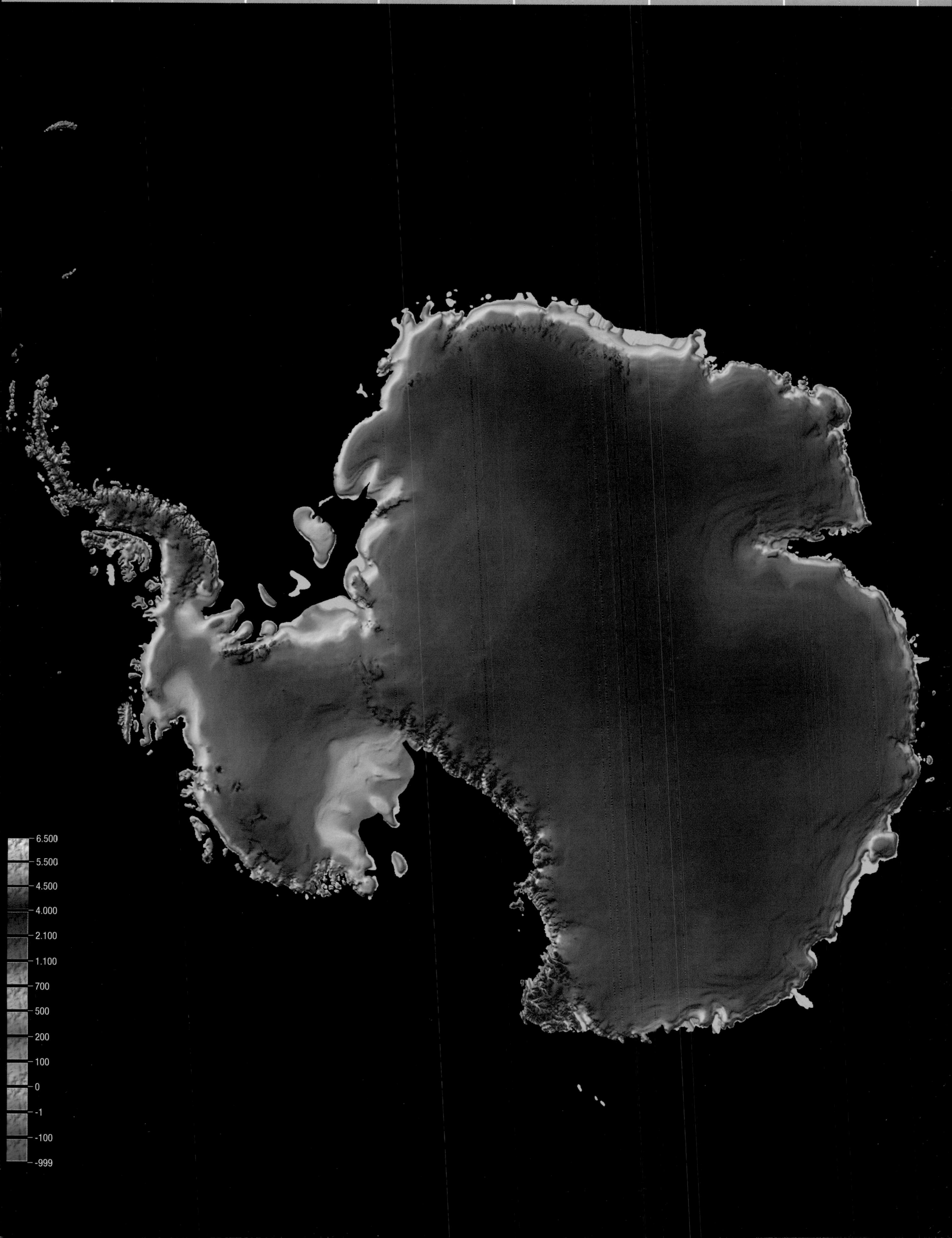
6.500
5.500
4.500
4.000
2.100
1.100
700
500
200
100
0
-1
-100
-999

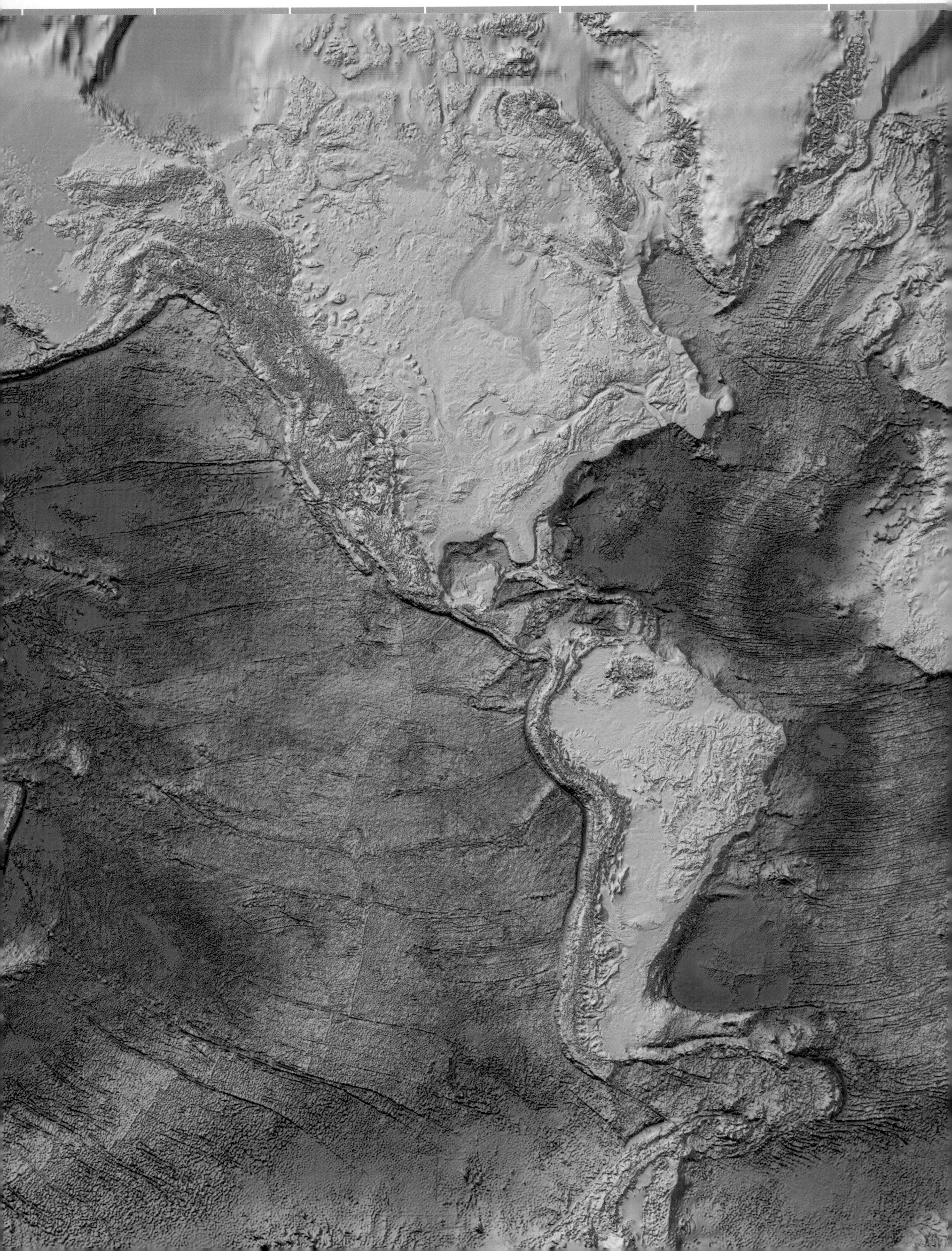

South Tasman Rise
Southeast Indian Ridge
50°S
150°W
160°W
170°W
180°
170°E
160°E
150°E
Basin
Perth
Plain
Broken Ridge
Diamantina Fracture Zone
Obi Trench
30°S

30

North Pole

Bathymetry

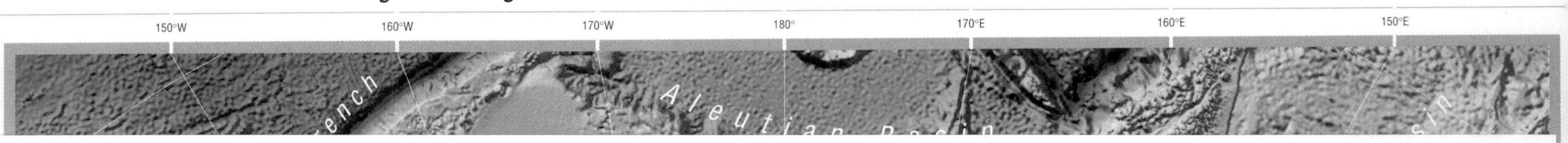

32

Atlantic ocean

Bathymetry

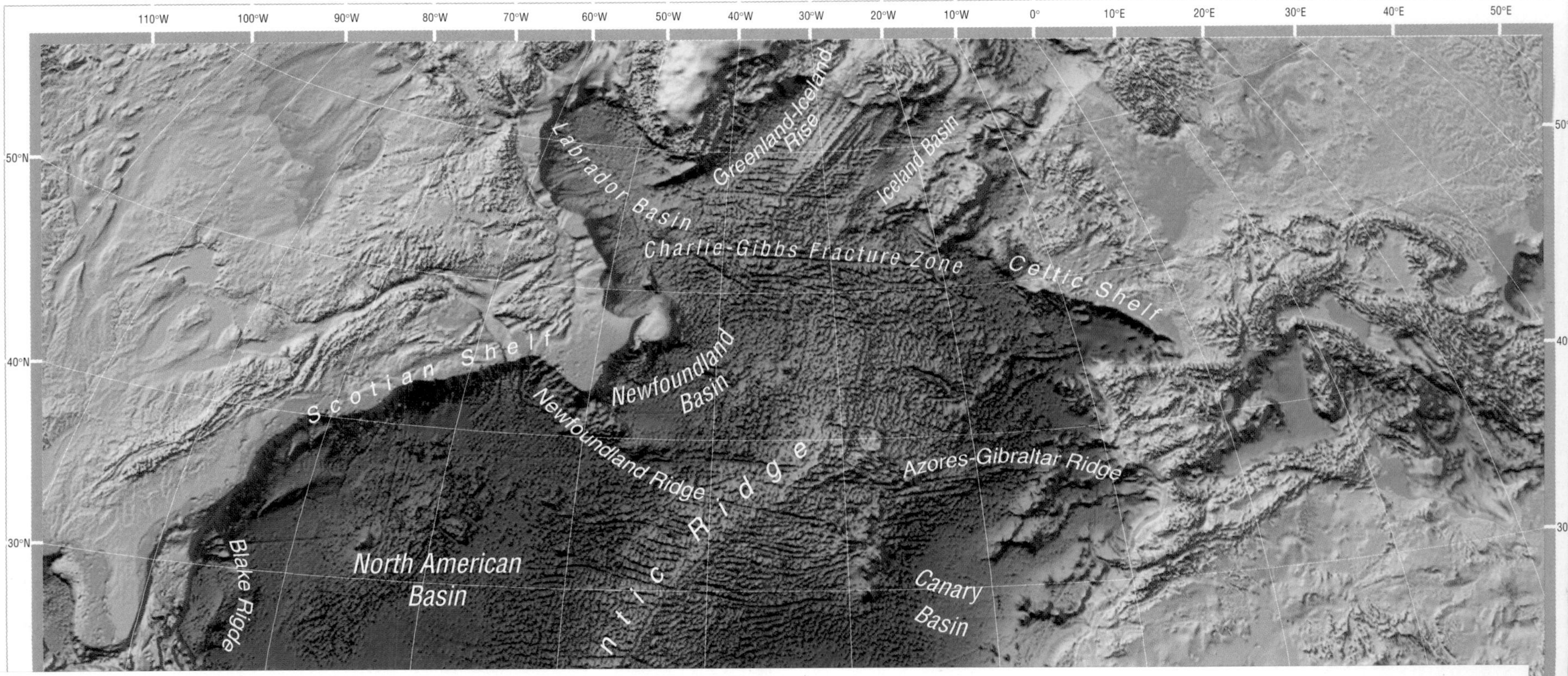

CLIMATOLOGY GEOLOGY AND BIOGEOGRAPHY

Climatology

Climate zones

Climate regions

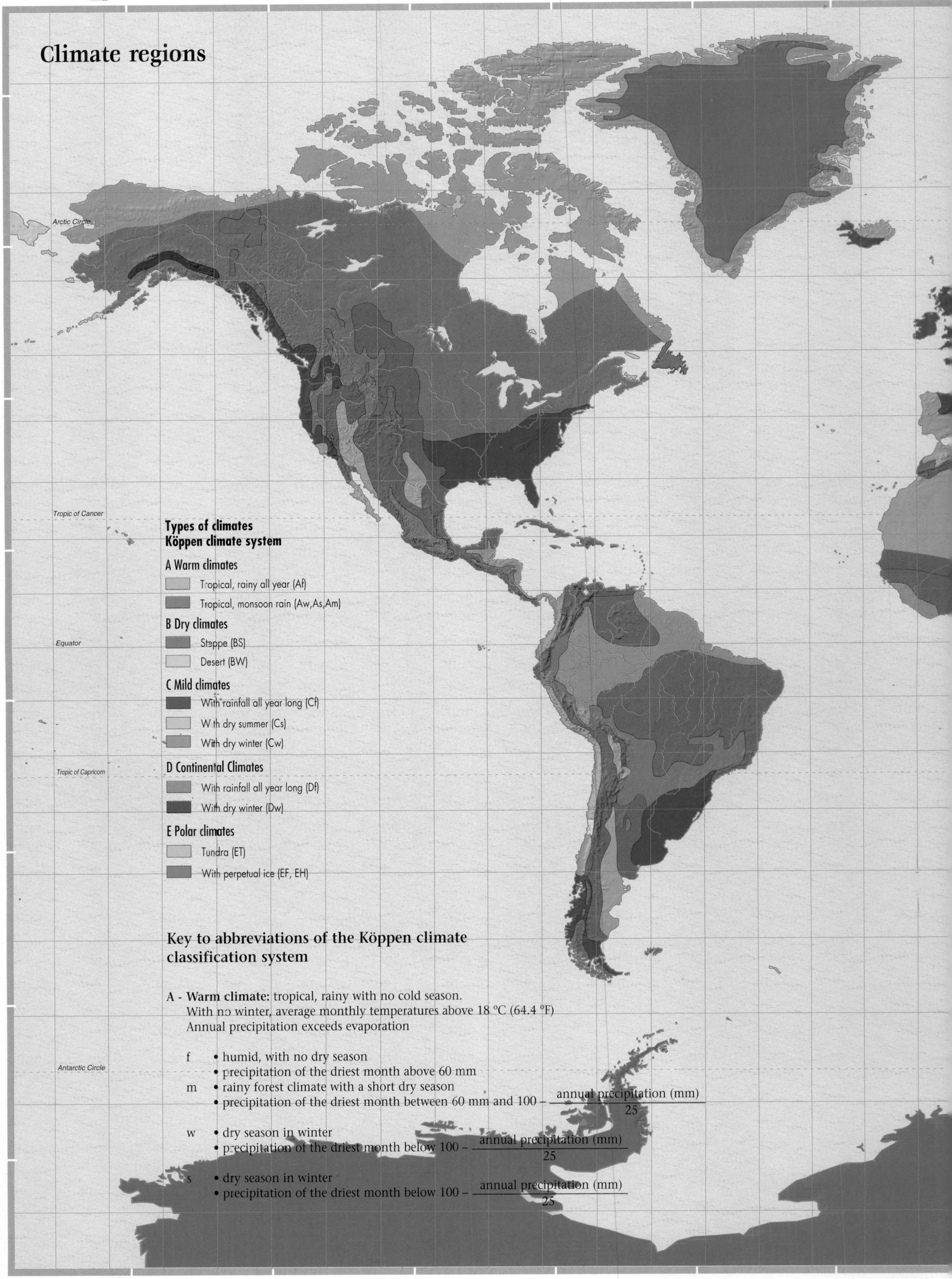

Key to abbreviations of the Köppen climate classification system

A - **Warm climate:** tropical, rainy with no cold season.
With no winter, average monthly temperatures above 18 °C (64.4 °F)
Annual precipitation exceeds evaporation

f
- humid, with no dry season
- precipitation of the driest month above 60 mm

m
- rainy forest climate with a short dry season
- precipitation of the driest month between 60 mm and $100 - \frac{\text{annual precipitation (mm)}}{25}$

w
- dry season in winter
- precipitation of the driest month below $100 - \frac{\text{annual precipitation (mm)}}{25}$

s
- dry season in winter
- precipitation of the driest month below $100 - \frac{\text{annual precipitation (mm)}}{25}$

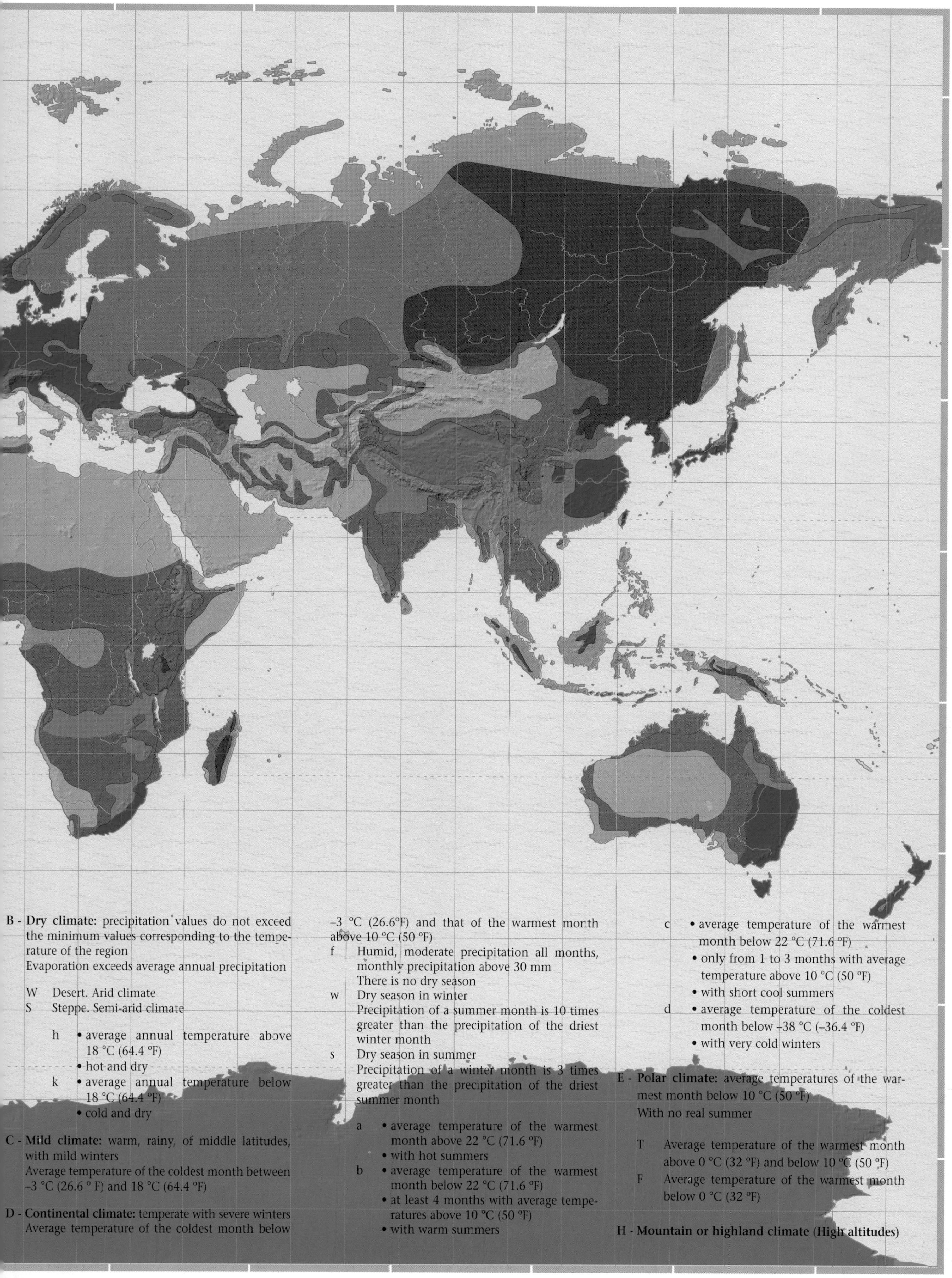

B - Dry climate: precipitation values do not exceed the minimum values corresponding to the temperature of the region
Evaporation exceeds average annual precipitation

W Desert. Arid climate
S Steppe. Semi-arid climate

h • average annual temperature above 18 °C (64.4 °F)
• hot and dry
k • average annual temperature below 18 °C (64.4 °F)
• cold and dry

C - Mild climate: warm, rainy, of middle latitudes, with mild winters
Average temperature of the coldest month between –3 °C (26.6 ° F) and 18 °C (64.4 °F)

D - Continental climate: temperate with severe winters
Average temperature of the coldest month below –3 °C (26.6°F) and that of the warmest month above 10 °C (50 °F)

f Humid, moderate precipitation all months, monthly precipitation above 30 mm
There is no dry season
w Dry season in winter
Precipitation of a summer month is 10 times greater than the precipitation of the driest winter month
s Dry season in summer
Precipitation of a winter month is 3 times greater than the precipitation of the driest summer month

a • average temperature of the warmest month above 22 °C (71.6 °F)
• with hot summers
b • average temperature of the warmest month below 22 °C (71.6 °F)
• at least 4 months with average temperatures above 10 °C (50 °F)
• with warm summers
c • average temperature of the warmest month below 22 °C (71.6 °F)
• only from 1 to 3 months with average temperature above 10 °C (50 °F)
• with short cool summers
d • average temperature of the coldest month below –38 °C (–36.4 °F)
• with very cold winters

E - Polar climate: average temperatures of the warmest month below 10 °C (50 °F)
With no real summer

T Average temperature of the warmest month above 0 °C (32 °F) and below 10 °C (50 °F)
F Average temperature of the warmest month below 0 °C (32 °F)

H - Mountain or highland climate (High altitudes)

Climatology

Climate graphs and annual precipitation

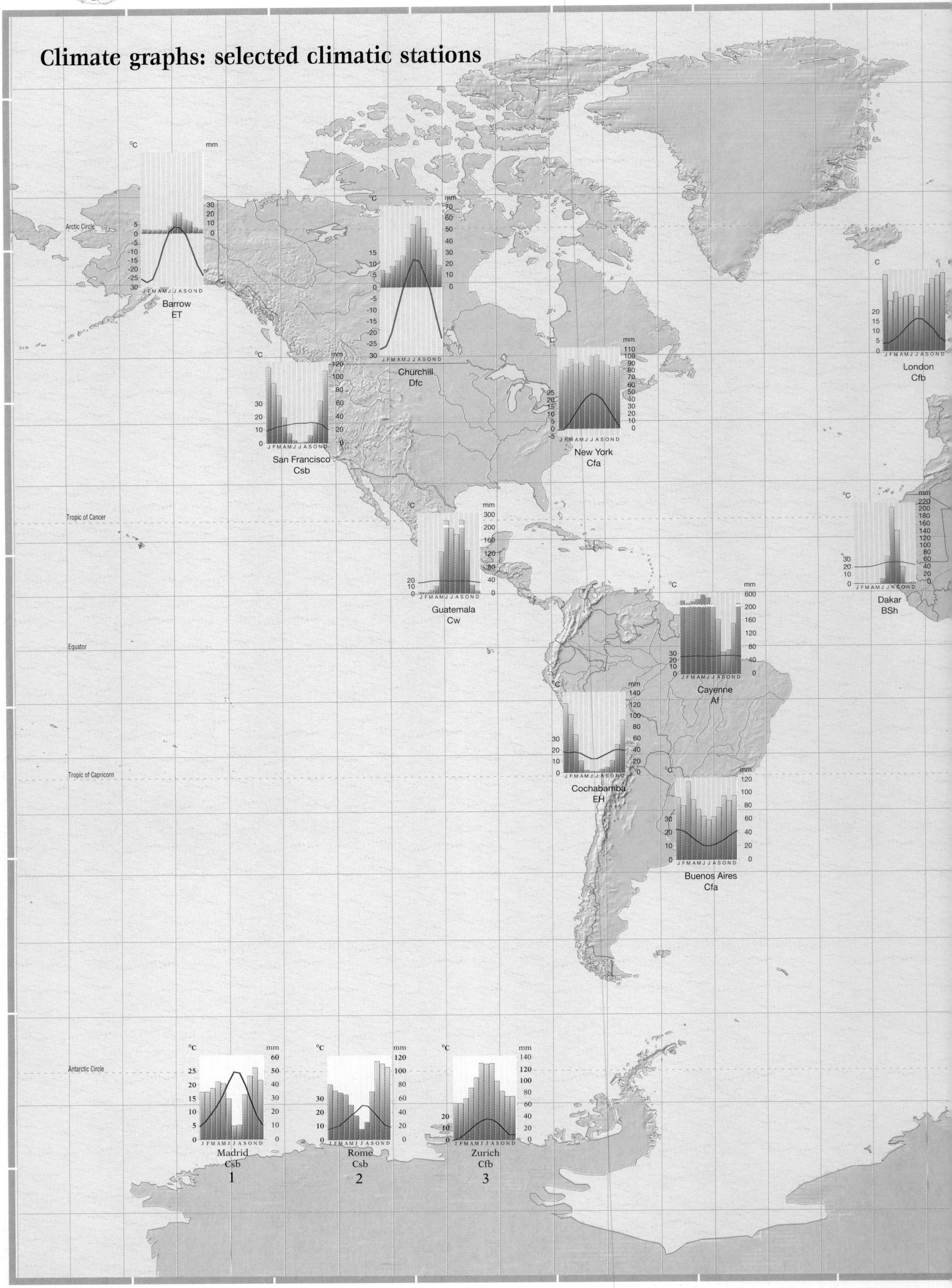

NOTE: The abreviations of each climate graph correspond to the Köppen climate system, on the previous page.

Stockholm
Dfb
Sankt Peterburg
Dfb
Tomsk
Dfc
Anadyr
Eh
Seoul
Dwb
Alger
Csa
Cairo
BWh
Riyadh
Dwh
New Delhi
Bsh
Calcutta
Aw
Chiang Mai
Aw
Kinshasa
Aw
Nairobi
Cw
Johannesburg
Cwb
Townsville
Aw
Cape Town
Csb
°C
mm
Average annual rainfall
Average annual rainfall (mm)
Below 200
From 200 to 500
From 500 to 1,000
From 1,000 to 2,000
From 2,000 to 3,000
Above 3,000

Climatology

Temperatures and ocean currents

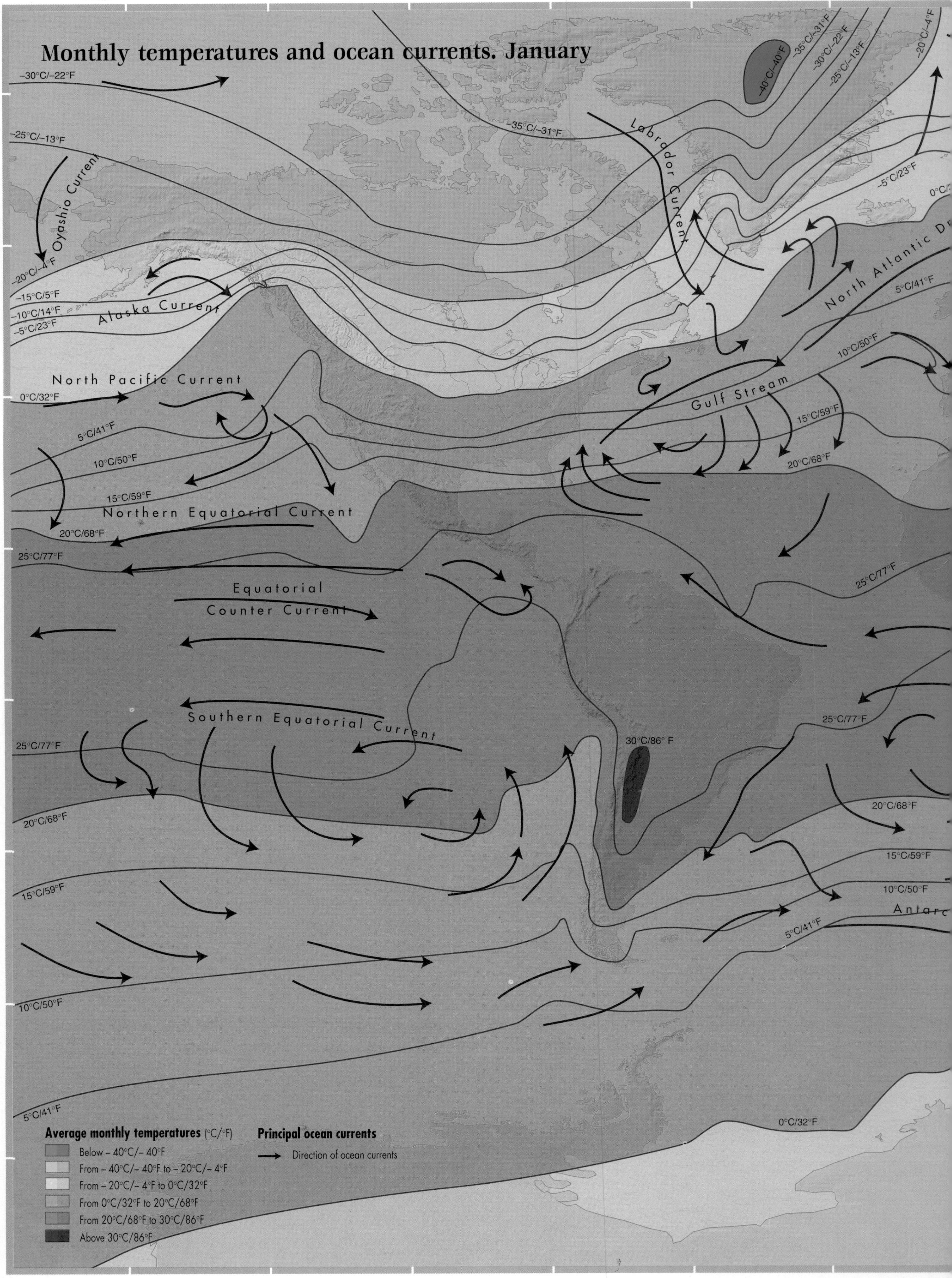

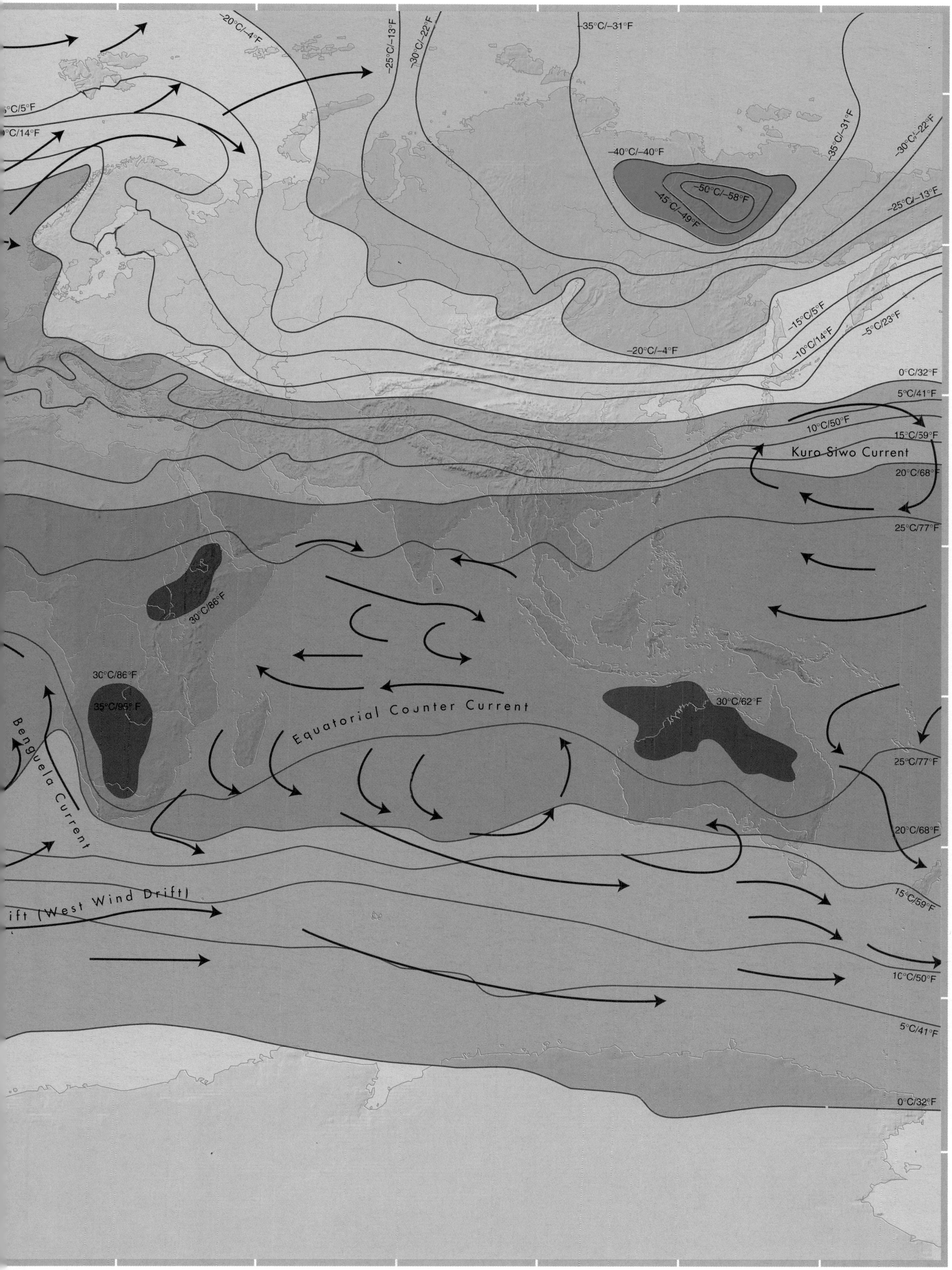

–20°C/–4°F
–25°C/–13°F
–30°C/–22°F
–35°C/–31°F
–40°C/–40°F
–45°C/–49°F
–50°C/–58°F
–35°C/–31°F
–30°C/–22°F
–25°C/–13°F
–20°C/–4°F
–15°C/5°F
–10°C/14°F
–5°C/23°F
0°C/32°F
5°C/41°F
10°C/50°F
15°C/59°F
Kuro Siwo Current
20°C/68°F
25°C/77°F
30°C/86°F
30°C/86°F
35°C/95°F
Benguela Current
Equatorial Counter Current
30°C/62°F
25°C/77°F
20°C/68°F
15°C/59°F
(West Wind Drift)
10°C/50°F
5°C/41°F
0°C/32°F

Precipitation, pressure and winds

Monthly precipitation, atmospheric pressure and prevailing winds. January

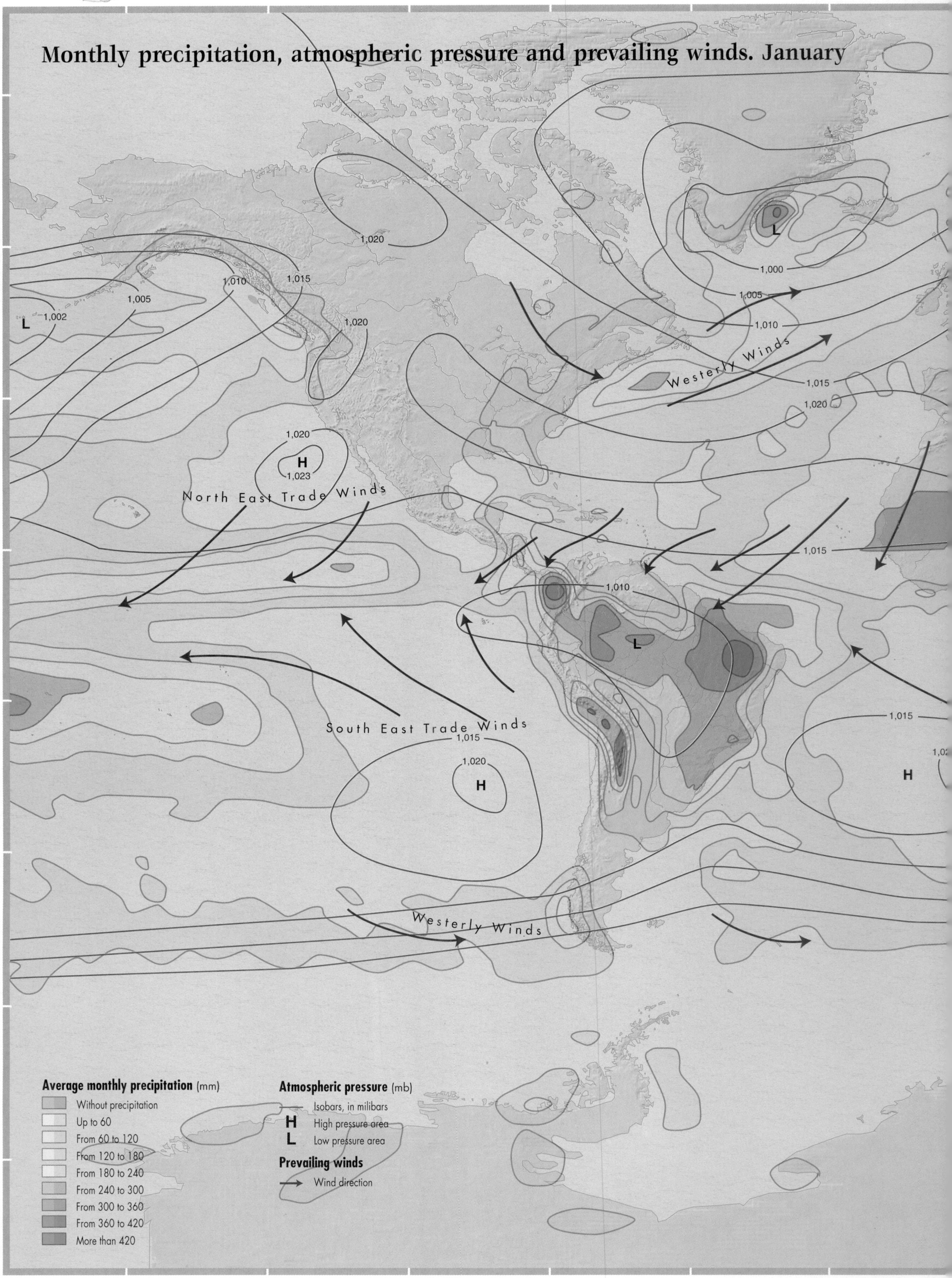

North East Trade Winds
H
1,035
1,030
1,025
1,020
1,010
1,005
1,002
L
North East Monsoon
North East Monsoon
North West Monsoon
1,010
1,005
L
1,010
L
South East Trade Winds
1,015
1,020
H
1,020
1,010
1,005
1,000
Westerly Winds

Climatology

Temperatures and ocean currents

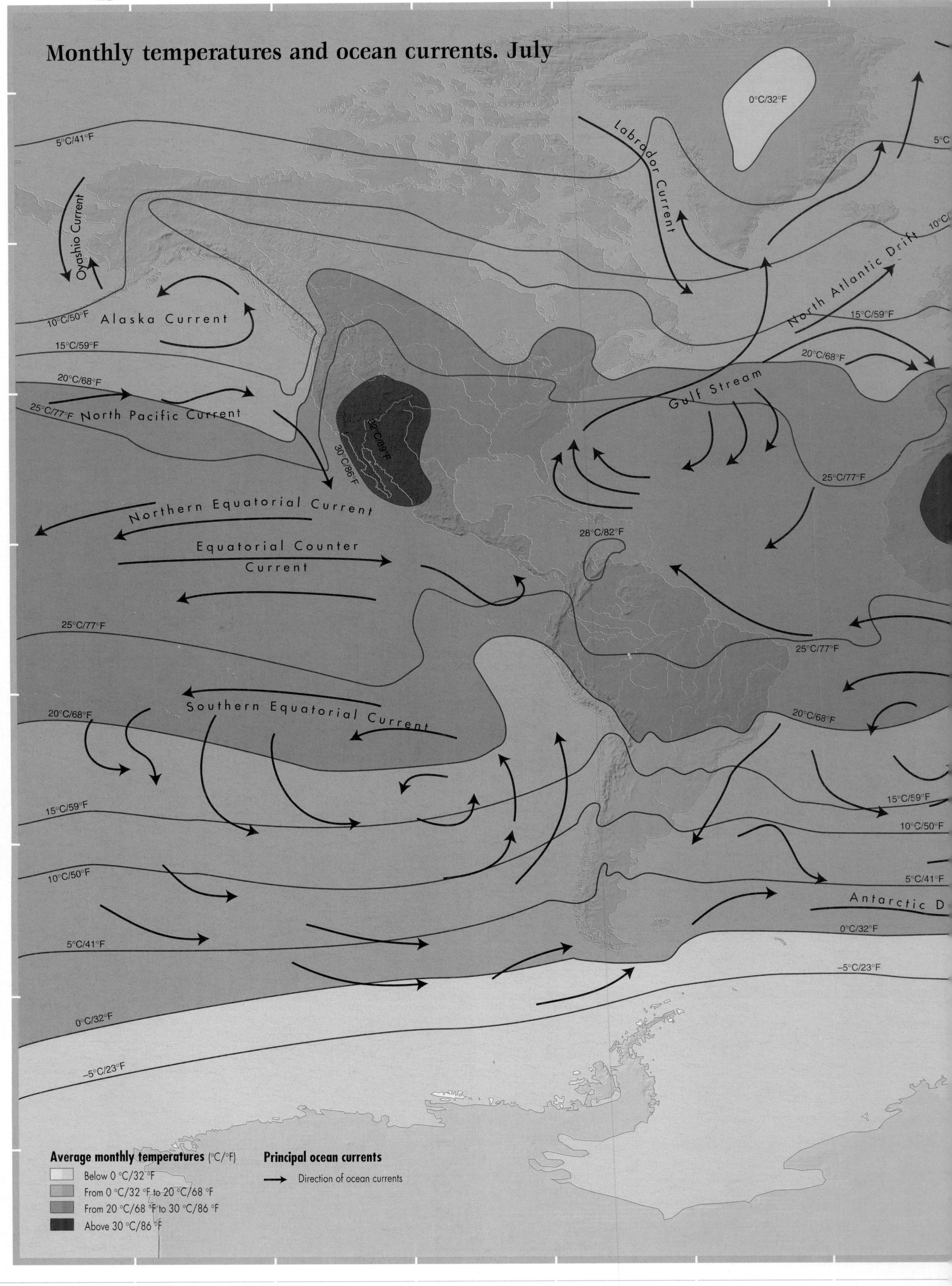

5°C/41°F
10°C/50°F
20°C/68°F
15°C/59°F
20°C/68°F
25°C/77°F
Kuro Siwo Current
32°C/89°F
32°C/89°F
30°C/86°F
28°C/82°F
28°C/82°F
28°C/82°F
25°C/77°F
20°C/68°F
10°C/50°F
15°C/59°F
10°C/50°F
uela Current
est Wind Drift)
5°C/41°F
0°C/32°F
–5°C/23°F

Climatology

Precipitation, pressure and winds

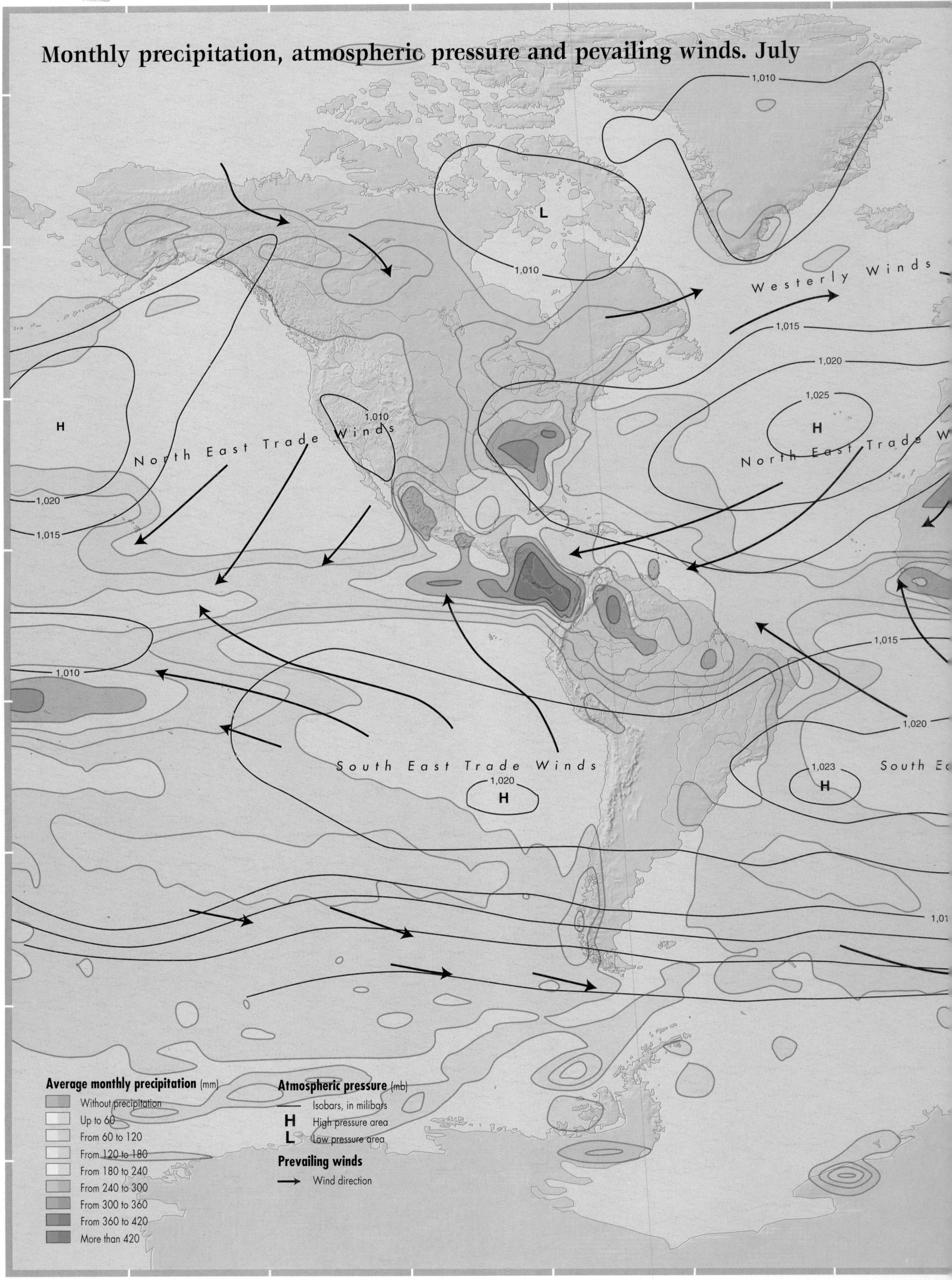

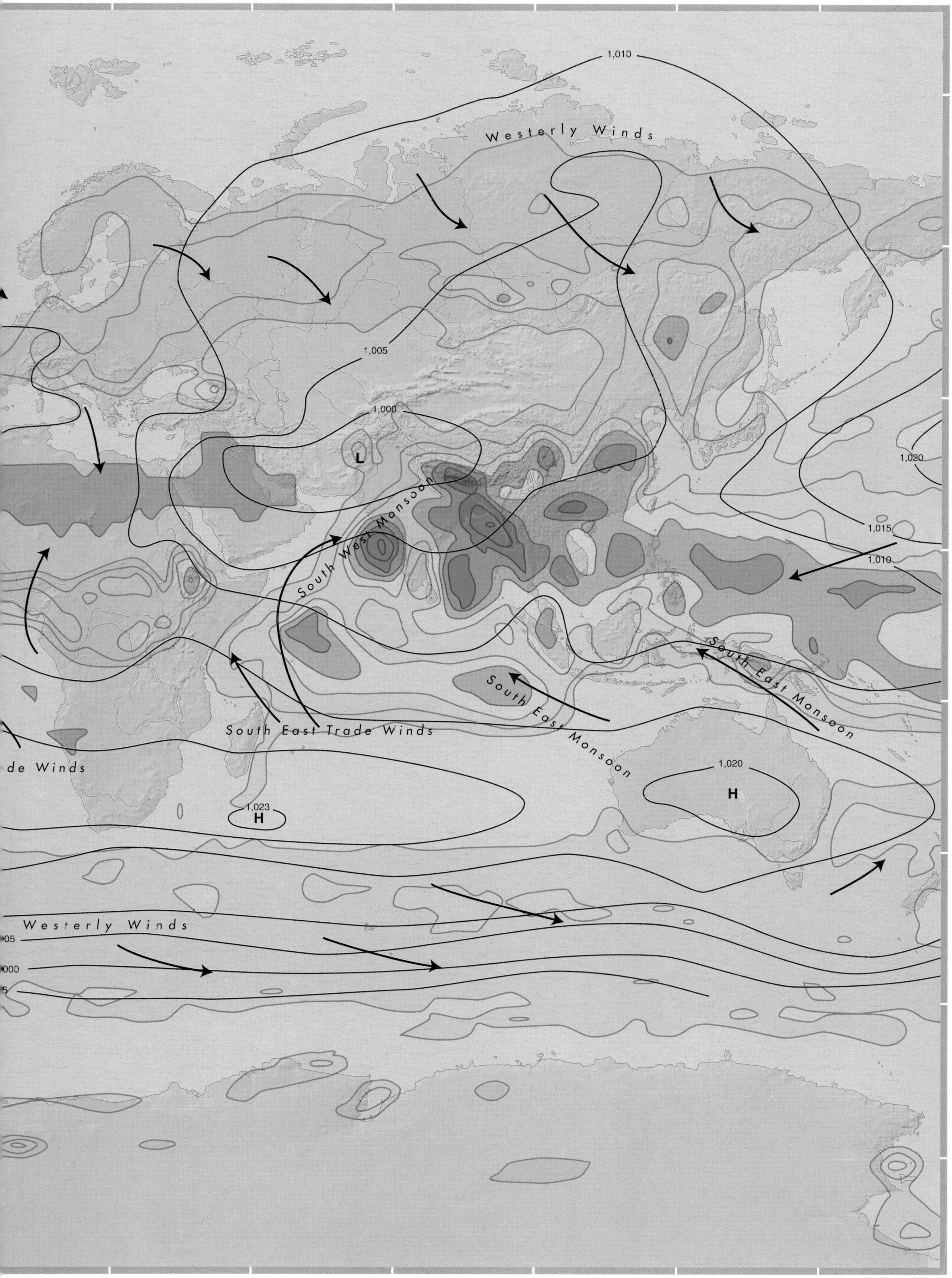
1,010
Westerly Winds
1,005
1,000
L
1,020
1,015
1,010
South West Monsoon
South East Monsoon
South East Monsoon
South East Trade Winds
de Winds
1,020
H
1,023
H
Westerly Winds
05
000
5

Geology

Plate tectonics

- —— Transforming fault
- ▬ Ridge (area where new ocean floor crust is forming)
- ⦙⦙⦙⦙ Trough (graben)
- ⟶ Direction of continental plate movement
- ⟶ Direction of movement of continental plate boundaries
- ▭ New ocean floor crust

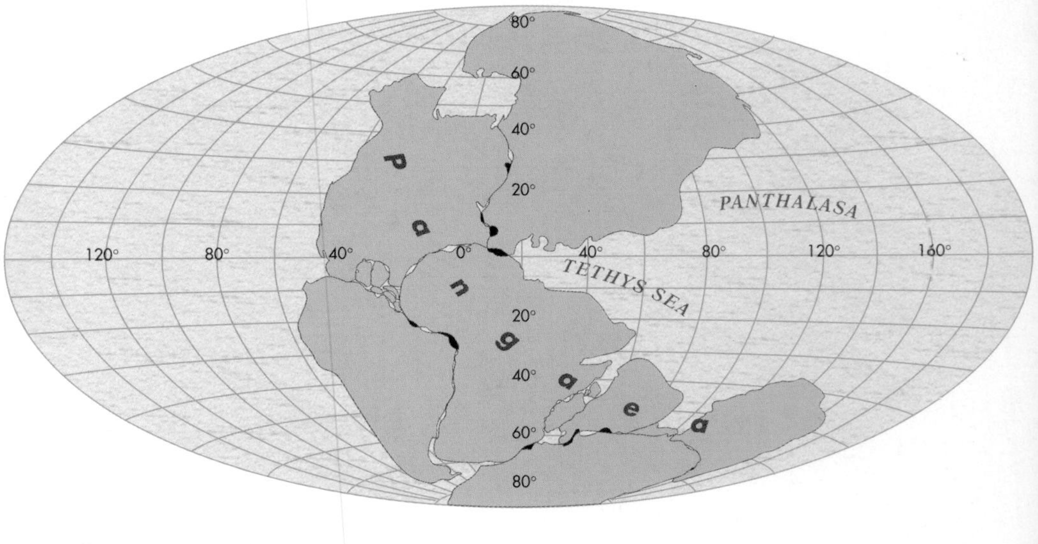

200 million years ago (Triassic)

- A single continent called Pangaea can be observed
- Panthalasa is the present Pacific Ocean, and Tethys Sea, which separates Africa from Eurasia, is the Mediterranean Sea
- The magnetic poles are displaced with regard to their present-day positions

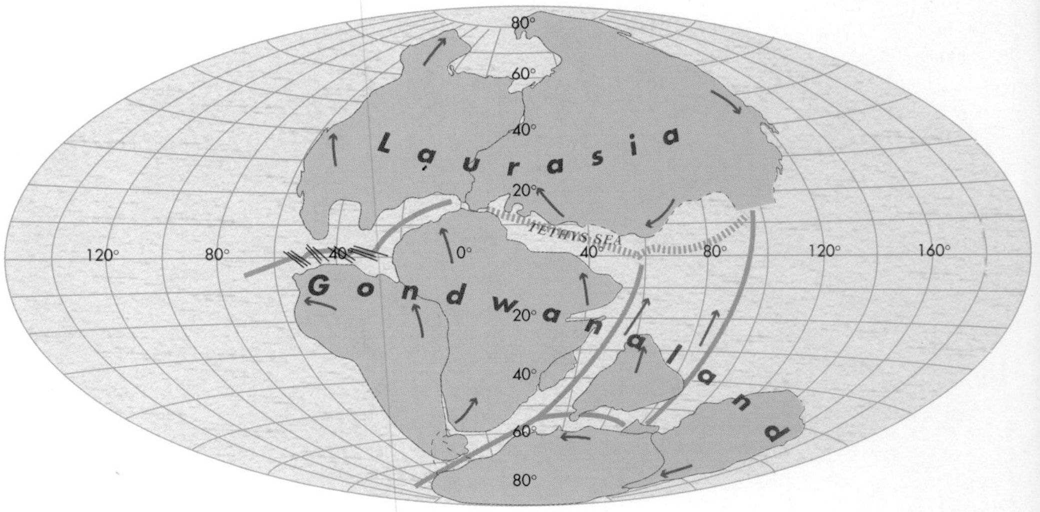

180 million years ago (end of the Triassic-Jurassic)

- The continent of Pangaea divides into Laurasia, which moves towards the north, and Gondwanaland, which moves towards the sou
- The Tethys Sea is closing up
- India separates from the Africa-South America-Antarctica group and slips northward
- The separation of the Africa-South America group from that of Antarctica-Australia begins

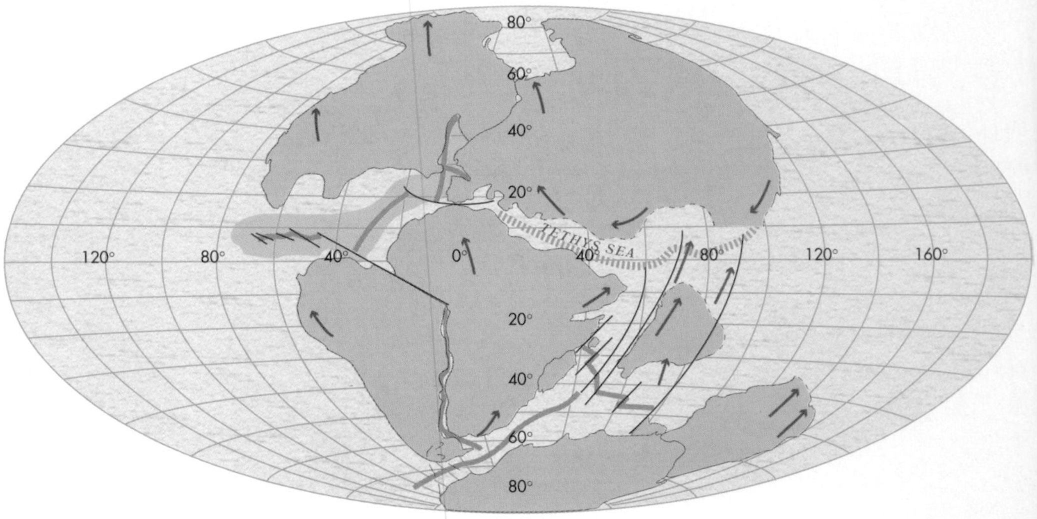

135 million years ago (end of the Jurassic)

- The Atlantic and Indian Oceans are very well-developed
- Africa begins to separate from South America, India continues its approach towards Asia
- A hot-spot in India forms the Deccan Plateau, and another in South America forms the ridges of Walvis and Río Grande

Geological time

AGE (in millions of years)	EON	ERA	SYSTEM	SERIE	LENGTH (millions of years)	CHARACTERISTICS
4500	ARCHAIC					• Formation of the planet Earth • End of the great meteorite bombardment
3800					2,000	• Plate tectonics • First fossils known (cianobacterias) • Cooling of rocks • Oldest rock known • Rigid lithosphere • First confirmed glaciation
2500	PROTEROZOIC	PALEOPROTEROZOIC			1,930	• Oldest fossil animal known, organisms capable of metabolizing oxygen • Appearance of bacterias • First metazoos • Asintian orogeny • Formation of the continent of Pangaea 1
		MESOPROTEROZOIC				
		PALEOPROTEROZOIC				
540	PHANEROZOIC	PALEOZOIC	CAMBRIAN	Lower (Georsian)	65	• Caledonian orogeny • Fragmentation of the continent of Pangaea 1 • First shelled animals • Cambrian explosion
				Middle (Acadian)		
				Upper (Post-Damian)		
500			ORDOVICIAN	Lower	67	• First fish • Animals-vertebrates and tetrapods
				Upper		
440			SILURIAN	Llandoverian	30	• Ordovician-Silurian glaciation • First jawed fish
				Wenlockian		
				Ludlowian		
				Pridolian		
410			DEVONIAN	Lower	48	• First terrestial plants • First insects • First seed-producing plants • First amphibians
				Middle		
				Upper		
360			CARBONIFEROUS	Lower Tournaisian Viséan	74	• First trees • Hercynian orogeny • First Hercynian granites • First flying insects • Formation of the continent of Pangaea 2
				Upper Namurian Westphalian Stephanian		
290			PERMIAN	Lower	41	• Permian crisis, extinction of the trilobites
245				Upper		

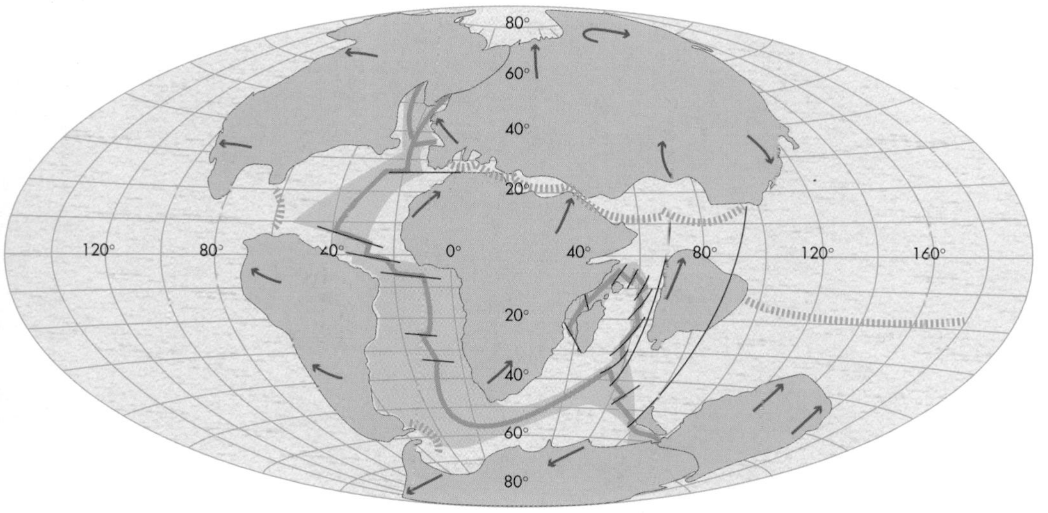

million years ago (end of the Cretaceous)

- South America and Africa progressively move apart and North and South America approach one another
- Madagascar separates from Africa when a rift area appears
- The Mediterranean begins to take shape

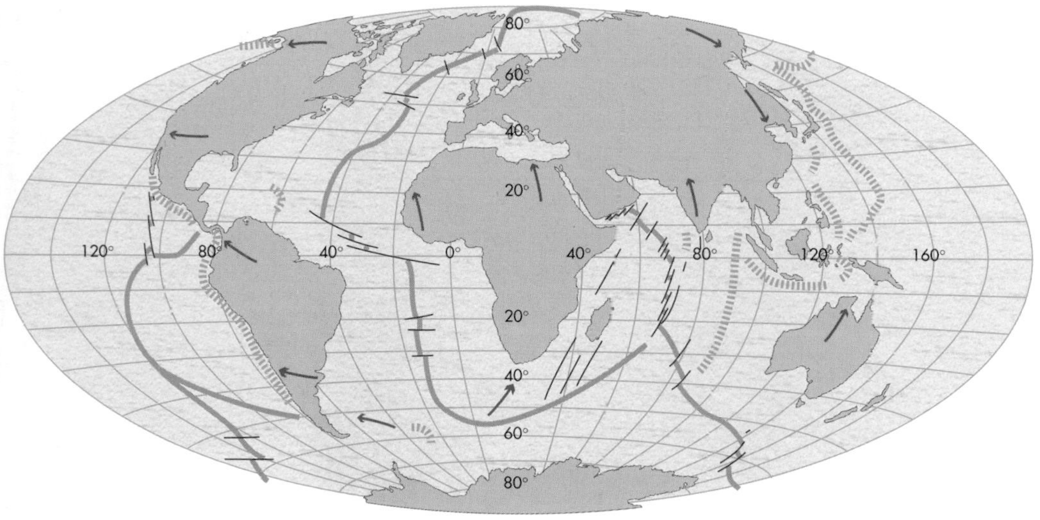

resent-day earth (Cenozoic)

- Creation of almost half of the ocean floor
- India joins Asia and the Himalaya is upfolded
- Australia separates from Antarctica
- Laurasia is completely broken up when the Atlantic Ocean joins the Arctic

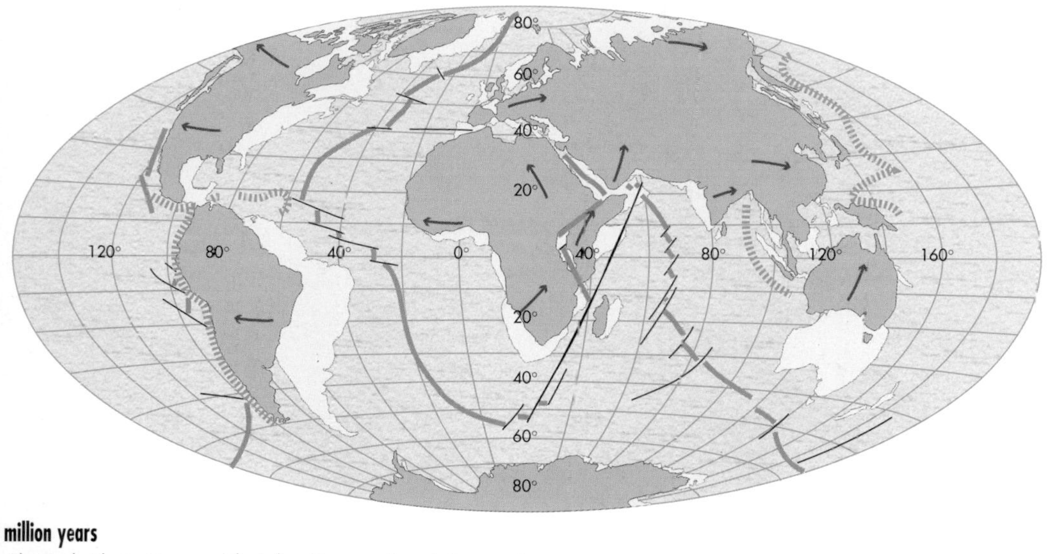

50 million years

- The South Atlantic Ocean and the Indian Ocean continue their expansion
- Australia moves toward the north, almost touching the Euroasian plate
- Eastern Africa splits off and the rest of the continent continues its drift towards the north closing up the Bay of Biscay and deforming the Mediterranean
- Antarctica does not move

AGE (in millions of years)	EON	ERA	SYSTEM	SERIE	LENGTH (millions of years)	CHARACTERISTICS
245	PHANEROZOIC	MESOZOIC	TRIASSIC	Lower (Buntsandstein)	37	• First mammals • First dinosaurs • Alpine orogenies (Alpine, Laramic)
				Middle (Muschelkalk)		
				Upper (Keuper)		
210			JURASSIC	Lower (Lias)	64	• Fragmentation of the continent of Pangea 2 • First birds
				Middle (Dogger)		
				Upper (Malm)		
146			CRETACEOUS	Lower	77.6	• First flowering plants • First mammals with placenta • Largest marine transgression in history • Extinction of dinosaurs and ammonites
				Upper		
65		CENOZOIC	PALEOGENE	Paleocene Eocene Lower Middle Upper Oligocene	42.7	• Expansion of mammals • First primates with prehensile hand and stereoscopic vision • Development of the Antarctic polar icecap • Formation of the first glacier icesheets in time in the Phanerozoic • Disecation of the Mediterranean Sea • Messinien crisis • First hominid, Homo Habilis
23			NEOGENE	Miocene Lower Middle Upper Pliocene Lower Upper	21.9	
1.8			QUATERNARY	Pleistocene Lower Middle Upper Holocene	1.8	• Expansion and evolution of Homo Sapiens • Ice Age, first Pleistocenic glaciations • Large mammals and birds
0						• End of the Ice Age

Phanerozoic time scale

ERA	PERIOD	BASE AGE (in millions of years)
CENOZOIC	Quaternary Pleistocene	1.8
	Tertiary Pliocene Miocene Oligocene Eocene Palaeocene	 7 23 33 54 65
MESOZOIC	Cretaceous Jurassic Triassic	146 210 245
PALEOZOIC	Permian Carboniferous Devonian Silurian Ordovician Cambrian	290 360 410 440 500 540

Geology

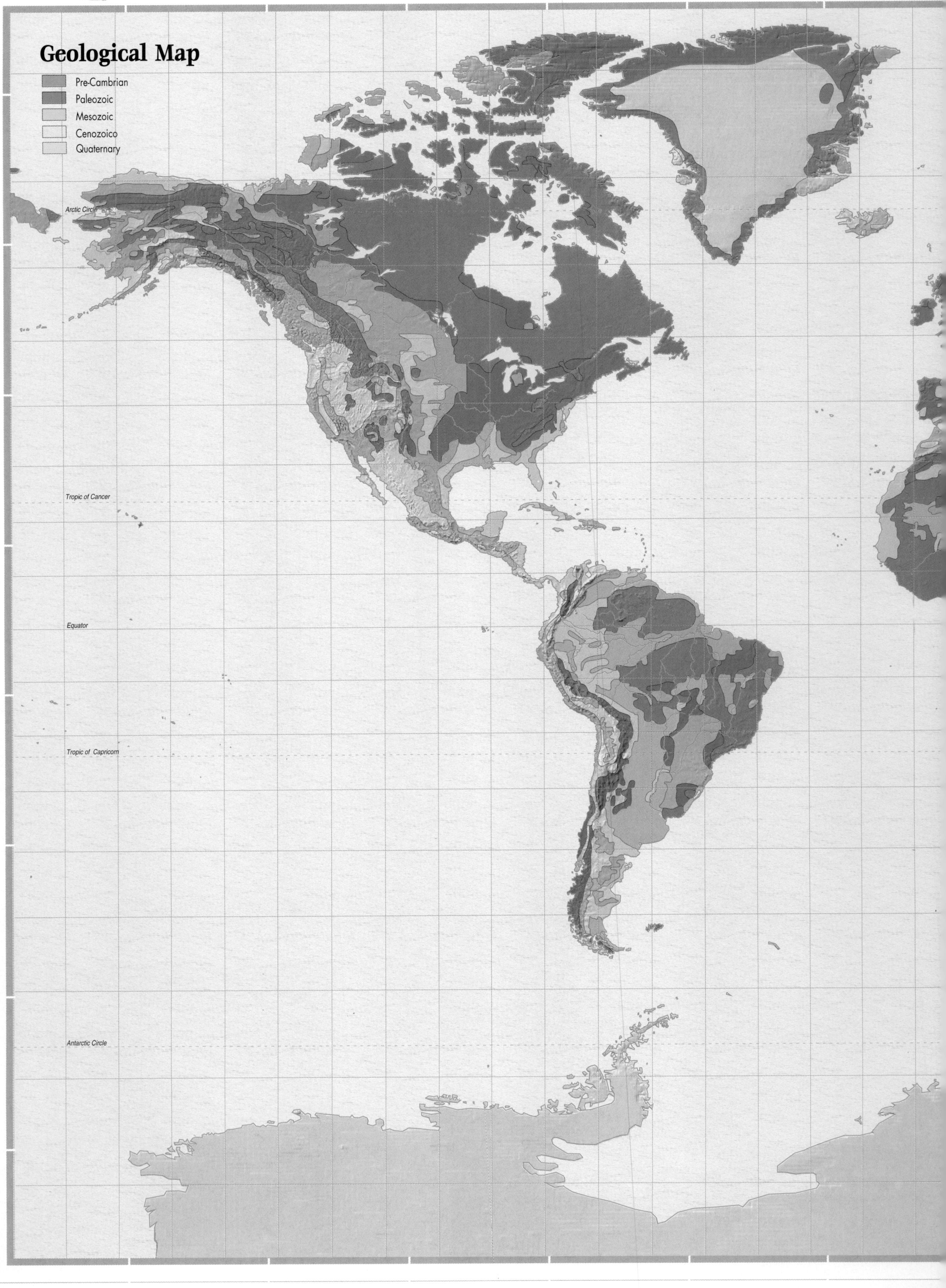
Geological Map
Pre-Cambrian
Paleozoic
Mesozoic
Cenozoico
Quaternary
Arctic Circle
Tropic of Cancer
Equator
Tropic of Capricorn
Antarctic Circle

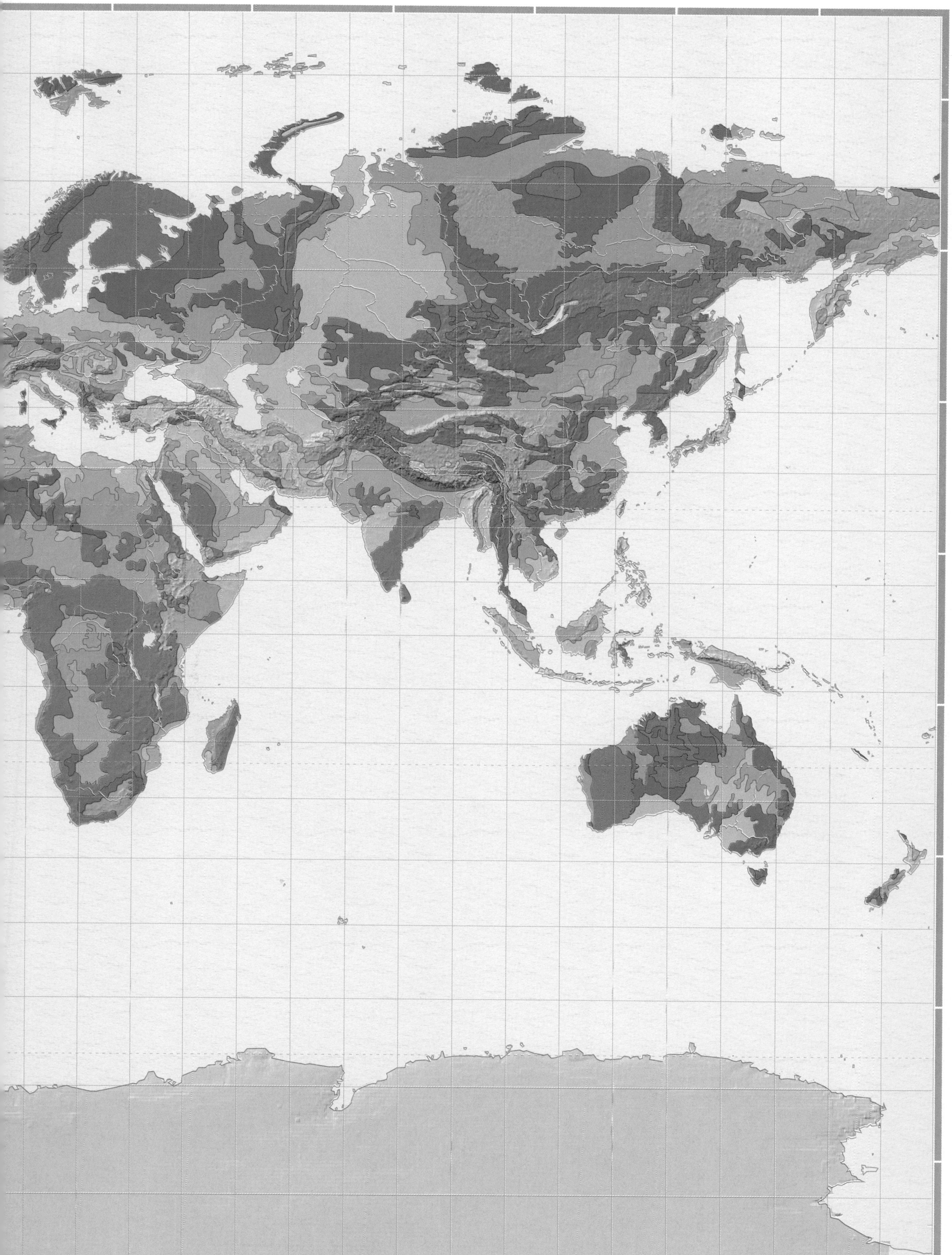

Lithological map

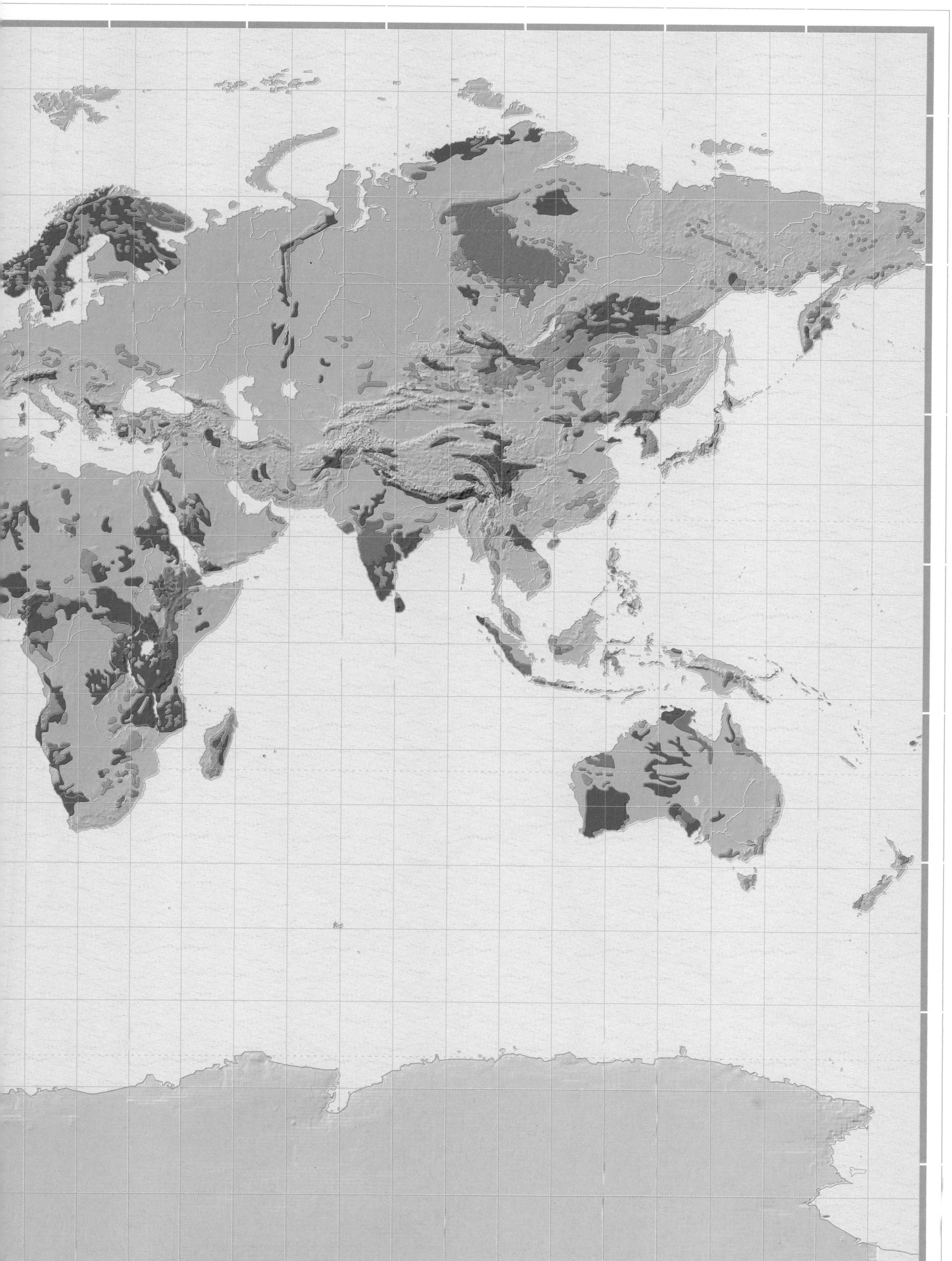

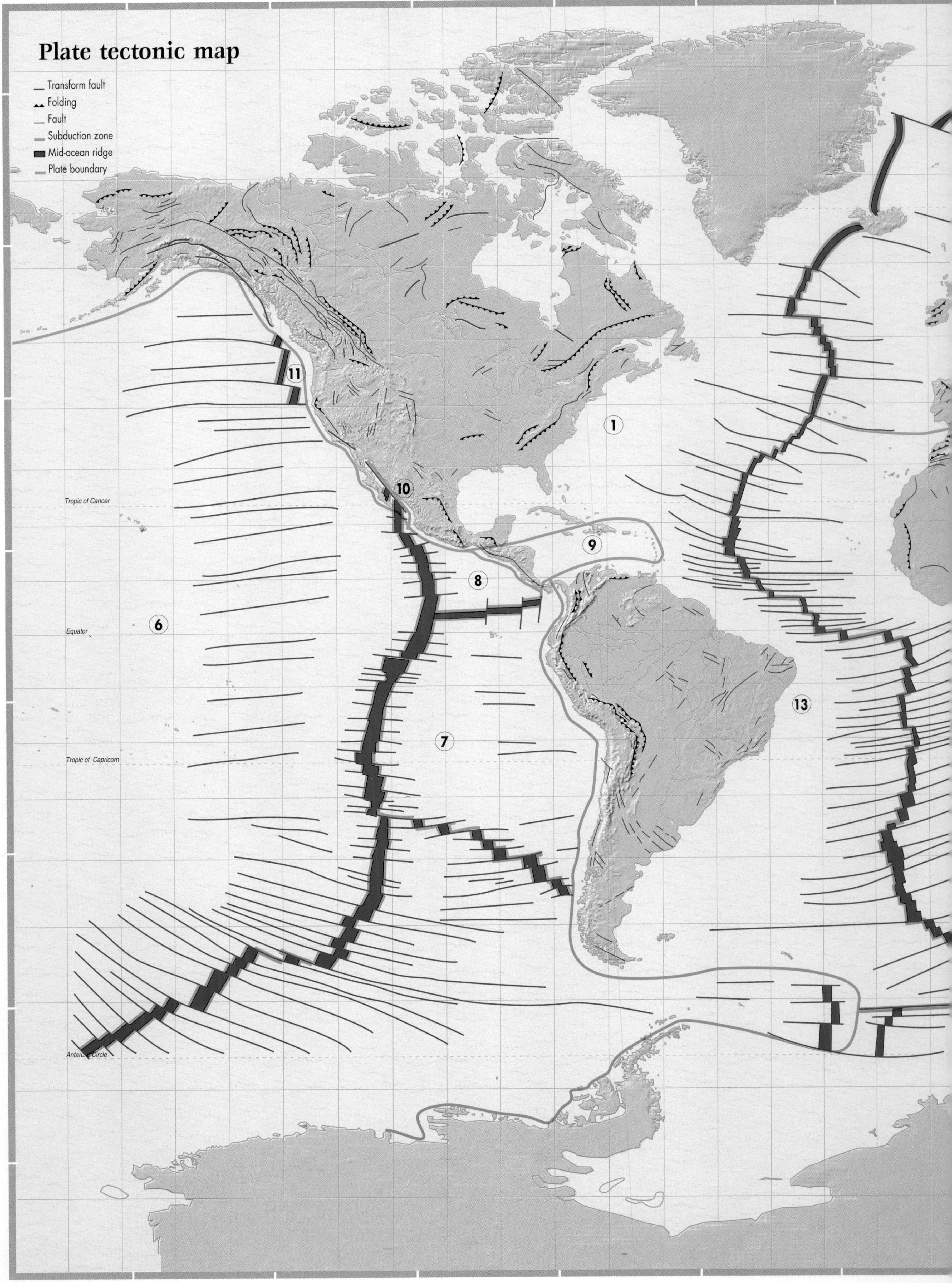
Plate tectonic map
Transform fault
Folding
Fault
Subduction zone
Mid-ocean ridge
Plate boundary
Tropic of Cancer
Equator
Tropic of Capricorn
Antarctic Circle
1
6
7
8
9
10
11
13

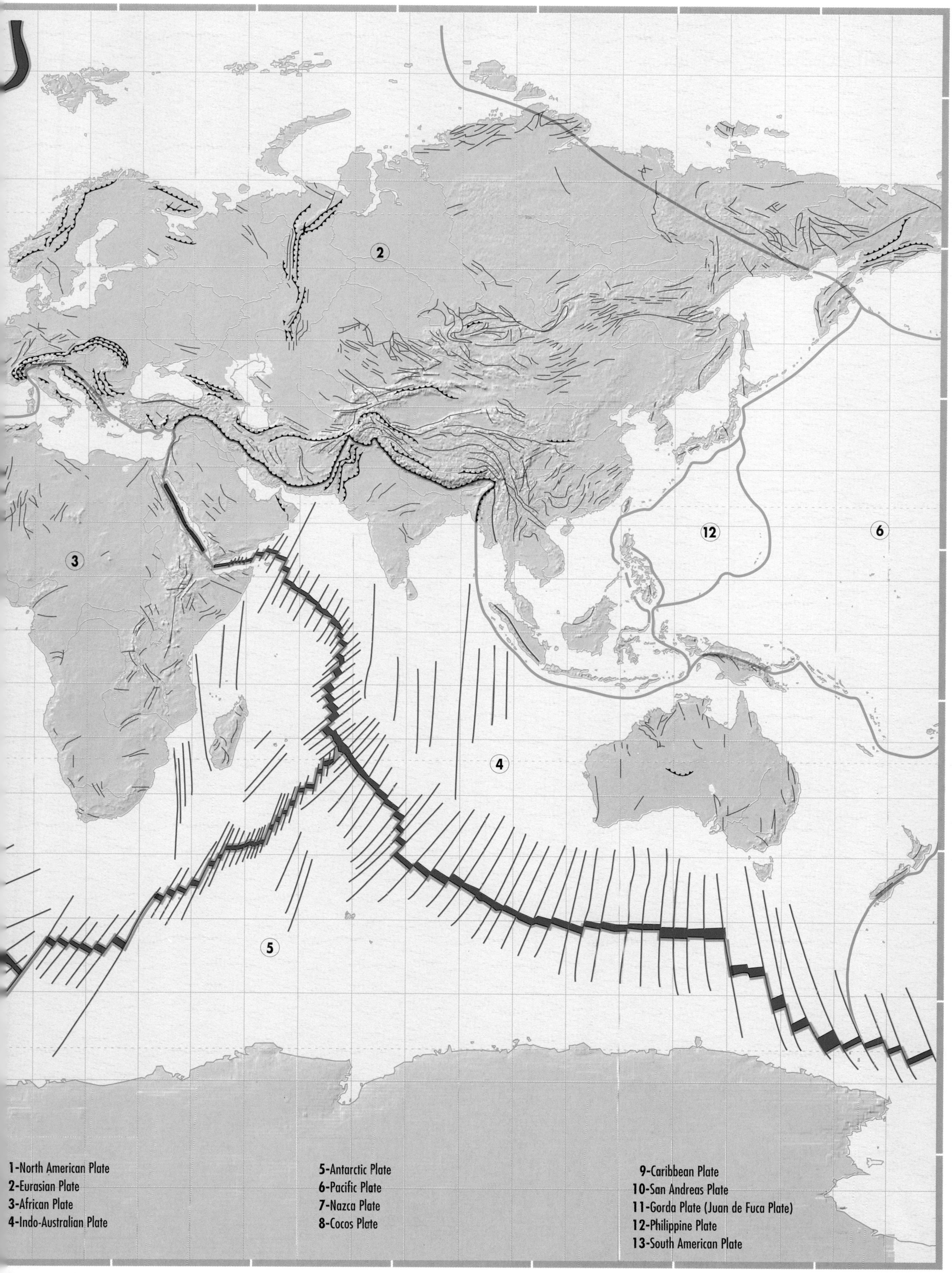

1-North American Plate
2-Eurasian Plate
3-African Plate
4-Indo-Australian Plate
5-Antarctic Plate
6-Pacific Plate
7-Nazca Plate
8-Cocos Plate
9-Caribbean Plate
10-San Andreas Plate
11-Gorda Plate (Juan de Fuca Plate)
12-Philippine Plate
13-South American Plate

Geomorphological map
Plains
Hills and low plateaus
Depressions or basins
High plateaus
Scattered mountains
Mountains
Arctic Circle
Tropic of Cancer
Equator
Tropic of Capricorn
Antarctic Circle

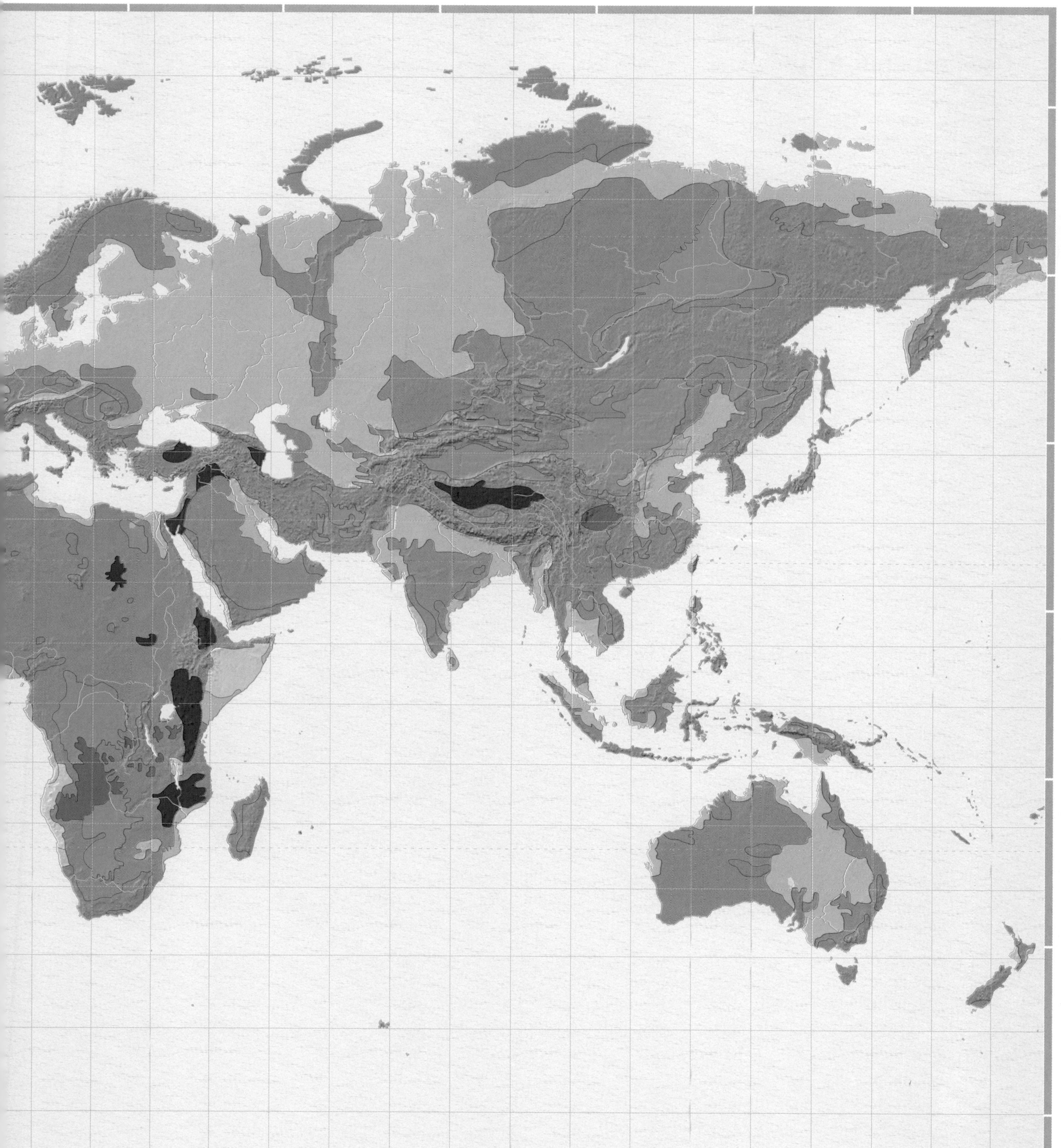

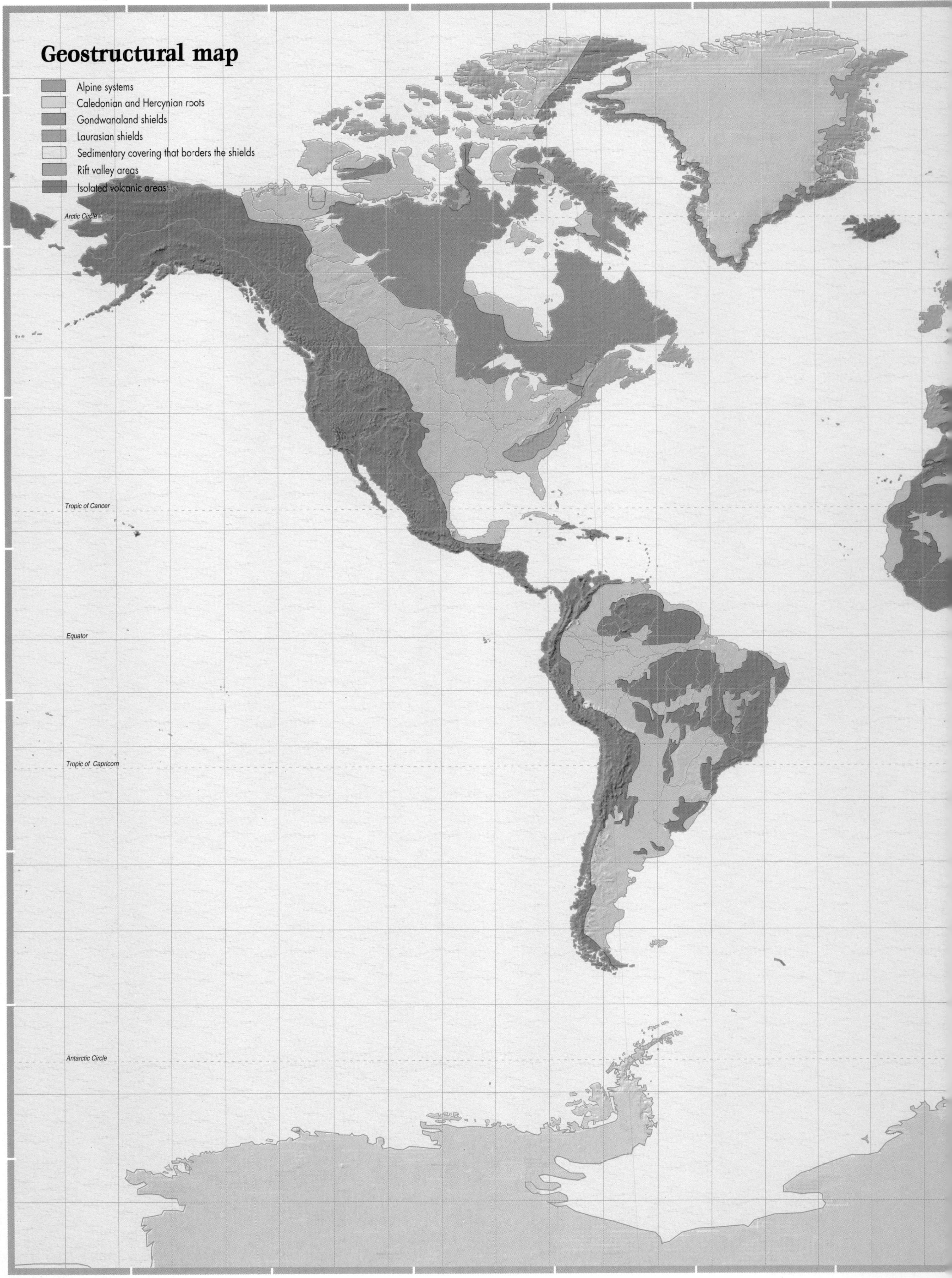
Geostructural map
Alpine systems
Caledonian and Hercynian roots
Gondwanaland shields
Laurasian shields
Sedimentary covering that borders the shields
Rift valley areas
Isolated volcanic areas
Arctic Circle
Tropic of Cancer
Equator
Tropic of Capricorn
Antarctic Circle

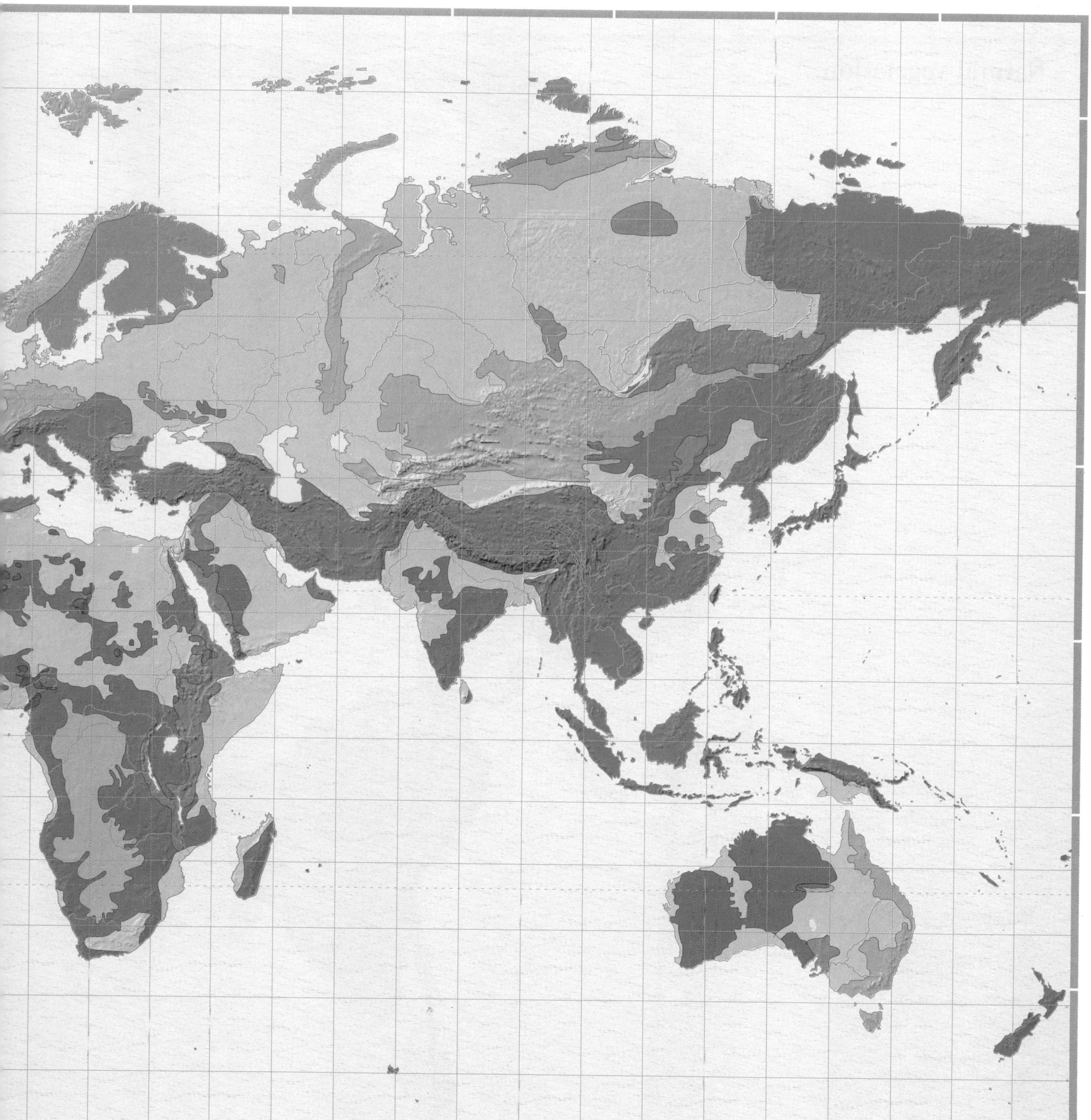

DEMOGRAPHY AND SOCIAL INDICATORS

Population
Population distribution

Total present-day population

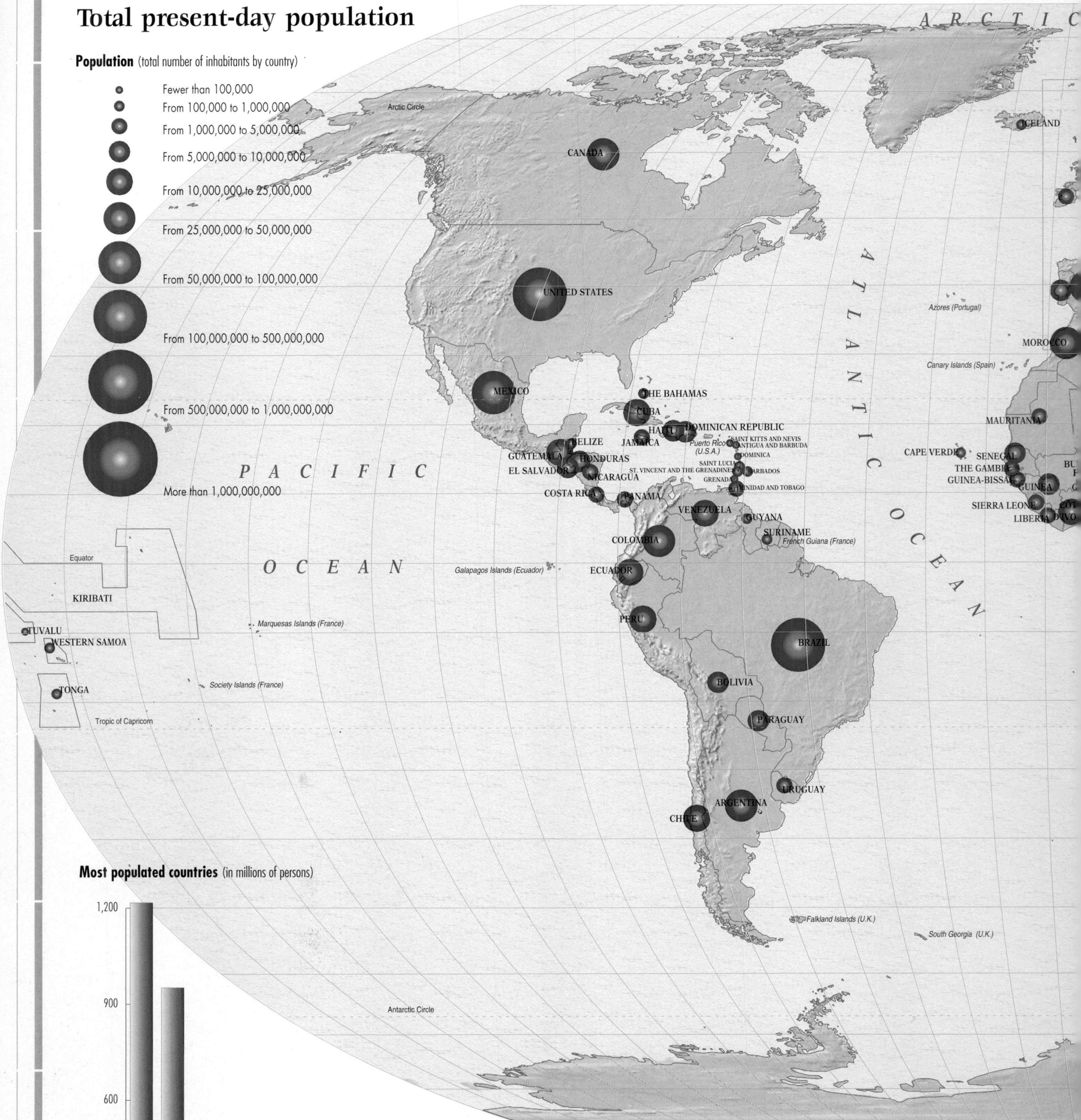

Most populated countries (in millions of persons)

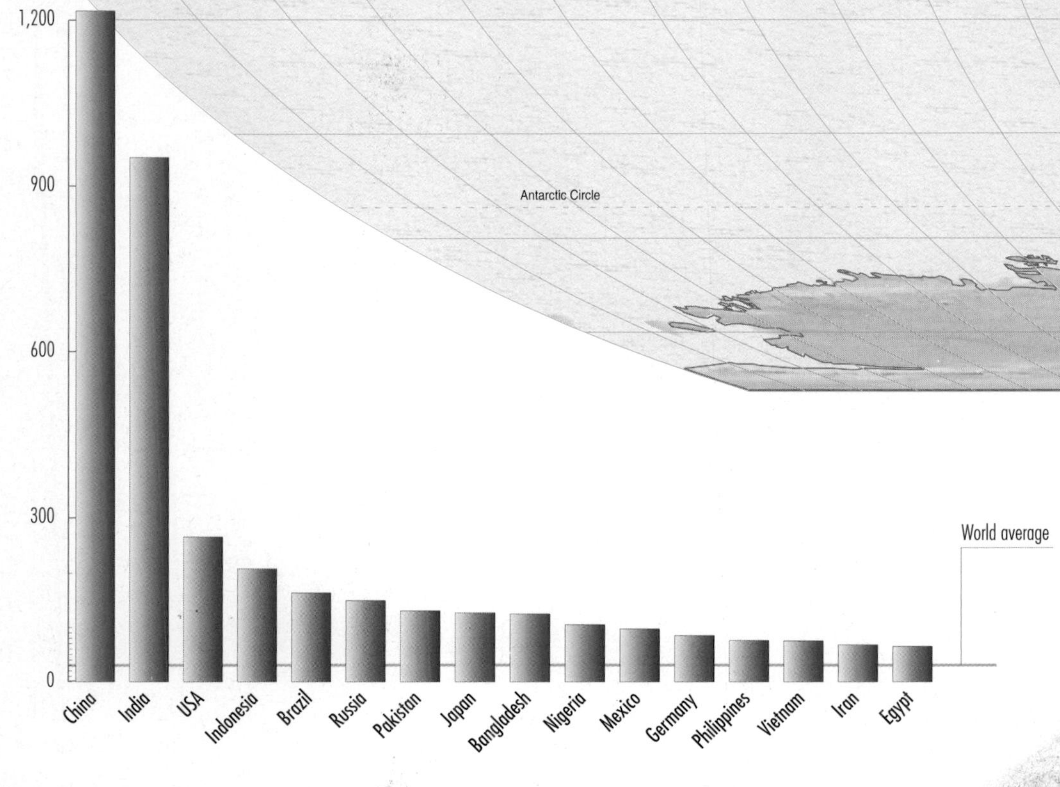

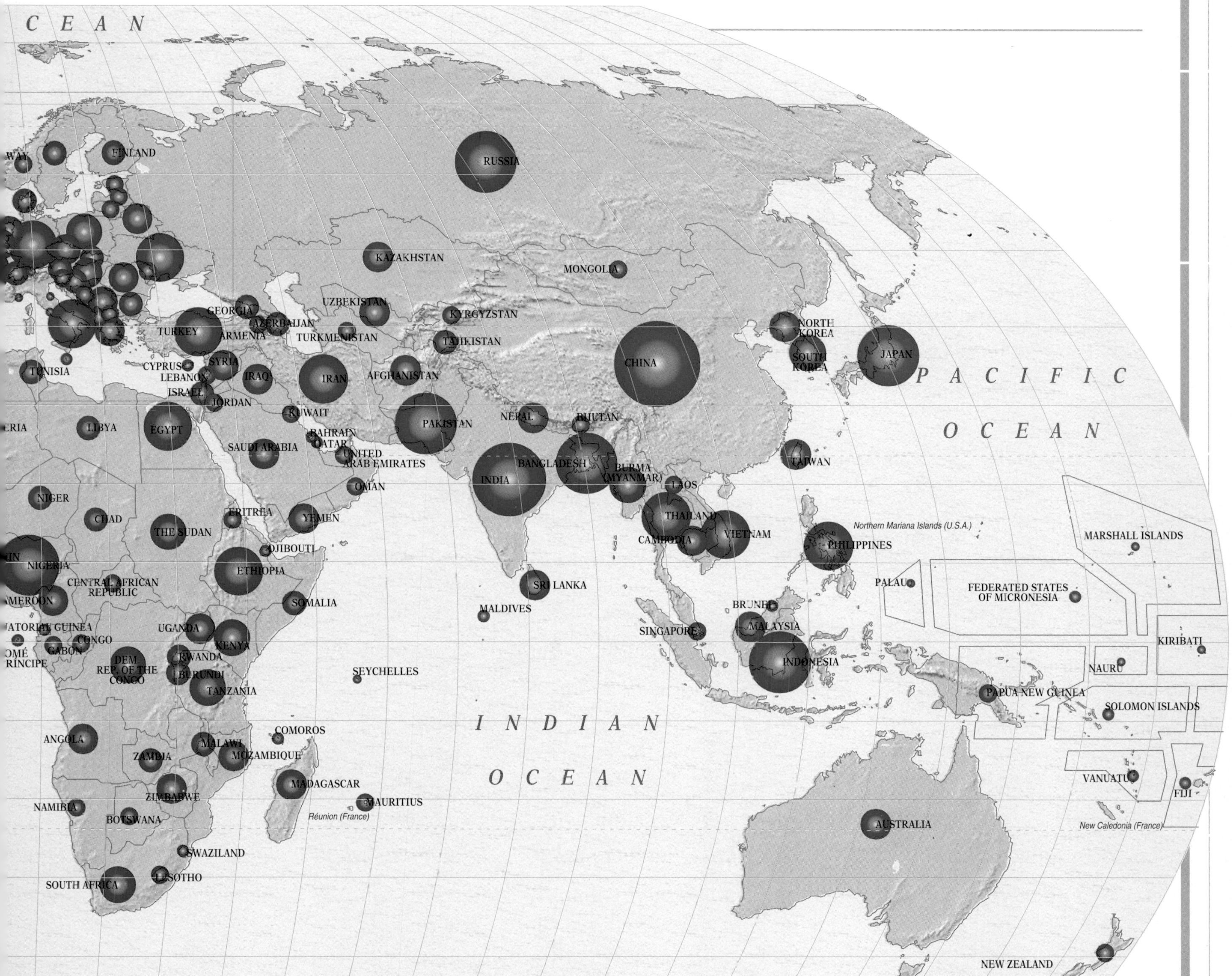

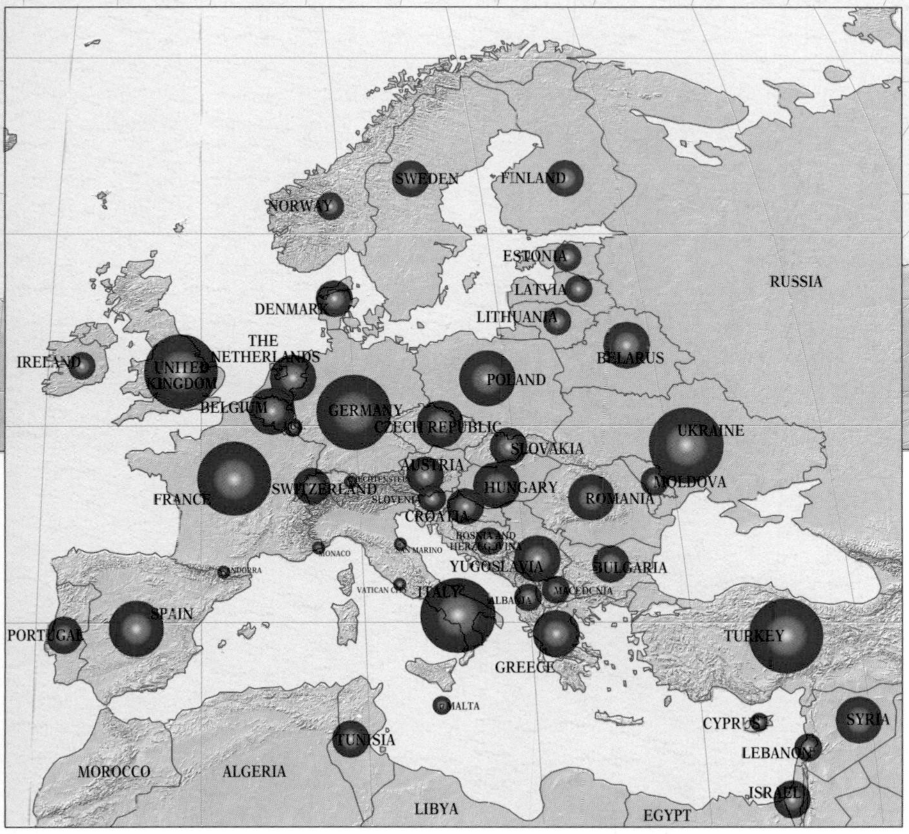

Population growth by continent (in millions of persons / years)

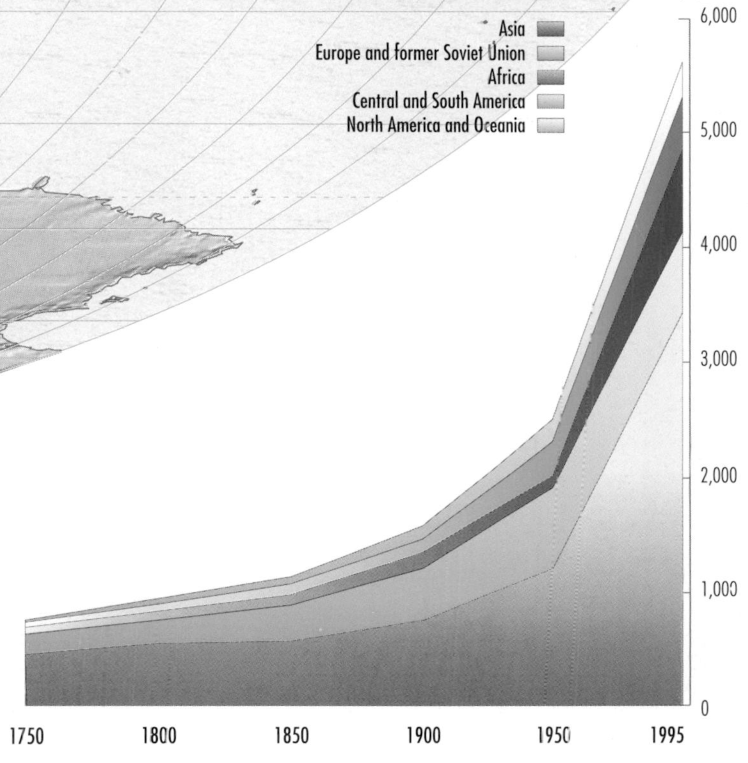

Population
Population distribution

Total population in the year 2020 (projections)

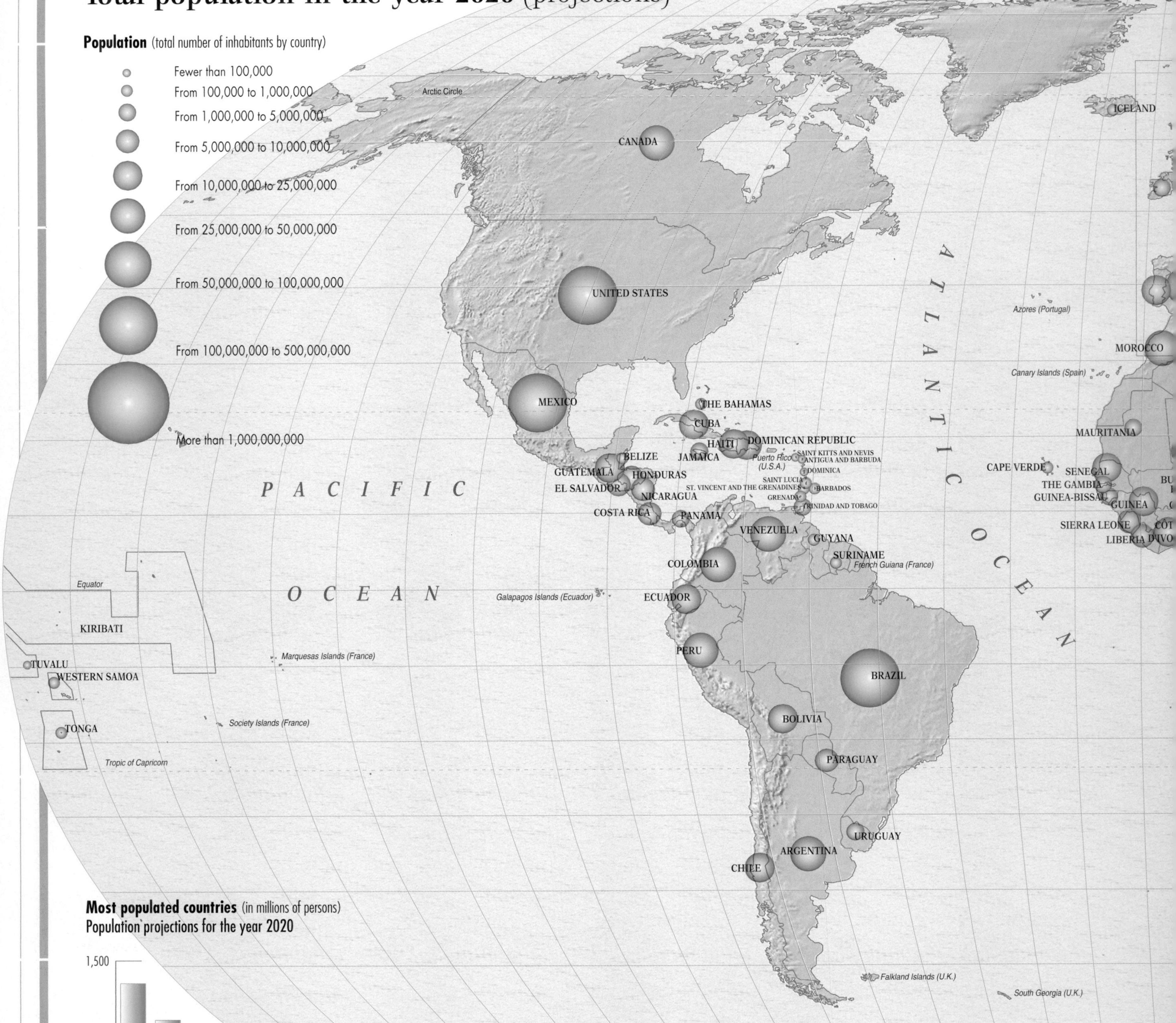

Most populated countries (in millions of persons)
Population projections for the year 2020

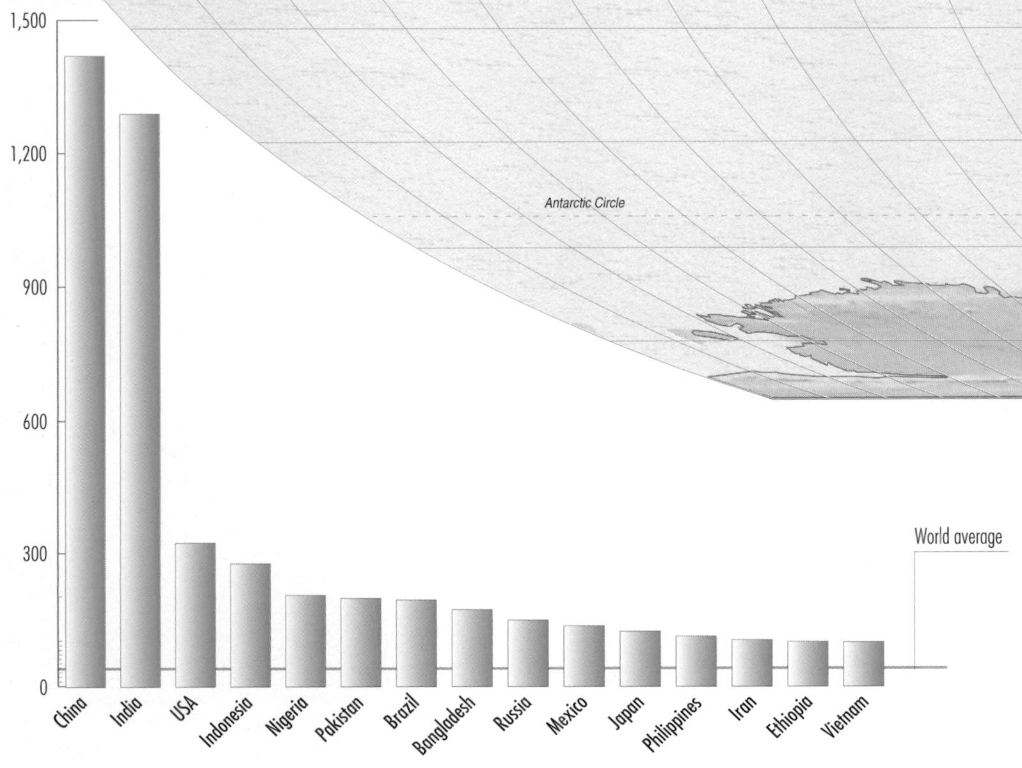

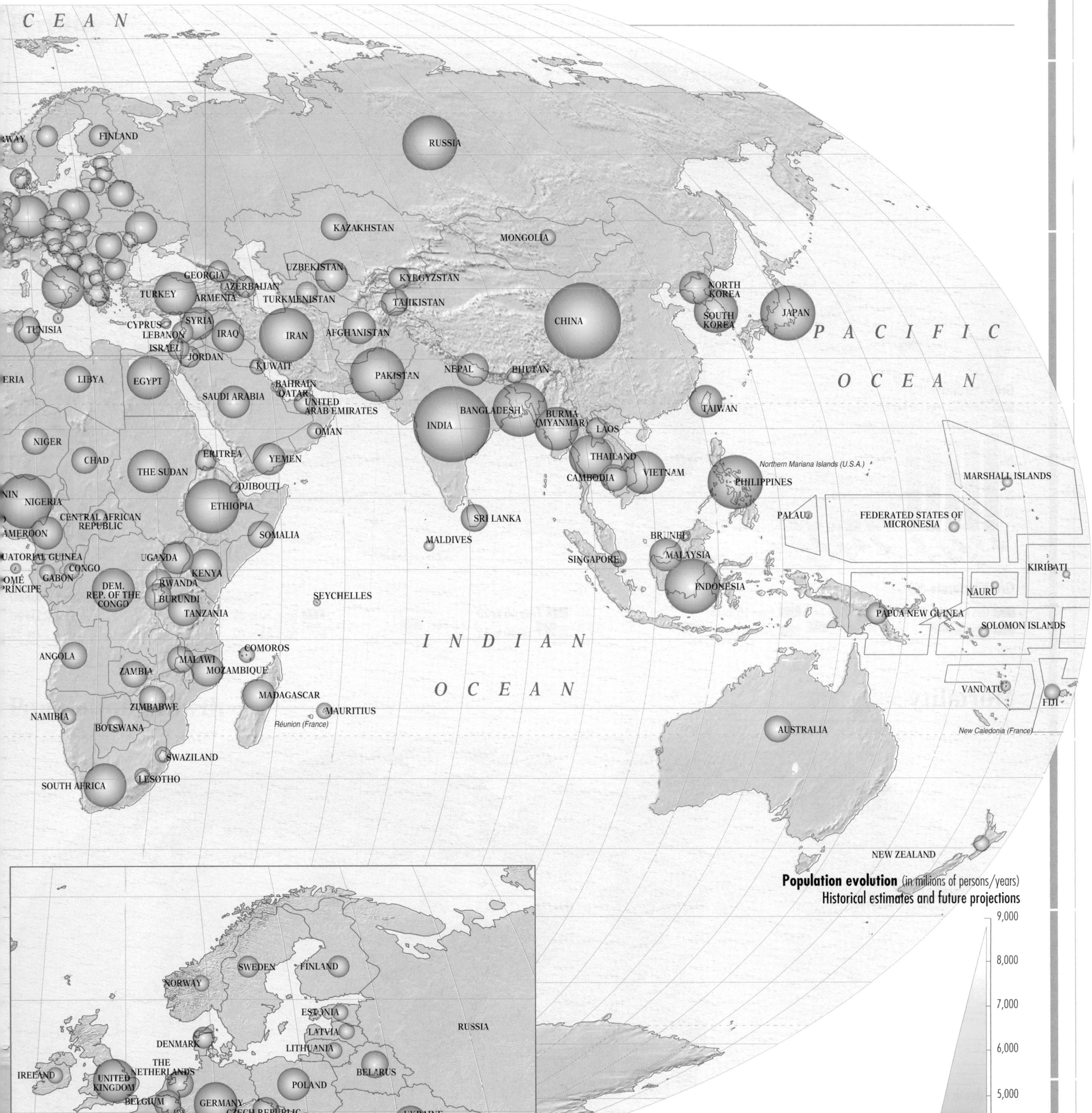

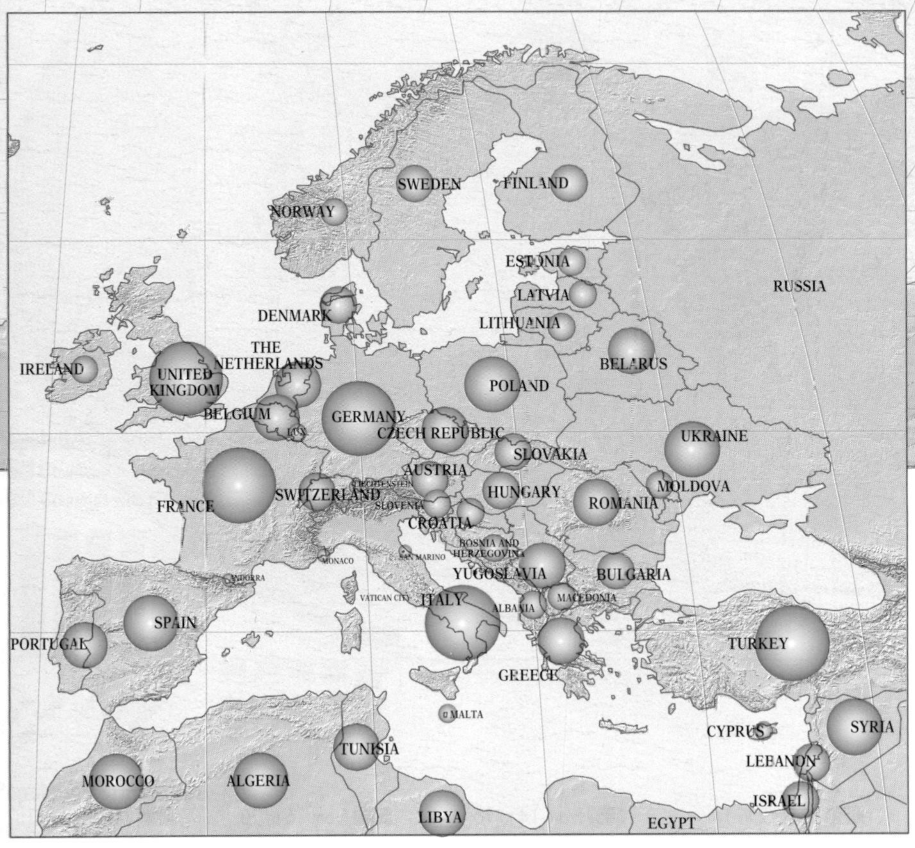

Population evolution (in millions of persons/years)
Historical estimates and future projections

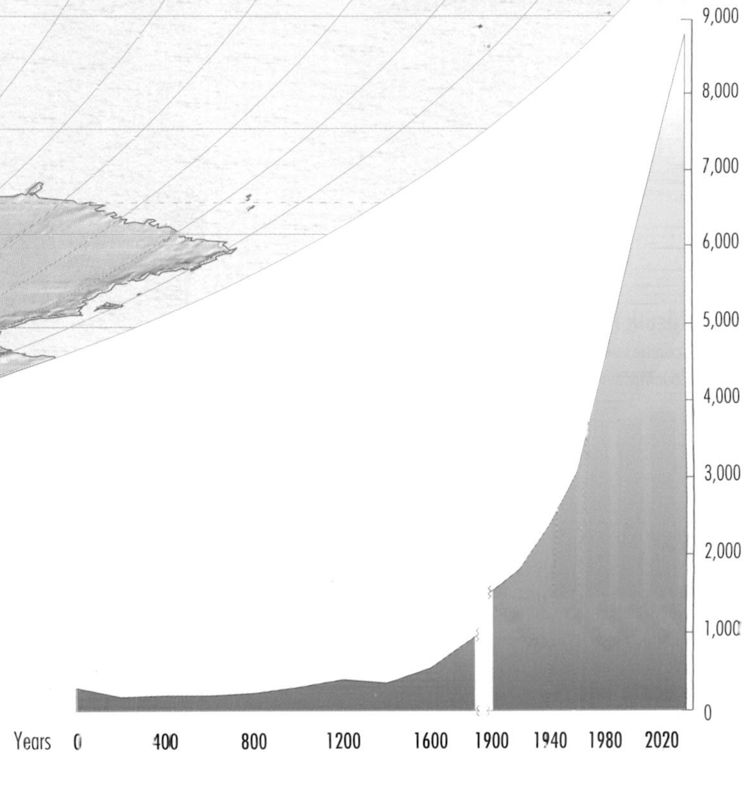

Population

Population distribution

Population density by country

Population density (persons per sq km)

- Fewer than 5
- From 5 to 10
- From 10 to 15
- From 15 to 25
- From 25 to 35
- From 35 to 50
- From 50 to 75
- From 75 to 100
- From 100 to 150
- From 150 to 200
- From 200 to 300
- From 300 to 500
- More than 500

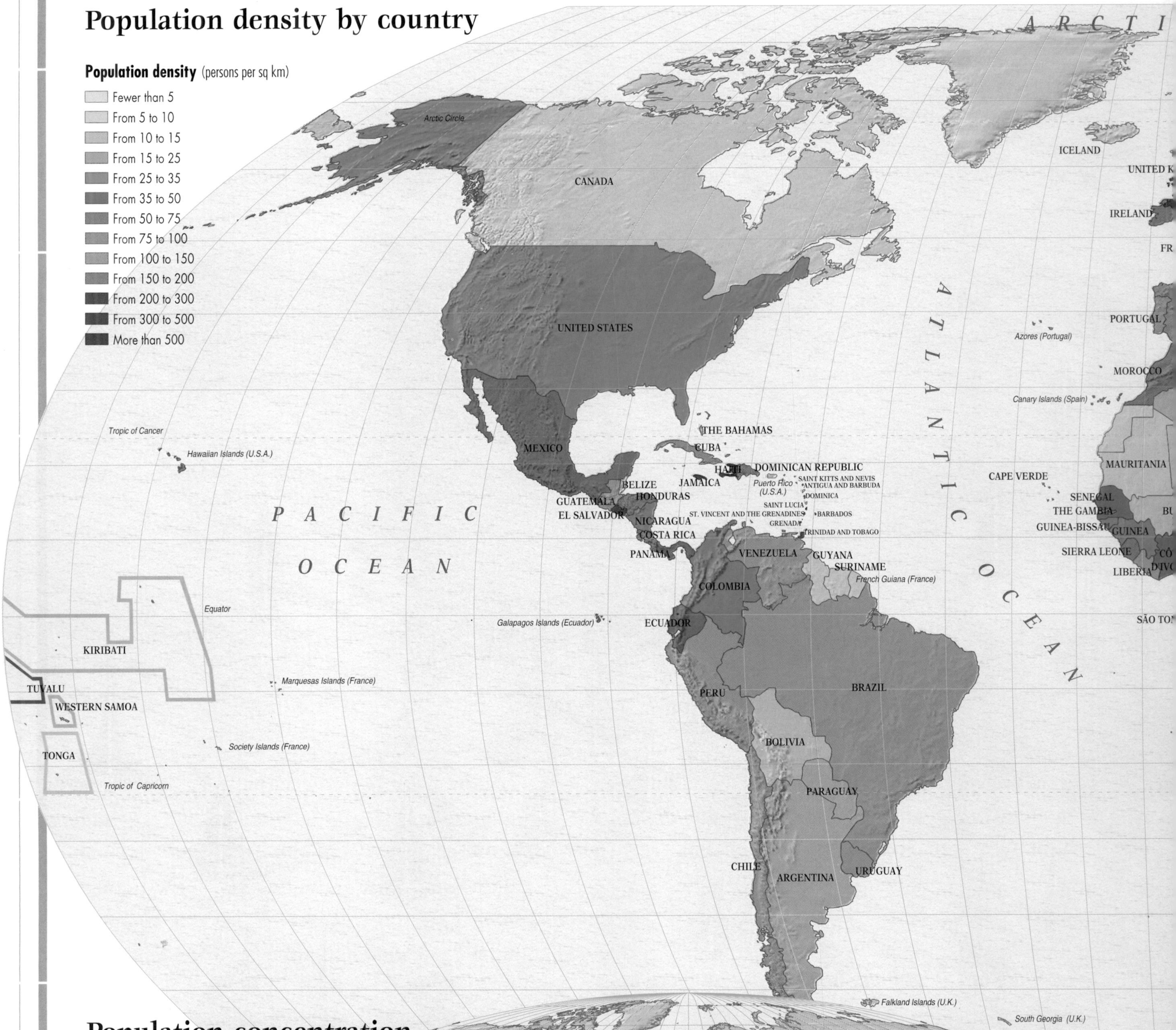

Population concentration

Most populated cities

- City with over 100,000 inhabitants

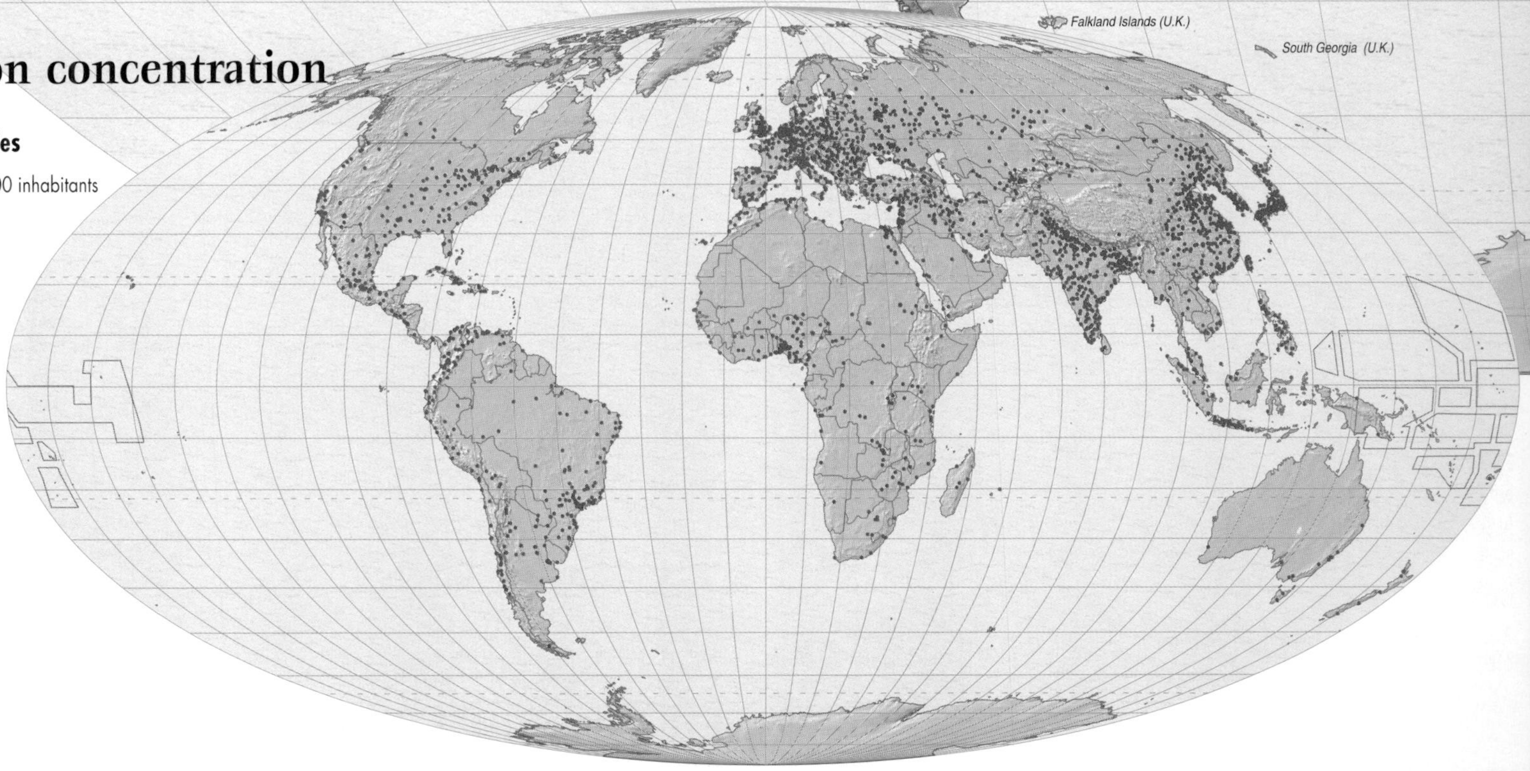

OCEAN
SWEDEN
FINLAND
ESTONIA
LATVIA
LITHUANIA
RUSSIA
POLAND
BELARUS
GERMANY
CZECH REPUBLIC
SLOVAKIA
UKRAINE
AUSTRIA
HUNGARY
MOLDOVA
SLOVENIA
CROATIA
BOSNIA AND HERZEGOVINA
ROMANIA
YUGOSLAVIA
BULGARIA
MACEDONIA
ALBANIA
ITALY
GREECE
GEORGIA
AZERBAIJAN
ARMENIA
TURKEY
KAZAKHSTAN
MONGOLIA
UZBEKISTAN
KYRGYZSTAN
TURKMENISTAN
TAJIKISTAN
NORTH KOREA
SOUTH KOREA
JAPAN
TUNISIA
MALTA
CYPRUS
SYRIA
LEBANON
ISRAEL
IRAQ
IRAN
AFGHANISTAN
CHINA
PACIFIC
OCEAN
JORDAN
KUWAIT
PAKISTAN
NEPAL
BHUTAN
LIBYA
EGYPT
BAHRAIN
QATAR
UNITED ARAB EMIRATES
BANGLADESH
TAIWAN
SAUDI ARABIA
INDIA
BURMA (MYANMAR)
LAOS
OMAN
NIGER
CHAD
ERITREA
YEMEN
THAILAND
Northern Mariana Islands (U.S.A)
THE SUDAN
CAMBODIA
DJIBOUTI
VIETNAM
PHILIPPINES
ETHIOPIA
CENTRAL AFRICAN REPUBLIC
SRI LANKA
MARSHALL ISLANDS
PALAU
FEDERATED STATES OF MICRONESIA
CAMEROON
SOMALIA
BRUNEI
MALDIVES
MALAYSIA
UGANDA
CONGO
KENYA
SINGAPORE
GABON
DEM. REP. OF THE CONGO
RWANDA
BURUNDI
INDONESIA
PAPUA NEW GUINEA
NAURU
KIRIBATI
SEYCHELLES
TANZANIA
SOLOMON ISLANDS
COMOROS
INDIAN
OCEAN
ANGOLA
MALAWI
ZAMBIA
MOZAMBIQUE
VANUATU
NAMIBIA
ZIMBABWE
MADAGASCAR
MAURITIUS
Réunion (Fr.)
New Caledonia (France)
FIJI
BOTSWANA
SWAZILAND
AUSTRALIA
SOUTH AFRICA
LESOTHO
NEW ZEALAND
Kerguelen Islands (France)
Population density by regions
Population density (persons per sq km)
Fewer than 1
From 1 to 2
From 2 to 5
From 5 to 10
From 10 to 15
From 15 to 20
From 20 to 30
From 30 to 40
From 40 to 50
From 50 to 75
From 75 to 100
From 100 to 150
From 150 to 250
More than 250

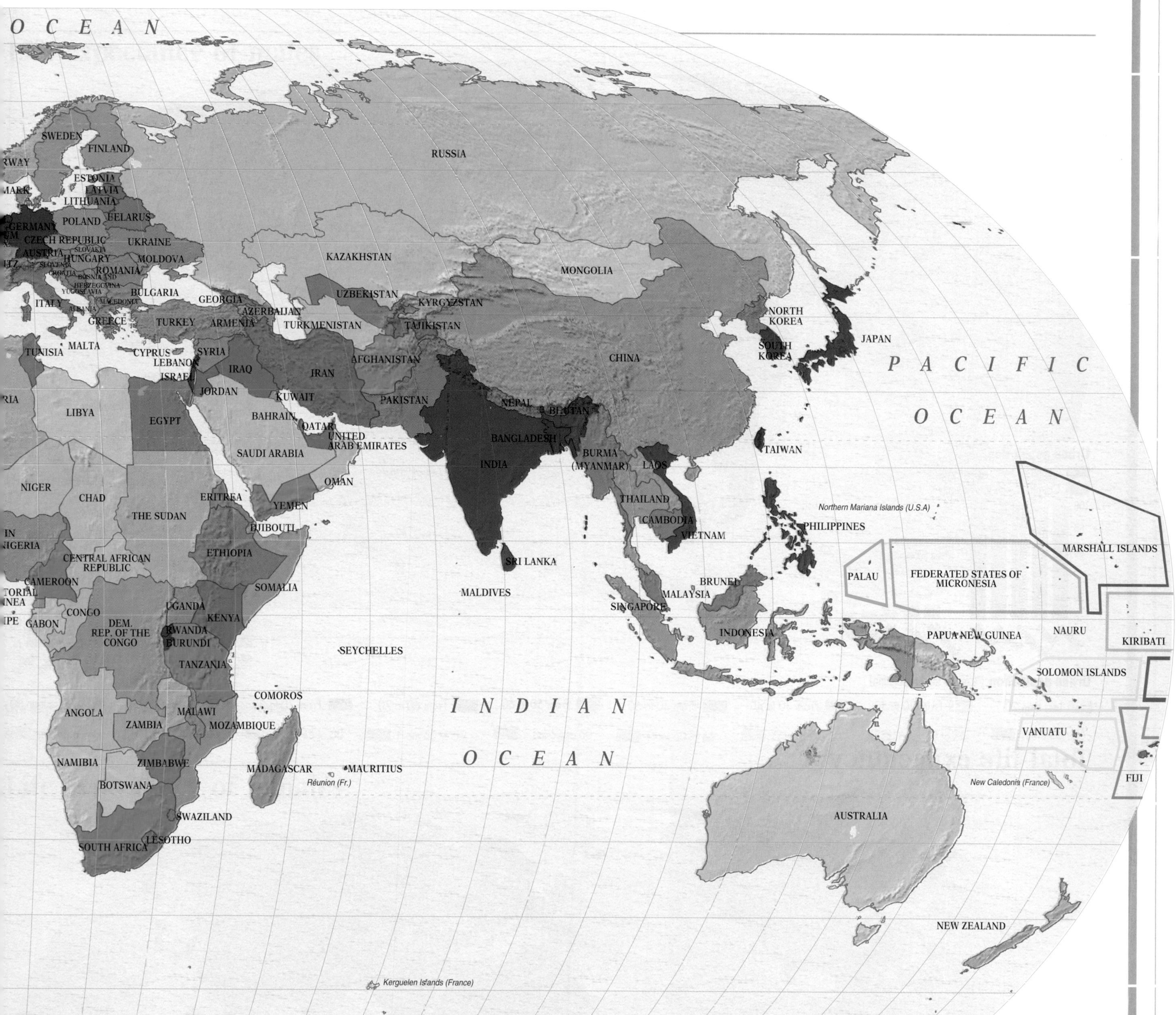

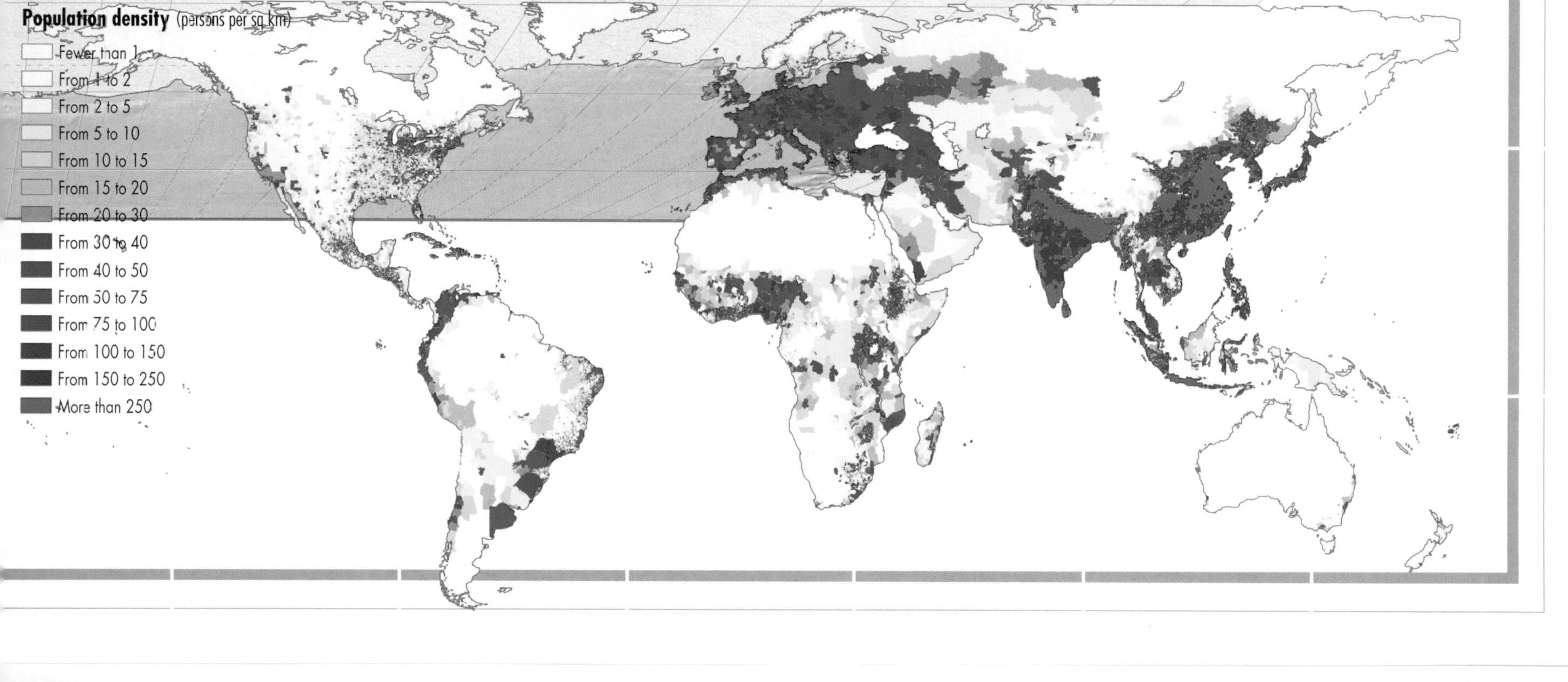

Population structure

Composition of the population by age groups (%)

Population under 15 years of age
Population from 15 to 64 years of age
Population over 64 years of age

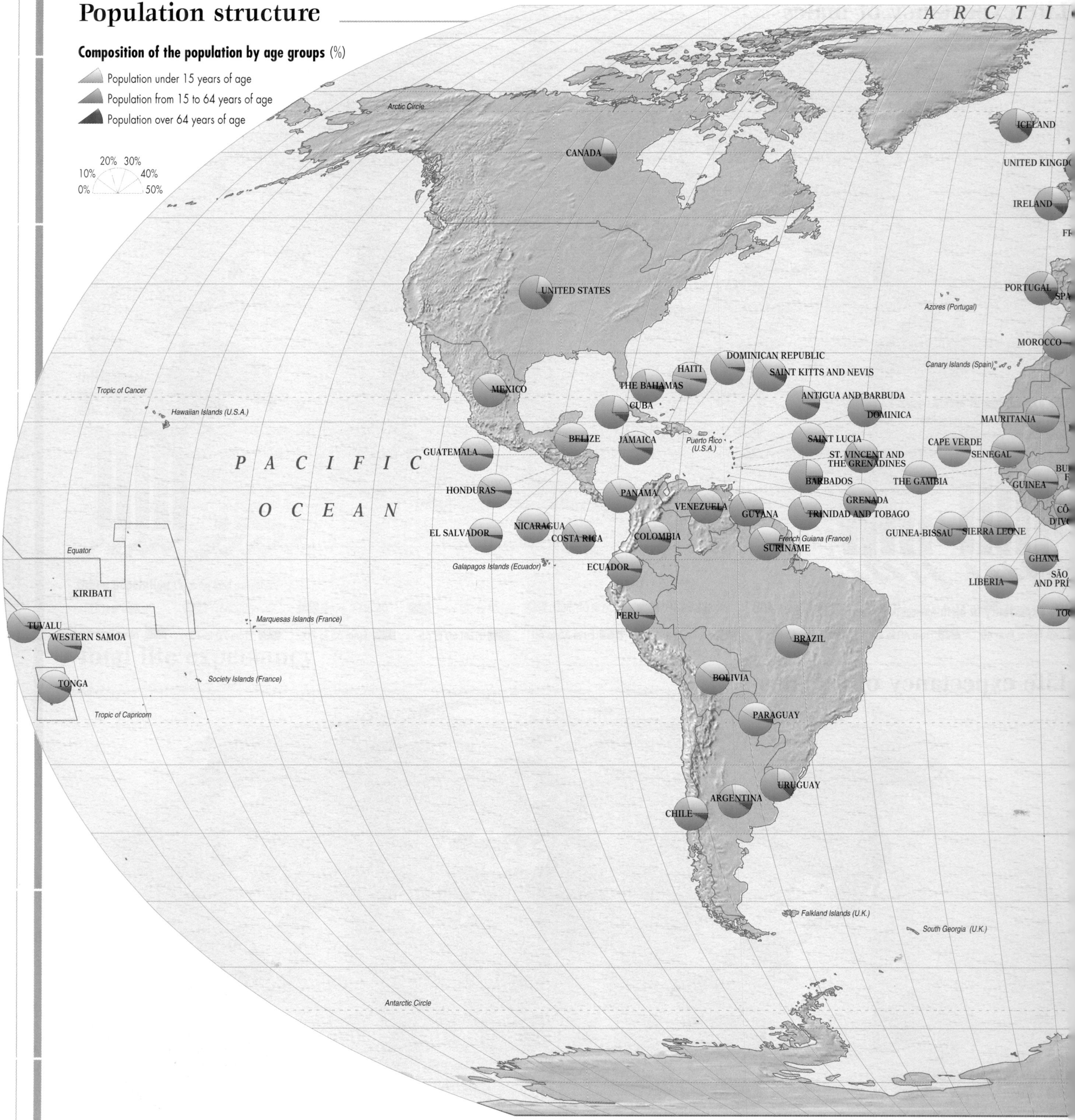

Age groups by continent (% of the total population)

	Population under 15 years of age (%)	Population from 15 to 64 years of age (%)	Population over 64 years of age (%)
World total	32%	61%	7%
Asia	32%	63%	5%
Africa	46%	51%	3%
Europe	19%	67%	14%
North America	22%	65%	13%
South and Central America	33%	62%	5%
Oceania	26%	64%	10%

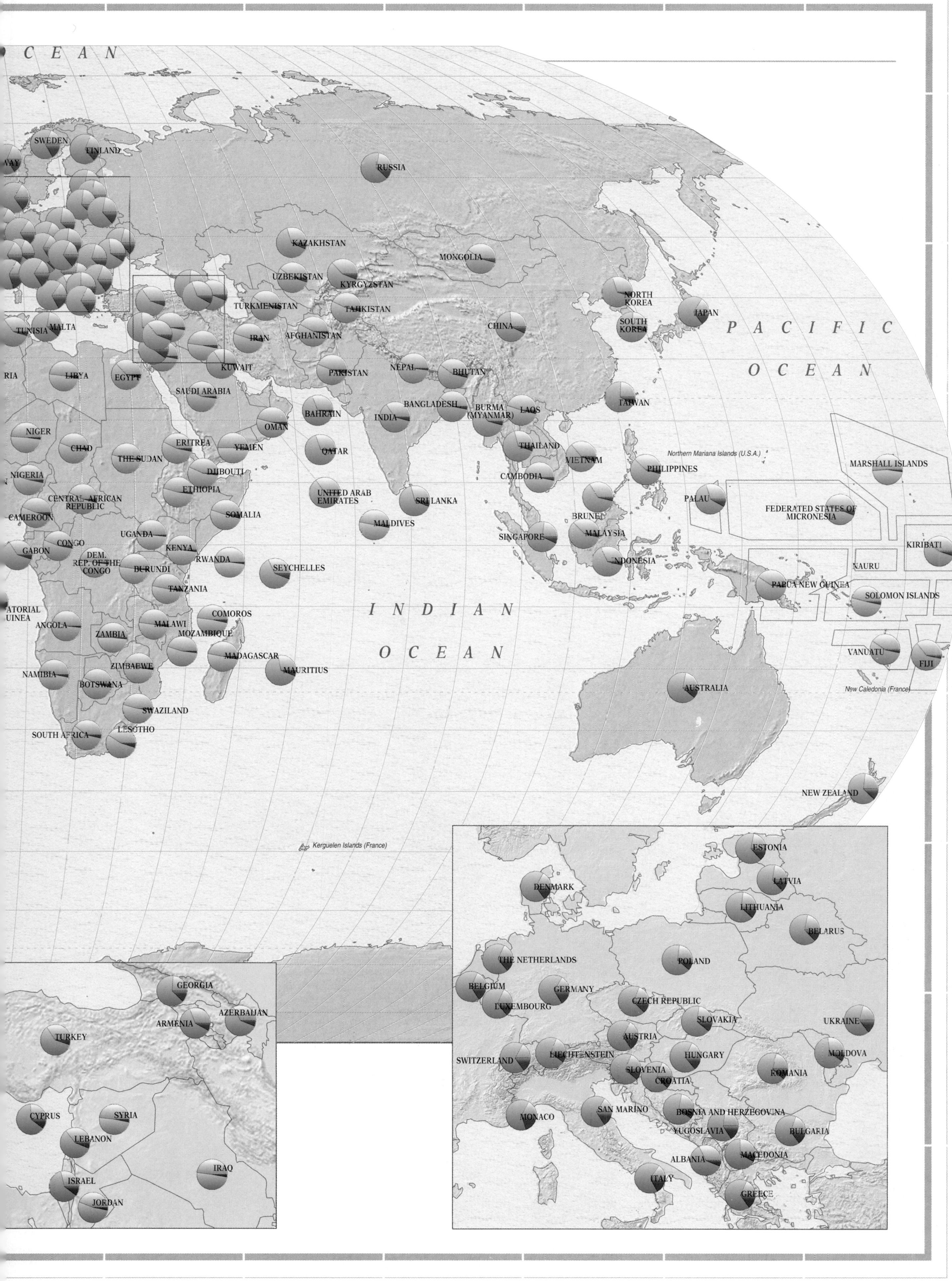
C E A N
SWEDEN
FINLAND
RUSSIA
KAZAKHSTAN
MONGOLIA
UZBEKISTAN
KYRGYZSTAN
TURKMENISTAN
TAJIKISTAN
NORTH KOREA
SOUTH KOREA
JAPAN
TUNISIA
MALTA
IRAN
AFGHANISTAN
CHINA
P A C I F I C
O C E A N
LIBYA
EGYPT
KUWAIT
PAKISTAN
NEPAL
BHUTAN
SAUDI ARABIA
TAIWAN
BANGLADESH
BURMA (MYANMAR)
LAOS
BAHRAIN
INDIA
OMAN
NIGER
CHAD
ERITREA
YEMEN
QATAR
THAILAND
VIETNAM
Northern Mariana Islands (U.S.A.)
MARSHALL ISLANDS
THE SUDAN
DJIBOUTI
CAMBODIA
PHILIPPINES
NIGERIA
ETHIOPIA
UNITED ARAB EMIRATES
SRI LANKA
PALAU
FEDERATED STATES OF MICRONESIA
CENTRAL AFRICAN REPUBLIC
CAMEROON
SOMALIA
MALDIVES
BRUNEI
MALAYSIA
SINGAPORE
UGANDA
CONGO
GABON
KENYA
DEM. REP. OF THE CONGO
RWANDA
BURUNDI
SEYCHELLES
INDONESIA
KIRIBATI
NAURU
TANZANIA
PAPUA NEW GUINEA
SOLOMON ISLANDS
I N D I A N
O C E A N
COMOROS
ANGOLA
ZAMBIA
MALAWI
MOZAMBIQUE
VANUATU
FIJI
MADAGASCAR
ZIMBABWE
MAURITIUS
NAMIBIA
BOTSWANA
AUSTRALIA
New Caledonia (France)
SWAZILAND
SOUTH AFRICA
LESOTHO
NEW ZEALAND
Kerguelen Islands (France)
ESTONIA
LATVIA
DENMARK
LITHUANIA
BELARUS
THE NETHERLANDS
POLAND
BELGIUM
GERMANY
LUXEMBOURG
CZECH REPUBLIC
UKRAINE
SLOVAKIA
AUSTRIA
MOLDOVA
SWITZERLAND
LIECHTENSTEIN
HUNGARY
SLOVENIA
ROMANIA
CROATIA
MONACO
SAN MARINO
BOSNIA AND HERZEGOVINA
YUGOSLAVIA
BULGARIA
ALBANIA
MACEDONIA
ITALY
GREECE
GEORGIA
AZERBAIJAN
ARMENIA
TURKEY
CYPRUS
SYRIA
LEBANON
IRAQ
ISRAEL
JORDAN

Social and economic indicators
Food intake and infant mortality

Consumption of calories

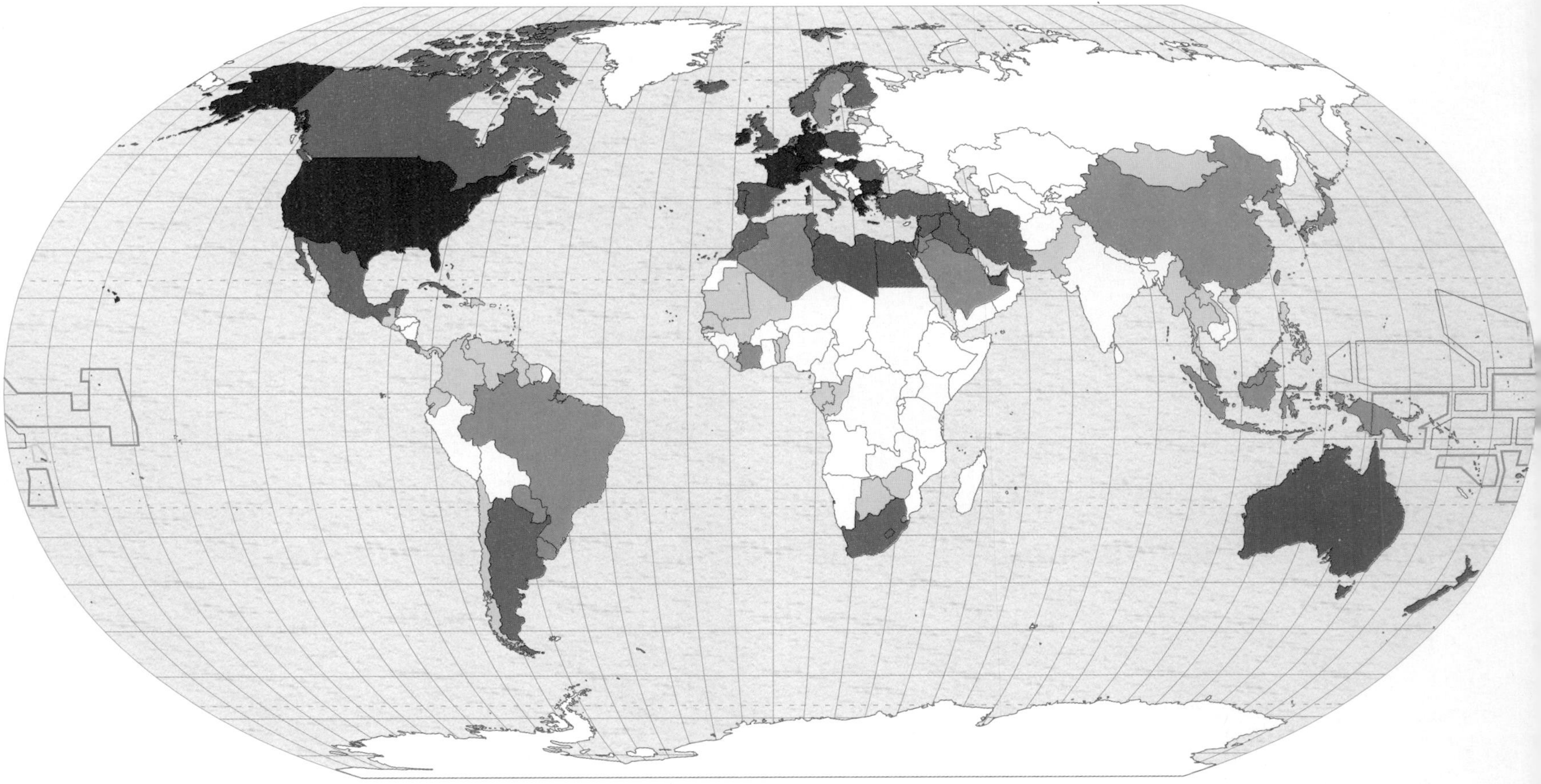

Caloric intake (per person per day)

- Fewer than 2,000
- From 2,000 to 2,250
- From 2,250 to 2,500
- From 2,500 to 3,000
- From 3,000 to 3,250
- From 3,250 to 3,500
- More than 3,500

Food aid

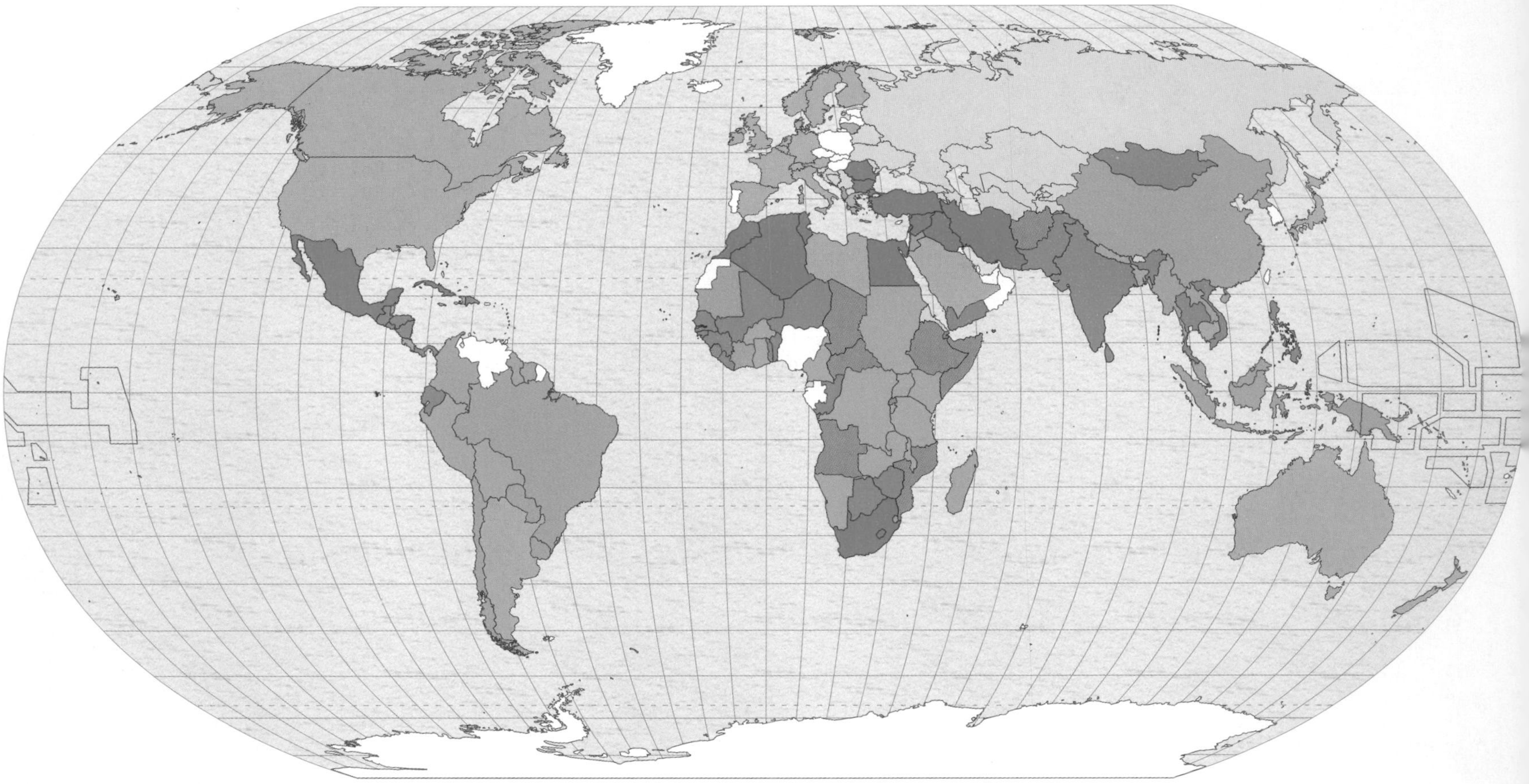

Food received (in tons)

- Fewer than 1,000
- From 1,000 to 2,000
- From 2,000 to 2,300
- From 2,300 to 2,500
- From 2,500 to 3,000
- More than 3,000
- Donor countrie

Production of food resources

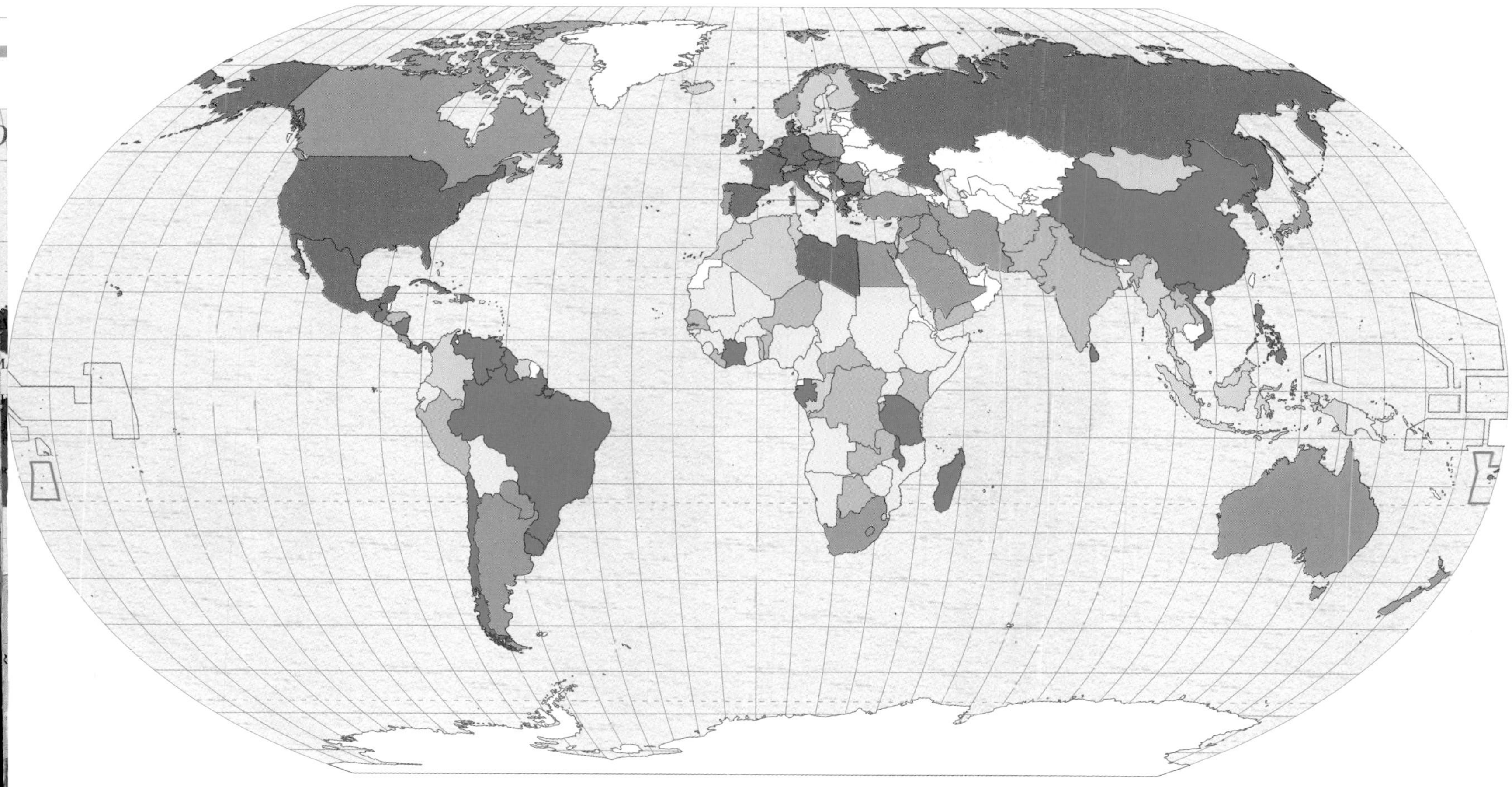

Production of food resources (percentage)

Less than 50 | From 90 to 100 | From 100 to 110 | From 110 tc 120 | From 120 to 130 | More than 130

Infant mortality rate

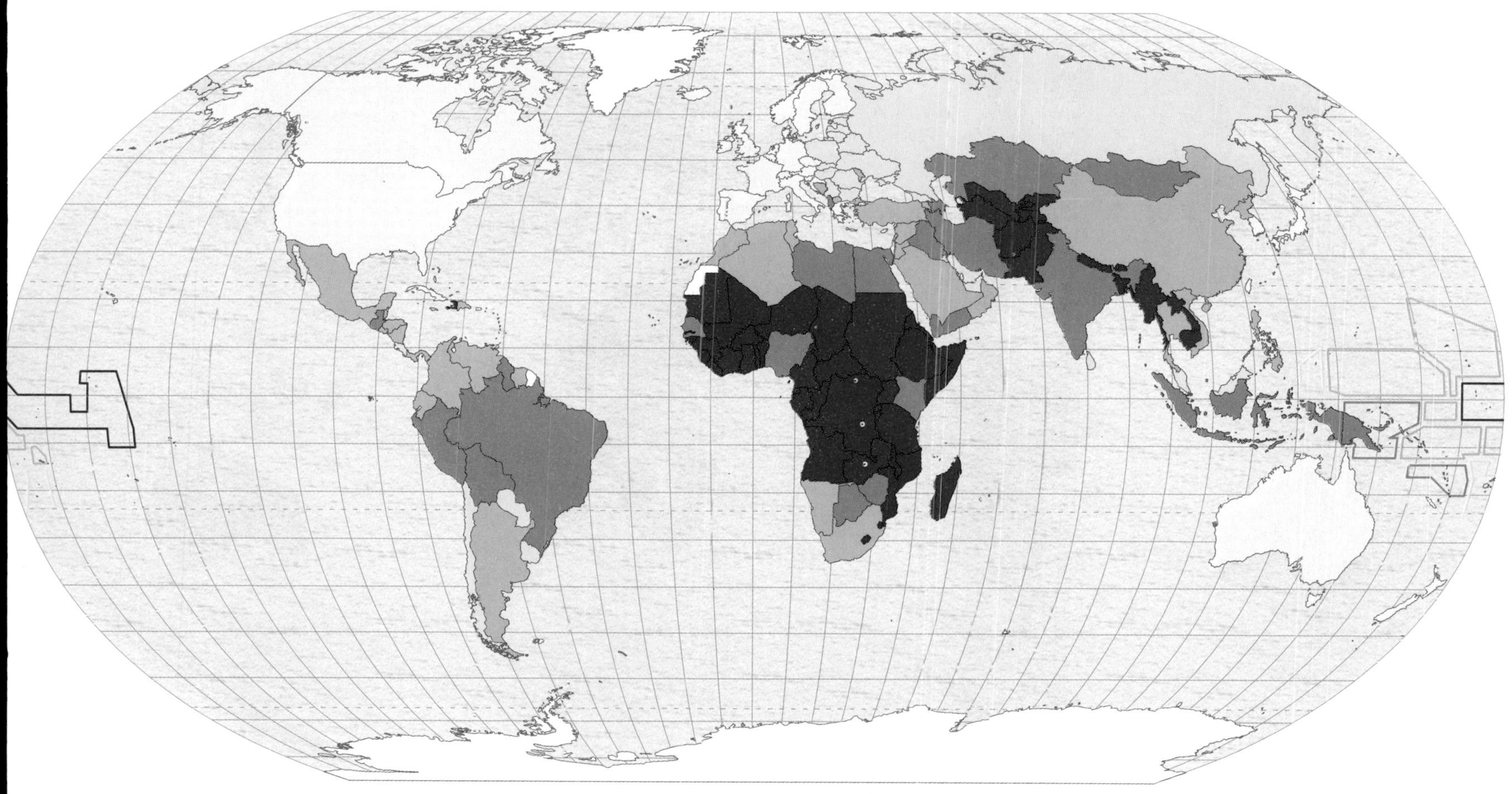

Number of infant deaths (per 1,000 live births)

Fewer than 10 | From 10 to 25 | From 25 to 50 | From 50 to 75 | From 75 to 100 | More than 100

Social and economic indicators

Macro-economic indicators

Inflation

Inflation rate (percentage)

- Less than 1
- From 1 to 5
- From 5 to 10
- From 10 to 25
- From 25 to 50
- From 50 to 100
- From 100 to 1,000
- More than 1,000

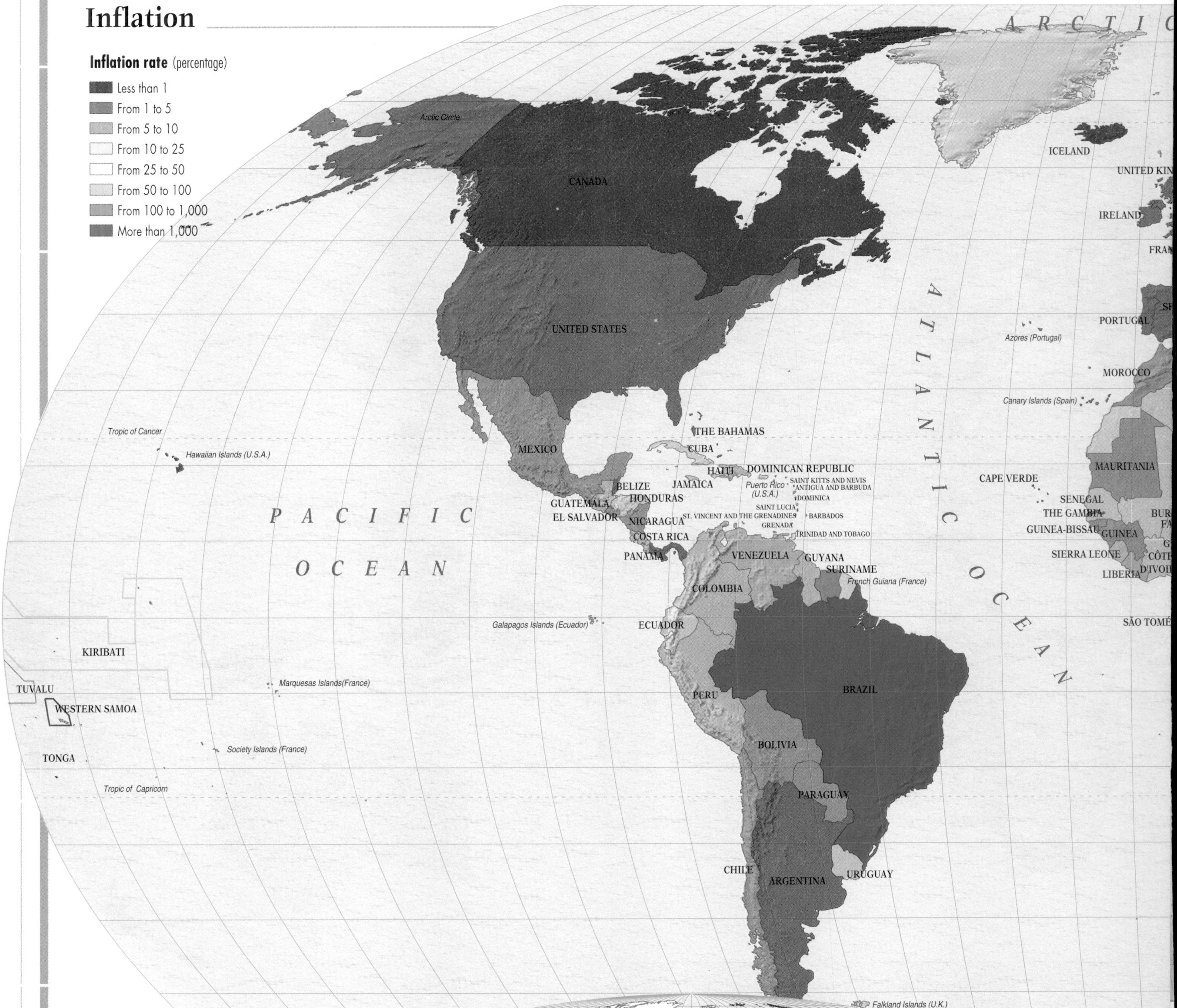

Economic growth

Economic growth rate (percentage)

- From -50 to -10
- From -10 to 0
- From 0 to 2
- From 2 to 3
- From 3 to 4
- From 4 to 5
- From 5 to 6
- From 6 to 7
- From 7 to 10
- More than 10

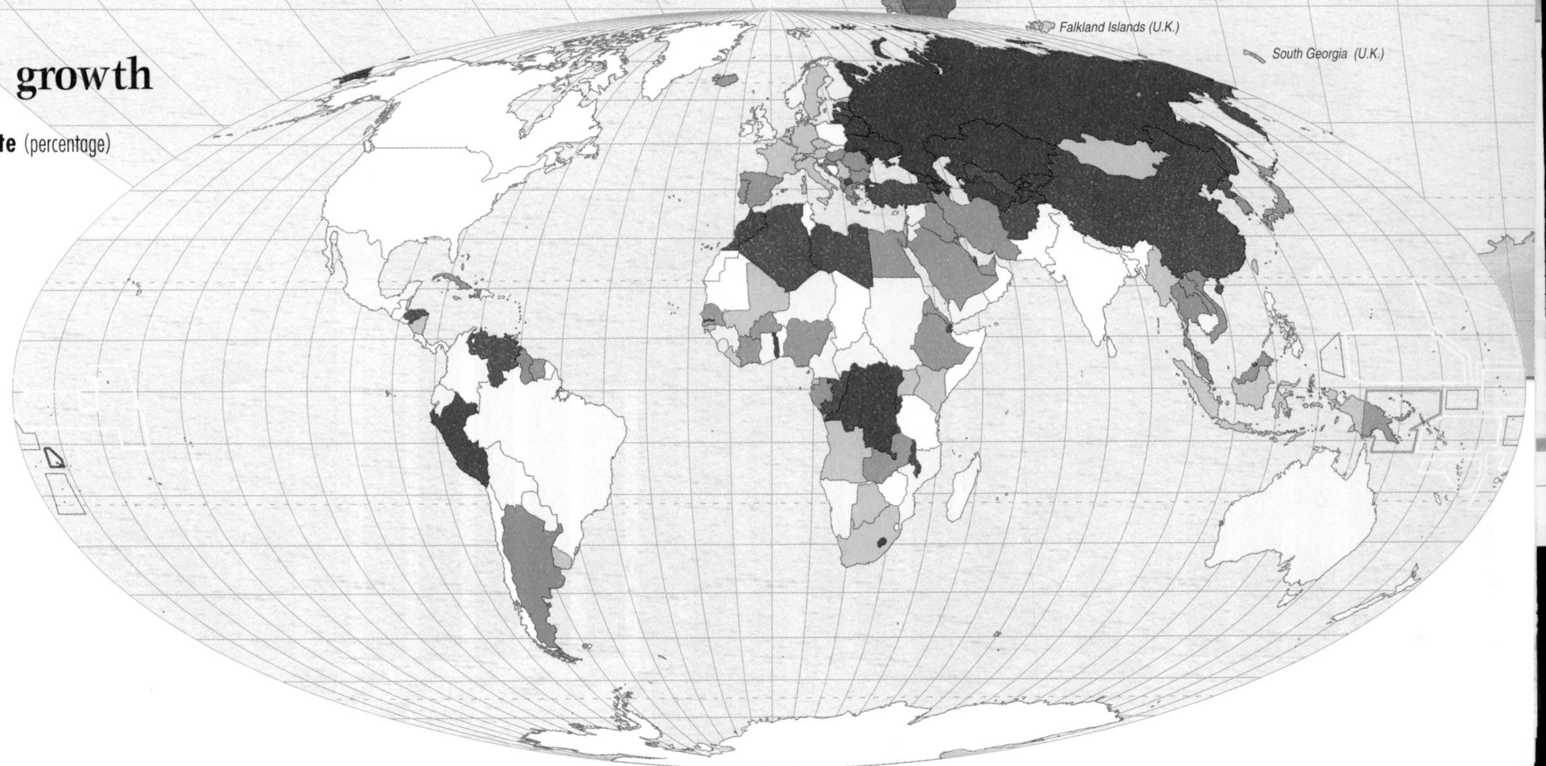

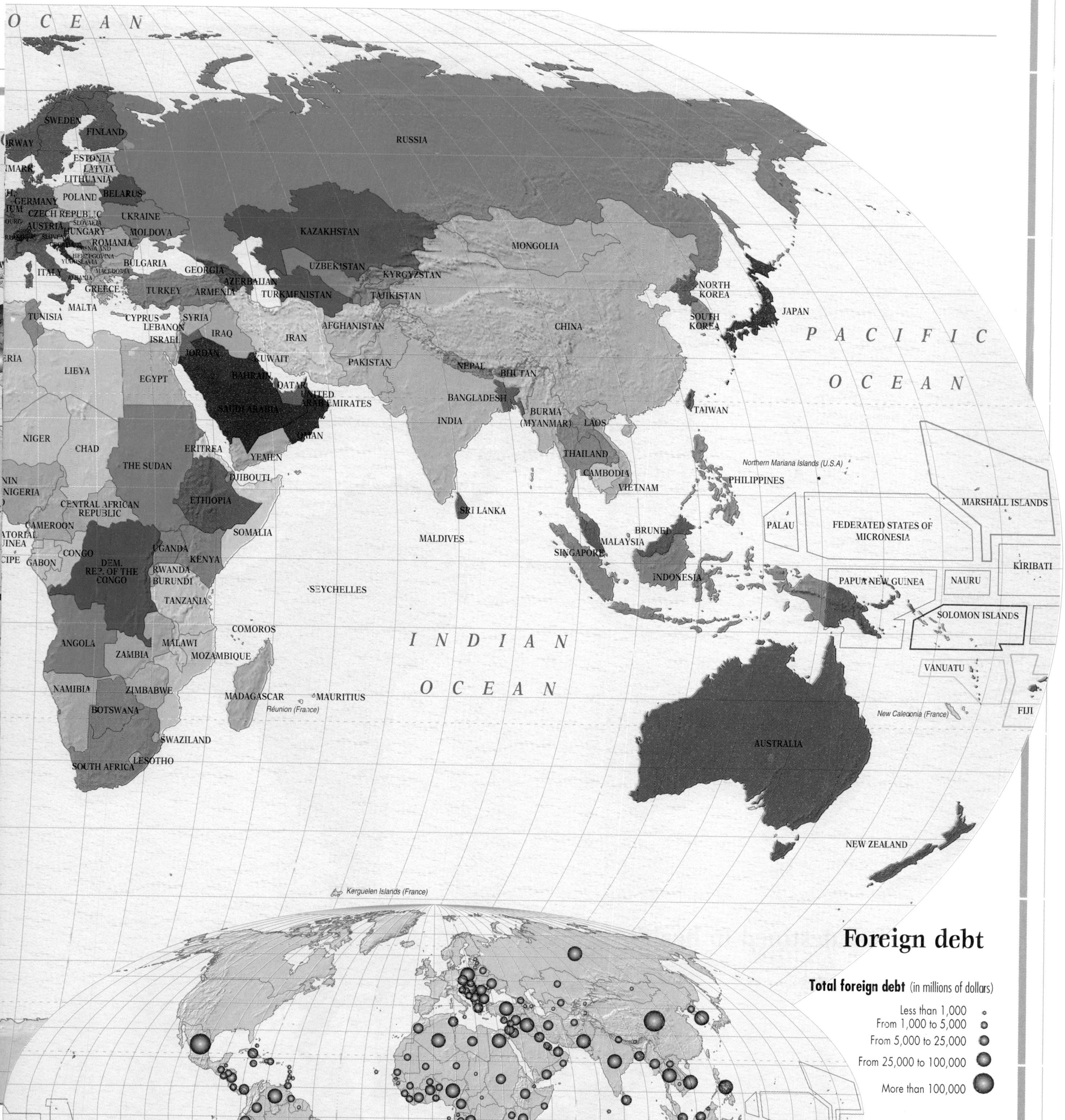

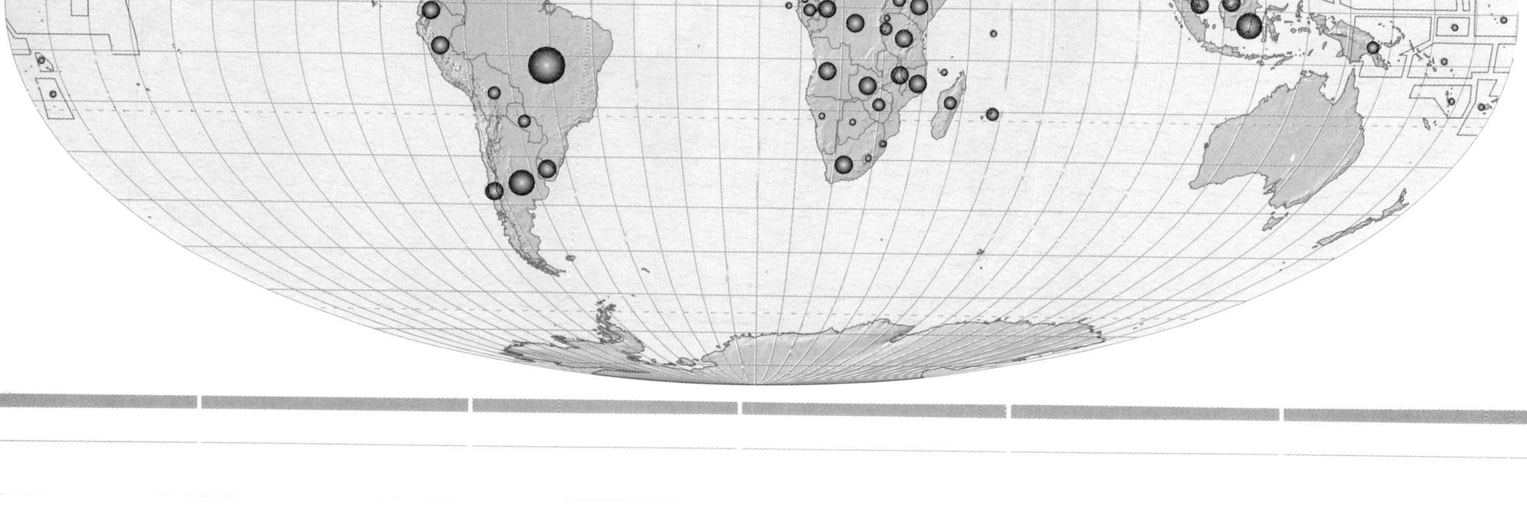

Foreign debt

Total foreign debt (in millions of dollars)

- Less than 1,000
- From 1,000 to 5,000
- From 5,000 to 25,000
- From 25,000 to 100,000
- More than 100,000

BASIC ECONOMIC ACTIVITIES

Basic economic activities
Agricultural land surface area

Cultivated land surface area

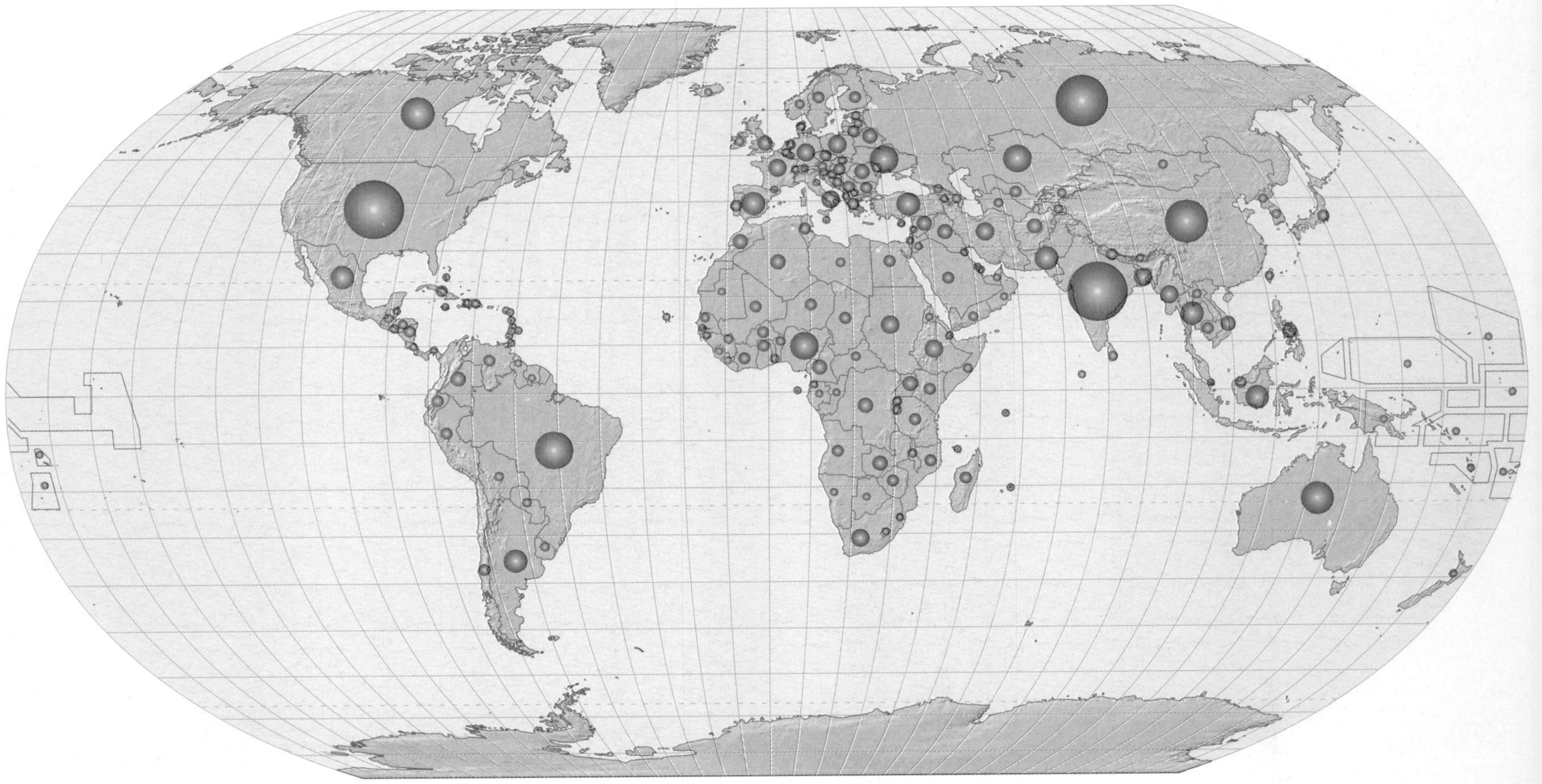

Total cultivated land surface area (in sq km)

- Less than 7,500
- From 7,500 to 25,000
- From 25,000 to 50,000
- From 50,000 to 100,000
- From 100,000 to 200,000
- From 200,000 to 300,00
- From 1,500,000 to 2,000,000
- From 1,000,000 to 1,500,000
- From 750,000 to 1,000,000
- From 500,000 to 750,000
- From 400,000 to 500,000
- From 300,000 to 400,0C

Ratio of cultivated surface area to total surface area

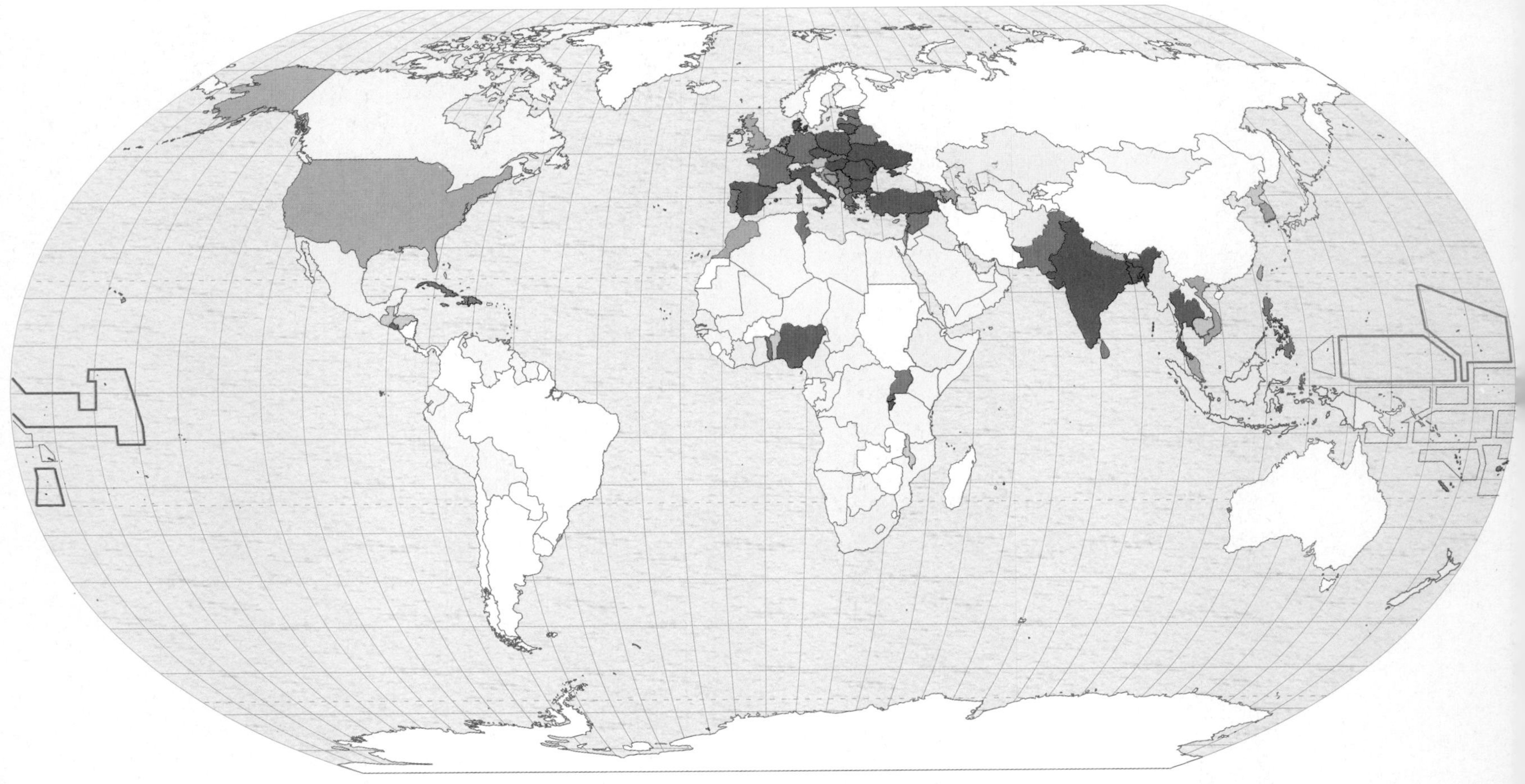

Cultivated area in percentages of the total surface area

- Less than 5
- From 5 to 10
- From 10 to 15
- From 15 to 20
- From 20 to 25
- From 25 to 35
- From 35 to 50
- From 50 to

Irrigated land surface area

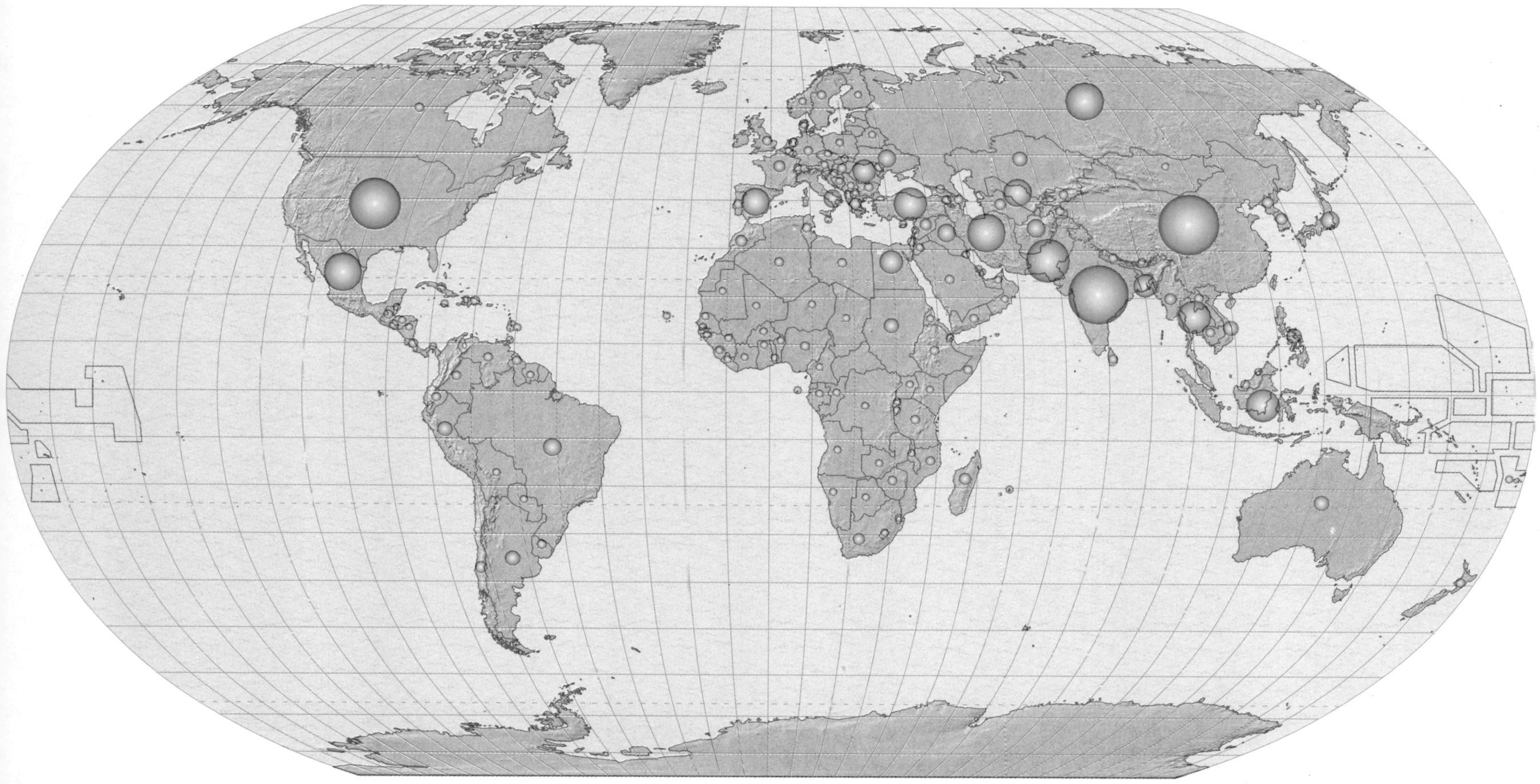

Total irrigated land surface area (in sq km)

- Less than 1,000
- From 1,000 to 10,000
- From 10,000 to 15,000
- From 15,000 to 25,000
- From 25,000 to 30,000
- From 30,000 to 35,000
- From 400,000 to 500,000
- From 200,000 to 400,000
- From 100,000 to 200,00
- From 50,000 to 100,000
- From 40,000 to 50,000
- From 35,000 to 40,000

Ratio of irrigated surface area to total cultivated surface area

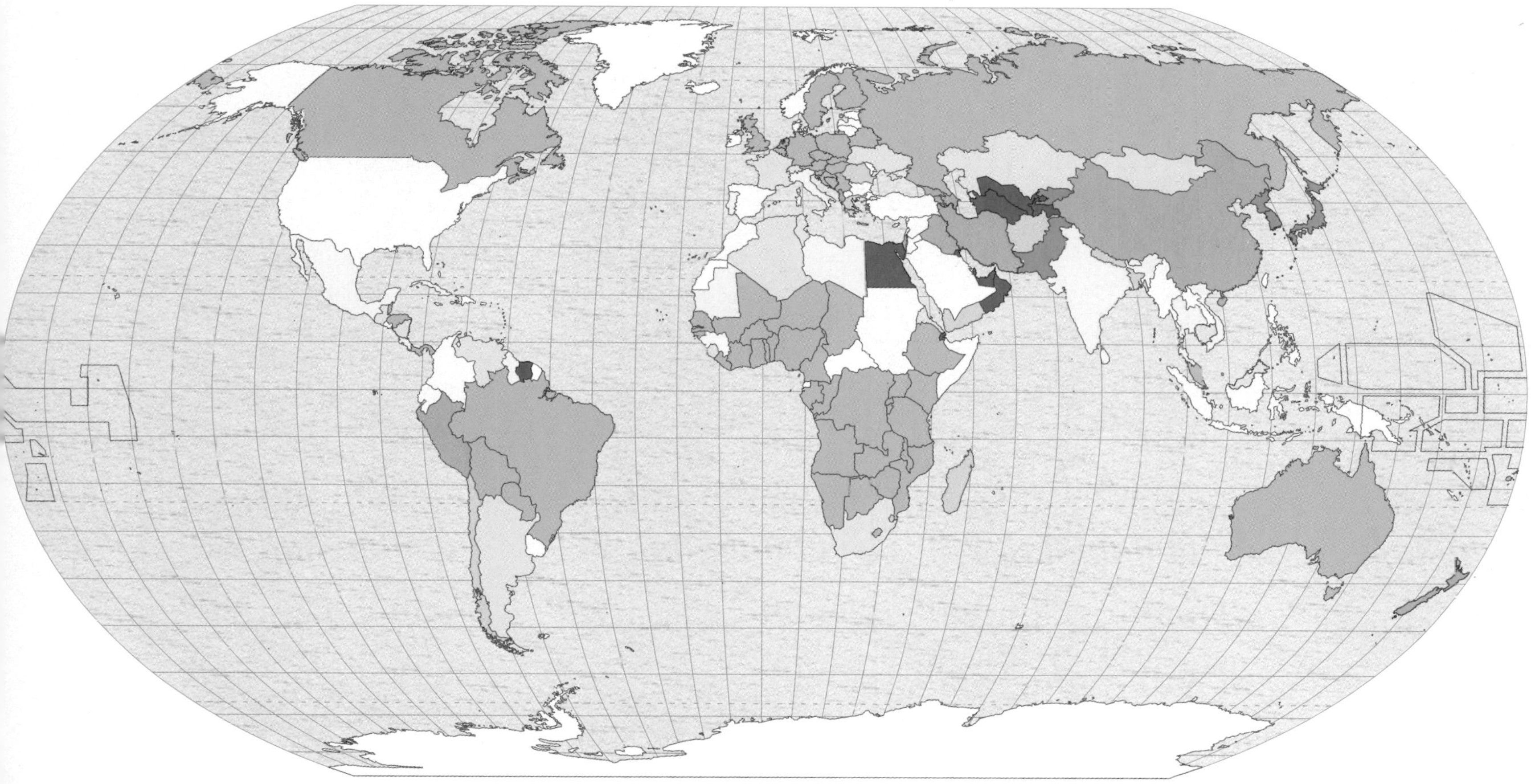

Ratio of irrigated surface area to total cultivated surface area

- Less than 5
- From 5 to 10
- From 10 to 20
- From 20 to 30
- From 30 to 40
- From 40 to 60
- From 60 to 80
- From 80 to 100

Basic economic activities

Agriculture

Harvesters/Threshers

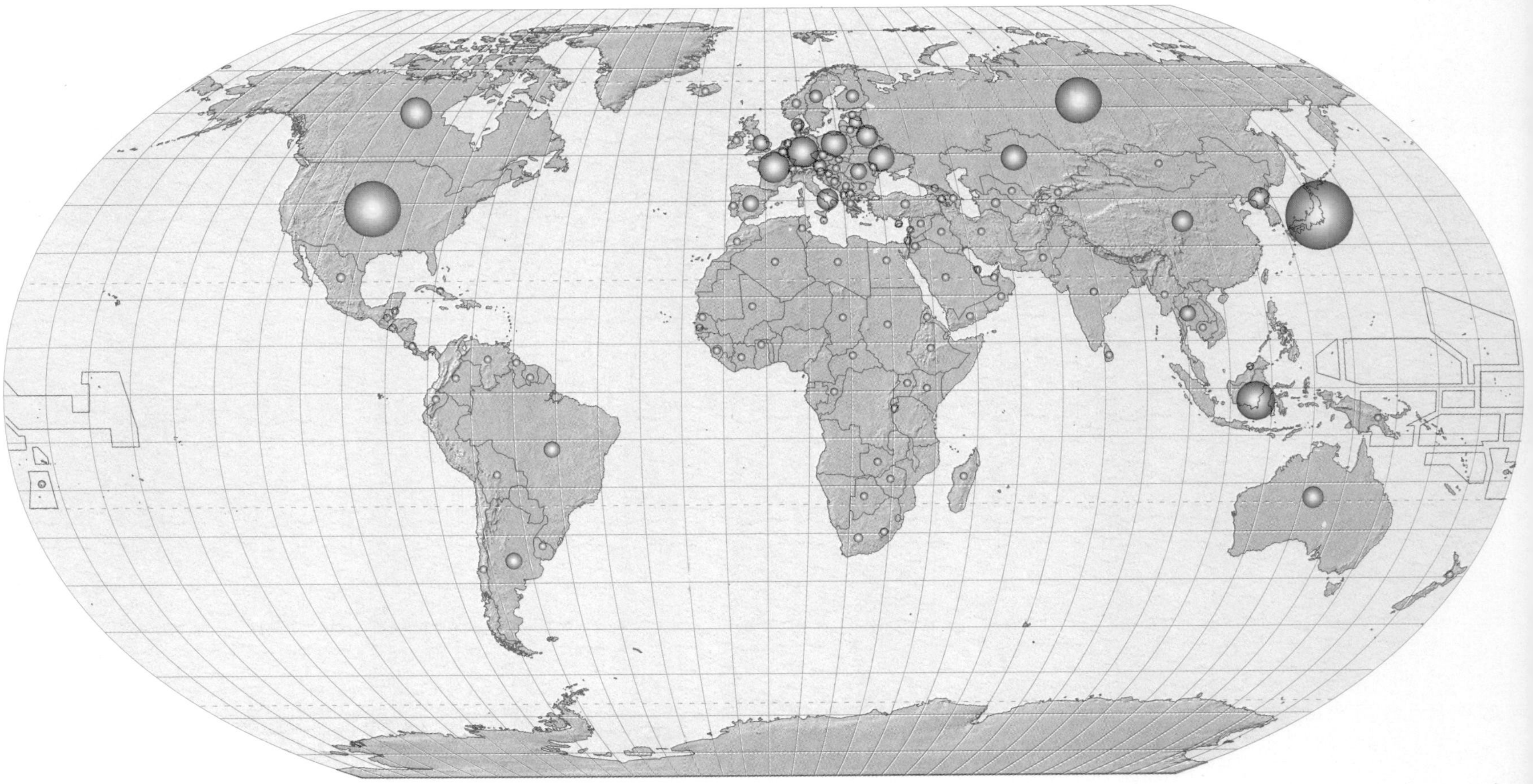

Harvesters/Threshers (in thousands of units)

- Fewer than 10
- From 10 to 20
- From 20 to 40
- From 40 to 50
- From 50 to 75
- From 75 to 1
- From 1,000 to 1,250
- From 500 to 1,000
- From 300 to 500
- From 200 to 300
- From 100 to 200

Tractors

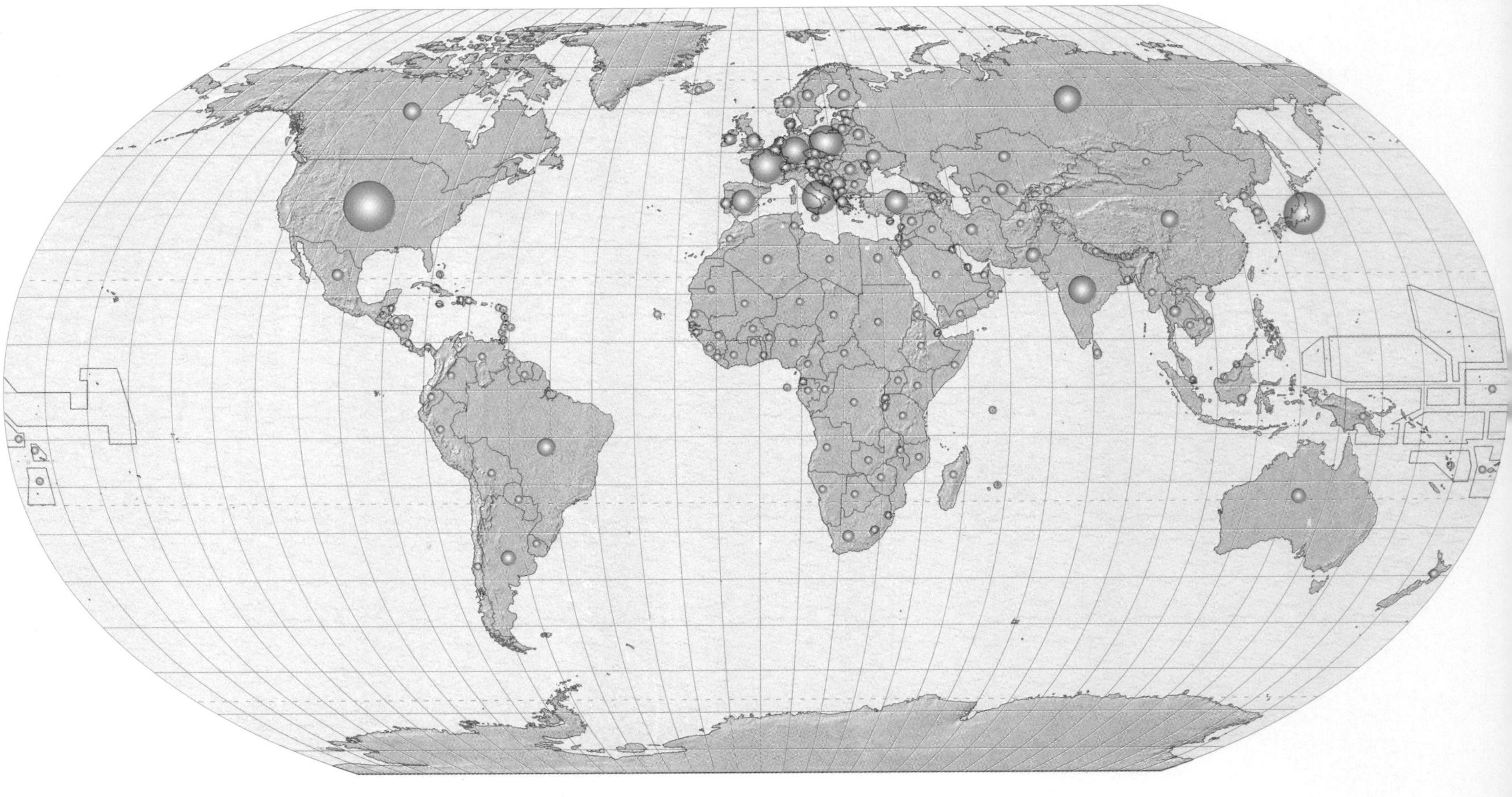

Tractors (in thousands of units)

- Fewer than 50
- From 50 to 100
- From 100 to 250
- From 250 to 500
- From 500 to 75
- From 2,500 to 5,000
- From 1,500 to 2,500
- From 1,300 to 1,500
- From 1,000 to 1,300
- From 750 to 1,

Mechanical milking machines

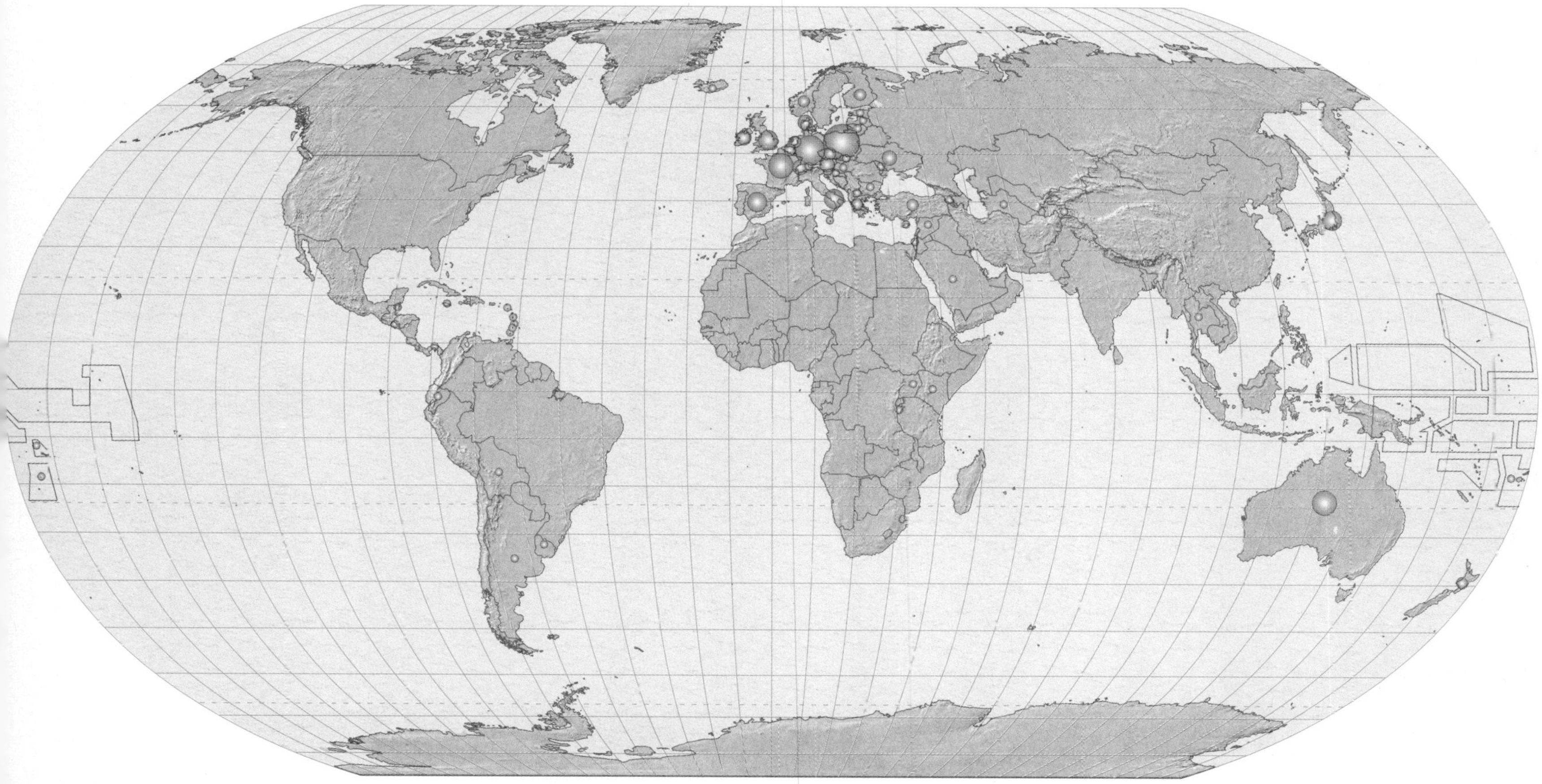

Mechanical milking machines (in thousands of units)

Fewer than 10 · From 10 to 50 · From 50 to 100 · From 100 to 175 · From 175 to 200 · From 200 to 250 · From 250 to 600

NOTE: Data about mechanical milking machines for Canada and United States is not available.

Pesticides

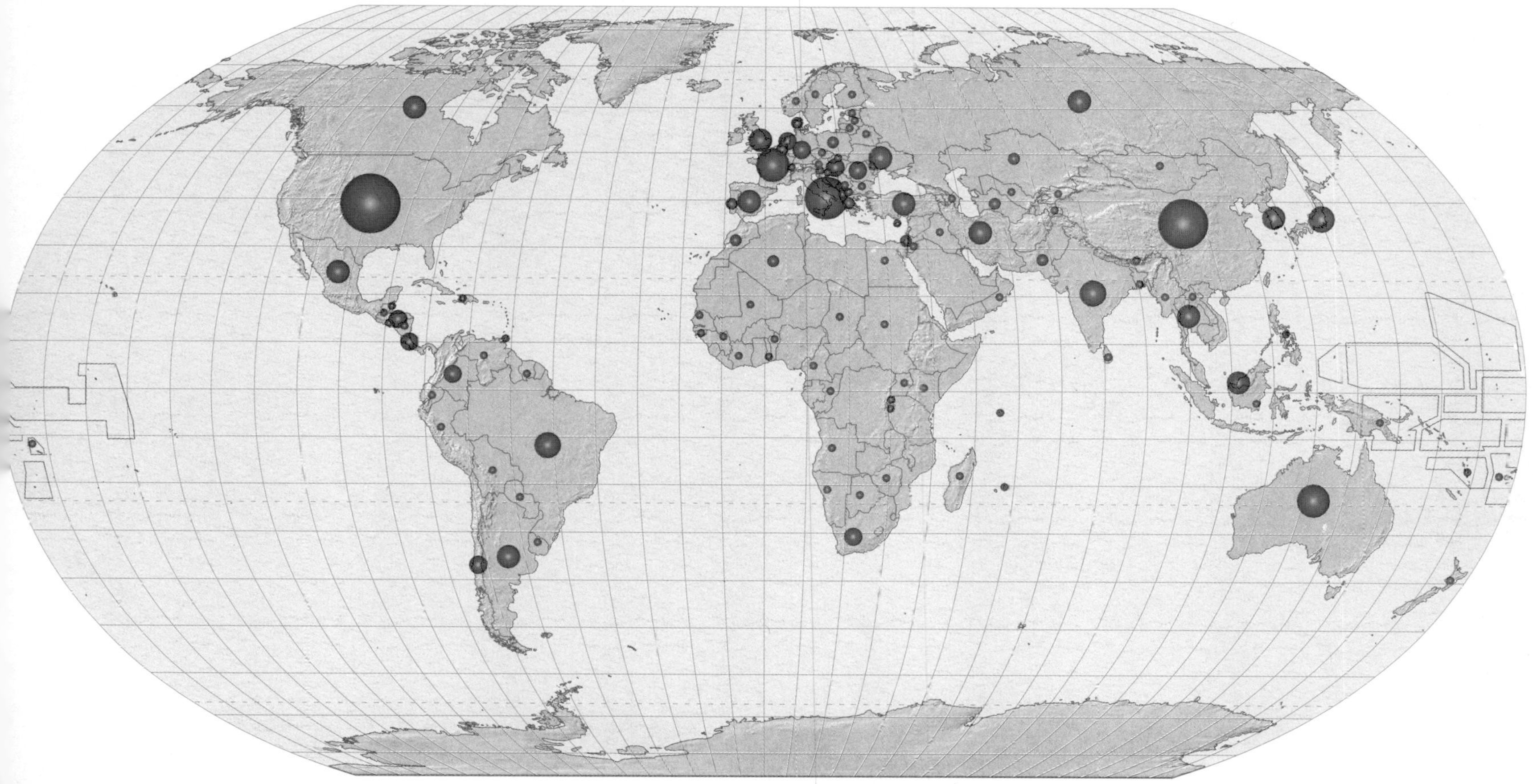

Pesticides (in thousands of tons of active ingredients)

Fewer than 5 · From 5 to 10 · From 10 to 25 · From 25 to 50 · From 50 to 100 · From 100 to 150 · From 150 to 200 · From 200 to 250 · From 250 to 400

Basic economic activities

Agriculture

Cereals

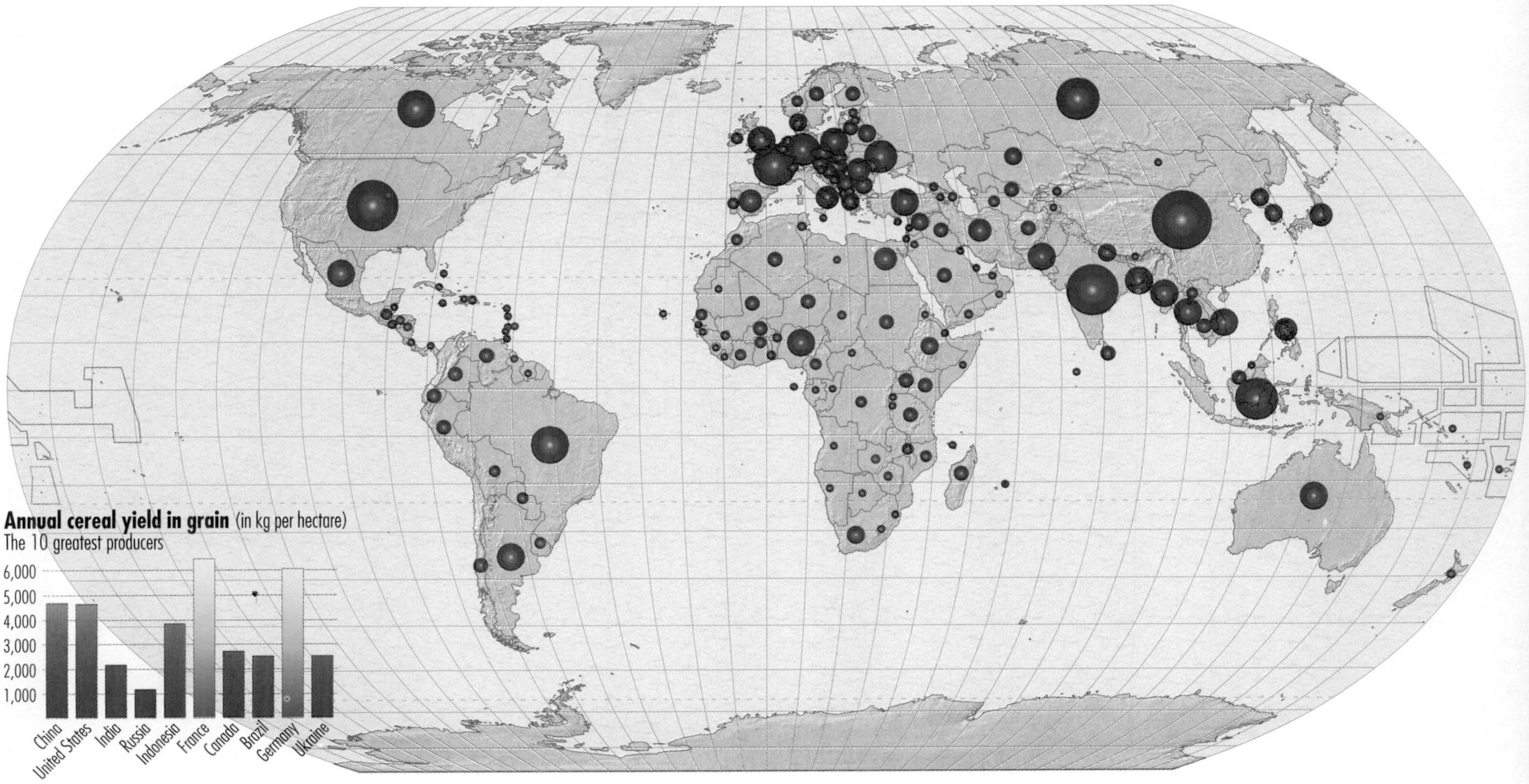

Cereals (in millions of tons)

- Less than 0,5
- From 0.5 to 1
- From 1 to 2
- From 2 to 5
- From 5 to 10
- From 10 to 2
- From 300 to 450
- From 75 to 300
- From 50 to 75
- From 40 to 50
- From 30 to 40
- From 20 to

Wheat

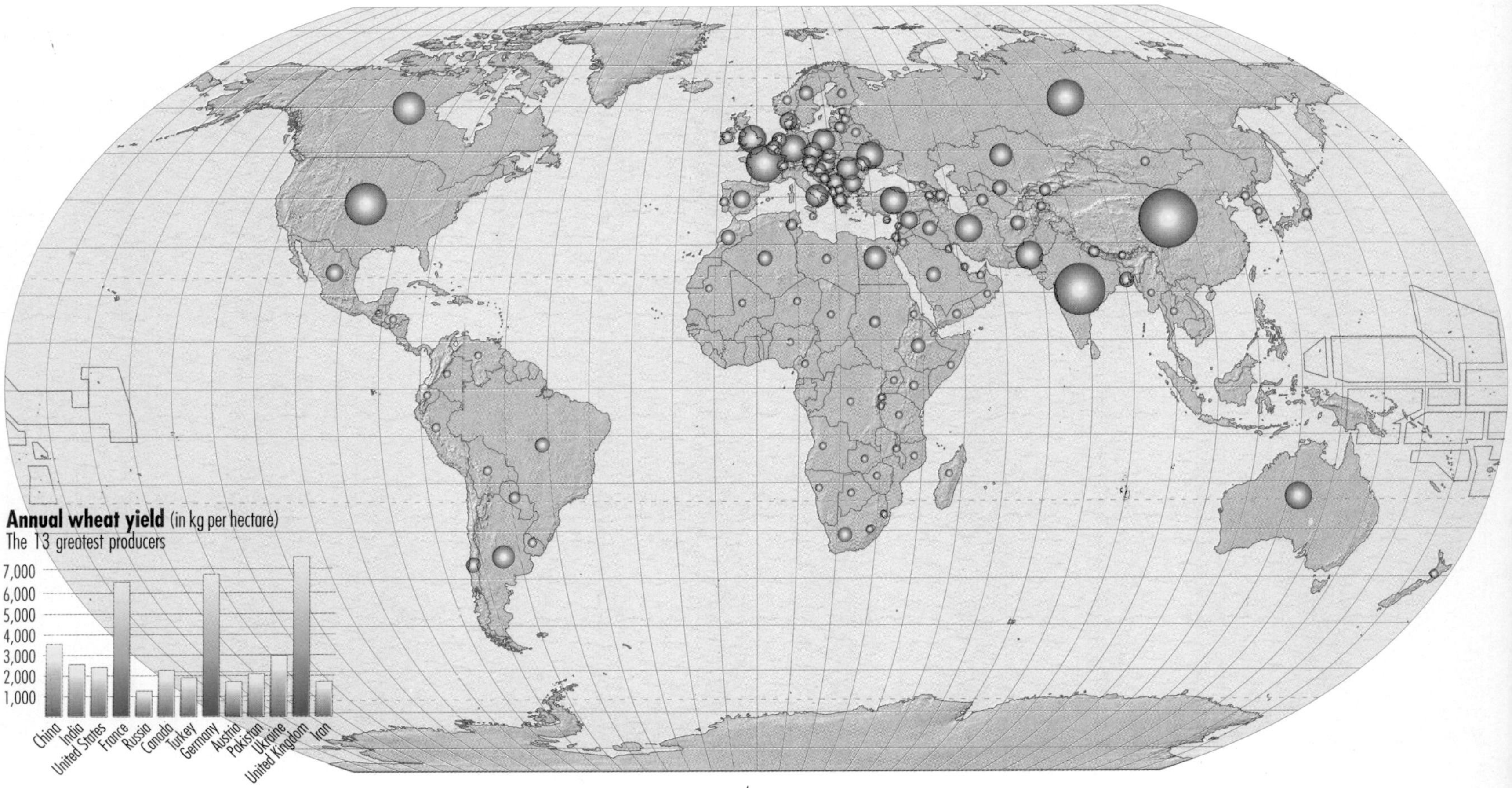

Wheat (in millions of tons)

- Lees than 0.1
- From 0.1 to 0.5
- From 0.5 to 1
- From 1 to 2,5
- From 2.5 to 5
- From 5 to 1
- From 75 to 105
- From 60 to 75
- From 50 to 60
- From 30 to 50
- From 20 to 30
- From 10 to 2

Barley

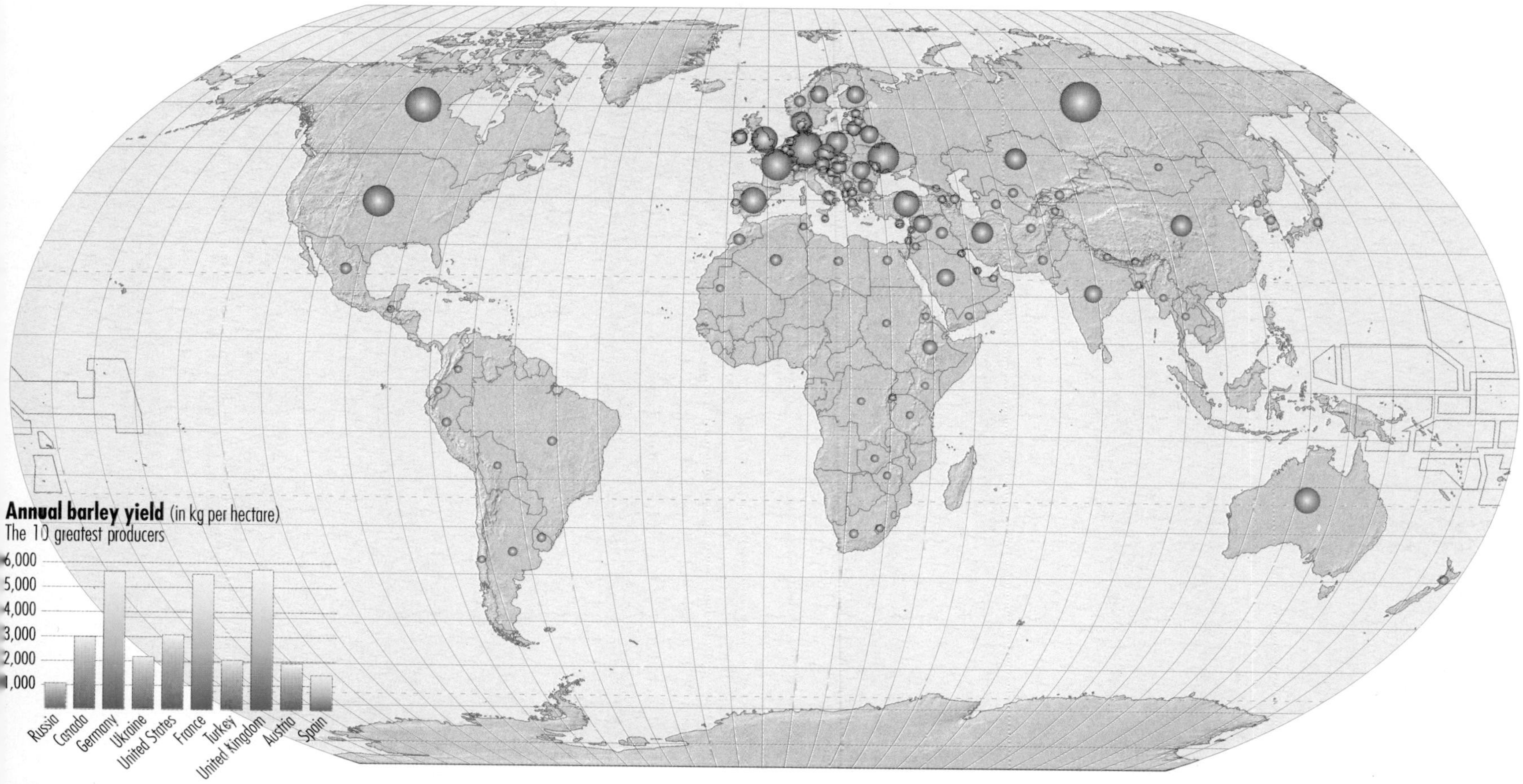

Barley (in millions of tons)

Less than 0.1 · From 0.1 to 0.5 · From 0.5 to 1 · From 1 to 1.5 · From 1.5 to 2.5 · From 2.5 to 5 · From 5 to 7.5 · From 7.5 to 10 · From 10 to 15 · From 15 to 16

Corn

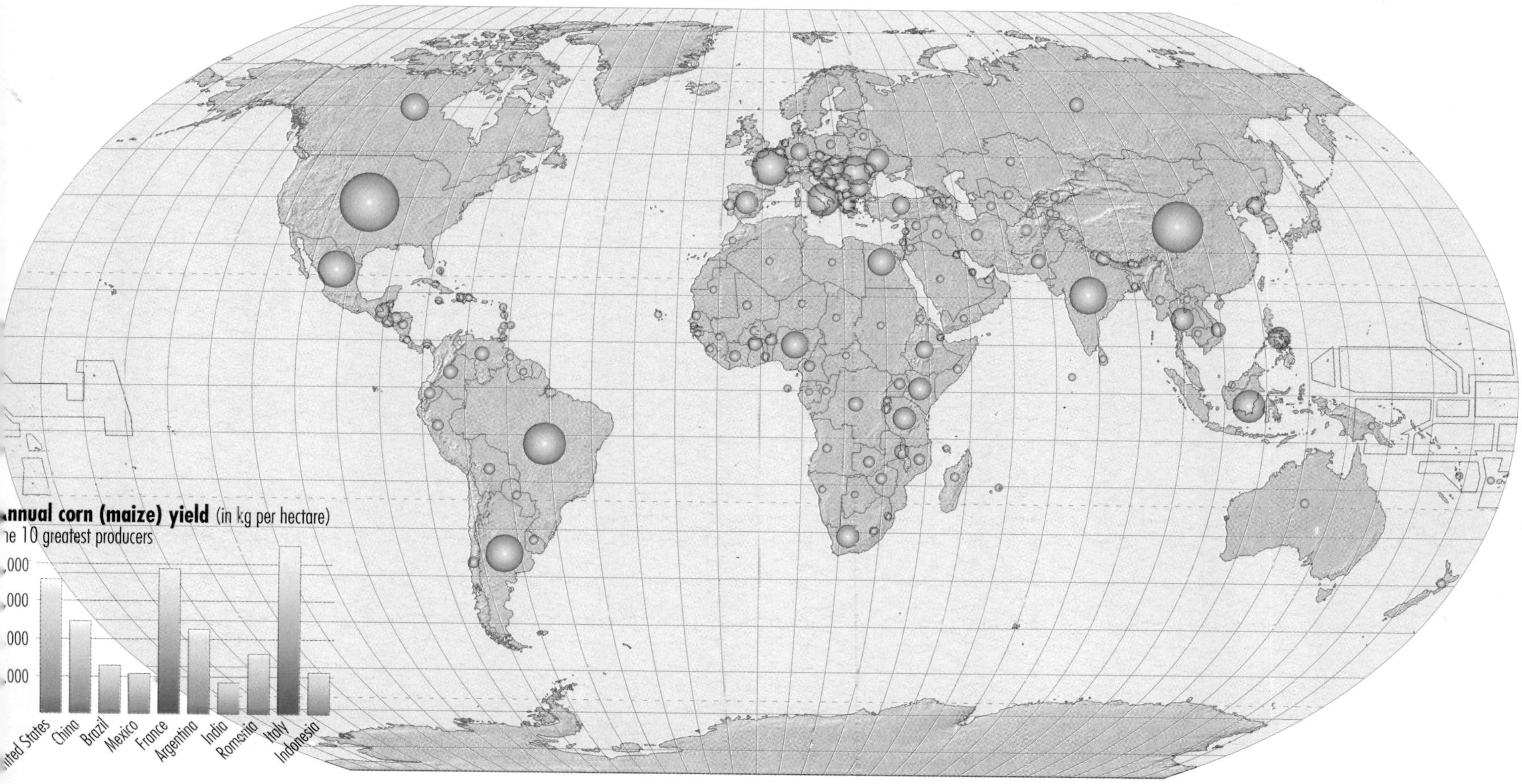

orn (maize) (in millions of tons)

Less than 0.1 · From 0.1 to 0.5 · From 0.5 to 1 · From 1 to 1.75 · From 1.75 to 2.5 · From 2.5 to 5

From 150 to 200 · From 100 to 150 · From 25 to 100 · From 10 to 25 · From 7.5 to 10 · From 5 to 7.5

Basic economic activities

Agriculture

Oats

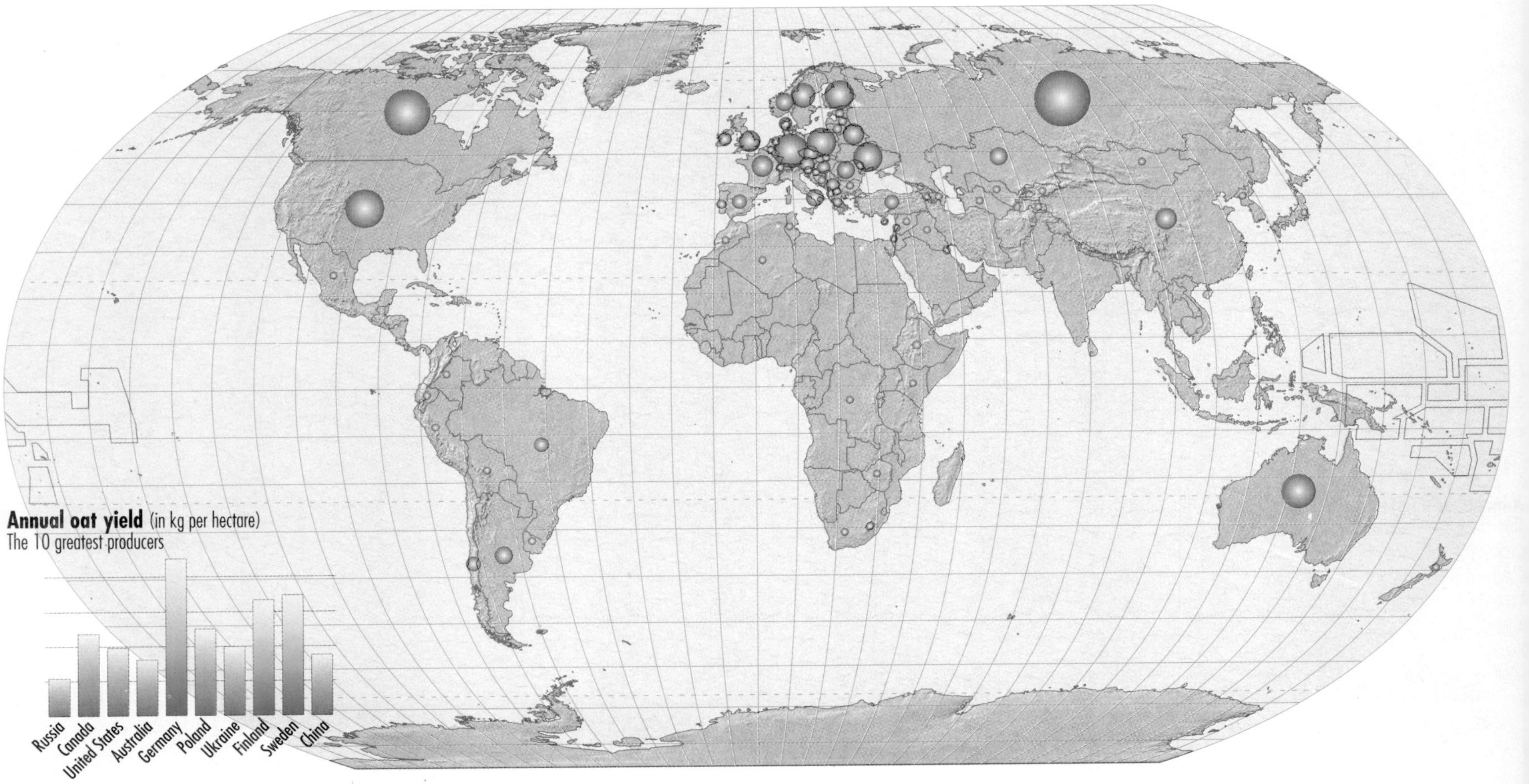

Annual oat production (in millions of tons)

- Less than 50
- From 50 to 100
- From 100 to 150
- From 150 to 250
- From 250 to 500
- From 500 to 750
- From 5,000 to 10,000
- From 2,500 to 5,000
- From 2,000 to 2,500
- From 1,500 to 2,000
- From 1,000 to 1,500
- From 750 to 1,00

Rice

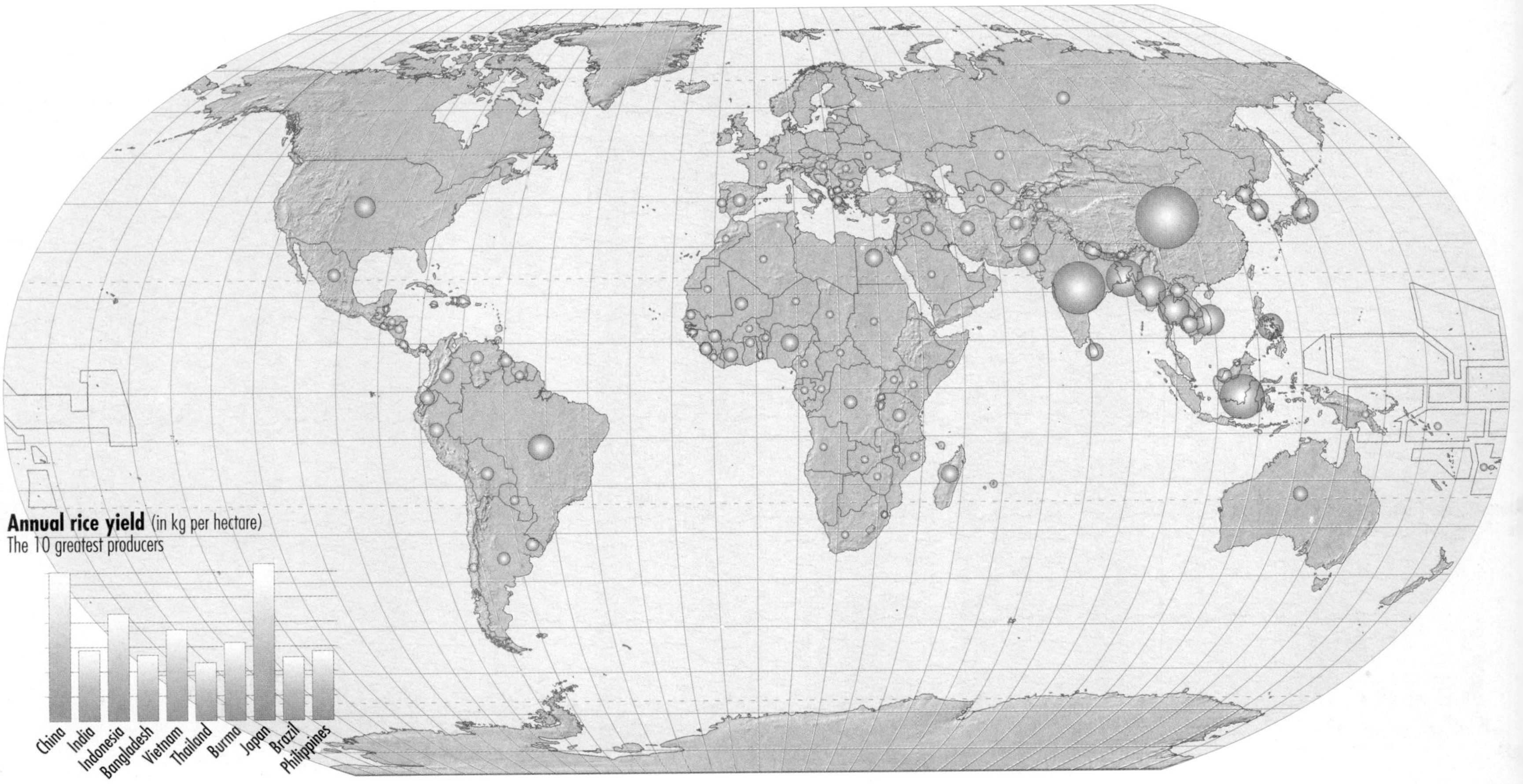

Annual rice production (in millions of tons)

- Less than 0.1
- From 0.1 to 0.25
- From 0.25 to 1
- From 1 to 1.25
- From 2.5 to 5
- From 5 to 1
- From 175 to 200
- From 100 to 175
- From 45 to 100
- From 25 to 45
- From 20 to 25
- From 10 to

Millet

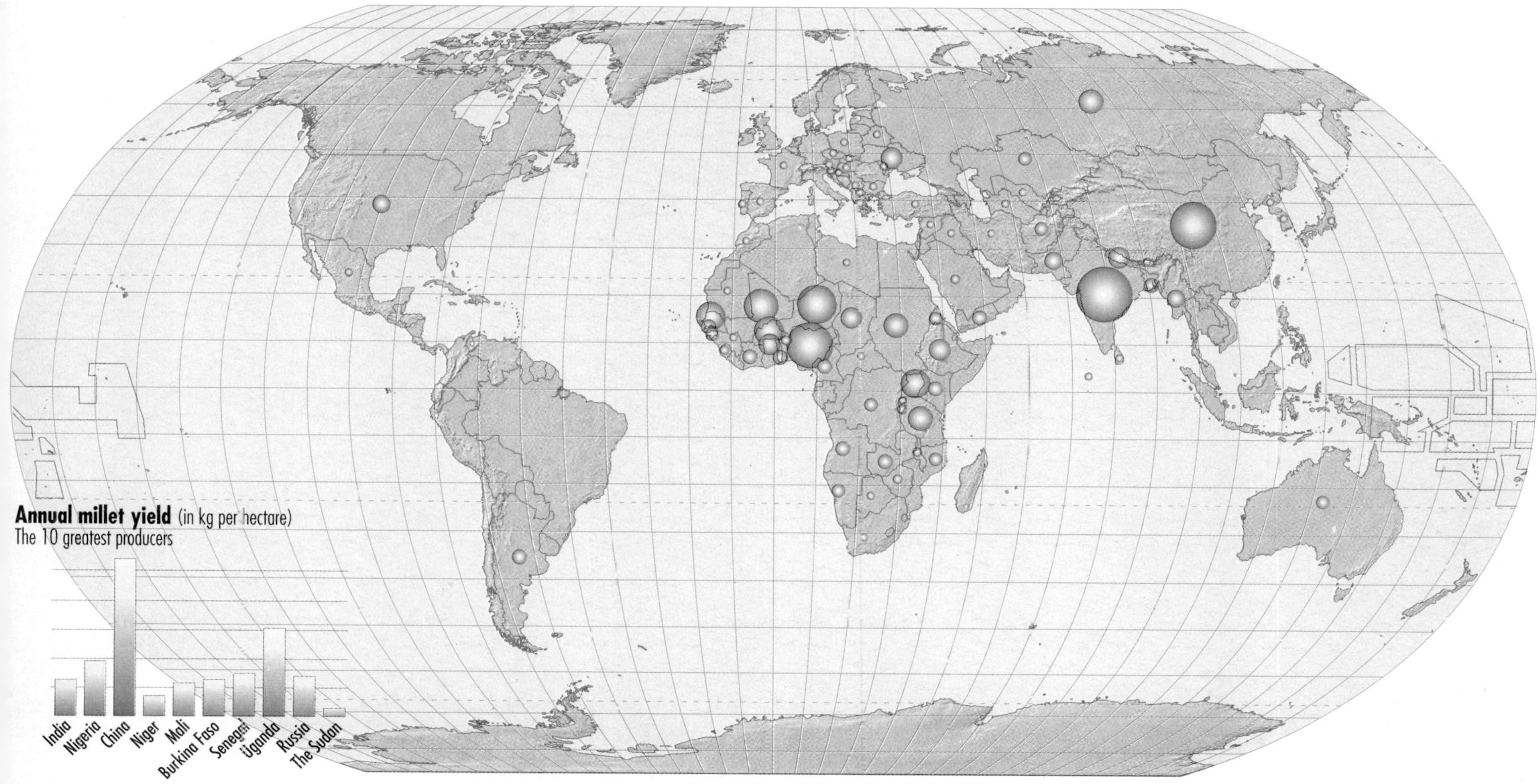

Annual millet production (in thousands of tons)

- Less than 10
- From 10 to 25
- From 25 to 50
- From 50 to 100
- From 100 to 200
- From 200 to 300
- From 5,000 to 10,000
- From 2,500 to 5,000
- From 1,000 to 2,500
- From 750 to 1,000
- From 500 to 750
- From 300 to 500

Sorghum

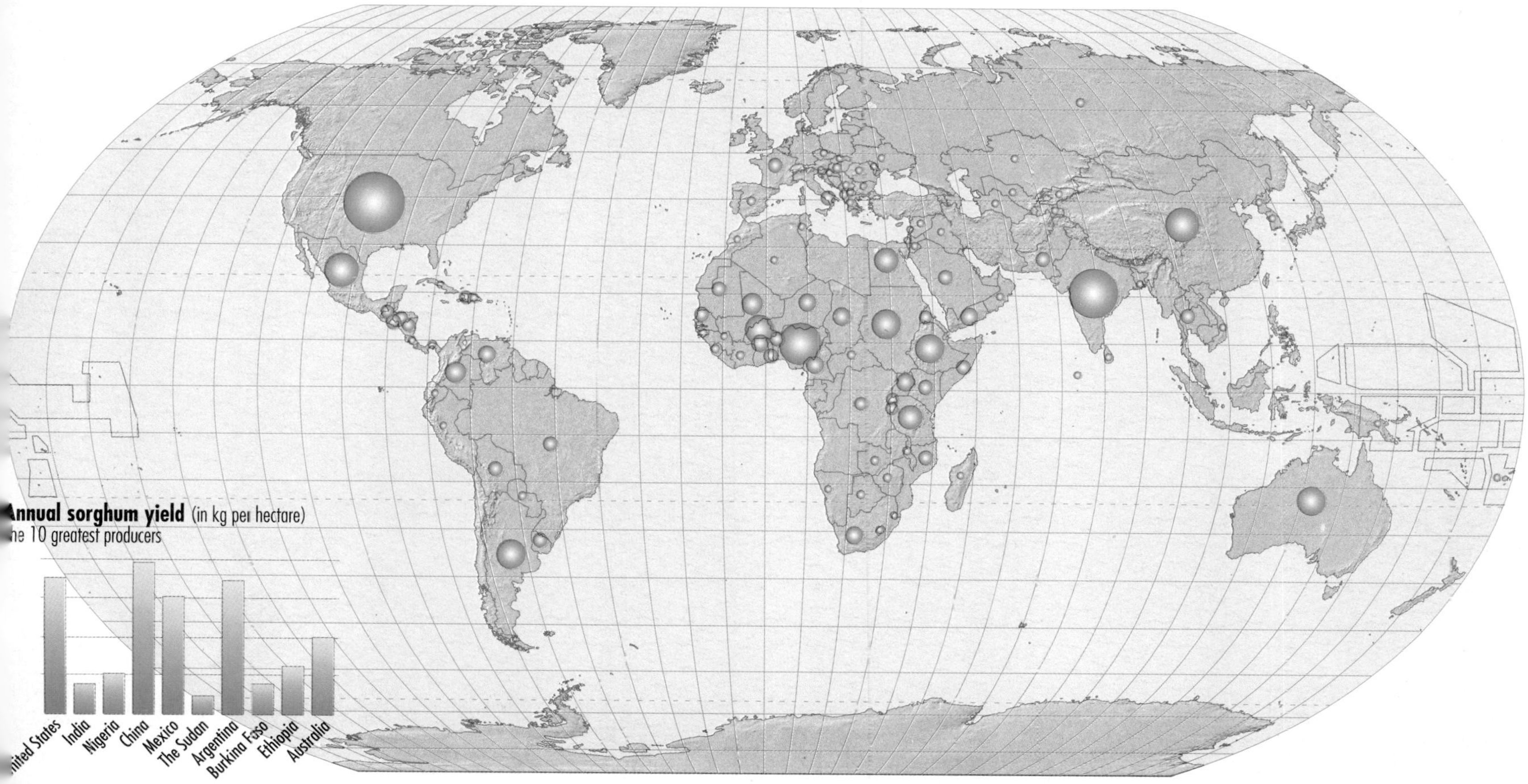

Annual sorghum production (in thousands of tons)

- Less than 10
- From 10 to 50
- From 50 to 100
- From 100 to 250
- From 250 to 500
- From 500 to 750
- From 10,000 to 12,000
- From 7,500 to 10,000
- From 5,000 to 7,500
- From 2,500 to 5,000
- From 1,000 to 2,500
- From 750 to 1,000

Basic economic activities
Agriculture

Oilseed crops

Annual production of oilseed crops (in thousands of tons oil equivalent)

- Less than 25
- From 25 to 50
- From 50 to 100
- From 100 to 250
- From 250 to 500
- From 500 to 1,000
- From 1,000 to 1,500
- From 1,500 to 2,500
- From 2,500 to 5,000
- From 5,000 to 7,500
- From 7,500 to 10,000
- From 10,000 to 15,000

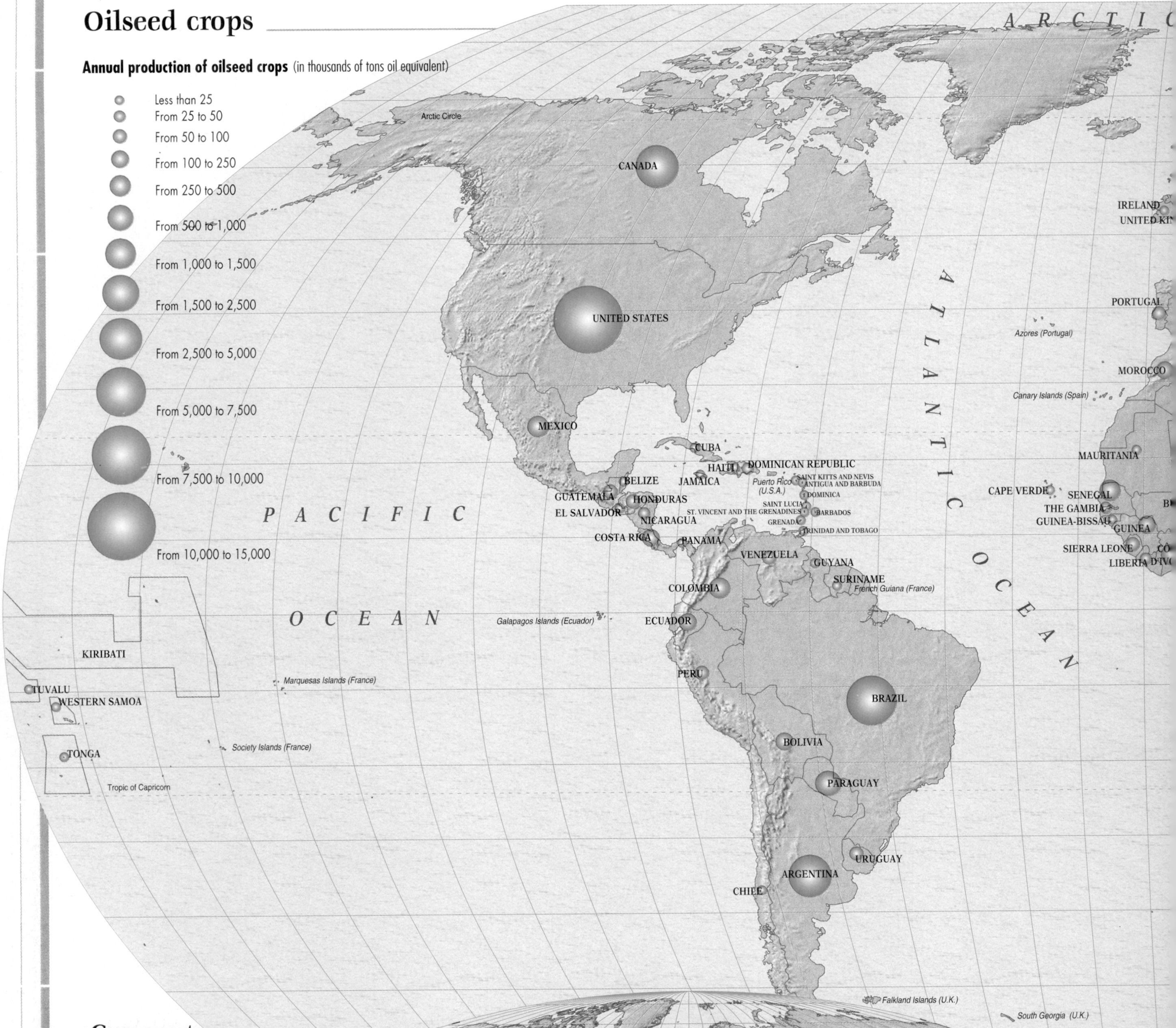

Coconuts

Annual production of coconuts (in thousands of tons)

- Less than 25
- From 25 to 100
- From 100 to 250
- From 250 to 500
- From 500 to 1,000
- From 1,000 to 7,500
- From 7,500 to 10,000
- From 10,000 to 12,500
- From 12,500 to 15,000

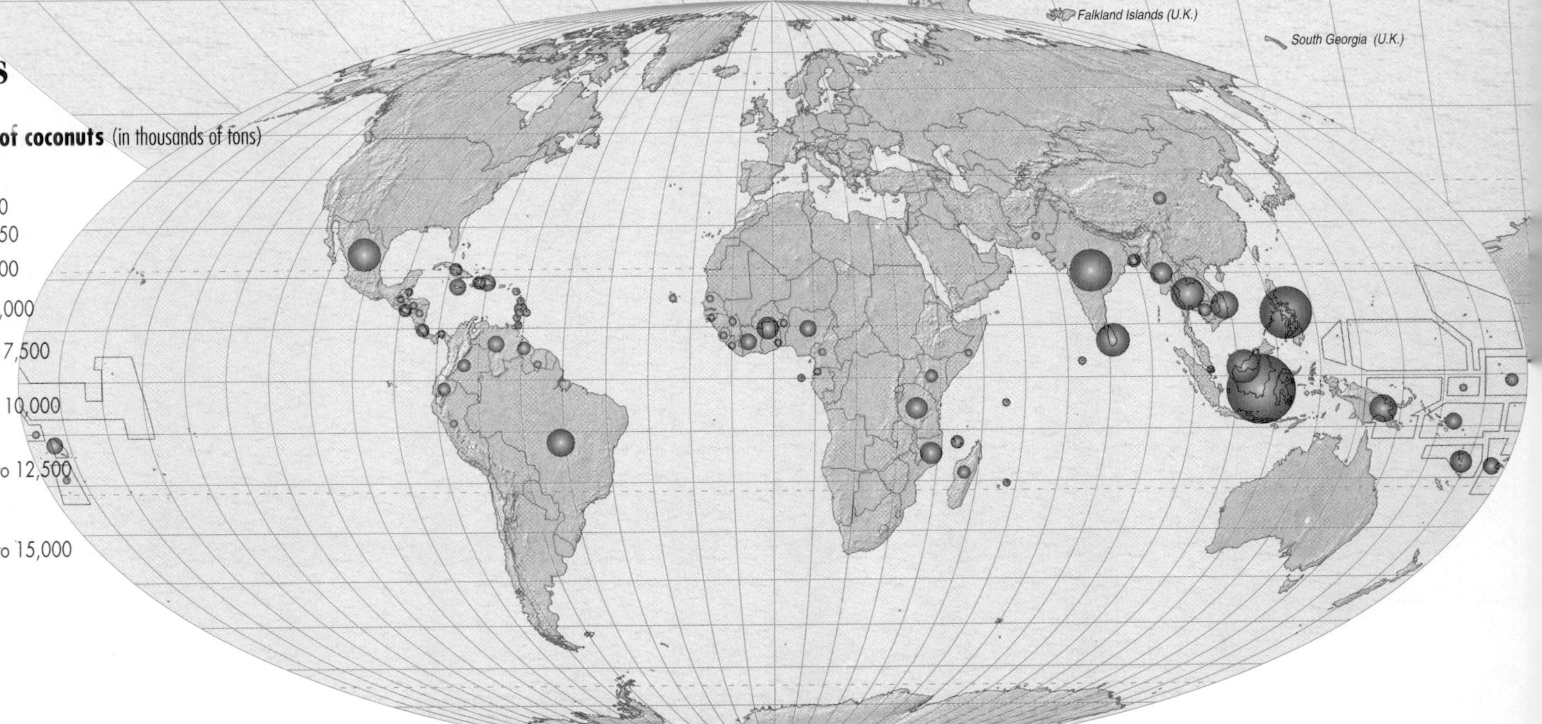

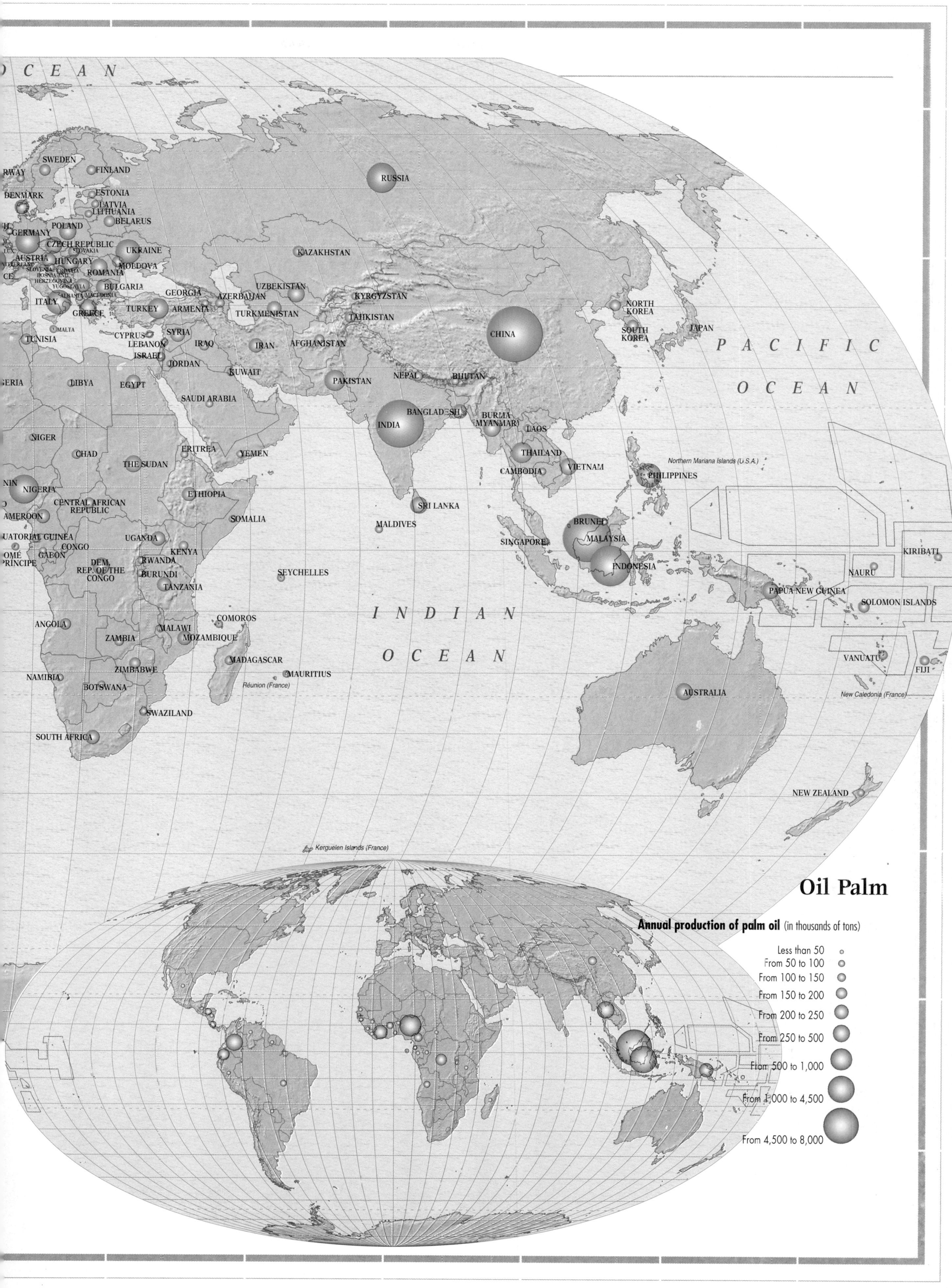
Oil Palm
Annual production of palm oil (in thousands of tons)
Less than 50
From 50 to 100
From 100 to 150
From 150 to 200
From 200 to 250
From 250 to 500
From 500 to 1,000
From 1,000 to 4,500
From 4,500 to 8,000
PACIFIC OCEAN
INDIAN OCEAN
SWEDEN
FINLAND
DENMARK
ESTONIA
LATVIA
LITHUANIA
BELARUS
POLAND
GERMANY
CZECH REPUBLIC
SLOVAKIA
UKRAINE
AUSTRIA
HUNGARY
MOLDOVA
SLOVENIA
CROATIA
ROMANIA
BOSNIA AND HERZEGOVINA
YUGOSLAVIA
BULGARIA
ALBANIA
MACEDONIA
ITALY
GREECE
MALTA
TUNISIA
RUSSIA
KAZAKHSTAN
GEORGIA
AZERBAIJAN
ARMENIA
UZBEKISTAN
TURKEY
TURKMENISTAN
KYRGYZSTAN
TAJIKISTAN
CYPRUS
SYRIA
LEBANON
ISRAEL
IRAQ
IRAN
AFGHANISTAN
JORDAN
KUWAIT
LIBYA
EGYPT
SAUDI ARABIA
PAKISTAN
NEPAL
BHUTAN
INDIA
BANGLADESH
CHINA
NORTH KOREA
SOUTH KOREA
JAPAN
BURMA (MYANMAR)
LAOS
THAILAND
CAMBODIA
VIETNAM
PHILIPPINES
Northern Mariana Islands (U.S.A.)
NIGER
CHAD
THE SUDAN
ERITREA
YEMEN
NIGERIA
ETHIOPIA
CENTRAL AFRICAN REPUBLIC
SOMALIA
SRI LANKA
MALDIVES
BRUNEI
MALAYSIA
SINGAPORE
INDONESIA
KIRIBATI
NAURU
PAPUA NEW GUINEA
SOLOMON ISLANDS
UGANDA
CONGO
KENYA
GABON
DEM. REP. OF THE CONGO
RWANDA
BURUNDI
TANZANIA
SEYCHELLES
COMOROS
ANGOLA
ZAMBIA
MALAWI
MOZAMBIQUE
MADAGASCAR
MAURITIUS
Réunion (France)
ZIMBABWE
NAMIBIA
BOTSWANA
SWAZILAND
SOUTH AFRICA
AUSTRALIA
VANUATU
FIJI
New Caledonia (France)
NEW ZEALAND
Kerguelen Islands (France)

Basic economic activities
Agriculture

Soybeans

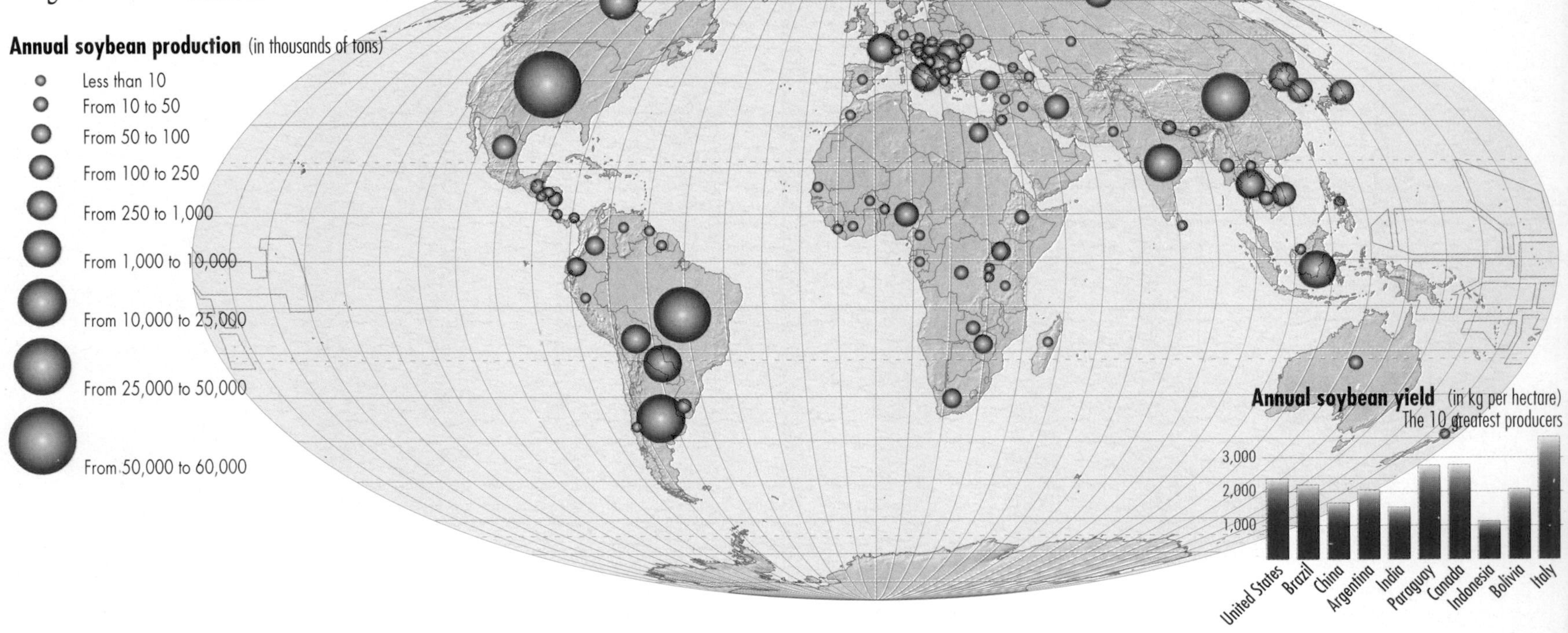

Cottonseeds

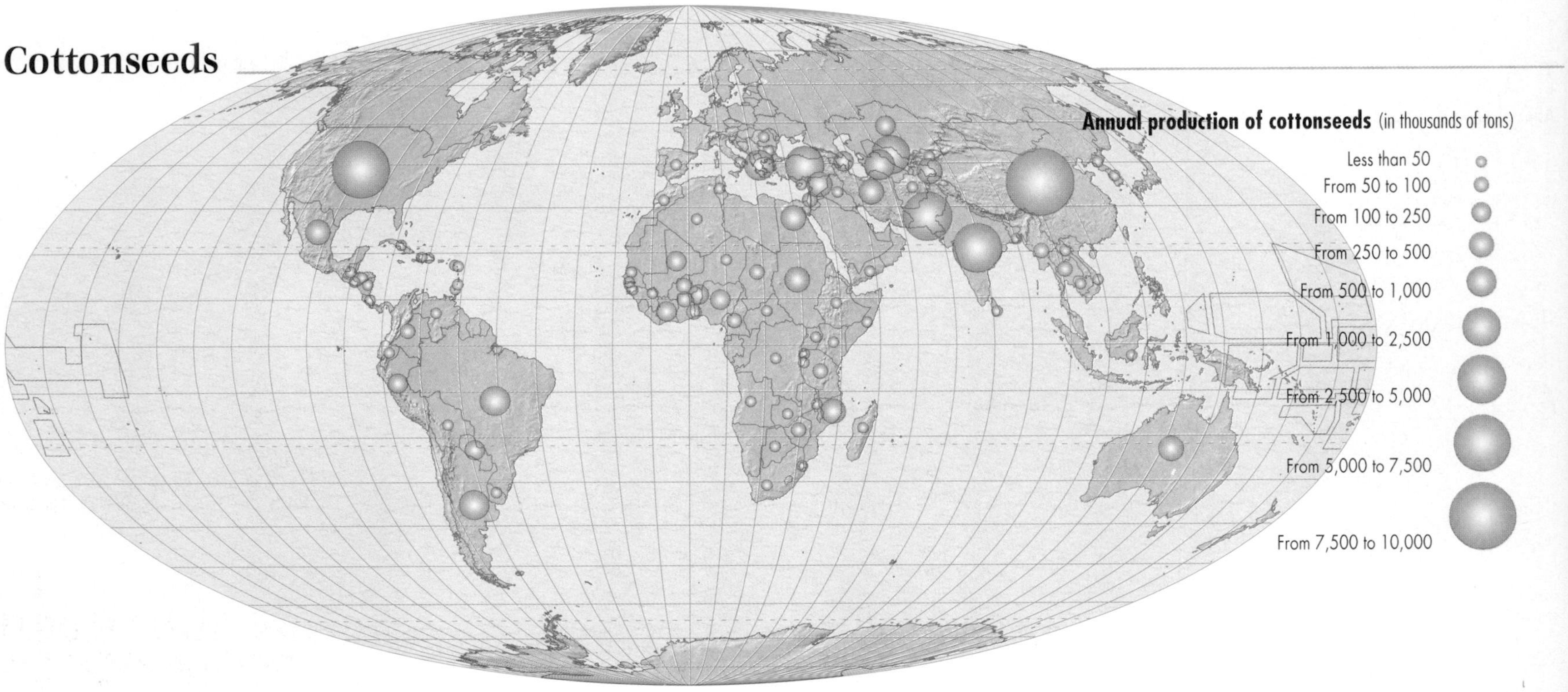

Peanuts

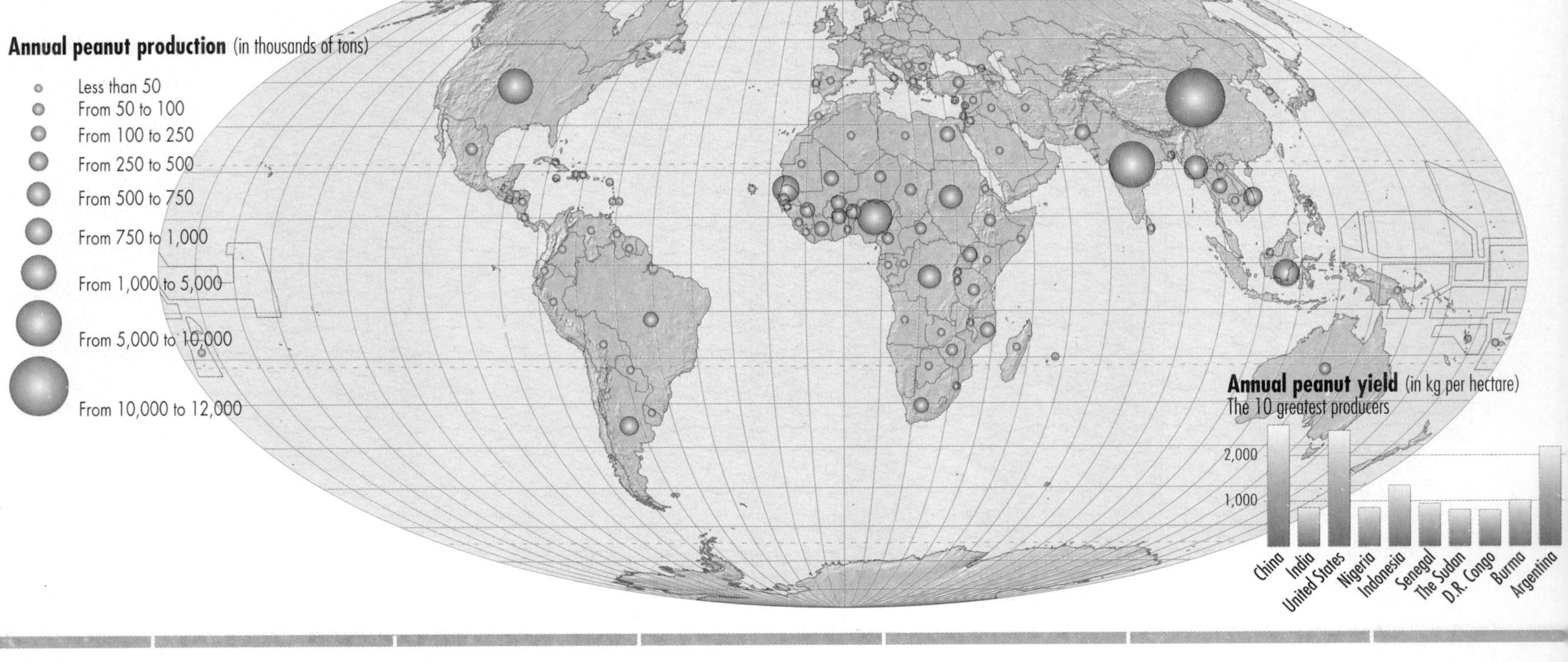

Rapeseeds
Annual rapeseed production (in thousands of tons)
Less than 50
From 50 to 100
From 100 to 250
From 250 to 500
From 500 to 1,000
From 1,000 to 2,500
From 2,500 to 5,000
From 5,000 to 7,500
From 7,500 to 10,000
Annual rapeseed yield (in kg per hectare)
The 10 greatest producers
3,000
2,000
1,000
China
Canada
India
Germany
France
Poland
United Kingdom
Czech Republic
Australia
Denmark
Sunflower seeds
Annual production of sunflower seeds (in thousands of tons)
Less than 100
From 100 to 500
From 500 to 750
From 750 to 1,000
From 1,000 to 1,500
From 1,500 to 2,000
From 2,000 to 4,000
From 4,000 to 5,000
From 5,000 to 6,000
Annual sunflower seed yield (in kg per hectare)
The 10 greatest producers
2,000
1,000
Argentina
Russia
Ukraine
France
United States
India
China
Romania
Turkey
Hungary
Olives
Annual olive production (in thousands of tons)
Less than 10
From 10 to 25
From 25 to 50
From 50 to 100
From 100 to 300
From 300 to 500
From 500 to 1,500
From 1,500 to 3,000
From 3,000 to 3,500

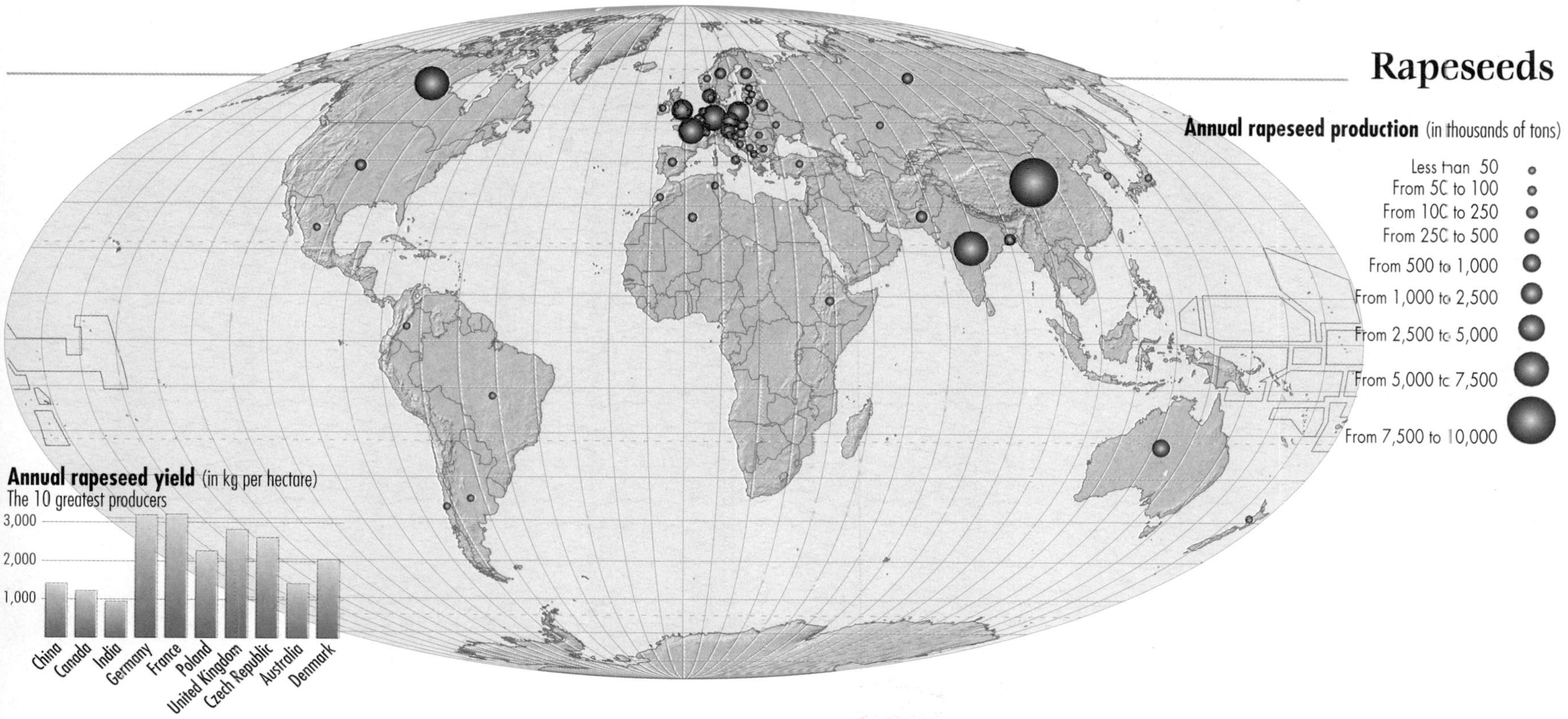

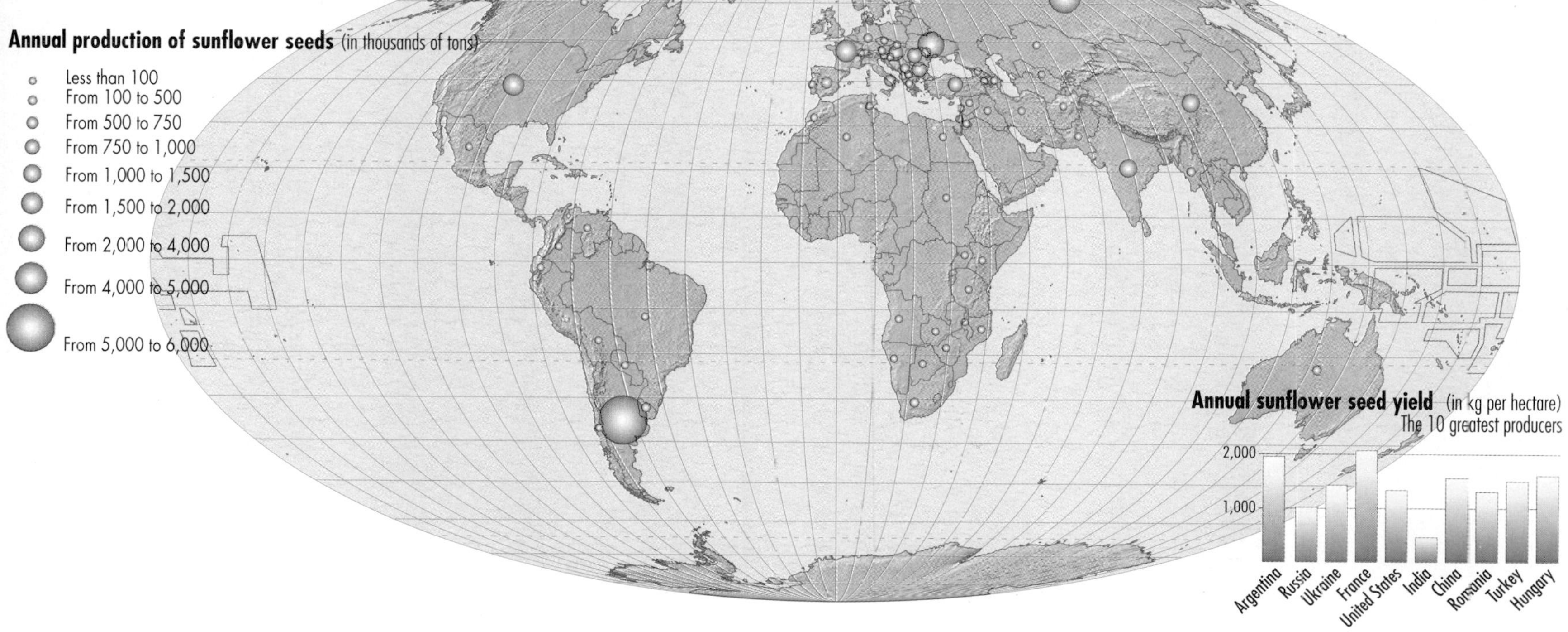

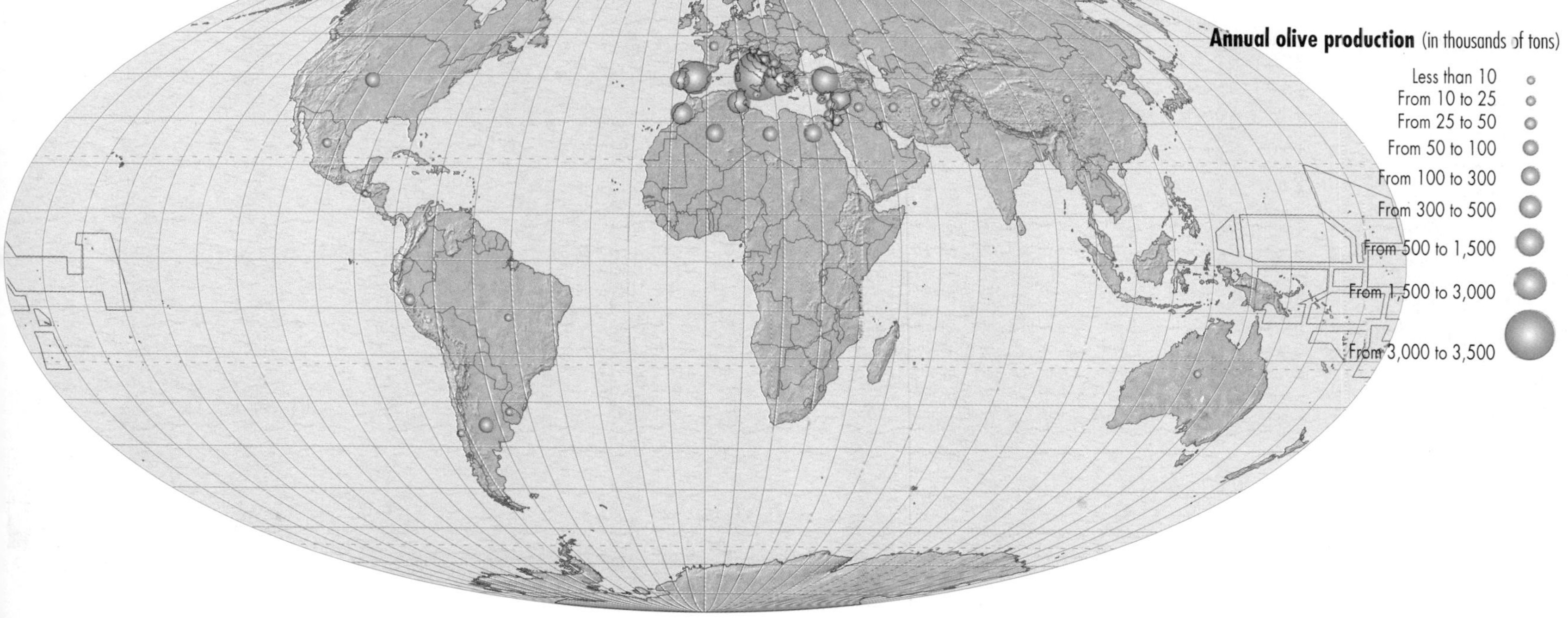

Basic economic activities
Agriculture

Vegetables

Annual vegetable production
(in millions of tons)

- Less than 0.1
- From 0.1 to 0.25
- From 0.25 to 0.5
- From 0.5 to 1
- From 1 to 1.5
- From 1.5 to 2.5
- From 2.5 to 5
- From 5 to 10
- From 10 to 20
- From 20 to 40
- From 40 to 65
- From 65 to 210

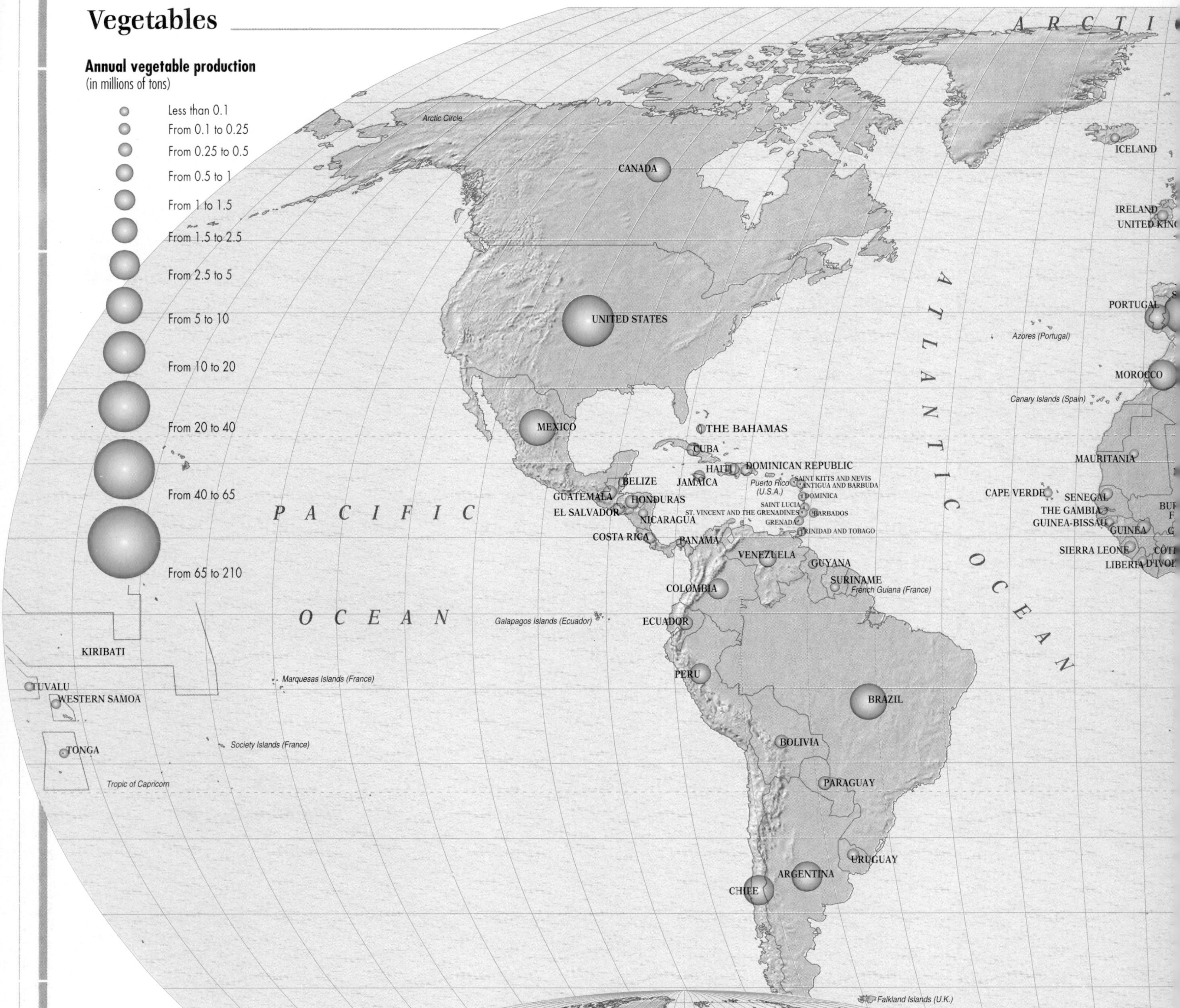

Tomatoes

Annual tomato production
(in thousands of tons)

- Less than 15
- From 15 to 50
- From 50 to 250
- From 250 to 500
- From 500 to 1,000
- From 1,000 to 2,000
- From 2,000 to 4,000
- From 4,000 to 8,000
- From 8,000 to 15,000

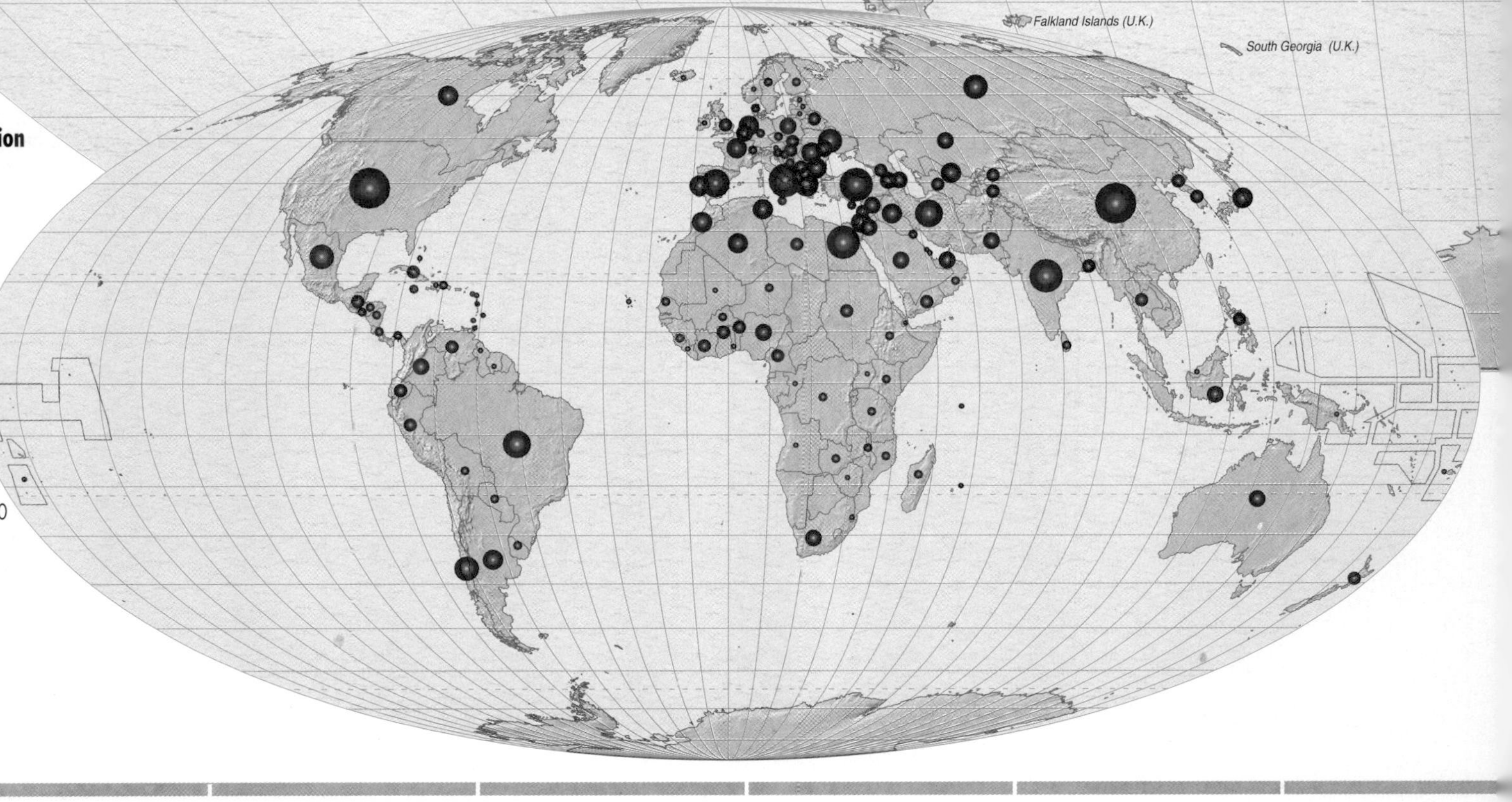

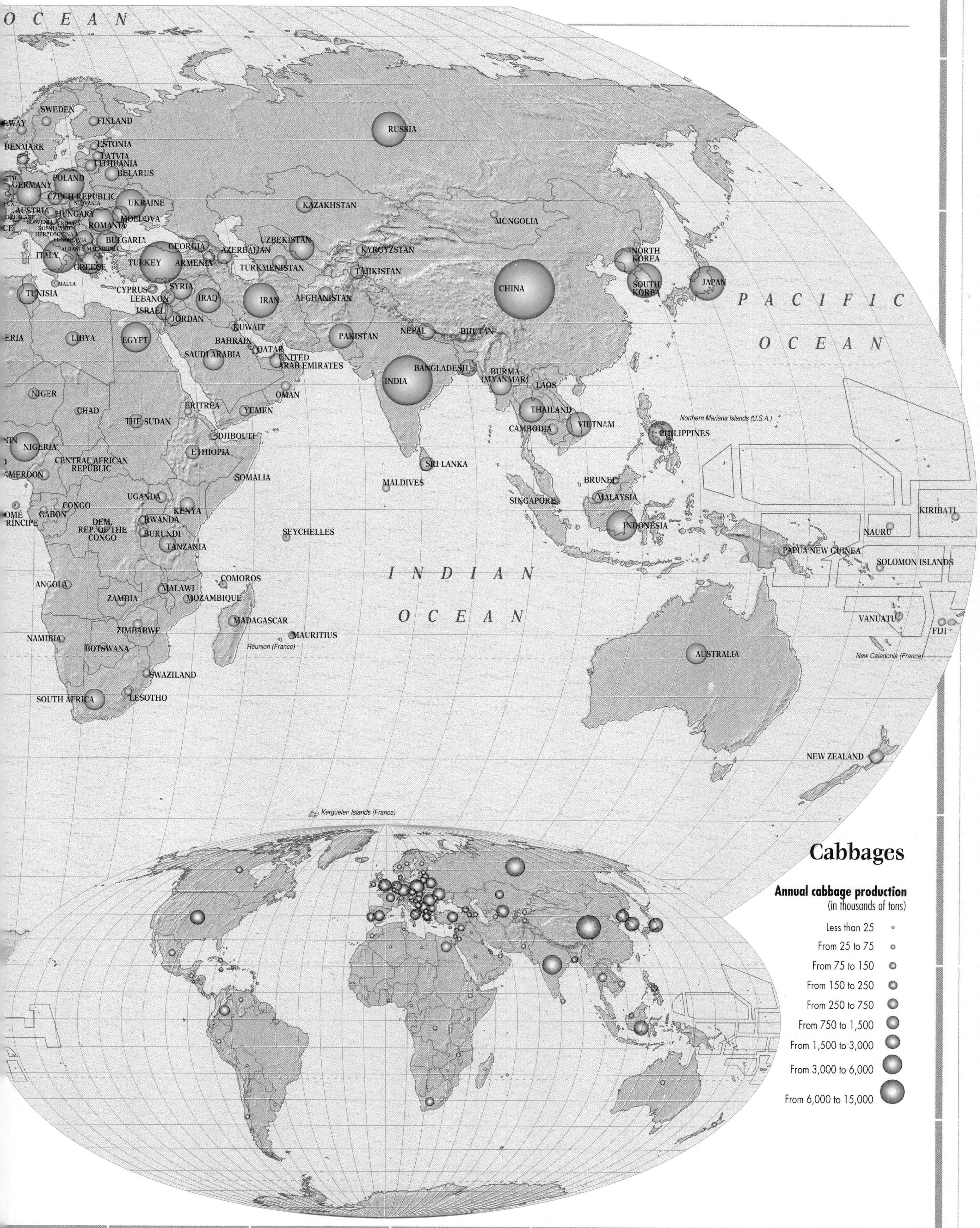

Cabbages

Annual cabbage production
(in thousands of tons)

- Less than 25
- From 25 to 75
- From 75 to 150
- From 150 to 250
- From 250 to 750
- From 750 to 1,500
- From 1,500 to 3,000
- From 3,000 to 6,000
- From 6,000 to 15,000

Basic economic activities

Agriculture

Dried fruits and nuts

Annual production of dried fruits and nuts (in thousands of tons)

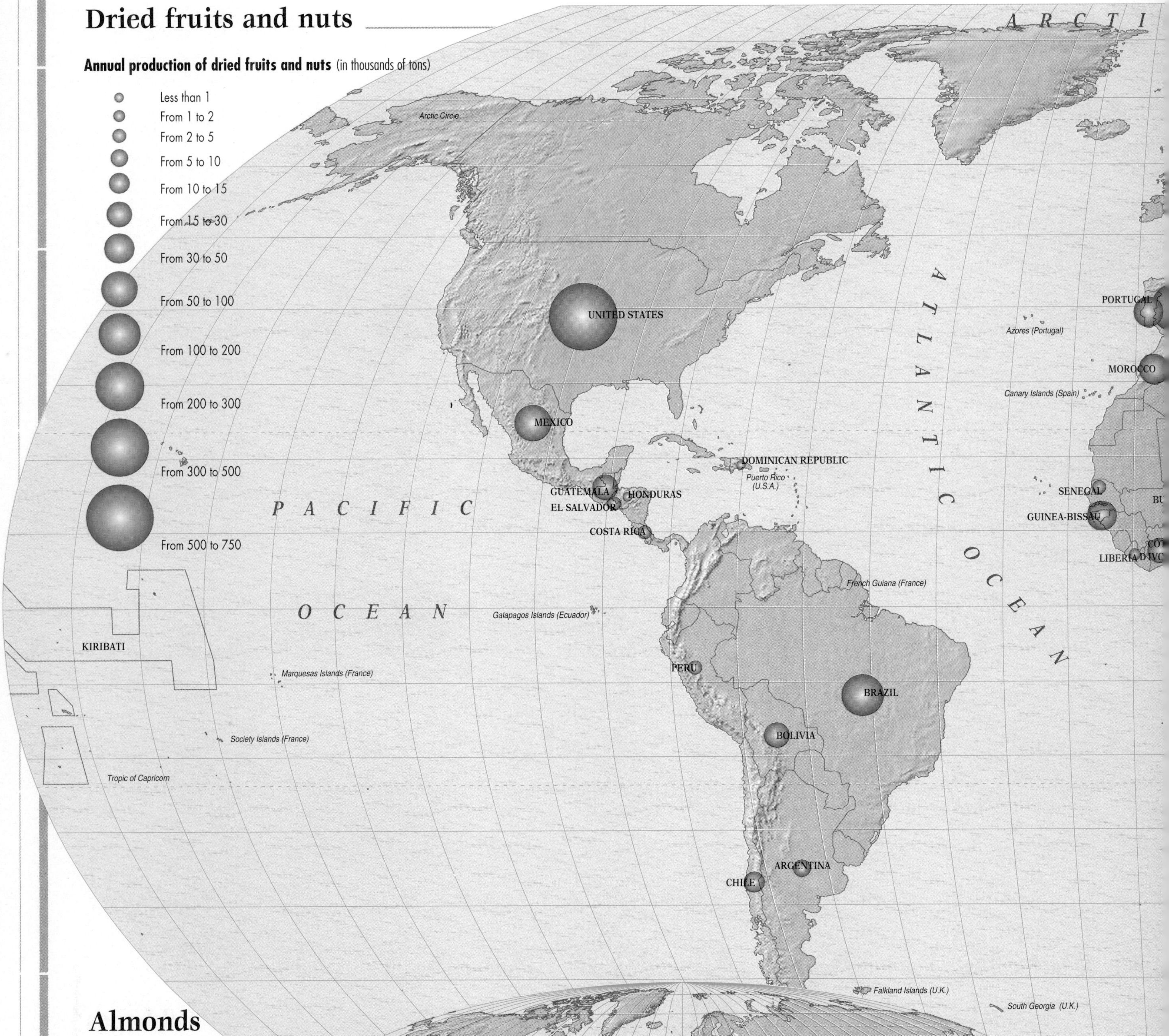

Almonds

Annual almond production (in thousands of tons)

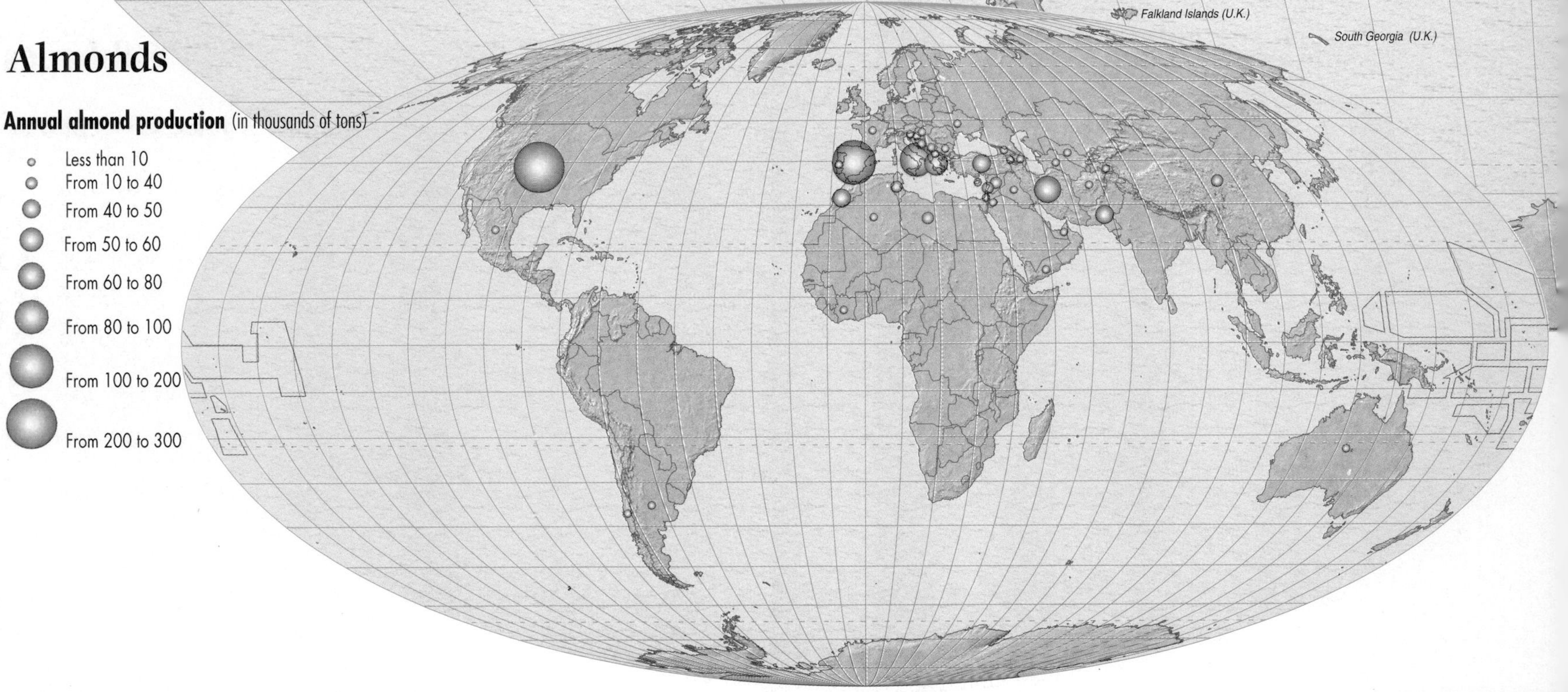

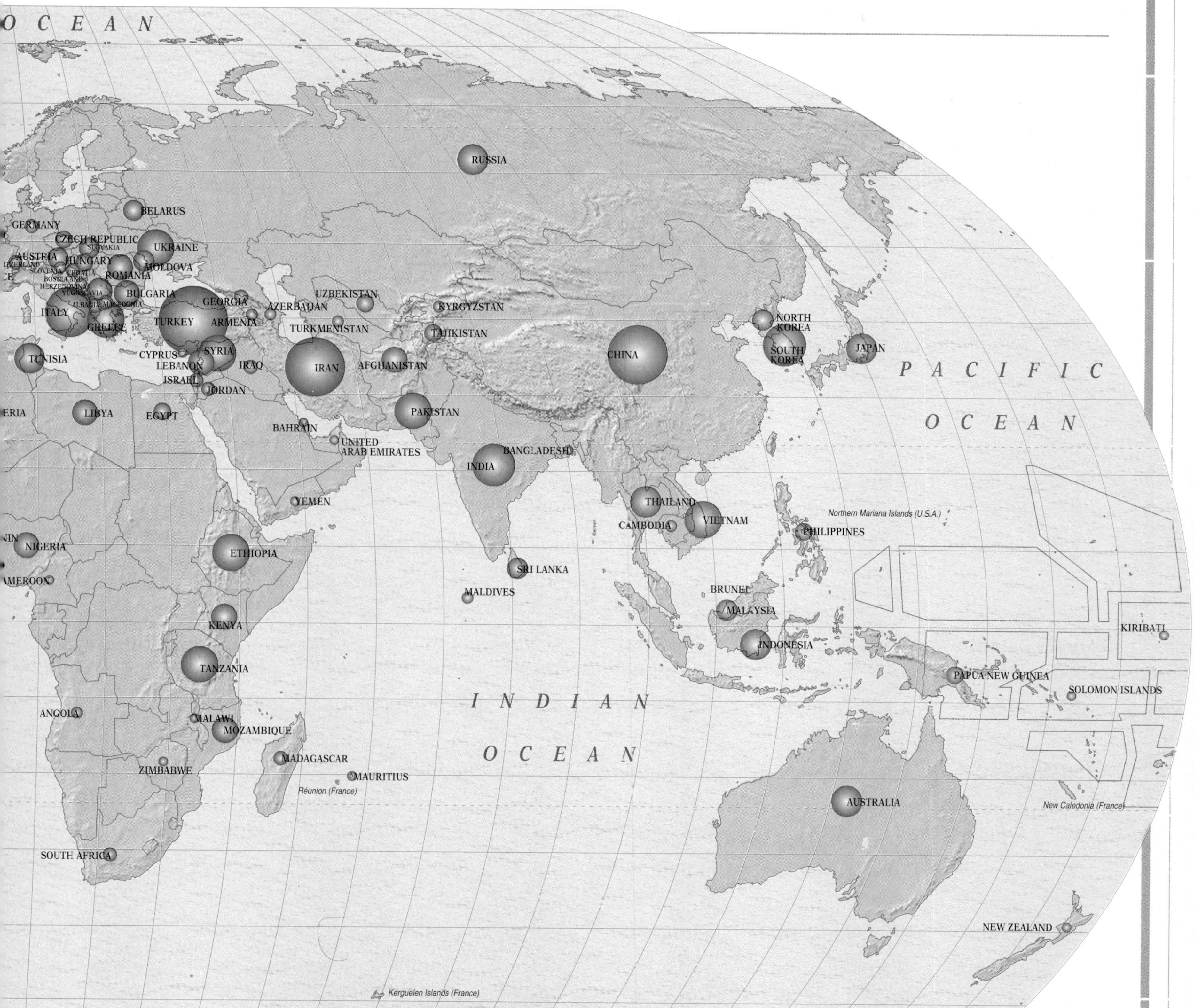
OCEAN
RUSSIA
BELARUS
GERMANY
CZECH REPUBLIC
SLOVAKIA
UKRAINE
AUSTRIA
HUNGARY
MOLDOVA
ROMANIA
BULGARIA
ITALY
GREECE
GEORGIA
AZERBAIJAN
TURKEY
ARMENIA
UZBEKISTAN
KYRGYZSTAN
TURKMENISTAN
TAJIKISTAN
TUNISIA
CYPRUS
SYRIA
LEBANON
IRAQ
ISRAEL
IRAN
AFGHANISTAN
JORDAN
CHINA
NORTH KOREA
SOUTH KOREA
JAPAN
PACIFIC
OCEAN
LIBYA
EGYPT
PAKISTAN
BAHRAIN
UNITED ARAB EMIRATES
BANGLADESH
INDIA
YEMEN
THAILAND
VIETNAM
CAMBODIA
Northern Mariana Islands (U.S.A.)
PHILIPPINES
NIGERIA
ETHIOPIA
SRI LANKA
MALDIVES
BRUNEI
MALAYSIA
KENYA
INDONESIA
KIRIBATI
TANZANIA
PAPUA NEW GUINEA
SOLOMON ISLANDS
INDIAN
OCEAN
ANGOLA
MALAWI
MOZAMBIQUE
MADAGASCAR
ZIMBABWE
MAURITIUS
Réunion (France)
AUSTRALIA
New Caledonia (France)
SOUTH AFRICA
NEW ZEALAND
Kerguelen Islands (France)

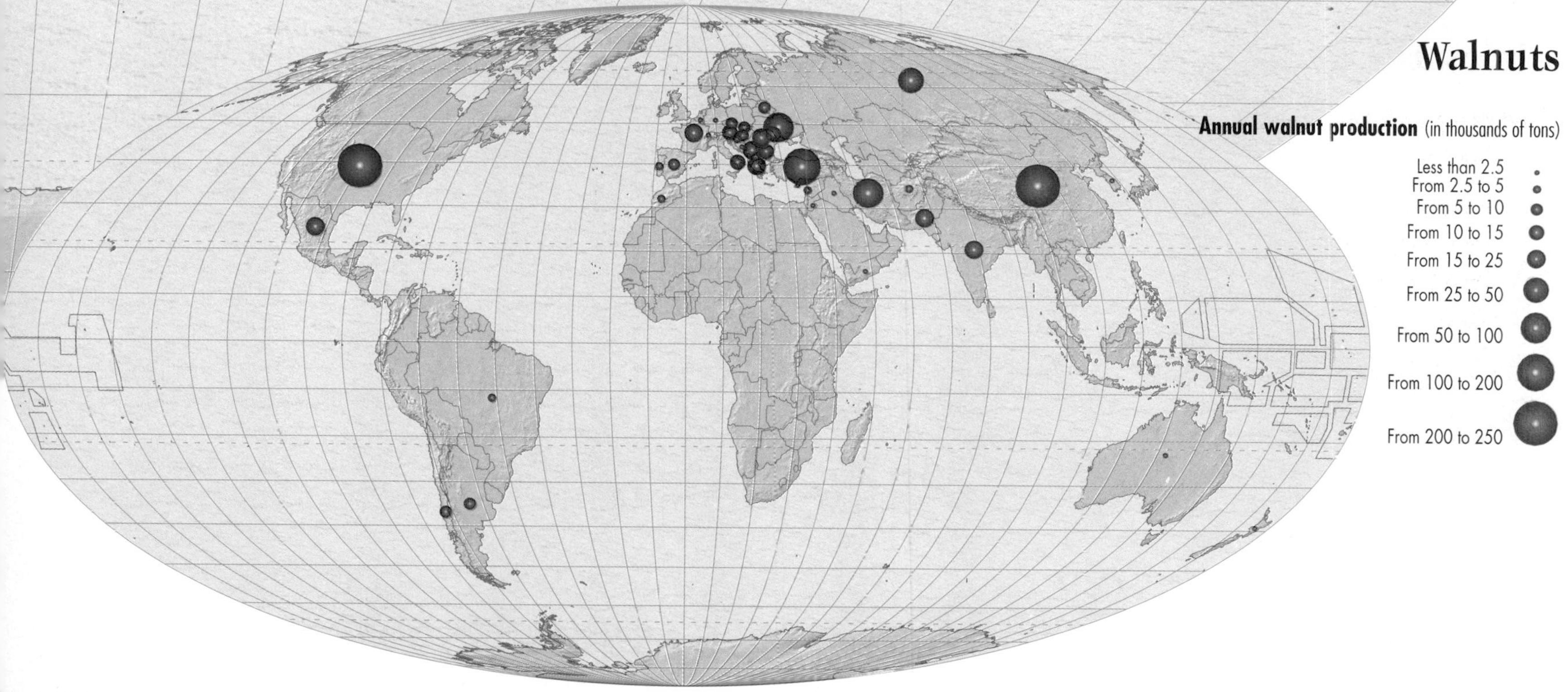
Walnuts
Annual walnut production (in thousands of tons)
Less than 2.5
From 2.5 to 5
From 5 to 10
From 10 to 15
From 15 to 25
From 25 to 50
From 50 to 100
From 100 to 200
From 200 to 250

Basic economic activities

Agriculture

Fruits

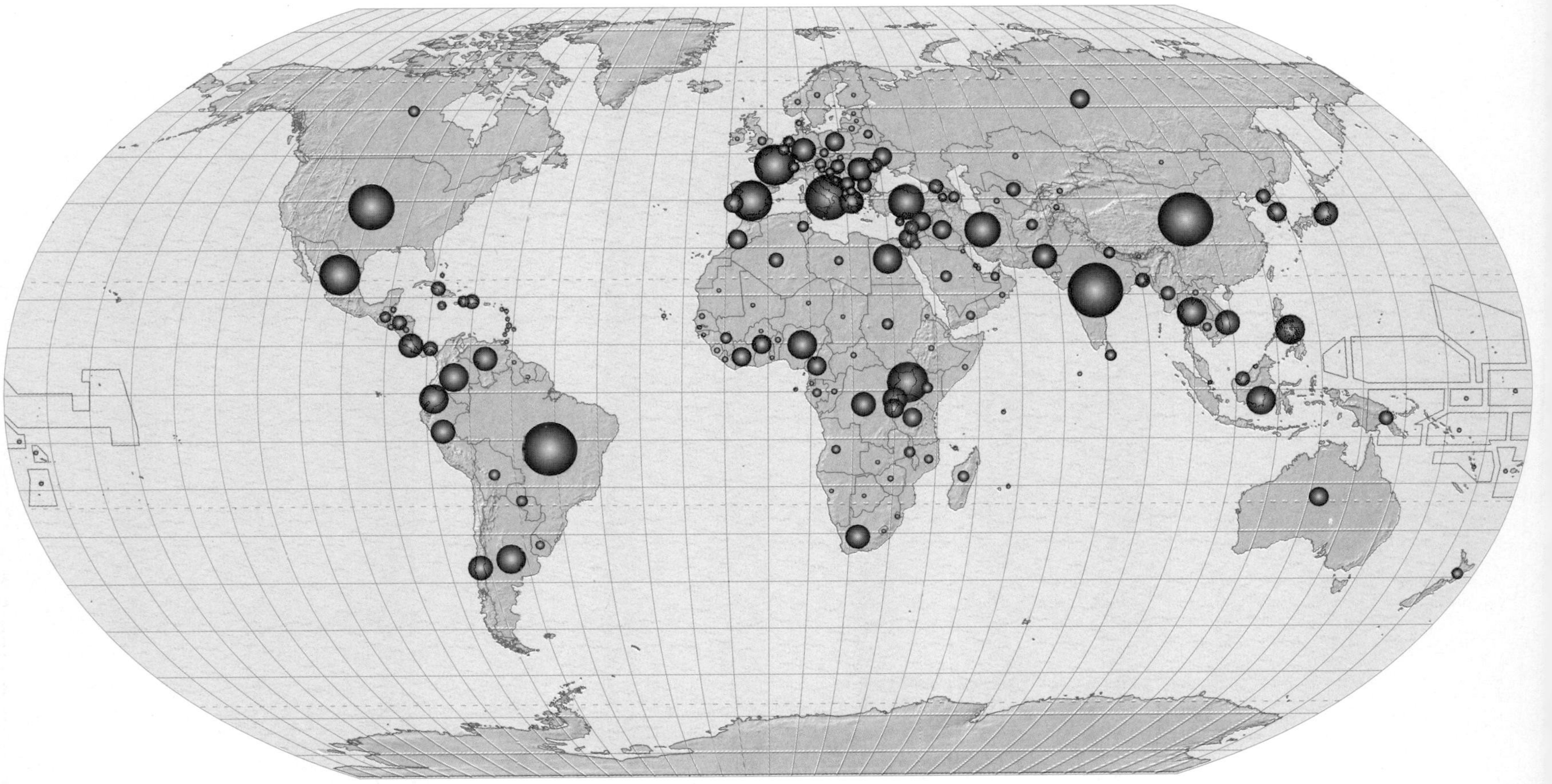

Annual fruit production (in millions of tons)

- Less than 0.1
- From 0.1 to 0.25
- From 0.25 to 0.5
- From 0.5 to 1
- From 1 to 1.5
- From 1.5 to 2
- From 30 to 45
- From 15 to 30
- From 10 to 15
- From 7.5 to 10
- From 5 to 7.5
- From 2.5 to 5

Oranges

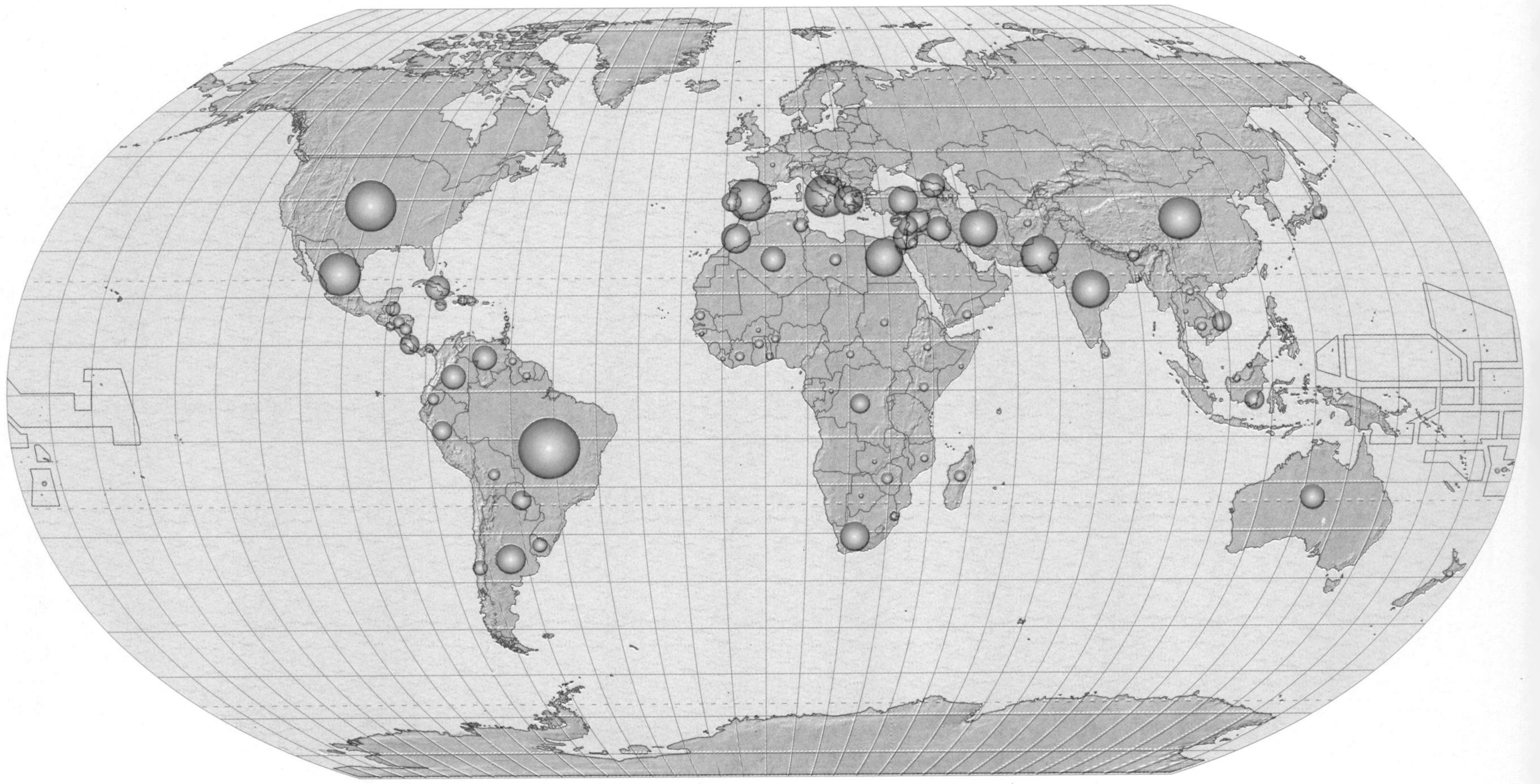

Annual orange production (in thousands of tons)

- Less than 10
- From 10 to 25
- From 25 to 50
- From 50 to 100
- From 100 to 150
- From 150 to 25
- From 15,000 to 20,000
- From 10,000 to 15,000
- From 2,000 to 10,000
- From 1,000 to 2,000
- From 500 to 1,000
- From 250 to 5

Lemons

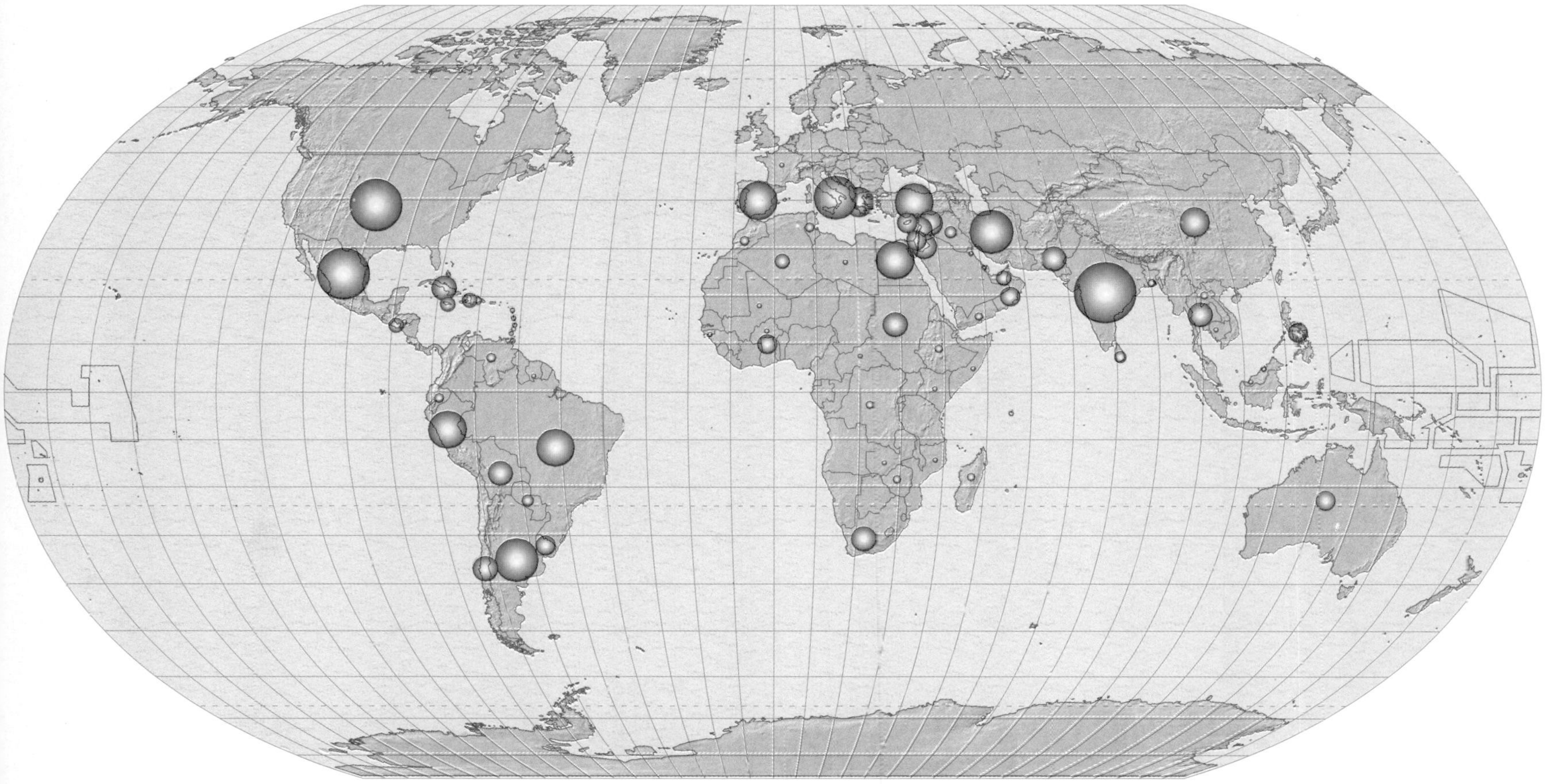

Annual lemon production (in thousands of tons)

- Less than 5
- From 5 to 10
- From 10 to 15
- From 15 to 20
- From 20 to 25
- From 25 to 50
- From 1,000 to 1,750
- From 750 to 1,000
- From 500 to 750
- From 250 to 500
- From 100 to 250
- Form 50 to 100

Tangerines

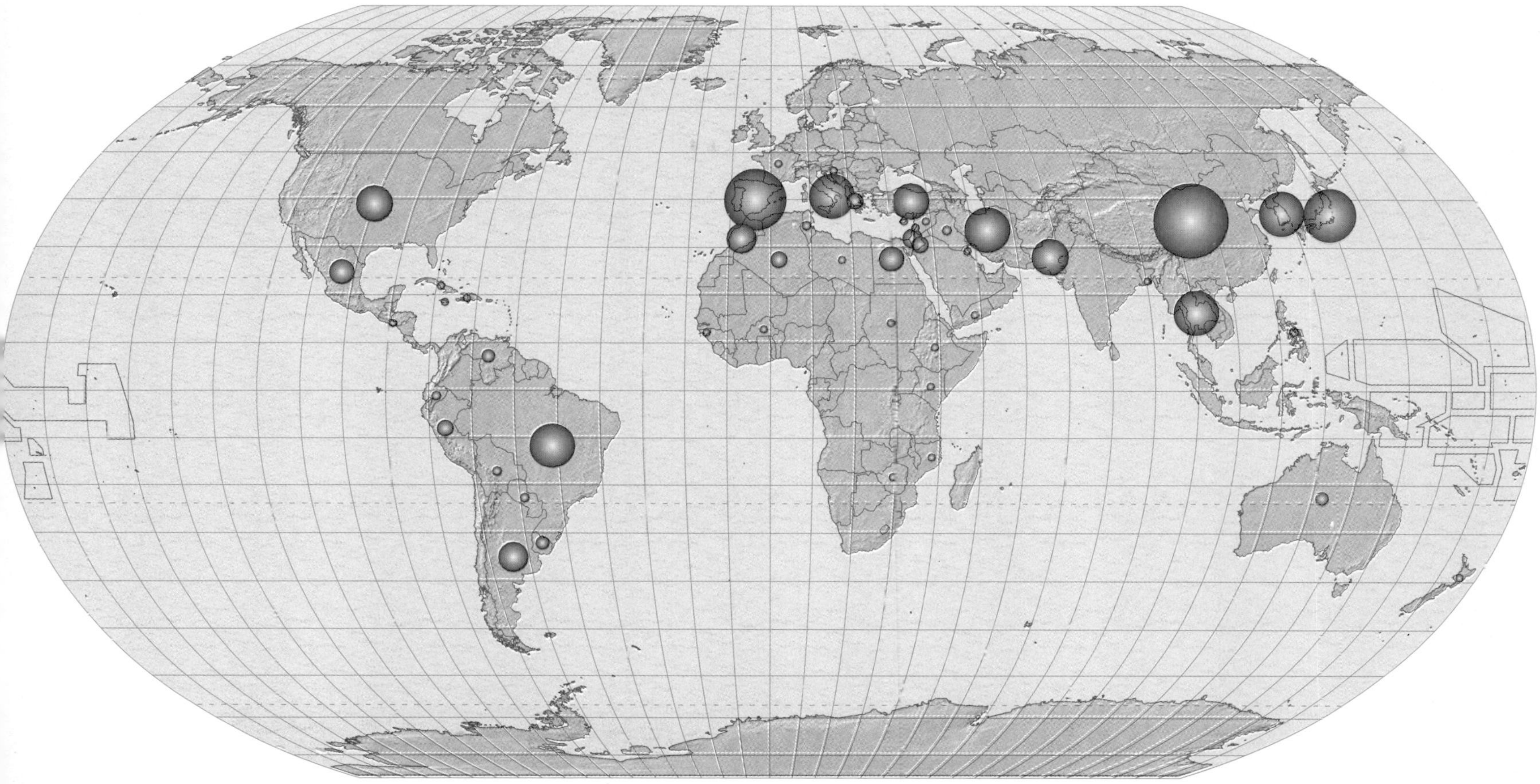

Annual tangerine production (in thousands of tons)

- Less than 25
- From 25 to 50
- From 50 to 75
- From 75 to 100
- From 100 to 200
- From 200 to 300
- From 2,000 to 6,000
- From 1,000 to 2,000
- From 750 to 1,000
- From 500 to 750
- From 400 to 500
- From 300 to 400

Basic economic activities
Agriculture

Apples

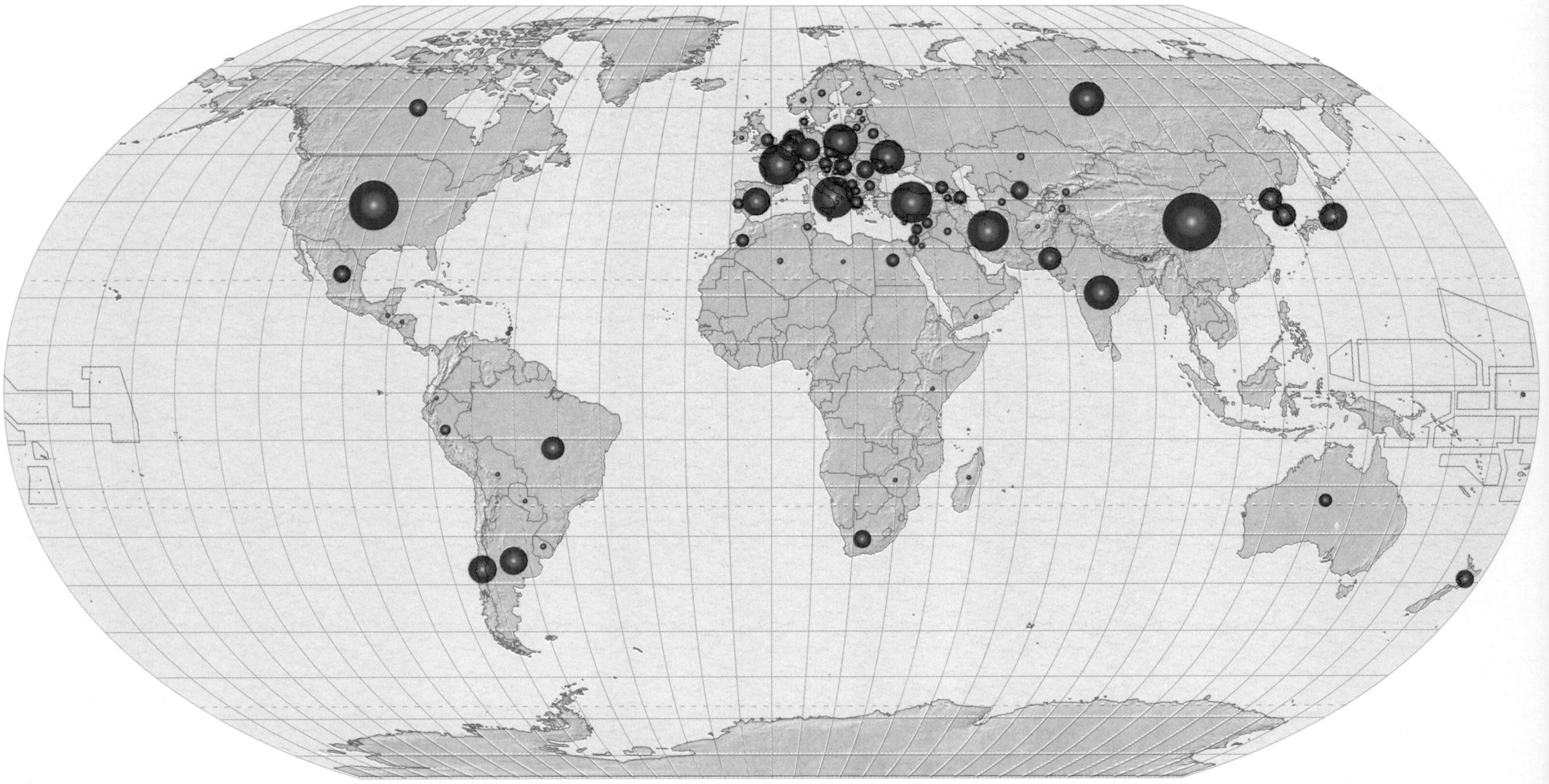

Annual apple production (in thousands of tons)

- Less than 25
- From 25 to 50
- From 50 to 100
- From 100 to 250
- From 250 to 350
- From 350 to 50
- From 5,000 to 15,000
- From 2,500 to 5,00C
- From 1,500 to 2,500
- From 1,000 to 1,500
- From 750 to 1,000
- From 500 to 75

Pears

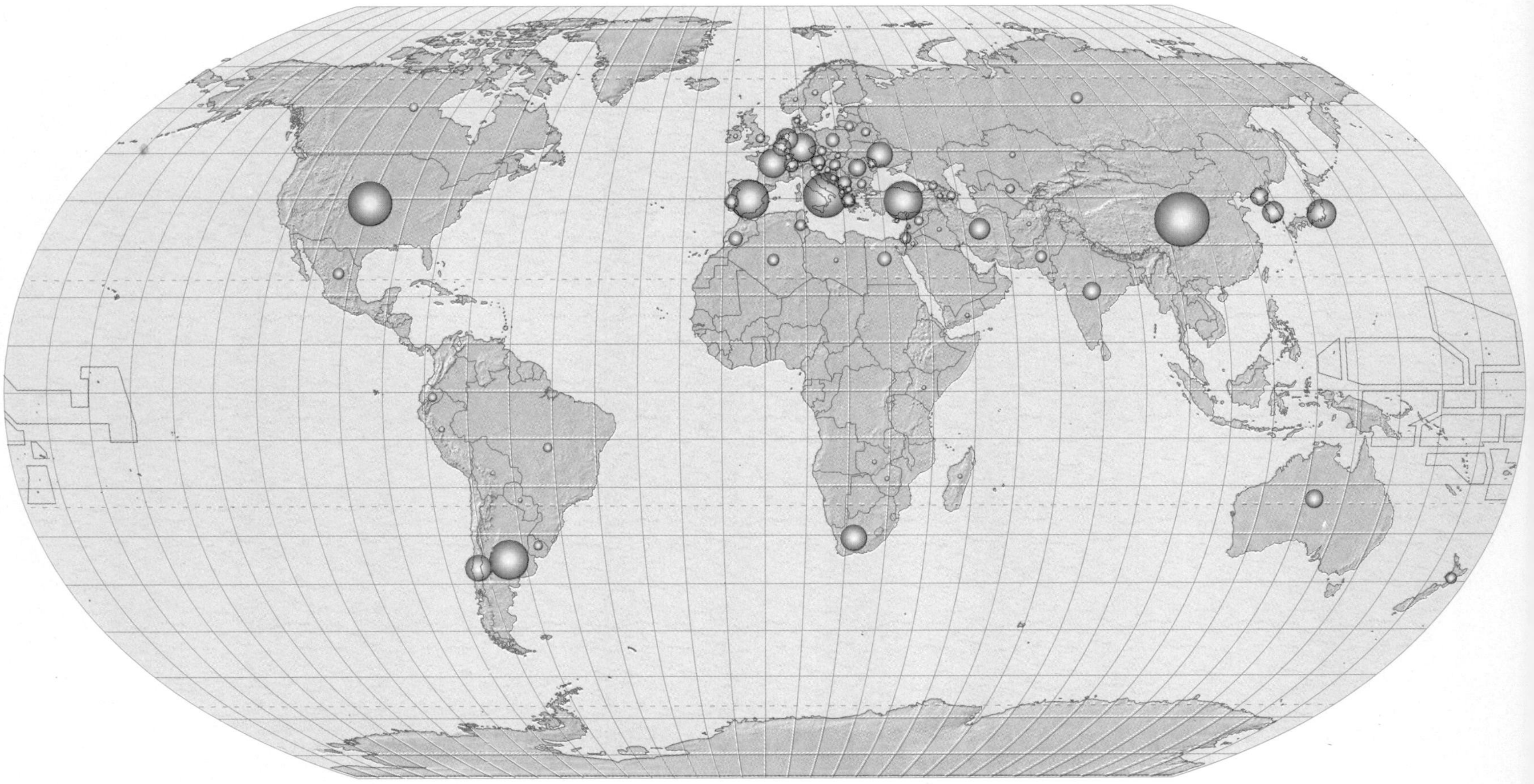

Annual pear production (in thousands of tons)

- Less than 5
- From 5 to 10
- From 10 to 25
- From 25 to 50
- From 50 to 100
- From 100 to 1
- From 1,000 to 6,000
- From 600 to 1,000
- From 400 to 600
- From 250 to 400
- From 200 to 250
- Fom 150 to 2C

Grapes

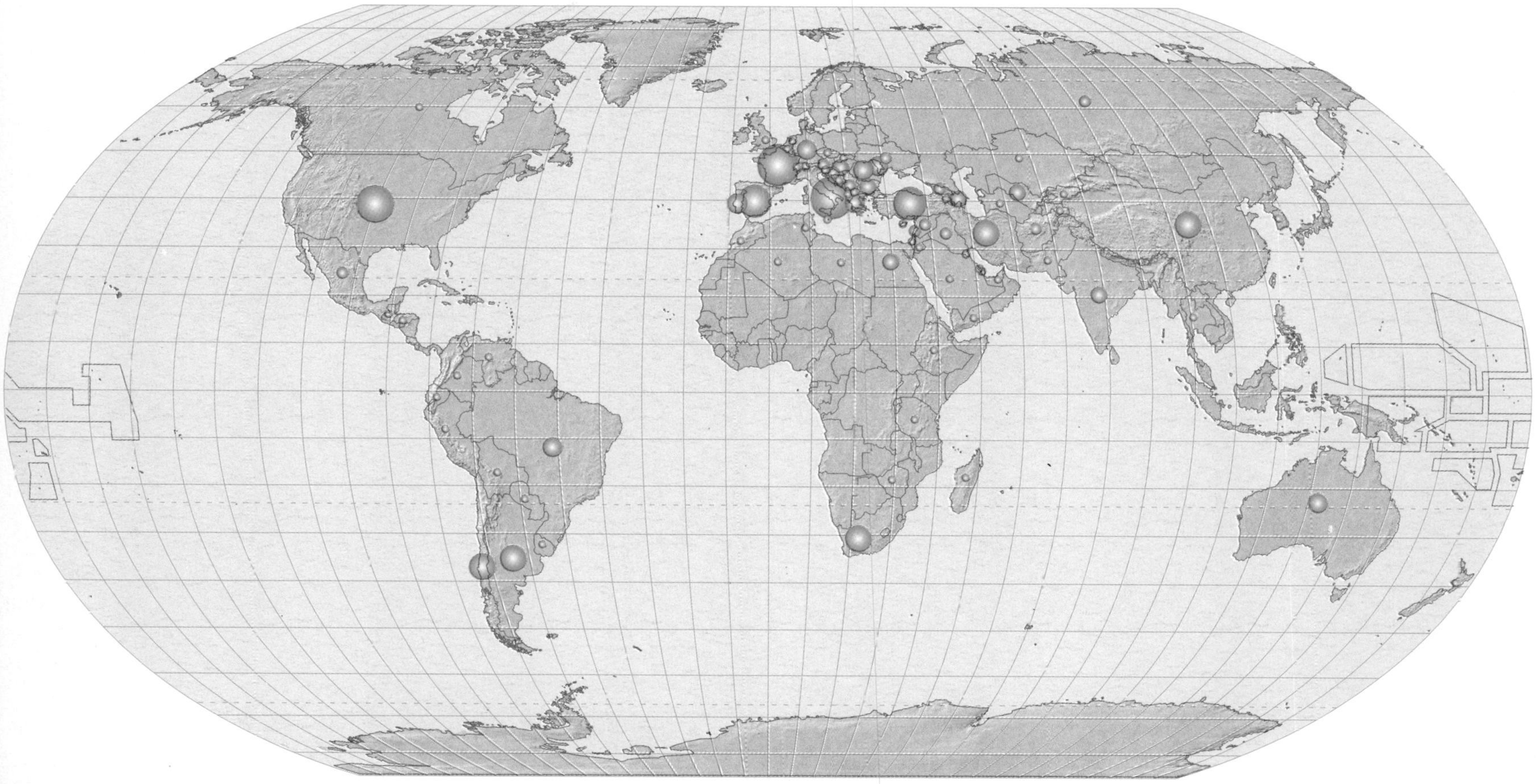

Annual grape production (in thousands of tons)

- Less than 250
- From 250 to 500
- From 500 to 750
- From 750 to 1,500
- From 1,500 to 3,000
- From 3,000 to 5,000
- From 5,000 to 7,000
- From 7,000 to 8,500

Peaches and nectarines

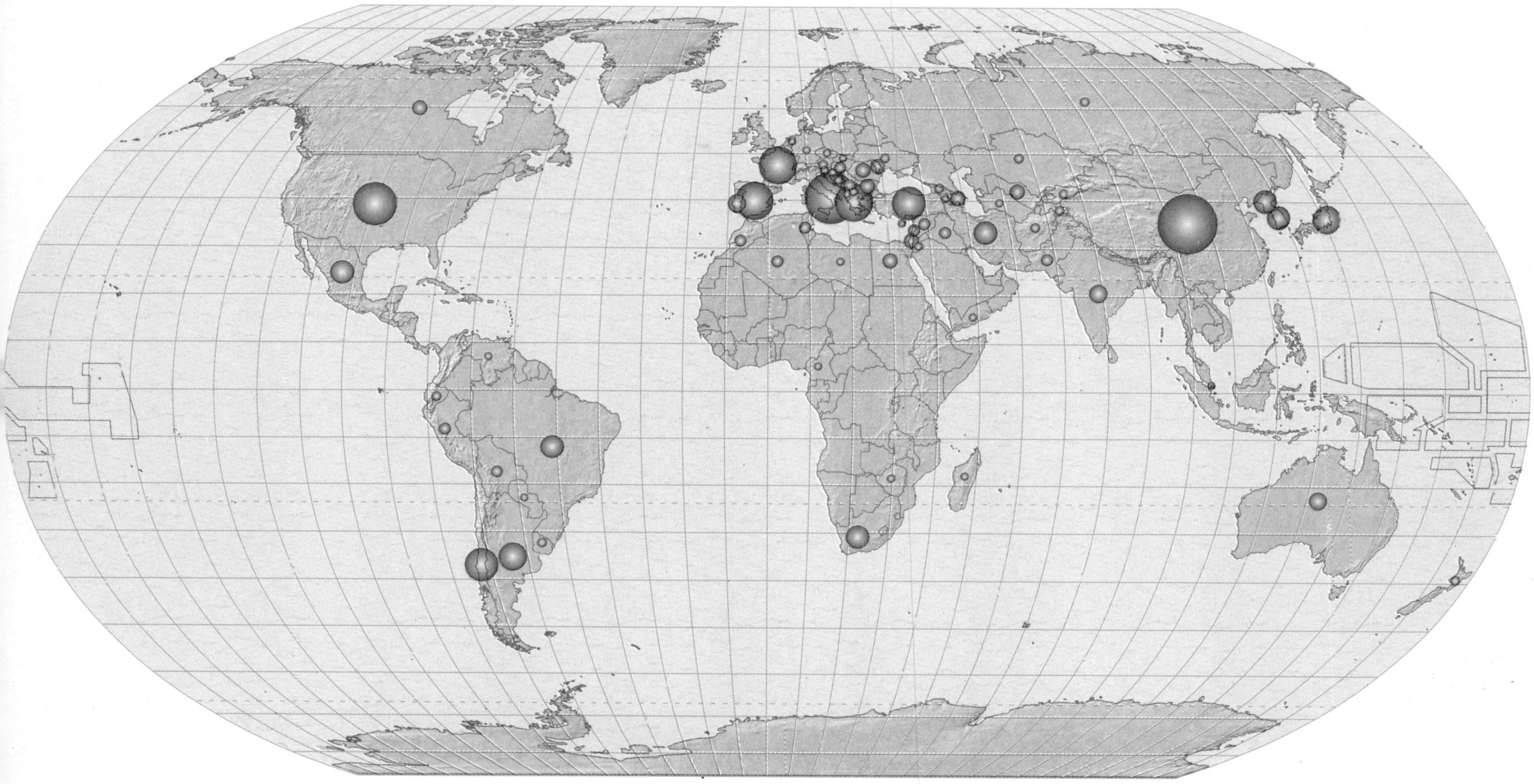

Annual peach and nectarine production (in thousands of tons)

- Less than 10
- From 10 to 25
- From 25 to 50
- From 50 to 75
- From 75 to 100
- From 100 to 150
- From 2,000 to 2,500
- From 1,500 to 2,000
- From 1,000 to 1,500
- From 500 to 1,000
- From 250 to 500
- From 150 to 250

Basic economic activities
Agriculture

Plums

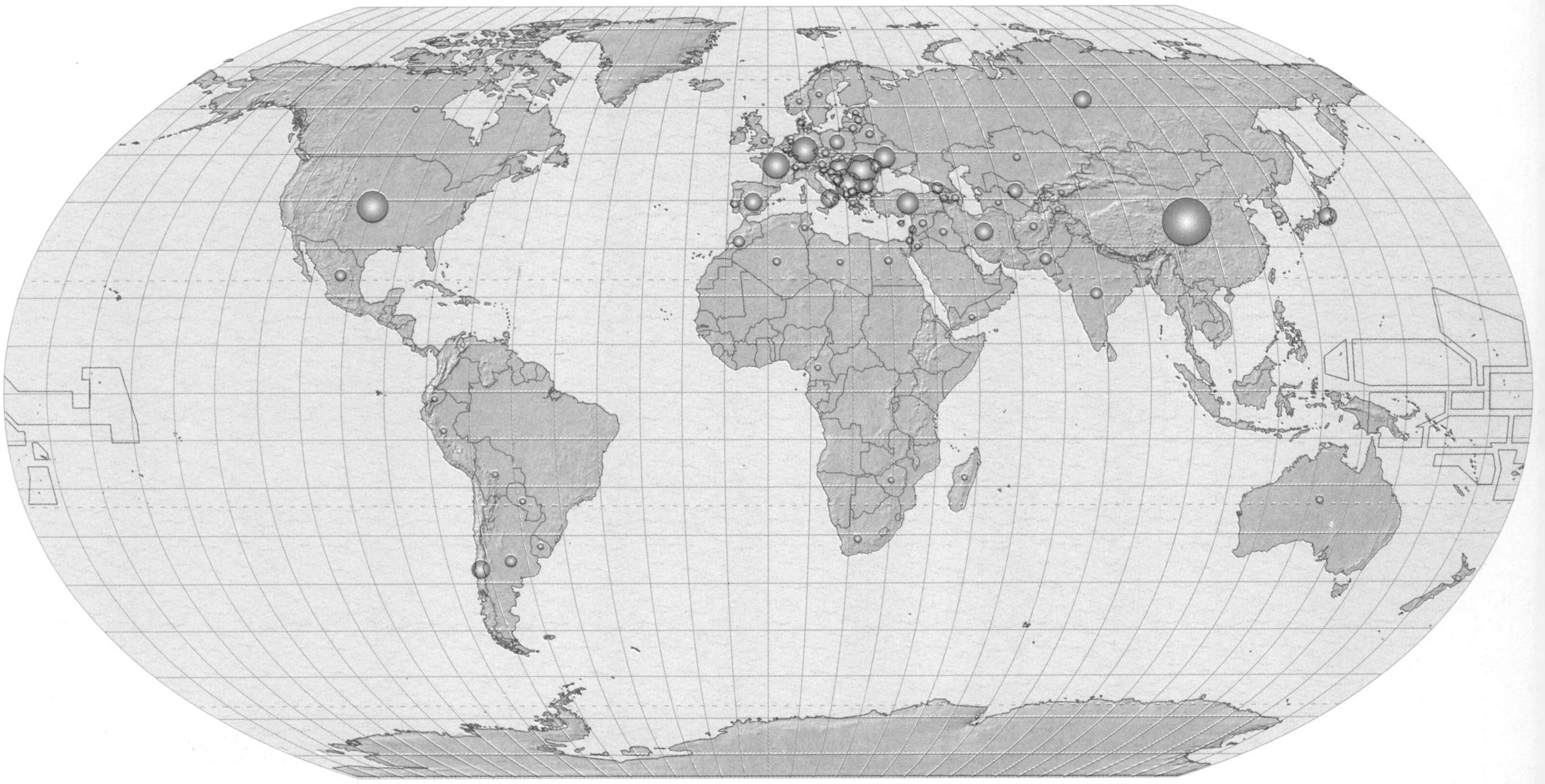

Annual plum production (in thousands of tons)

Less than 15 · From 15 to 50 · From 50 to 75 · From 75 to 100 · From 100 to 150 · From 150 to 250 · From 250 to 500 · From 500 to 1,000 · From 1,000 to 2,C

Bananas and plantains

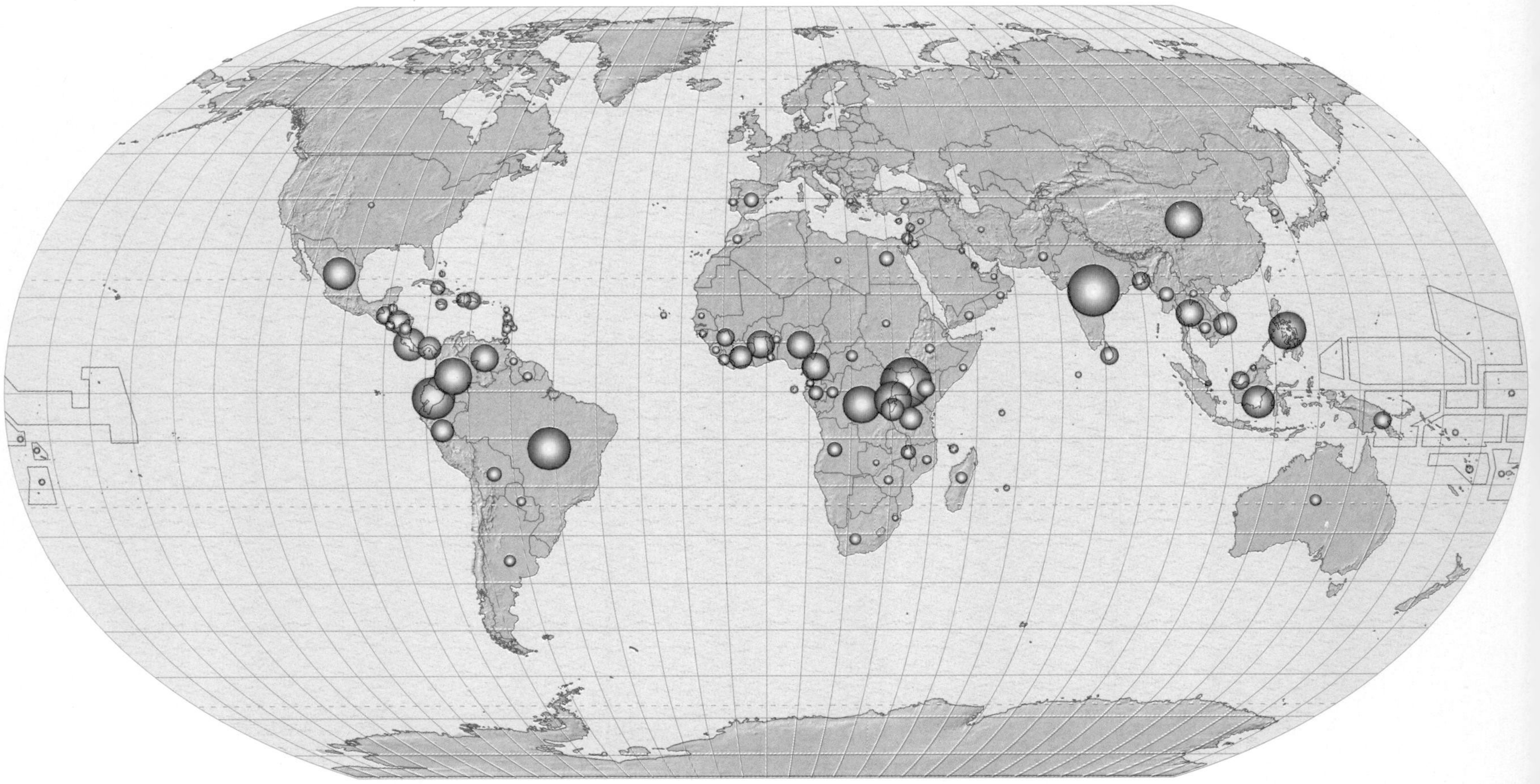

Annual banana production (in thousands of tons)

Less than 10 · From 10 to 50 · From 50 to 100 · From 100 to 250 · From 250 to 500 · From 500 to 1,000

From 7,500 to 12,000 · From 5,000 to 7,500 · From 2,500 to 5,000 · From 2,000 to 2,500 · From 1,500 to 2,000 · From 1,000 to 1,5(

Pineapples

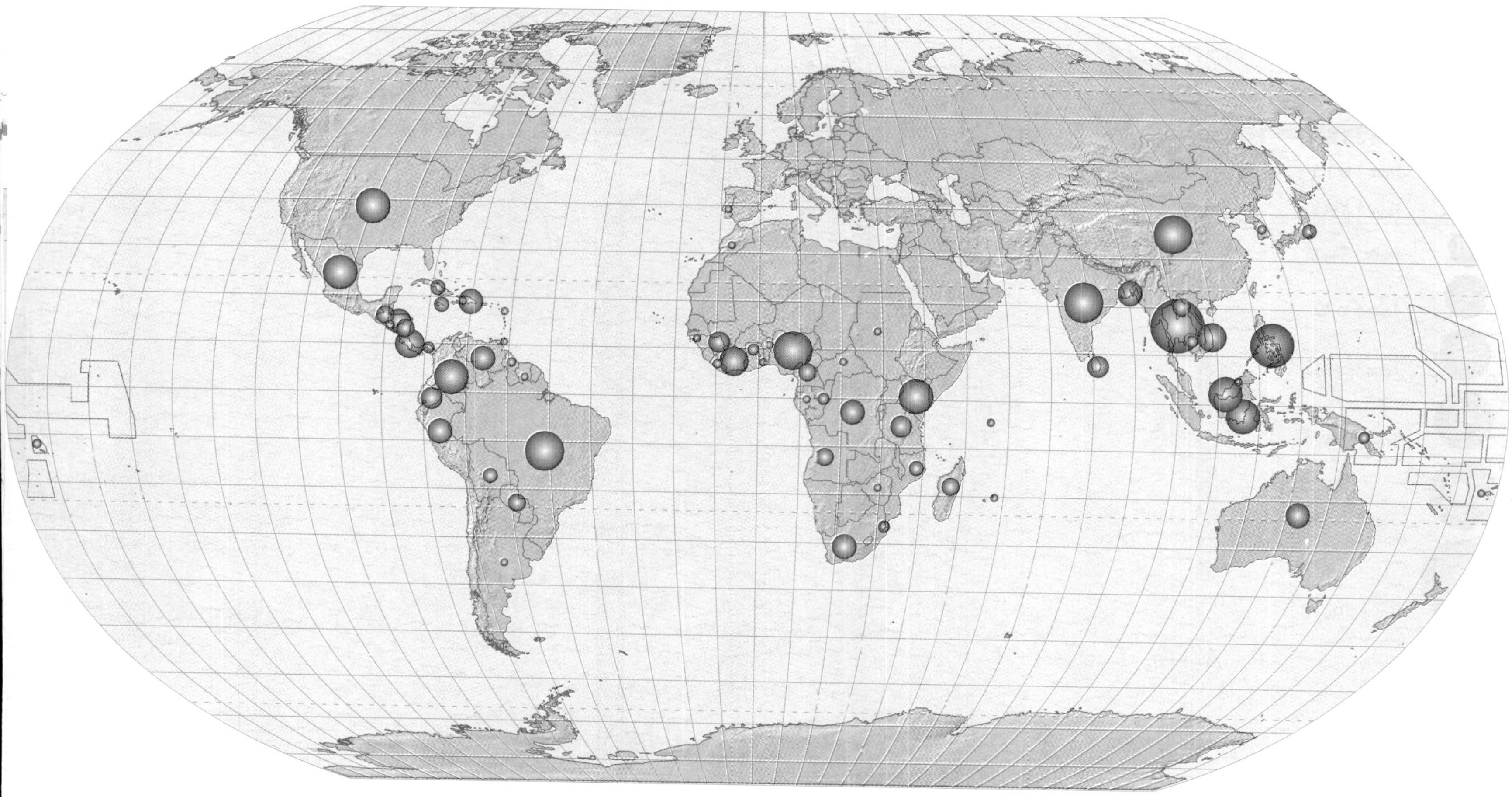

Annual pineapple production (in thousands of tons)

- Less than 5
- From 5 to 10
- From 10 to 15
- From 15 to 25
- From 25 to 50
- From 50 to 100
- From 2,000 to 2,500
- From 1,000 to 2,000
- From 500 to 1,000
- From 250 to 500
- From 150 to 250
- From 100 to 150

Mangoes

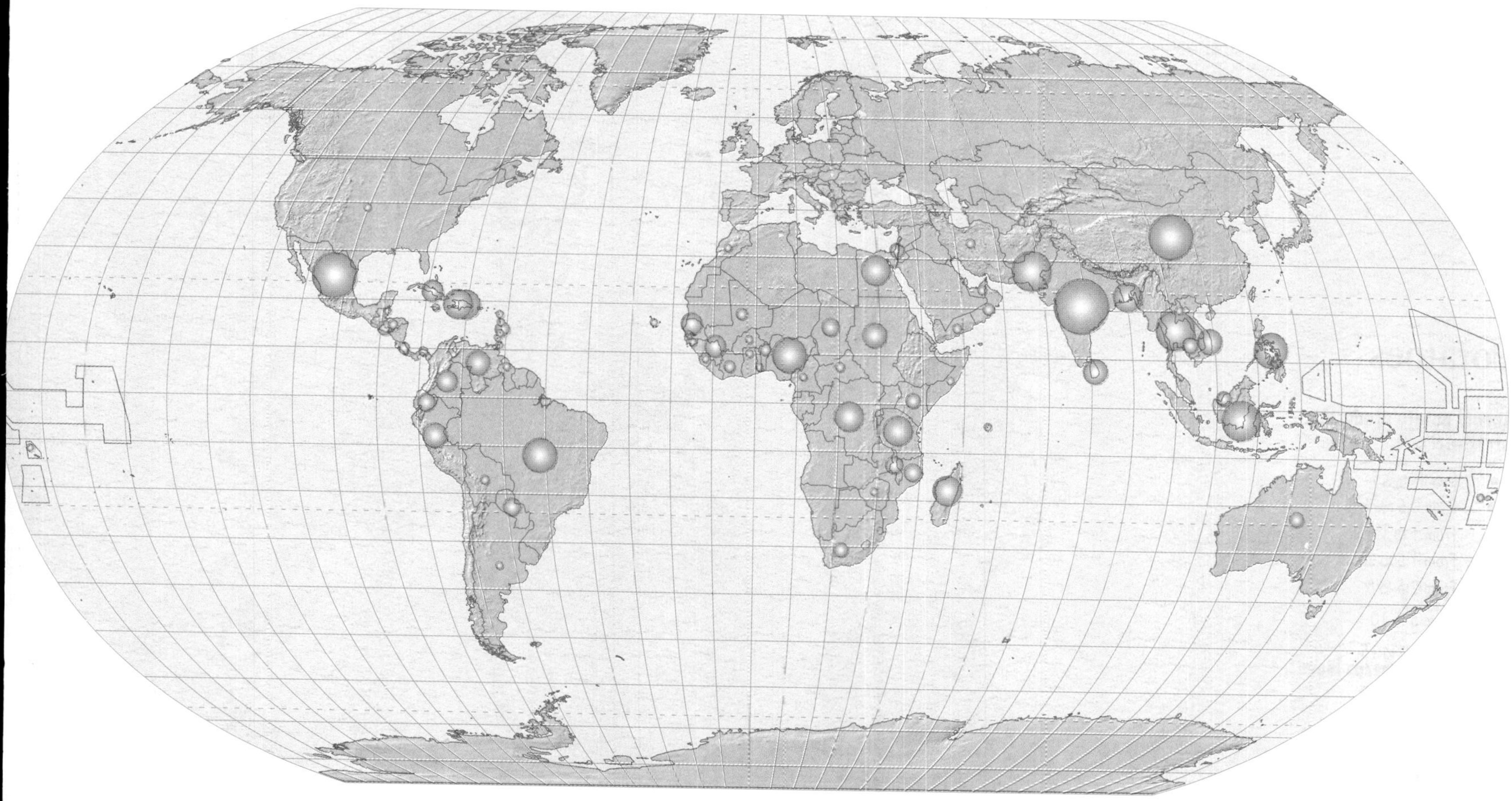

Annual mango production (in thousands of tons)

- Less than 5
- From 5 to 10
- From 10 to 15
- From 15 to 30
- From 30 to 60
- From 60 to 100
- From 2,000 to 10,000
- From 1,000 to 2,000
- From 500 to 1,000
- From 250 to 500
- From 150 to 250
- From 100 to 150

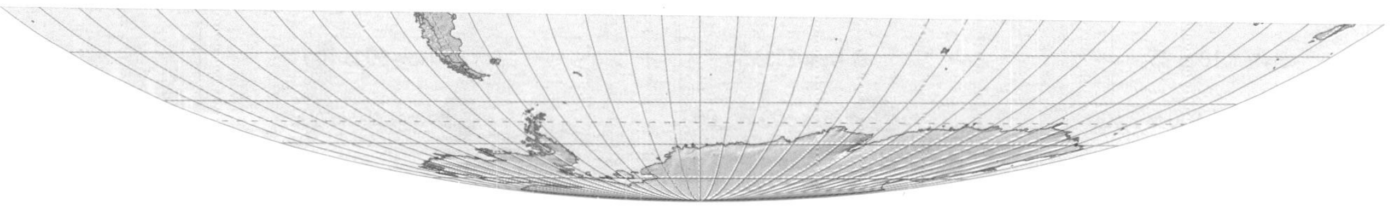

INDUSTRY COMERCE AND TRANSPORT

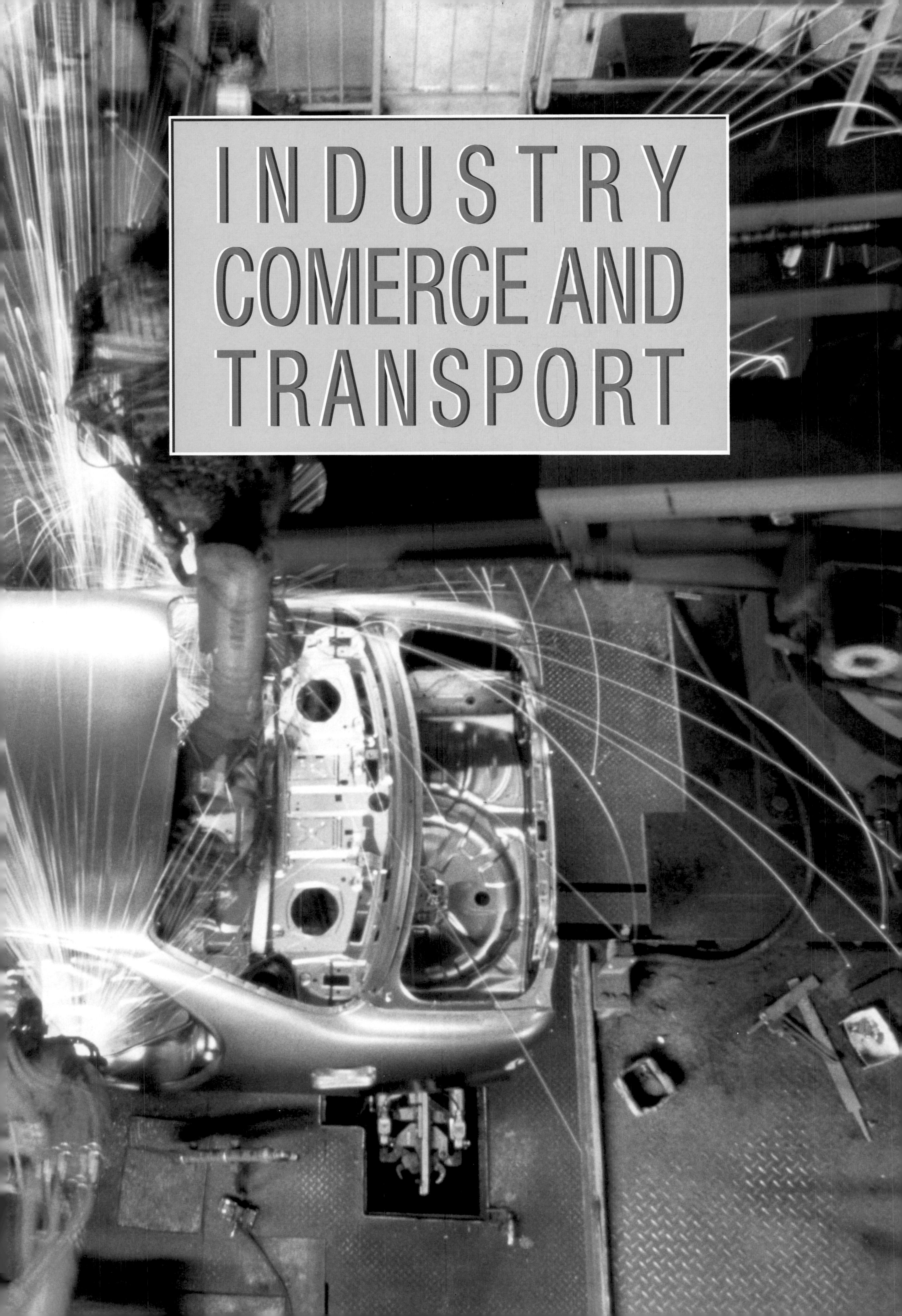

Mining and energy
Energy resources: location

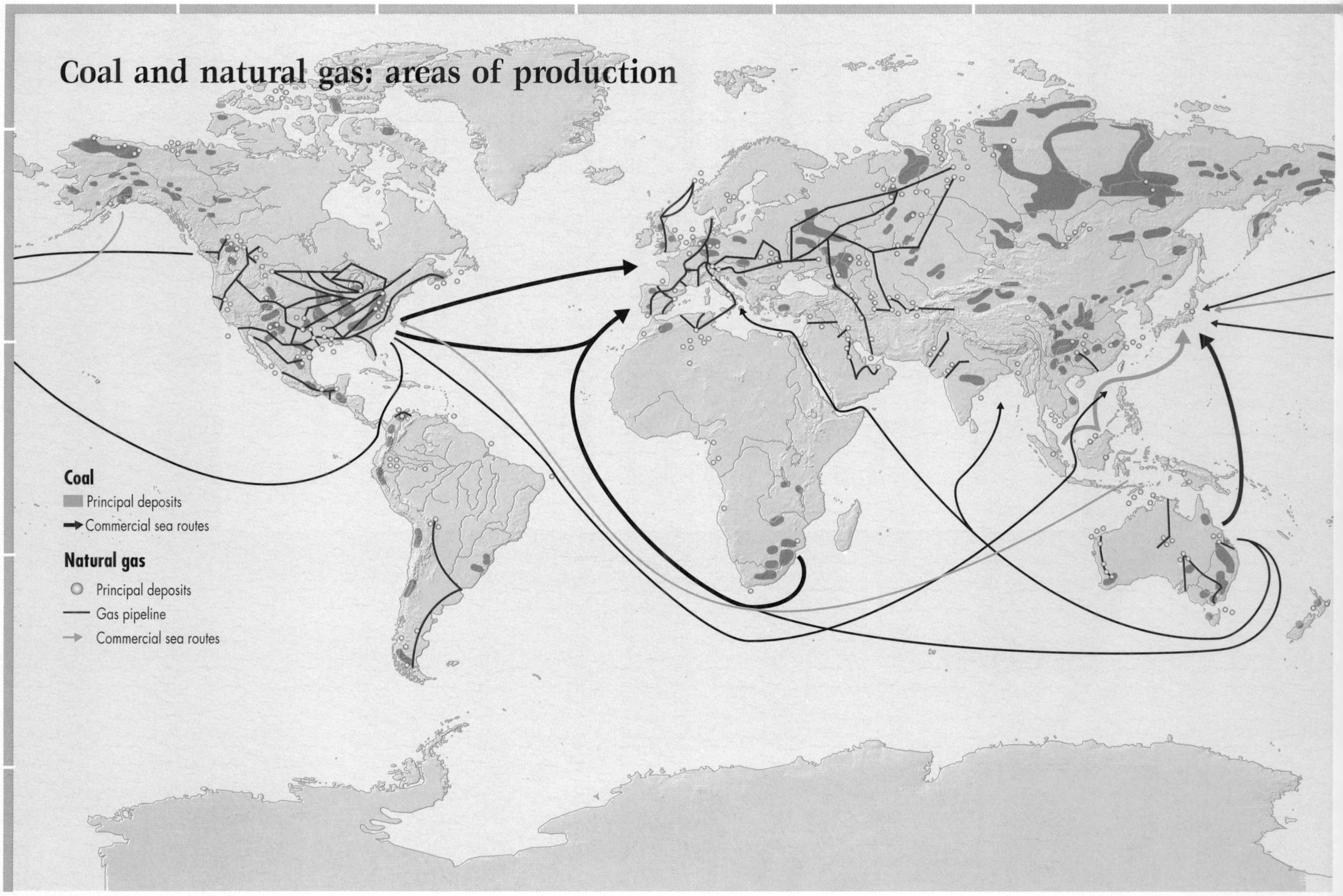

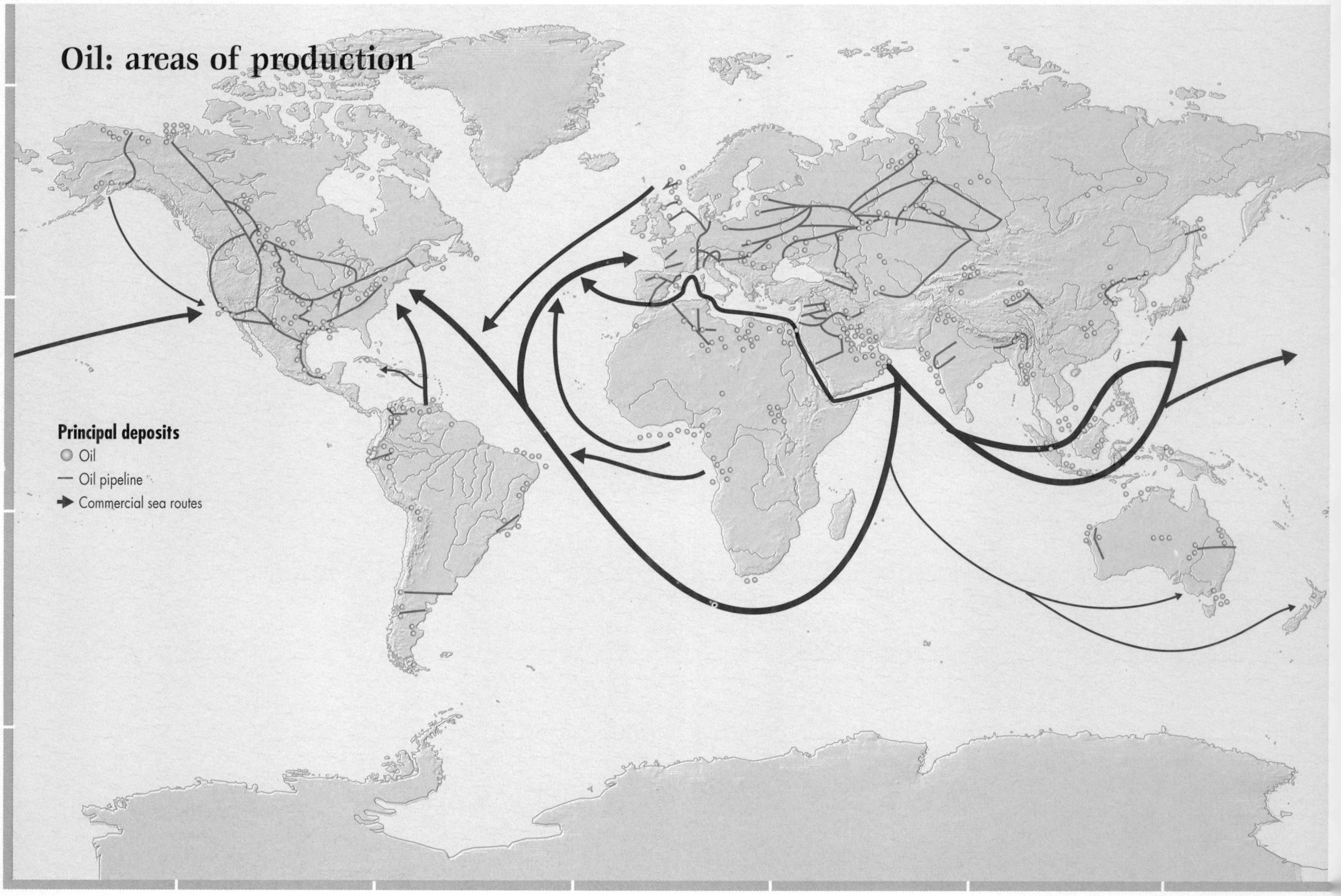

Renewable energy: geothermal and solar

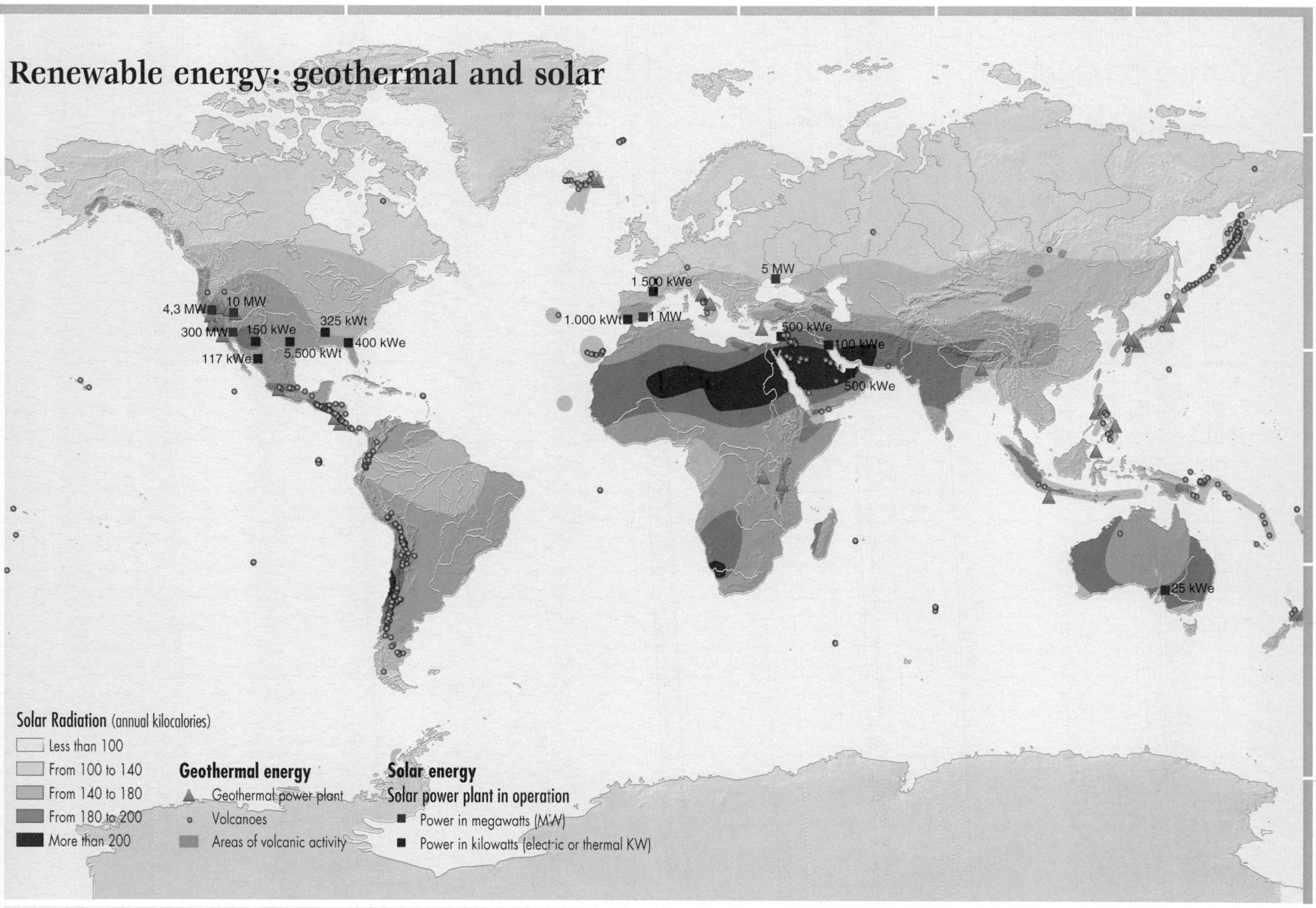

Nuclear energy

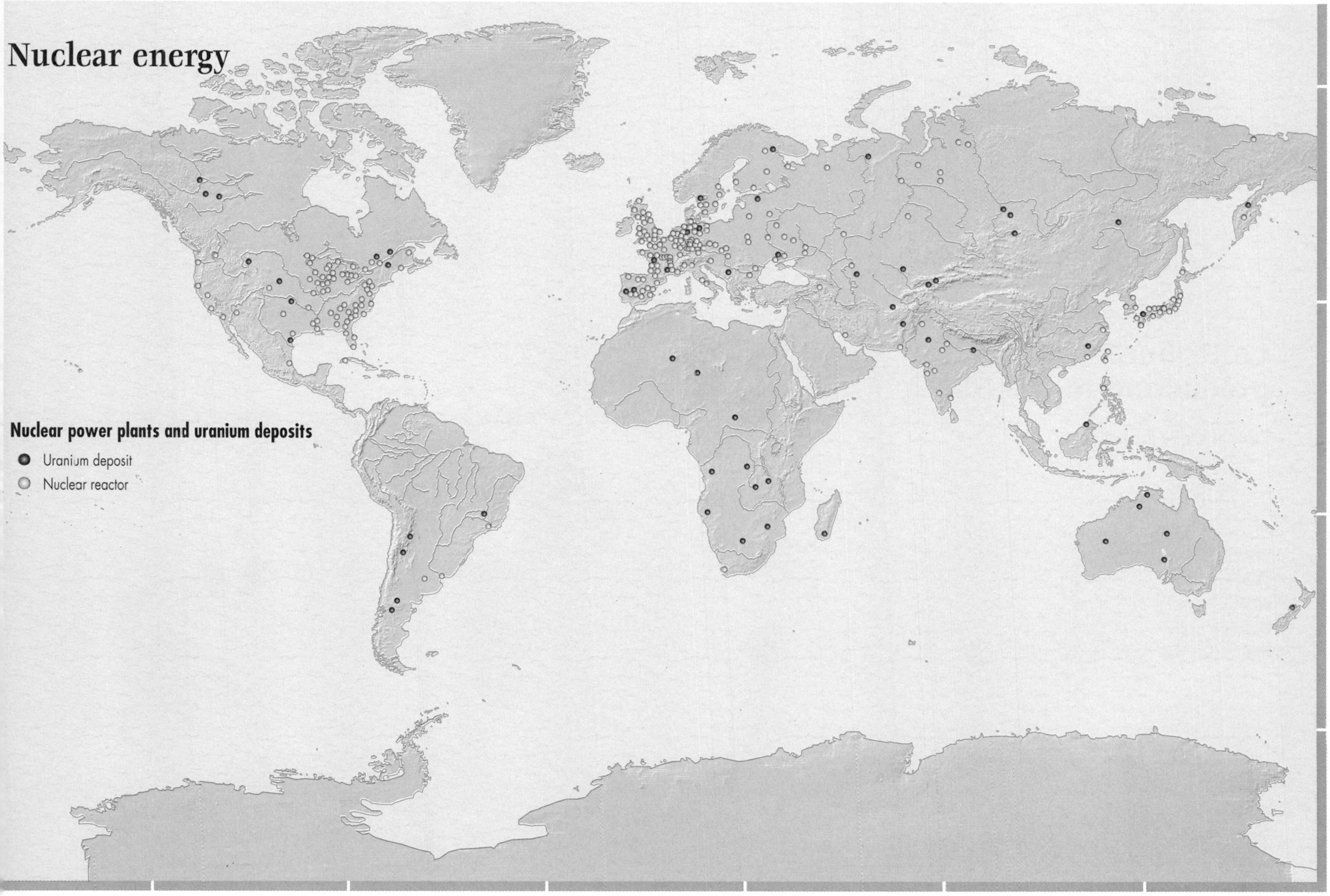

Mining and energy

Mineral resources: production

Mining production

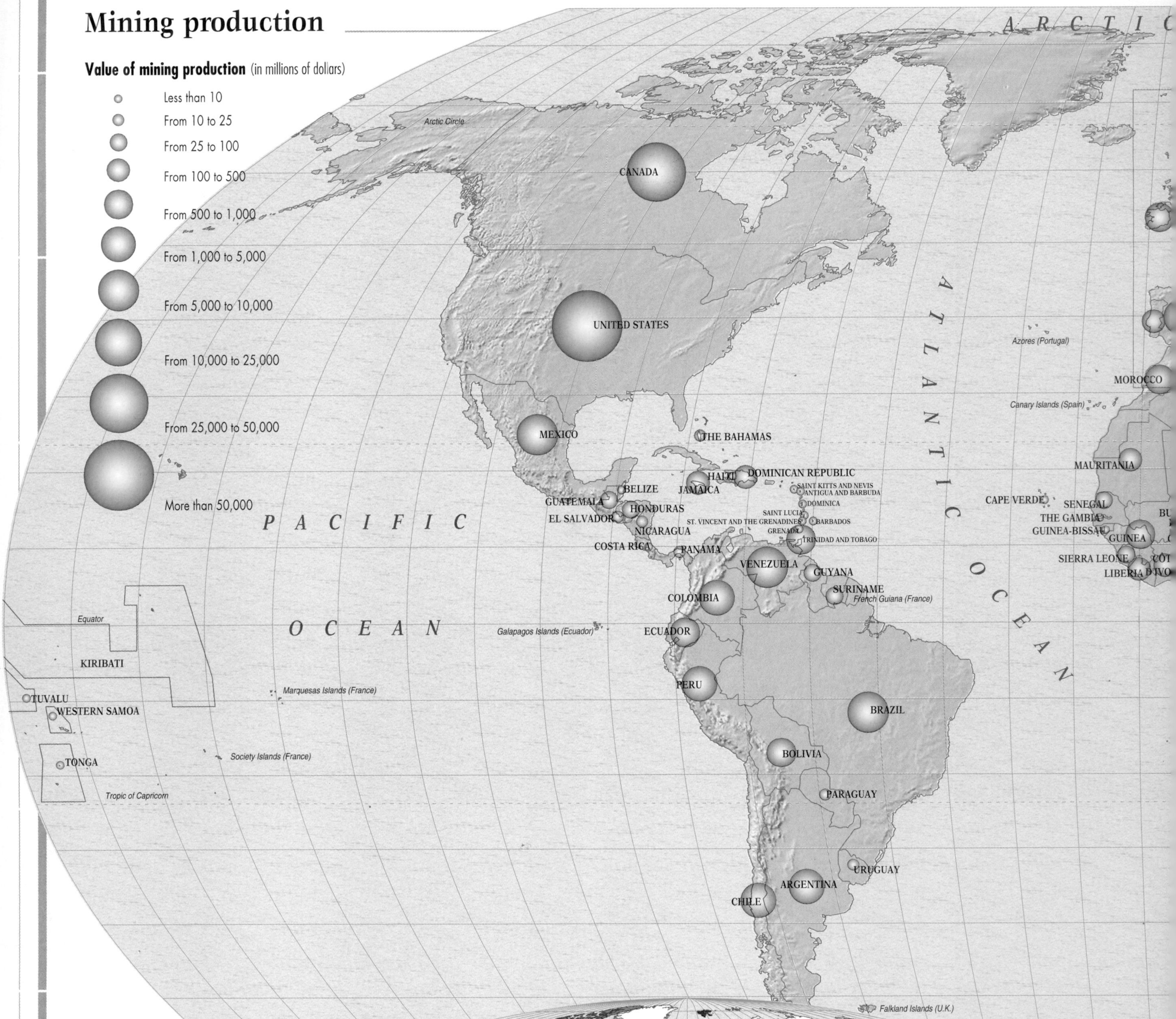

Contribution of mining production to the GDP

Value of mining production
(% of the GDP)

- Less than 0.5
- From 0.5 to 1
- From 1 to 2.5
- From 2.5 to 5
- From 5 to 10
- From 10 to 25
- From 25 to 50
- More than 50

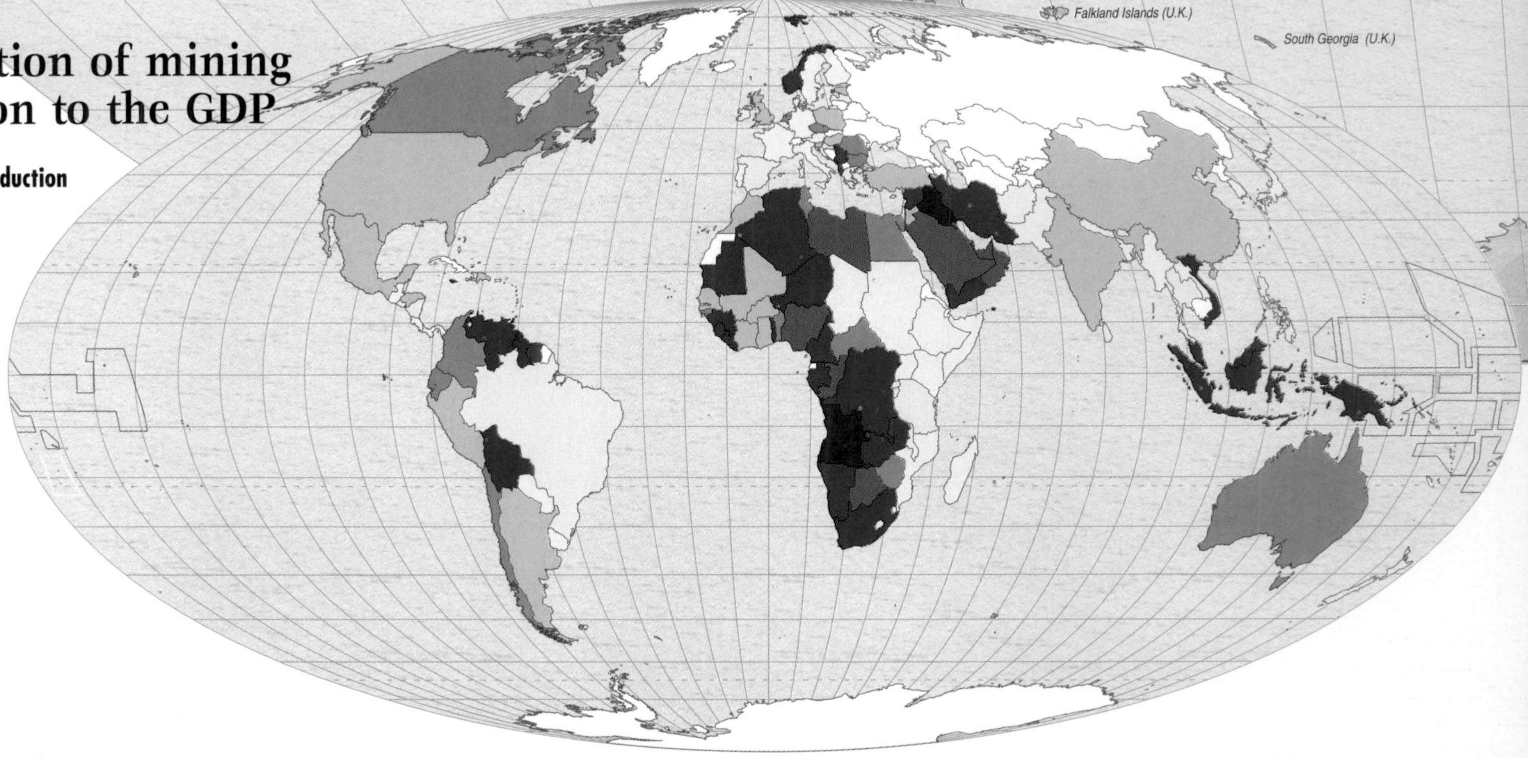

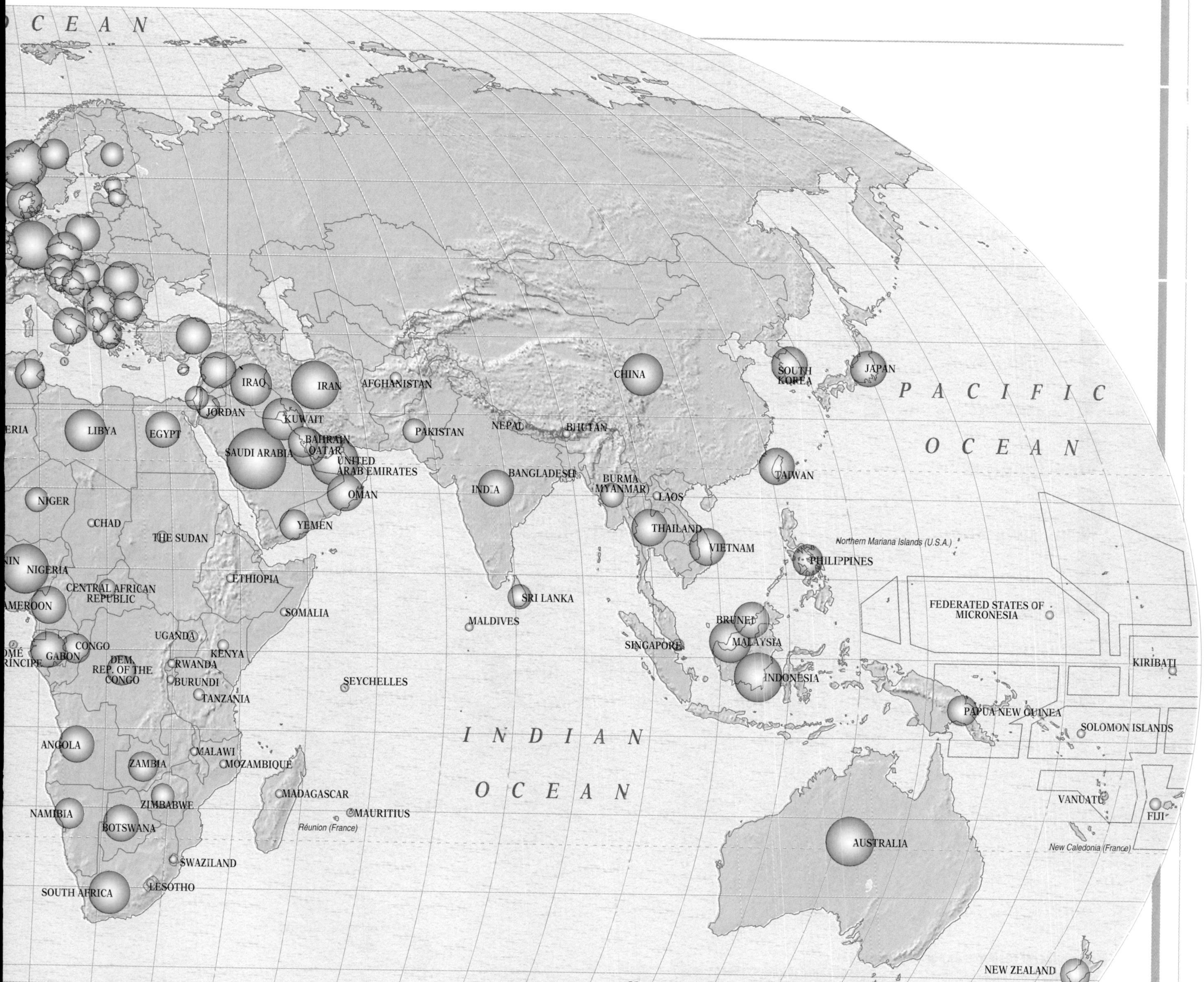

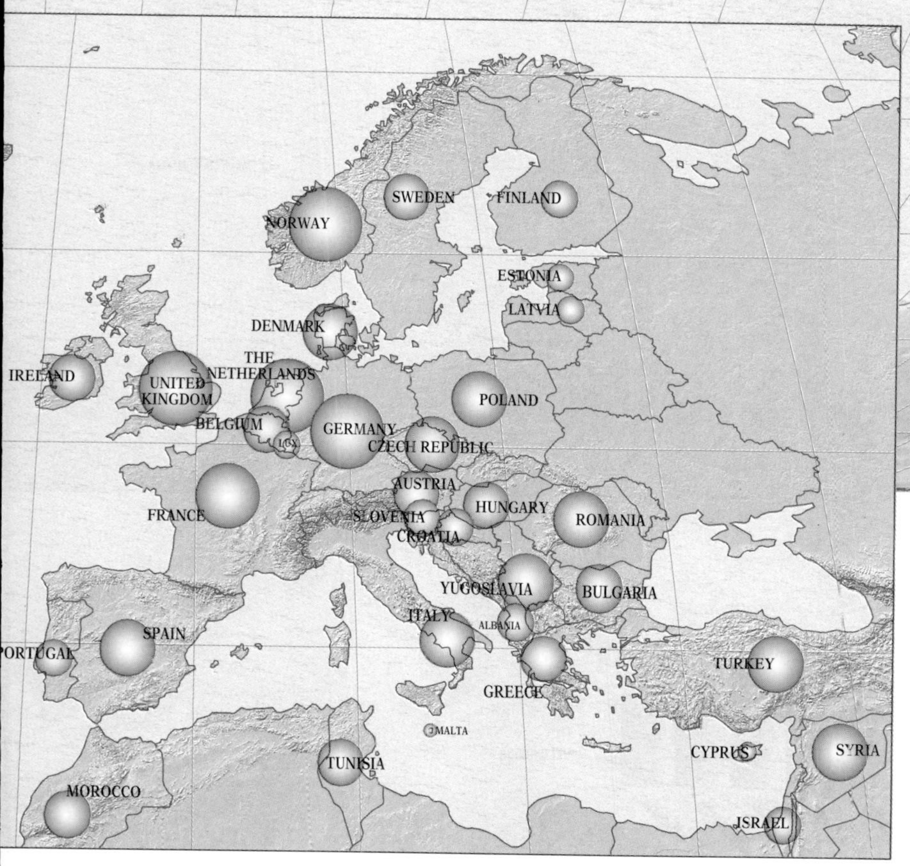

Major mineral resource producing countries
(Value of production in millions of dollars)

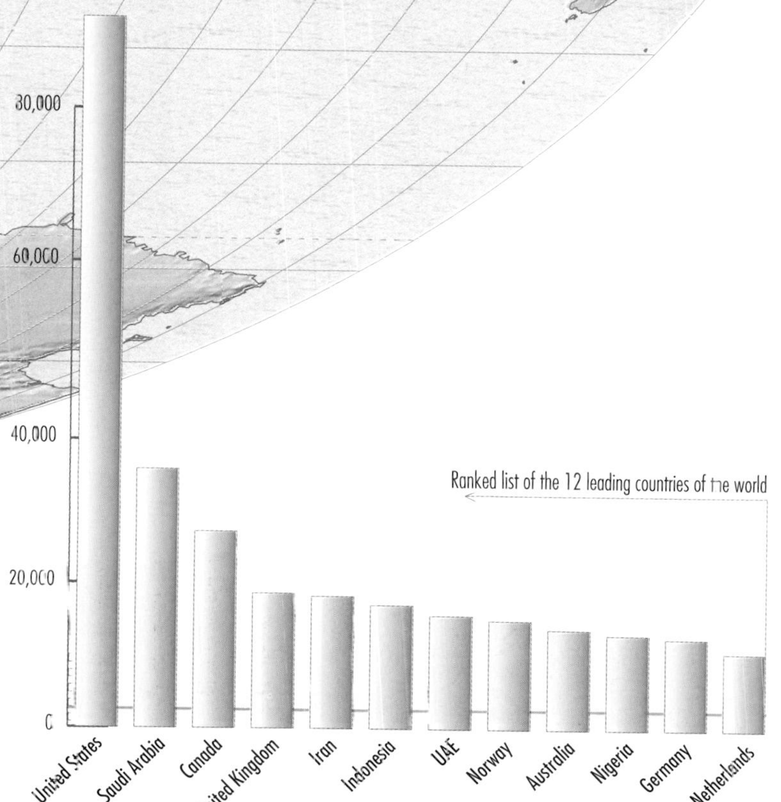

Mining and energy
Rock and industrial mineral production

Potash

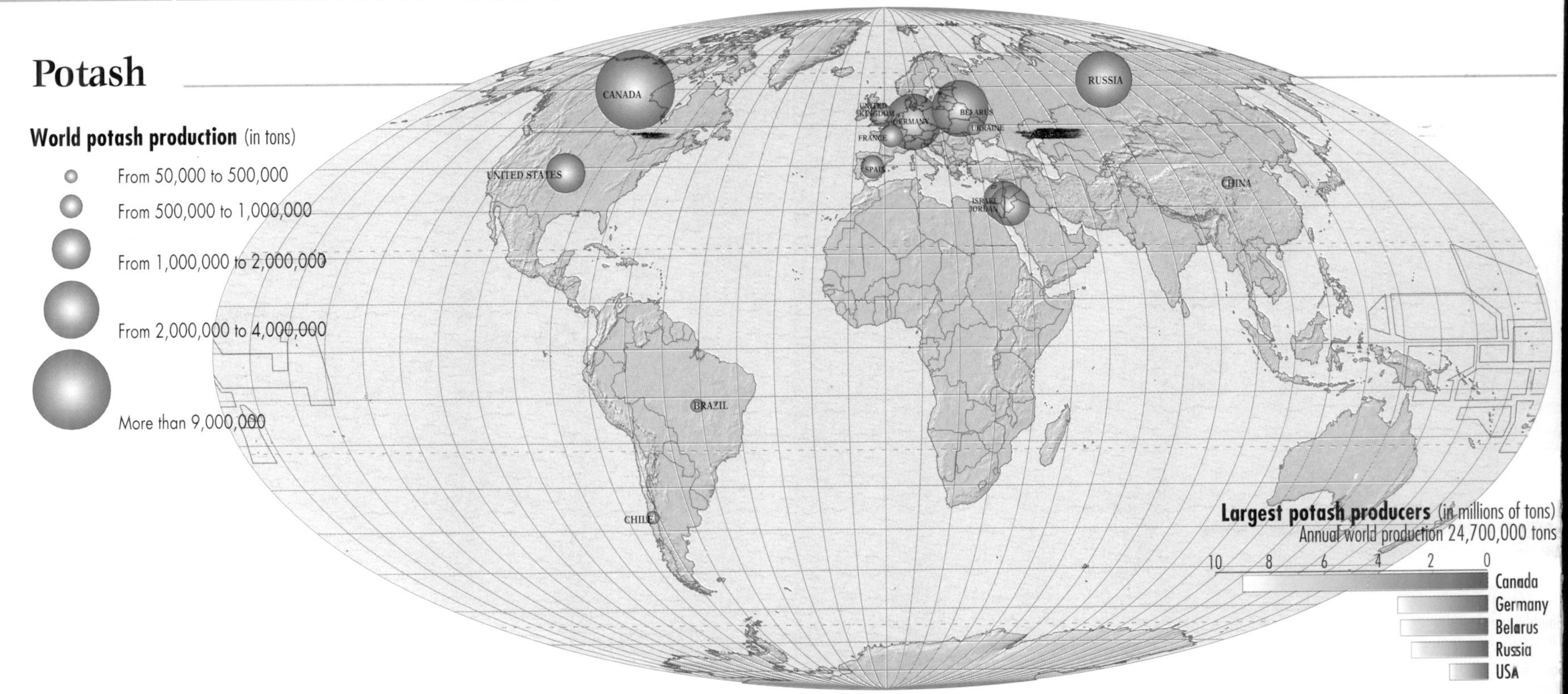

Salt

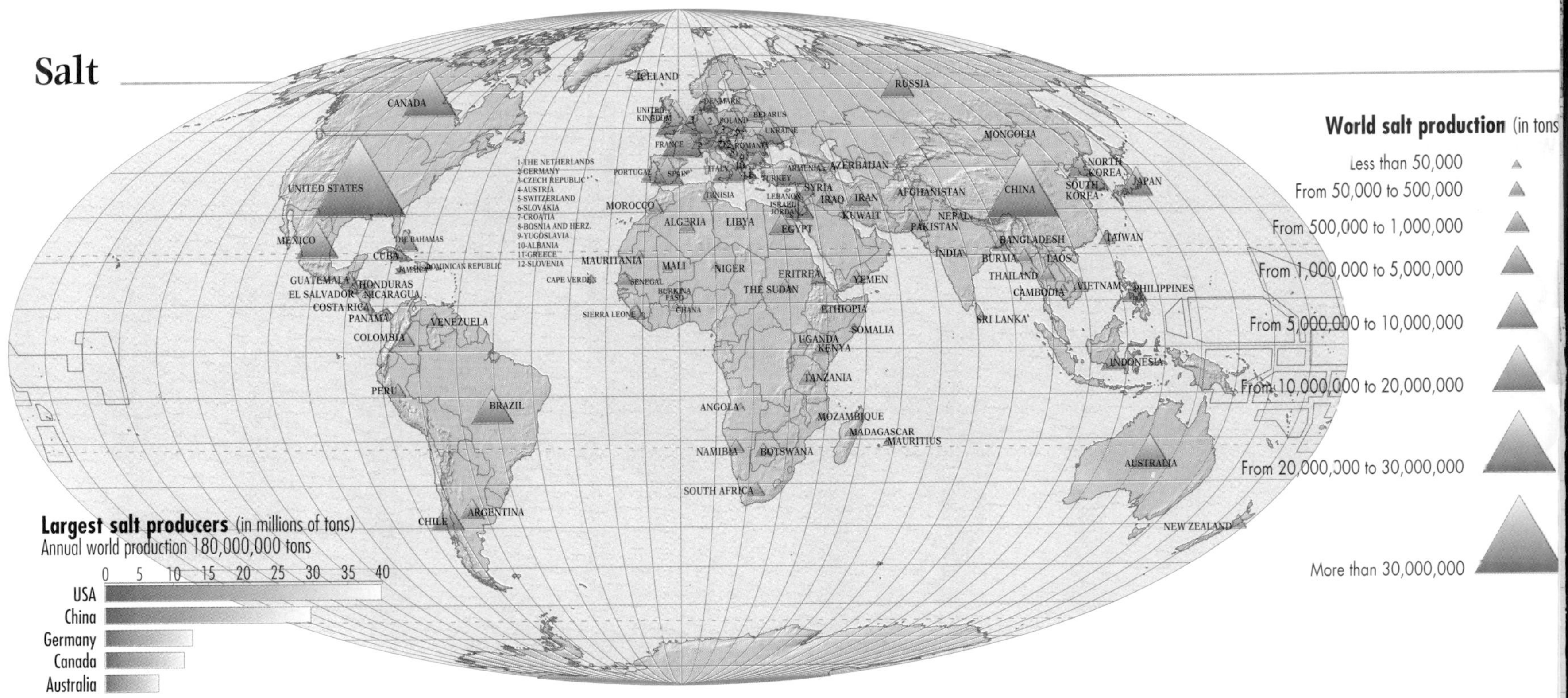

Sodium sulfate

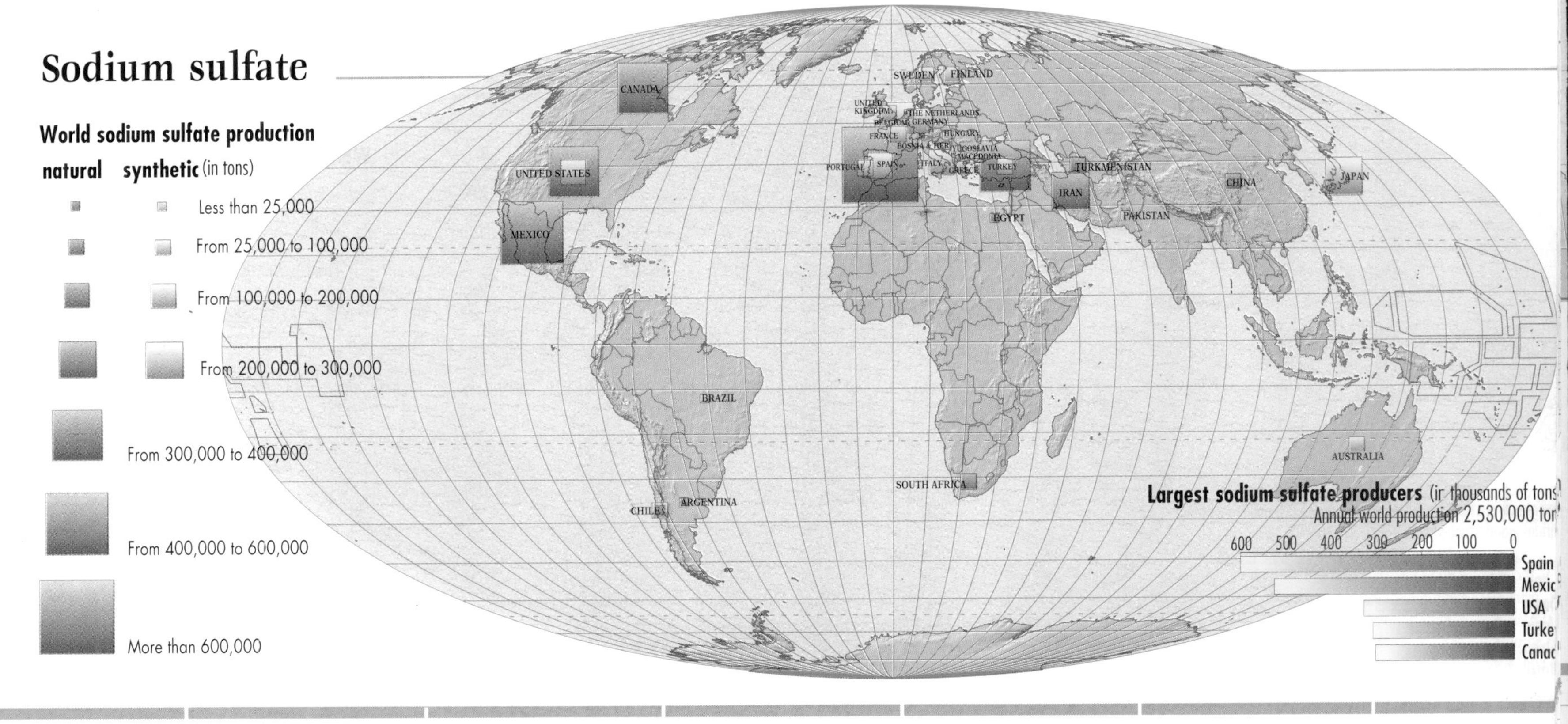

Talc, pyrophyllite and steatite

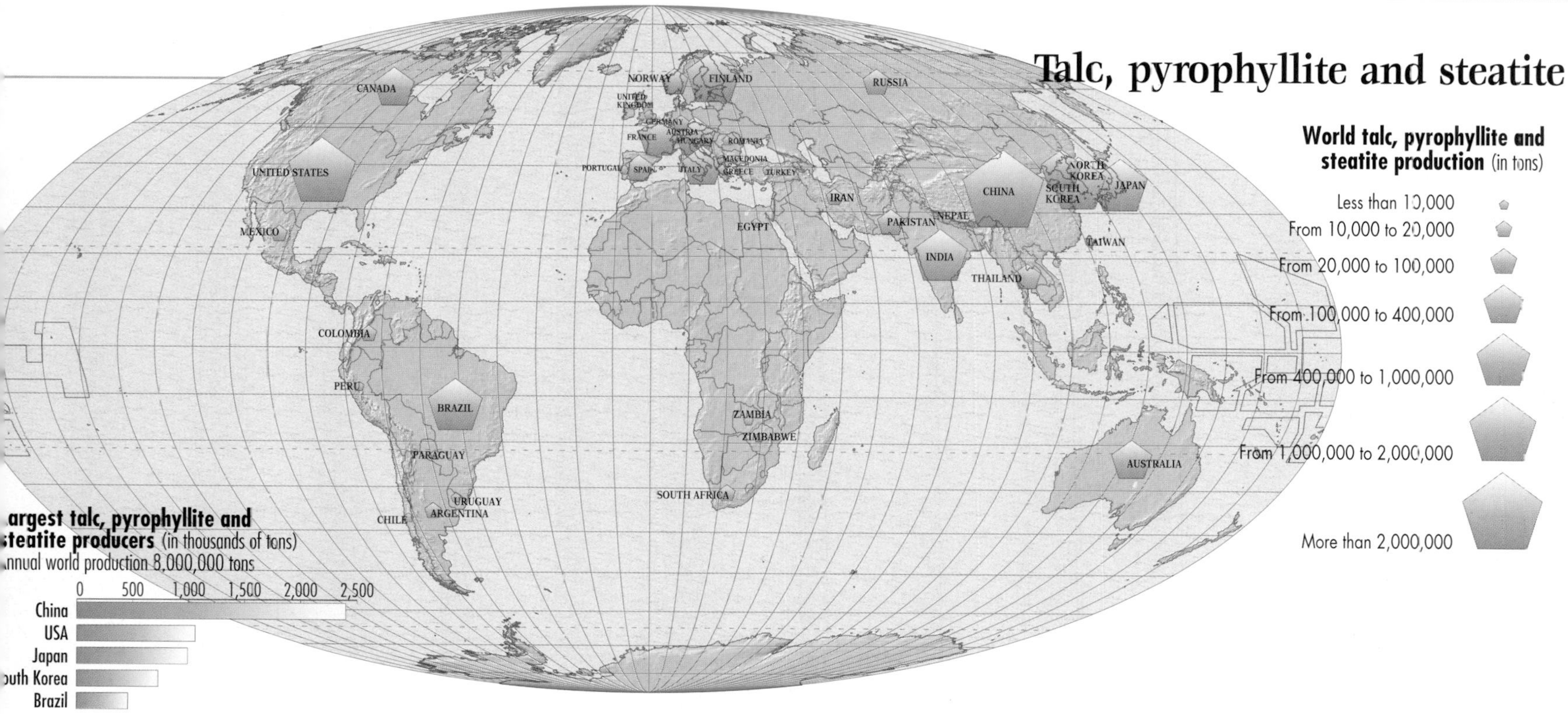

Titanium

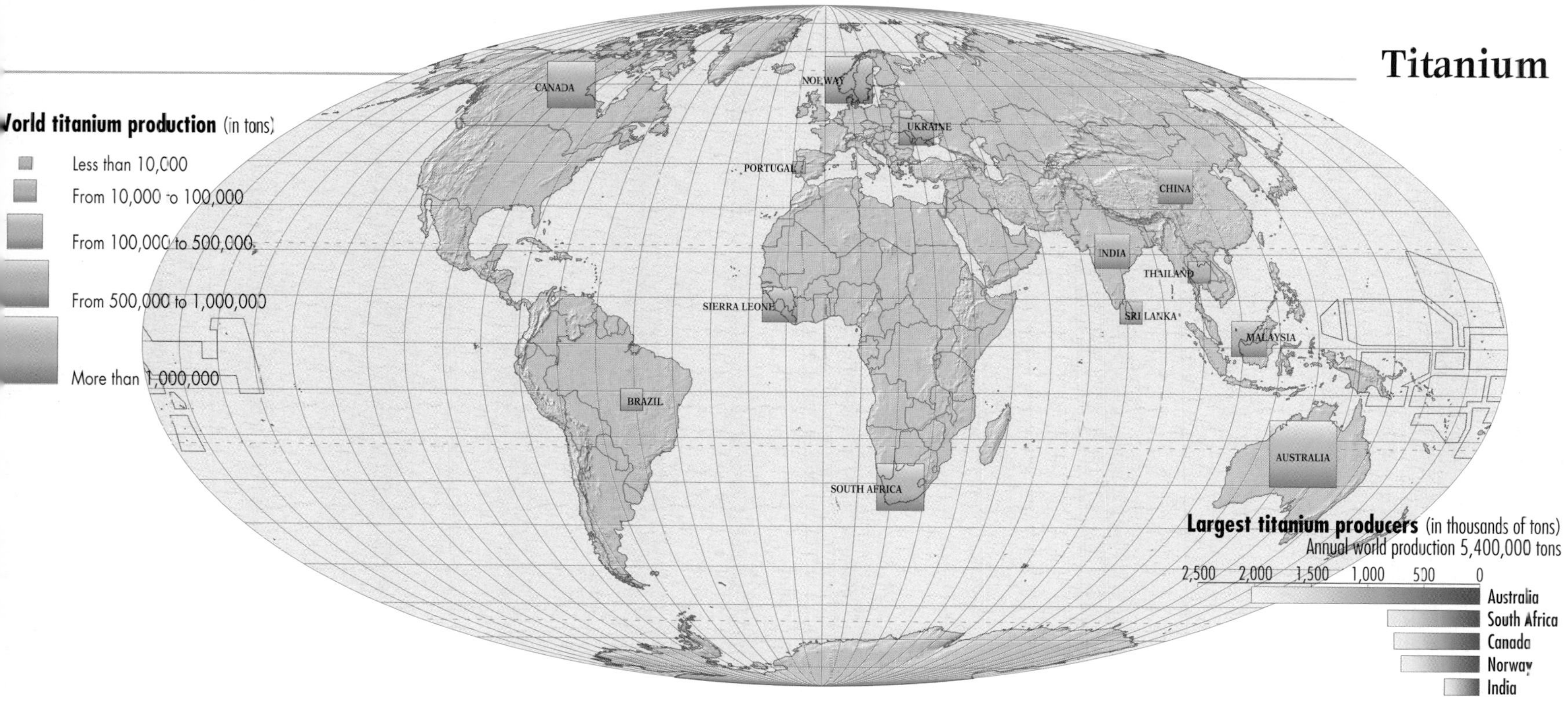

Gypsum

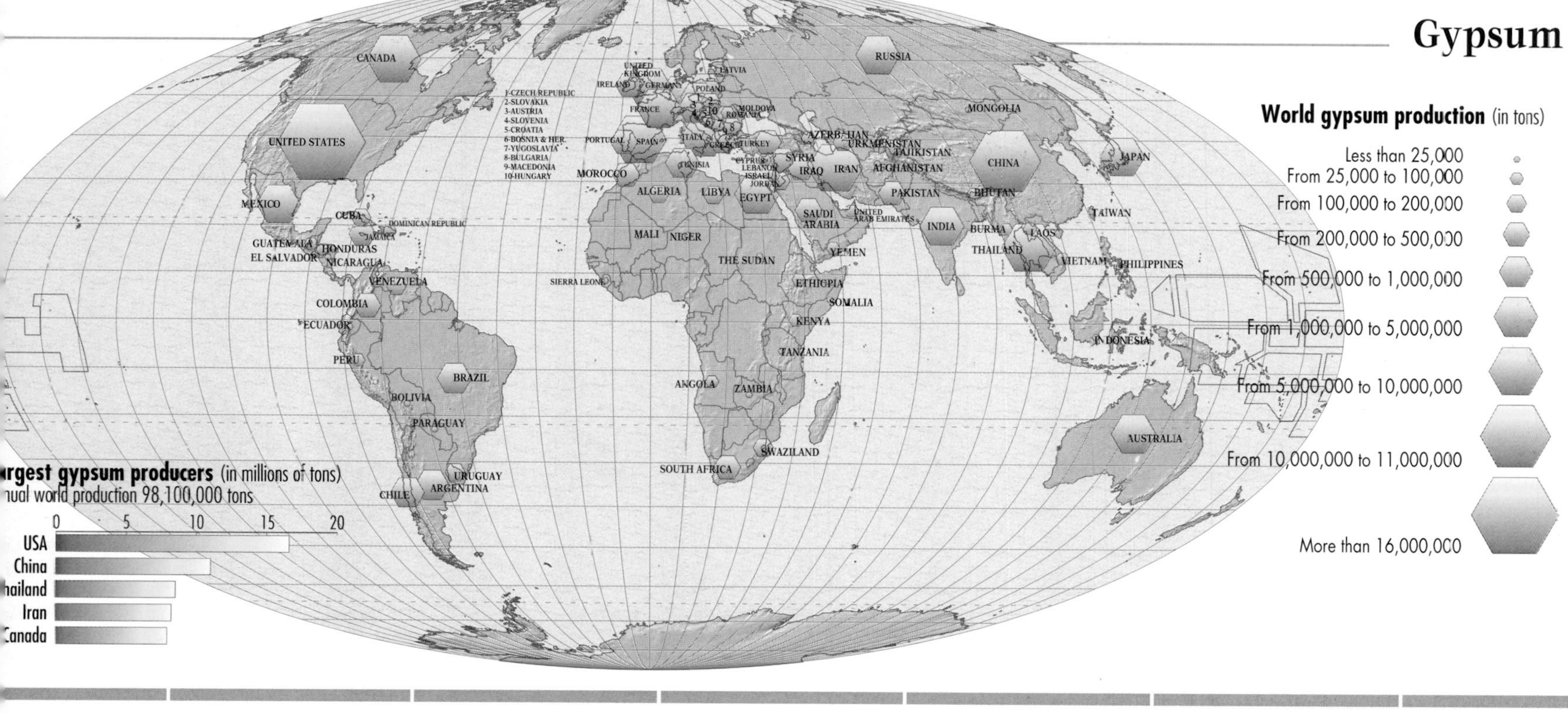

Mining and energy

Energy source mineral resources: fossil fuels

Coal consumption

Total consumption (toe)

- Less than 1,000
- From 1,000 to 10,000
- From 10,000 to 100,000
- From 100,000 to 1,000,000
- From 1,000,000 to 5,000,000
- From 5,000,000 to 10,000,000
- From 10,000,000 to 50,000,000
- From 50,000,000 to 100,000,000
- From 100,000,000 to 500,000,000
- More than 500,000,000

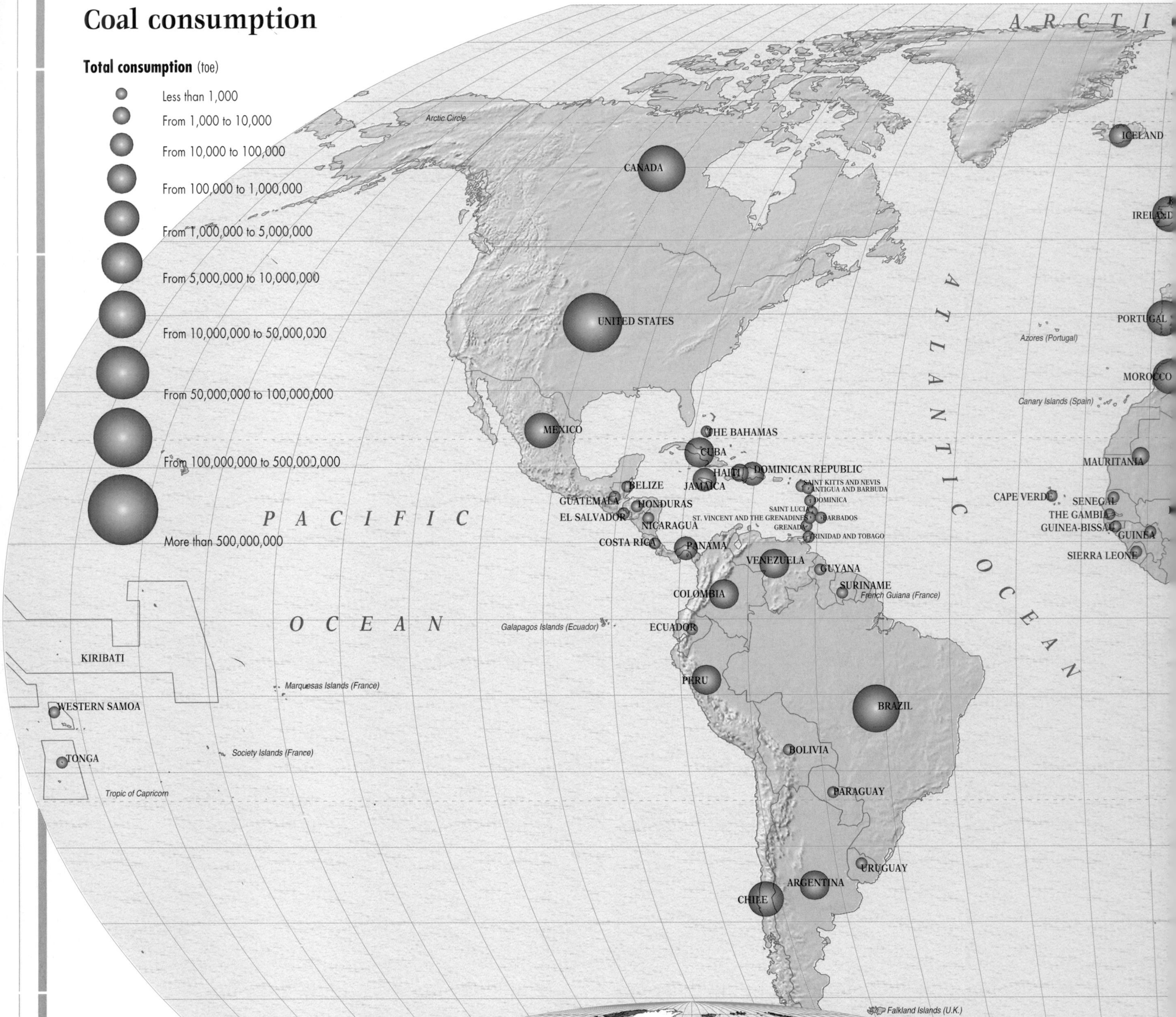

Coal consumption per person

Consumption per person (koe per person)

- Less than 1
- From 1 to 10
- From 10 to 100
- From 100 to 500
- From 500 to 1,000
- From 1,000 to 2,000
- More than 2,000

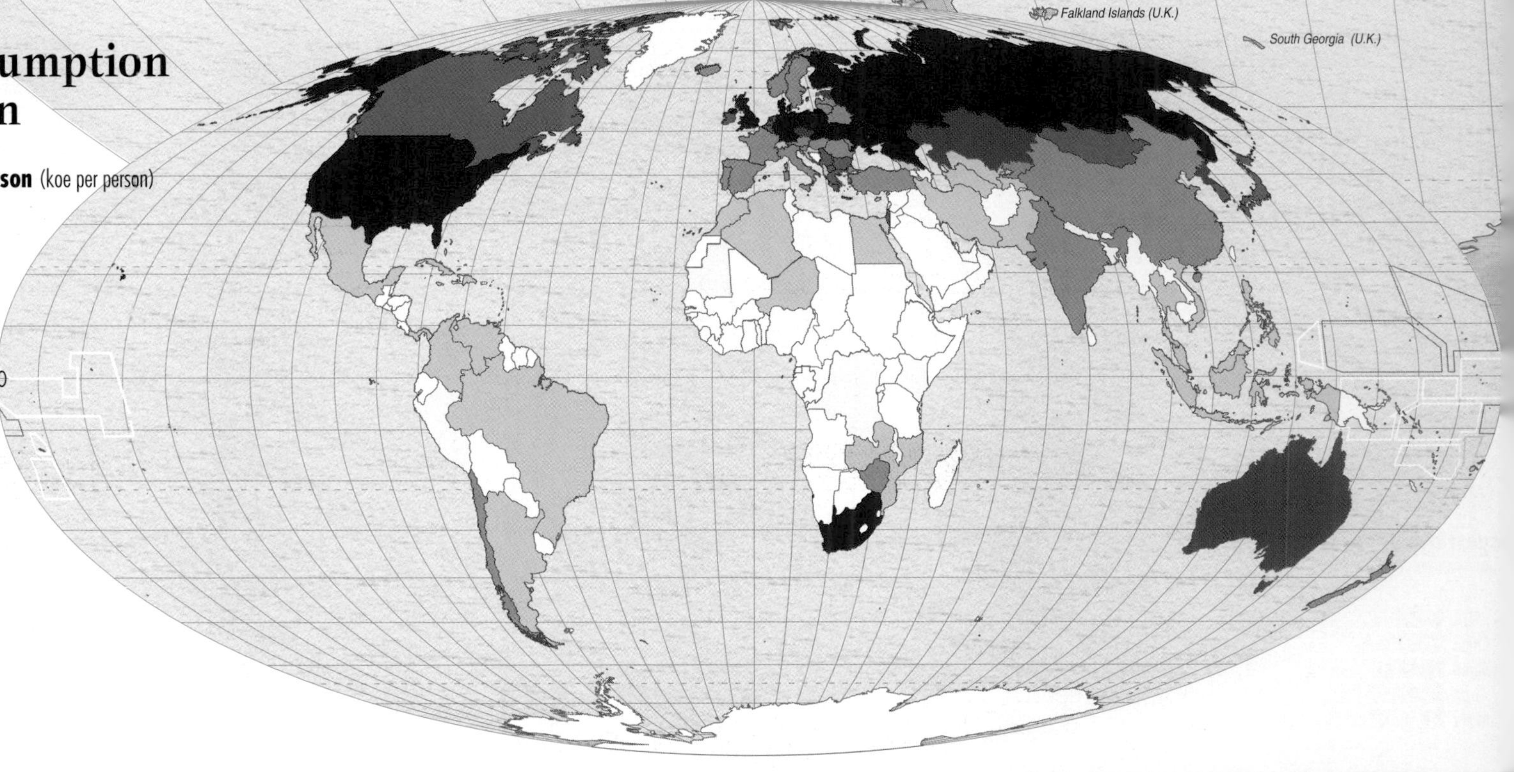

NOTE: The data corresponding to South Africa on all three maps includes Botswana, Lesotho, Namibia and Swaziland.

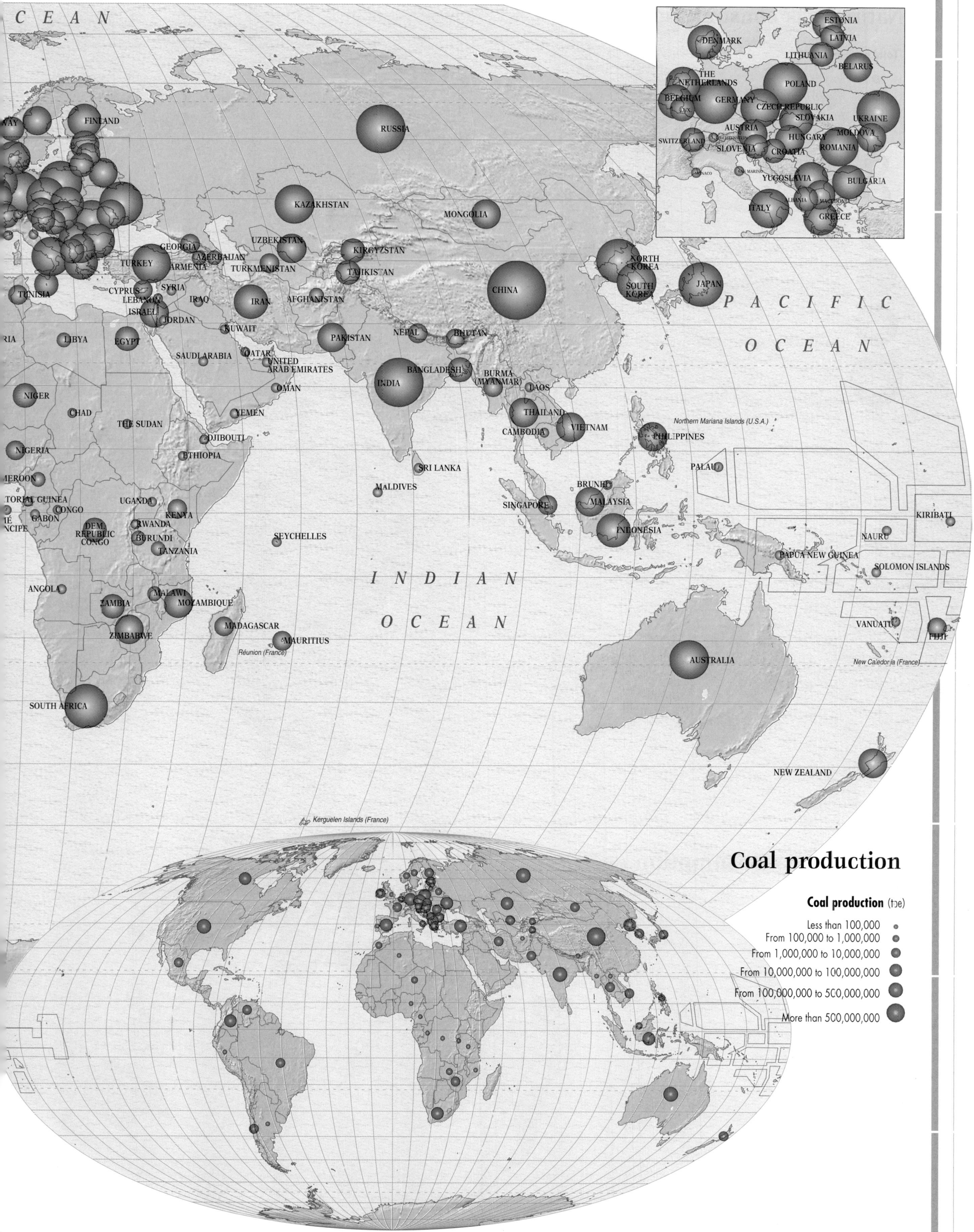

Coal production

Coal production (toe)

- Less than 100,000
- From 100,000 to 1,000,000
- From 1,000,000 to 10,000,000
- From 10,000,000 to 100,000,000
- From 100,000,000 to 500,000,000
- More than 500,000,000

Mining and energy

Energy source mineral resources: fossil fuels

Oil consumption

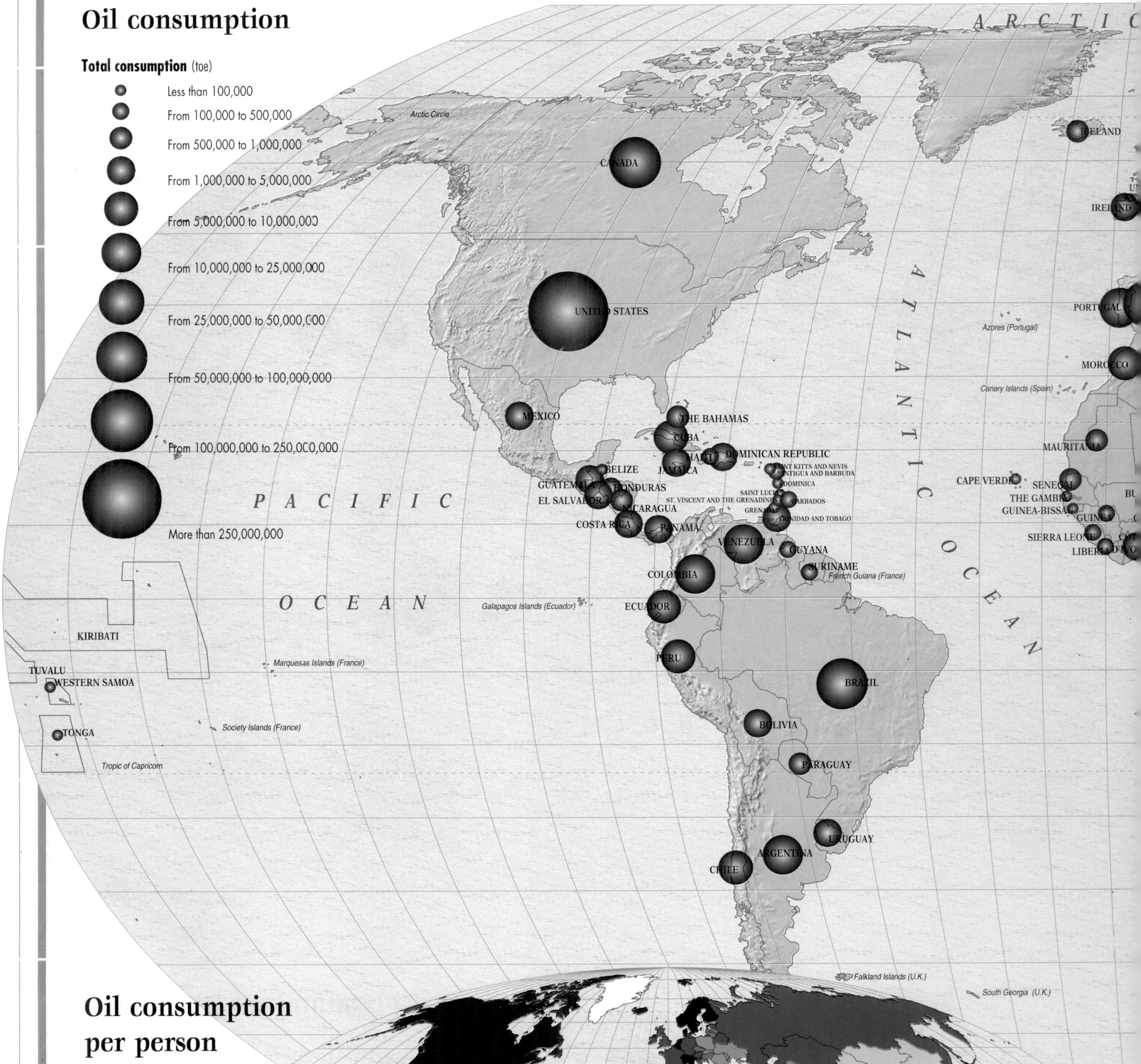

Oil consumption per person

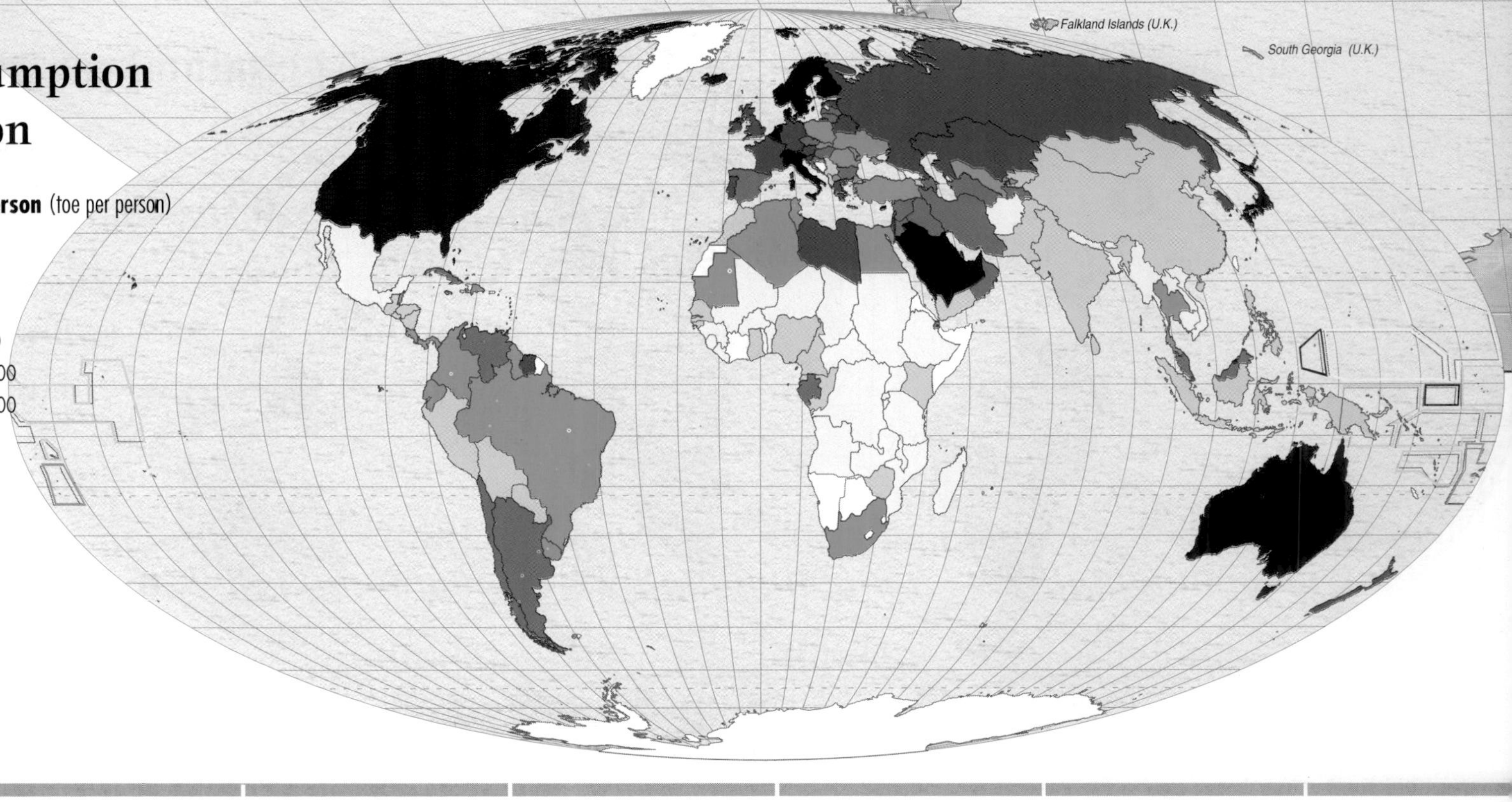

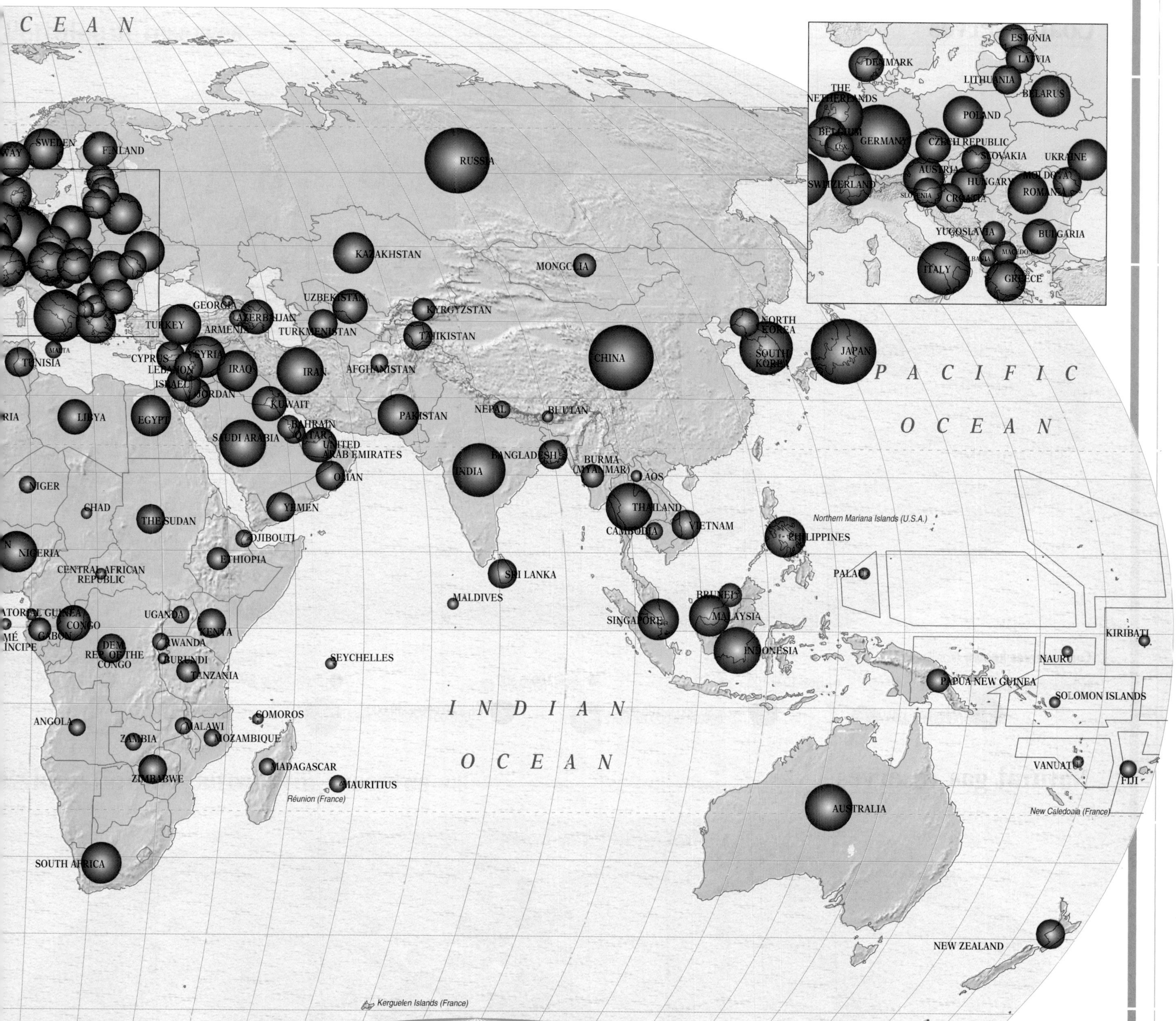

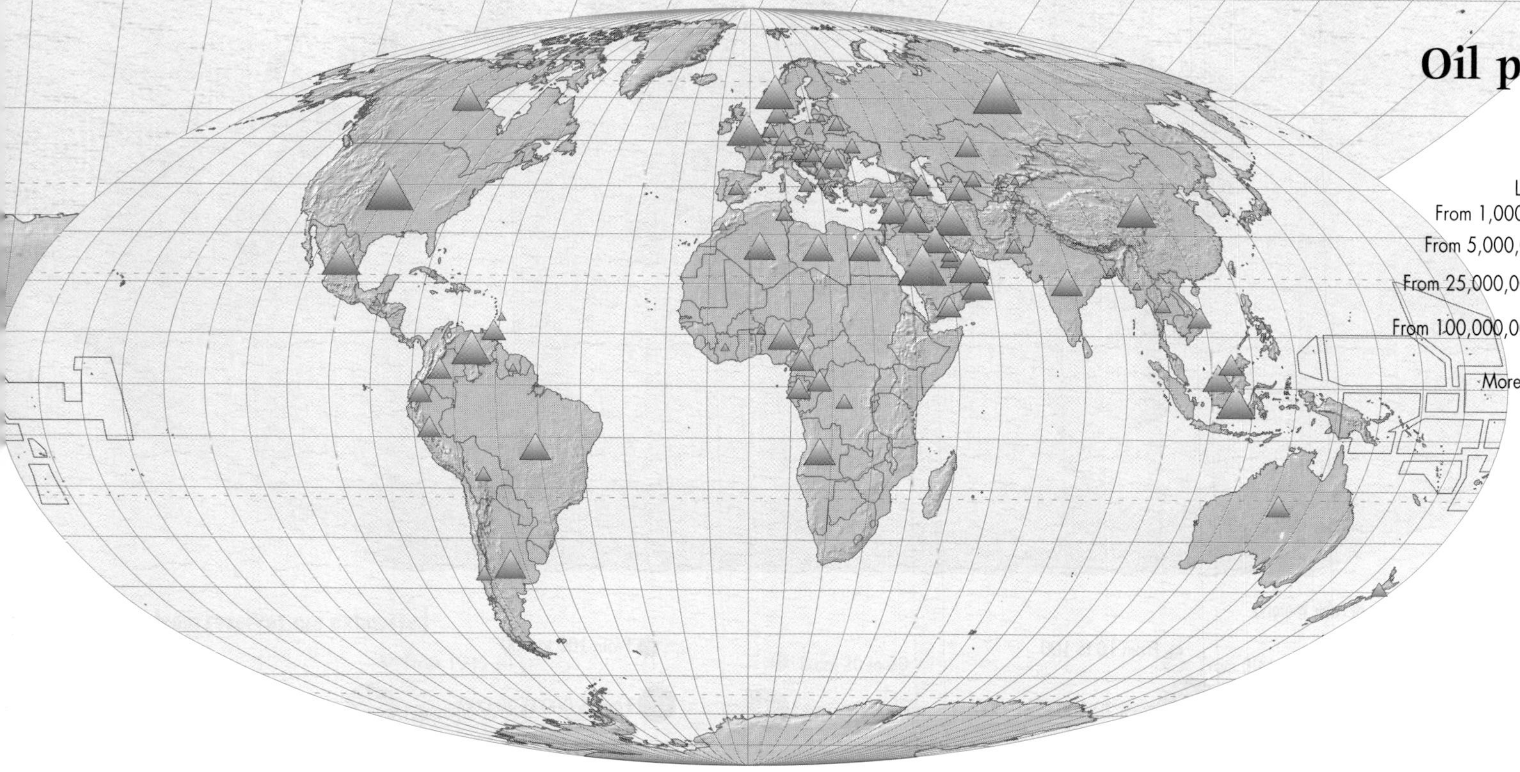

Oil production

Oil production (toe)

Less than 1,000,000
From 1,000,000 to 5,000,000
From 5,000,000 to 25,000,000
From 25,000,000 to 100,000,000
From 100,000,000 to 250,000,000
More than 250,000,000

Manufacturing

Textiles, clothing, leather and footwear

Value of production

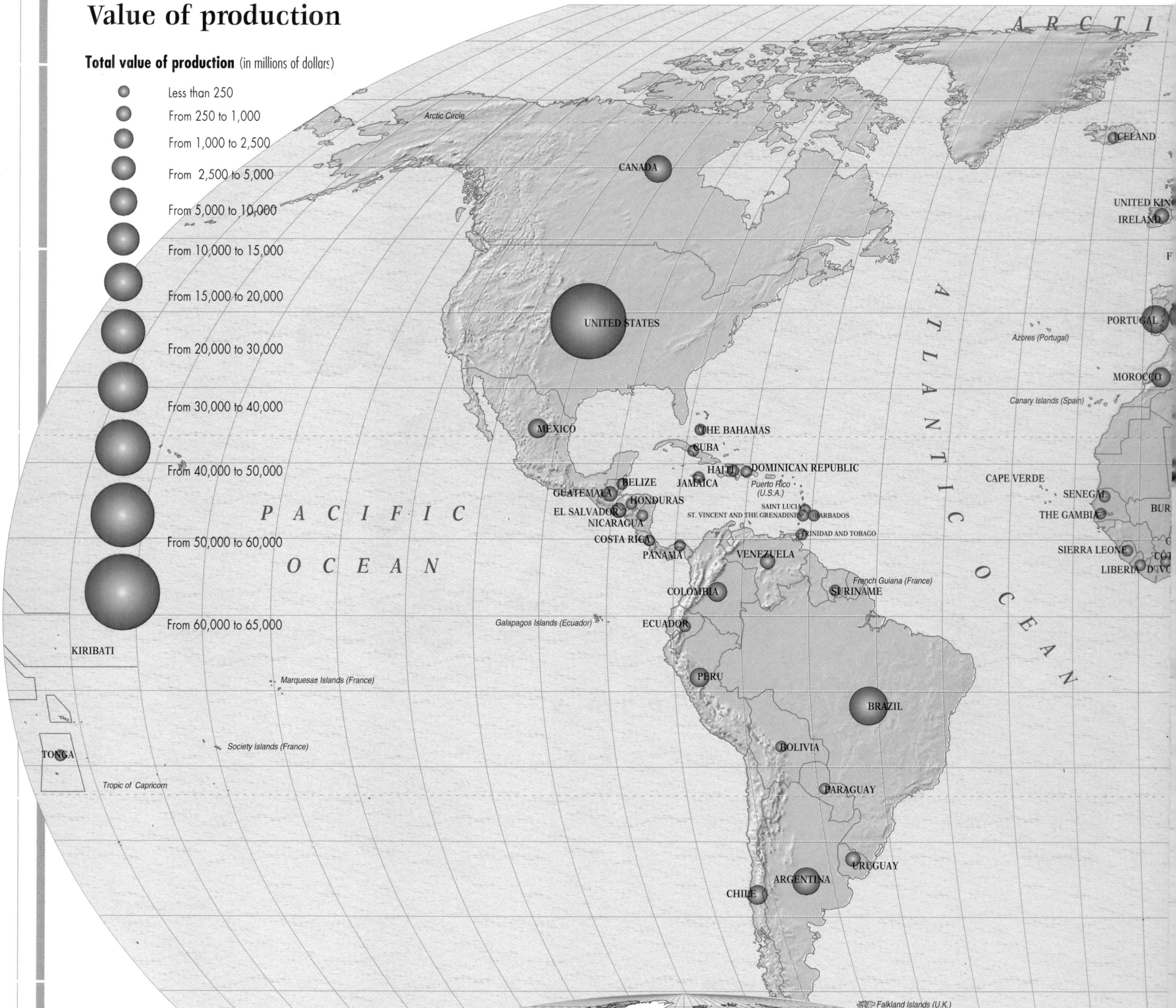

Relative participation

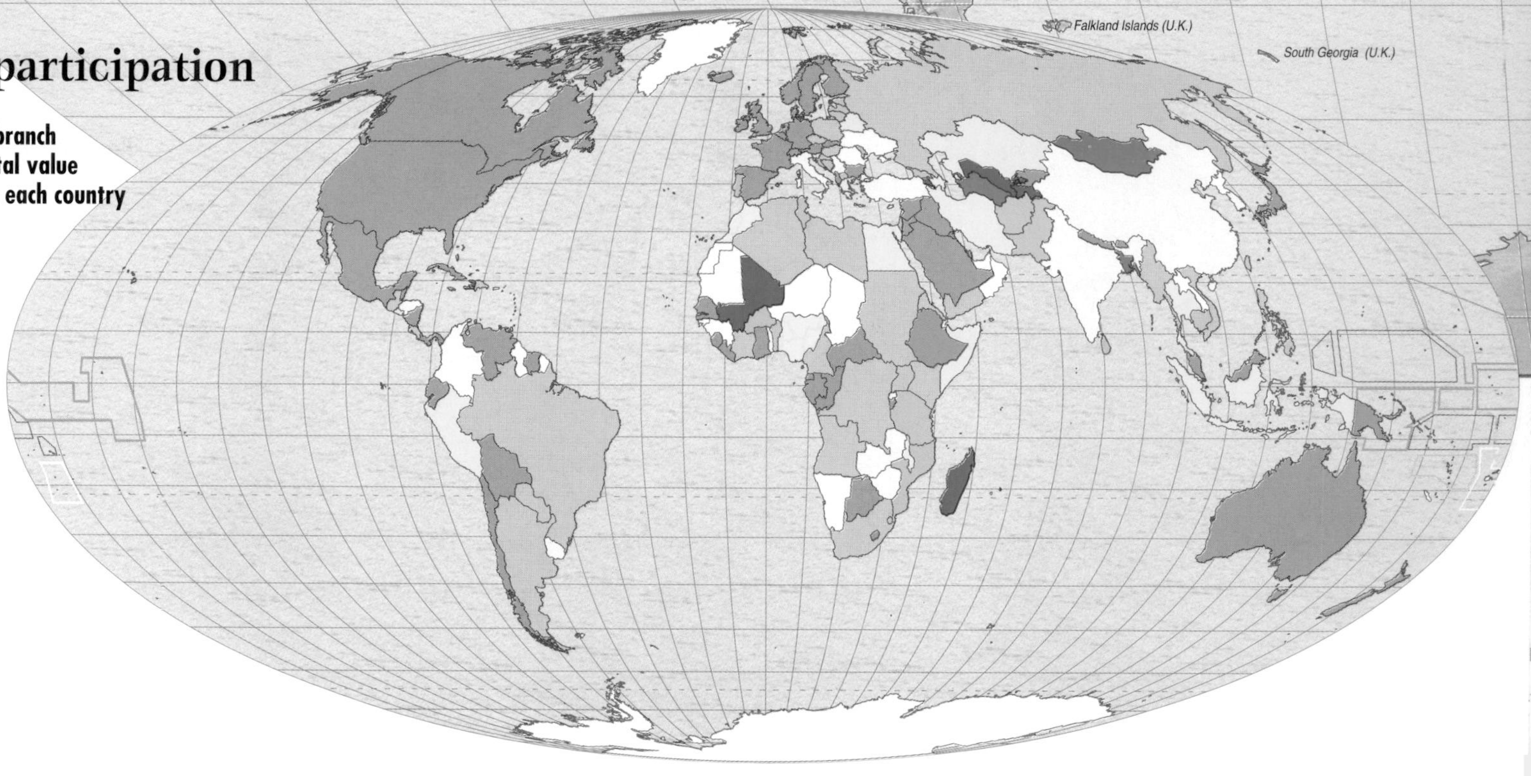

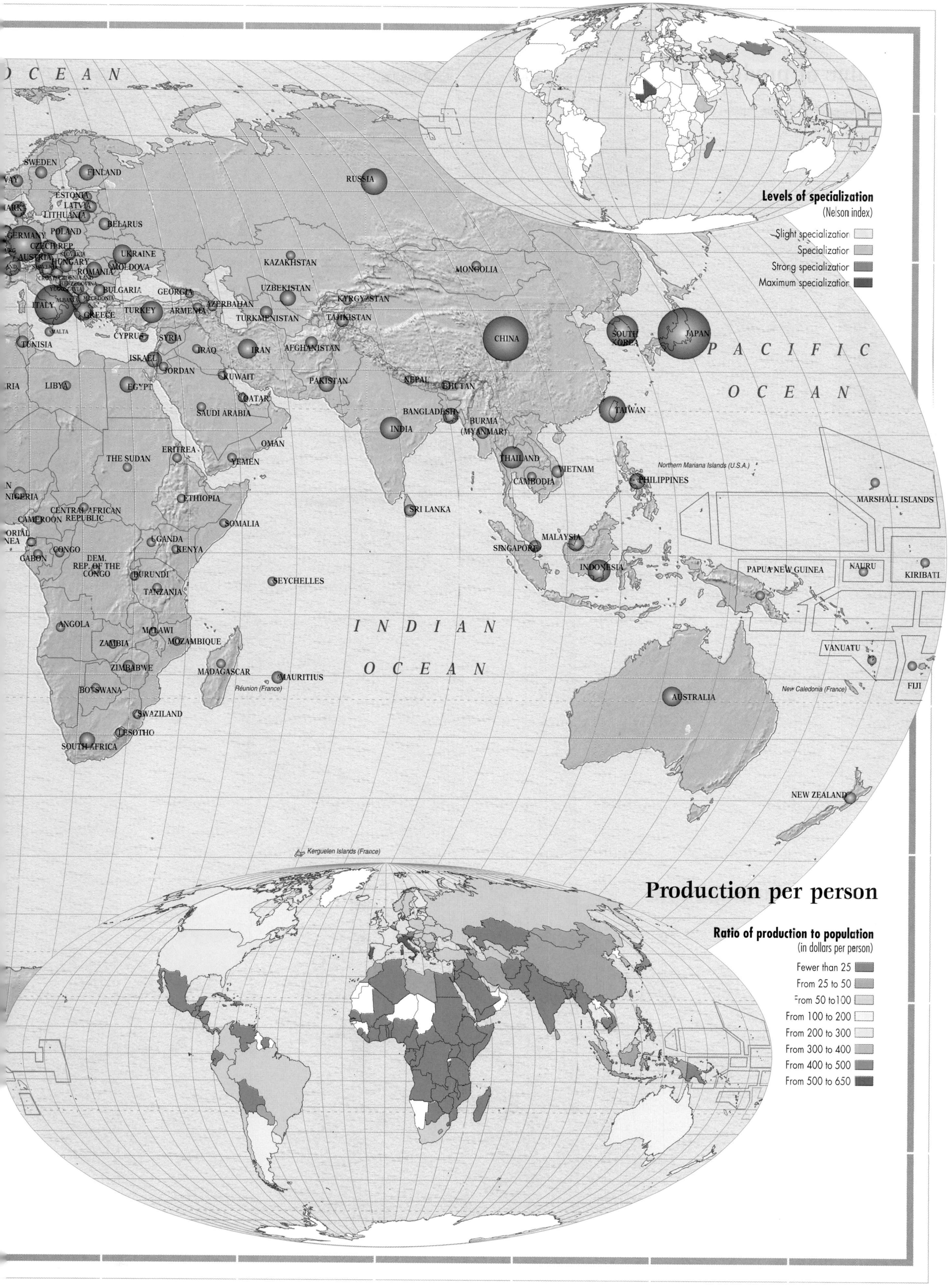
Levels of specialization
(Nelson index)
Slight specialization
Specialization
Strong specialization
Maximum specialization
Production per person
Ratio of production to population
(in dollars per person)
Fewer than 25
From 25 to 50
From 50 to 100
From 100 to 200
From 200 to 300
From 300 to 400
From 400 to 500
From 500 to 650
OCEAN
PACIFIC
OCEAN
INDIAN
OCEAN
SWEDEN
FINLAND
ESTONIA
LATVIA
LITHUANIA
RUSSIA
BELARUS
POLAND
GERMANY
CZECH REP.
AUSTRIA
HUNGARY
UKRAINE
MOLDOVA
ROMANIA
BULGARIA
ITALY
GREECE
MALTA
TURKEY
GEORGIA
ARMENIA
AZERBAIJAN
KAZAKHSTAN
UZBEKISTAN
TURKMENISTAN
KYRGYZSTAN
TAJIKISTAN
MONGOLIA
CHINA
SOUTH KOREA
JAPAN
TUNISIA
CYPRUS
SYRIA
IRAQ
IRAN
AFGHANISTAN
ISRAEL
JORDAN
KUWAIT
QATAR
SAUDI ARABIA
PAKISTAN
NEPAL
BHUTAN
BANGLADESH
INDIA
BURMA (MYANMAR)
TAIWAN
LIBYA
EGYPT
OMAN
YEMEN
ERITREA
THE SUDAN
THAILAND
VIETNAM
CAMBODIA
PHILIPPINES
Northern Mariana Islands (U.S.A.)
MARSHALL ISLANDS
NIGERIA
CENTRAL AFRICAN REPUBLIC
CAMEROON
ETHIOPIA
SOMALIA
SRI LANKA
MALAYSIA
SINGAPORE
UGANDA
KENYA
CONGO
GABON
DEM. REP. OF THE CONGO
BURUNDI
TANZANIA
SEYCHELLES
INDONESIA
PAPUA NEW GUINEA
NAURU
KIRIBATI
ANGOLA
ZAMBIA
MALAWI
MOZAMBIQUE
ZIMBABWE
MADAGASCAR
MAURITIUS
Réunion (France)
BOTSWANA
SWAZILAND
LESOTHO
SOUTH AFRICA
VANUATU
FIJI
New Caledonia (France)
AUSTRALIA
NEW ZEALAND
Kerguelen Islands (France)

Manufacturing
Machinery and transport equipment

Value of production

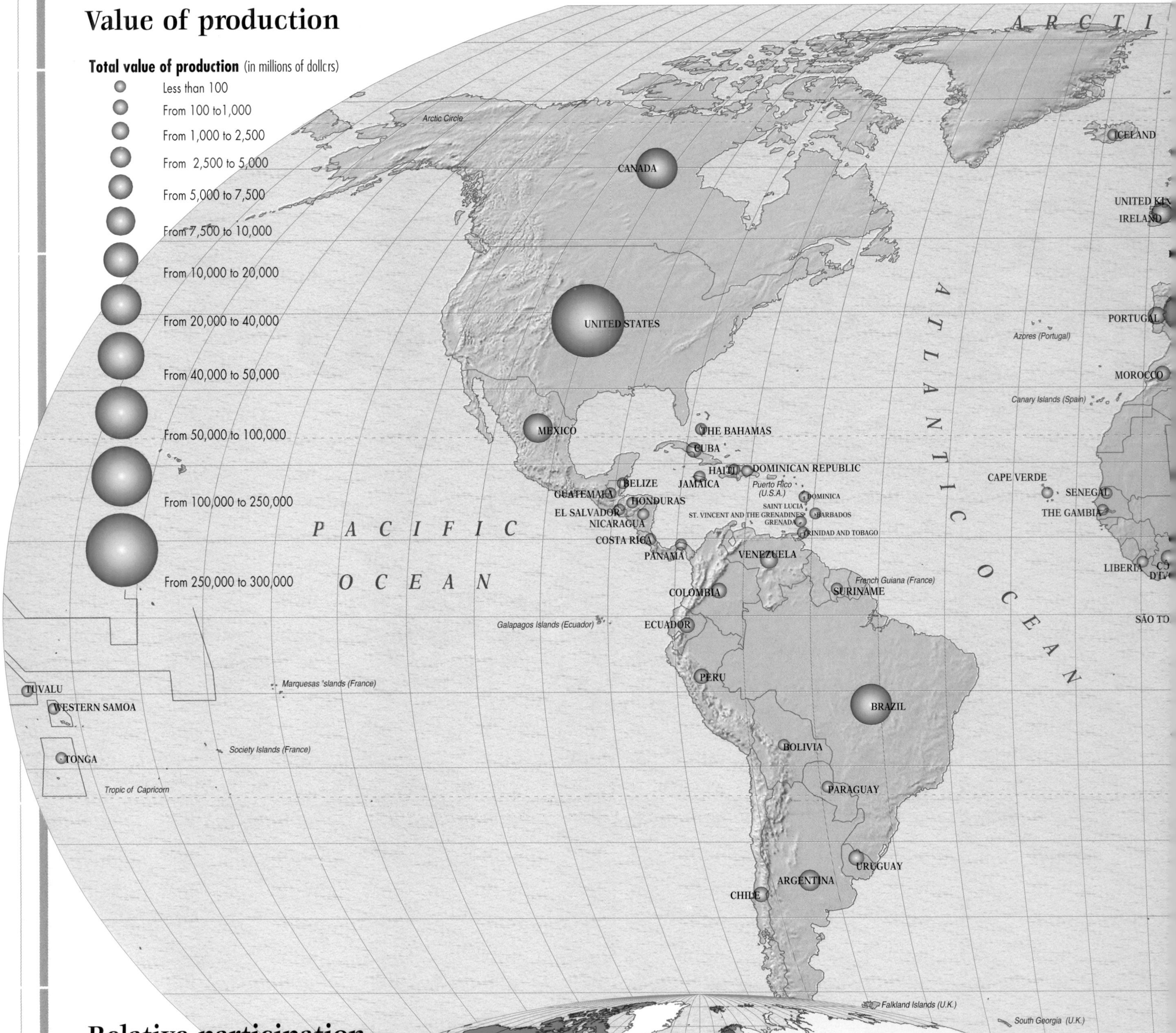

Relative participation

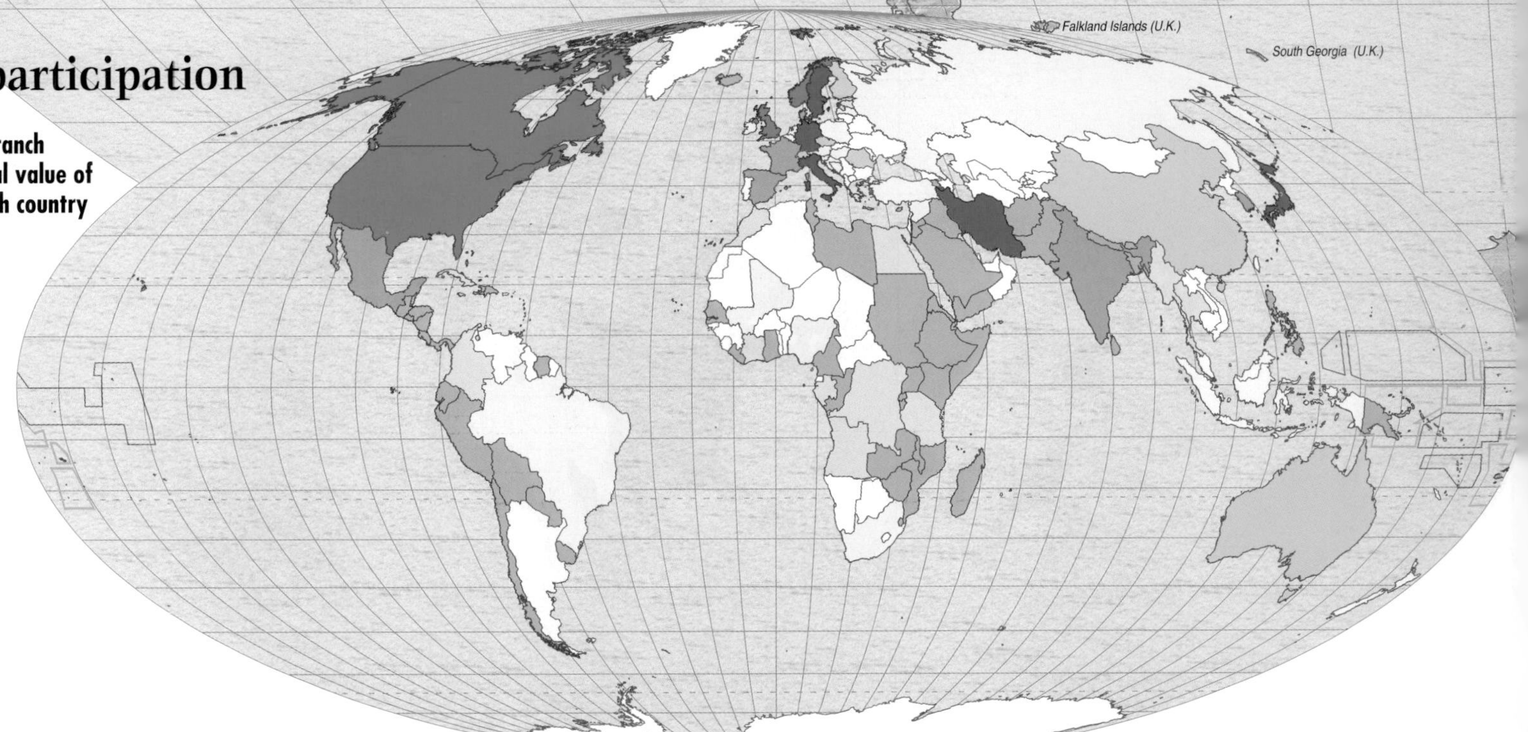

NOTE: Countries in which the data corresponding to *metallurgy and metal products, machinery and transport equipment* and *electrical, electronical and optical equipment* is shown grouped together.

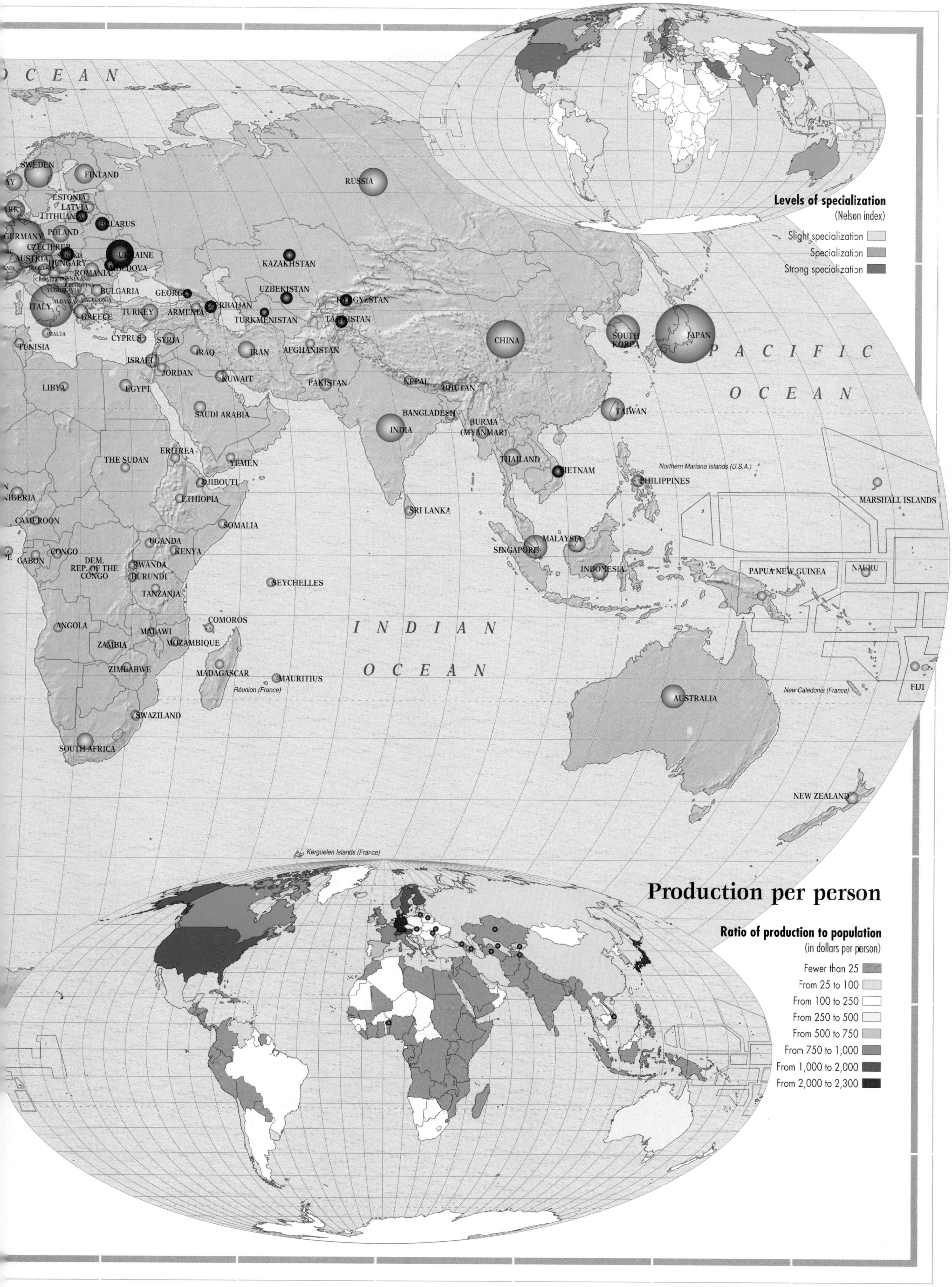

Levels of specialization
(Nelson index)
Slight specialization
Specialization
Strong specialization
SWEDEN
FINLAND
RUSSIA
ESTONIA
LATVIA
LITHUANIA
BELARUS
GERMANY
POLAND
CZECH REP.
AUSTRIA
HUNGARY
UKRAINE
MOLDOVA
ROMANIA
KAZAKHSTAN
BULGARIA
GEORGIA
UZBEKISTAN
KYRGYZSTAN
ITALY
GREECE
TURKEY
ARMENIA
AZERBAIJAN
TURKMENISTAN
TAJIKISTAN
MALTA
CYPRUS
SYRIA
TUNISIA
ISRAEL
IRAQ
IRAN
AFGHANISTAN
JORDAN
KUWAIT
LIBYA
EGYPT
PAKISTAN
NEPAL
BHUTAN
CHINA
SOUTH KOREA
JAPAN
PACIFIC
OCEAN
SAUDI ARABIA
BANGLADESH
TAIWAN
INDIA
BURMA (MYANMAR)
ERITREA
THE SUDAN
YEMEN
THAILAND
VIETNAM
Northern Mariana Islands (U.S.A.)
PHILIPPINES
DJIBOUTI
ETHIOPIA
SRI LANKA
MARSHALL ISLANDS
CAMEROON
SOMALIA
UGANDA
KENYA
MALAYSIA
SINGAPORE
CONGO
GABON
DEM. REP. OF THE CONGO
RWANDA
BURUNDI
INDONESIA
PAPUA NEW GUINEA
NAURU
SEYCHELLES
TANZANIA
COMOROS
ANGOLA
MALAWI
ZAMBIA
MOZAMBIQUE
INDIAN
OCEAN
ZIMBABWE
MADAGASCAR
MAURITIUS
Réunion (France)
New Caledonia (France)
FIJI
AUSTRALIA
SWAZILAND
SOUTH AFRICA
NEW ZEALAND
Kerguelen Islands (France)
Production per person
Ratio of production to population
(in dollars per person)
Fewer than 25
From 25 to 100
From 100 to 250
From 250 to 500
From 500 to 750
From 750 to 1,000
From 1,000 to 2,000
From 2,000 to 2,300

Manufacturing
Electrical, electronical and optical equipment

Value of production

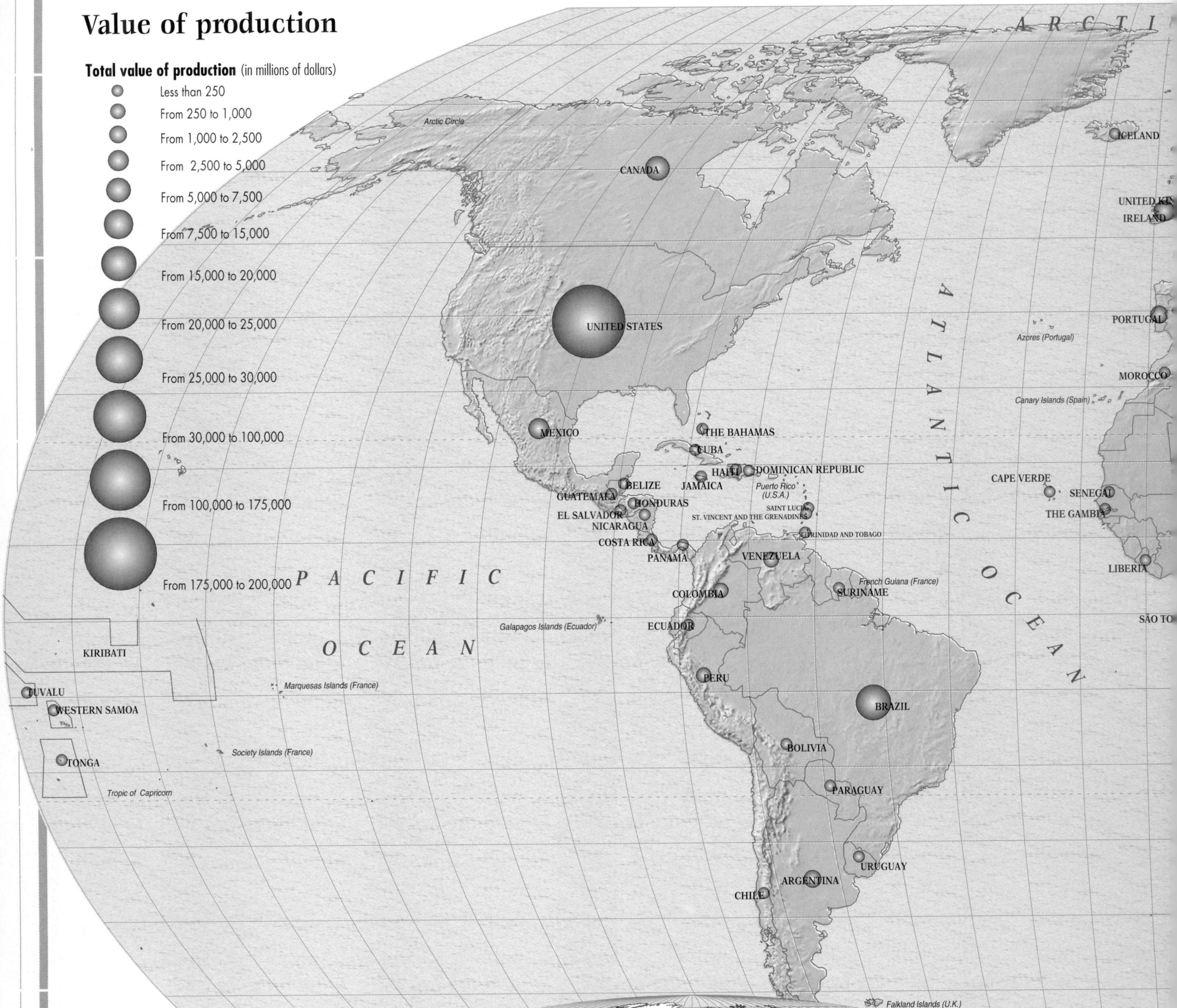

Relative participation

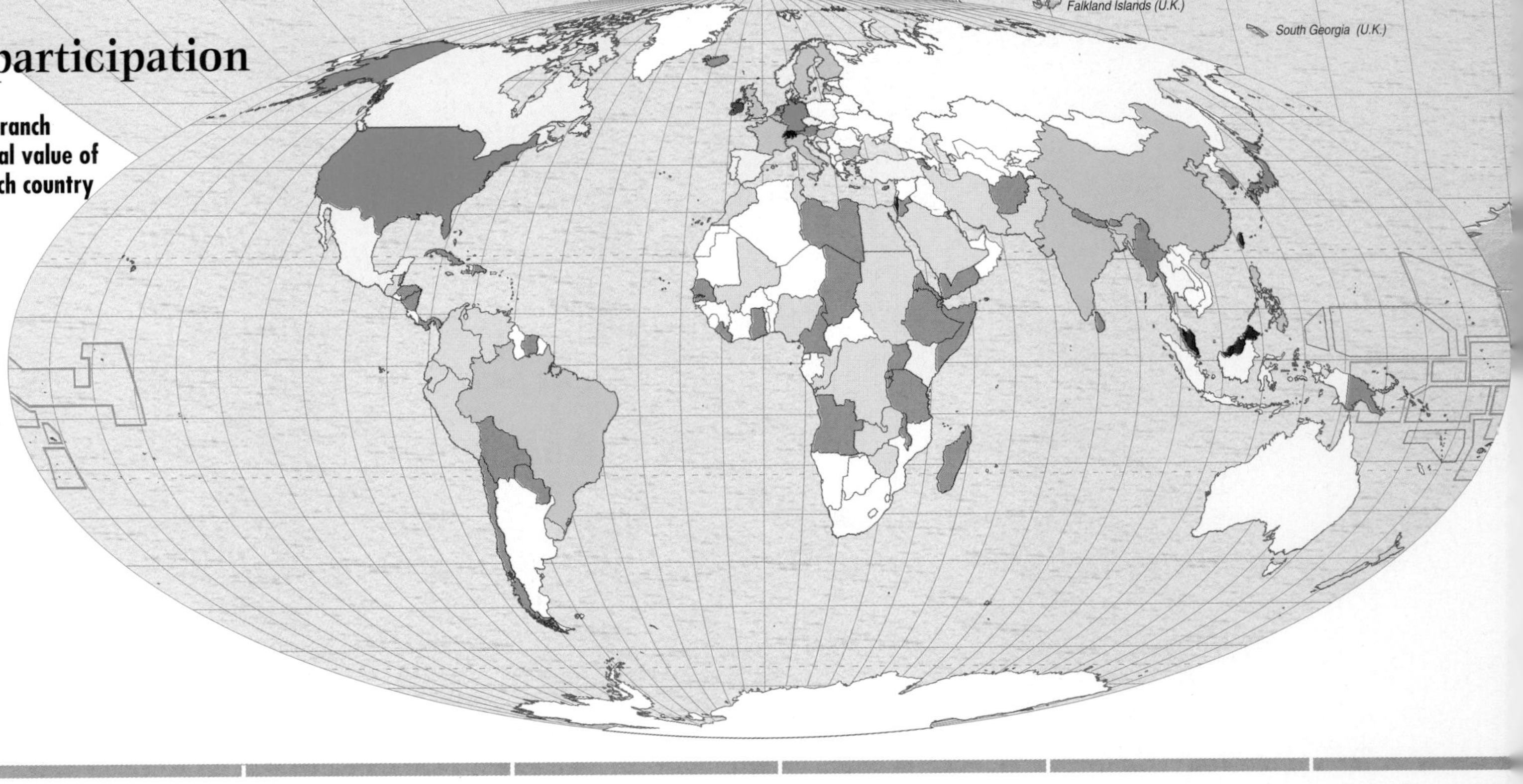

NOTE: Countries in which the data corresponding to *metallurgy and metal products, machinery and transport equipment* and *electrical, electronical and optical equipment* is shown grouped together.

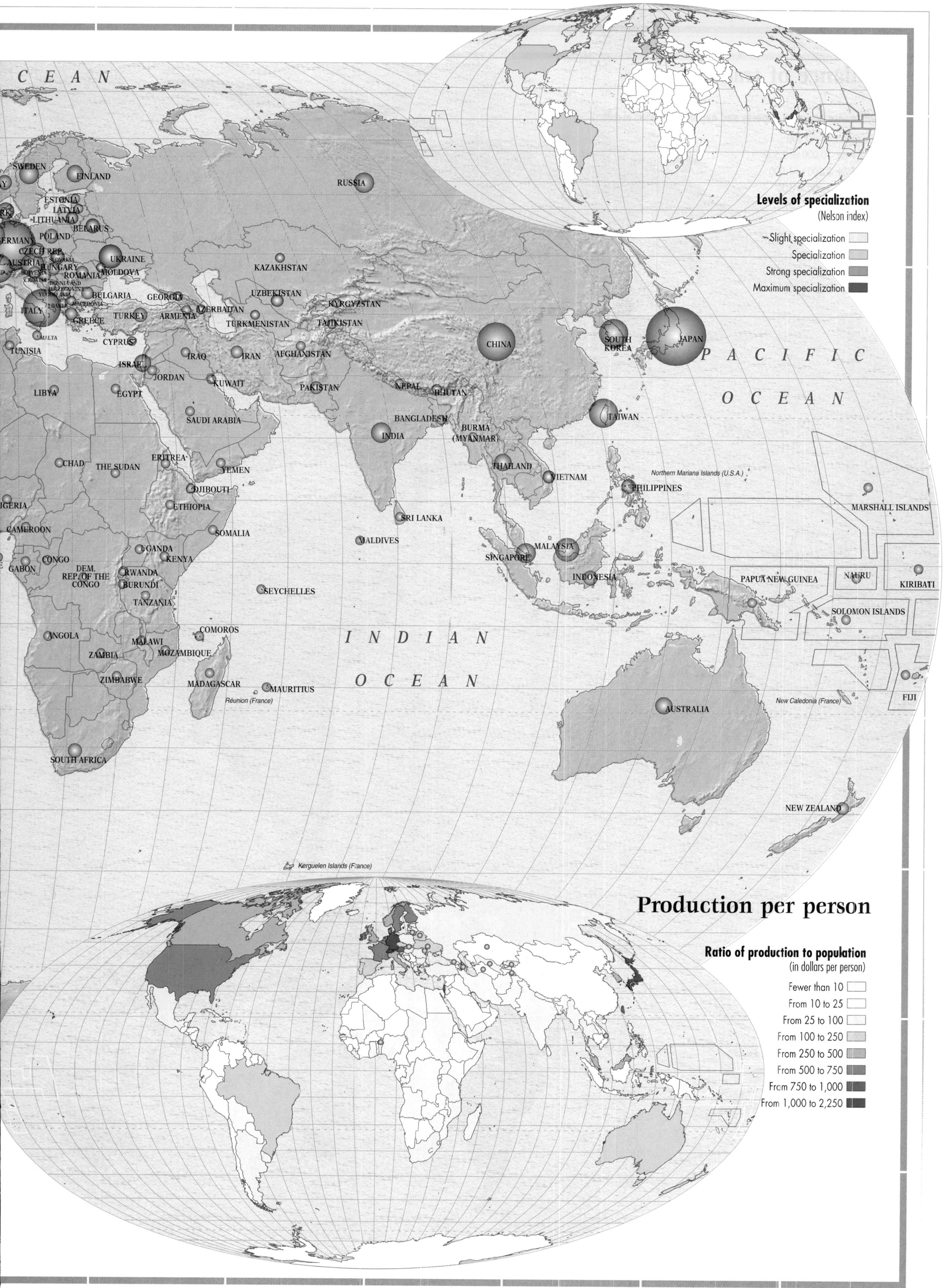
Levels of specialization
(Nelson index)
Slight specialization
Specialization
Strong specialization
Maximum specialization
Production per person
Ratio of production to population
(in dollars per person)
Fewer than 10
From 10 to 25
From 25 to 100
From 100 to 250
From 250 to 500
From 500 to 750
From 750 to 1,000
From 1,000 to 2,250
PACIFIC OCEAN
INDIAN OCEAN
SWEDEN
FINLAND
RUSSIA
ESTONIA
LATVIA
LITHUANIA
BELARUS
POLAND
CZECH REP.
UKRAINE
MOLDOVA
ROMANIA
KAZAKHSTAN
UZBEKISTAN
KYRGYZSTAN
BULGARIA
GEORGIA
AZERBAIJAN
ARMENIA
TURKMENISTAN
TAJIKISTAN
ITALY
GREECE
TURKEY
MALTA
CYPRUS
TUNISIA
IRAQ
IRAN
AFGHANISTAN
ISRAEL
JORDAN
KUWAIT
PAKISTAN
NEPAL
BHUTAN
CHINA
SOUTH KOREA
JAPAN
LIBYA
EGYPT
SAUDI ARABIA
BANGLADESH
INDIA
BURMA (MYANMAR)
TAIWAN
CHAD
THE SUDAN
ERITREA
YEMEN
THAILAND
VIETNAM
Northern Mariana Islands (U.S.A.)
PHILIPPINES
DJIBOUTI
ETHIOPIA
SRI LANKA
MARSHALL ISLANDS
CAMEROON
SOMALIA
MALDIVES
UGANDA
KENYA
MALAYSIA
SINGAPORE
CONGO
GABON
DEM. REP. OF THE CONGO
RWANDA
BURUNDI
TANZANIA
INDONESIA
PAPUA NEW GUINEA
NAURU
KIRIBATI
SEYCHELLES
SOLOMON ISLANDS
COMOROS
ANGOLA
MALAWI
ZAMBIA
MOZAMBIQUE
ZIMBABWE
MADAGASCAR
MAURITIUS
Réunion (France)
AUSTRALIA
New Caledonia (France)
FIJI
SOUTH AFRICA
NEW ZEALAND
Kerguelen Islands (France)

AFRICA

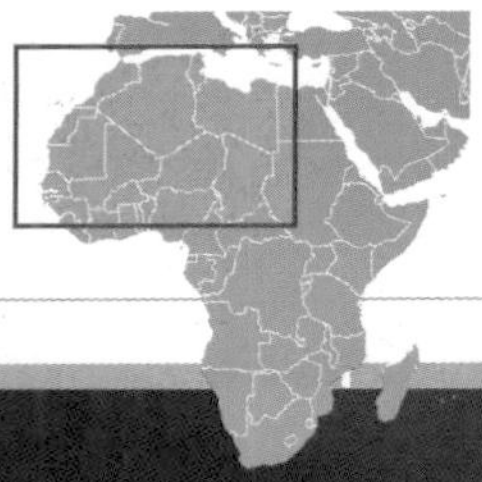

Africa
Northwest

This satellite image of the northwestern part of the African continent reveals the strongly contrasting landscapes which characterize Africa. The band that runs east-west north of the Equator stands out because of its heavy vegetation, while north of Lake Chad —lower half of the page on the right— the Sahara Desert begins with the Grand Erg de Bilma. In this zone north of Lake Chad, we can see the triangle formed by the mountains of Hoggar in the north, Tibesti in the

ast, and Aïr in the west, which enclose the well-nown region of Ténéré.
ollowing the coast from west to east —the upper part f the image— first can be seen the abrupt Moroccan oast, sinuous due to the proximity of the Atlas Mountain Range. Farther east, the Gulf of Gabès, facing the island of Sicily, and the Gulf of Sirte farther south, break the African coastline in the north. The coastline continues towards the east and the image allows us to see the Gulf of Alexandria, where the city of that name lies next to the right-hand cut-off point. The western coastline, with the Canary Islands visible offshore, descends gently towards the southwest until it reaches the sharply pointed tip of Cape Verde.

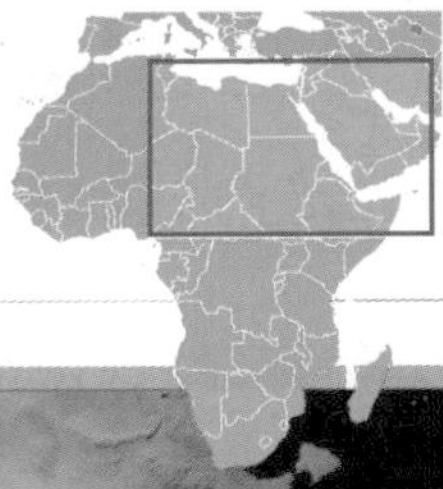

Africa
Northeast

A continuation of the satellite image on the previous page shows the northeastern part of Africa and the Arabian Peninsula, this last part of the continent of Asia.

Following the coastline of the Mediterranean Sea from west to east, the Gulf of Gabès can be seen, where the coastline turns down gently towards the south to the Gulf of Sirte. From here it turns back brusquely towards the north and continues eastward until it reaches the Nile Delta.

The change in color towards greenish tones indicates the presence of croplands flooded by

the waters of the Nile River. The course of the river can be followed perfectly from north to south, with long Lake Nasser visible in its middle reaches.

To the right of the Nile, the Peninsula of Sinai can be seen, bordered on the west by the Gulf of Suez, and the Gulf of Aqaba on the east. Both gulfs announce the Red Sea, that, as can be seen in the satellite image, extends from here towards the south until it finds the opening to the Indian Ocean by way of the Gulf of Aden.

The lower part of the image allows us to see the equatorial zone, densely covered with vegetation, and the spurs of the Ethiopian Highlands west of the Nile, dotted with small lakes and rivers that favour the presence of a varied, dense and rich vegetation.

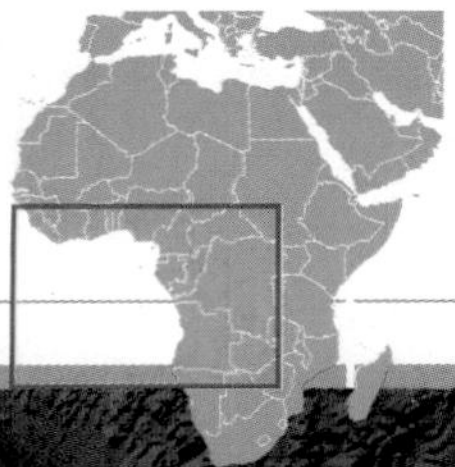

Africa
West Central

This is an image of Equatorial Africa, showing its Atlantic watershed. The green tones reflect the abundant vegetation of the equatorial rainforests that cover this part of the African continent.

The Atlantic coastline north of the Equator follows an east-west direction and is characterized by the presence of many large masses of surface waters on the continent near the coast. To cite those of greatest

size and going from west to east, Lake Kossow can be seen first, farther to the east and of greater size, Lake Volta and in the center of the Gulf of Guinea, the Mouths of the River Niger, forming a great delta. From here, the coastline follows a north-south direction with the mouth of the Congo River clearly visible, its discharge marked by the light blue-colored stain. On the right-hand page the most notable feature is the Congo Basin. East of the river, oriented north-south, there is a partial view of the region of the Great Lakes, located in an area of very rough terrain. To the south, small Lake Kariba can be seen.

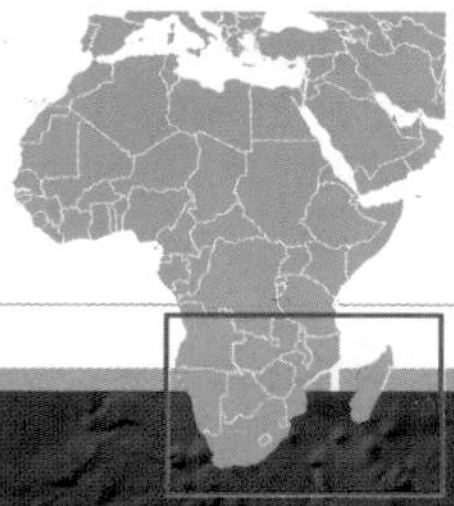

Africa
South

This is the last of the satellite images of the African continent. Also visible are the great island of Madagascar, between this and the continent the Comoros Islands, to the east of Madagascar, the island of Réunion, and Mauritius, the easternmost of all.

The western coastline of the continent, bathed by the Atlantic Ocean, draws a line in a southeasterly direction until it reaches the Cape of Good Hope, a feature in the form of an inverted "j" on which lies Cape Town, the capital of the Republic of South

Africa. Towards the east can be seen Cape Agulhas, the very tip of the continent, in the area of confluence between the Atlantic and Indian Oceans. From here the coastline turns up in a northeasterly direction. The climatic differences between this coast and the west coast are notable and the result is the greater presence of continuous currents of surface waters and of vegetation. Moving northward, the Limpopo, Lundi Save and Zambeze (Zambezi) Rivers can be seen. Following the course of the Zambeze upriver, we find Lake Cobova Bassa and Lake Kariba farther west. On the island of Madagascar, separated from the continent by the Mozambique Channel, besides its enormous size we can observe the rich vegetation that completely covers the island.

Africa
Bathymetry

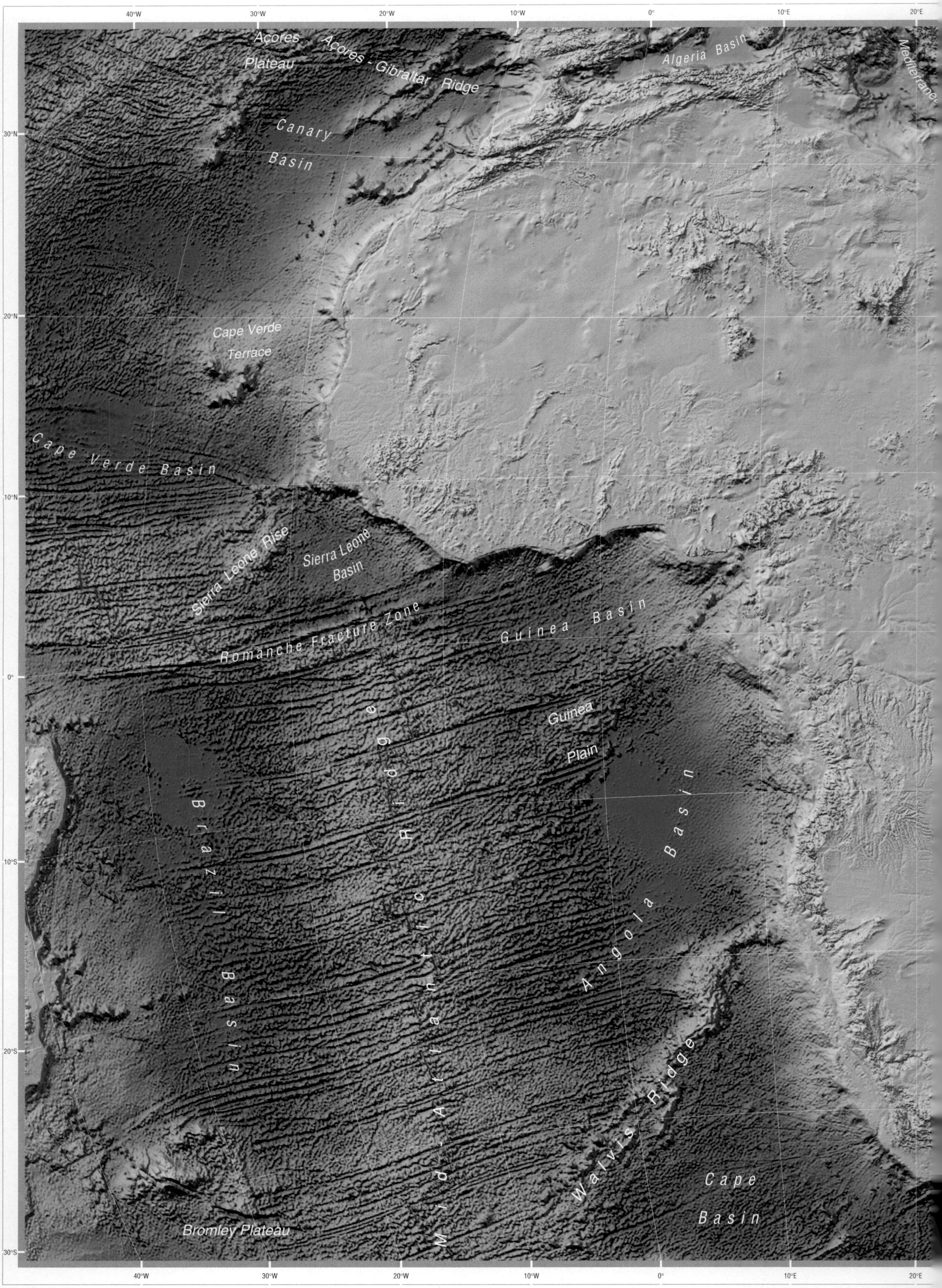

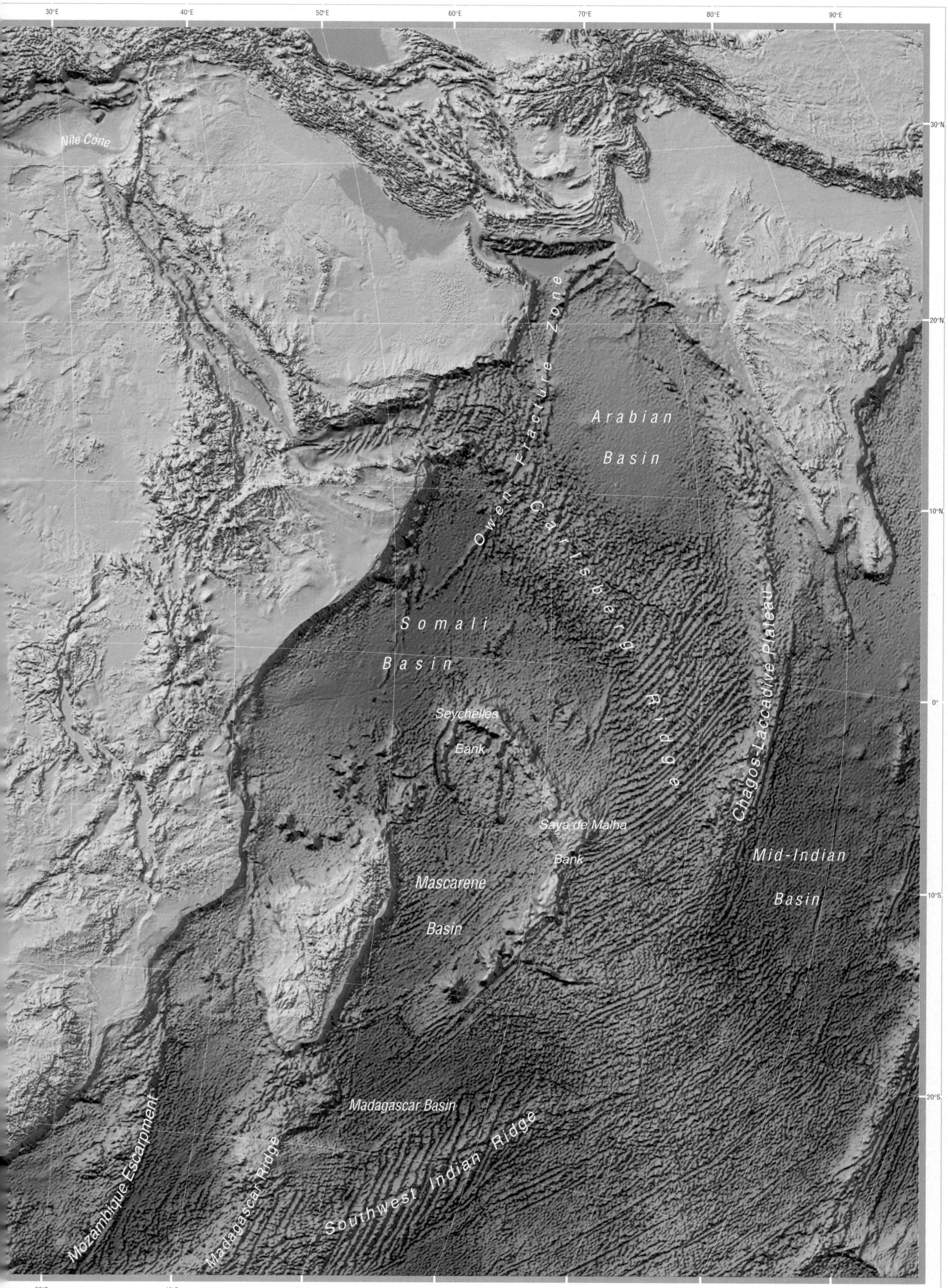
30°E
40°E
50°E
60°E
70°E
80°E
90°E
30°N
20°N
10°N
0°
10°S
20°S
Nile Cone
Owen Fracture Zone
Arabian Basin
Carlsberg Ridge
Somali Basin
Seychelles Bank
Chagos-Laccadive Plateau
Saya de Malha Bank
Mid-Indian Basin
Mascarene Basin
Madagascar Basin
Southwest Indian Ridge
Madagascar Ridge
Mozambique Escarpment

Africa
Physical map

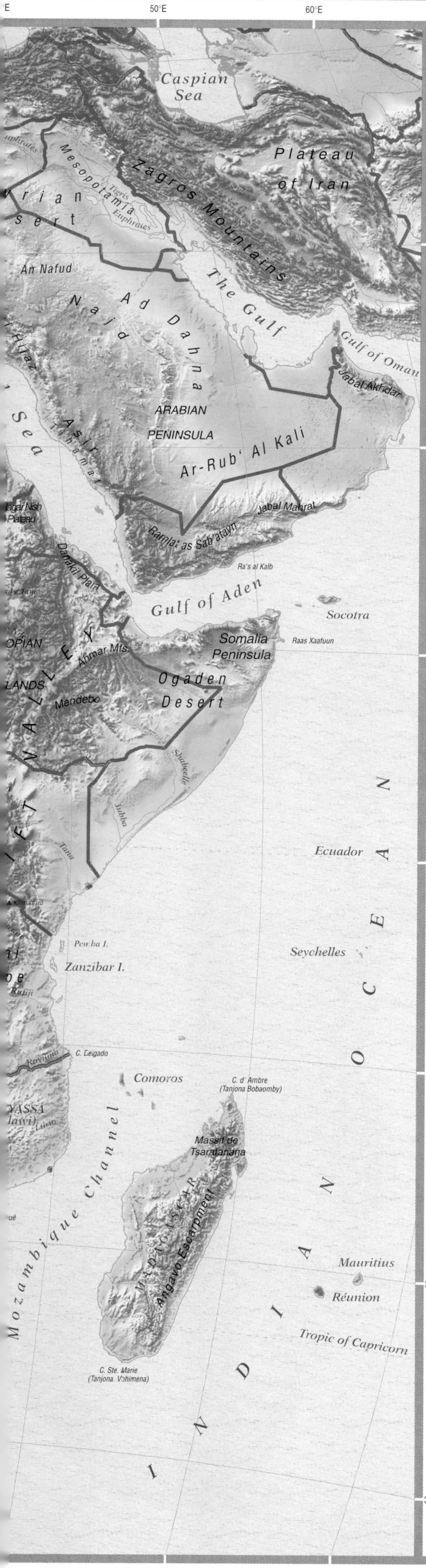

Major rivers of Africa

Length (km)

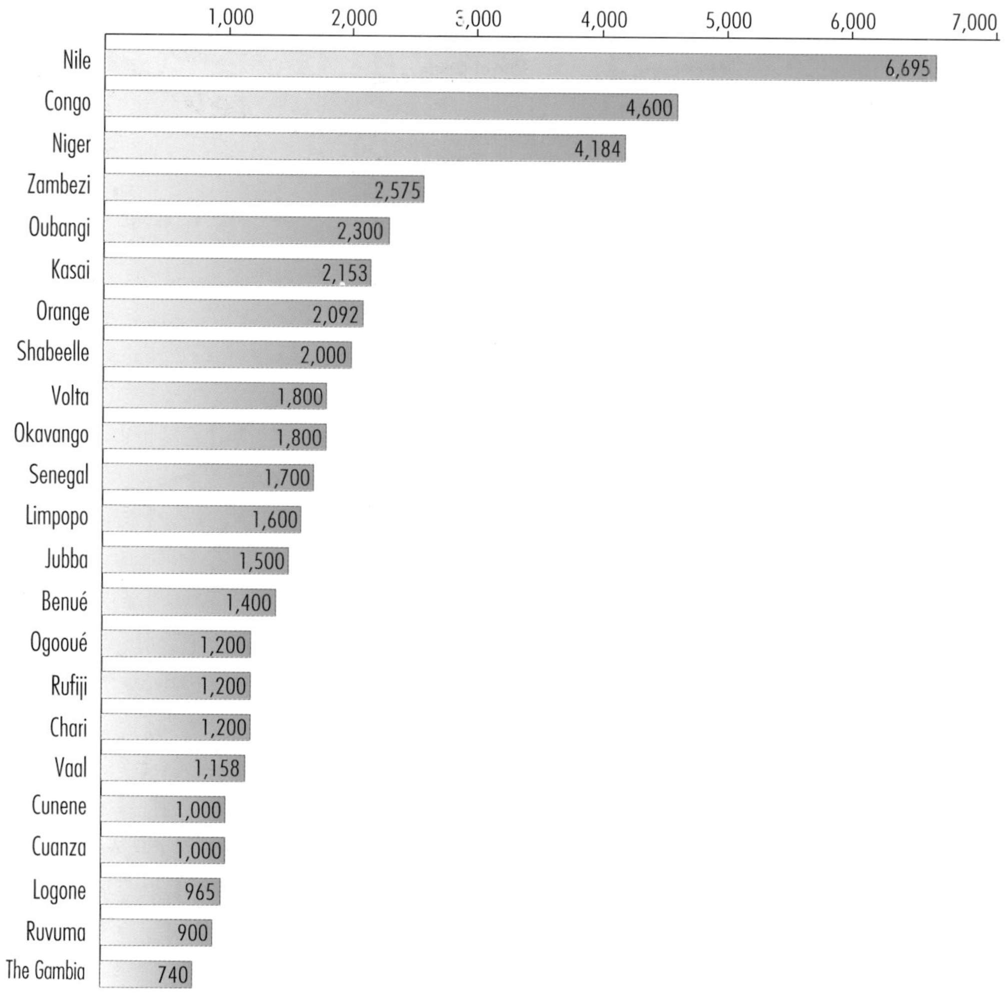

Drainage basin (sq km)

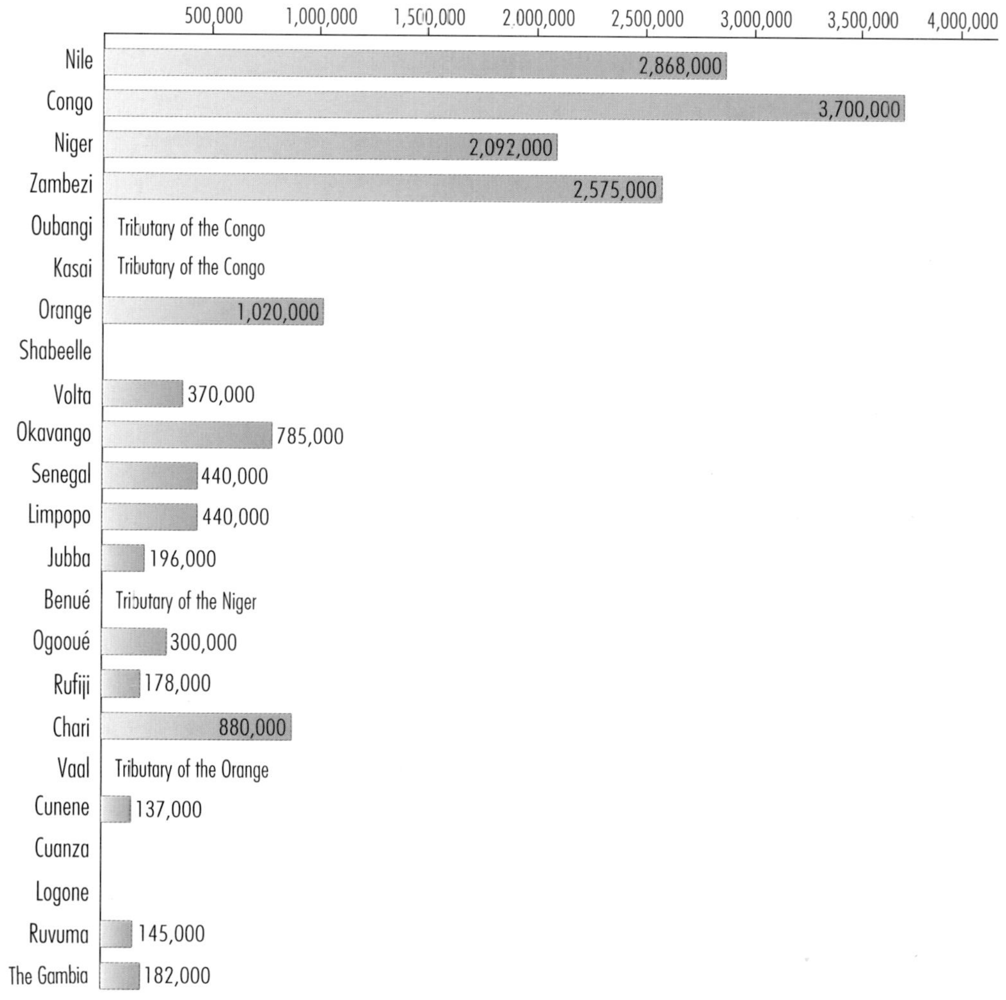

Africa

Northwest Africa

ATLANTIC OCEAN

Mediterranean

MOROCCO

Western Sahara

MAURITANIA

MALI

SENEGAL

THE GAMBIA

GUINEA-BISSAU

GUINEA

SIERRA LEONE

CÔTE D'IVOIRE

BURKINA FASO

GHANA

SPAIN

Atlas Mountains

SAHARA

Niger Basin

DAKAR

NOUAKCHOTT

BAMAKO

CONAKRY

FREETOWN

OUAGADOUGOU

NIAMEY

RABAT

Dar-el-Beida (Casablanca)

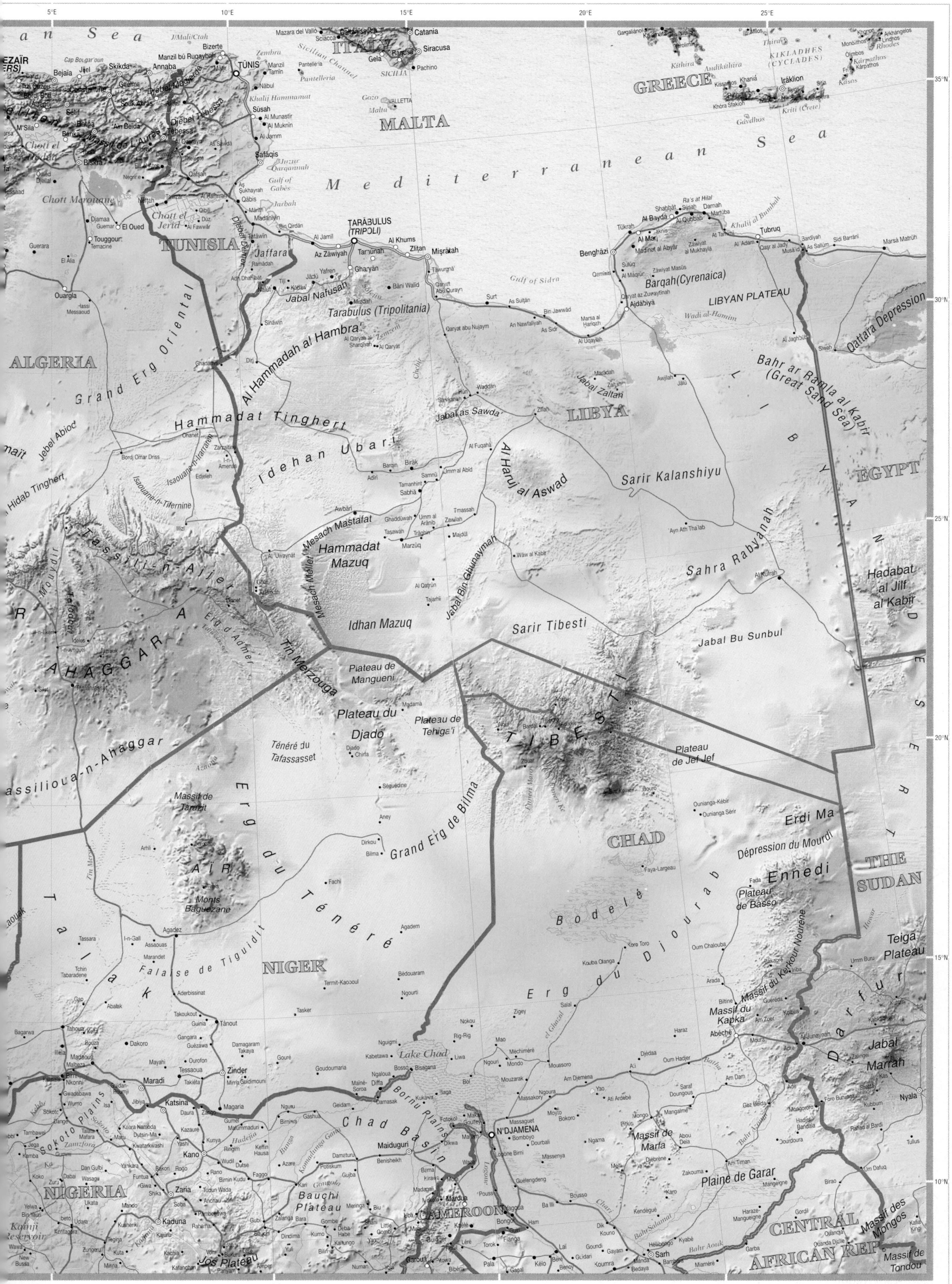
5°E
10°E
15°E
20°E
25°E
35°N
30°N
25°N
20°N
15°N
10°N
M e d i t e r r a n e a n S e a
ITALY
SICILIA
Catania
Siracusa
Sicilian Channel
Pantelleria
MALTA
VALLETTA
GREECE
KIKLADHES (CYCLADES)
Iráklion
Kriti (Crete)
Rhodes
Kárpathos
TUNISIA
TÛNIS
Bizerte
Sûsah
Şafâqis
Gulf of Gabès
Qâbis
Jarbah
ALGERIA
Annaba
Skikda
Constantine
Sétif
Biskra
Tebessa
Chott Merouane
Touggourt
El Oued
Ouargla
Grand Erg Oriental
TARĀBULUS (TRIPOLI)
Az Zāwiyah
Al Khums
Zlīţan
Mişrātah
Jabal Nafusah
Tarabulus (Tripolitania)
Al Hammadah al Hambra
Gulf of Sidra
Surt
Benghāzī
Ajdābiyā
Barqah(Cyrenaica)
LIBYAN PLATEAU
Darnah
Tubruq
Al Bayḑā
Khalij al Bumbah
LIBYA
Jabal Zaltan
Jabal as Sawda'
Hammadat Tinghert
Idehan Ubari
Sabhā
Al Haruj al Aswad
Sarir Kalanshiyu
Bahr ar Ramla al Kabir (Great Sand Sea)
Qattara Depression
Siwah
EGYPT
L I B Y A N D E S E R T
Sahra Rabyanah
Al Kufrah
Hadabat al Jilf al Kabir
Hammadat Mazuq
Mesach Mastafat
Murzūq
Idhan Mazuq
Jabal Bin Ghunaymah
Sarir Tibesti
Jabal Bu Sunbul
Tassili-n-Ajjer
Tin Merzouga
Erg d'Admer
A H A G G A R
Tassilioua-n-Ahaggar
Plateau de Mangueni
Plateau du Djado
Plateau de Tehiga'i
Ténéré du Tafassasset
T I B E S T I
Plateau de Jef Jef
Erdi Ma
Massif de Taraïzit
Erg du Ténéré
Grand Erg de Bilma
Bilma
Aïr
Monts Baguezane
Agadez
Falaise de Tiguidit
Talak
NIGER
CHAD
Dépression du Mourdi
Ennedi
Plateau de Basso
Faya-Largeau
Bodélé
Erg du Djourab
Massif du Kapka
Abéché
THE SUDAN
Teiga Plateau
Darfur
Jabal Marrah
Nyala
Zinder
Maradi
Katsina
Kano
Zaria
Kaduna
Jos Plateau
NIGERIA
Sokoto Plains
Bauchi Plateau
Maiduguri
Lake Chad
Chad Basin
Bornu Plains
N'DJAMENA
CAMEROON
Massif de Marfa
Plaine de Garar
Sarh
CENTRAL AFRICAN REP.
Massif des Mongos
Massif de Tondou
Kainji Reservoir

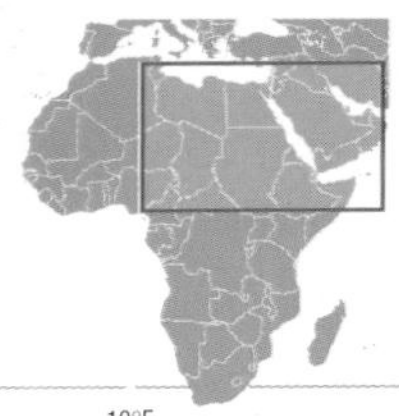

Africa

Northeast Africa

0 100 200 300 400 500 Km
0 40 80 120 140 180 200 220 miles

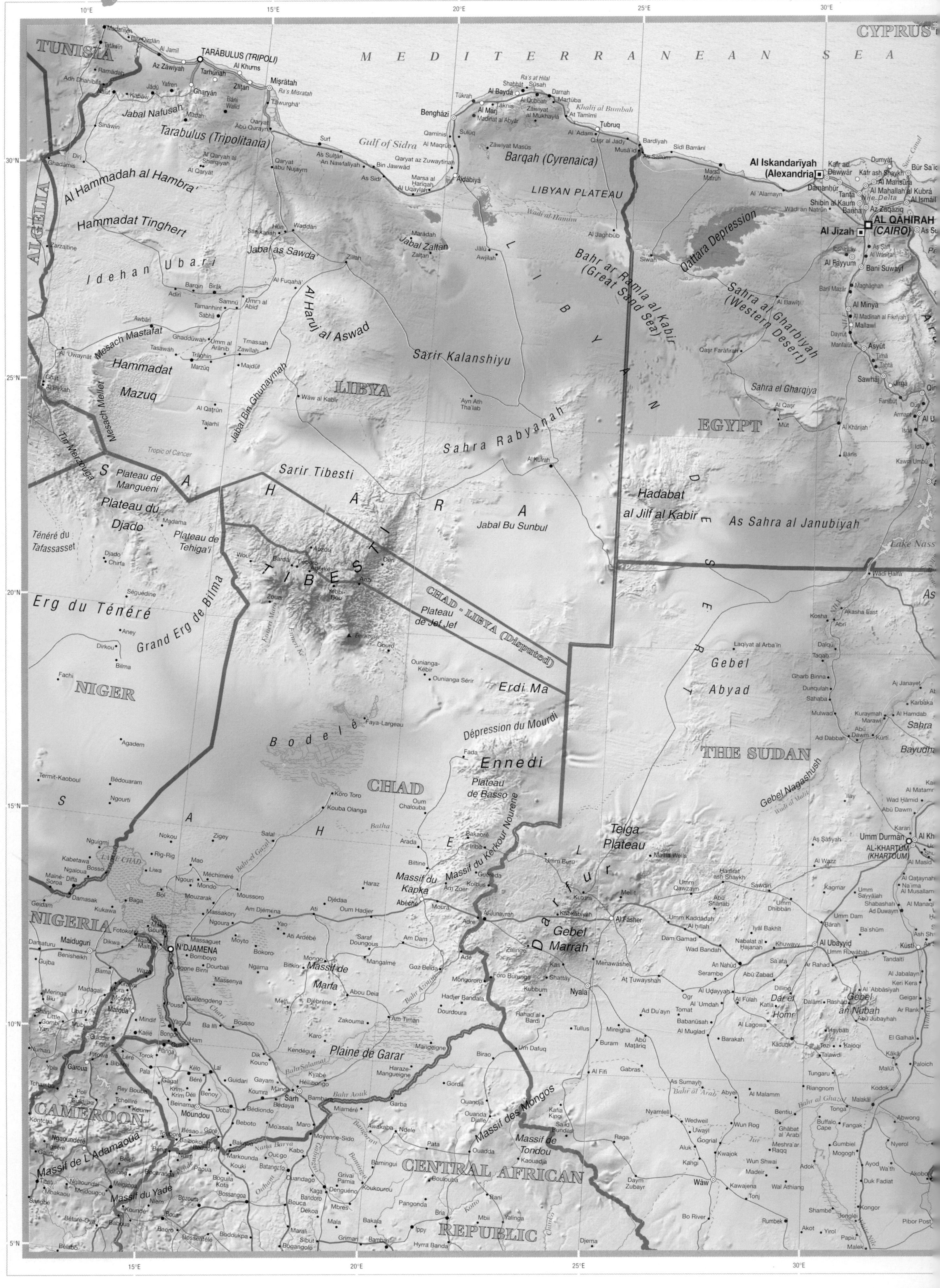

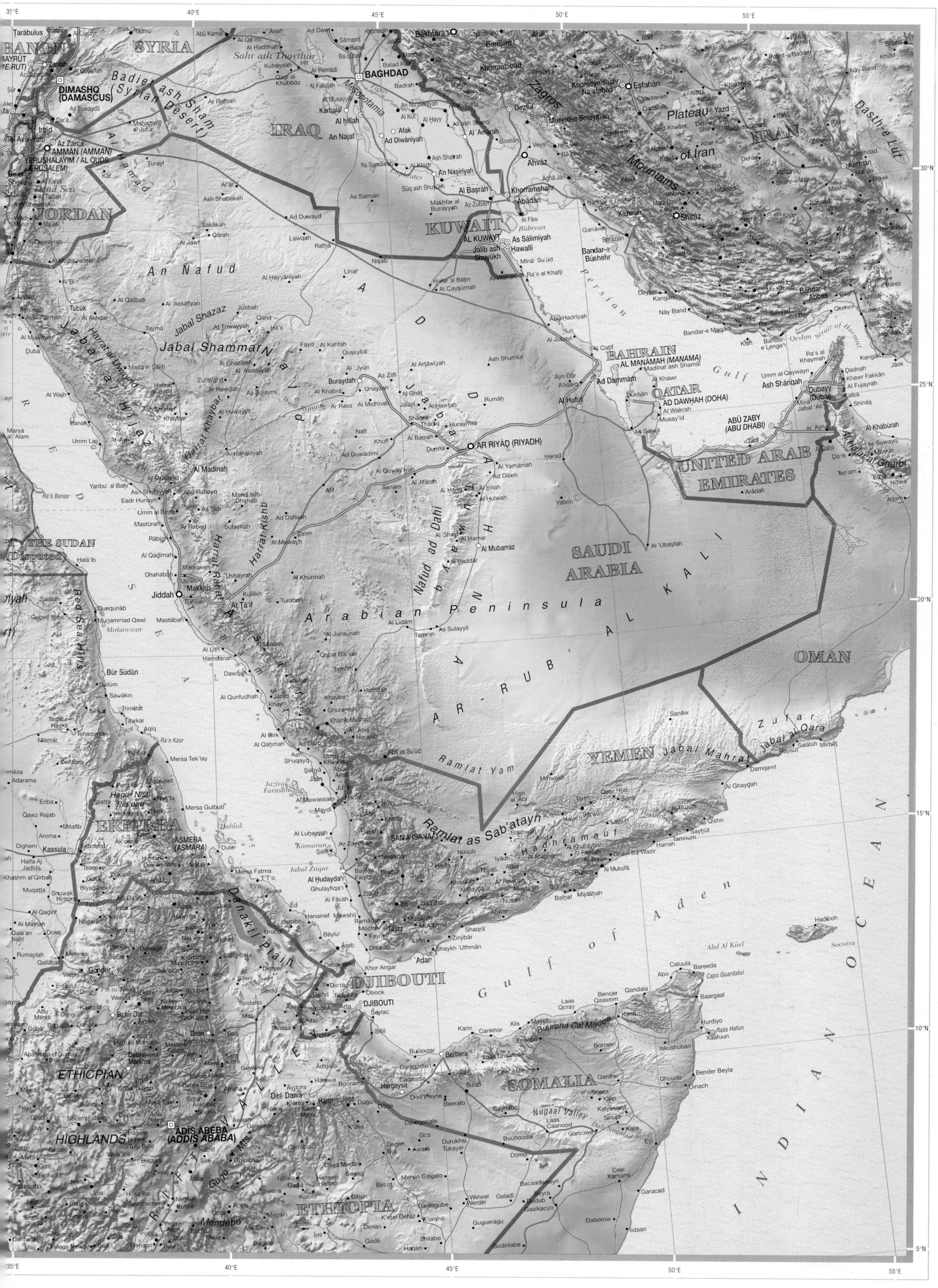

SYRIA
IRAQ
KUWAIT
IRAN
JORDAN
BAHRAIN
QATAR
UNITED ARAB EMIRATES
SAUDI ARABIA
OMAN
YEMEN
ERITREA
DJIBOUTI
SOMALIA
ETHIOPIA
THE SUDAN (Disputed)
BAGHDAD
DIMASHQ (DAMASCUS)
AMMAN (AMMAN)
YERUSHALAYIM / AL QUDS (JERUSALEM)
AL KUWAYT
AL MANĀMAH (MANAMA)
AD DAWḨAH (DOHA)
ABŪ ZABY (ABU DHABI)
AR RIYĀḌ (RIYADH)
ṢAN'Ā' (SANA)
ASMERA (ASMARA)
DJIBOUTI
ADIS ABEBA (ADDIS ABABA)
Badiet ash Sham (Syrian Desert)
Al Hamad
An Nafud
Jabal Shammar
Najd
Jabal Shazaz
Harrat al Uwayrid
Jabal al Ḩijāz
Harrat Khaybar
Harrat Kishb
Harrat Rahat
Ad Dahnā'
Jabal Ṭuwayq
Nafud ad Dahi
Arabian Peninsula
Ar Rub' al Khali
Ramlat Yam
Ramlat as Sab'atayn
Ḩaḑramawt
Jabal Mahrat
Jabal al Qara
Zufar
Al Ḩajar al Gharbī
Zagros Mountains
Plateau of Iran
Dasht-e Lut
Mesopotamia
Persian Gulf
Strait of Hormuz
Red Sea
Red Sea Hills
Gulf of Aden
INDIAN OCEAN
Danakil Plain
Rift Valley
ETHIOPIAN HIGHLANDS
Haga Nish Plateau
Nugaal Valley
Buuraha Cal Madow
Gugu Mts.
Socotra
Capo Guardafui
Raas Hafun
35°E
40°E
45°E
50°E
55°E
30°N
25°N
20°N
15°N
10°N
5°N

Africa

West Central Africa

10°W
5°W
0°
5°E

SIERRA LEONE
GUINEA
LIBERIA
CÔTE D'IVOIRE
GHANA
TOGO
BENIN
NIGERIA

CONAKRY
FREETOWN
MONROVIA
Abidjan
YAMOUSSOUKRO
ACCRA
LOMÉ
PORTO-NOVO
Lagos
Ibadan
Cotonou
Kumasi
Bouaké
Korhogo
Man
Daloa
Takoradi
Cape Coast
Tema

Guinea Highlands
Lac de Kossou
Volta Basin
Lake Volta
Ashanti Uplands
Kwahu Plateau
Akwapim Togo Range
Mont Bouorou
Toura Mountains
Plateau of Yorubaland
Cape Palmas
Cape Three Points
Cape Saint Paul
Bight of Benin
Niger Delta
Mouths of the Niger

Gulf of Guinea

ATLANTIC OCEAN

SÃO TOMÉ AND PRÍNCIPE
São Tomé
Palé
Annobón

5°N
0°
16°N
7°55′S
16°S

Cape Verde (inset)

24°W
Santo Antão
Ribeira Grande
Mindelo
São Vicente
Santa Luzia
São Nicolau
Castilhiano
Barril
Sal
Pedra Lume
Santa Maria
Boa Vista
Sal Rei
Curral Velho
BARLAVENTO (WINDWARD) ISLANDS
ATLANTIC OCEAN
SOTAVENTO (LEEWARD) ISLANDS
Maio
Santo Antonio
Tarrafal
Santiago Maior
PRAIA
Fajãzinha
São Filipe
Fajã
Brava
Fogo
Santiago
0 50 100 km
0 20 40 60 miles

CAPE VERDE

Ascension I.

Ascension Island (inset)

14°20′W
North Point
Georgetown
The Peak
Portland Point
South Point
0 5 10 km
0 2 4 6 miles

Ascension (St. Helena)

St. Helena Island (inset)

5°40′W
JAMESTOWN
Longwood
Diana's Peak
Blue Hill
Sandy Bay
0 5 10 km
0 2 4 6 miles

St. Helena I.

St. Helena (UNITED KINGDOM)

Tristan da Cunha (inset)

12°15′W
37°05′S
Edinburgh
Anchorstock Point
Queen Mary's Peak
Sandy Point
Stonyhill Point
0 5 10 km
0 2 4 6 miles

Tristan da Cunha (St. Helena)

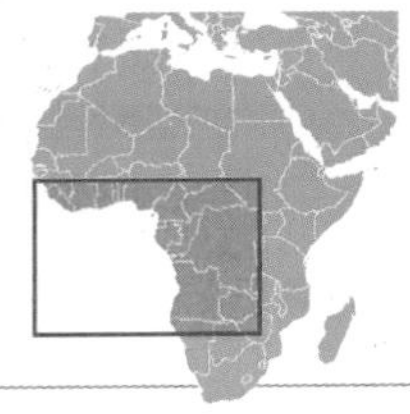

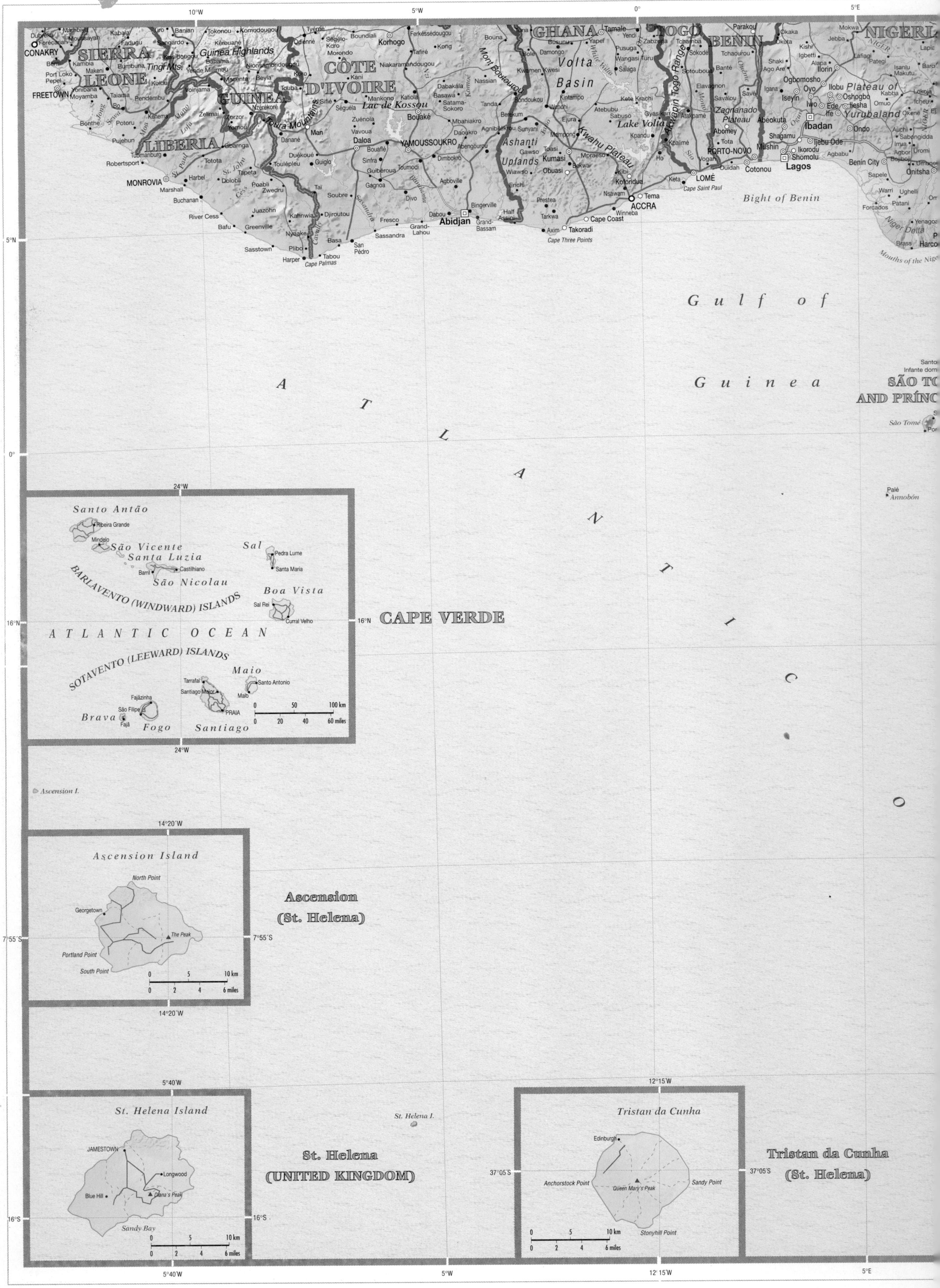

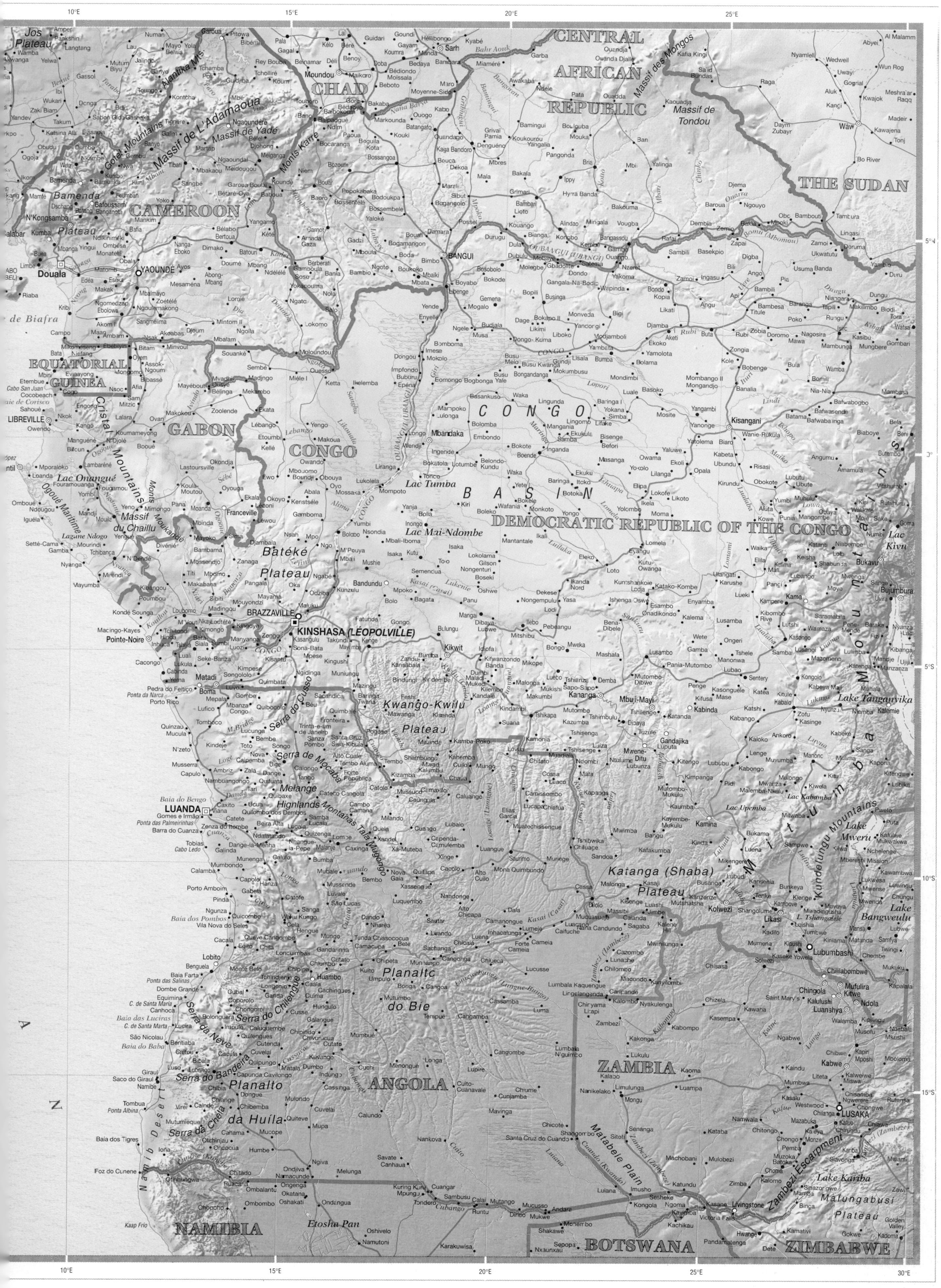
10°E
15°E
20°E
25°E
30°E
5°N
0°
5°S
10°S
15°S
CENTRAL AFRICAN REPUBLIC
CHAD
CAMEROON
EQUATORIAL GUINEA
GABON
CONGO
DEMOCRATIC REPUBLIC OF THE CONGO
THE SUDAN
ANGOLA
ZAMBIA
NAMIBIA
BOTSWANA
ZIMBABWE
CONGO BASIN
Jos Plateau
Massif de L'Adamaoua
Massif de Yade
Massif des Mongos
Massif de Tondou
Gotel Mountains
Alantika Mts.
Monts Karre
Bamenda Plateau
Cristal Mountains
Monts Birougou
Massif du Chaillu
Batéké Plateau
Kwango-Kwilu Plateau
Serra do Cusso
Serra de Mocaba
Melange Highlands
Montanhas Tala Mugongo
Planalto do Bie
Planalto da Huíla
Serra da Neve
Serra do Chilengue
Serra da Chela
Serra do Bandeira
Namib Desert
Etosha Pan
Katanga (Shaba) Plateau
Kundelungu Mountains
Mitumba Mountains
Matabele Plain
Zambezi Escarpment
Matungabusi Plateau
Lac Tumba
Lac Mai-Ndombe
Lake Tanganyika
Lac Kivu
Lake Mweru
Lake Bangweulu
Lake Kariba
Lac Upemba
Lac Kabamba
Lac Onangué
de Biafra
Baia do Bengo
Baia dos Tigres
YAOUNDÉ
Douala
LIBREVILLE
BANGUI
BRAZZAVILLE
KINSHASA (LÉOPOLVILLE)
LUANDA
LUSAKA
Pointe-Noire
Matadi
Kisangani
Mbandaka
Kananga
Mbuji-Mayi
Lubumbashi
Kolwezi
Likasi
Ndola
Kitwe
Livingstone
Lobito
Benguela
Huambo
Sarh
Moundou
Bukavu
Bujumbura
Kalemie
Kamina
Kikwit
Bandundu
Tshikapa
Cabinda

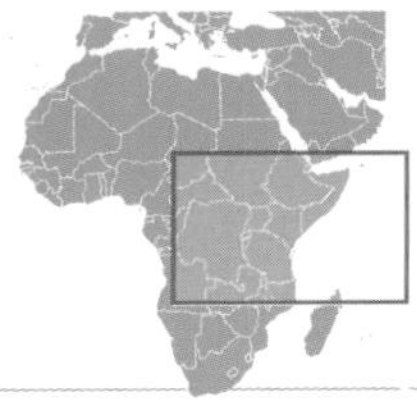

Africa

East Central Africa

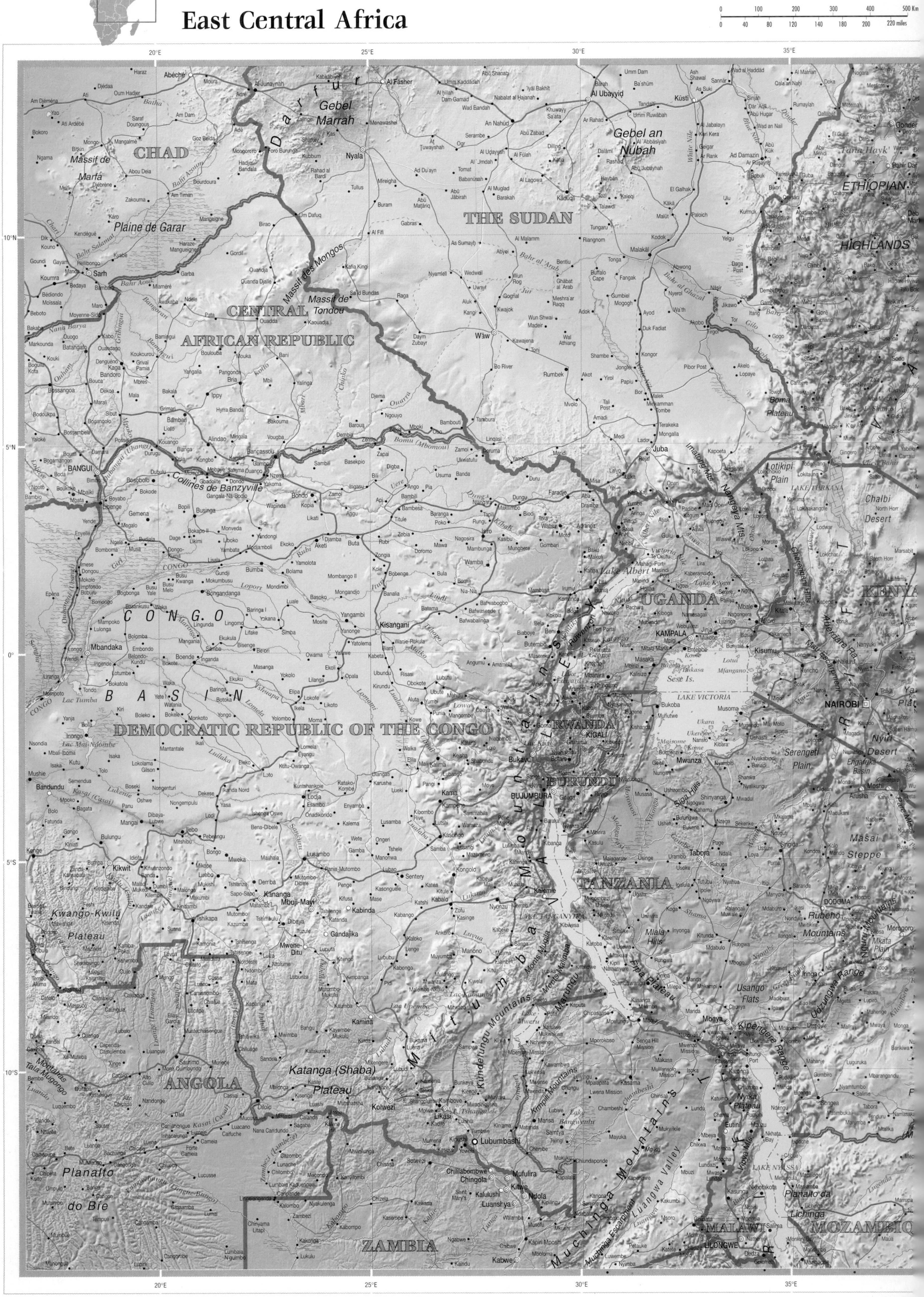

40°E
45°E
50°E
55°E
60°E
10°N
5°N
0°
5°S
10°S
YEMEN
Ta'izz
Adan
Shaykh 'Uthmān
Zinjibār
Mocha
Bab el Mandeb
Gulf of Aden
ERITREA
Aseb
DJIBOUTI
Golfe de Tadjourah
DJIBOUTI
Obock
Tadjoura
Dikhil
Seylac
Danakil Plain
'Abd Al Kūrī
Socotra
Caluula
Bareeda
Raas Caseyr
Capo Guardafui
Abo
Qandala
Baargaal
Bender Cassim
Laas Qoray
Buuraha Cal Madow
Erigabo
Mayd
Xiis
Raas Khaanziir
Karin
Berbera
Bullaxaar
Laas Dhaareed
Sheikh
Hargeysa
Burao
Oodweyne
Beerato
Hafun Bay North
Raas Hafun
Hafun Bay South
Xaafuun
Hurdiyo
Iskushuban
Borrama
Qardho
Bender Beyla
Dhuudo
Dinach
Ceel Afweyne
Nugaal Valley
Garoowe
Eyl
Dirē Dawa
Harer
Jijiga
Ahmar Mts.
Dibile
Degeh Bur
Āwarē
Gos
Tukayel
Durukhsi
Buuhoodle
Domo
Laas Caanood
Garacad
Bacaadweyn
Ceel Xamurre
Gaalkacyo
Beyra
Galadi
Dudub
Dusa Mareb
ETHIOPIA
Werder
Warder
Shilabo
Gode
K'ebri Dehar
Denan
Imi
Wabi Shebele
Aldo Range
Guguerago
Dabarow
Iidaan
Hobyo
Godinlabe
Dhusa Mareeb
El Ābrēd
Ceeldheere
Sinadhago
Feerfeer
Mustahil
Beledweyne
El Dere
Beled Weyne
El Cohole
Ceel Buur
Xarardheere
Jilgley
Bulo Berde
Ceel Dheere
Mereeg
Dolo Odo
Luuq
Waajid
Tayeeglow
Xuddur
SOMALIA
Baydhabo
Yageg
Buur Hakaba
Wanle Weyne
Jawhar
Mahadday Weyn
Itala
Warshiikh
MUQDISHO
(MOGADISHU)
Jannaale
Qoryooley
Marka
Awara Plain
Boji Plain
Ngangerabeli Plain
Bardheere
Diinsoor
Jilib
Kamsuuma
Jamaame
Kismaayo
Afmadow
Kolbio
Buur Gaabo
Raas Jumbo
Kiunga
Pate
Lamu
Formosa Bay
Malindi
Mombasa
Pemba
Zanzibar
DAR ES SALAAM
Mafia
Kilwa Kivinje
Kilwa Masoko
Lindi
Mtwara
Ras Rawura
Cabo Delgado
Vamizi
Mocimboa da Praia
Mucojo
Macomia
Ibo
Quissanga
Pemba
Mecúfi
Lúrio
Baía de Memba
Cabo Melamo
Nacala
INDIAN OCEAN
Inner Islands
Grand'Anse
Praslin
Silhouette
VICTORIA
Mahé
Poivre Atoll
Amirante Islands
Alphonse Group
SEYCHELLES
Aldabra Atoll
Assomption
Cosmoledo Atoll
Astove
Aldabra Group
Providence Atoll
Farquar Group
Farquhar Atoll
Mitsamiouli
Grande Comore
(Njazidia)
MCRONI
Foumbouni
COMOROS
Mohéli
(Mwali)
Sima
Anjouan
(Nzwani)
Mamoutzou
Sada
Mayotte
Glorieuses
Mozambique Channel
Tanjon'i Bobaomby
Andranovondrona
Antsirahana
Sadjoavato
Baie d'Ambaro
Ampisikinana
Nossy-Be
Ambilobe
Iharana
Ambanja
MADAGASCAR
Bemanevika
Sambava
Analalava

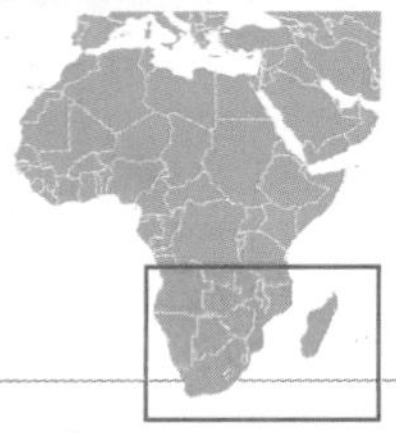

Africa

South of Africa

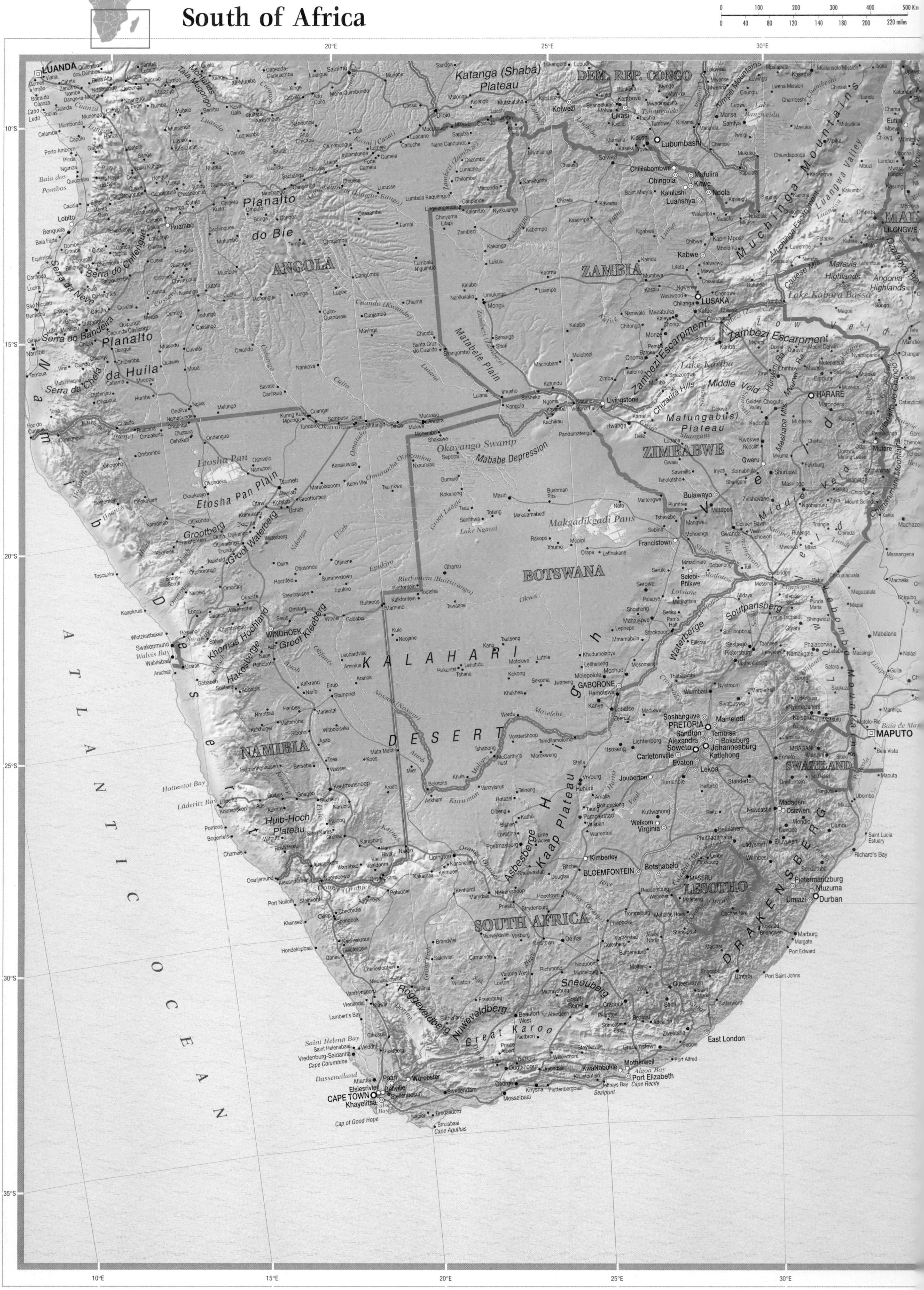

40°E
45°E
50°E
55°E
10°S
15°S
20°S
25°S
TANZANIA
SEYCHELLES
COMOROS
MOZAMBIQUE
MADAGASCAR
MAURITIUS
Aldabra Atoll
Cosmoledo Atoll
Assumption
Astove
Aldabra Group
Providence Atoll
Farquhar Atoll
Farquar Group
Planalto dos Macondes
(Makonde Plateau)
Lindi
Mtwara
Ras Rawura
Cabo Delgado
Vamizi
Mocímboa da Praia
Mucojo
Ibo
Quissanga
Pemba
Mecúfi
Lúrio
Baía de Memba
Cabo Melamo
Nacala
Mossuril
Moçambique
Nampula
Lumbo
Mogincual
Angoche
Moma
Pebane
Quelimane
Chinde
Blantyre
Zomba
Serra Chiperone
Serra Namuli
MORONI
Grande Comore (Njazídja)
Mitsamiouli
Fomboni
Mohéli Mwali
Anjouan (Nzwani)
Mamoutzou
Dzaoudzi
Mayotte
Glorieuses
Mozambique Channel
Ile Juan de Nova
Tanjona Vilanandro
Tanjon'i Bobaomby
Antsiranana
Massif de Tsaratanana
Nossy-Bé
Sambava
Antalaha
Mahajanga
Ambato Boeny
Tanjon'i Masoala
Maroantsetra
Toamasina
TANANARIVE
Antsirabe
Fianarantsoa
Ambositra
Mananjary
Manakara
Vohipeno
Farafangana
Vangaindrano
Bongolava
Plateau du Bemaraha
Ankaratra
Betsimisaraka Escarpment
Angavo Escarpment
Massif du Makay
Massif Ruiniforme de l'Isalo
Ribaon Manambo
Beamangarana
Mahafaly Massif
Morondava
Morombe
Toliara
Betioky
Beloha
Ampanihy
Amboasary
Ambovombe
Tolañaro
Tanjon'i Vohimena
Tropic of Capricorn
Iles Mascareignes (Mascarene Islands)
PORT LOUIS
Curepipe
Mahébourg
Mauritius
Saint-Denis
Saint Paul
Saint-André
Saint-Pierre
Réunion (FRANCE)
INDIAN OCEAN
Ilha do Bazaruto
Vilanculos
Ilha Benguerua
Inhambane
55°30'E
21°S
Réunion (FRANCE)
La Port
Saint-Benoit
Mat
Galets
Cirque de Chaos
St-Étienne
l'Est
Remparts
Saint-Louis
Le Tampon
Saint-Joseph
0 10 20 km
0 4 8 12 miles

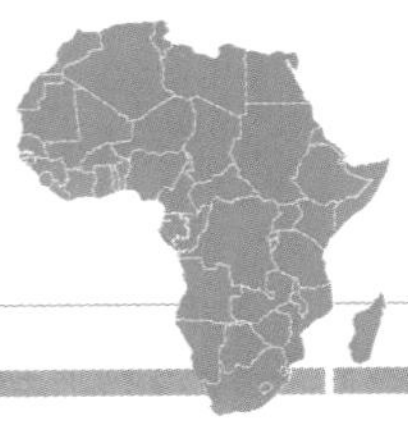

Gabon

Official name: Gabonese Republic

Form of government: republic; multiparty presidential regime

Capital: Libreville

Official language: French

Monetary unit: CFA franc

Religious affiliation: Christian (96.2%), traditional religions (2.9%), Muslim (0.8%), other (0.1%)

Ethnic composition of the population: Fang (35%), Mpongwe (15.1%), Mbete (14.2%), Punu (11.5%), others (23.5%)

Area: 267,667 sq km

Total population: 1,173,000 inhabitants

Population density: 4.4 persons per sq km

An Atlantic coast state of West Africa, Gabon is crossed through the center by the Equator. Physically, the country consists of two natural regions: a sedimentary coastal plain formed by alluvial deposits, and an interior tableland with elevations below 1,400 m. Its rivers flow into the Atlantic Ocean. The most important is the Ogooué River, with a basin that includes most of the territory of the country. The climate of Gabon is equatorial, hot and wet with abundant rainfall throughout the year. The population registers one of the lowest average densities in Africa, and the great majori of its inhabitants live in rural areas. The Fang ethn group predominates over others. Subsistence farmin employs a great number of its economically activ population. However, herding and fishing are mo productive. The lumbering of valuable woods, main ebony, is in the hands of foreign companies. There a mines of manganese, uranium and natural gas. Th industrial sector hardly exists. Gabon is a developi country that is economically dependent on France.

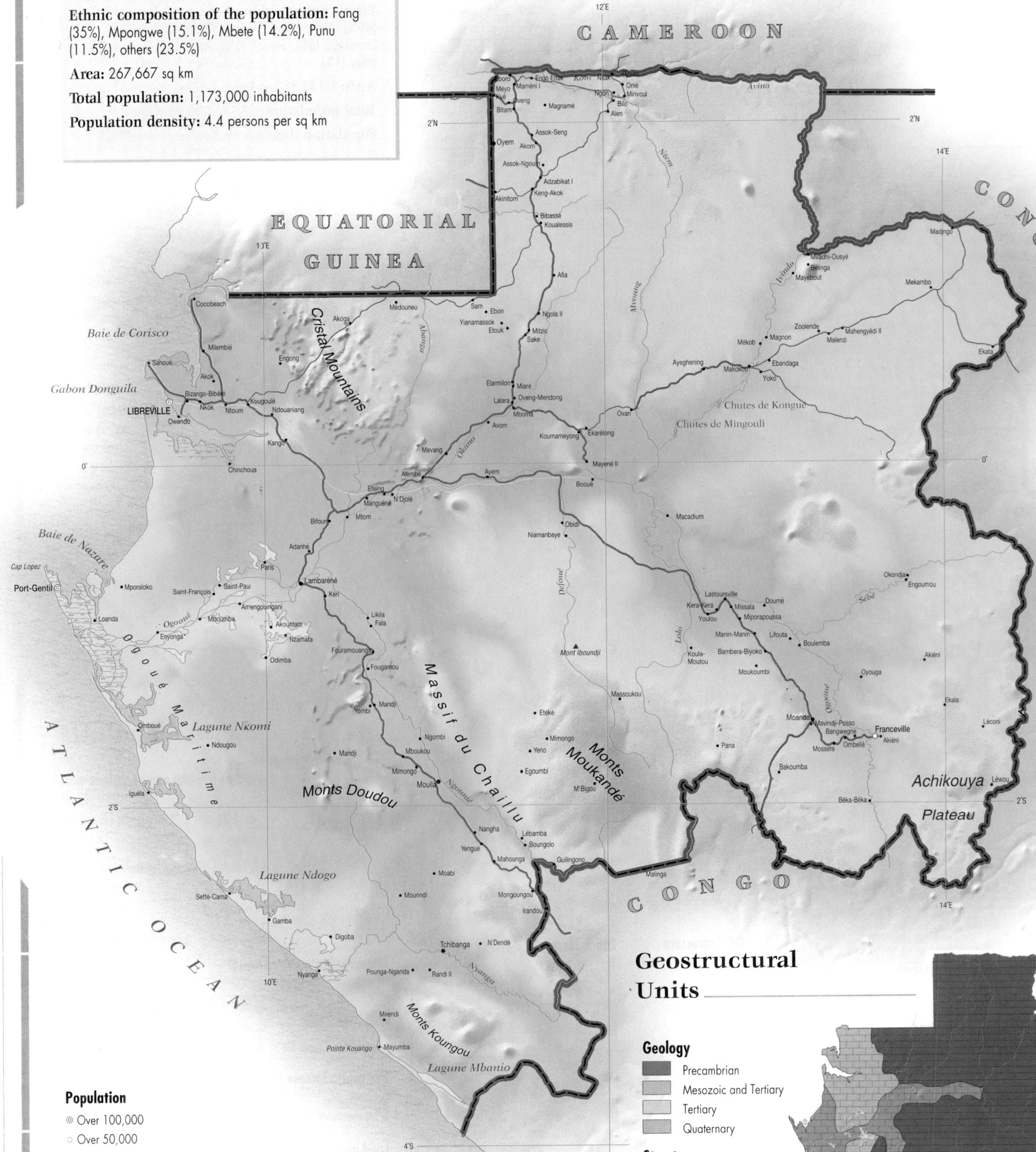

Population

◎ Over 100,000

○ Over 50,000

• Over 10,000

· Under 10,000

0 25 50 75 km

0 10 20 30 40 50 miles

Geostructural Units

Geology

Precambrian

Mesozoic and Tertiary

Tertiary

Quaternary

Structures

Shields

Sedimentary covering

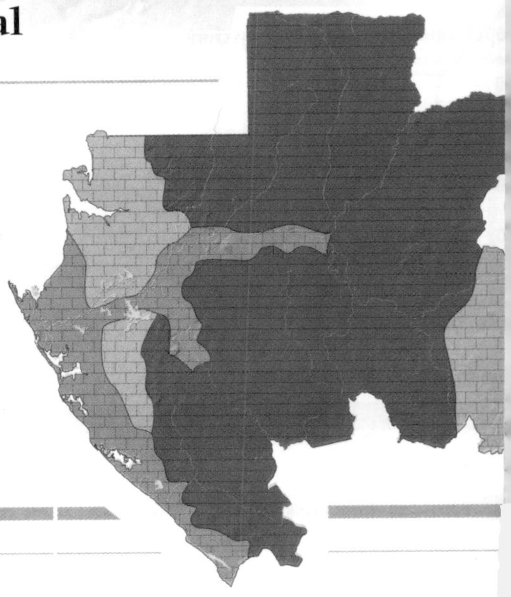

Mining

Non-energy source mineral resources
Metals
- Iron ore (unexploited)
- Manganese
- Gold
- Lead (unexploited)

Rocks and industrial minerals
- Diamonds

Mineral fuel resources
Fossil fuels
- Natural gas

Radioactive fuels
- Uranium

Energy-related installations
- Hydroelectric power plant
- Thermal power plant
- Refinery
- Oil pipeline

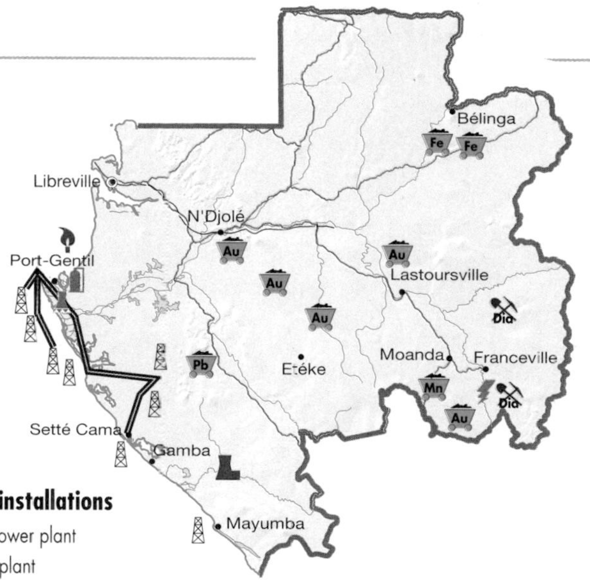

Vital statistics

0‰ 10‰ 20‰ 30‰ 40‰ 50‰ 60‰
Birth rate(‰)
Death rate(‰)
Population growth rate(%)
-1% 0% 1% 2% 3% 4%
Minimum and maximum world values | Average world value

Population age distribution

34% | 61% | 5%
0 years | 15 years | 60 years

Literacy (% of population over15)

63.2% | 73.7% | 53.3%
0% | 100%
Total literate population | Male literacy | Female literacy

Population evolution and projection
in millions of persons

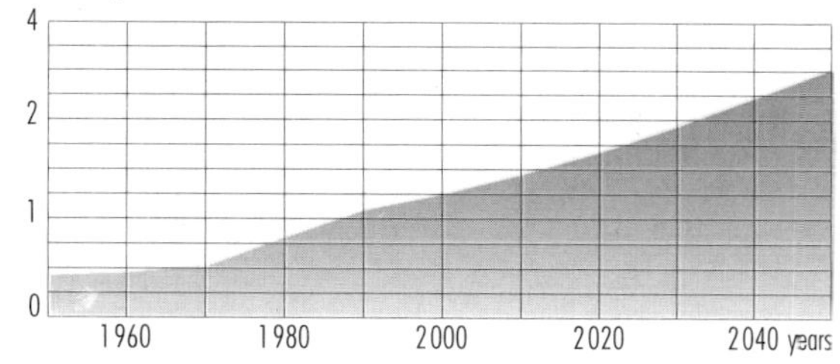

GDP structure
4,691 million dollars

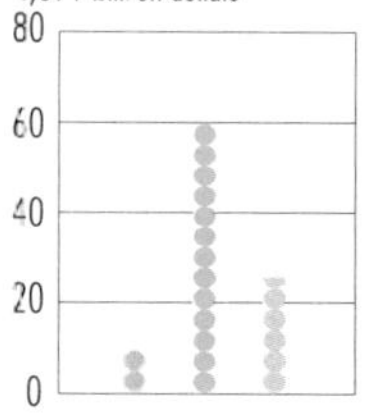

Labor force
606,000 persons

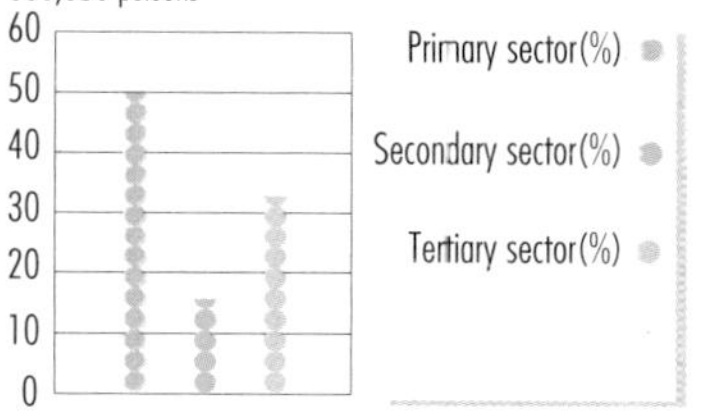

Per capita income (GDP per person)

$4,265.98/head
$77/person (world minimum: Mozambique) (world maximum:Japan) $37,075/person

Land use

0% | 100%
Forests and jungles **78%** | Cropland **2%** | Other **2%**
Meadows and pastures **18%**

Gambia, The

Population evolution and projection
millions of persons

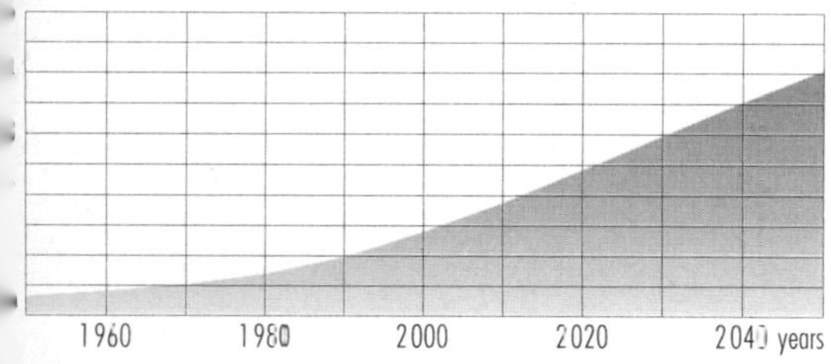

GDP structure
million dollars

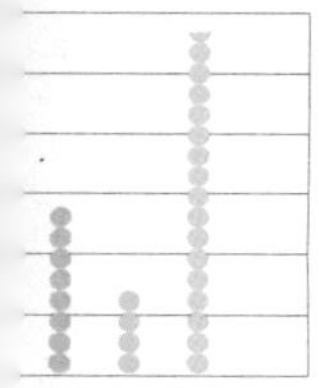

Labor force
531,000 persons

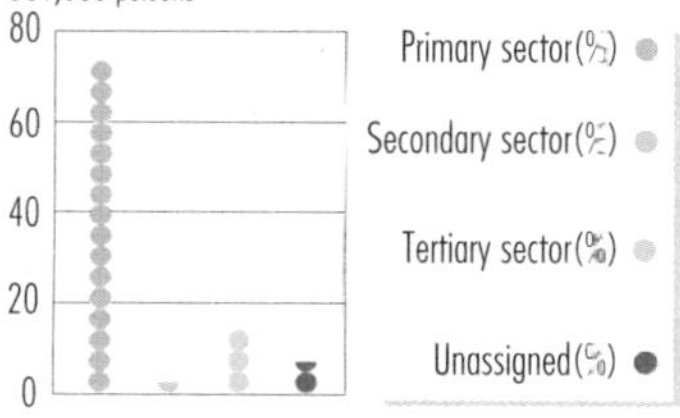

Population age distribution

47% | 51% | 2%
0 years | 15 years | 60 years

Vital statistics

0‰ 10‰ 20‰ 30‰ 40‰ 50‰ 60‰
Birth rate(‰)
Death rate(‰)
Population growth rate(%)
-1% 0% 1% 2% 3% 4%
Minimum and maximum world values | Average world value

Literacy (% of population over15)

38.6% | 52.8% | 24.9%
0% | 100%
Total literate population | Male literacy | Female literacy

Per capita income (GDP per person)

$308.71/person
$77/person (world minimum: Mozambique) (world maximum:Japan) $37,075/person

Land use

0% | 100%
Forests and jungles **14.5%** | Cropland **17%** | Other **59%**
Meadows and pastures **9.5%**

Official name: Republic of The Gambia
Form of government: republic under multiparty democratic rule
Capital: Banjul (Bathurst)
Official language: English
Monetary unit: dalasi
Religious affiliation: Muslim (95.4%), Christian (3.7%), Traditional beliefs and other (0.9%)
Ethnic composition of the population: Mandinka (42%), Fula (18%), Wolof (16%), Dyola (10%), Serahuli (9%), Ogras (4%); non Gambian (1%)
Area: 10,689 sq km
Total population: 1,205,000 inhabitants
Population density: 112.7 persons per sq km

The smallest state of the whole continent, The Gambia is formed by a narrow strip oriented in a west-east direction and enclosed in the Republic of Senegal. The course of the Gambia River is the backbone of its territory. Almost all the country is occupied by a sandy plateau, except in the east, where small hills rise separated from each other by narrow valleys. The climate, which is tropical and dry, has a short season of heavy rains, more noticeable on the coast. The population is located in the rural areas, while urban areas are scarcely developed. Gambians profess the Muslim religion. Several languages are spoken in the country: English (the official language), Mandinka, Fula and Wolof. Subsistence farming (cassava, millet, sorghum, rice) employs half of the population and extends along the banks of the Gambia River; peanuts are the most important export crop. Fishing and herding also have a certain economic weight. The few industries are located in the cities.

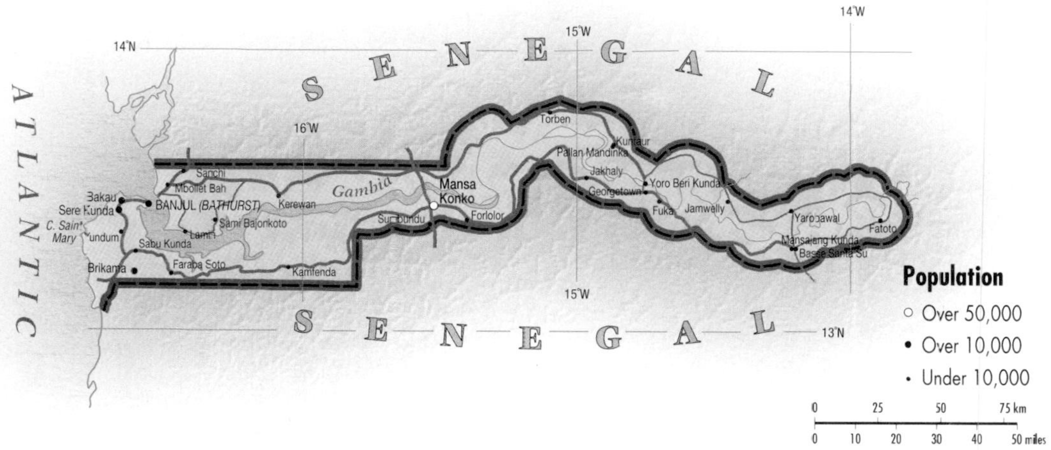

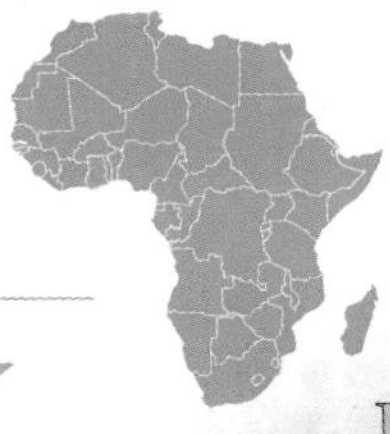

Ghana

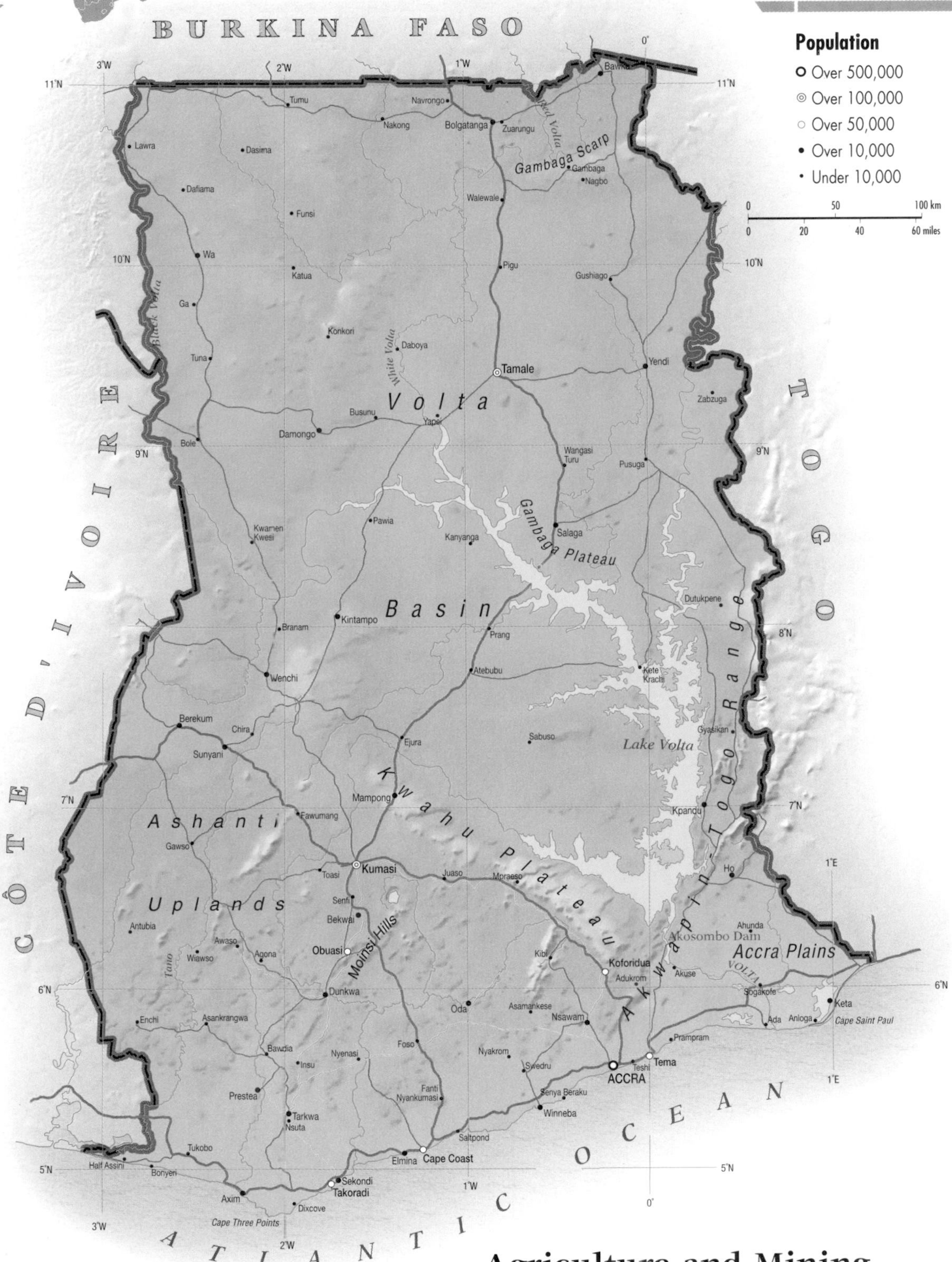

Population

- Over 500,000
- Over 100,000
- Over 50,000
- Over 10,000
- Under 10,000

Official name: Republic of Ghana

Form of government: constitutional democracy

Capital: Accra

Official language: English

Monetary unit: cedi

Religious affiliation: Christian (62.6%), traditional beliefs (21.4%), Muslim (15.7%), other (0.3%)

Ethnic composition of the population: black African: Akan (44%), Mossi-Dagomba (16%), Ewe (13%), Ga (8%), European and other (0.2%)

Area: 238,533 sq km

Total population: 17,698,000 inhabitants

Population density: 74.2 persons per sq km

Population evolution and projection

in millions of persons

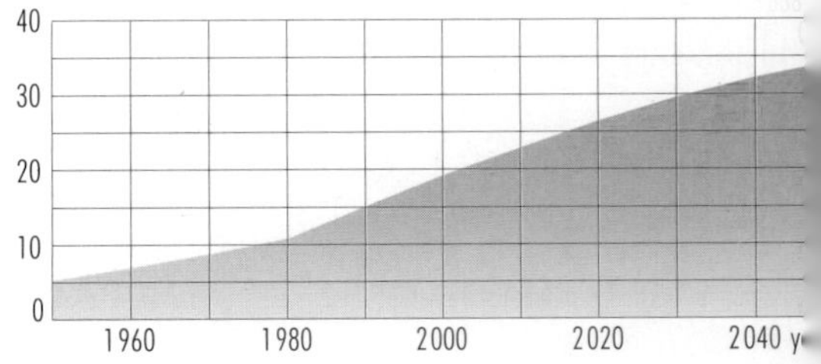

GDP structure

6,315 million dollars

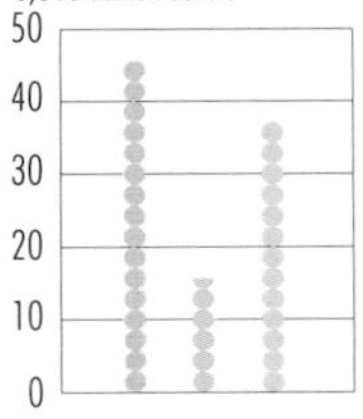

Labor force

7,900,000 persons

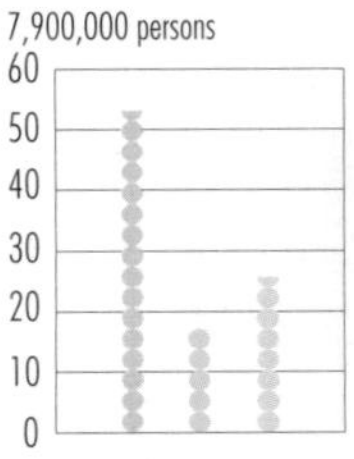

Primary sector(%)

Secondary sector(%)

Tertiary sector(%)

Population age distribution

Vital statistics

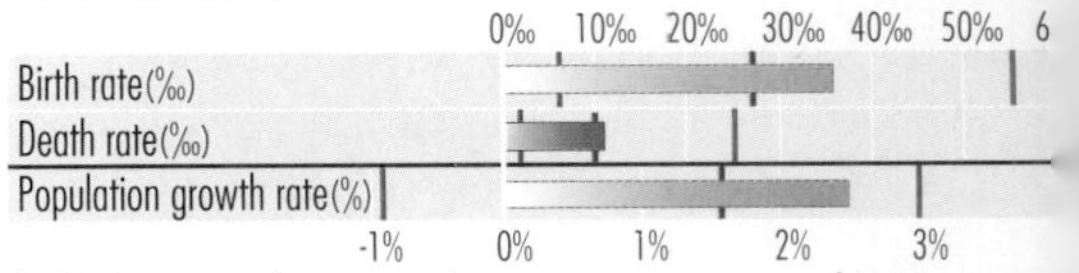

Global minimun and maximum value

Global average

Literacy (% of population over15)

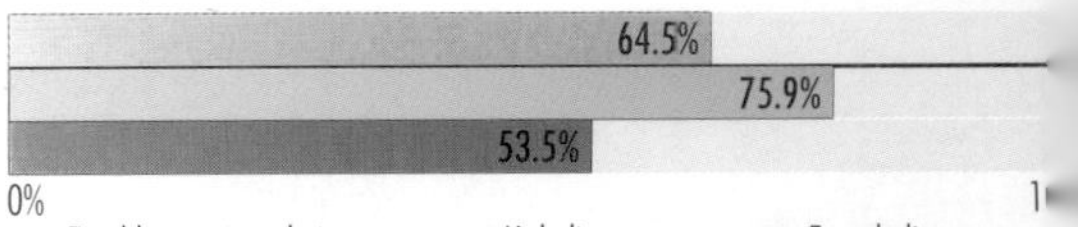

Total literate population

Male literacy

Female literacy

Per capita income (GDP per person)

$397.78/person

$77/person (world minimum: Mozambique) (world maximum:Japan) $37,075/pe

Unemployment (% of total population economically active)

10%

0%

Land use

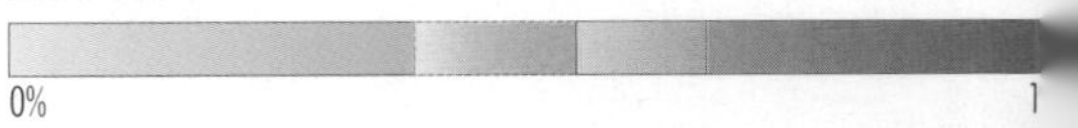

Forests and jungles 37%

Cropland 12%

Other

Meadows and pastures 15%

Agriculture and Mining

Non-energy source mineral resources

Metals

Bauxite Manganese Gold

Rocks and industrial minerals

Limestone Diamonds Salt

Mineral fuel resources

Fossil fuels

Petroleum

Energy-related installations

Refinery Hydroelectric power plant

Most of Ghana's flat territory corresponds to the basin of the Volta River, that traverses the country from northwest to southeast on the way to its mouth in the Atlantic Ocean. The climate is subequatorial, alternating dry periods with two rainy seasons (April-June and September-October). The influence of the hot Saharian air masses reduces precipitation in the northern half of the country. The average temperatures oscilate between the 26 ºC of the coast and the 29 ºC of the interior. The population, of Sudanic-Guinean descent, is experiencing very rapid growth. It is made up of more than 50 tribes, among which the Akan, Mossi-Dagomba, Ewe and Ga are the most notable. The official language is English. Protestantism is practiced by the majority. Ghanese agriculture produces subsistence crops (rice and other cereals, cassava) and crops for export (cocoa, coffee, oil palm, copra, bananas, peanuts, cotton, sugar cane). The underground holds great riches in gold, diamonds, manganese and bauxite. The only industries belong to the food, paper, textile and petrochemical sectors.

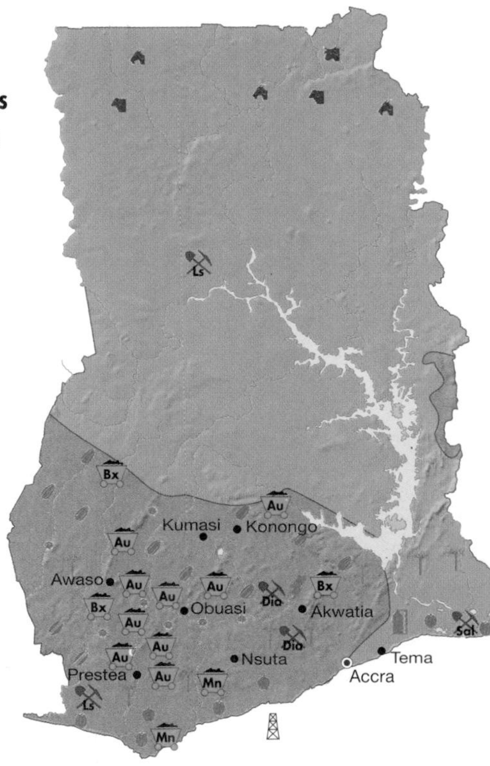

Types of agriculture and livestock production

- Subsistence farming (sorghum, millet, corn, rice)
- Forest
- Fruits and vegetables
- Coconut tree
- Oil palm
- Coffee
- Cocoa
- Cola-nut
- Cattle
- Sheep
- Goats

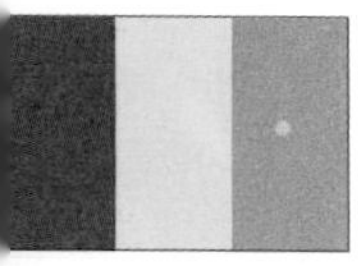

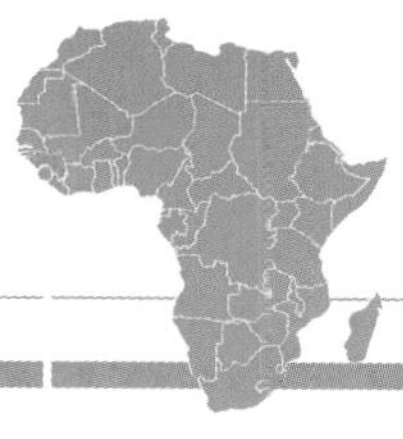

Ǝuinea is an Atlantic Coast republic of West Africa. Four ;eographical areas can be distinguished: lowland Guinea, hat occupies the western plains of the Atlantic Coast; ighland Guinea, located on the plains of the Niger River; he mountain ranges of Fouta Djallon, that make up niddle Guinea; and the forest region of the southeast. 'he climate is tropical, characterized by the alternation of dry season with a wet one. Most of the population is istributed irregularly throughout the rural zones. Various ethnic groups populate the country, among which the Peuhl and the Malinke are most notable. Traditional beliefs continue to be practiced, although the Islamic religion is predominant. Since World War II, bauxite and iron ore mining have experienced an important expansion, joining the traditional mining of gold and diamonds. Agriculture has entered a decline. Besides possessing important mineral resources that are exploited inadequately, Guinea has great hydroelectric potential.

Official name: Republic of Guinea
Form of government: republic
Capital: Conakry
Official language: French
Monetary unit: Guinean franc
Religious affiliation: Muslim (85%), traditional beliefs (5%), Christian (1.5%), other (8.5%)
Ethnic composition of the population: Peuhl (40%), Malinke (30%), Susu (20%), small tribes (10%)
Area: 245,857 sq km
Total population: 7,412,000 inhabitants
Population density: 30.1 persons per sq km

'opulation evolution and projection

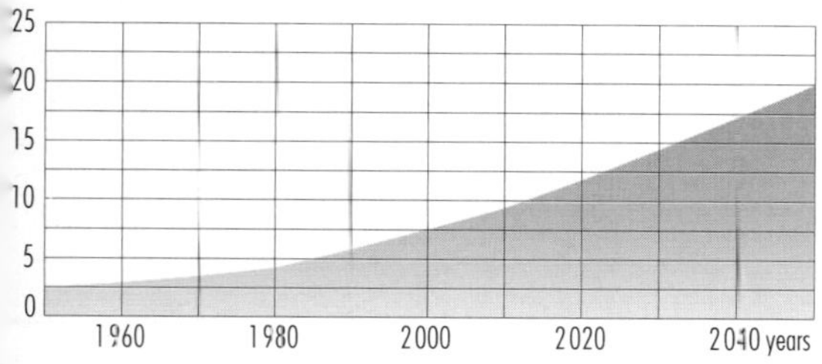

Population age distribution

Vital statistics

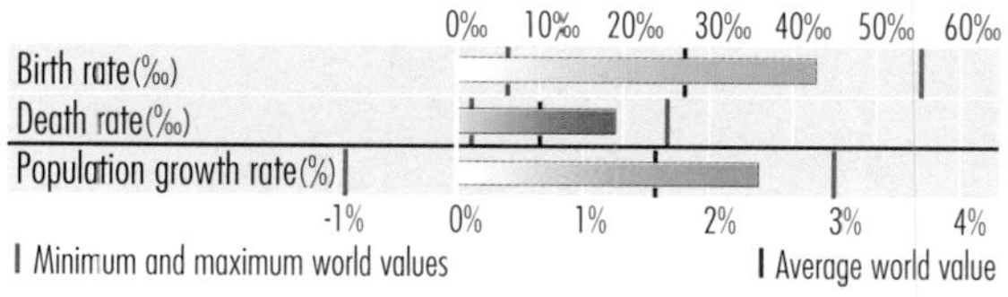

ƏDP structure

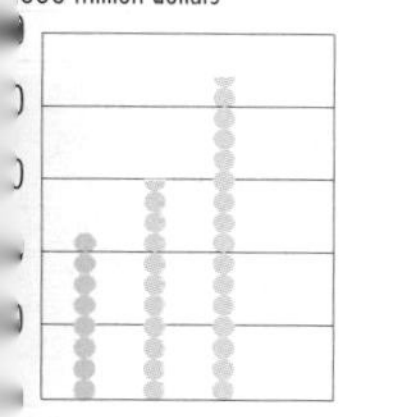

Labor force

Literacy (% of population over15)

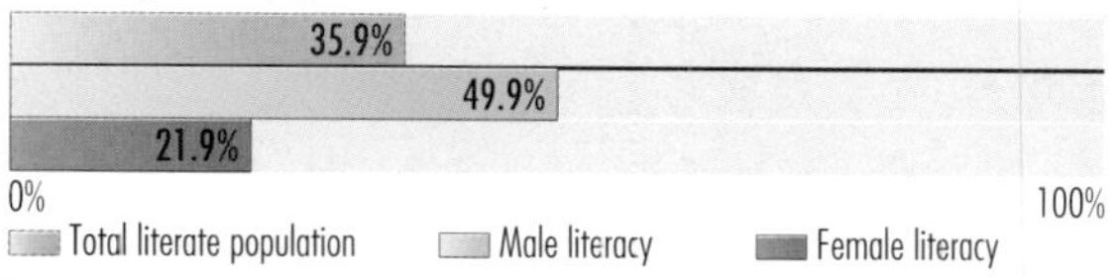

Per capita income (GDP per person)

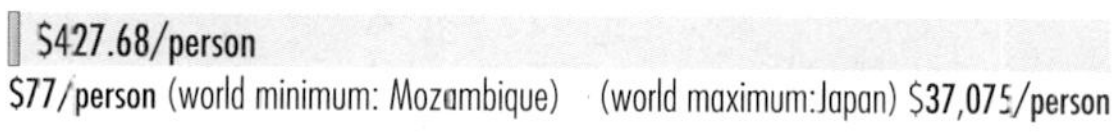

Land use

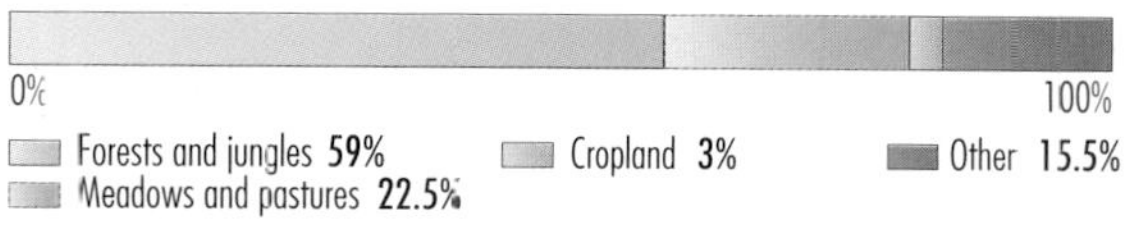

'opulation

- Over 500,000
- Over 50,000
- Over 10,000
- Under 10,000

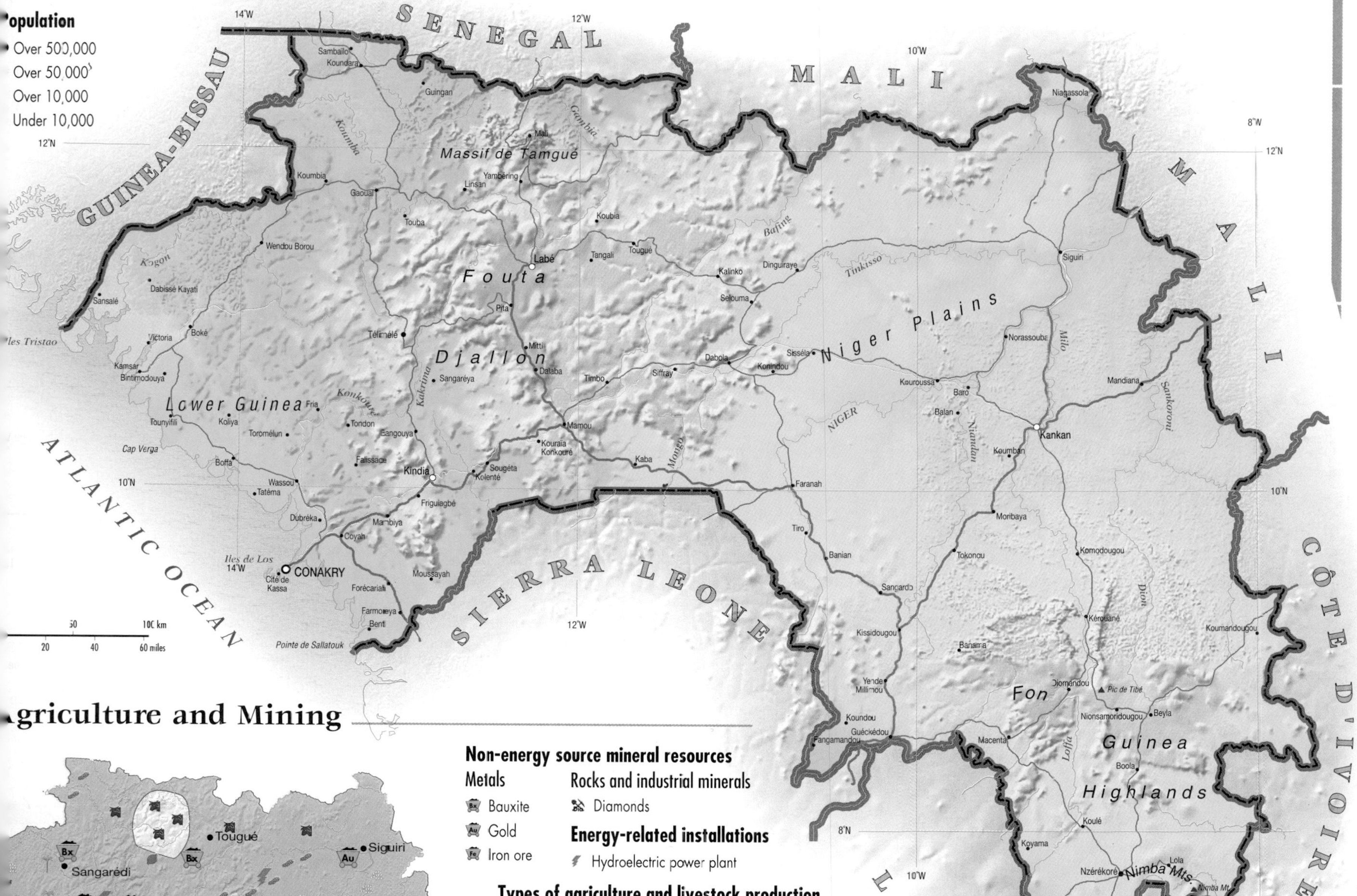

Agriculture and Mining

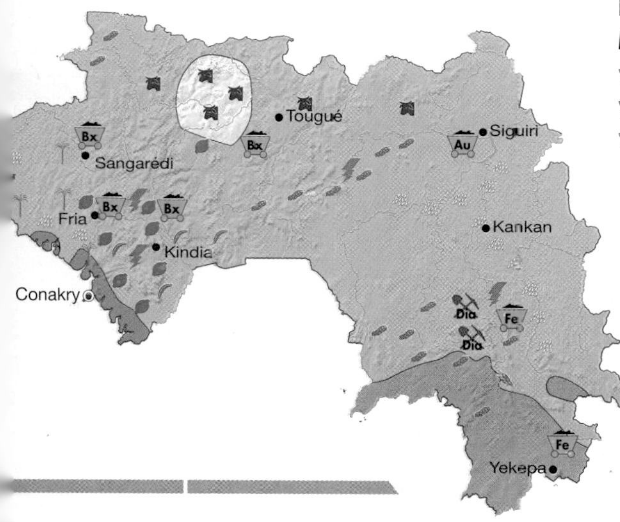

Non-energy source mineral resources

Metals
- Bauxite
- Gold
- Iron ore

Rocks and industrial minerals
- Diamonds

Energy-related installations
- Hydroelectric power plant

Types of agriculture and livestock production
- Subsistence farming (cassava, sorghum, corn, bananas)
- Herding
- Forest
- Swamplands
- Rice
- Citrus fruits
- Bananas
- Peanuts
- Oil palm
- Coffee
- Tea
- Cattle

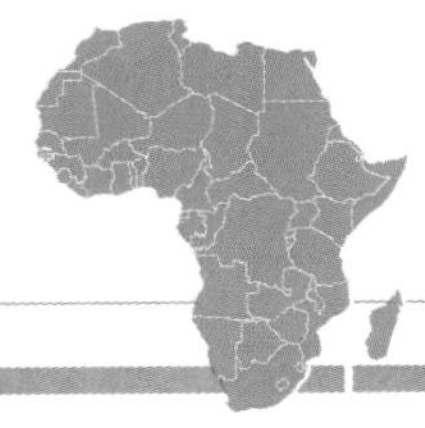

Guinea-Bissau

Guinea-Bissau has a tropical climate with high temperatures throughout the year and very heavy rains during the six months of summer. The people belong to the Semi-Bantu groups, within the Guinean subgroup; the most important are the Balanta, Fula, Mandyako, Mandinga and Pepel. The backward economy of the country is based on agriculture, divided between a subsistence crop (rice) and other plantation crops, the most important being peanuts and to a lesser degree, coconut groves, sugar cane, oil palm and rubber. Small factories for processing of agricultural and forestry products constitute the small industrial sector. There are no important resources underground, although recently, deposits of bauxite and petroleum have been discovered.

Official name: Republic of Guinea-Bissau

Form of government: republic

Capital: Bissau

Official language: Portuguese

Monetary unit: Guinea-Bissau peso

Religious affiliation: traditional beliefs (5.4%), Muslim (38%), Christian (8%)

Ethnic composition of the population: African: Balanta (30%), Fula (20%), Mandyako (14%), Mandinga (13%), Pepel (7%); European and mulatto (1%)

Area: 36,125 sq km

Total population: 1,151,000 inhabitants

Population density: 31.9 persons per sq km

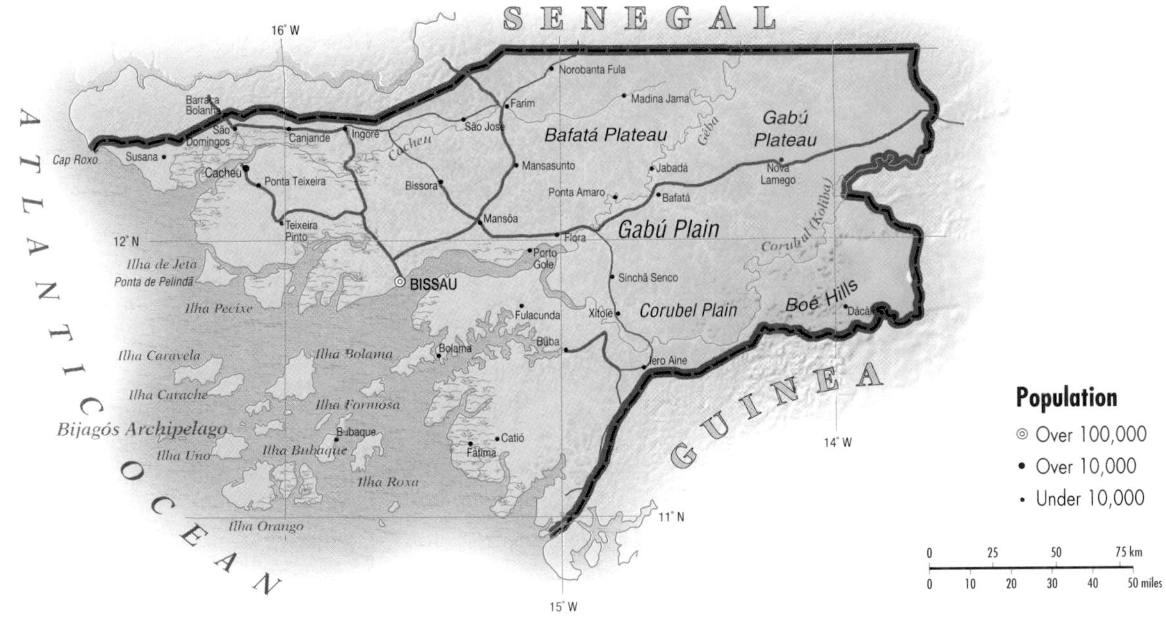

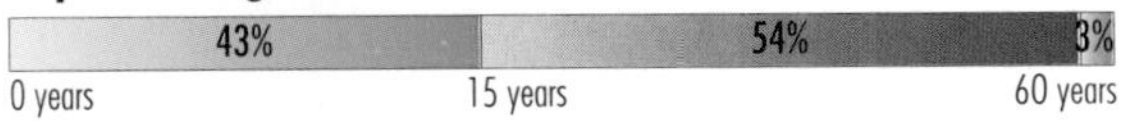

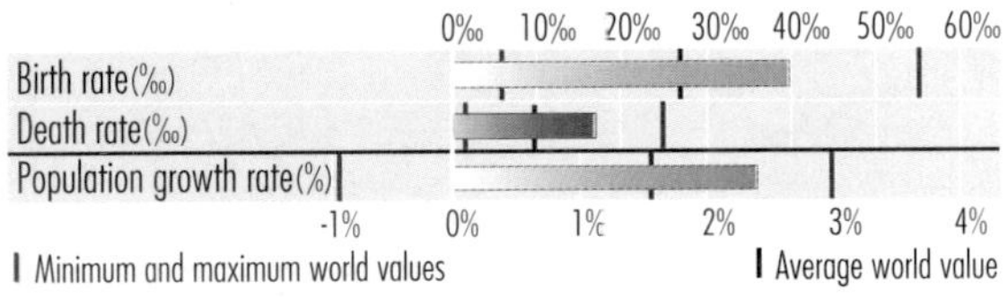

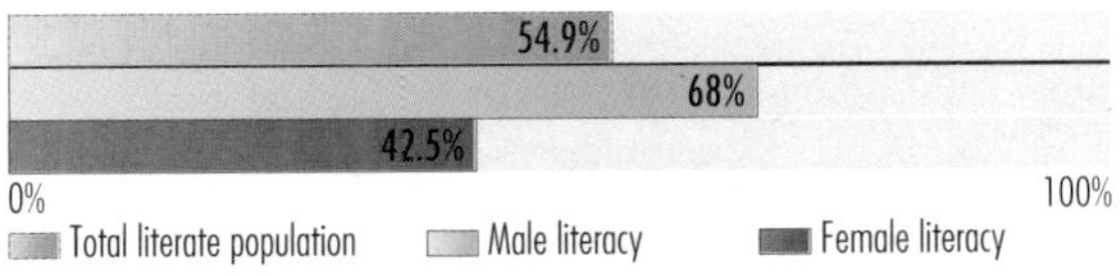

Per capita income (GDP per person)

$202.43/person

$77/person (world minimum: Mozambique) (world maximum:Japan) $37,075/person

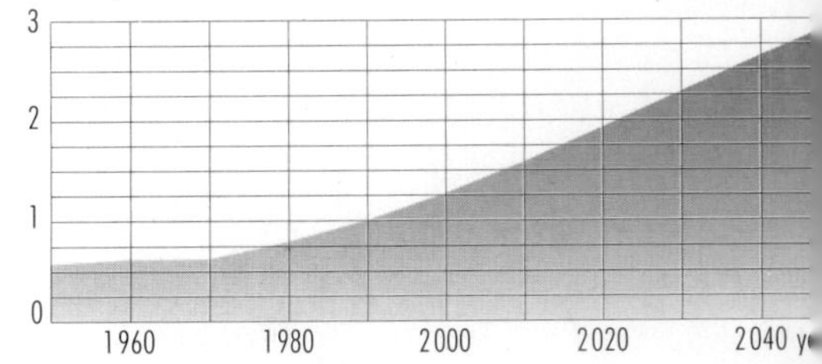

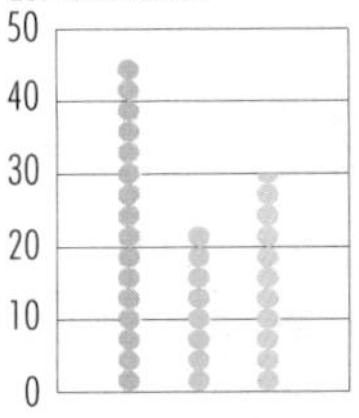

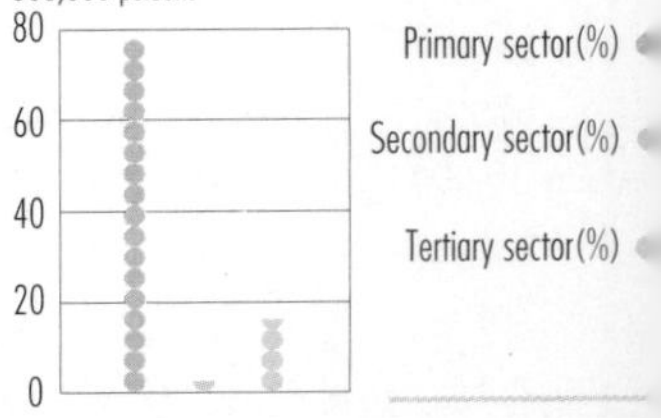

Kenya

A state of East Africa, Kenya's territory is made up of the following geomorphological regions: to the east it has low tablelands; in the west rise the highlands, in which central zone the eastern border of the Rift Valley is formed by the Aberdare Range and the western one by the Mau Escarpment.

In the western and southern regions ancient volcanic formations abound. Despite its equatorial latitude, the elevation of the western part of the country favours a mild and regular climate characterized by the small variation in temperature and the succession of various seasons (differenciated by the amount of precipitation, dependent on the Trade Winds).

In the northeastern region, there is a tendency toward a desert climate, with higher temperatures, marked thermal variations and scant rainfall. The coastal strip has an equatorial climate, with heavy rains.

Most of the Kenyans live in rural areas. The population is composed of Bantu descent, that form the most numerous group, and another group of Nilo-Chamite origin.

Among the Bantu tribes the Kikuyu, Luhya, Luo and Kamba are the most notable, while the principal Nilo-Chamite tribe, a nomadic one, is that of the Kisii.

Most of the economically active population work in agriculture, the main economic activity of the country. Coffee, tea, cotton, sugar cane and sisal are grown on the plantations. Subsistence farming, practiced according to archaic methods, is dedicated to growing corn, wheat, millet, potatoes, sweet potatoes, oats, sesame and barley. The Europeans raise beef cattle, while the nomadic shepherds herd sheep for wool and also goats. Industry centers on the processing of agricultural products, although there are also factories of fertilizers and insecticides as well as an oil refinery. The discovery of a great deposit of lead and silver and the exploitation of a deposit of fluorite has recently encouraged the development of mining. Another growing source of income is tourism, that is attracted by the great national parks of Tsavo, Amboseli and The Aberdares.

Official name: Republic of Kenya

Form of government: republic

Capital: Nairobi

Official language: Swahili, English

Monetary unit: Kenya shilling

Religious affiliation: Christian (73%), traditional beliefs (19%), Muslim (6%), other (2%)

Ethnic composition of the population: Kikuyu (22%), Luhya (14%), Luo (13%), Kalenjin (12%), Kamba (11%), Kisii (6%), Meru (6%), Asian, European and Arab (1%), other (15%)

Area: 582,646 sq km

Total population: 28,177,000 inhabitants

Population density: 48.4 persons per sq km

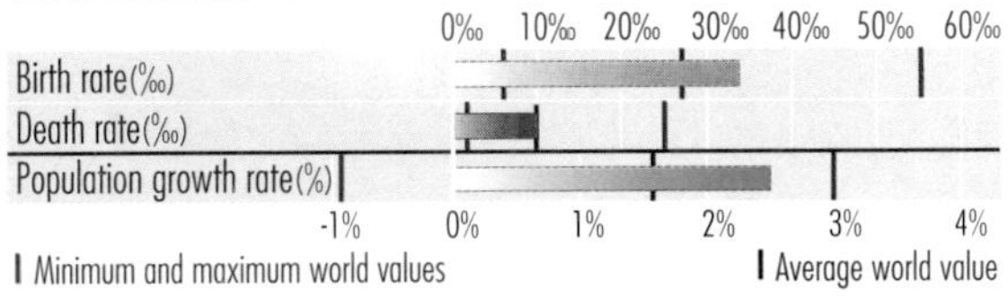

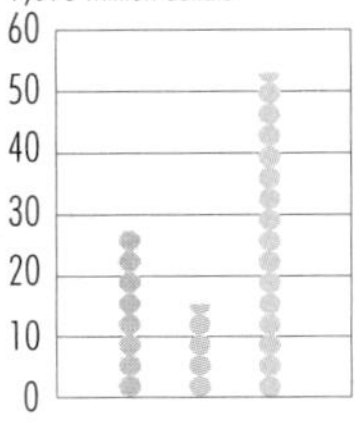

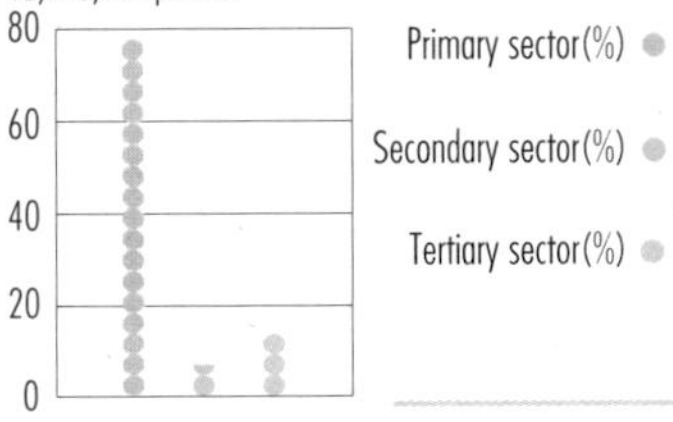

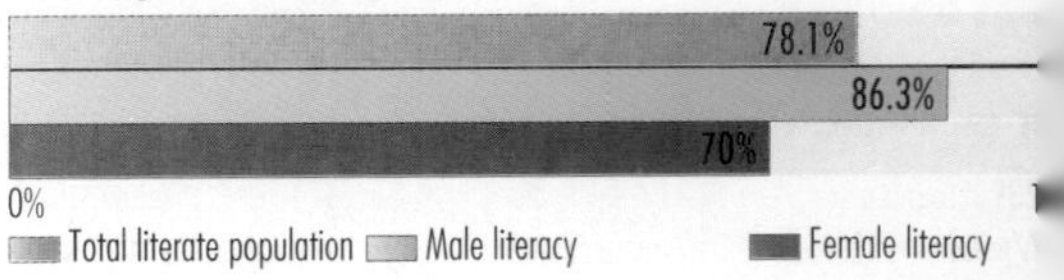

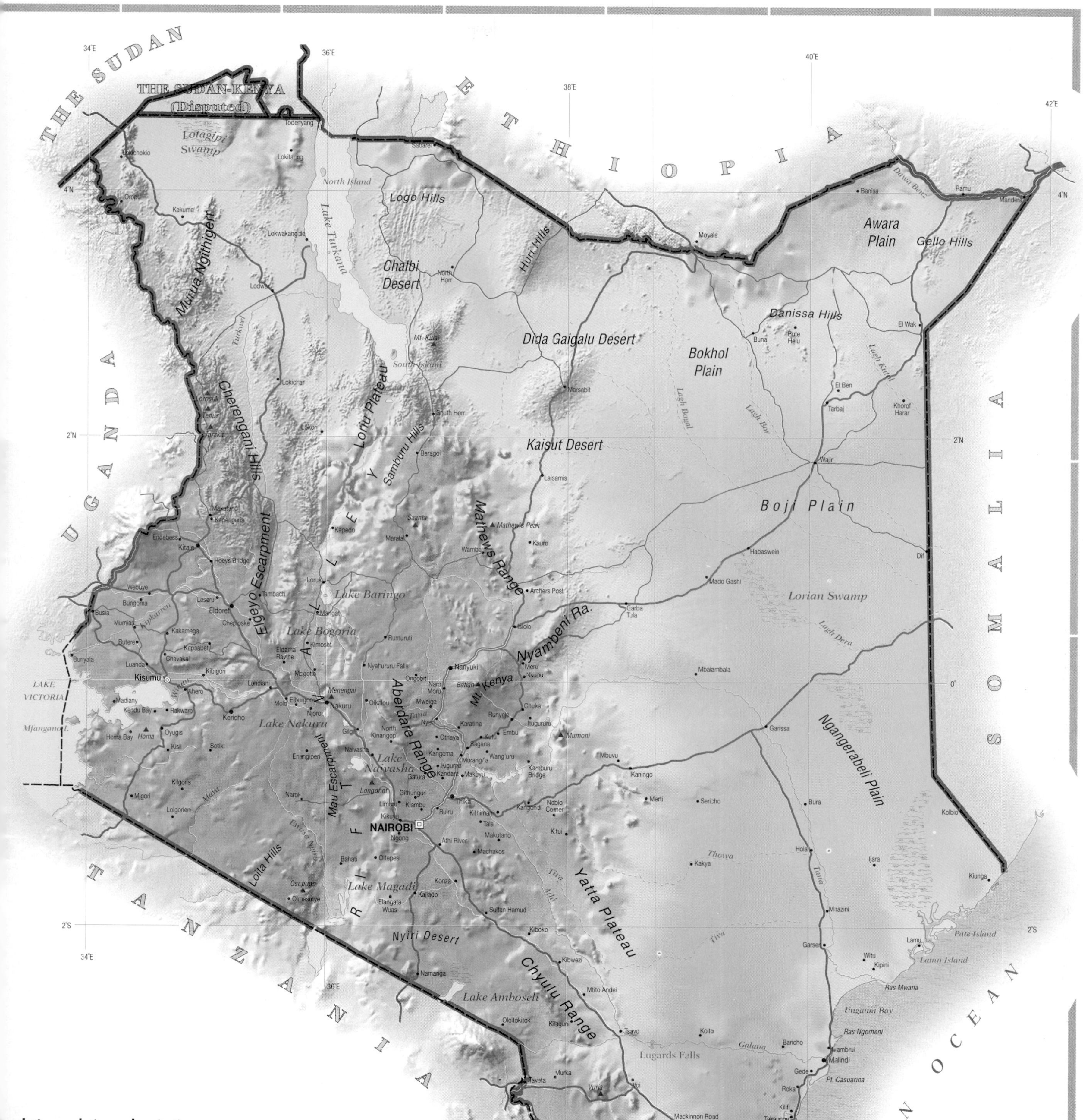

Population evolution and projection

millions of persons

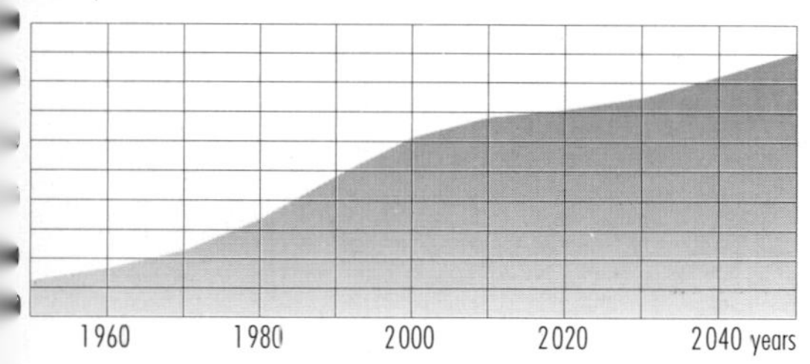

Population age distribution

48% | 50% | 2%

years | 15 years | 60 years

Per capita income (GDP per person)

239.3/person

/person (world minimum: Mozambique) (world maximum: Japan) $37,075/person

Unemployment (% of total population economically active)

35%

0% | 50%

Land use

0% | 100%

Forests and jungles 4% | Cropland 4% | Other 85%

Meadows and pastures 7%

Mining and Energy

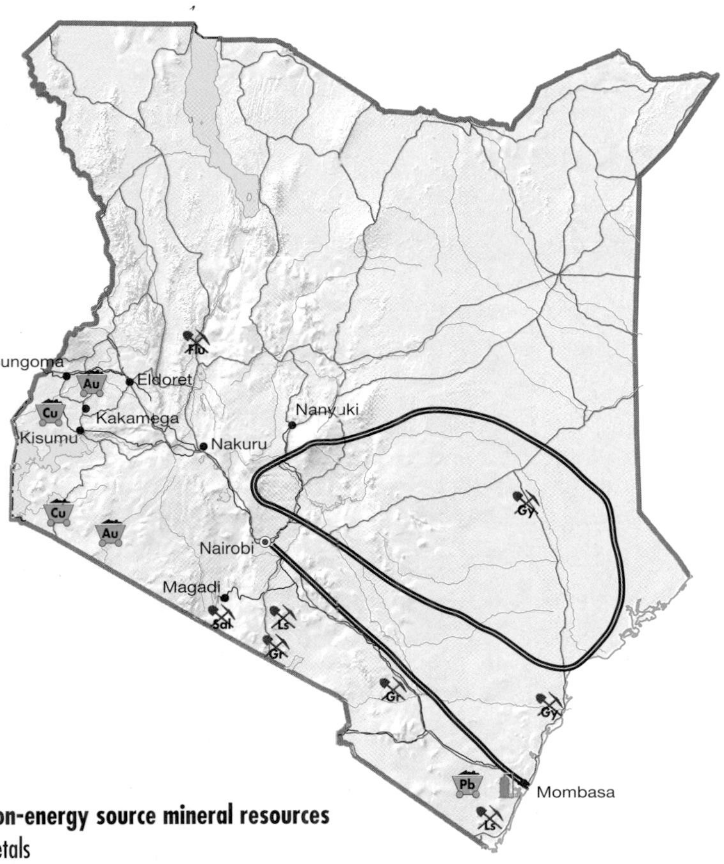

Non-energy source mineral resources

Metals

Copper Gold Lead

Rocks and industrial minerals

Limestone Graphite Gypsum

Fluorine Salt

Energy-related installations

Refinery

Oil pipeline

Geostructural units

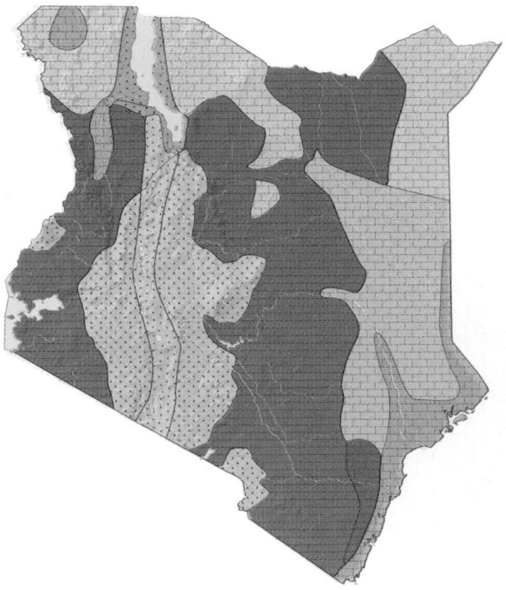

Geology

Precambrian

Paleozoic

Mesozoic

Tertiary

Quaternary

Structures

Shields

Sedimentary covering

Areas of the Rift Valley

Volcanic areas

Agriculture

Types of agriculture and livestock production

Commercial and plantation farming

Subsistence farming (corn, sorghum, millet, cassava, bananas, vegetables)

Nomadic herding
(zebus, goats, sheep, camels)

Forest/brush

Swamplands

Rice

Coconut tree

Cotton

Sisal

Coffee

Tea

Sugar cane

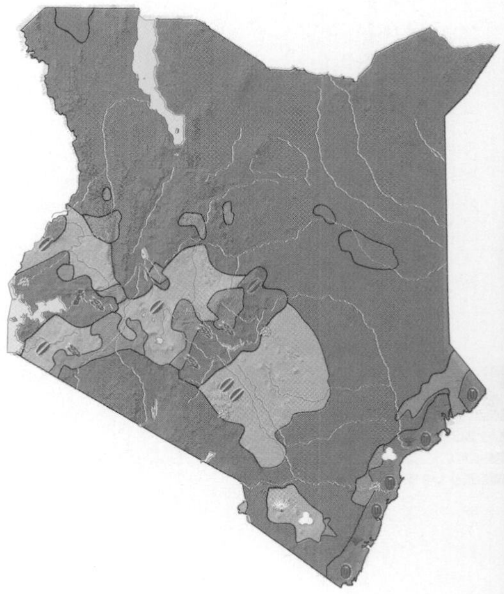

Industry

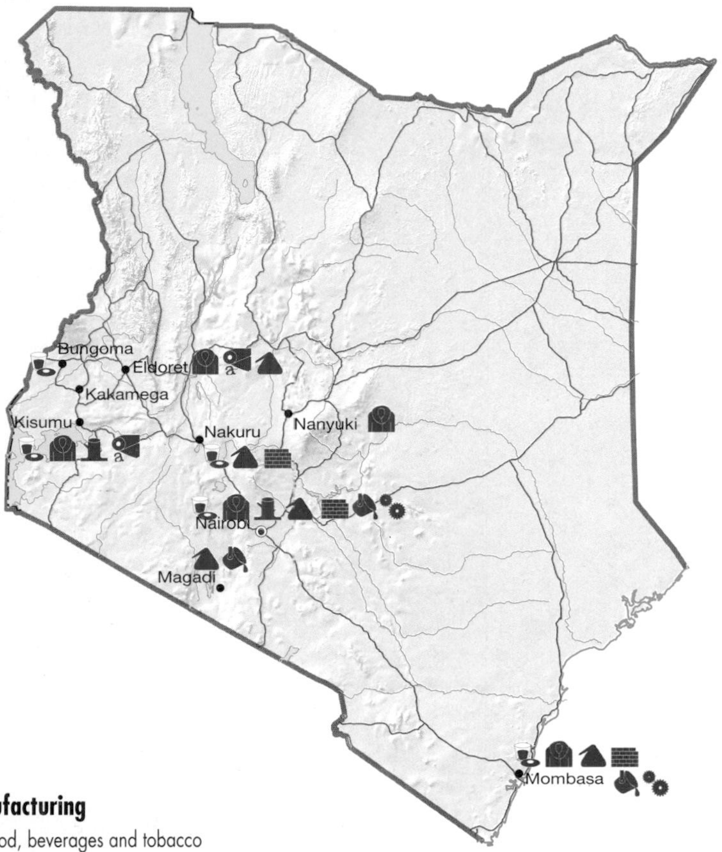

Manufacturing

Food, beverages and tobacco

Textile, clothing, leather and footwear

Wood, cork and furniture

Paper and graphic arts

Chemical products

Building materials, glass and cement

Metallurgy and metal products

Machinery and transport equipment

Natural spaces

Protected natural spaces

1 Lakes of the Rift Valley
2 Lake Turkana and Sibiloi
3 Nasalot and the south of Lake Turkana
4 Marsabit
5 Maralal
6 Samburu, Buffalo Spring and Shaba
7 Lake Victoria
8 Ruma
9 Lake Nakuru
10 Lake Naivasha
11 Mount Kenya
12 The Aberdares
13 Meru, Bisandi, Rahole and Kora
14 Nairobi
15 Eastern preserves
16 Masai Mara
17 Amboseli
18 Tsavo
19 Taita Hills

Lesotho

Lesotho is a small kingdom surrounded by the Republic of South Africa. The principal landform is the Basuto Highland, which practically coincides with the borders of the territory. It has a continental-type climate, with great thermal variation, above all in the areas with higher elevations, where very much colder temperatures are recorded. Between the months of October and April the bulk of the annual precipitation falls. The population is Sotho and the official languages are English and Sotho (Bantu dialect). The Roman Catholic and Protestant religions are predominant. Most of the population live in rural areas. Agricultural production is destined for domestic consumption; corn, wheat, barley and fruit trees are grown, although these last in a lesser proportion. A great deal of the territory is covered by pastures which benefit ranching. The greatest number of livestock are sheep, followed by goats. There are deposits of diamonds. There is hardly any industry. Lesotho exports wool, wood, food and chemical products. It is a country which is dependent on foreign aid, since its balance of trade is negative.

Official name: Kingdom of Lesotho
Form of government: constitutional monarchy
Capital: Maseru
Official language: Sotho, English
Monetary unit: loti
Religious affiliation: Roman Catholic (43.5%), Protestant (29.8%), Anglican (11.5%), other Christian (8%), traditional beliefs (6.2%), other (1%)
Ethnic composition of the population: Sotho (99.7%), European (0.08%), Asian (0.04%)
Area: 30,355 sq km
Total population: 1,971,000 inhabitants
Population density: 64.9 persons per sq km

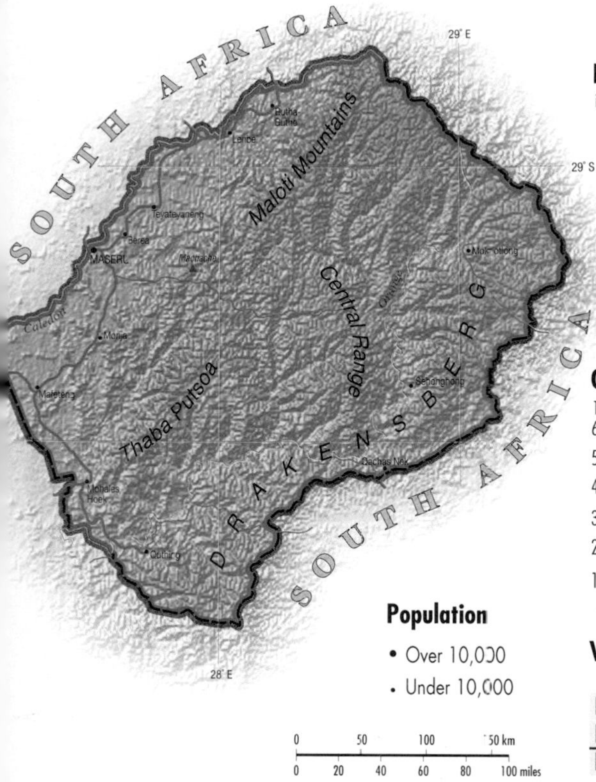

Population evolution and projection

in millions of persons

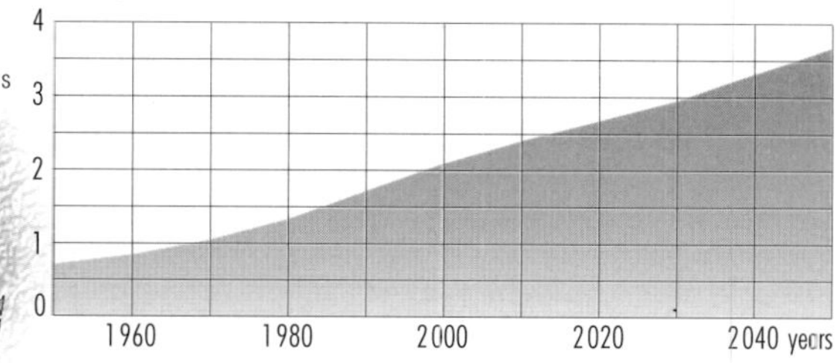

GDP structure

1,029 million dollars

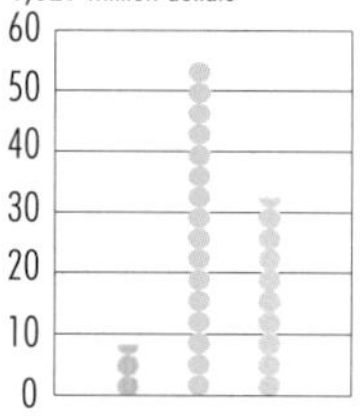

Labor force

808,000 persons

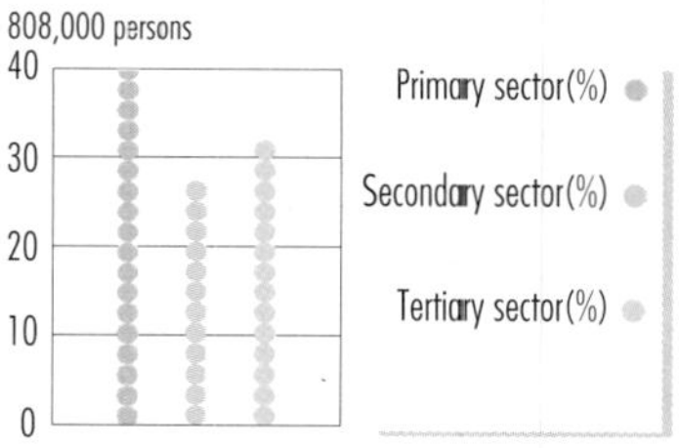

Vital statistics

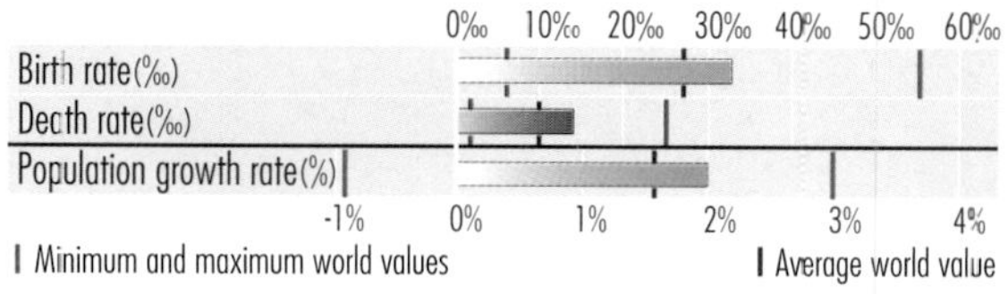

Population age distribution

Literacy (% of population over 15)

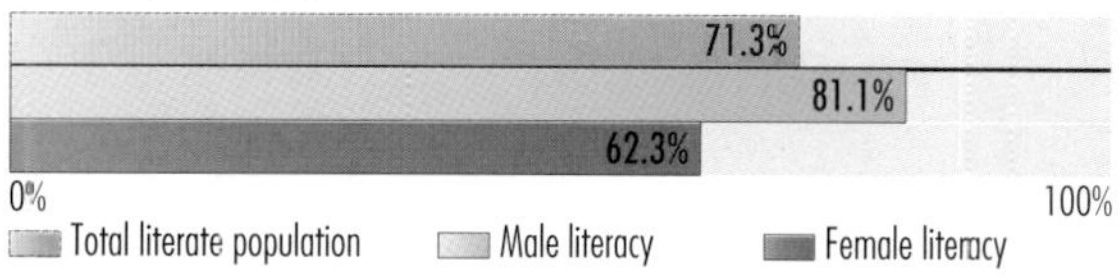

Per capita income (GDP per person)

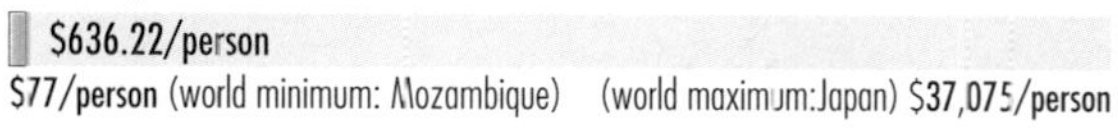

Land use

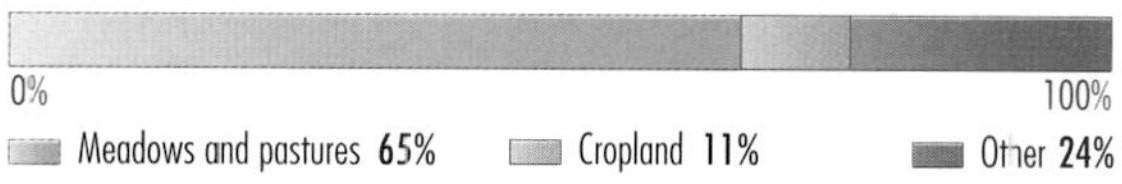

Liberia

Official name: Republic of Liberia
Form of government: republic
Capital: Monrovia
Official language: English
Monetary unit: Liberian dollar
Religious affiliation: Christian (67.7%), Muslim (13.8%), traditional beliefs and other (18.5%)
Ethnic composition of the population: Indigenous African tribes: (95%): Kpelle, Bassa, Grebo, Gio, Kru, Mano; descendents of slaves (5%)
Area: 99,067 sq km
Total population: 2,110,000 inhabitants
Population density: 21.3 persons per sq km

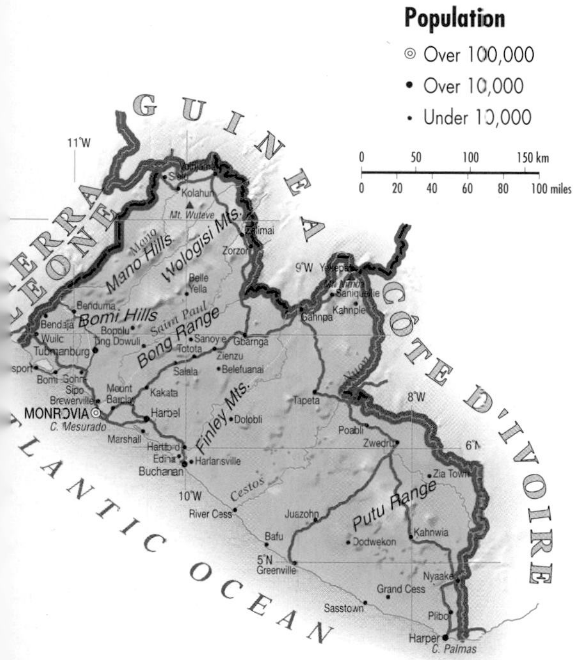

Population evolution and projection

in millions of persons

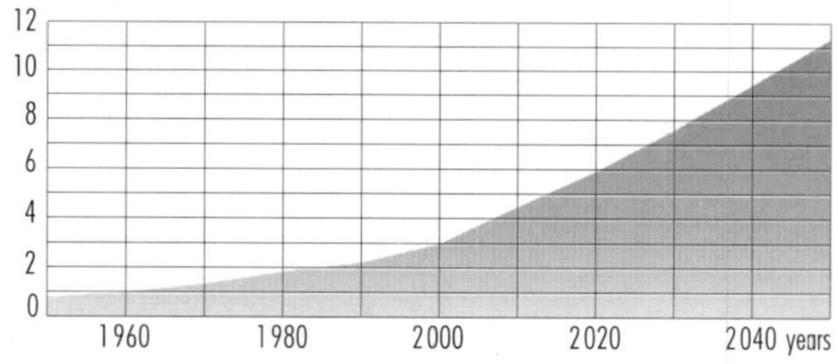

GDP structure

1,194 million dollars

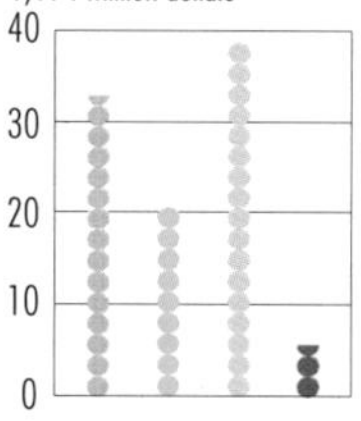

Labor force

1,168,000 persons

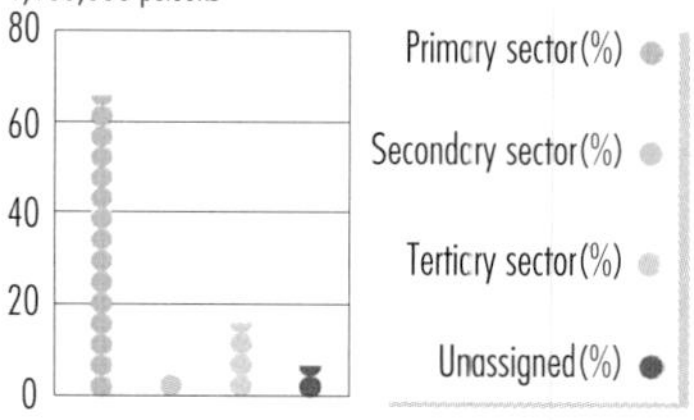

Literacy (% of population over 15)

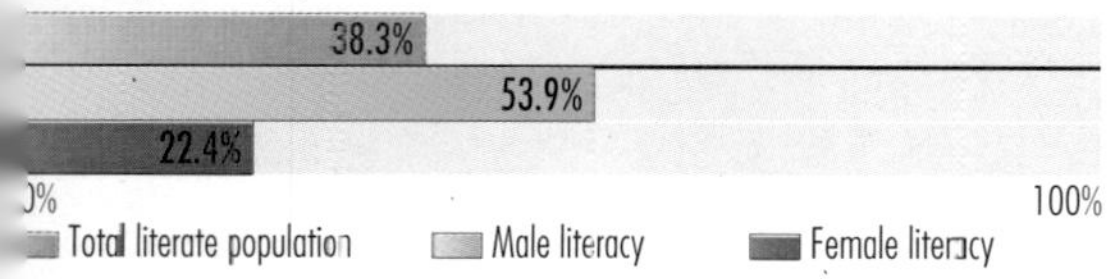

Vital statistics

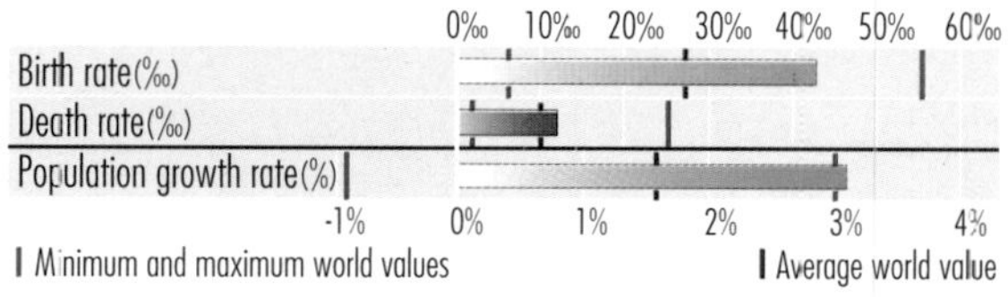

Population age distribution

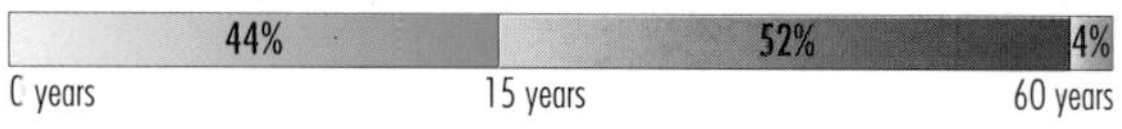

Per capita income (GDP per person)

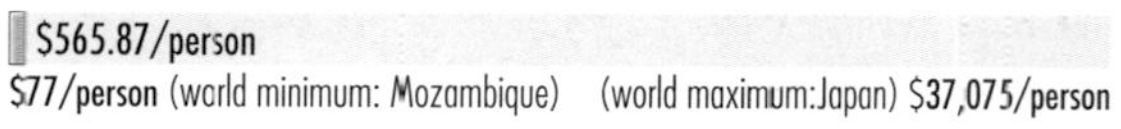

Libya

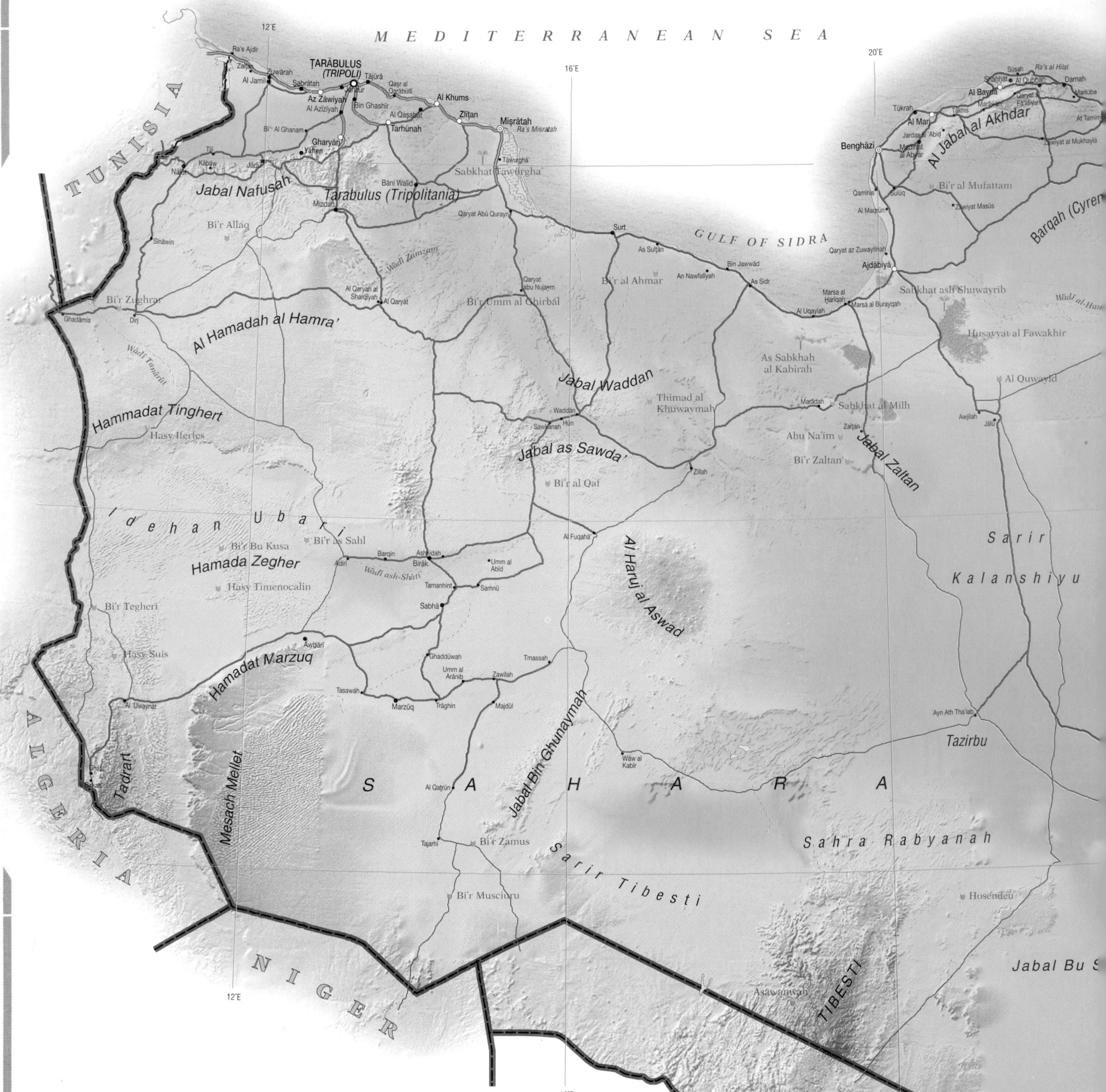

Population

- Over 500,000
- Over 100,000
- Over 50,000
- Over 10,000
- Under 10,000

0 50 100 150 km
0 20 40 60 80 100 miles

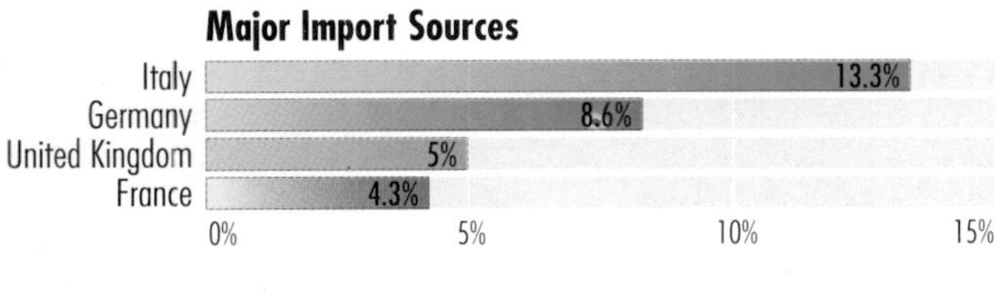

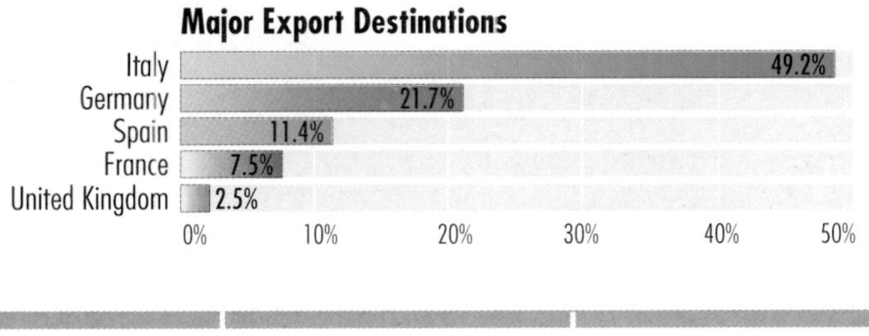

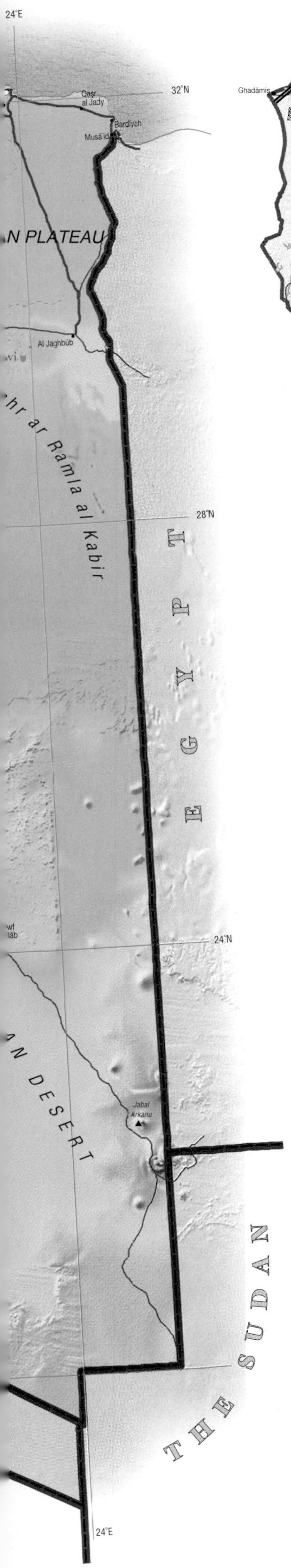

Industry and Mining

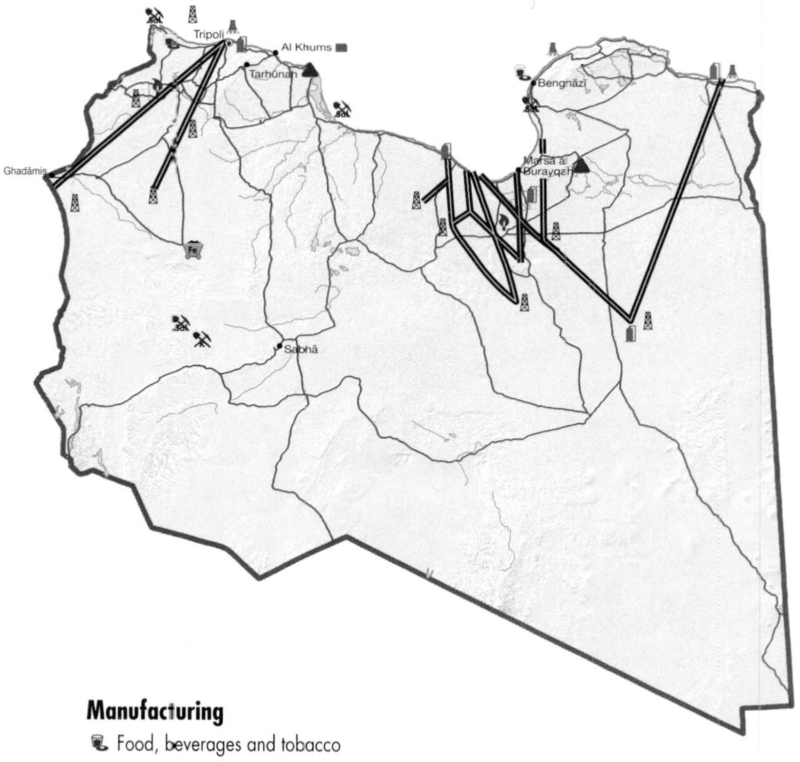

Manufacturing
- Food, beverages and tobacco
- Chemical products
- Building materials, glass and cement

Non-energy source mineral resources

Metals
- Iron ore

Rocks and industrial minerals
- Potash (unexploited)
- Salt

Mineral fuel resources
- Natural gas
- Petroleum

Energy-related installations
- Thermal power plant
- Refinery
- Gas pipeline
- Oil pipeline

Agriculture

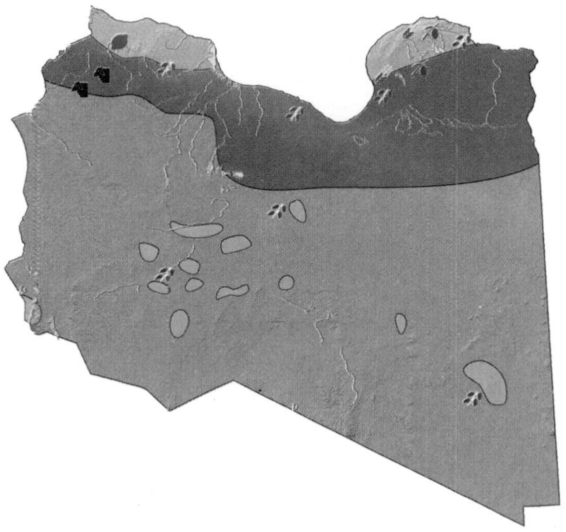

Types of agriculture and livestock production
- Polyculture (grapevines, olive trees, citrus fruits, fruit trees, horticulture, cereals)
- Intensive farming in oases
- Nomadic Herding
- Desert
- Wheat
- Citrus fruit
- Dates
- Olives
- Sheep

Official name: Socialist People's Libyan Arab Jamahiriya
Form of government: socialist republic
Capital: Tarabulus (Tripoli)
Official language: Arabic
Monetary unit: Libyan dinar
Religious affiliation: Muslim majority
Area: 1,757,000 sq km
Total population: 5,648,359 inhabitants
Population density: 3.1 persons per sq km

Population evolution and projection
in millions of persons

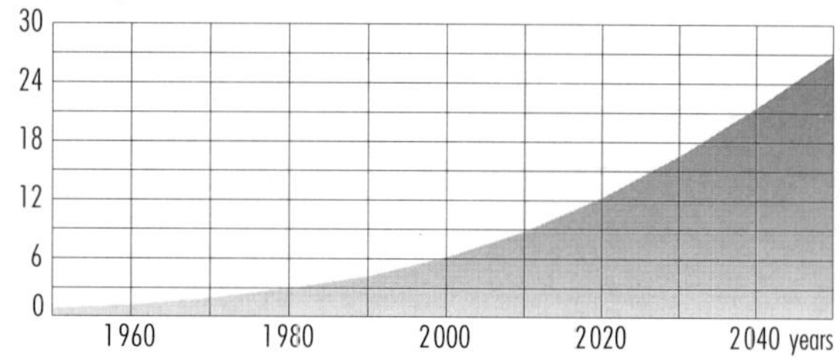

Vital statistics

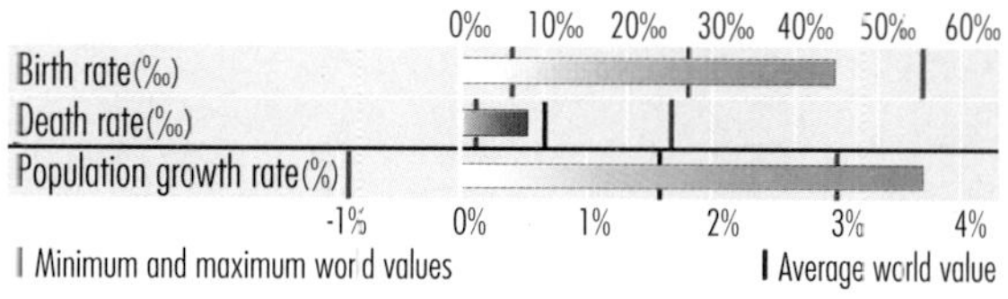

| Minimum and maximum world values | | Average world value

Literacy (% of population over 15)

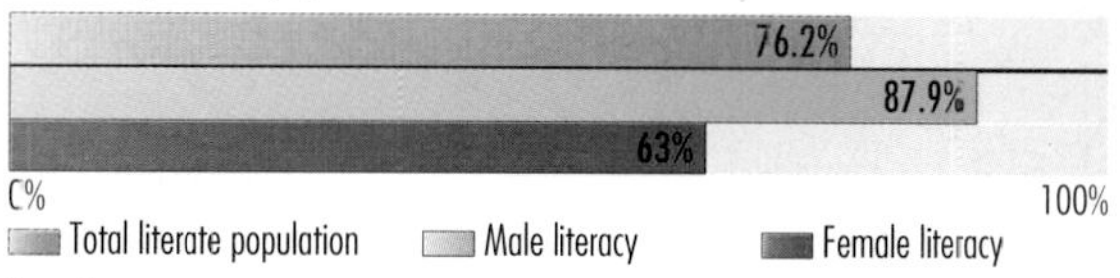

Total literate population · Male literacy · Female literacy

Land use

Meadows and pastures **8%** · Cropland **2%** · Other **90%**

GDP structure
29,240 million dollars

Labor force
925,000 persons

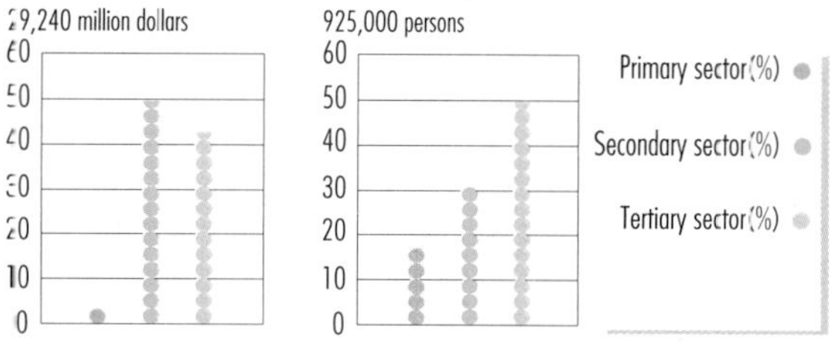

Libya is a Mediterranean state of the north of Africa. From north to south it has the following landforms: a coastal plain, a steppe tableland and the Sahara Desert. On the coast it has a Mediterranean climate, with mild winters and hot summers. Towards the interior the tropical desert dominates and the climate becomes dry and hot, with a marked daily thermal oscillation. Most of the population inhabit rural areas. Libya is a country with great ethnic complexity, in which mainly Arabs and Berbers live together, although there are other ethnic groups. The major and official religion is Islam. The official language is Arabic. Agriculture provides one of the principal economic resources. Among the crops cultivated, barley, wheat, tomatoes and olives are most important. Herding (sheep and goats) and fishing also have a certain importance. Libya receives large revenues from the exploitation of its fields of petroleum and natural gas. Industry, which is scarcely developed, is concentrated in the cities (Tripoli, Bengasi).

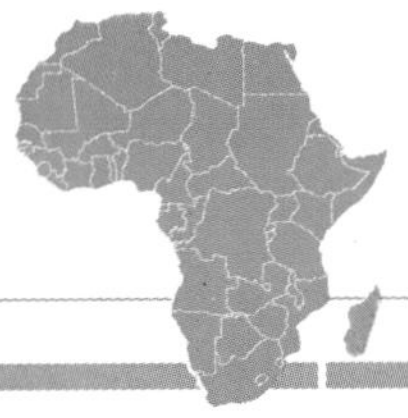

Madagascar

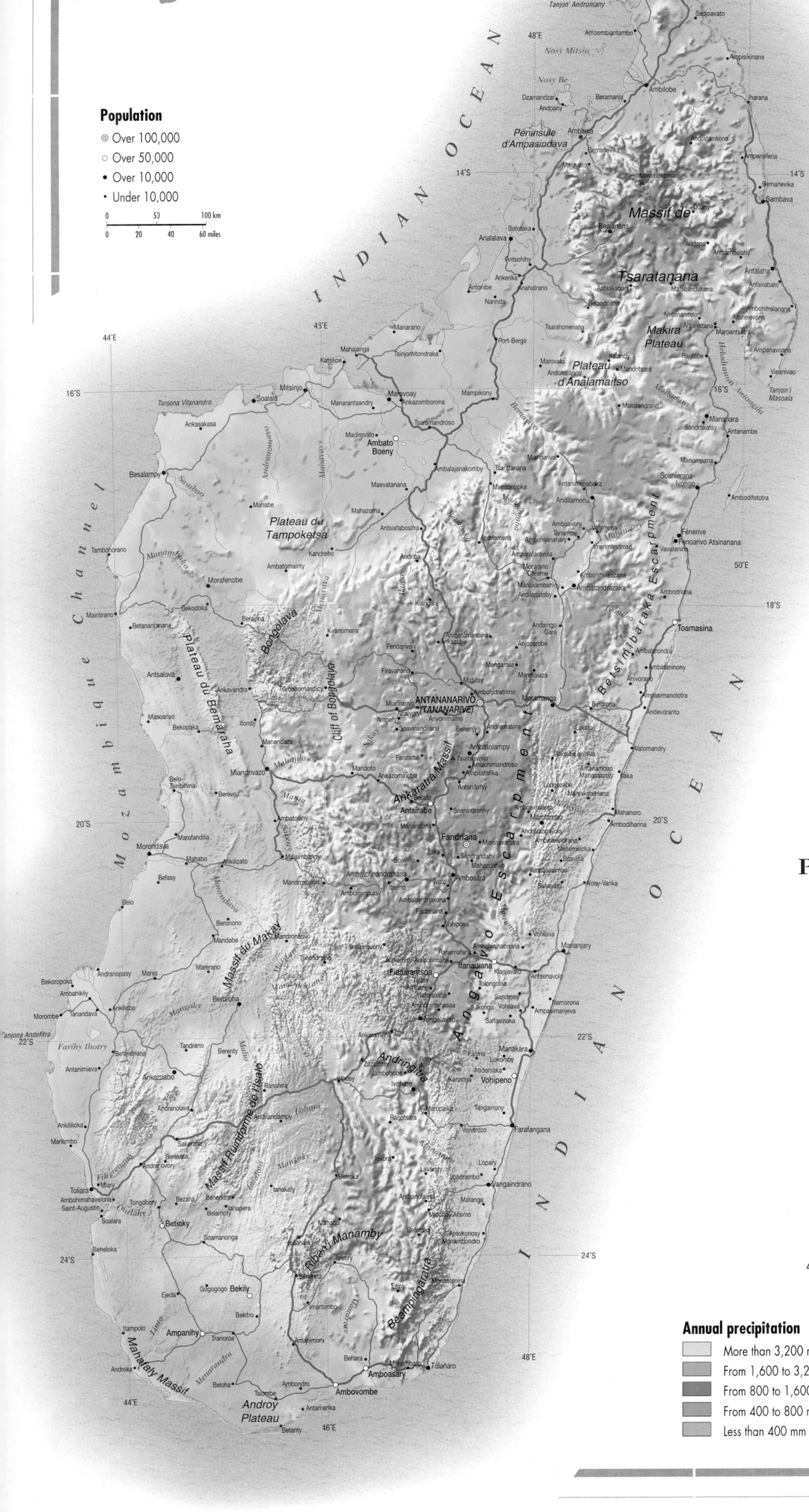

An island republic located in the Indian Ocean, the landforms of Madagascar are divided into three geographical areas: the extensive central highlands, the western coastal plain, wide and gentle, and the eastern coastal plain, narrow and separated from the plateau by high crags.

The climatic conditions vary according to the zone. The eastern regions have a tropical climate, wet and with high average temperatures. The western regions, extremely dry, possess a very marked dry season. On the central plateau, the climate is temperate, while on the coast higher temperatures are registered. The average amount of rainfall descends from north to south.

The mixture of Malay-Polynesian, African, and Arab peoples has originated the present-day population. The Malagasies constitute the principal native group of the country. There also exists population belonging to African ethnic groups —above all in the center— and Arabs —in the west—, along with Indian, Pakistani and Chinese minorities. The most important foreign group in the country is that of the French, who are the political elite. Roman Catholicism predominates; traditional beliefs are also practiced; a minority declare themselves to be Muslim.

Agriculture is the most important activity in the Malagasy economy. Crops are grown for individual consumption (rice, sweet potatoes, corn (maize), sorghum, different varieties of beans and pumpkins) and for export, coffee, fundamentally, in addition to vanilla, tropical fruits, cotton, pepper, essences for perfumes and sugar cane. With regard to livestock, cattle predominate over goats. Important mineral reserves exist (mica, graphite and bauxite) and deposits of petroleum have been discovered. The manufacturing of textiles and food products are the most notable industrial activities.

Precipitation

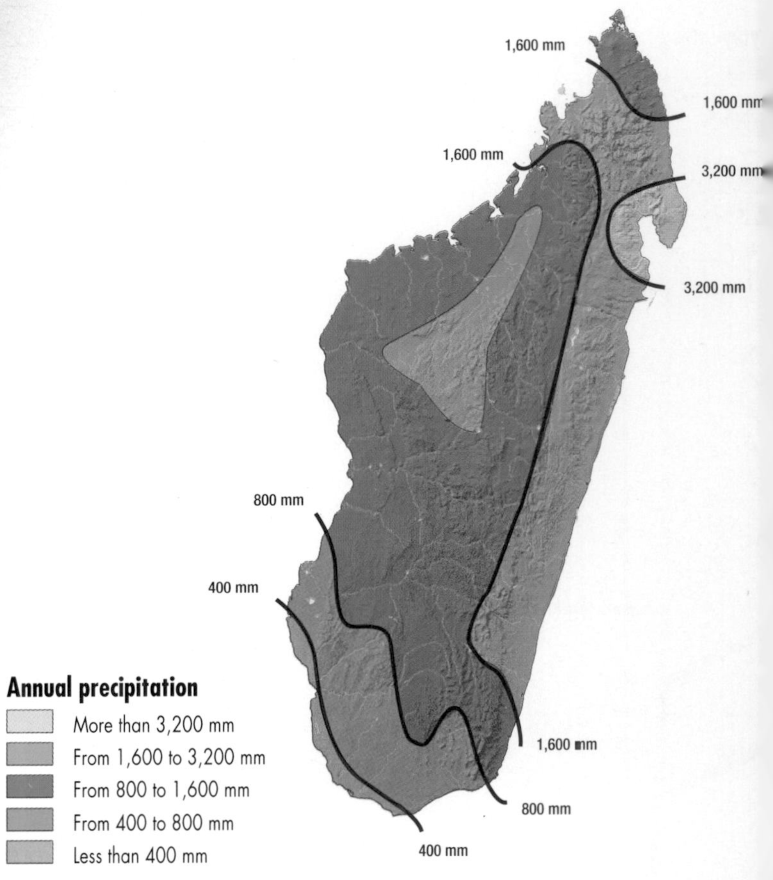

Industry and Mining

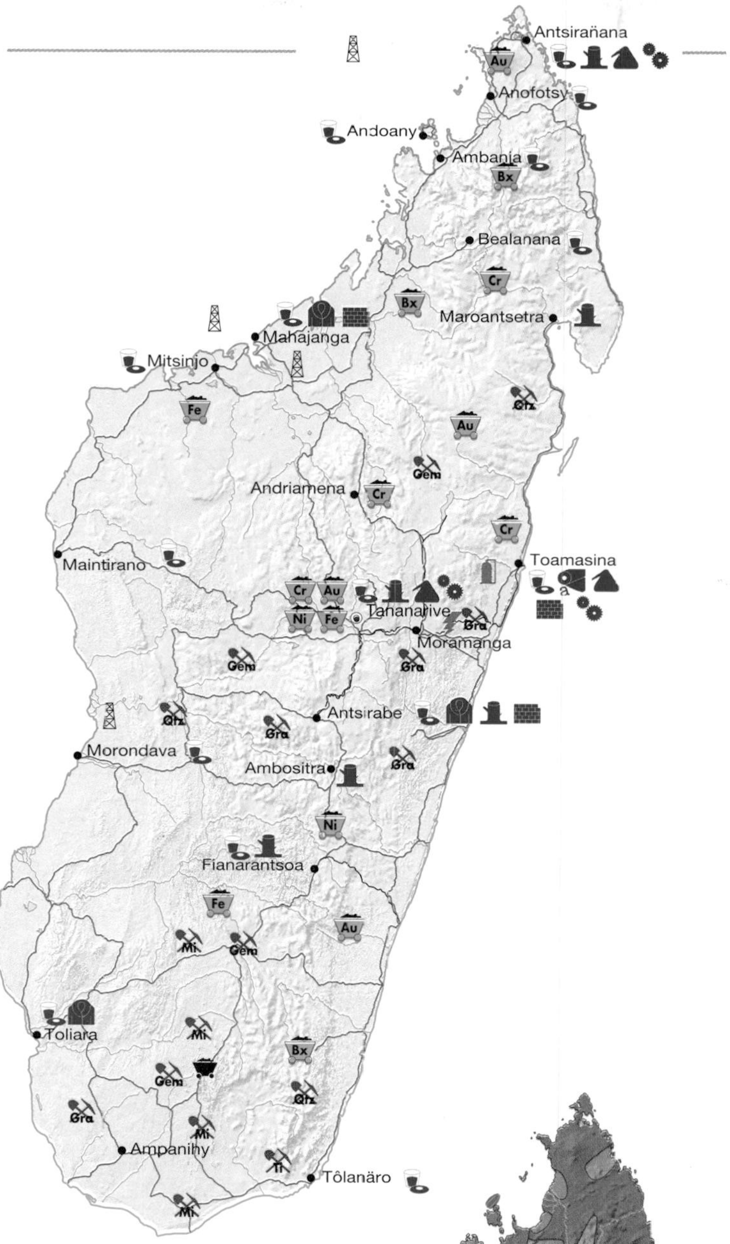

Non energy source mineral resources

Metals

- Bauxite
- Chromite
- Iron ore
- Nicke
- Gold

Rocks and industrial minerals

- Quartzite
- Gemstones
- Graphite
- Mica
- Titanium

Mineral fuel resources

- Coal
- Petroleum

Energy-related installations

- Hydroelectric power plcnt
- Refinery

Manufacturing

- Food and beverages and tobacco
- Textile, clothing, leather and footwear
- Wood, cork and furniture
- Paper and graphic arts
- Chemical products
- Building materials, glass and cement
- Machinery and transport equipment

Official name: Republic of Madagascar
Form of government: republic
Capital: Antananarivo (Tananarive)
Official language: Malagasy, French
Monetary unit: Malagasy franc
Religious affiliation: Christian (51%), traditional beliefs (47%), Muslim (1.7%), other (0.3%)
Ethnic composition of the population: Malagasy (98.9%), Comorian (0.3%), Indian and Pakistani (0.2%), French (0.2%), Chinese (0.1%), other (0.3%)
Area: 587,041 sq km
Total population: 13,671,000 inhabitants
Population density: 23.3 persons per sq km

Agriculture

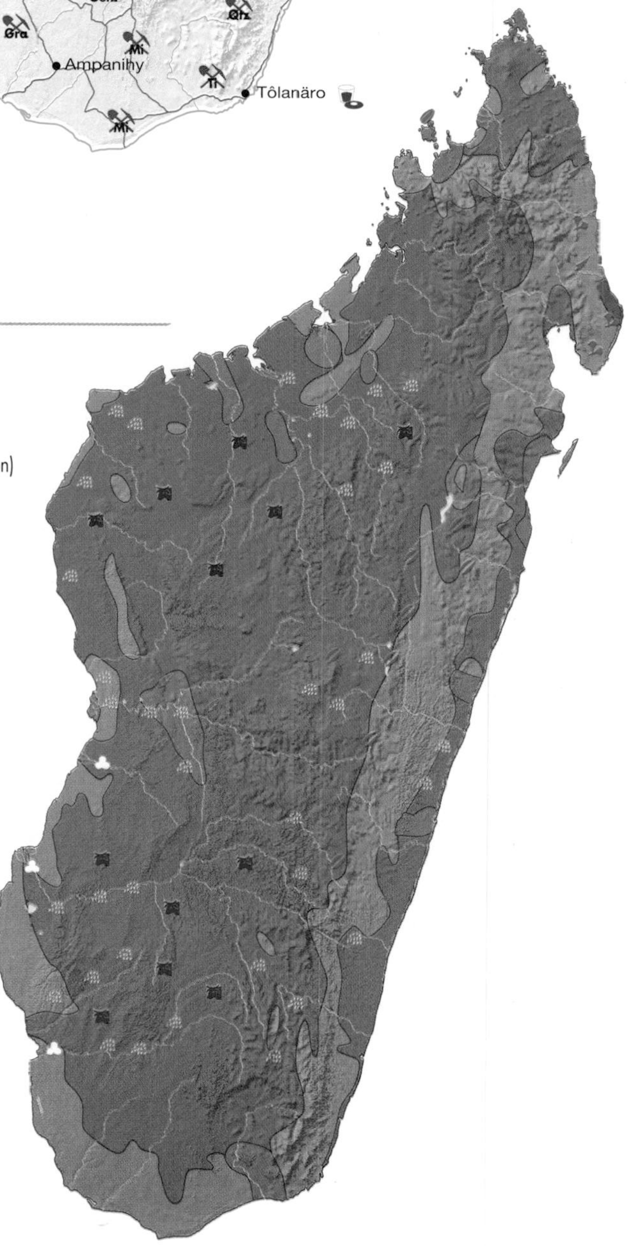

Types of agriculture and livestock production

- Commercial and plantation farming (coffee, cocoa, sugar cane, vanilla, coconuts, sisal, cotton)
- Subsistence farming and herding (rice, corn (maize), cassava, potatoes, peanuts)
- Forest/brush
- Swamplands
- Rice
- Oil Palm
- Cotton
- Sisal
- Coffee
- Cocoa
- Tobacco
- Cloves
- Vanilla
- Cattle

Population evolution and projection

in millions of persons

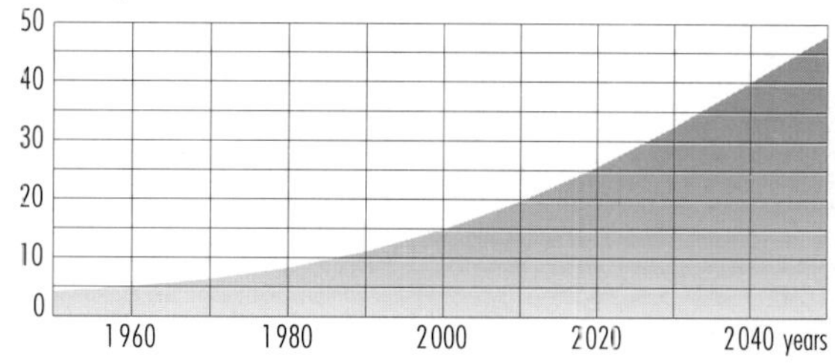

GDP structure

3,198 million dollars

Labor force

6,785,000 persons

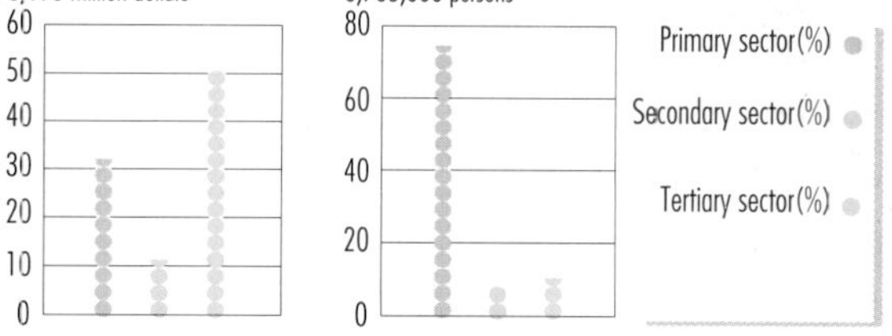

Population age distribution

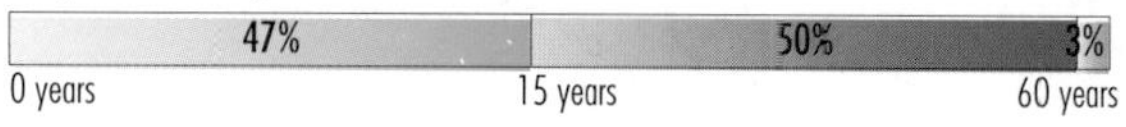

Vital statistics

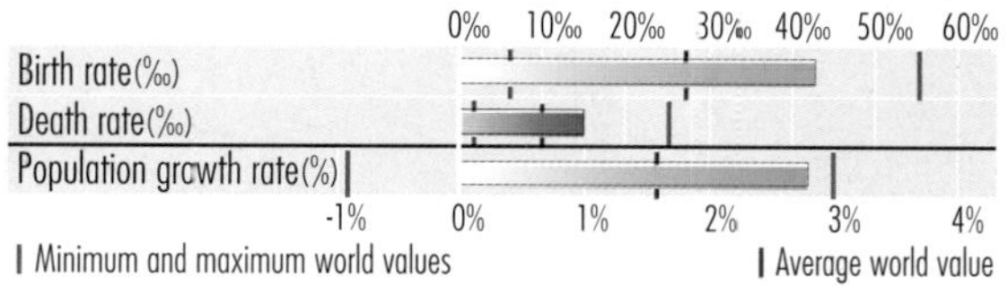

Literacy (% of population over15)

Per capita income (GDP per person)

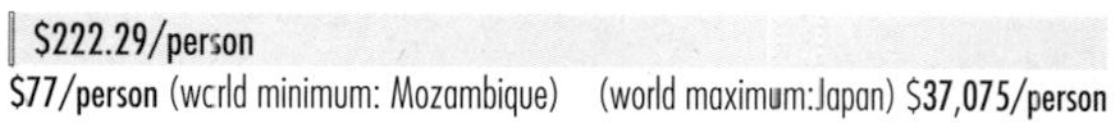

Land use

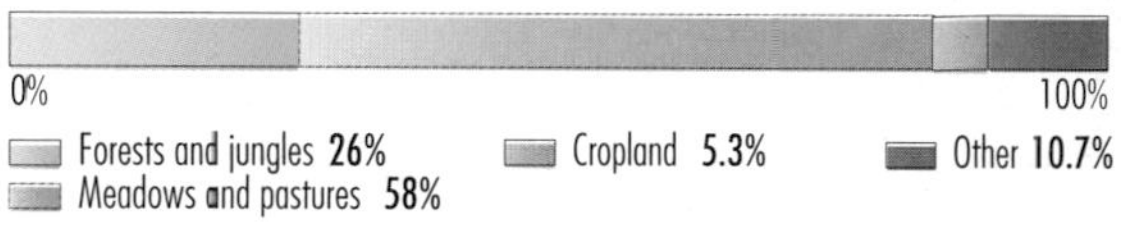

Malawi

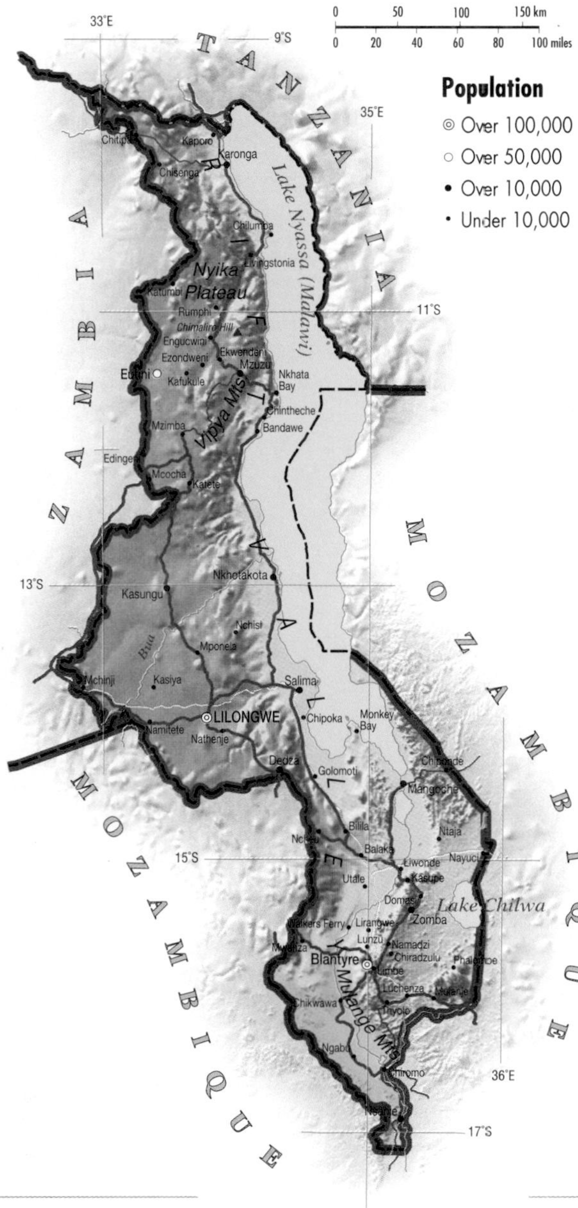

Malawi is a state of southeastern Africa which lies along the southern sector of the tectonic Rift Valley occupied by Lake Nyassa (or Lake Malawi). Its climate is tropical and has two seasons. The rains, more abundant in the south, come in summer. A large part of the population live in rural areas. Tribes of the Bantu linguistic group make up the whole of its inhabitants. The economy of Malawi is in a state of extreme underdevelopment. It is based on farming and livestock-raising, that include subsistence crops (maize, rice, etc.) and plantation crops (tobacco, tea, cotton, etc.).

Official name: Republic of Malawi
Form of government: multiparty democracy
Capital: Lilongwe
Official language: Chewa (English)
Monetary unit: Malawi kwacha
Religious affiliation: Christian (64.5%): Protestant (34.5%), Roman Catholic (30%); traditional beliefs (19%), Muslim (16.2%), other (0.3%)
Ethnic composition of the population: Maravi (58.3%), Lomwe (18.4%), Yao (13.2%), Ngoni (6.7%), other (3.4%)
Area: 118.484 sq km
Total population: 9,453,000 inhabitants
Population density: 79.8 persons per sq km

Population evolution and projection

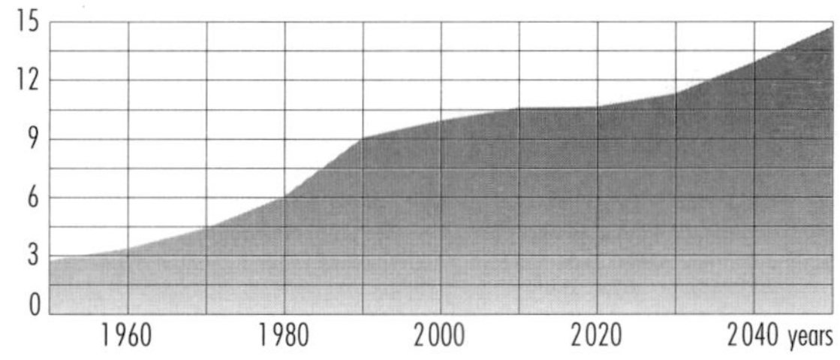

Population age distribution

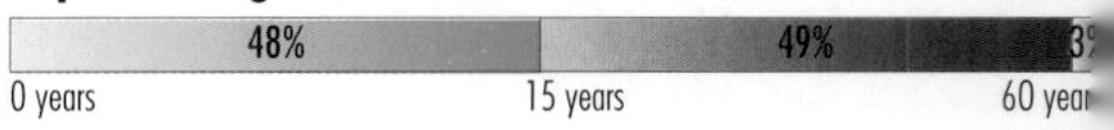

GDP structure

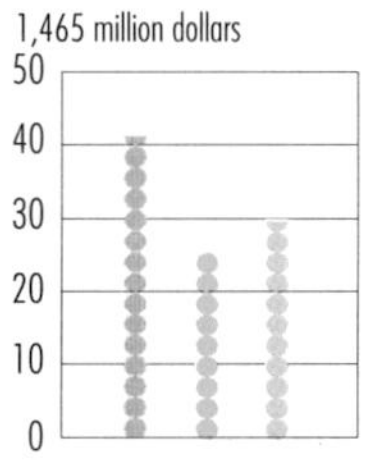

Labor force

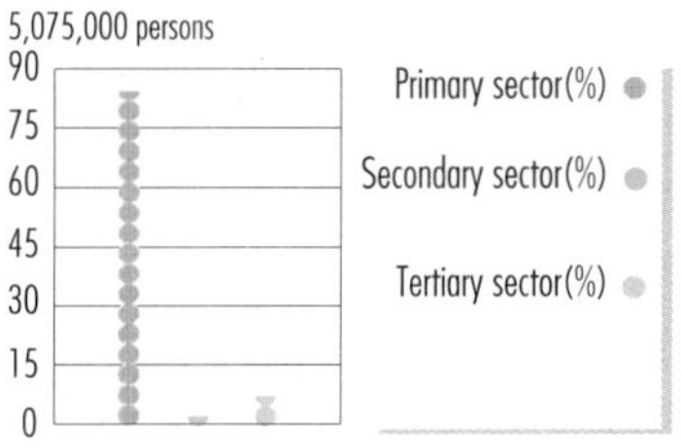

Literacy (% of population over15)

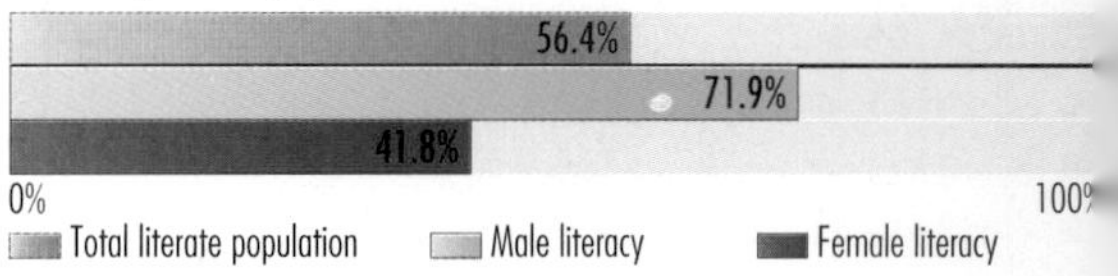

Per capita income (GDP per person)

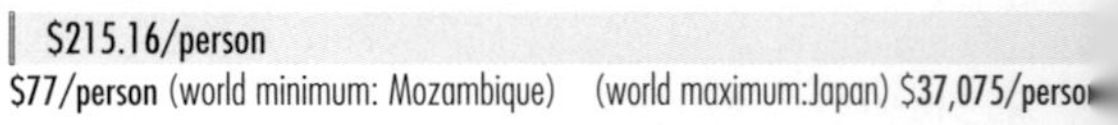

Vital statistics

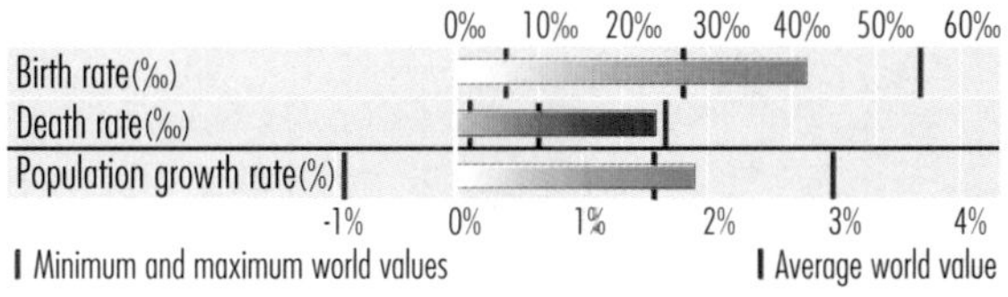

Land use

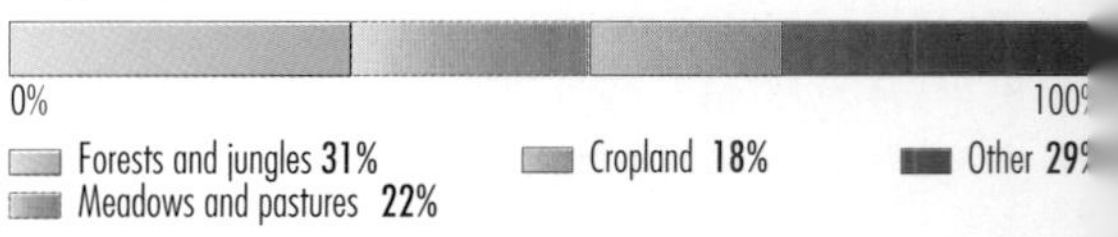

Mali

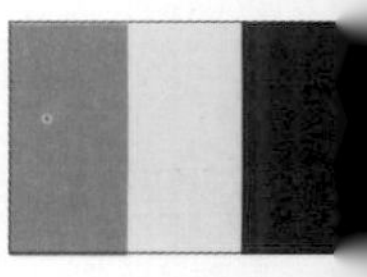

Agriculture

Types of agriculture and livestock production

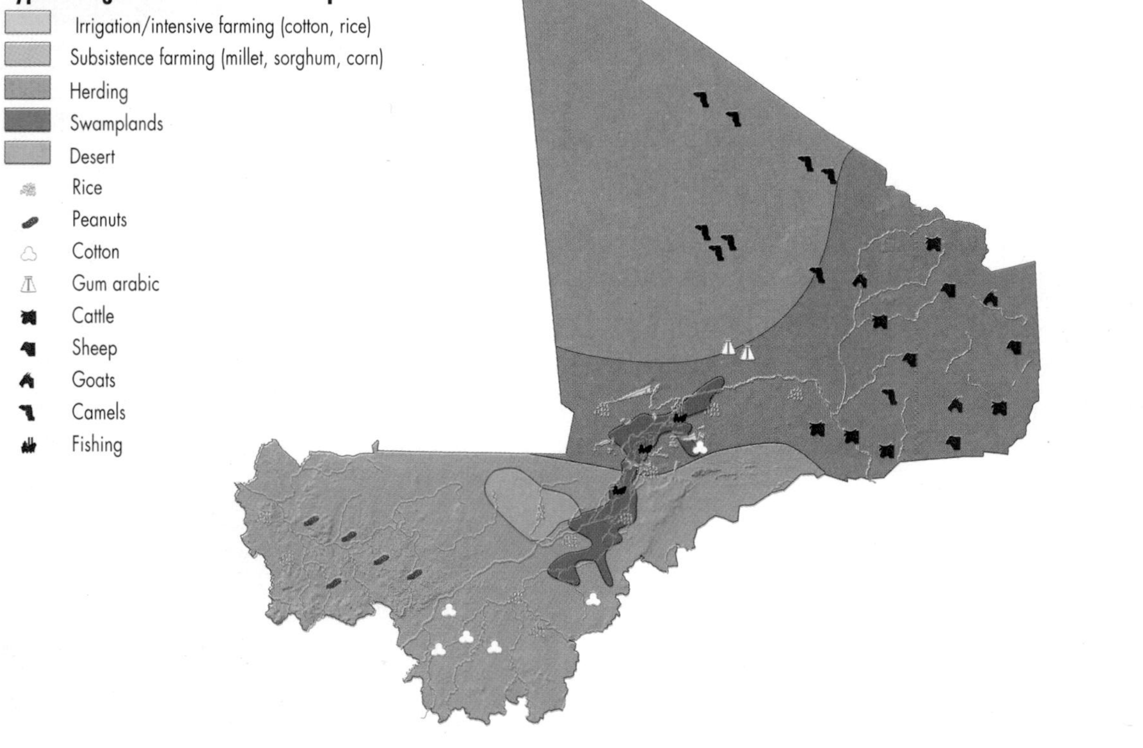

Mali is a republic of West Africa. In the north of the country there extends a region formed by plains that penetrate into the Sahara Desert. To the south lies the Sudanese region, where some small hills stand. Among these, the Mandinga Mountains, located between the Senegal and Falémé Rivers, are most notable.

Mali has a hot climate that varies depending on the latitude. In the north, in the Saharian zone, a desert climate prevails; in the central zone, the Sahel, milder temperatures and a greater amount of rainfall are registered; and in the south, where rainfall is more abundant, temperatures are markedly uniform.

It is a sparsely populated country, rural in nature, that has experienced high population growth in recent years. In Saharian regions and in the Sahel, white population predominates (Arabs, Tuaregs). The principal black ethnic group of importance is that of the Songhai. Agriculture constitutes the primary economic sector in Mali. As their basic food, the people depend upon the cultivation of cereals, while products destined for export include peanuts and cotton. Fishing and herding (sheep and goats) have a certain importance. The small amount of industry is limited to the processing of the products of farming and herding. Saharian rock salt represents the most notable mining venture.

Official name: Republic of Mali
Form of government: republic
Capital: Bamako
Official language: French
Monetary unit: CFA franc
Religious affiliation: Muslim (90%), traditional beliefs (9%), Christian (1%)
Ethnic composition of the population: Mande (50%), Peulh (17%), Voltaic (12%), Songhai (6%), Tuareg and Moor (10%), other (5%)
Area: 1,248,574 sq km
Total population: 9,653,000 inhabitants
Population density: 7.7 persons per sq km

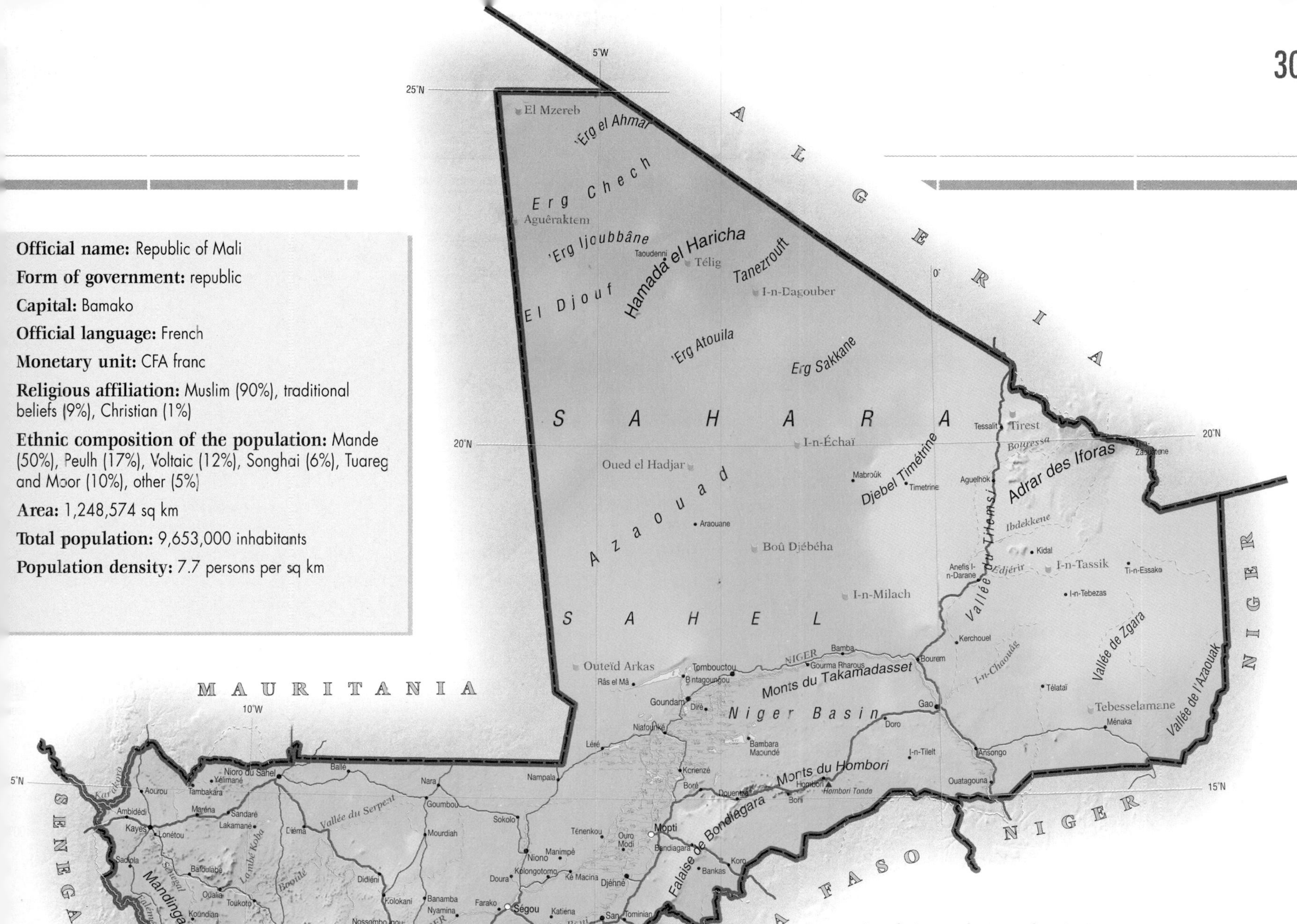

Industry and Mining

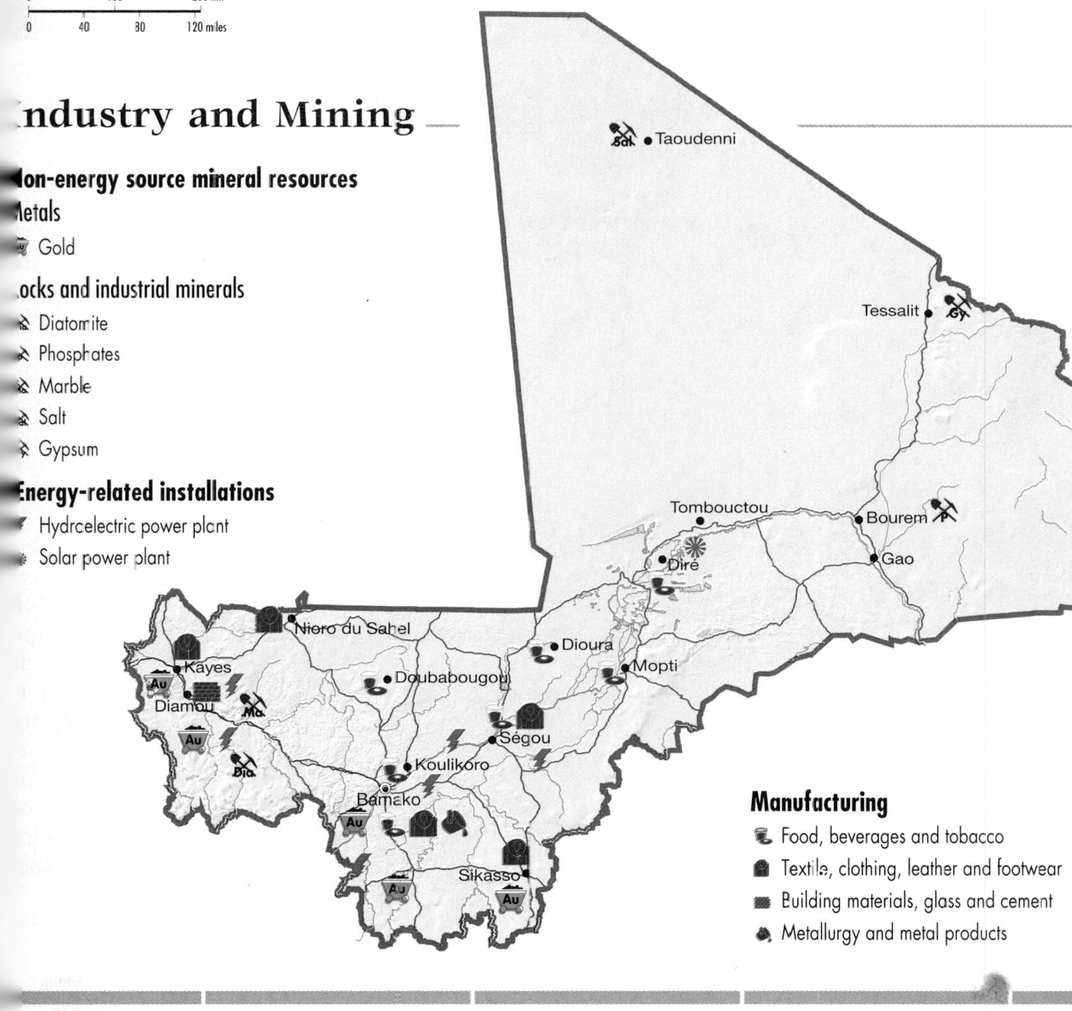

Population evolution and projection

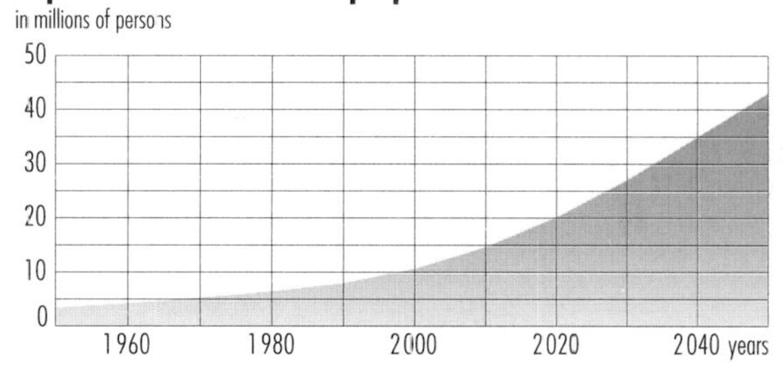

GDP structure / **Labor force**

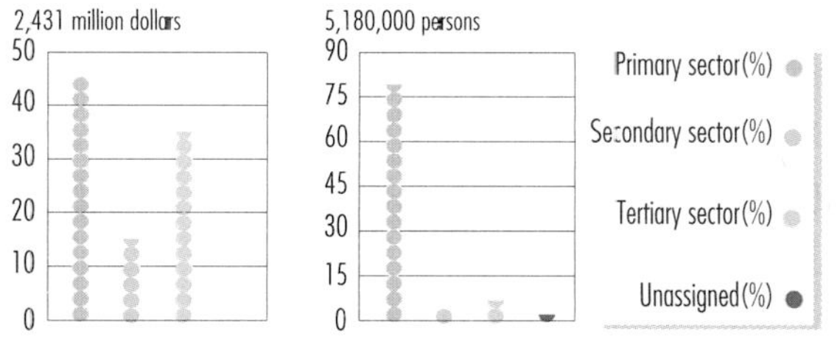

Population age distribution

Vital statistics

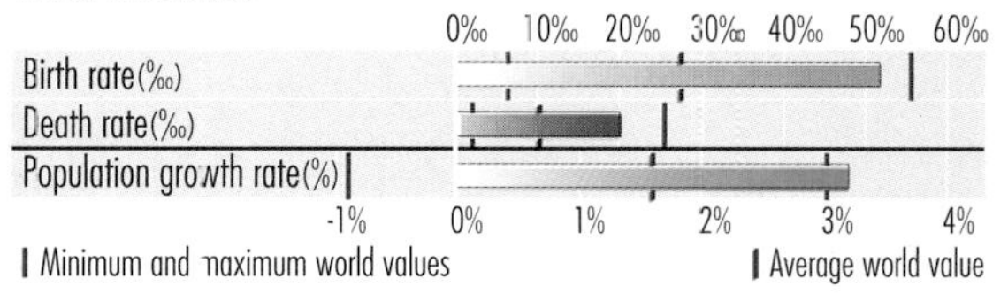

Literacy (% of population over 15)

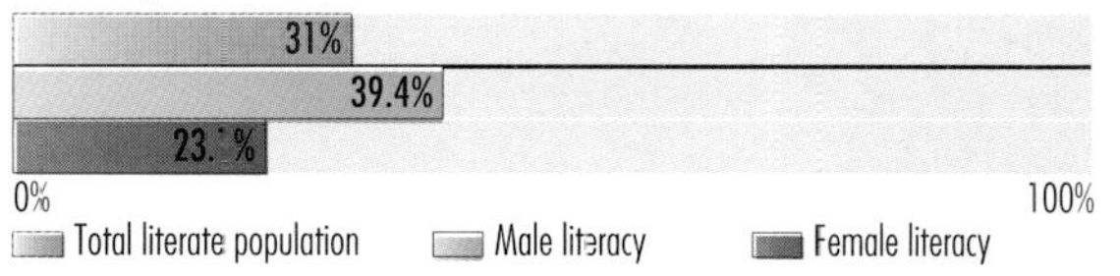

Per capita income (GDP per person)

$284.26/person
$77/person (world minimum: Mozambique) (world maximum: Japan) $37,075/person

Land use

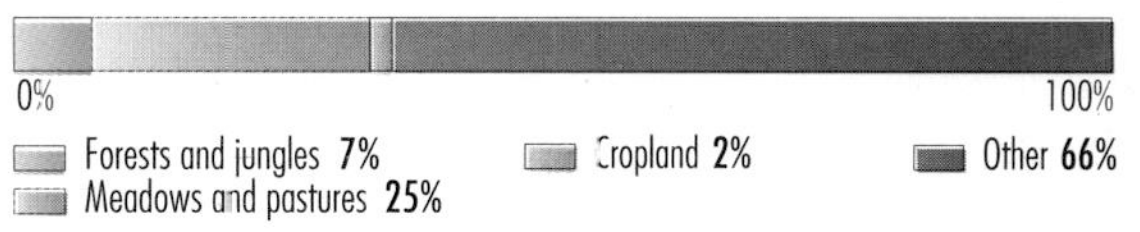

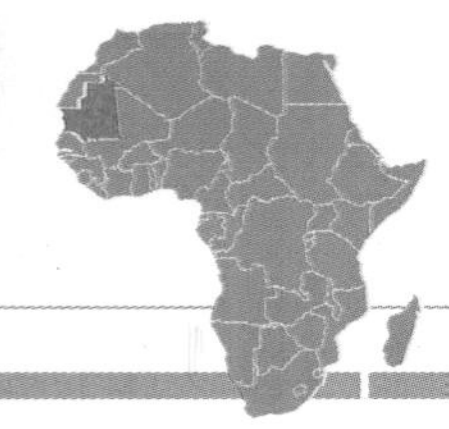

Mauritania

Official name: Islamic Republic of Mauritania
Form of government: republic
Capital: Nouakchott
Official language: Arabic
Monetary unit: ouguiya
Religious affiliation: Muslim majority
Area: 1,030,700 sq km
Total population: 2,336,000 inhabitants
Population density: 2.3 persons per sq km

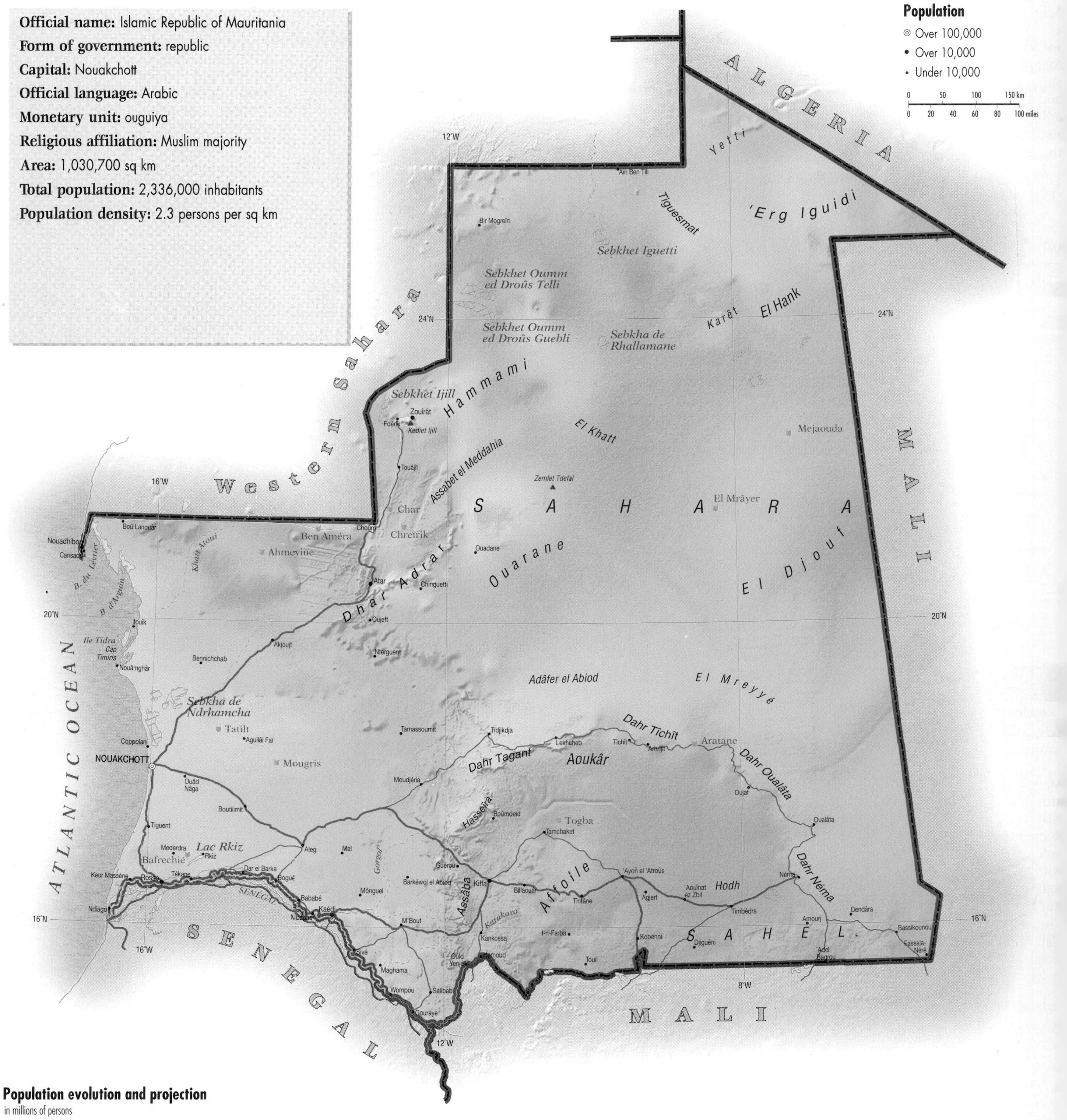

Population evolution and projection

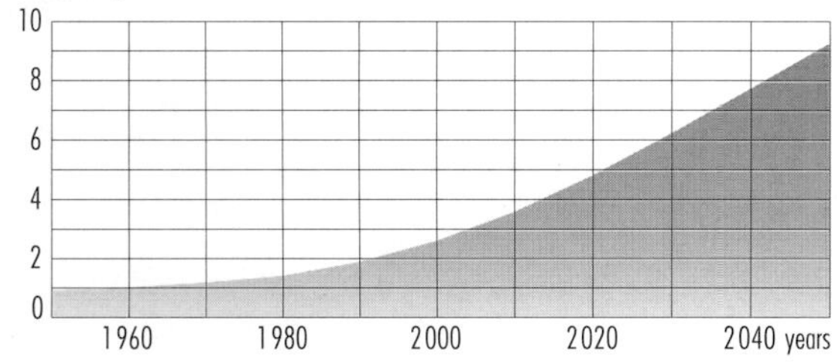

Population age distribution

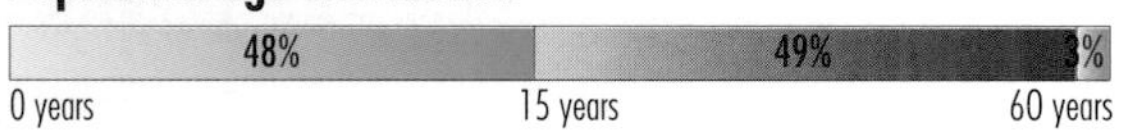

Unemployment (% of total population economically active)

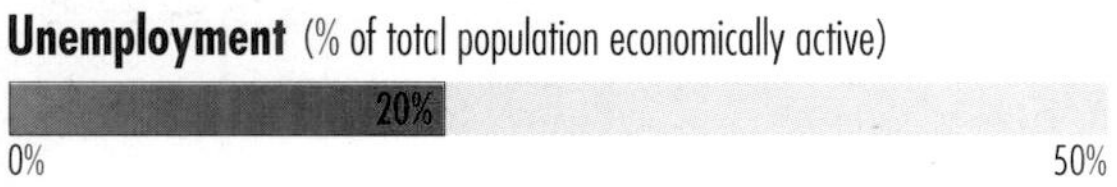

GDP structure

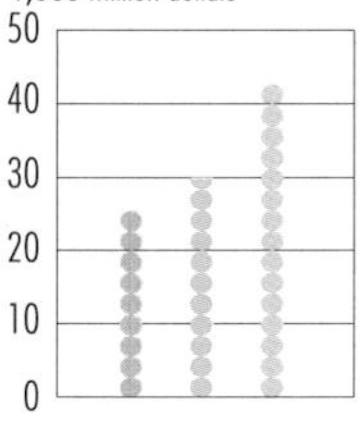

Labor force

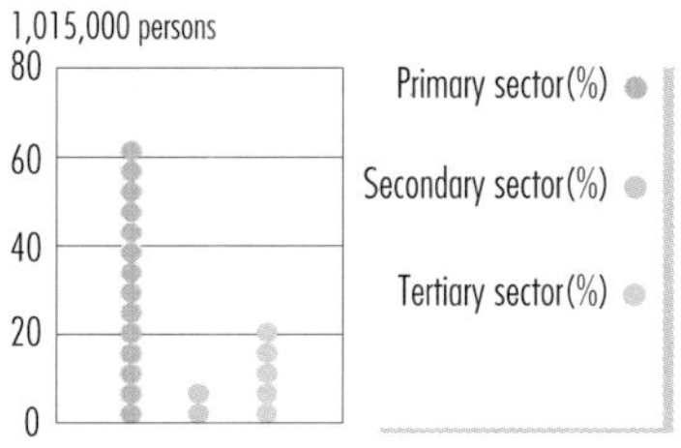

Vital statistics

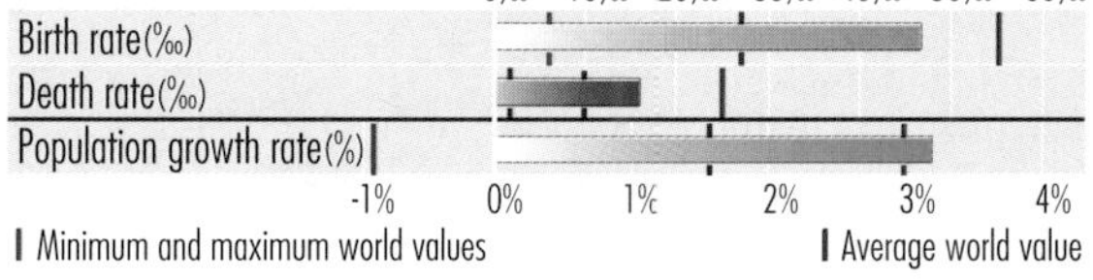

Literacy (% of population over15)

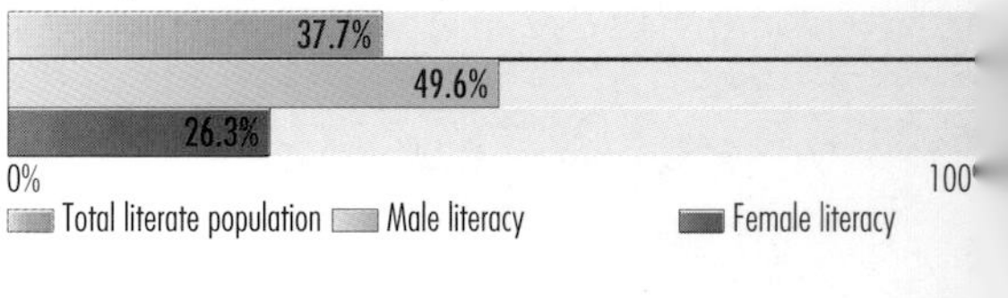

Per capita income (GDP per person)

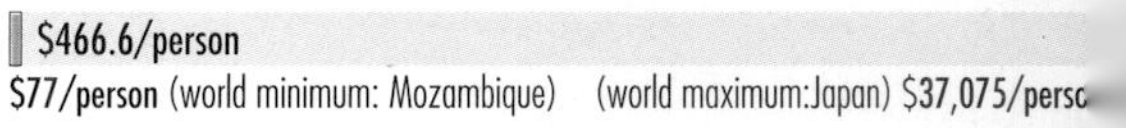

Land use

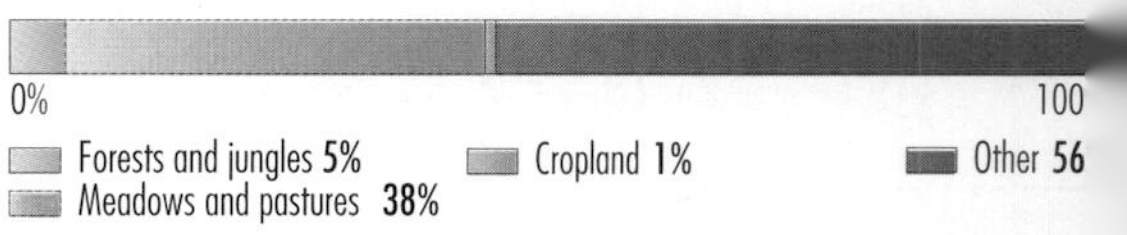

Mauritania is a republic of Northwestern Africa. It has extensive lowland plains, covered by sand dunes and rocks. Mauritanian territory includes the western tip of the Sahara Desert in the northern half and a band of the steppe or desert fringe of the Sahel in the south. It has an arid tropical climate, with marked daily thermal variations and two seasons, a winter dry season and another wetter season. Most of the territory is uninhabited. The bulk of the population is concentrated in the southern lowland region, while the only settlements in the northeast are found in the oases. The majority of the Mauritanians are racially moor and black. Pastures and forests cover a surface area greater than that of farmlands. Among the main crops the most important are millet, sorghum, corn (maize), rice and potatoes. On the banks of the Senegal River, there are plantations of sugar cane and peanuts. Livestock husbandry constitutes the principal activity of the primary sector (sheep and goats, dromedaries). The development of fishing contributes derivatives such as flours and canned goods. Mining (iron ore, copper, salt and phosphates) represents a growing field, and the industrial sector includes factories of manufactured goods and those related to mining. The per capita income of Mauritania figures among the lowest in Africa. Only a third of the roads can be utilized year round. Navigation of the Senegal River connects the cultivated riverbanks with the Senegalese port of Saint Louis.

Vegetation and Precipitation

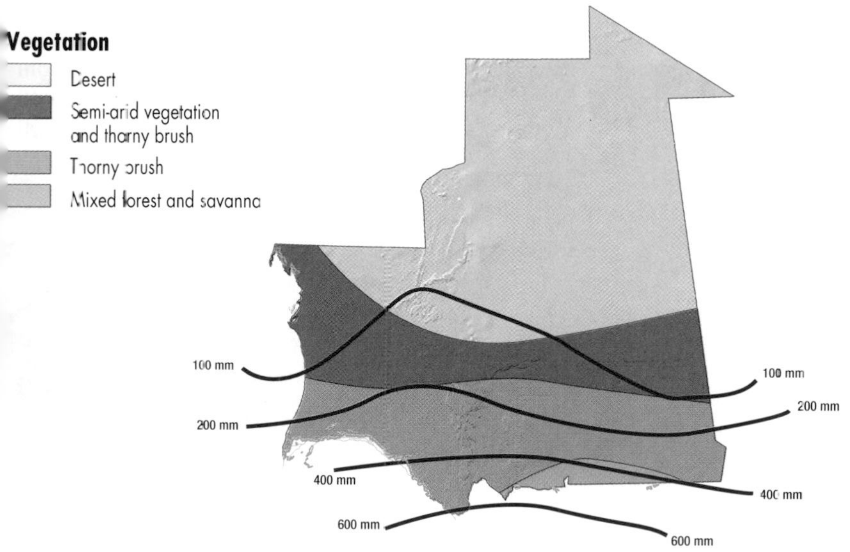

Industry and Mining

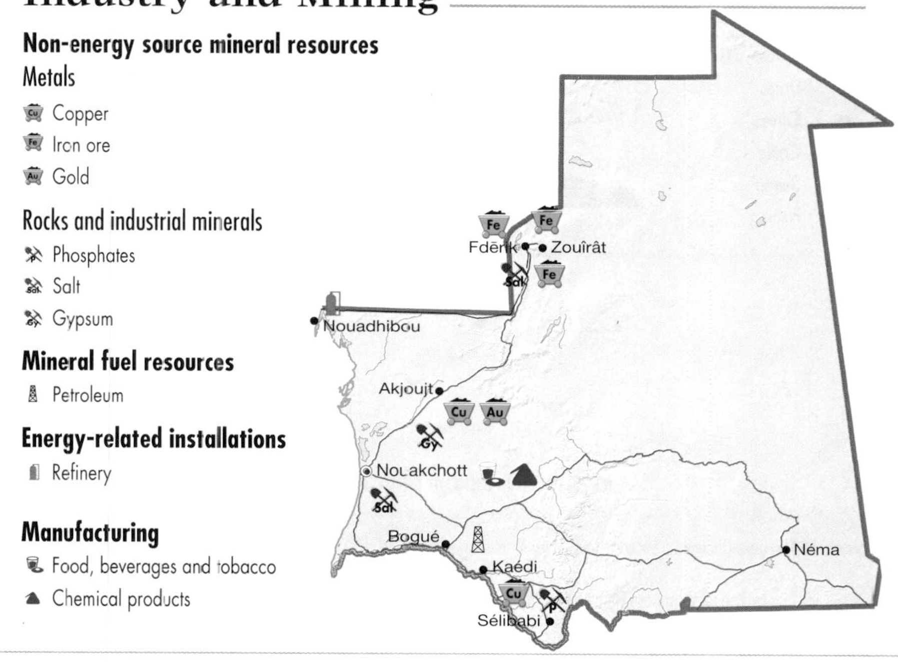

Mauritius

Mauritius is a small island state located in the archipelago of the Mascareñas. It is made up of the island of the same name and its dependencies: Rodrigues, Agalega and St. Brandon. Mauritius is of volcanic origen; lavas formed mountainous landforms, with a central plateau where a series of fertile valleys are found. Coral reefs configure the terrain of its coastlines. Rural population predominates over urban population. The major religious beliefs are Hinduism and Roman Catholicism, while English and Creole are spoken. The agricultural sector constitutes the basis of the economy. Sugar cane, the main crop of the country, in addition to corn, tea, bananas, potatoes, coconuts, vanilla and tobacco are cultivated. Livestock production covers the country's domestic needs. Cattle and goats are the most numerous livestock. Recently, development of the fishing industry has begun. Industry is centered on the manufacture of fabric and clothing and on the distillation of rum. The service sector employs most of the economically active population.

Official name: Republic of Mauritius
Form of government: parliamentary democracy
Capital: Port Louis
Official language: English
Monetary unit: Mauritian rupee
Religious affiliation: Hindu (50.6%), Roman Catholic (27.2%), Muslim (16.3%), Protestant (5.2%), Buddhist (0.3%), other (0.4%)
Ethnic composition of the population: Indo-Mauritian (68%), Creole (27%), Sino-Mauritian (3%), Franco-Mauritian (2%)
Area: 2,040 sq km
Total population: 1,140,000 inhabitants
Population density: 558.8 persons per sq km

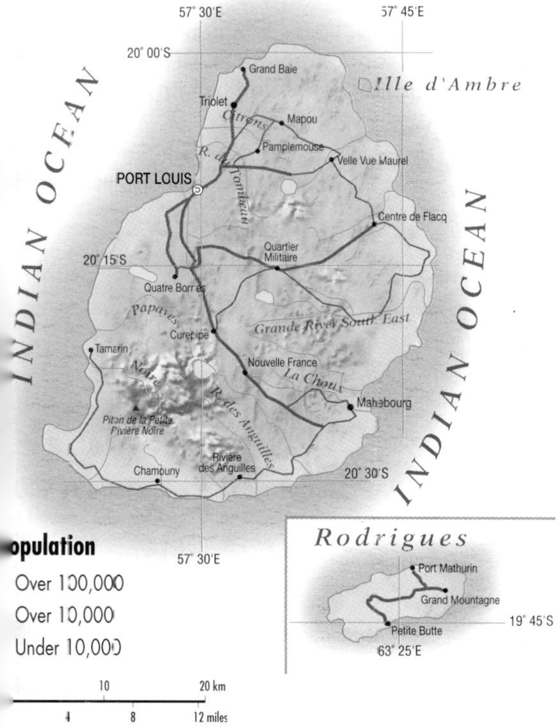

Population evolution and projection

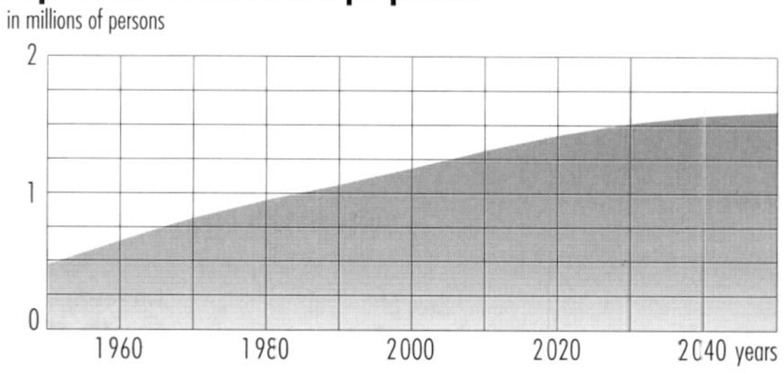

GDP structure / **Labor force**

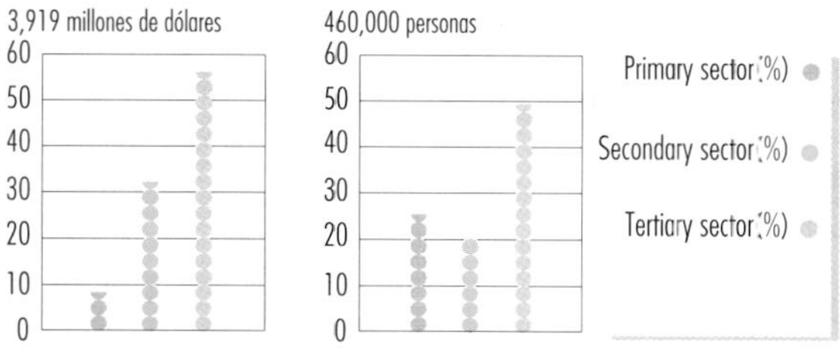

Population age distribution

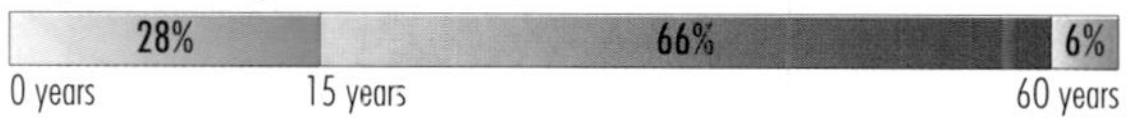

Literacy (% of population over15)

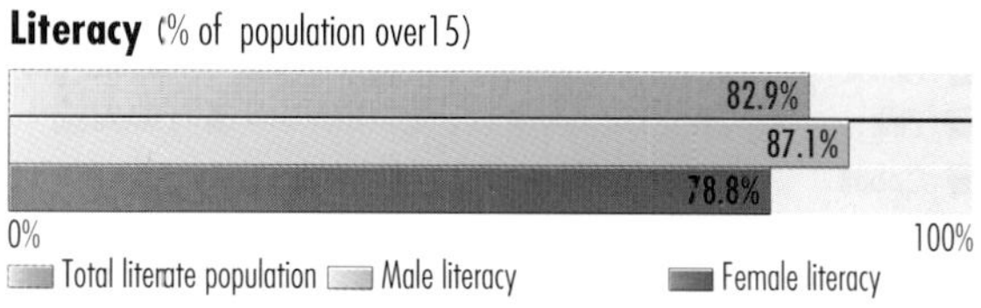

Per capita income (GDP per person)

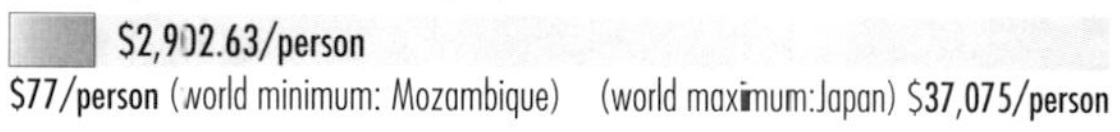

Land use

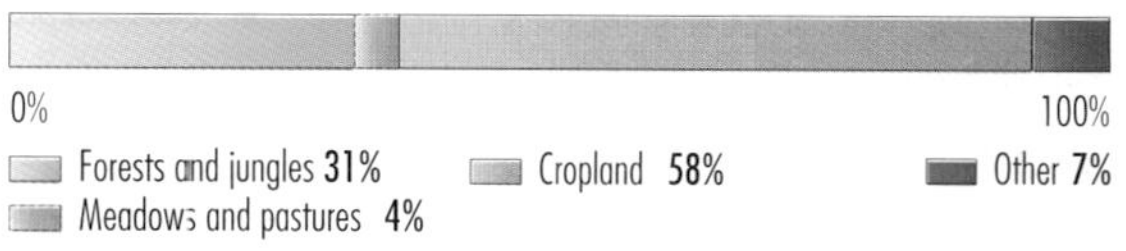

Population

- Over 1,000,000
- Over 100,000
- Over 10,000
- Under 10,000

0 50 100 150 km
0 20 40 60 80 100 miles

Industry

Manufacturing

- Food, beverages and tobacco
- Textiles, clothing, leather and footwear
- Wood, cork and furniture
- Paper and graphic arts
- Chemical products
- Building materials, glass and cement
- Metallurgy and metal products
- Machinery and transport equipment

Agriculture

Types of agriculture and livestock production

- Irrigation/intensive farming (bananas, wheat, fruit, citrus fruits)
- Subsistence farming (sorghum, millet, corn, cassava)
- Forest/brush
- Swampland
- Rice
- Cashew nuts
- Coconuts
- Cotton
- Sisal
- Sugar cane
- Tea
- Tobacco
- Cattle
- Sheep
- Goats
- Fishing

Namibia

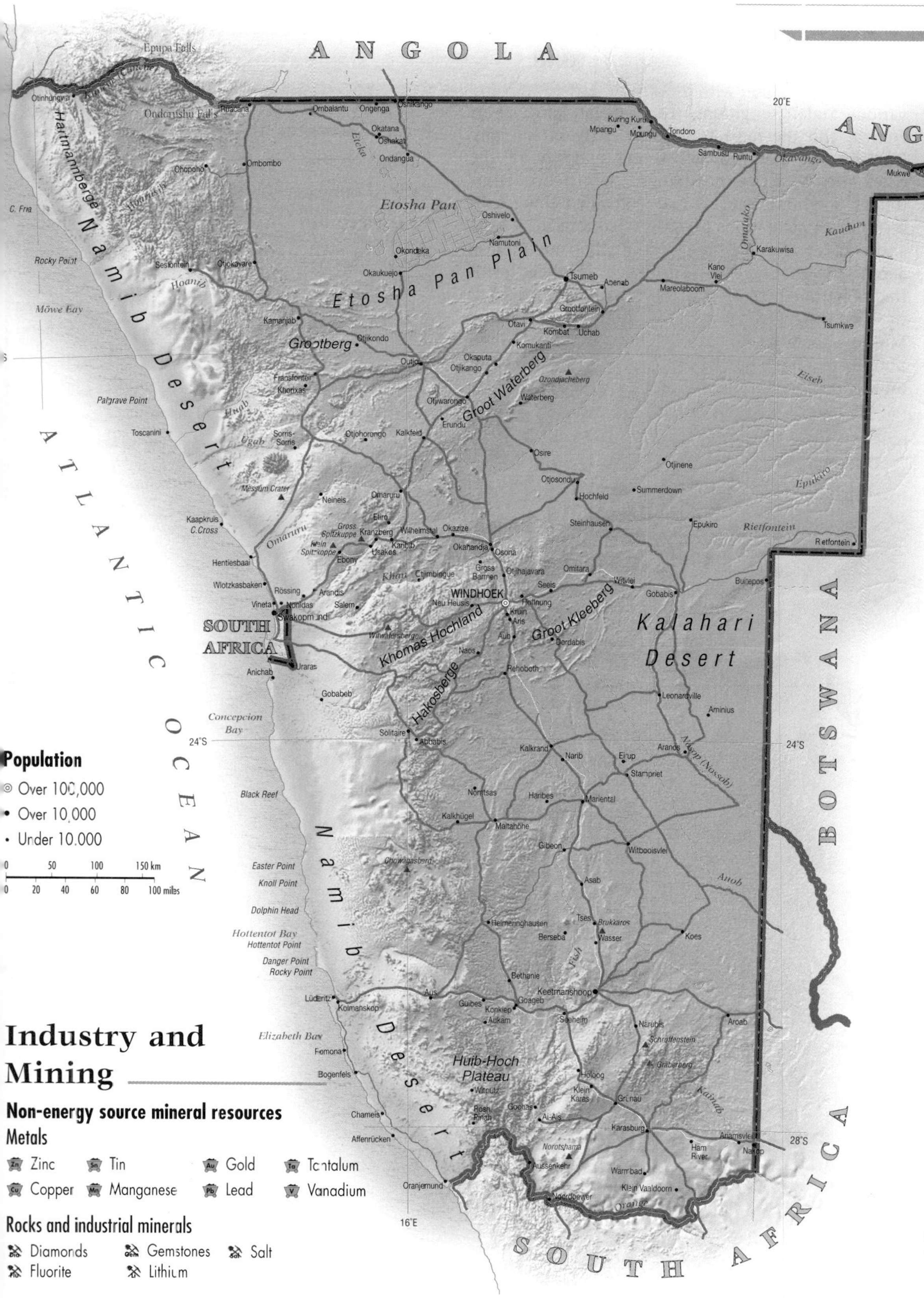

Population

- Over 100,000
- Over 10,000
- Under 10,000

0 50 100 150 km
0 20 40 60 80 100 miles

Official name: Republic of Namibia
Form of government: republic
Capital: Windhoek
Official language: English
Monetary unit: Namibian dollar
Religious affiliation: Lutheran (51.2%), Roman Catholic (19.8%), Dutch Reformed (6.1%), Anglican (5%), other (17.9%)
Ethnic composition of the population: Ovambo (47.4%), Kavango (8.8%), Herero (7.1%), Damara (7.1%), white (6.1%), Nama (4.6%), other (18.9%)
Area: 825,118 sq km
Total population: 1,677,000 inhabitants
Population density: 2 persons per sq km

Industry and Mining

Non-energy source mineral resources

Metals

Zinc, Tin, Gold, Tantalum, Copper, Manganese, Lead, Vanadium

Rocks and industrial minerals

Diamonds, Gemstones, Salt, Fluorite, Lithium

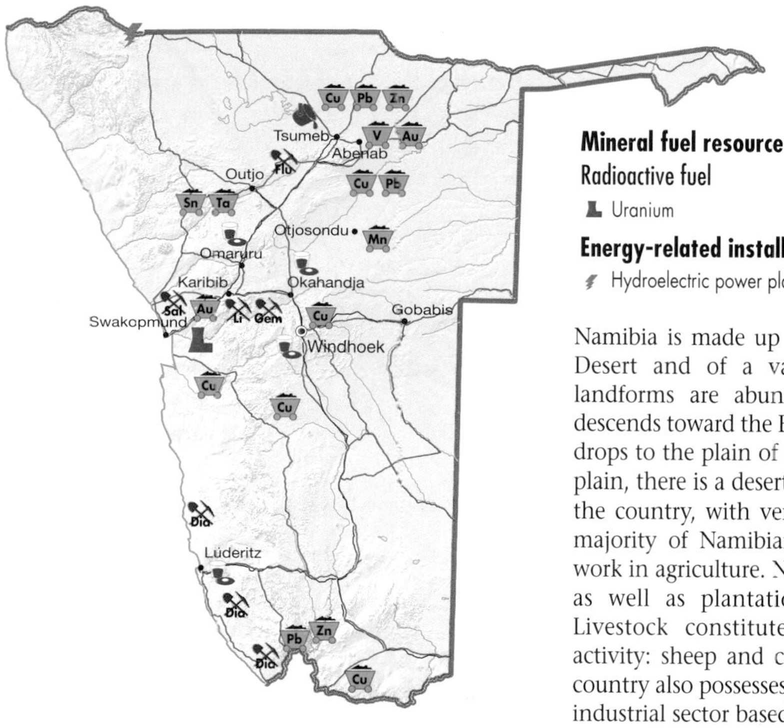

Mineral fuel resources

Radioactive fuel

Uranium

Energy-related installations

Hydroelectric power plant

Manufacturing

Food, beverages and tobacco

Metallurgy and metal products

Namibia is made up of the coastal plain of the Namib Desert and of a vast plateau, where mountainous landforms are abundant. In the north, the plateau descends toward the Etosha Pan Plain, while to the east it drops to the plain of the Kalahari Desert. On the coastal plain, there is a desert climate and it is arid in the rest of the country, with very marked thermal variations. The majority of Namibians live in traditional villages and work in agriculture. Namibia produces subsistence crops, as well as plantation crops (cotton and tobacco). Livestock constitute the most productive primary activity: sheep and cattle are the most important. The country also possesses important mineral reserves and an industrial sector based principally on metallurgy. It has a railroad system and an extensive network of paved roads.

Population evolution and projection

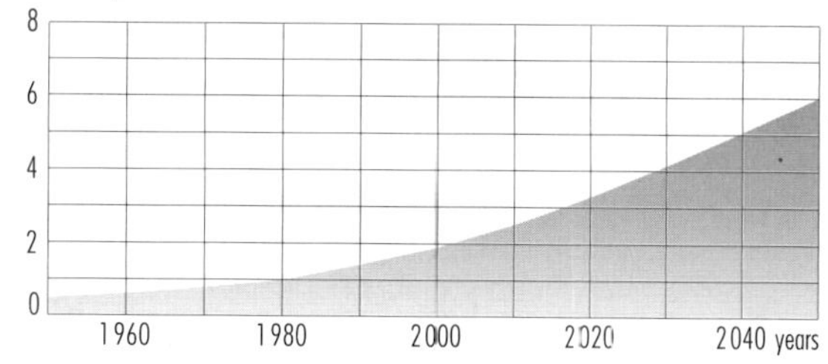

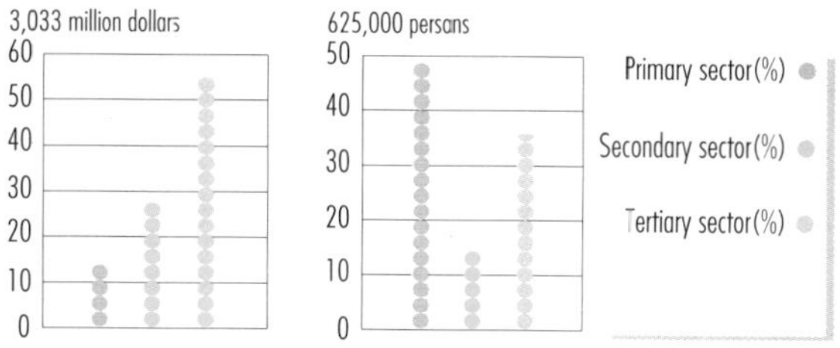

Population age distribution

47% | 50% | 3%

0 years — 15 years — 60 years

Vital statistics

0‰ 10‰ 20‰ 30‰ 40‰ 50‰ 60‰

Birth rate(‰)
Death rate(‰)
Population growth rate(%)

-1% 0% 1% 2% 3% 4%

I Minimum and maximum world values — I Average world value

Literacy (% of population over15)

72.5%
74.2%
70.8%

0% — 100%

Total literate population — Male literacy — Female literacy

Per capita income (GDP per person)

$1,546.8/person

$77/person (world minimum: Mozambique) (world maximum Japan) $37,075/person

Unemployment (% of total population economically active)

35%

0% — 50%

Land use

0% — 100%

Forests and jungles 22% — Cropland 1% — Other 13%
Meadows and pastures 64%

Nigeria

Nigeria is a state of western Africa which extends throughout a wide range of latitudes, a circumstance which confers great variety in landscapes to its territory.
It possesses a long coastline. Plains extend across the north and in the interior is the Jos Plateau. The Niger and Benuvé Rivers, among others, flow through Nigerian soil; the country also has part of Lake Chad and some volcanic lakes.
Nigeria has a hot and humid climate, with temperatures that vary little year-round and abundant rainfall, especially in the coastal zone. It is the most populated country of the African continent and is inhabited by more than 200 ethnic groups, each maintaining their own native language, although the official language is English. In the interior animist beliefs are practiced, but Roman Catholicism has become the major religion.
Agriculture constitutes the most important sector in the economy of Nigeria, which possesses an exceptional diversity of production for western Africa. Subsistence crops, along with other plantation crops (oil palm, peanuts, etc.) are important.
Nigeria is one of the most important countries in production and exportation of crude oil, and one of the most industrially developed countries of the whole continent. The secondary sector encompasses three branches: industries based on agriculture, heavy industry, and capital equipment. Nigeria is equipped with a planned and relatively widespread highway network, and has an important railroad system, with two mainline arteries that connect the ports of Lagos-Apapa and Port Harcourt.

Official name: Federal Republic of Nigeria
Form of government: federal republic (oct. 98)
Capital: Lagos/Abuja
Official language: English
Monetary unit: naira
Religious affiliation: Christian (49%), Muslim (45%), other (6%)
Ethnic composition of the population: Hausa (21.3%), Yoruba (21.3%), Ibo (18%), Fulani (11.2%), Ibibio (5.6%), Kanuri (4.2%), Edo (3.4%), Tiu (2.2%), Ijaw (1.8%), Busa (1.7%), Nupe (1.2%), other (8.1%)
Area: 923,768 sq km
Total population: 103,912,000 inhabitants
Population density: 112.5 persons per sq km

Agriculture

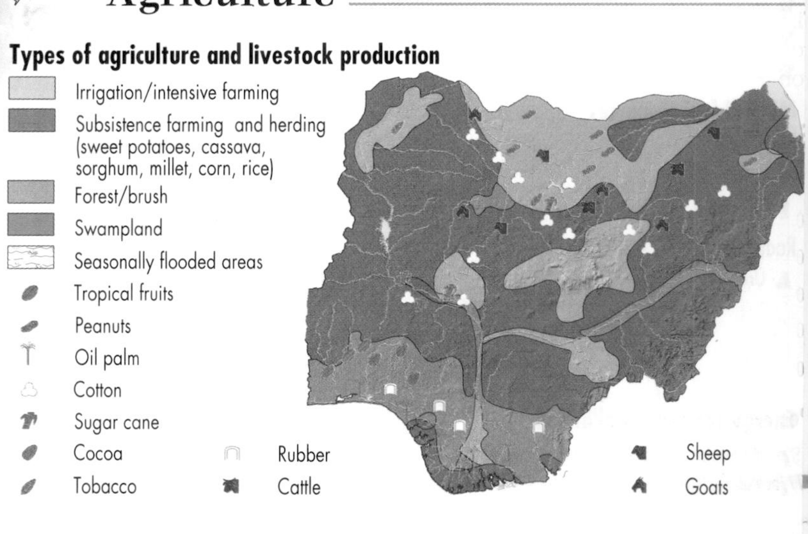

Industry and Mining

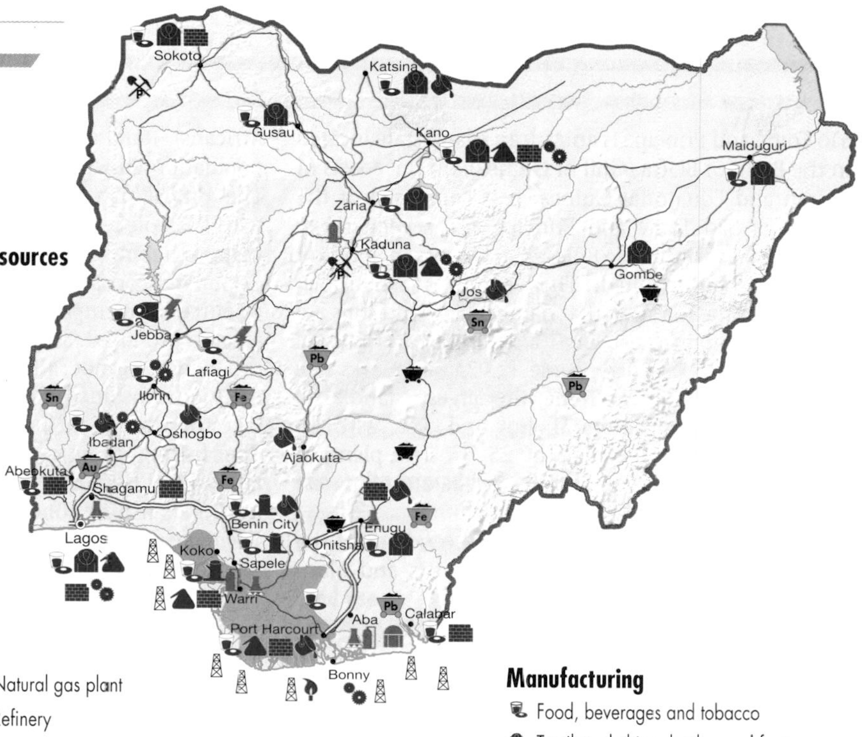

Non-energy source mineral resources

Metals

- Tin
- Gold
- Iron ore
- Lead

Rocks and industrial minerals

- Phosphates

Mineral fuel resources

- Coal
- Natural gas
- Petroleum
- Oil field

Energy-related installations

- Hydroelectric power plant
- Natural gas plant
- Thermal power plant
- Refinery

Manufacturing

- Food, beverages and tobacco
- Textiles, clothing, leather and footwear
- Wood, cork and furniture
- Paper and graphic arts
- Chemical products
- Building materials, glass and cement
- Metallurgy and metal products
- Machinery and transport equipment

Population evolution and projection
in millions of persons

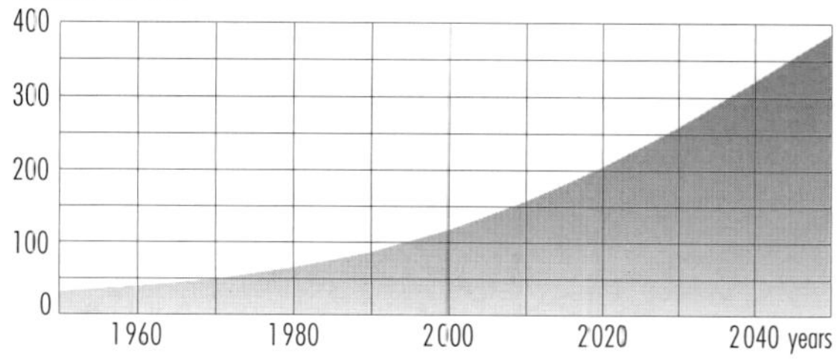

GDP structure
40,477 million dollars

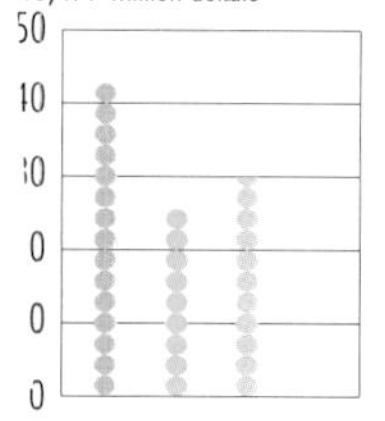

Labor force
43,059,000 persons

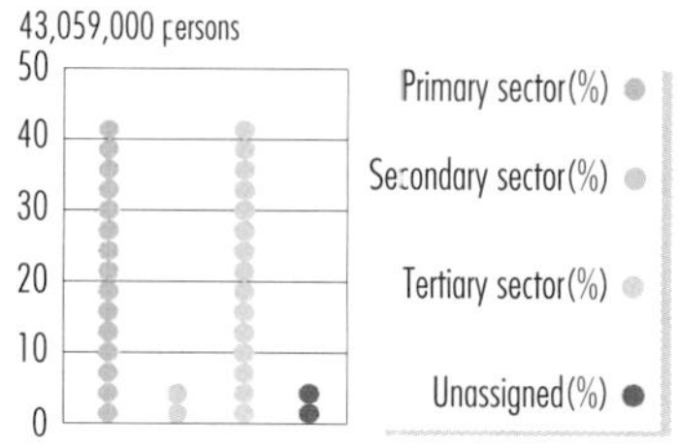

Population age distribution

45% | 52% | 3%
0 years | 15 years | 60 years

Vital statistics

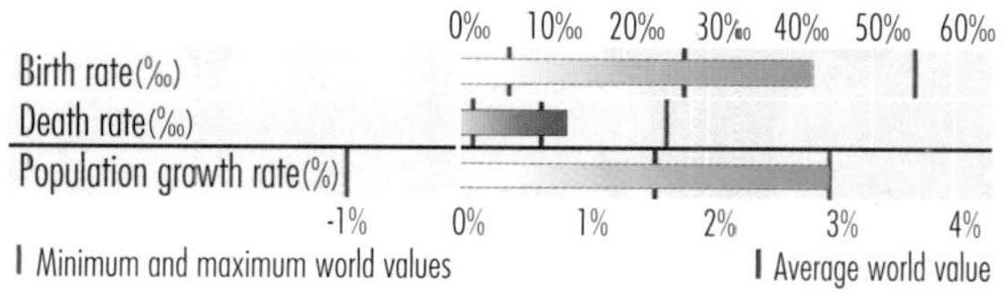

Literacy (% of population over15)

57.1%
67.3%
47.3%

% — 100%

Total literate population | Male literacy | Female literacy

Per capita income (GDP per person)

$317.48/person

77/person (world minimum: Mozambique) (world maximum: Japan) $37,075/person

Land use

0% — 100%

Forests and jungles 15.5% | Cropland 35.5% | Other 8%
Meadows and pastures 41%

Unemployment (% of total population economically active)

28%

0% — 50%

Population

- Over 100,000
- Over 10,000
- Under 10,000

Rwanda

Rwanda is a republic of central Africa located in the region of the Great Lakes. Most of its territory is made up of highlands.

Rwanda registers one of the highest population densities in Africa. The population is composed of two principal ethnic groups: the Hutus and the Tutsis, the first being the majority group that represents approximately 90% of the total population. The official languages are Rwandi and French. Rural settlement predominates. Most of the Ruandi people work in farming, above all of subsistence crops (sweet potatoes, cassava, sorghum, millet, etc.) that do not cover the needs of the population. Industrial plantations of coffee, tea, tobacco and cotton exist, producing cash crops for export. Herding is practiced according to archaic methods; the most numerous kinds of livestock are cattle and goats. Fishing activities are carried out in Lake Kivu, and constitute an important source of food for domestic consumption.

Official name: Rwandese Republic
Form of government: presidential republic
Capital: Kigali
Official language: Rwanda, French
Monetary unit: Rwanda franc
Religious affiliation: Roman Catholic (65%), traditional beliefs (17%), Protestant (9%), Muslim (9%)
Ethnic composition of the population: Hutu (90%), Tutsi (9%), Twa (1%)
Area: 26,338 sq km
Total population: 6,853,000 inhabitants
Population density: 260.2 persons per sq km

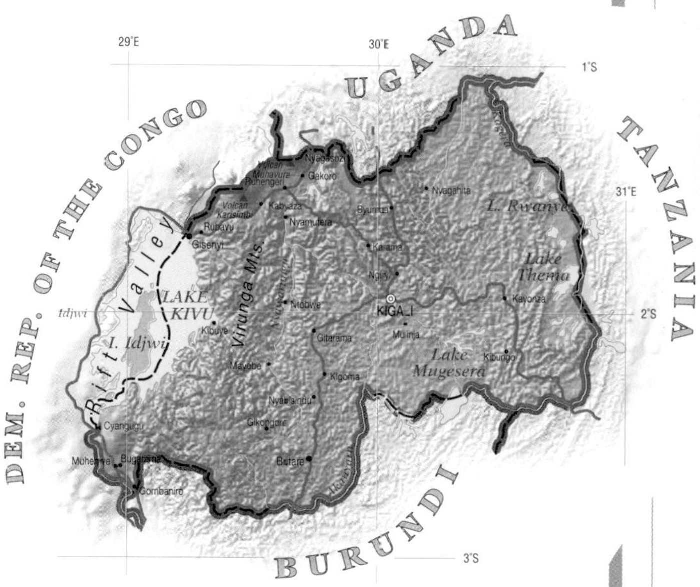

GDP structure
1,128 million dollars

Labor force
4,099,000 persons

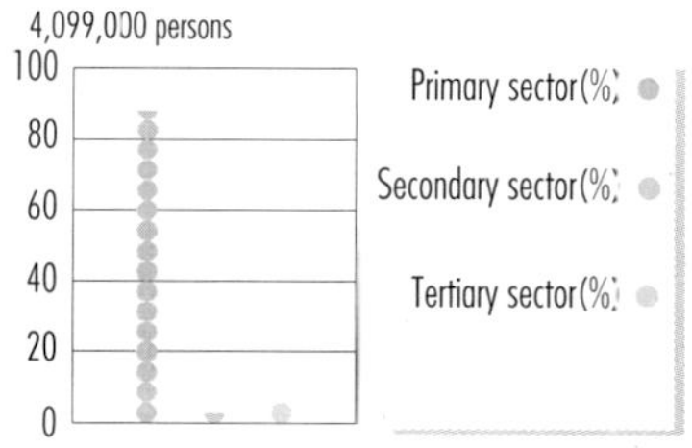

Per capita income (GDP per person)

$218.73/person

7/person (world minimum: Mozambique) (world maximum: Japan) $37,075/person

Population evolution and projection
in millions of persons

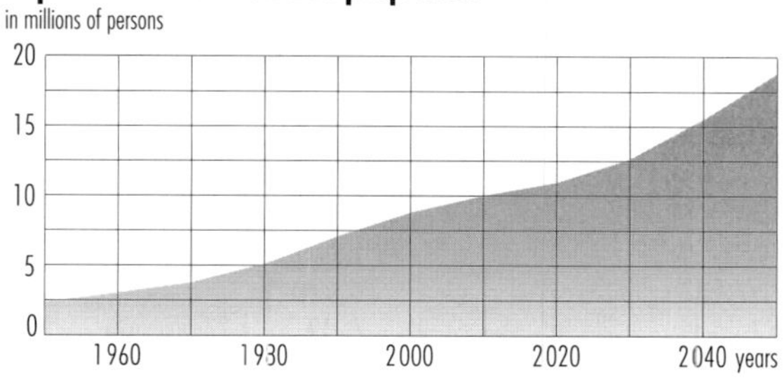

Population age distribution

51% | 47% | 2%
0 years | 15 years | 60 years

Vital statistics

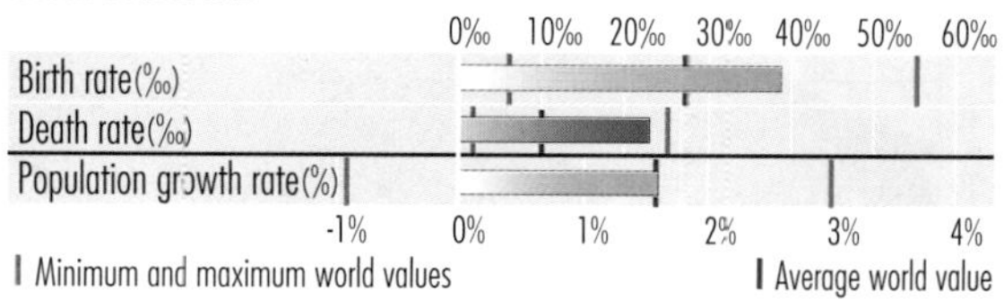

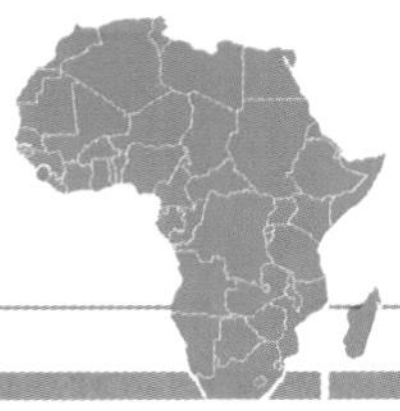

Sierra Leone

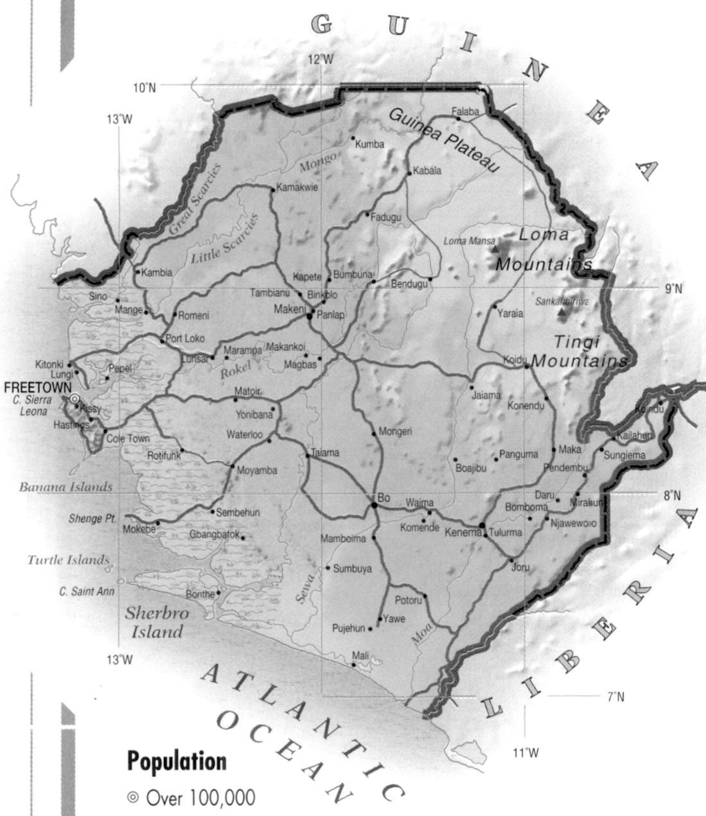

Population

◎ Over 100,000

• Over 10,000

· Under 10,000

Sierra Leone is a republic of West Africa that has three well-differentiated geographical zones: the mountainous region in the northeast, the central area where tablelands and hills predominate, and the coastal plain with low straight coastlines. It has a tropical climate, hot and wet, with a rainy season in summer, influenced by the Trade Winds. A large part of the population, whose principal ethnic groups are the Mende (Mandinga) and the Temne, inhabit rural zones. The economy is developing; the primary sector absorbs the majority of the economically active population. Oil palm, coffee, and cocoa are included among the main plantation crops, and among those of subsistence the most important are rice, corn and sorghum. Fishing has greater importance than livestock production. Sierra Leone figures among the principal producers of diamonds worldwide. Industry is centered on the processing of farming and livestock products. Raw minerals (rutile, bauxite, iron ore, etc.) are exported, in addition to coffee, cocoa and palm kernels.

Official name: Republic of Sierra Leone

Form of government: constitutional democracy

Capital: Freetown

Official language: English

Monetary unit: leone

Religious affiliation: Muslim (60%), traditional beliefs (30%), Christian (10%)

Ethnic composition of the population: Native tribes: Temne (30%), Mende (30%), other (39%); Creole, European, Lebanese and Asian (1%)

Area: 71,740 sq km

Total population: 4,793,000 inhabitants

Population density: 66.8 persons per sq km

GDP structure

824 million dollars

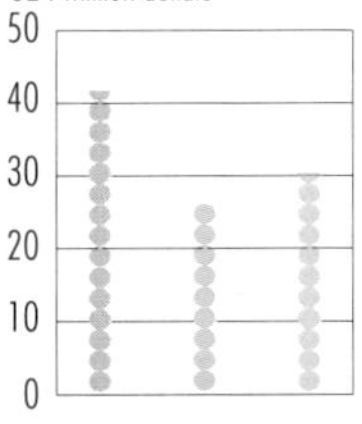

Labor force

1,638,000 persons

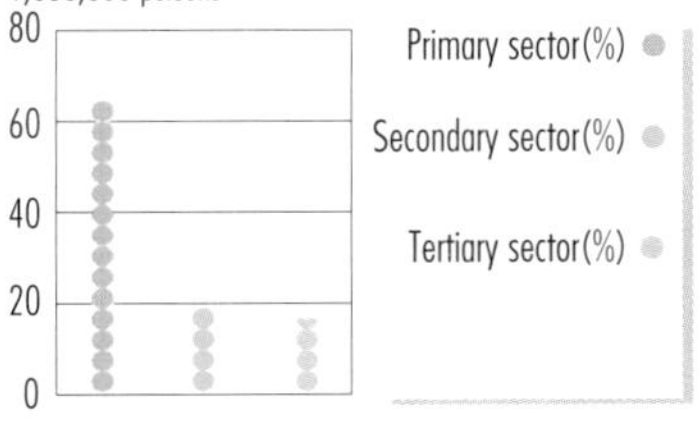

Literacy (% of population over15)

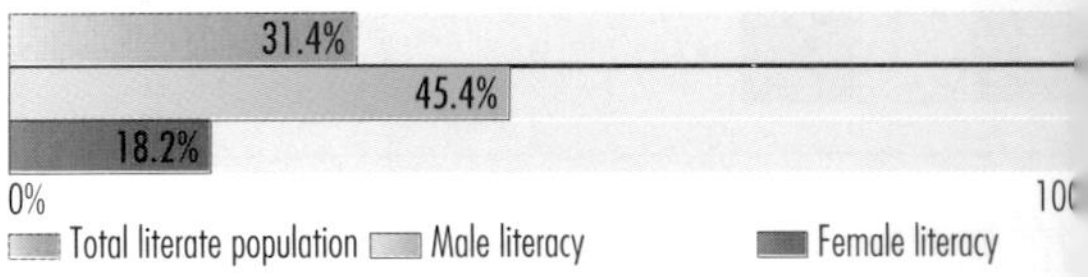

Population evolution and projection

in millions of persons

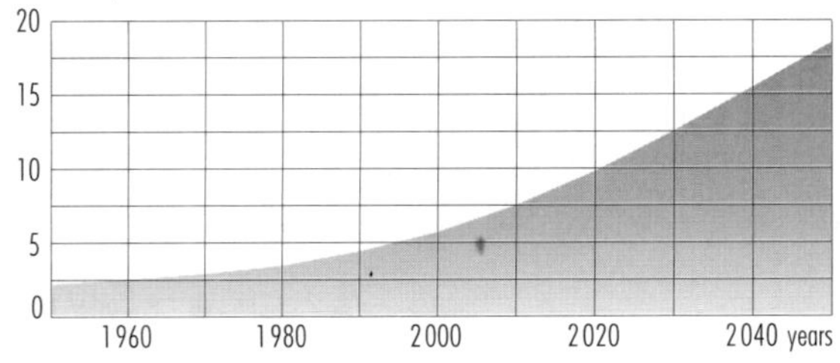

Population age distribution

Per capita income (GDP per person)

| $134.98/person

$77/person (world minimum: Mozambique) (world maximum:Japan) $37,075/pers

Vital statistics

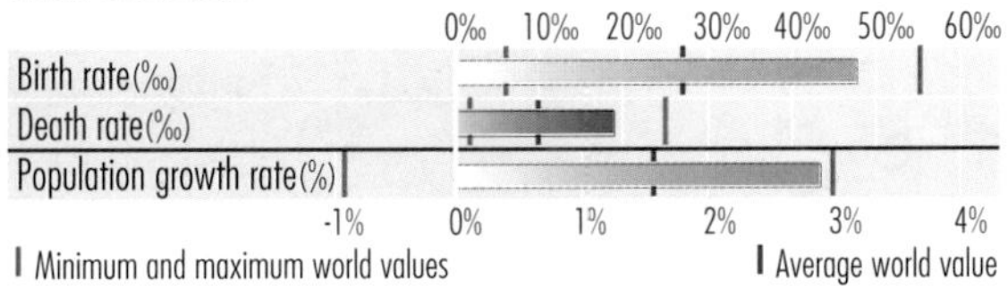

Land use

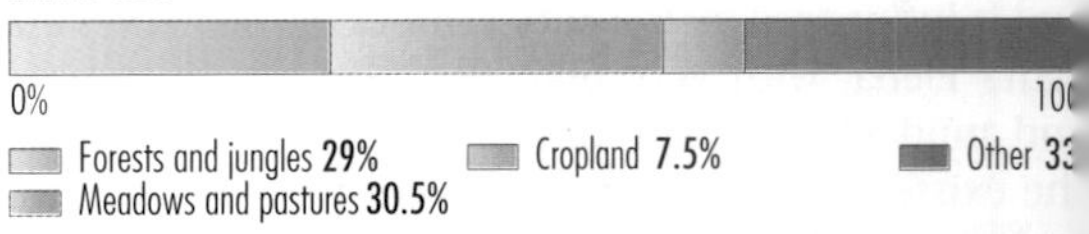

Somalia

Somalia is a state of East Africa, with most of its surface area occupied by the Ethiopian Highlands, which descend towards the Indian Ocean. In its northern part there are tablelands of higher altitude, interrupted by valleys and depressions. Somali territory possesses two regular watercourses, the Jubba and the Shabeelle, in addition to numerous wadis (seasonal watercourses, with flow frequently interrupted). It has a hot and very dry climate, with minimal seasonal variations and scanty precipitation. It is a sparsely populated country, where the greater part of its inhabitants practice a pastoral way of life. The Somali population is composed of a great number of tribal groups: the Dir in the north, the Darod in the center, the Ishak in the northwest; and the Hawija, Digil and Rahanwen in the south. The primary sector absorbs the majority of the economically active population. Subsistence crops are grown (sorghum, millet, cassava, etc.), as well as plantation crops (banana, sugar cane and peanuts, among others). Another economic activity is pastoral herding, seasonally migratory, in which goats are the most important type of livestock. The fishing industry contributes large captures of tuna and sharks. Somalia figures among the principal world producers of frankincense and myrrh. Manufacturing, which has traditionally been dedicated to the processing of agricultural products, has developed a sector composed of chemical factories, recasting and sheet-metal working. Raw materials are exported, while industrial equipment, fuels and quality food products are imported.

Mining and Energy

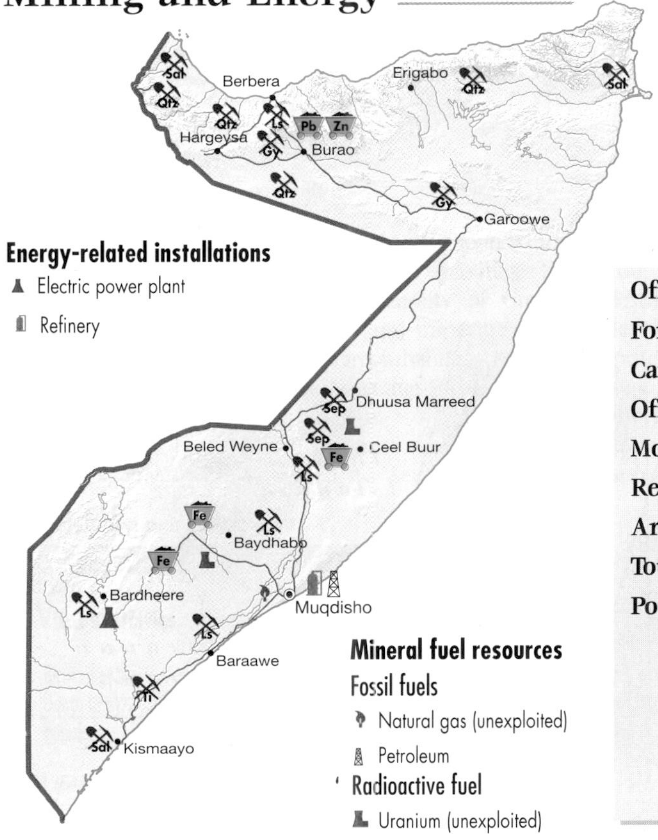

Non-energy source mineral resources

Metals

- Zinc (unexploited)
- Lead (unexploited)
- Iron ore (unexploited)

Rocks and industrial minerals

- Limestone
- Sepiolite
- Quartzite (unexploited)
- Titanium (unexploitec
- Salt
- Gypsum

Official name: Somalia

Form of government: none

Capital: Muqdisho (Mogadishu)

Official language: Somali, Arabic

Monetary unit: Somali shilling

Religious affiliation: Muslim majority

Area: 637,000 sq km

Total population: 9,639,000 inhabitants

Population density: 15.1 persons per sq km

Population evolution and projection

in millions of persons

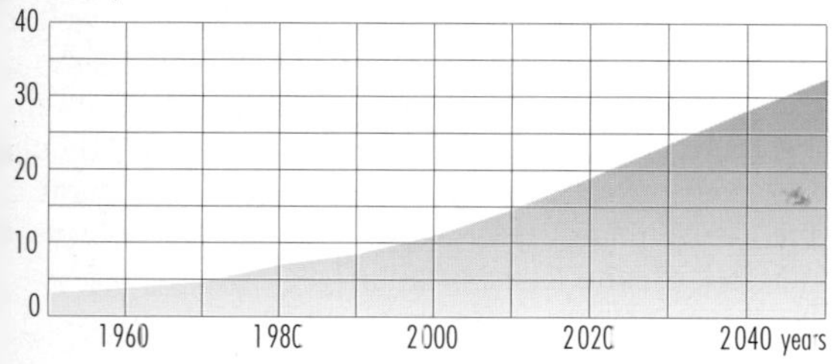

GDP structure

835 million dollars

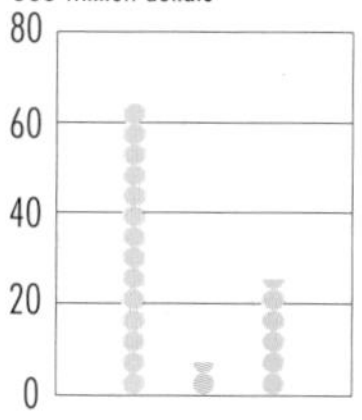

Labor force

4,153,000 persons

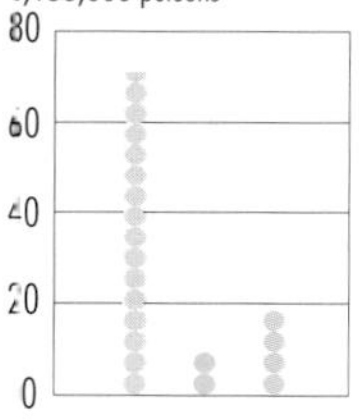

Primary sector(%)
Secondary sector(%)
Tertiary sector(%)

Land use

0% — 100%

Forests and jungles 14%
Meadows and pastures 46%
Cropland 2%
Other 38%

Population age distribution

45% | 51% | 4%

0 years — 15 years — 60 years

Population

- Over 500,000
- Over 50,000
- Over 10,000
- Under 10,000

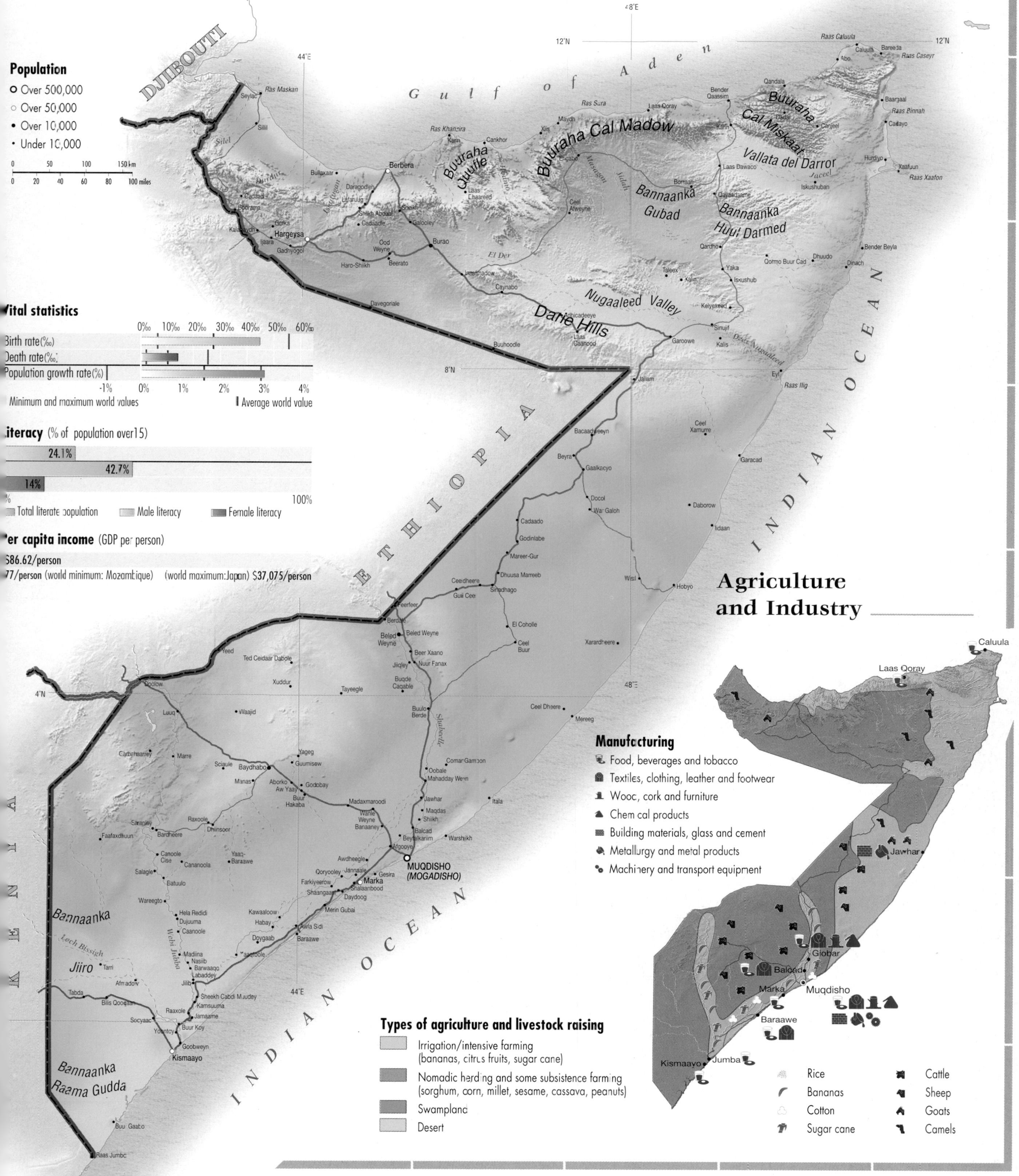

Vital statistics

0‰ 10‰ 20‰ 30‰ 40‰ 50‰ 60‰
Birth rate(‰)
Death rate(‰)
Population growth rate(%)
-1% 0% 1% 2% 3% 4%

Minimum and maximum world values | Average world value

Literacy (% of population over15)

24.1%
42.7%
14%

0% — 100%

Total literate population | Male literacy | Female literacy

Per capita income (GDP per person)

$86.62/person

$77/person (world minimum: Mozambique) (world maximum:Japan) $37,075/person

Agriculture and Industry

Manufacturing

- Food, beverages and tobacco
- Textiles, clothing, leather and footwear
- Wood, cork and furniture
- Chemical products
- Building materials, glass and cement
- Metallurgy and metal products
- Machinery and transport equipment

Types of agriculture and livestock raising

- Irrigation/intensive farming (bananas, citrus fruits, sugar cane)
- Nomadic herding and some subsistence farming (sorghum, corn, millet, sesame, cassava, peanuts)
- Swampland
- Desert

Rice | Cattle
Bananas | Sheep
Cotton | Goats
Sugar cane | Camels

South Africa

South Africa is a republic of austral Africa. The interior is a large plateau bordered by higher landforms to the east and south of Cape Province and by the Drakensberg Mountains between Lesotho and the southeastern coast of the Indian Ocean. The high plateau gives way to peripheral low regions. In the north of the region of the Orange river is found a part of the Kalahari Desert. Except in eastern area, rains are scarce and irregular in South African territory. The north of the country, the center and the area to the north of Cape Town have a continental climate; the meridional coast has a Mediterranean-type climate. Great racial diversity exists, originating a numerous mestizo community, which is called "colored". Black groups make up the majority of the population of South Africa, followed in number by the whites and the Oriental minority. Farming and ranching have lost economic weight, although they allow the country to supply its own needs. Agriculture is characterized by the variety of crops grown and livestock production is based on an important number of cattle and sheep Nevertheless, the great economic wealth of the Stat derives from its plentiful mining resources, notabl from the extraction of diamonds and gold, as well a from the quarrying of the deposits of uranium, amon the greatest in the world. The food, textile, iron an steel and chemical industries have been strengthene and developed. South Africa is the economic giant o the African continent, and possesses a widesprea network of land transportation.

Agriculture

Types of agriculture and livestock raising

- Polyculture (grapevines, citrus fruits, fruit trees, horticulture)
- Irrigation/intensive farming (wheat, alfalfa, corn (maize), cotton)
- Subsistence farming and herding
- Ranching (cattle, sheep, goats)
- Forest/brush
- Desert
- Urban area

- Fruit trees
- Citrus fruits
- Grapevines
- Bananas
- Sugar cane
- Oil-producing crops
- Tea
- Tobacco
- Cattle
- Sheep
- Goats
- Pigs

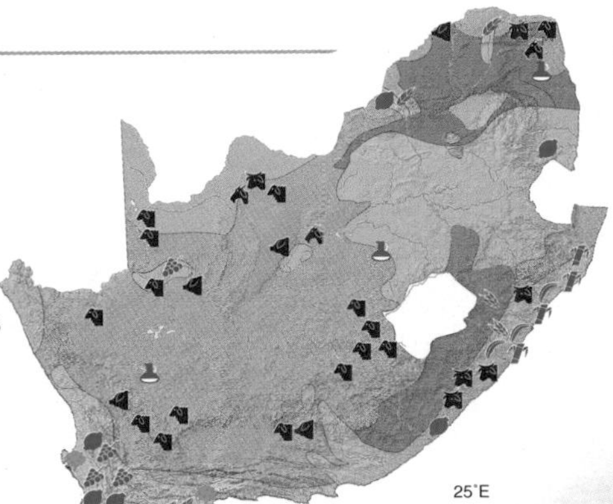

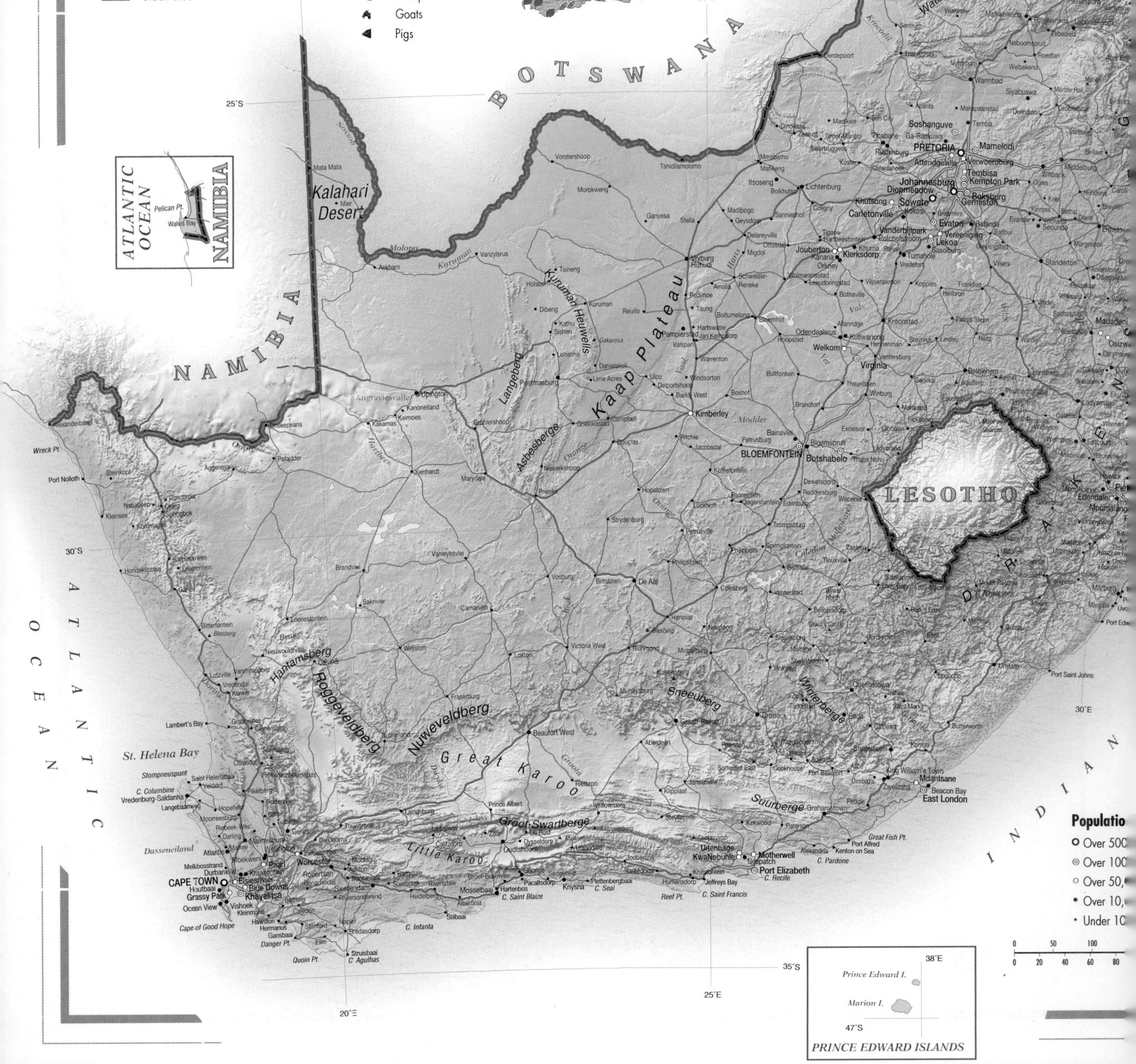

Mining and Energy

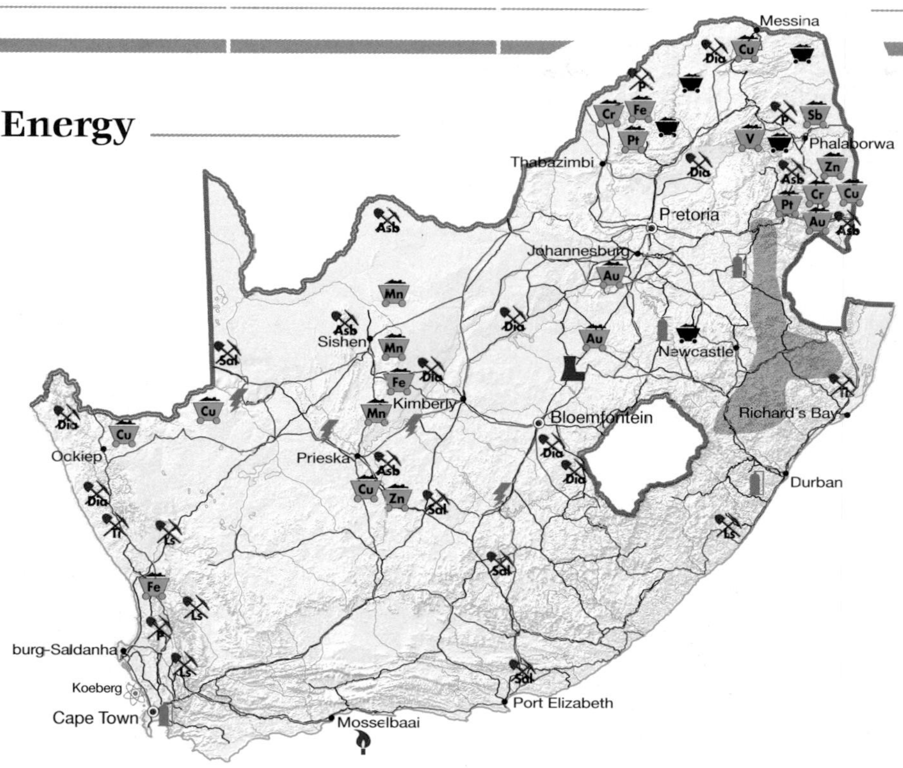

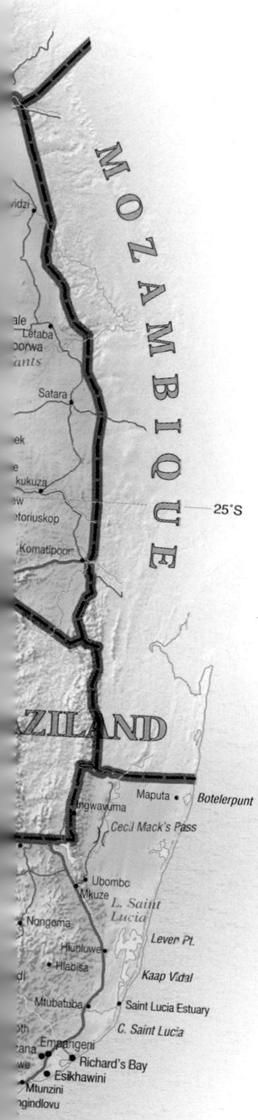

Non-energy source mineral resources

Metals

- Antimony
- Zinc
- Copper
- Chromite
- Iron ore
- Manganese
- Gold
- Platinum
- Vanadium

Energy-related installations

- Hydroelectric power plant
- Refinery
- Nuclear reactor

Rocks and industrial minerals

- Asbestos
- Limestone
- Diamonds
- Phospates
- Salt
- Titanium

Mineral fuel resources

Fossil fuels

- Coal
- Coal deposit
- Natural gas

Radioactive fuel

- Uranium

Official name: Republic of South Africa
Form of government: republic
Capital: Pretoria/Cape Town/Bloemfontein
Official language: Afrikans, English, Ndebele, Pedi, Sotho, Swazi, Tsonga, Tswana, Venda, Xhosa, Zulu
Monetary unit: rand
Religious affiliation: Christian (78%), traditional beliefs (10.5%), Hindu (1.7%), other (9.8%)
Ethnic composition of the population: black (75.2%), white (13.6%), colored (8.6%), Indian (2.6%)
Area: 1,223,200 sq km
Total population: 41,743,000 inhabitants
Population density: 34.1 persons per sq km

Population evolution and projection
in millions of persons

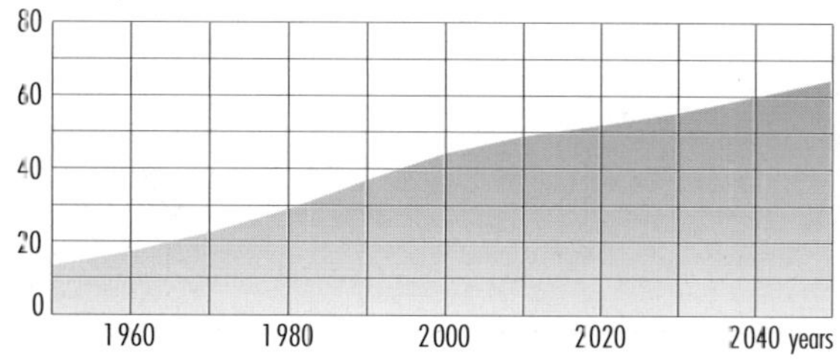

GDP structure
136,035 million dollars

Labor force
15,817,000 persons

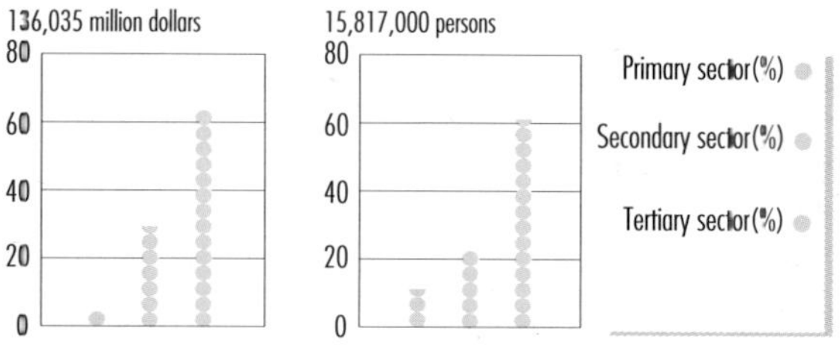

Population age distribution

40% | 56% | 4%

0 years — 15 years — 60 years

Vital statistics

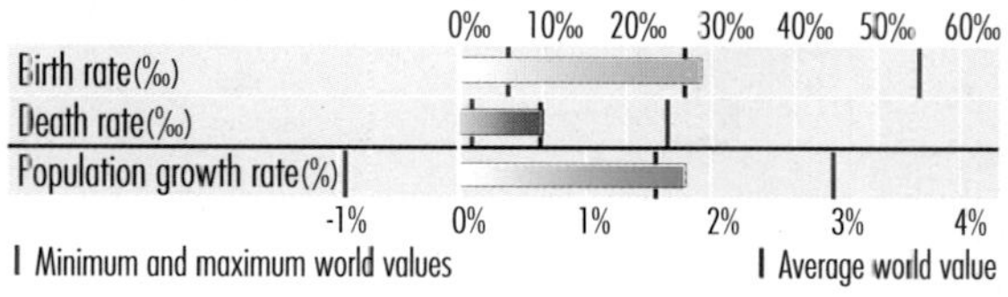

I Minimum and maximum world values — I Average world value

Literacy (% of population over 15)

81.8%
81.9%
81.7%

0% — 100%

Total literate population / Male literacy / Female literacy

Per capita income (GDP per person)

$2,829.21/person

$77/person (world minimum: Mozambique) (world maximum: Japan) $37,075/person

Unemployment (% of total population economically active)

32.6%

0% — 50%

Land use

0% — 100%

Forests and jungles 3% / Cropland 11% / Other 21% / Meadows and pastures 65%

Industry

Manufacturing

- Food, beverages and tobacco
- Textiles, clothing, leather and footwear
- Wood, cork and furniture
- Paper and graphic arts
- Chemical products
- Building materials, glass and cement
- Metallurgy and metal products
- Machinery and transport equipment
- Electrical, electronical and optical equipment

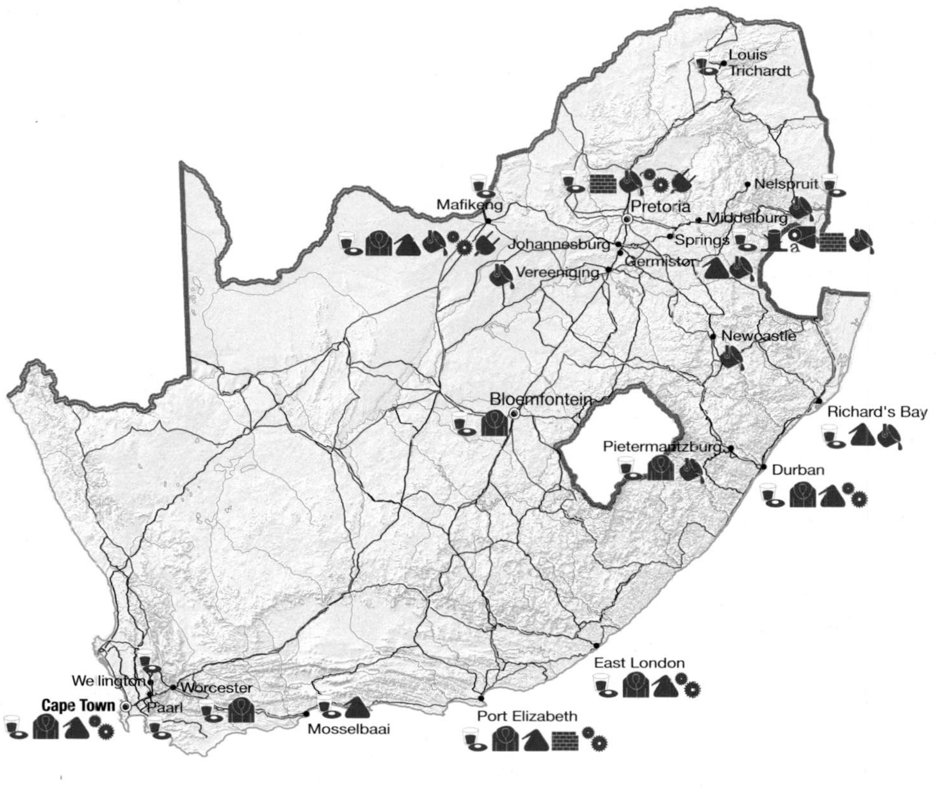

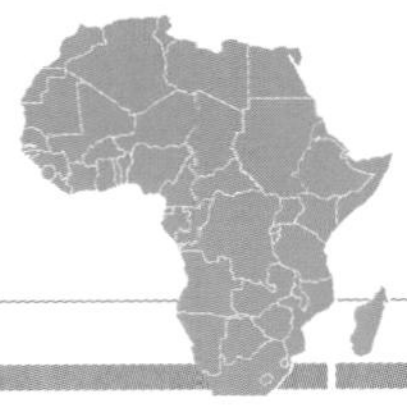

Sudan, The

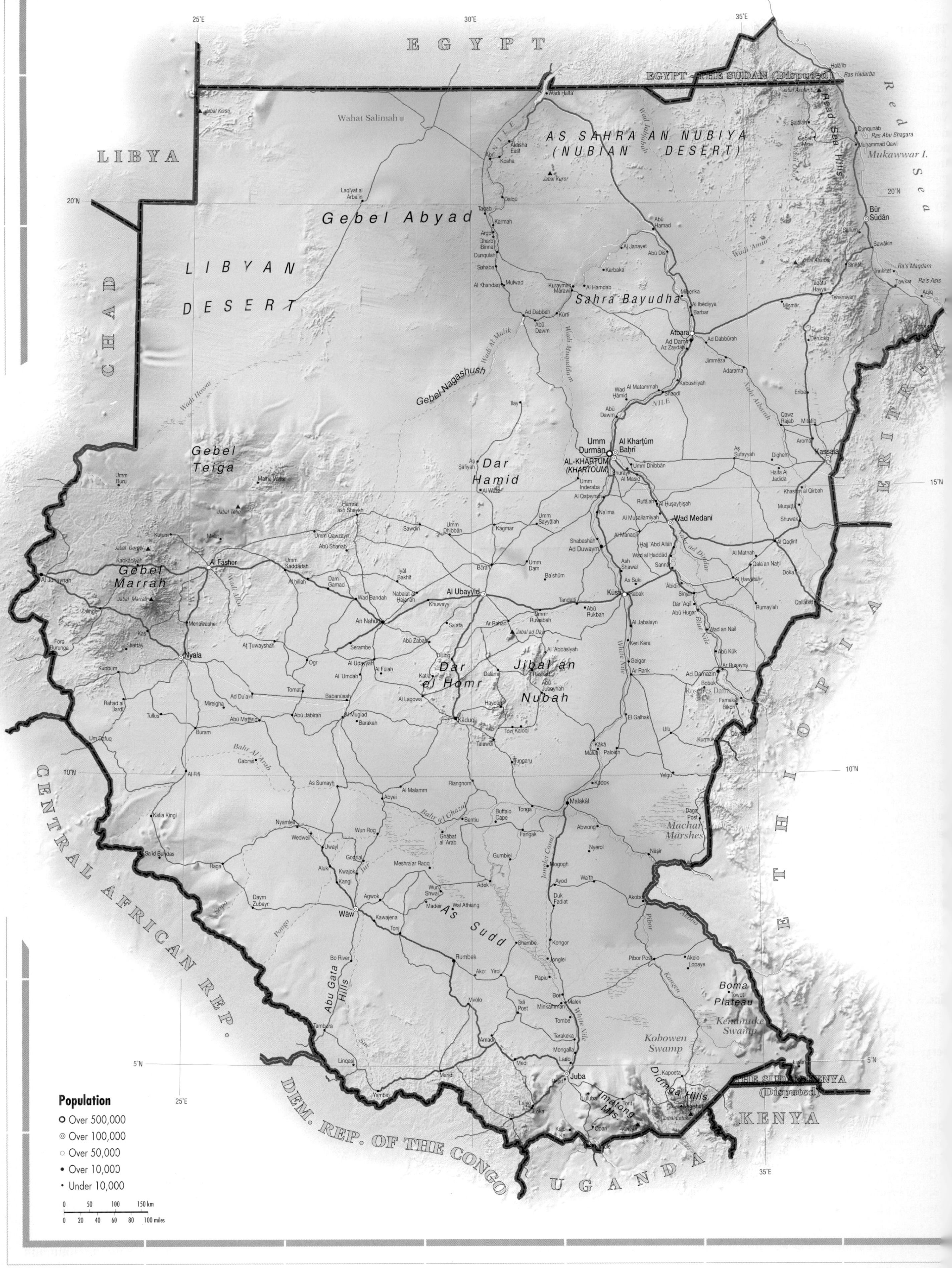

EGYPT
LIBYA
CHAD
EGYPT - THE SUDAN (Disputed)
Red Sea
ERITREA
ETHIOPIA
KENYA
UGANDA
DEM. REP. OF THE CONGO
CENTRAL AFRICAN REP.
THE SUDAN - KENYA (Disputed)
25°E
30°E
35°E
20°N
15°N
10°N
5°N
LIBYAN DESERT
Gebel Abyad
AS SAHRA AN NUBIYA (NUBIAN DESERT)
Sahra Bayudha
Wahat Salimah
Gebel Nagashush
Gebel Teiga
Gebel Marrah
Dar Hamid
Dar el Homr
Jibal an Nubah
As Sudd
Machar Marshes
Boma Plateau
Kenamuke Swamp
Kobowen Swamp
Didinga Hills
Imatong Mts.
Abu Gata Hills
Red Sea Hills
Mukawwar I.
Wadi Halfa
Dunqulah
Karmah
Kurayma
Marawi
Ad Dabbah
Atbara
Ad Damir
Shandi
Umm Durman
Al Khartum Bahri
AL-KHARTUM (KHARTOUM)
Wad Medani
Kassala
Bur Sudan
Sawakin
Tawkar
Al Qadarif
Sinnar
Kusti
Rabak
Al Ubayyid
Al Fasher
Nyala
Al Junaynah
Zalingei
An Nahud
Dilling
Kaduqli
Malakal
Bentiu
Waw
Rumbek
Bor
Juba
Yei
Torit
Kapoeta
Yambio
Tambura
Raga
Aweil
Kafia Kingi
Ad Damazin
Ar Rusayris
Kurmuk
Nasir
Akobo
Pibor Post
Kodok
Nile
White Nile
Blue Nile
Bahr al Ghazal
Bahr al Arab
Wadi Howar
Wadi al Malik
Jonglei Canal
Population
Over 500,000
Over 100,000
Over 50,000
Over 10,000
Under 10,000
0 50 100 150 km
0 20 40 60 80 100 miles

The Sudan is a Central African republic, the state with the largest land area in Africa. In the south and east there are wide clay plains and great swamps. The region of the Red Sea, in the east, has rougher terrain. Mountain ranges rise in the south, on the border with Uganda, while the western region is covered with sand dunes and has several volcanoes. The Nile River flows across the country in a north-south direction. It has a very hot climate that varies according to the region: in the north it is continental tropical, and in the south, where more abundant precipitation also falls, it has equatorial characteristics. The population is characterized by its diversity, as more than 500 ethnic groups live together in Sudanese territory. The geographical location of the country makes it form part of the Arab world and that of black Africa. The inhabitants of the north share the Arabic language and Islam; those of the south, of the black race, practice traditional beliefs or are Christians. All together, they make up a young population —a large percent are under 15 years of age— with a low population density that increases along the Nile, in the provinces of Geriza and Khartoum. Arabic is the official language, but another 32 tongues are also spoken. The Sudan, one of the most poverty-stricken countries in the world, has a developing economy in which agriculture is the main resource; the majority of the economically active population is engaged in agricultural work. Especially important as a commercial crop is cotton, which represents half of the country's exports. Among subsistence crops, the most notable are wheat, corn and cassava. The most productive area of Sudan is the central region, where irrigation projects have been carried out. The food shortage that the country suffers has been aggravated by the massive arrival of refugees and the country's heavy dependence on the cultivation of cotton. It possesses few mining, hydroelectric or petroleum resources. Only a small percent of the population works in manufacturing, primarily dedicated to the processing of agricultural products.

Official name: Republic of the Sudan
Form of government: republic
Capital: Al-Kharṭūm (Khartoum)
Official language: Arabic
Monetary unit: Sudanese dinar
Religious affiliation: Muslim (74.7%), traditional beliefs (17.1%), Christian (8.2%)
Ethnic composition of the population: Sudanese Arab (49%), Dinka (11.5%), Nuba (8%), Beja (6.5%), Nuer (5%), Azande (2.7%), Bari (2.5%), foreign (2%), other (12.5%)
Area: 2,503,890 sq km
Total population: 31,065,000 inhabitants
Population density: 12.4 persons per sq km

Agriculture

Types of agriculture and livestock raising
- Irrigation/intensive farming (fruits, vegetables, tobacco, cereals)
- Subsistence farming (cotton, tobacco, coffee, peanuts)
- Subsistence farming and herding (sorghum, wheat, cassava, corn, legumes)
- Forest/brush
- Desert
- Swampland
- Peanuts
- Sesame
- Cotton
- Sugar cane
- Gum arabic
- Cattle
- Sheep
- Goats
- Camels
- Oasis

Population evolution and projection
in millions of persons

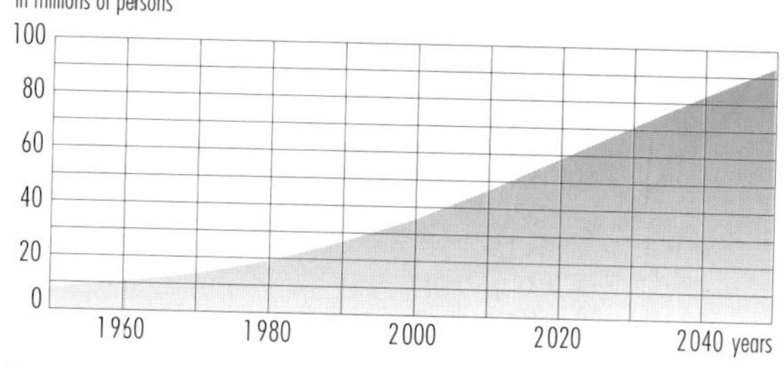

GDP structure
6,380 million dollars

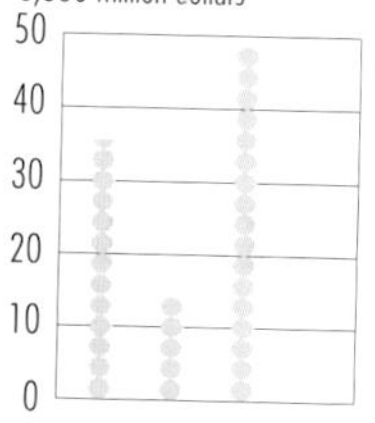

Labor force
10,073,000 persons

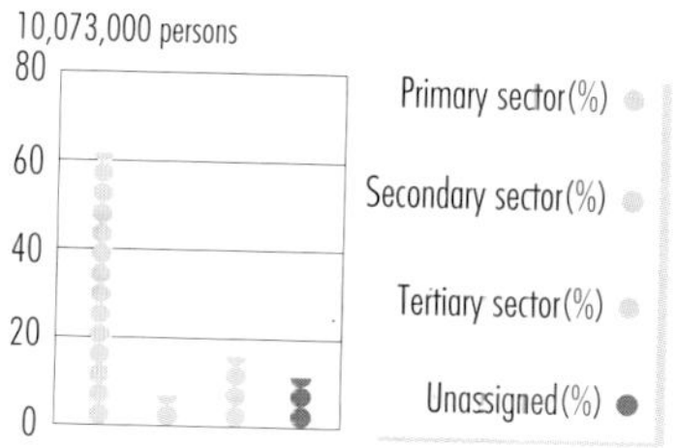

Population age distribution

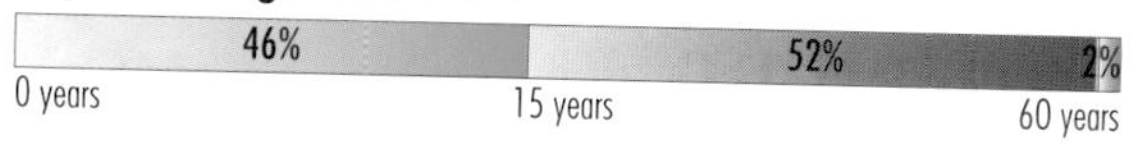

Vital statistics

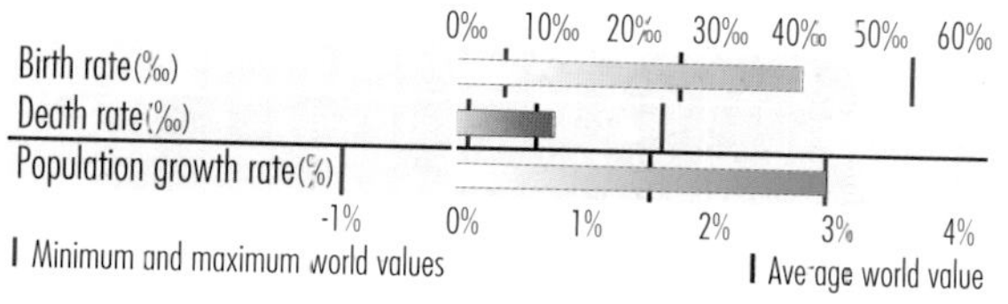

I Minimum and maximum world values | Average world value

Literacy (% of population over 15)

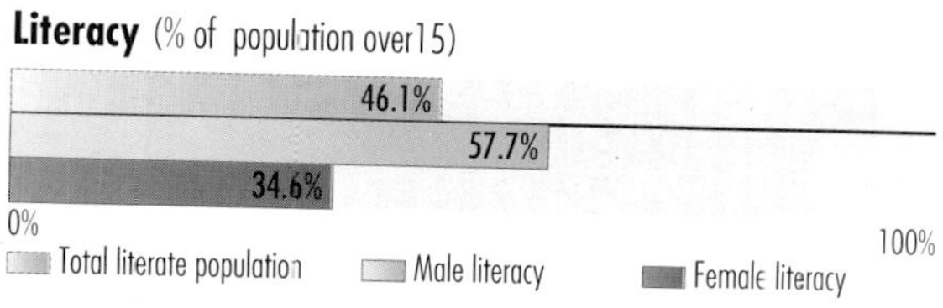

Total literate population | Male literacy | Female literacy

Per capita income (GDP per person)
$205.37/person
$77/person (world minimum: Mozambique) (world maximum: Japan) $37,075/person

Unemployment (% of total population economically active)

Land use

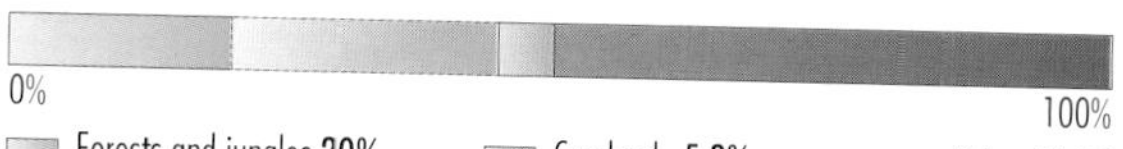

Forests and jungles 20% | Cropland 5.2% | Other 50.8%
Meadows and pastures 24%

Industry and Mining

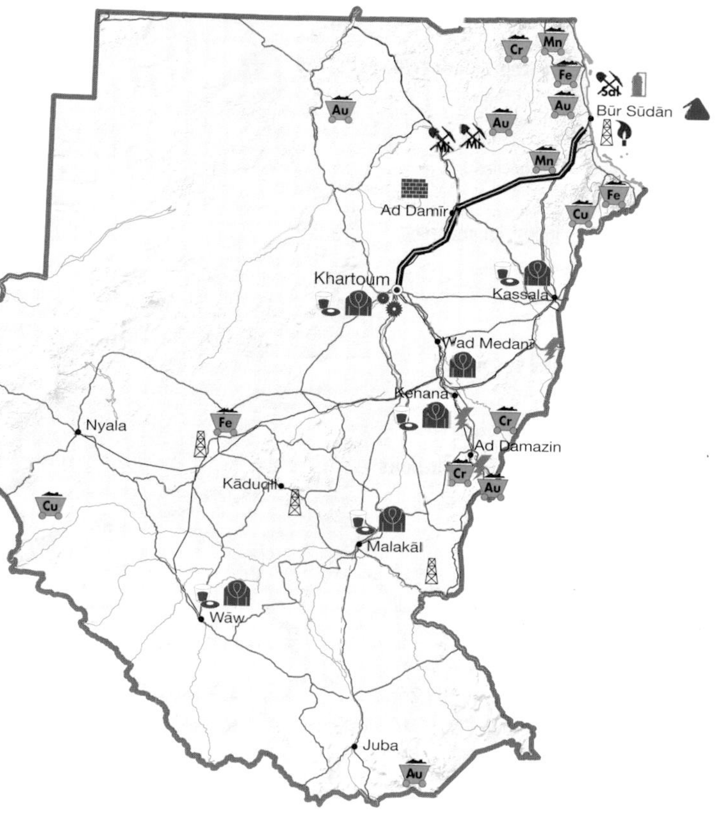

Non-energy source mineral resources
Metals
- Copper (unexploited)
- Chromite
- Iron ore (unexploited)
- Manganese
- Gold

Rocks and industrial minerals
- Mica
- Salt

Mineral fuel resources
- Natural gas
- Petroleum

Energy-related installations
- Hydroelectric power plant
- Refinery
- Oil pipeline

Manufacturing
- Food, beverages and tobacco
- Textiles, clothing, leather and footwear
- Chemical products
- Building materials, glass and cement
- Machinery and transport equipment

Forests and jungles 47% | Cropland 4% | Other 9%
Meadows and pastures 40%

AMERICA

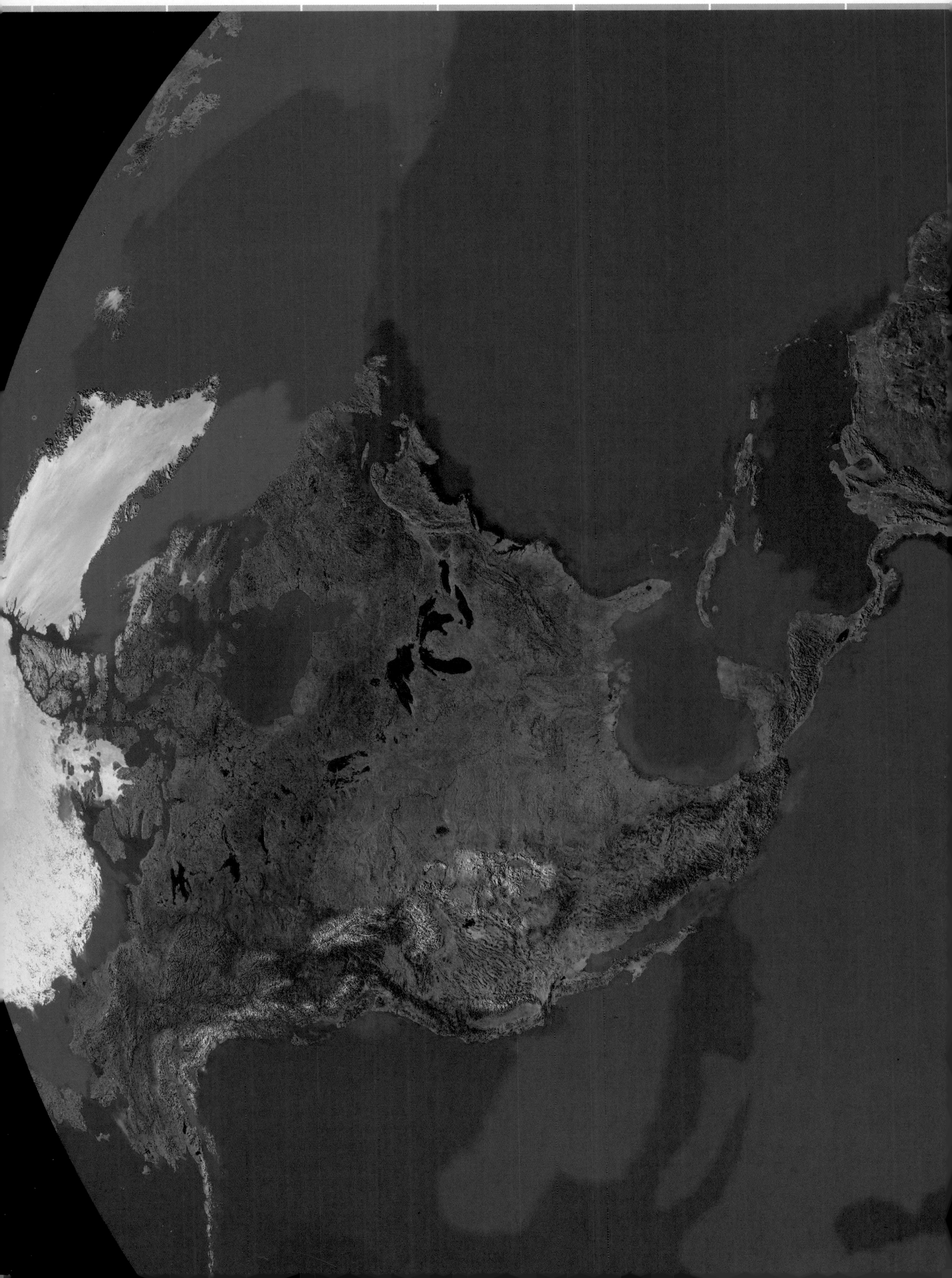

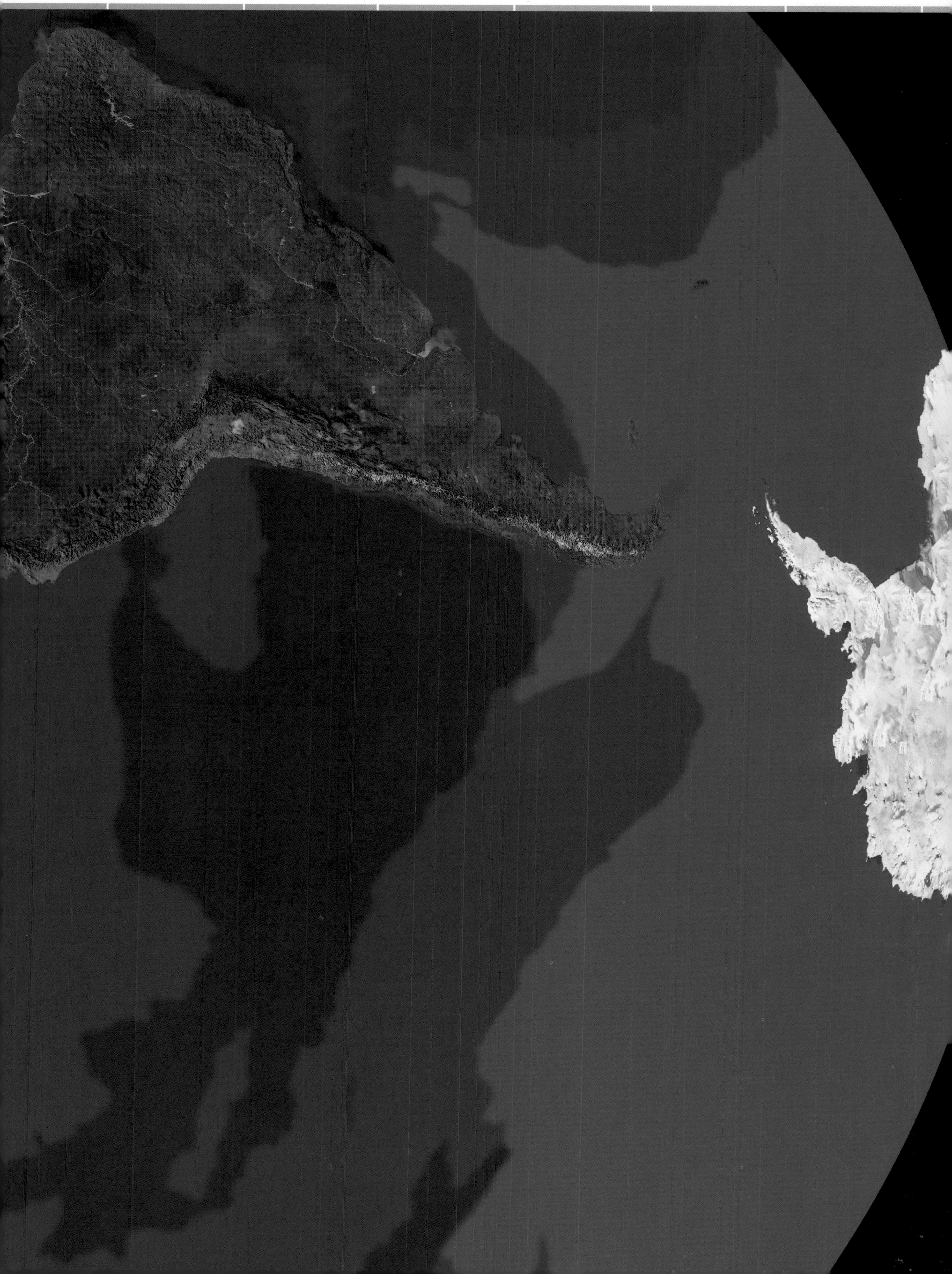

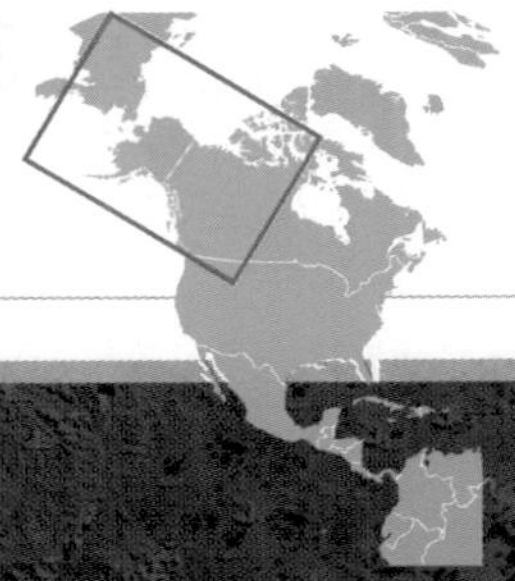

America
West of North America

Following the image from left to right, first, the northeastern tip of Asia, the Arctic Ocean and the icecap that covers its water, Alaska and the northeastern tip of Canada can be seen.
In Alaska, Bering Strait separates America from Asia and

acts as a passageway between the Pacific Ocean and the Arctic Ocean. Seward Peninsula marks the narrowest point of this passage; north of this are visible Kotzebue Sound and to the south, Norton Sound. In the far south, Alaska Peninsula stretches out into the Pacific by means of the Aleutian Islands. Toward the east is found the Gulf of Alaska, with a rugged coastline full of islands, like the Alexander Archipelago and Queen Charlotte Islands, in the far southeast of the gulf.

Inland, moving from west to east, the Great Bear, Great Slave and Athabasca Lakes can be seen. South of the first are found the Mackenzie Mountains. Following the coastline of the gulf, the Coast Mountains and farther inland, the beginning of the Rocky Mountains are visible.

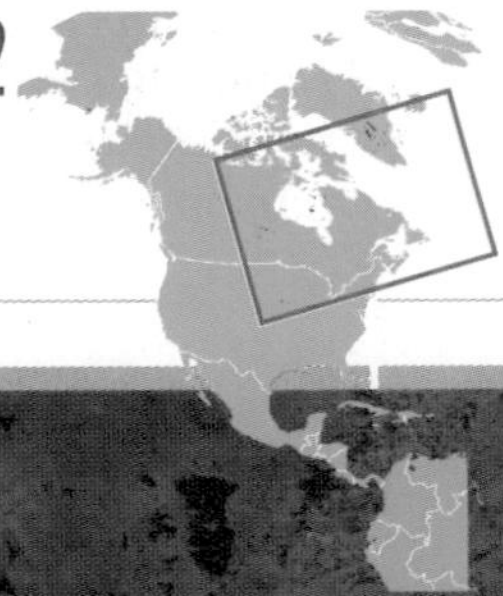

America

East of North America

This peculiar satellite image shows the capricious orography of the Canadian Northeast and the band bordering the United States, in the Great Lakes region. The intense green color of the image corresponds to the presence of rich forest

vegetation. The portion of land in the shape of an inverted triangle on the page on the right corresponds to Greenland, with a blue-white color that shows the areas covered by ice.
On the left page, Hudson Bay can be seen in the center of the image with its extension toward the south in James Bay. Hudson Strait communicates the Bay with the Sea of Labrador, the threshhold of the Atlantic Ocean. North of this strait, Baffin Island can be seen. On the east, the Labrador Peninsula and the island of Newfoundland. In the south, after the continental band is the Great Lakes region, with Lake Superior, the largest and the one with the northernmost location.

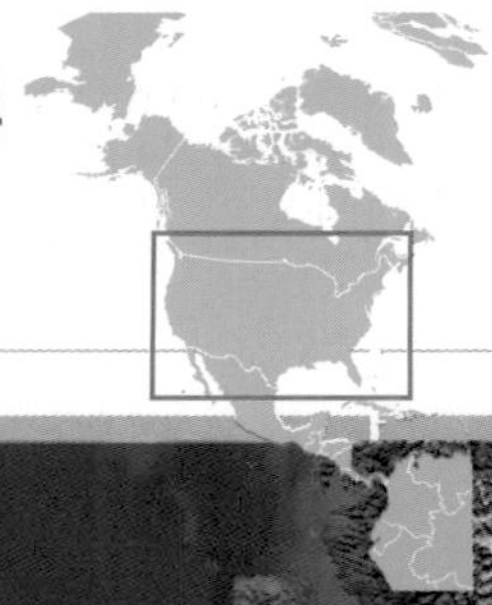

America
The United States

The west coast that can be seen in the image begins in southern Alaska and reaches to the peninsula of Baja California. From north to south can be seen, first, Vancouver Island, Mendocino Cape, the westernmost tip; Inner San Francisco Bay, and just before the very

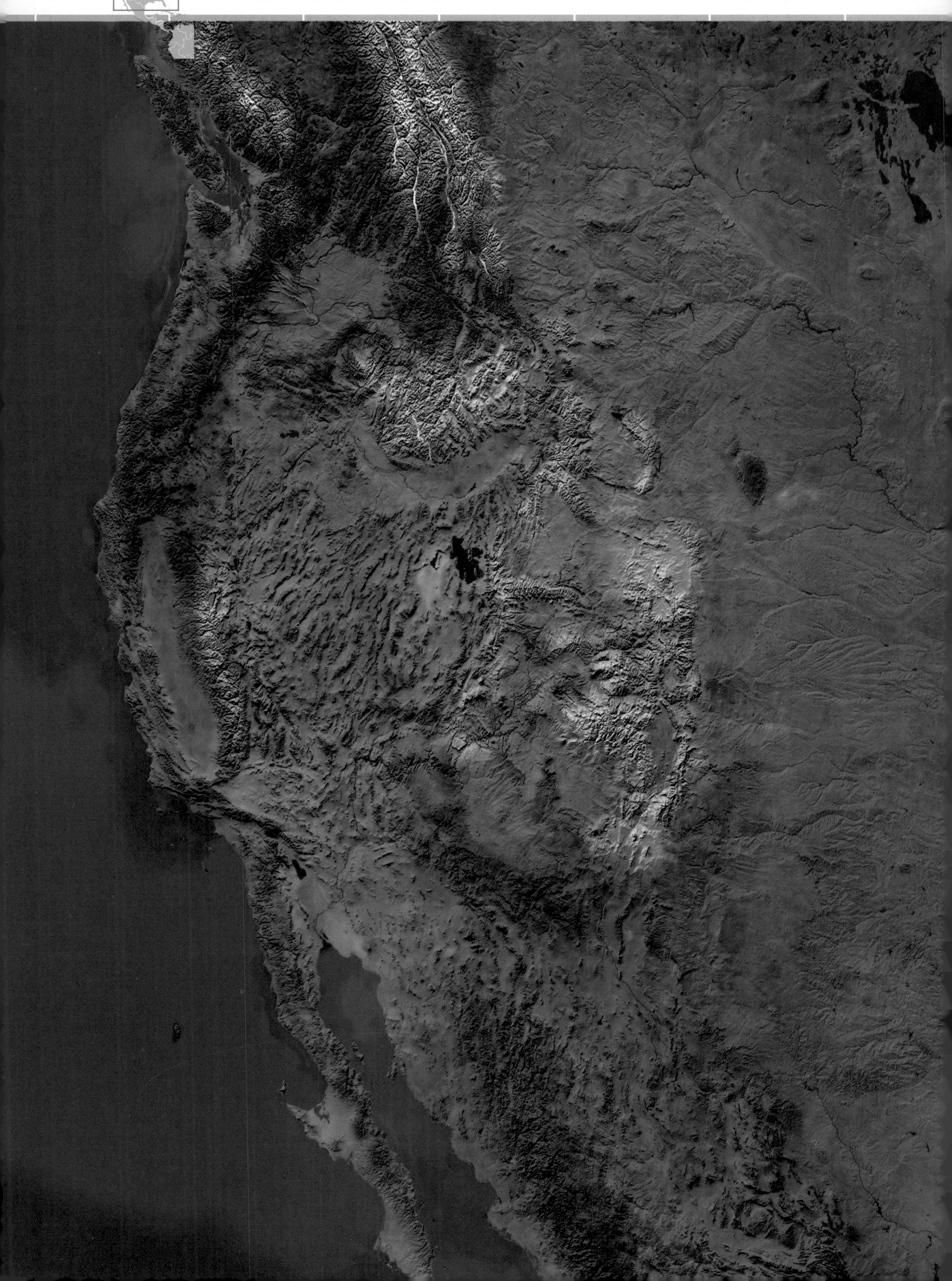

long peninsula of Baja California, Arguello Point can be seen. Inland, the Rocky Mountains are notable, very visible because of their white tones. West of that mountain chain is the Great Salt Lake and the desert of the same name, in an ocher color. Parallel to the coast and oriented in a north-south direction, are the Cascade Range and farther south, Sierra Nevada. The eastern zone is differentiated from the western regions because of its lower altitude and the number of rivers. In the north can be seen the Gulf of Saint Lawrence; to the south, Prince Edward Island and the peninsula of Nova Scotia. In the south, the peninsula of Florida, the Bahama Islands and the Gulf of Mexico are visible. In the center of this last, the delta of the Mississippi River can be seen.

America

Central America

The image shows in great detail the strip of land that separates the Pacific and Atlantic Oceans and which connects the continents of North and South America. In the east, the Bahama Islands and the Greater Antilles: Cuba, Jamaica, Hispaniola —where Haiti and

he Dominican Republic are located— and Puerto ico can be seen. On the continent the tip of the eninsula of Baja California and the Gulf of California re visible. To the east, in Mexican territory, the Sierra Madre Occidental can be seen parallel to the coast; to the south, the Sierra Madre del Sur. Between them Chapala Lake is notable, very near the city of Guadalajara. In the east is the Sierra Madre Oriental. Continuing toward the south, now in Central American territory, the Yucatan peninsula which closes the Gulf of Mexico in the south is prominent. In its final stretch, the strip of land narrows into the Isthmus of Panama, giving way to South America. At the very bottom of the image is the Galapagos Islands Archipelago, under the sovereignty of Ecuador.

America

North of South America

This is the northwestern region of South America in which the Amazon Basin is notable for the intensity of its green color. From the western mountains to the Atlantic Ocean extends this basin populated with innnumerable and varied vegetal and faunal

species that constitute one of the greatest natural reserves of mankind.
In the west, the Andes mountain range runs through the southern continent from north to south and forms a barrier in which many of its peaks exceed six thousand meters in altitude above sea level. In its northern sector are clearly distinguished, in the shape of a trident, the different alignments that form it: the Western, Central and Eastern mountain ranges.
On the northern coast, between the peninsula of La Guajira —on the left— and Paraguaná —right— is Lake Maracaibo, open in the north to the Gulf of Venezuela. Farther east, can be seen part of the Lesser Antilles, among which is notable, due to its size, the island of Trinidad, near the delta of the Orinocco River.

America

Center of South America

The peculiar shape of South America requires a partition that prevents us from seeing the imposing Andes Mountain Range in all its north-south length. In this image of the central zone the Andean elbow is visible, past which the range takes an almost

straight north-south direction and the different ranges that form this Andean colossus are clearly distinguished. Focusing attention on this elbow, a border zone between Peru, Bolivia and Chile, we see Lake Titicaca, of greater size, and Lake Poopó, this last located right on the Bolivian altiplano. Farther south, the turquoise-blue-colored area corresponds to the salt works of Coipasa and Uyuni. In the interior, in the center of the image, the Paraguay river can be seen oriented in a north-south direction. Farther east, the Paraná River is visible, and close to the lower cut-off point of the image, the confluence of both rivers. The tributaries of the Paraná, originating in the eastern ranges, are visible, interrupted by numerous dams and reservoirs.

America

South of South America

As we descend towards the south, the continent becomes narrower and the coastline more broken. The proximity of the Andes to the Pacific and the bioclimatic conditions of these latitudes provoke this peculiar aspect of the lands near Antarctica. At a

nedium height in the image, the island of Chiloé can e seen, apparent because of its size; on its southern order, the Boca de Guafo serves as a passageway to the Gulf of Corcovado; behind this last, the Archipelago of he Chonos is visible. The coast continues to the Great Island of Tierra del Fuego, separated from the continent by the Straits of Magellan. Small Staten Island finalizes this broken coastline of Tierrra del Fuego on the east. Further out in the Atlantic, the Falkland Islands and South Georgia Islands can be seen on the lower far right of the page. On the east coast, the Peninsula of Valdés, in the shape of a hammer, and the estuary of Río de la Plata at the mouth of the Paraná and Uruguay Rivers can be distinguished. Toward the north, Mirim and Patos Lakes are visible.

America
Digital terrain model

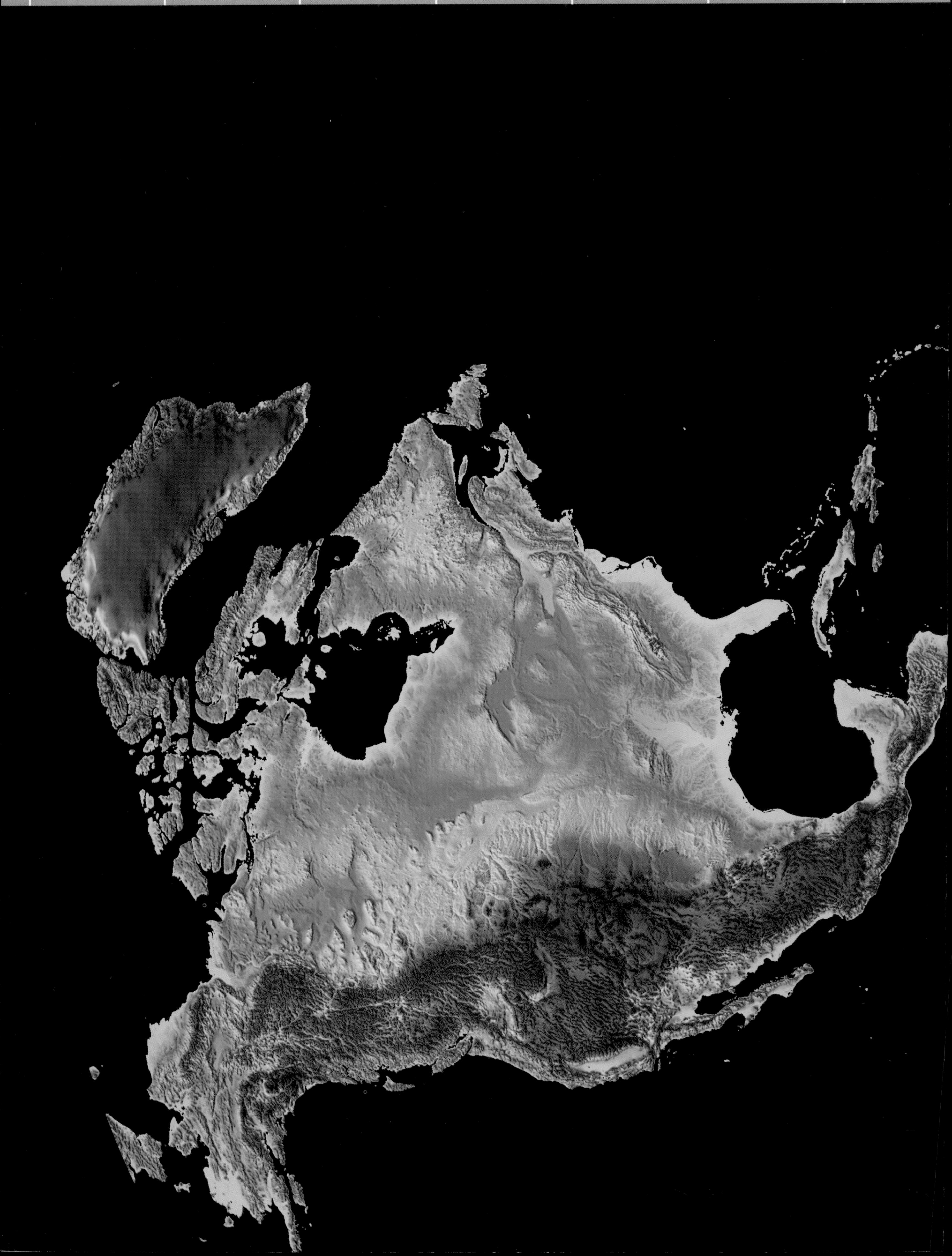

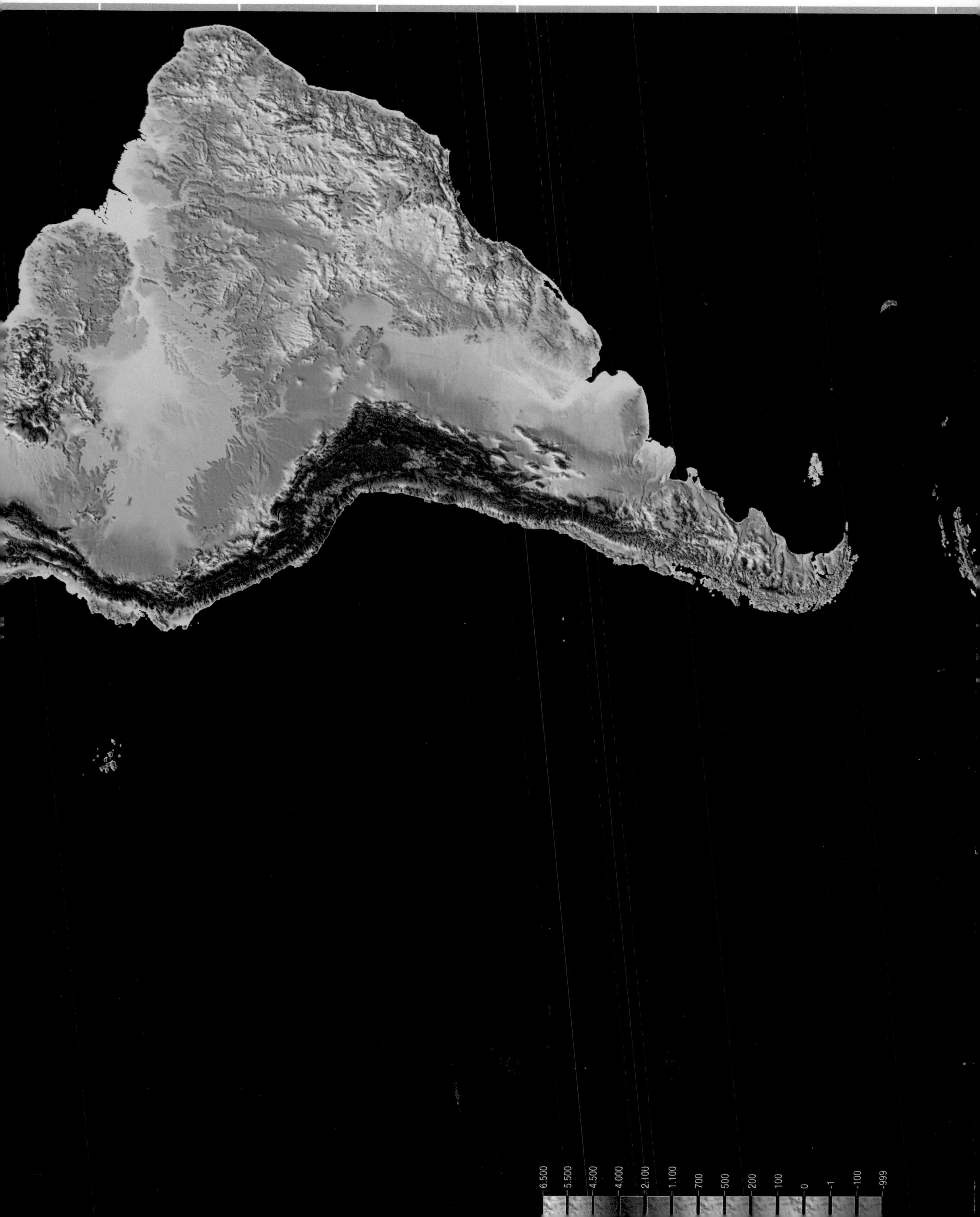
6.500
5.500
4.500
4.000
2.100
1.100
700
500
200
100
0
-1
-100
-999

North America
Digital terrain model

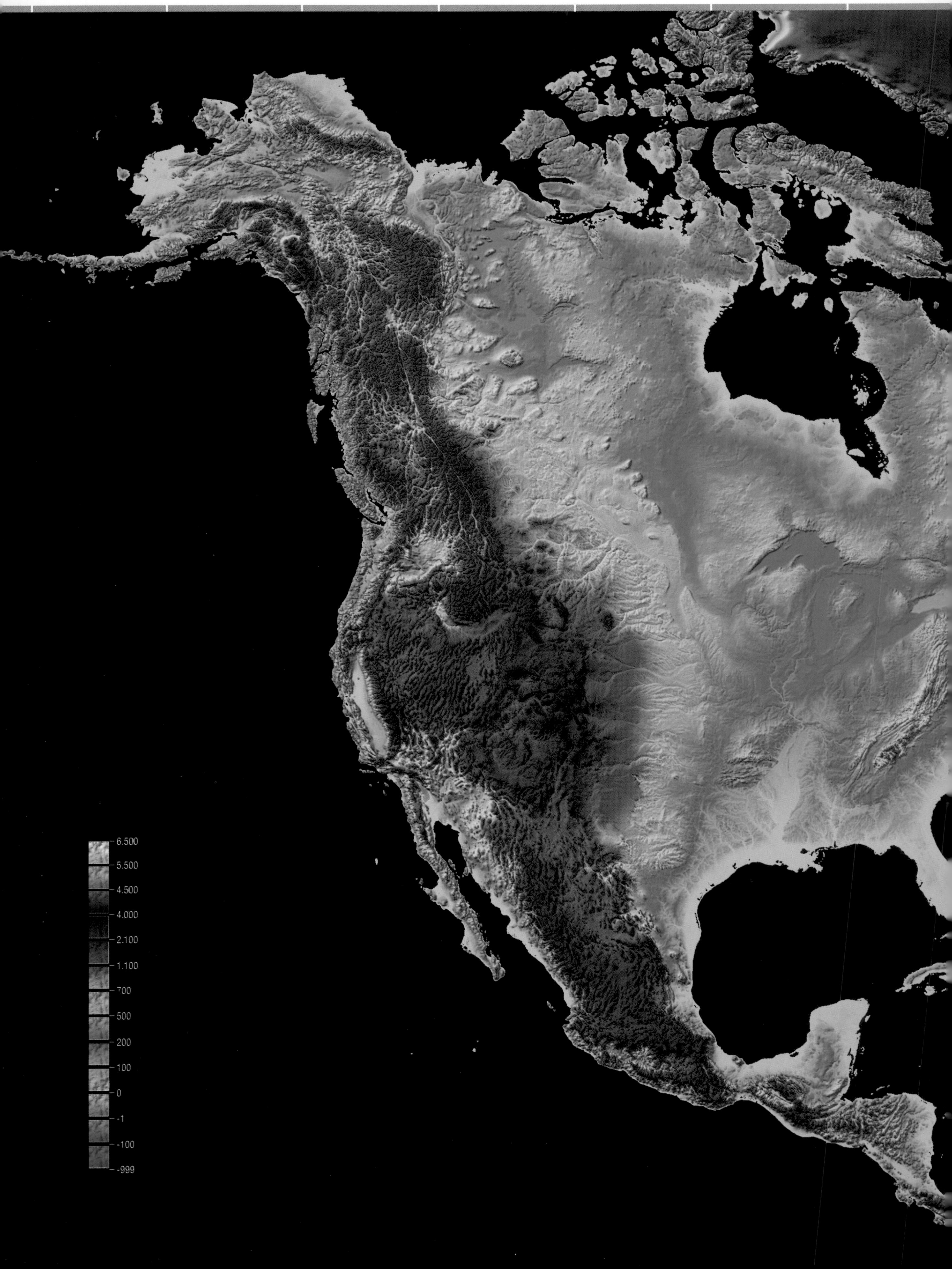

N
W
E
S
W
S
N
E
S
E
W
N

North America
Bathymetry

60°W
50°W
40°W
30°W
20°W
10°W
0°
Baffin Basin
Greenland-Iceland Basin
Iceland Basin
Reykjanes Ridge
Rockall Bank
Celtic Shelf
Labrador Basin
Charlie-Gibbs Fracture Zone
Mid-Atlantic Ridge
Açores-Gibraltar Ridge
Açores Plateau
Grand Bank
Newfoundland Basin
Newfoundland Ridge
30°N
Guyot Great
Meteor
Georges Bank
Kelvin Seamount
Yakutat Seamount
North American Basin
20°N
Blake Plateau
Blake Ridge
Mexico Basin
Bahama Basin
Campeche Bank
10°N
Puerto Rico Ridge
Cayman Trench
Venezuela Basin
Guiana Basin
Colombia Basin
America Trench
0°
atemala Basin
Cocos Ridge
Panama Basin
90°W
80°W
70°W
60°W
50°W
40°W

South America
Digital terrain model

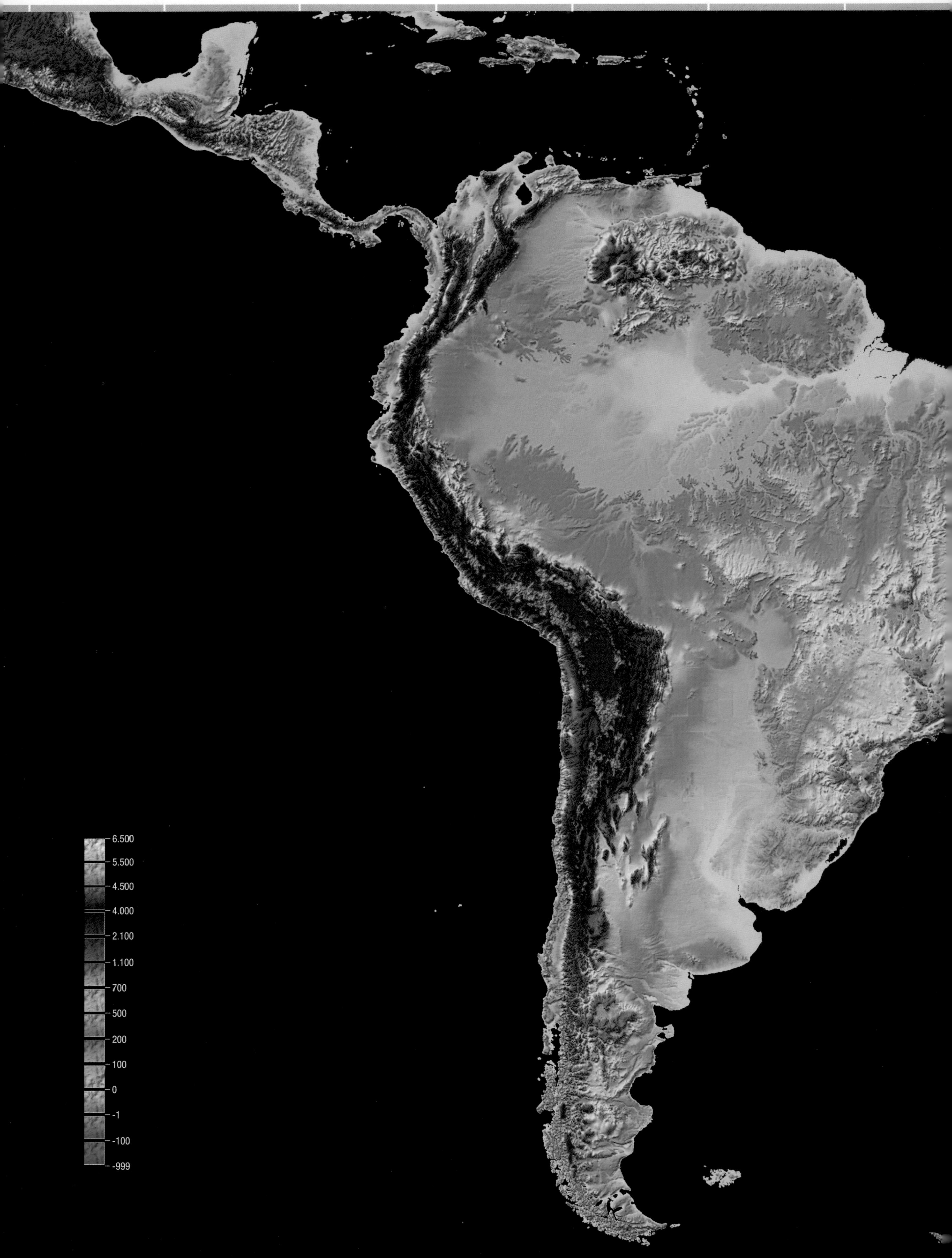

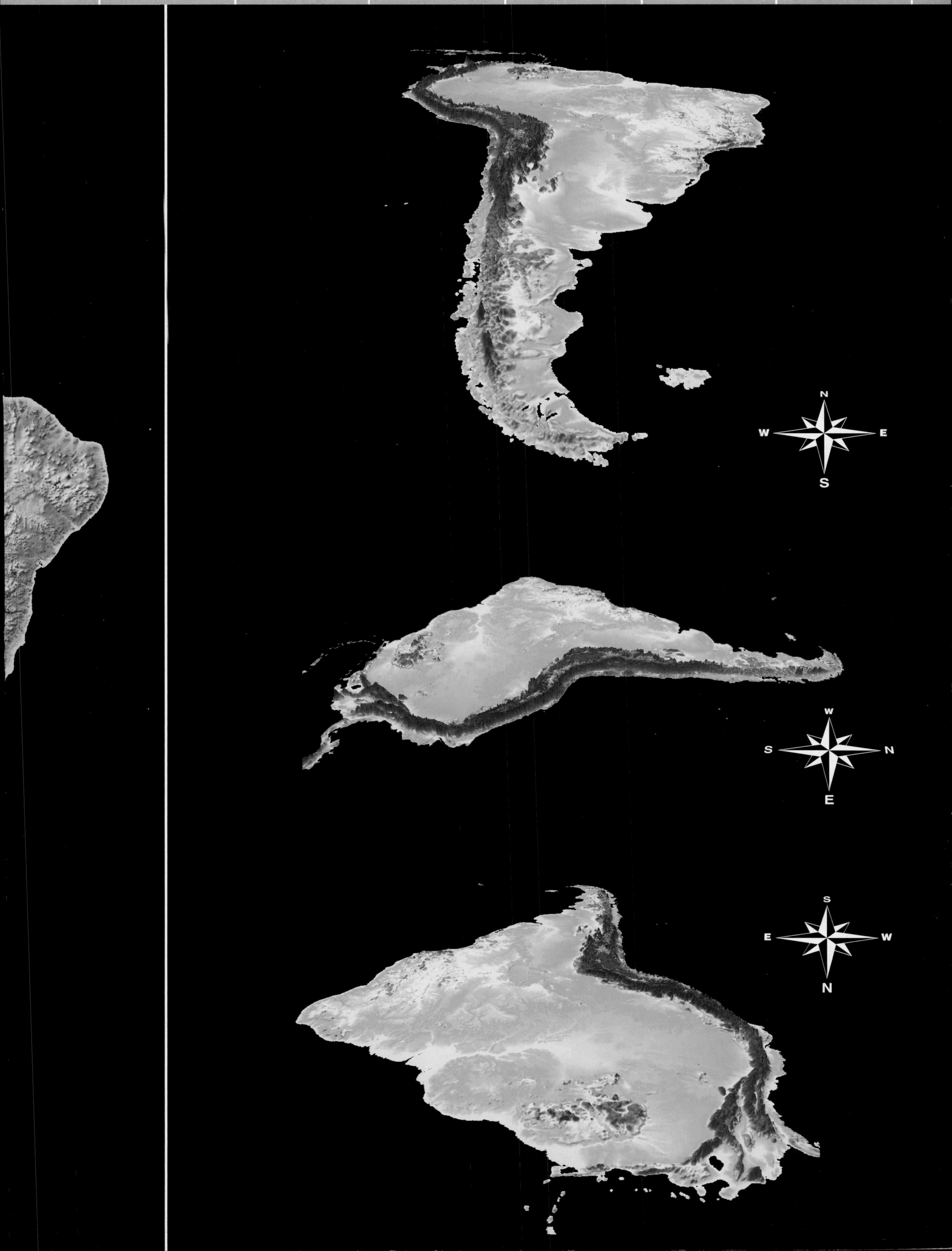
N
W
E
S
W
S
N
E
S
E
W
N

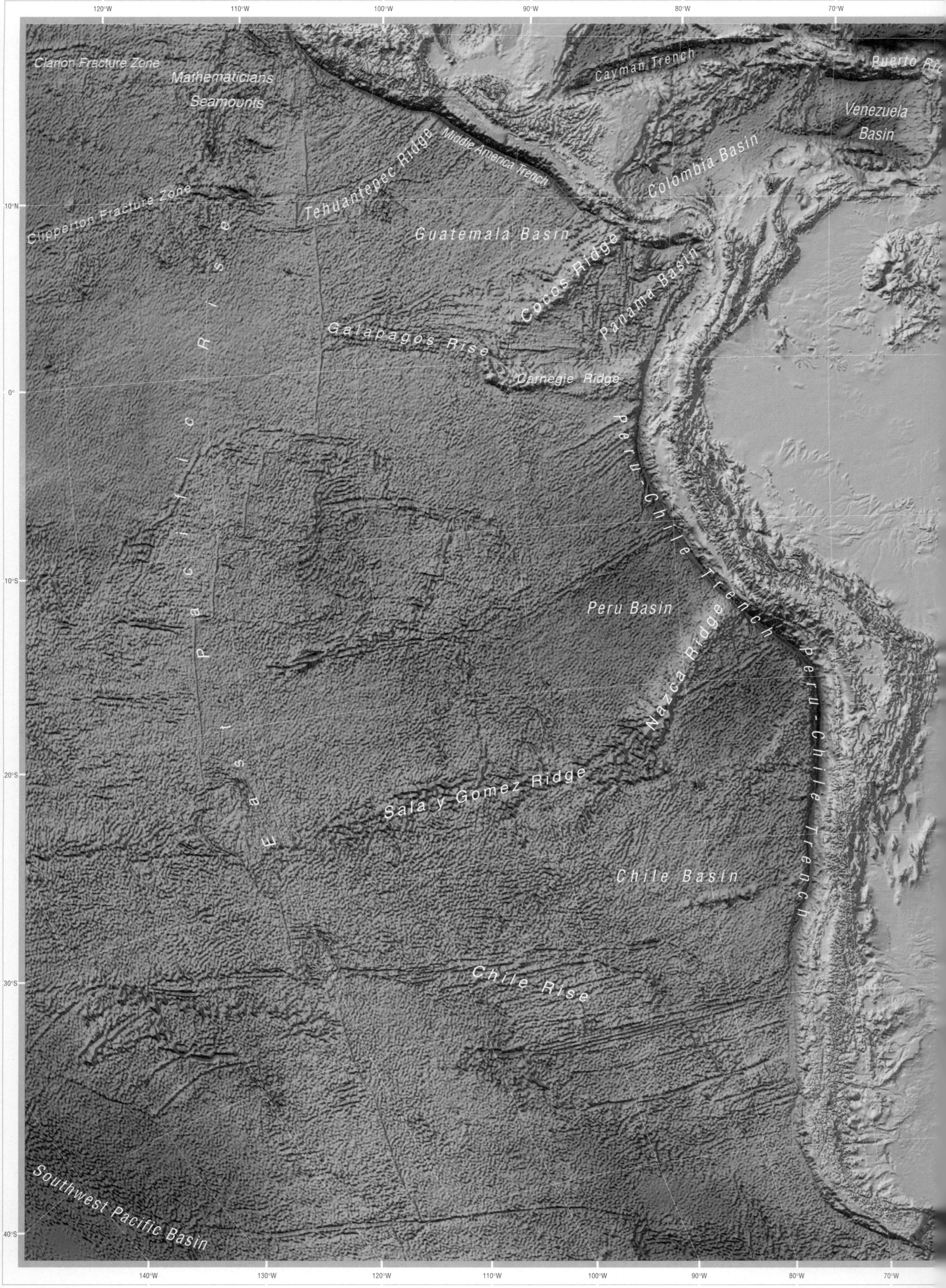

South America

Bathymetry

Clarion Fracture Zone
Mathematicians Seamounts
Cayman Trench
Puerto Ri
Venezuela Basin
Colombia Basin
Middle America Trench
Tehuantepec Ridge
Clipperton Fracture Zone
Guatemala Basin
Cocos Ridge
Panama Basin
Galapagos Rise
Carnegie Ridge
East Pacific Rise
Peru-Chile Trench
Peru Basin
Nazca Ridge
Sala y Gomez Ridge
Chile Basin
Chile Rise
Southwest Pacific Basin

Cape Verde Terrace
Atlantic Ridge
Cape Verde Basin
Guiana Basin
Sierra Leone Rise
Sierra Leone Basin
Romanche Fracture Zone
Guinea Basin
Brazil Basin
Mid-Atlantic Ridge
Angola Basin
Bromley Plateau
Walvis Ridge
Argentine Basin
Cape Basin
Falkland Plateau
Cape Rise
Bank
South Georgia Ridge
50°W
40°W
30°W
20°W
10°W
0°
10°N
10°S
20°S
30°S
40°S
10°E
20°E

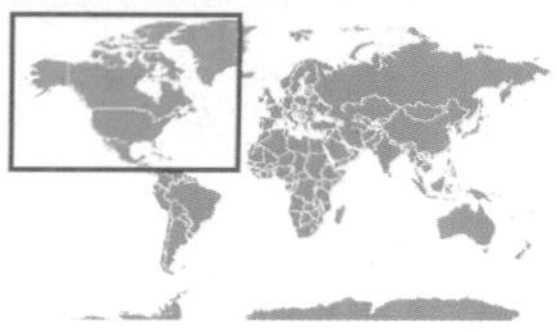

North and Central America
Physical map

South America
Physical map

Caribbean Sea
Greater Antilles
Lesser Antilles
La Española (Hispaniola)
Jamaica
Puerto Rico
Punta Gallinas
Pen. de Guajira
Pen. de Paraguaná
Golfo de Venezuela
Nevado de Sta. Marta
Lago de Maracaibo
Cordillera de Mérida
Cordillera de la Costa
Llanos del Orinoco
Orinoco
Apure
Capanaparo
Punta Barima
Golfo de los Mosquitos
Panama Canal
Península de Azuero
Gulf of Panama
Cabo Corrientes
Bahía de Buenaventura
Cordillera Occidental
Cordillera Central
Cordillera Oriental
Cabo Manglares
Cabo San Francisco
Bahía de Manta
La Puntilla
Golfo de Guayaquil
Punta Pariñas
Punta Aguja
Guiana Highlands
Serra Pacaraima
Serra Parima
Montes Curupira
Serra Tumucumaque
Cabo Orange
Cabo do Norte
Araguari
Baía de Marajó
Cabo Gurupi
Baía de São Marcos
Equator
Amazon
AMAZON BASIN
Negro
Japurá
Putumayo
Napo
Marañón
Ucayali
Juruá
Purus
Madeira
Tapajós
Xingu
Tocantins
Araguaia
Cabo de São Roque
Serra do Cachimbo
Serra Formosa
Sa dos Gradaús
Sa da Ibiapaba
Planalto da Borborema
Serra da Tabatinga
São Francisco
Represa de Sobradinho
Ponta do Manguinho
Cord. Huamaní
CORDILLERA DE LOS ANDES
Cordillera Occidental
Cordillera Oriental
Cordillera Real
Cord. de Carabaya
Altiplano
Punta Chilca
Península de Paracas
Punta Parada
Punta Coles
Madre de Dios
Beni
Las Yungas
Llanos de Mojos
Llanos de Guarayos
Chapada dos Parecis
Planalto do Mato Grosso
Llanos de Chiquitos
Serra do Roncador
Sa do Caiapó
Serra de Maracaju
Serra Geral de Goiás
Chapada Diamantina
Cabo Santo Antonio
Baía de Todos os Santos
Brazilian Highlands
Serra do Espinhaço
Serra da Mantiqueira
Ponta da Baleia
Ponta de Monsarás
Cabo de São Tomé
Cabo Frio
Ponta de Juatinga
Tropic of Capricorn
Gran Chaco
Pilcomayo
Bermejo
Paraná
Paranapanema
Sa de Paranapiacaba
Serra do Mar
Serra Geral
Uruguay
Cabo de Santa Marta Grande
Lagoa dos Patos
Lagoa Mirim
Cuchilla Grande
Cabo Polonia
Mesopotamia
Laguna Mar Chiquita
Sierra de Córdoba
Salado
Aconcagua
Pampa
Río de la Plata
Cabo San Antonio
Colorado
Negro
Bahía de Anegada
Golfo San Matías
Meseta de Somuncurá
Península Valdés
Punta Ninfas
Punta Tetas
Desierto de Atacama
Cordillera Domeyko
Cabo Bascuñán
Punta Lavapié
Isla Grande de Chiloé
Golfo Corcovado
Archipiélago de los Chonos
Península de Taitao
Golfo de Penas
Cabo Dos Bahías
Golfo de San Jorge
Cabo Tres Puntas
Punta Medanosa
Gran Altiplanicie Central
Patagonia
Bahía Grande
Archipiélago Reina Adelaida
Falkland Islands (Islas Malvinas)
Isla Grande de Tierra de Fuego
Cabo de Hornos (Cape Horn)
PACIFIC OCEAN
ATLANTIC OCEAN
20°N
10°N
0°
10°S
20°S
30°S
40°S
50°S
80°W
70°W
60°W
50°W
40°W
100°W
90°W
30°W
20°W

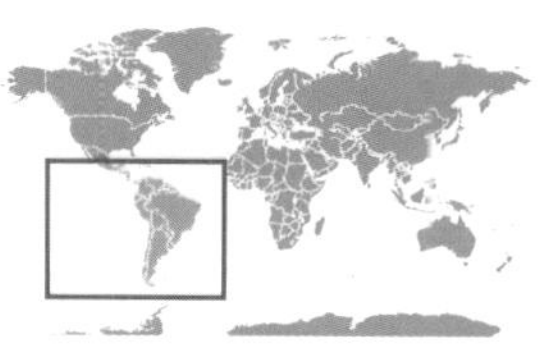

America
Northwest USA

110°W
108°W
106°W
104°W
102°W
100°W
98°W
96°W
94°W
50°N
48°N
46°N
44°N
42°N
40°N
38°N
SASKATCHEWAN
MANITOBA
ONTARIO
MINNESOTA
NORTH DAKOTA
SOUTH DAKOTA
MONTANA
WYOMING
NEBRASKA
COLORADO
KANSAS
C A N A D A
U N I T E D S T A T E S
G R E A T P L A I N S
R O C K Y M O U N T A I N S
CENTRAL LOWLAND
Saskatoon
Regina
Winnipeg
Brandon
Moose Jaw
Swift Current
Yorkton
Great Sand Hills
Cypress Hills
Missouri Coteau
Touchwood Hills
Duck Mt.
Riding Mt.
Manitoba Escarpment
Moose Mt.
LAKE WINNIPEGOSIS
LAKE MANITOBA
LAKE WINNIPEG
Lake of the Woods
Souris Plain
Plateau du Coteau du Missouri
Williston Basin
Lake Sakakawea
Fort Peck Lake
Missouri Plateau
Bearpaw Mts.
Judith Mts.
Riding Mt.
BADLANDS
Black Hills
Rapid City
Bismarck
Mandan
Fargo
Grand Forks
Minot
Williston
Jamestown
Devils Lake
Red River Valley
Aberdeen
Pierre
Sioux Falls
Lake Oahe
Coteau des Prairies
Sioux City
Billings
Big Horn Basin
Big Horn Mountains
Shoshone Basin
Wind River Range
GREAT DIVIDE
Red Desert
BASIN
Laramie Range
Casper
Cheyenne
Rock Springs
Pine Ridge
SAND HILLS
North Platte
Lincoln
Kearney
Grand Island
Scottsbluff
Park Range
Front Range
Sawatch Range
ROAN PLATEAU
Book Cliffs
Denver
Aurora
Lakewood
Boulder
Fort Collins
Greeley
Colorado Springs
Pueblo
Grand Junction
Smoky Hills
Salina
Wichita
Garden City
Hutchinson

America
Southwest USA

0 50 100 150 200 250 km
0 20 40 60 80 100 120 140 miles

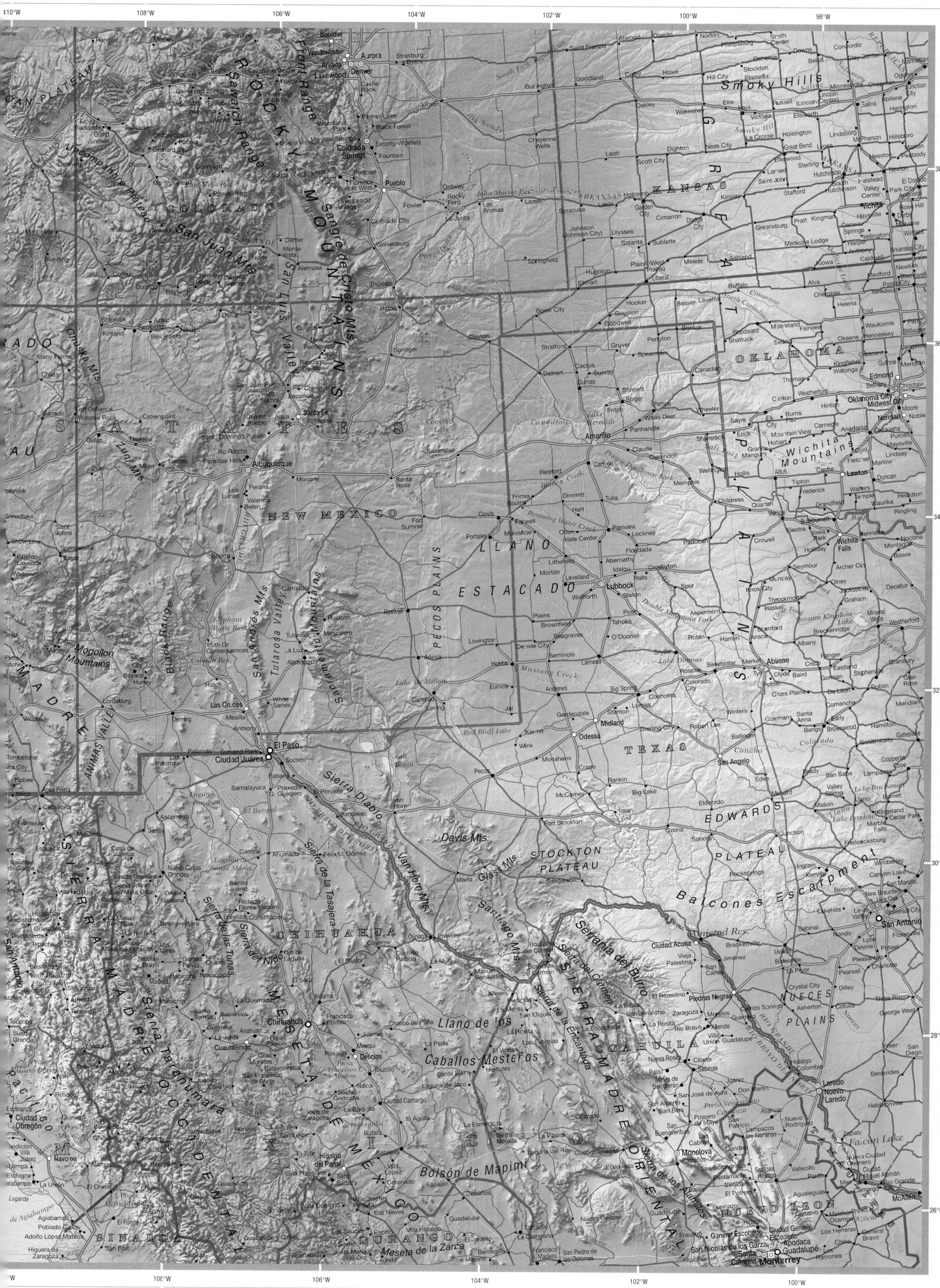
110°W
108°W
106°W
104°W
102°W
100°W
98°W
38°N
36°N
34°N
32°N
30°N
28°N
26°N
ROCKY MOUNTAINS
Sawatch Range
Front Range
Sangre de Cristo Mts.
San Juan Mts.
San Luis Valley
Uncompahgre Plateau
COLORADO
Denver
Boulder
Aurora
Colorado Springs
Pueblo
Smoky Hills
GREAT PLAINS
KANSAS
Wichita
Salina
OKLAHOMA
Oklahoma City
Wichita Mountains
Amarillo
Lubbock
LLANO ESTACADO
PECOS PLAINS
NEW MEXICO
Albuquerque
Santa Fe
Las Cruces
Roswell
Chuska Mts.
Zuni Mts.
Mogollon Mountains
Black Range
San Andres Mts.
Tularosa Valley
Sacramento Mountains
El Paso
Ciudad Juárez
Midland
Odessa
San Angelo
Abilene
TEXAS
EDWARDS PLATEAU
STOCKTON PLATEAU
Balcones Escarpment
Davis Mts.
Glass Mts.
San Antonio
Laredo
Nuevo Laredo
NUECES PLAINS
Sierra Diablo
Van Horn Mts.
Santiago Mts.
CHIHUAHUA
Chihuahua
Llano de los Caballos Mesteños
Bolsón de Mapimí
MESETA DE MÉXICO
SIERRA MADRE OCCIDENTAL
Sierra Tarahumara
SIERRA MADRE ORIENTAL
Serranía del Burro
COAHUILA
Monclova
NUEVO LEON
Monterrey
DURANGO
Meseta de la Zarca
SINALOA
Ciudad Obregón
Navojoa
Hidalgo del Parral
Delicias
Cuauhtémoc

America
Southeast USA

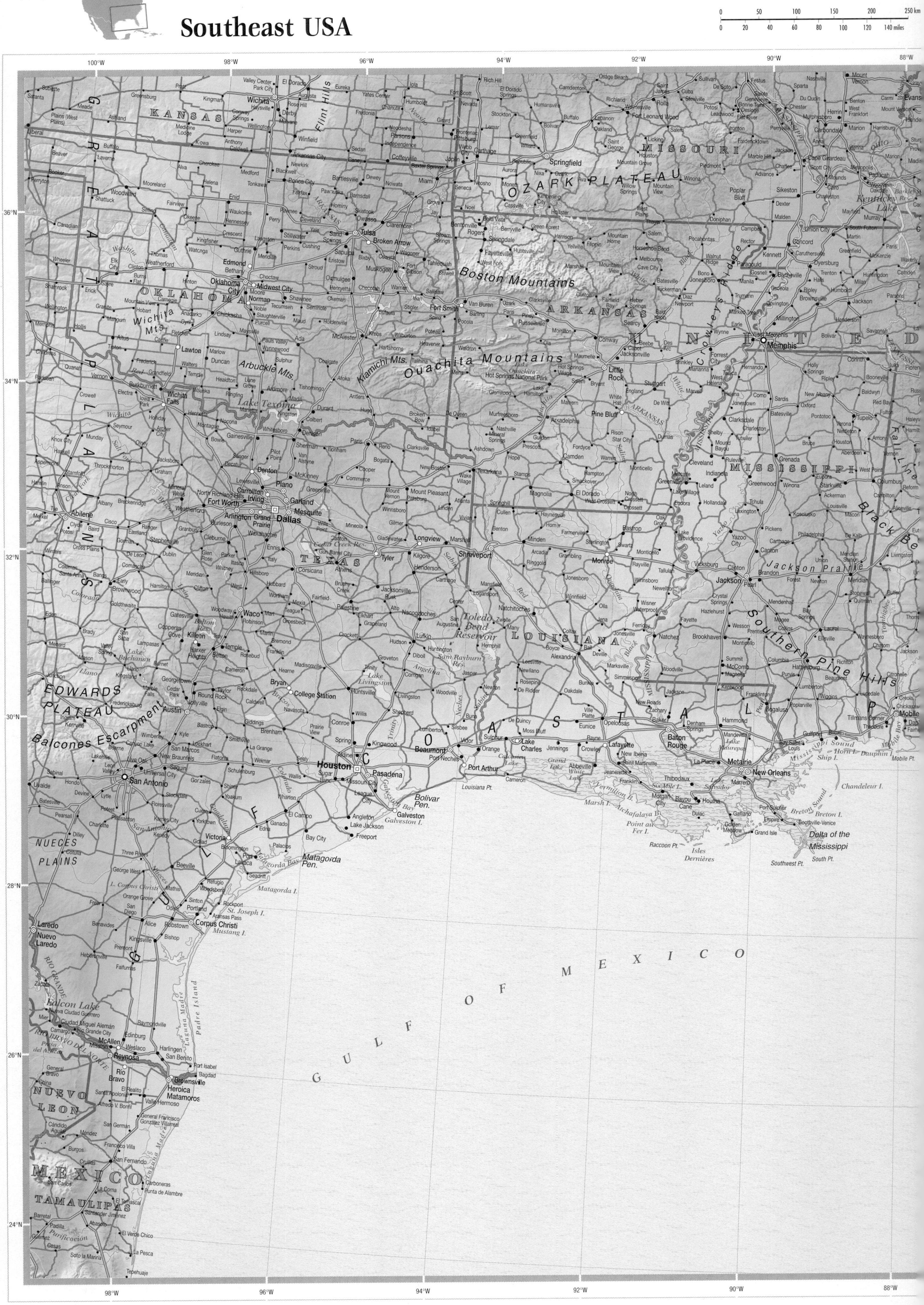

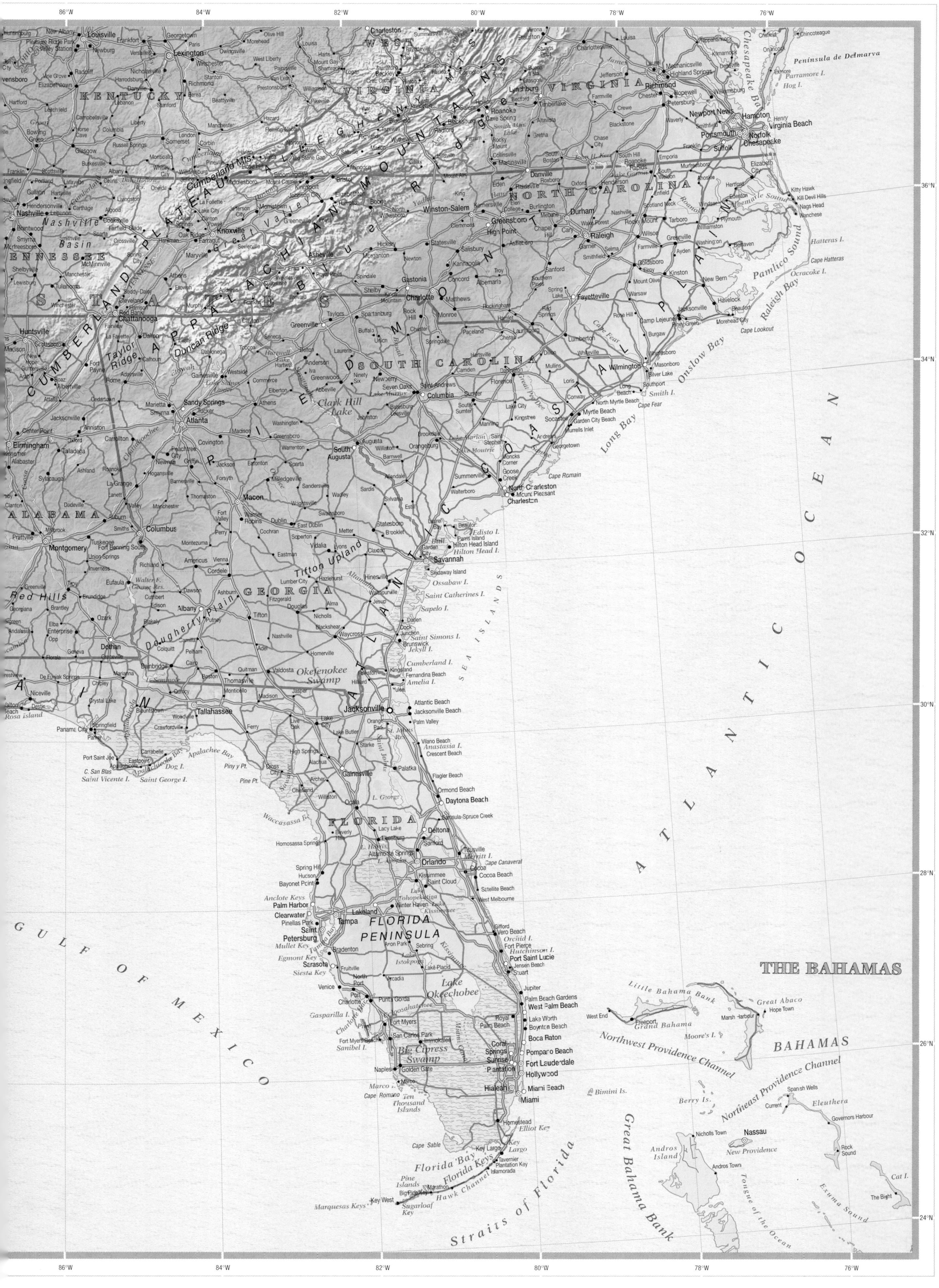

86°W
84°W
82°W
80°W
78°W
76°W
36°N
34°N
32°N
30°N
28°N
26°N
24°N
KENTUCKY
VIRGINIA
WEST VIRGINIA
NORTH CAROLINA
SOUTH CAROLINA
GEORGIA
ALABAMA
FLORIDA
TENNESSEE
UNITED STATES
CUMBERLAND PLATEAU
APPALACHIAN MOUNTAINS
ALLEGHENY MTS
Blue Ridge
PIEDMONT
ATLANTIC COASTAL PLAIN
Great Valley
Nashville Basin
Cumberland Mts.
Taylor Ridge
Duncan Ridge
Tifton Upland
Dougherty Plain
Red Hills
Okefenokee Swamp
Clark Hill Lake
SEA ISLANDS
FLORIDA PENINSULA
Lake Okeechobee
Big Cypress Swamp
Ten Thousand Islands
Florida Bay
Florida Keys
Straits of Florida
GULF OF MEXICO
ATLANTIC OCEAN
THE BAHAMAS
BAHAMAS
Little Bahama Bank
Great Bahama Bank
Grand Bahama
Great Abaco
Northwest Providence Channel
Northeast Providence Channel
Tongue of the Ocean
Exuma Sound
Andros Island
New Providence
Eleuthera
Berry Is.
Bimini Is.
Cat I.
Freeport
Nassau
Chesapeake Bay
Peninsula de Delmarva
Albemarle Sound
Pamlico Sound
Raleigh Bay
Onslow Bay
Long Bay
Cape Hatteras
Cape Lookout
Cape Fear
Cape Romain
Cape Canaveral
Cape Sable
Apalachee Bay
Louisville
Lexington
Knoxville
Chattanooga
Nashville
Huntsville
Birmingham
Montgomery
Columbus
Atlanta
Macon
Augusta
Savannah
Charleston
North Charleston
Columbia
Charlotte
Greensboro
Winston-Salem
Durham
Raleigh
Fayetteville
Wilmington
Richmond
Norfolk
Virginia Beach
Chesapeake
Newport News
Hampton
Portsmouth
Roanoke
Lynchburg
Asheville
Greenville
Spartanburg
Myrtle Beach
Jacksonville
Tallahassee
Gainesville
Ocala
Daytona Beach
Orlando
Tampa
Saint Petersburg
Clearwater
Lakeland
Sarasota
Fort Myers
Naples
Palm Beach Gardens
West Palm Beach
Boca Raton
Fort Lauderdale
Hollywood
Hialeah
Miami
Miami Beach
Homestead
Key Largo
Key West
Panama City
Albany
Dothan
Valdosta
Brunswick
Hilton Head Island

America

Northern South America

0 100 200 300 400 500 Km
0 40 80 120 140 180 200 220 miles

ATLANTIC OCEAN
BARBADOS
BRIDGETOWN
THE GRENADINES
TRINIDAD AND TOBAGO
GUYANA
GEORGETOWN
SURINAME
PARAMARIBO
French Guyana
Cayenne
Kourou
Serra Tumucumaque
Kamoa Mts.
Serra Iricoumé
Eilerts de Haan
Boa Vista
Macapá
Planalto Maracanaguará
Belém
São Luís
Santarém
Manaus
Teresina
Marabá
Imperatriz
Serra do Tapará
Serra dos Carajás
Serra das Cordilheiras
Serra das Alpercatas
Serra do Tiracambu
Serra do Cachimbo
Serra Formosa
Serra dos Apiacás
Serra do Tombador
Chapada dos Parecis
Serra do Roncador
Serra Geral de Goiás
Serra do Penitente
Serra do Uruçuí
Serra da Tabatinga
Serra Dois Irmãos
Serra da Ibiapaba
Chapada Diamantina
BRAZILIAN HIGLANDS
Itaituba
Parnaíba
Petrolina
Juazeiro
Barreiras
Vitória da Conquista
10°N
5°N
0°
5°S
10°S
60°W
55°W
50°W
45°W

America

Central South America

0 100 200 300 400 500 km
0 40 80 120 140 180 200 220 miles

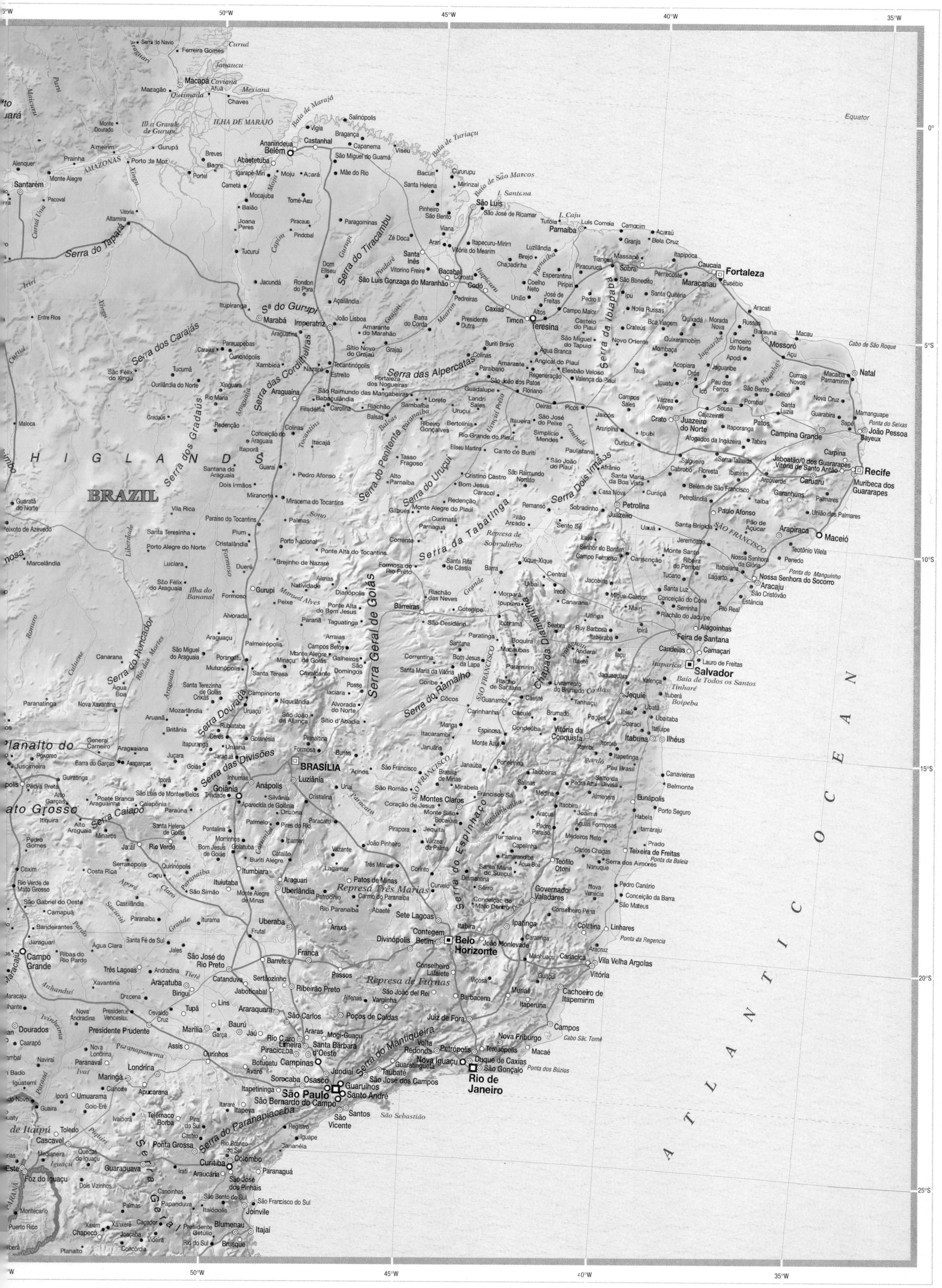
50°W
45°W
40°W
35°W
0°
5°S
10°S
15°S
20°S
25°S
Equator
BRAZIL
H I G H L A N D S
A T L A N T I C   O C E A N
ILHA DE MARAJÓ
AMAZONAS
Macapá
Belém
Santarém
São Luís
Fortaleza
Teresina
Natal
João Pessoa
Recife
Maceió
Aracaju
Salvador
BRASÍLIA
Goiânia
Belo Horizonte
Vitória
Rio de Janeiro
São Paulo
Curitiba
Campo Grande
Campina Grande
Feira de Santana
Petrolina
Juazeiro
Montes Claros
Uberlândia
Uberaba
Campinas
Santos
Londrina
Maringá
Florianópolis
Joinvile
Blumenau
Foz do Iguaçu
Marabá
Imperatriz
Mossoró
Caruaru
Ilhéus
Vitória da Conquista
Juiz de Fora
Serra do Tapajós
Serra dos Carajás
Serra das Cordilheiras
Serra do Tiracambu
Serra das Alpercatas
Serra da Ibiapaba
Serra Geral de Goiás
Serra da Tabatinga
Serra do Espinhaço
Serra do Mar
Serra da Mantiqueira
Serra do Paranapiacaba
Serra Geral
Serra Dourada
Serra das Divisões
Serra Caiapó
Serra do Roncador
Serra dos Gradaús
Serra do Penitente
Serra do Uruçuí
Serra Dois Irmãos
Serra do Ramalho
Chapada Diamantina
Represa de Sobradinho
Represa Três Marias
Represa de Furnas
Planalto do Mato Grosso
Baía de Todos os Santos
Baía de Marajó
Baía de São Marcos
Cabo de São Roque
Cabo São Tomé
Ilha do Bananal
SÃO FRANCISCO

America

Southern South America

0 100 200 300 400 500 Km
0 40 80 120 140 180 200 220 miles

85°W 80°W 75°W 70°W 65°W

25°S 30°S 35°S 40°S 45°S 50°S

P A C I F I C O C E A N

CHILE

ARGENTINA

CORDILLERA DE LOS ANDES

SANTIAGO

Copiapó
Huasco
La Serena
Coquimbo
Ovalle
Viña del Mar
Valparaíso
San Antonio
Rancagua
Talca
Talcahuano
Concepción
Chillán
Los Ángeles
Temuco
Valdivia
Osorno
Puerto Montt
San Carlos de Bariloche
Castro
Ancud
Golfo Corcovado
Golfo de Penas
Península de Taitao
Península Skyring
Estrecho de Magallanes
Punta Arenas
Península Brunswick
Península Brecknock
Cordillera Darwin
Península Hardy
Península de Mitre
Isla Grande de Tierra del Fuego
Río Gallegos
Comodoro Rivadavia
Golfo de San Jorge
Gran Bajo de San Julián
Bahía Grande
Gran Altiplanicie Central
Meseta de Montemayor
Meseta de Somuncurá
Altiplanicie del Payún
Altiplanicie de Hakelhuincul
Bajo de Santa Rosa
Neuquén
General Roca
San Rafael
Mendoza
San Juan
La Rioja
Catamarca
San Luis
Trelew
Puerto Madryn
Falso Cabo de Hornos
Cabo de Hornos

95°W 90°W 85°W 80°W 75°W 70°W

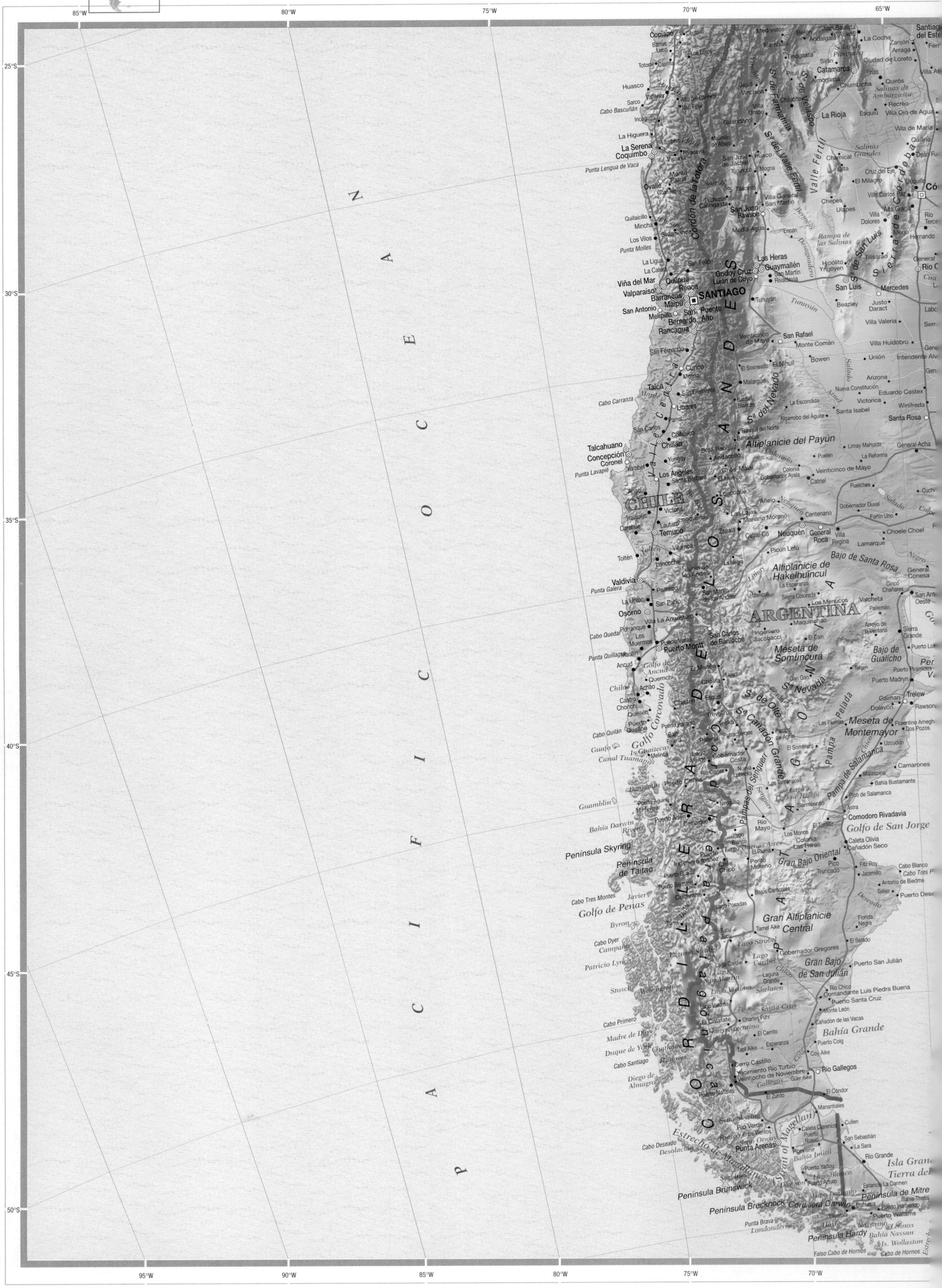

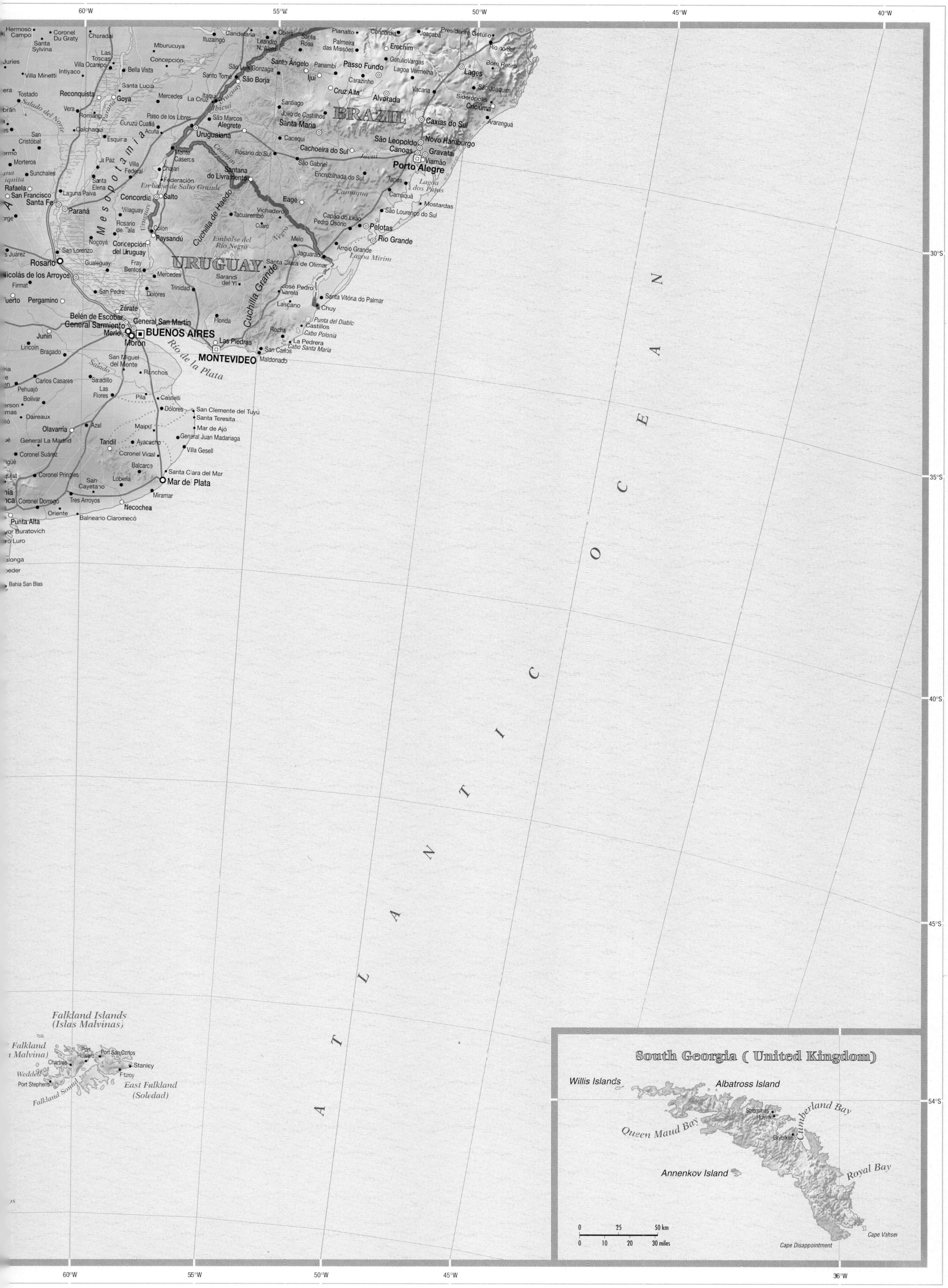

60°W
55°W
50°W
45°W
40°W
36°W
30°S
35°S
40°S
45°S
54°S
BRAZIL
URUGUAY
A T L A N T I C O C E A N
BUENOS AIRES
MONTEVIDEO
Porto Alegre
Caxias do Sul
Novo Hamburgo
São Leopoldo
Canoas
Gravataí
Viamão
Pelotas
Rio Grande
Lagoa dos Patos
Lagoa Mirim
Santa Maria
Passo Fundo
Erechim
Lages
Criciúma
Araranguá
Uruguaiana
Alegrete
São Borja
Santana do Livramento
Bagé
Rivera
Tacuarembó
Melo
Paysandú
Salto
Concordia
Paraná
Santa Fe
Rosario
San Nicolás de los Arroyos
Pergamino
Zárate
Belén de Escobar
General San Martín
General Sarmiento
Merlo
Morón
Río de la Plata
Las Piedras
Maldonado
Punta del Diablo
Chuy
Cuchilla Grande
Cuchilla de Haedo
Embalse del Río Negro
Mesopotamia
Salado
Carlos Casares
Olavarría
Tandil
Azul
Dolores
San Clemente del Tuyú
Mar del Plata
Necochea
Miramar
Tres Arroyos
Coronel Dorrego
Punta Alta
Bahía San Blas
Falkland Islands (Islas Malvinas)
Stanley
East Falkland (Soledad)
Falkland Sound
Port Howard
Port San Carlos
Fitzroy
Chartres
Port Stephens
South Georgia (United Kingdom)
Willis Islands
Albatross Island
Cumberland Bay
Queen Maud Bay
Annenkov Island
Royal Bay
Grytviken
Cape Disappointment
Cape Vahsel
0 25 50 km
0 10 20 30 miles

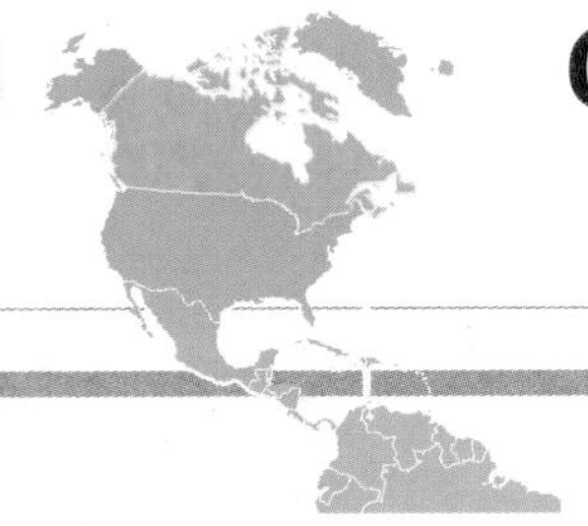

Canada

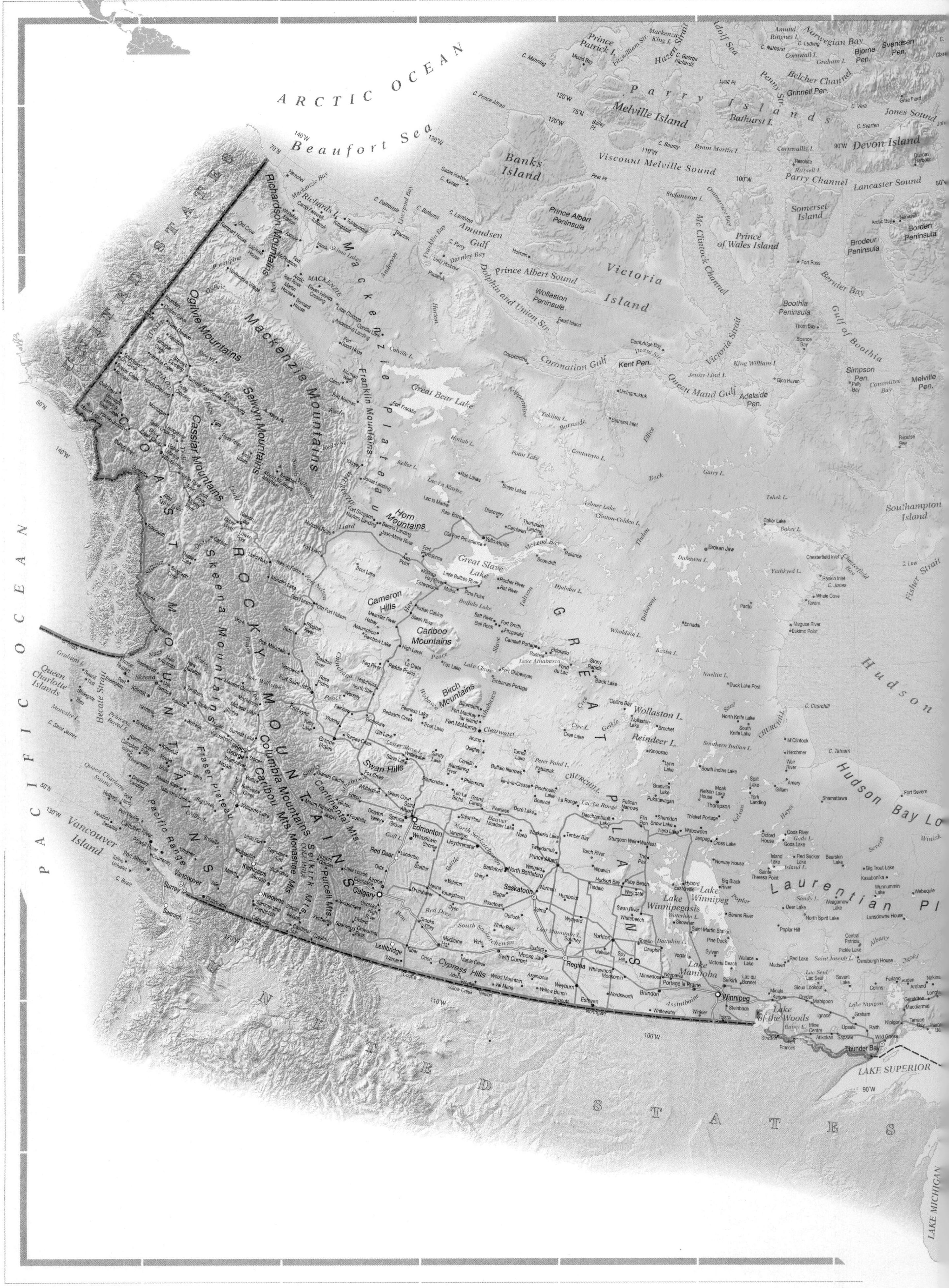
ARCTIC OCEAN
Beaufort Sea
PACIFIC OCEAN
UNITED STATES
U N I T E D   S T A T E S
Prince Patrick I.
Melville Island
Parry Islands
Banks Island
Viscount Melville Sound
Devon Island
Jones Sound
Lancaster Sound
Parry Channel
Somerset Island
Prince of Wales Island
Victoria Island
Amundsen Gulf
Prince Albert Sound
Wollaston Peninsula
Dolphin and Union Str.
Coronation Gulf
Kent Pen.
Victoria Strait
Queen Maud Gulf
Boothia Peninsula
Gulf of Boothia
Brodeur Peninsula
Borden Peninsula
Bernier Bay
Simpson Pen.
Melville Pen.
Adelaide Pen.
Southampton Island
Hudson Bay
Hudson Bay Lowland
Great Bear Lake
Great Slave Lake
Lake Athabasca
Wollaston L.
Reindeer L.
Lake Winnipeg
Lake Winnipegosis
Lake Manitoba
Lake of the Woods
LAKE SUPERIOR
LAKE MICHIGAN
Mackenzie Mountains
Richardson Mountains
Ogilvie Mountains
Selwyn Mountains
Cassiar Mountains
Skeena Mountains
ROCKY MOUNTAINS
COAST MOUNTAINS
Columbia Mountains
Cariboo Mts.
Fraser Plateau
Monashee Mts.
Selkirk Mts.
Purcell Mts.
Continental Mts.
Pacific Range
Mackenzie Plateau
Franklin Mountains
Horn Mountains
Cameron Hills
Caribou Mountains
Birch Mountains
Swan Hills
Cypress Hills
GREAT PLAINS
Laurentian Plateau
Queen Charlotte Islands
Hecate Strait
Vancouver Island
Whitehorse
Yellowknife
Edmonton
Calgary
Saskatoon
Regina
Winnipeg
Vancouver
Surrey
Saanich
Kelowna
Kamloops
Prince George
Red Deer
Lethbridge
Medicine Hat
Moose Jaw
Prince Albert
Brandon
Thunder Bay
Thompson
Fort McMurray
Grande Prairie
Inuvik
140°W
130°W
120°W
110°W
100°W
90°W
70°N
60°N
50°N

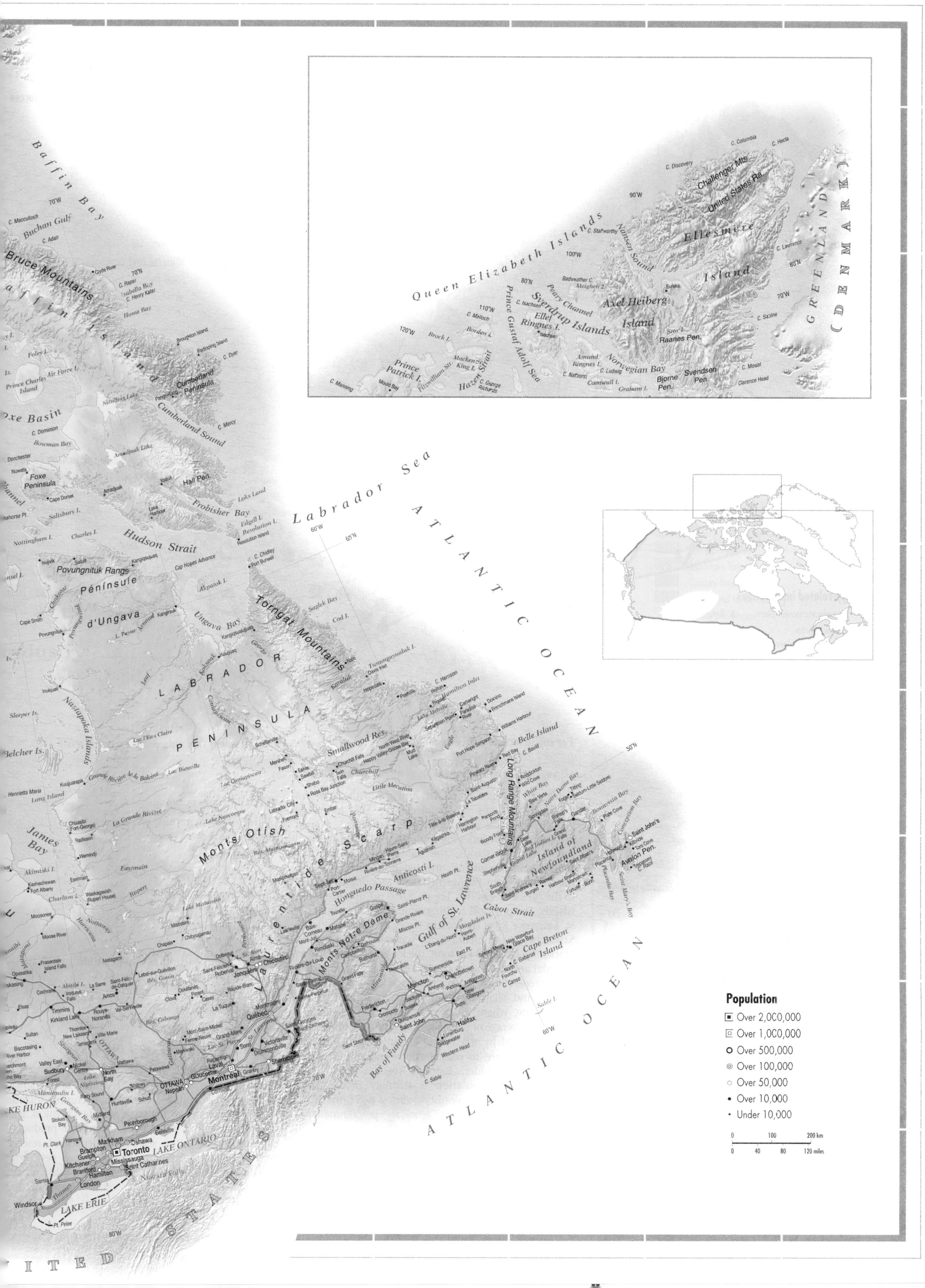
Baffin Bay
Buchan Gulf
Bruce Mountains
Baffin Island
Cumberland Peninsula
Cumberland Sound
Foxe Basin
Foxe Peninsula
Hall Pen.
Frobisher Bay
Hudson Strait
Labrador Sea
ATLANTIC OCEAN
Péninsule d'Ungava
Povungnituk Range
Ungava Bay
Torngat Mountains
LABRADOR PENINSULA
Nastapoka Islands
Belcher Is.
Smallwood Res.
Churchill
Hamilton Inlet
Belle Isle
Long Range Mountains
Island of Newfoundland
Avalon Pen.
Saint John's
Gander
Corner Brook
James Bay
Monts Otish
Laurentide Scarp
Anticosti I.
Honguedo Passage
Gulf of St. Lawrence
Cabot Strait
Cape Breton Island
Monts Notre Dame
Bay of Fundy
Halifax
Moncton
Saint John
Fredericton
Charlottetown
Québec
Chicoutimi
Montréal
OTTAWA
Laval
Sherbrooke
Sudbury
Toronto
Mississauga
Hamilton
London
Windsor
Kitchener
Brampton
Oshawa
Peterborough
LAKE HURON
LAKE ONTARIO
LAKE ERIE
UNITED STATES
Queen Elizabeth Islands
Ellesmere Island
Axel Heiberg Island
Sverdrup Islands
Challenger Mts.
United States Ra.
Nansen Sound
Peary Channel
Ellef Ringnes I.
Amund Ringnes I.
Norwegian Bay
Prince Gustaf Adolf Sea
Prince Patrick I.
Borden I.
Mackenzie King I.
Hazen Strait
Bjorne Pen.
Svendsen Pen.
GREENLAND (DENMARK)
C. Columbia
C. Hecla
Population
Over 2,000,000
Over 1,000,000
Over 500,000
Over 100,000
Over 50,000
Over 10,000
Under 10,000
0 100 200 km
0 40 80 120 miles

Mexico

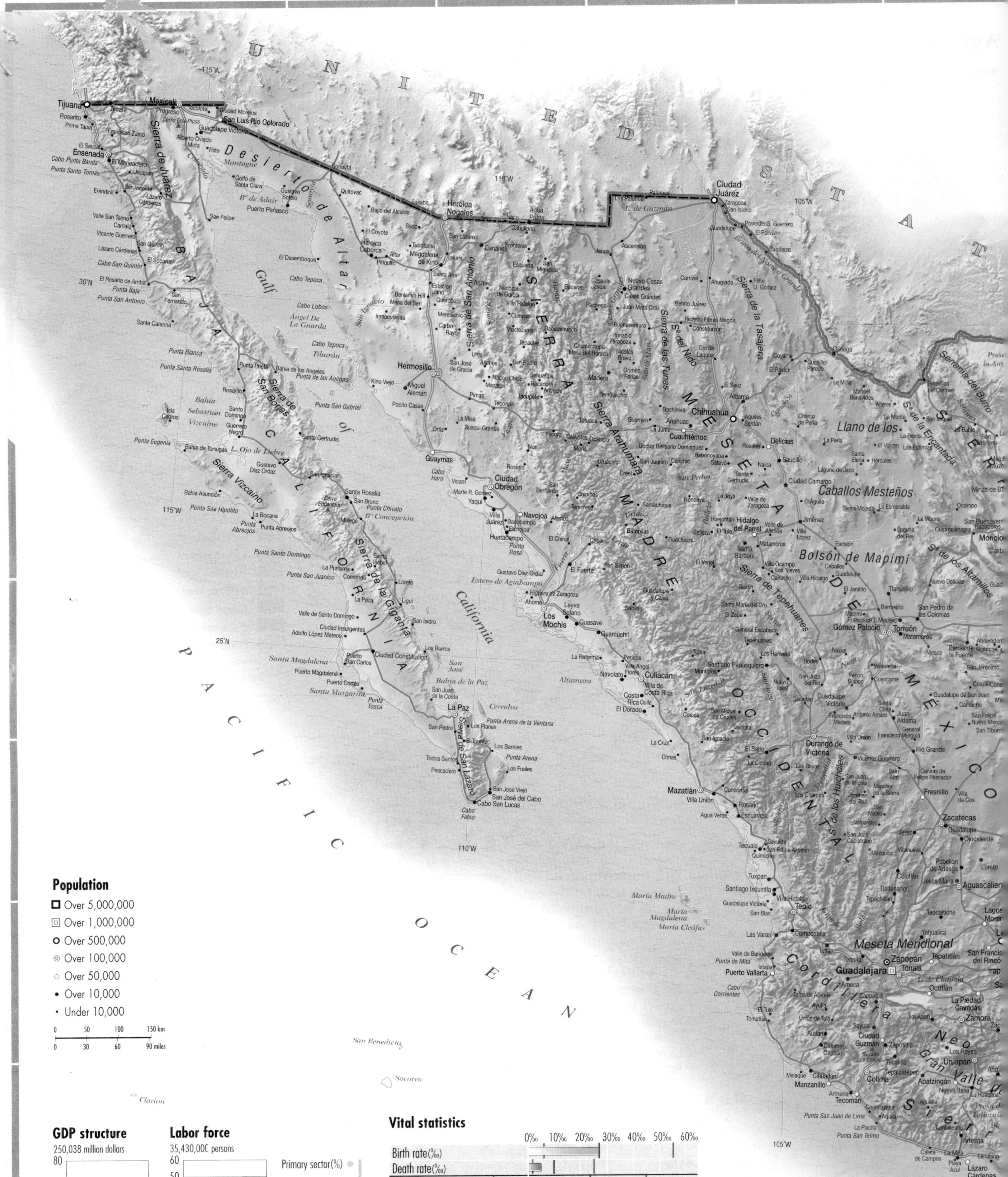
UNITED STATES
PACIFIC OCEAN
Gulf of California
BAJA CALIFORNIA
SIERRA MADRE OCCIDENTAL
MESETA CENTRAL
Desierto de Altar
Bolsón de Mapimí
Llano de los Caballos Mesteños
Meseta Meridional
Cordillera Neo Gran Valle
Tijuana
Mexicali
Ensenada
Heroica Nogales
Ciudad Juárez
Hermosillo
Chihuahua
Guaymas
Ciudad Obregón
Los Mochis
Culiacán
La Paz
Mazatlán
Durango de Victoria
Torreón
Zacatecas
Tepic
Puerto Vallarta
Guadalajara
Zapopan
Colima
Manzanillo
Socorro
San Benedicto
Clarion
115°W
110°W
105°W
30°N
25°N
Population
Over 5,000,000
Over 1,000,000
Over 500,000
Over 100,000
Over 50,000
Over 10,000
Under 10,000
0 50 100 150 km
0 30 60 90 miles

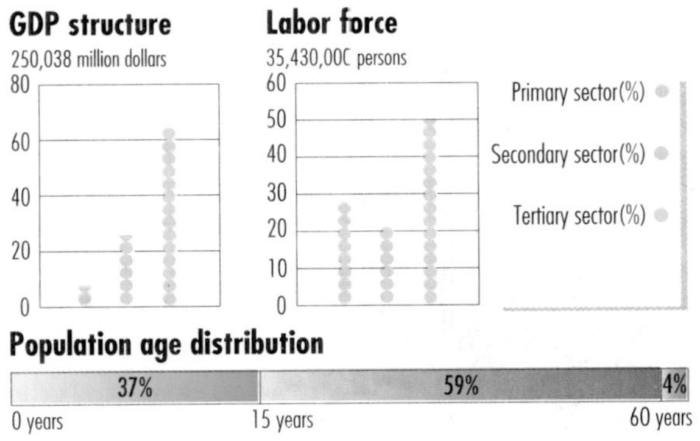
GDP structure
250,038 million dollars
Labor force
35,430,00C persons
Primary sector(%)
Secondary sector(%)
Tertiary sector(%)
Population age distribution
37%
59%
4%
0 years
15 years
60 years

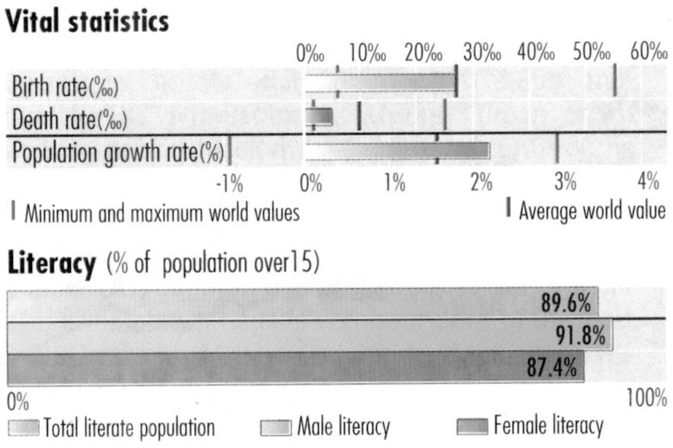
Vital statistics
0‰ 10‰ 20‰ 30‰ 40‰ 50‰ 60‰
Birth rate(‰)
Death rate(‰)
Population growth rate(%)
-1% 0% 1% 2% 3% 4%
Minimum and maximum world values
Average world value
Literacy (% of population over15)
89.6%
91.8%
87.4%
0%
100%
Total literate population
Male literacy
Female literacy

Mexico is a republic of North America. The Mexican plateau occupies almost one half of its territory. Surrounding this plateau are the mountain ranges of the Sierra Madre Occidental and the Sierra Madre Oriental (Peña Nevada, 3,664 m). The Cordillera Neovolcánica range crosses 880 km in an east-west direction; it is one of the most important volcanic formations in the world. In the south rise the mountain ranges of Sierra Madre del Sur and the Sierra Madre of Chiapas. The Yucatan Peninsula, with unlike landform features, is made up of a calcareous plateau with elevations below 500 m. Among the fluvial watercourses — unimportant— is the Río Grande or Bravo del Norte (3,540 km). The drainage systems form notable catch-basins with no outlet to the sea. Mexico is located in subtropical and tropical latitudes, but the altitude of the land acts as a climatic distorting factor. The north of the plateau has a dry and desert climate, with mean annual temperatures between 20-25 °C and precipitation below 400 mm. The south of the plateau and the Cordillera Neovolcnica are more temperate zones, with average temperatures of less than 20 °C and a level of rainfall close to 750 mm. The extreme south and the Pacific coast, totally tropical in climate, have average temperatures above 25 °C and wide pluviometric ranges (between 800 and 1,600 mm annually). More than half of the Mexican people are mestizos and descend from the fusion of Spaniards and the indigenous people. Almost a third of the census corresponds to the native population, divided in several ethnolinguistic branches. Mexican demography shows great population growth. Inter-regional inequities have favored migrations, interior —from the country to urban areas— as well as exterior ones — towards the United States (USA). The capital (Mexico City) is among the most populated cities on the planet. In Mexico, modern businesses co-exist alongside handicraft methods of production. The principal source of income derives from the exportation of petroeum and from mining (silver, cinnabrium, sulphur, fluorite, iron ore, lead, zinc, copper, antimony, uranium). Mexican industry includes above all, the textile, chemical and mechanical construction branches. Farming employs almost a third of the economically active population, but its productivity is less than that from ranching. The ejido, a system that awards the property of the land to the peasant, but without the right to sell it or rent it out, survives. Mexico's economy is burdened by the weight of its foreign debt to the United States, although this has been reduced considerably in the last few years.

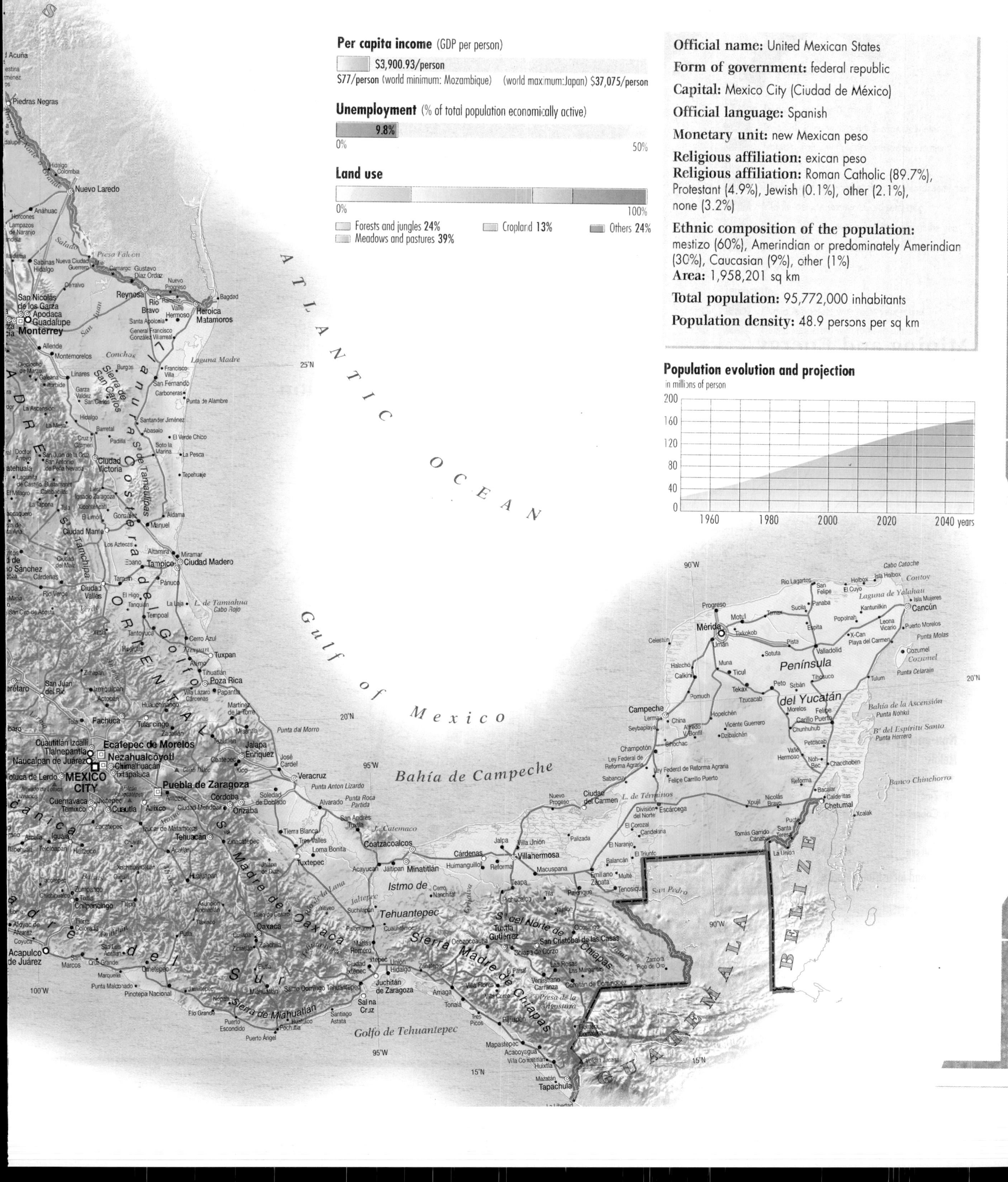

Per capita income (GDP per person)

$3,900.93/person

$77/person (world minimum: Mozambique) (world maximum: Japan) $37,075/person

Unemployment (% of total population economically active)

9.8%

0% — 50%

Land use

0% — 100%

Forests and jungles 24% · Cropland 13% · Others 24% · Meadows and pastures 39%

Official name: United Mexican States
Form of government: federal republic
Capital: Mexico City (Ciudad de México)
Official language: Spanish
Monetary unit: new Mexican peso
Religious affiliation: exican peso
Religious affiliation: Roman Catholic (89.7%), Protestant (4.9%), Jewish (0.1%), other (2.1%), none (3.2%)
Ethnic composition of the population: mestizo (60%), Amerindian or predominately Amerindian (30%), Caucasian (9%), other (1%)
Area: 1,958,201 sq km
Total population: 95,772,000 inhabitants
Population density: 48.9 persons per sq km

Population evolution and projection

in millions of person

200 · 160 · 120 · 80 · 40 · 0

1960 · 1980 · 2000 · 2020 · 2040 years

Panama

Panama is a republic of Central America. A discontinuous mountain system runs through the country from west to east, while low plains occupy the interior of the tectonic depressions (grabens). In the central part is the Panama Canal zone, under U.S. jurisdiction. It has regular watercourses, short and with steep slopes, above all on the Atlantic watershed. The rivers that flow into the Gulf of Panama have greater lengths and amounts of water-flow. The climate is equatorial, hot and wet, acquiring temperate characteristics at higher elevations. Abundant precipitations are recorded, mainly in the Atlantic Coast regions.

In general, the Panamanian population lives in rural areas and is distributed iregularly throughout the territory. Mestizos are predominant, living together with minorities of blacks and whites. Small percentages of Chinese, Japanese and Arab immigraints also exist and there are still indigenous groups, such as the Chocos, the Guayimi and the Cuna.

Farming produces subsistence crops, among which the most important are cereals, cassava, yams and other root crops, potatoes, legumes and vegetables. Cash crops for export are also grown (bananas, sugar cane and coffee). Livestock-raising, fishing production and forestry contribute considerable income. Manufacturing, a sector which is not very active, is dedicated above all to food-processing and the chemical branch; nevertheless, the free port of Colón is encouraging industrial development.

Official name: Republic of Panama
Form of government: presidential republic
Capital: Panamá
Official language: Spanish
Monetary unit: balboa
Religious affiliation: Roman Catholic (80%), Protestant (10%), Muslim (5%), Bāha'ī (1%), Hindu (0.3%), Jewish (0.3%), other (3.4%)
Ethnic composition of the population: mestizo (64%), black and mulatto (14%), white (10%), Amerindian (8%), Asian (4%)]
Area: 75,517 sq km
Total population: 2,655,000 inhabitants
Population density: 35.2 persons per sq km

Population evolution and projection

in millions of persons

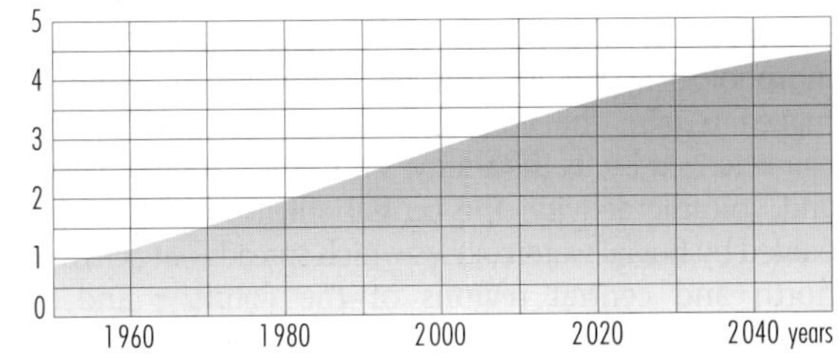

Population age distribution

Vital statistics

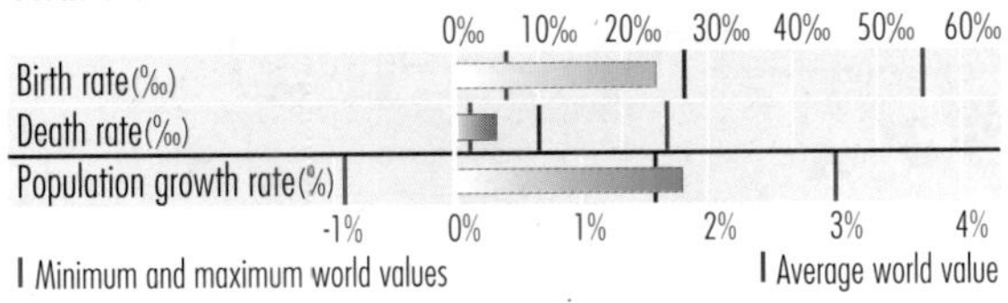

Per capita income (GDP per person)

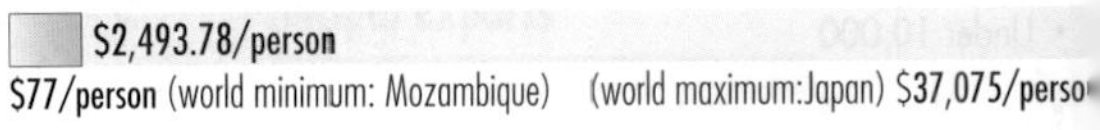

GDP structure

7,413 million dollars

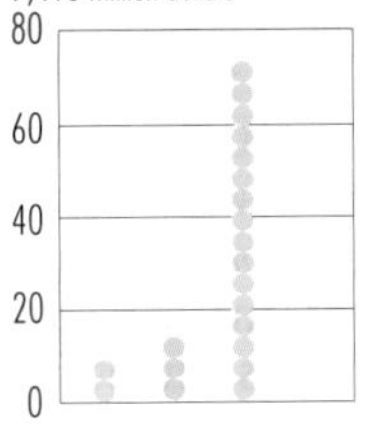

Labor force

1,030,000 persons

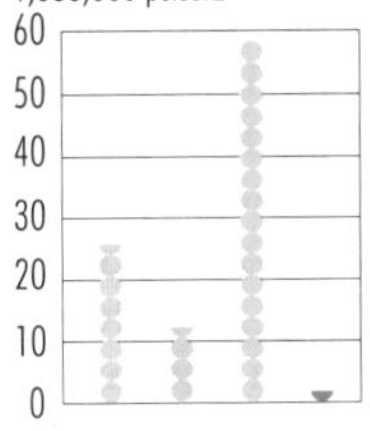

Primary sector(%)
Secondary sector(%)
Tertiary sector(%)
Unassigned(%)

Unemployment (% of total population economically active)

Literacy (% of population over15)

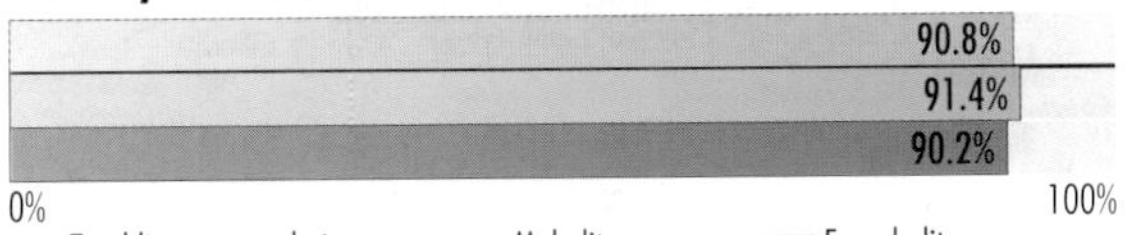

Land use

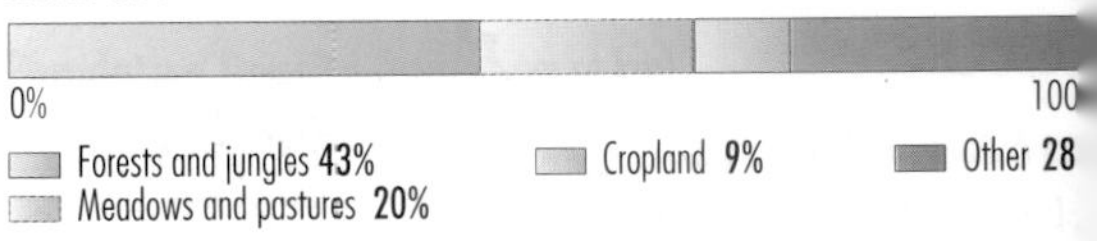

Agriculture

Types of agriculture and livestock production

- Commercial and plantation farming (sugar cane, bananas, coffee, cocoa, tobacco, hemp)
- Ranching and some subsistence farming (rice, corn, root crops, legumes)
- Forest/brush/forestry
- Swamplands
- Corn (maize)
- Rice
- Citrus fruits
- Bananas
- Coconut trees
- Sugar cane
- Coffee
- Tobacco
- Cattle
- Pigs
- Fishing

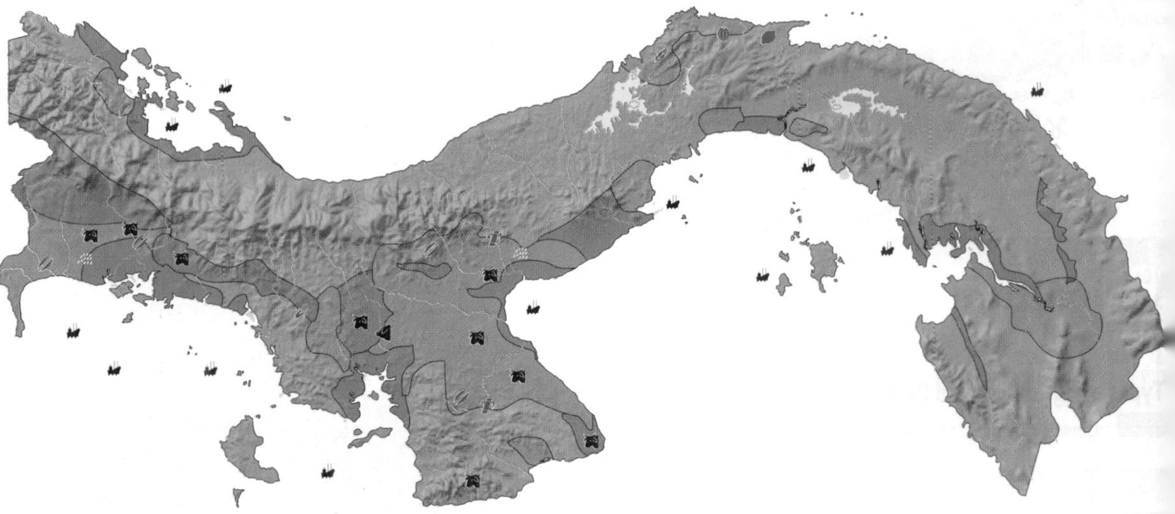

Industry and Minig

Non-energy source mineral resources

Metals

Copper, Gold, Manganese

Energy-related installations

- Electric power plant
- Hydroelectric power plant
- Oil pipeline
- Refinery

Manufacturing

- Food, beverages and tobacco
- Textiles, clothing, leather and footwear
- Chemical products
- Building materials, glass and cement
- Metallurgy and metal products
- Machinery and transport equipment

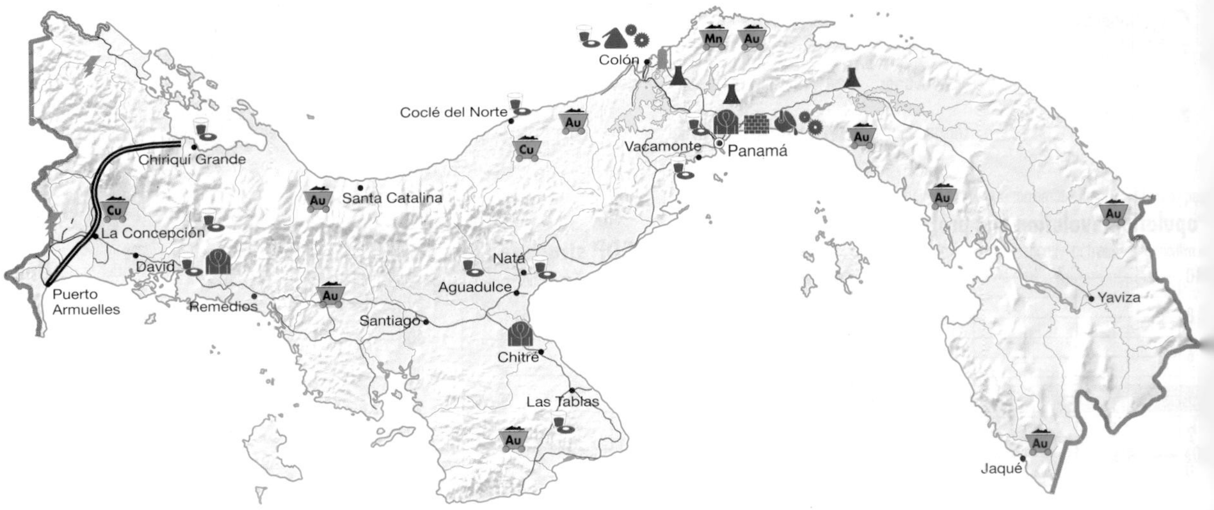

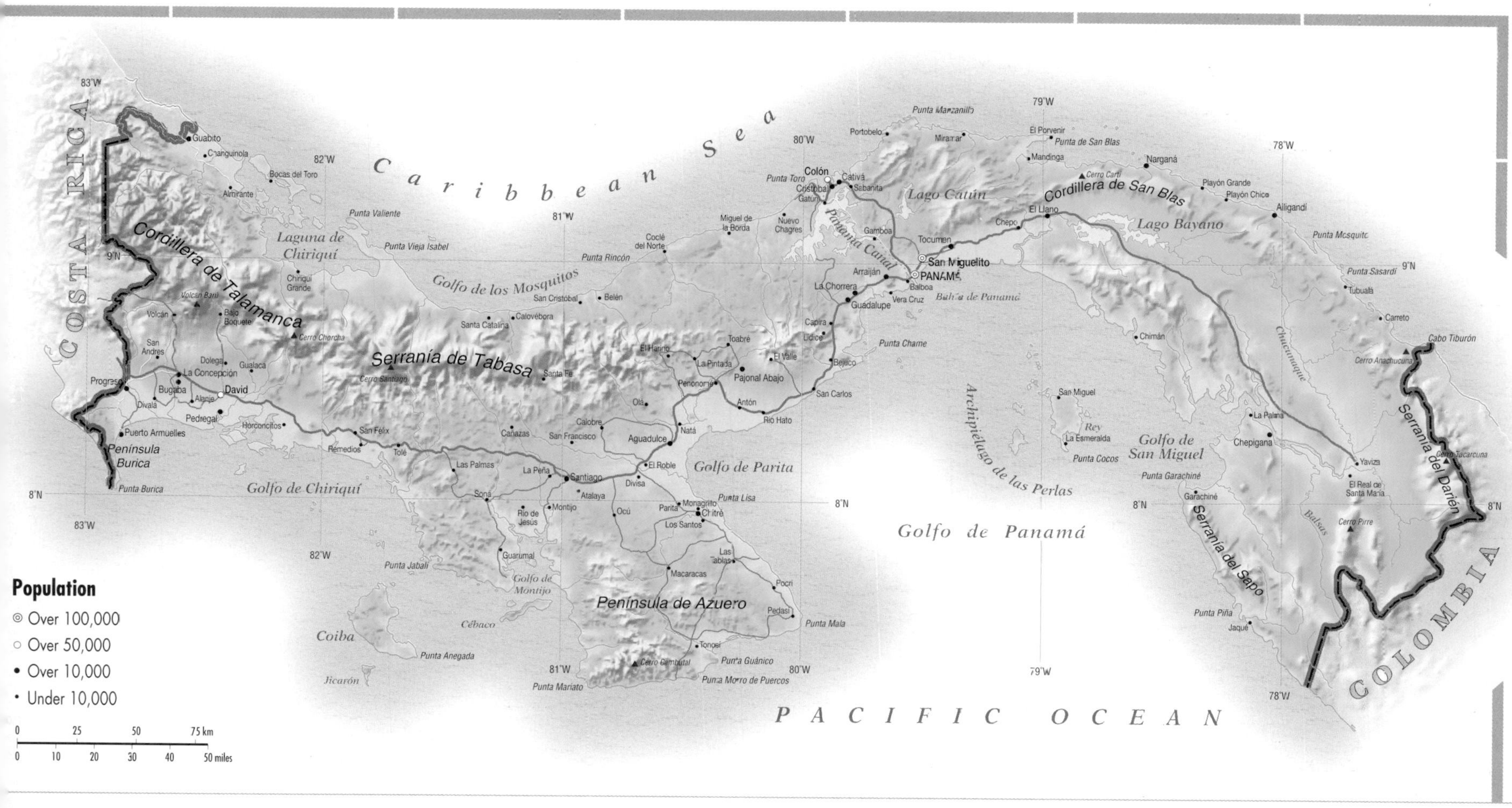

Population

- ◎ Over 100,000
- ○ Over 50,000
- • Over 10,000
- · Under 10,000

0 25 50 75 km
0 10 20 30 40 50 miles

Saint Kitts and Nevis

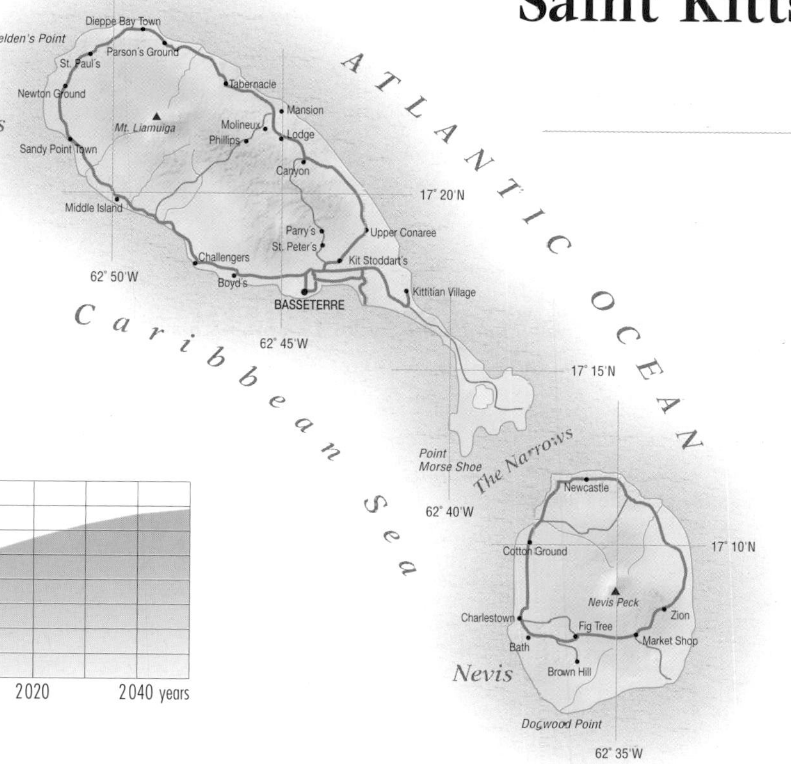

Population

- • Over 10,000
- · Under 10,000

0 5 10 km
0 20 40 60 miles

Official name: Federation of Saint Kitts and Nevis
Form of government: constitutional monarchy
Capital: Basseterre
Official language: English
Monetary unit: Eastern Caribbean dollar
Religious affiliation: Protestant (76.4%), Roman Catholic (10.7%), other (12.9%)
Ethnic composition of the population: black (94.9%), mixed/white/Indo-Pakistani (5.1%)
Area: 269 sq km
Total population: 41,369 inhabitants
Population density: 153.8 persons per sq km

opulation evolution and projection
thousands of persons

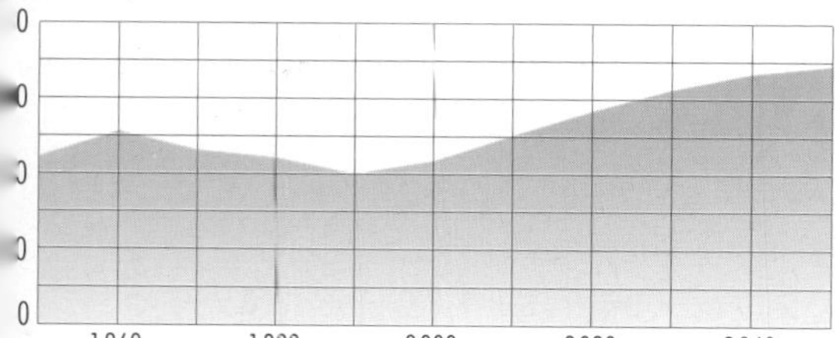

DP structure
5 million dollars

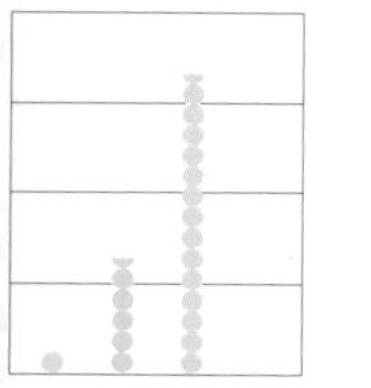

Labor force
17,100 persons

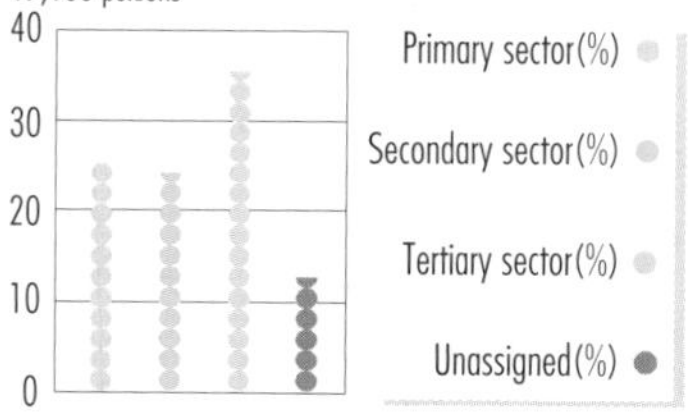

pulation age distribution

tal statistics

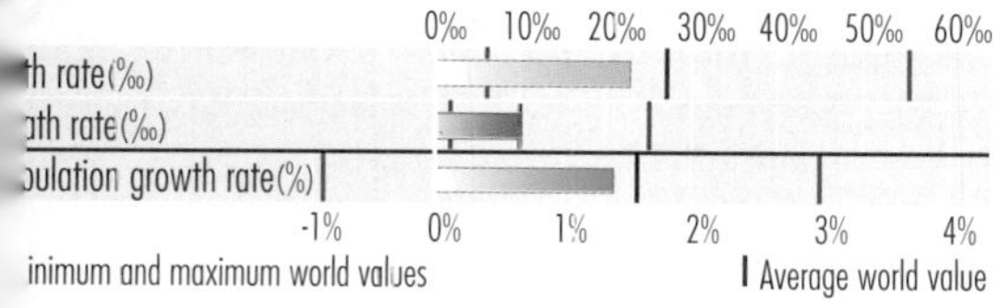

Literacy (% of population over15)

Unemployment (% of total population economically active)

Land use

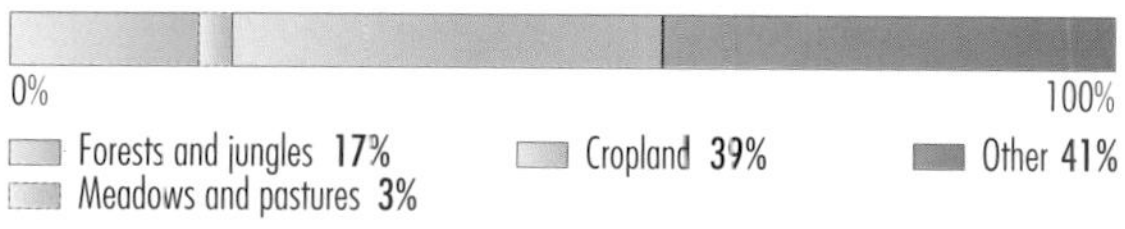

An island state of the Caribbean Sea, Saint Kitts and Nevis is associated with the United Kingdom. It is composed of the islands of Saint Kitts and Nevis, in the Lesser Antilles (Leeward group). Saint Kitts is the largest of the populated islands, and has a volcanic mountain chain in the shape of a semi-circle, within which extends a fertile plain.

Practically the whole island of Nevis consists of a mountain bordered by coral reefs. Saint Kitts has a more temperate climate, while Nevis enjoys a tropical one, softened by ocean breezes.

The major population group is made up of persons of the black race.

Cotton and sugar cane are produced, part of which are exported. There are also crops of cereals, coconuts, various fruits and vegetables, and there exists a small agricultural processing industry. The balance of trade is negative.

Saint Lucia

Saint Lucia is an island state of the Caribbean made up of the island of that name and belonging to the Windward group of the Lesser Antilles, south of Martinique. It has mountainous terrain of volcanic origin. On the southwestern coast rise the volcanoes Gros Piton and Petit Piton. A mountain chain crosses the interior of the island, with a maximum elevation that corresponds to Mt. Gimie. It possesses fertile valleys, watered by the rivers that descend from the mountains. Saint Lucia has a tropical climate, moderated by the Trade Winds from the northeast. The island has a high population density.

The official language is English and Roman Catholicism is practiced. The economy has traditionally depended on agriculture, although a third of the economically active population works in the services sector. Saint Lucia exports bananas, coconut oil and tobacco. Livestock production is based on sheep and cattle. Fishing is also practiced. The industrial sector, scarcely diversified at all, is dedicated to the processing of food products.

Official name: Saint Lucia
Form of government: parliamentary democracy
Capital: Castries
Official language: English
Monetary unit: Eastern Caribbean dollar
Religious affiliation: Roman Catholic (79%), Protestant (15.5%), other (5.5%)
Ethnic composition of the population: African descent (90.3%), mixed (5.5%), East Indian (3.2%), Caucasian (0.8%)
Area: 617 sq km
Total population: 157,862 inhabitants
Population density: 255.9 persons per sq km

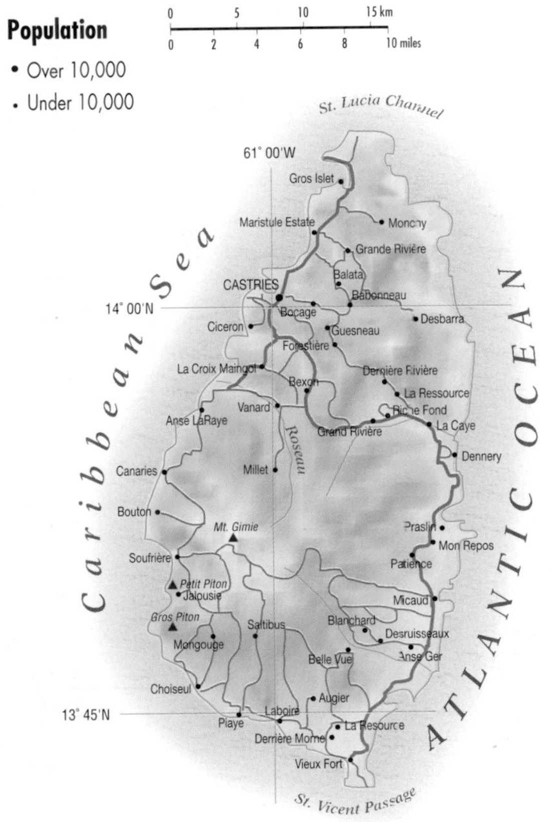

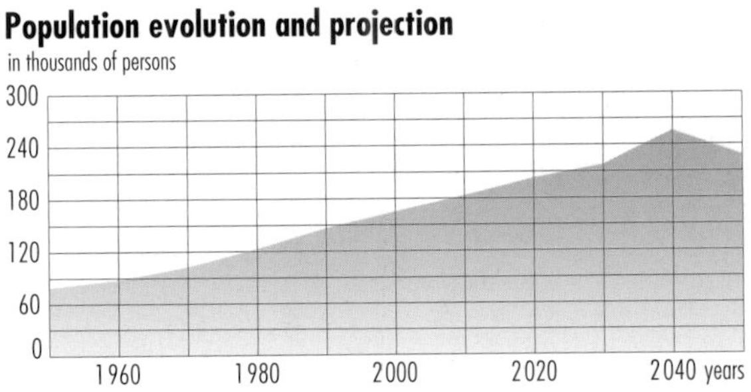

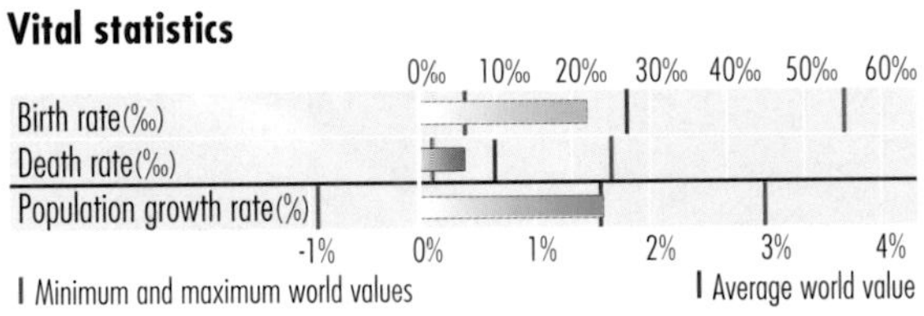

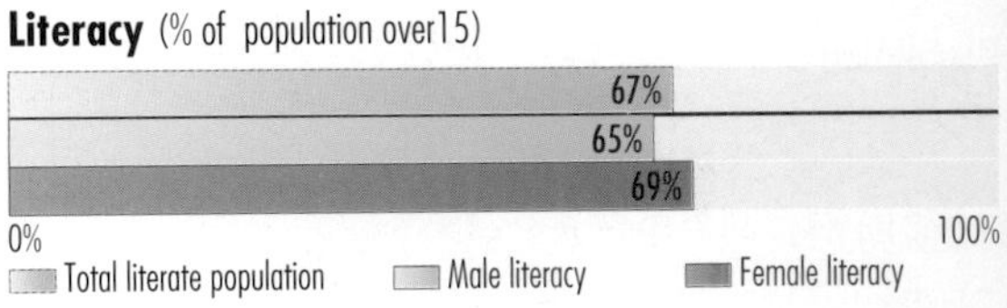

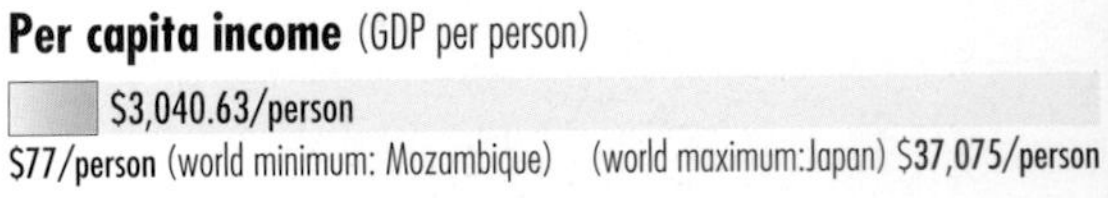

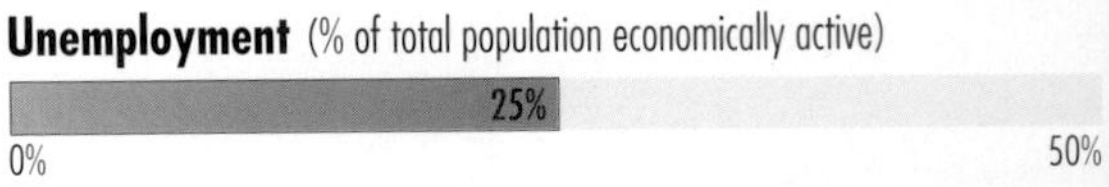

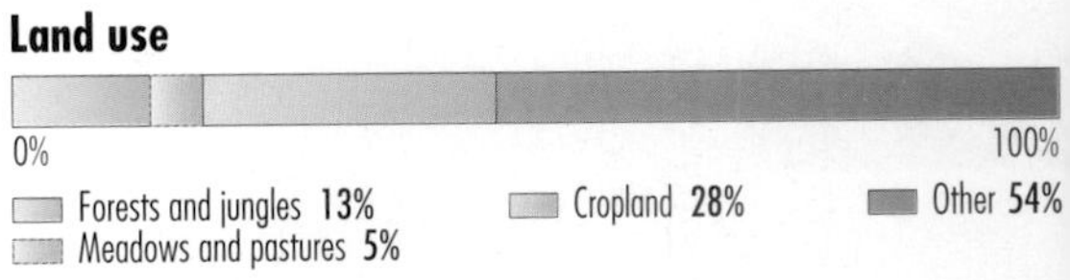

Saint Vincent and the Grenadines

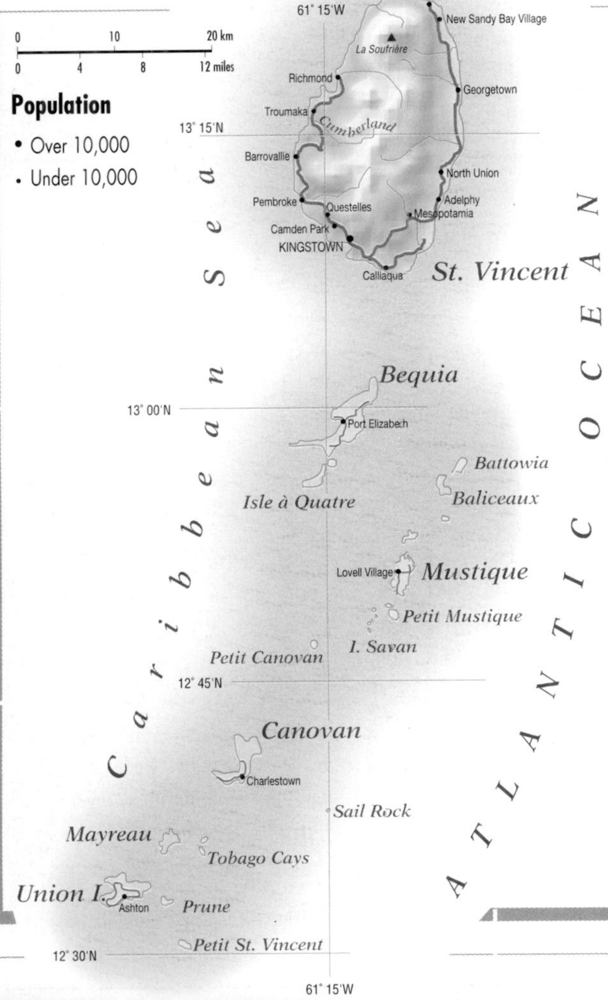

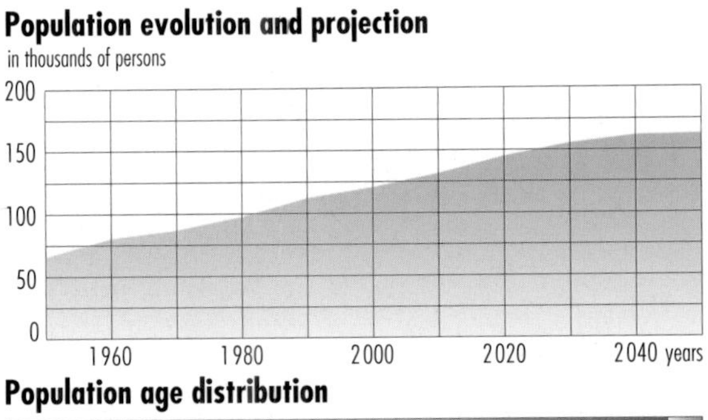

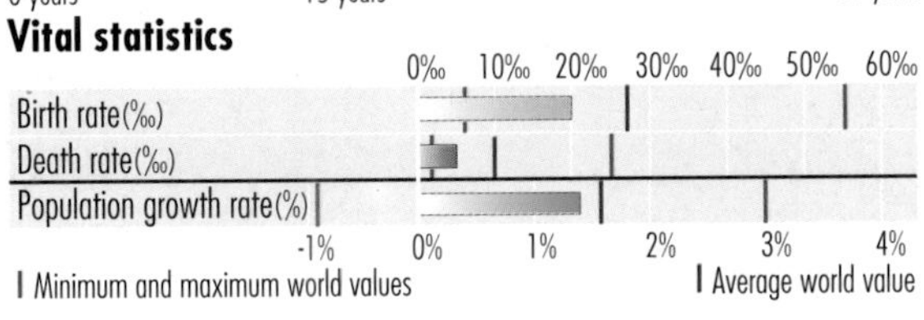

Official name: Saint Vincent and the Grenadines
Form of government: constitutional monarchy
Capital: Kingstown
Official language: English
Monetary unit: Eastern Caribbean dollar
Religious affiliation: Protestant (80.5%), Roman Catholic (11.6%), other (7.9%)
Ethnic composition of the population: black (65.5%), mulatto (19%), East Indian (5.5%), white (3.5%), Amerindian/black(2.%), other (4.5%)
Area: 389 sq km
Total population: 118,344 inhabitants
Population density: 304.2 persons per sq km
GDP: 254 million dollars

An island state of the Caribbean Sea, it is located in the archipelago of the Lesser Antilles (Windward group). It is composed of the islands of Saint Vincent and the western Grenadines, lands of volcanic origen. The mountains of the interior are heavily forested. The volcano La Soufrière (1,234 m high) occupies most of the territory of Saint Vincent and last went into eruption in 1979. The tropical climate registers mild temperatures throughout the year. Hurricanes frequently hit the islands. The country is governed by a constitution monarchy. The official language is English. The religion practiced by the majority are Protestantism and Roma Catholicism. Farming, the main traditional econom activity, is based on the cultivation of bananas, followe by that of plantains and sweet potatoes. The beauty of i beaches and its mild climate have attracted tourists fro abroad, so that more than half of the economical active population work in the services sector.

Argentina

Population
Over 2,000,000
Over 1,000,000
Over 500,000
Over 100,000
Over 50,000
Over 10,000
Under 10,000
0 100 200 km
0 40 80 120 miles
BOLIVIA
PARAGUAY
BRAZIL
URUGUAY
CHILE
ANDES
ATLANTIC OCEAN
PACIFIC OCEAN
PATAGONIA
PAMPA
GRAN CHACO
Chaco Central
Chaco Austral
BUENOS AIRES
Córdoba
Rosario
Mendoza
San Miguel de Tucumán
Salta
San Salvador de Jujuy
Santa Fe
Paraná
Corrientes
Resistencia
Formosa
Posadas
Mar del Plata
La Plata
Bahía Blanca
Neuquén
Santiago del Estero
Catamarca
La Rioja
San Juan
San Luis
Río Cuarto
Santa Rosa
San Rafael
Comodoro Rivadavia
Trelew
Rawson
Viedma
Río Gallegos
Ushuaia
Río Grande
San Carlos de Bariloche
Puna de Atacama
Salinas Grandes
Salinas de Ambargasta
Laguna Mar Chiquita
Río de la Plata
Bahía Samborombón
Bahía Blanca
Golfo San Matías
Golfo San Jorge
Península Valdés
Meseta de Somuncurá
Meseta de Montemayor
Altiplanicie del Payún
Gran Bajo Oriental
Gran Altiplanicie Central
Lago Colhué Huapí
Lago Buenos Aires
Lago Strobel
Lago Cardiel
Lago San Martín
Lago Fagnano
Estrecho de Magallanes
Estrecho de Le Maire
Los Estados
Cataratas del Iguazú (Iguazú Falls)
25°S
30°S
35°S
40°S
45°S
50°S
55°S
55°W
60°W
65°W
70°W

Agriculture

Types of agriculture and livestock production

- Cereal farming (corn, wheat) and ranching
- Irrigation/intensive farming
- Commercial and plantation farming (cotton, sugar cane, grapevines, fruits tobacco)
- Ranching (cattle, sheep, horses, pigs)
- Ranching (sheep)
- Forest/brush
- Swamplands
- Wheat
- Corn (maize)
- Rice
- Fruit and vegetables
- Fruit trees
- Citrus fruits
- Grapevines
- Potatoes
- Alfalfa
- Cotton
- Flax
- Sugar cane
- Mate
- Tobacco
- Quebracho
- Cattle
- Sheep
- Goats
- Pigs
- Horses
- Llamas
- Fishing

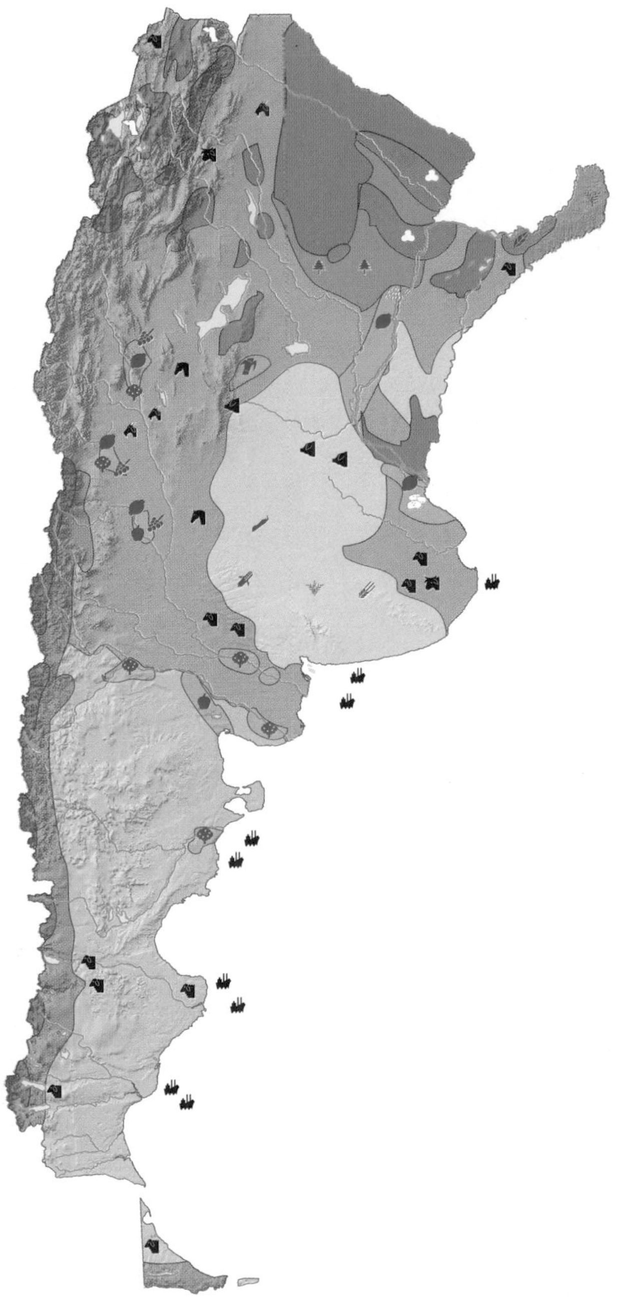

Argentina is a state of South America, the second largest of the continent, with more than 4,000 km of Atlantic coastline. Several geomorphological regions can be distinguished in its territory. Great stepped plains occupy the north (Chaco), center (Pampa) and south (Patagonia). The Andes —a volcanic mountain range— covers all the western flank of the country and in its central part has the highest mountains of the continent (Cerro Aconcagua, 6,959 m; Bonete, 6,872 m). La Puna of Atacama is an enormous plateau set at an altitude of 3,800 m, enclosed by the northernmost Andean mountain ranges.

The two rivers that are longest and with greatest water-flow, the Paraná and Uruguay, flow into the great estuary of Río de la Plata. The principal watercourses of Patagonia are much shorter (Colorado, Negro, Chubut, Santa Cruz, Gallegos).

The climate owes its marked variety to two factors: the great latitudinal differences —from the tropical zone to the extreme southern regions— and the differences in altitude from sea level to the highest Andean peaks.

In the north, a humid tropical climate characterizes the province of Misiones and the region of Mesopotamia (between the Paraná and Uruguay Rivers). In the Chaco rainy summers follow dry winters.

The Pampa registers warm temperatures moderated by the humidity of the Atlantic winds and rains. The Cuyo —the farthest inland and driest part of the Pampa— has desert landscapes or dry ones characteristic of a Mediterranean climate. In the Puna, even more desert like, low temperatures are predominant. Patagonia has a humid and temperate climate in the north, but the temperatures become more extreme in the south.

The population of Argentina is composed, in its immense majority, of descendents of European immigrants, above all Spanish and Italians, but also of French, Germans Poles, and Russians, not to mention Arabs; the rest are mestizo and indigenous peoples. The city of Buenos Aires concentrates one third of the population, while large interior areas remain uninhabited.

Argentina possesses immense natural wealth. The Pampa is among the most fertile lands on the planet and supports millions of heads of cattle and sheep. The deposits of minerals and hydrocarbons had not been exploited until recently.

Industry is very diversified (food products, mechanical textiles, iron and steel, electrical, graphics, chemical sectors)

Vegetation

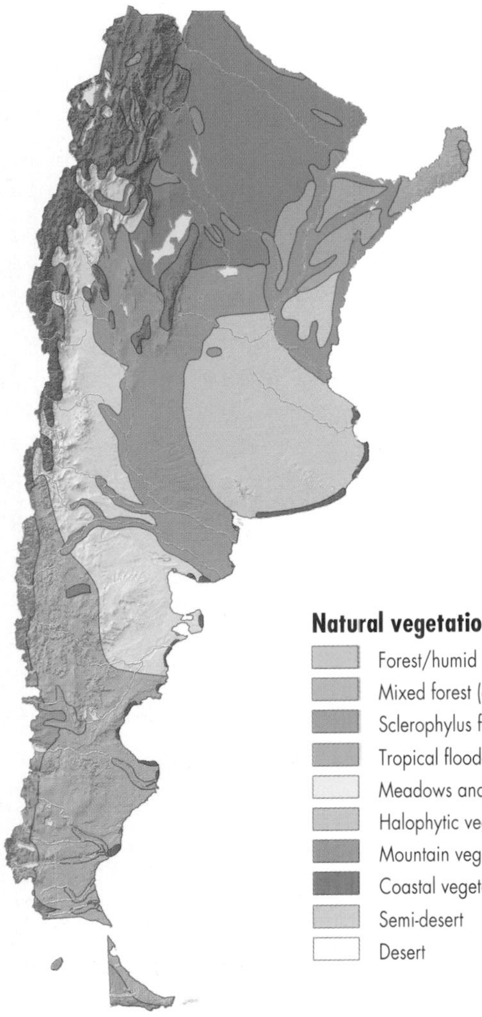

Natural vegetation

- Forest/humid savanna
- Mixed forest (deciduous, evergreen)
- Sclerophylus forest/clear forest
- Tropical flood-plain vegetation
- Meadows and pastures
- Halophytic vegetation
- Mountain vegetation
- Coastal vegetation
- Semi-desert
- Desert

Population

Major Import Sources

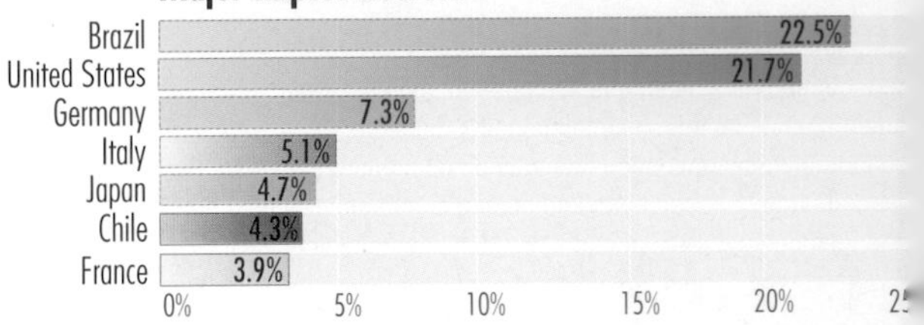

Major Export Destinations

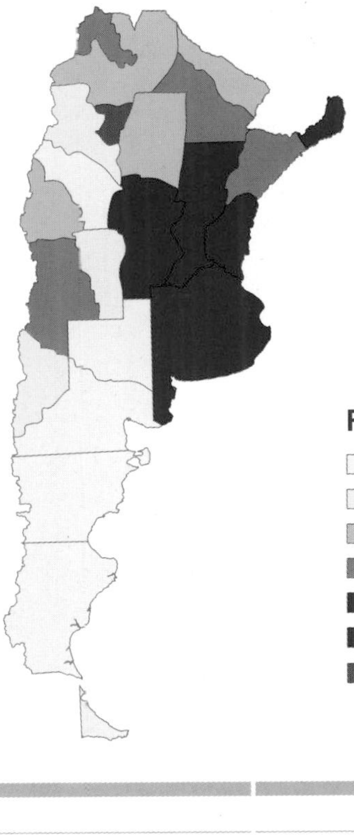

Population density (persons per sq km)

- Fewer than 2
- From 2 to 4
- From 4 to 6
- From 6 to 10
- From 10 to 25
- From 25 to 50
- More than 50

Mining and Energy

Non-energy source mineral resources

Metals

- Zinc
- Copper
- Tin
- Iron ore
- Manganese
- Molybdenum
- Gold
- Silver
- Lead

Rocks and industrial minerals

- Boron
- Sodium sulphate
- Gypsum

Mineral fuel resources

Fossil fuels

- Coal
- Natural gas
- Petroleum

Radioactive fuel

- Uranium

Energy-related installations

- Hydroelectric power plant
- Nuclear reactor
- Refinery
- Gas pipeline
- Oil pipeline

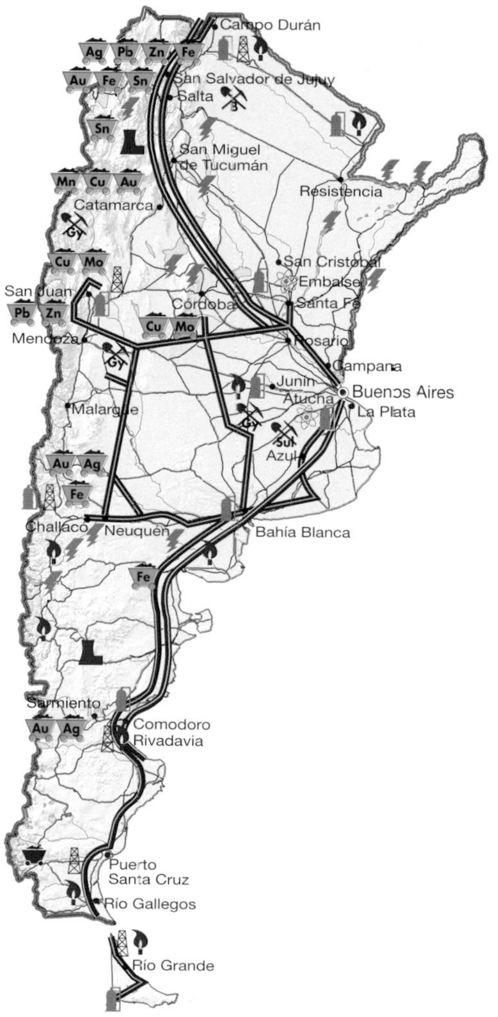

Official name: Argentine Republic
Form of government: republic
Capital: Buenos Aires
Official language: Spanish
Monetary unit: new Argentine peso
Religious affiliation: Roman Catholic (90%), Protestant (2%), Jewish (2%), other (6%)
Ethnic composition of the population: white (85%), mestizo, Amerindian and other non-white groups (15%)
Area: 2,780,400 sq km
Total population: 34,673,000 inhabitants
Population density: 12.5 persons per sq km

Industry

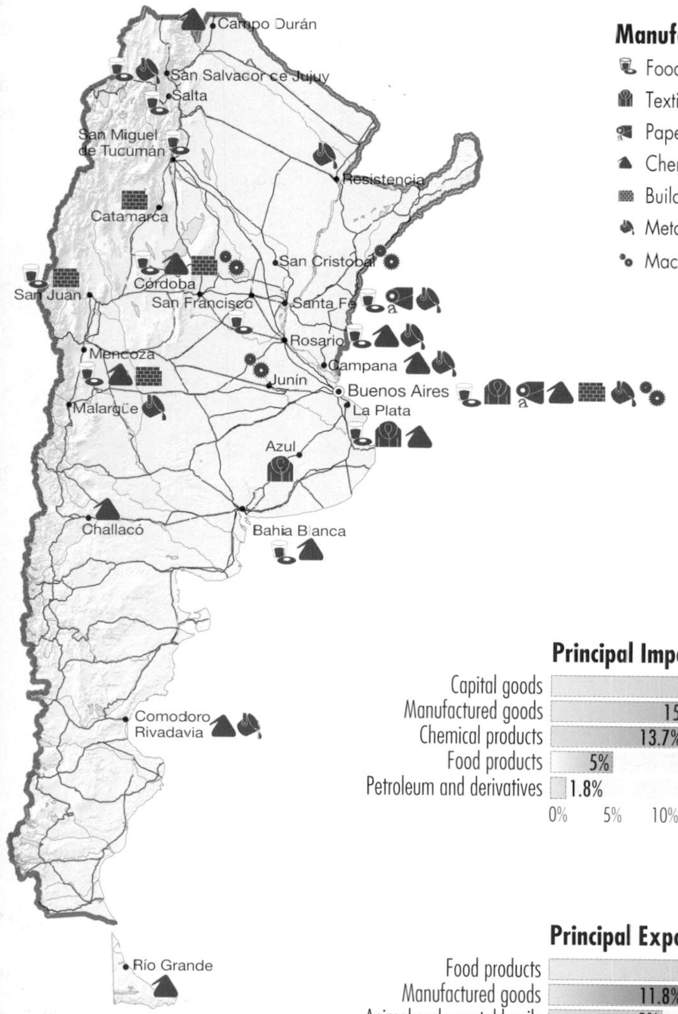

Manufacturing

- Food, beverages and tobacco
- Textiles, clothing, leather and footwear
- Paper and graphic arts
- Chemical products
- Building materials, glass and cement
- Metallurgy and metal products
- Machinery and transport equipment

Principal Imports

Product	%
Capital goods	47.8%
Manufactured goods	15.1%
Chemical products	13.7%
Food products	5%
Petroleum and derivatives	1.8%

Principal Exports

Product	%
Food products	44.1%
Manufactured goods	11.8%
Animal and vegetable oils	9%
Petroleum and derivatives	8.5%
Capital goods	7.5%

Population evolution and projection
in millions of persons

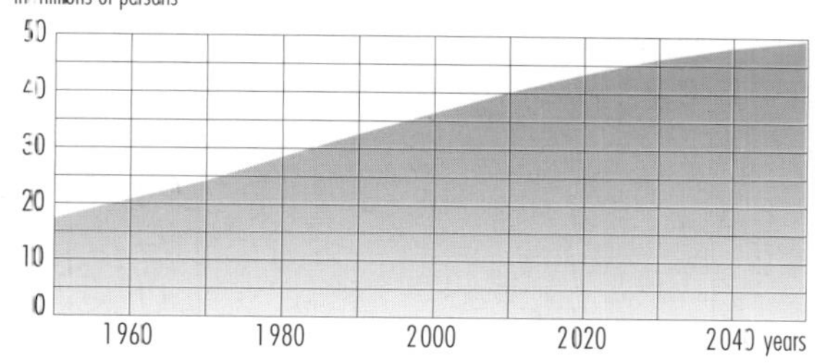

GDP structure
281,060 million dollars

Labor force
13,225,000 persons

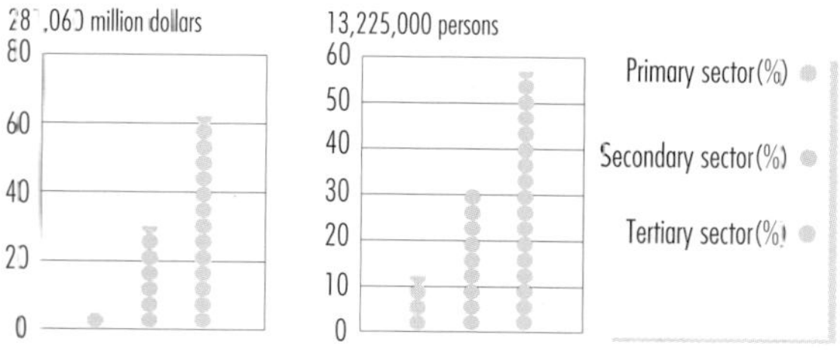

Population age distribution

28% | 62% | 10%
0 years — 15 years — 60 years

Vital statistics

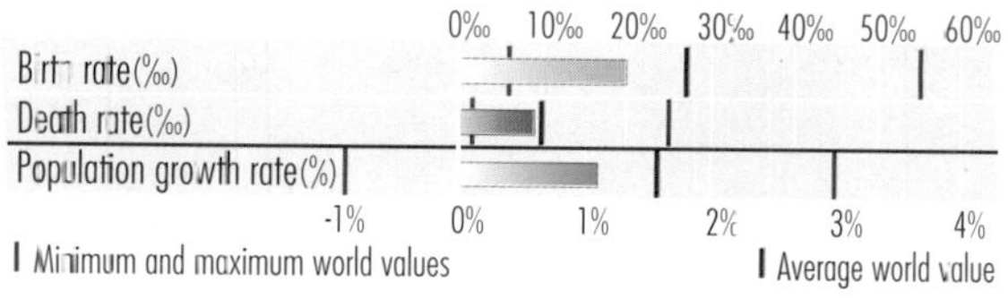

Literacy (% of population over15)

Total literate population 96.2%
Male literacy 96.2%
Female literacy 96.2%
0% — 100%

Per capita income (GDP per person)

$7,037.17/person
$77/person (world minimum: Mozambique) (world maximum: Japan) $37,075/person

Unemployment (% of total population economically active)

12%
0% — 50%

Land use

0% — 100%
Forests and jungles 21.6%
Meadows and pastures 51.9%
Cropland 9.9%
Other 16.6%

Bolivia

Official name: Republic of Bolivia
Form of government: presidential republic
Capital: La Paz/Sucre
Official language: Aymara, Quechua, Spanish
Monetary unit: boliviano
Religious affiliation: Roman Catholic (92.5%), Baha'i (2.6%), other (4.9%)
Ethnic composition of the population: Quechua (30%), Aymara (25%), mestizo (25-30%), European (5-15%)
Area: 1,098,581 sq km
Total population: 7,165,000 inhabitants
Population density: 6.5 persons per sq km

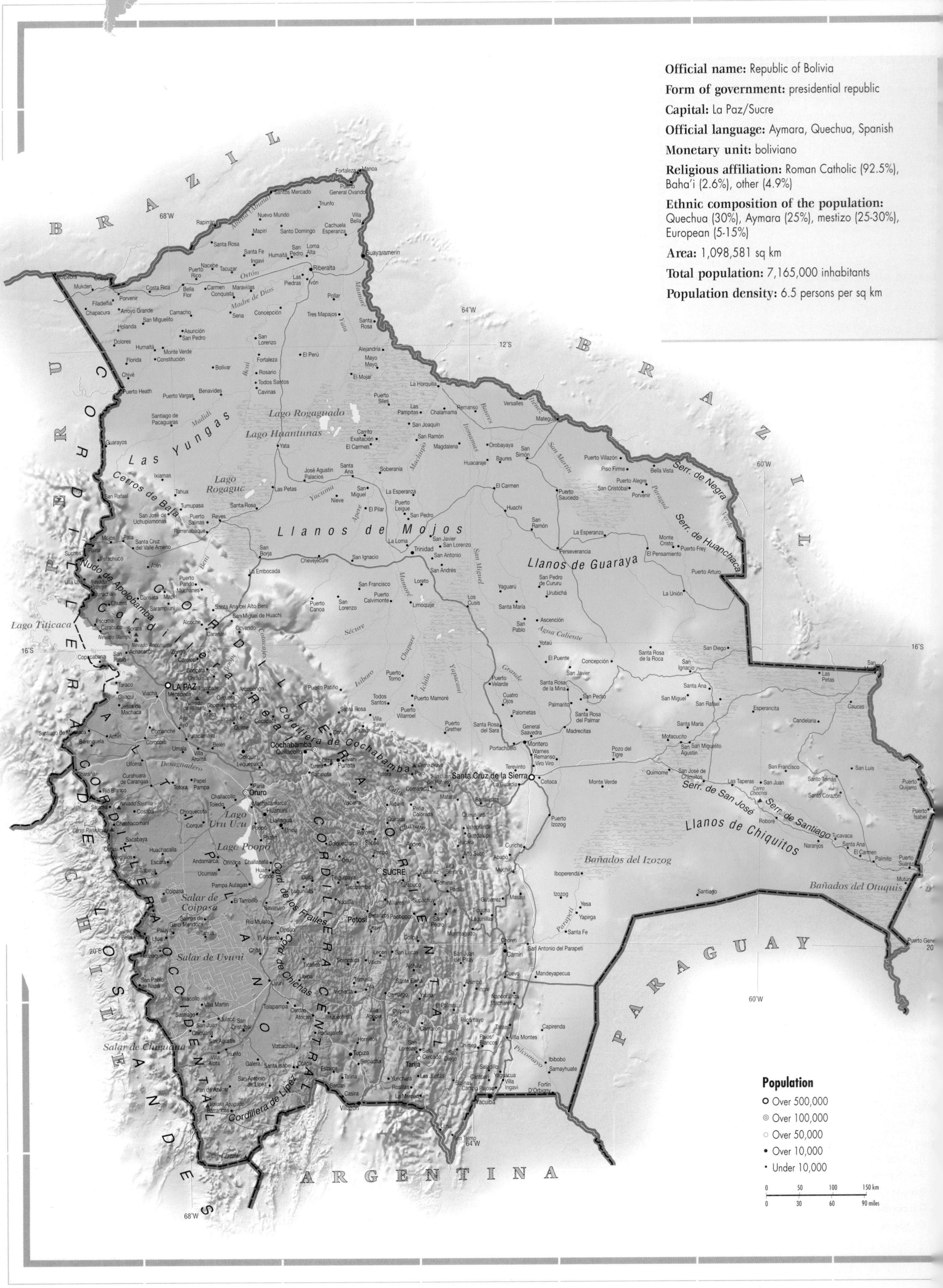

Bolivia is a landlocked state of South America. The Andes traverse its territory from north to south divided in three chains: the Cordillera Occidental, the Cordillera Central and the Cordillera Oriental (Nevado Illampú 6,485 m), that enclose the extensive valley of Cochabamba. Between the first two mountain ranges lies the Altiplano, a plateau that is 700 km in length, 500 km in width and with an average altitude of 3,500 m, where numerous rivers arise (Desaguadero R.) and the great lakes of Titicaca and Poopó are found. In the northwest of the country are found the Yungas, transition lands irrigated by tributaries of the Amazon (Madre de Dios, Beni, Mamoré) and of the Paraguay River. The climate has different traits depending on the altitude: very hot in the eastern zone, rainy in the north (Amazon sector) and in the Andean range, and arid on the Altiplano (with a rainy season from October to March).

More than half of the Bolivians spring from two Amerindian ethnolinguistic branches: Quechua and Aymara. Almost a third of the population is mestizo, while the descendents of Europeans are a minority. The urban settlement rate is among the lowest in Latin America.

Farming employs more than a third of the working population, but only a small part of the land is suitable for cultivation, and so insufficient to satisfy the domestic food demand. Mining of the country's very rich mineral reserves constitutes a basic source of income (petroleum, natural gas, iron ore, gold, silver, tin). Industry, which is not very well-developed, centers on the petroleum refineries and on the branches of food products and textiles. The Bolivian economy is weighed down by the burden of an enormous foreign debt.

Population evolution and projection

in millions of persons

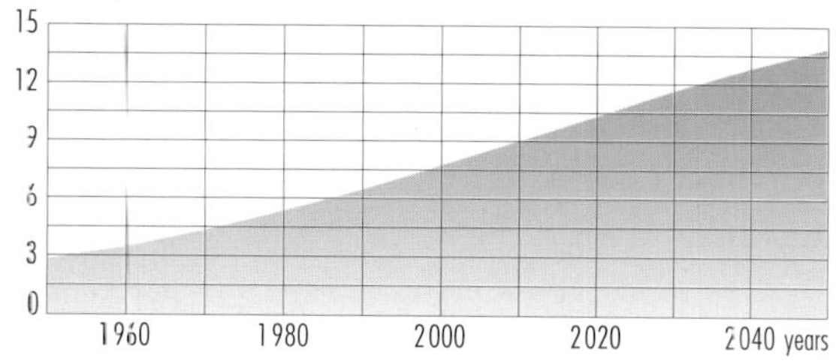

GDP structure

6,131 million dollars

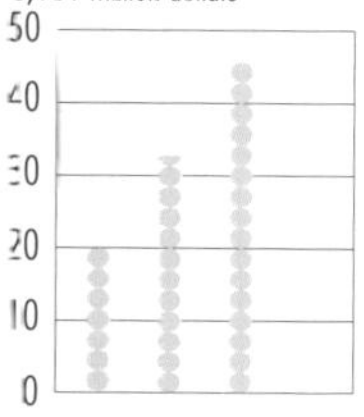

Labor force

2,900,000 persons

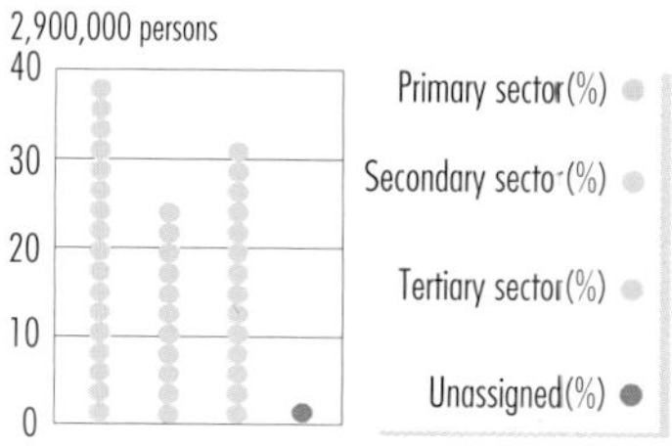

Agriculture

Types of agriculture and livestock production

- Commercial and plantation farming (sugar cane, rice, corn, wheat, cotton, citrus fruits, bananas...)
- Herding (sheep, llamas, alpacas) and some subsistence farming (corn, wheat, potatoes, forage crops, cinchona-tree)
- Pastures and highland farming (potatoes, barley, cinchona-tree, dry French beans)
- Forest/brush/forestry
- Non-arable lands (high mountains, swamplands, saline soils)
- Wheat
- Corn
- Barley
- Rice
- Fruit trees
- Vegetables
- Citrus fruits
- Bananas
- Vegetable oilseeds
- Potatoes
- Beans
- Cotton
- Sugar cane
- Coffee
- Cattle

Vital statistics

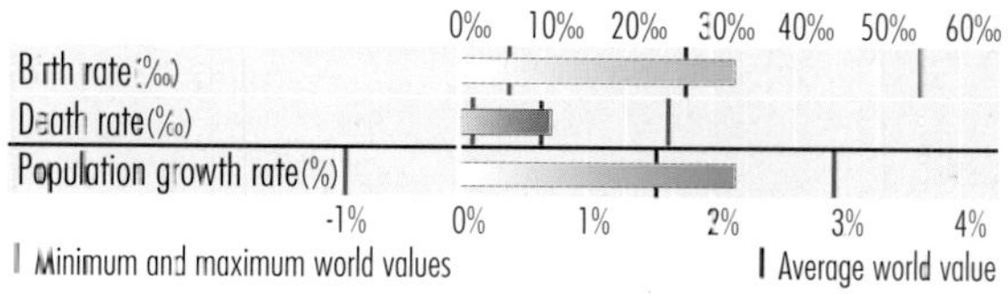

Literacy (% of population over15)

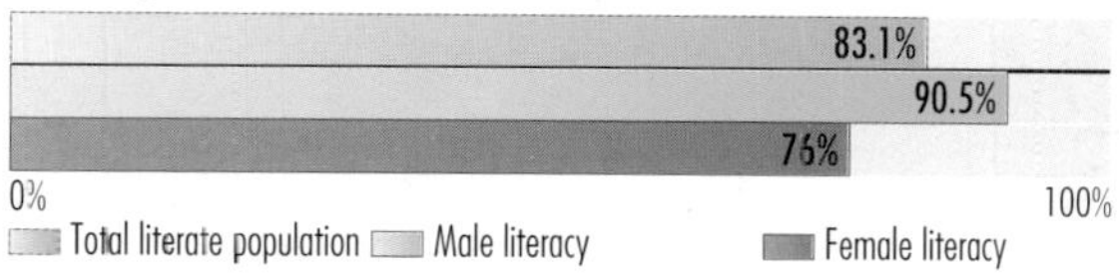

Per capita income (GDP per person)

$763.71/person

$77/person (world minimum: Mozambique) (world maximum:Japan) $37,075/person

Unemployment (% of total population economically active)

Land use

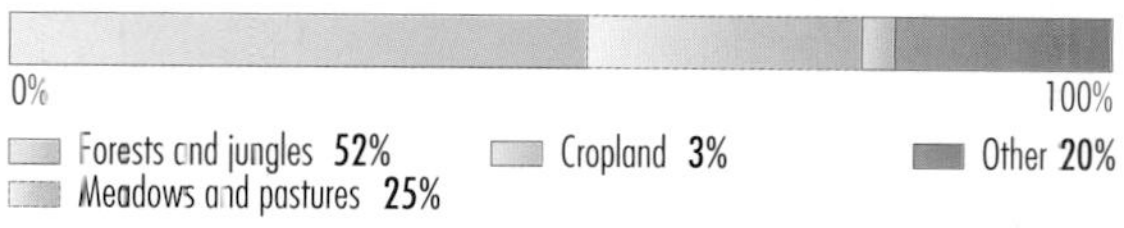

Industry and Mining

Non-energy source mineral resources

Metals

- Antimony
- Zinc
- Copper
- Tin
- Iron ore
- Manganese
- Gold
- Silver
- Lead
- Wolfram
- Area of concentration of tin mines

Rocks and industrial minerals

- Sulphur
- Boron
- Gemstones
- Lithium
- Potash

Mineral fuel resources

Fossil fuels

- Natural gas
- Petroleum

Radioactive fuel

- Uranium

Energy-related installations

- Hydroelectric power plant
- Thermal power plant
- Refinery
- Gas pipeline
- Oil pipeline

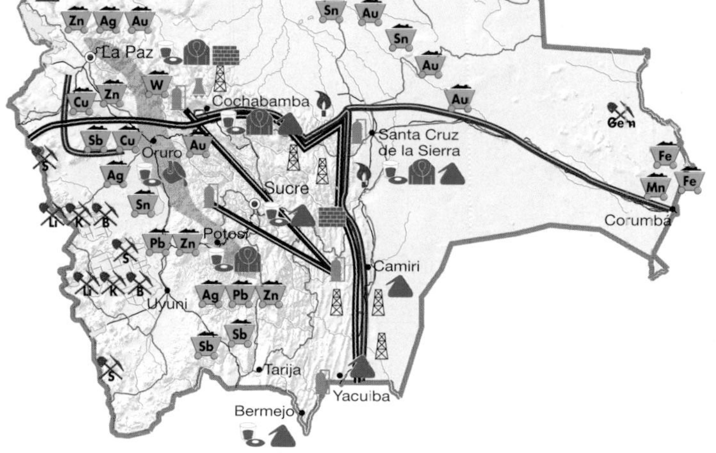

Manufacturing

- Food, beverages and tobacco
- Textiles, clothing, leather and footwear
- Chemical products
- Building materials, glass and cement
- Metallurgy and metal products

Principal imports

Principal exports

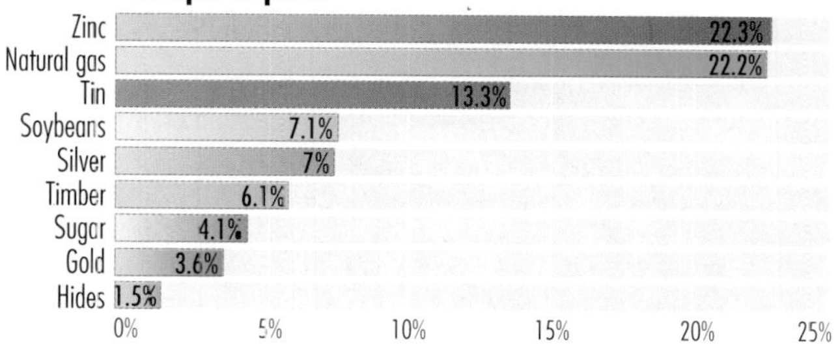

Brazil

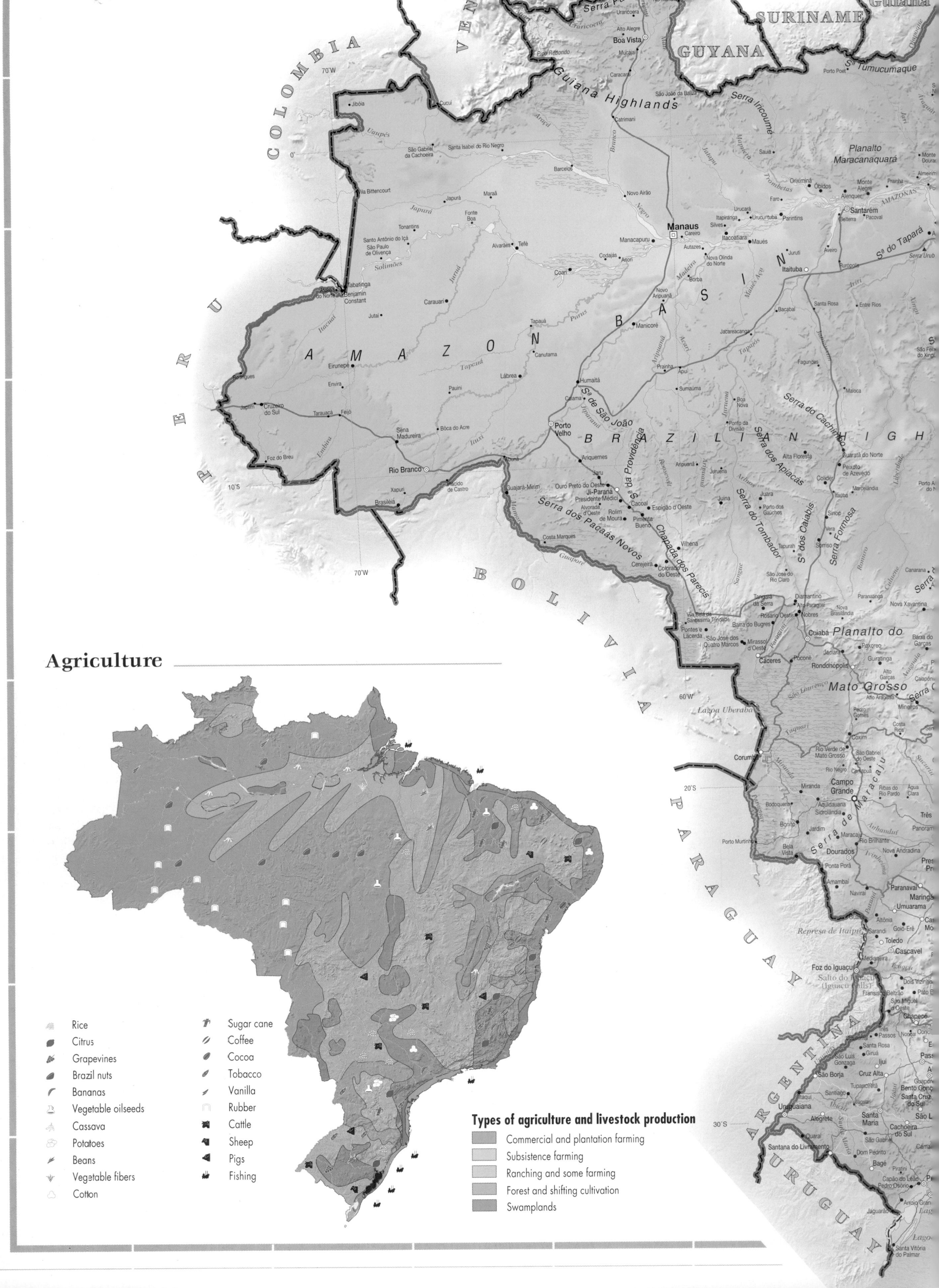
VENEZUELA
COLOMBIA
PERU
BOLIVIA
PARAGUAY
ARGENTINA
URUGUAY
GUYANA
SURINAME
French Guiana
Serra Paracaima
Guiana Highlands
Serra Iricoumé
Sª Tumucumaque
Planalto Maracanaquará
AMAZON BASIN
BRAZILIAN HIGH
Sª do Tapará
Sª de São João
Sª da Providência
Serra dos Pacaás Novos
Chapada dos Parecis
Serra do Cachimbo
Serra dos Apiacás
Serra do Tombador
Sª dos Caiabis
Serra Formosa
Planalto do Mato Grosso
Serra de Maracaju
Lagoa Uberaba
Represa de Itaipu
Salto do Iguaçu (Iguaçu Falls)
Boa Vista
Manaus
Santarém
Porto Velho
Rio Branco
Cuiabá
Campo Grande
Corumbá
Foz do Iguaçu
Cruzeiro do Sul
Tabatinga
Benjamin Constant
São Gabriel da Cachoeira
Santa Isabel do Rio Negro
Barcelos
Tefé
Coari
Manacapuru
Parintins
Óbidos
Itaituba
Humaitá
Ariquemes
Ji-Paraná
Vilhena
Guajará-Mirim
Cáceres
Rondonópolis
Dourados
Ponta Porã
Uruguaiana
Alegrete
Santana do Livramento
Santa Maria
70°W
60°W
0°
10°S
20°S
30°S
Agriculture
Rice
Citrus
Grapevines
Brazil nuts
Bananas
Vegetable oilseeds
Cassava
Potatoes
Beans
Vegetable fibers
Cotton
Sugar cane
Coffee
Cocoa
Tobacco
Vanilla
Rubber
Cattle
Sheep
Pigs
Fishing
Types of agriculture and livestock production
Commercial and plantation farming
Subsistence farming
Ranching and some farming
Forest and shifting cultivation
Swamplands

Official name: República Federativa do Brazil
Form of government: federal republic
Capital: Brasília
Official language: Portuguese
Monetary unit: real
Religious affiliation: Roman Catholic (76%), evangelical Protestant (11%), other (13%)
Ethnic composition of the population: Caucasian (55%), mixed Caucasian and African (38%), African (6%), other (1%)
Area: 8,511,996 sq km
Total population: 162,661,000 inhabitants
Population density: 19.1 persons per sq km

Brazil is one of the largest countries in the world and the most extensive of South America. Its territory encompasses lands included between the Equator and the Tropic of Capricorn. The long coastlines of the Atlantic Ocean, to the east, have gentle landform features and great bays (Ilha Grande, Todos os Santos). This region lacks important relief, as almost half of the territory is below an altitude of 200 m. In the center-south and east rise the highlands (Mato Grosso, Goiás), plateaus that mark the water divide between the Amazon River Basin and that of the Rio de la Plata. Parallel to the coast there are some mountain ranges (Pico da Bandeira, 2,890 m), as well as in the north, on the frontier with Venezuela and the Guayanas. The basin of the Amazon and its principal tributaries (more than seven million square kilometers) includes more than half of the land area of Brazil. Linked to the river is the greatest tropical rainforest on the planet (8.3 million sq km), although it is threatened by farming, ranching and mining activities, which have destroyed a tenth of its original surface area. The climate has tropical and torrid traits, with very high average temperatures (between 25-30 °C), a high level of humidity in the air and abundant precipitations that can reach apto 2,000 mm annually. The differences in altitude are the cause of significant regional variations (increasing dryness and milder temperatures in the highlands).

Brazilian society is distinguished by its interracial character: the majority of its members are Caucasian, that live together with the mixed Caucasian and African, black (descended from African slaves) and Asian (made up mostly of Japanese) groups. The birth rate is high and, therefore, the country has a high population growth rate. The population is distributed very unevenly, with vast interior areas practically uninhabited and great human concentrations in the cities of the southern coast (Sao Paulo, Rio de Janeiro, Belo Horizonte).

Brazil enjoys enviable macroeconomical figures that raise its GDP to the leading positions in the world classification. Large revenues are obtained from plantation farming (coffee, sugar, cocoa), forestry (rubber) and mining (bauxite, iron ore, gold, precious stones). The industrial sector, quite well-developed, centers on metallurgy, iron-and-steel working and the production of weaponry. The flow of tourists is constant thanks to the beauties of the country. Sao Paulo has an active stock and financial market. Its immense natural wealth has not been enough to remove Brazil from the list of developing countries. Its macroeconomic structure, oriented towards exportation, is excessively subject to the fluctuation of prices in the international market. Most of the capital invested comes from foreign companies or is controlled by speculators. Inflation, the flight of capital and the large foreign debt prevent the country from destining its own funds to the renovation of the industrial structure or to the development of programs of formation and social assistance suitable for a great number of the population that live below poverty level. Urban misery is clearly visible in the agglomerations of fabelas (huts) that surround the modern and centrally-located neighbourhoods of the great cities.

Ecosystems

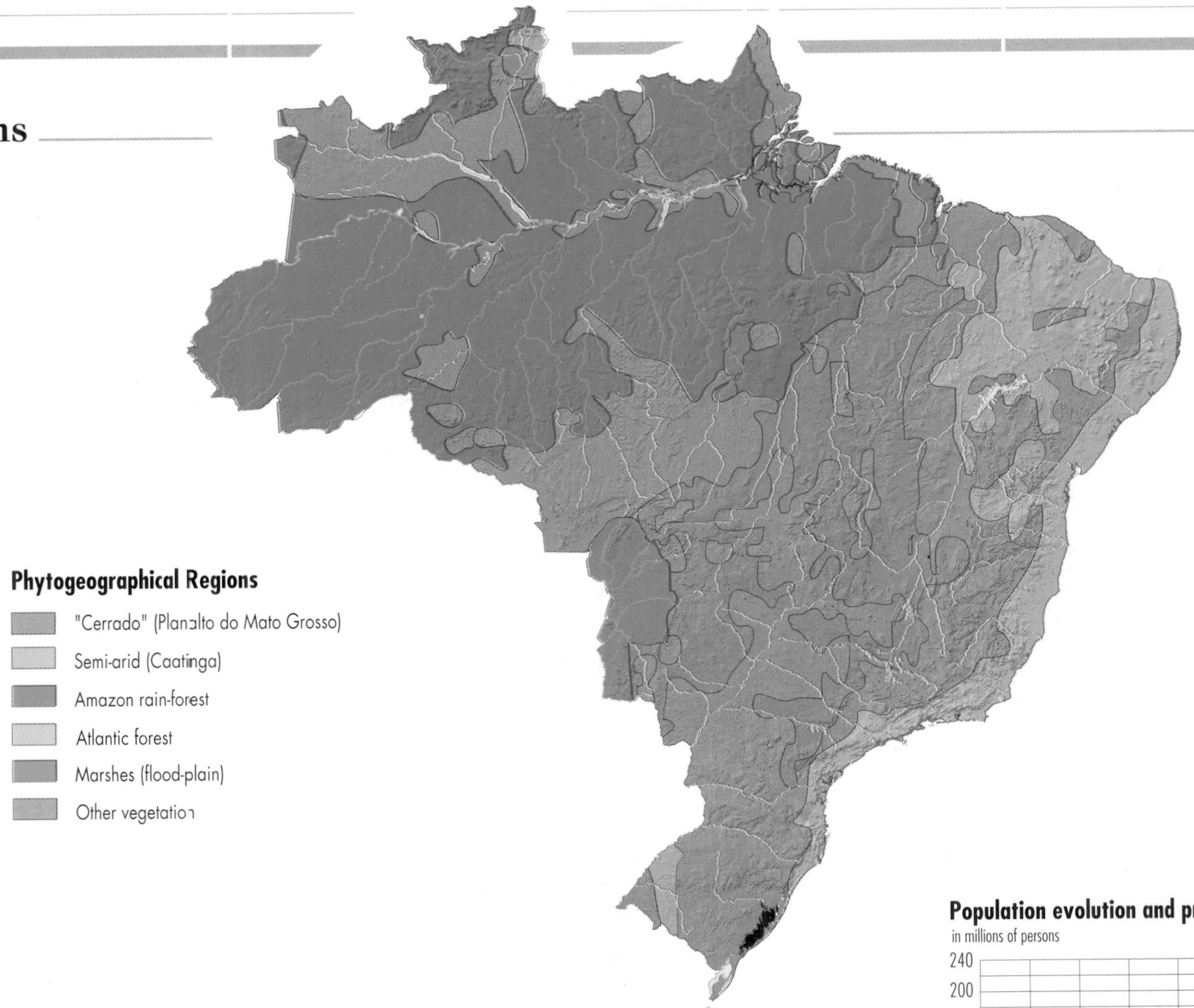

Vegetation

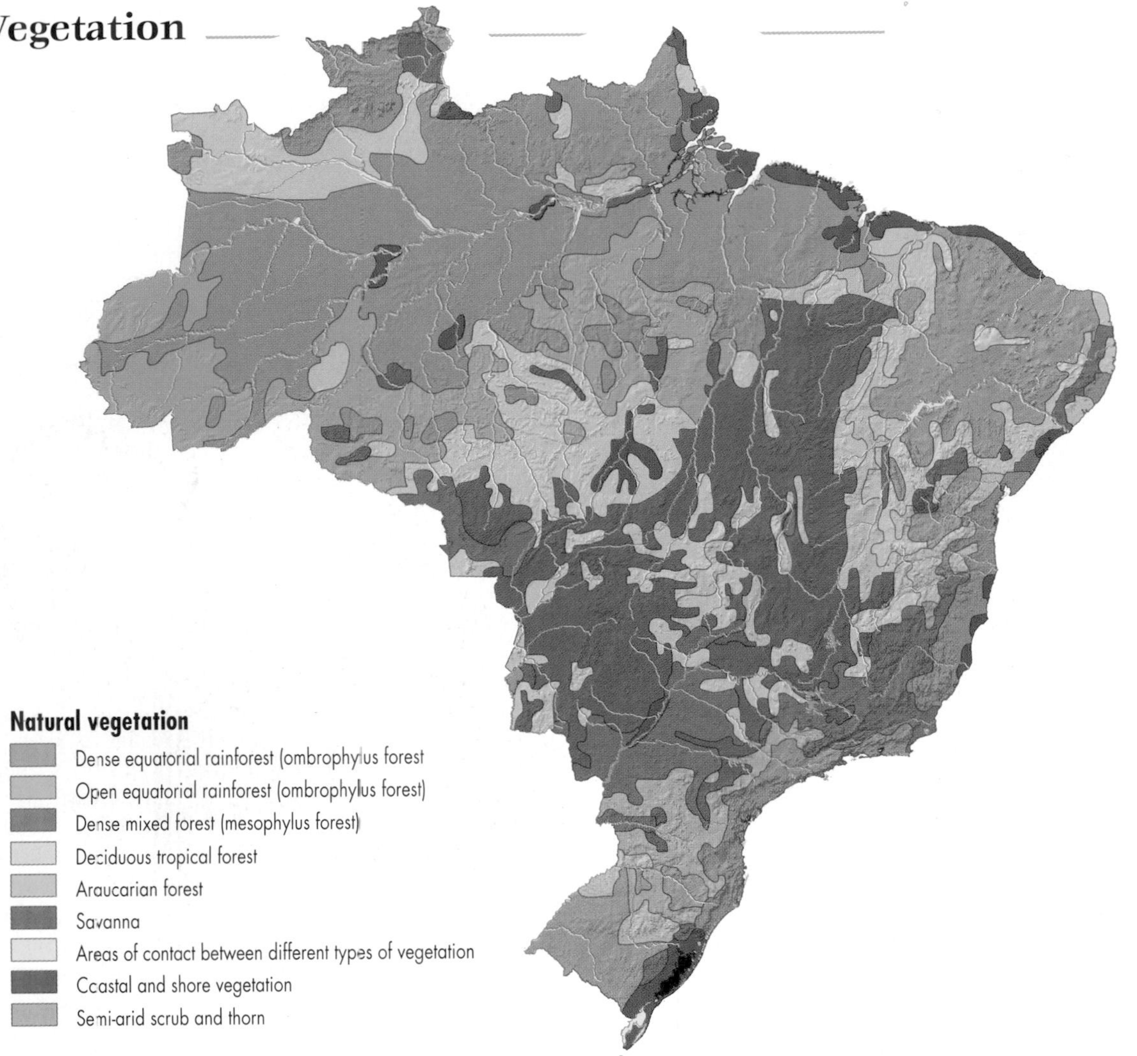

Principal Imports

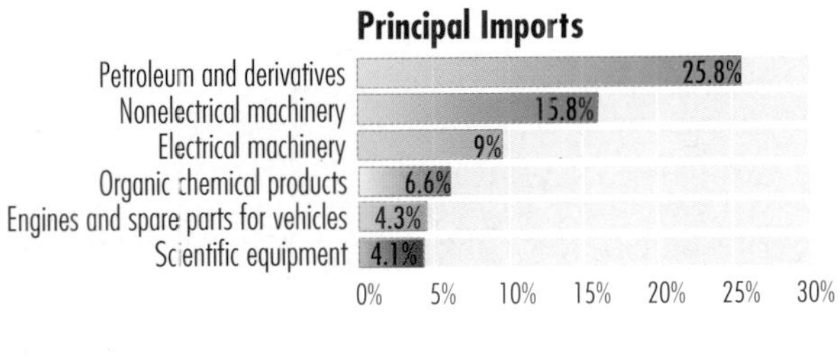

Principal Exports

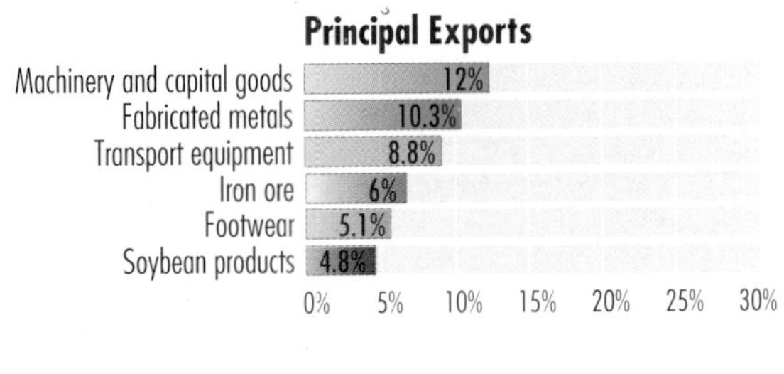

Population evolution and projection

in millions of persons

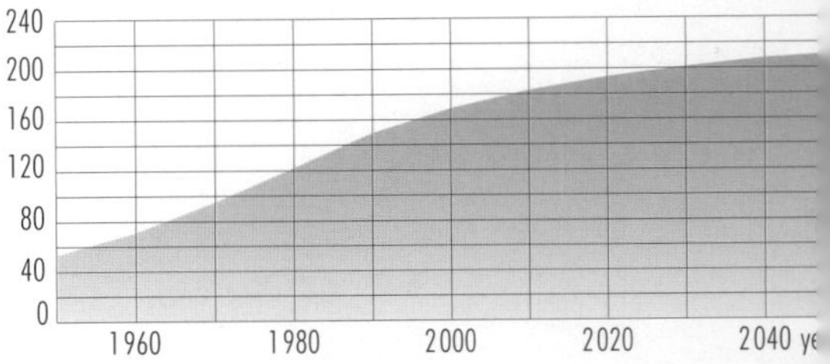

GDP structure

688,085 million dollars

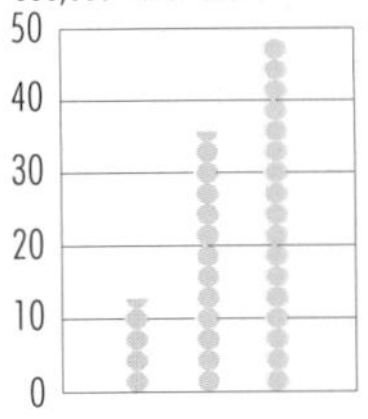

Labor force

71,021,000 persons

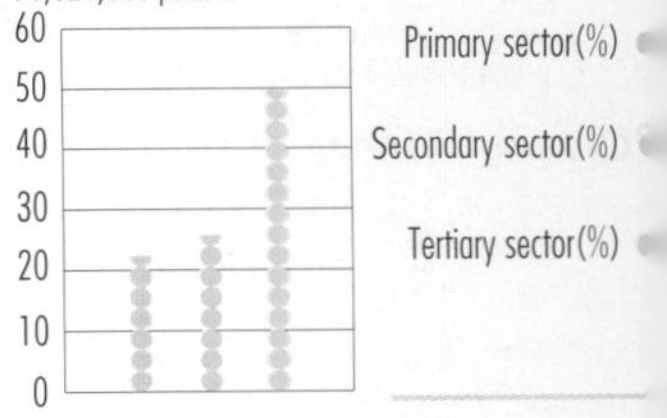

Population age distribution

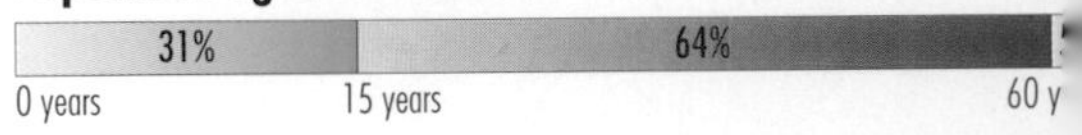

Vital statistics

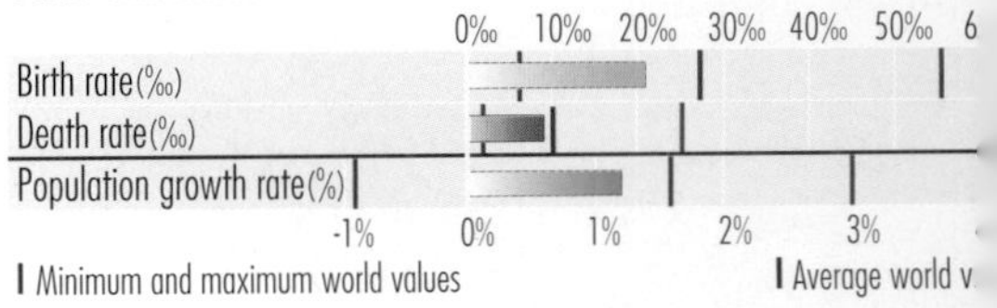

Literacy (% of population over15)

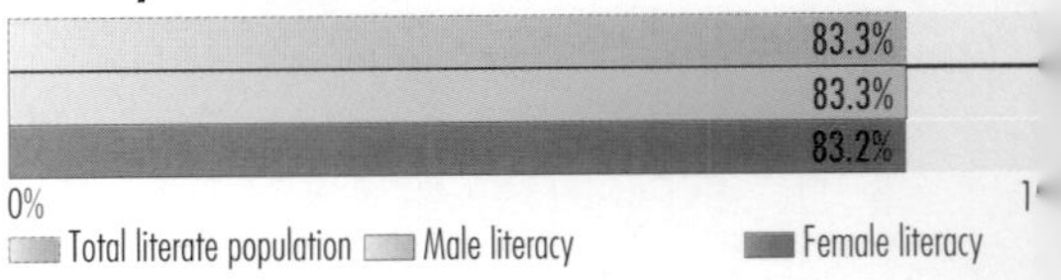

Per capita income (GDP per person)

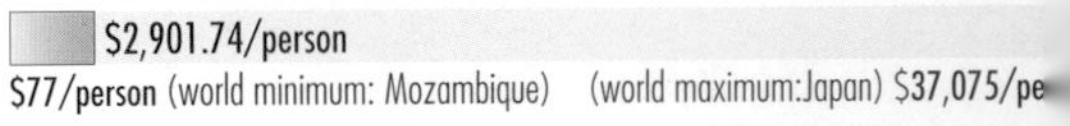

$77/person (world minimum: Mozambique) (world maximum:Japan) $37,075/pe

Unemployment (% of total population economically active)

Land use

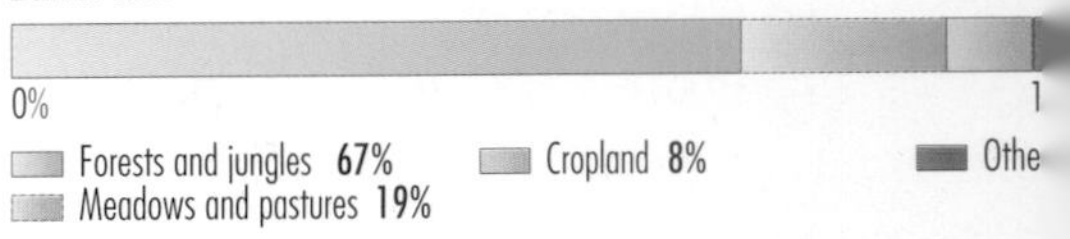

Industry, Mining and Energy

Non-energy source mineral resources

Metals

- Bauxite
- Zinc
- Copper
- Chromite
- Tin
- Iron ore
- Manganese
- Nickel
- Gold
- Lead

Rocks and industrial minerals

- Asbestos
- Kaolin
- Diamonds
- Phosphates
- Graphite
- Gypsum

Mineral fuel resources

- Coal
- Natural gas
- Petroleum

Energy-related installations

- Hydroelectric power plant
- Nuclear reactor
- Refinery
- Gas pipeline
- Oil pipeline

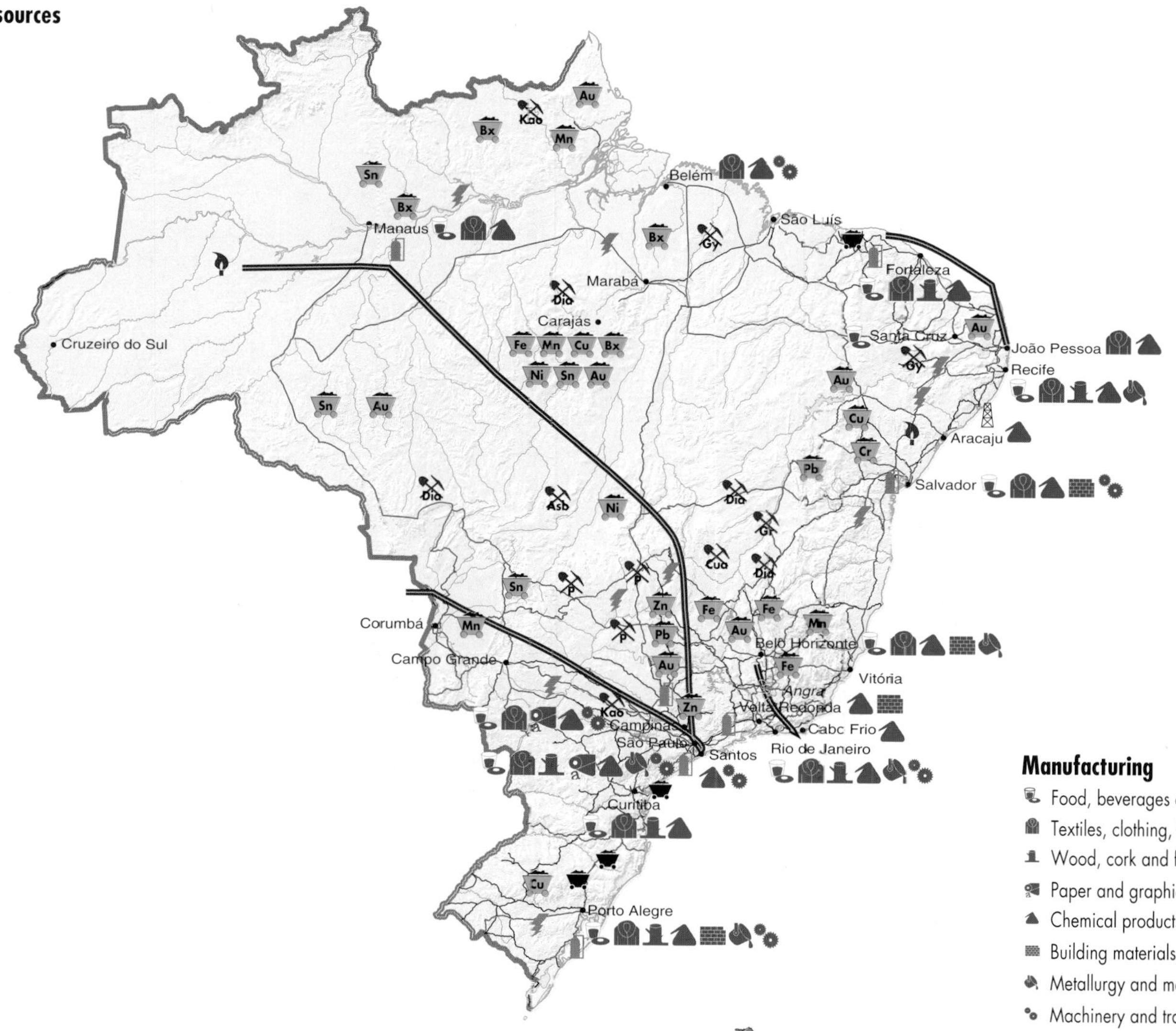

Manufacturing

- Food, beverages and tobacco
- Textiles, clothing, leather and footwear
- Wood, cork and furniture
- Paper and graphic arts
- Chemical products
- Building materials, glass and cement
- Metallurgy and metal products
- Machinery and transport equipment

Population

Population density (persons per sq km)

- Fewer than 2
- From 2 to 5
- From 5 to 25
- From 25 to 100
- More than 100

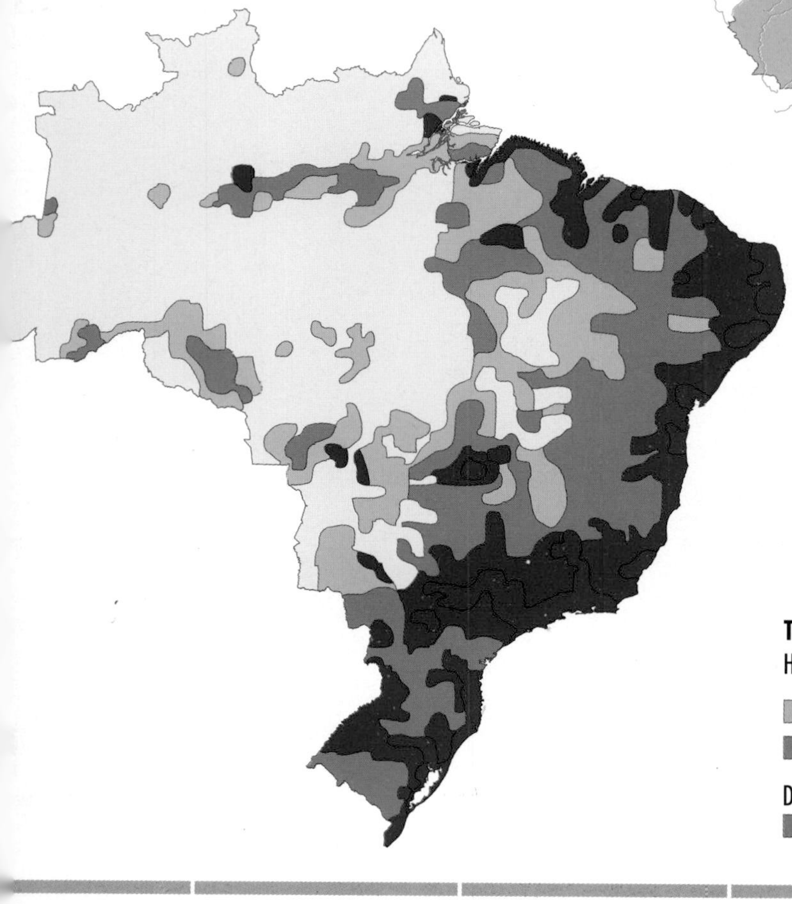

Climates

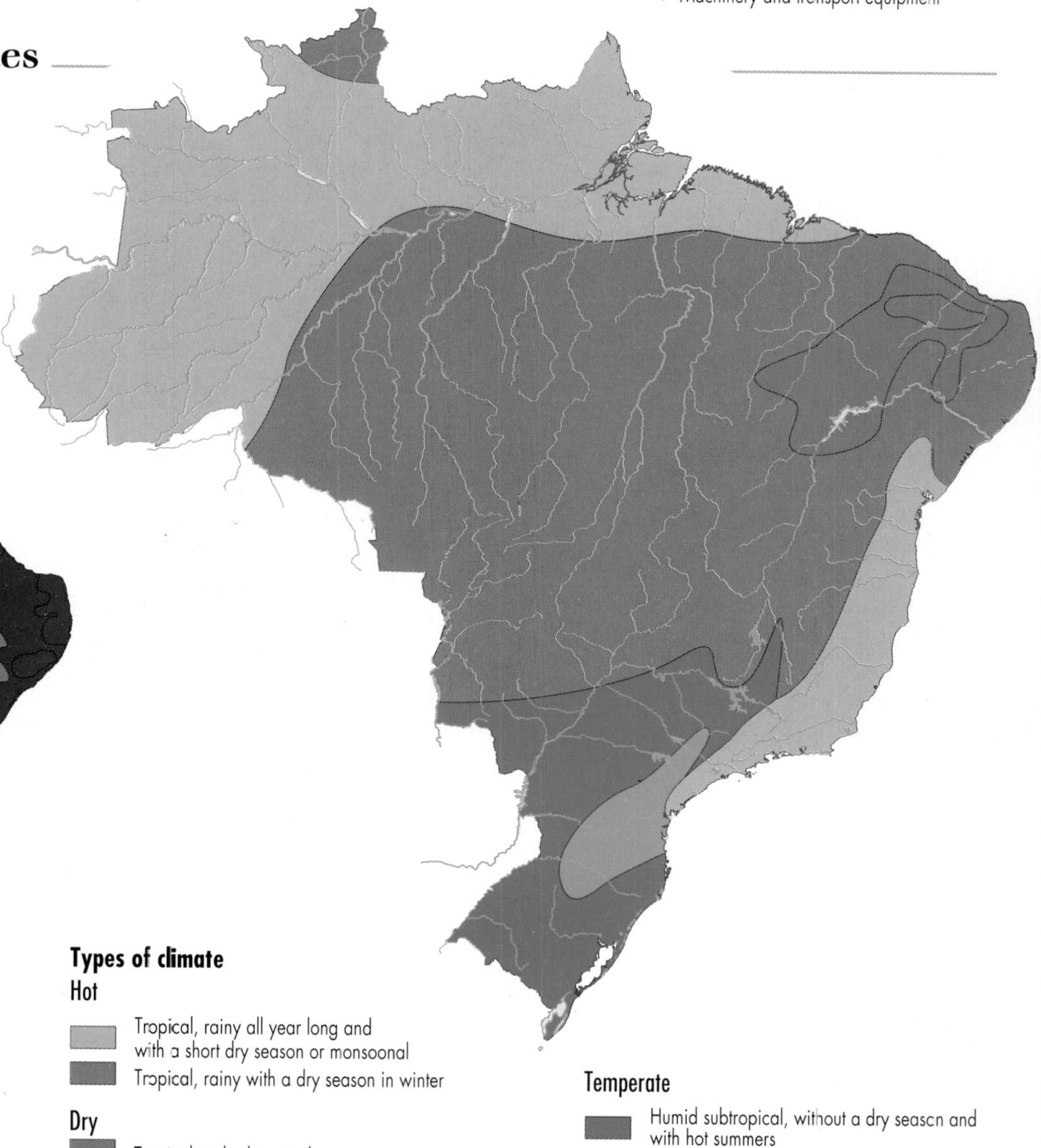

Types of climate

Hot

- Tropical, rainy all year long and with a short dry season or monsoonal
- Tropical, rainy with a dry season in winter

Dry

- Tropical and subtropical steppe

Temperate

- Humid subtropical, without a dry season and with hot summers
- Marine west coast temperate

Chile

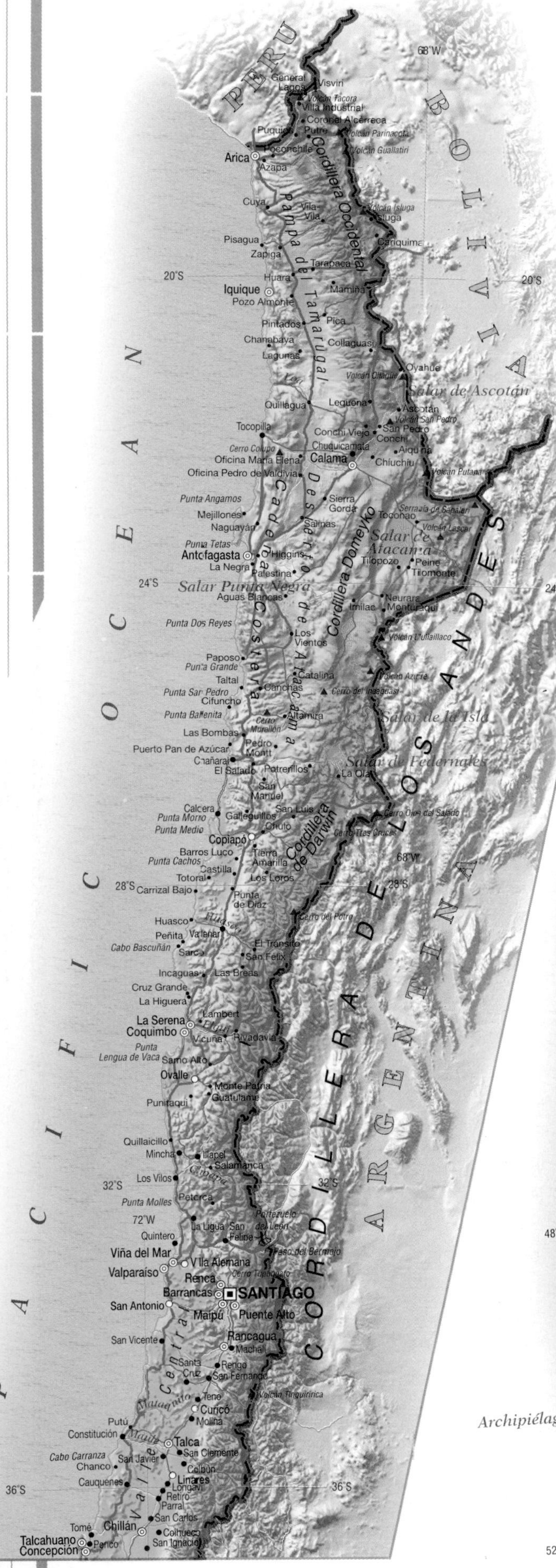

Chile is a republic of South America with coasts on the Pacific Ocean, extending north to south between 18º and 56º south latitude. Its territory —a narrow strip between the Andes and the sea— has a markedly linear lay-out, with more than 4,000 km of length and an average width of 200 km. Chilean terrain, very abrupt, has several geomorphological units, all oriented in an east-west direction. The Andes form a mountain barrier along all its eastern border and include numerous volcanoes. Parallel to the coastline runs the Coastal chain, very eroded by streams and rivers. Between the two mountain chains lies the Central Valley, the north of which is occupied by the Atacama Desert. In the far south appears the Tierra del Fuego island chain, with elevations above 2,000 m. The rivers —short and with plentiful water-flow— have their sources in the Andes or in the Coastal range, and flow in an east-west direction towards the Pacific. Chile has extreme climatic variations according to the region, due to the differences in latitude. In the north, the Atacama Desert has an arid tropical climate. In the central region, which has typically Mediterranean climatic traits, dry summers are followed by mild winters. Farther south the characteristics of a marine west coast climate dominate, with high amounts of precipitation and moderate temperatures. In Tierra del Fuego, near the continent of Antarctica, freezing rains and winds are constants. Differences in altitude also provoke local variations.

Most Chileans descend from the interbreeding of Spanish colonists and the aboriginal peoples. The Amerindian minority is a small percentage of the population. In Chile there are hardly any blacks, in contrast to other Latinoamerican countries. The high birth rate generates important population growth, although it has been contained during recent years. A little less than half of the population is concentrated in the megalopolis of Santiago, the capital of the nation. Mining, the country's main source of revenues, has immense resources (copper, saltpetre, nitrates, phosphates, petroleum and natural gas). Agricultural production is oriented towards exportation and the fishing industry is consolidating itself, favored by the demand and Japanese investments. Industry has developed new branches (canning, petrochemicals). The Chilean economy, historically dependent on foreign capital, above all British, has opted in the last few decades for a privatization of different sectors, facilities for foreign investment, containing inflation, the freezing of salaries, payment of foreign debt, cutting public spending, etc. These measures have favored agrarian and industrial modernization; but, on the other side of the scales, the dependence on foreign capital continues to exist, a growing polarization between classes is taking place and more than a third of the population is socially unprotected.

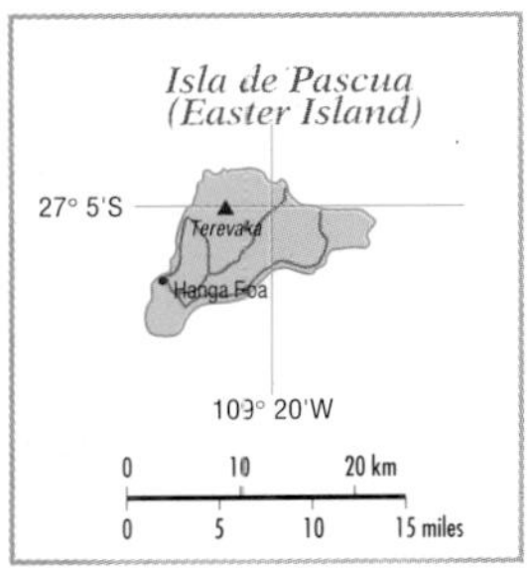

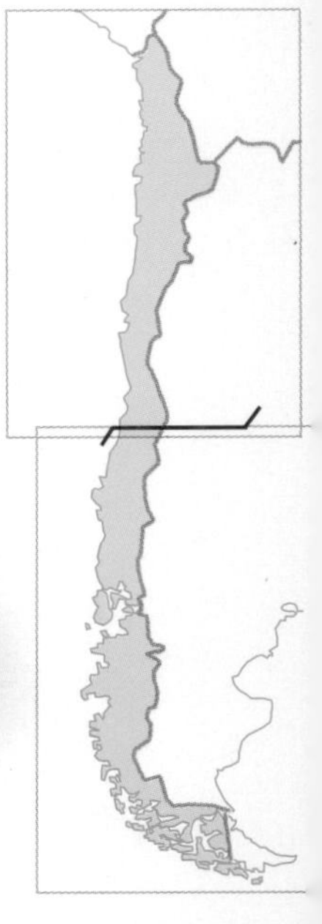

Agriculture

Types of agriculture and livestock production

- Cereal farming (corn, rice, oats, wheat, barley)
- Irrigation/intensive farming
- Sheep-herding
- Forest/brush
- Non-arable land (deserts, high mountains, glaciers)
- Corn (maize)
- Rice
- Fruits and vegetables
- Apples
- Peaches
- Citrus fruits
- Potatoes
- Grapevines
- Tobacco
- Cattle
- Sheep
- Goats
- Fishing

Industry and Mining

Non-energy source mineral resources

Metals

- Zinc
- Copper
- Iron ore
- Manganese
- Molybdenum
- Gold
- Silver
- Lead

Rocks and industrial minerals

- Litium
- Magnesite
- Nitrates
- Salt

Mineral fuel resources

- Coal
- Natural gas
- Petroleum

Energy-related installations

- Electric power plant
- Hydroelectric power plant
- Refinery

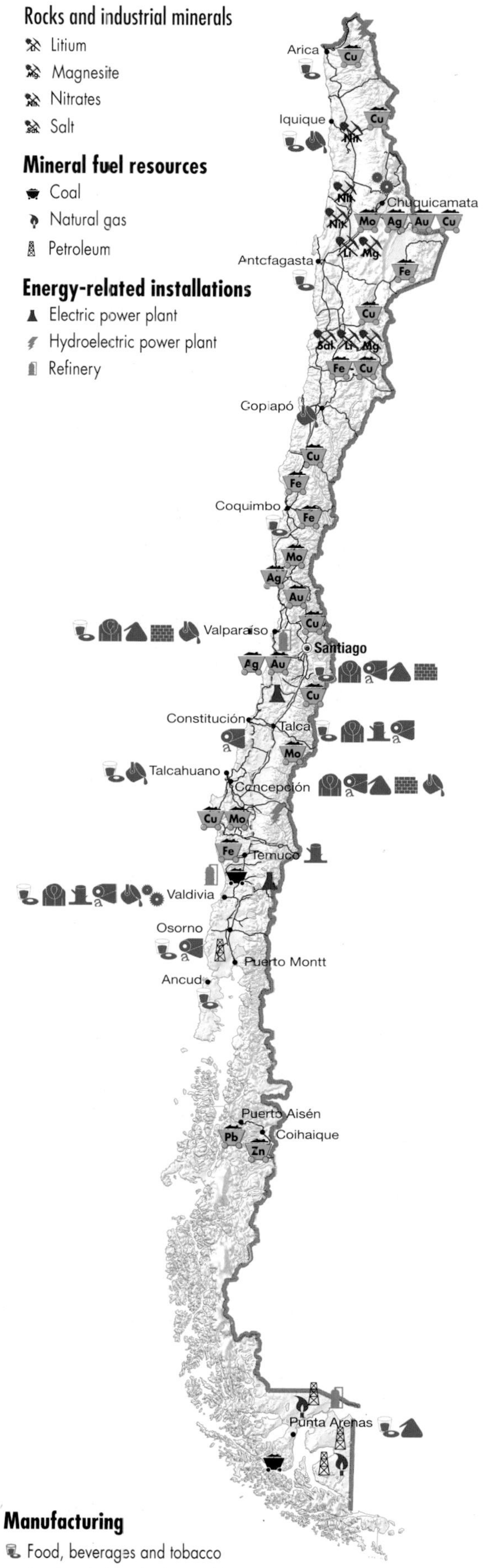

Manufacturing

- Food, beverages and tobacco
- Textiles, clothing, leather and footwear
- Wood, cork and furniture
- Paper and graphic arts
- Chemical products
- Building materials, glass and cement
- Metallurgy and metal products
- Machinery and transport equipment

Official name: Republic of Chile
Form of government: presidential republic
Capital: Santiago
Official language: Spanish
Monetary unit: new Chilean peso
Religious affiliation: Roman Catholic (80.7%), Protestant (6.1%), Jewish (0.2%), atheist and nonreligious (12.8%), other (0.2%)
Ethnic composition of the population: European and European/Amerindian (95%), Amerindian (3%), other (2%)
Area: 756,626 sq km
Total population: 14,333,000 inhabitants
Population density: 18.9 persons per sq km

Population evolution and projection

in millions of persons

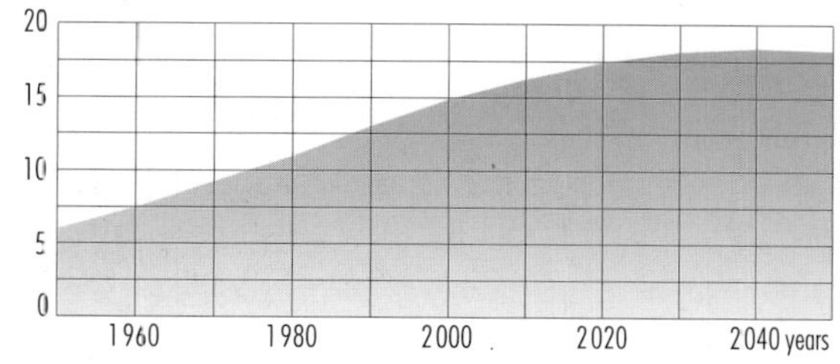

GDP structure

67,297 million dollars

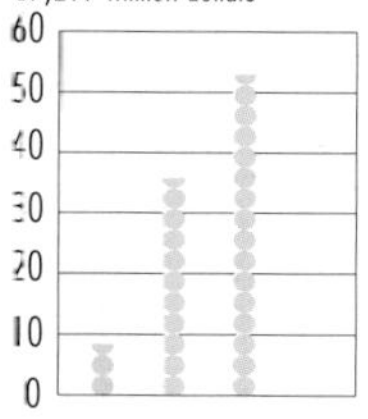

Labor force

5,468,000 persons

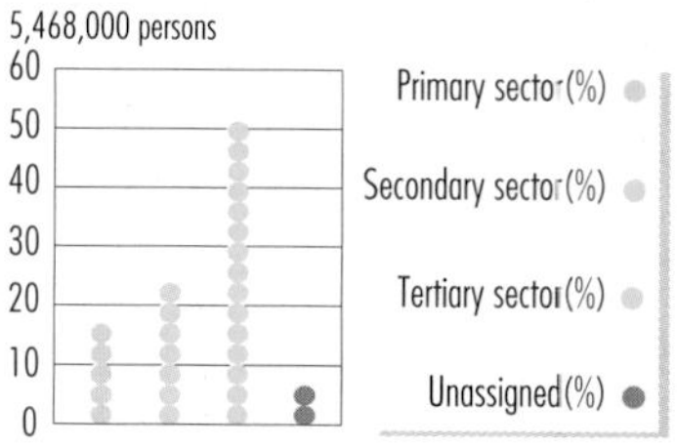

Population age distribution

29% | 64% | 7%

0 years · 15 years · 60 years

Vital statistics

0‰ 10‰ 20‰ 30‰ 40‰ 50‰ 60‰

- Birth rate (‰)
- Death rate (‰)
- Population growth rate (%)

-1% 0% 1% 2% 3% 4%

I Minimum and maximum world values · I Average world value

Literacy (% of population over 15)

- Total literate population: 95.2%
- Male literacy: 95.4%
- Female literacy: 95%

0% – 100%

Per capita income (GDP per person)

$2,961.69/person

$77/person (world minimum: Mozambique) (world maximum: Japan) $37,075/person

Unemployment (% of total population economically active)

6%

0% – 50%

Land use

0% – 100%

- Forests and jungles 21%
- Meadows and pastures 16%
- Cropland 7%
- Other 56%

Colombia

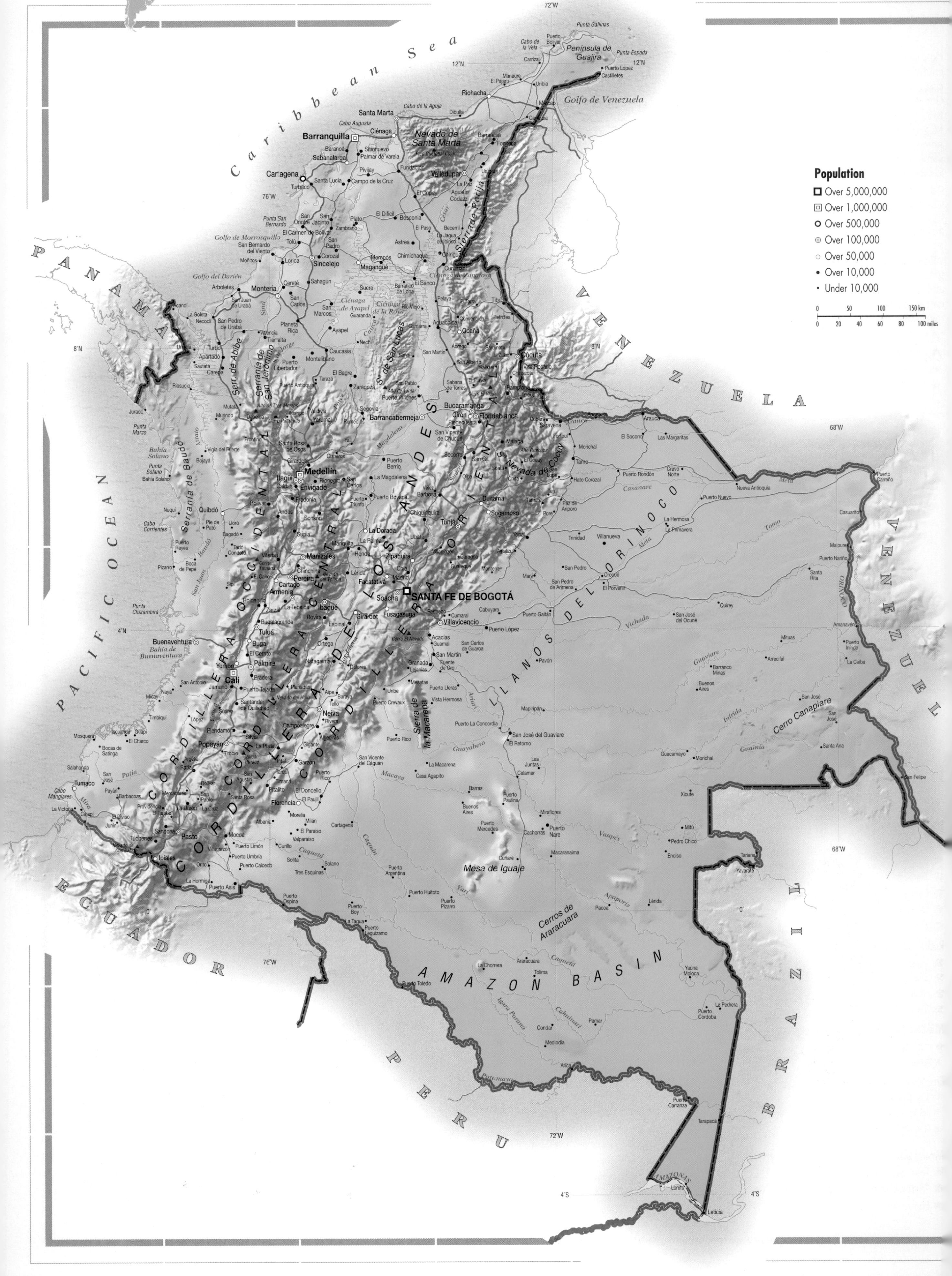
Population
Over 5,000,000
Over 1,000,000
Over 500,000
Over 100,000
Over 50,000
Over 10,000
Under 10,000
0 50 100 150 km
0 20 40 60 80 100 miles
Caribbean Sea
PACIFIC OCEAN
PANAMA
VENEZUELA
ECUADOR
PERU
BRAZIL
SANTA FE DE BOGOTÁ
Medellín
Cali
Barranquilla
Cartagena
Santa Marta
Bucaramanga
Cúcuta
Manizales
Pereira
Armenia
Ibagué
Villavicencio
Pasto
Popayán
Neiva
Montería
Sincelejo
Valledupar
Riohacha
Tunja
Quibdó
Florencia
Leticia
Península de Guajira
Golfo de Venezuela
Golfo de Morrosquillo
Golfo del Darién
Nevado de Santa Marta
Sierra de Perijá
CORDILLERA OCCIDENTAL
CORDILLERA CENTRAL
CORDILLERA ORIENTAL
LOS ANDES
Serranía de Baudó
Nevado de Cocuy
LLANOS DEL ORINOCO
Sierra de la Macarena
Mesa de Iguaje
Cerro Canapiare
Cerros de Araracuara
AMAZON BASIN
Magdalena
Cauca
Meta
Guaviare
Caquetá
Putumayo
Vaupés
Apaporis
Orinoco
Amazonas
72°W
68°W
76°W
12°N
8°N
4°N
0°
4°S

Colombia is a republic of South America. Its physical environment is dominated by the Andes, that traverse the country from north to south forming three branches: the Occidental, Central and Oriental mountain ranges. Between them extend two great valleys: that of the Magdalena River and that of the Cauca River, open in the north. The coasts have low or irregular relief, swampy in some zones. East of the Oriental range are located the lowlands that form part of the Amazon River Basin. The country has a rich hydrographic system. The climate is characterized by great variation: the low areas enjoy a wet tropical-equatorial climate; gradually, as the land gains altitude, the temperatures fall, until reaching the cold and perpetual snows covering the high mountain tops. Each valley has its own micro-climate. With an elevated annual growth rate, Colombia has a high population density, although it is distributed irregularly. The population is composed of groups of mulattos (in the Caribbean regions), mestizos (in the Andes valleys), Andean indigenous groups (enclaves at high elevations in the Andes mountain range) and Amerindian tribes (in the Amazon rainforest). The country has great mineral wealth, with emeralds and petroleum being especially important. The fertility of its soils and the variety of climates make possible the existence of vast coffee plantations —of which Colombia is one of the main producers— cotton, bananas and other crops destined for export, in addition to the farming dedicated to subsistence. The manufacturing sector (textiles, iron and steel industry, chemicals and processing) is presently experiencing a phase of growth. In Colombia, large amounts of "black" money circulates, illegal profits generated by the exportation of cocaine. The struggle against the mafias is bleeding the country dry humanly and economically, and has a negative influence on tourism and industry. The enormous sums of drug money have also promoted a financial sector. Colombia is a country of great social, economic and territorial contrasts.

Official name: Republic of Colombia
Form of government: republic
Capital: Santa Fe de Bogotá
Official language: Spanish
Monetary unit: peso colombiano
Religious affiliation: Roman Catholic (93.1%), other (6.9%)
Ethnic composition of the population: mestizo (58%), white (20%), mulatto (14%), black (4%), mixed black-Amerindian (3%), Amerindian (1%)
Area: 1,141,748 sq km
Total population: 36,813,000 inhabitants
Population density: 32.2 persons per sq km

Agriculture

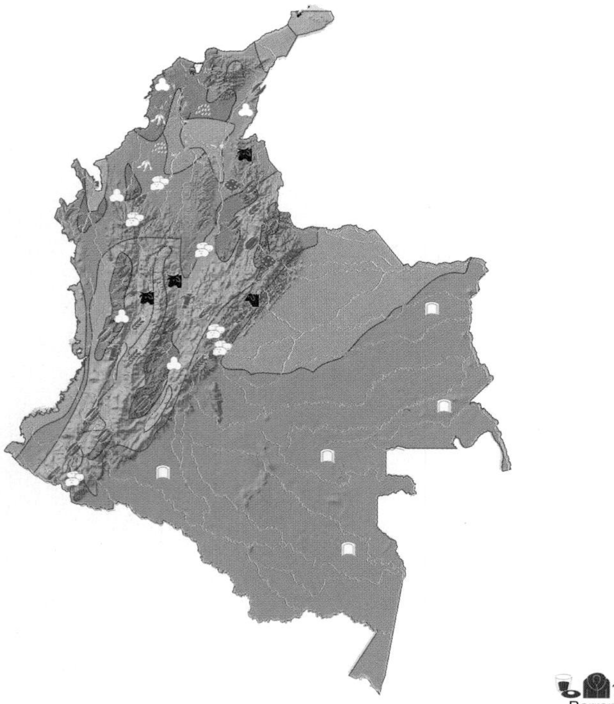

Types of agriculture and livestock production

- Commercial and plantation farming (cotton, tobacco, bananas, coffee, sugar cane)
- Pastures and highland farming (cereals, corn, potatoes, forage crops, cattle)
- Ranching
- Forest/forestry and Shifting cultivation
- Non-arable land (deserts, swamps)

Corn (maize)	Sugar cane
Rice	Coffee
Sorghum	Cocoa
Fruits	Tobacco
Bananas	Rubber
Yucca	Cattle
Potatoes	Sheep
Cotton	

Population evolution and projection

in millions of persons

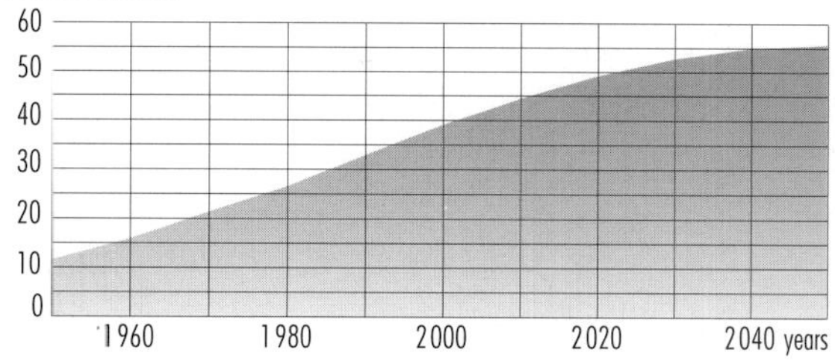

GDP structure

76,112 mill on dollars

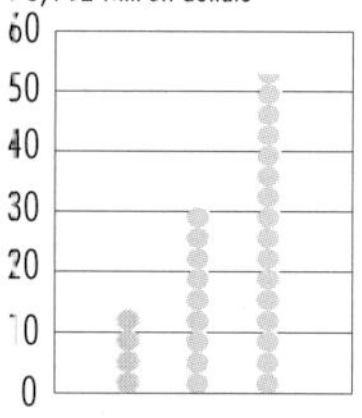

Labor force

14,513,000 persons

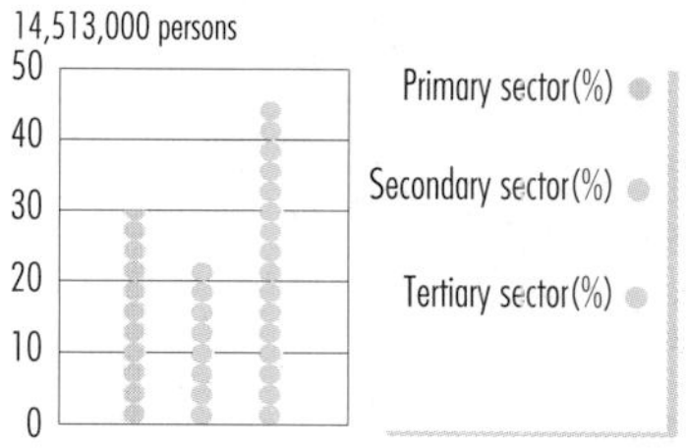

Population age distribution

Vital statistics

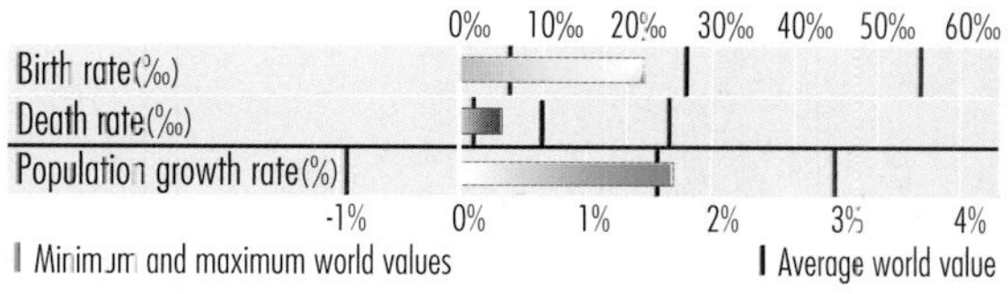

Literacy (% of population over15)

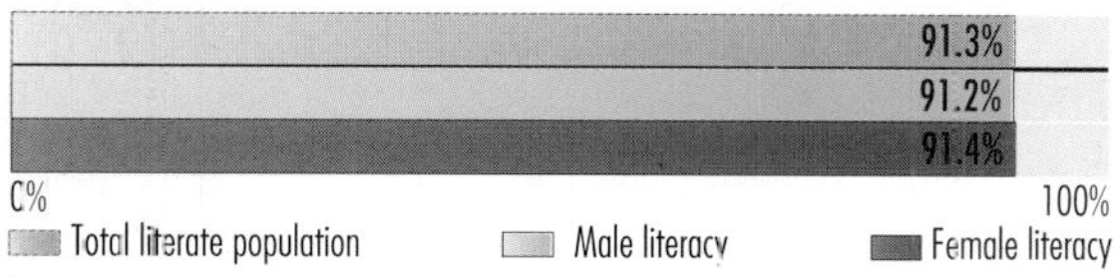

Per capita income (GDP per person)

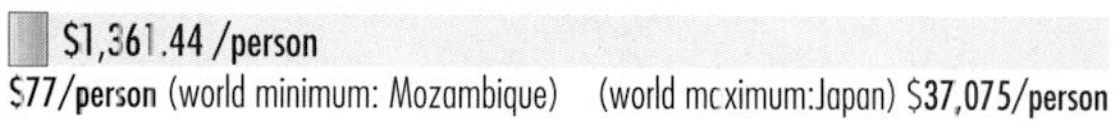

Unemployment (% of total population economically active)

Land use

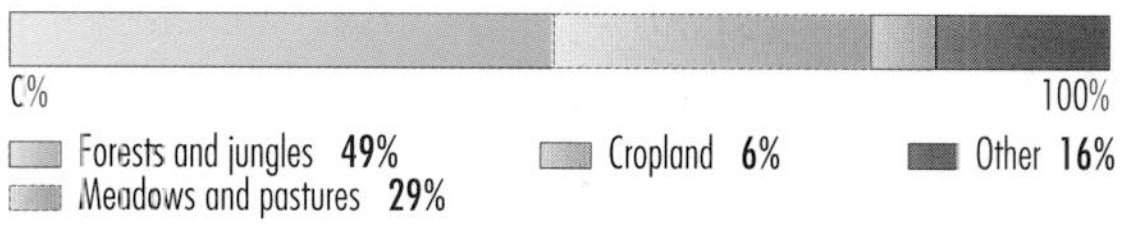

Industry and Mining

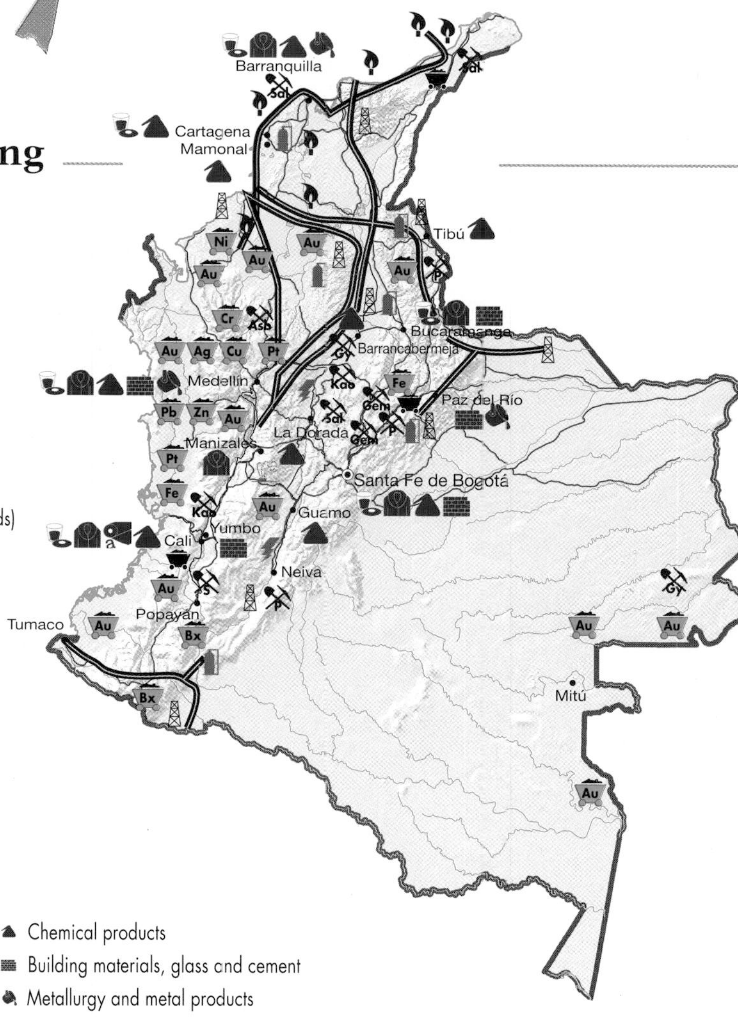

Non-energy source mineral resources

Metals

Bauxite	Nickel
Zinc	Gold
Copper	Silver
Chromite	Platinum
Iron ore	Lead

Rocks and industrial minerals

Asbestos	Gemstones (emeralds)
Sulphur	Salt
Kaolin	Gypsum
Phosphates	

Mineral fuel resources

- Coal
- Petroleum
- Natural gas

Energy-related installations

- Geothermal power plant
- Hydroelectric power plant
- Refinery

Manufacturing

- Food, beverages and tobacco
- Textiles, clothing, leather and footwear
- Paper and graphic arts
- Chemical products
- Building materials, glass and cement
- Metallurgy and metal products

Ecuador

Official name: Republic of Ecuador

Form of government: republic

Capital: Quito

Official language: Spanish

Monetary unit: sucre

Religious affiliation: Roman Catholic (93%), other (7%)

Ethnic composition of the population: mestizo (55%), Amerindian (25%), white (10%), black (10%)

Area: 272,045 sq km

Total population: 11,466,000 inhabitants

Population density: 42.1 persons per sq km

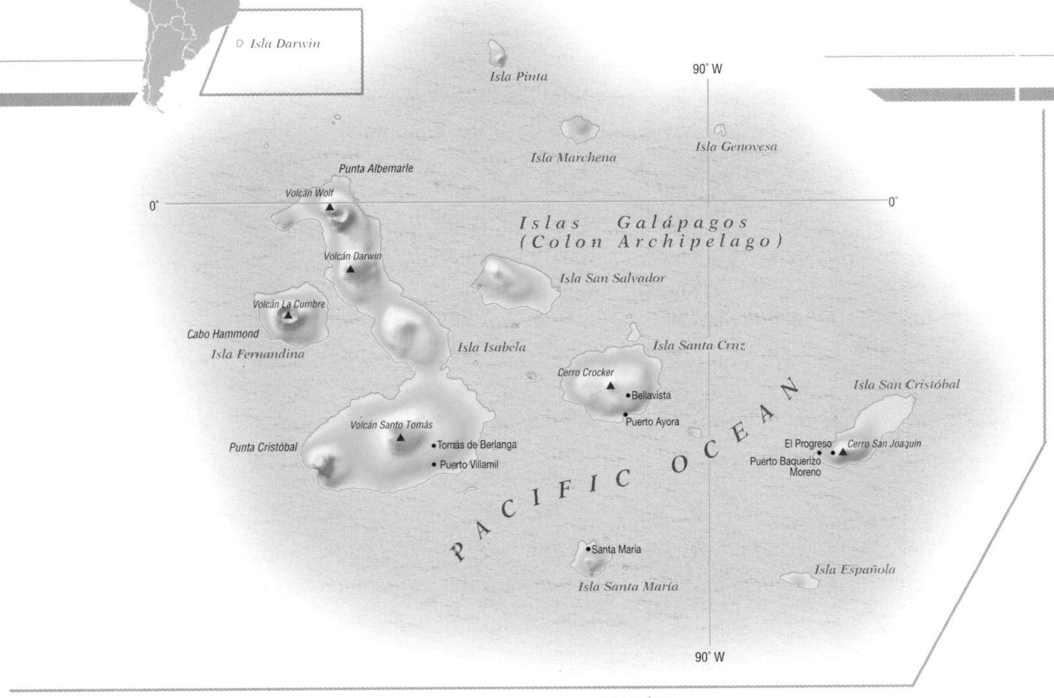

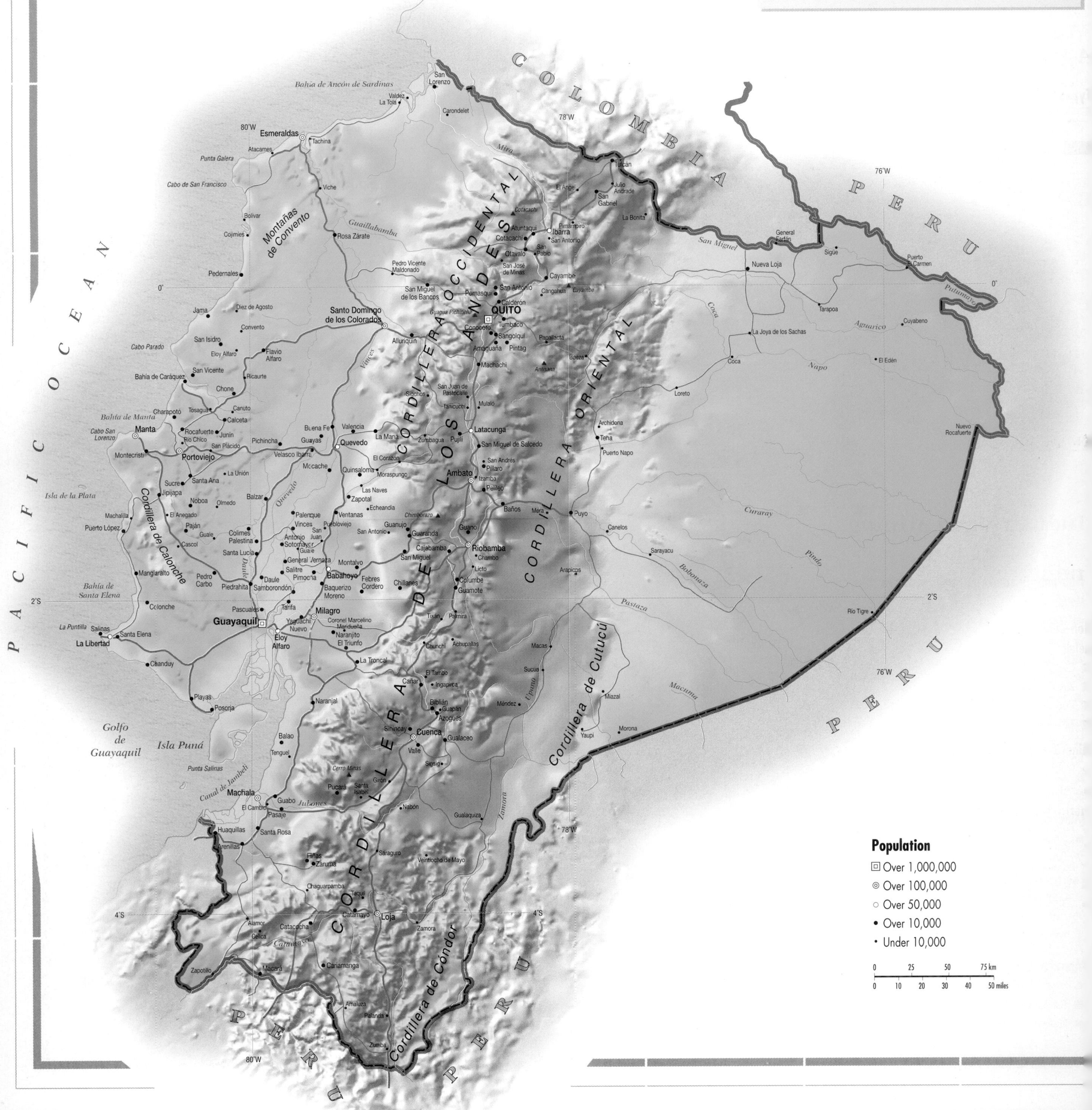

:cuador is a West Coast state of South America that ncludes the Galapagos Islands or Colón Archipelago. Three geomorphological regions can be distinguished: he coast forms an alluvial plain that extends from the Andes to the sea; the Mountain range is an integral part of the Andes mountains and is divided into two chains separated by a tectonic trough oriented lengthwise, formed of valleys and plateaus where a large part of the population is settled in the interior; lastly, the eastern egion is composed of plateaus that descend to a vast plain bathed by the tributaries of the Amazon-Marañón. The Galapagos Islands are of volcanic origen and contain more than a hundred volcanic cones. In general, Ecuador has an equatorial climate, hot and wet, although it shows variation depending on the altitude and the influence of he Peru (Humboldt) Current, a cold ocean current that cools the affected zones.

The population is composed of Amerindians, among whom he Jibaros are noteworthy, and mestizos, as well as a minority of Creole whites. The climatic conditions and the physical conditions of the terrain determine where human settlements are located, with the eastern region —the most inaccessible— the least populated.

A third of the working population is dedicated to farming. Ecuador is among the world's leading producers of bananas; coffee, sugar cane, rice and tropical fruits are also cultivated. In the mountains livestock-raising has a certain importance. Fishing and forestry are fields in expansion. From the decade of the 70's on, manufacturing has experimented a manifest reorientation with the development of important petroleum fields, in spite of the intervention of foreign monopolies. A great reserve of natural gas has also been detected. Industrial production encompasses the branches of food products, consumer goods, textiles, petrochemicals, and pharmaceuticals. Ecuador's balance of trade is in equilibrium, but its dependence on foreign markets and the necessity of importing technology hinders greater economic development.

Population evolution and projection
in millions of persons

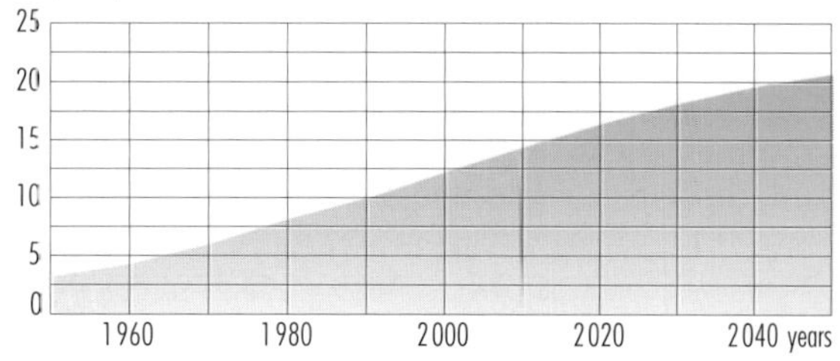

GDP structure
17,939 million dollars

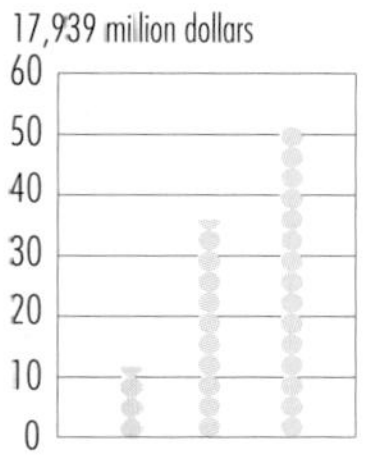

Labor force
4,098,000 persons

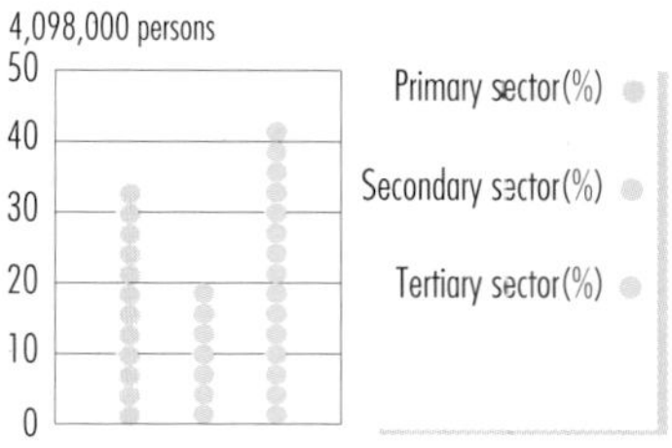

Population age distribution

36% | 60% | 4%
0 years | 15 years | 60 years

Vital statistics

0‰ 10‰ 20‰ 30‰ 40‰ 50‰ 60‰
Birth rate(‰)
Death rate(‰)
Population growth rate(%)
-1% 0% 1% 2% 3% 4%
I Minimum and maximum world values
I Average world value

Literacy (% of population over15)

90.1%
92%
88.2%
0% 100%
Total literate population · Male literacy · Female literacy

Per capita income (GDP per person)

$1,152.71/person
$77/person (world minimum: Mozambique) (world maximum: Japan) $37,075/person

Unemployment (% of total population economically active)

7.1%
0% 50%

Land use

0% 100%
Forests and jungles 45% · Cropland 11% · Other 26%
Meadows and pastures 18%

Agriculture

Types of agriculture and livestock production

- Commercial and plantation farming (bananas, coffee, cocoa, rice, sugar cane, cotton)
- Mixed farming (subsistence and commercial) (barley, legumes, corn, wheat, potatoes, fruits, vegetables)
- Forest/forestry and shifting cultivation
- Non-arable land (deserts, swamps)
- Rice
- Citrus fruits
- Bananas
- Cotton
- Sugar cane
- Coffee
- Cocoa
- Sheep
- Pigs
- Fishing

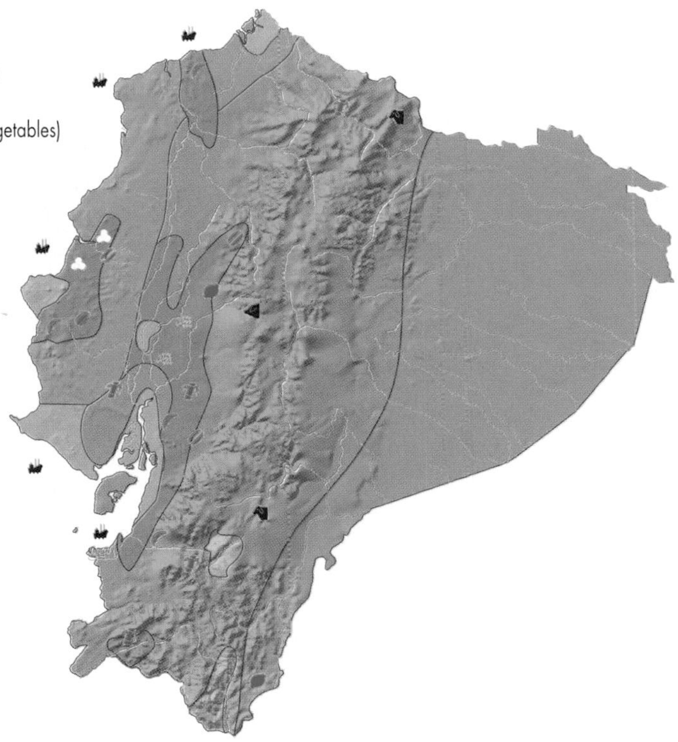

Industry and Mining

Non-energy source mineral resources

Metals

- Cadmium
- Zinc
- Copper
- Tin
- Iron ore
- Gold
- Silver
- Lead

Mineral fuel resources

- Natural gas
- Petroleum

Energy-related installations

- Hydroelectric power plant
- Thermal power plant
- Refinery
- Gas pipeline
- Oil pipeline

Manufacturing

- Food, beverages and tobacco
- Textiles, clothing, leather and footwear
- Paper and graphic arts
- Chemical products
- Building materials, glass and cement

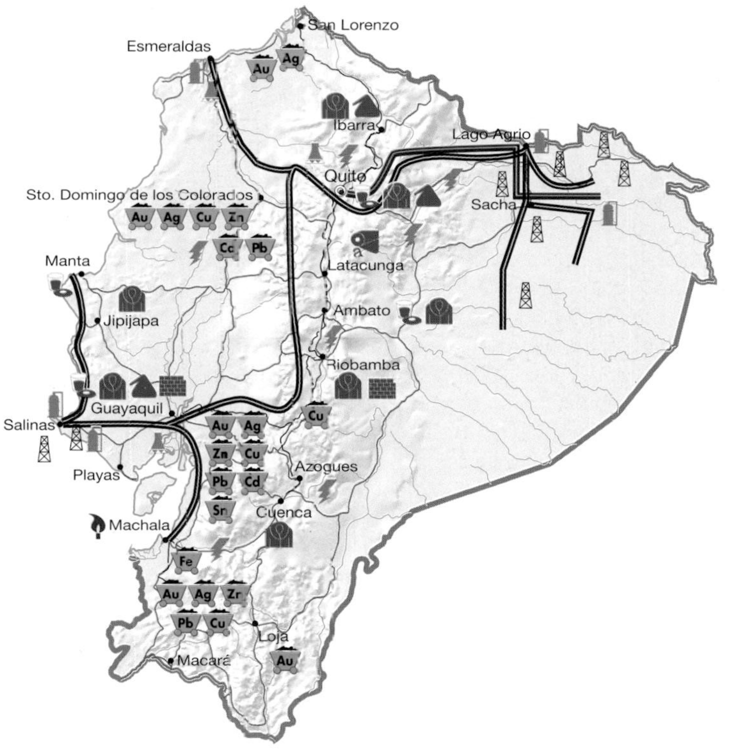

Guyana

Population
- ○ Over 50,000
- • Over 10,000
- · Under 10,000

Guyana is a republic of South America. Flatlands are predominant in its territory; the only important mountainous landform, the Pacaraima mountain chain, is found in the central western part of the country. The Acarai mountains, in the south, has lower elevations. Its hydrographic system consists of rivers with abundant water-flow. The population is composed of Asians, blacks and mestizos, along with a minority of whites. The weak economy of the country suffers from the lack of basic structures and services; nevertheless, great efforts are being made in the farming and industrial sectors. Farming centers above all on the cultivation of sugar cane. Fishing and livestock production, as well as the exploitation of forest resources, are poorly developed. Guyana is among the world's main producers of bauxite. The industry is limited to the processing of agricultural and livestock products and refineries. Coastal transportation is by means of roads; the access to inland areas is by river.

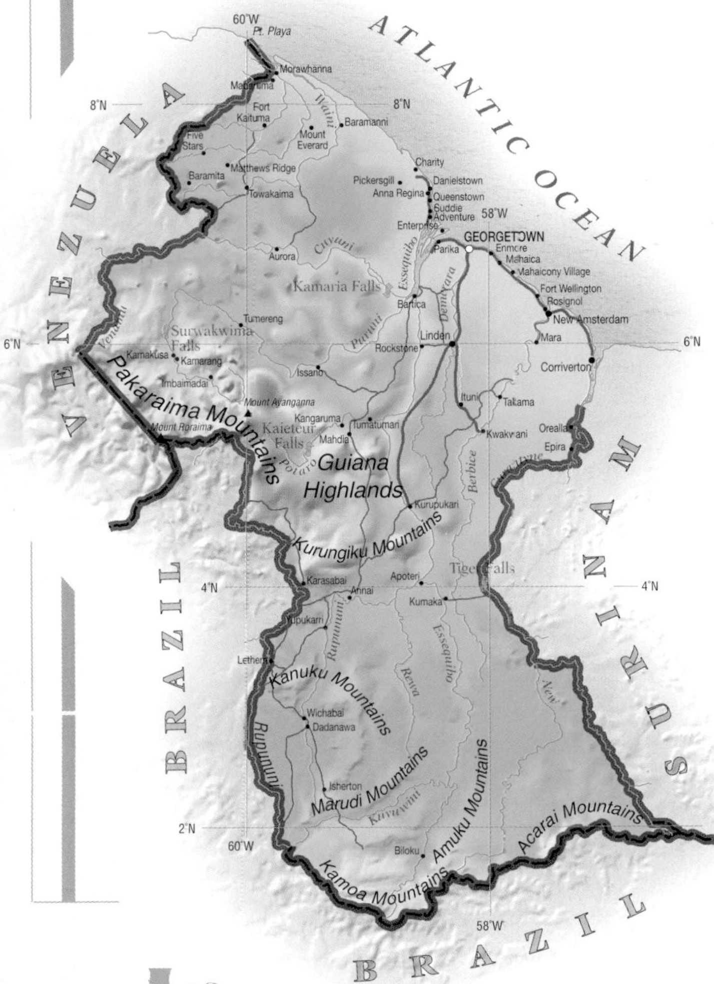

Population evolution and projection

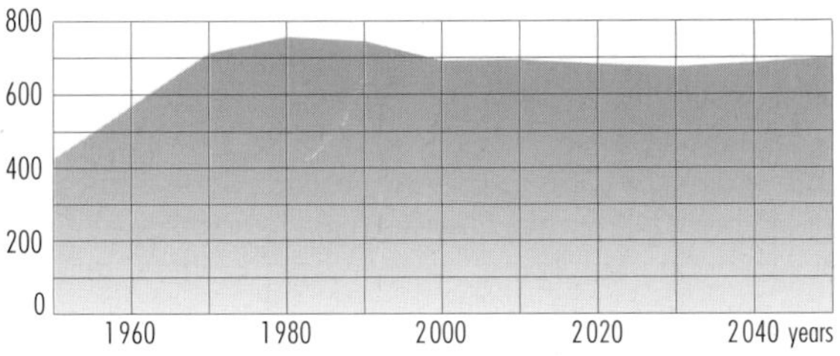

GDP structure

595 million dollars

Labor force

342,000 persons

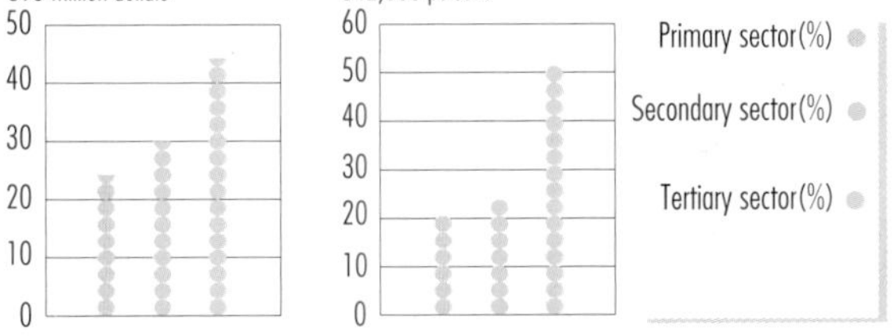

Population age distribution

0 years – 15 years	15 years – 60 years	60 years –
33%	62%	5%

Vital statistics

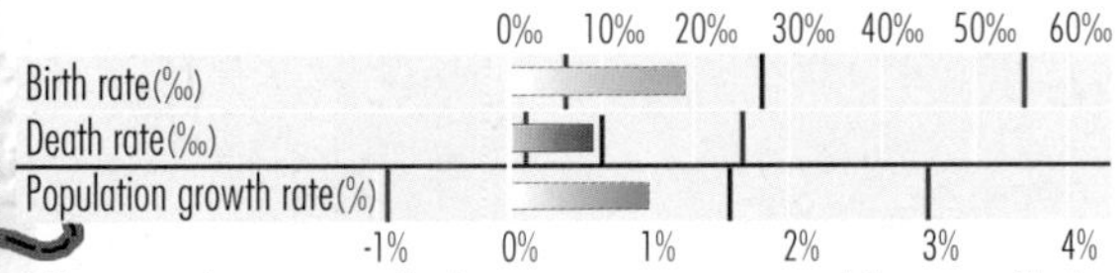

Official name: Cooperative Republic of Guyana

Form of government: presidential republic

Capital: Georgetown

Official language: English

Monetary unit: Guyana dollar

Religious affiliation: Christian (52%), Hindu (34%), Muslim (9%), other (5%)

Ethnic composition of the population: East Indian (51%), black and mixed (43%), Amerindian (4%), European and Chinese (2%)

Area: 215,083 sq km

Total population: 712,091 inhabitants

Population density: 3.3 persons per sq km

Literacy (% of population over15)

Total literate population	Male literacy	Female literacy
98.1%	98.6%	97.5%

Per capita income (GDP per person)

$400.22/person

$77/person (world minimum: Mozambique) (world maximum:Japan) $37,075/person

Unemployment (% of total population economically active)

12%

Land use

Forests and jungles **83%**
Meadows and pastures **6%**
Cropland **3%**
Other 8%

Paraguay

Paraguay is a state of South America composed of plains, with some low altitude mountainous landforms. Crossed from north to south by the Paraguay River, the country is divided in two halves: to the west extends the Gran Chaco, an extensive plain; to the east, the vital core of the population is settled on a spur of the Brazilian Mato Grosso Highlands. It possesses many watercourses, among which the Paraguay, Paran· and Pilcomayo Rivers are the most important. The climate is subtropical, with high temperatures that in winter vary between 18 ∫ and 21 ∫C and in summer between 25 ∫ and 40 ∫C. The moist winds from the Atlantic are responsible for large amounts of precipitation, especially in summer months, which diminishes in the westernmost region of the Chaco.

Paraguay shows great ethnic homogeneity. Mestizos are predominant, although there also exist minorities of Amerindians and a low percentage of whites. Small in number, the population is irregularly distributed, as the Chaco is almost uninhabited while half of the country's inhabitants are concentrated in the capital. It is a developing country that is fundamentally dedicated to farming (cassava, corn, sugar cane, bananas, tobacco, soybeans, matÈ and several vegetable oil-producing crops.) Paraguay is poor in minerals and manufacturing has experienced little development, limiting itself to the processing of farm and livestock products and those of forestry. The Itaip` dam constitutes one of the most ambitious projects launched by Paraguay, fruit of a treaty with Brazil.

Industry and Mining

Non-energy source mineral resources

Metals
- Copper
- Iron ore
- Manganese

Rocks and industrial minerals
- Feldspar
- Mica
- Ochre
- Talc

Energy-related installations
- Hydroelectric power plant
- Refinery

Manufacturing
- Food, beverages and tobacco
- Textiles, clothing, leather and footwear
- Wood, cork and furniture
- Chemical products

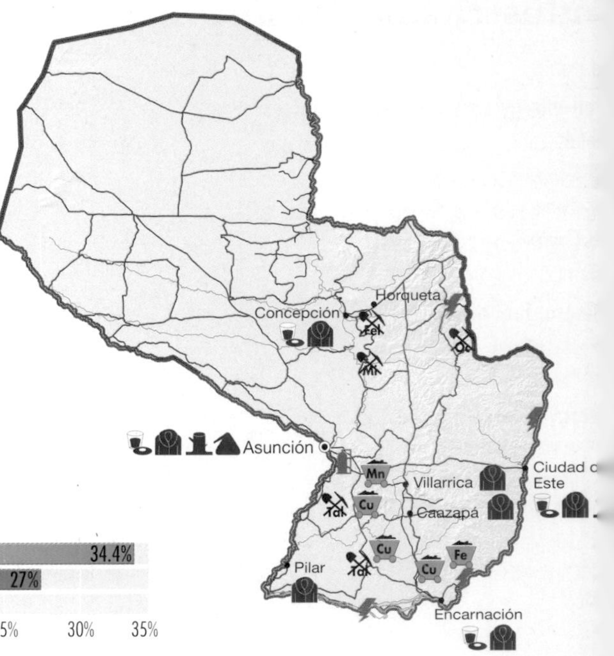

Principal Imports

Item	%
Capital goods	34.4%
Manufactured goods	27%
Food products	15.3%

Principal Exports

Item	%
Petroleum	50.9%
Natural gas	40%
Petroleum derivates	5.6%

Population evolution and projection
in millions of persons

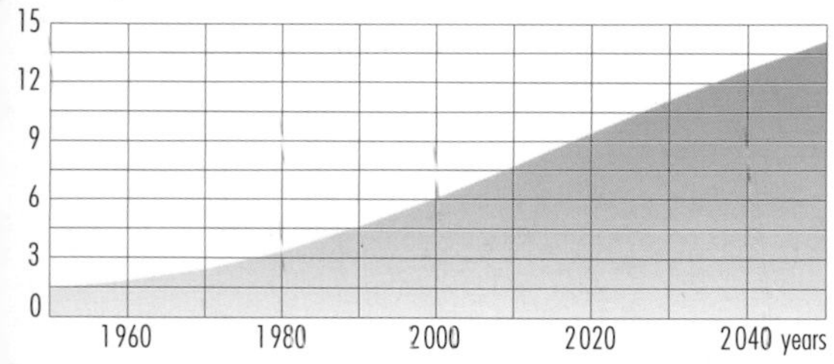

GDP structure
7,743 million dollars

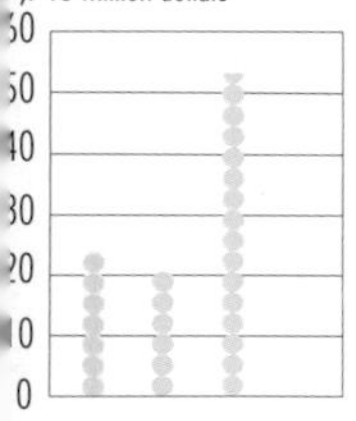

Labor force
1,810,000 persons

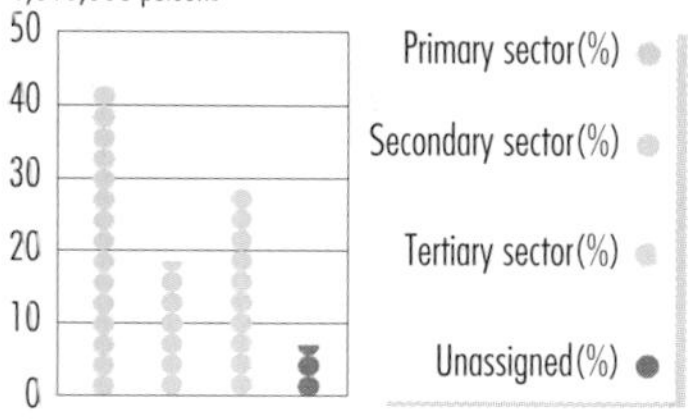

Vital statistics

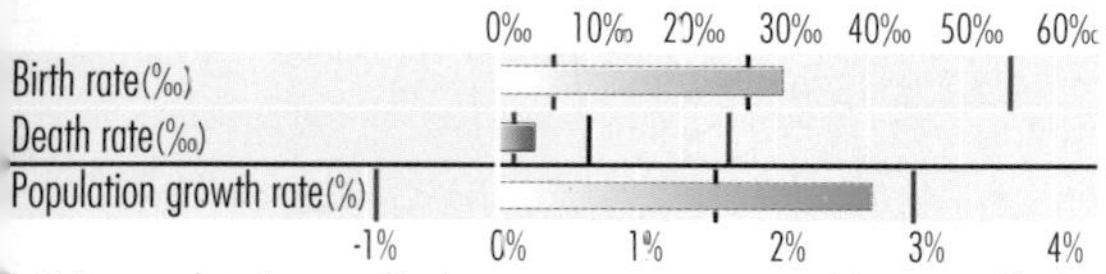

Population age distribution

41% (0 years – 15 years) | 55% (15 years – 60 years) | 4% (60 years)

Literacy (% of population over15)

- 92.1% Total literate population
- 93.5% Male literacy
- 90.6% Female literacy

0% – 100%

Per capita income (GDP per person)

$1,269.98/person

$77/person (world minimum: Mozambique) (world maximum: Japan) $37,075/person

Unemployment (% of total population economically active)

11.2%

0% – 50%

Land use

Forests and jungles 31.6%
Meadows and pastures 54.6%
Cropland 5.6%
Other 8.2%

0% – 100%

Official name: Republic of Paraguay
Form of government: presidential republic
Capital: Asunción
Official language: Guaraní, Spanish
Monetary unit: guaraní
Religious affiliation: Roman Catholic (93.1%), other (6.9%)
Ethnic composition of the population: mestizo (95%), Caucasian and Amerindian (5%)
Area: 406,752 sq km
Total population: 5,504,000 inhabitants
Population density: 13.5 persons per sq km

Population

Population density (persons per sq km)

- Fewer than 5
- From 5 to 10
- From 10 to 25
- From 25 to 50
- More than 50

Population
- Over 500,000
- Over 100,000
- Over 50,000
- Over 10,000
- Under 10,000

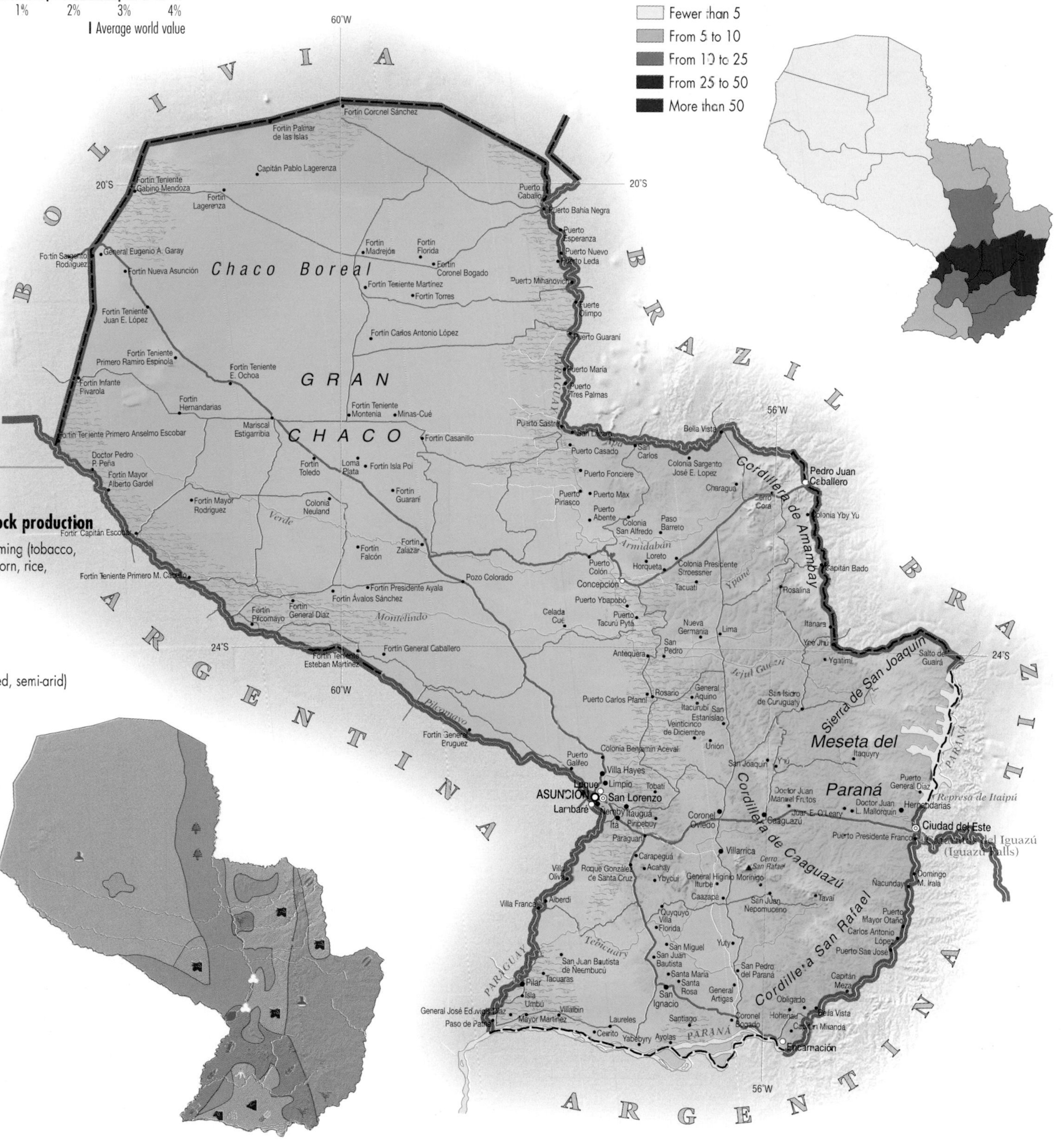

Agriculture

Types of agriculture and livestock production

- Commercial and plantation farming (tobacco, cotton, bananas, sugar cane, corn, rice, vegetable oil seeds, coffee)
- Ranching
- Forest/forestry and sshifting cultivation (cassava)
- Non-arable land (poorly drained, semi-arid)
- Wheat
- Corn
- Rice
- Citrus fruits
- Vegetable oil-seeds
- Cassava
- Cotton
- Sugar cane
- Coffee
- Maté
- Tobacco
- Quebracho
- Cattle
- Sheep
- Pigs

Peru

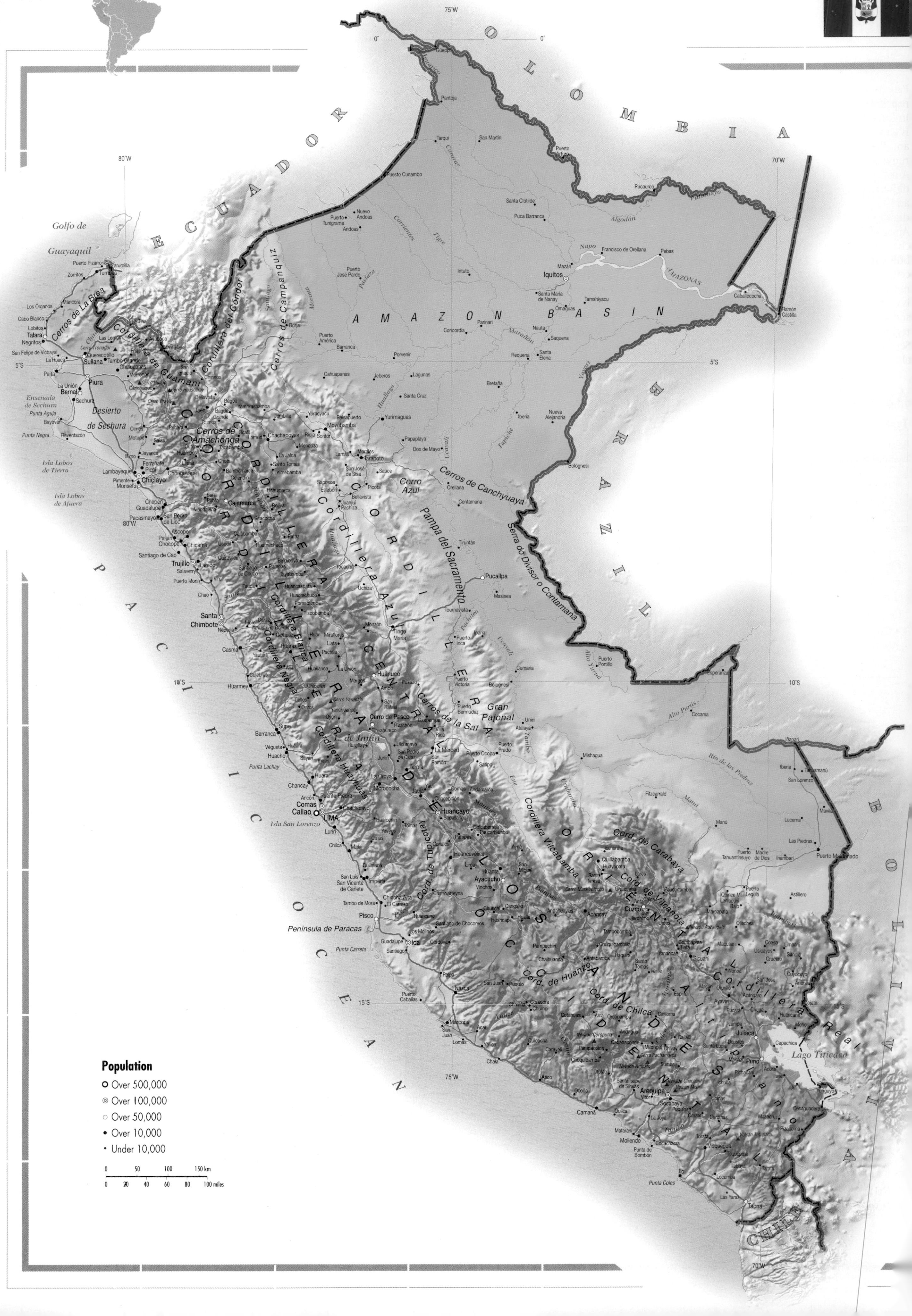
COLOMBIA
ECUADOR
BRAZIL
BOLIVIA
CHILE
PACIFIC OCEAN
AMAZON BASIN
CORDILLERA OCCIDENTAL
CORDILLERA CENTRAL
CORDILLERA ORIENTAL
LOS ANDES
Golfo de Guayaquil
Cerros de La Brea
Cordillera de Guamani
Cordillera del Condor
Cerros de Campanquiz
Cerros de Amachonga
Desierto de Sechura
Ensenada de Sechura
Punta Aguja
Punta Negra
Isla Lobos de Tierra
Isla Lobos de Afuera
Cordillera Azul
Cerro Azul
Cerros de Canchyuaya
Pampa del Sacramento
Serra do Divisor o Contamana
Cordillera Blanca
Cordillera Negra
Cerros de la Sal
Gran Pajonal
L. de Junín
Cordillera Huayhuash
Cordillera Vilcabamba
Cord. de Carabaya
Cord. de Vilcanota
Cord. de Huanzo
Cord. de Chilca
Cord. de Turpicotay
Cordillera Real
Lago Titicaca
Isla San Lorenzo
Península de Paracas
Punta Carreta
Punta Lachay
Punta Coles
AMAZONAS
Napo
Putumayo
Algodón
Marañón
Huallaga
Ucayali
Tigre
Corrientes
Pastaza
Morona
Yavarí
Alto Purús
Río de las Piedras
Manú
Alto Yuruá
Tambo
Urubamba
Apurímac
Mantaro
Iquitos
Pucallpa
Piura
Sullana
Talara
Tumbes
Chiclayo
Cajamarca
Trujillo
Chimbote
Huaraz
Huánuco
Cerro de Pasco
Tingo María
Huancayo
Huancavelica
Ayacucho
LIMA
Callao
Comas
Pisco
Ica
Nazca
Cuzco
Abancay
Puerto Maldonado
Juliaca
Puno
Arequipa
Moquegua
Tacna
Mollendo
Chala
Camaná
Tarapoto
Moyobamba
Chachapoyas
Yurimaguas
Jaén
Lambayeque
Pacasmayo
Huacho
Barranca
Cañete
Chincha Alta
80°W
75°W
70°W
0°
5°S
10°S
15°S
Population
Over 500,000
Over 100,000
Over 50,000
Over 10,000
Under 10,000
0 50 100 150 km
0 20 40 60 80 100 miles

Peru is an Andean state of South America. The great regional geomorphological diversity can be summarized in three great areas: the coastal region or region of Chala is an arid plain between the western border of the Andes and the ocean; the Peruvian Andes or region of Yungas runs through the country from north to south; and the Amazon plain or Quechua region encompasses two very different parts, the lower zone of the Andean water-shed and the low rainforest. The rivers belong to three drainage basins: that draining into the Pacific, the Amazon Basin and that of Lake Titicaca. The climate is characterized by its extreme contrasts. In general, it has hot temperatures in the north and temperate ones in the center and south. In the Andes it is defined as a tropical mountain climate, with temperatures falling as elevation is gained. On the peaks, low temperatures and perpetual snow are registered. The rainforest has an equatorial regime.

Several ethnic communities make up the population: almost half belong to the Amerindian group (especially Quechuas). Mestizos also abound and in a smaller measure, groups of whites and blacks. Peru's inhabitants are distributed throughout the territory quite irregularly, since the Andean region is heavily populated, while there are scarcely any residents in the rainforest. Efforts have been made to stimulate the economy of the country, proceeding from the public sector to a greater extent than from private initiatives. Irrigation projects have enabled the number of agricultural products produced to be enlarged. While the domestic market consumes cereals, the products destined for export include cotton, sugar cane and coffee. Livestock production (sheep, cattle and llamas) is important as well as that of rubber and various woods. Fishing represents an important influx of foreign currency. Industry has experienced a certain growth, especially the iron and steel industry and petroleum refineries; the textile sector is going through a period of increasing prosperity. Mining (copper, petroleum, etc.) would produce greater profits if practically all of it were not in foreign hands. The basic infrastructure of the transportation network is generally deficient.

Official name: Republic of Peru
Form of government: presidential republic
Capital: Lima
Official language: Quechua, Spanish, Aymara
Monetary unit: nuevo sol
Religious affiliation: Roman Catholic (92.5%), Protestant (5.5%)
Ethnic composition of the population: Amerindian (45%), mestizo (37%), white (15%), black, Japanese, Chinese and other (3%)
Area: 1,285,216 sq km
Total population: 24,523,000 inhabitants
Population density: 19.1 persons per sq km

Agriculture

Types of agriculture and livestock production

- Irrigation/intensive farming (coffee, rice, sugar cane, cotton)
- Commercial and plantation farming
- Ranching and subsistence farming (potatoes, corn, wheat, forage crops)
- Pastures and highland farming
- Forest/forestry and shifting cultivation
- Non-crable land (coastal desert)
- Rice
- Citrus fruits
- Grapevines
- Potatoes
- Cotton
- Sugar cane
- Coffee
- Cocoa
- Rubber
- Cattle
- Sheep
- Pigs
- Alpacas
- Llamas
- Fishing

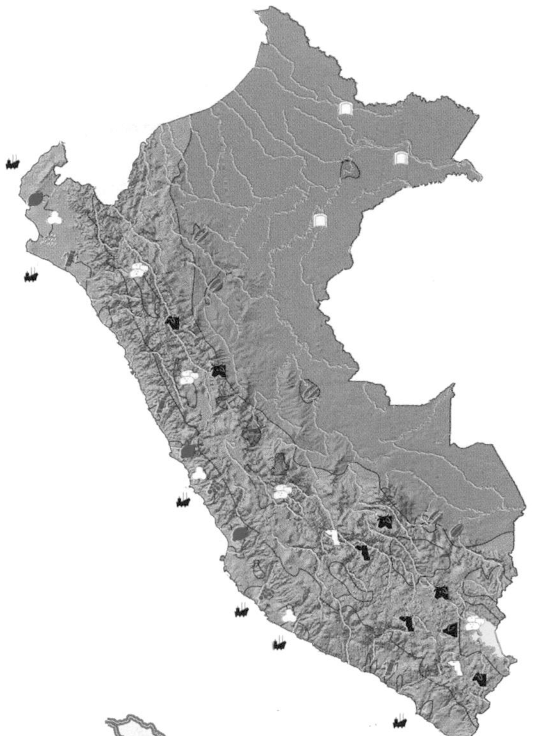

Industry and Mining

Non-energy source mineral resources

Metals

- Zinc
- Gold
- Copper
- Silver
- Tin
- Lead
- Iron ore
- Wolfram
- Molybdenum

Mineral fuel resources

- Natural gas
- Petroleum

Energy-related installations

- Hydroelectric power plant
- Refinery
- Oil pipeline

Manufacturing

- Food, beverages and tobacco
- Textiles, clothing, leather and footwear
- Paper and graphic arts
- Chemical products
- Building materials, glass and cement
- Metallurgy and metal products
- Machinery and transport equipment

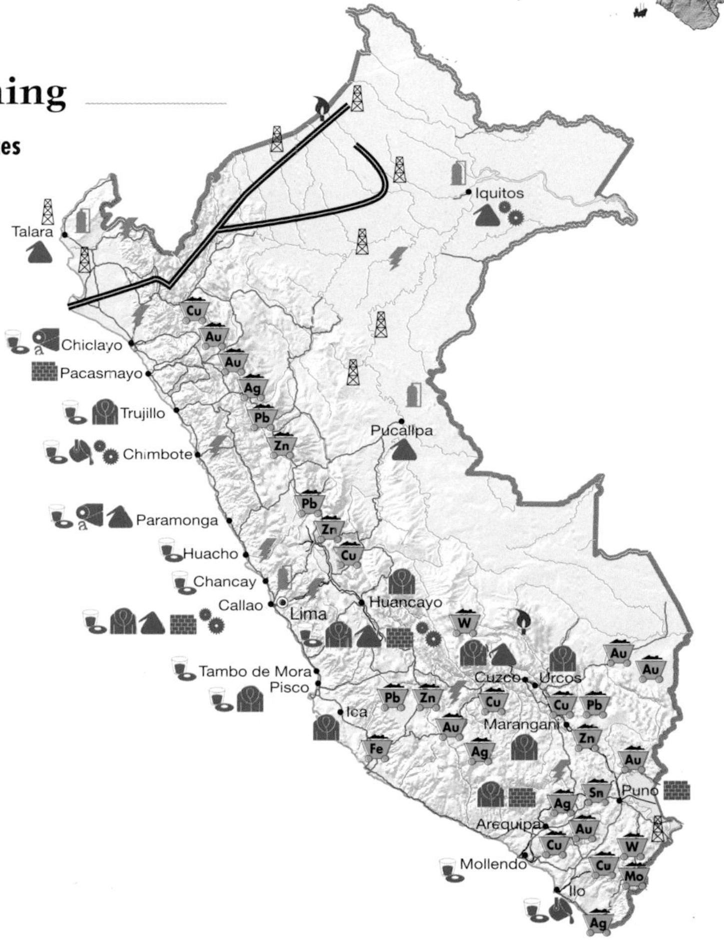

Population evolution and projection

in millions of persons

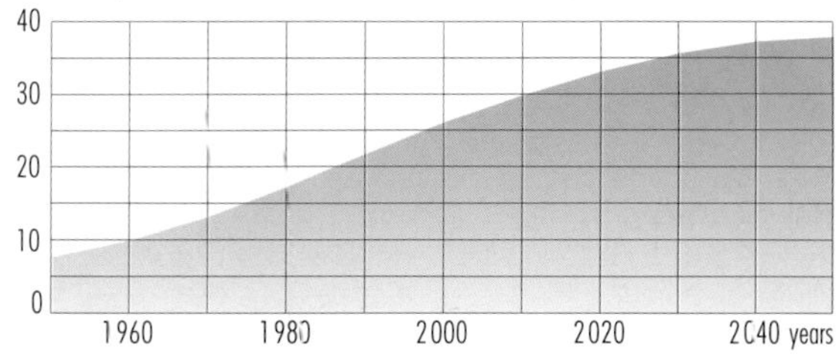

GDP structure

57,424 million dollars

Labor force

8,414,000 persons

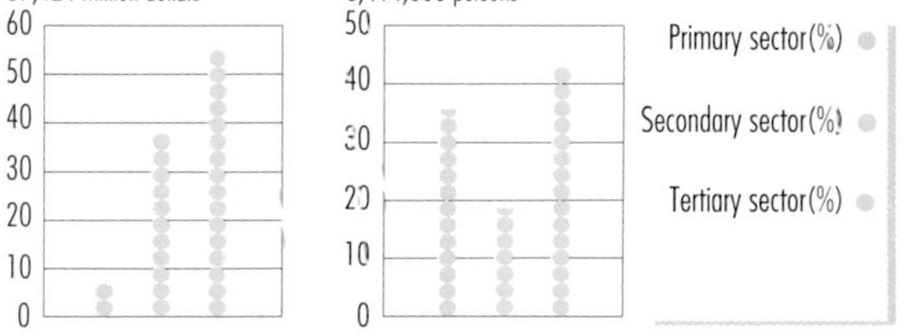

Population age distribution

Vital statistics

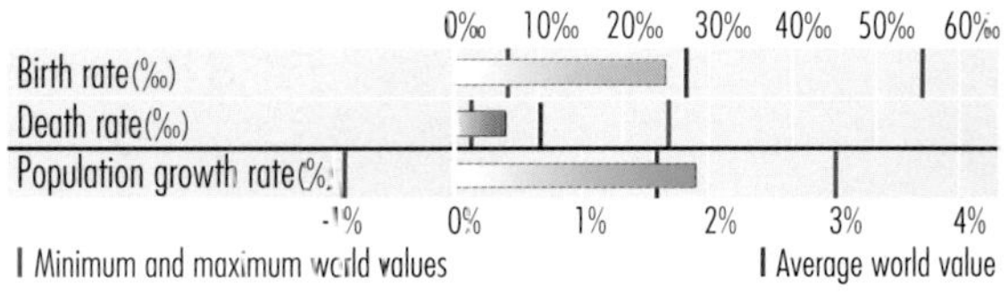

I Minimum and maximum world values I Average world value

Literacy (% of population over 15)

Total literate population Male literacy Female literacy

Per capita income (GDP per person)

$1,387.67/person

$77/person (world minimum: Mozambique) (world maximum: Japan) $37,075/person

Unemployment (% of total population economically active)

Land use

Forests and jungles 55% Cropland 3% Other 21%
Meadows and pastures 21%

Suriname

Population evolution and projection
in thousands of persons

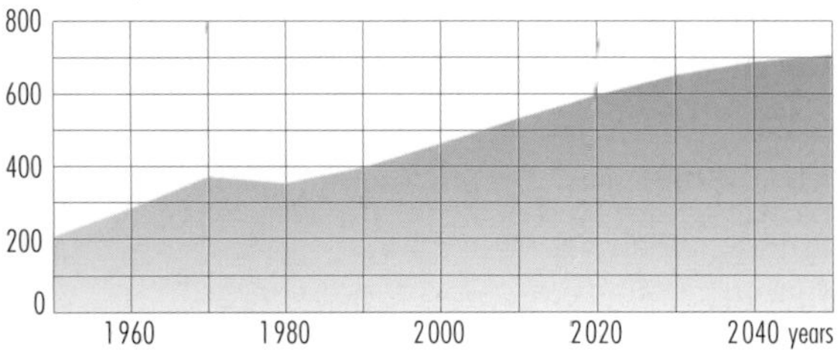

GDP structure
335 million dollars

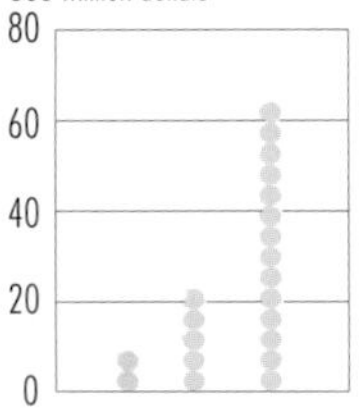

Labor force
148,000 persons

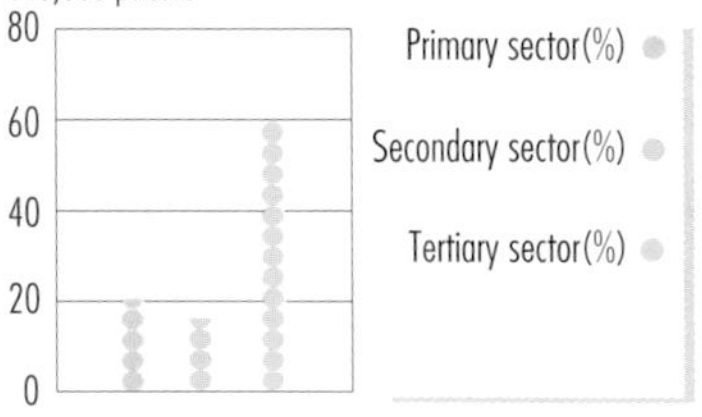

Population age distribution

The state of Suriname is in northern South America. From north to south it is composed of a vast coastal plain, a large central highland and several mountain chains. Surinam has a humid equatorial climate, with average temperatures above 20 °C, few variations in temperature and abundant precipitation. Its population is composed of groups of Creoles, Asians (from India, Indonesia and China), Amerindians and Samaracca or Bush Negros (descendents of black slaves). The country has a low population density and its inhabitants are distributed unevenly throughout the territory. Farming activity is based on subsistence crops (rice, corn, vegetables and tropical fruits). On the plantations, sugar cane, citrus fruits, coconut trees, coffee, cocoa and various vegetable oilseed crops are grown. The large deposits of bauxite represent the principal mineral reserve; an associated industry has developed near these. The manufacturing industry of agricultural products is also noteworthy.

Official name: Republic of Suriname
Form of government: republic
Capital: Paramaribo
Official language: Dutch
Monetary unit: Suriname guilder
Religious affiliation: Hindu (26%), Roman Catholic (21.6%), Muslim (18.6%), Protestant (18%), other (15.8%)
Ethnic composition of the population: Asian Indian (37%), Creole (31%), Javanese (15.3%), African (Bush Negro) (10.3%), Amerindian (2.6%), Chinese (1.7%), European (1%), other (1.1%)
Area: 163,820 sq km
Total population: 436,418 inhabitants
Population density: 2.7 persons per sq km

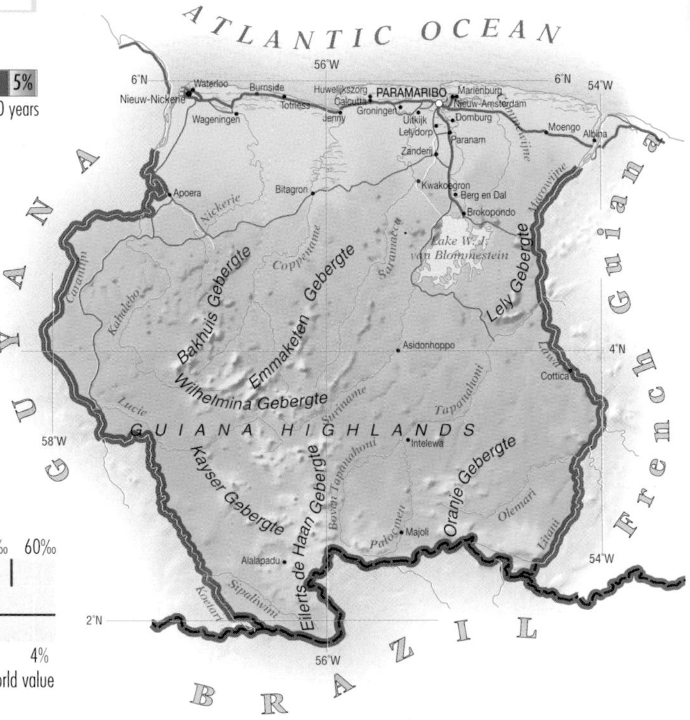

Population
○ Over 50,000
• Over 10,000
· Under 10,000

0 50 100 km
0 30 60 miles

Vital statistics

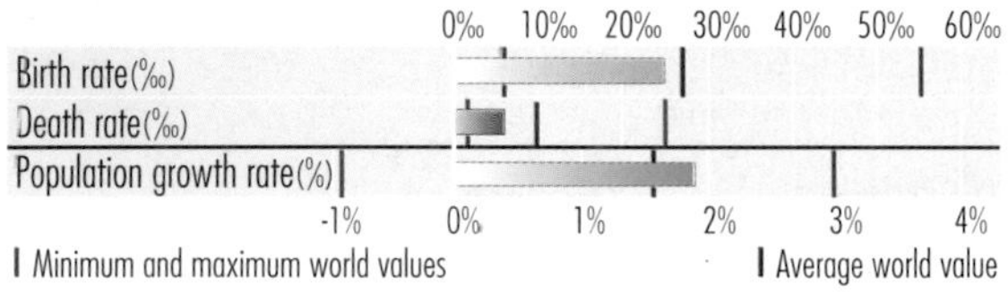

Literacy (% of population over15)

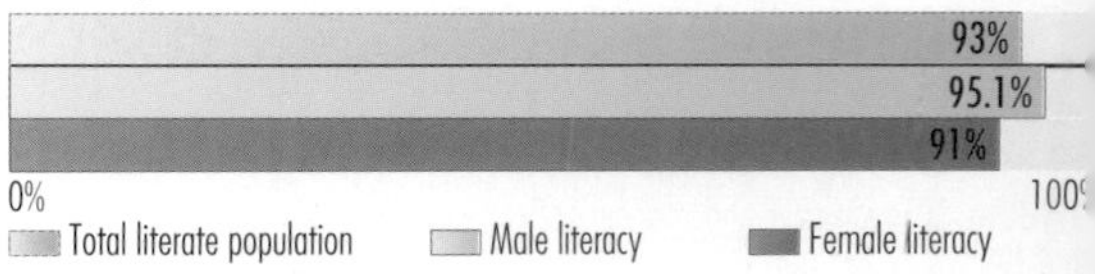

Per capita income (GDP per person)

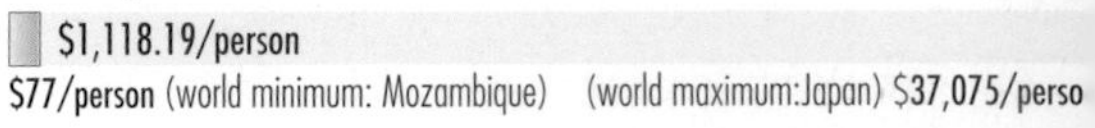

Land use

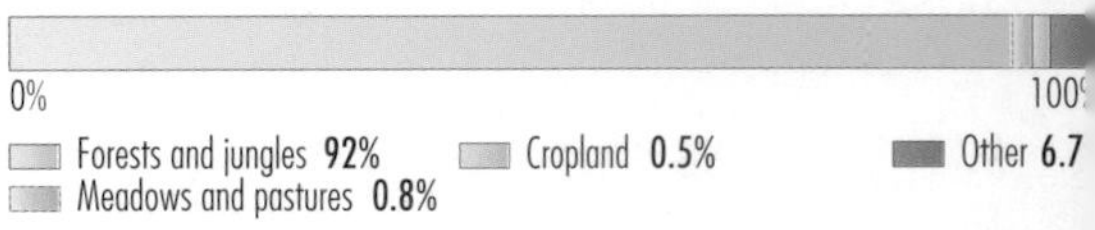

Trinidad and Tobago

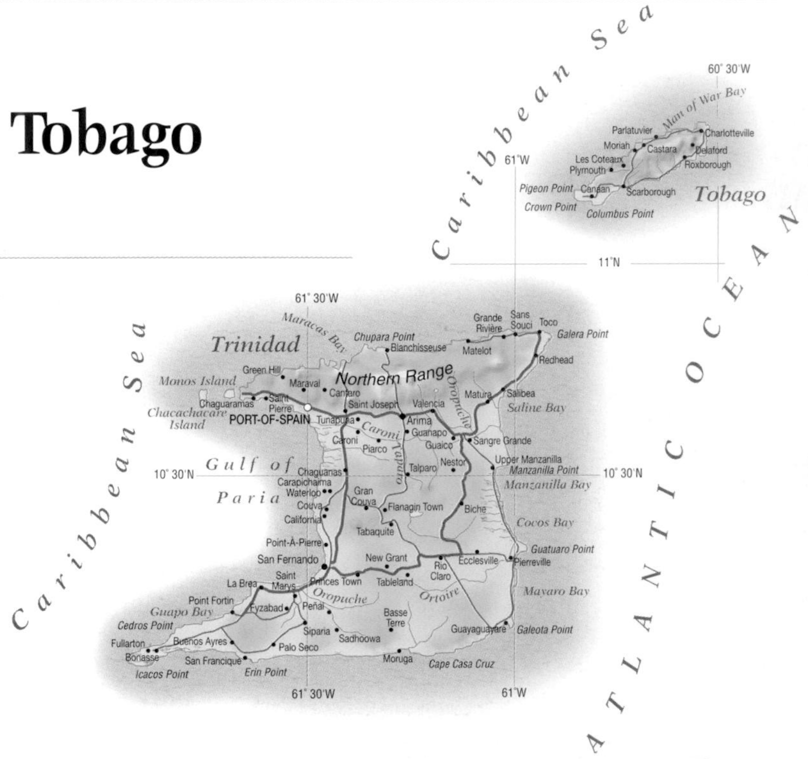

Population
○ Over 50,000
• Over 10,000
· Under 10,000

0 10 20 30 km
0 5 10 15 20 miles

Official name: Republic of Trinidad and Tobago
Form of government: parliamentary democracy
Capital: Port-of-Spain
Official language: English
Monetary unit: Trinidad and Tobago dollar
Religious affiliation: Roman Catholic (29.4%), Hindu (23.8%), Anglican (10.9%), Muslim (5.8%), other (30.1%)
Ethnic composition of the population: black (43%), East Indian (40%), mixed (14%), white (1%), Chinese(1%), other (1%)
Area: 5,128 sq km
Total population: 1,272,000 inhabitants
Population density: 248 persons per sq km

Trinidad and Tobago is an island state of South America. Trinidad, the larger of the two islands, has a mountainous region in the north, while the rest of the territory includes gentle landforms with alluvial plains. The island of Tobago is formed by low hills. The hydrography consists of short rivers. The climate is tropical, hot and very humid, with abundant rainfall. The population is made up of blacks, East Indians, mestizos, Chinese and Europeans. Trinidad and Tobago has one of the highest average population densities of South America. The economy centers on the extraction of petroleum and on its associated industry, which also works with imported crude oil. The deposits of natural gas found on the coast and the natural asphalt (tar) are of great importance. Other noteworthy industries are those of consumer goods and food products. Agricultural activities produce subsistence crops (rice, vegetables, etc.) and plantation crops (sugar cane and cocoa, among others). The tourist industry brings considerable foreign currency into the country.

Jruguay is a southern state of South America. In general he terrain is flat, with some rolling hills of low elevation cuchillas). In the east is located the Cuchilla Grande ınd from the center towards the frontier with Brazil, the Cuchilla de Haedo. It has an important hydrographic ystem (the Uruguay, Queguay Grande, Negro and Yaguarin Rivers). Uruguay has a temperate climate, semi-humid and very unstable, with abundant rainfall. Whites make up most of the population, along with a minority of mestizos and blacks.

Livestock production includes sheep, cattle, pigs and horses. An industry has developed which is dedicated to the processing of livestock products (meat, dairy products, wool, leather, etc.). Despite the fact that crops have been diversified in farming, productivity is not very high. Tourism contributes important foreign currency to the country. The Uruguayan economy remains in a state of crisis, since it possesses a structure based on the latifundium and industrial investment is low.

Official name: Oriental Republic of Uruguay
Form of government: republic
Capital: Montevideo
Official language: Spanish
Monetary unit: Uruguayan peso
Religious affiliation: Roman Catholic (66%), Protestant (2%), Jewish (0.8%), nonreligious and atheist (31.2%)
Ethnic composition of the population: white (88%), mestizo (8%), black (4%)
Area: 176,215 sq km
Total population: 3,239,000 inhabitants
Population density: 18.4 persons per sq km

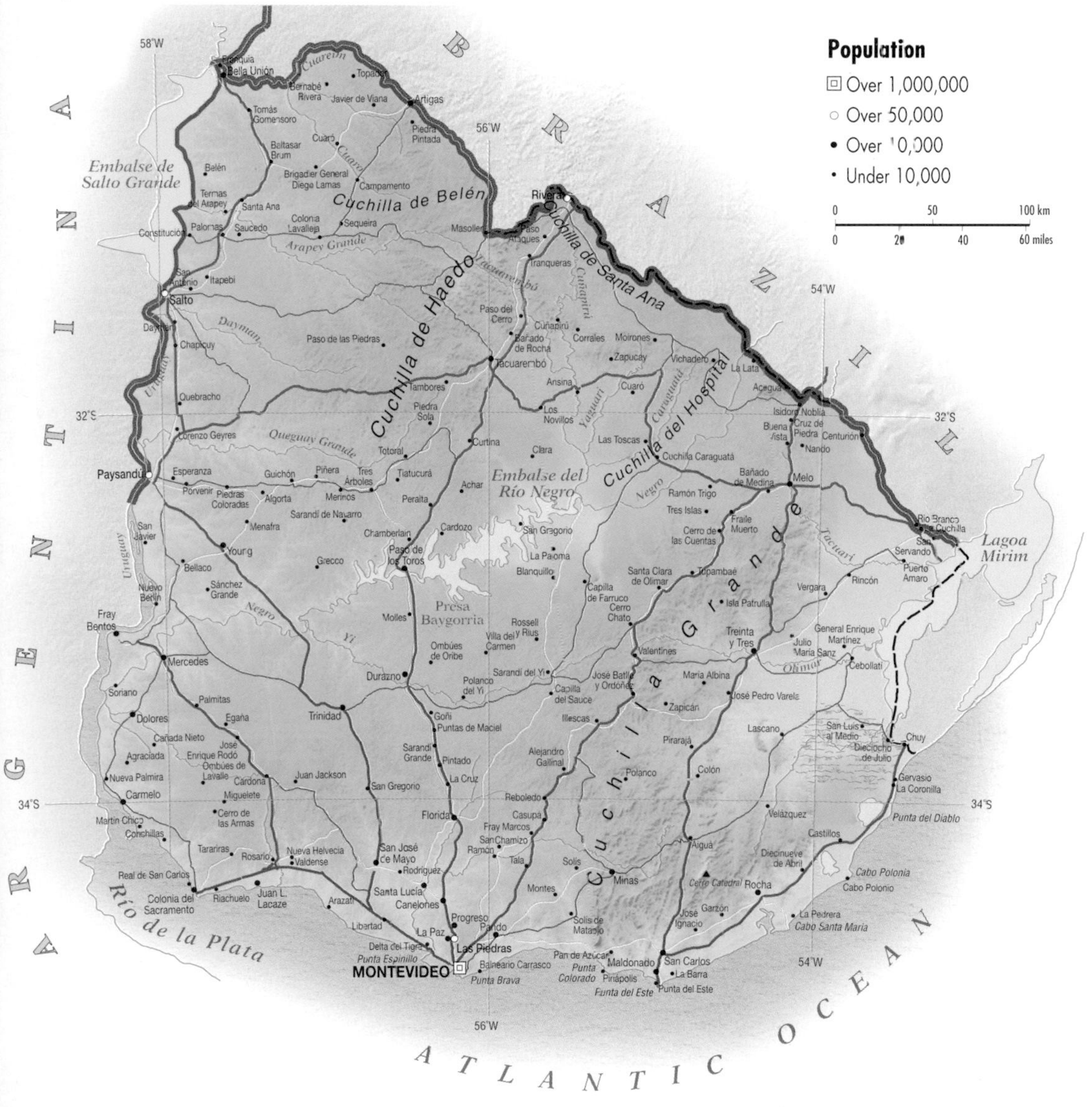

Population evolution and projection
in millions of persons

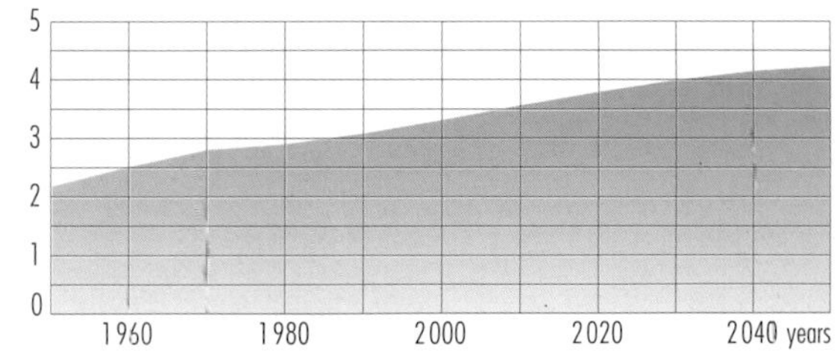

GDP structure
17,847 million dollars

Labor force
1,414,000 persons

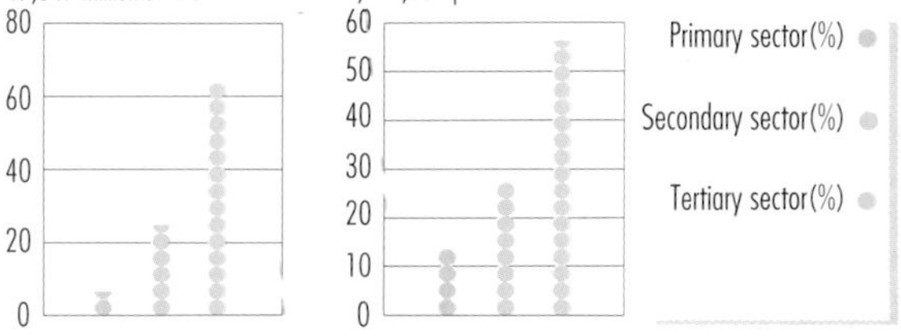

Population age distribution

25%	63%	12%
0 years	15 years	60 years

Vital statistics

0‰ 10‰ 20‰ 30‰ 40‰ 50‰ 60‰
Birth rate(‰)
Death rate(‰)
Population growth rate(%)
-1% 0% 1% 2% 3% 4%
I Minimum and maximum world values I Average world value

Literacy (% of population over15)

97.3%
96.9%
97.7%
0% 100%
Total literate population / Male literacy / Female literacy

Per capita income (GDP per person)

$3,800.55/person
$77/person (world minimum: Mozambique) (world maximum:Japan) $37,075/person

Unemployment (% of total population economically active)

9%
0% 50%

Land use

0% 100%
Forests and jungles 4% Cropland 8% Other 10%
Meadows and pastures 78%

Agriculture, Industry and Mining

Types of agriculture and livestock production

- Irrigation/intensive farming
- Commercial and plantation farming (fruits, grapevines)
- Ranching and farming (wheat, corn, barley, flax, rice, sugar cane, vegetable oilseed crops: peanuts, sunflower seeds)
- Ranching
- Forest/brush
- Apples
- Citrus fruits
- Grapevines
- Vegetable oilseeds crops
- Sugar cane
- Sugar beets
- Cattle
- Sheep
- Fishing

Non-energy source mineral resources

Metals

- Iron ore
- Titanium
- Gold

Rocks and industrial minerals

- Limestone
- Marble

Energy-related installations

- Hydroelectric power plant
- Refinery
- Oil pipeline

Manufacturing

- Food, beverages and tobacco
- Textiles, clothing, leather and footwear
- Chemical products
- Building materials, glass and cement
- Machinery and transport equipment

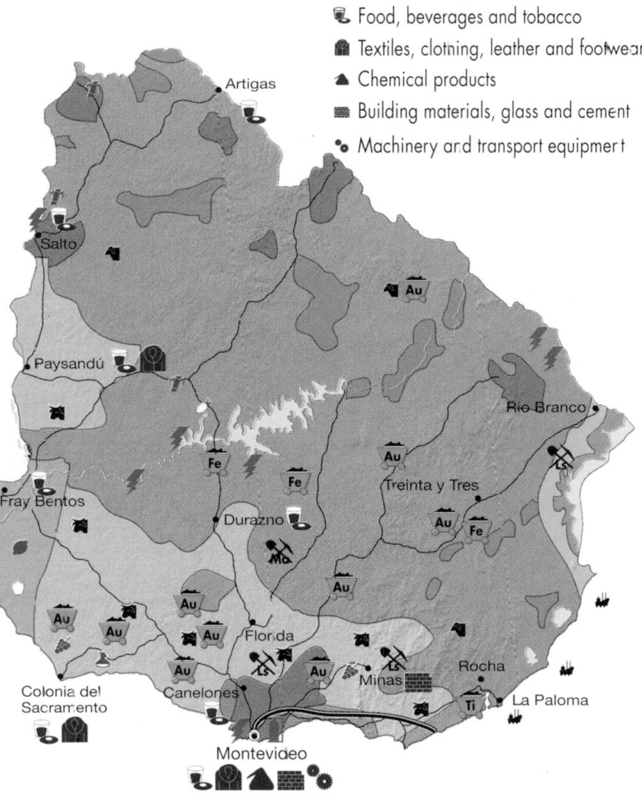

Venezuela

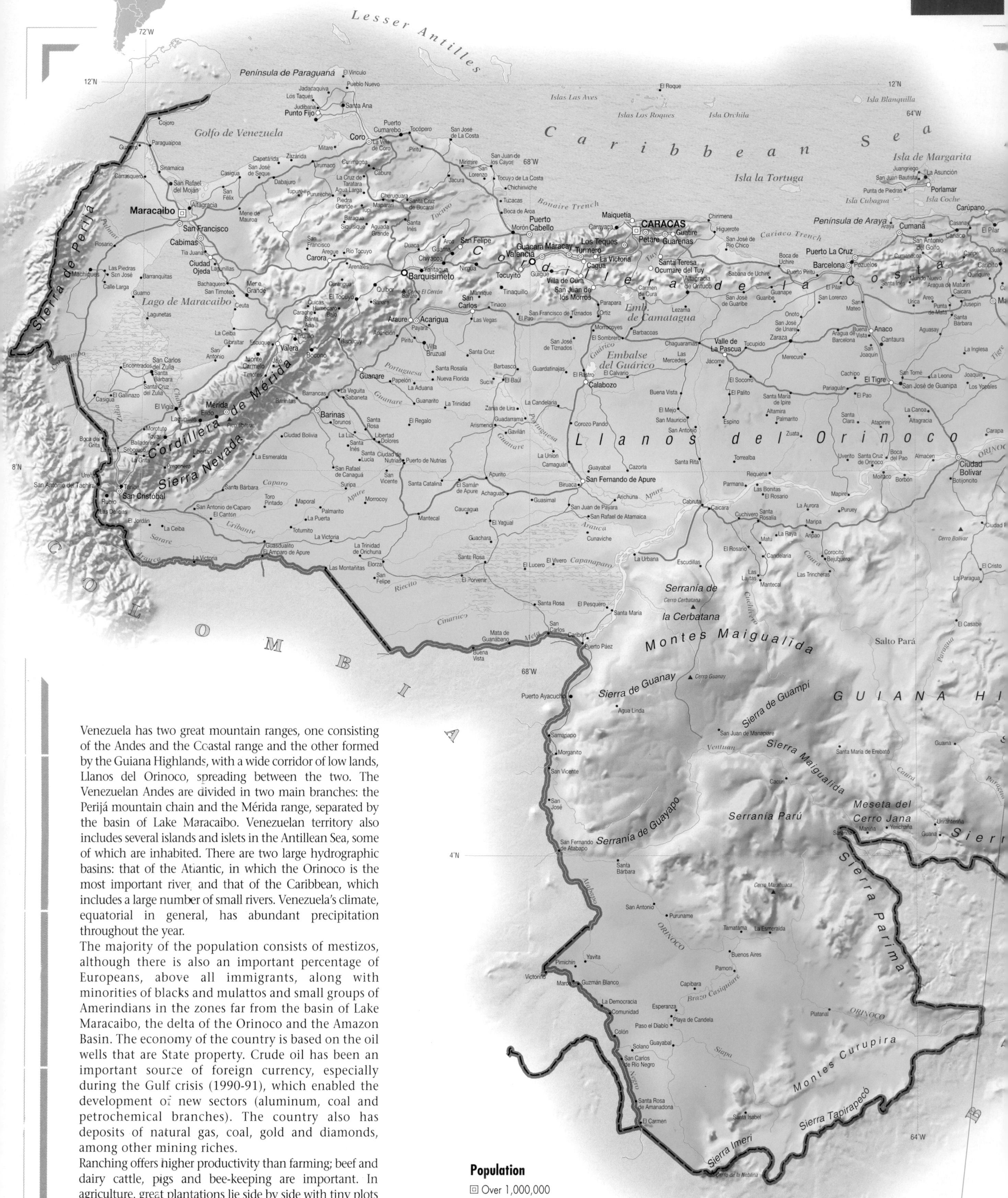

Population

- Over 1,000,000
- Over 500,000
- Over 100,000
- Over 50,000
- Over 10,000
- Under 10,000

0 50 100 km
0 20 40 60 miles

Venezuela has two great mountain ranges, one consisting of the Andes and the Coastal range and the other formed by the Guiana Highlands, with a wide corridor of low lands, Llanos del Orinoco, spreading between the two. The Venezuelan Andes are divided in two main branches: the Perijá mountain chain and the Mérida range, separated by the basin of Lake Maracaibo. Venezuelan territory also includes several islands and islets in the Antillean Sea, some of which are inhabited. There are two large hydrographic basins: that of the Atlantic, in which the Orinoco is the most important river, and that of the Caribbean, which includes a large number of small rivers. Venezuela's climate, equatorial in general, has abundant precipitation throughout the year.

The majority of the population consists of mestizos, although there is also an important percentage of Europeans, above all immigrants, along with minorities of blacks and mulattos and small groups of Amerindians in the zones far from the basin of Lake Maracaibo, the delta of the Orinoco and the Amazon Basin. The economy of the country is based on the oil wells that are State property. Crude oil has been an important source of foreign currency, especially during the Gulf crisis (1990-91), which enabled the development of new sectors (aluminum, coal and petrochemical branches). The country also has deposits of natural gas, coal, gold and diamonds, among other mining riches.

Ranching offers higher productivity than farming; beef and dairy cattle, pigs and bee-keeping are important. In agriculture, great plantations lie side by side with tiny plots (minifundios); cereals, cocoa, tobacco, cotton and sugar cane are grown. Governmental policy has encouraged basic iron and steel industry, while the development of light industry (food products, textiles, etc.) is due mostly to private initiative. Another source of income is contributed by the tourist industry, with the lure of its Caribbean beaches and national parks.

Vital statistics

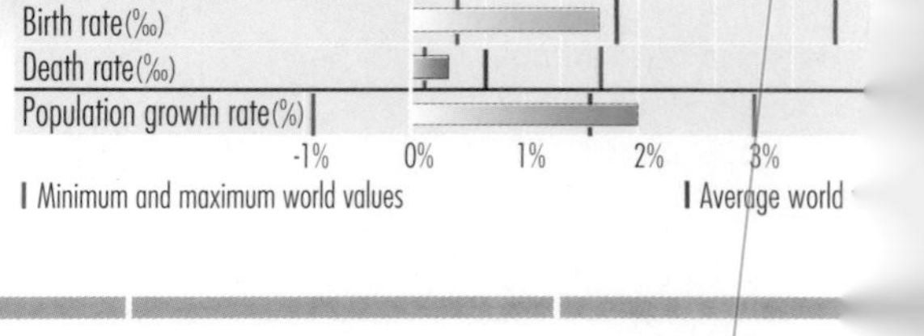

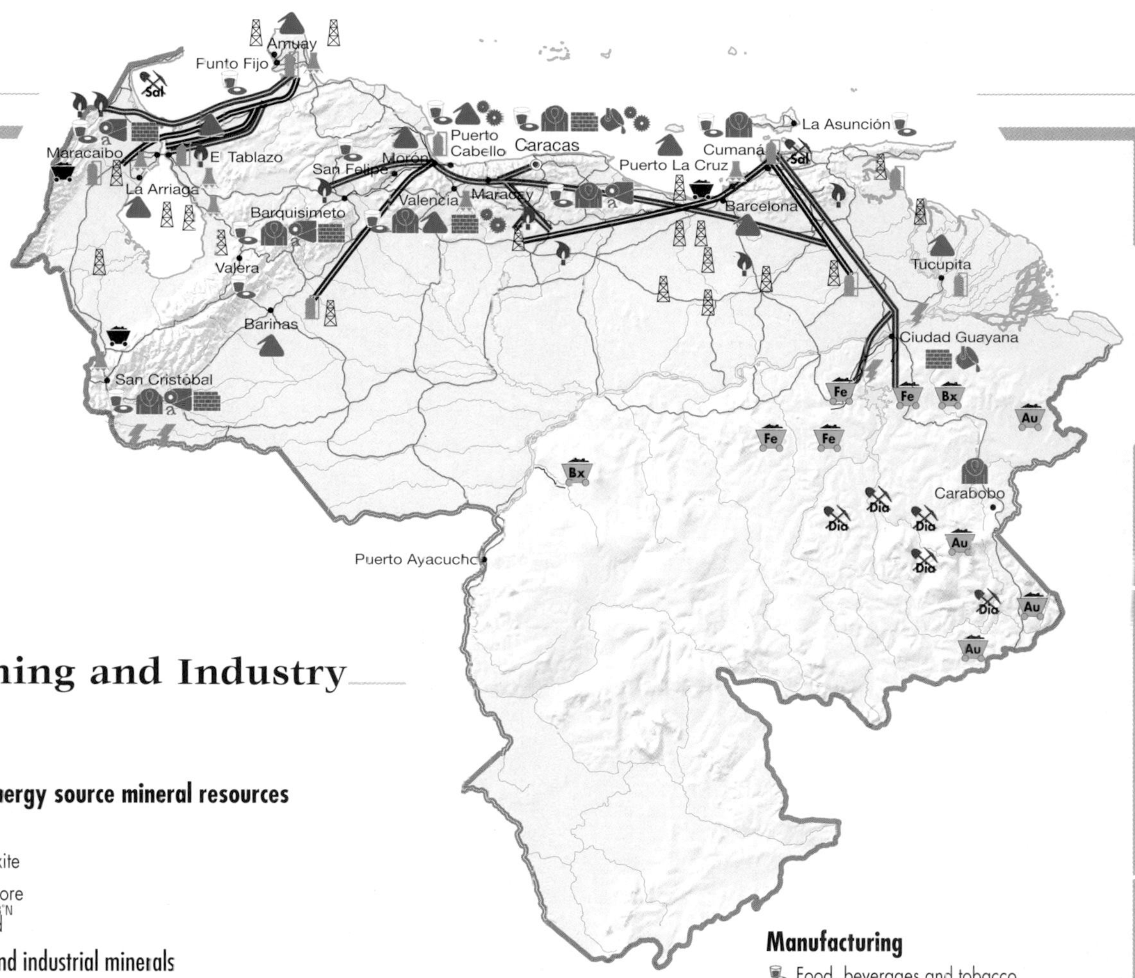

Mining and Industry

Non-energy source mineral resources

Metals
- Bauxite
- Iron ore
- Gold

Rocks and industrial minerals
- Diamonds
- Salt

Mineral fuel resources
- Coal
- Natural gas
- Petroleum

Energy-related installations
- Hydroelectric power plant
- Thermal power plant
- Refinery
- Gas pipeline
- Oil pipeline

Manufacturing
- Food, beverages and tobacco
- Textiles, clothing, leather and footwear
- Paper and graphic arts
- Chemical products
- Building materials, glass and cement
- Metallurgy and metal products
- Machinery and transport equipment

Literacy (% of population over15)

Total literate population	91.1%
Male literacy	91.8%
Female literacy	90.3%

0% — 100%

Per capita income (GDP per person)

$2,680.07/person

$77/person (world minimum: Mozambique) (world maximum: Japan) $37,075/person

Unemployment (% of total population economically active)

9%

0% — 50%

Official name: Republic of Venezuela
Form of government: republic
Capital: Caracas
Official language: Spanish
Monetary unit: bolívar
Religious affiliation: Roman Catholic (92.1%), other (7.1%)
Ethnic composition of the population: mestizo (67%), white (21%), black (10%), Amerindian (2%)
Area: 912,050 sq km
Total population: 21,983,000 inhabitants
Population density: 24.1 persons per sq km

Agriculture

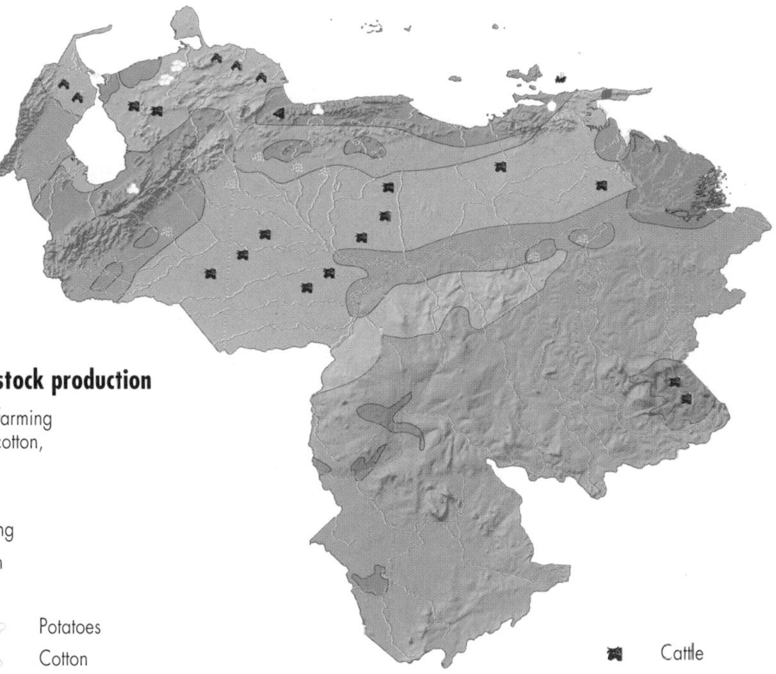

Types of agriculture and livestock production
- Commercial and plantation farming (cocoa, bananas, tobacco, cotton, coffee, sugar cane)
- Ranching and some farming
- Pastures and highland farming
- Forest and shifting cultivation
- Swamplands

- Corn
- Rice
- Apples
- Citrus fruits
- Bananas
- Potatoes
- Cotton
- Sugar cane
- Coffee
- Tobacco
- Cattle
- Goats
- Pigs
- Fishing

Population evolution and projection
in millions of persons

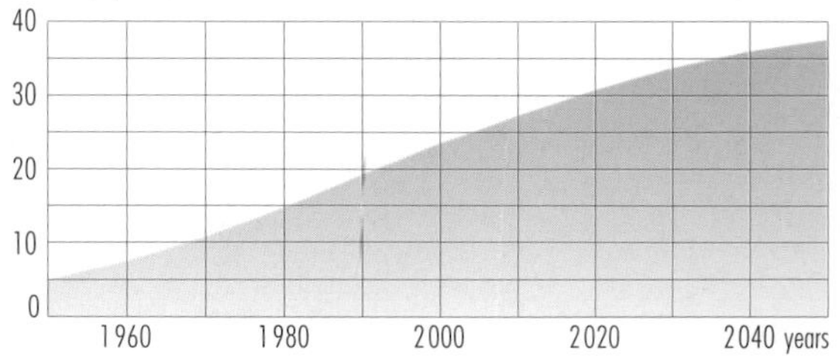

GDP structure
75,016 million dollars

Labor force
8,222,000 persons

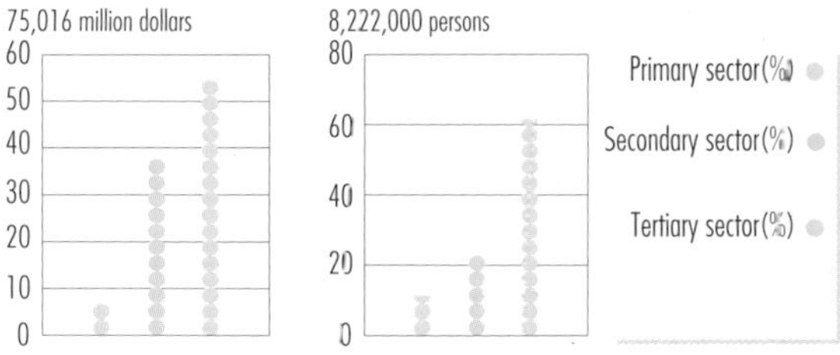

Population age distribution

ASIA

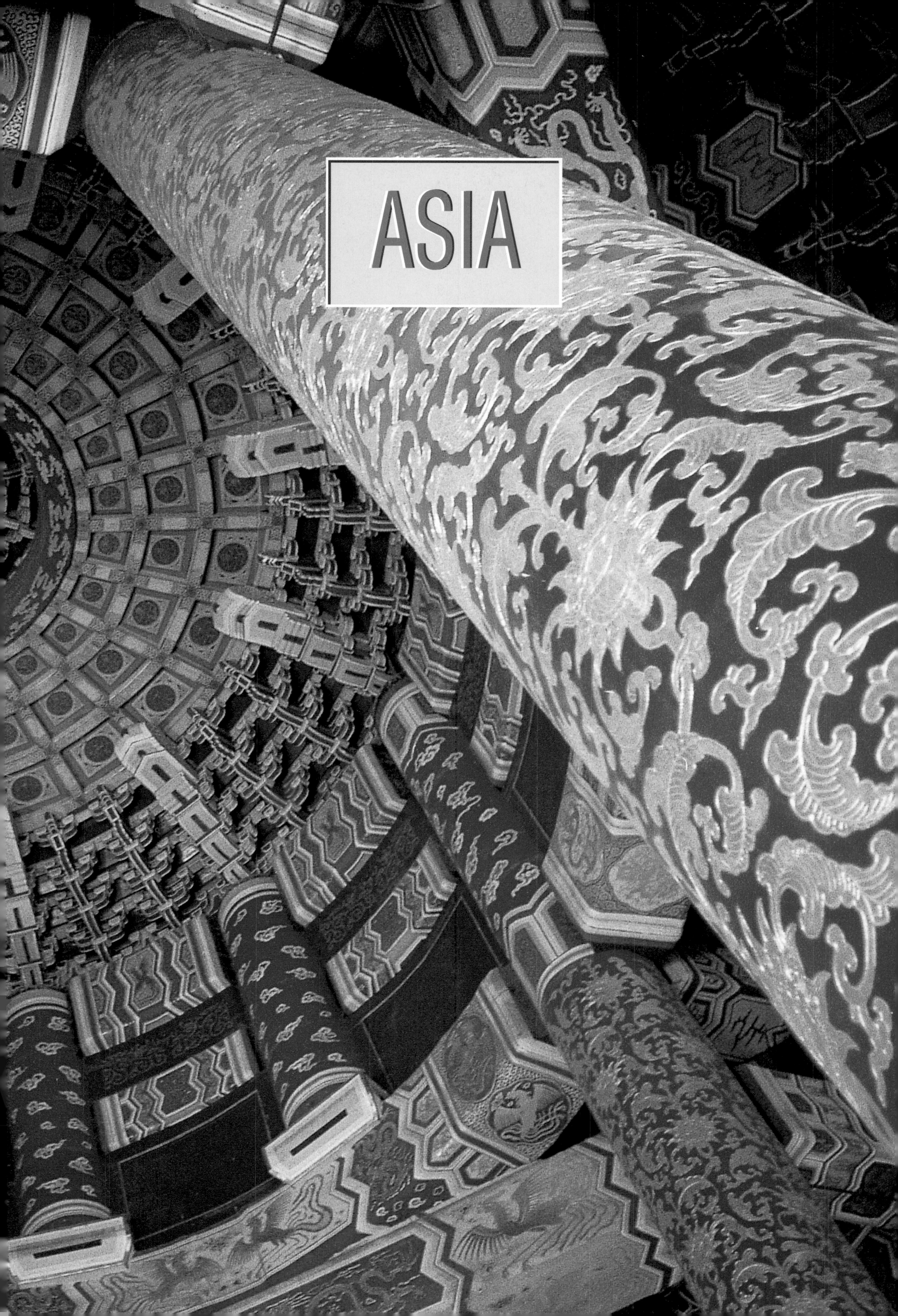

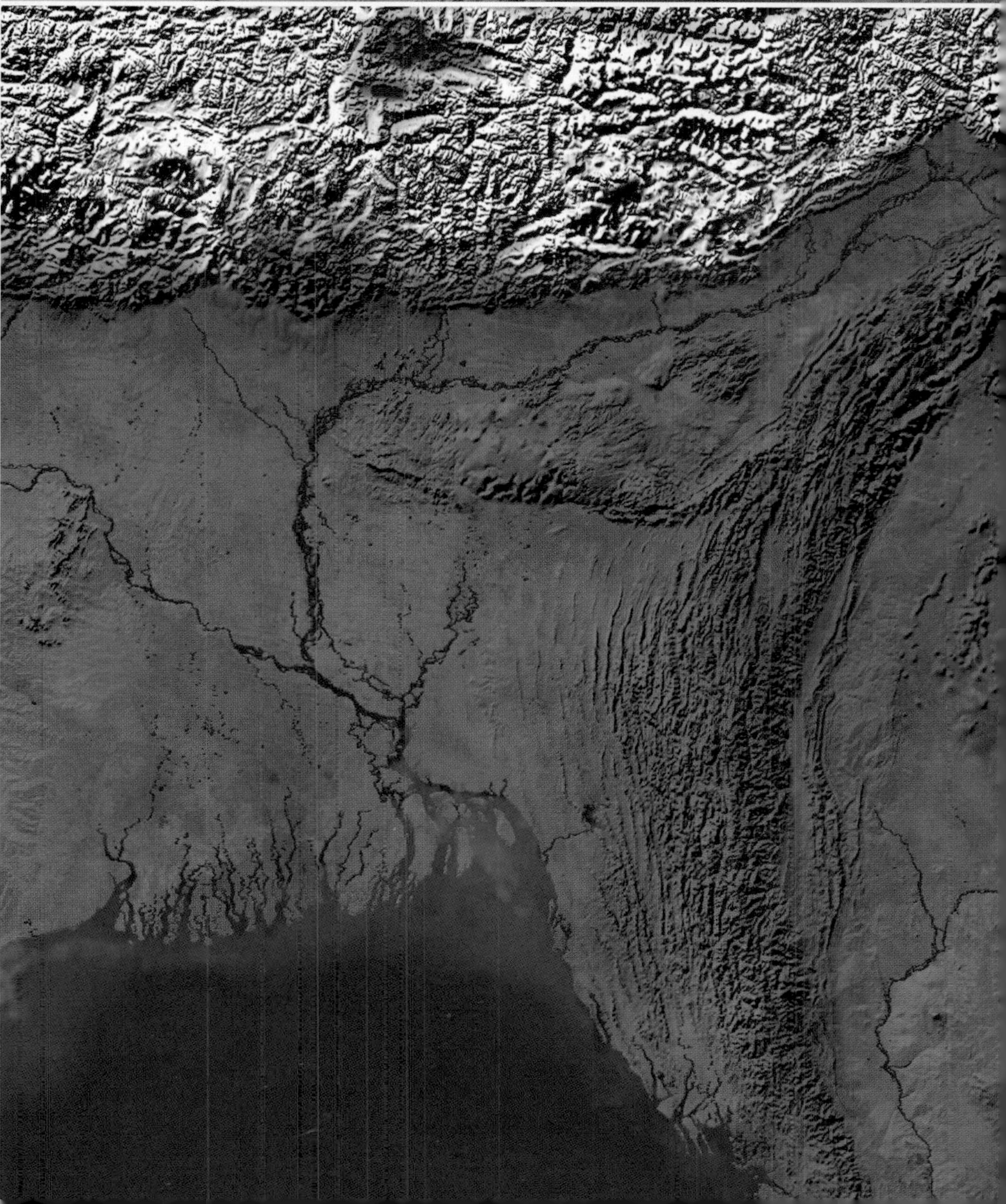

Asia
Northwest

The satellite image shows how the division between Asia and Europe is really more cultural than physical. The Ural Mountains, in the center of the image oriented in a north-south direction, are the mountain barrier that has traditionally been emphasized as the separation between the two continents: to the west, Europe, and to the east, Asia. Further south, the Caspian Sea and below it the Elburz Mountains complete the group of landform features that separate both continents.

On the page to the right, the Western Siberian Plain extends across the north, west of the Urals, with strong coloring in green tones that denote the presence of abundant vegetation and moisture. South of the Ural Mountains extends the Kirgiz Steppe, reaching to the environs of the Aral Sea. Here, the former level of this sea's waters can be observed in the light ocher-colored area that surrounds it. In the lower part of the image, the great elevation of the Hindu Kush and of the Karakorum Range is notable. North of these, the Tian Shan Mountains extend from west to east in an almost straight alignment. Just above them is almond-shaped Lake Issyk-kul'. Further north, and separated by the desert of Sary Ishikotrau, is Lake Balkhash.

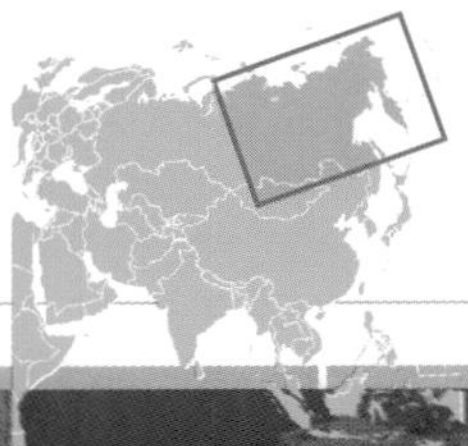

Asia
Northeast

This image of the Asian northeast corresponds to Russian Siberia, which spreads from east to west, north of Lake Baikal —lower part of the left page. In the upper part of the image, the Arctic Ocean and the enormous icecap that covers a great part of its waters can be seen. In the east, the Sea of Okhotsk stands out, bordered on its eastern shore by the Kamchatka Peninsula. Following the Arctic coastline from west to east, first to be seen is the Yamal Peninsula, bordered on its eastern side by

he Bay of Obskaya; farther east, the mouth of the Yenisey River is visible in the gulf of the same name. Very near the icecap is the Taymyr Peninsula and a little farther east, the delta of the Lena River. Near the coast are found the New Siberian Islands and in the far east, the Peninsula of Chukotskiy, separated from the lands of Alaska by Bering Strait. Moving in a southerly direction from here, we find Navarin Point, the Kamchatka Peninsula and at the southern tip of this, the Kuril Islands. In the interior are visible the courses of the Yenisey River in the west and the Lena River in the center of the image, and following the winding course of the Lena River, the Verkhoyansk Range, which extends in a north-south direction.

Asia
Southeast

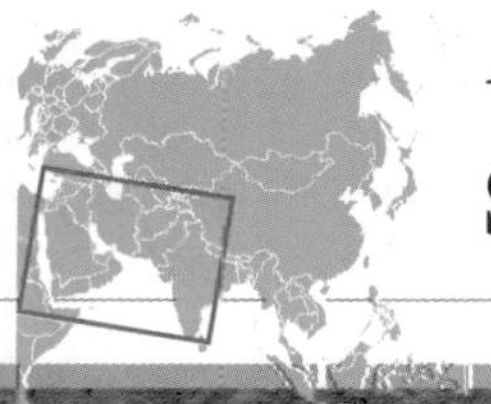

The continental continuity between Europe and Asia can be observed clearly in this image of the Asian southwest. This physical reality is used as an argument by different specialists to consider Europe as a peninsula of Asia; in other cases, the continent of Eurasia is spoken of, in a clear allusion to this physical continuity of both emerged land masses. The rugged relief of this part of Asia is arranged from east to west in a continous succession of mountains and mountain ranges that start with the Taurus

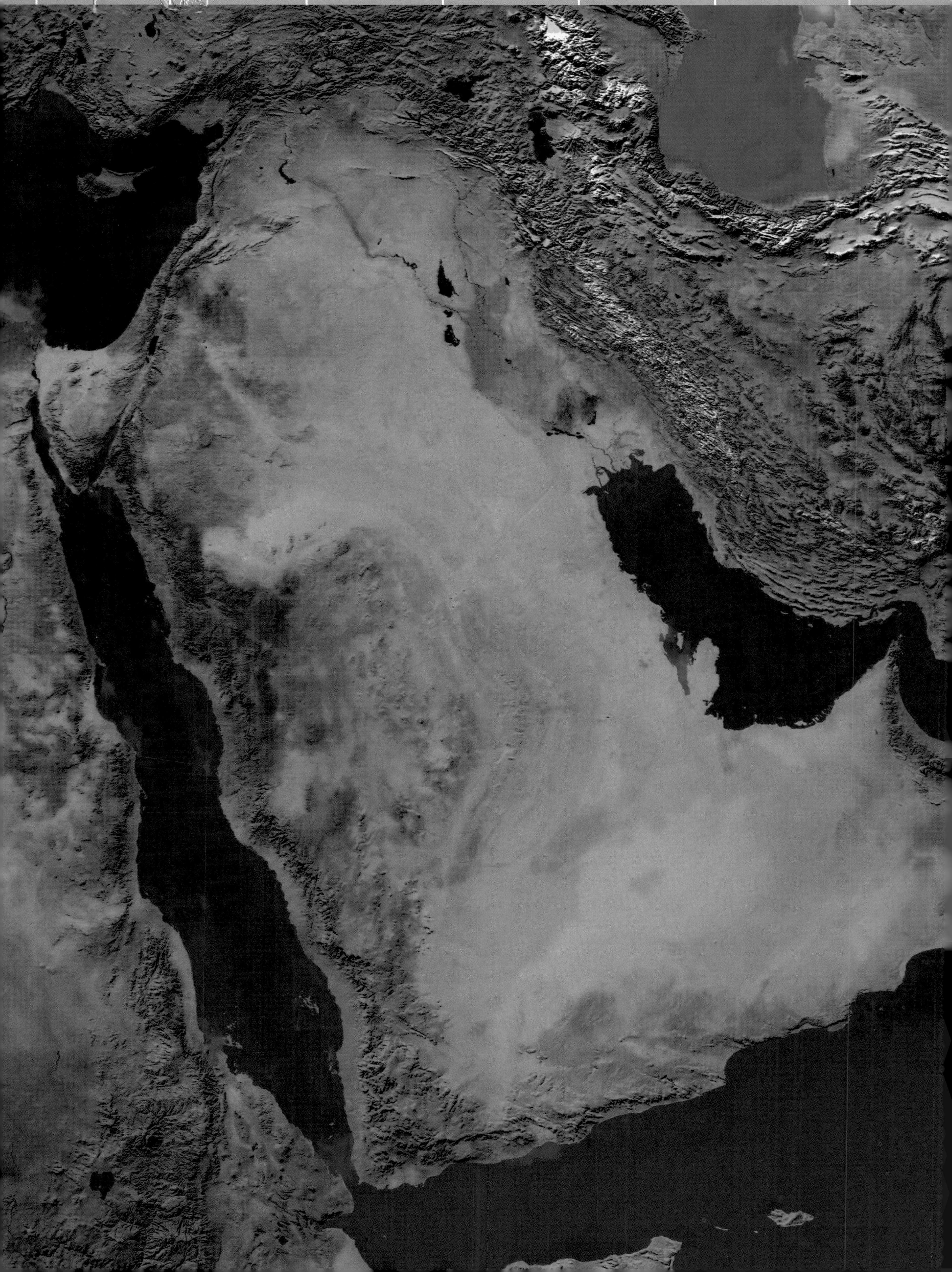

Mountains on the Mediterranean coast of Turkey, and reach the great mountain range of Himalaya in the north of Nepal, Bhutan and India. This continuous chain of mountains splits into two before reaching the Caspian Sea. South of this sea, the Elburz Mountains are visible; the Zagros Mountains descend across the northeast of the Arabian Peninsula with spurs continuing north of the Persian Gulf to the Strait of Hormuz.
Both alignments meet again in the east in the Hindu Kush and Karakorum Mountains —the great whitish mass in the upper center of the right page— which are the western threshold of the Great Himalaya where the highest point on earth is found: Mt. Everest.

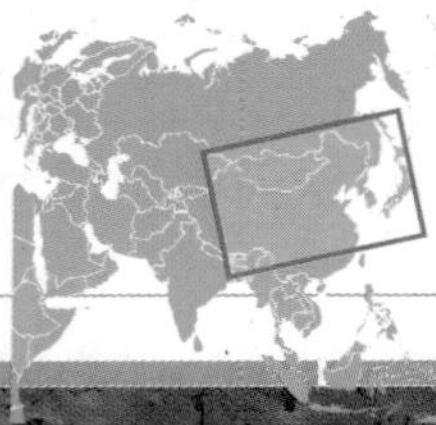

Asia
East of central Asia

In this satellite image of the Asian continent, the Hangayn Mountains in the far upper left, Lake Baikal in the upper center of the image, the eastern coast of the continent, the Archipelago of Japan and the Himalaya can be observed clearly. Following the

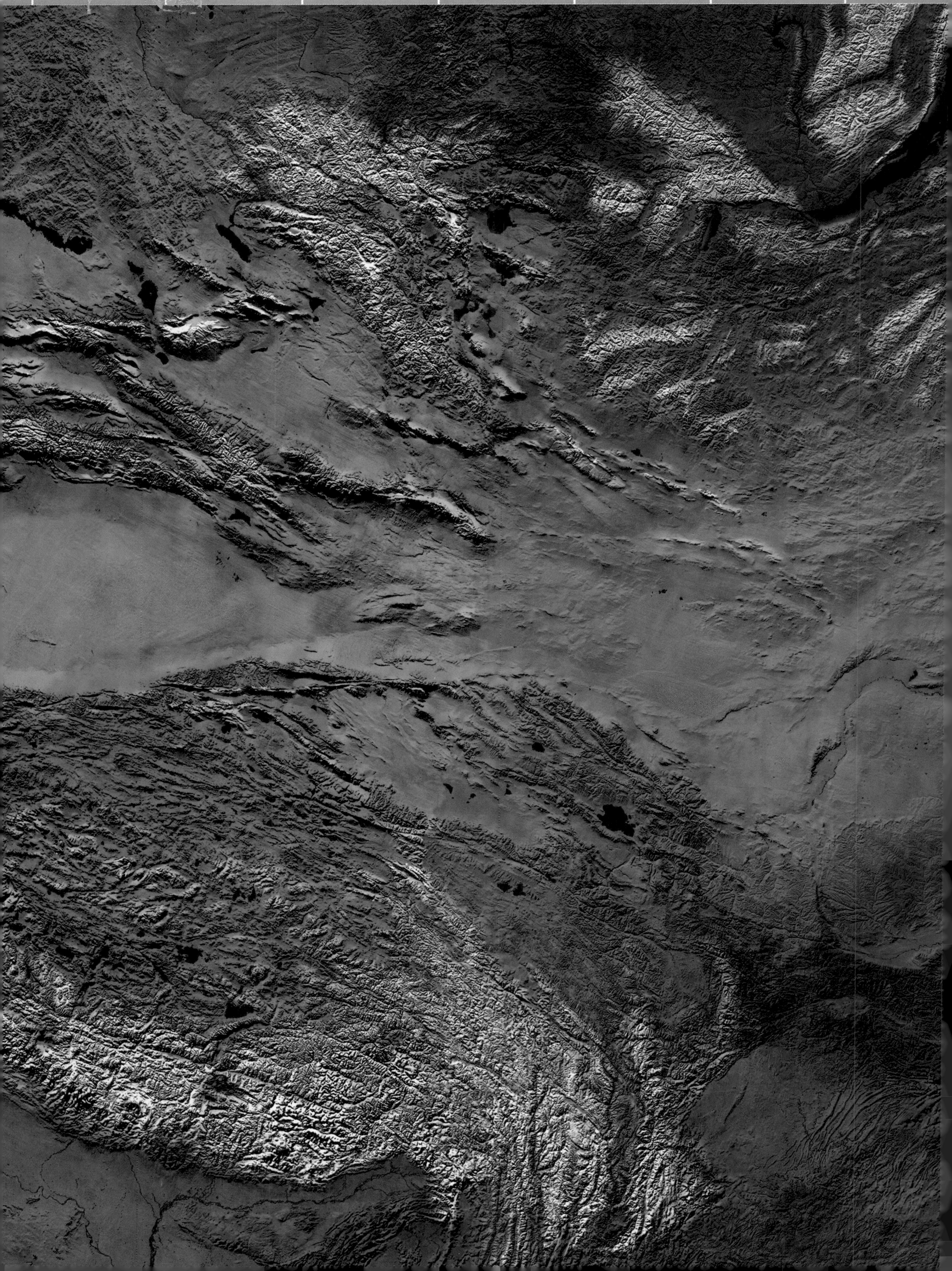

coast from north to south, on the right margin of the image, the group of islands in the shape of an arc which form Japan can be seen first. To the north are the Russian island of Sakhalin and the strait of Tartaria which connects the Sea of Japan with the Sea of Okhotsk in the north. In the south, facing the island of Kyushu, the southernmost of the great islands, is the Peninsula of Korea where North Korea and South Korea are located.
The Korea Strait separates the two groups and serves to communicate with the East China Sea and the Yellow Sea that enters the continent in the form of a large gulf. In the lower left quadrant, the great whitish mass corresponding to the mountain range of the Himalaya and of Tibet is visible.

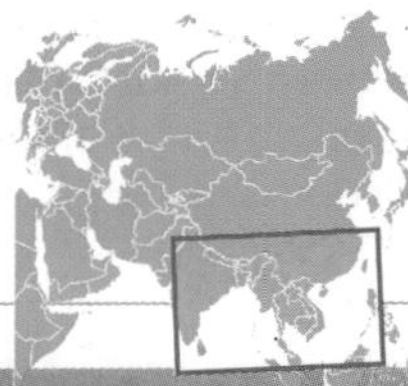

Asia

Continental Southeast Asia

This is a satellite image that covers, from west to east, from India to the Phillipines. In the north, in the upper part of the image, the Himalaya can be seen, and in the south the Peninsula of Malaysia.

The Himalaya stands out because of its coloring in

tones of white that denote the presence of perpetual snows. South of this great mountain range can be observed the abrupt slope that drops to the valleys of the Ganges River on the left and the Brahmaputra River on the right. Further south can be seen the saw-toothed coastline of the Mouths of the Ganges, where this river flows into the Gulf of Bengal.

In the lower center of the image can be seen the beginning of the very long peninsula of Malaysia and on its right the enormously wide peninsula of Indochina traversed from north to south by the Mekong River, which at its mouth forms several deltas known as the Mouths of the Mekong. On the right margin can be seen the island of Taiwan near the coast of China, and further south, the Phillipine Islands.

Asia
Digital terrain model and perspectives

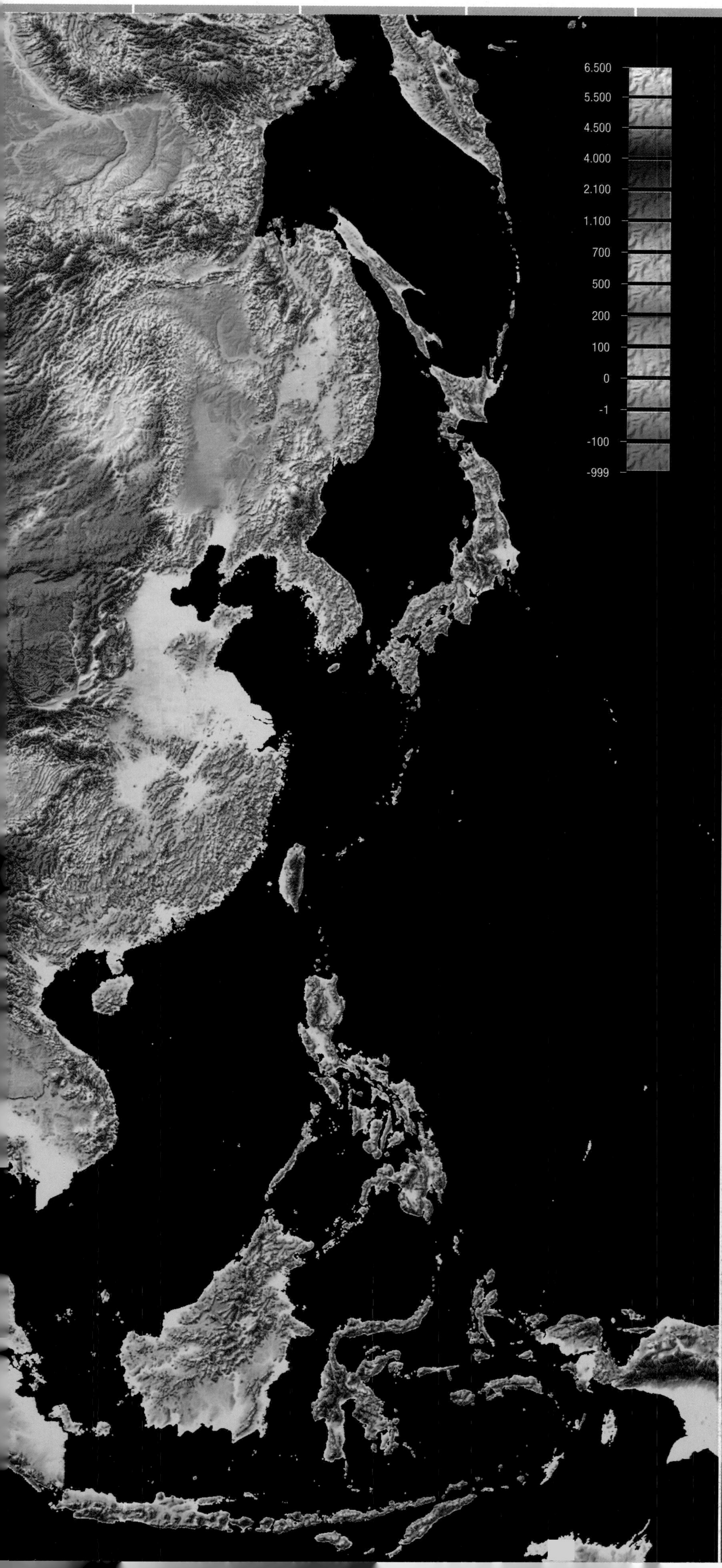
6.500
5.500
4.500
4.000
2.100
1.100
700
500
200
100
0
-1
-100
-999

N
W
E
S
W
S
N
E
S
E
W
N
E
N
S
W

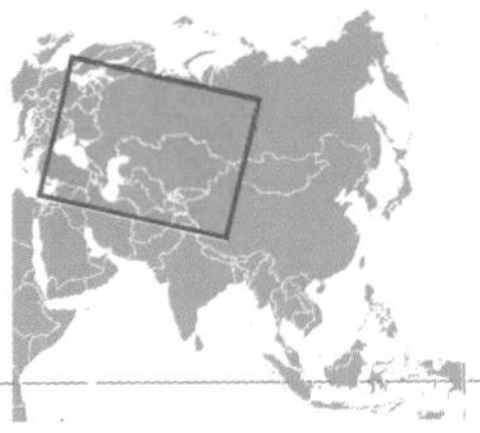

Asia

Northwest Asia

0 100 200 300 400 500 Km
0 40 80 120 140 180 200 220 miles

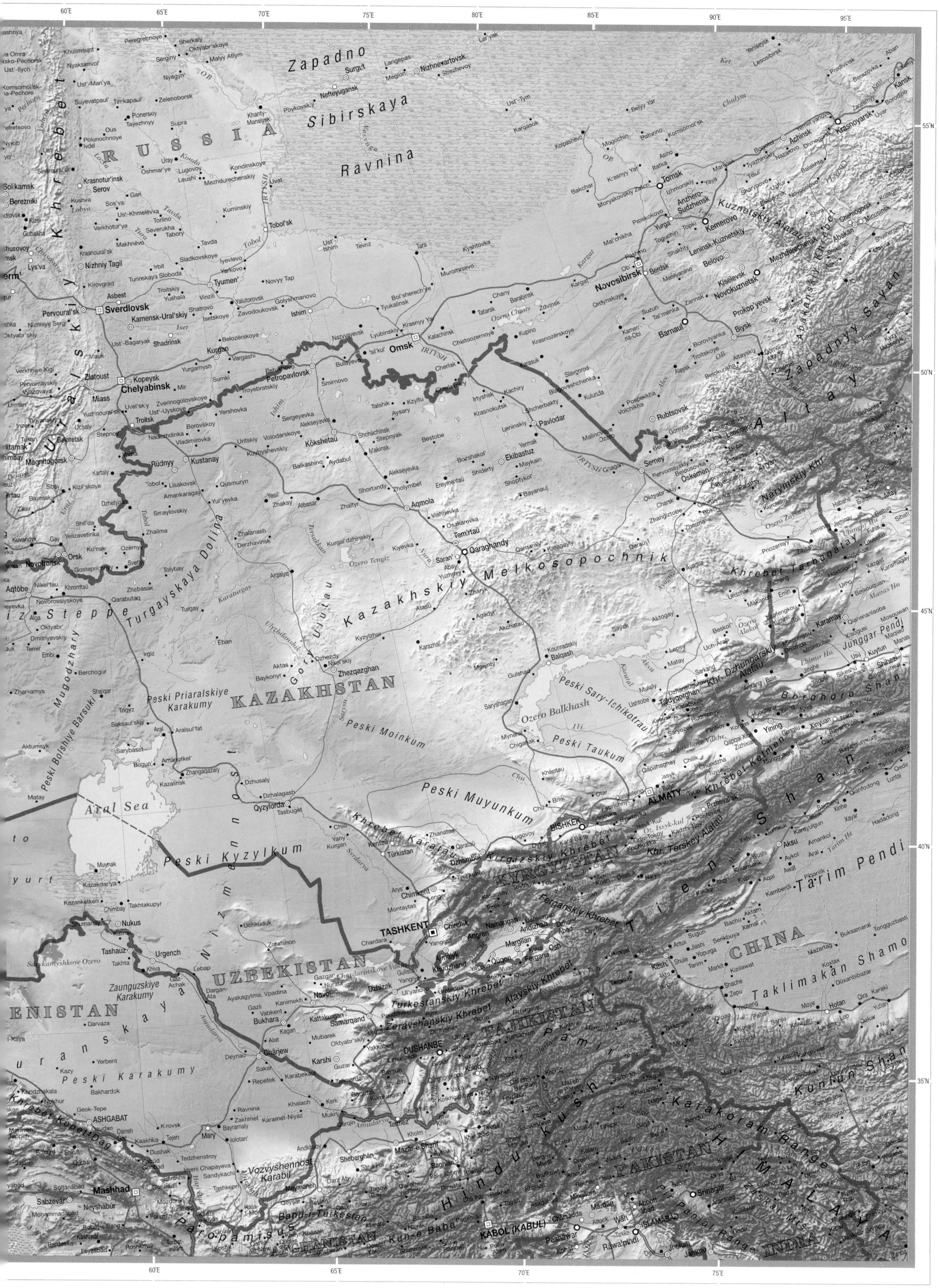
60°E
65°E
70°E
75°E
80°E
85°E
90°E
95°E
55°N
50°N
45°N
40°N
35°N
RUSSIA
KAZAKHSTAN
UZBEKISTAN
KYRGYZSTAN
TAJIKISTAN
AFGHANISTAN
PAKISTAN
INDIA
CHINA
Zapadno
Sibirskaya
Ravnina
Ural'skiy Khrebet
Kazakhskiy Melkosopochnik
Turgayskaya Dolina
Mugodzhary
Peski Priaral'skiye Karakumy
Peski Moinkum
Peski Muyunkum
Peski Kyzylkum
Peski Karakumy
Peski Taukum
Peski Sary-Ishikotrau
Peski Bol'shiye Barsuki
Ozero Balkhash
Ozero Tengiz
Aral Sea
Ulutau
Zaunguzskiye Karakumy
Turanskaya Nizmennost'
Khrebet Kopet-Dag
Vozvyshennost' Karabil
Band-i-Turkestan
Paropamisus
Kuh-e Baba
Hindu Kush
Pamir
Karakoram Range
HIMALAYA
Zaskar Mts.
Pir Panjal Range
Kunlun Shan
Taklimakan Shamo
Tarim Pendi
Tien Shan
Junggar Pendi
Borohoro Shan
Khrebet Tarbagatay
Narymskiy Khr.
Altay
Zapadnyy Sayan
Abakanskiy Khrebet
Kuznetskiy Alatau
Khr. Dzhungarskiy Alatau
Khrebet Karatau
Kirgizskiy Khrebet
Khr. Terskey Alatau
Ferganskiy Khrebet
Turkestanskiy Khrebet
Zeravshanskiy Khrebet
Alayskiy Khrebet
Khrebet Ketmen
Sverdlovsk
Chelyabinsk
Omsk
Novosibirsk
Tomsk
Kemerovo
Novokuznetsk
Barnaul
Krasnoyarsk
Tyumen'
Tobol'sk
Kurgan
Petropavlovsk
Kustanay
Kökshetau
Aqmola
Pavlodar
Semey
Oskemen
Qaraghandy
Zhezqazghan
Qyzylorda
Balqash
Taldyqorghan
ALMATY
BISHKEK
TASHKENT
Chimkent
Türkistan
Dzhambul
Namangan
Andizhan
Fergana
Osh
Khudzhand
Samarqand
Bukhara
Navoi
Karshi
Chärjew
Urgench
Nukus
Tashauz
DUSHANBE
Termez
Mazar-e Sharif
Meymaneh
Mary
ASHGABAT
Mashhad
KABOL (KABUL)
Peshawar
ISLAMABAD
Rawalpindi
Srinagar
Kashi
Yarkant
Hotan
Aksu
Yining
Karamay
Shihezi
Magnitogorsk
Orsk
Novotroitsk
Aqtöbe
Rüdnyy
Ekibastuz
Biysk
Gorno-Altaysk
Abakan
Minusinsk
Kansk
Achinsk
Nizhniy Tagil
Zlatoust
Miass
Troitsk
Ishim
Surgut
Nizhnevartovsk
Nefteyugansk
Khanty-Mansiysk
IRTYSH
OB'
Chu
Ili
Syrdarya
Amudarya
Ishim
Tobol
Ural
Aral Sea

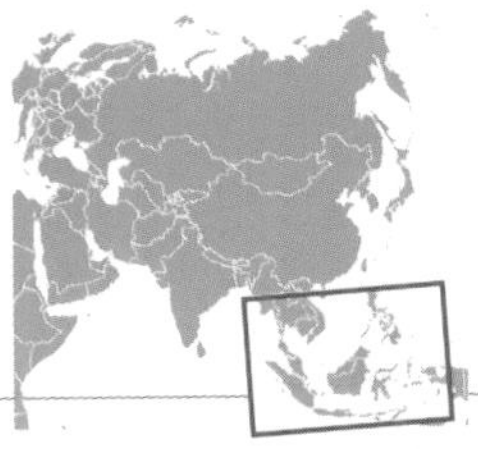

Asia

Islands of southeast Asia

0 100 200 300 400 500 Km
0 40 80 120 140 180 200 220 miles

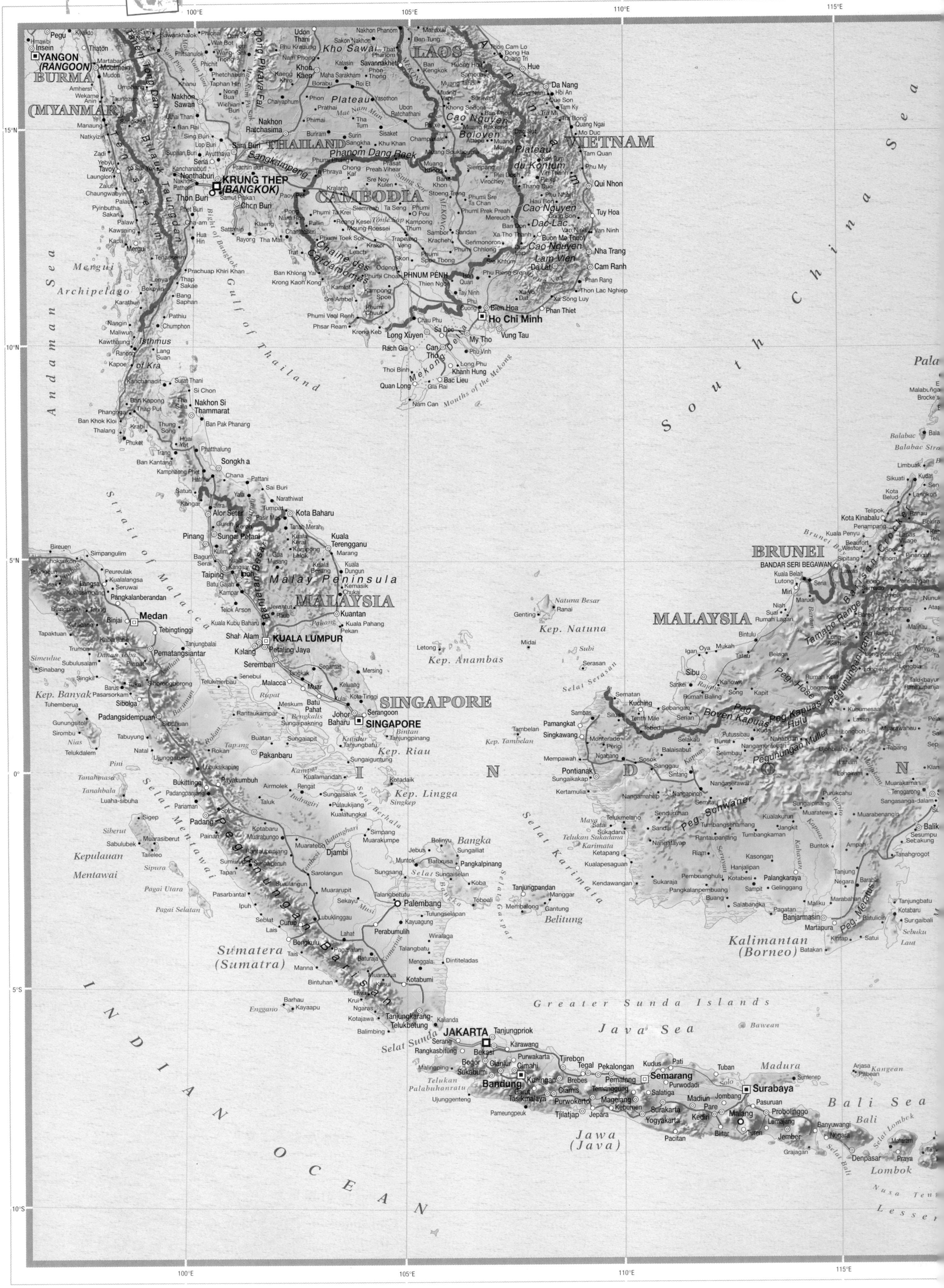

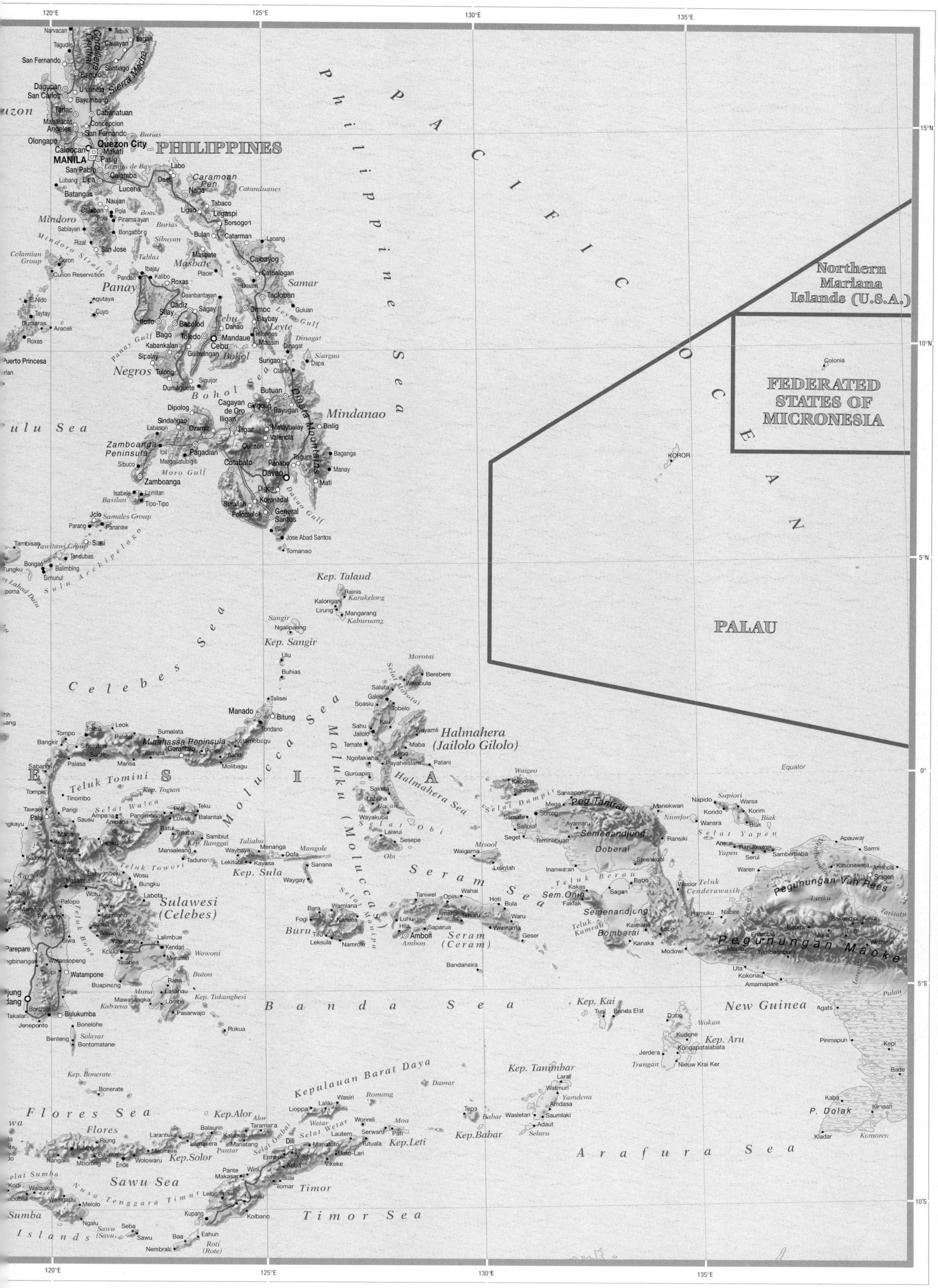
120°E
125°E
130°E
135°E
15°N
10°N
5°N
0°
5°S
10°S
PHILIPPINES
PACIFIC OCEAN
Philippine Sea
Northern Mariana Islands (U.S.A.)
FEDERATED STATES OF MICRONESIA
Colonia
KOROR
PALAU
Luzon
San Fernando
Dagupan
San Carlos
Baguio
Tarlac
Cabanatuan
Angeles
San Fernando
Olongapo
Caloocan
Quezon City
MANILA
Makati
Pasig
Calamba
Lucena
Batangas
Cordillera Central
Sierra Madre
Mindoro
Calamian Group
Mindoro Strait
Culion Reservation
Burias
Caramoan Pen.
Catanduanes
Naga
Legaspi
Sorsogon
Masbate
Sibuyan
Tablas
Panay
Roxas
Iloilo
Bacolod
Negros
Cebu
Bohol
Samar
Catbalogan
Calbayog
Tacloban
Leyte
Ormoc
Leyte Gulf
Dinagat
Siargao
Surigao
Bohol Sea
Mindanao
Diwata Mountains
Cagayan de Oro
Iligan
Butuan
Bislig
Zamboanga Peninsula
Zamboanga
Moro Gulf
Cotabato
Davao
Davao Gulf
General Santos
Basilan
Samales Group
Jolo
Tawitawi Group
Sulu Archipelago
Sulu Sea
Puerto Princesa
Celebes Sea
Kep. Talaud
Kep. Sangir
Morotai
Halmahera (Jailolo Gilolo)
Ternate
Manado
Bitung
Minahassa Peninsula
Gorontalo
Teluk Tomini
Kep. Togian
Molucca Sea
Maluku (Moluccas)
Halmahera Sea
Selat Obi
Obi
Kep. Sula
Taliabu
Mangole
Sulawesi (Celebes)
Teluk Tawori
Teluk Bone
Buton
Muna
Wowoni
Kep. Tukangbesi
Banda Sea
Buru
Seram (Ceram)
Ambon
Seram Sea
Selat Manipa
Bandanaira
Waigeo
Selat Dampier
Sorong
Misool
Peg. Tamrau
Manokwari
Semenandjung Doberai
Teluk Berau
Sem. Onin
Semenandjung Bombarai
Fakfak
Kaimana
Teluk Kamrau
Teluk Cenderawasih
Numfor
Biak
Supiori
Selat Yapen
Yapen
Serui
Sarmi
Jayapura
Pegunungan Van Rees
Pegunungan Maoke
New Guinea
Kep. Kai
Tual
Kep. Aru
Dobo
Kep. Tanimbar
Yamdena
Saumlaki
Selaru
Kep. Babar
Damar
Kepulauan Barat Daya
Wetar
Romang
Moa
Kep. Leti
Selat Wetar
Selat Ombai
Timor
Dili
Kupang
Roti (Rote)
Sawu (Savu)
Timor Sea
Arafura Sea
P. Dolak
Kep. Alor
Alor
Kep. Solor
Flores
Flores Sea
Sawu Sea
Nusa Tenggara Timur
Sumba
Selat Sumba
Kep. Bonerate
Salayar
Equator

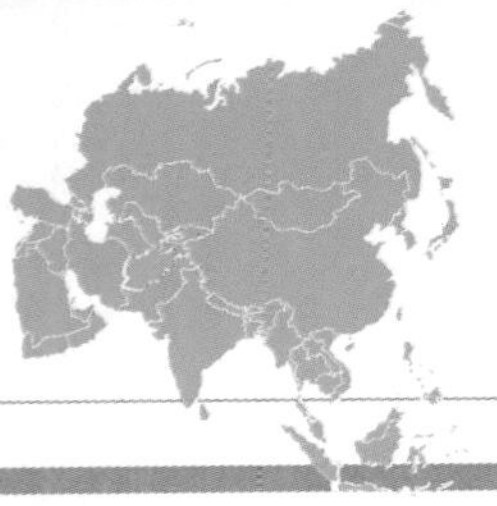

Afghanistan

Located in the southwest of Asia, Afghanistan's territory consists of large plateaus and considerable elevations, and it is crossed in an east-west direction by the Hindu Kush Mountains. The Amudar'ya, Kabul, Helmand and Hari Rud are its principal rivers. The climate, arid and continental, is very harsh, with an annual rainfall of less than 300 mm except in the peaks of the Eastern Hindu Kush.

Among the Afghan people, two great ethnic groups can be distinguished: the Pashtun or Pathan, the main ethnic group, a nomadic people with an eastern Iranian language who inhabit the south of the country, and the Tadzhik, sedentary and of Persian origin. A third racial group, much more in the minority, the Uzbek, inhabits the north of the country (Afghan Turkestan). Some semi-nomadic communities exist and the urban sector is not very developed. Most of the people live in rural areas and work in farming; the lands that are not irrigated are communal property. Cereals, fruit trees and dried fruits are the main crops. Other economic resources are crafts (carpet-making), the natural gas deposits of the north of the country and a modest petrochemical industry. Great mineral riches (coal, iron ore, chrome) remain unexploited. Industry has a small number of textile and food product factories. The scarcity of basic road infrastructure makes the traditional caravans continue to be the main means of domestic transportation.

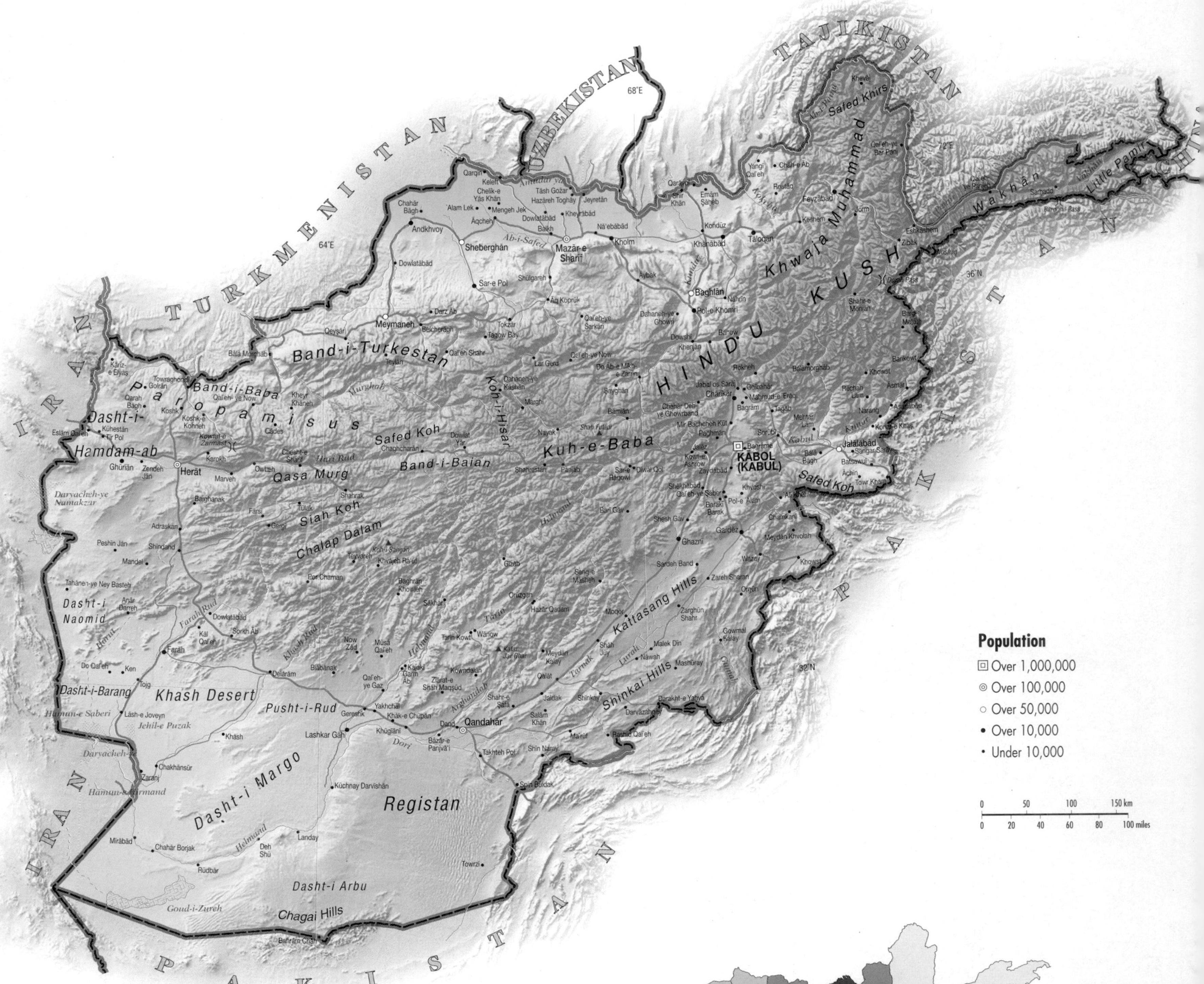

Population

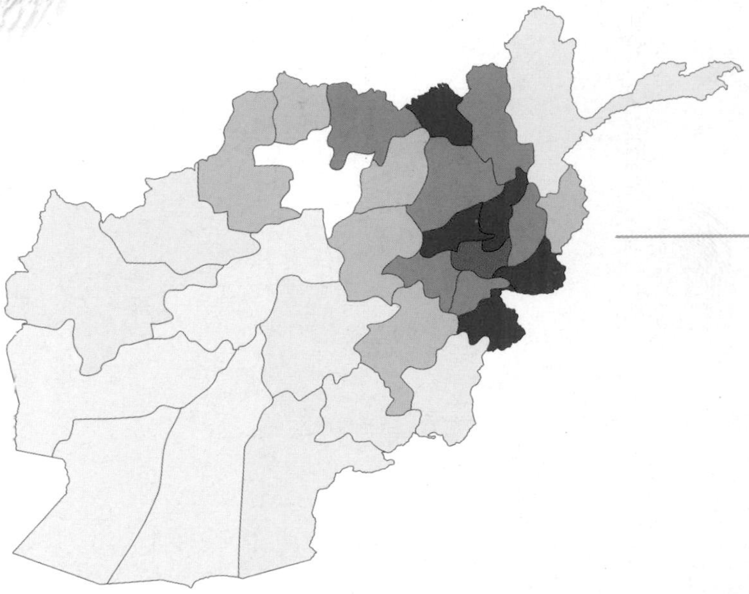

Population density (persons pr sq km)

- Fewer than 5
- From 10 to 15
- From 15 to 30
- From 30 to 50
- From 50 to 75
- From 75 to 150
- More than 150
- Data unavailable

Agriculture

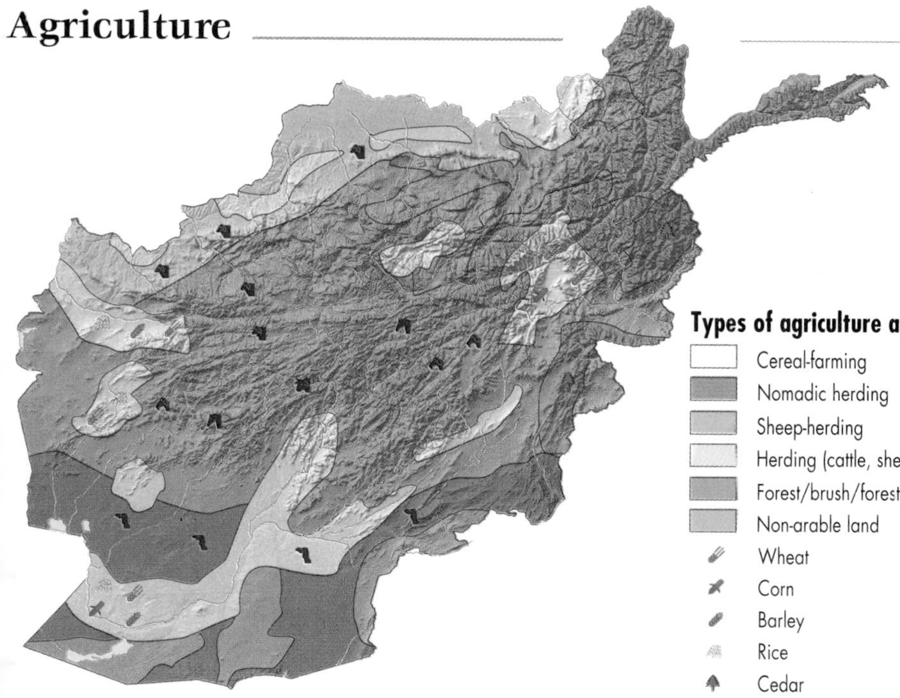

Types of agriculture and livestock production

- Cereal-farming
- Nomadic herding
- Sheep-herding
- Herding (cattle, sheep, horses)
- Forest/brush/forestry
- Non-arable land

Wheat	Cattle
Corn	Sheep
Barley	Goats
Rice	Horses
Cedar	Camels

Official name: Islamic State of Afghanistan (Pashtu)
Form of government: Transitional government
Capital: Kabul (Kābol)
Official language: Pashto, Dari
Monetary unit: afghani
Religious affiliation: Muslim (99%), other (1%)
Ethnic composition of the population: Pashtun (35%), Tadzhik (25%), Uzbek (6%), Hazara (19%), minority groups (15%)
Area: 652,225 sq km
Total population: 22,664,000 inhabitants
Population density: 34.7 persons per sq km

Geostructural units

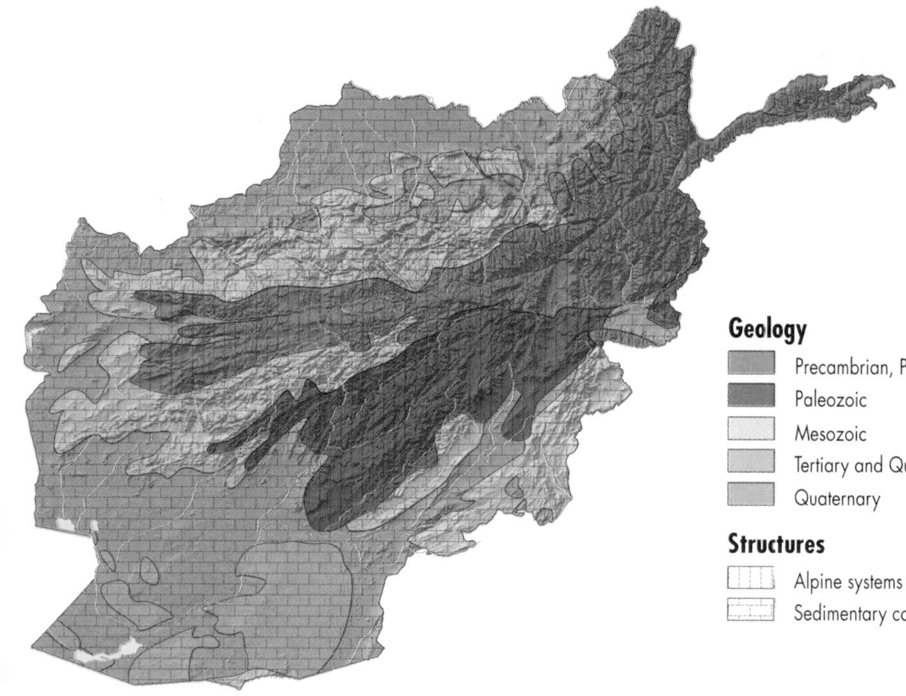

Geology

- Precambrian, Paleozoic and Mesozoic
- Paleozoic
- Mesozoic
- Tertiary and Quaternary
- Quaternary

Structures

- Alpine systems
- Sedimentary covering

Population evolution and projection

in millions of persons

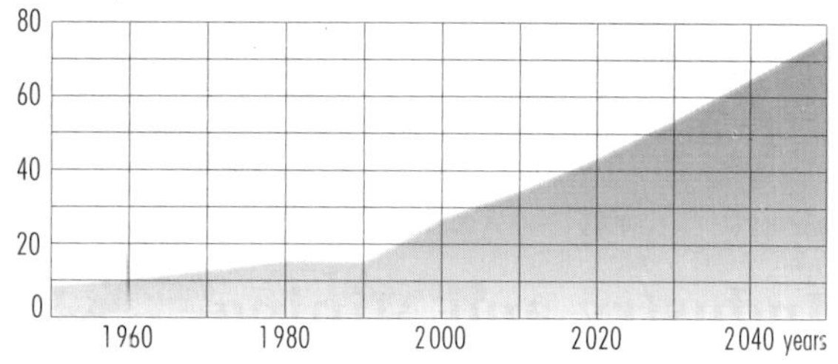

GDP structure

5,870 million dollars

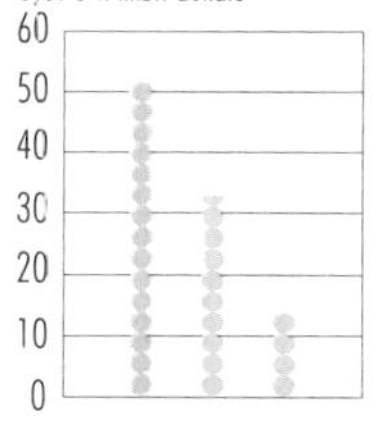

Labor force

7,877,000 persons

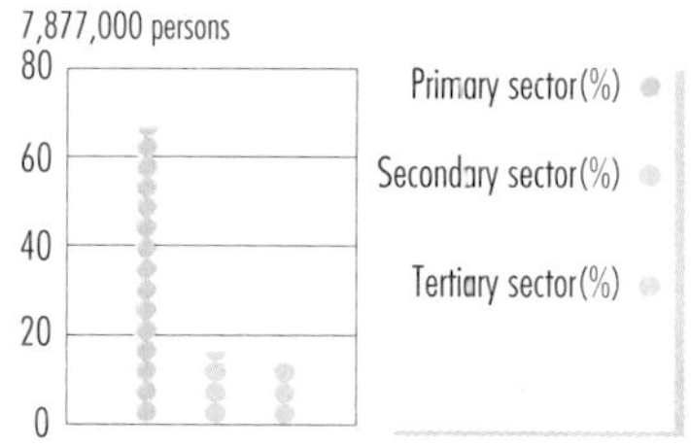

Industry and Mining

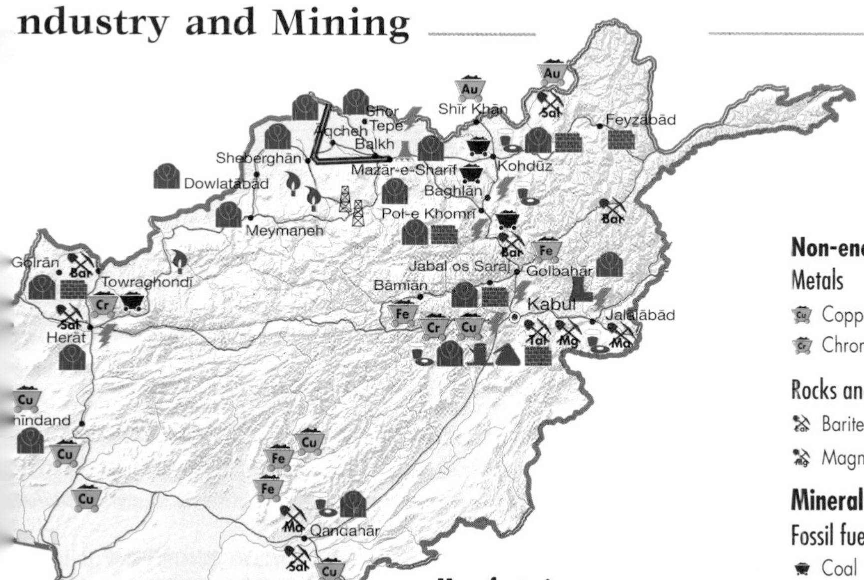

Manufacturing

- Food, beverages and tobacco
- Textiles, clothing, leather and footwear
- Wood, cork and furniture
- Paper and graphic arts
- Chemical products
- Building materials, glass and cement

Non-energy source mineral resources

Metals

- Copper
- Iron ore
- Chromite
- Gold

Rocks and industrial minerals

- Barite
- Marble
- Talc
- Magnesite
- Salt

Mineral fuel resources

Fossil fuels

- Coal
- Natural gas
- Petroleum

Radioactive fuel

- Uranium

Energy-related installations

- Hydroelectric power plant
- Thermal power plant
- Gas pipeline

Population age distribution

Vital statistics

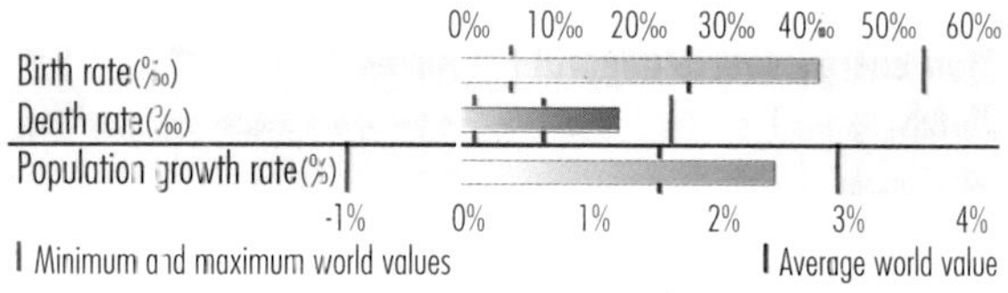

Literacy (% of population over 15)

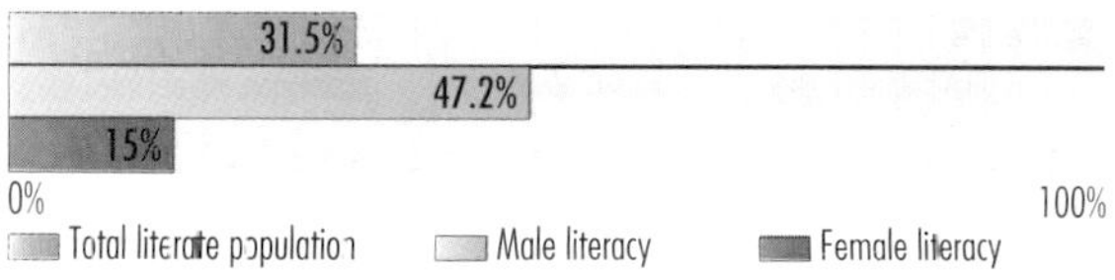

Per capita income (GDP per person)

$259/person
$77/person (world minimum: Mozambique) (world maximum: Japan) $37,075/person

Land use

Forests and jungles 3% | Cropland 12% | Other 39% | Meadows and pastures 46%

China

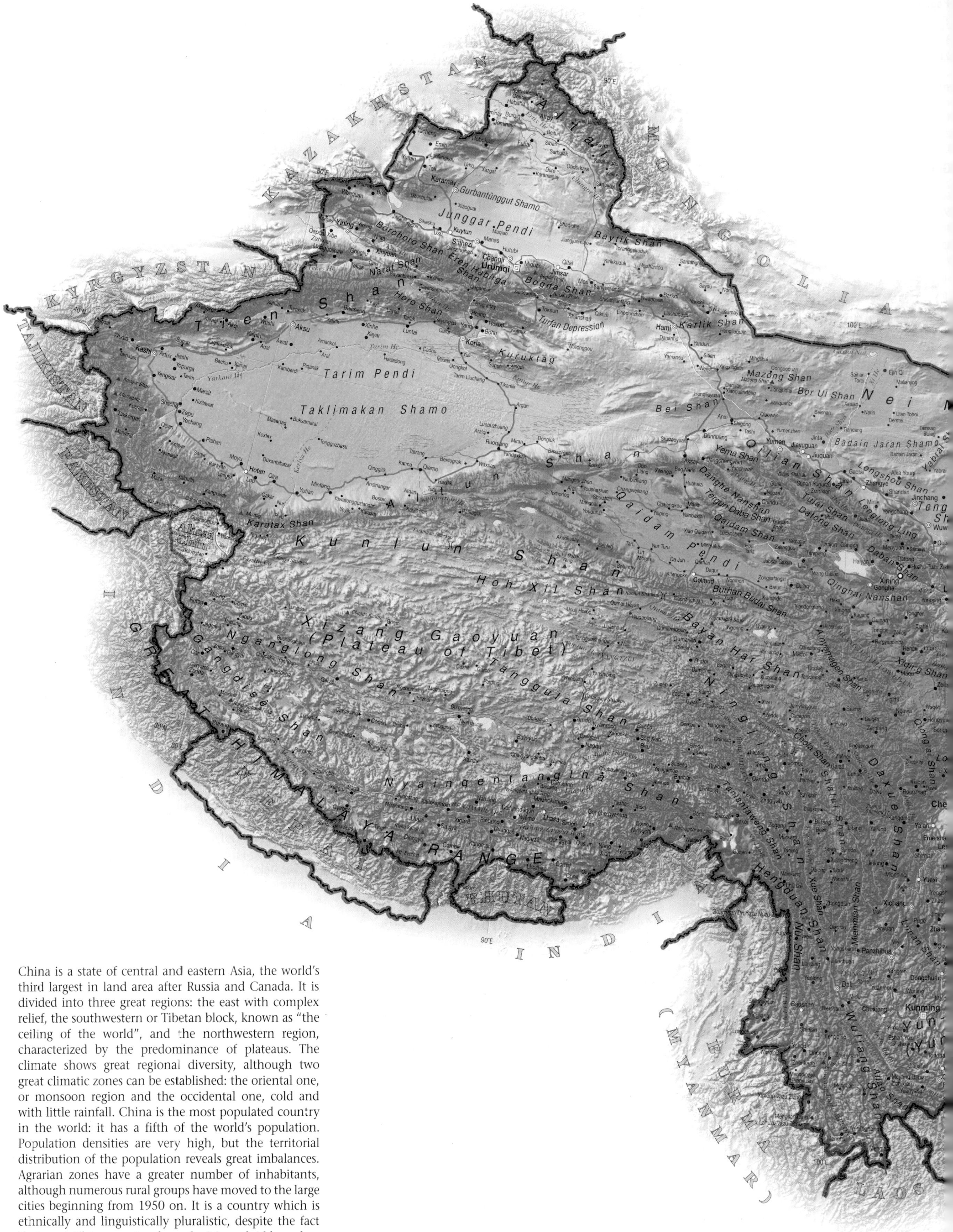

China is a state of central and eastern Asia, the world's third largest in land area after Russia and Canada. It is divided into three great regions: the east with complex relief, the southwestern or Tibetan block, known as "the ceiling of the world", and the northwestern region, characterized by the predominance of plateaus. The climate shows great regional diversity, although two great climatic zones can be established: the oriental one, or monsoon region and the occidental one, cold and with little rainfall. China is the most populated country in the world: it has a fifth of the world's population. Population densities are very high, but the territorial distribution of the population reveals great imbalances. Agrarian zones have a greater number of inhabitants, although numerous rural groups have moved to the large cities beginning from 1950 on. It is a country which is ethnically and linguistically pluralistic, despite the fact that most Chinese spring from the Mongoloid branch.

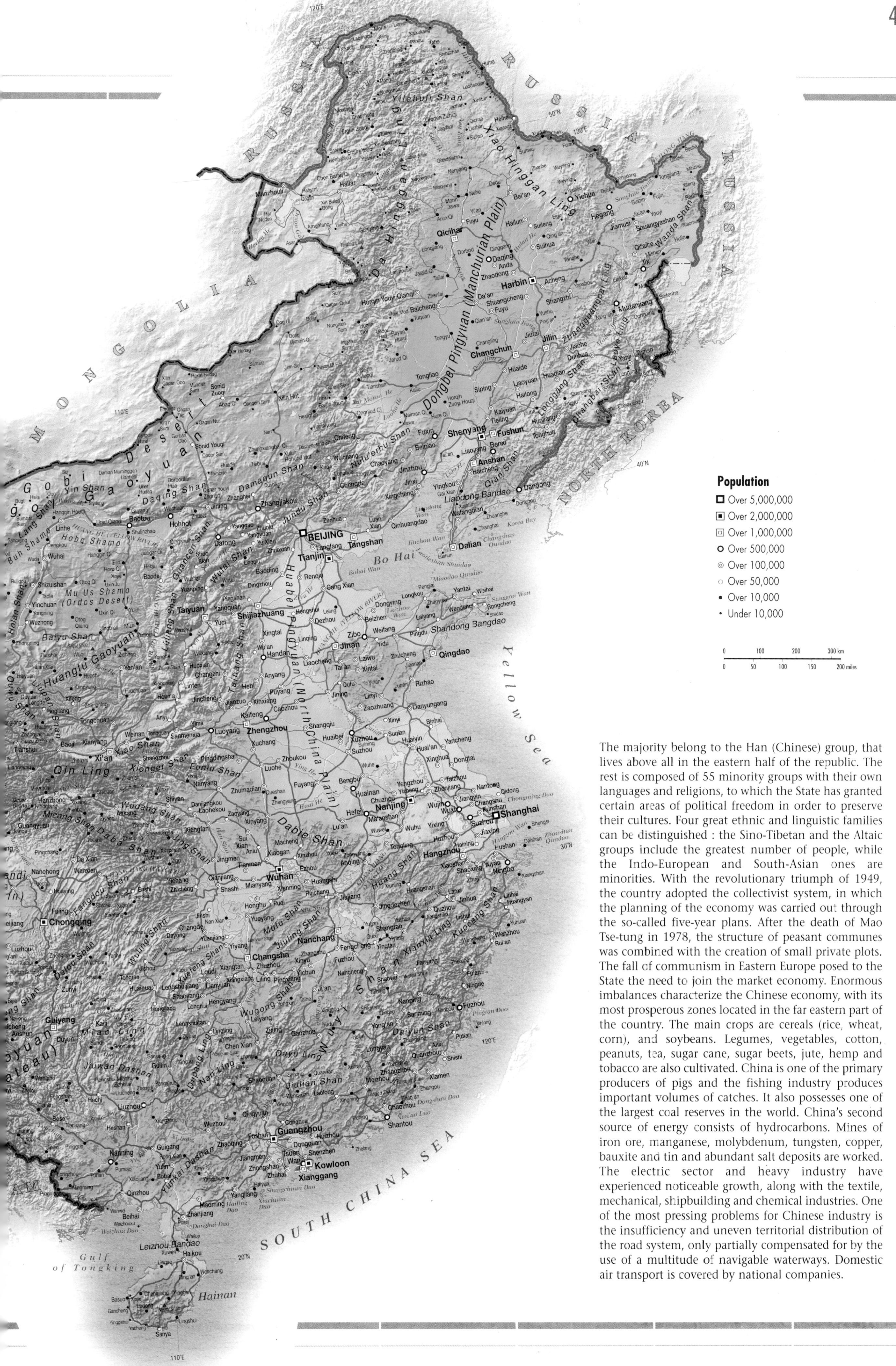

The majority belong to the Han (Chinese) group, that lives above all in the eastern half of the republic. The rest is composed of 55 minority groups with their own languages and religions, to which the State has granted certain areas of political freedom in order to preserve their cultures. Four great ethnic and linguistic families can be distinguished : the Sino-Tibetan and the Altaic groups include the greatest number of people, while the Indo-European and South-Asian ones are minorities. With the revolutionary triumph of 1949, the country adopted the collectivist system, in which the planning of the economy was carried out through the so-called five-year plans. After the death of Mao Tse-tung in 1978, the structure of peasant communes was combined with the creation of small private plots. The fall of communism in Eastern Europe posed to the State the need to join the market economy. Enormous imbalances characterize the Chinese economy, with its most prosperous zones located in the far eastern part of the country. The main crops are cereals (rice, wheat, corn), and soybeans. Legumes, vegetables, cotton, peanuts, tea, sugar cane, sugar beets, jute, hemp and tobacco are also cultivated. China is one of the primary producers of pigs and the fishing industry produces important volumes of catches. It also possesses one of the largest coal reserves in the world. China's second source of energy consists of hydrocarbons. Mines of iron ore, manganese, molybdenum, tungsten, copper, bauxite and tin and abundant salt deposits are worked. The electric sector and heavy industry have experienced noticeable growth, along with the textile, mechanical, shipbuilding and chemical industries. One of the most pressing problems for Chinese industry is the insufficiency and uneven territorial distribution of the road system, only partially compensated for by the use of a multitude of navigable waterways. Domestic air transport is covered by national companies.

India

The external boundaries of India as depicted in the maps are neither correct nor authentic to lower right area
Population
Over 5,000,000
Over 2,000,000
Over 1,000,000
Over 500,000
Over 100,000
Over 50,000
Over 10,000
Under 10,000
0 100 200 km
0 40 80 120 miles
GREAT HIMALAYA
Karakoram Range
Ladakh Range
Zaskar Mts
Pir Panjal Range
Siwalik Range
Thar or Great Indian Desert
Aravalli Range
GANGES PLAIN
INDIA
Vindhya Range
Satpura Range
Mahadeo Hills
Ajanta Range
Deccan
Plateau
Balaghat Range
Western Ghats
Eastern Ghats
Chota Nagpur Plateau
Kaimur Range
Rajmahal Hills
Nilgiri Hills
Palni Hills
Gulf of Kachchh
Kathiawar
Gulf of Khambhat
Arabian Sea
Laccadive Sea
Malabar Coast
Coromandel Coast
Bay of
INDIAN OCEAN
SRI LANKA
Gulf of Mannar
Palk Strait
Delhi
NEW DELHI
Bombay
Calcutta
Madras
Bangalore
Hyderābād
Ahmadābād
Kānpur
Lucknow
Nāgpur
Pune
Jaipur
Surat
Indore
Bhopāl
Srinagar
Amritsar
Ludhiāna
Chandīgarh
Agra
Vārānasi
Allahābād
Patna
Jabalpur
Rānchi
Cuttack
Visākhapatnam
Vijayawada
Madurai
Cochin
Trivandrum
Mangalore
Mysore
Coimbatore
Sholāpur
Baroda
Rājkot
Jodhpur
Kota
Gwalior
Jammu
Cape Comorin
Mouths of the Godavari
Mouths of the Krishna
35°N
30°N
25°N
20°N
15°N
10°N
70°E
75°E
80°E
85°E
90°E

Agriculture

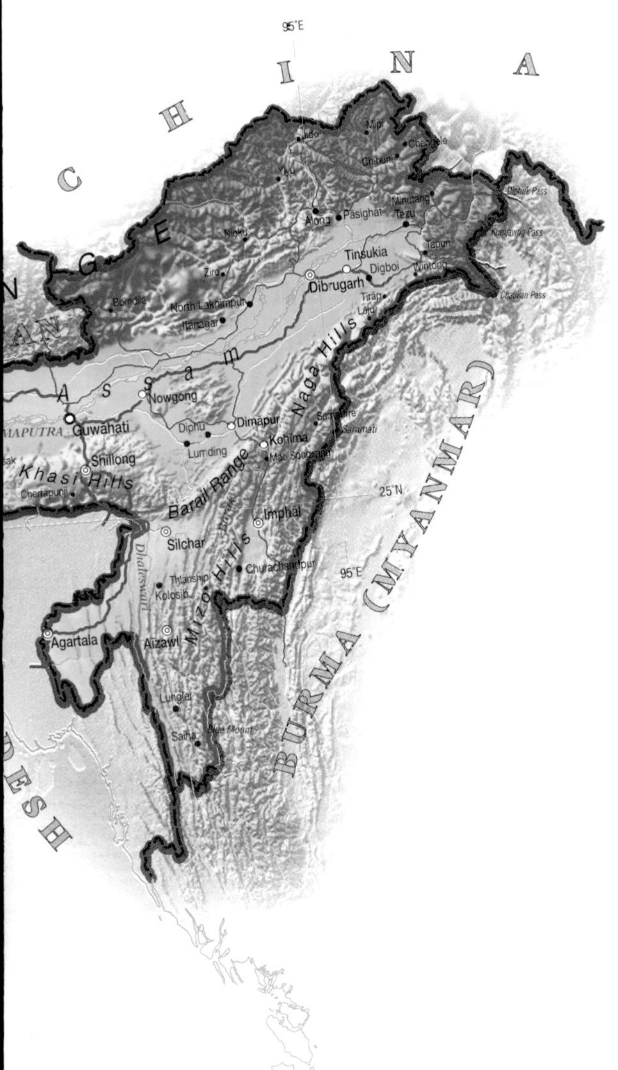

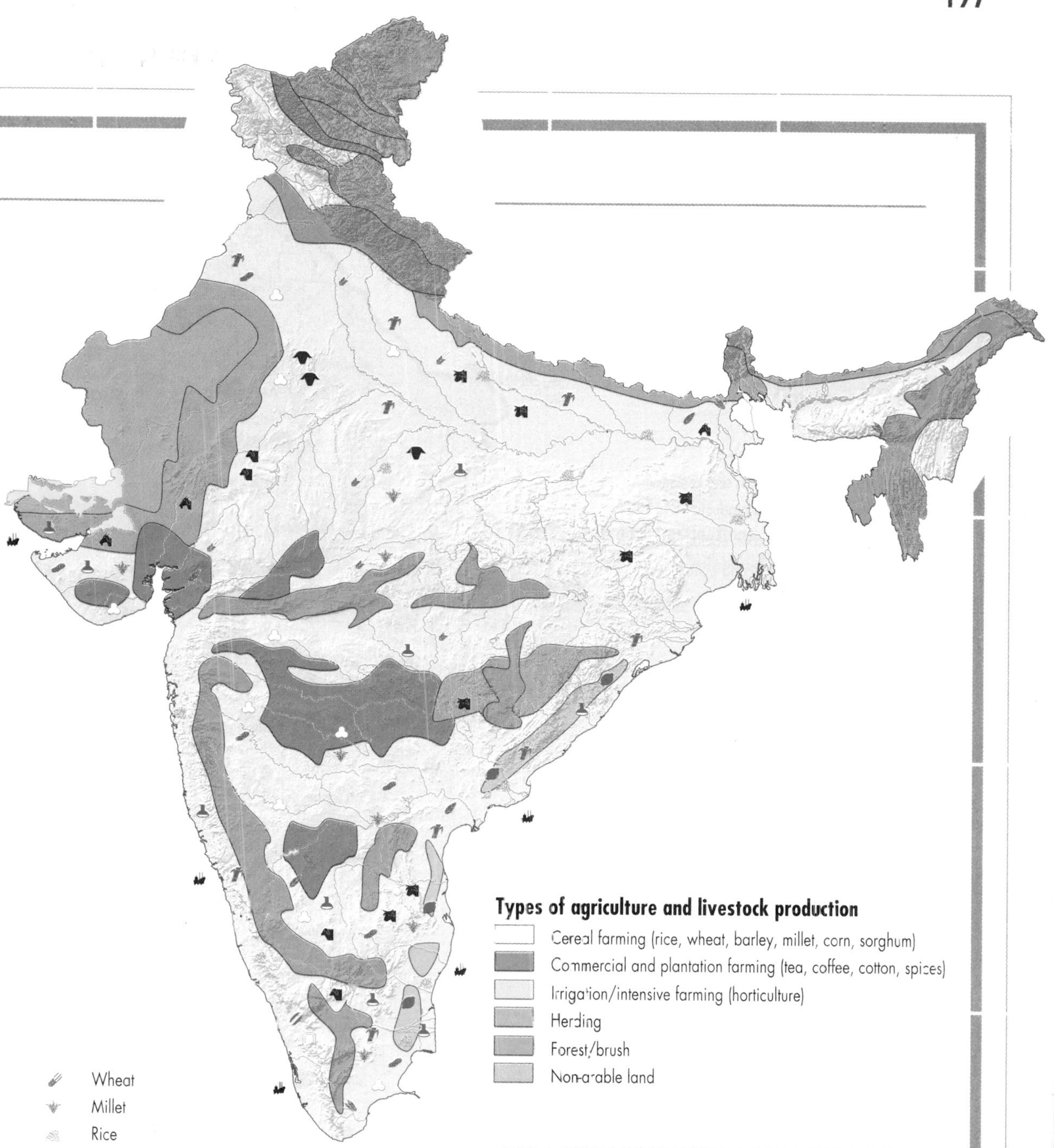

Official name: Bharat, Republic of India

Form of government: federal republic

Capital: New Delhi

Official language: Hindi, English

Monetary unit: Indian rupee

Religious affiliation: Hindu (80.3%), Muslim (11%), Christian (2.4%), Sikh (2%), Buddhist (0.7%), Jain (0.5%), Zoroastrian (0.01%), other (3.1%)

Ethnic composition of the population: Indo-European (72%), Dravidian (25%), Mongoloid and other (3%)

Area: 3,165,596 sq km

Total population: 952,108,000 inhabitants

Population density: 300.8 persons per sq km

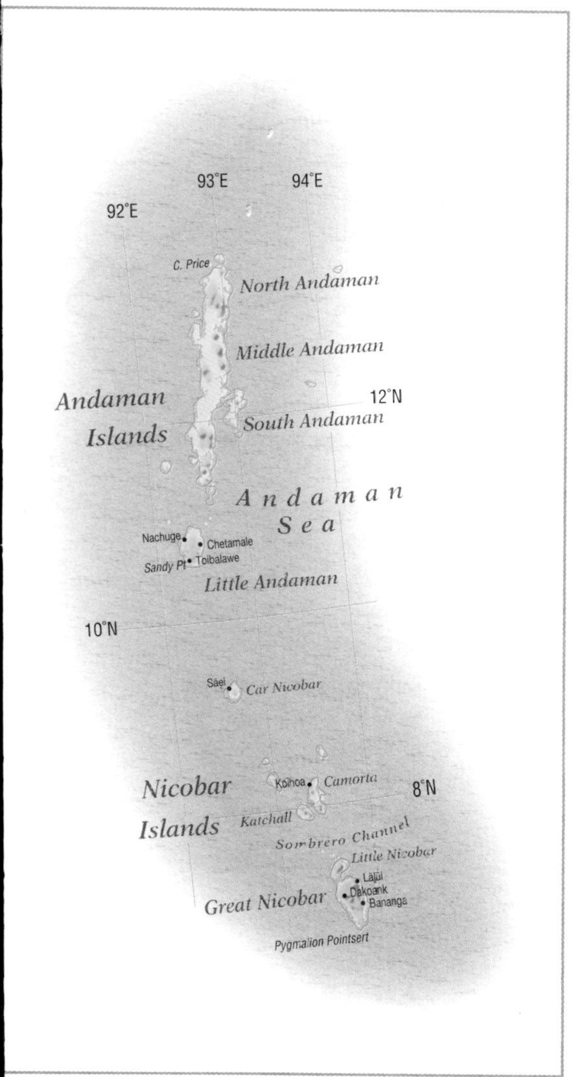

India's physical geography consists of three basic features: the Himalayan Mountains, the Indo-Ganges river plain and the Deccan Plateau. The climate has tropical and subtropical characteristics, except in the mountainous regions of the north. The monsoon winds cause abundant precipitation in some areas, such as on the western coast, while rainfall is scarce in the northwestern regions of the country. After China, India is the most heavily populated state in the world. The population comes from the successive invasions that the country has suffered throughout history. At the present, two great ethnic groups predominate: the Negroid or Dravidian group and the white or Indo-European one (the major group). The yellow races are concentrated in the Northeast. The ancestral division of its inhabitants into castes constitutes one of the most characteristic aspects of Indian society. In recent years, urban dwelling has increased, but most of the population live in rural areas. The country registers a high infant mortality rate; living conditions are miserable and primitive and life expectancy is short. India has the typical problems of a developing economy. Its economy is of the mixed type, and is based on farming, oriented mainly towards the production of rice, wheat, corn, cotton, jute, tea, coffee, sugar cane, rubber and tobacco. The fishing industry is not very well-developed. The number of livestock is the greatest in the world, but milk production is low and the consumption of meat is forbidden by the Hindu religion. Coal and iron ore constitute the principal mining resources of the country, which also has great potential in hydroelectric energy. Manufacturing has developed in recent years, dedicated to the food product and textile branches, and heavy industry has also been implanted. Other products and sectors in growth are the aluminum industry and shipbuilding. The movie-making industry is important to mention, as India is the second-ranking country in film production, while there are also numerous small handicraft industries.

Kuwait

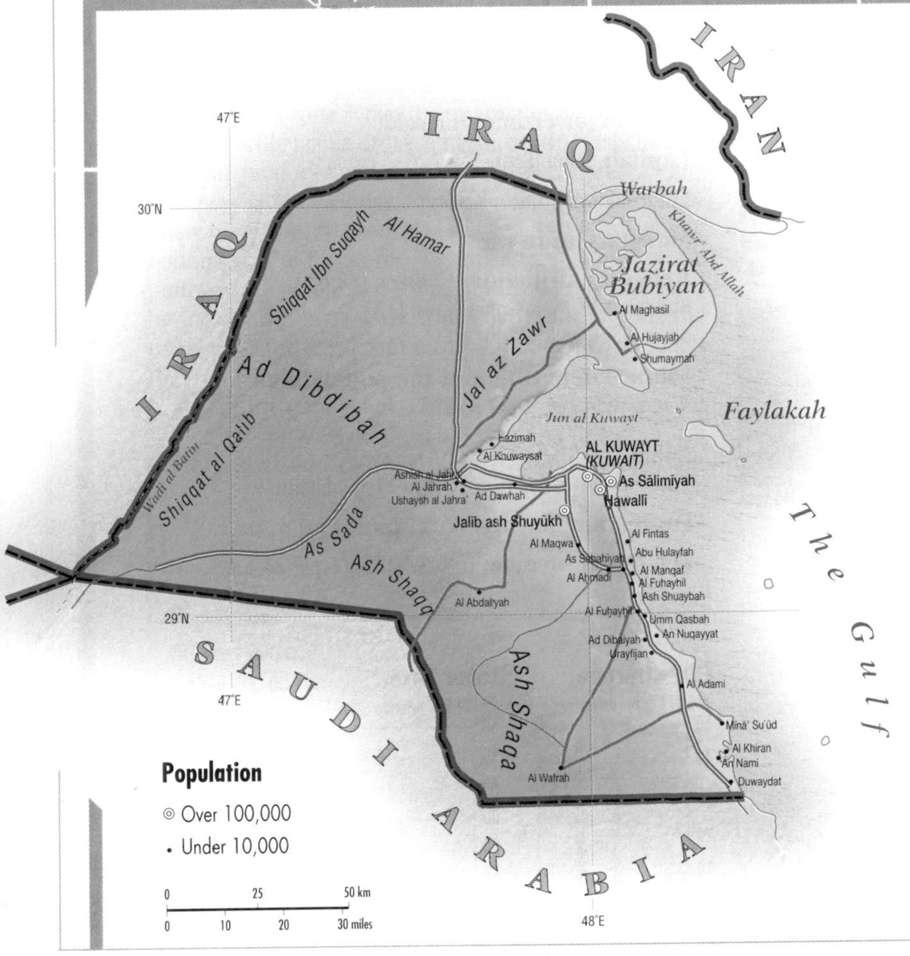

Population

- Over 100,000
- Under 10,000

0 25 50 km
0 10 20 30 miles

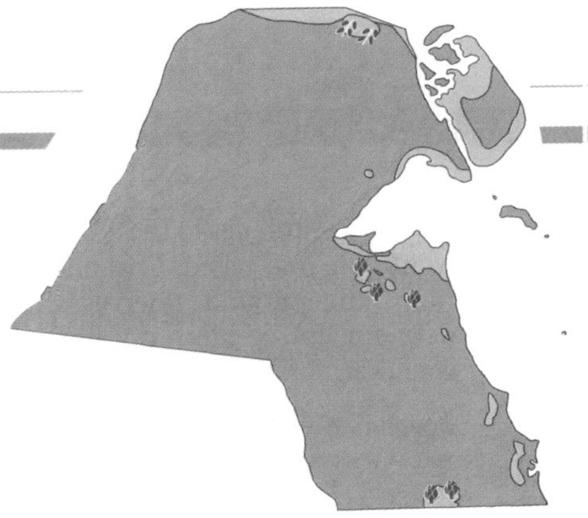

Agriculture

Types of agriculture and livestock production

- Irrigation/intensive farming
- Nomadic herding
- Desert
- Urban area
- Vegetables
- Dates

Industry and Mining

Mineral fuel resources

Fossil fuels

- Natural gas (gas fields)
- Petroleum (oil fields)

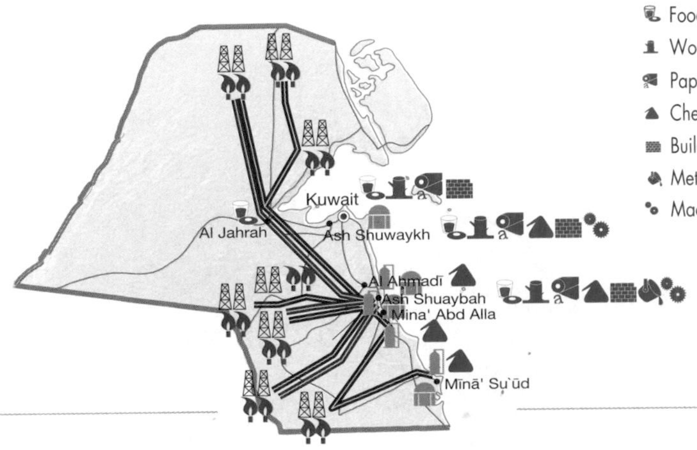

Energy-related installations

- Natural gas plant
- Refinery
- Gas pip
- Oil pipe

Manufacturing

- Food, beverages and tobacco
- Wood, cork and furniture
- Paper and graphic arts
- Chemical products
- Building materials, glass and cement
- Metallurgy and metal products
- Machinery and transport equipment

Kyrgyzstan

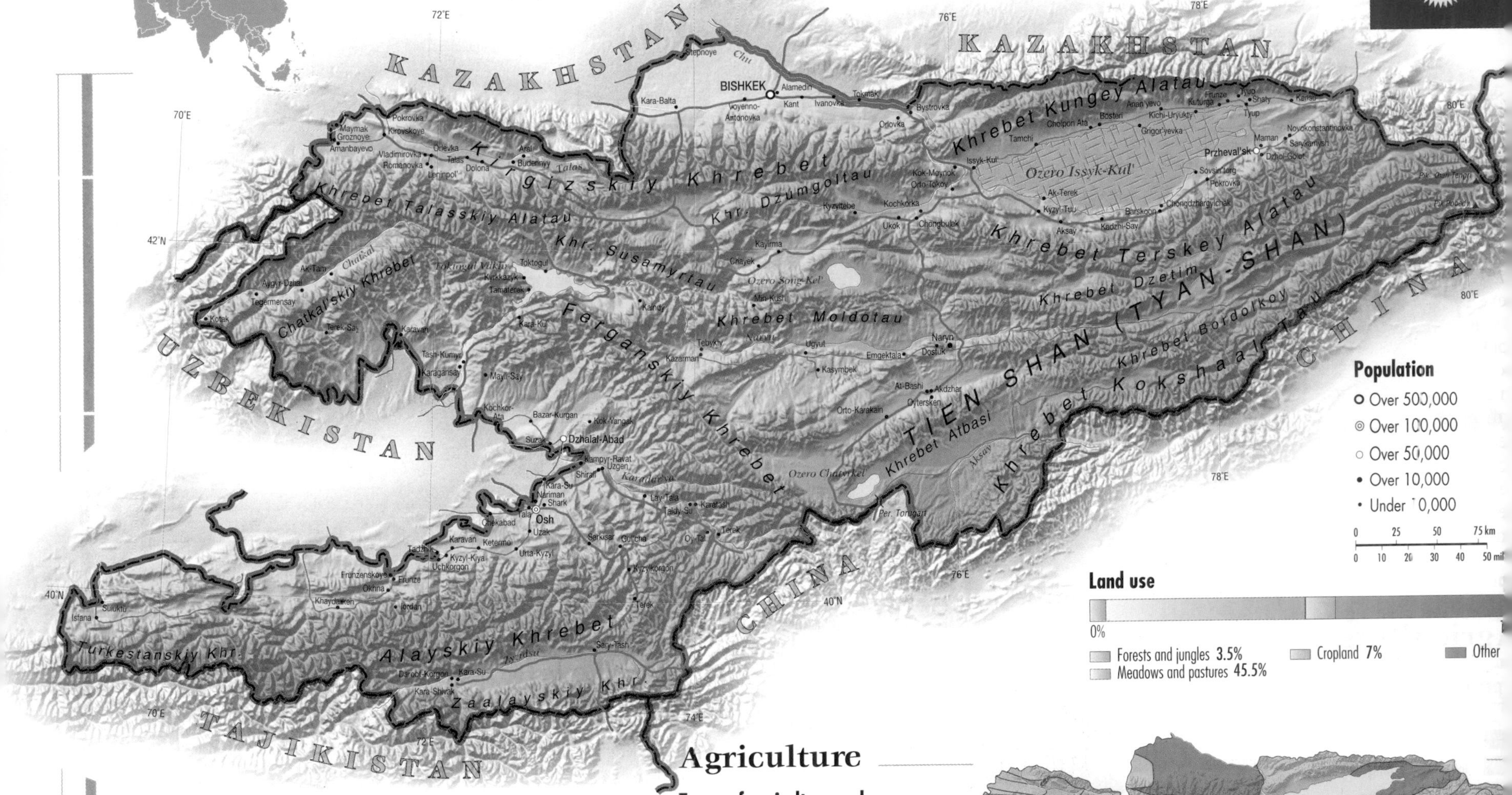

Population

- Over 500,000
- Over 100,000
- Over 50,000
- Over 10,000
- Under 10,000

0 25 50 75 km
0 10 20 30 40 50 mi

Land use

0%

Forests and jungles 3.5%
Meadows and pastures 45.5%
Cropland 7%
Other

Population evolution and projection

in millions of persons

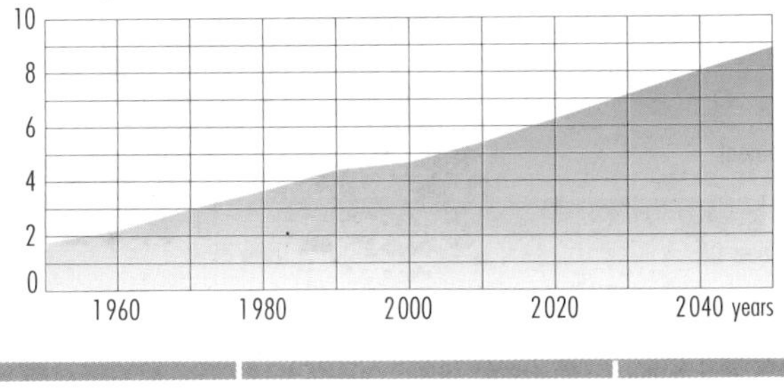

Agriculture

Types of agriculture and livestock production

- Cropland (cereals, forage crops)
- Irrigation/intensive farming (barley, rice, wheat, root crops)
- Stock raising (sheep, cattle, goats, astrakhan)
- Non-arable land (mountainous areas)

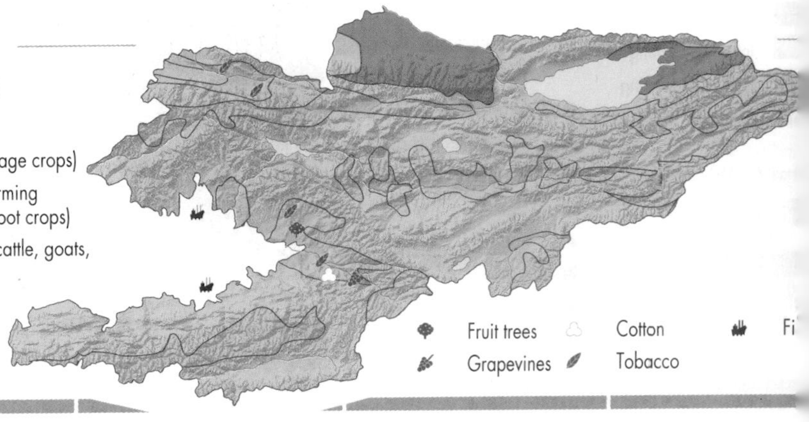

- Fruit trees
- Grapevines
- Cotton
- Tobacco
- Fi

.ocated in western Asia, Kuwait forms part of the Arabian 'eninsula. The desert bury the tabular-shaped landforms of the country. It has no rivers, only torrential watercourses hat remain dry most of the year. Off the coast (the Persian Gulf) numerous islands and islets rise from the sea. Its lesert climate, extremely hot, registers very marked daily .nd seasonal variations in temperature. Rainfall is xtremely scarce. The indigenous population, of the outhern Arab race, comprises fewer than half of the inhabitants of the kingdom of Kuwait, where groups originally from neighboring Arab countries, Asia, eastern Africa and Europe have concentrated. The working population makes up almost 42% of the total. Traditional economic activities (fishing, the pearl trade) have been pushed aside by the extremely profitable petrochemical industry: Kuwait is among the principal world producers of petroleum and natural gas, and has great oil pipelines for the export of its hydrocarbons.

Official name: State of Kuwait
Form of government: constitutional monarchy
Capital: Kuwait (Al Kuwayt)
Official language: Arabic
Monetary unit: Kuwaiti dinar
Religious affiliation: Muslim majority
Area: 17,818 sq km
Total population: 1,950,000 inhabitants
Population density: 109.4 persons per sq km

'opulation evolution and projection

millions of persons

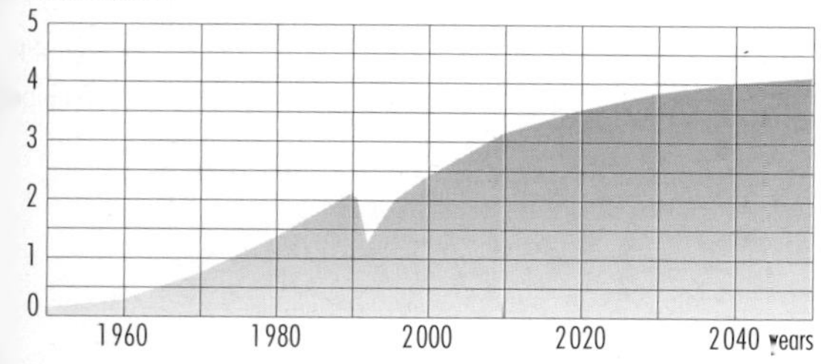

DP structure

,650 million dollars

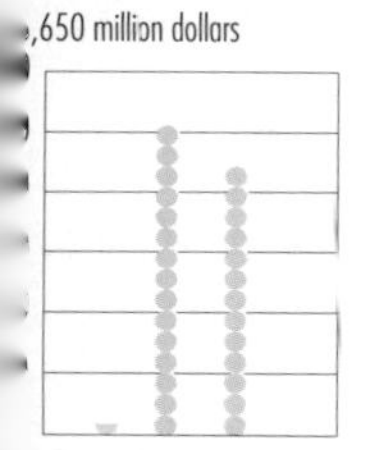

Labor force

818,000 persons

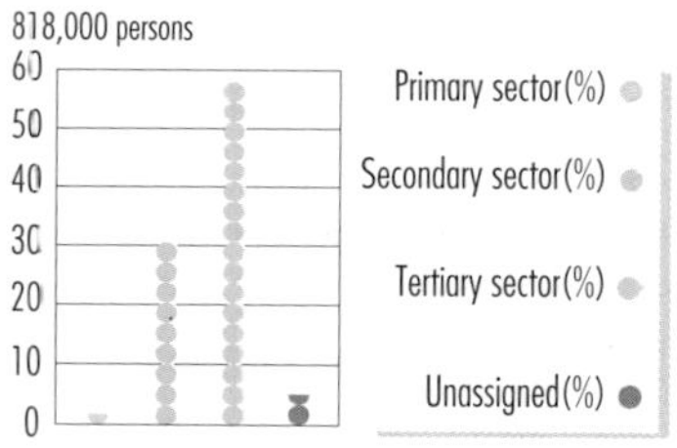

Population age distribution

Vital statistics

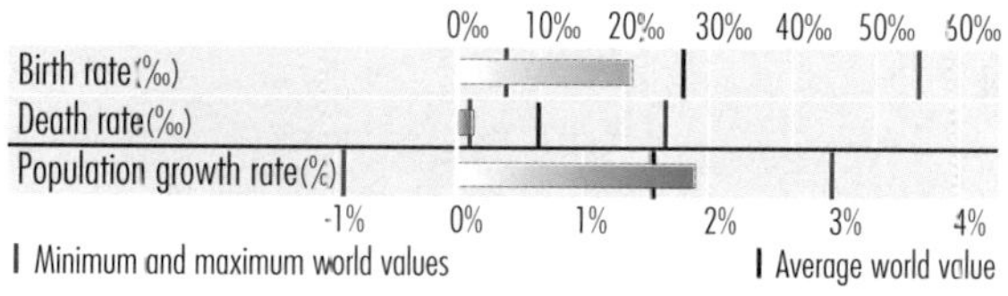

Literacy (% of population over15)

Per capita income (GDP per person)

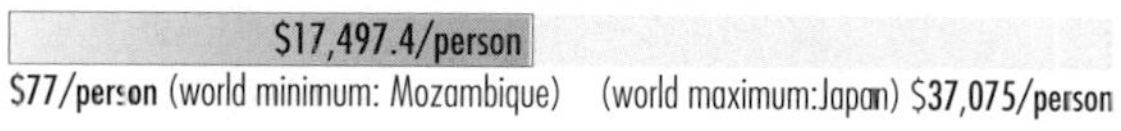

Land use

·cated in central Asia, Kyrgyzstan has very rugged relief. ·e most important mountain ranges are the Pamir-Alay layskiy) (with altitudes above 4,000 m), the Tien Shan here the Pobedy peaks, 7,439 m in altitude, and the ·an-Tengri, 6,995 m, rise), and the Farghona ·rganskiy), which crosses the center of the country from ·utheast to northwest). The Naryn river, tributary of the ·rdarya, constitutes its principal fluvial watercourse. To · north is found the great lake basin of Issyk-Kul, set at altitude of more than 1,600 m. The country has a high ·untain climate, except on the river plains of Naryn, ·d it is characterized by temperate summers and very ·rsh winters. Rainfall fluctuates between 100 m and 500 ·n annually. In the Farghona mountain chain, this ·erage rises to 750-1,000 mm annually. The population ·oncentrated in the far western and northern parts of · country (slopes of the Farghona, the northern water- ·d of the Tien Shan Mountains, the valley of the Chu ·l shores of Lake Issyk-Kul). The Kyrgyz, the major ethnic group, spring from the Turco-Mongol branch and profess the Islamic religion. They live alongside Russian, Uzbek and Ukrainian minorities.

Sheep and cattle raising, favored by the abundance and quality of pastures, has been the mainstay of the Kyrgyzstan economy for centuries, with seasonal migratory herding still being practiced in the areas of higher elevation. The irrigation projects carried out during the Soviet period enabled agricultural development (cotton, cereals, sugar beets, tobacco, vegetables, fruit trees), but the abusive use of pesticides and other chemical substances has created grave problems of soil pollution. The mineral resources are limited to small deposits of coal, petroleum and natural gas. There are textile, food product, cement and mechanical construction factories in some cities of the country, but the industrial sector in not very highly developed and most of the consumer goods have to be imported from other Central Asian Muslim republics.

Official name: Kyrgyz Republic
Form of government: republic
Capital: Bishkek
Official language: Kyrgyz; Russian
Monetary unit: som
Religious affiliation: Muslim (70%), Russian Orthodox
Ethnic composition of the population: Kyrgyz (52.4%), Russian (21.5%), Uzbek (12.9%), Ukrainian (2.5%), German (2.4%), other (3.8%)
Area: 198,500 sq km
Total population: 4,530,000 inhabitants
Population density: 22.8 persons per sq km
GDP: U.S. $3,028 million
Per capita income: U.S. $827.81 per person

›ulation age distribution

›al statistics

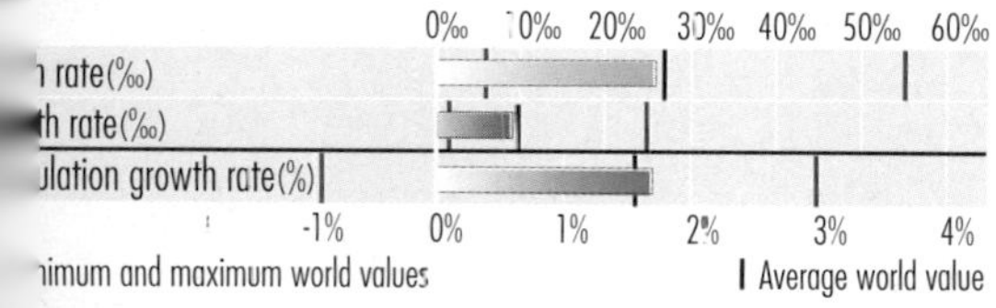

racy (% of population over15)

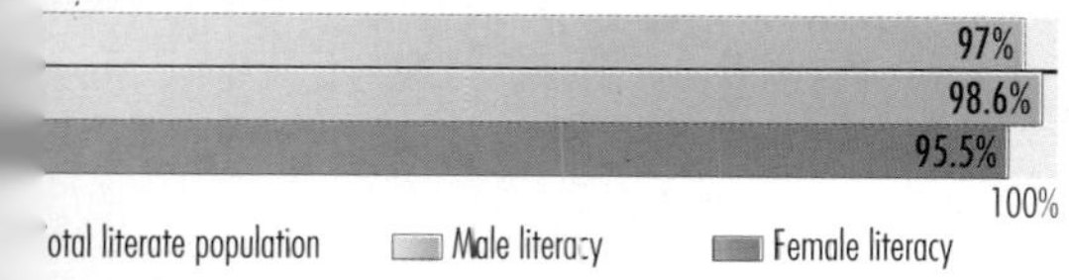

mployment (% of total population economically active)

Industry and Mining

Non-energy source mineral resources

Metals

- Antimony
- Mercury
- Lead
- Zinc
- Gold

Manufacturing

- Food, beverages and tobacco
- Textiles, clothing, leather and footwear
- Wood, cork and furniture
- Paper and graphic arts
- Chemical products
- Building materials, glass and cement
- Metallurgy and metal products
- Machinery and transport equipment

Mineral fuel resources

Fossil fuels

- Coal
- Natural gas
- Petroleum

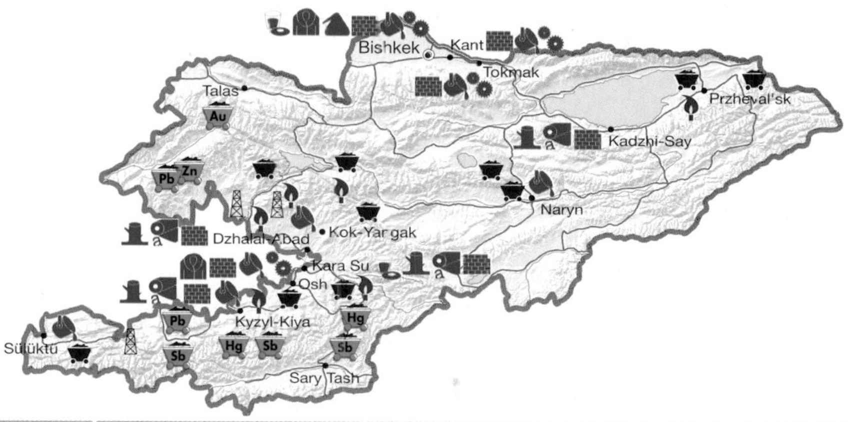

Laos

Laos is a state of Southeast Asia located on the Peninsula of Indochina. Its territory, which is very mountainous, is divided into two natural regions: an area of high rugged mountain ranges in the north, and the Mekong River plain in the south, with much gentler terrain. The monsoons are the conditioning factor in the climate of Laos, which is subequatorial with a dry season (October-April) and a rainy one (May-October). The temperatures are high and very constant all year long, but there are daily thermal variations during the dry season. In high mountain areas larger amounts of precipitation are recorded; in the low lands, rainfall does not exceed an annual average of 1,300 mm. The Laotian population, although modest in number, reveals notable ethnic complexity. The Lao-Lum, the most numerous ethnic group, live in the valleys of the Mekong River. In the upper valleys live the Lao-Theung, and the Lao-Soung inhabit the high mountain areas. The cities are concentrated in the Mekong valley, and in them the groups of Chinese, Pakistanis, Vietnamese and French have a decisive social weight. The major religion of the State is Buddhism, although Islam and animist religions are also professed; the official language is Lao. The primary sector, which produces large amounts of corn (maize), cassava, potatoes, sweet potatoes, rice, coffee, lacquer, opium and teak wood, is predominant in the country's economy. Industry is limited to the extraction of minerals (tin, gypsum, zinc, coal and iron ore), saw-mills and rice mills. Because of its low domestic production, Laos depends on the economic aid of other countries.

Official name: Lao People's Democratic Republic
Form of government: communist state
Capital: Vientiane (Viangchan)
Official language: Lao
Monetary unit: new kip
Religious affiliation: Buddhist (57.8%), tribal religions (33.6%), Christian (1.8%), Muslim (1%), atheist (1%), other (4.8%)
Ethnic composition of the population: Lao-Lum (68%), Lao-Theung (22%), Lao-Soung (9%), other (1%)
Area: 236,800 sq km
Total population: 4,976,000 inhabitants
Population density: 21 persons per sq km

Agriculture

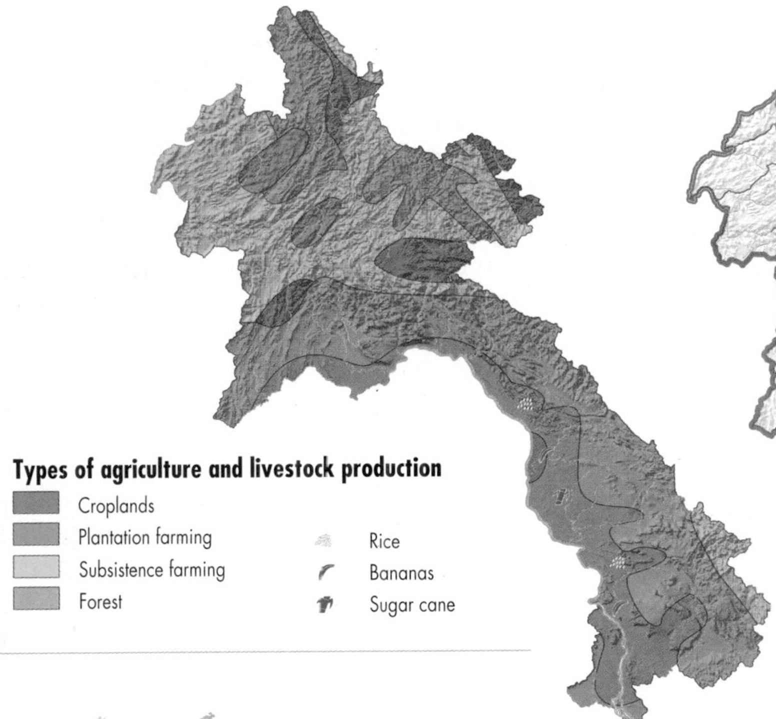

Industry and Mining

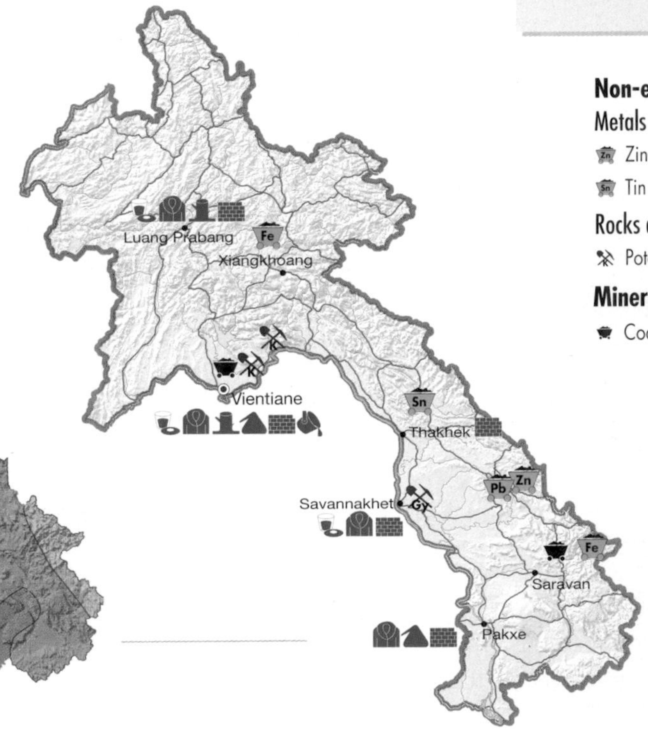

Non-energy source mineral resources

Metals

- Zinc
- Iron ore
- Tin
- Lead

Rocks and industrial minerals

- Potash
- Gypsum

Mineral fuel resources

- Coal

Manufacturing

- Food, beverages and tobacco
- Textiles, clothing, leather and footwear
- Wood, cork and furniture
- Chemical products
- Building materials, glass and cement
- Metallurgy and metal products

Lebanon

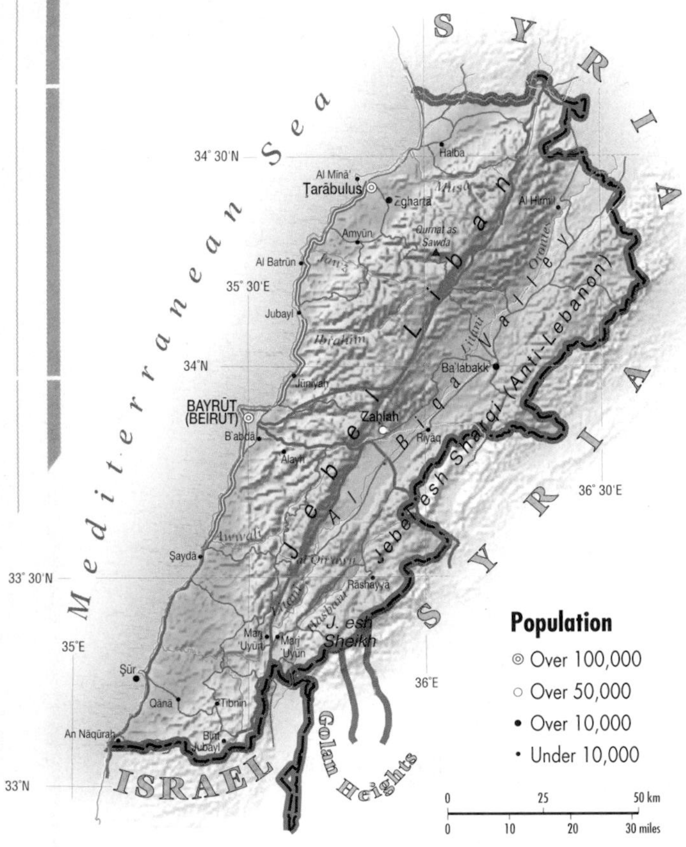

A Mediterranean state of western Asia, Lebanon is divided into four natural regions: the western coastal plain, the calcareous mountain range of Lebanon (Jebel Liban), the Bekaa Valley (Al-Biqa) and the minor mountain chains of the Anti-Lebanon (Jebel esh Sharqi) and Hermon (Jebel esh Sheikh). The coastline has a Mediterranean climate of mild winters and long hot summers. The Bekaa plain has continental characteristics. In the mountainous zones of the interior, mild summers are followed by fairly harsh winters. In Lebanon, Maronite Christians, Sunnite and Shi'ite Muslim live alongside each other, along with small communities of Greeks, Armenians, Syrians, Protestants and Jews. The population is unevenly distributed within the territory. Lebanese farming, limited by the ruggedness of the terrain, is sustained by the large magnitude springs that descend from its mountain ranges. The flat irrigated lands produce wheat, grapevines, olive trees and fruits. In spite of the good domestic road system, sufficient industrial production to satisfy the needs of the population has not developed.

Official name: Lebanese Republic
Form of government: republic
Capital: Beirut (Bayrūt)
Official language: Arabic
Monetary unit: Lebanese pound
Religious affiliation: Muslim (70%), Christian (30%)
Ethnic composition of the population: Arab (95%), Armenian (4%), other (1%)
Area: 10,230 sq km
Total population: 3,776,000 inhabitants
Population density: 369.1 persons per sq km

Population evolution and projection

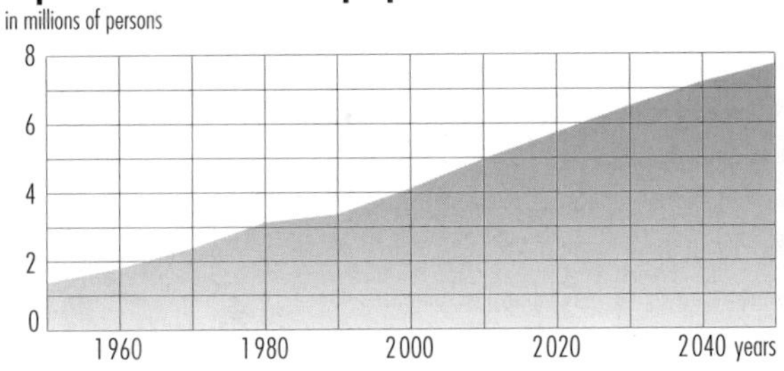

GDP structure

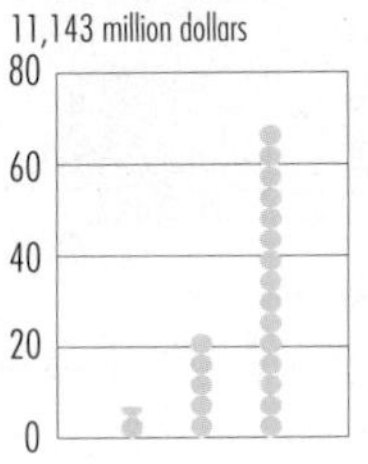

Labor force

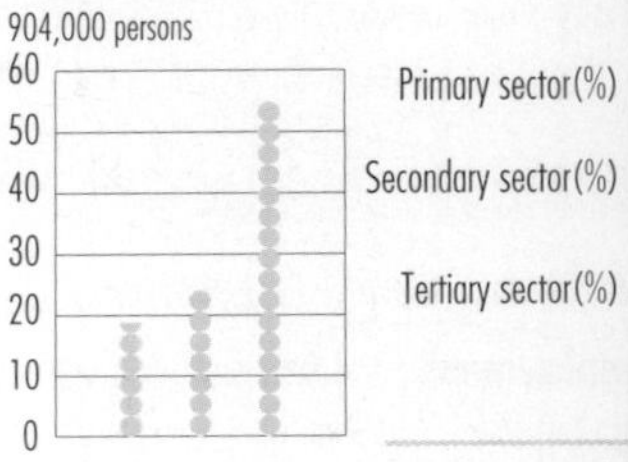

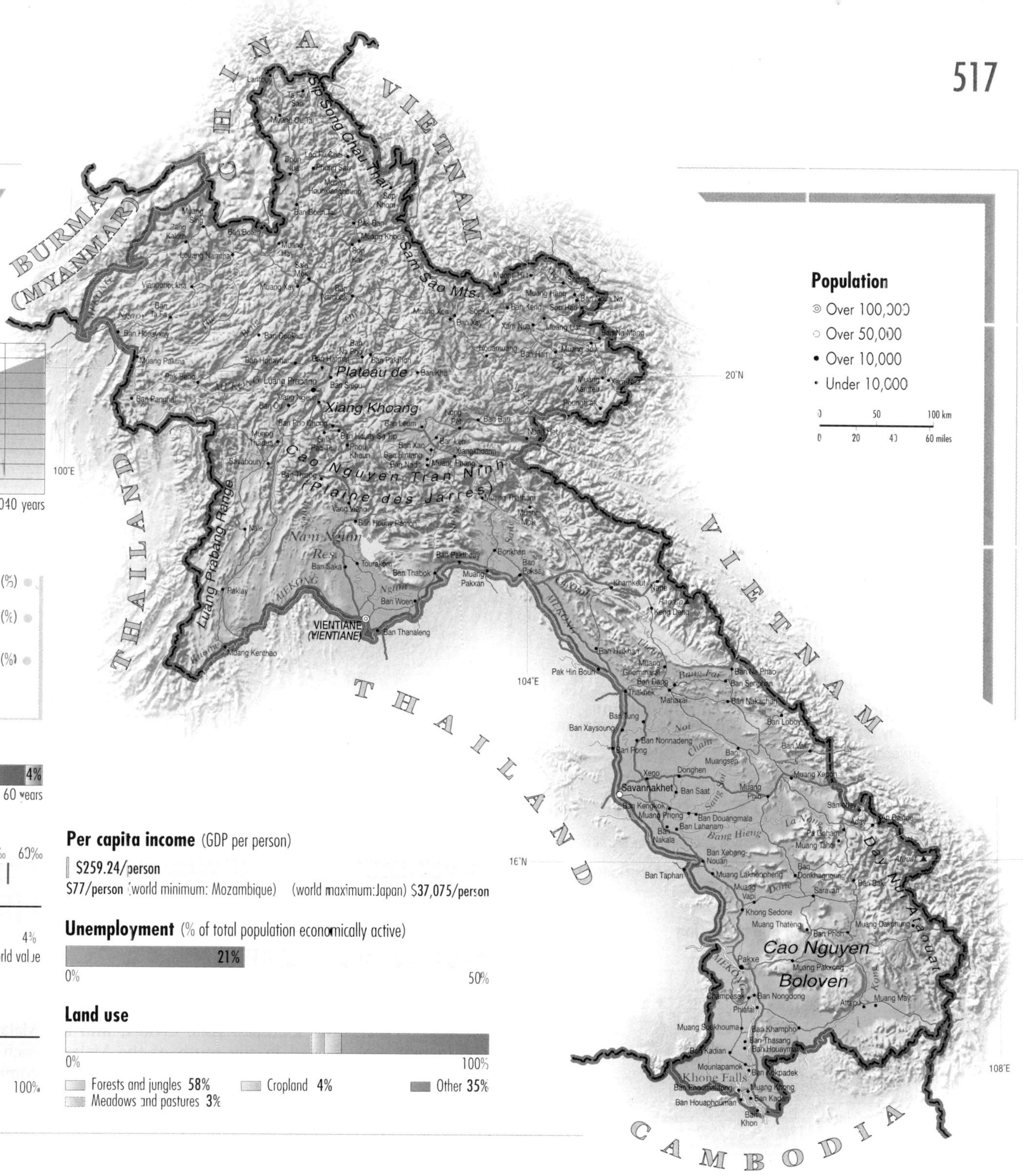

Population
- Over 100,000
- Over 50,000
- Over 10,000
- Under 10,000

0 50 100 km
0 20 40 60 miles

Population evolution and projection
in millions of persons

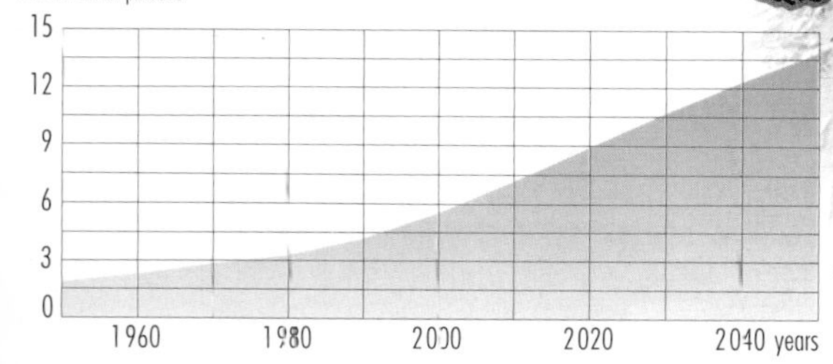

GDP structure
1,760 million dollars

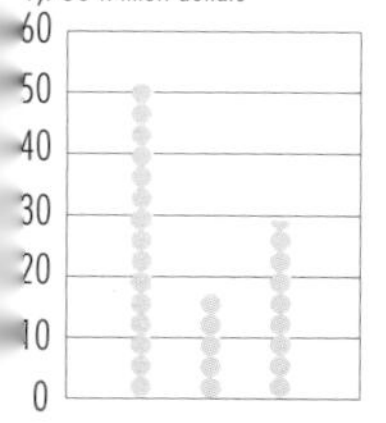

Labor force
2,316,000 persons

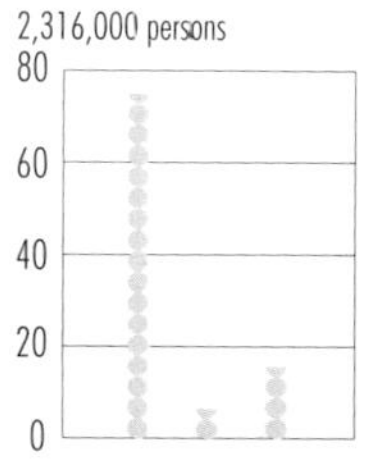

Primary sector(%)
Secondary sector(%)
Tertiary sector(%)

Population age distribution
45% | 51% | 4%
0 years 15 years 60 years

Vital statistics
0‰ 10‰ 20‰ 30‰ 40‰ 50‰ 60‰
Birth rate(‰)
Death rate(‰)
Population growth rate(%)
-1% 0% 1% 2% 3% 4%
Minimum and maximum world values | Average world value

Literacy (% of population over 15)
56.6%
69.4%
44.4%
0% 100%
Total literate population | Male literacy | Female literacy

Per capita income (GDP per person)
$259.24/person
$77/person (world minimum: Mozambique) (world maximum: Japan) $37,075/person

Unemployment (% of total population economically active)
21%
0% 50%

Land use
0% 100%
Forests and jungles 58%
Meadows and pastures 3%
Cropland 4%
Other 35%

Agriculture

Types of agriculture and livestock production
- Croplands
- Perennial crops
- Irrigation/intensive farming
- Nomadic herding (sheep, goats)
- Forest/brush
- Urban area
- Cereals
- Vegetables
- Fruit trees
- Citrus fruits
- Grapevines
- Olive trees

Industry and Mining

Non-energy source mineral resources
Metals
- Iron ore

Rocks and industrial minerals
- Salt

Energy-related installations
- Hydroelectric power plant
- Refinery
- Oil pipeline

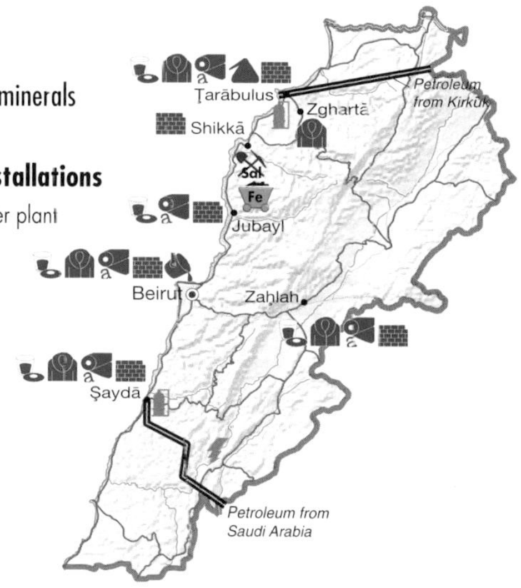

Manufacturing
- Food, beverages and tobacco
- Textiles, clothing, leather and footwear
- Paper and graphic arts
- Chemical products
- Building materials, glass and cement
- Metallurgy and metal products

Population age distribution
36% | 58% | 6%
0 years 15 years 60 years

Vital statistics
0‰ 10‰ 20‰ 30‰ 40‰ 50‰ 60‰
Birth rate(‰)
Death rate(‰)
Population growth rate(%)
-1% 0% 1% 2% 3% 4%
Minimum and maximum world values | Average world value

Literacy (% of population over 15)
92.4%
94.7%
90.3%
0% 100%
Total literate population | Male literacy | Female literacy

Per capita income (GDP per person)
$746.82/person
$77/person (world minimum: Mozambique) (world maximum: Japan) $37,075/person

Unemployment (% of total population economically active)
35%
0% 50%

Land use
0% 100%
Forests and jungles 8%
Meadows and pastures 1%
Cropland 30%
Other 61%

Saudi Arabia

Population

- Over 500,000
- Over 100,000
- Over 50,000
- Over 10,000
- Under 10,000

0 50 100 150 km
0 20 40 60 80 100 miles

Agriculture

Types of agriculture and livestock production

- Irrigation/intensive farming
- Nomadic herding
- Pastures
- Forest/brush
- Desert

- Cereals
- Fruit trees
- Vegetables
- Dates
- Coffee
- Sheep
- Goats
- Camels
- Oasis

Principal Imports

Item	Share
Transport equipment	21%
Machinery	19.4%
Metal and metal products	9.1%

0% 5% 10% 15% 20% 25%

Principal Exports

Item	Share
Petroleum	78.1%
Petroleum derivatives	13.2%
Other	8.7%

0% 10% 20% 30% 40% 50% 60% 70% 80%

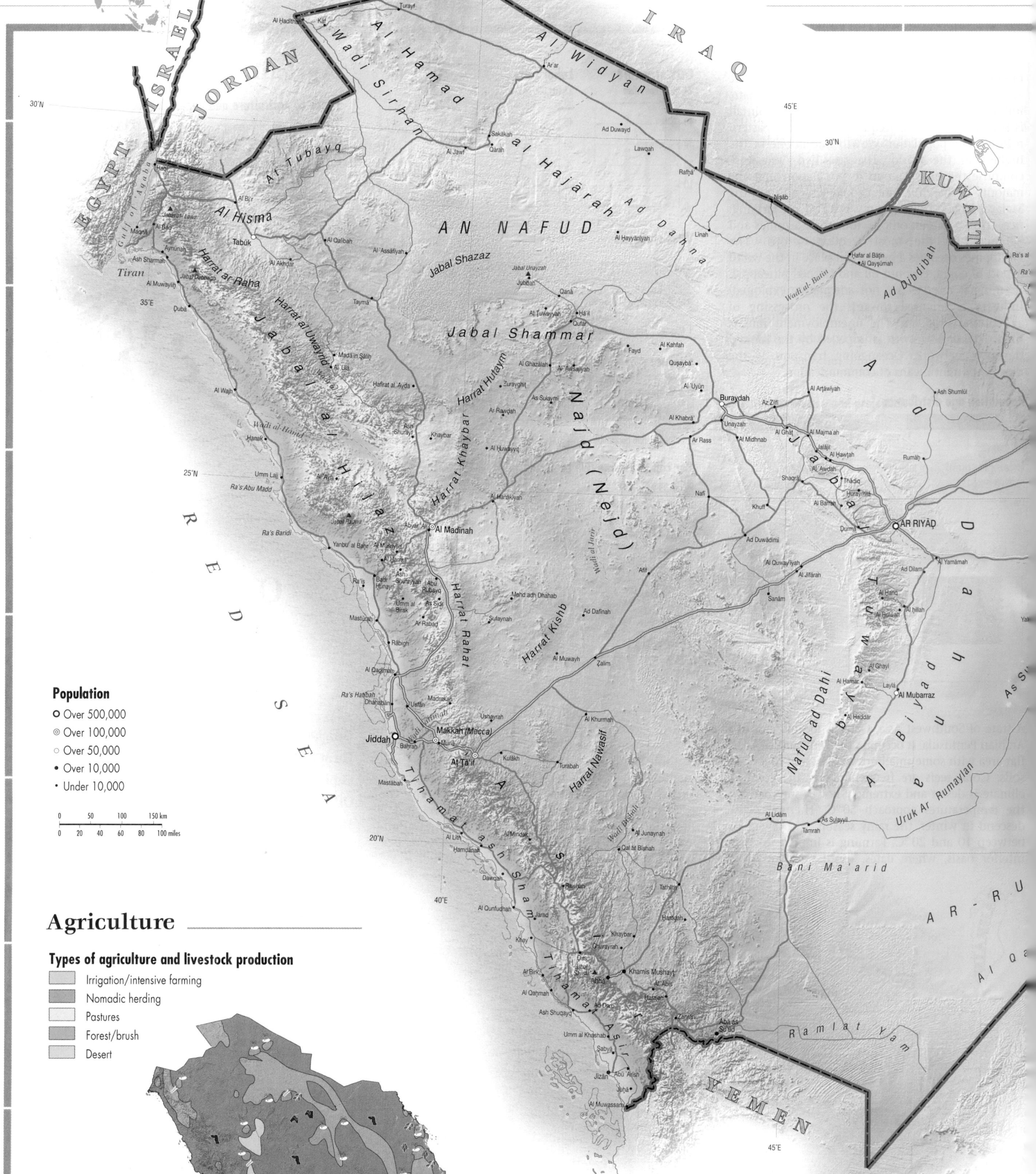

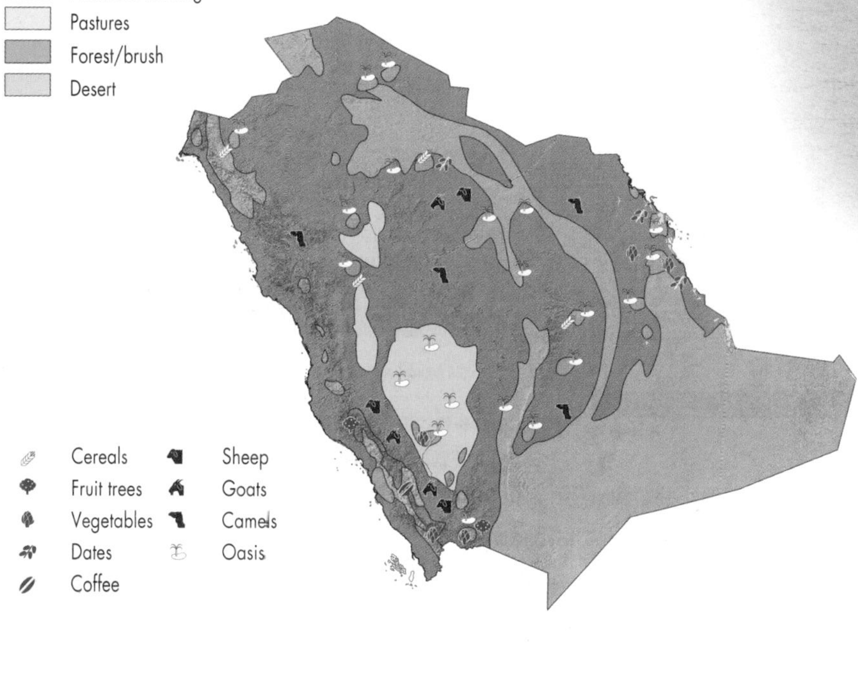

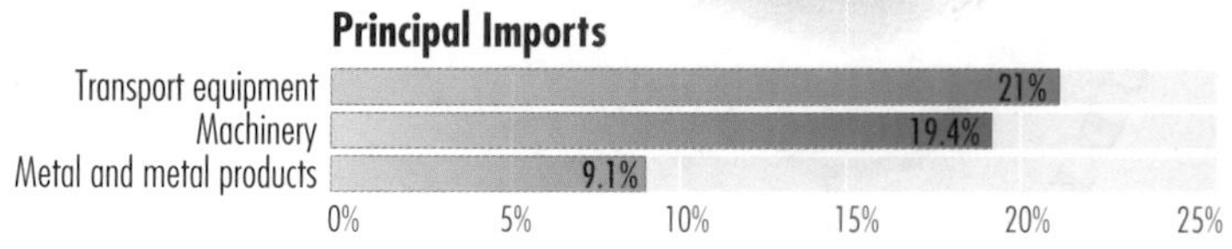

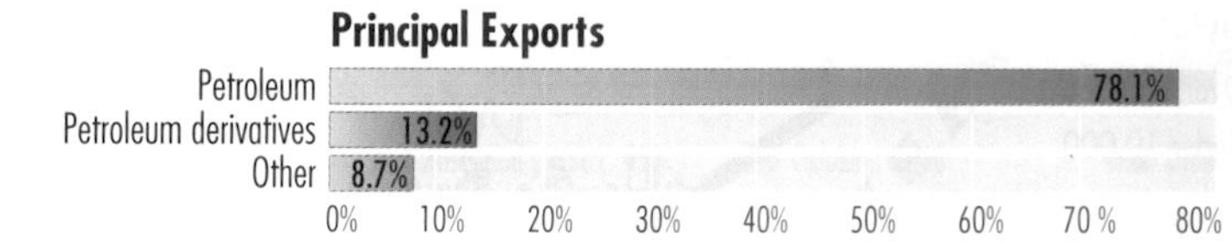

Industry and Mining

Non-energy source mineral resources

Metals

Zinc · Iron ore · Silver · Copper · Gold · Lead

Rocks and industrial minerals

Gypsum

Mineral fuel resources

Fossil fuels

Natural Gas · Petroleum

Energy-related installations

Solar power plant · Gas pipeline · Natural gas plant · Oil pipeline · Refinery

Manufacturing

Food, beverages and tobacco

Textiles, clothing, leather and footwear

Paper and graphic arts

Chemical products

Building materials, glass and cement

Metallurgy and metal products

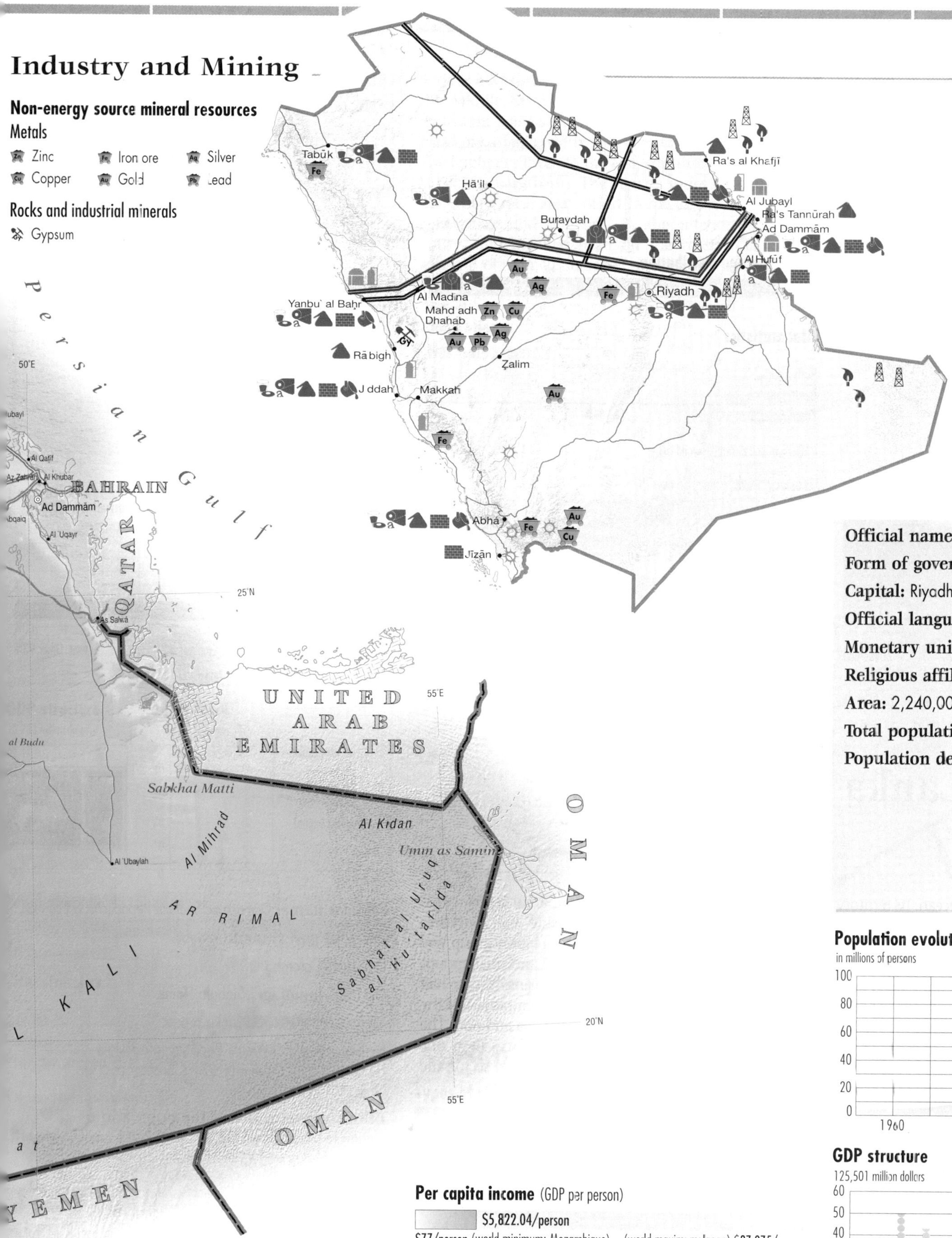

Official name: Kingdom of Saudi Arabia
Form of government: monarchy
Capital: Riyadh (Ar Riyad)
Official language: Arabic
Monetary unit: Saudi riyal
Religious affiliation: Muslim majority
Area: 2,240,000 sq km
Total population: 19,409,000 inhabitants
Population density: 8.7 persons per sq km

Population evolution and projection
in millions of persons

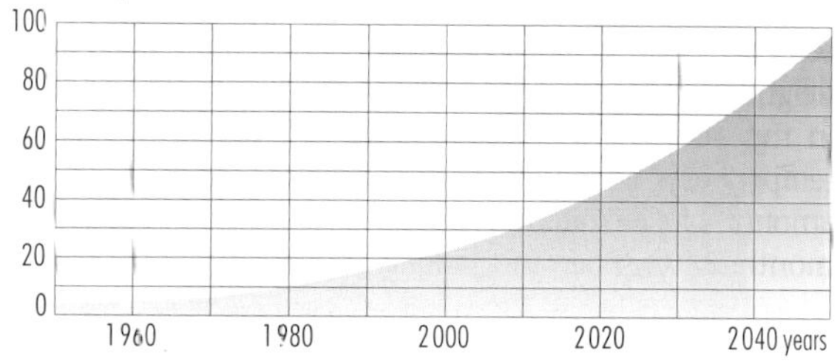

GDP structure
125,501 million dollars

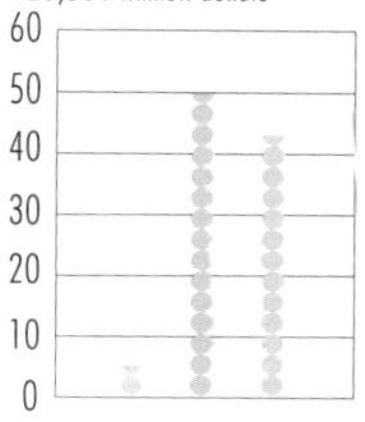

Labor force
5,960,000 persons

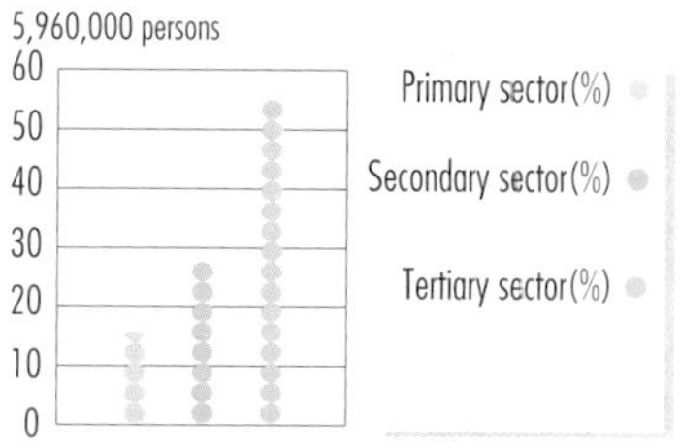

Per capita income (GDP per person)

$5,822.04/person

$77/person (world minimum: Mozambique) (world maximum: Japan) $37,075/person

Unemployment (% of total population economically active)

6.5%

0% 50%

Land use

0% 100%

Forests and jungles 1% · Cropland 1% · Other 59% · Meadows and pastures 39%

Population age distribution

43% · 55% · 2%

0 years · 15 years · 60 years

Vital statistics

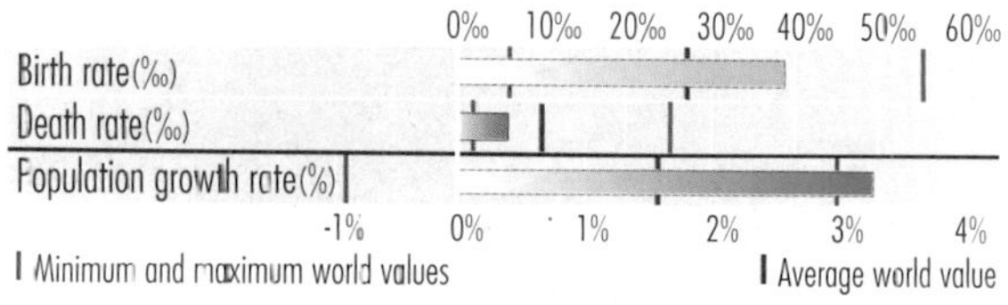

Literacy (% of population over 15)

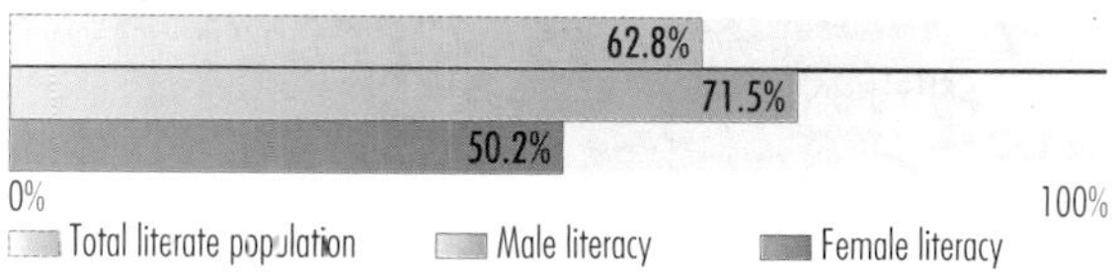

ituated in the southwest of Asia, Saudi Arabia spreads ut over a large part of the Arabian peninsula. Three-ourths of Saudi land area consist of great desert regions. Vith an arid tropical climate, temperatures of 50 °C an be reached in summer, although clear climatic ifferences can be observed between north and south ue to the differences in latitude: in the north and orthwest of the country, rainfall does not surpass 100 nm annually (in inland areas long periods of absolute rought elapse), while in the south the influence of the nonsoons provokes an average annual rainfall of etween 150-300 mm.

lost of the Saudi population is of the Arab race, lthough the presence of the Muslim holy places has ncouraged the settlement of small Asian and African ommunities. The native Bedouins, traditionally nomadic shepherds, have experienced a rapid change in settlement patterns towards urban dwelling fomented by the development of the petrochemical industry. Nevertheless, a good part of the population continues to work in farming and herding.

Saudi Arabia, one of the principal petroleum producers and exporters in the world, holds beneath its territory a fourth of the world's crude oil reserves. With the enormous financial resources that are produced by petroleum export, efforts have been made to achieve a diversification of economic activities. Modern prospecting has discovered extremely varied mineral wealth (iron ore, silver, gold, copper and crystallized salt). The development of domestic and foreign transportation networks makes the cohesion of the territory possible.

EUROPE

The Mediterranean Sea, seen from the satellite, ratifies its primitive name of Mare Nostrum (Our Sea). Closed in the east, it was witness to the development of classical cultures and millenary cities have been settled on its shores since then. From the Strait of Gibraltar, known in ancient

times as the Columns of Hercules, moving towards the east, the image allows us to see the continuous succession of islands and peninsulas that populate the Mediterranean: The Balearic Islands, Corsica, Sardinia, and Sicily. South of this last is the island of Malta, of modest dimensions. East of the Italian Peninsula, the Adriatic Sea rises to the Gulf of Venice, and on its eastern shore, displays a rugged broken coastline due to the nearness of the Dinaric Alps that run along it from north to south. Continuing towards the east, the Peloponese Peninsula and the island of Crete form the Aegean Sea, dotted with small islands. Towards the northeast, the small Sea of Marmara serves as a passageway to reach the Black Sea. In the far eastern part, near the Turkish coast, the island of Cyprus can be seen.

Europe
Digital terrain model

Bathymetry

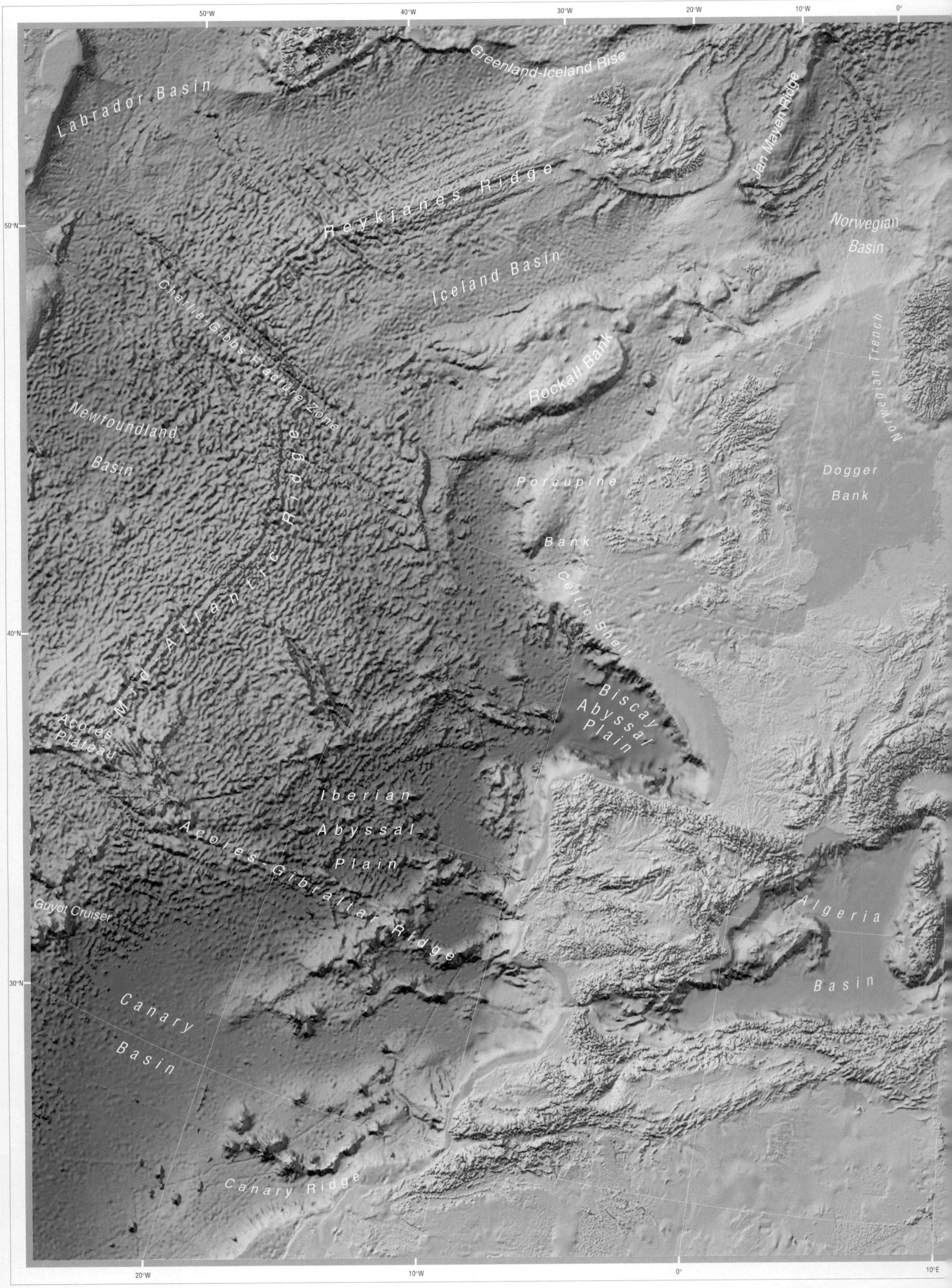
50°W
40°W
30°W
20°W
10°W
0°
50°N
40°N
30°N
20°W
10°W
0°
10°E
Greenland-Iceland Rise
Labrador Basin
Jan Mayen Ridge
Reykjanes Ridge
Norwegian Basin
Iceland Basin
Charlie-Gibbs Fracture Zone
Norwegian Trench
Rockall Bank
Newfoundland Basin
Mid-Atlantic Ridge
Dogger Bank
Porcupine Bank
Celtic Shelf
Biscay Abyssal Plain
Açores Plateau
Iberian Abyssal Plain
Açores-Gibraltar Ridge
Guyot Cruiser
Algeria Basin
Canary Basin
Canary Ridge

20°E
30°E
40°E
50°E
60°E
70°E
80°E
50°N
40°N
30°N
Ionian Basin
Mediterranean Ridge
Cyprus Basin
Nile Cone
Messina Abyssal Plain
20°E
30°E
40°E

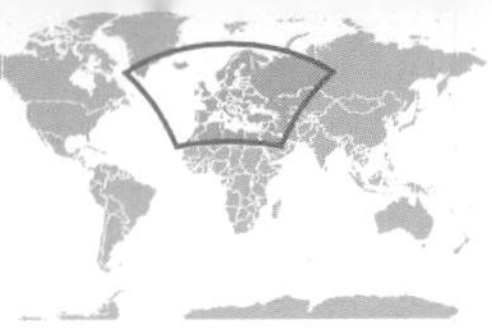

Europe
Physical map

20°E
30°E
40°E
50°E
60°E
70°E
80°E
O C E A N
North Cape
Varanger Peninsula
Barents Sea
Kolguyev Island
Mys Kanin Nos
Mys Svjatoj Nos
Kanin Peninsula
Chesha Bay
Malozemelskaya Tundra
Pechora
Usa
Pechora Basin
Timan Ridge
Ural Mountains
WEST SIBERIAN PLAIN
Ob
Irtysh
Konda
Tabda
Tura
Tobol
Ishim
Lake Chany
Ishim Steppe
Inari
Lake Imandra
Kola Peninsula
Ponoi
White Sea
Mezen
Vashka
Pinega
Izhma
Kjølen (Kölen)
Lake Pya
Lake Top
Gulf of Bothnia
Lake Vyg
Onega
Northern Dvina
Vychegda Lowland
Sysola
Northern Uvals
Kama
Kama Reservoir
Upper Kama Upland
Lake Seg
White Sea-Baltic Canal
Lake Onega
Lake Region
Saimaa
Lake Ladoga
Svir
Yug
Sukhona
Aland Islands
Gulf of Finland
Neva
Volkhov
Valdai Hills
Rybinsk Reservoir
Unzha
Vetluga
Gorky Reservoir
Volga
Vyatka
Ufa
Belaya
Ural
Miass
Iset
Turgai Upland
Tobol
Lake Tengiz
Lake Peipus
Lake Ilmen
Lovat
Gulf of Riga
Gotland
Öland
Baltic Sea
Western Dvina
Smolensk-Moscow Upland
Klyazma
Oka
Moscow Basin
Kuybyshev Reservoir
Sura
Samara
Obshchiy Syrt
Mugodzhari
EAST EUROPEAN PLAIN
Central Russian Upland
Oka-Don Plain
Tsna
Volga Upland
Volgograd Reservoir
Kirghiz Steppe
Uil
Emba
Aral Sea
Turan Lowlands
Neman
Baltic Plains
Berezina
Dnieper
Pripet Marshes
Pripet
Desna
Oskol
Khoper
Medveditsa
Don
Caspian Depression
Vistula
Bug
Oder
Silesia Plain
Sudeten
Moravian Upland
Gorin
San
Dnieper Plain
Kremenchuk Reservoir
Donets Ridge
Donets
Dnieper Upland
Donets Basin
Don Upland
Tsimlyansk Reservoir
Yergeni Hills
Ustyurt Plateau
Volyn-Podolian Upland
Dniester
Southern Bug
Ingulets
Kakhovka Reservoir
Azov Upland
Lake Manych Gudilo
Kuban Lowland
Nogay Steppe
Kuma
Caspian Sea
Garabogazköl Aylagy
Carpathian Mountains
Moldavia Plateau
Siret
Prut
Black Sea Lowland
Sea of Azov
Stavropol Plateau
Terek
Great Hungarian (Alföld)
Tisza
Danube
Transylvanian Plateau
Mures
Drava
Transylvanian Alps
Crimea Peninsula
Caucasus Mountains
Sava
Danube Plain
Black Sea
Lesser Caucasus
Mingechevir Reservoir
Lake Sevan
Dinaric Alps
Morava
Balkan Mountains
Kuzey Anadolu Dağları
Elburz Mountains
Adriatic Sea
Maritsa
Rhodope Mts.
Balkan Peninsula
Vardar
Sea of Marmara
Sakarya
Kızılırmak
Lake Van
Lake Urmia
Dasht-e-Kavir
Anatolia Plateau
Lake Tuz
Taurus Mountains
Namak Lake
Plateau of Iran
Zagros Mountains
C. Sta. Maria di Leuca
Pindus Mts.
Aegean Sea
Ionian Islands
Mesopotamia
Tigris
Euphrates
Tharthar Lake
C. Spartivento
Peloponnesus
Cyclades
Ionian Sea
Sicily
C. Correnti
Cyprus
Syrian Desert
Razzaza Lake
Crete
The Gulf
MEDITERRANEAN SEA
Ra's Amir
Ra's Misratah
Gulf of Sidra
Nile Delta
Libyan Plateau
Sinai Peninsula
Nile
Najd
50°N
40°N
30°N

Europe
Political map

20°E
30°E
40°E
50°E
60°E
70°E
80°E
50°N
40°N
30°N
FINLAND
Murmansk
Oulu (Uleåborg)
Umeå
Kuopio
Joensuu
Sundsvall
Söderhamn
Tampere (Tammerfors)
Turku (Abo)
HELSINKI (HELSINGFORS)
SWEDEN
Uppsala
Västerås
Örebro
Norrköping
Linköping
Jönköping
STOCKHOLM
TALLINN
ESTONIA
Tartu
Pskov
LATVIA
RIGA (RIGA)
Liepāja
Šiaulia
Daugavpils
Klaipėda
Panevėžys
LITHUANIA
RUSSIA
Kaliningrad
Kaunas
VILNIUS
Alytus
Słupsk
Gdynia
Gdańsk
Koszalin
Elbląg
Olsztyn
Grudziądz
Toruń
Bydgoszcz
Gorzów Wielkopolski
Włocławek
Płock
Poznań
POLAND
WARSZAWA (WARSAW)
Białystok
Hrodna
Zielona Góra
Kalisz
Łódź
Radom
Legnica
Wrocław
Częstochowa
Kielce
Lublin
Katowice
Rzeszów
Liberec
Hradec Kralove
Ostrava
Olomouc
Kraków
Tarnów
Brno
Košice
SLOVAKIA
BRATISLAVA
Miskolc
WIEN (VIENNA)
Győr
BUDAPEST
Debrecen
Graz
Székesfehérvár
HUNGARY
Pécs
Subotica
Szeged
Maribor
LJUBLJANA
ZAGREB
Sombor
Osijek
CROATIA
Banja Luka
Tuzla
Šabac
BEOGRAD (BELGRADE)
Zenica
SARAJEVO
Mostar
Split
Kruševac
Niš
Čačak
YUGOSLAVIA
Priština
Titograd
Prizren
SKOPJE
Gostivar
MACEDONIA
Prilep
Bitola
TIRANË
ALBANIA
Pescara
Foggia
Bari
Napoli
Salerno
Taranto
Lecce
ITALY
Cosenza
Catanzaro
Messina
Reggio di Calabria
Catania
Siracusa
Sicily
GREECE
Thessaloníki
Lárisa
Vólos
ATHÍNAI (ATHENS)
Pátrai
Kalamáta
Khaniá
Iráklion
Ierápetra
Crete
Ródhos
Sankt Peterburg
Petrozavodsk
Belomorsk
Segezha
Severodvinsk
Arkhangel'sk
Novgorod
Velikiye Luki
Smolensk
Vitsyebsk
Orsha
MINSK
Barysaw
Mahilyow
BELARUS
Babruysk
Baranavichy
Homyel'
Pinsk
Mazyr
Brest
Chernihiv
KYYIV (KIEV)
Zhytomyr
Rovno
Luts'k
UKRAINE
Khmel'nytskyy
Vinnytsya
Bila Tserkva
Cherkasy
Ternopil'
L'viv
Ivano-Frankivs'k
Uzhhorod
Chernivtsi
Kam'yanets'-Podil's'kyy
Sumy
Kharkiv
Poltava
Kremenchuk
Kirovohrad
Dnipropetrovs'k
Kryvyy Rih
Nikopol'
Zaporizhzhya
Kramators'k
Pavlograd
Donets'k
Luhans'k
Makiyivka
Mariupol'
Melitopol'
Berdyans'k
Taganrog
Rostov
Novocherkassk
Shakhty
Mykolayiv
Kherson
Odesa
Tiraspol
CHIȘINĂU
Tighina
MOLDOVA
Bălți
Botoșani
Iași
Suceava
Satu Mare
Baia Mare
Oradea
Cluj-Napoca
Piatra Neamț
Bacău
Arad
Timișoara
Sibiu
Brașov
Galați
Brăila
Ploiești
Drobeta-Turnu Severin
Craiova
Pitești
BUCUREȘTI (BUCHAREST)
Constanța
ROMANIA
Ruse
Tolbukhin
Varna
Pleven
Shumen
Sliven
BULGARIA
SOFIYA (SOFIA)
Stara Zagora
Burgas
Plovdiv
Edirne
TURKEY
İstanbul
ANKARA
Simferopol'
Sevastopol'
Yevpatoriya
Kerch
Novorossiysk
Krasnodar
Sochi
Armavir
Stavropol'
Nevinnomyssk
Cherkessk
Pyatigorsk
Kislovodsk
Maykop
Nal'chik
Vladikavkaz
Groznyy
Makhachkala
Derbent
GEORGIA
TBILISI
ARMENIA
YEREVAN
AZERBAIJAN
BAKY (BAKU)
TEHRĀN
IRAN
MOSKVA (MOSCOW)
Obninsk
Kaluga
Tula
Serpukhov
Kolomna
Ryazan'
Novomoskovsk
Bryansk
Orël
Yelets
Lipetsk
Michurinsk
Tambov
Kursk
Voronezh
Staryy Oskol
Belgorod
T'ver
Sergiyev Posad
Kovrov
Vladimir
Murom
Arzamas
Nizhniy Novgorod
Ivanovo
Kostroma
Kineshma
Yaroslavl'
Rybinsk
Cherepovets
Vologda
Novocheboksarsk
Yoshkar-Ola
Kazan'
Izhevsk
Votkinsk
Sarapul
Neftekamsk
Naberezhnye Chelny
Al'met'yevsk
Dimitrovgrad
Oktyabr'skiy
Ufa
Sterlitamak
Salavat
Tol'yatti
Samara
Syzran'
Simbirsk
Saransk
Penza
Balakovo
Saratov
Kamyshin
Volgograd
Akhtubinsk
Astrakhan'
Elista
Orenburg
Orsk
Magnitogorsk
Chelyabinsk
Pervoural'sk
Sverdlovsk
Nizhniy Tagil
Kamensk-Ural'skiy
Kurgan
Perm'
Solikamsk
Berezniki
Glazov
Vyatka
Syktyvkar
Ukhta
Zheleznodorozhnyy
Kotlas
Nyandoma
Pechora
Serov
Tyumen'
Tobol'sk
Ishim
Omsk
Surgut
R U S S I A
KAZAKHSTAN
UZBEKISTAN
TURKMENISTAN
T U R K E Y
NICOSIA
CYPRUS
LEBANON
BAYRŪT (BEIRUT)
DIMASHQ (DAMASCUS)
SYRIA
ISRAEL
YERUSHALAYIM (JERUSALEM)
'AMMĀN (AMMAN)
JORDAN
BAGHDAD
IRAQ
KUWAIT
AL KUWAYT (KUWAIT)
AL QĀHIRAH (CAIRO)
EGYPT
SAUDI ARABIA
AR RIYĀD (RIYADH)

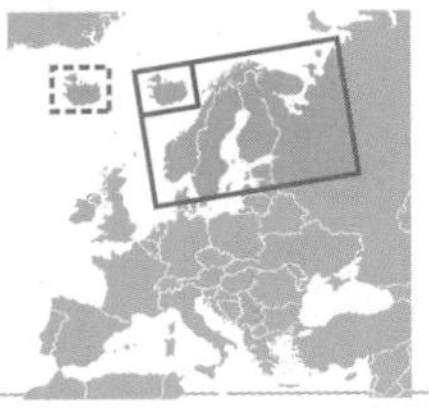

Europe

Northern Scandinavia

Barents Sea
White Sea
FINLAND
RUSSIA
ESTONIA
LATVIA
Gulf of Finland
Kolskiy Poluostrov
Poluostrov Kanim
Kanim Kamen
Ostrov Kolguyev
Cheshskaya Guba
Timanskiy Kryazh
Malozemelskaya Tundra
Pomorskiy Proliv
Terskiy Bereg
Kandalakshskaya Bereg
Kandalakshskaya Guba
Dvinskaya Guba
Onezhskaya Guba
Poluostrov Onezhskiy
Zimniy Bereg
Kryazh Vetreni Poyas
Andomskaya Vozvyshennost
Onezhskoye Ozero
Ladozhskoye Ozero
Northern European Plain
Valdayskaya Vozvysh.
Vepsovskaya Vozvysh.
Rybinskoye Vdkhr.
Beloye Oz.
Ozero Ilmen
Lake Peipus
Lake Pskov
Maanselkä
Suomenselkä
Salpausselkä
LAKE REGION
Saimaa
Inarijärvi
Oulujärvi
Ozero Imandra
Ozero Topozero
Ozero Vygozero
Ozero Segozero
Murmansk
Arkhangel'sk
Severodvinsk
Sankt Peterburg
Petrozavodsk
Vologda
Yaroslavl'
Cherepovets
Rybinsk
Novgorod
Pskov
Kostroma
Ivanovo
HELSINKI (HELSINGFORS)
TALLINN
Tampere
Oulu
Kuopio
Lappeenranta
Narva
Tartu
Pärnu
Vyborg
Kandalaksha
Apatity
Monchegorsk
Kem'
Belomorsk
Onega
Mezen'
Kotlas
Pinega
Kargopol'
Tikhvin
Tver
NORDKAPP (NORTH CAPE)
Varangerhalvøya
Poluostrov Rybachiy
70°N
68°N
66°N
64°N
62°N
60°N
58°N
24°E
26°E
28°E
30°E
32°E
34°E
36°E
38°E
40°E
42°E
44°E
46°E
48°E
50°E
52°E
54°E

Europe

Northeast Europe

0 50 100 150 200 250 km
0 20 40 60 80 100 120 140 miles

30°E
32°E
34°E
36°E
38°E
40°E
42°E
44°E
46°E
48°E
56°N
54°N
52°N
50°N
48°N
46°N
RUSSIA
UKRAINE
MOSKVA (MOSCOW)
Sea of Azov
lack Sea
Crimean Peninsula
Rybinskoye Vdkhr.
Gorkovskoye Vdkhr.
Kuybyshevskoye Vdkhr.
Volgogradskoye Vdkhr.
Tsimlyanskoye Vdkhr.
Kremenchugskoye Vdkhr.
Kakhovskoye Vdkhr.
Valdayskaya Vozvyshennost
Smolensko-Moskovskaya Vozvyshennost
Sredne Russkaya Vozvyshennost
Kalachskaya Vozvyshennost
Privolzhskaya Vozvyshennost
Dnieprovskaya Nizmennost
Prichernomorskaya Nizmennost
Donetskiy Kryazh
Priazovskaya Vozvyshennost
Prikubanskaya Nizmennost
Stavropolskaya Vozvyshennost
Salsko-Manichskaya Griada
Prikaspiyskaya Nizmennost
Vyatskiy Uval
Dubravnaya Nizmennost
VOLGA
OKA
DON
DNEPR
Vologda
Cherepovets
Rybinsk
Yaroslavl'
Kostroma
Ivanovo
Vladimir
Nizhniy Novgorod
Dzerzhinsk
Kazan'
Cheboksary
Yoshkar-Ola
Tver'
Tula
Kaluga
Ryazan'
Smolensk
Bryansk
Orël
Kursk
Lipetsk
Voronezh
Tambov
Penza
Saransk
Simbirsk
Tol'yatti
Syzran'
Saratov
Engel's
Belgorod
Kharkiv
Sumy
Poltava
Chernihiv
Kremenchuk
Dnipropetrovs'k
Zaporizhzhya
Kryvyy Rih
Donets'k
Luhans'k
Mariupol'
Melitopol'
Berdyans'k
Kherson
Mykolayiv
Rostov
Taganrog
Novocherkassk
Shakhty
Volgograd
Volzhskiy
Kamyshin
Balakovo
Elista
Stavropol'
Armavir
Kerch

Europe

Southwest Europe

0 50 100 150 200 250 km
0 20 40 60 80 100 120 140 miles

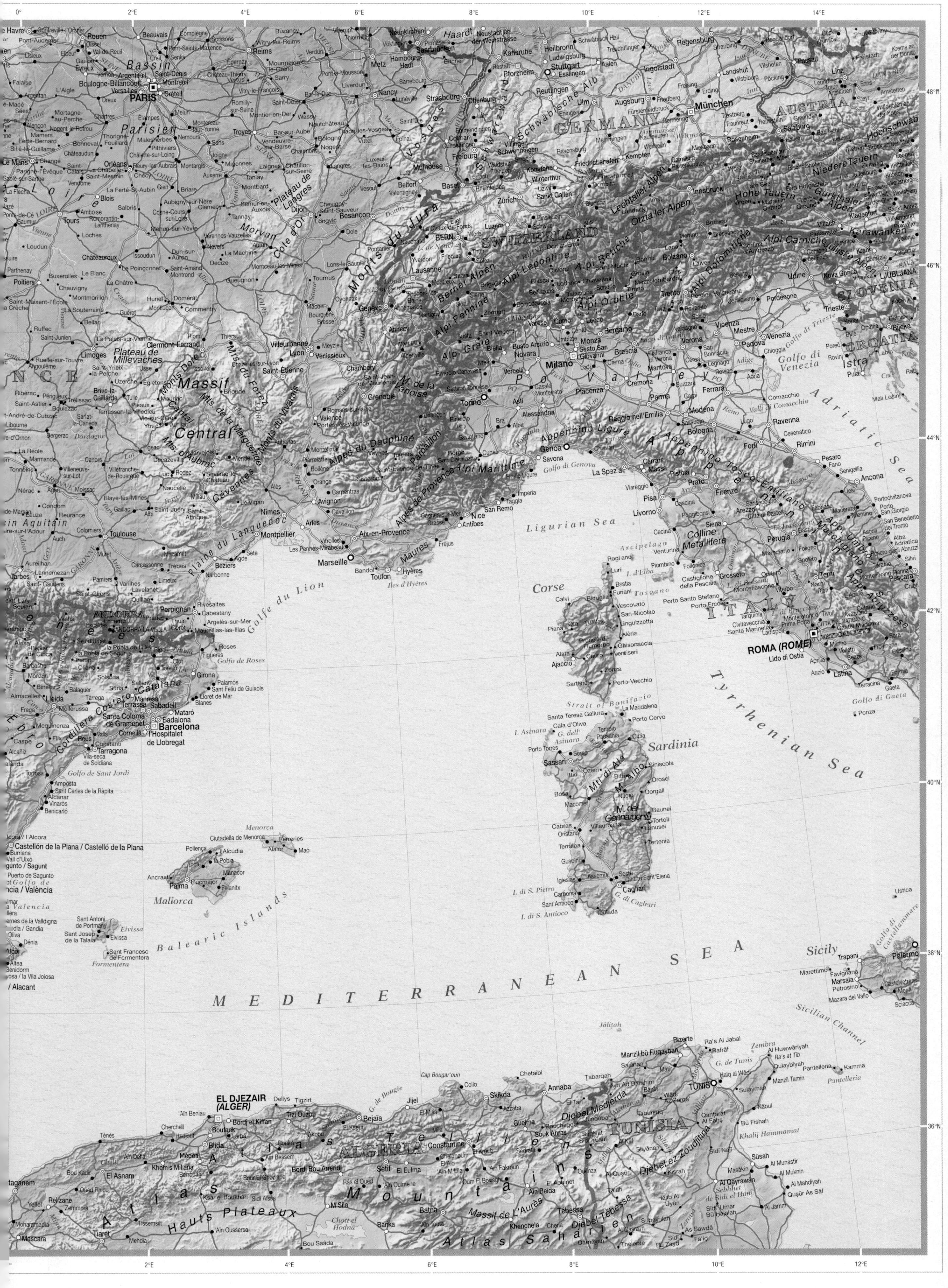
MEDITERRANEAN SEA
Ligurian Sea
Tyrrhenian Sea
Adriatic Sea
Golfe du Lion
Sicilian Channel
Balearic Islands
GERMANY
SWITZERLAND
AUSTRIA
SLOVENIA
CROATIA
ITALY
ALGERIA
TUNISIA
ANDORRA
PARIS
BERN
ROMA (ROME)
EL DJEZAIR (ALGER)
TUNIS
LJUBLJANA
München
Milano
Torino
Genova
Marseille
Barcelona
Lyon
Toulouse
Montpellier
Firenze
Bologna
Venezia
Zürich
Stuttgart
Palermo
Cagliari
Ajaccio
Corse
Sardinia
Sicily
Menorca
Mallorca
Eivissa
Formentera
Massif Central
Bassin Parisien
Monts du Jura
Alpi Dolomitiche
Appennino Ligure
Appennino Tosco-Emiliano
Atlas Mountains
Tell Atlas
Atlas Saharien
Hauts Plateaux
Pianura Padana
Golfo di Genova
Golfo di Venezia
Strait of Bonifacio
Castellón de la Plana / Castelló de la Plana
Tarragona
Sassari
Nice
Toulon
Annaba
Constantine
Bizerte
Pantelleria
Trapani
Marsala
Livorno
Pisa
Perugia
Ancona
Rimini
Ravenna
Verona
Padova
Trieste
Strasbourg
Dijon
Grenoble
Avignon
Nîmes
Genève
Lausanne
Basel
Innsbruck
Salzburg
Bolzano

Europe
Southeast Europe

0 50 100 150 200 250 km
0 20 40 60 80 100 120 140 miles

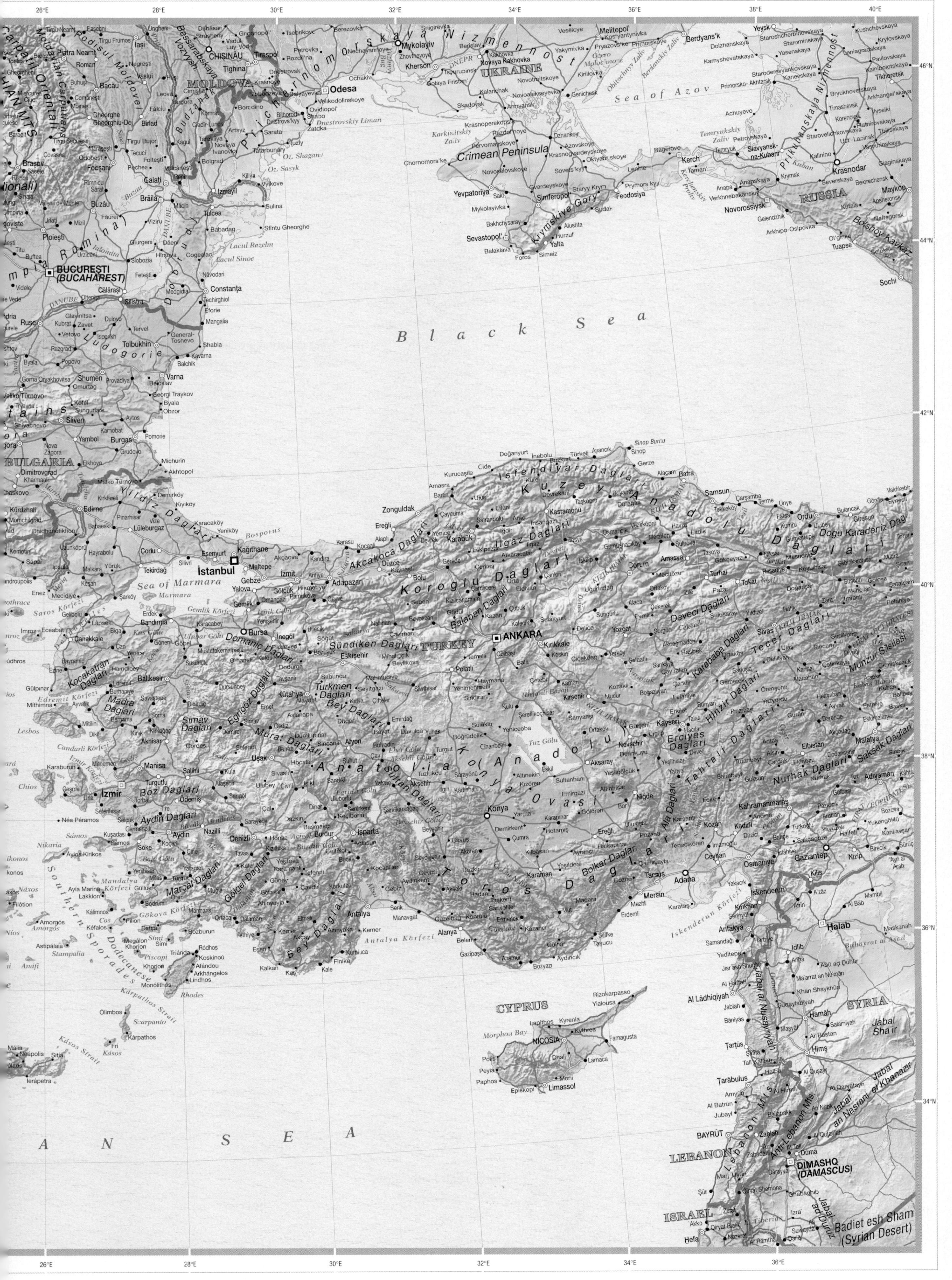
26°E
28°E
30°E
32°E
34°E
36°E
38°E
40°E
46°N
44°N
42°N
40°N
38°N
36°N
34°N
Black Sea
Sea of Azov
Sea of Marmara
Bosporus
Crimean Peninsula
Krymskiye Gory
Karkinitskiy Zaliv
Dnestrovskiy Liman
Temryukskiy Zaliv
Kerchenskiy Proliv
Prichernomorskaya Nizmennost
Prikubanskaya Nizmennost
Bolshoy Kavkaz
UKRAINE
RUSSIA
MOLDOVA
BULGARIA
TURKEY
CYPRUS
SYRIA
LEBANON
ISRAEL
CHIŞINĂU
BUCUREŞTI (BUCHAREST)
ANKARA
NICOSIA
DIMASHQ (DAMASCUS)
BAYRŪT
Odesa
Mykolayiv
Kherson
Melitopol'
Berdyans'k
Yeysk
Krasnodar
Novorossiysk
Kerch
Feodosiya
Simferopol'
Sevastopol'
Yevpatoriya
Yalta
Sochi
Tuapse
Maykop
Galaţi
Brăila
Constanţa
Tulcea
Ploieşti
Iaşi
Bacău
Varna
Burgas
Shumen
Sliven
Edirne
İstanbul
İzmit
Bursa
Balıkesir
İzmir
Manisa
Aydın
Denizli
Burdur
Isparta
Antalya
Alanya
Konya
Eskişehir
Kütahya
Afyon
Uşak
Zonguldak
Kastamonu
Samsun
Ordu
Giresun
Amasya
Tokat
Sivas
Yozgat
Kayseri
Kırşehir
Niğde
Aksaray
Adana
Mersin
Tarsus
Gaziantep
Kahramanmaraş
Malatya
Adıyaman
İskenderun
Antakya
Halab
Hamāh
Ḥimş
Al Lādhiqīyah
Ţarţūs
Ţarābulus
Limassol
Larnaca
Famagusta
Paphos
Rhodes
Kárpathos
Sâmos
Chios
Lesbos
Black Sea
Kuzey Anadolu Dağlari
Koroglu Daglari
Toros Daglari
Anatolia
Konya Ovasi
Tuz Gölü
Sea of Azov
Southern Sporades
Dodecanese
Kárpathos Strait
Kásos Strait
Antalya Körfezi
Iskenderun Körfezi
Jabal an Nuşayrīyah
Lebanon Mts
Anti-Lebanon Mts
Badiet esh Sham (Syrian Desert)
A N   S E A

Albania

Albania is a republic of southeastern Europe. It is an essentially mountainous country in which four areas can be distinguished: the Albanian Alps (Bjeshkete Nemuna), located in the north; a series of mountain chains, plains and small hills that rise in the center; the high plateaus predominating in the Albanian Epirus or southern region; and the coastal plain, formed by a swampy area. The climate is Mediterranean on the coast and acquires continental traits towards the interior. Among its inhabitants, the majority are Albanians. There are minorities of Greeks, Turks, Gypsies and Slavs. Rural settlement predominates over urban settlement. Albania, one of the poorest countries of Europe, has experienced a certain industrial development since World War II, but continues to be dependent on farming (cereals, fig trees, olive trees, grapevines, cotton, tobacco and mulberry trees). Industry is based on the exploitation of the deposits of iron, copper, chrome and nickel. Its fragile economic development is in part a consequence of the isolation in which the country has been immersed for decades.

Official name: Republic of Albania
Form of government: emerging democracy
Capital: Tiranë
Official language: Albanian
Monetary unit: lek
Religious affiliation: Muslim (70%), Albanian Orthodox (20%), Roman Catholic (10%)
Ethnic composition of the population: Albanian (95%), Greek (3%), other (2%)
Area: 28,748 sq km
Total population: 3,249,000 inhabitants
Population density: 113 persons per sq km

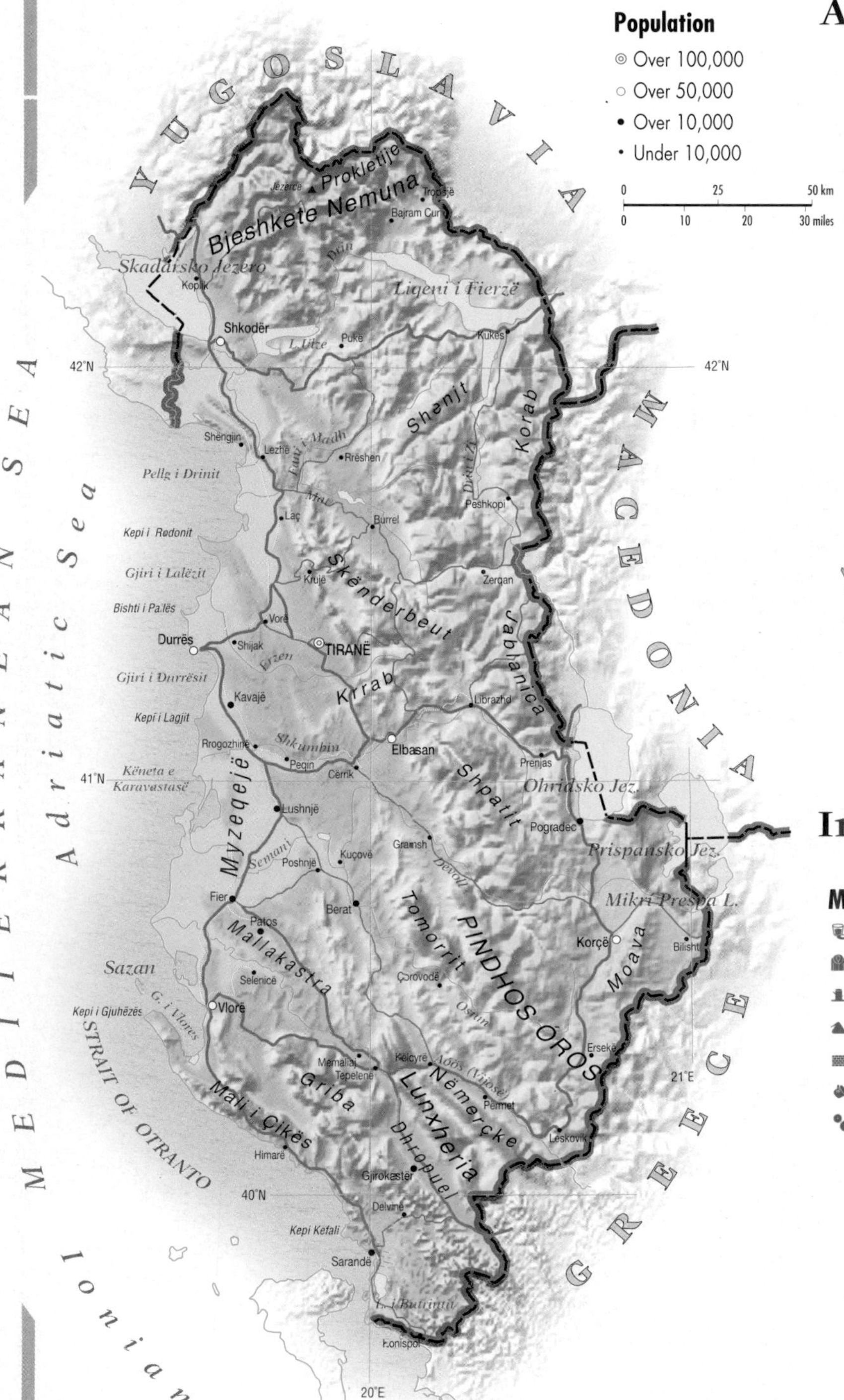

Agriculture

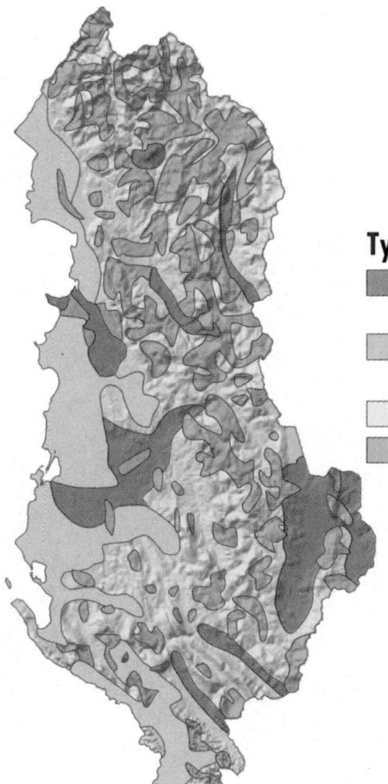

Types of agriculture and livestock production

- Croplands (cereals, potatoes, vegetables) and animal husbandry
- Perennial crops (citrus fruits, grapevines, olive trees)
- Grasslands and pastures
- Forest/brush

Population evolution and projection
in millions of persons

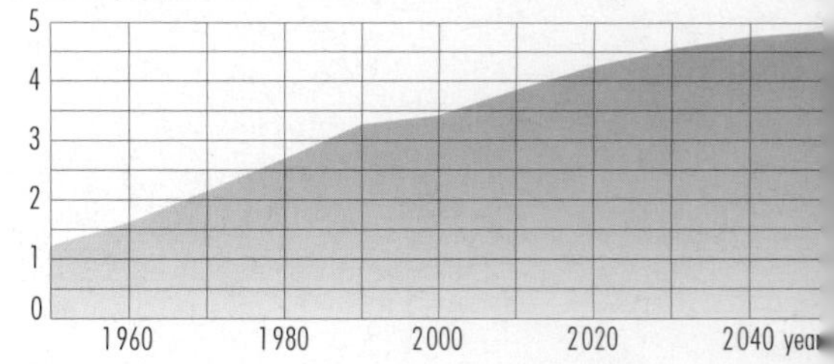

Industry

Manufacturing

- Food, beverages and tobacco
- Textiles, clothing, leather and footwear
- Wood, cork and furniture
- Chemical products
- Building materials, glass and cement
- Metallurgy and metal products
- Machinery and transport equipment

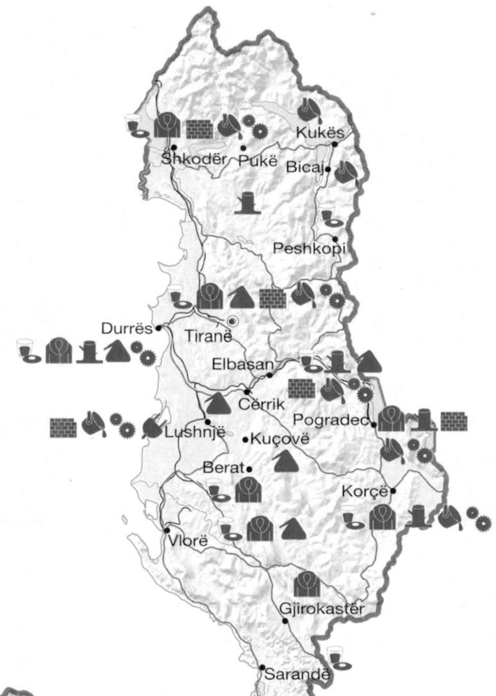

Energy-related installations

- Hydroelectric power plant
- Refinery

GDP structure
2,192 million dollars

Labor force
1,658,000 persons

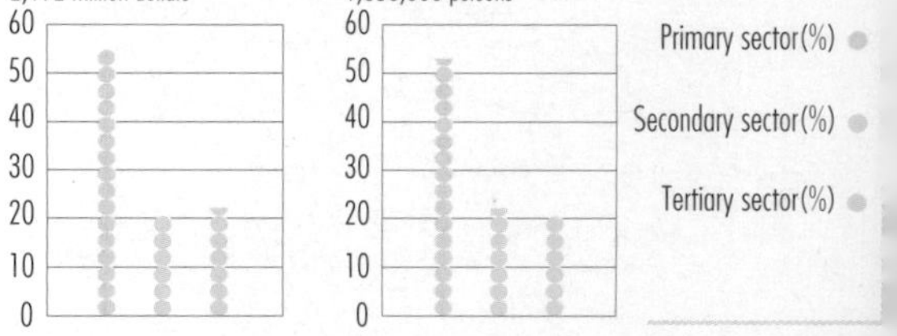

Population age distribution

32% | 62% | 6%
0 years | 15 years | 60 years

Vital statistics

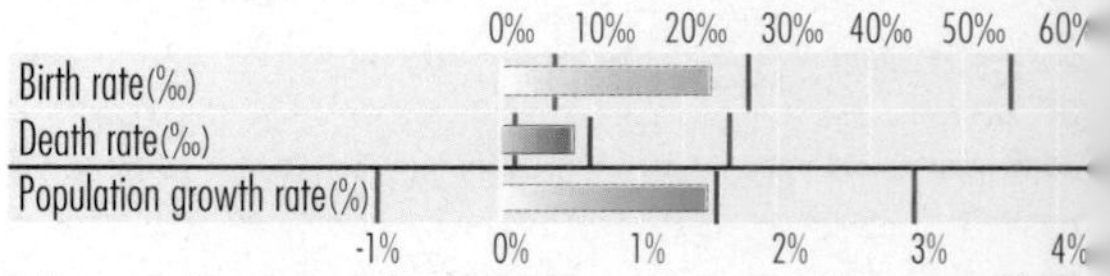

| Minimum and maximum world values | Average world value

Literacy (% of population over15)

100% | 100% | 100%
0% — 100%
Total literate population | Male literacy | Female literacy

Per capita income (GDP per person)

$360.11/person
$77/person (world minimum: Mozambique) (world maximum:Japan) $37,075/person

Unemployment (% of total population economically active)

18%
0% — 50%

Land use

0% — 100%
Forests and jungles 38% | Cropland 25% | Other 22%
Meadows and pastures 15%

Mining and Energy

Non-energy source mineral resources

Metals

- Bauxite
- Copper
- Chromite
- Iron ore
- Nickel

Mineral fuel resources

- Coal
- Natural gas
- Petroleum

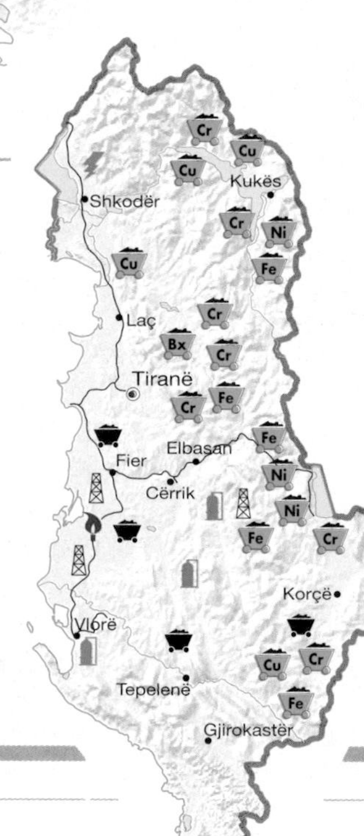

Andorra

Andorra is a European state situated on the southern slope of the eastern Pyrenees Mountains. It is formed by mountainous landforms, worn down by fluvial and glacial erosion. The Valira valley represents the principal geomorphological axis towards which other lesser valleys run. The rivers have a niveo-pluvial regime and steep slopes. The climate of Andorra corresponds to the Mediterranean high mountain type, with variations depending on the altitude. The precipitation —more abundant in summer— falls in the form of snow in winter. The population, composed of Spanish (the majority), Andorrans and French, is mainly employed in the tertiary sector. The inexistence of customs duties and direct taxes has attracted foreign capital, encouraging the creation of trade and promoting the banking sector. The tourist industry provides a great deal of income, while stock raising and farming are not very dynamic activities. Despite having a seasonal economy and depending to a great extent on imports, Andorra ranks as one of the most commercially active countries in the world.

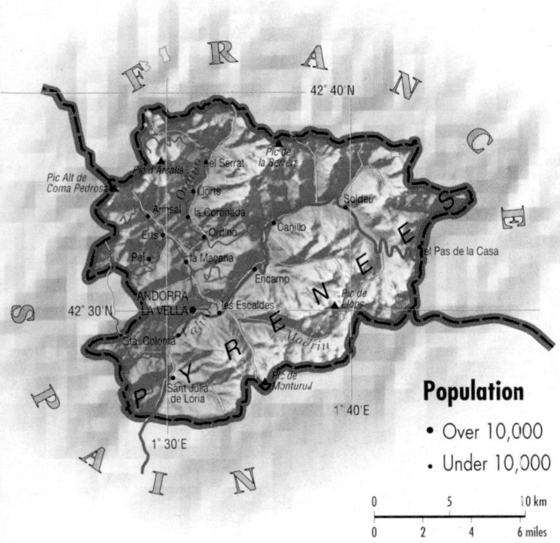

Official name: Principality of Andorra

Form of government: parliamentary democracy

Capital: Andorra la Vella

Official language: Catalan

Monetary unit: French franc, Spanish peseta

Religious affiliation: Roman Catholic (90%), other (10%)

Ethnic composition of the population: Spanish (61%), Andorran (30%), French (6%), other (3%)

Area: 468 sq km

Total population: 72,766 inhabitants

Population density: 155.5 persons per sq km

GDP: U.S.$1,060 million

Population evolution and projection

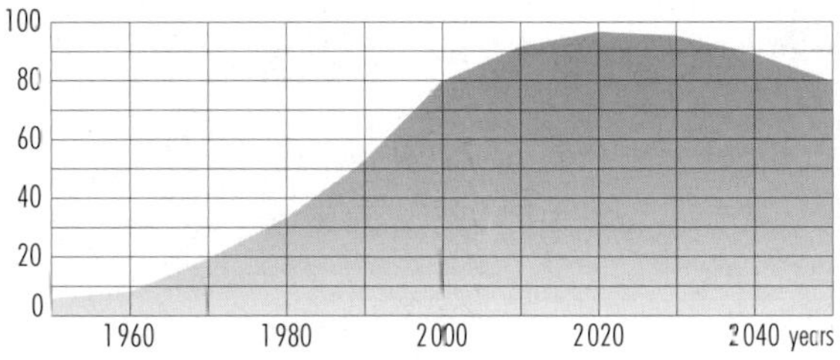

Labor force

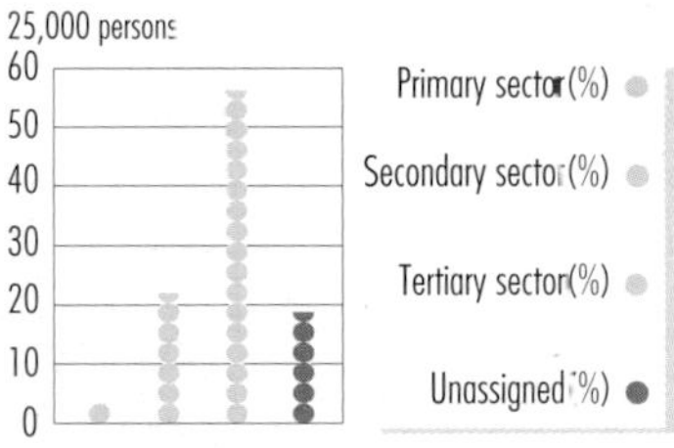

Population age distribution

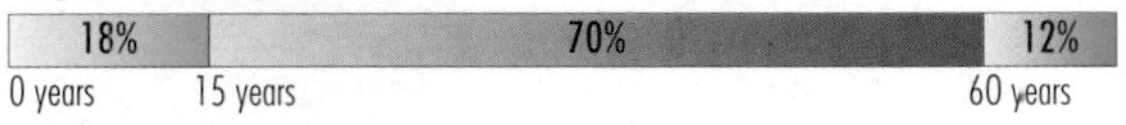

Vital statistics

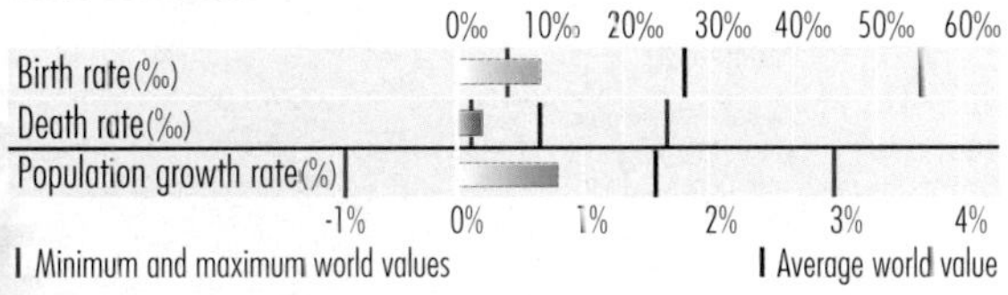

Literacy (% of population over15)

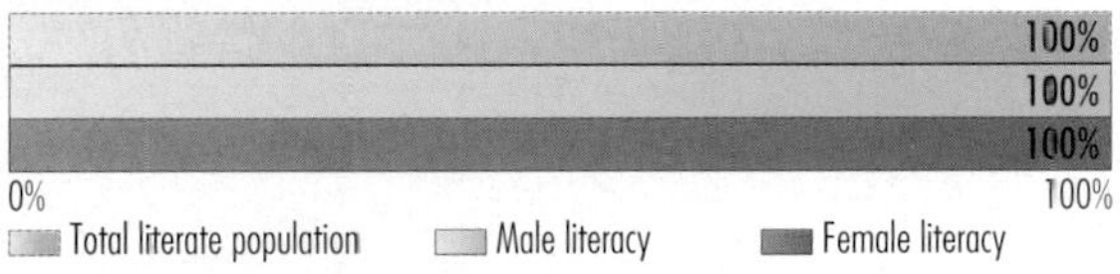

Per capita income (GDP per person)

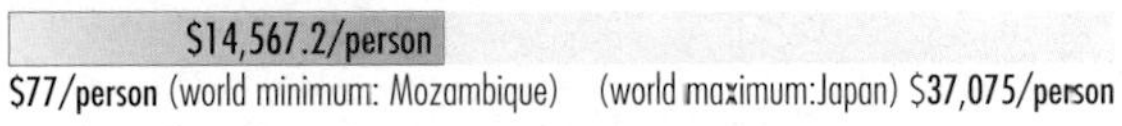

Land use

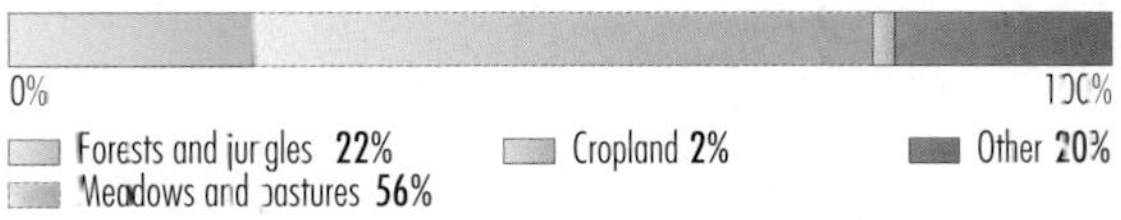

Principal Imports

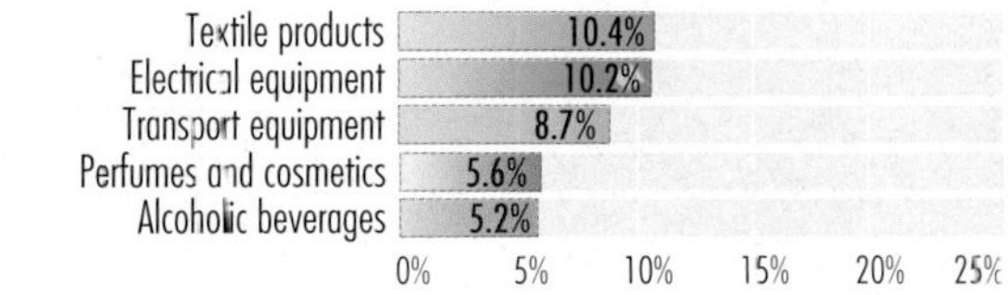

Principal Exports

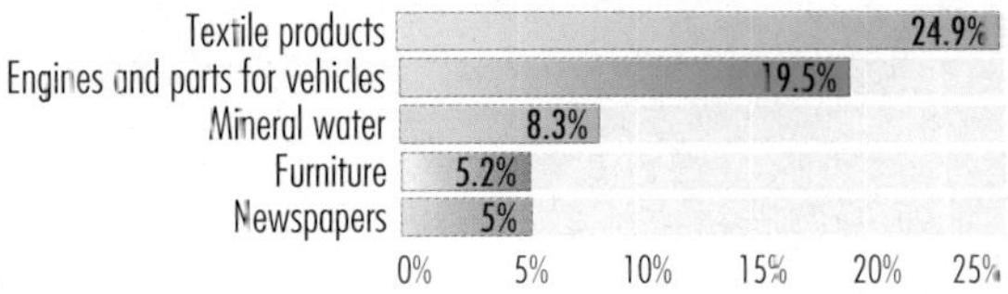

Austria

Austria is an Alpine and Danubian state of Central Europe in which three natural regions can be distinguished: western Austria, characterized by its high Alpine mountain landscape; the sub-Alpine area and the borders of the Bohemian Forest (Böhmer Wald) in the north, which form an area of valleys, plains and plateaus, through which east and west Europe are communicated; and finally, the eastern region of the country with relief that is not so rugged. The Danube basin drains almost all the territory; other drainage basins belong to the Rhine and the Elba.

Its location in the interior of the continent, situation in a temperate zone, and its terrain are conditioning factors for the climate. Three climatic environments can be distinguished: the alpine or mountain regime is characteristic of the western and central regions of the country, while the continental climate corresponds to the eastern part. In the rest of the territory there is an environment of transition, with marine west coast and continental influences.

Progressive aging defines Austrian demography, along with the high degree of urban dwelling, heavy concentration and ethnic homogeneity. Almost all the population is made up of Germanic people with Slavs and Jews constituting small minorities.

Austria is one of the most highly-developed European nations. The iron and steel industry, petrochemical, paper, food products, and electronic industries are important. It possesses abundant mining and energy-producing wealth, that nevertheless, do not cover its domestic needs. The tourist industry contributes important revenues. Forestry and livestock-producing activities predominate over farming. The primary sector occupies a low percentage of the working population, the majority of which are employed in the tertiary sector.

The strategical geographic location of Austria converts it into a corridor between Eastern and Western Europe. Modern communication networks run through the country. Austria enjoys a high standard of living and its unemployment rate is low.

Population evolution and projection

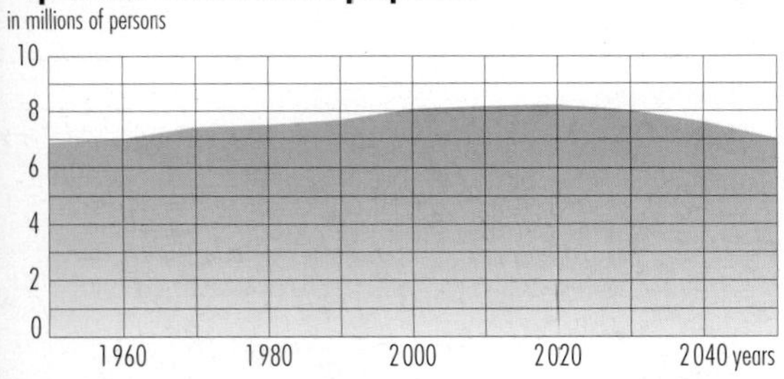

Land use

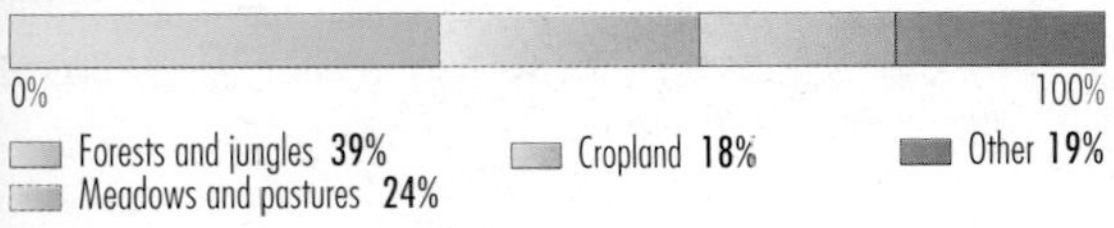

GDP structure

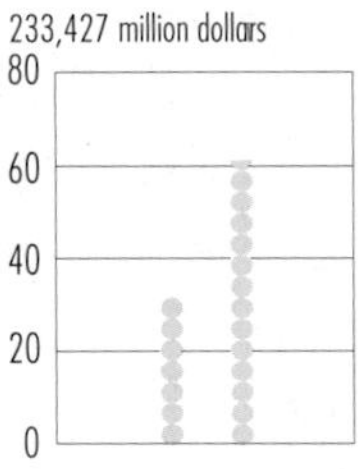

Labor force

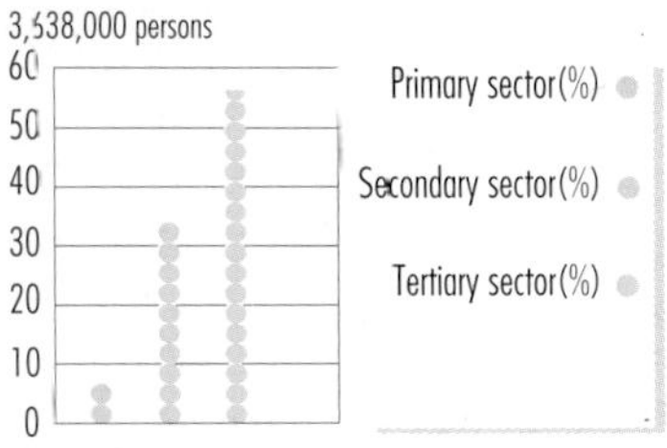

Literacy (% of population over15)

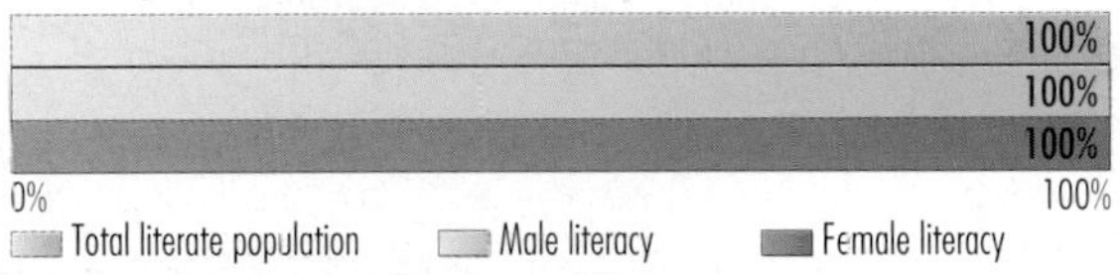

Vital statistics

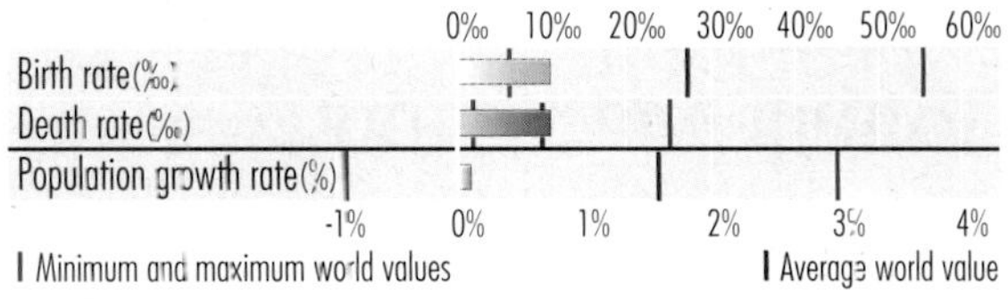

Per capita income (GDP per person)

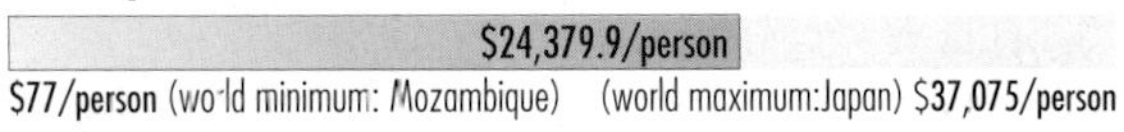

Unemployment (% of total population economically active)

Population age distribution

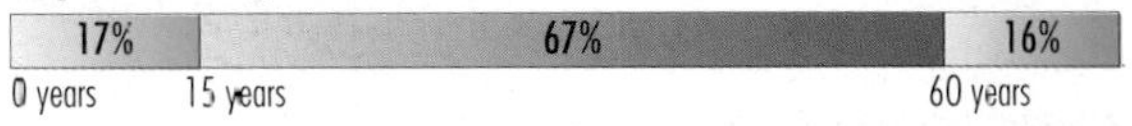

Official name: Republic of Austria
Form of government: federal republic
Capital: Vienna (Wien)
Official language: German
Monetary unit: Austrian schilling
Religious affiliation: Roman Catholic (78.3%), nonreligious and atheist (8.3%), Lutheran-Reformed (4.9%), Muslim (2.1%), Jewish (0.1%), other (2.8%), unknown (3.5%)
Ethnic composition of the population: German (99.4%), Croatian (0.3%), Slovenian (0.2%), other (0.1%)
Area: 83,859 sq km
Total population: 8,023,000 inhabitants
Population density: 95.7 persons per sq km

Population
- Over 1,000,000
- Over 100,000
- Over 50,000
- Over 10,000
- Under 10,000

0 25 50 75 km
0 10 20 30 40 50 miles

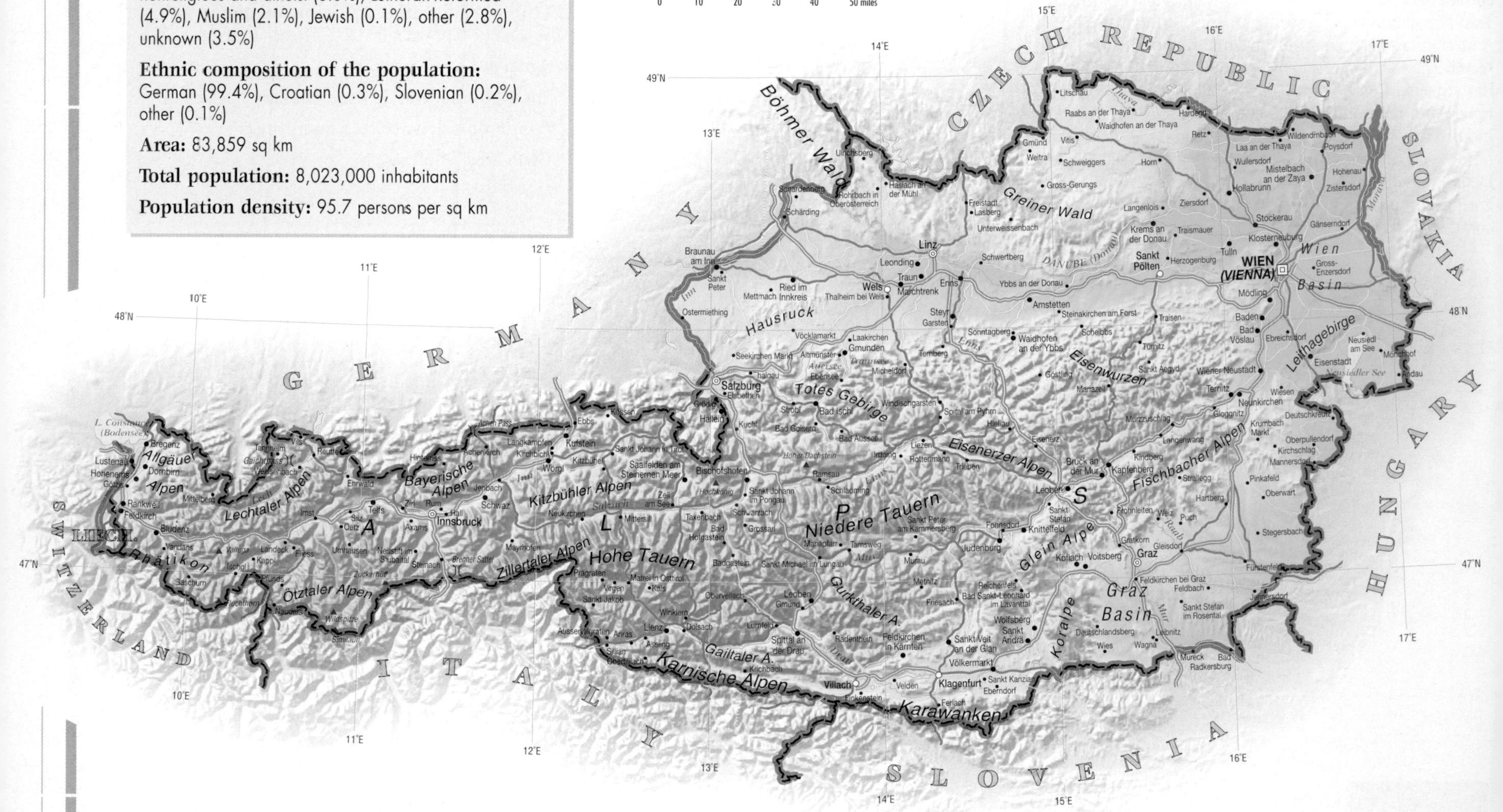

Agriculture and Industry

Types of agriculture and livestock production
- Cereal-farming (wheat, barley, corn)
- Croplands (cereals, sugar beets, forage crops)
- Perennial crops and croplands
- Highland pastures
- Grasslands
- Forests
- Non-arable land
- Urban area

- Apples
- Potatoes
- Sugar beets
- Cattle
- Pigs

Manufacturing
- Food, beverages and tobacco
- Textiles, clothing, leather and footwear
- Wood, cork and furniture
- Paper and graphic arts
- Chemical products
- Building materials, glass and cement
- Metallurgy and metal products
- Machinery and transport equipment
- Electrical, electronical and optical equipment

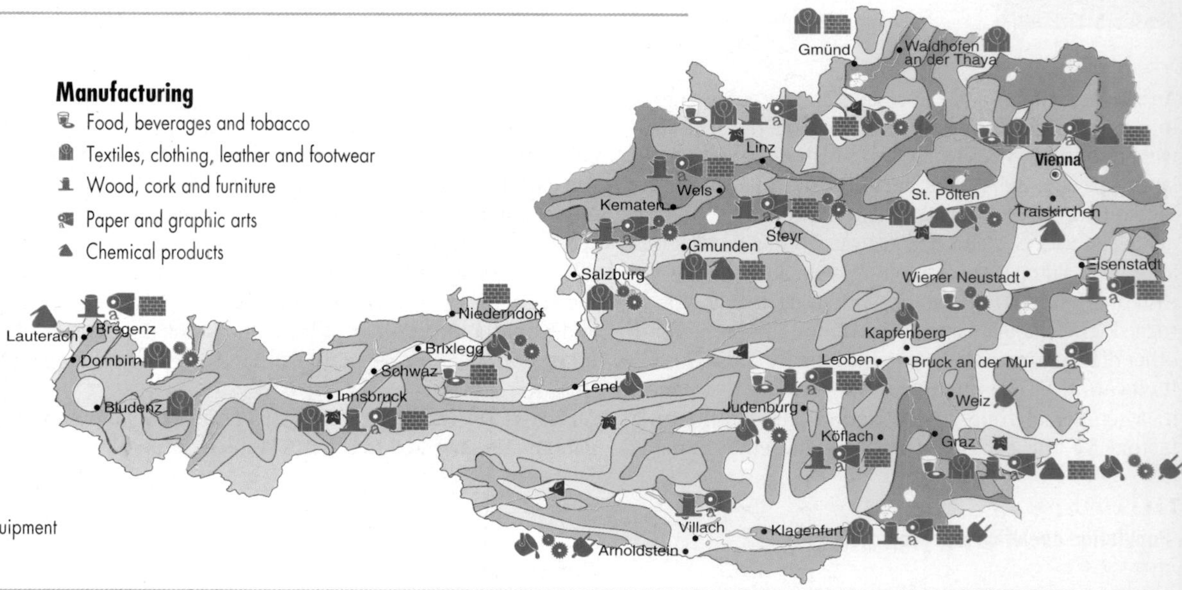

Mining and Energy

Non-energy source mineral resources

Metals
- Antimony
- Zinc
- Copper
- Iron ore
- Manganese
- Lead
- Wolfram

Rocks and industrial minerals
- Kaolin
- Dolomite
- Graphite
- Magnesite
- Salt
- Talc
- Gypsum

Mineral fuel resources
- Coal
- Natural gas
- Petroleum

Energy-related installations
- Hydroelectric power plant
- Refinery

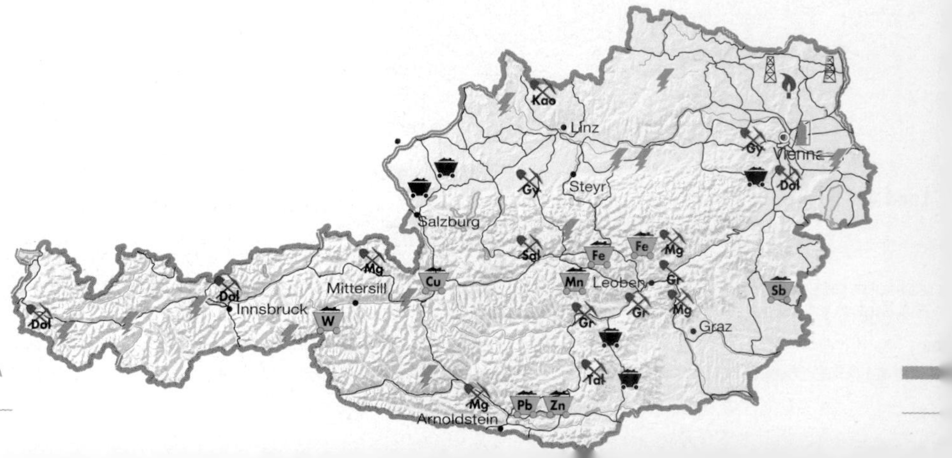

Belarus

Belarus is a republic of northeastern Europe. Also called White Russia, it possesses a flat territory, with heavy quagmires. The hills of the Belarusian chain rise in the north and in the south lies Polesia, a swampy area. It has an important hydrographic network of glacial origin. With a continental climate, it has cold winters and cool wet summers. Most of the population is composed of Belarusians, an ethnic group belonging to the Eastern Slavs. There also exists a minority of Russians and a smaller percentage of Poles, Ukrainians and Jews.

Farming is basically oriented towards the production of cereals, flax, potatoes, and sugar beets; livestock production is important because of its cattle. The country has many forests and a great quantity of peat. The industrial sector is the backbone of a good deal of national production; worthy of mention are the mechanical, petrochemical, electronical, textile, paper and data-processing branches. The river and railroad networks facilitate the development of the Belarusian economy.

Official name: Republic of Belarus
Form of government: republic
Capital: Minsk
Official language: Belarusian, Russian
Monetary unit: Belarusian rubel
Religious affiliation: predominantly Belarusian Orthodox with a Roman Catholic minority
Ethnic composition of the population: Belarusian (77.9%), Russian (13.2%), Polish (4.1%), Ukrainian (2.9%), other (1.9%)
Area: 207,595 sq km
Total population: 10,416,000 inhabitants
Population density: 50.2 persons per sq km
Per capita income: U.S.$2,812.01 per person

Population age distribution

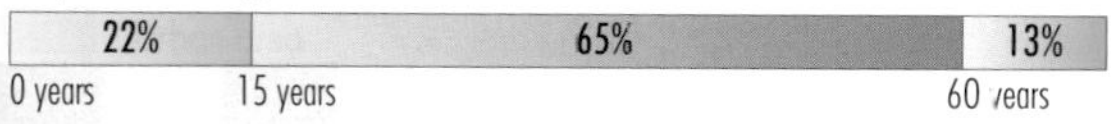

Vital statistics

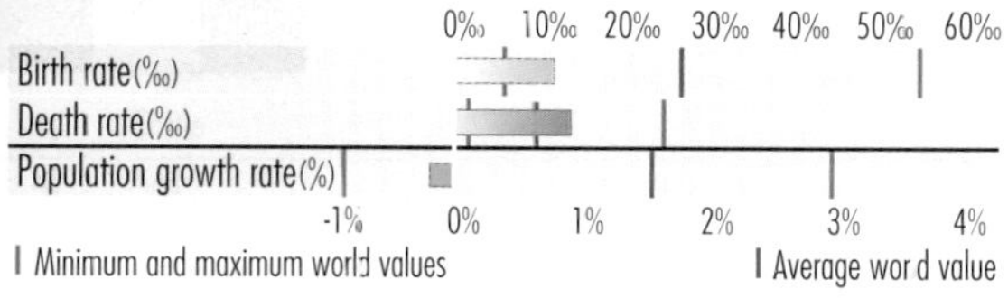

Literacy (% of population over15)

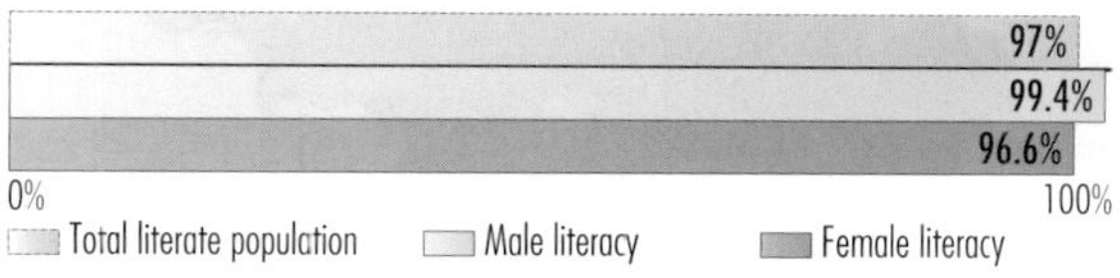

Per capita income (GDP per person)

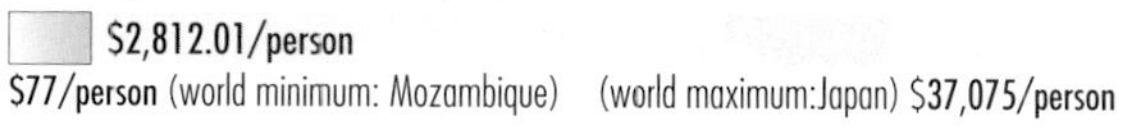

Population evolution and projection

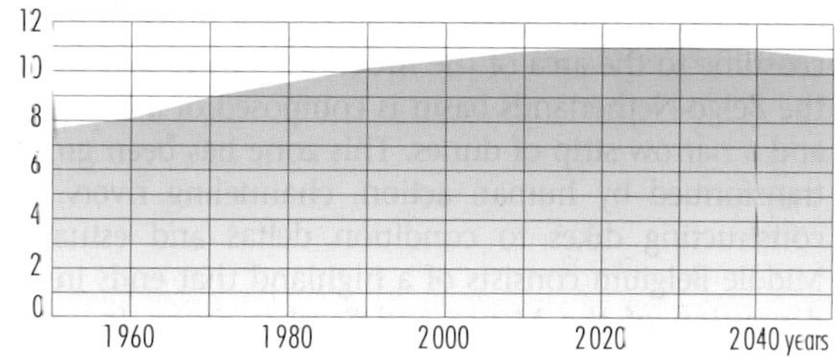

GDP structure

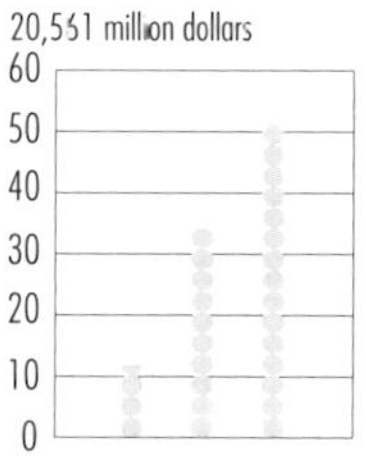

Labor force

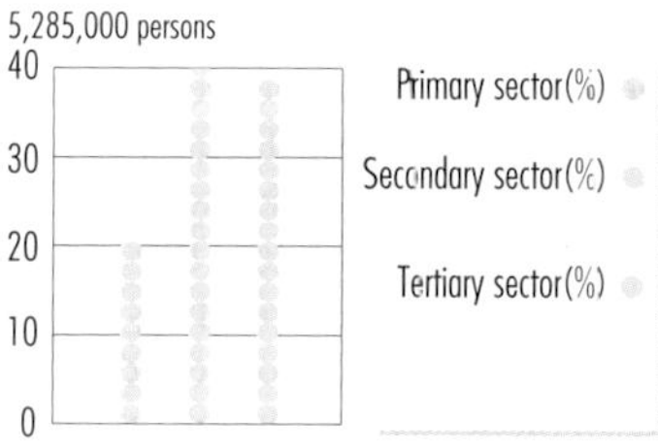

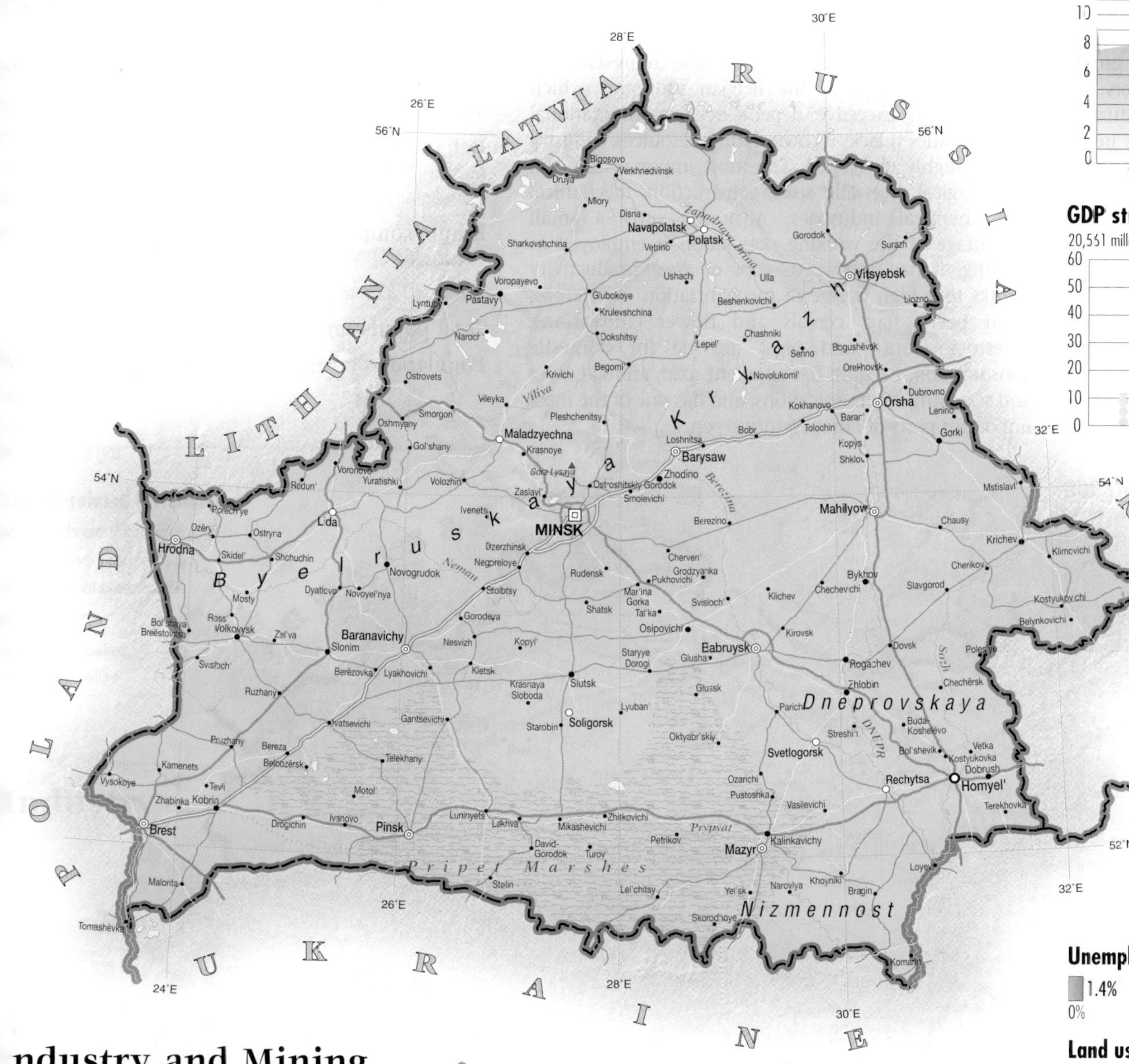

Population

- Over 1,000,000
- Over 500,000
- Over 100,000
- Over 50,000
- Over 10,000
- Under 10,000

0 50 100 km
0 20 40 60 miles

Unemployment (% of total population economically active)

Land use

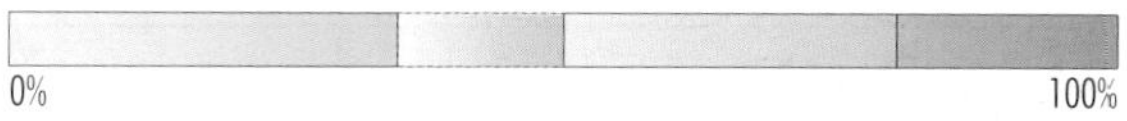

Forests and jungles **35%** Cropland **30%** Other **20%**
Meadows and pastures **15%**

Industry and Mining

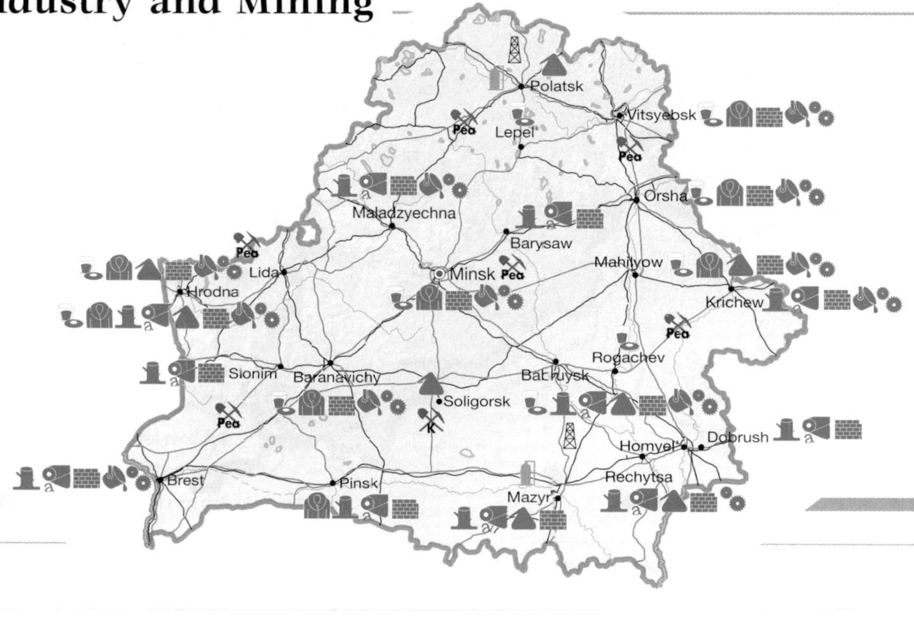

Non-energy source mineral resources
Rocks and industrial minerals
- Potash
- Peat

Mineral fuel resources
- Petroleum

Energy-related installations
- Refinery

Manufacturing
- Food, beverages and tobacco
- Textiles, clothing, leather and footwear
- Wood, cork and furniture
- Paper and graphic arts
- Chemical products
- Building materials, glass and cement
- Metallurgy and metal products
- Machinery and transport equipment

Denmark

Official name: Kingdom of Denmark
Form of government: constitutional monarchy
Capital: Copenhagen (København)
Official language: Danish
Monetary unit: Danish krone
Religious affiliation: Evangelical Lutheran (88.2%), other Christian (1.6%), Muslim (1.3%), other (8.9%)
Ethnic composition of the population: Danish (96.5%), Asian (1.5%), other Scandinavian (0.5%), British (0.2%), German (0.2%), other (1.1%)
Area: 43,094 sq km
Total population: 5,250,000 inhabitants
Population density: 121.8 persons per sq km

Denmark is a state of northern Europe with coasts on the Baltic Sea (east) and on the North Sea (north and west). Its territory includes the Peninsula of Jutland and more than 500 islands. The Faroe Islands archipelago —in the Atlantic— and Greenland are under Danish sovereignty. Flat landforms are predominant. The coasts, with gulfs and fiords, were carved out by glacial erosion. The Danish climate corresponds to a regime of transition between the marine west coast and continental types, with cool summers and relatively cold winters. The population, which is very homogeneous, is composed of Danes; however, there is a German-speaking minority. In Greenland, Danes live alongside Eskimos. Denmark has the highest population density in Scandinavia, although its inhabitants are distributed unevenly. Almost a third of the population is concentrated in Copenhagen, the capital. Denmark ranks among the most highly developed countries of Europe. Agriculture bases its excellent productivity on the fertility of the soil, the medium and large size of land Holdings and the high technical level of the farmers. Agricultural production is oriented towards stockraising (forage crops), important for its meat production. Fishing also represents another important source of income. In the industrial sector, the food products (canned fish, flours, dairy products), mechanical, chemical and ship-building branches are specially significant. Denmark's balance of payments is negative, due to the need to import fuels. The country enjoys an excellent network of terrestrial and maritime transport.

Population evolution and projection
in millions of persons

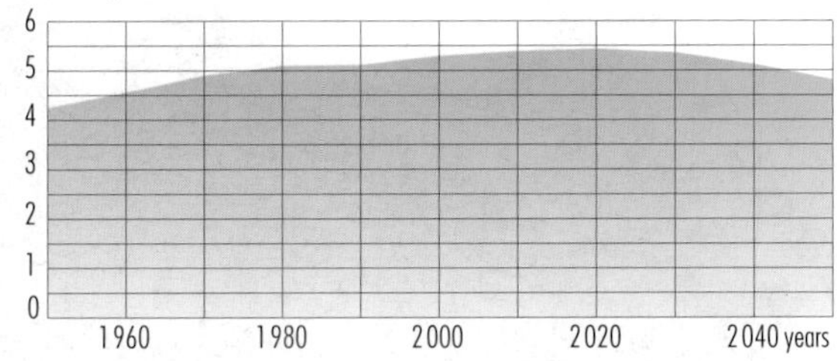

Vital statistics

0‰ 10‰ 20‰ 30‰ 40‰ 50‰ 60‰
Birth rate(‰)
Death rate(‰)
Population growth rate(%)
-1% 0% 1% 2% 3% 4%

| Minimum and maximum world values | Average world value

GDP structure
172,220 million dollars

Labor force
2,902,000 persons

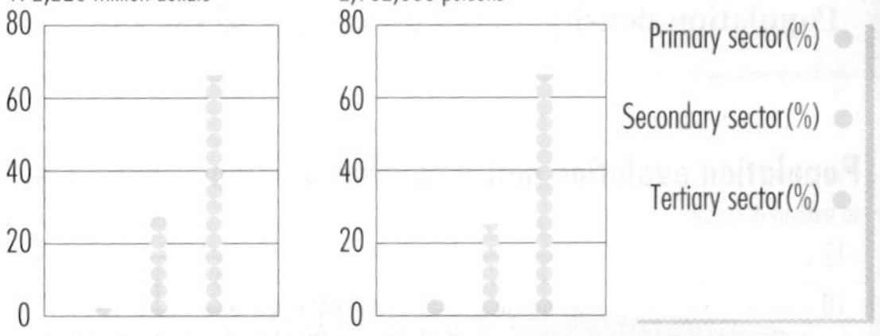

Population age distribution

17%	68%	15%

0 years — 15 years — 60 years

Literacy (% of population over15)

	0% – 100%
Total literate population	100%
Male literacy	100%
Female literacy	100%

Per capita income (GDP per person)

$28,076.2/person

$77/person (world minimum: Mozambique) (world maximum:Japan) $37,075/person

Unemployment (% of total population economically active)

12.3% (scale 0% – 50%)

Land use

0% – 100%

Forests and jungles 12%
Meadows and pastures 6%
Cropland 61%
Other 21%

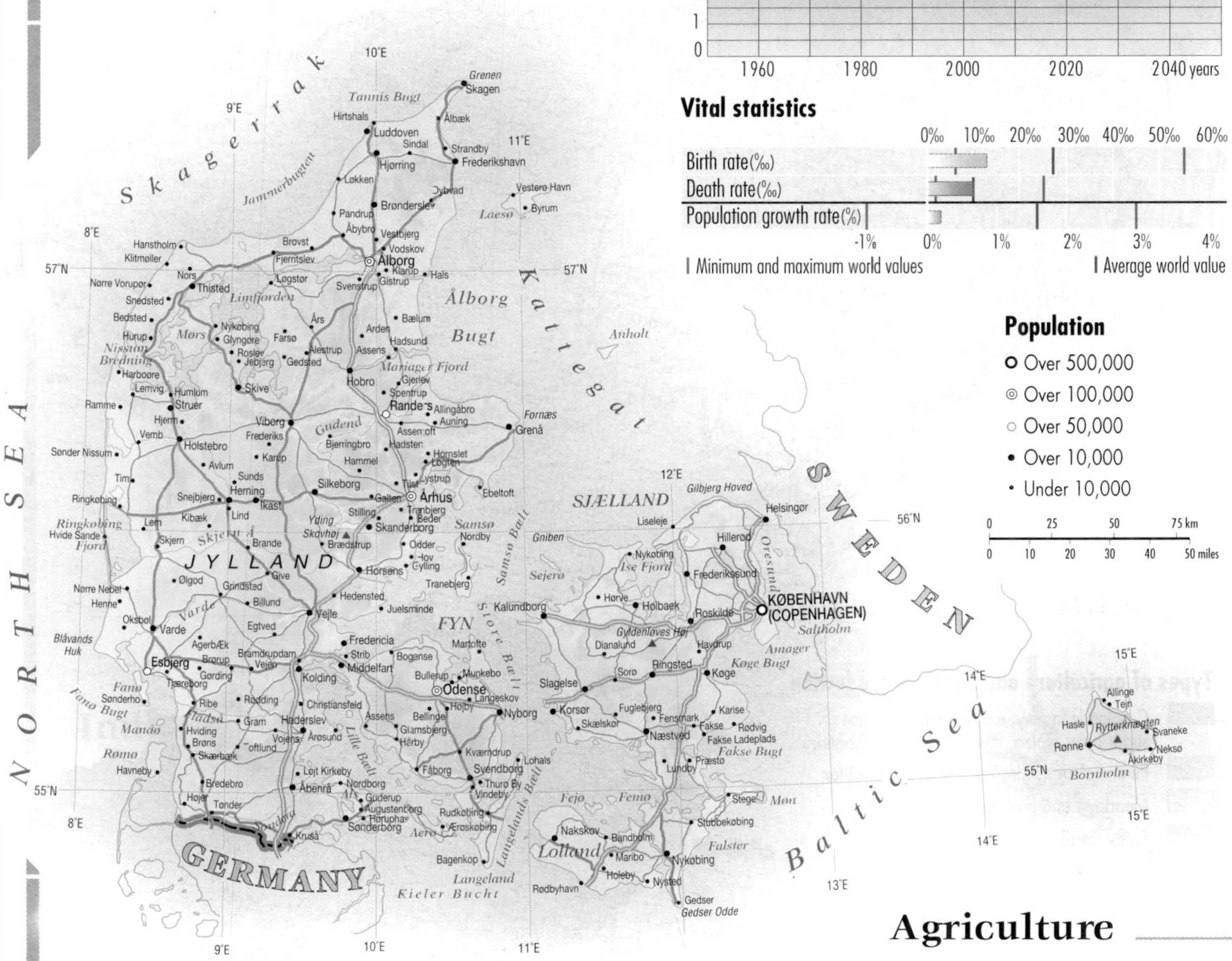

Population
Over 500,000
Over 100,000
Over 50,000
Over 10,000
Under 10,000

Agriculture

Types of agriculture and livestock production

- Croplands
- Meadows
- Forest/brush
- Non-arable land
- Urban area
- Apples
- Potatoes
- Sugar beets
- Cattle
- Pigs
- Fishing

Industry and Mining

Non-energy source mineral resources
Rocks and industrial minerals
- Limestone
- Salt

Mineral fuel resources
Fossil fuels
- Natural gas
- Petroleum
- Gas and oil field

Manufacturing
- Food, beverages and tobacco
- Textiles, clothing, leather and footwear
- Wood, cork and furniture
- Paper and graphic arts
- Chemical products
- Building materials, glass and cement
- Metallurgy and metal products
- Machinery and transport equipment
- Electrical, electronical and optical equipment

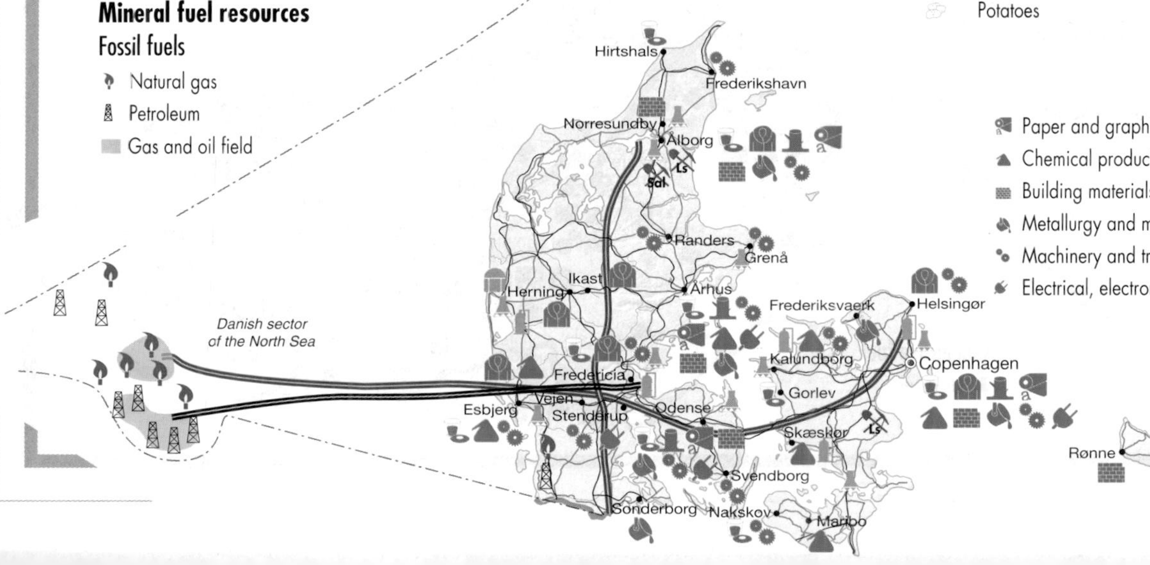

Energy-related installations
- Thermal power plant
- Natural gas plant
- Refinery
- Gas pipeline
- Oil pipeline

Official name: Republic of Estonia
Form of government: republic
Capital: Tallinn
Official language: Estonian
Monetary unit: Estonian kroon
Religious affiliation: Lutheran
Ethnic composition of the population: Estonian (61.5%), Russian (30.3%), Ukrainian (3.17%), Belarusian (1.8%), Finnish (1.1%), other (2.13%)
Area: 45,226 sq km
Total population: 1,459,000 inhabitants
Population density: 32.3 persons per sq km
Per capita income: U.S.$3,221 per person

A state of northern Europe, Estonia is the smallest of the Baltic Republics, which were part of the Soviet Union until 1991. It possesses more than 3,500 km of coastline and nearly 1,500 islands. Its terrain is flat, with small hills that rise no higher than 400 m in altitude. Coastal rivers —short and with little water flow— traverse the territory; inland lakes abound. The climate is continental, moderated by ocean influence, with harsh winters and short mild summers. Estonians represent more than half of the population and Russians nearly a third. There are small Ukrainian and Belarusian minorities. Settlement is concentrated in the cities, especially in Tallinn, the capital of the State, where a third of the inhabitants of the country reside. The economy is based on farming, stock raising —meat and dairy milk— and fishing, although other industries exist (food products, chemical, electronical and component assembly) which are more vital for its economy. Estonia lacks petroleum and supplies itself with fuel resources by importing them from Russia.

Population
- ◎ Over 100,000
- ○ Over 50,000
- • Over 10,000
- · Under 10,000

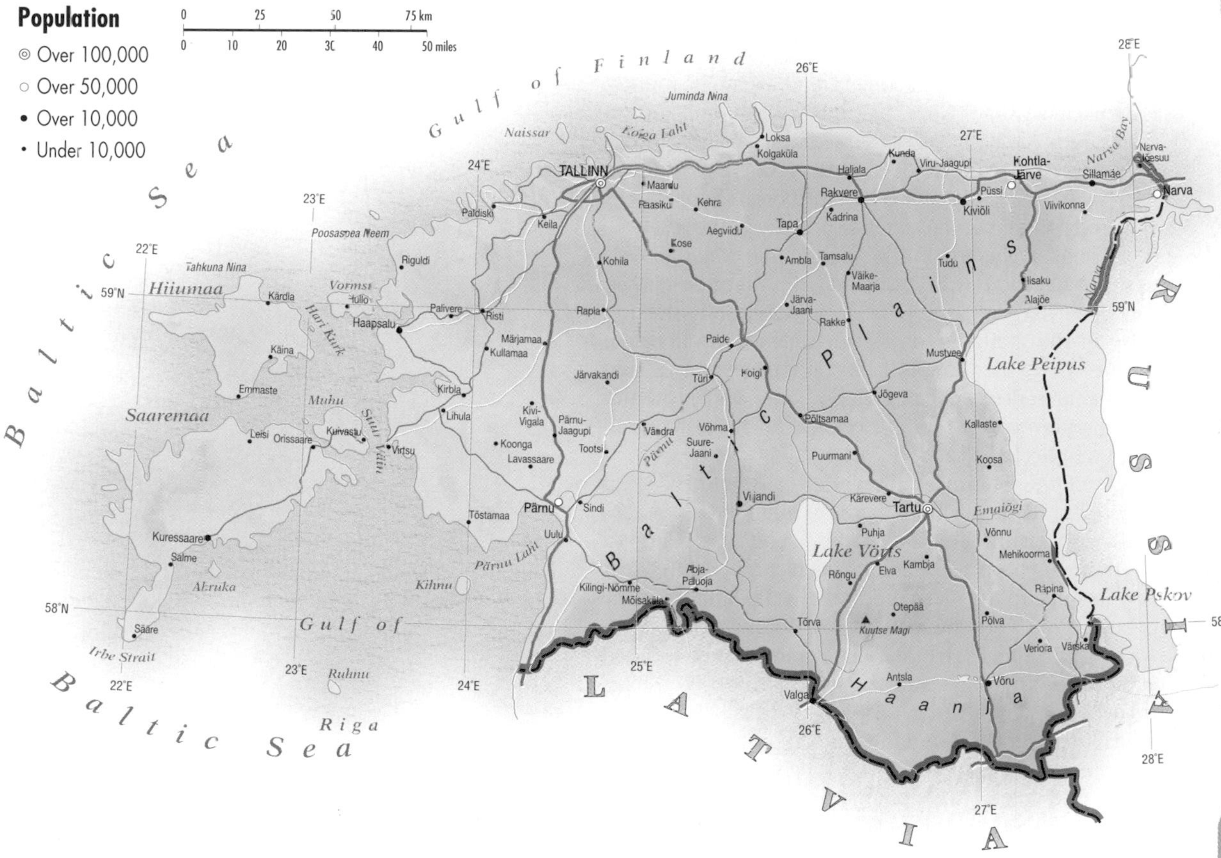

Population evolution and projection

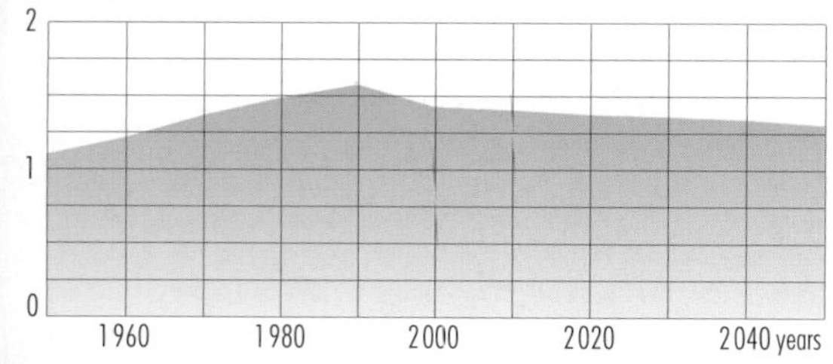

GDP structure

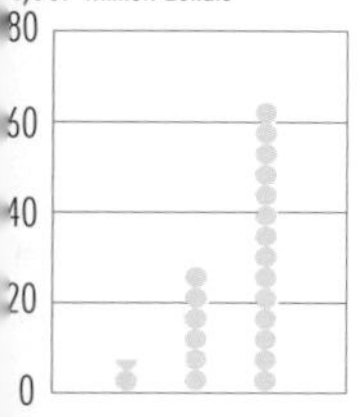

Labor force

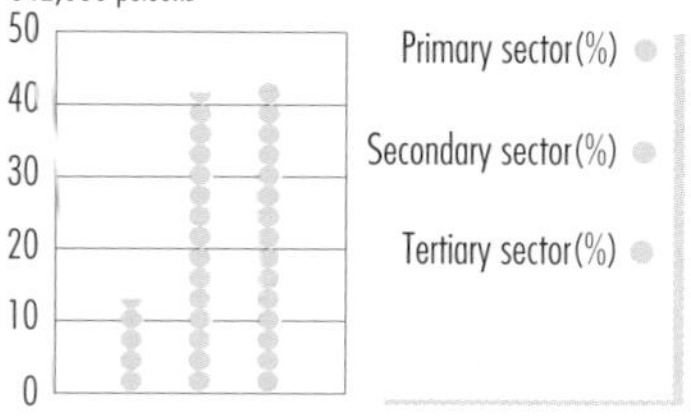

Population age distribution

Vital statistics

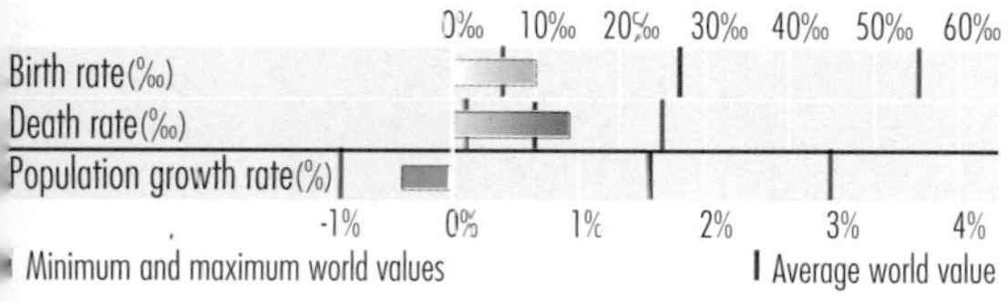

Literacy (% of population over15)

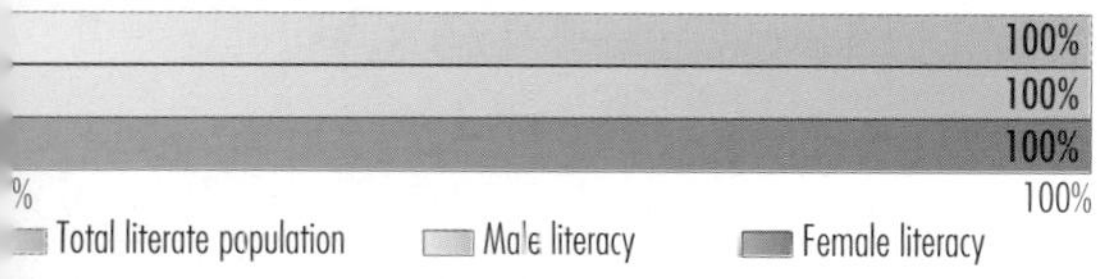

Unemployment (% of total population economically active)

Land use

Forests and jungles **45%**
Meadows and pastures **8%**
Cropland **26%**
Other **21%**

Industry and Mining

Non-energy source mineral resources
- Phosphates

Mineral fuel resources
- Uranium

Energy-related installations
- Nuclear reactor

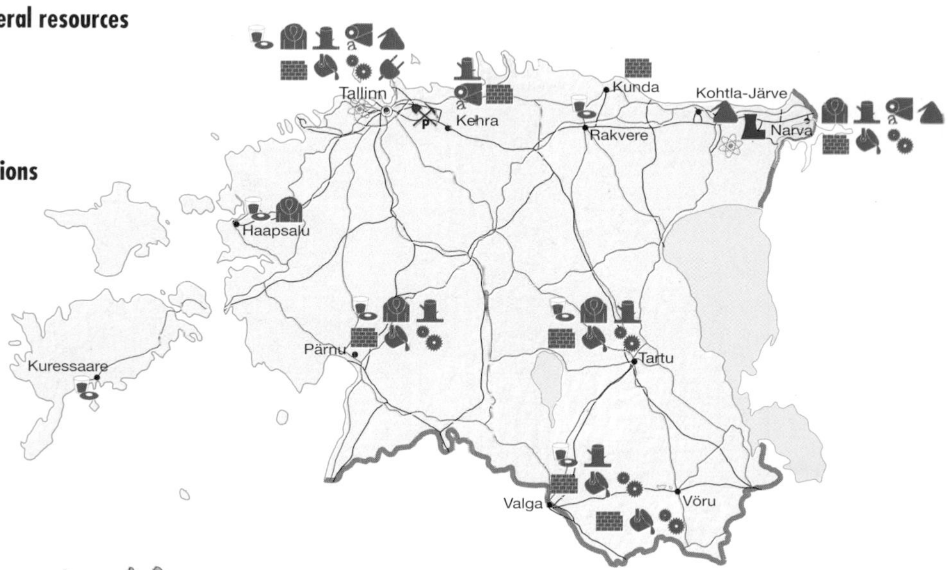

Manufacturing
- Food, beverages and tobacco
- Textiles, clothing, leather and footwear
- Wood, cork and furniture
- Paper and graphic arts
- Chemical products
- Building materials, glass and cement
- Metallurgy and metal products
- Machinery and transport equipment
- Electrical, electronical and optical equipment

Agriculture

Types of agriculture and livestock production
- Croplands (flax) and animal husbandry
- Irrigation/intensive farming
- Meadows and pastures
- Forest/brush

Finland

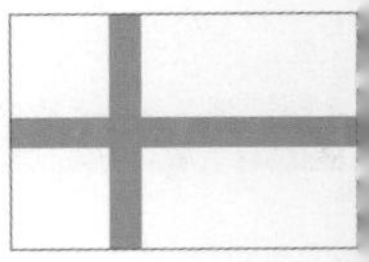

Finland is a republic of northern Europe with coasts on the Baltic Sea. It is the northernmost country of the continent, since almost a fourth of its land area lies within the Arctic Circle. The crystalline rock of the Scandinavian Shield constitutes the foundation of very flat terrain, averaging less than 200 m in altitude. The moraine deposits form hills in the north and southeast, as well as low folds that act like natural dikes between the more than 188,000 lakes. Among these, Lakes Inari, Päijänne and Saimaa must be mentioned, these last grouping together on the lacustrine plateau of the southeast. The lakes occupy a tenth of Finnish soil. The highest peak is Mount Haltia, in the northwest of the country (1,338 m). The rivers are grouped in five drainage basins: Kemijoki and Oulujoki (north), Kokemäenjoki (southwest), Kymijoki (south) and Vuoksa (flows into Lake Ladoga). Dense forests occupy three-fourths of the territory, one third of them growing in swampy soil. Finland is situated in the boreal region, but its very wet climate is not as harsh due to the cyclonic depressions originating in the Atlantic that penetrate in a west-east direction, with cool or slightly warm air masses, depending on the season. There is significant variation between the southern zones and Lapland, the northern region where the amount of rainfall decreases and temperatures descend considerably. The whole country remains snow-covered for a good deal of the year (up to seven months in Lapland).

People of the Finnish ethnic group constitute the great majority of the population; there are minorities of Swedes —less than a tenth of the population— and Laps, scarcely a few thousand people. The annual population growth rate is very low due to the marked descent in the birth rate. The population is concentrated on the southwestern coast, where the capital, Helsinki, has more than a million inhabitants. In other cities more than 100,000 people reside: Tampere, Turku, Espoo, Vantaa and Oulu. Agricultural activity (oats and wheat crops) has a negligible effect on the Finnish economy; livestock husbandry (beef cattle and pigs) and poultry raising have greater importance. Copper, zinc, gold and chrome are extracted from Finland's mines. In the secondary sector, the fur, wood —Finland is an important world exporter of conglomerated wood— and paper industries have achieved a high level of development. Other note-worthy industries are mechanical construction (located in Helsinki, Vaasa, Turku and Hamina), steel mills (in Tampere and other centers) and the chemical industry (sodium hydroxide and sulphuric acid are produced.). The dense and modern network of transport facilitates commercial interchange.

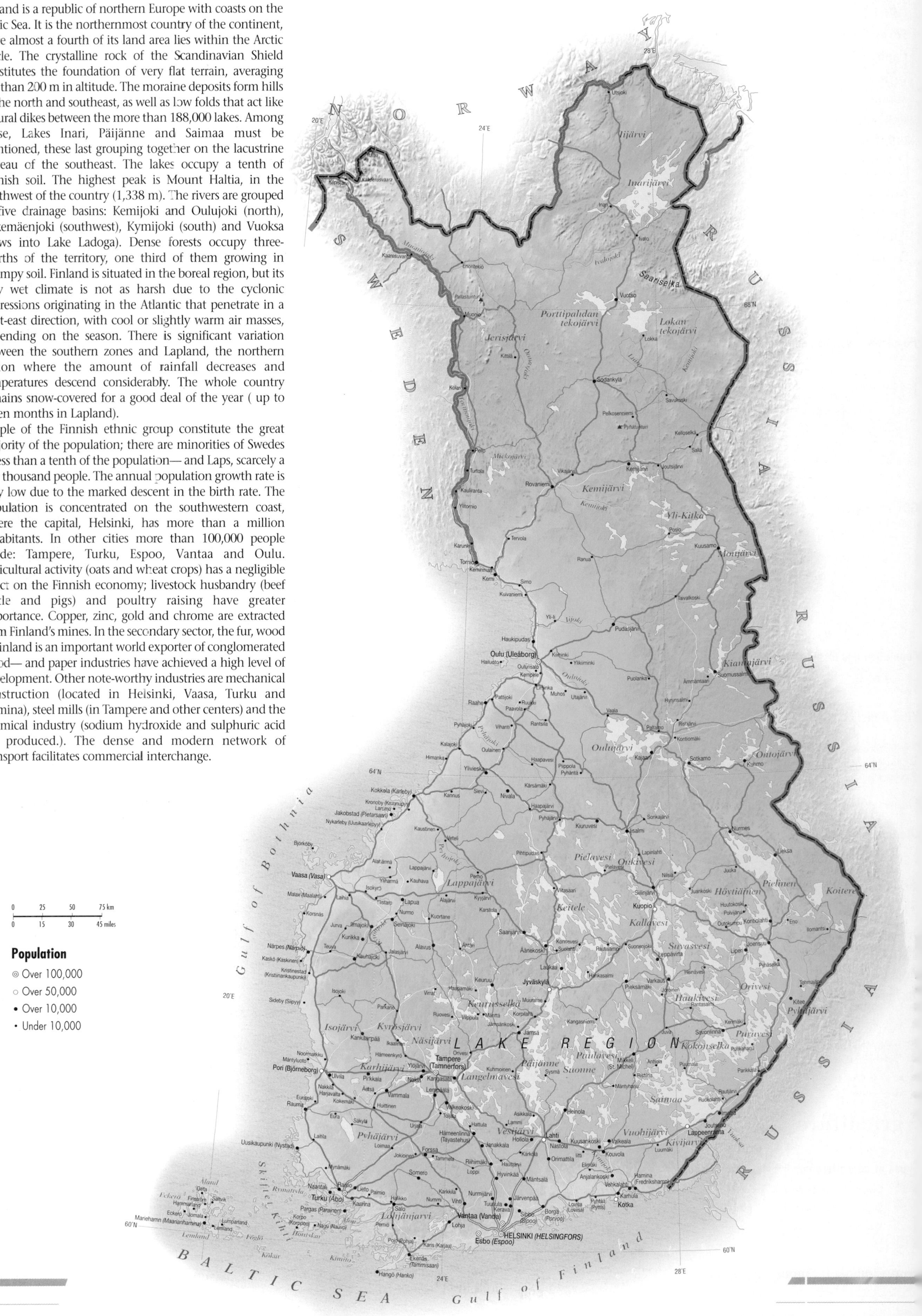

Agriculture

Types of agriculture and livestock production

- Cereal farming (wheat, rye, oats, barley)
- Croplands (cereals, oilseeds, turnips, potatoes)
- Nomadic herding
- Meadows
- Forest
- Urban area
- Apples
- Potatoes
- Sugar beets
- Cattle
- Sheep
- Pigs
- Reindeer
- Fishing

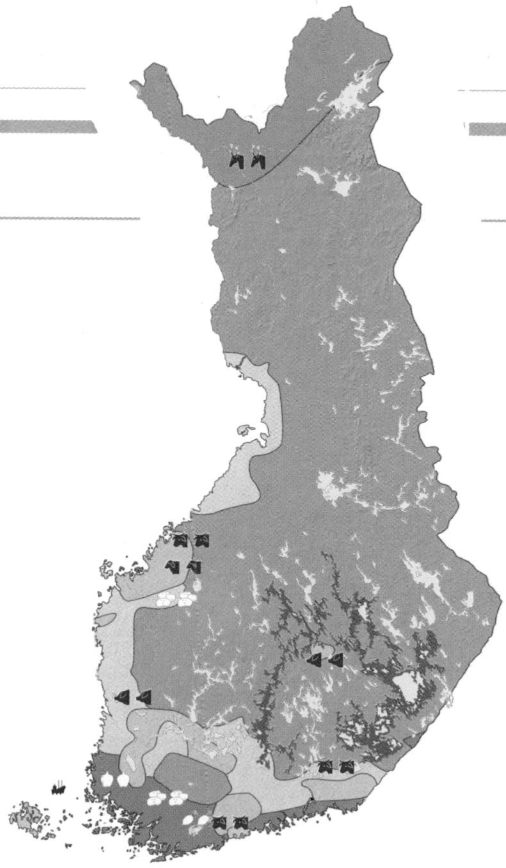

Official name: Republic of Finland
Form of government: parliamentary republic
Capital: Helsinki (Helsingfors)
Official language: Finnish, Swedish
Monetary unit: Finnish markka
Religious affiliation: Evangelical Lutheran (87.3%), Finnish (Greek) Orthodox (1.1%), nonreligious (10.6%), other (1%)
Ethnic composition of the population: Finnish, Swedish, Lap, Gypsy, Tartar
Area: 338,145 sq km
Total population: 5,105,000 inhabitants
Population density: 15.1 persons per sq km

Mining and energy

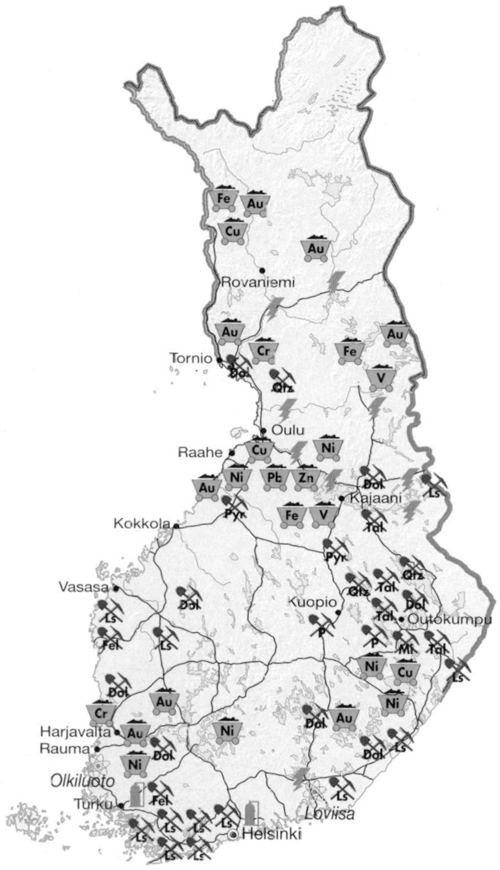

Non-energy source mineral resources

Metals

- Zinc
- Copper
- Chromite
- Iron ore
- Nickel
- Gold
- Lead
- Vanadium

Rocks and industrial minerals

- Limestone
- Quartzite
- Dolomite
- Feldspar
- Phosphates
- Mica
- Pyrites
- Talc

Energy-related installations

- Hydroelectric power plant
- Nuclear reactor
- Refinery

Population evolution and projection

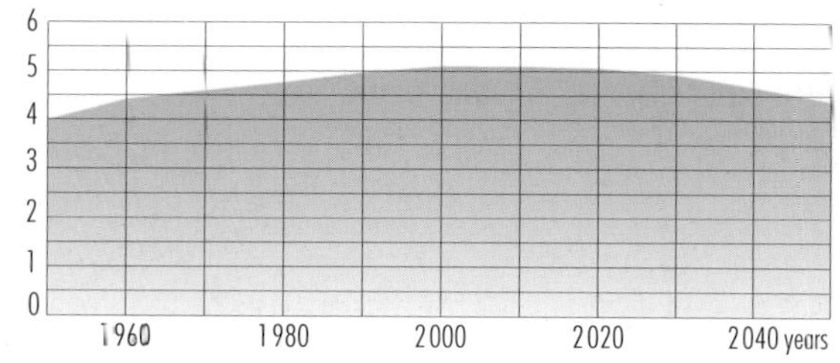

GDP structure

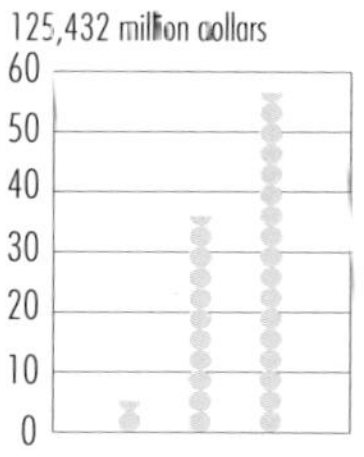

Labor force

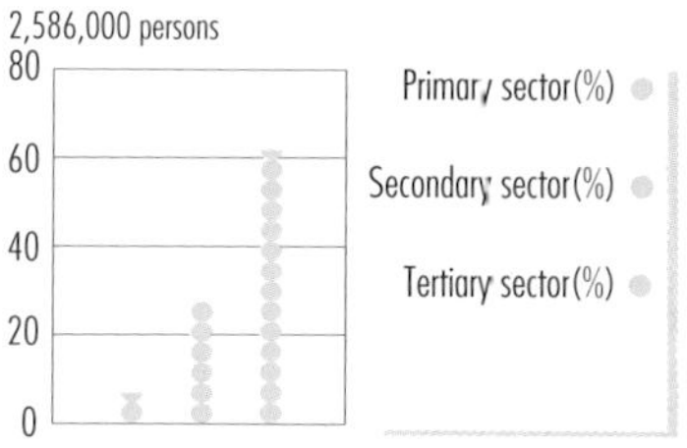

Population age distribution

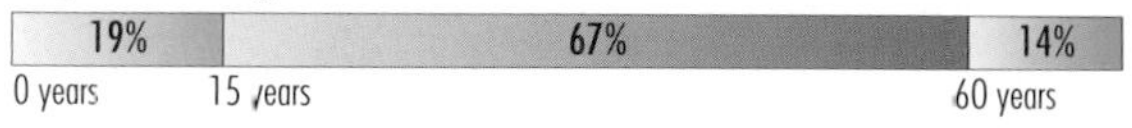

Vital statistics

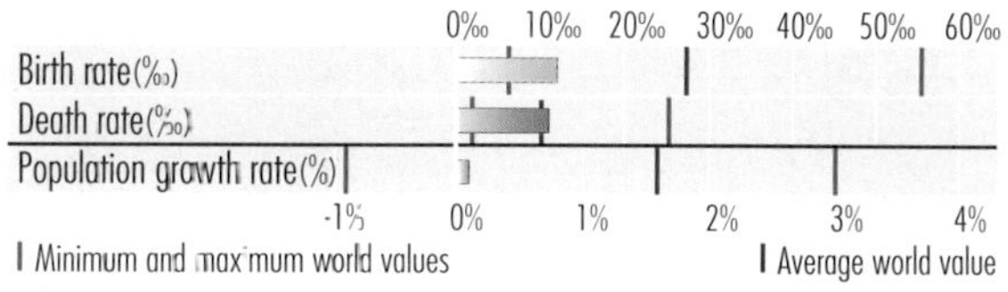

Literacy (% of population over15)

Per capita income (GDP per person)

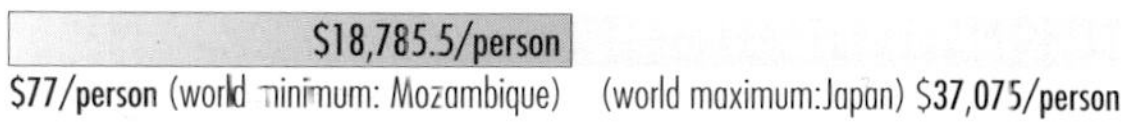

Unemployment (% of total population economically active)

Usos del suelo

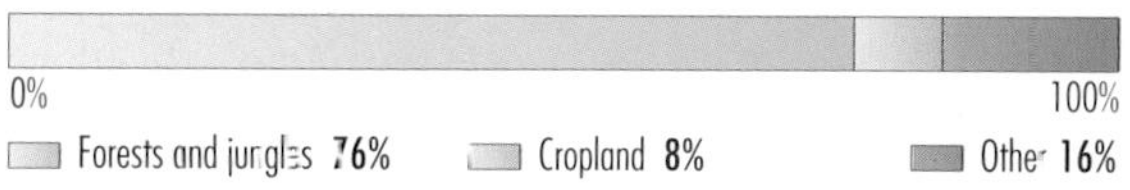

Industry

Manufacturing

- Food, beverages and tobacco
- Textiles, clothing, leather and footwear
- Wood, cork and furniture
- Paper and graphic arts
- Chemical products
- Building materials, glass and cement
- Metallurgy and metal products
- Machinery and transport equipment

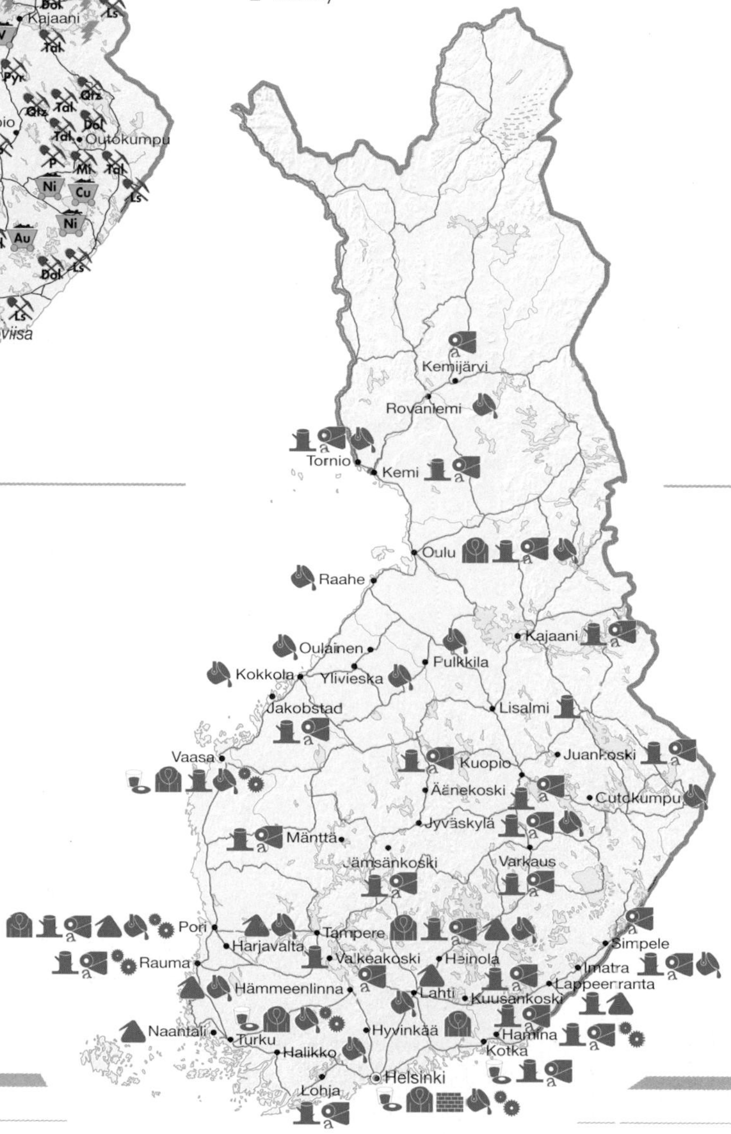

France

Official name: French Republic
Form of government: republic
Capital: Paris
Official language: French
Monetary unit: French franc
Religious affiliation: Roman Catholic (76.4%), other Christian (3.7%), atheist (3.4%), Muslim (3%), other (13.5%)
Ethnic composition of the population: French (93.6%), German (2.3%), Breton (1%), Catalan (0.4%), Arabic (2.5%), other (3.9%)
Area: 543,965 sq km
Total population: 58,298,814 inhabitants
Population density: 107.2 persons per sq km

Population evolution and projection

in millions of persons

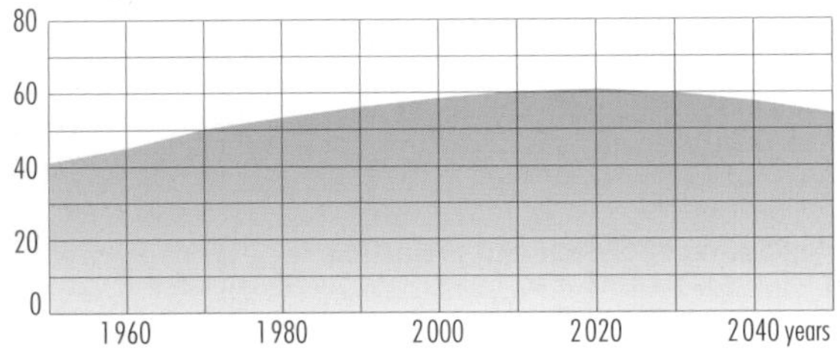

GDP structure

1,536,089 million dollars

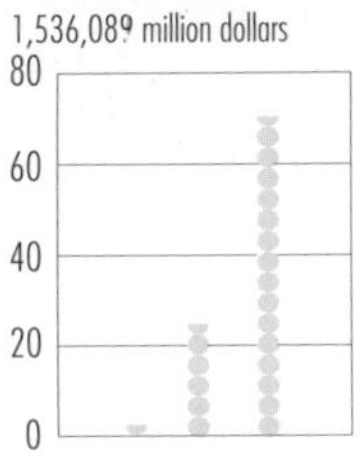

Labor force

25,506,000 persons

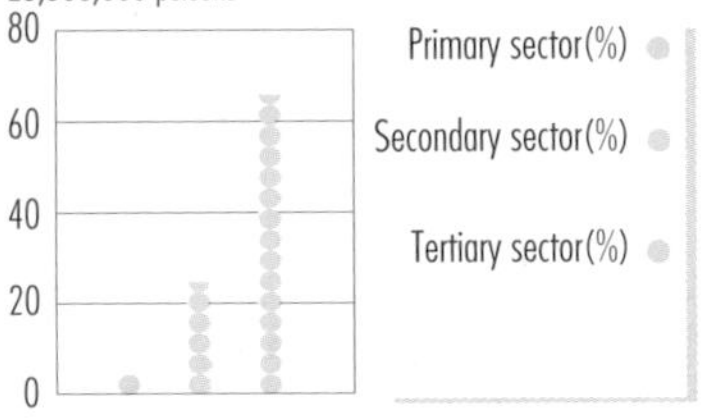

Population age distribution

0 years – 15 years	15 years – 60 years	60 years –
19%	65%	16%

Vital statistics

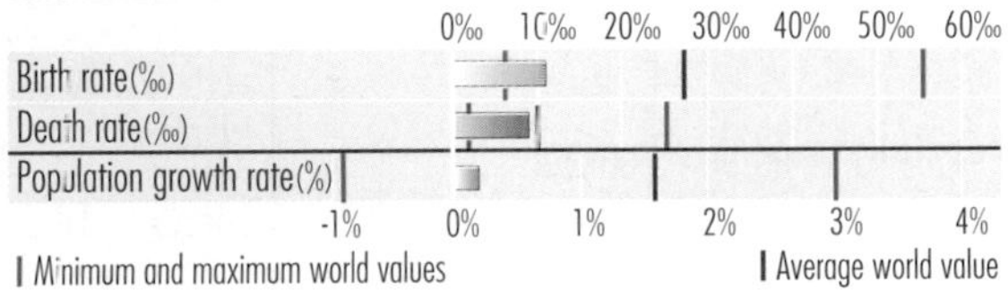

Literacy (% of population over15)

Total literate population	99%
Male literacy	98.9%
Female literacy	98.7%

0% – 100%

Per capita income (GDP per person)

$22,623.1/person

$77/person (world minimum: Mozambique) (world maximum:Japan) $37,075/person

Unemployment (% of total population economically active)

12.6%

0% – 50%

Land use

0% – 100%

Forests and jungles **27%**
Meadows and pastures **23%**
Cropland **34%**
Other **16%**

France is a state of the European Union, with coasts on the Atlantic and the Mediterranean Sea. Its terrain can be divided into three great units: plains, old mountain ranges or massifs and young mountain ranges. The plains of Artois, the Paris basin and others in the north and west of the country occupy two-thirds of France's total land area, with average altitudes below 350 m. The Paris basin is cut by the Seine, Loire, Meuse and Moselle Rivers, that communicate it with the plains of the Loire and of Aquitaine (watered by the Garonne and the Adour Rivers). The old massifs can be grouped into three sets: the Massif Central (Puy de Sancy, 1,858 m), the Armorican Massif and the Vosges Mountains. There are three young mountain ranges, uplifted by the Alpine folding: the Pyrenees, the Alps and the Jura. The Pyrenees, a natural barrier between France and Spain, extend for a distance of 450 km (Vignemale, 3,298 m). The Alps rise between France, Italy and Switzerland and in their French sector have the highest mountain of western Europe (Mont Blanc, 4,810 m) and enormous glaciers. The Jura Mountains penetrate into Switzerland and Germany (Reculet, 1,720 m). The Atlantic coastal areas have a marine west coast climate, with moderate temperatures, abundant precipitation and fogs and mists caused by the high humidity. On the eastern plains, continental climate traits are registered, to a greater extent towards the south, with great thermal oscillations between summer and winter and less rainfall. The southeast of the country has Mediterranean features, mild winters and very hot summers, with small amounts of precipitation.

France ranks among the European states with the greatest ethnic variety, due to the fact that it has received very large numbers of immigrants in recent decades. The great majority of its inhabitants are of French origin, but there are North African minorities (Algerians, Moroccans, Tunisians), Portuguese, Spanish, Italian and those of former overseas colonies. Three-fourths of the population —whose distribution is very uneven— reside in the cities, that have a radial structure, with a network of medium-sized centers surrounding a few megalopolis. (Paris, Lyon, Marseille).

Agriculture bases its high productivity on mechanization, crop specialization and the increase in the size of farms. Wheat, corn (maize), sugar beets, potatoes, vineyards, fruit trees, legumes and vegetables are harvested. Stock raising is oriented toward the production of cattle for meat and dairy products. The fishing industry has important fishing banks. In France, one of the world's great economic powers, the State controls key sectors such as finances, energy, communications, and heavy industry. The mining industry extracts coal, iron ore, bauxite, potash salts, zinc, lead and gold. The scarcity of petroleum is compensated for with nuclear energy. Industry, which is highly developed, encompasses all sectors; specially noteworthy are the iron and steel, automobile, aeronautical, weapons, mechanical, electrical and chemical production. The economically active population tends to concentrate in the tertiary sector (services). The French transport and communication system is one of the most modern and efficient in the world.

Mining and Energy

Non-energy source mineral resources

Metals

- Bauxite
- Zinc
- Copper
- Iron ore
- Gold
- Silver
- Lead
- Wolfram

Rocks and industrial minerals

- Sulphur
- Barite
- Fluorite
- Potash
- Salt
- Talc

Mineral fuel resources

Fossil fuels

- Coal
- Natural gas
- Petroleum

Radioactive fuel

- Uranium

Energy-related installations

- Hydroelectric power plant
- Nuclear reactor
- Refinery

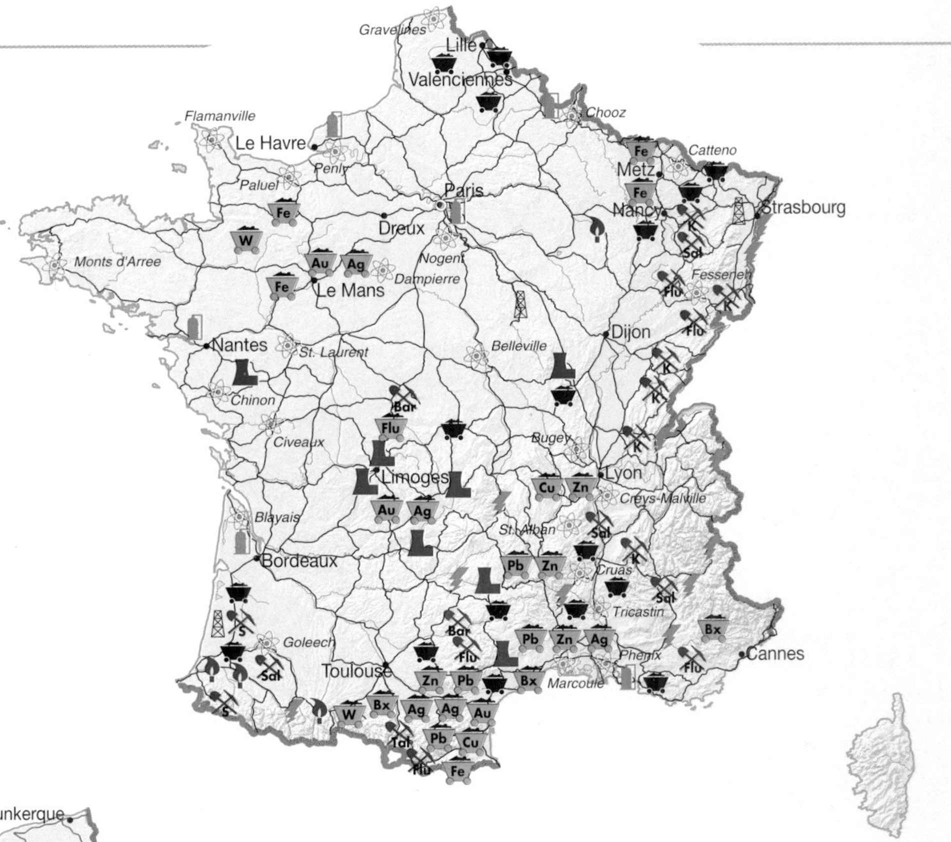

Industry

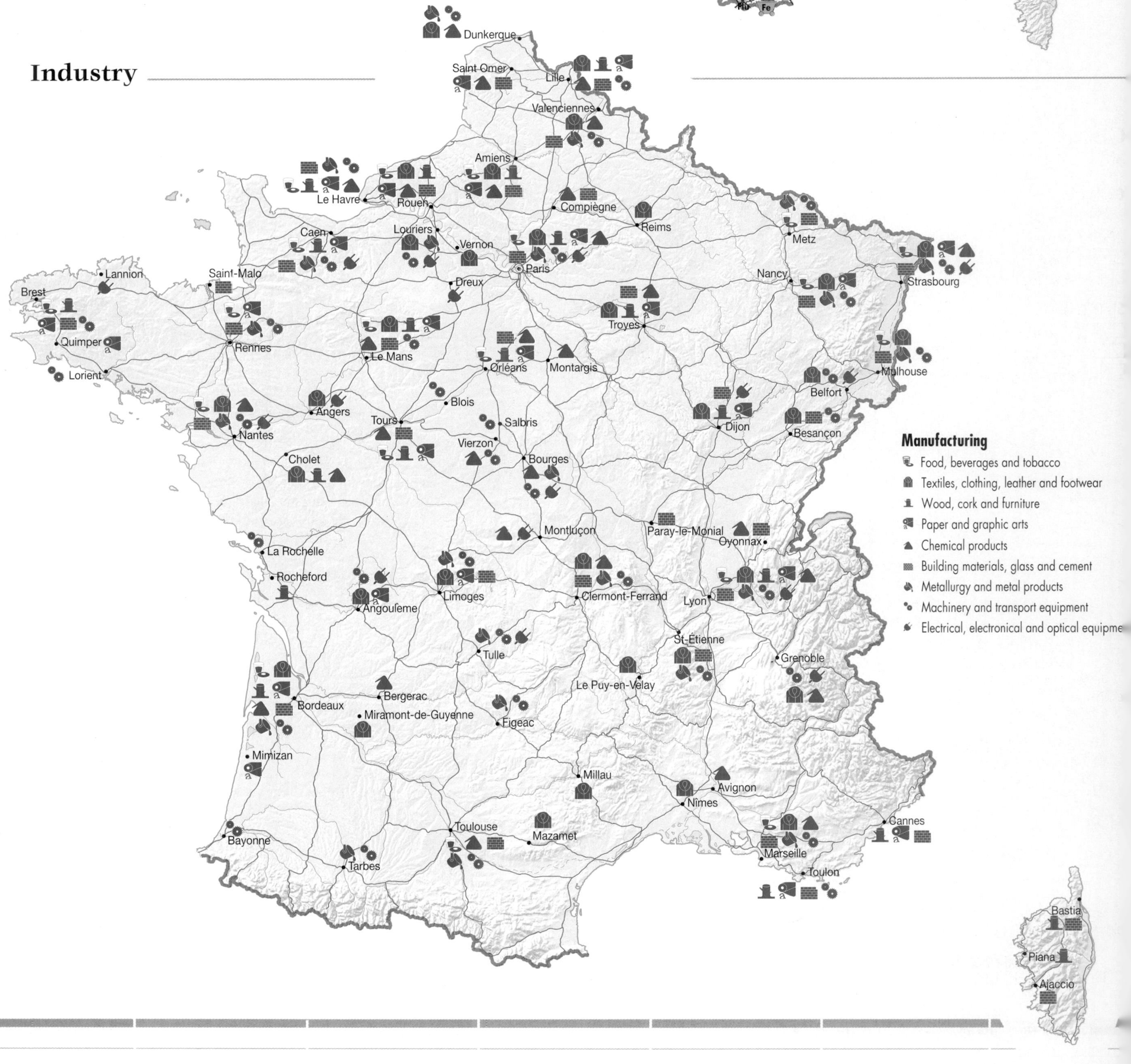

Manufacturing

- Food, beverages and tobacco
- Textiles, clothing, leather and footwear
- Wood, cork and furniture
- Paper and graphic arts
- Chemical products
- Building materials, glass and cement
- Metallurgy and metal products
- Machinery and transport equipment
- Electrical, electronical and optical equipme

Agriculture

Types of agriculture and livestock production

- Cereal farming (wheat, barley, oats, rye, corn)
- Croplands (cereals, sugar beets, forage crops)
- Mixed farming (grapes, olive trees, citrus fruits, fruit trees, horticulture and cereals)
- Intensive farming
- Highland pastures
- Forest/brush
- Urban area
- Rice
- Fruits and vegetables
- Apples
- Vineyards
- Vegetable oilseeds
- Olive trees
- Potatoes
- Vegetable fibers (flax)
- Sugar beets
- Tobacco
- Cattle
- Sheep
- Pigs
- Fishing

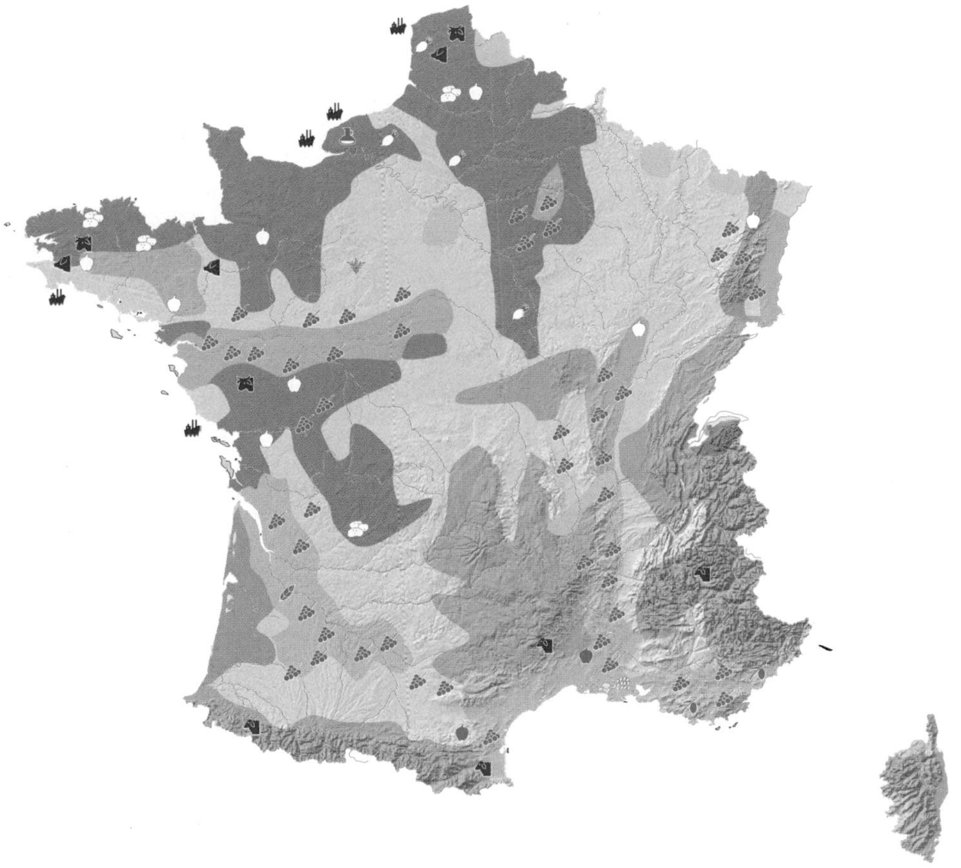

Geostructural units

Geology

- Paleozoic
- Mesozoic
- Tertiary
- Tertiary and Quaternary

Structures

- Caledonian and Hercynian roots
- Alpine systems
- Sedimentary covering

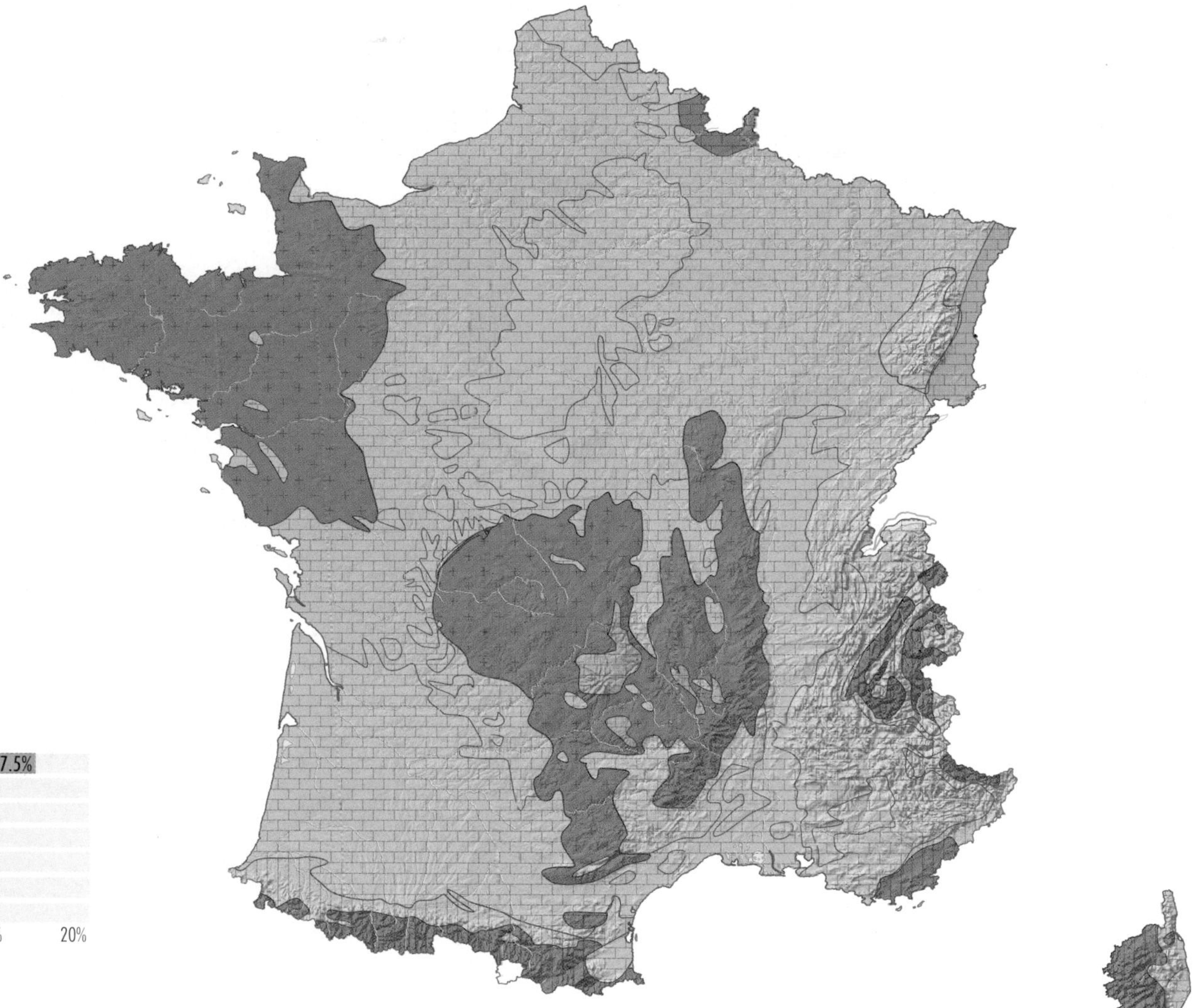

Major Import Sources

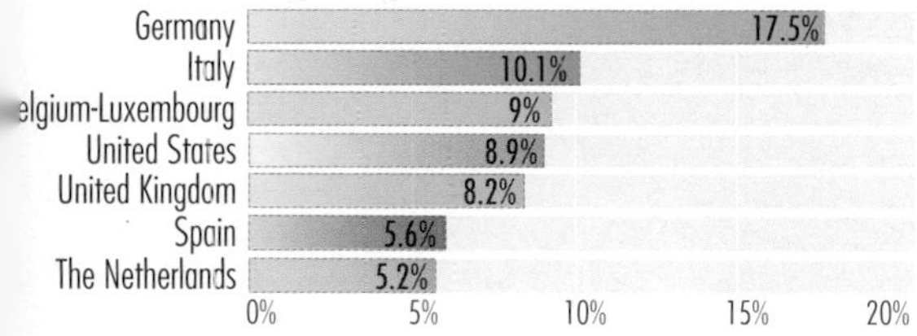

Major Export Destinations

Principal Imports

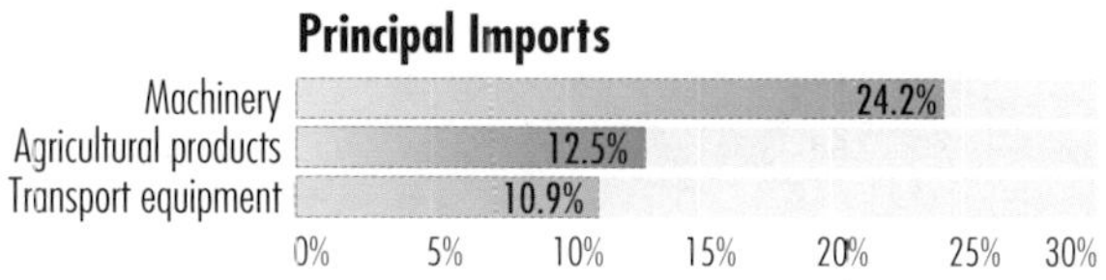

Principal Exports

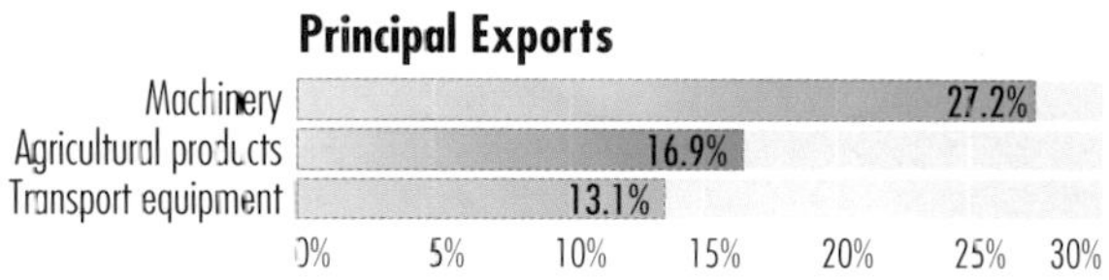

Germany

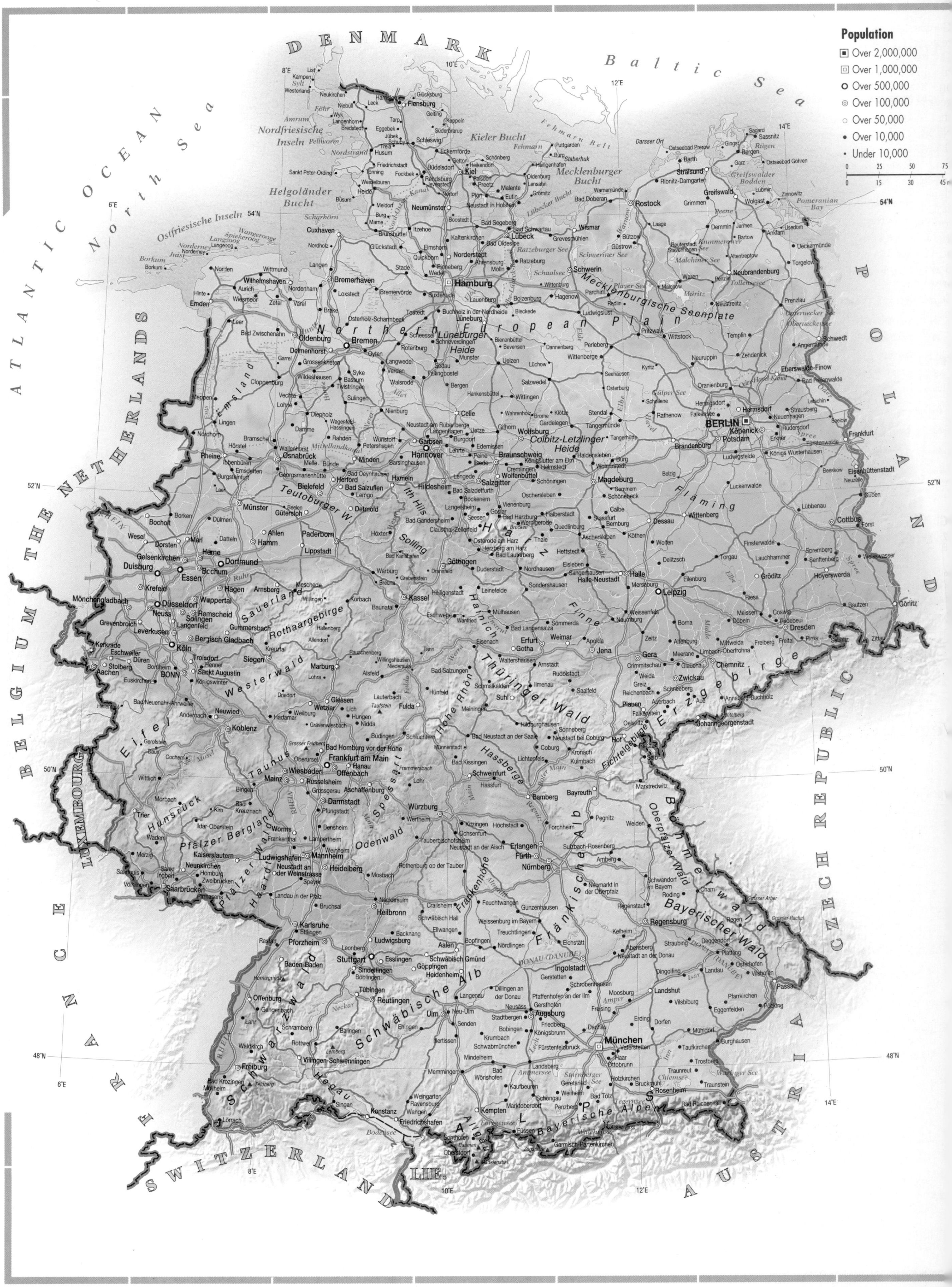
Population
Over 2,000,000
Over 1,000,000
Over 500,000
Over 100,000
Over 50,000
Over 10,000
Under 10,000
0 25 50 75
0 15 30 45
DENMARK
Baltic Sea
North Sea
ATLANTIC OCEAN
THE NETHERLANDS
BELGIUM
LUXEMBOURG
FRANCE
SWITZERLAND
LIE.
AUSTRIA
CZECH REPUBLIC
POLAND
54°N
52°N
50°N
48°N
6°E
8°E
10°E
12°E
14°E
BERLIN
Hamburg
München
Köln
Frankfurt am Main
Stuttgart
Dresden
Leipzig
Hannover
Bremen
Kiel
Rostock
Nürnberg

Germany is a state in central Europe in which three natural regions can be distinguished: the plains of northern Germany, a transition zone formed by a varied system of massifs and depressions in central and southern Germany, and a pre-alpine and alpine region in the south. The general slope of the lands, from south to north, determines that the majority of the rivers have their mouths in the North Sea —the Rhine (Rhein), Ems, Weser, and Elba Elbe)—, except the Danube (Donau), which flows into the Black Sea, and the Oder, which flows into the Baltic. Germany has a transition climate between the temperate climate of western Europe and the continental climate of eastern Europe. In the north, the presence of the sea is the conditioning factor for summers that are not as warm as in the south. Regular precipitation falls throughout the year, heavier in the mountains than in the basins.
Germans have a heterogeneous origin; the Nordic type predominates and Alpine and Dinaric traits abound, but Celtic, Mediterranean and Slavic characteristics are also found among its population. The agricultural sector produces cereals, vegetables, fruit trees and tobacco. The country has important livestock production, especially pigs and cattle. Forest resources are exploited and winter tourism, in the southern area above all, provides important revenues. German industry constitutes one of the principal economic motors of Europe, in spite of the difficulties that have arisen in the adaptation of the planned economy of the former East Germany to a free market system after re-unification. The cities are active industrial centers; the most important branches are textiles, paper, electrochemical, watch-making, the mechanical industry, metallurgy, etc. The ports not only fulfill a commercial function, but also powerful sectors such as the naval, mechanical, automobile and petroleum (refined and derivatives) have developed in them. Important mining centers (lignite, copper and iron) are found in the northernmost part of Germany; the mountains situated between the Ardennes and the Hessen depression hold the great mining and industrial basins of Ruhr and Aachen.

Official name: Federal Republic of Germany
Form of government: federal republic
Capital: Berlin
Official language: German
Monetary unit: Deutsche mark
Religious affiliation: Protestant (45%), Roman Catholic (37%), unaffiliated and other (18%)
Ethnic composition of the population: German (95.1%), Turkish (2.3%), Italian (0.7%), Greek (0.4%), Polish (0.4%), other (1.1%)
Area: 356,959 sq km
Total population: 83,536,000 inhabitants
Population density: 234 persons per sq km

Population evolution and projection
in millions of persons

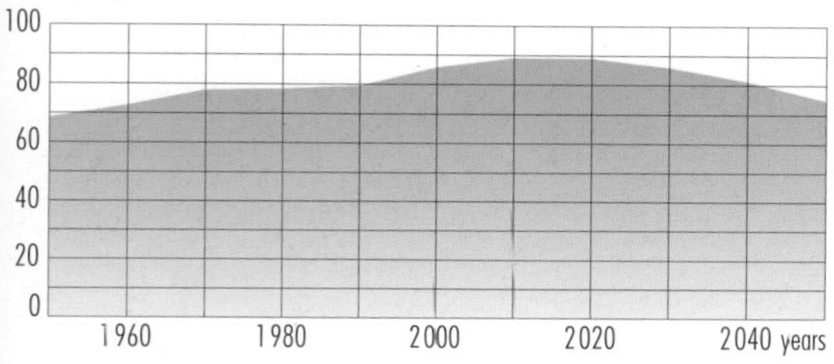

GDP structure
2,415,764 million dollars

Labor force
40,127,000 persons

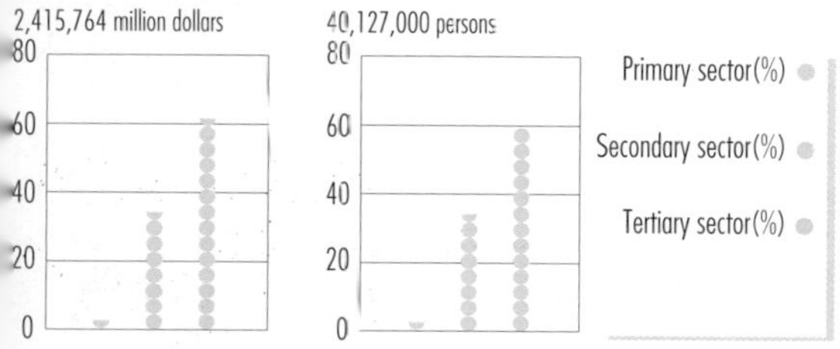

Population age distribution

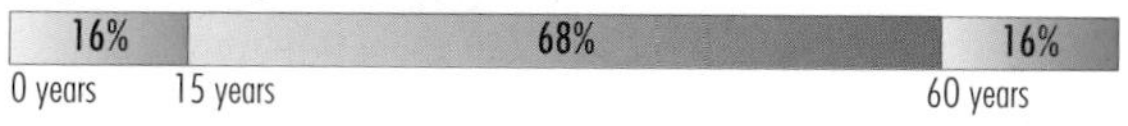

Vital statistics

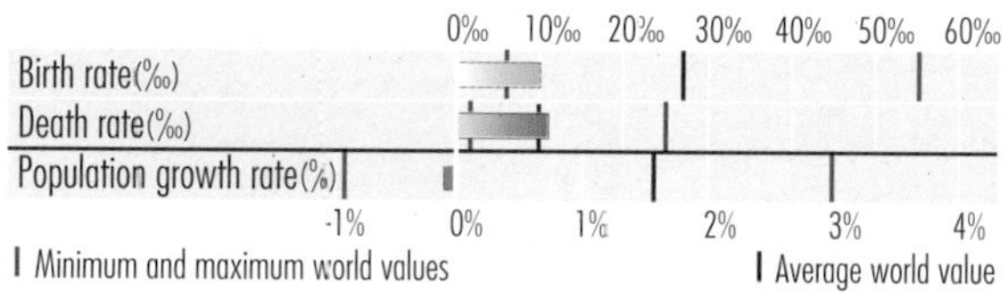

Literacy (% of population over15)

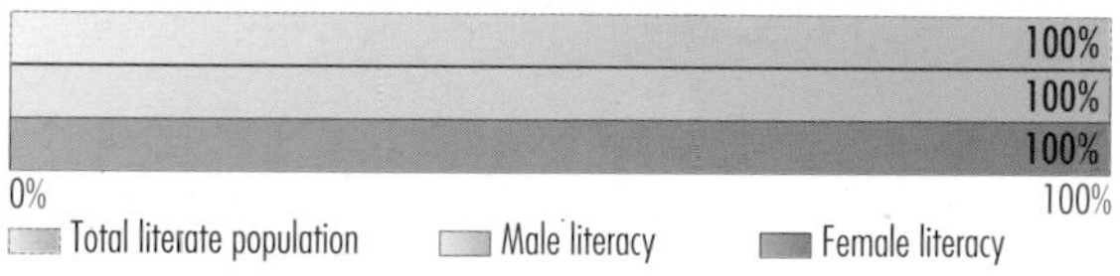

Per capita income (GDP per person)

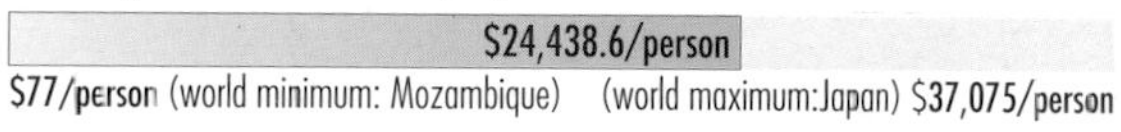

Unemployment (% of total population economically active)

Land use

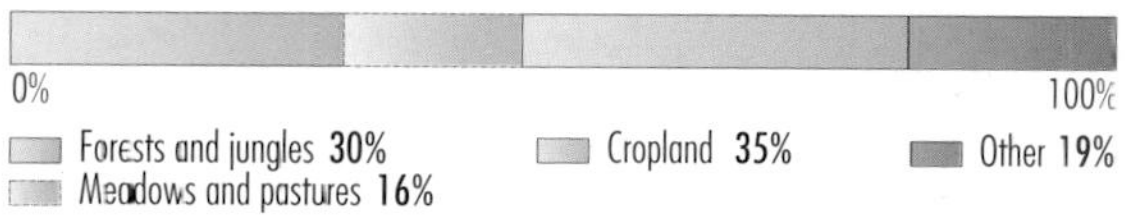

Population

Population density (persons per sq km)

- Fewer than 125
- From 125 to 175
- From 175 to 225
- From 225 to 325
- From 325 to 425
- From 425 to 750
- From 750 to 2,000
- More than 2,000

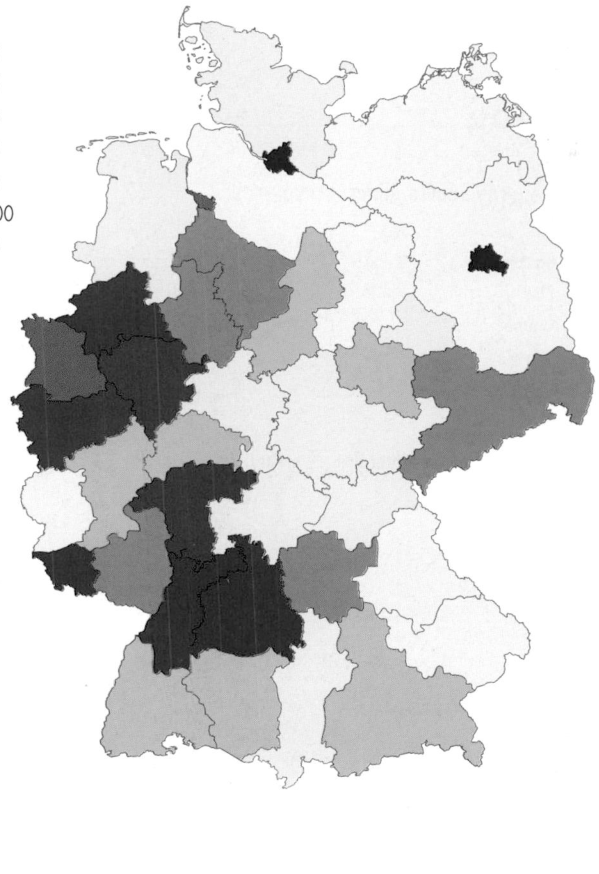

Vegetation

Types of Vegetation

- Mixed forest
- Deciduous forest
- Mesophytic oak forest
- Mesophytic beech forest
- Mesophytic forest
- Semi-xerophytic pine forest
- Halophytic grassland (prairie)
- Pastures
- Riverine vegetation

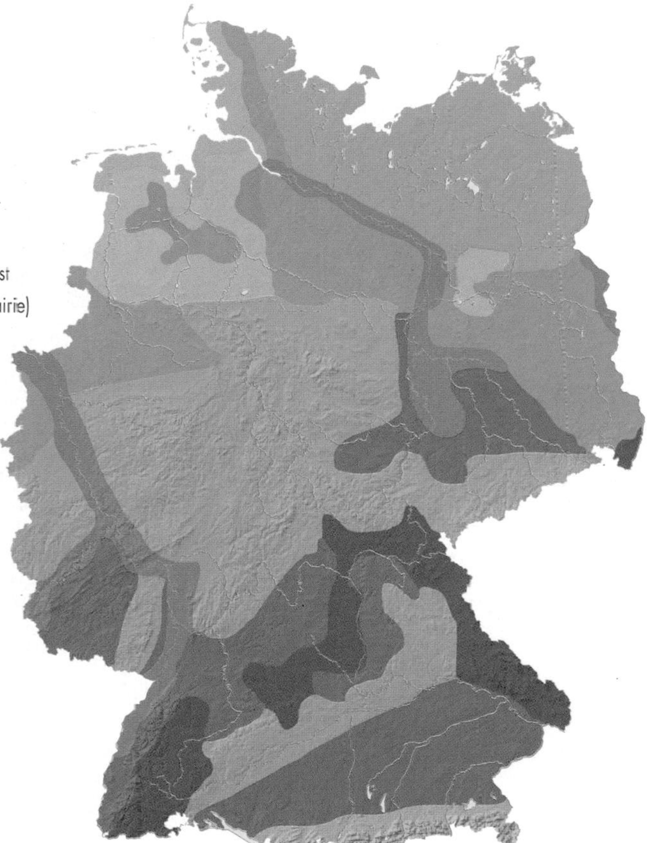

Energy

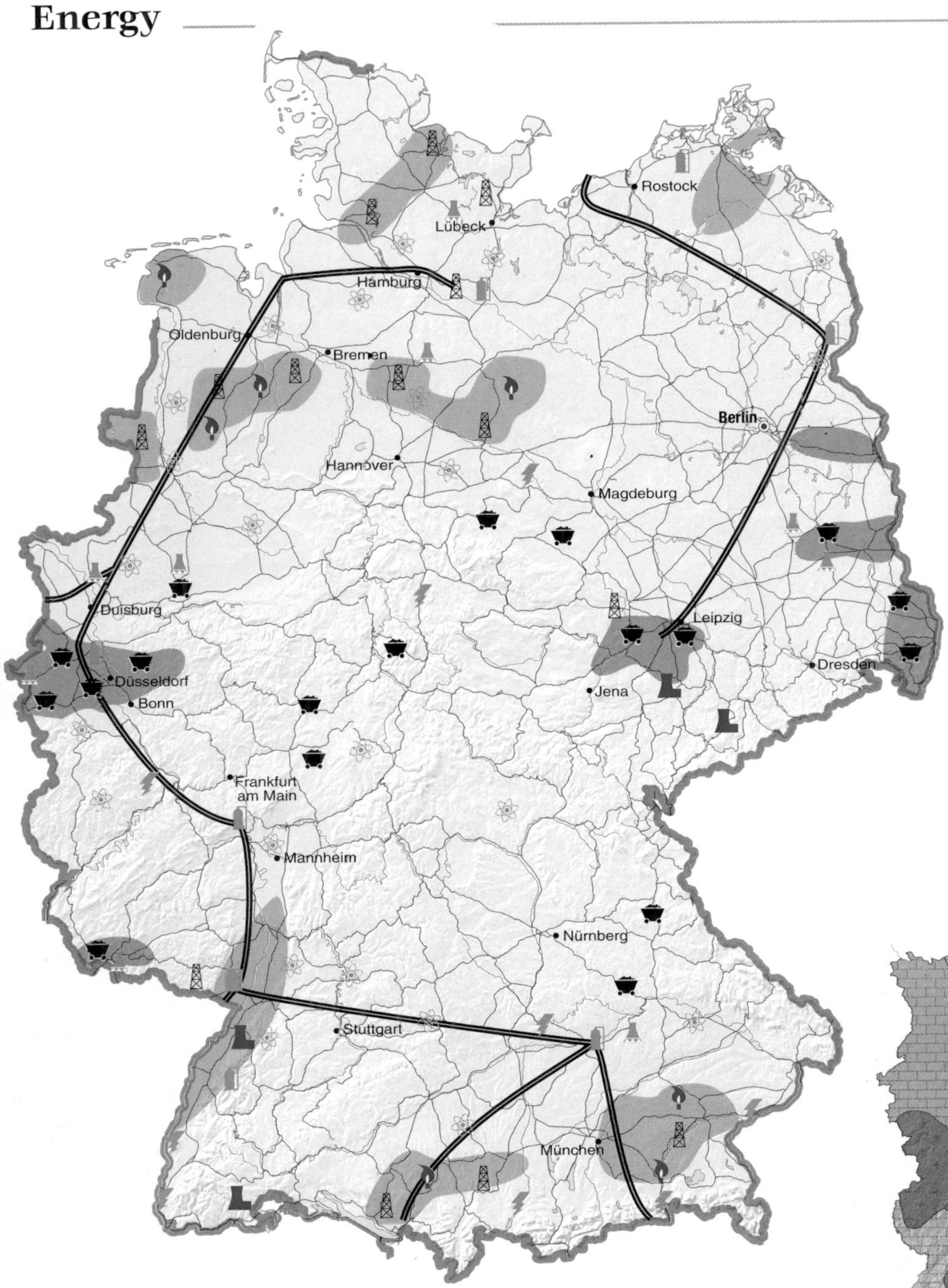

Mineral fuel resources

Fossil fuels

- Coal
- Natural gas
- Petroleum
- Coal fields
- Natural gas or oil field

Radioactive fuel

- Uranium

Energy-related installations

- Hydroelectric power plant
- Nuclear reactor
- Thermal power plant
- Refinery
- Oil pipeline

Geostructural units

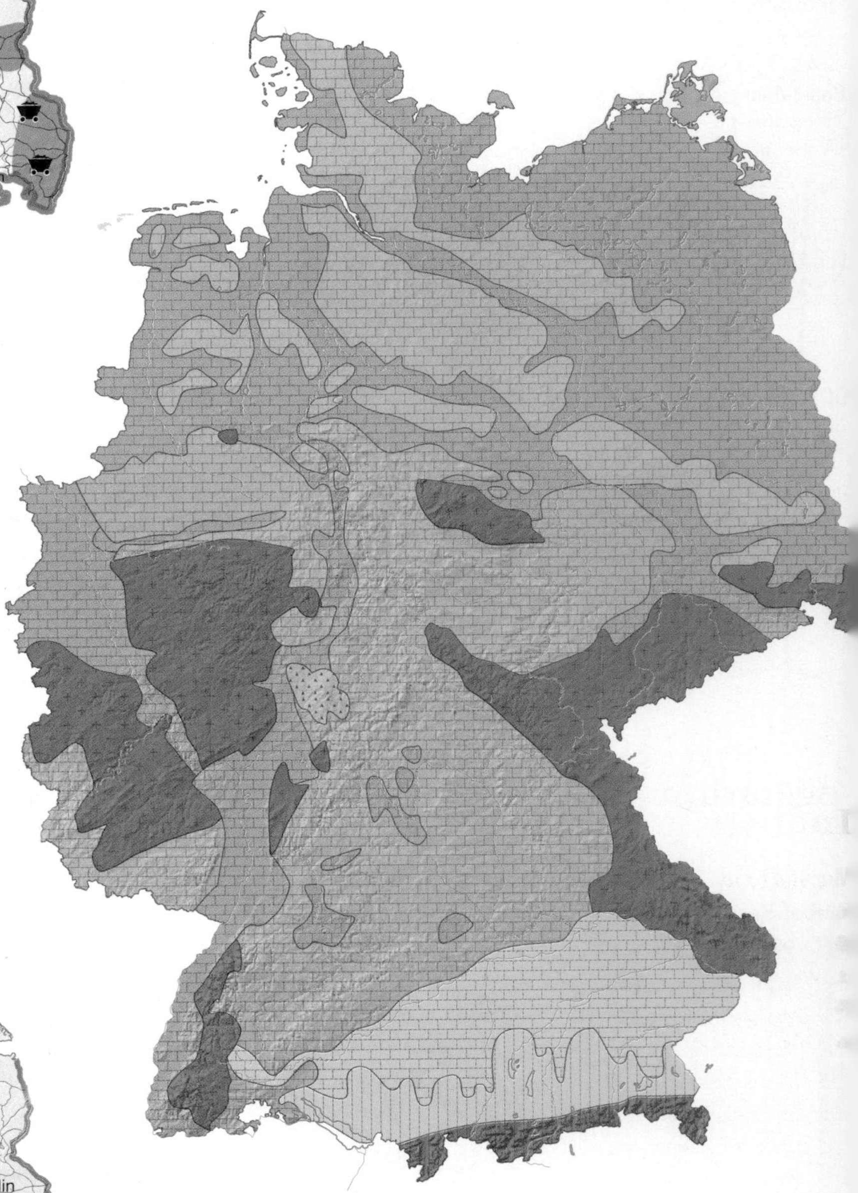

Geology

- Paleozoic
- Mesozoic
- Tertiary
- Quaternary

Structures

- Caledonian and Hercynian roc
- Alpine systems
- Sedimentary covering
- Volcanic areas

Mining

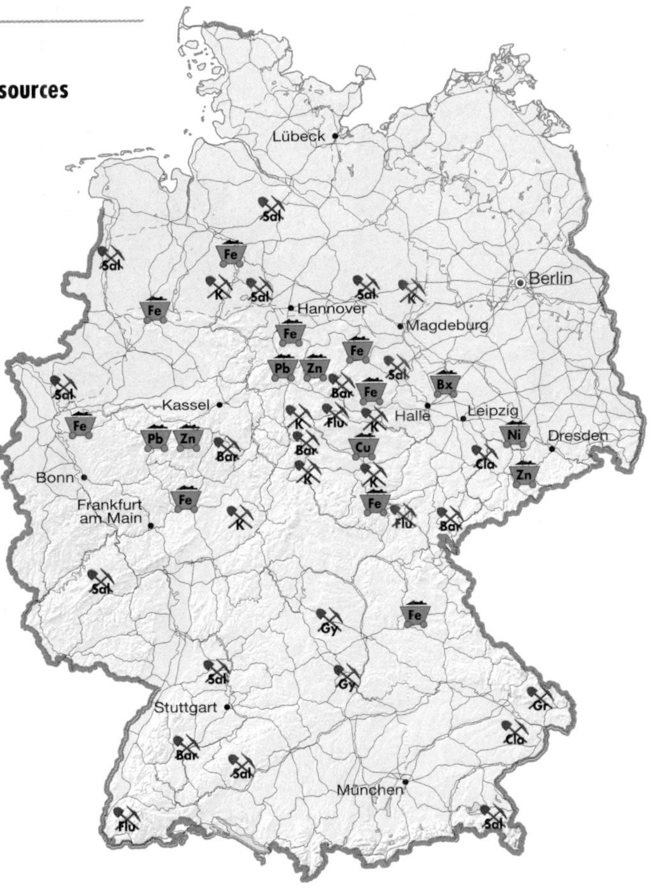

Non-energy source mineral resources

Metals

- Bauxite
- Zinc
- Copper
- Iron ore
- Nickel
- Lead

Rocks and industrial minerals

- Clays
- Barite
- Fluorite
- Graphite
- Potash
- Salt
- Gypsum

Agriculture

Types of agriculture and livestock production

- Cereal-farming (barley, wheat, rye)
- Croplands (cereals, sugar beets, hops, potatoes, fruit trees)
- Perennial crops (vineyards)
- Highland pastures
- Forests
- Urban area
- Apples
- Grapevines
- Vegetable oilseed crops
- Potatoes
- Vegetable fibers
- Sugar beets
- Hops
- Tobacco
- Cattle
- Sheep
- Pigs
- Fishing

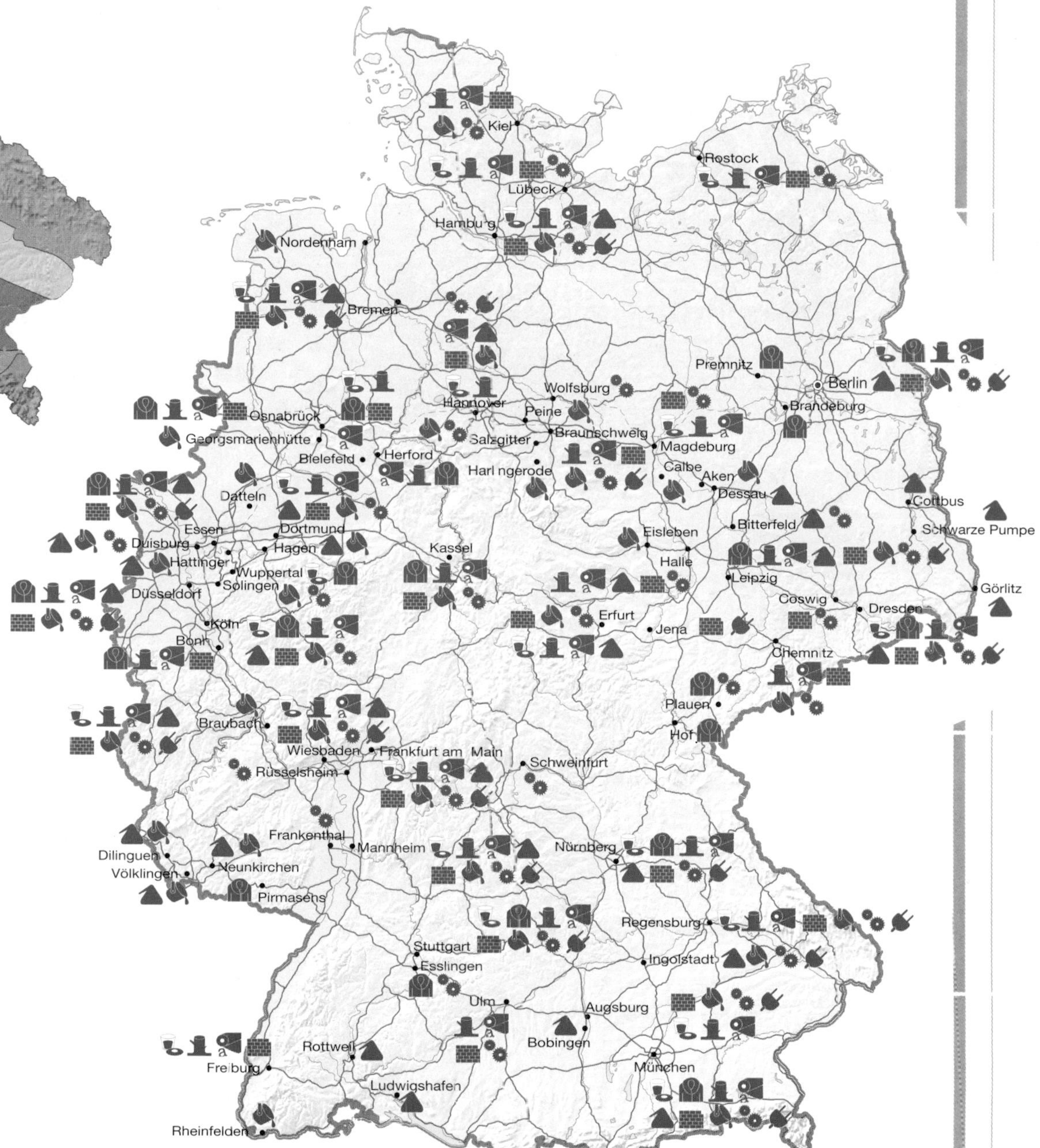

Industry

Manufacturing

- Food, beverages and tobacco
- Textiles, clothing, leather and footwear
- Wood, cork and furniture
- Paper and graphic arts
- Chemical products
- Chemical products
- Building materials, glass and cement
- Metallurgy and metal products
- Machinery and transport equipment
- Electrical, electronical and optical equipment

Major Import Sources

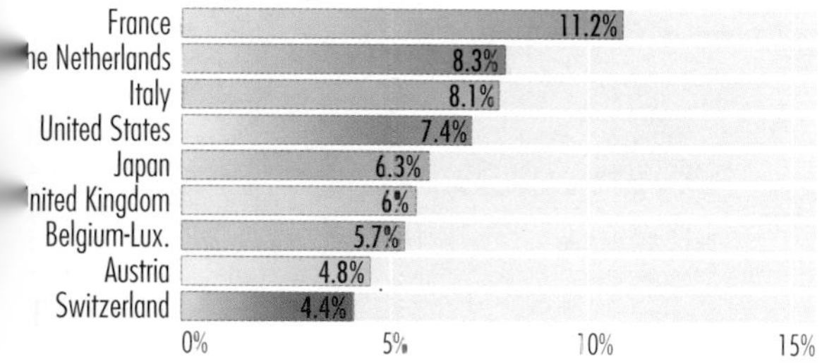

Major Export Destinations

Principal Imports

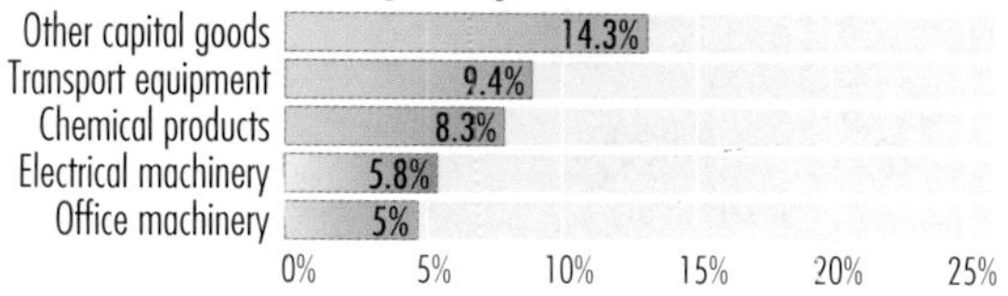

Principal Exports

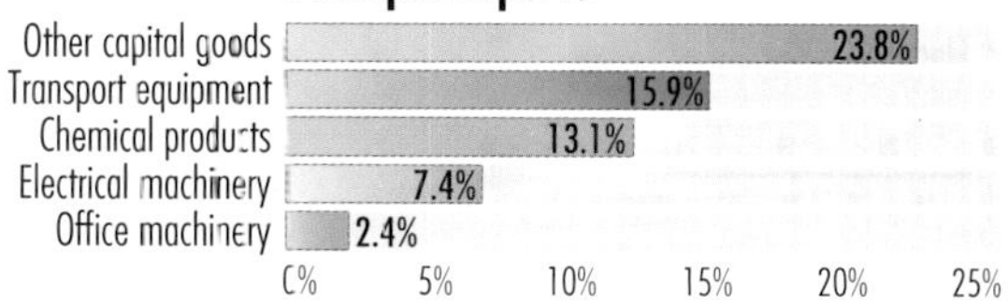

Hungary

Hungary is a landlocked state of eastern Europe that occupies the Carpathian Basin (situated on the Pannonian Plain). Most of the land area is below 200 m in altitude; the highest Hungarian peaks (Mátra Mountains) only reach 1,015 m. The Great Plain encompasses the central part of the country, watered by the Danube and Tisza Rivers (main watercourses). In the west, the Little Plain has its natural borders in the Sopron and Köszeg Massifs (Eastern Alps). Lake Balaton occupies a tectonic trough and is characterized by its shallow depth (an average of 3.5 m). The climate is continental, although it is influenced by air masses of Mediterranean origin. Regional variations are scarcely registered: the humid seasons run from May to June and from October to November, with short warm summers and long cold winters. The average annual temperature ranges between the 11 °C of the plain and the 8 °C of the mountains. The Hungarian ethnic group (Magyars) comprises most of the population. A fifth of the inhabitants are concentrated in Budapest, the capital. Agriculture is based on the techniques of intensive farming practiced in cooperatives (wheat, corn, oats, barley, rye, rice, potatoes, beets, tobacco, vineyards). The conditions of the terrain favor extensive ranching. Light industries are numerically predominant, very widely spread throughout the country (chemical, food-processing, textile branches). The tourist industry is experiencing moments of expansion. The transport and communication network requires substantial improvement.

Official name: Republic of Hungary
Form of government: republic
Capital: Budapest
Official language: Hungarian
Monetary unit: forint
Religious affiliation: Roman Catholic (67.5%), Calvinist (20%), Lutheran (5%), atheist and other (7.5%)
Ethnic composition of the population: Hungarian [Magyar] (89.9%), Gypsy (4%), German (2.6%), Serb (2%), Slovak (0.8%), Rumanian (0.7%)
Area: 93,033 sq km
Total population: 10,003,000 inhabitants
Population density: 107.5 persons per sq km

Mining and Energy

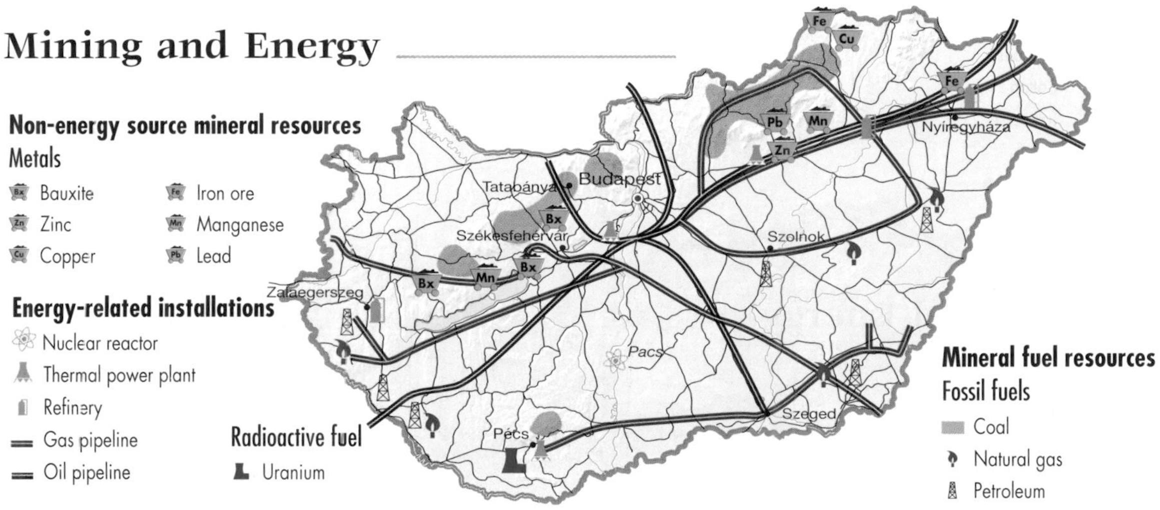

Population evolution and projection

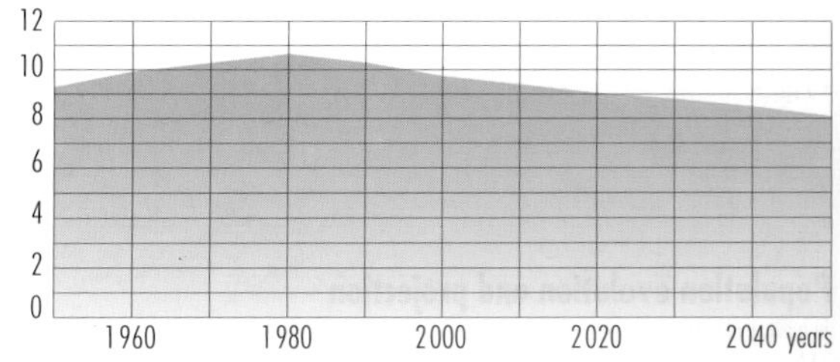

Vital statistics

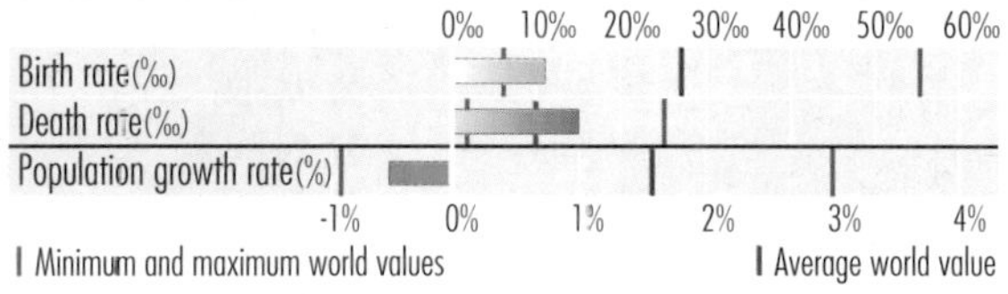

Per capita income (GDP per person)

$77/person (world minimum: Mozambique) (world maximum: Japan) $37,075/person

GDP structure

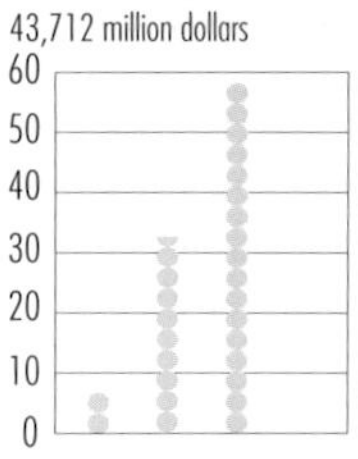

Labor force

Unemployment (% of total population economically active)

Literacy (% of population over15)

Land use

Population age distribution

Population

- Over 2,000,000
- Over 100,000
- Over 50,000
- Over 10,000
- Under 10,000

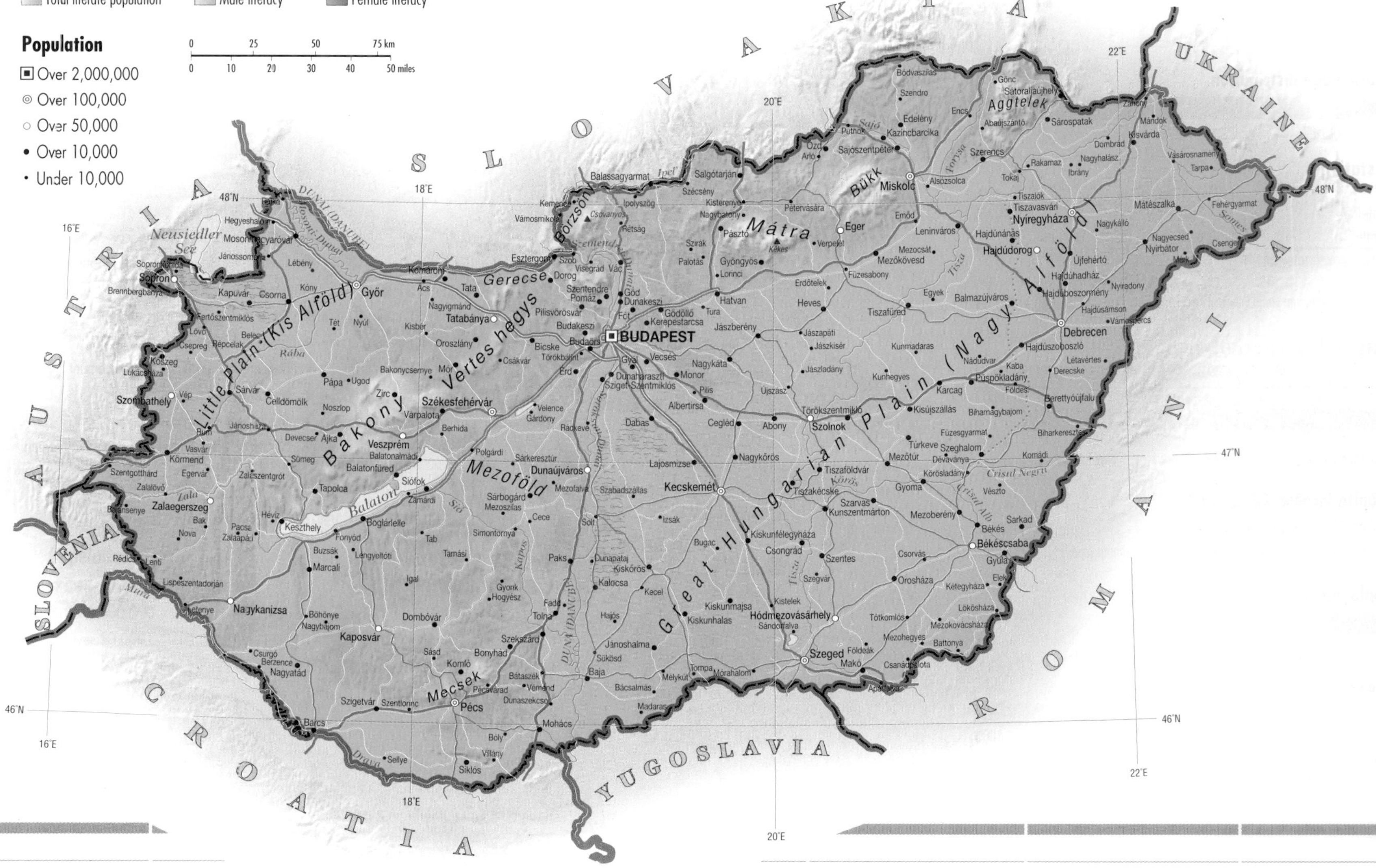

Industry and Agriculture

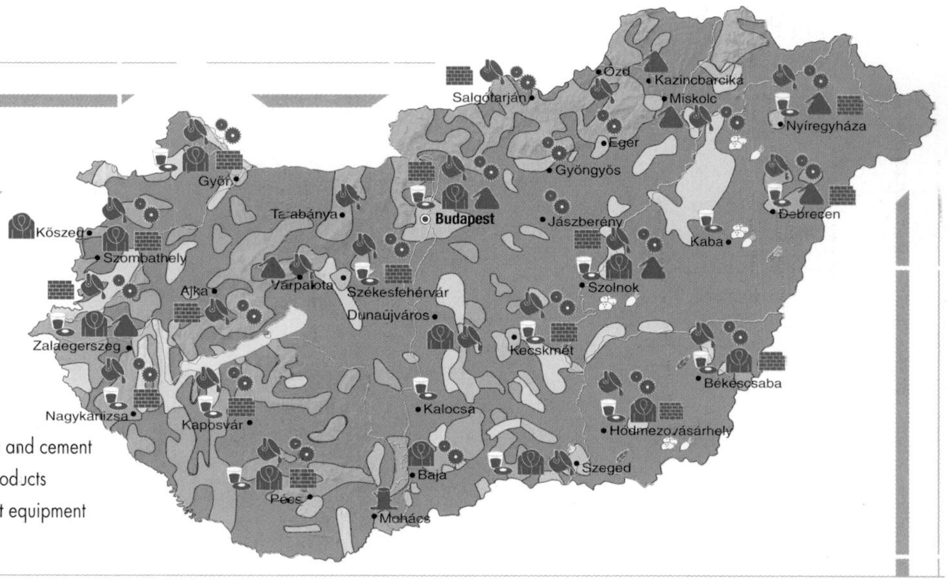

Types of agriculture and livestock production

- Croplands (cereals, forage crops, root crops, sunflowers) and animal husbandry
- Perennial crops (grapevines) and vegetables
- Meadows and pastures
- Forest/brush
- Urban area
- Sugar beets
- Potatoes
- Tobacco

Manufacturing

- Food, beverages and tobacco
- Textiles, clothing, leather and footwear
- Wood, cork and furniture
- Chemical products
- Building materials, glass and cement
- Metallurgy and metal products
- Machinery and transport equipment

Iceland

Iceland is an island state situated in the North Atlantic. Of volcanic origin, the present-day relief, modified by the action of the ice that covers almost all the island, has been shaped by Quaternary faults and sunken blocks. It possesses many rivers, small lakes, glaciers, geysers and thermal springs. The climate of the north has extremely cold average temperatures, while in the southern region, the warm current of the Gulf Stream confers certain nuances characteristic of a marine west coast climate. The people are very homogeneous, descendants of the colonists that arrived on the island towards the 9th century B.C. The greatest population density is registered in the area of the capital, Reykjavik, while a large part of the territory remains almost uninhabited. The fishing catches and the manufacture of fish products constitute one of the mainstays of the economy. The waters of the volcanic underground make it possible to create greenhouses for the cultivation of vegetables, besides being utilized for home heating. The main crops are forage crops, hay and potatoes.

Official name: Republic of Iceland

Form of government: constitutional republic

Capital: Reykjavik

Official language: Icelandic

Monetary unit: Icelandic króna

Religious affiliation: Protestant (96.3%), Roman Catholic (0.9%), nonreligious (1.4%), other (1.4%)

Ethnic composition of the population: Icelandic (96.1%), Danish (0.8%), Swedish (0.5%), persons born in the United States (0.5%), German (0.3%), other (1.8%)

Area: 102,819 sq km

Total population: 270,292 inhabitants

Population density: 2.6 persons per sq km

Population evolution and projection

in thousands of persons

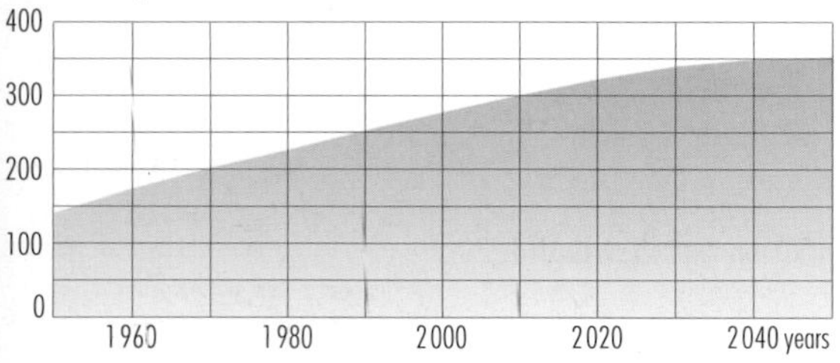

GDP structure

7,052 million dollars

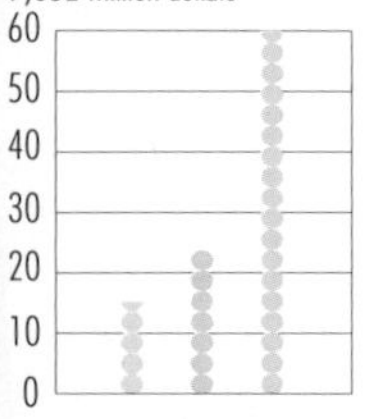

Labor force

151,000 persons

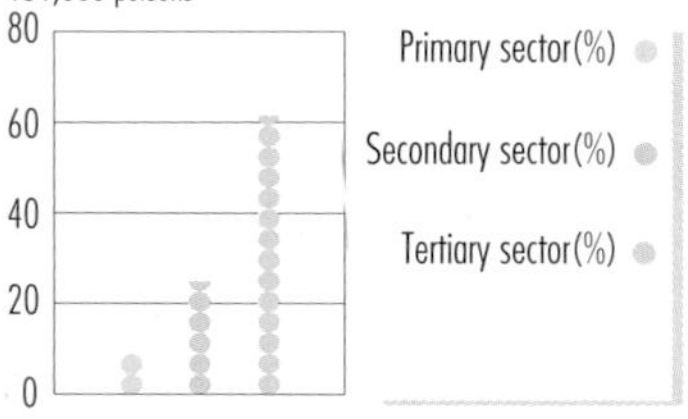

Population age distribution

0 years–15 years	15 years–60 years	60 years–
24%	65%	11%

Vital statistics

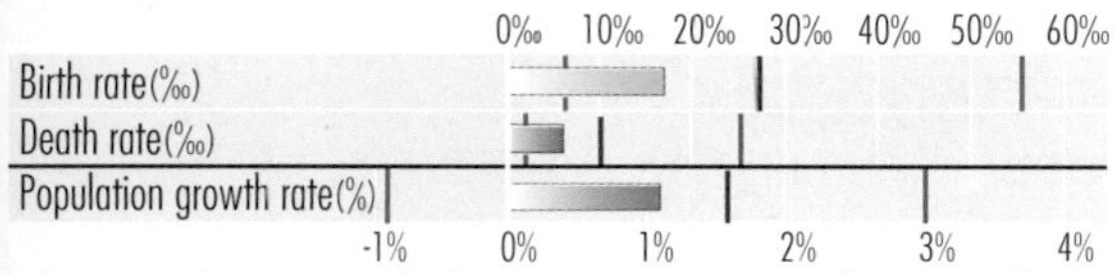

| Minimum and maximum world values | | Average world value

Literacy (% of population over15)

Total literate population	100%
Male literacy	100%
Female literacy	100%

Per capita income (GDP per person)

$22,568.2/person

$77/person (world minimum: Mozambique) (world maximum:Japan) $37,075/person

Land use

- Forests and jungles 1%
- Cropland 1%
- Other 78%
- Meadows and pastures 20%

Unemployment (% of total population economically active)

7% (scale 0%–50%)

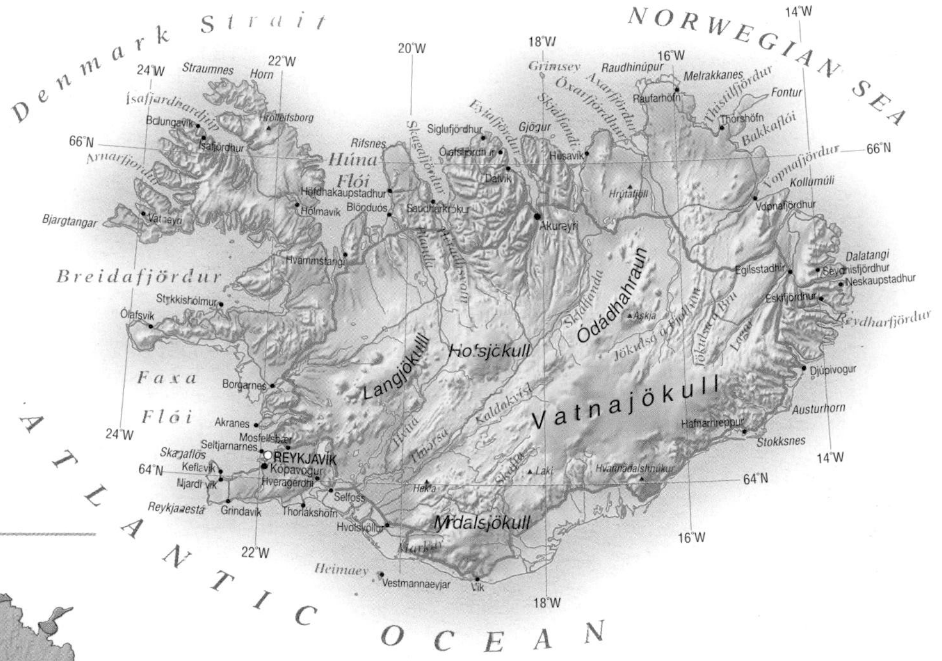

Agriculture, Industry and Mining

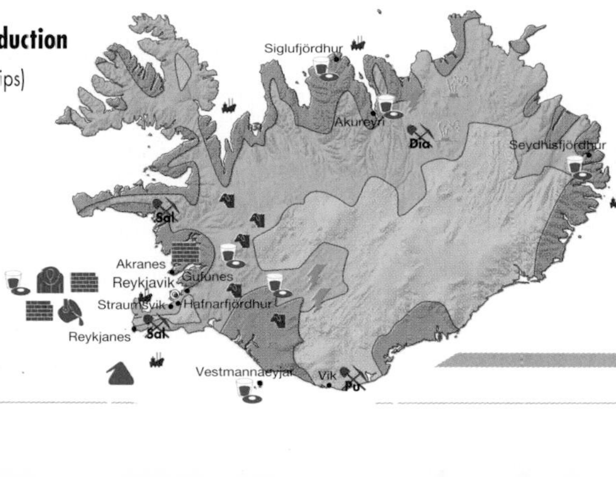

Types of agriculture and livestock production

- Croplands (Forage crops, potatoes, turnips)
- Highland pastures and farming
- Non-arable lands
- Sheep
- Fishing

Non-energy source mineral resources

Rocks and industrial minerals

- Diatomite
- Pumice stone
- Salt

Manufacturing

- Food, beverages and tobacco
- Textiles, clothing, leather and footwear
- Chemical products
- Building materials, glass and cement
- Metallurgy and metal products

Energy-related installations

- Geothermal power plant
- Hydroelectric power plant

Ireland

Ireland is a republic of northwestern Europe that occupies more than three-fourths of the island of Ireland, the second in area and the westernmost of the British Isles. Its territory includes the islands of Achill and Clare and also the Aran Islands archipelago. The Irish coasts have a very rugged outline, with fiords, estuaries and peninsulas formed by the erosive action of the Quaternarian glaciers. The relief consists of a great central plain surrounded by groups of low altitude hills. The river courses, all short in length, feed numerous swamps and lakes; the Shannon River deserves mention because of its length (198 km). The country has a marine west coast climate, influenced by the mild winds proceeding from the southwest and the Gulf Stream (of warm waters). It rains all year long —the regional precipitation varies between 600 and 1,500 mm— and the average temperatures oscillate between 0 ºC (winter) and 16 ºC (summer). The population has Celtic roots and reveals ethnic homogeneity, but has been reduced over the last two centuries by emigration (especially towards the USA). English is more wide-spread than the Gaelic language, native to the country. The great majority of the Irish profess Roman Catholicism. The farming and livestock production sector constitutes one of the basis of the national economy, and is organized according to the model of family farms. Cereals, beets and potatoes are grown. Extensive livestock raising has become extremely important, especially that of cattle and sheep. Sea fishing is scarcely developed, which is not the case of river fishing, with large catches of salmon. Ireland possesses few mineral resources; therefore, its sources of energy depend on importation. Industry is centered on textile and food-processing factories, but has begun to spread to the chemical and electrical branches. The tourist industry —a growing activity— sustains a dense network of hotels and of services. The European Union has granted very large loans to Ireland so than it can overcome its territorial imbalances and the traditional foreign economic dependence on the United Kingdom.

Official name: Éire (Ireland)
Form of government: parliamentary republic
Capital: Dublin
Official language: Gaelic, English
Monetary unit: Irish pound
Religious affiliation: Roman Catholic (93.1%), Anglican (2.8%), Presbyterian (0.4%), other (3.7%)
Ethnic composition of the population: Irish (96%)
Area: 70,285 sq km
Total population: 3,567,000 inhabitants
Population density: 50.8 persons per sq km

0 25 50 75 km
0 15 30 45 miles

Population
- ◎ Over 100,000
- ○ Over 50,000
- • Over 10,000
- · Under 10,000

Population evolution and projection
in millions of persons

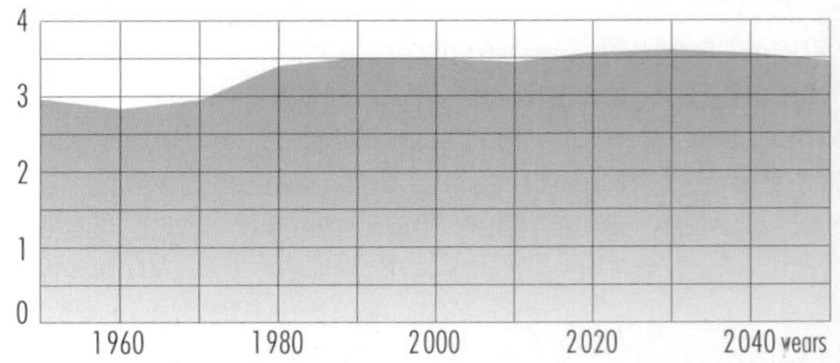

GDP structure
60,780 million dollars

Labor force
1,388,000 persons

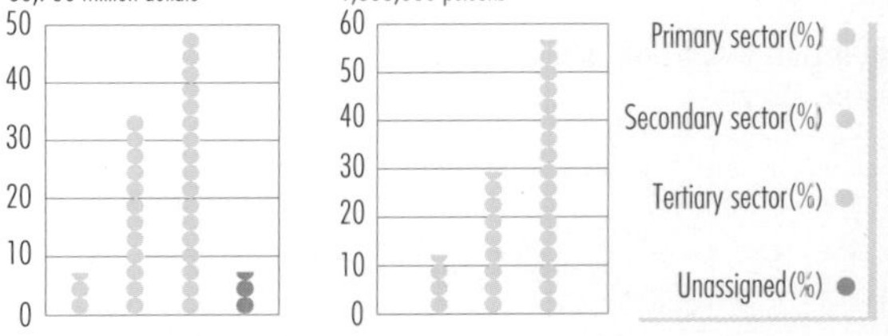

Population age distribution

24%	64%	12%
0 years	15 years	60 years

Vital statistics

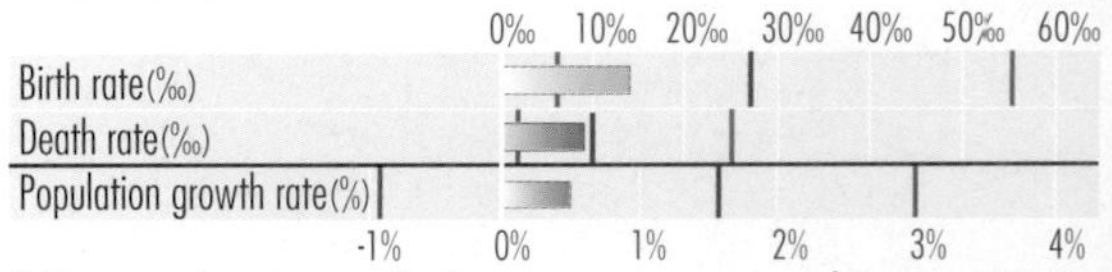

I Minimum and maximum world values
I Average world value

Types of agriculture and livestock production
- Cereal-farming (barley, wheat, oats)
- Croplands (cereals, forage crops, potatoes)
- Meadows
- Highland pastures
- Extensive livestock raising
- Urban area

Literacy (% of population over15)

Total literate population	Male literacy	Female literacy
100%	100%	100%

0% – 100%

Per capita income (GDP per person)

$14,522/person

$77/person (world minimum: Mozambique) (world maximum:Japan) $37,075/person

Unemployment (% of total population economically active)

16%

0% – 50%

Land use

0% – 100%

- Forests and jungles 5%
- Meadows and pastures 71%
- Cropland 14%
- Other 10%

Industry, mining and agriculture

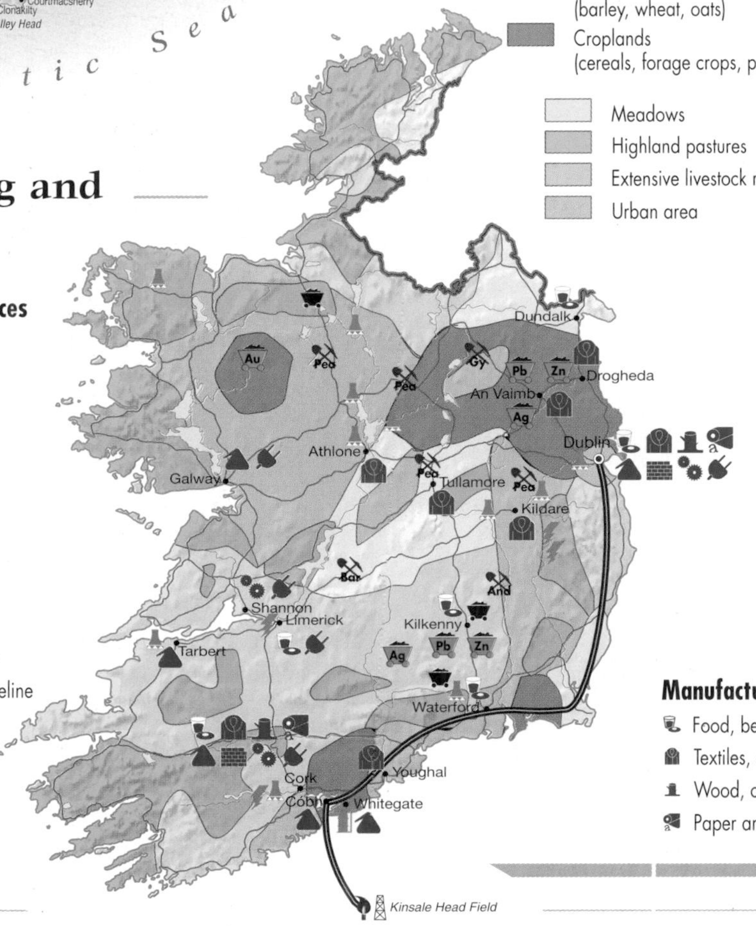

Non-energy source mineral resources

Metals
- Zinc
- Gold
- Silver
- Lead

Rocks and industrial minerals
- Andalusite
- Peat
- Barite
- Gypsum

Mineral fuel resources
- Coal
- Natural gas
- Petroleum

Energy-related installations
- Hydroelectric power plant
- Refinery
- Thermal power plant
- Gas pipeline

Manufacturing
- Food, beverages and tobacco
- Textiles, clothing, leather and footwear
- Wood, cork and furniture
- Paper and graphic arts
- Chemical products
- Building materials, glass and cement
- Machinery and transport equipment
- Electrical, electronical and optical equipment

Italy

Official name: Repubblica Italiana, Italian Republic
Form of government: parliamentary republic
Capital: Roma (Rome)
Official language: Italian
Monetary unit: lire
Religious affiliation: Roman Catholic (83.2%), nonreligious (13.6%), atheist (2.6%), other (1.9%)
Ethnic composition of the population: Italian (94.1%), Sardinian (2.7%), Rhaetian (1.3%), other (0.6%)
Area: 301,303 sq km
Total population: 57,460,000 inhabitants
Population density: 190.7 persons per sq km

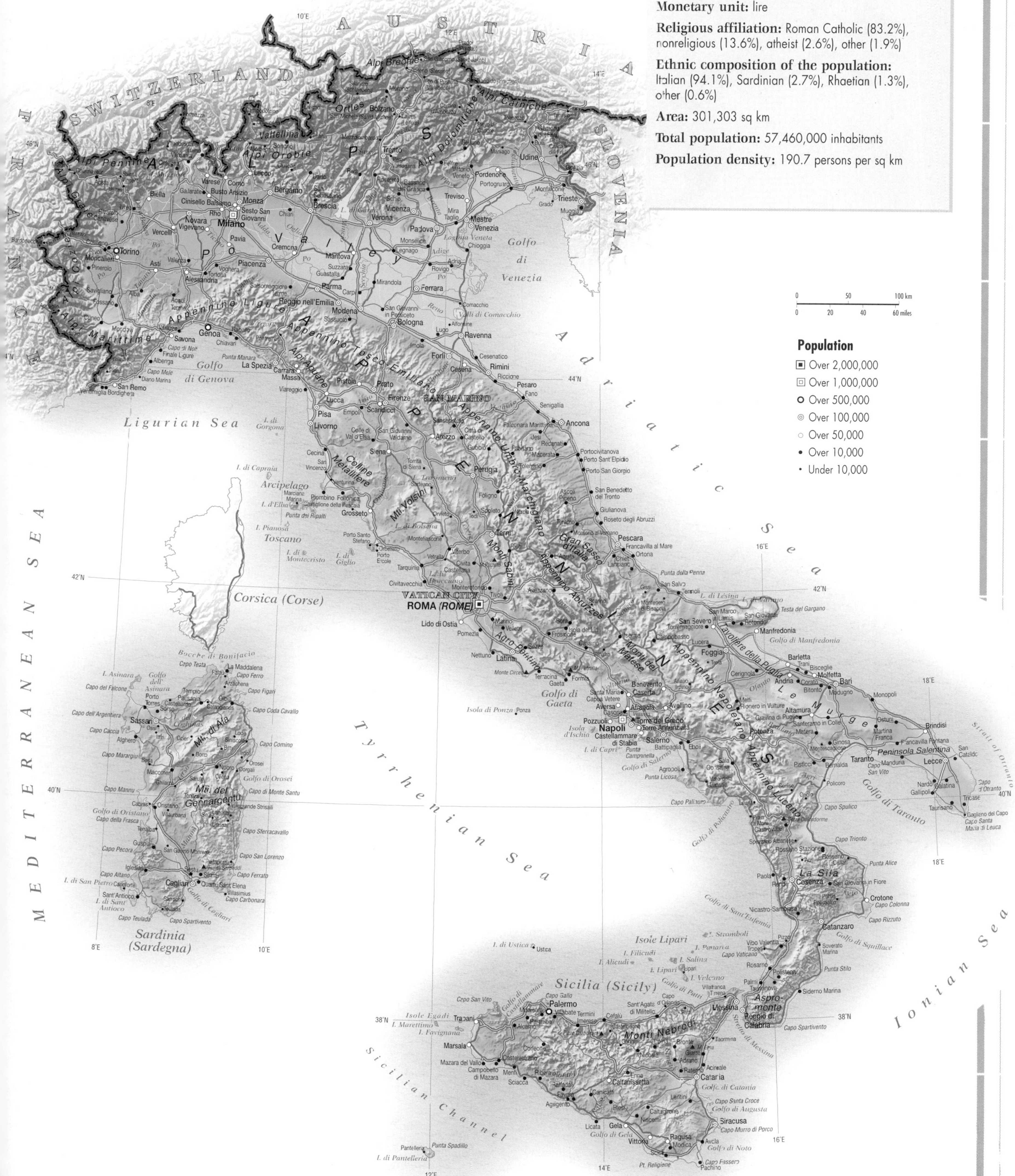

Population
- ▣ Over 2,000,000
- ◻ Over 1,000,000
- o Over 500,000
- ◎ Over 100,000
- ○ Over 50,000
- • Over 10,000
- · Under 10,000

Population

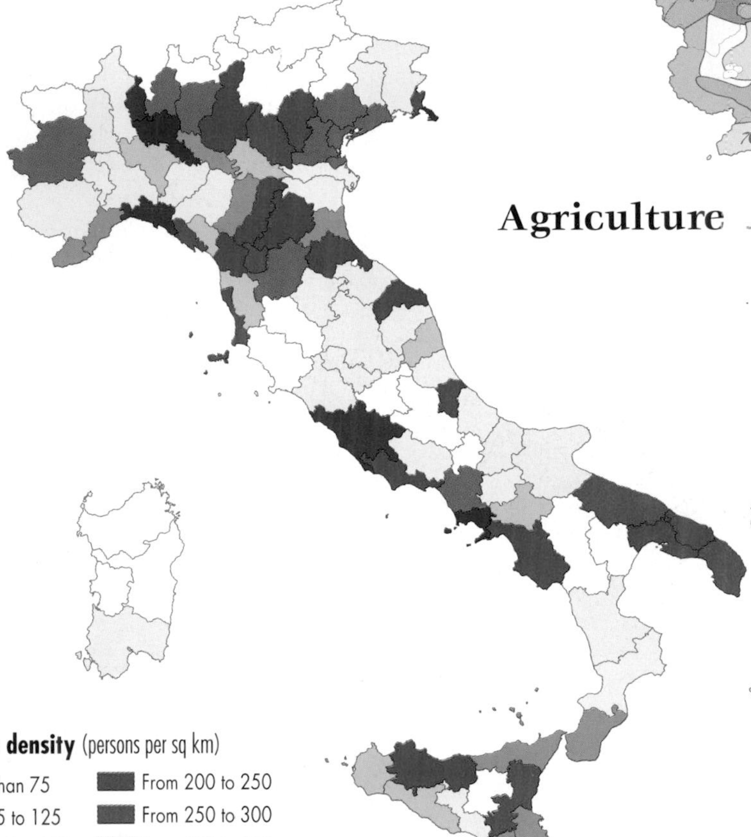

Population density (persons per sq km)

- Fewer than 75
- From 75 to 125
- From 125 to 150
- From 150 to 175
- From 175 to 200
- From 200 to 250
- From 250 to 300
- From 300 to 500
- From 500 to 1,000
- More than 1,000

Agriculture

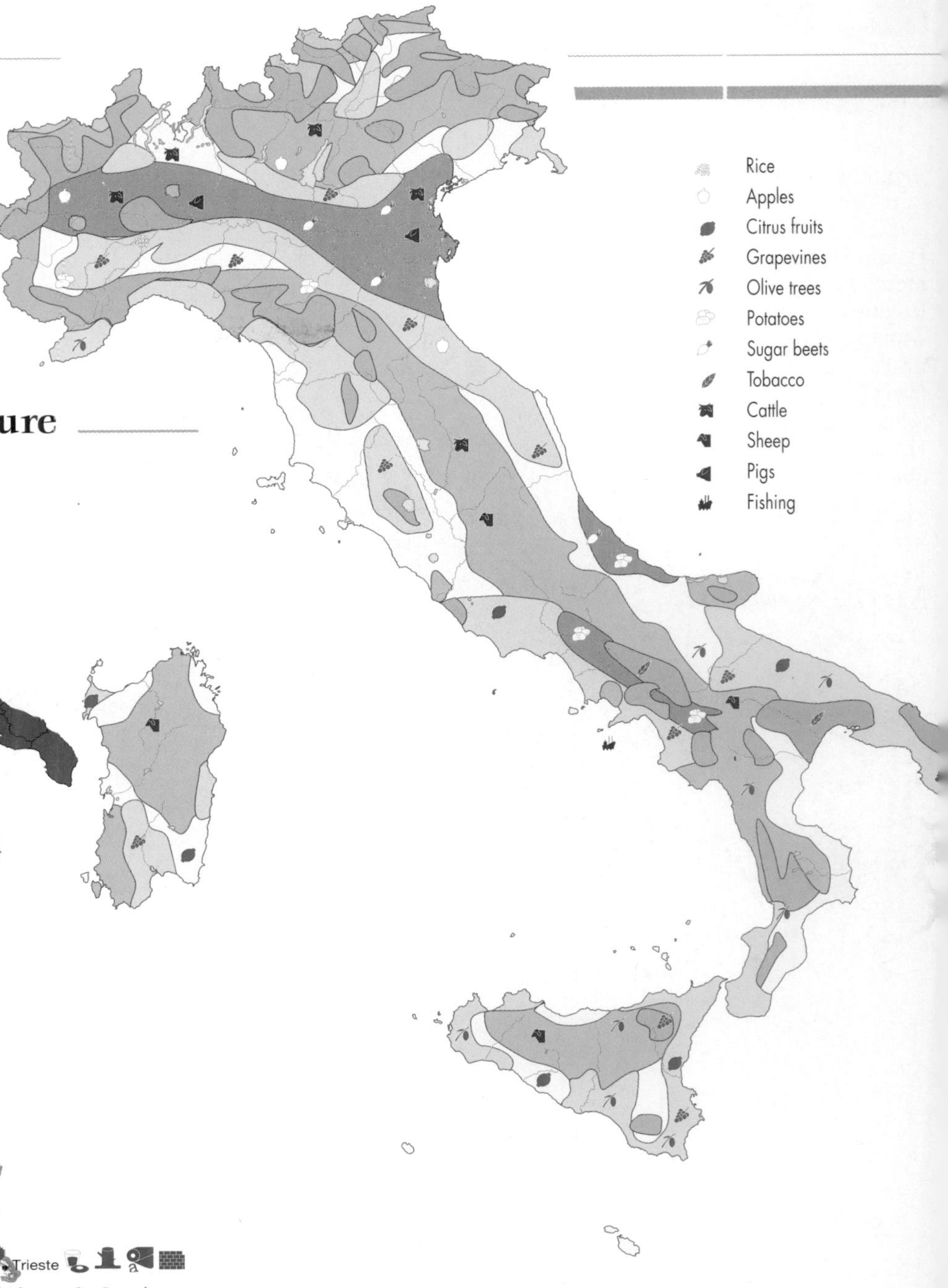

- Rice
- Apples
- Citrus fruits
- Grapevines
- Olive trees
- Potatoes
- Sugar beets
- Tobacco
- Cattle
- Sheep
- Pigs
- Fishing

Types of agriculture and livestock production

- Cereal farming (wheat, corn)
- Croplands (cereals, forage crops, fruit trees, industrial crops)
- Mixed crops (grapevines, olive trees, citrus fruits, fruit trees, vegetables, and cerea
- Plantation farming
- Highland pastures
- Forest/brush
- Non-arable land
- Urban area

Manufacturing

- Food, beverages and tobacco
- Textiles, clothing, leather and footwear
- Wood, cork and furniture
- Paper and graphic arts
- Chemical products
- Building materials, glass and cement
- Metallurgy and metal products
- Machinery and transport equipment
- Electrical, electronical and optical equipment

Italy is a republic of southern Europe that is divided into various physical regions. In continental Italy, the Alps and the Po depression of Padana plain are found. Peninsular Italy is dominated by the Appennines, a mountain chain that forms its backbone in a lengthwise direction. It also includes several islands —among which are Sicily and Sardinia— that comprise insular Italy. A western water-shed, draining into the Ligurian and Tyrrhenian Seas, and an eastern or Adriatic one can be distinguished in its drainage system. The shape and orography of the Italian Peninsula do not favor the existence of important river basins, although the Po River in continental Italy is worthy of mention. Italy's climate is Mediterranean and has marked variations. The Po depression has a transition climate between the Mediterranean and continental types.

The country has a high population density. Its cities concentrate most inhabitants, which are distributed irregularly throughout the territory, since almost half of the total population reside in the north.

Fruit-growing and horticultural farming constitute one of the economic mainstays of the country. Among other crops, Italy produces and exports citrus fruits, wine, olive oil, tomatoes and fruits. It is poor in mineral resources but exploits its deposits of natural gas. In addition, it has hydroelectric, geothermal and solar energy. Another important source of foreign currency is the tourist industry. However, industry, trade and highly developed tertiary activities (design, art, business administration and finance) are the principal motors of the nation's economy. Italy reveals strong social and economic contrasts between the north —with a powerful industrial fabric— and the south, that remains controlled by local Mafia, and is hard hit by unemployment and endemic underdevelopment.

Geostructural units

Mining and Energy

Non-energy source mineral resources

Metals
- Bauxite
- Copper
- Mercury
- Zinc
- Iron ore
- Lead

Rocks and industrial minerals
- Clays
- Pyrite
- Sulphur
- Potash
- Barite
- Salt
- Feldspar
- Talc

Mineral fuel resources

Fossil fuels
- Coal
- Natural gas
- Natural gas field
- Petroleum

Radioactive fuel
- Uranium

Energy-related installations
- Geothermal power plant
- Hydroelectric power plant
- Nuclear reactor
- Refinery
- Gas pipeline

Population age distribution

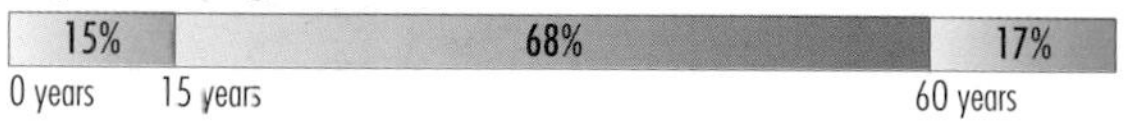

Vital statistics

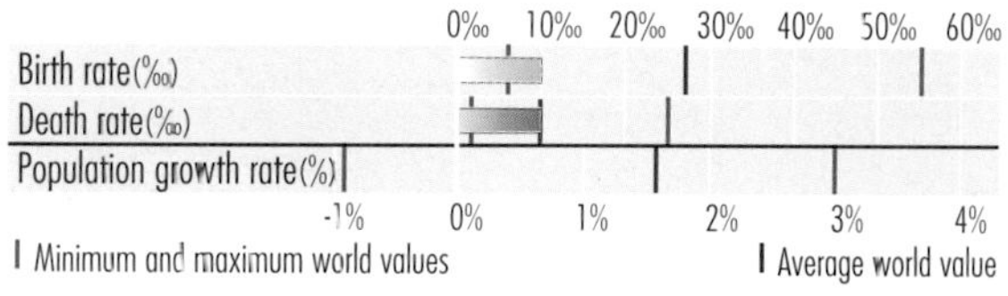

Literacy (% of population over15)

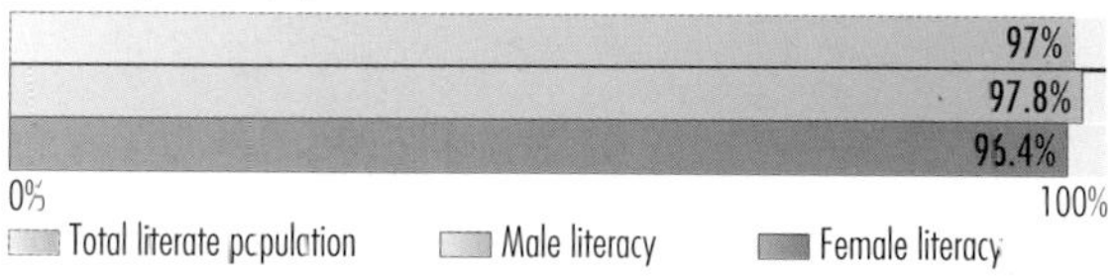

Per capita income (GDP per person)

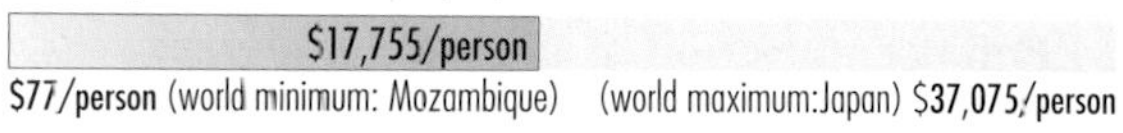

Unemployment (% of total population economically active)

Land use

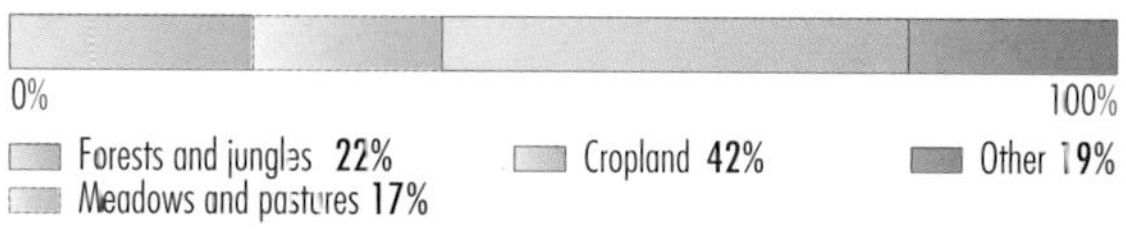

Population evolution and projection

in millions of persons

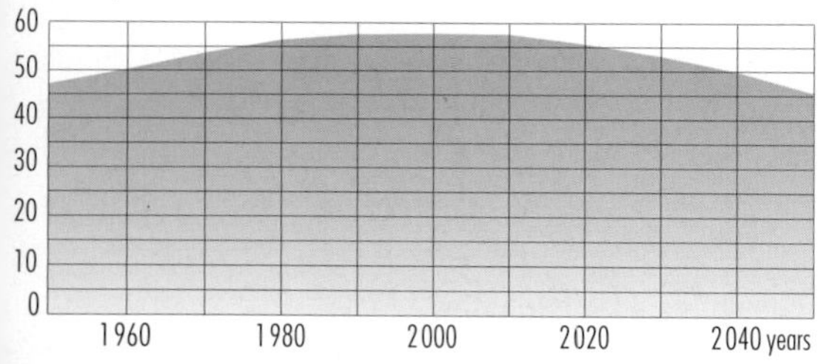

GDP structure

1,085,932 million dollars

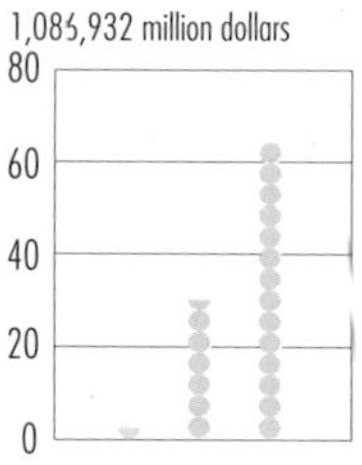

Labor force

24,865,000 persons

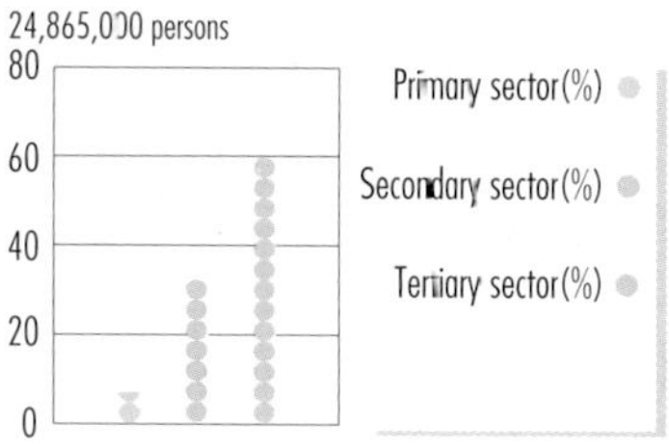

Latvia

Latvia is a state of northern Europe. It is a flat territory, which becomes somewhat more rugged in the region of Livonia, in the northeast. It possesses a varied landscape, since it has small coastal dunes, some hills and numerous lake basins carved out by glaciers. The shoreline is composed of low sandy coasts, with many shoals. The gulf of Riga is important; into this gulf flows the Daugava or Western Dvina (one of the main rivers of the country, which provides with its flow the energy for several hydroelectric power plants). Latvia has a transition climate between marine west coast and continental, softened by the influence of the sea, with cool humid summers and winter temperatures that do not fall below –3 °C. Half of the population is composed of Latvians, besides a significant percentage of Russians and a minority of Belarusians and Ukrainians. It is a state with a high level of urban dwelling.

In its agriculture, the flax, forage crops, sugar beets, potatoes, and cereals are noteworthy. Cattle raising (with the production of milk and meat) along with that of pigs represent the main stock raising activities. Industry depends on the foreign supply of petroleum. Despite lacking raw materials, an iron and steel mill center has been established in the region of Riga, in which the most important are the naval construction, mechanical and railroad equipment production. Important chemical and petrochemical industries have also been developed in the surrounds of Ventspils, on the banks of the Venta River.

Official name: Republic of Latvia

Form of government: republic

Capital: Rīga

Official language: Latvian

Monetary unit: lats

Religious affiliation: Roman Catholic (20%), Lutheran (12%), Russian Orthodox (4%), Old Believer (2.8%), Baptist (0.2%), Jewish (0.2%), other or none (60.8%)

Ethnic composition of the population: Latvian (51.8%), Russian (33.8%), Belarusian (4.5%), Ukrainian (3.4%), Polish (2.3%), other (4.2%)

Area: 64,610 sq km

Total population: 2,469,000 inhabitants

Population density: 38.2 persons per sq km

Population
- Over 500,000
- Over 100,000
- Over 50,000
- Over 10,000
- Under 10,000

0 25 50 75 km
0 10 20 30 40 50 miles

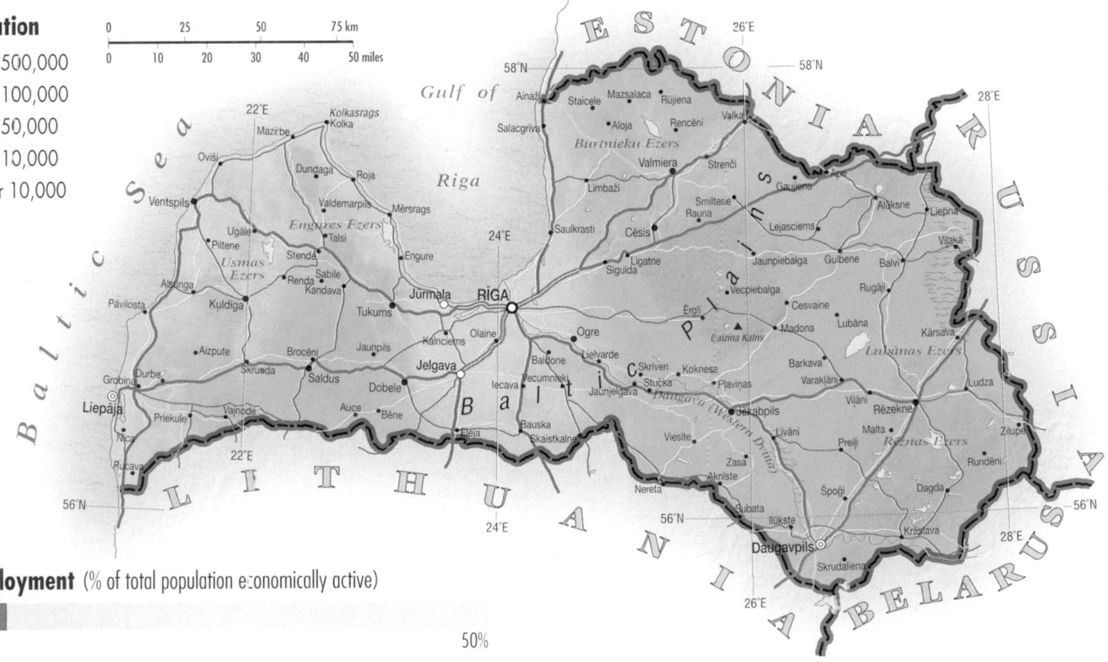

Unemployment (% of total population economically active)

6.5%

0% — 50%

Population age distribution

0 years–15 years	15 years–60 years	60 years–
22%	65%	13%

Literacy (% of population over15)

Total literate population	Male literacy	Female literacy
99.5%	99.8%	99.2%

0% — 100%

Per capita income (GDP per person)

$2,130.41/person

$77/person (world minimum: Mozambique) (world maximum:Japan) $37,075/person

Land use

Forests and jungles 44% Cropland 27% Other 17% Meadows and pastures 12%

0% — 100%

Population evolution and projection

in millions of persons

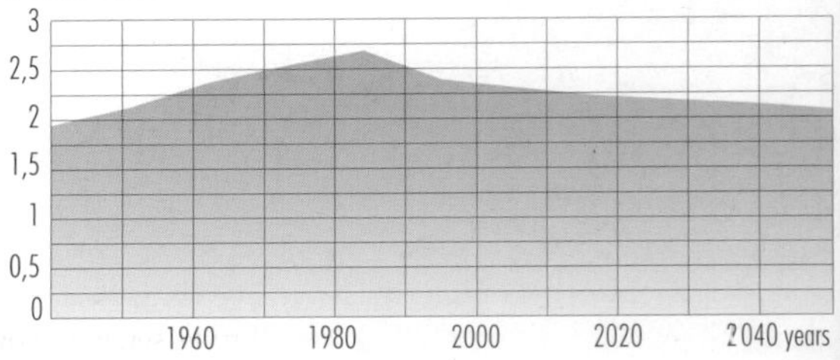

GDP structure

6,034 millones de dólares

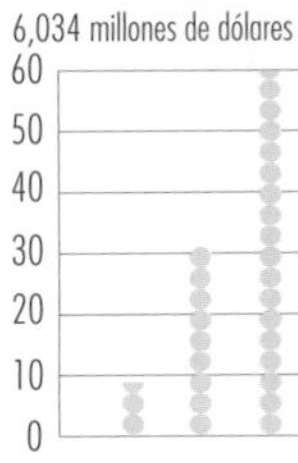

Labor force

1,408,000 persons

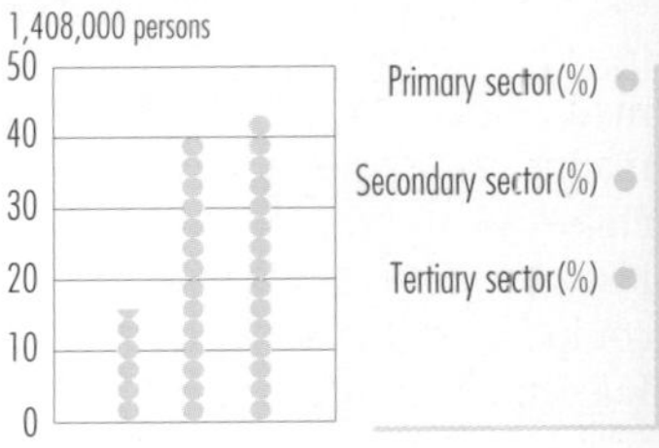

Vital statistics

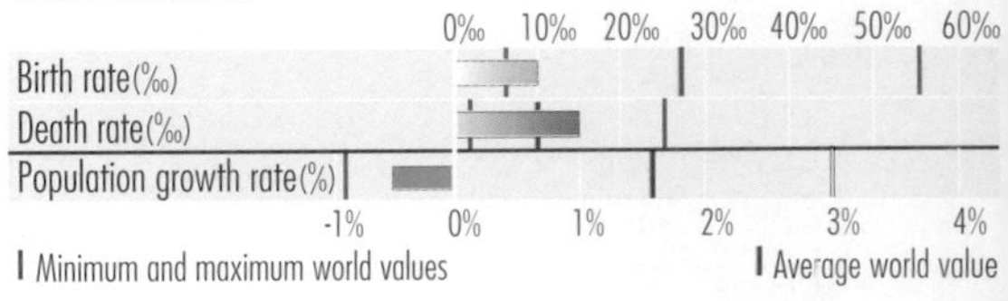

I Minimum and maximum world values I Average world value

Liechtenstein

Official name: Principality of Liechtenstein

Form of government: hereditary constitutional monarchy

Capital: Vaduz

Official language: German

Monetary unit: Swiss franc

Religious affiliation: Roman Catholic (81%), Protestant (7.3%), other (4.4%), not stated (7.3%)

Ethnic composition of the population: Liechtensteinian (61.7%), Swiss (15.7%), Austrian (7.4%), German (3.7%), other (11.5%)

Area: 160 sq km

Total population: 31,122 inhabitants

Population density: 194.5 persons per sq km

GDP: U.S.$978 million

An independent principality of central Europe, Liechtenstein is one of the smallest states in the world. Its territory extends parallel to the Rhine River, which forms its western border. Most of the country is occupied by the steep slopes of the Rhatikon Mountains, in the central Alps. It possesses many forests, meadows and pastures and is cut by numerous rivers, tributaries of the Rhine, that flow through the three largest valleys.

It has a continental climate, moderated by the warm winds from the south during the summer months. Most of the population are of German origin and practice Roman Catholicism.

In spite of the fertility of the valleys of the Principality, farming has lost relevance, due to the great development of industry. The industrial sector is based on metallurgy, textiles, mechanics and ceramics. Tourism and finance represent Liechtenstein's main sources of foreign currency.

Unemployment (% of total population economically active)

1.5%

0% — 50%

Population evolution and projection

in thousands of persons

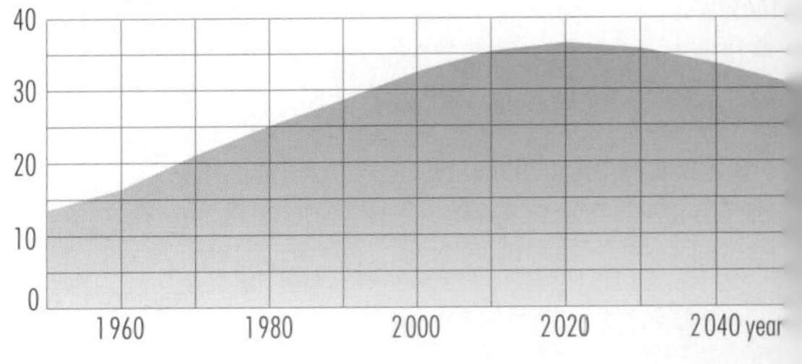

Labor force

15,100 persons

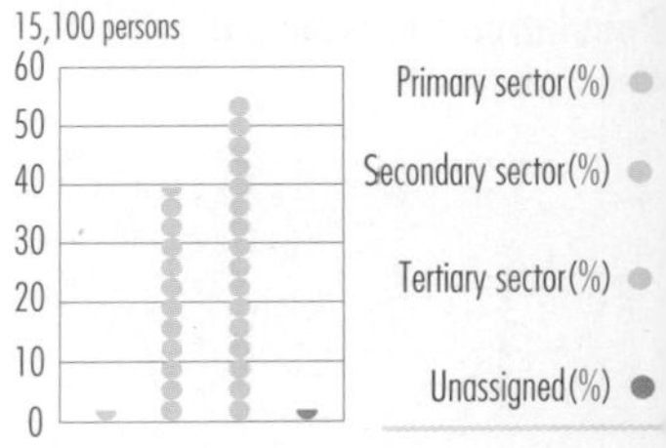

Population age distribution

0 years–15 years	15 years–60 years	60 years–
19%	71%	10%

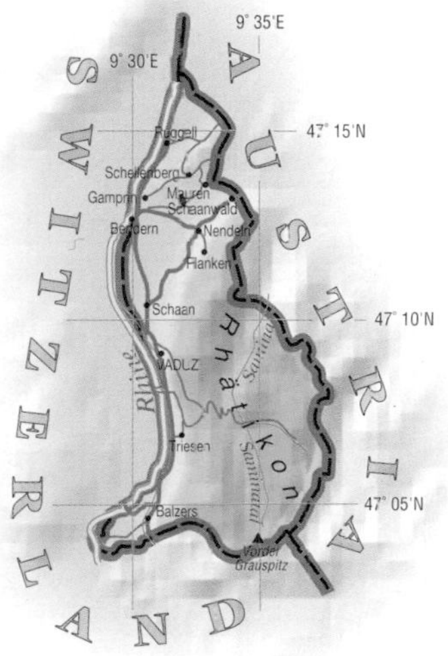

Population

- Under 10,000

0 5 10 km
0 2 4 6 miles

Literacy (% of population over15)

100%
100%
100%
0% 100%
Total literate population — Male literacy — Female literacy

Per capita income (GDP per person)

$31,424.7/person
$77/person (world minimum: Mozambique) (world maximum:Japan) $37,075/person

Land use

0% 100%
Forests and jungles **19%** — Cropland **25%** — Other **18%** — Meadows and pastures **38%**

Vital statistics

0‰ 10‰ 20‰ 30‰ 40‰ 50‰ 60‰
Birth rate(‰)
Death rate(‰)
Population growth rate(%)
-1% 0% 1% 2% 3% 4%
| Minimum and maximum world values — | Average world value

Lithuania

Lithuania is a state of northeastern Europe. It possesses a flat territory, although more rugged than that of the other two Baltic Republics (Estonia and Latvia) of the former Soviet Union. It extends over a sector of the Baltic-Russian flatland, partially modified by glacier erosion. In its eastern and southern region rise several hills of low altitude, separated by more than 3,000 lakes. The Nemunas is the principal river of the country; it flows into the Baltic Sea and like its tributaries, freezes over for three months of the year. Lithuania has a moderately continental climate in the interior, that becomes marine west coast towards the coast of the Baltic. In winter an average temperature of -4 °C is registered and in summer it reaches 17 °C on the average. Most of the population is composed of Lithuanians. In a lesser proportion, there are Russians, Poles, and a small minority of Jews. The Lithuanian population has a clear tendency towards urban dwelling. It is an agrarian country that produces cereals (wheat, rye), flax, potatoes and sugar beets. Stock raising is in the process of expansion, with specially important cattle raising —which has strengthened an associated food industry— and pig farming. Fishing also contributes important revenues. Coal and petroleum are obtained from mineral reserves. A great percentage of the working population is employed in the industrial sector. Together with the food industry, the metallurgical, mechanical engineering, chemical and textile sectors have developed. Since the disintegration of the former Soviet Union, the Lithuanian economy has experienced a profound crisis, which it is attempting to relieve with processes of privatization, liberalization of prices and reforms of the financial system.

Official name: Republic of Lithuania
Form of government: independent, democratic republic
Capital: Vilnius
Official language: Lithuanian
Monetary unit: litas
Religious affiliation: Roman Catholic (80%), Russian Orthodox, Old Believer, Lutheran, and nonreligious minorities
Ethnic composition of the population: Lithuanian (80.1%), Russian (8.6%), Polish (7.7%), Belarusian (1.5%), other (2.1%)
Area: 65,301 sq km
Total population: 3,646,000 inhabitants
Population density: 55.8 persons per sq km

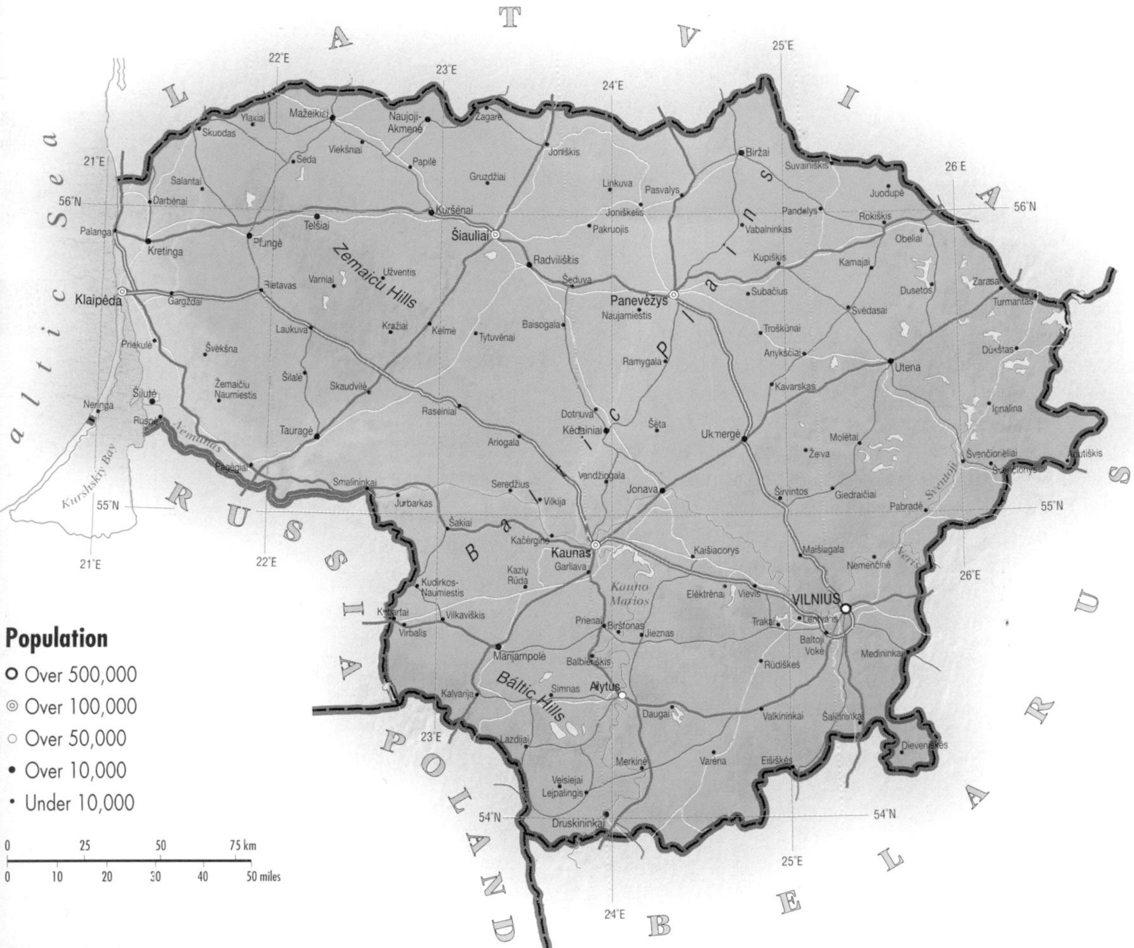

Population

- Over 500,000
- Over 100,000
- Over 50,000
- Over 10,000
- Under 10,000

0 25 50 75 km
0 10 20 30 40 50 miles

Population evolution and projection
in millions of persons

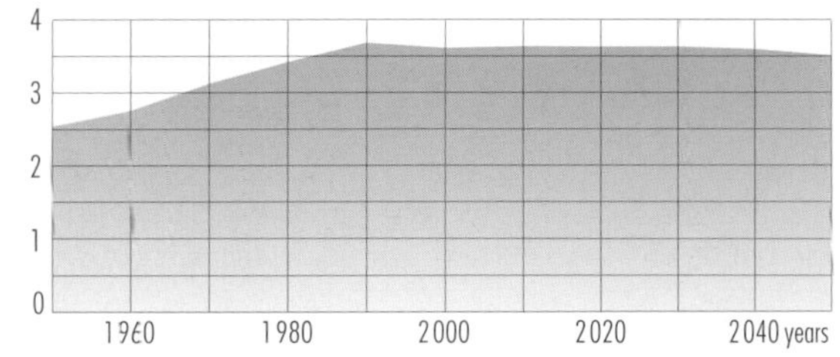

GDP structure
7,089 million dollars

Labor force
1,904,000 persons

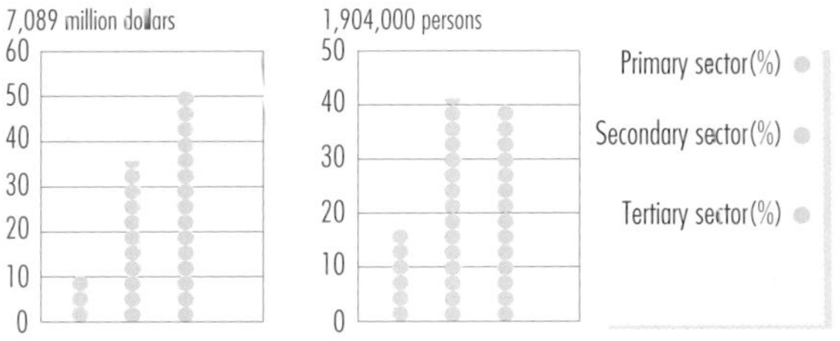

Population age distribution

23% — 65% — 12%
0 years — 15 years — 60 years

Vital statistics

0‰ 10‰ 20‰ 30‰ 40‰ 50‰ 60‰
Birth rate(‰)
Death rate(‰)
Population growth rate(%)
-1% 0% 1% 2% 3% 4%
| Minimum and maximum world values — | Average world value

Per capita income (GDP per person)

$1,341.19/person
$77/person (world minimum: Mozambique) (world maximum:Japan) $37,075/person

Unemployment (% of total population economically active)

4.5%
0% 50%

Land use

0% 100%
Forests and jungles **30.2%** — Cropland **47%** — Other **15.7%** — Meadows and pastures **7.1%**

Literacy (% of population over15)

98%
99.2%
97.8%
0% 100%
Total literate population — Male literacy — Female literacy

Luxembourg

Luxembourg is a state of western Europe. It is divided into two natural regions: in the north, on the Plateau de l'Ardenne, is located a cold and inhospitable forested area, the Oesling; in the south is found Gutland (Good land), situated on the tip of the Parisian plain. The country has a continental climate, with cold winters, especially in the more northerly regions. Most of the population reside in urban areas and there is a strong imbalance between the more densely populated areas (the southwest) and the less heavily populated ones (Oesling). Mechanization and the concentration of land holdings have benefited agricultural productivity (cereals, potatoes and grapes). A great deal of the domestic product proceeds from industry, manufacturing as well as mineral processing. Iron and steel production is important, and there are manufacturing industries of chemical products, machinery, glass and porcelain. Luxembourg enjoys a high standard of living.

Official name: Grand Duchy of Luxembourg

Form of government: constitutional monarchy

Capital: Luxembourg

Official language: Luxemburgian dialect, French, German

Monetary unit: Luxembourg franc

Religious affiliation: Roman Catholic (94.9%), Protestant (1.1%), other (4%)

Ethnic composition of the population: Luxembourger (69.7%), Portuguese (10.8%), Italian (5%), French (3.4%), Belgian (2.5%), German (2.2%), other (6.4%)

Area: 2,586 sq km

Total population: 415,870 inhabitants

Population density: 160.8 persons per sq km

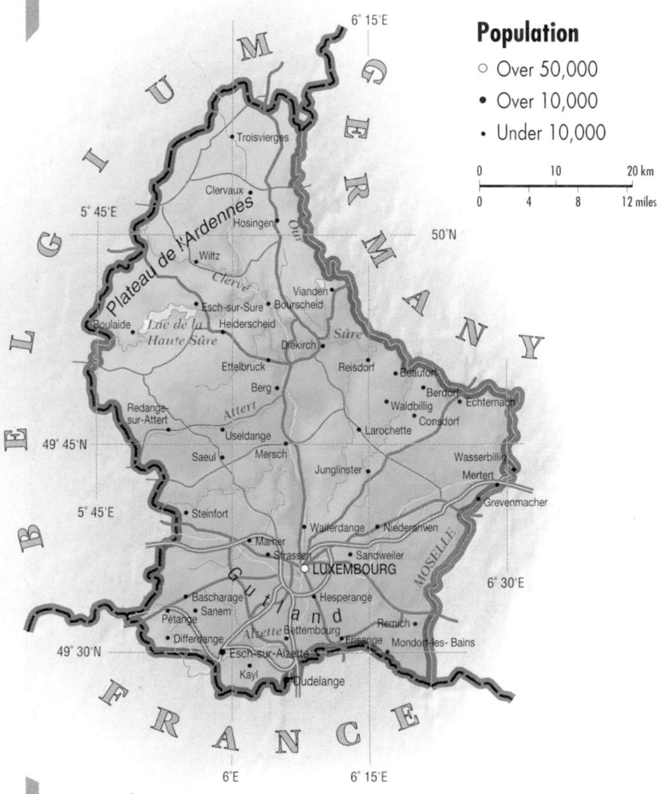

Population evolution and projection

in thousands of persons

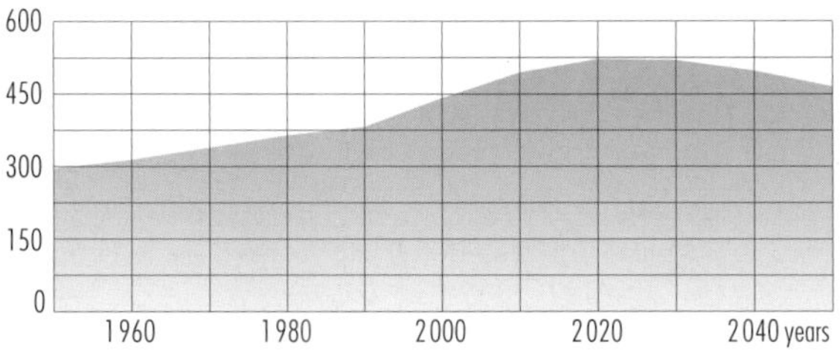

GDP structure

16,535 million dollars

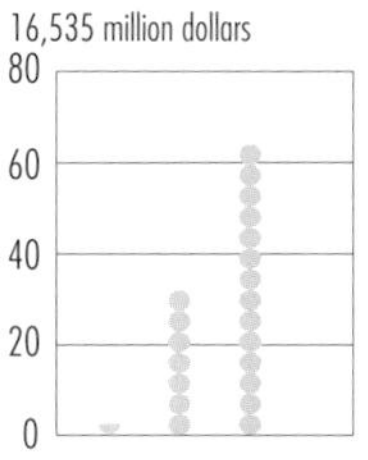

Labor force

171,000 persons

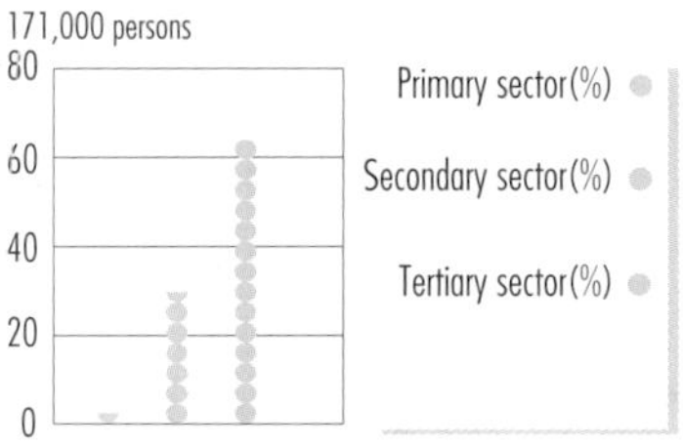

Population age distribution

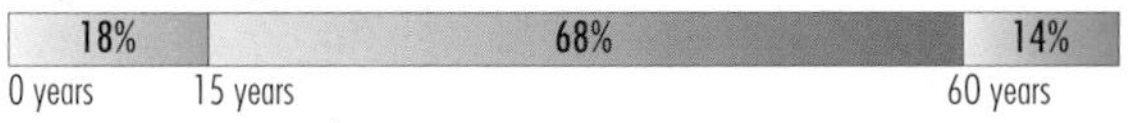

Vital statistics

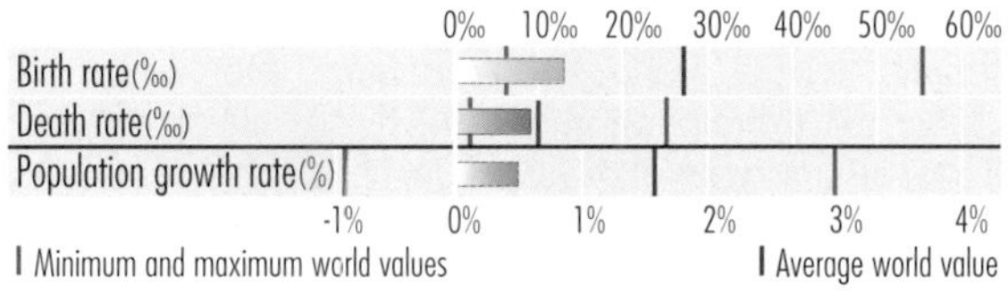

Literacy (% of population over15)

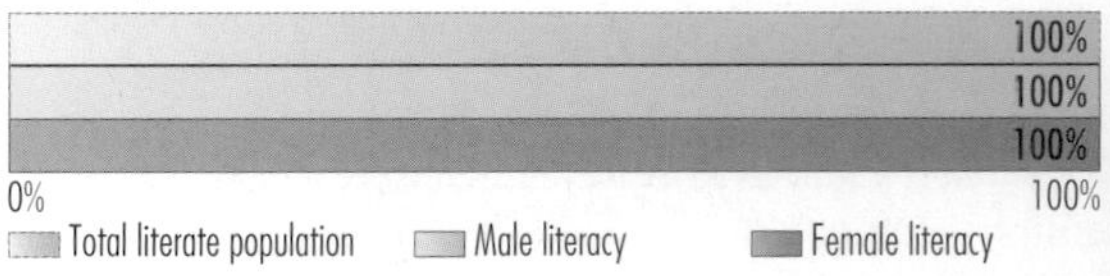

Per capita income (GDP per person)

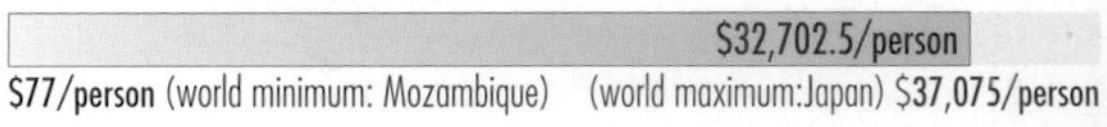

Unemployment (% of total population economically active)

Land use

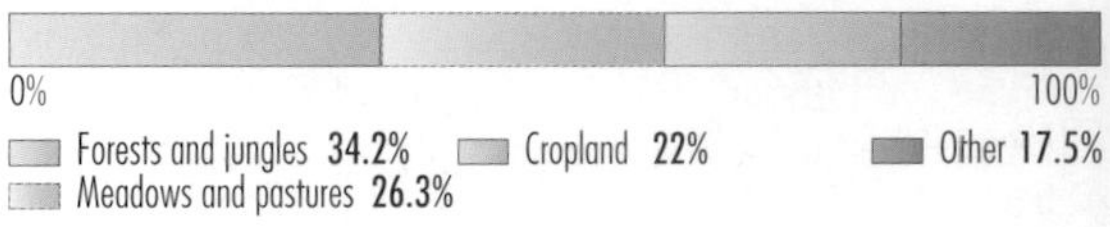

Macedonia

Macedonia is a republic of the southern Balkans, composed of several mountain ranges oriented in a northeast-southwesternly direction that mark the divide between the basins of the Aegean Sea and the Danube River. Its terrain is characterized by the presence of river basins surrounded by mountains, which decrease in height from west to east until the valley of the Vardar River joins that of the southern Morava. Lakes Ohridand Prespa are located in the far southwest. The valley of the Vardar and its tributaries represents the principal route of communication between the eastern Mediterranean and central Europe. Macedonia has a Mediterranean climate in the Vardar river valley, where there is little rainfall and an average annual temperature of 15 °C. Toward the west, the climate becomes continental and a greater amount of precipitation falls in the southwestern region, due to the proximity of the sea. The population groups together in the cultivated river basins and is predominantly composed of Macedonians. There is also an important Albanian minority and small percentages of Turks, Serbs, and Gypsies. Macedonian Orthodox Christianity, unrecognized by the other Orthodox communities, is the major religion. In the rich inland basins, important agrarian production is obtained, aided by the use of fertilizers, the extension of irrigated lands and the existence of great agroindustrial complexes. Mediterranean and subtropical species are grown (grapevines, tobacco, rice, cotton, poppies and sesame). Deposits of lead, zinc, chrome and iron ore exist. The secondary sector is based on the mechanical, textile, crystal, tobacco and iron and steel metallurgical industries.

Official name: Republic of Macedonia

Form of government: emerging democracy

Capital: Skopje

Official language: Macedonian

Monetary unit: Macedonian denar

Religious affiliation: Orthodox Christian (67%), Muslim (30%), other (3%)

Ethnic composition of the population: Macedonian (65%), Albanian (22%), Turkish (4%), Serb (2%), other (7%)

Area: 25,713 sq km

Total population: 2,104,000 inhabitants

Population density: 81.8 persons per sq km

Population evolution and projection

in millions of persons

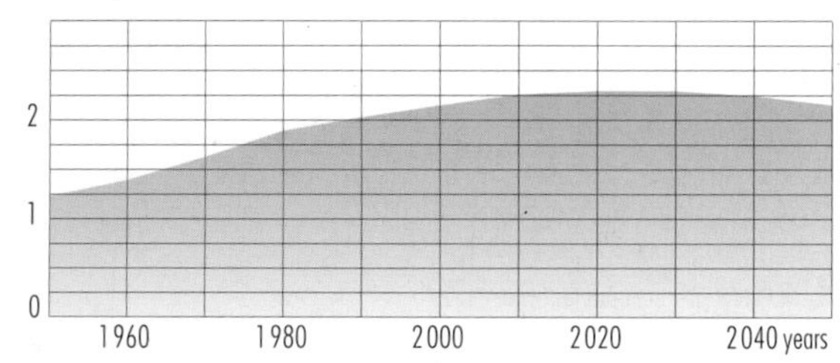

Population age distribution

GDP structure

1,975 million dollars

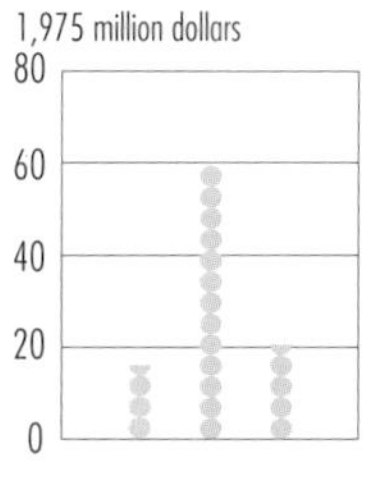

Labor force

970,000 persons

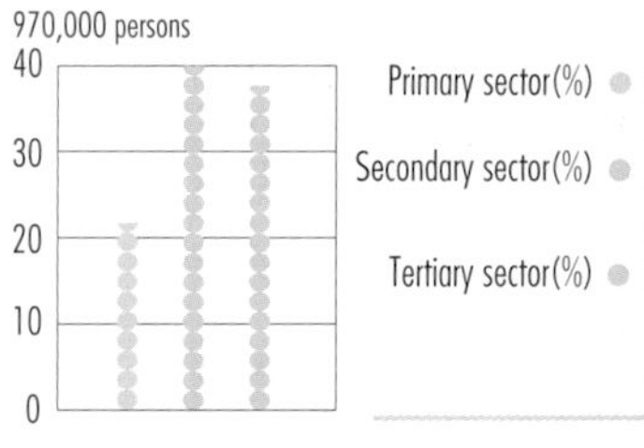

Land use

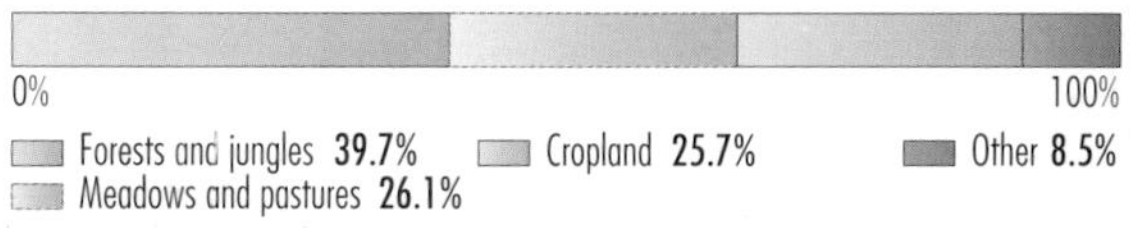

Vital statistics

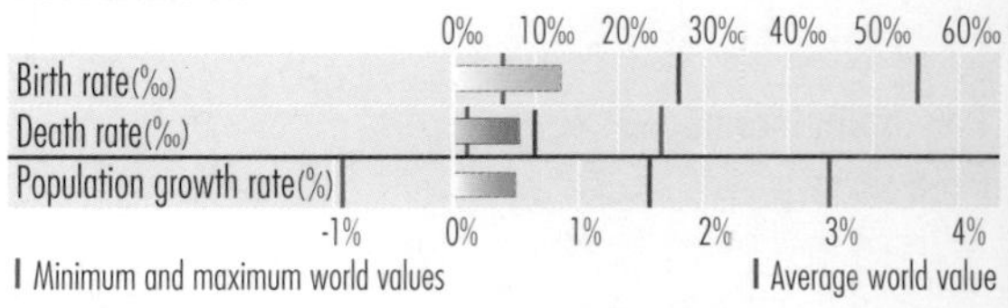

Unemployment (% of total population economically active)

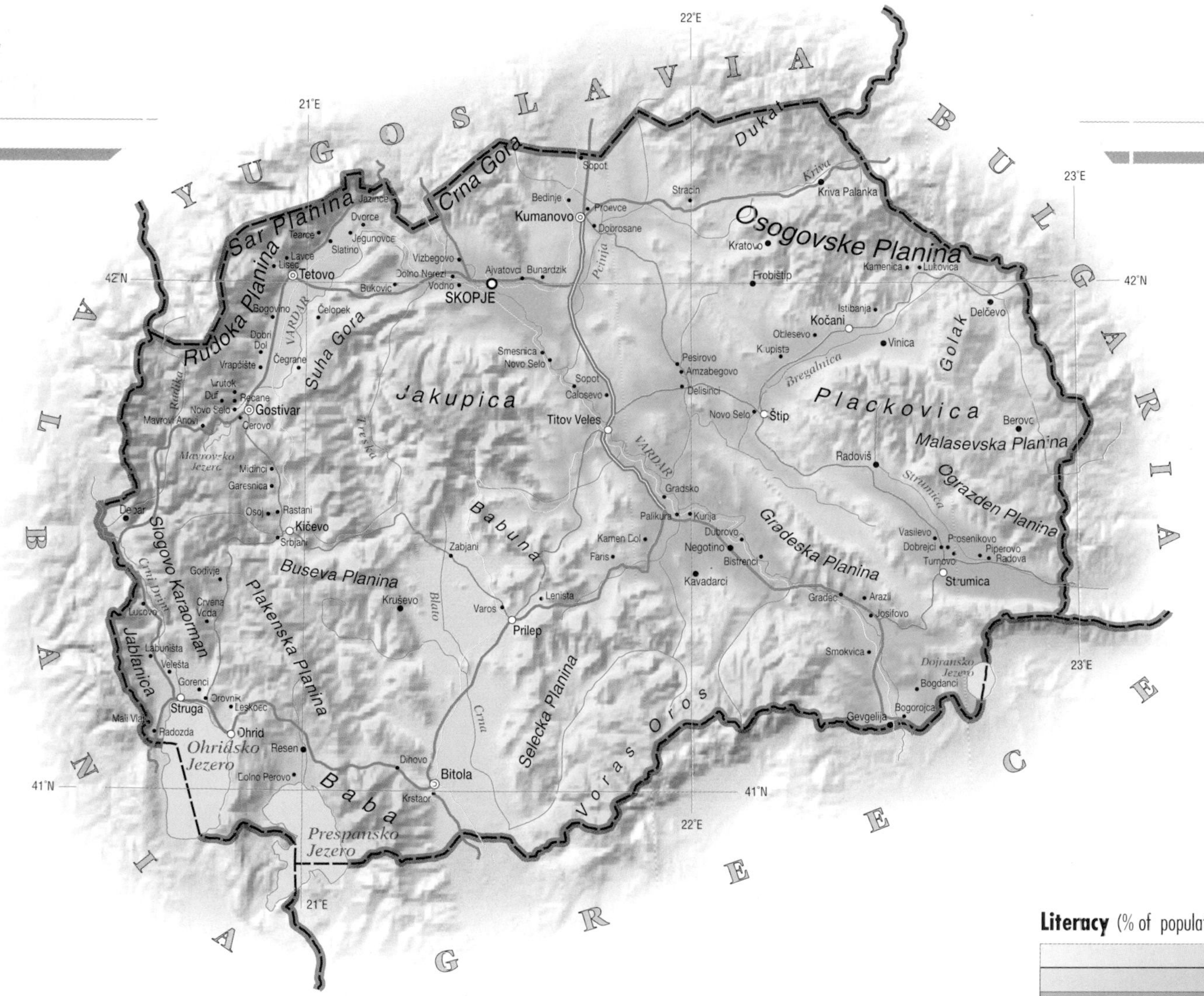

Population

- Over 500,000
- Over 100,000
- Over 50,000
- Over 10,000
- Under 10,000

0 20 40 km
0 5 10 15 20 25 miles

Literacy (% of population over15)

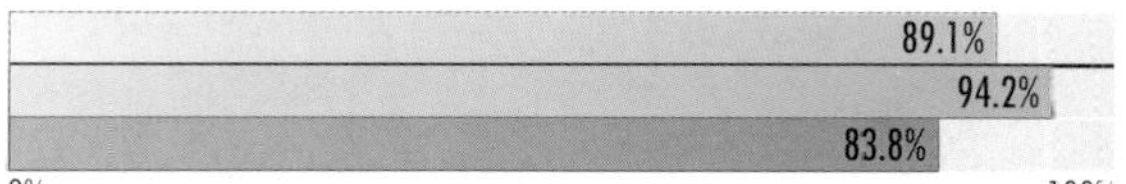

Total literate population · Male literacy · Female literacy

Per capita income (GDP per person)

$812.73/person

$77/person (world minimum: Mozambique) (world maximum:Japan) $37,075/person

Industry and Mining

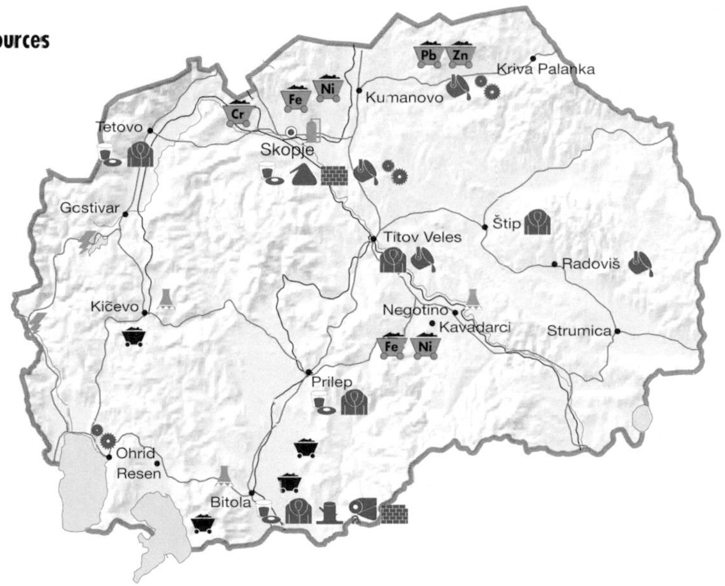

Non-energy source mineral resources

Metals

- Zinc
- Chromite
- Iron ore
- Nickel
- Lead

Mineral fuel resources

Fossil fuels

- Coal

Energy-related installations

- Hydroelectric power plant
- Thermal power plant
- Refinery

Manufacturing

- Food, beverages and tobacco
- Textiles, clothing, leather and footwear
- Wood, cork and furniture
- Paper and graphic arts
- Chemical products
- Building materials, glass and cement
- Metallurgy and metal products
- Machinery and transport equipment

Population

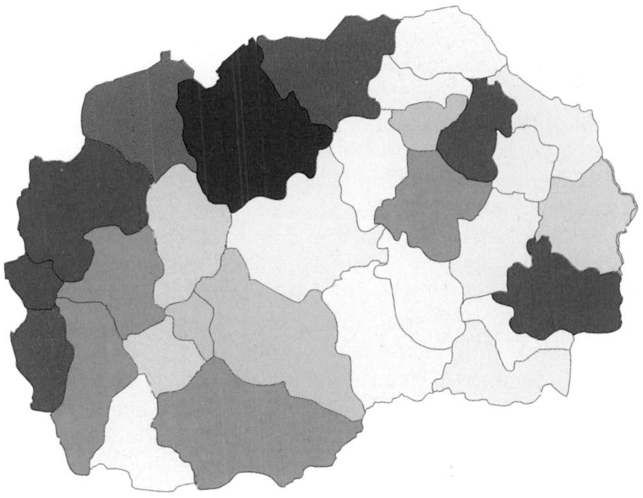

Population density (persons per sq km)

- Fewer than 30
- From 30 to 40
- From 40 to 50
- From 50 to 60
- From 60 to 75
- From 75 to 100
- From 100 to 125
- From 125 to 175
- More than 175

Agriculture

Types of agriculture and livestock production

- Croplands (corn, wheat, sunflowers, grapevines)
- Meadows and pastures
- Forest/brush
- Rice
- Cotton
- Tobacco

Malta

Malta is an island republic situated in the central Mediterranean Sea. It has a tabular-shaped geomorphology, sloping from southwest to northeast, and a rough terrain of low altitudes. There is a Mediterranean climate, with abundant rainfall in autumn and winter. Malta registers one of the highest population densities in the world. Its inhabitants, predominantly urban dwellers, are the result of the mixture of different peoples (Normans, Arabs, Spaniards, Sicilians and English). The tourist industry and the economic aid of UE, contribute important revenues. The industrial sector is progressively gaining in importance (naval construction, plastics, textiles, wood, building materials, etc.) and fishing and stock raising activities are increasing.

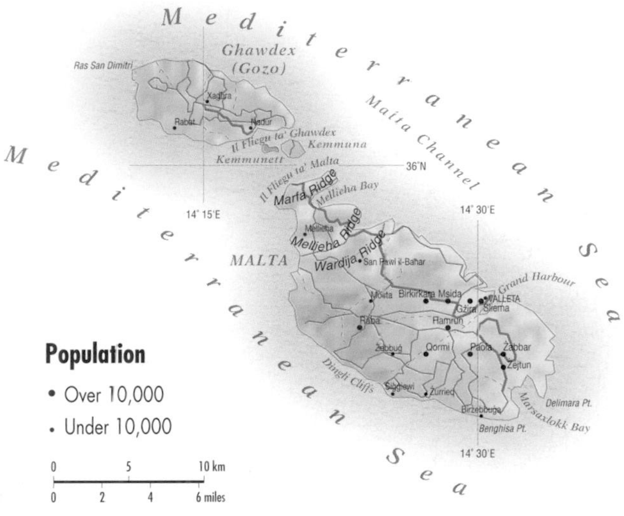

Population evolution and projection
in thousands of persons

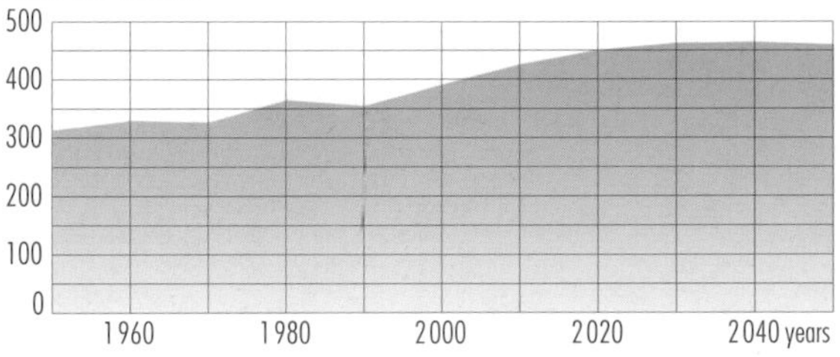

GDP structure
2,690 million dollars

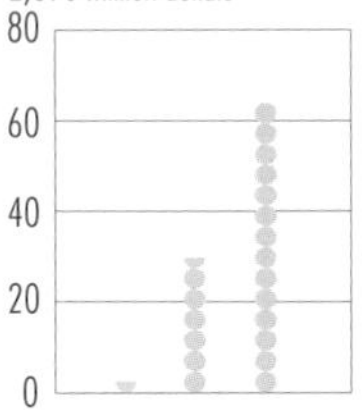

Labor force
135,000 persons

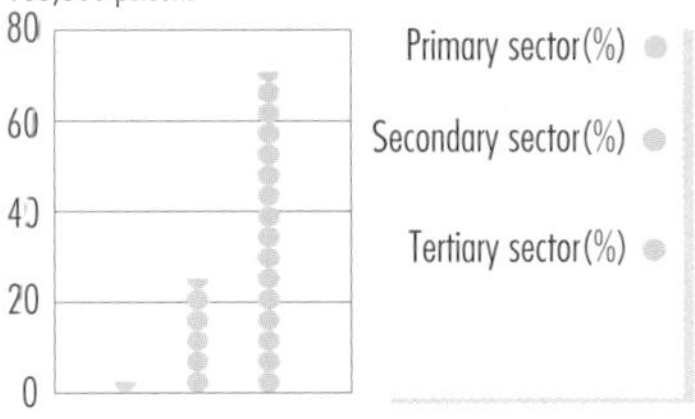

Population age distribution

Vital statistics

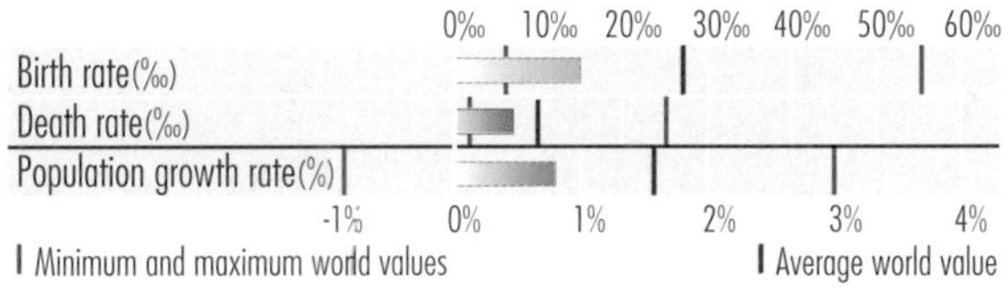

Land use

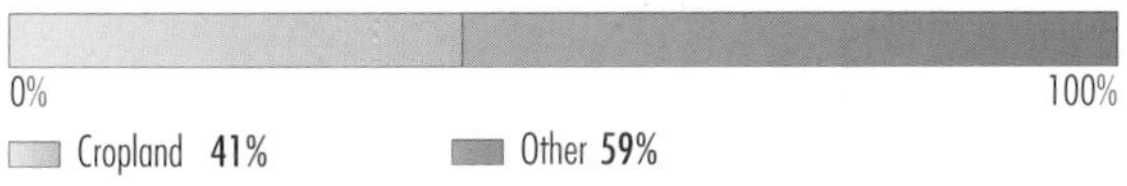

Official name: Republic of Malta
Form of government: parliamentary democracy
Capital: Valletta
Official language: Maltese, English
Monetary unit: Maltese lira
Religious affiliation: Roman Catholic (98.6%), other (1.4%)
Ethnic composition of the population: Maltese (95.7%), British (2.1%), other (2.2%)
Area: 316 sq km
Total population: 375,576 inhabitants
Population density: 1,188.5 persons per sq km

Literacy (% of population over15)

Per capita income (GDP per person)

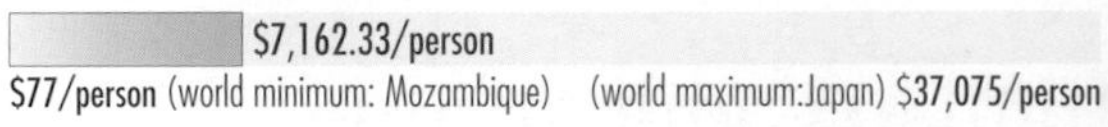

Unemployment (% of total population economically active)

Moldova

Moldova is a republic of southeastern Europe that formed part of the Soviet Union. The territory is composed of a fertile plain of loess, with its borders marked by the Dniester (Dnestr) and Prut Rivers. It includes only a small land area of the historical Moldava, in addition to the northern part of Besarabia and the southern area of Bucovina. It consists of flat relief interrupted toward the center and north by small hills and valleys, through which flow numerous rivers. Mild temperatures are registered, with increasingly warmer ones toward the south. Summers are long and warm and winters are short with low temperatures (below 0 °C). The amount of rainfall rises from south to north. The Moldovan population, of Orthodox religion and Romanian descent, form the largest ethnic group of the country. Important Ukrainian and Russian minorities exist, and a small percentage of Gagauz (Turkic-speaking Christians), Jews and Bulgarians. The economy is based on agriculture, which occupies a large part of the working population. In the north, cereals are grown (wheat, corn, sunflowers and sugar beets) and, in the south, grapevines, vegetables, and tobacco. The country does not possess raw materials or sources of energy, with the exception of small deposits of coal (lignite), but it has taken advantage of the potential of the Dniester (Dnestr) and Prut Rivers for the construction of hydroelectric power plants. A processing industry has been developed, in which the flour, canning, wine-making, sugar and tobacco sectors are noteworthy. Commercial interchanges are carried out mainly with the countries born from the disintegration of the Soviet Union, but Moldova is attempting to diversify its foreign trade and open its doors toward Western Europe.

Population evolution and projection
in millions of persons

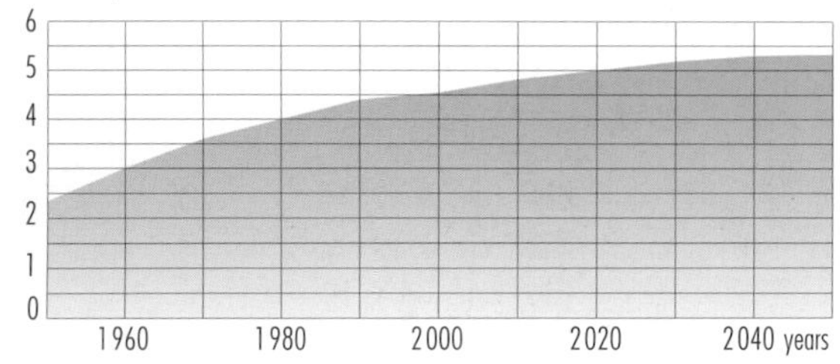

Vital statistics

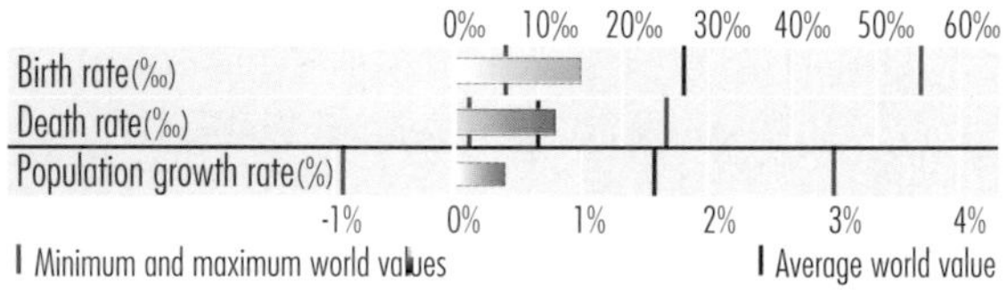

GDP structure
3,518 million dollars

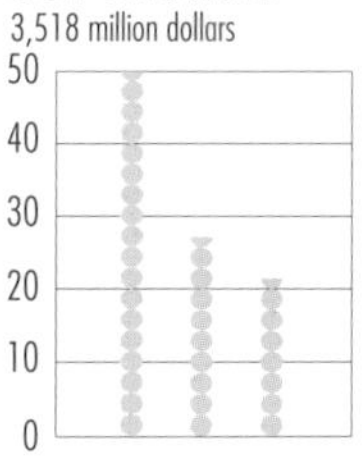

Labor force
2,172,000 persons

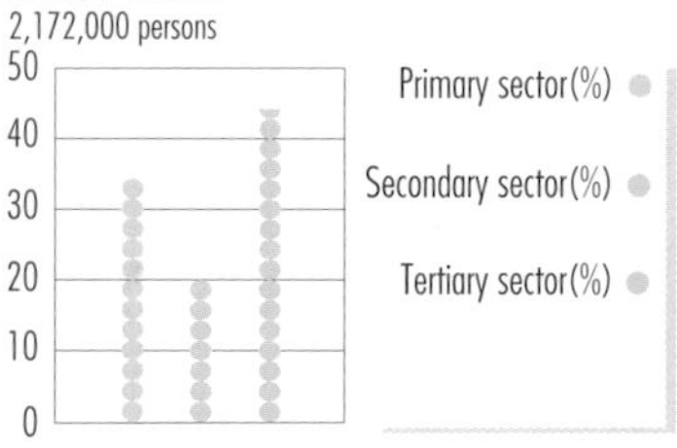

Population age distribution

Per capita income (GDP per person)

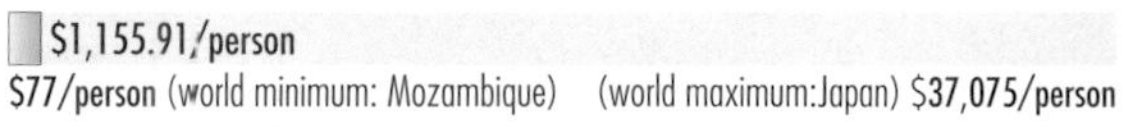

Official name: Republic of Moldova
Form of government: republic
Capital: Chişinău
Official language: Moldovan (Romanian dialect)
Monetary unit: Moldovan leu
Religious affiliation: Eastern Orthodox Christian (98.5%), Jewish (1.5%)
Ethnic composition of the population: Moldovan/Romanian (64.5%), Ukrainian (13.8%), Russian (13%), Gagauz (3.5%), Jewish (1.5%), Bulgarian (2%), other (1.7%)
Area: 33,700 sq km
Total population: 4,464,000 inhabitants
Population density: 132.5 persons per sq km

Literacy (% of population over15)

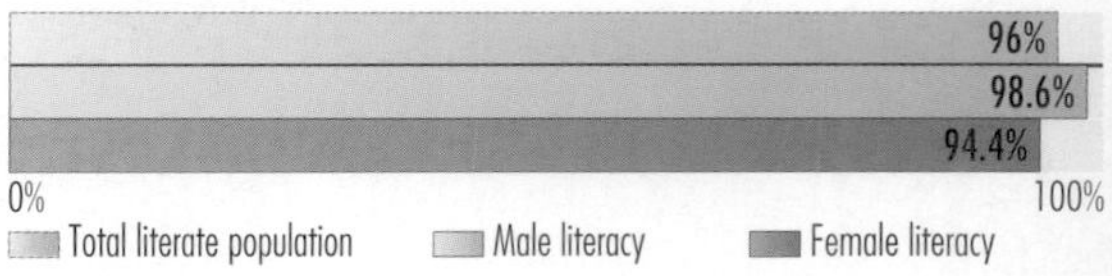

Unemployment (% of total population economically active)

Land use

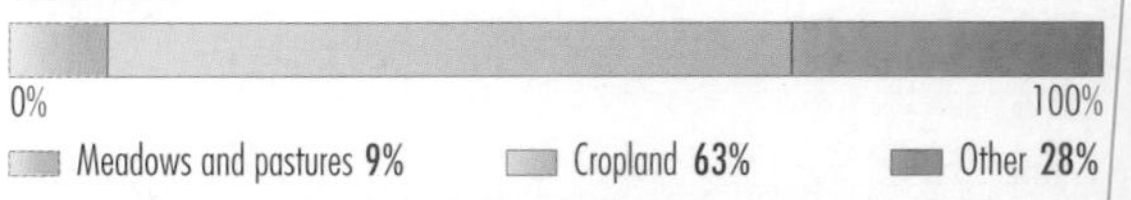

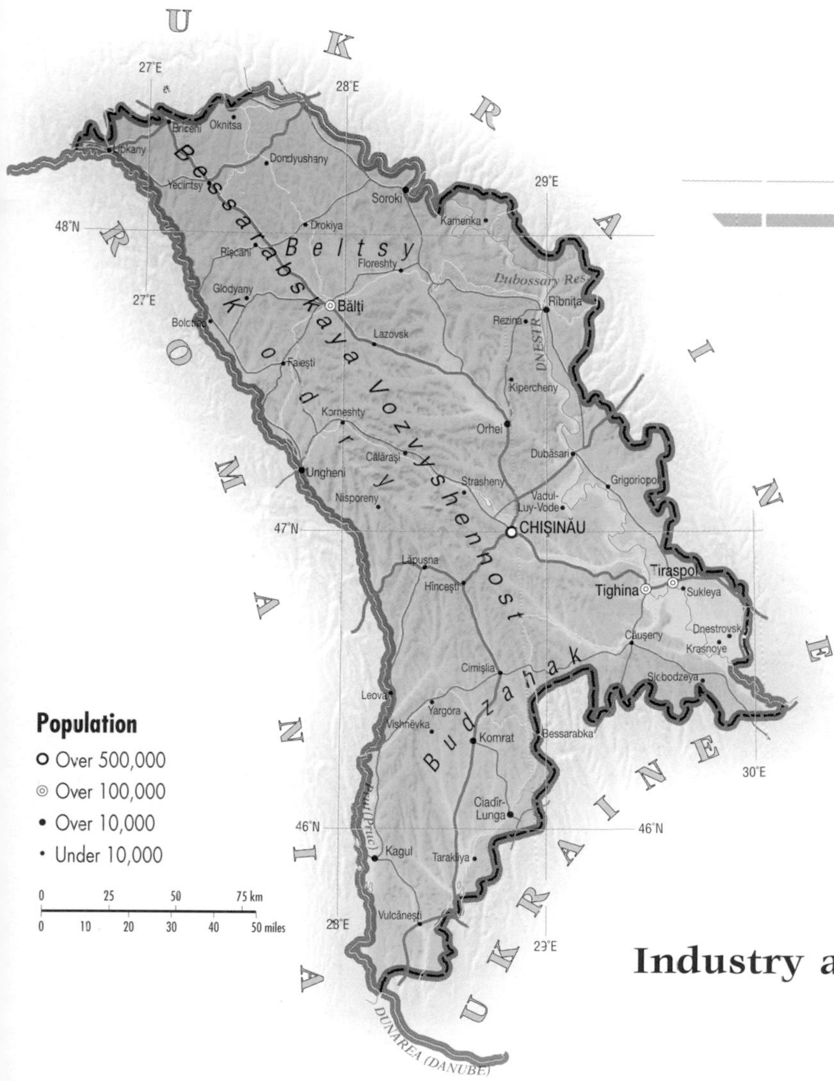

Population

- Over 500,000
- Over 100,000
- Over 10,000
- Under 10,000

0 25 50 75 km
0 10 20 30 40 50 miles

Agriculture

Types of agriculture and livestock production

- Cereal farming (wheat, rye, corn, barley)
- Forest/brush
- Vegetables
- Grapevines
- Sunflowers
- Sugar beets
- Tobacco
- Cattle
- Sheep
- Pigs

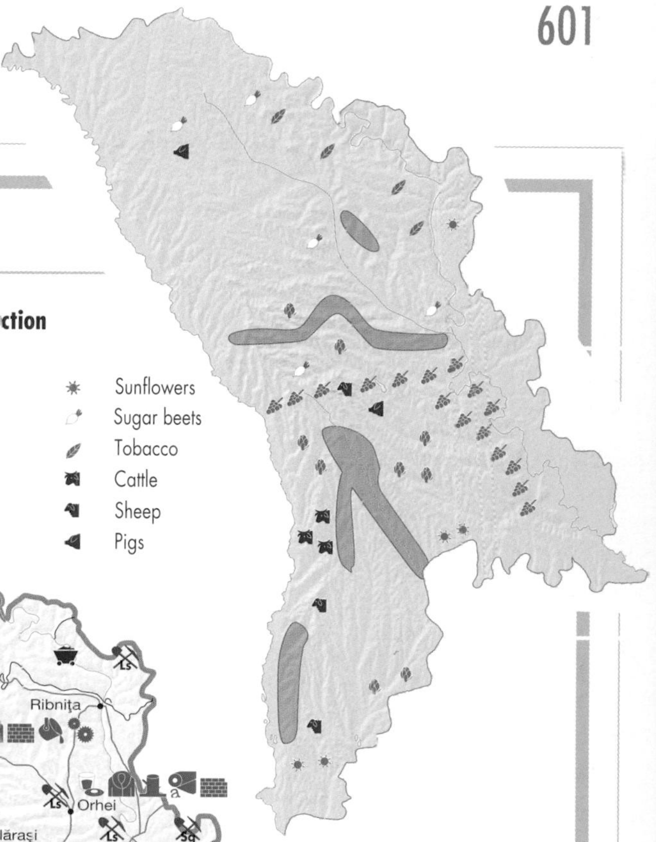

Industry and Mining

Manufacturing

- Food, beverages and tobacco
- Textiles, clothing, leather and footwear
- Wood, cork and furniture
- Paper and graphic arts
- Chemical products
- Building materials, glass and cement
- Metallurgy and metal products
- Machinery and transport equipment

Non-energy source mineral resources

Rocks and industrial minerals

- Sands and gravel
- Limestone

Mineral fuel resources

Fossil fuels

- Coal

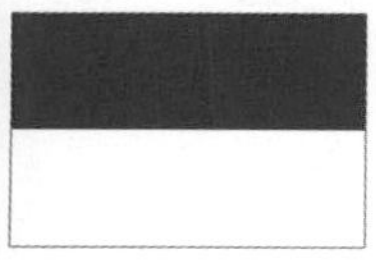

Monaco

Monaco is a small independent principality situated in the southeast of France. It is divided in nine districts, among which the most noteworthy are: Montecarlo, a tourist area where the famous casino is found; Monaco Ville, a highly urbanized area; Fontvielle, an industrial zone, and La Condamine, a commercial emporium next to the port.

It has a Mediterranean climate, with warm summers and mild winters. The geographical location and the mildness of the climate has encouraged the development of the tourist industry, one of the country's main sources of income.

Due to the exemption from payment of taxes, many foreign companies have established industries in Monaco, which produces perfumes, porcelain, chemical and food products, fabrics and precision instruments.

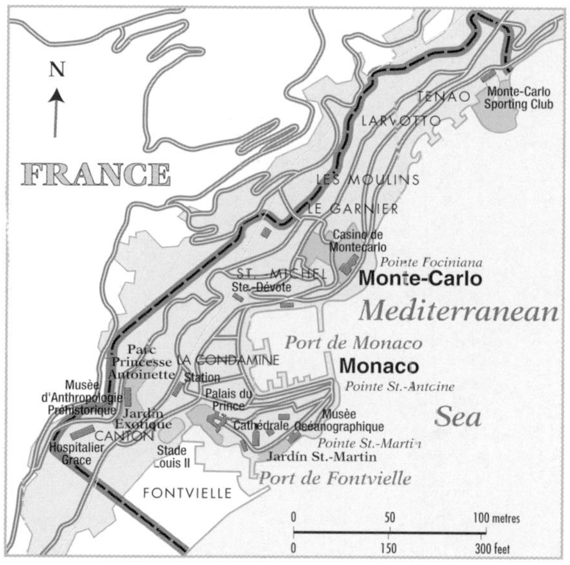

Official name: Principality of Monaco
Form of government: constitutional monarchy
Capital: Monaco
Official language: French
Monetary unit: French franc
Religious affiliation: Roman Catholic (95%)
Ethnic composition of the population: French (47%), Monagascan (16%), Italian (16%), other (21%)
Area: 1.95 sq km
Total population: 31,719 inhabitants
Population density: 16,266 persons per sq km
GDP: U.S.$280 million

Population evolution and projection

in thousands of persons

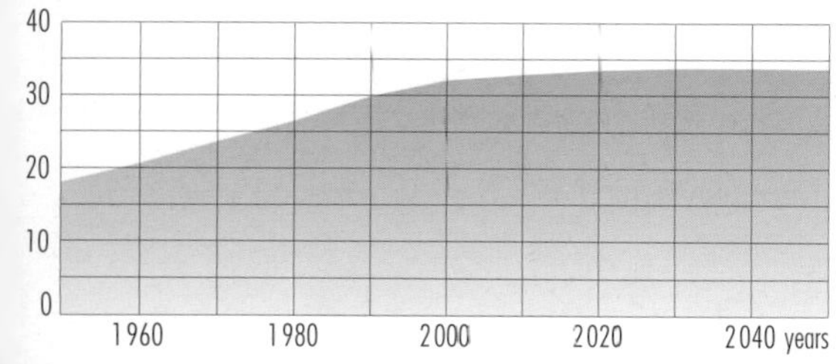

Population age distribution

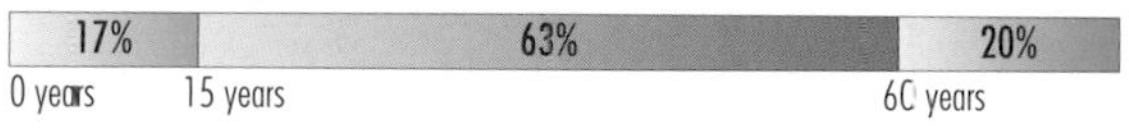

Per capita income (GDP per person)

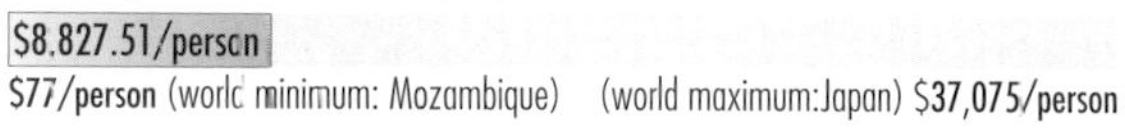

Labor force

2,600 persons

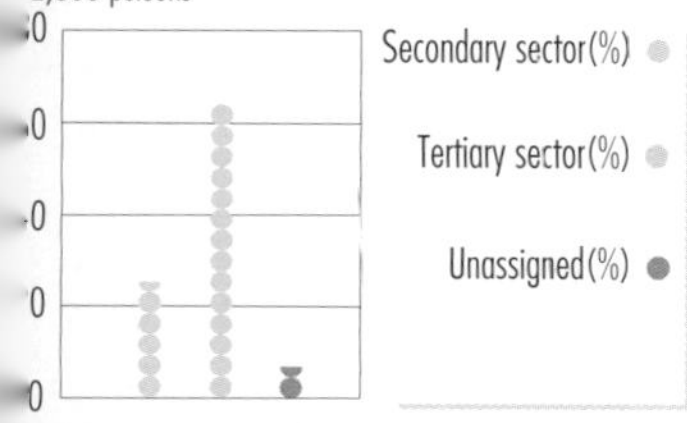

Vital statistics

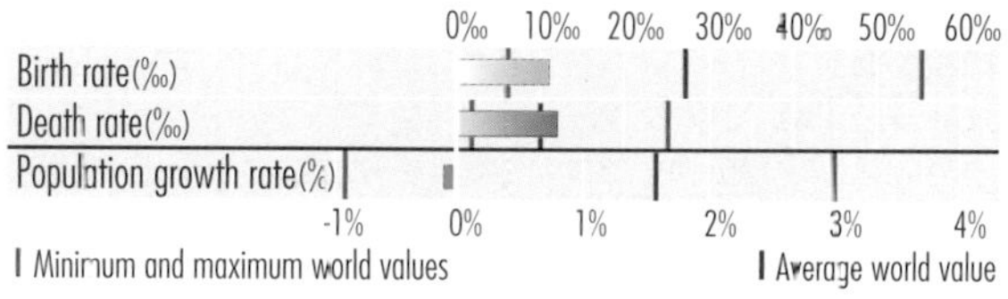

Land use

Principal places of origin of foreign visitors

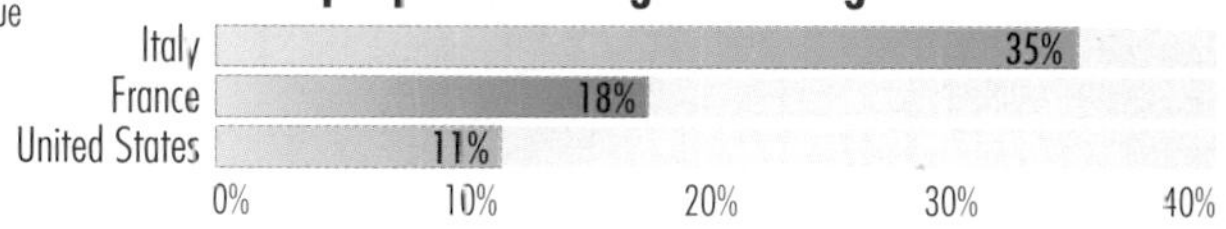

The Netherlands

The Netherlands is a state of western Europe comprising a territory of low flat lands. Despite the uniformity of the terrain, several landscape types can be distinguished: the wide sandy extensions of the south and east (regions of Brabant, Overijssel and Drenthe); the calcareous plateau of Limbourg, in the southeast; the alluvial soils of the coastal regions of the center and south (Holland and Zeeland) and of the territories gained from the sea in the northwest (polderlands); the peat bog soils, very abundant especially in the regions of the north; and the long strip of coastal dunes. The great surface area situated below sea level has been recovered with polders, canals and great dikes. The fluvial branches of the rivers — Schelde, Maas (Meuse), etc.— have been rerouted, channeled and drained. The Netherlands have a marine west coast climate with a small range of thermal variation and are struck frequently by strong winds, especially from the west. The total volume of precipitation is not very high.

The Netherlander (Germanic) ethnic group is predominant, with the major language, Dutch also of Germanic origin. Immigrants constitute a small percentage, with a number of Surinamese and those from former colonies, besides Turks, Moroccans, Belgians, etc. The population is distributed irregularly throughout the territory; the greatest concentrations are in the west, in the provinces of Zuid-Holland, Noord-Holland and Utrecht. The high degree of predominance of tertiary activities and an orientation towards the exterior characterize the Dutch economy. Export is favored by the geographical location of the country and by the highly developed means of transport and communication. To the textile and electrical appliance industries, chemical, petroleum, electro-mechanical, food product, paper, metallurgical and ship-building industries have been added. Farming (the cultivation of flowers above all), livestock husbandry (with an important cheese-making industry) and fishing also contribute important revenues. Important reserves of natural gas exist, used in part to meet domestic consumption. Other sources of energy are coal-fueled thermal energy, nuclear energy, hydroelectric and wind power.

Official name: Kingdom of The Netherlands

Form of government: constitutional monarchy

Capital: Amsterdam and The Hague (Amsterdam/'s-Gravenhage)

Official language: Dutch

Monetary unit: Netherlands guilder

Religious affiliation: Roman Catholic (33%), Dutch Reformed Church (15%), Calvinist (8%), Muslim (3.2%), other (1.8%), nonreligious (39%)

Ethnic composition of the population: Netherlander (96%), Moroccan, Turkish and other (4%)

Area: 41,526 sq km

Total population: 15,568,000 inhabitants

Population density: 374.9 persons per sq km

Population

- O Over 500,000
- ◎ Over 100,000
- ○ Over 50,000
- • Over 10,000
- · Under 10,000

Population evolution and projection

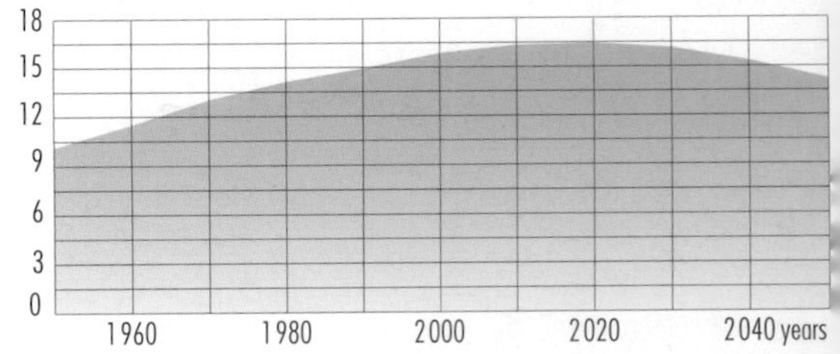

GDP structure

395,900 million dollars

Labor force

7,090,000 persons

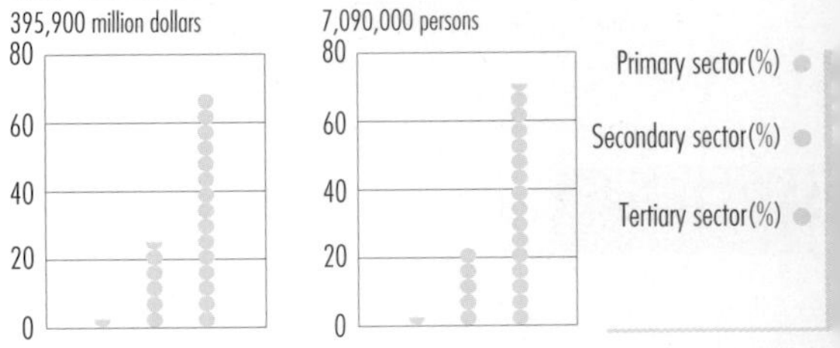

Population age distribution

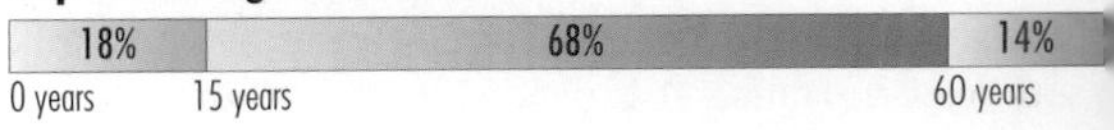

Vital statistics

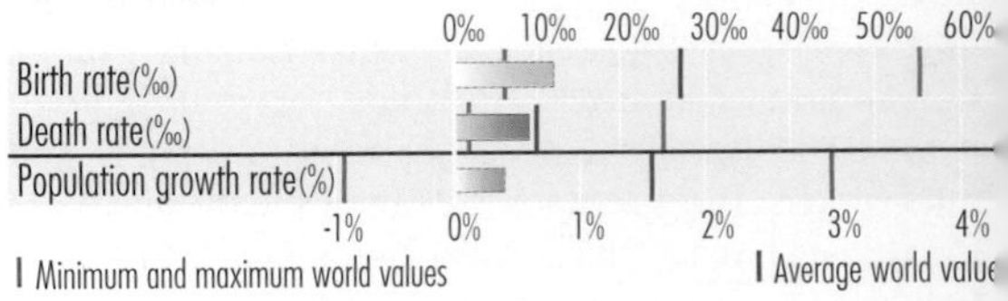

Literacy (% of population over15)

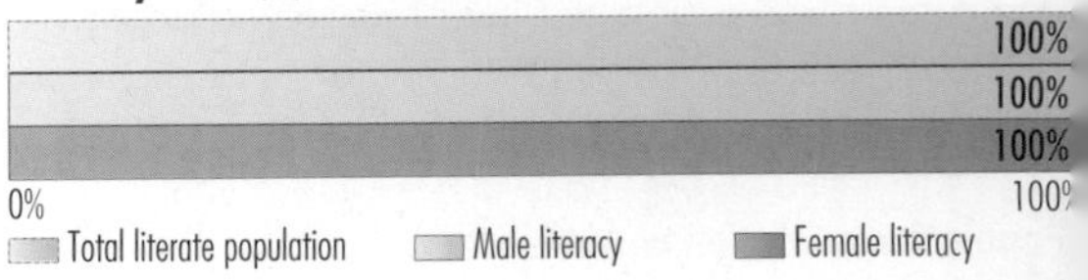

Per capita income (GDP per person)

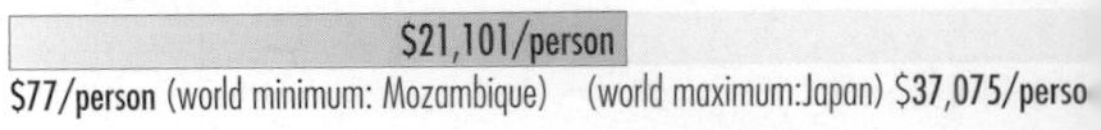

Unemployment (% of total population economically active)

Land use

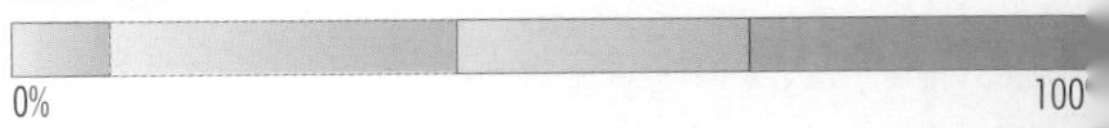

Industry

Manufacturing

- Food, beverages and tobacco
- Textiles, clothing, leather and footwear
- Wood, cork and furniture
- Paper and graphic arts
- Chemical products
- Building materials, glass and cement
- Metallurgy and metal products
- Machinery and transport equipment
- Electrical, electronical and optical equipment

Mining

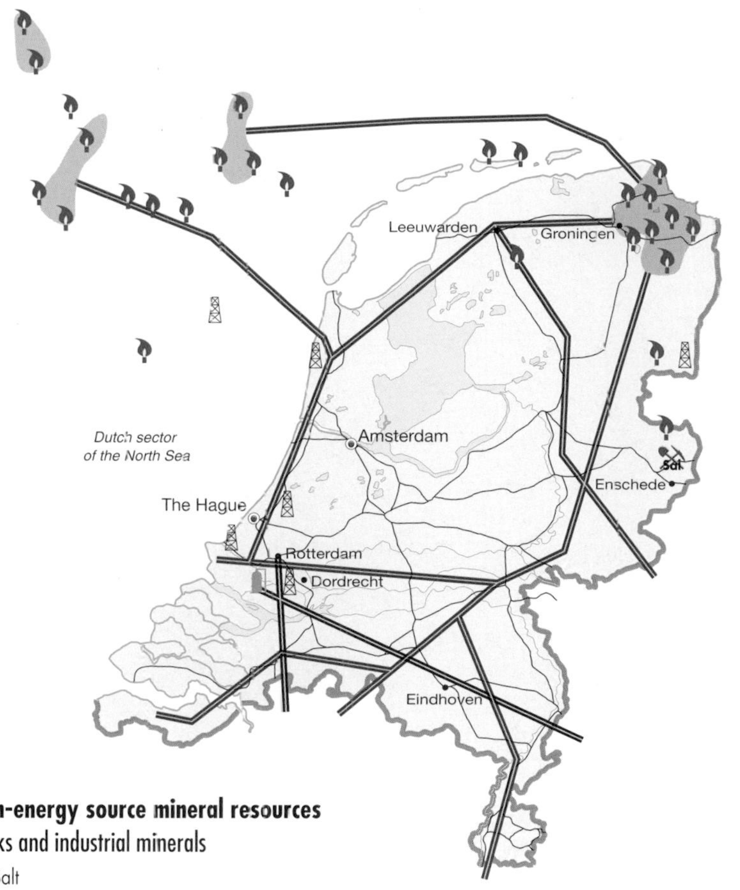

Non-energy source mineral resources

Rocks and industrial minerals

- Salt

Mineral fuel resources

Fossil fuels

- Natural gas
- Petroleum
- Gas and oil field

Energy-related installations

- Refinery
- Gas pipeline
- Oil pipeline

Sedimentary facies

Sedimentary layers

- Marine deposits
- River deposits
- Glacier deposits
- Peat bogs
- Lands recovered from the sea or the peat bogs

Structures

- Sedimentary covering

Agriculture

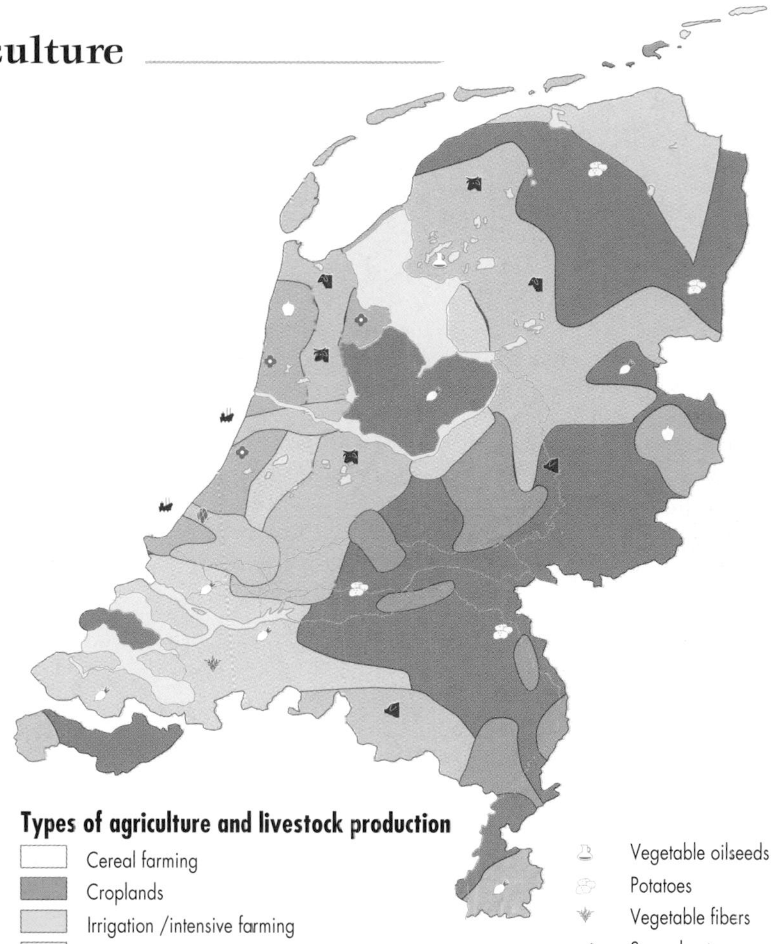

Types of agriculture and livestock production

- Cereal farming
- Croplands
- Irrigation /intensive farming
- Meadows and pastures
- Forests/brush
- Non-arable land
- Urban area
- Vegetables
- Apples
- Vegetable oilseeds
- Potatoes
- Vegetable fibers
- Sugar beets
- Flowers
- Cattle
- Sheep
- Pigs
- Fishing

Norway

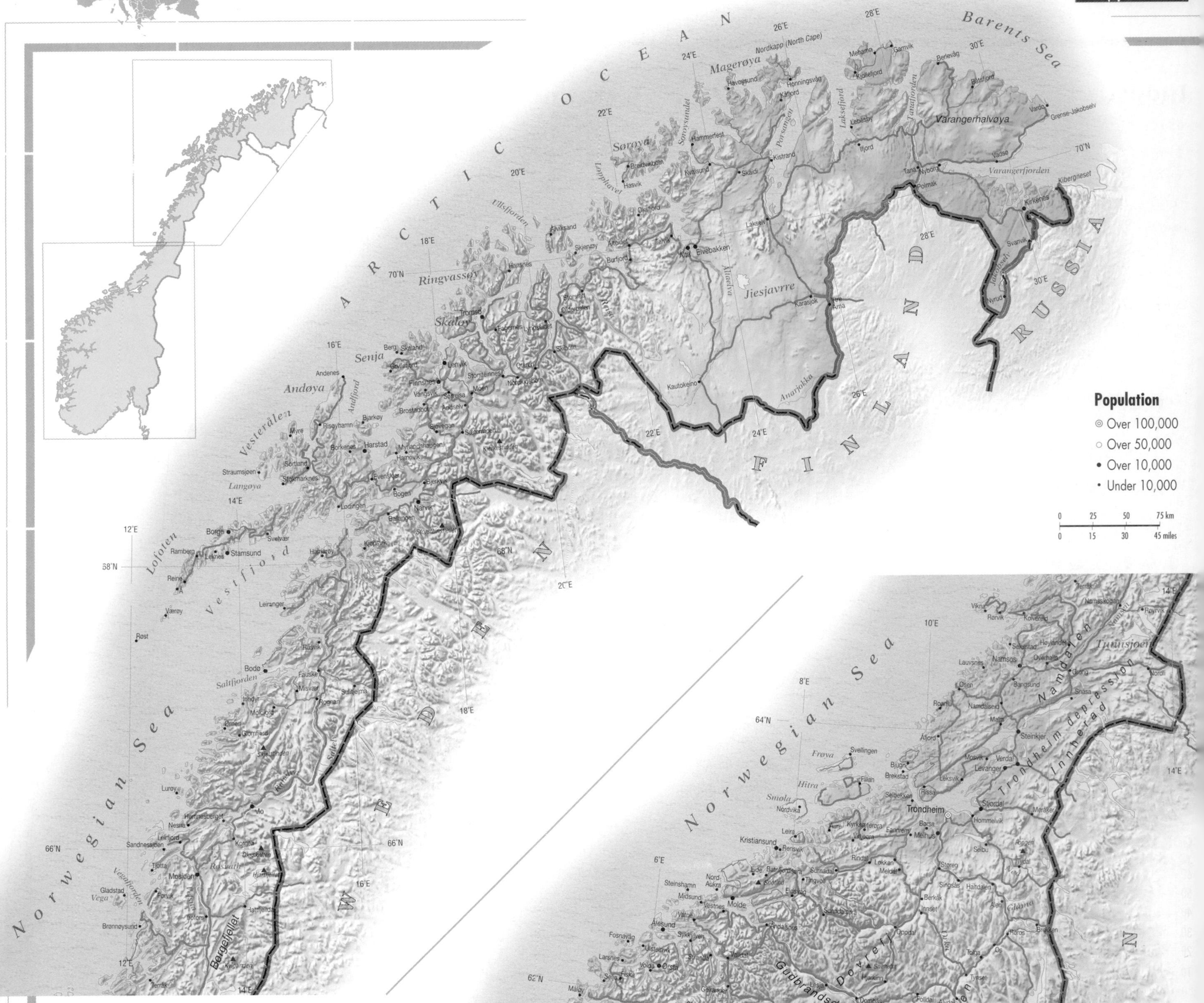

Norway is a state of northern Europe situated on the northwestern water-shed of the Scandinavian Peninsula. The country is very mountainous and coastal, with a shoreline that comprises narrow jagged fiords and thousands of islands, islets and shoals. The territory is divided into three regions: Finmark, the northernmost of the three, formed by a group of highlands; a narrow strip between the Norwegian Sea and Sweden, bordered by the Scandinavian Alps and the Trondheim depression; and the southern area, south of Trondheim, with more alpine landscape. The warm Gulf Stream and the winds from the west which bring moisture from the Atlantic make the climate of Norway milder. In general, the only winter temperatures registering below zero are recorded north of Trondheim. Summers are cool and rainy. Norway has a low population density, as well as a relatively homogeneous ethnic composition (except in Finmark, where enclaves of Finns and Laps are found). Its inhabitants are distributed very irregularly across the territory. Fishing ranks among Norway's main economic resources. An important food-processing industry has also developed, derived from the fish catches, and there are fish-hatcheries dedicated to raising salmon. Sheep, cattle, pig and reindeer husbandry have a greater economic weight than farming (cereals, fruits, vegetables, etc.). Forest resources have encouraged the consolidation of the lumbering industry. Important deposits of petroleum and natural gas exist, which have favored the growth of industrial activity, especially the chemical and steel-metallurgical branches.

Official name: Kingdom of Norway
Form of government: constitutional monarchy
Capital: Oslo
Official language: Norwegian
Monetary unit: Norwegian krone
Religious affiliation: Lutheran (87.9%), nonreligious (3.2%), other (8.9%)
Ethnic composition of the population: Norwegian (96.4%) Danish (0.4%), Swedish (0.3%), British (0.3%), Pakistani (0.3%), United States (0.2%), Irani (0.2%), other (1.9%)
Area: 323,878 sq km
Total population: 4,384,000 inhabitants
Population density: 13.5 persons per sq km

Agriculture

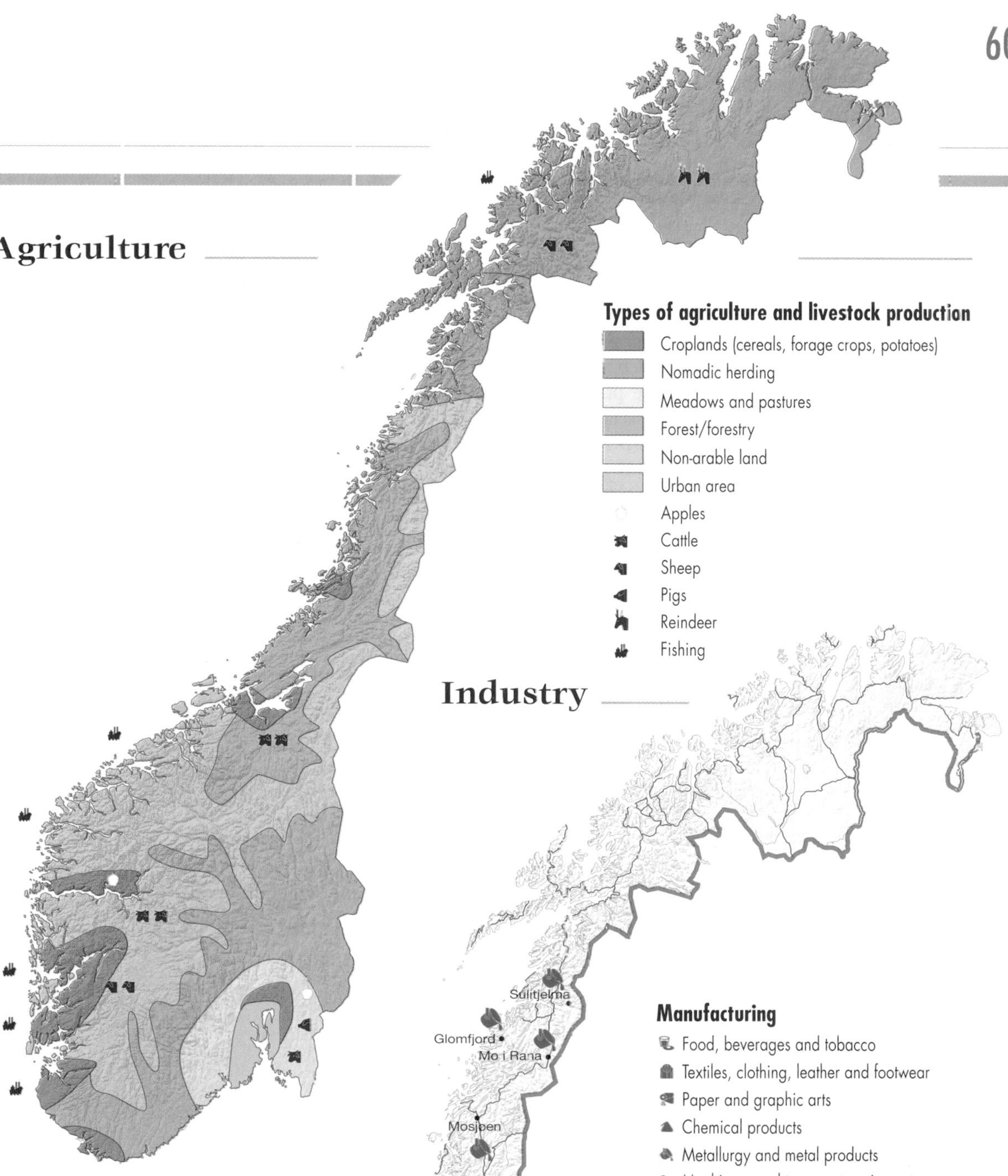

Mining and Energy

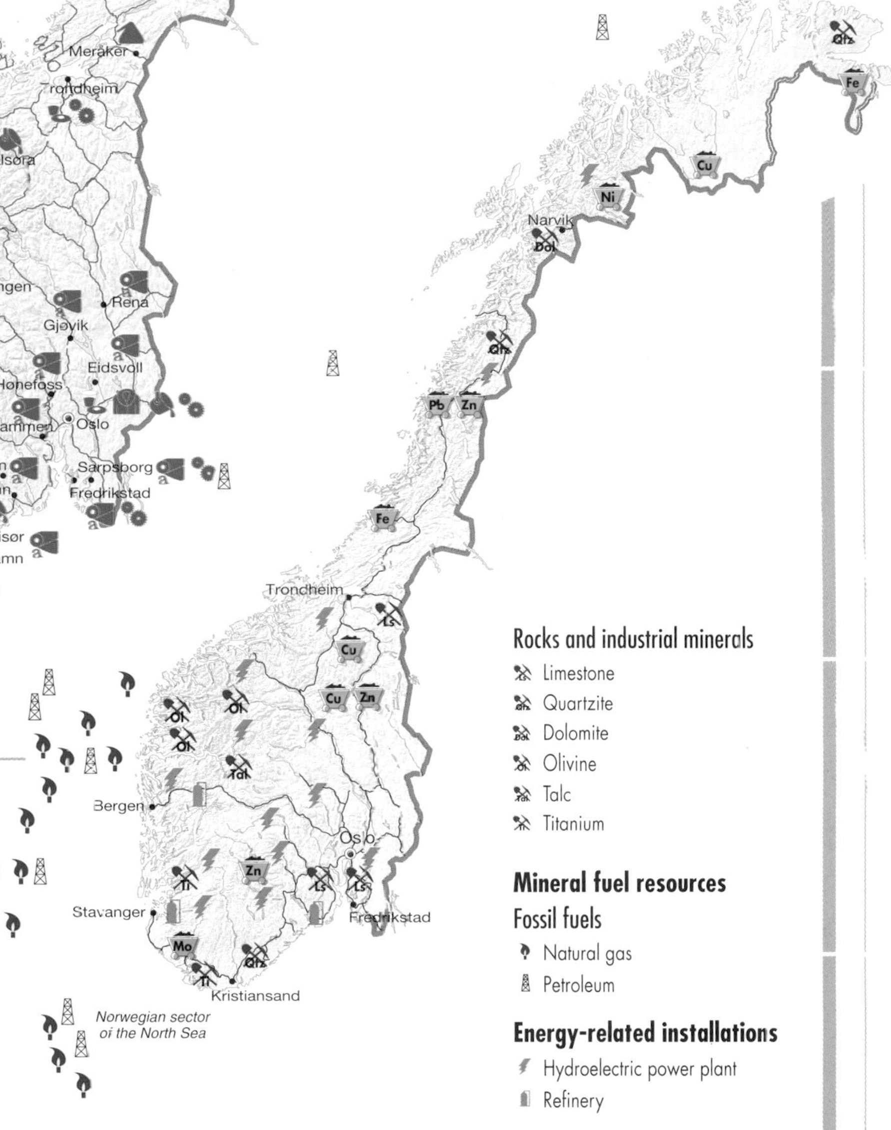

Population evolution and projection

in millions of persons

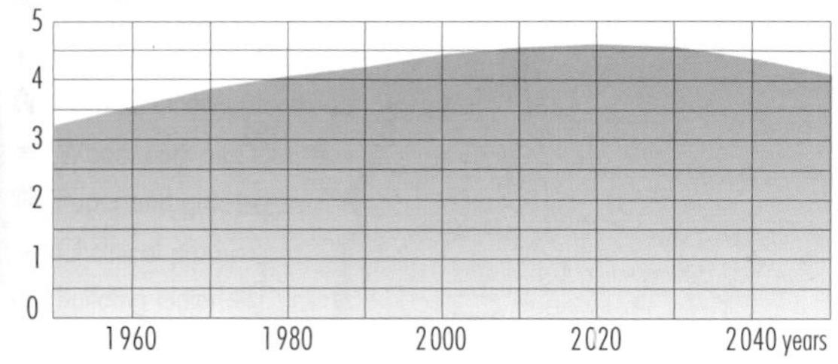

GDP structure

145,954 million dollars

Labor force

2,193,000 persons

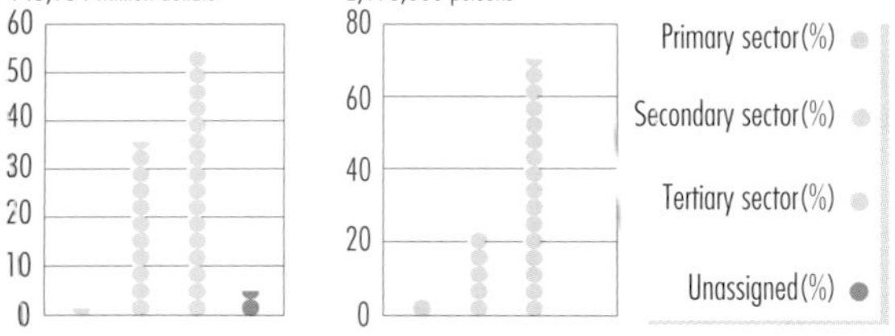

Population age distribution

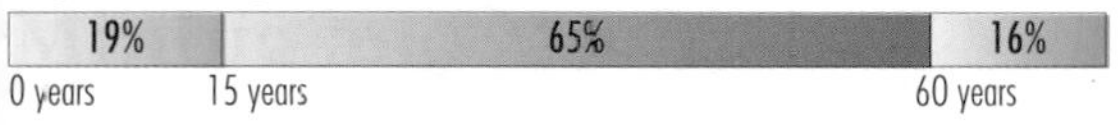

Vital statistics

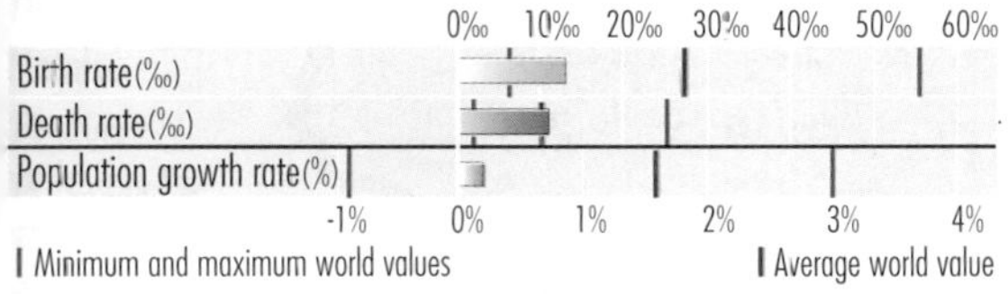

Literacy (% of population over15)

Per capita income (GDP per person)

Unemployment (% of total population economically active)

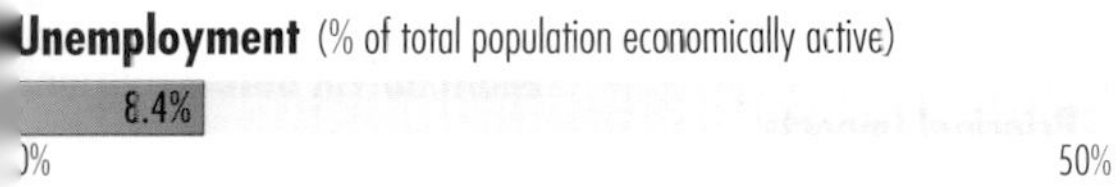

Land use

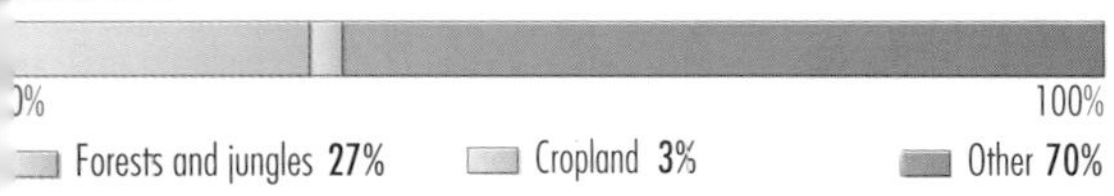

Portugal

Portugal is a republic of southwestern Europe that has three geomorphological elements: the old massif occupies most of the territory; the "orlas" constitute folded lands that extend from the mouth of the Douro River to the Sado, the coastal regions of the Alentejo and the Algarve; finally, the Tejo (Tagus)-Sado depression, framed by the lower basins of these rivers. The Azores and Madeira Islands archipelagos, both of volcanic origin, also belong to the Portuguese nation. The principal rivers have their origin in the interior of the peninsula —Tejo (Tagus), Douro, Guadiana and Minho (Miño)—, although exclusively Portuguese watercourses exist (the most important are the Vouga, the Mondego and the Sado). Portugal has a Mediterranean climate, with a marked summer drought. Its lengthwise orientation confers broad climatic variety to the country. The southern part and the coast enjoy a Mediterranean climate, the northwestern area receives strong Atlantic influences (marine west coast climate) and continental characteristics are apparent in the interior. Ethnic homogeneity defines the population of Portugal, which is distributed unevenly throughout the territory: the north and the coast register the highest demographic densities. Portugal's economic development is hindered by archaic agrarian structures, deficient systems of industrial production and the strong imbalance between the north and the coastal zone and the rest of the country. Ranking among the principal industrial sectors are textiles, footwear, lumbering, food-processing and ceramics. Forestry represents the most important field of the primary sector. Another noteworthy source of income is the tourist industry.

Official name: Portuguese Republic
Form of government: parliamentary democracy
Capital: Lisbon (Lisboa)
Official language: Portuguese
Monetary unit: escudo
Religious affiliation: Christian (96%), nonreligious (3.8%), Jewish (0.1%), Muslim (0.1%)
Ethnic composition of the population: predominantly Mediterranean with a minority of immigrants from independent former colonies
Area: 92,135 sq km
Total population: 9,865,000 inhabitants
Population density: 107.1 persons per sq km

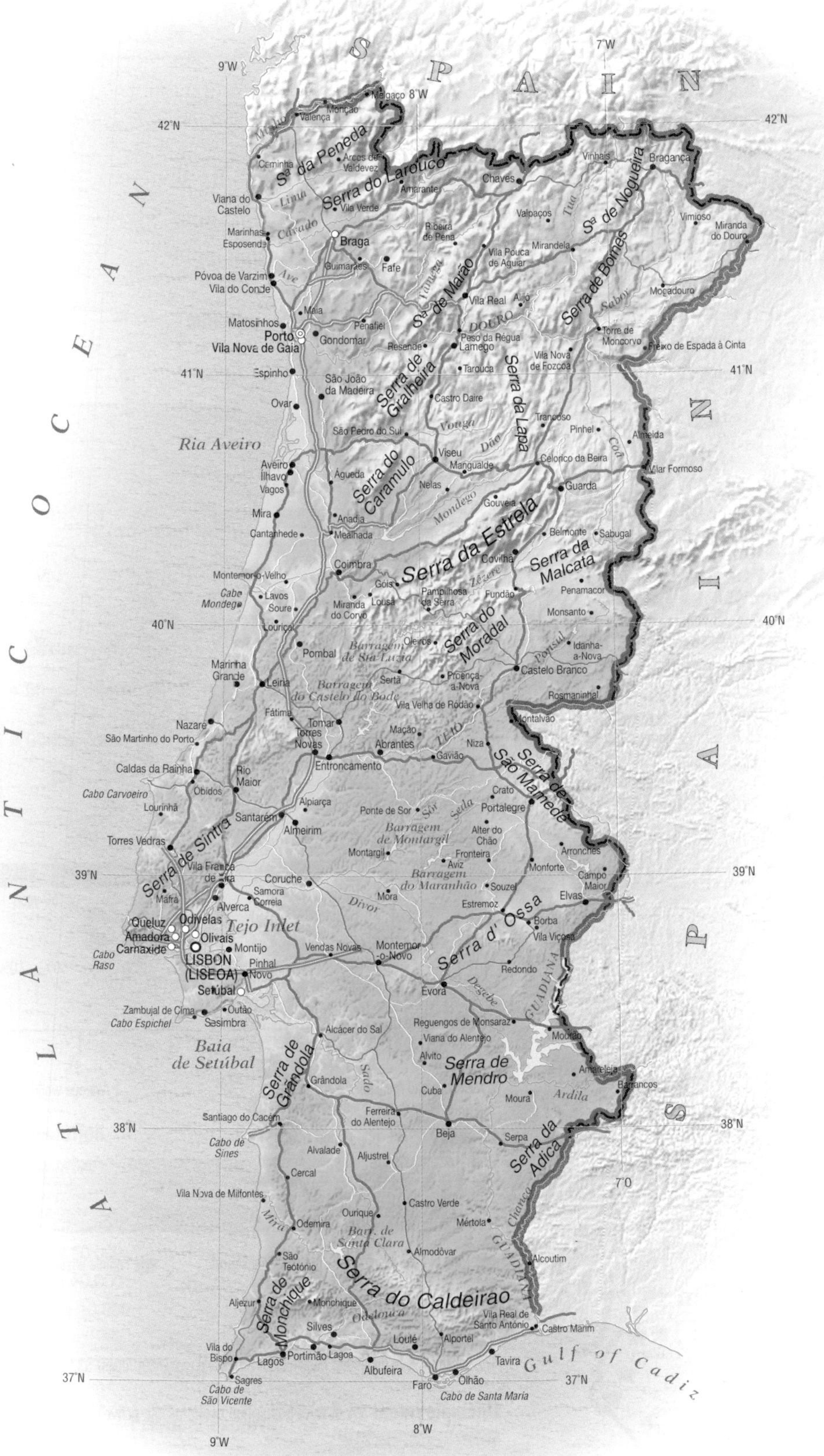

Population

- Over 500,000
- Over 100,000
- Over 50,000
- Over 10,000
- Under 10,000

0 25 50 75 km
0 10 20 30 40 50 miles

Population evolution and projection

in millions of persons

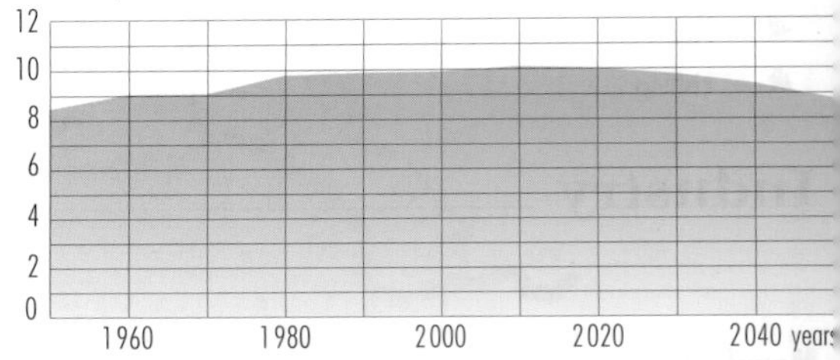

GDP structure

102,337 million dollars

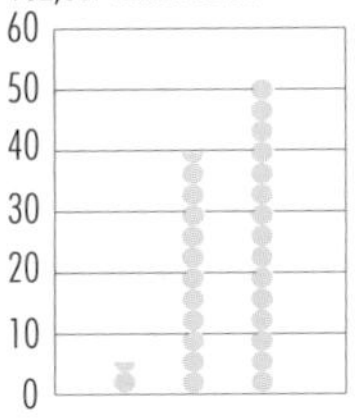

Labor force

4,861,000 persons

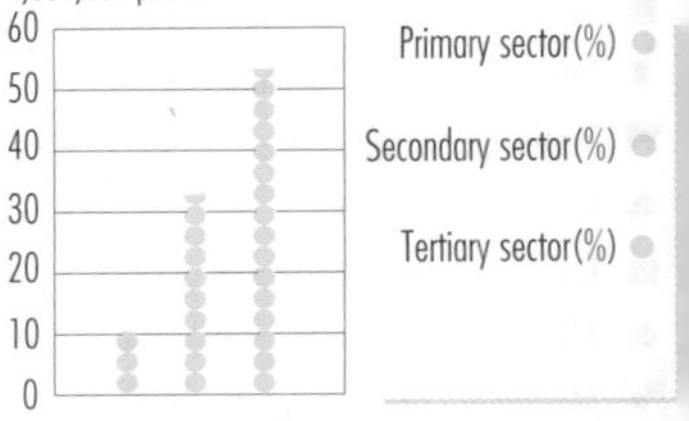

Population age distribution

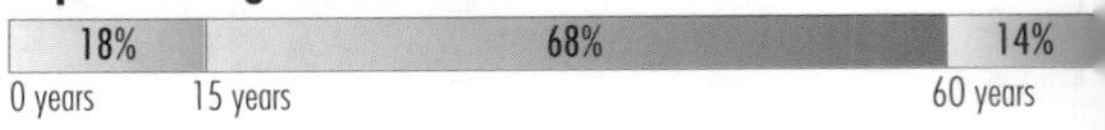

Vital statistics

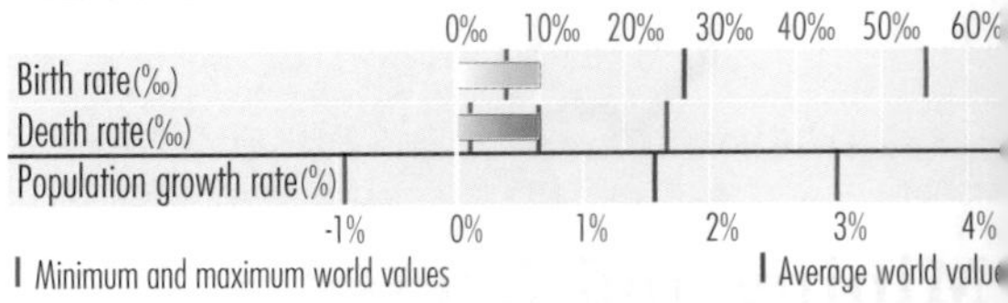

Literacy (% of population over15)

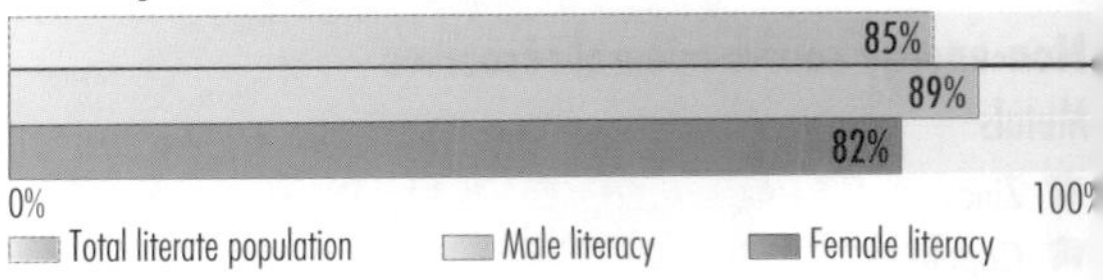

Geostructural units

Geology

- Paleozoic
- Mesozoic
- Tertiary
- Quaternary

Structures

- Caledonian and Hercynian roots
- Sedimentary covering

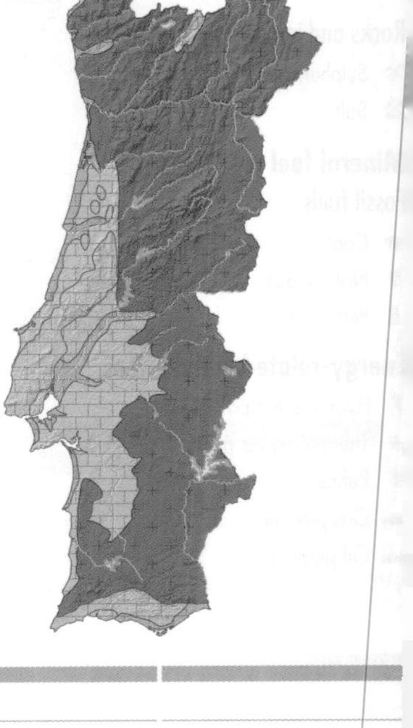

Per capita income (GDP per person)

$77/person (world minimum: Mozambique) (world maximum:Japan) $37,075/person

Land use

Forests and jungles 34% | Cropland 33% | Other 22.5%
Meadows and pastures 10.5%

Unemployment (% of total population economically active)

Agriculture and Industry

- Cereal-farming (wheat, rye, oats, corn)
- Croplands (cereals, potatoes, legumes)
- Mixed farming (grapevines, olive trees, citrus fruits, fruit trees, vegetables, cereals)
- Highland pastures
- Meadows and pastures
- Forests
- Urban area

- Rice
- Apples
- Citrus fruits
- Grapevines
- Olive trees
- Potatoes
- Sheep
- Pigs
- Fishing

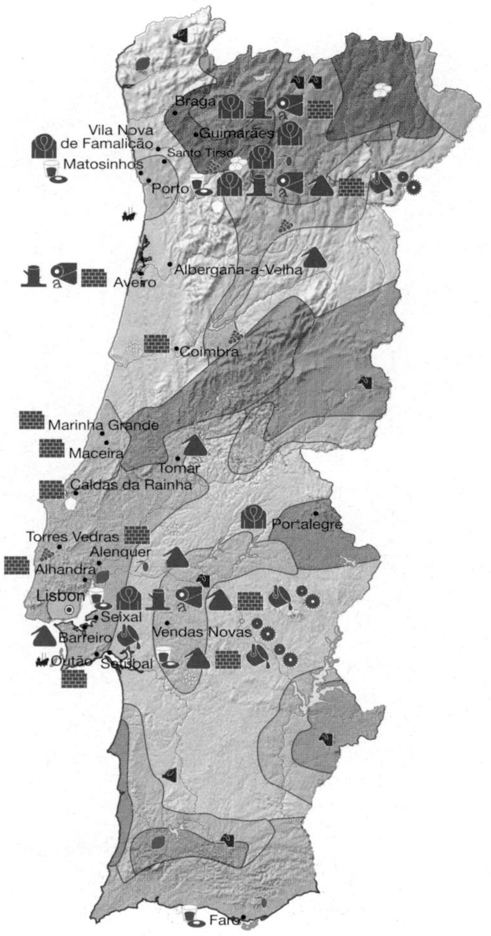

Manufacturing

- Food, beverages and tobacco
- Textiles, clothing, leather and footwear
- Wood, cork and furniture
- Paper and graphic arts
- Chemical products
- Building materials, glass and cement
- Metallurgy and metal products
- Machinery and transport equipment

Mining and Energy

Non-energy source mineral resources

Metals

- Zinc
- Copper
- Tin
- Iron ore
- Manganese
- Gold
- Silver
- Lead
- Wolfram

Rocks and industrial minerals

- Barite
- Feldspar
- Marble
- Salt
- Talc

Mineral fuel resources

Fossil fuels

- Coal
- Petroleum

Radioactive fuel

- Uranium

Energy-related installations

- Hydroelectric power plant
- Thermal power plant
- Refinery

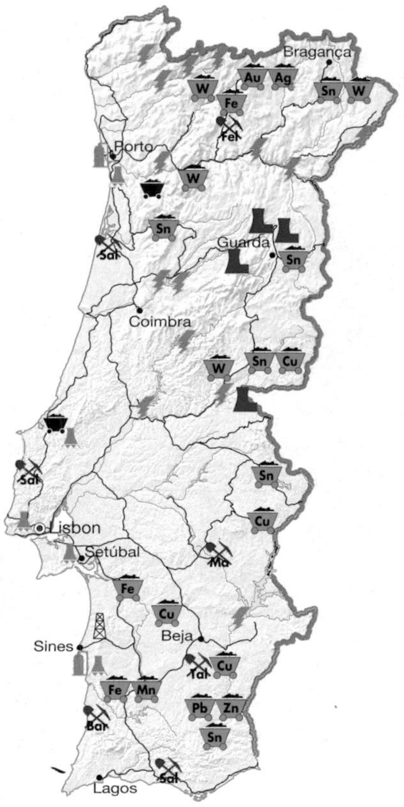

Romania

Romania is a Balkan state of eastern Europe. Four regions comprise its territory: the Carpathian Mountain Range, located in the center of the country and laid out in a U-shape open toward the northwest; the great plateau of Transylvania, situated in the interior of the Carpathians; the Plateau of Moldava, extending to the east; the extensive Danubian plains of the south. Romania has a continental climate, although the diversity of its physical environment favors the existence of significant variations. The regions of Transylvania and the Carpathians have harsher climates, while the shores of the Black Sea enjoy milder temperatures. Because of their culture and origin, the bulk of the population is homogeneous and is composed of a large majority of Romanians. There are minority groups of Hungarians and Germans, besides Serbs, Croats, Ukrainians, Turks, Gypsies and Jews. The Romanian language is derived from Latin. The distribution of the population within the territory does not reveal great imbalances, although the mountain areas show a lower demographic density. Romanian industry is disproportionate compared to the level of development of other productive sectors, absorbs a great deal of energy and lacks efficiency; the chemical, automotive, electronic and consumer goods sectors are the most important. Agriculture, with cereals as the most noteworthy crops, has also suffered a decrease in productivity, just as stock raising has, affected by the difficult situation in which the agricultural sector is immersed.

Official name: Romania
Form of government: republic
Capital: Bucharest (București)
Official language: Romanian
Monetary unit: Romanian leu
Religious affiliation: Romanian Orthodox (86.8%), Roman Catholic (5%), Greek Orthodox (3.5%), Muslim (0.2%), other (4.5%)
Ethnic composition of the population: Romanian (89.1%), Hungarian (8.8%), German (0.4%), Ukrainian, Serb, Croat, Russian, Turk and Gypsy (1.6%)
Area: 237,500 sq km
Total population: 21,657,000 inhabitants
Population density: 91.2 persons per sq km

Population evolution and projection
in millions of persons

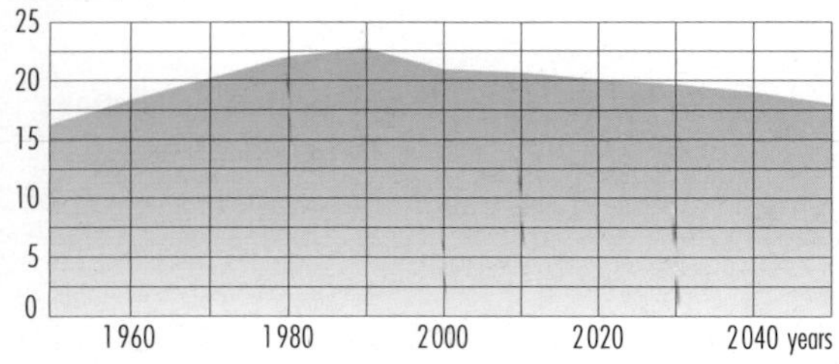

GDP structure
35,533 million dollars

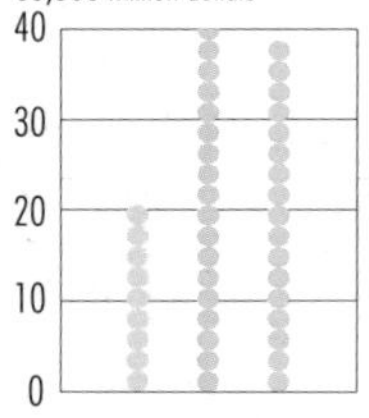

Labor force
10,703,000 persons

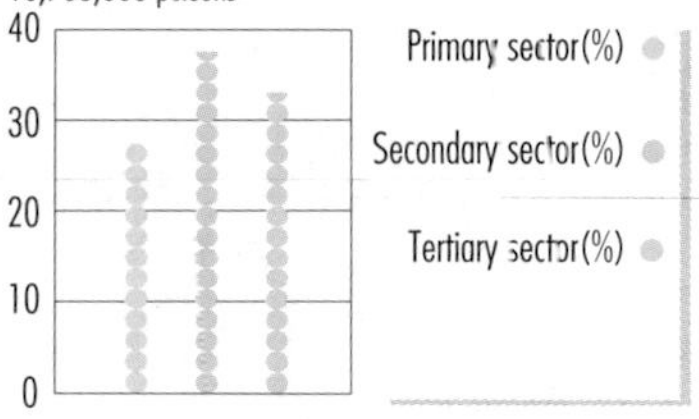

Population age distribution

21% | 67% | 12%
0 years | 15 years | 60 years

Land use

0% — 100%

Forests and jungles **28%** | Cropland **46%**
Meadows and pastures **19%** | Other **7%**

Literacy (% of population over15)

97% | 98% | 95%

0% — 100%

Total literate population | Male literacy | Female literacy

Vital statistics

0‰ 10‰ 20‰ 30‰ 40‰ 50‰ 60‰

Birth rate(‰)
Death rate(‰)
Population growth rate(%)

-1% 0% 1% 2% 3% 4%

| Minimum and maximum world values | Average world value

Per capita income (GDP per person)

$1,174.21/person

$77/person (world minimum: Mozambique) (world maximum:Japan) $37,075/person

Unemployment (% of total population economically active)

10.9%

0% — 50%

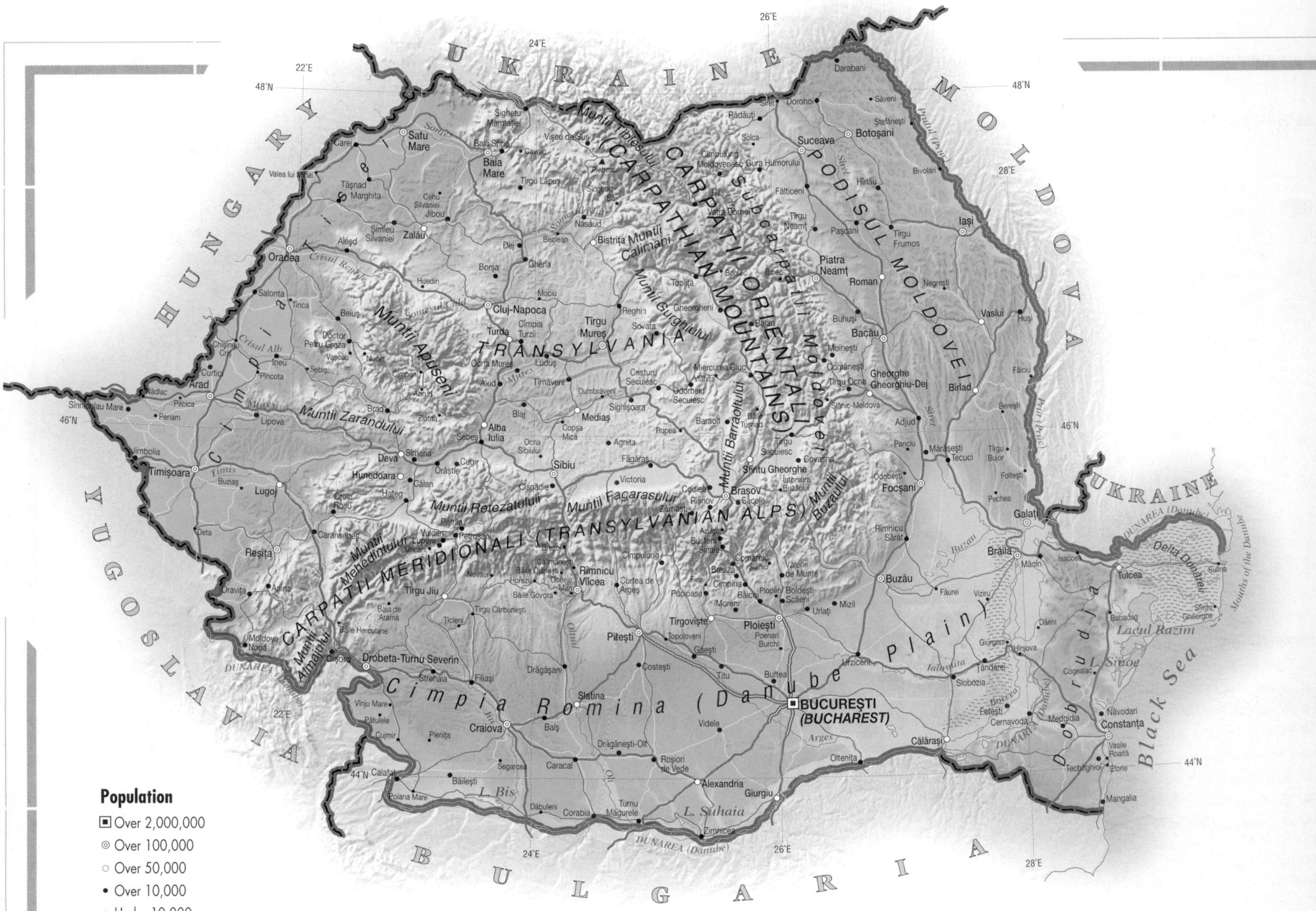

Population

- ▣ Over 2,000,000
- ◎ Over 100,000
- ○ Over 50,000
- • Over 10,000
- · Under 10,000

Agriculture

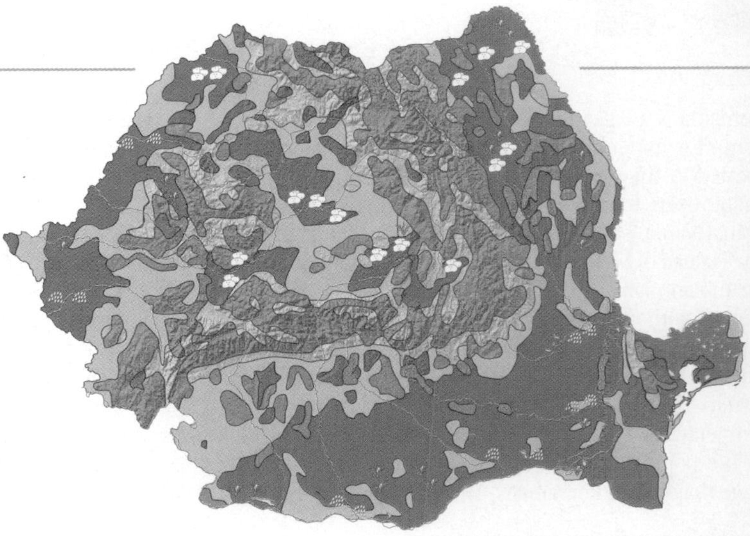

Types of agriculture and livestock production

- Croplands (wheat potatoes, sugar beets, rye) and stock raising
- Perennial crops (grapevines) and vegetables
- Meadows and pcstures
- Forest/brush
- Swampland
- Urban area
- Rice
- Potatoes
- Flax

Mining and Energy

Non-energy source mineral resources

Metals

- Bauxite
- Zinc
- Copper
- Iron ore
- Manganese
- Gold
- Silver
- Lead

Mineral fuel resources

Fossil fuels

- Coal
- Coal field
- Natural gas
- Petroleum

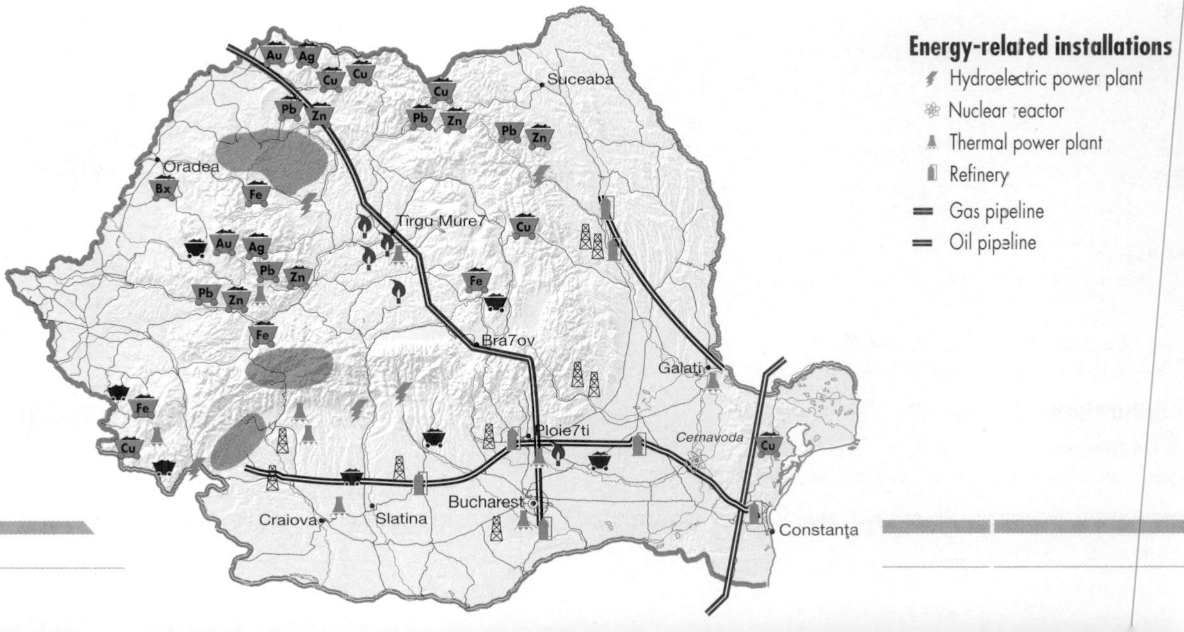

Energy-related installations

- Hydroelectric power plant
- Nuclear reactor
- Thermal power plant
- Refinery
- Gas pipeline
- Oil pipeline

Industry

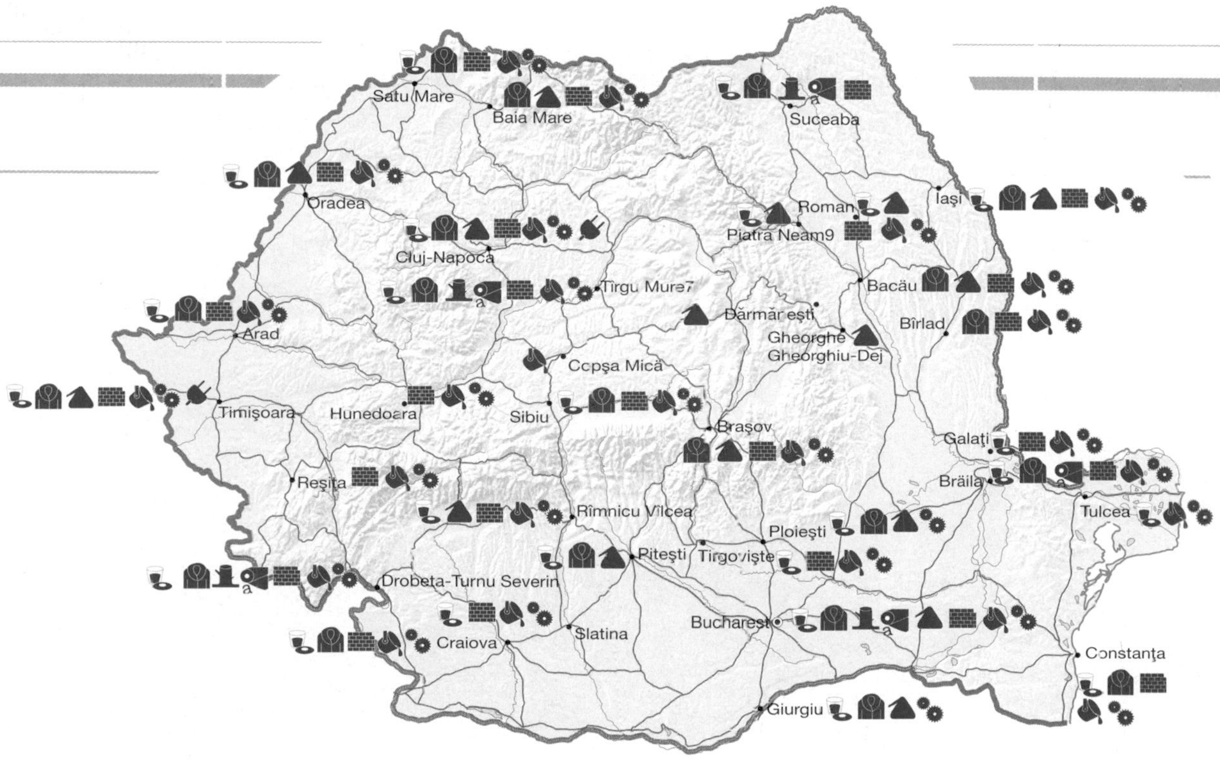

Manufacturing
- Food, beverages and tobacco
- Textiles, clothing, leather and footwear
- Wood, cork and furniture
- Paper and graphic arts
- Chemical products
- Building materials, glass and cement
- Metallurgy and metal products
- Machinery and transport equipment
- Electrical, electronical and optical equipment

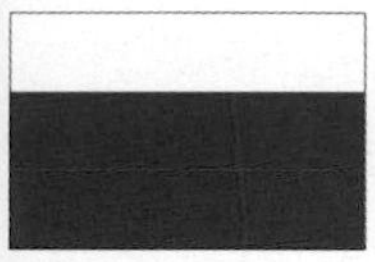

Russia

Russia is a state of eastern Europe and northern Asia, with coasts on the Baltic Sea (the west), the Arctic Ocean (the north) and the Pacific Ocean (the east). It is a federation comprising 21 autonomous republics. Its landform features are composed of an immense plain, lying between the Baltic Sea and the Yenisey River, which is dotted with small heights and numerous lakes and swamps. The Ural Mountains (Uralskiy Khrebet), of relatively narrow width and low altitude, cross the country from north to south, marking the dividing line between the North European Plain and the Siberian Plain (Sibirskaya Ravnina), which forms part of the continent of Asia. South of the European plain rise the Caucasus Mountains, with the highest peaks of Europe (Mount Elbrus, 5,642 m). On the eastern tip of the Siberian Plain appear mountain ranges of volcanic origin (Kliuchevskaya Sopka, 4,750 m). The country possesses a vast drainage basin, with great watercourses and lakes; the most important rivers are the Obi (Ob) (5,410 km in length), in the region of Siberia, and the Volga River (3,531 km in length), in the European part. Russia's climate, continental in type, suffers great thermal contrasts, seasonally as well as daily. The intermediate seasons —spring and autumn— are very brief, the opposite of summer and winter, periods in which extreme temperatures are reached (average winter temperature of –51.2 ºC in Verkhoyansk, Siberia). Precipitation, generally scanty, is approximately 400 to 600 mm annually, except in the Caucasian regions, where the altitude is a incrementing factor; snow lasts for many months. Russia has very low population density, due to the fact that Siberia is hardly inhabited. Four-fifths of the country's inhabitants are concentrated in the European part. More than 100 ethnic groups of diverse languages and origins inhabit the Federation, in which Russians are numerically predominant. The official language is Russian, and the major religion is Eastern Orthodox, but Islam, Roman Catholicism and Buddhism are also professed. The Russian economy has inherited the productive stagnation of the former Soviet Union and faces grave problems (obsolete technology, negative growth, inflation and unemployment). The standard of living of the population has worsened alarmingly.

Official name: Russian Federation
Form of government: federation
Capital: Moscow (Moskva)
Official language: Russian
Monetary unit: ruble
Ethnic composition of the population: Russian (81.5%), Tatar (3.8%), Ukrainian (3%), Chuvash (1.2%), Bashkir (0.9%), Belarusian (0.8%), Moldavan (0.7%), other (8.1%)
Area: 17,075,400 sq km
Total population: 148,178,000 inhabitants
Population density: 8.7 persons per sq km

Agriculture

Types of agriculture and livestock production
- Cereal farming (wheat, barley, oats, corn)
- Croplands (cereals, forage crops, potatoes, sugar beets)
- Intensive farming
- Plantation farming
- Subsistence farming and forest
- Nomadic herding, reindeer husbandry and hunting
- Pastures
- Forest
- Non-arable land
- Urban area
- Vegetables
- Grapevines
- Vegetable oilseeds
- Potatoes
- Vegetable fibers
- Cotton
- Sugar beets
- Tea
- Tobacco
- Cattle
- Sheep
- Pigs
- Reindeer
- Hunting (furs)
- Fishing

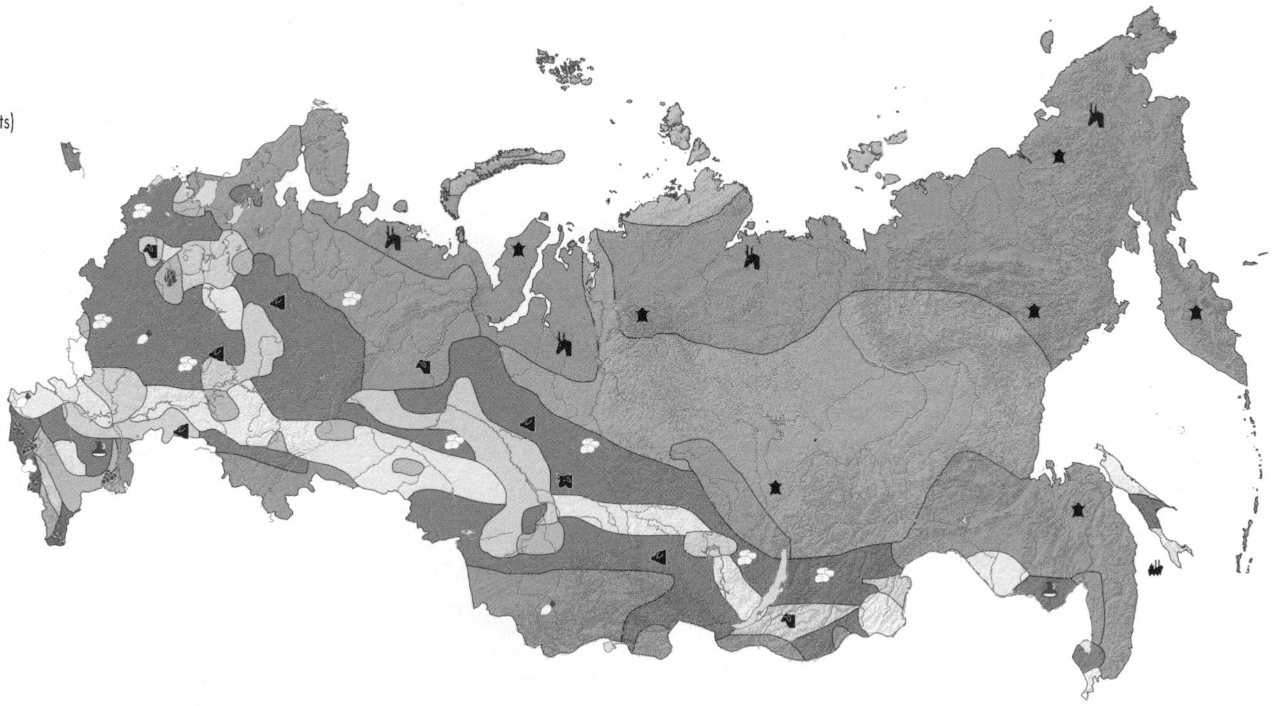

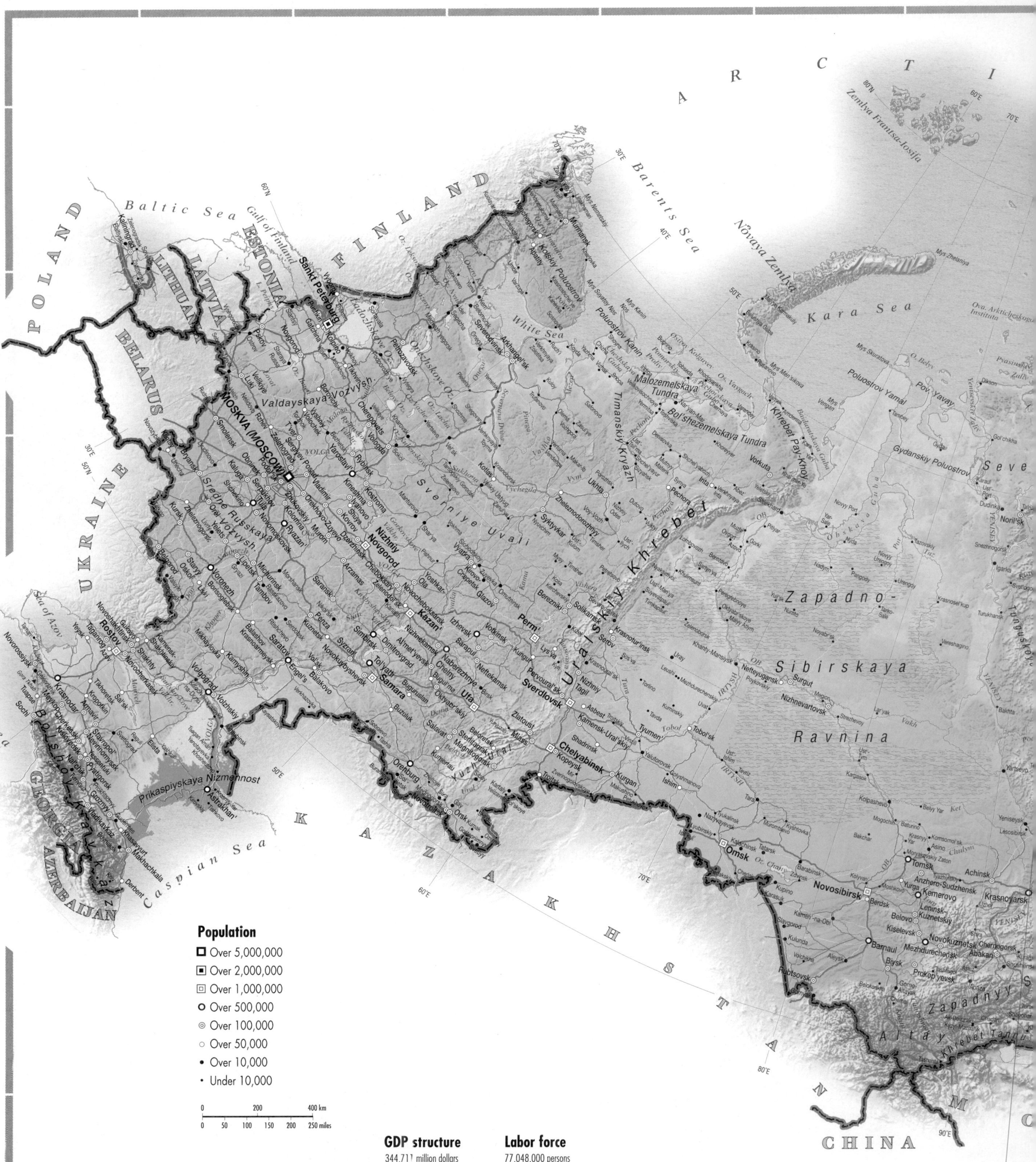

A R C T I
Zemlya Frantsa-Iosifa
Barents Sea
Novaya Zemlya
Kara Sea
White Sea
Baltic Sea
Gulf of Finland
FINLAND
POLAND
ESTONIA
LATVIA
LITHUANIA
BELARUS
UKRAINE
GEORGIA
AZERBAIJAN
K A Z A K H S T A N
CHINA
Black Sea
Sea of Azov
Caspian Sea
Sankt Peterburg
MOSKVA (MOSCOW)
Valdayskaya Vozvyshennost'
Sredne Russkaya Vozvyshennost'
Severnye Uvaly
Nizhniy Novgorod
Kazan'
Samara
Saratov
Volgograd
Astrakhan'
Rostov
Krasnodar
Voronezh
Perm'
Ufa
Sverdlovsk
Chelyabinsk
Orenburg
Omsk
Novosibirsk
Barnaul
Kemerovo
Tomsk
Krasnoyarsk
Arkhangel'sk
Murmansk
Kol'skiy Poluostrov
Poluostrov Kanin
Malozemel'skaya Tundra
Bol'shezemel'skaya Tundra
Timanskiy Kryazh
Khrebet Pay-Khoy
Vorkuta
Ural'skiy Khrebet
Poluostrov Yamal
Gydanskiy Poluostrov
Zapadno-Sibirskaya Ravnina
Prikaspiyskaya Nizmennost
Bol'shoy Kavkaz
Altay
Zapadnyy Sayan
Population
Over 5,000,000
Over 2,000,000
Over 1,000,000
Over 500,000
Over 100,000
Over 50,000
Over 10,000
Under 10,000
0 200 400 km
0 50 100 150 200 250 miles

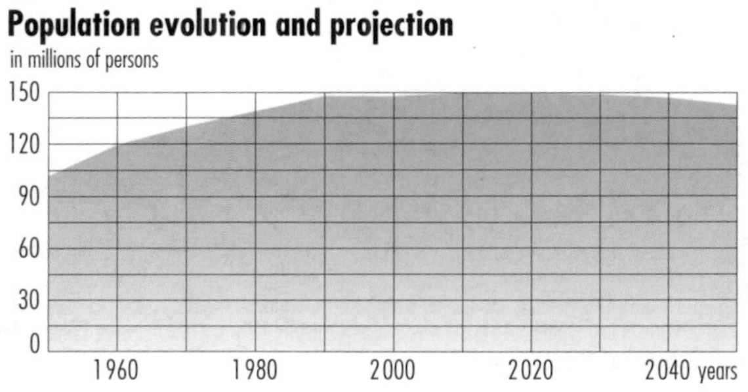

Population evolution and projection
in millions of persons
150
120
90
60
30
0
1960
1980
2000
2020
2040 years

GDP structure
344,711 million dollars
60
50
40
30
20
10
0
Labor force
77,048,000 persons
50
40
30
20
10
0
Primary sector(%)
Secondary sector(%)
Tertiary sector(%)
Unassigned(%)

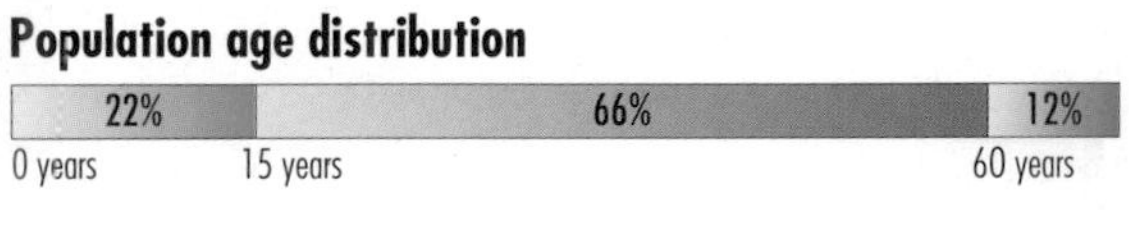

Population age distribution
22%
66%
12%
0 years
15 years
60 years

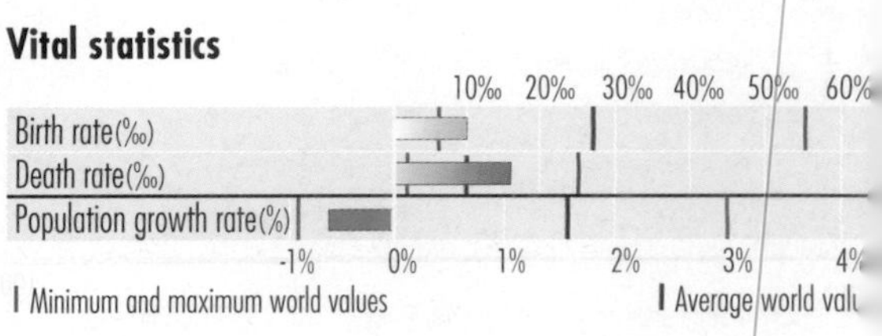

Vital statistics
10‰ 20‰ 30‰ 40‰ 50‰ 60‰
Birth rate(‰)
Death rate(‰)
Population growth rate(%)
-1% 0% 1% 2% 3% 4%
Minimum and maximum world values
Average world value

Literacy (% of population over15)

Total literate population	98%
Male literacy	100%
Female literacy	97%

0% — 100%

Per capita income (GDP per person)

$2,351.22/person

$77/person (world minimum: Mozambique) (world maximum:Japan) $37,075/person

Unemployment (% of total population economically active)

7.1%

0% — 50%

Land use

0% — 100%

Forests and jungles 45%
Meadows and pastures 15%
Cropland 8%
Other 32%

OCEANIA

Oceania

Australia and New Zealand

As can be seen in the image, Australia is the great territory around which Oceania is comprised; the island of Tasmania and New Zealand, moved from their real positions, complete the photographic mosaic of this page.

North of Australia the Gulf of Carpentaria is notable, closed on its eastern flank by Cape York Peninsula, with the cape of that name found on its northern tip. East of the cape and following the coastline in a southeasterly direction is the Great Barrier Reef that ends at the point where the coastline takes a southwesterly direction. Visible in the interior is the Great Dividing Range that traverses Australia from north to south. After passing Bass Strait, and moving in a westerly direction, Kangaroo Island, the Gulf of Spencer and the Great Australian Bight are found. In New Zealand, North Island and South Island can be seen separated by Cook Strait; south of this last island and separated from it by Foveaux Strait, Stewart Island is visible.

Oceania
Digital terrain model

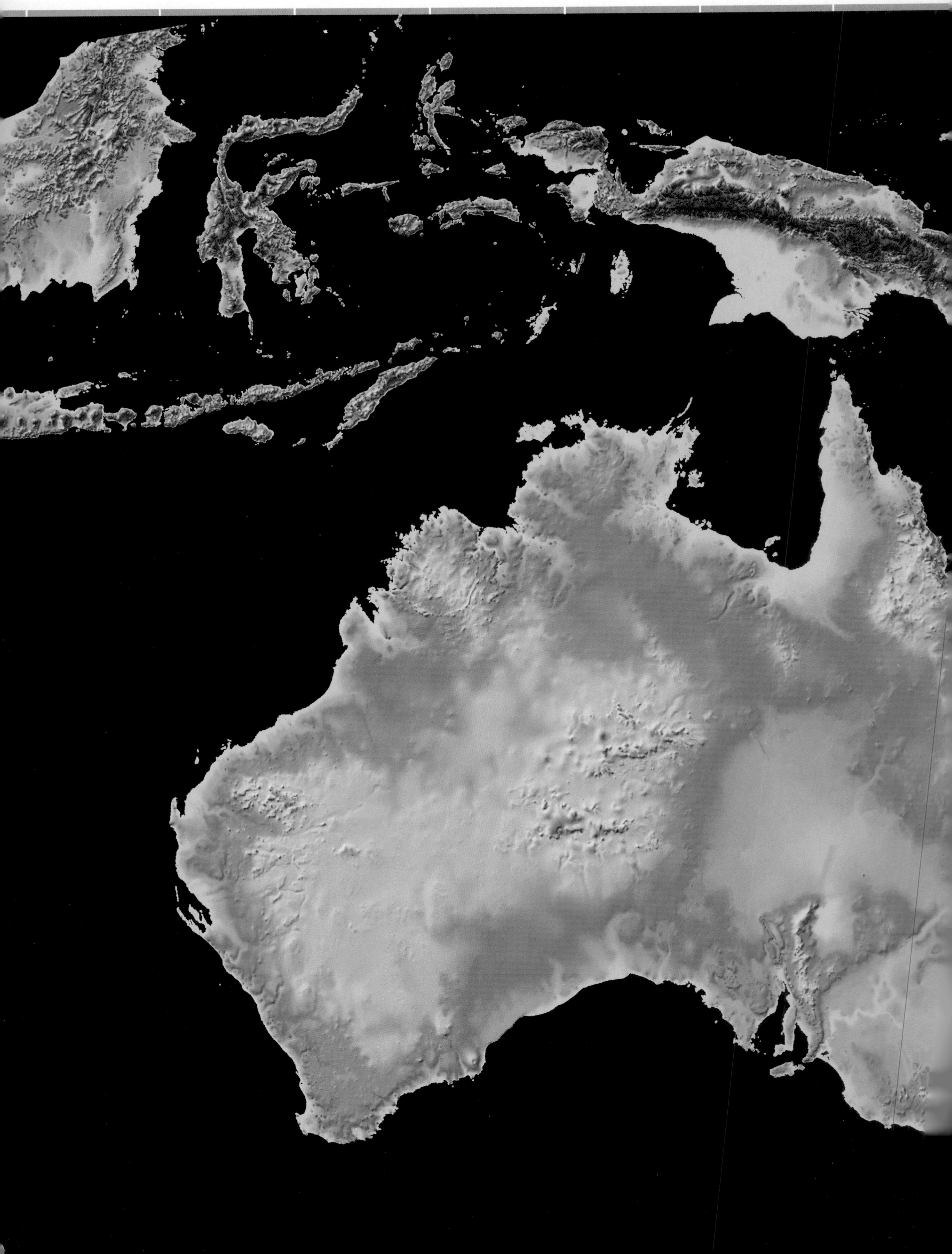

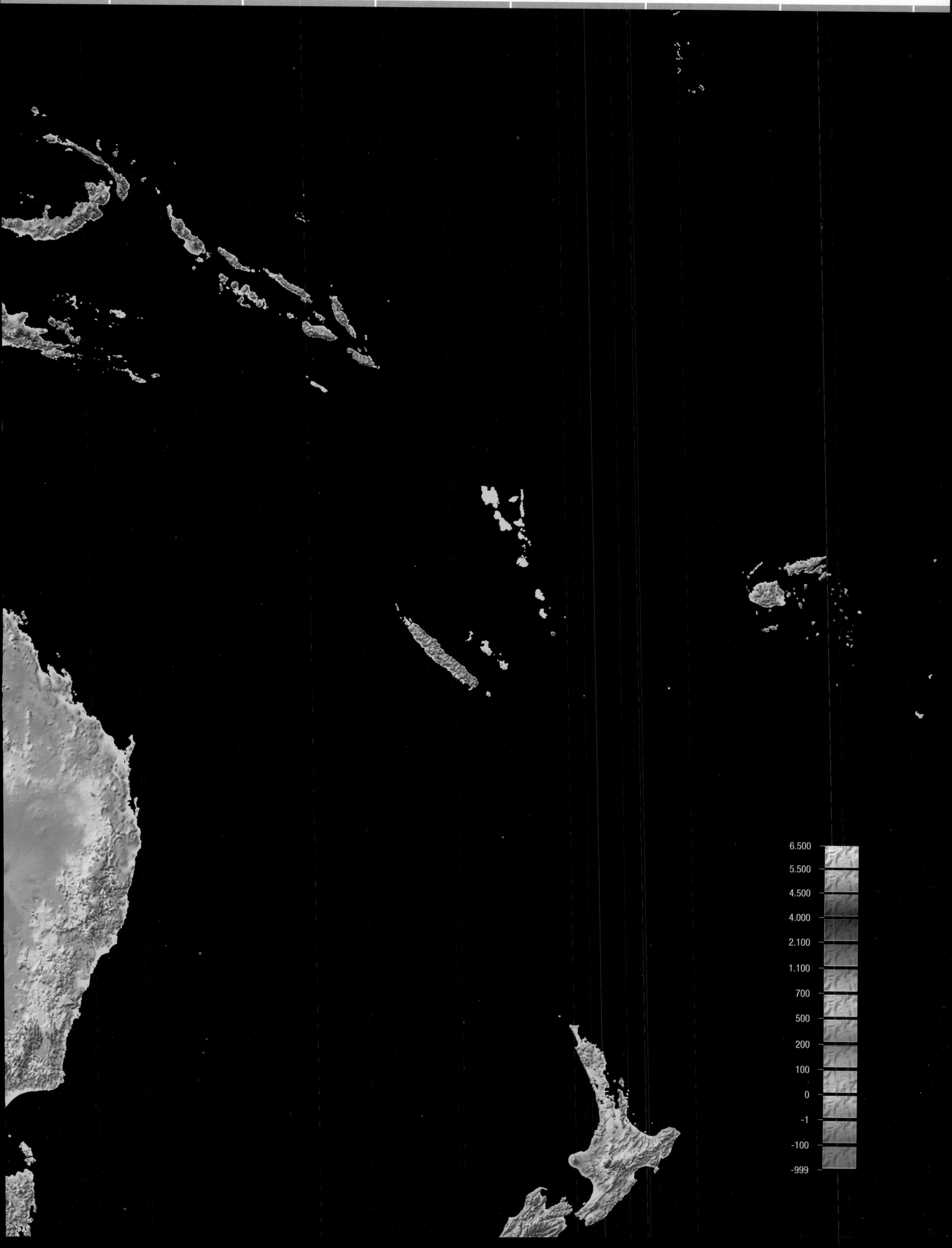
6.500
5.500
4.500
4.000
2.100
1.100
700
500
200
100
0
-1
-100
-999

Oceania
Bathymetry

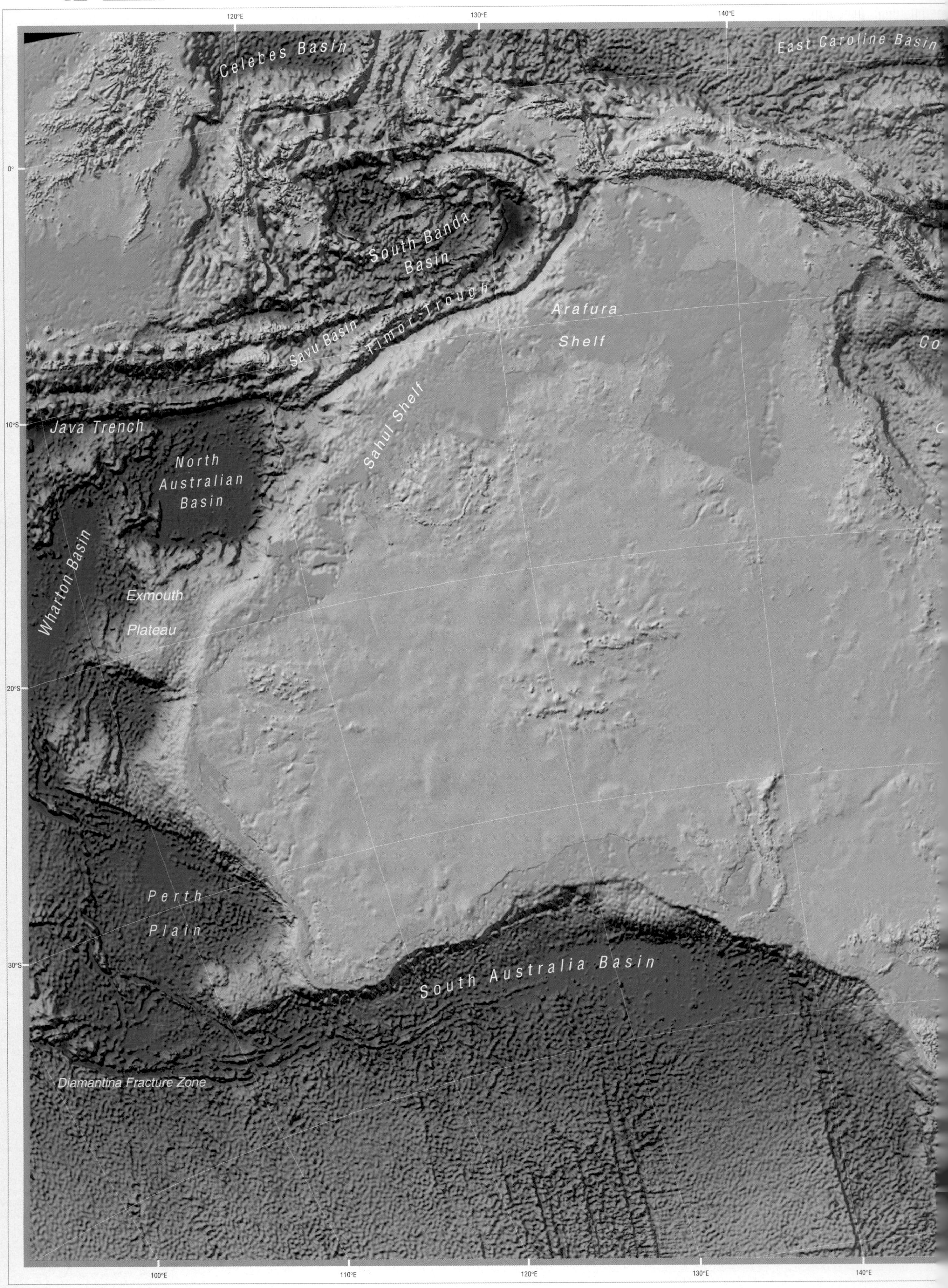

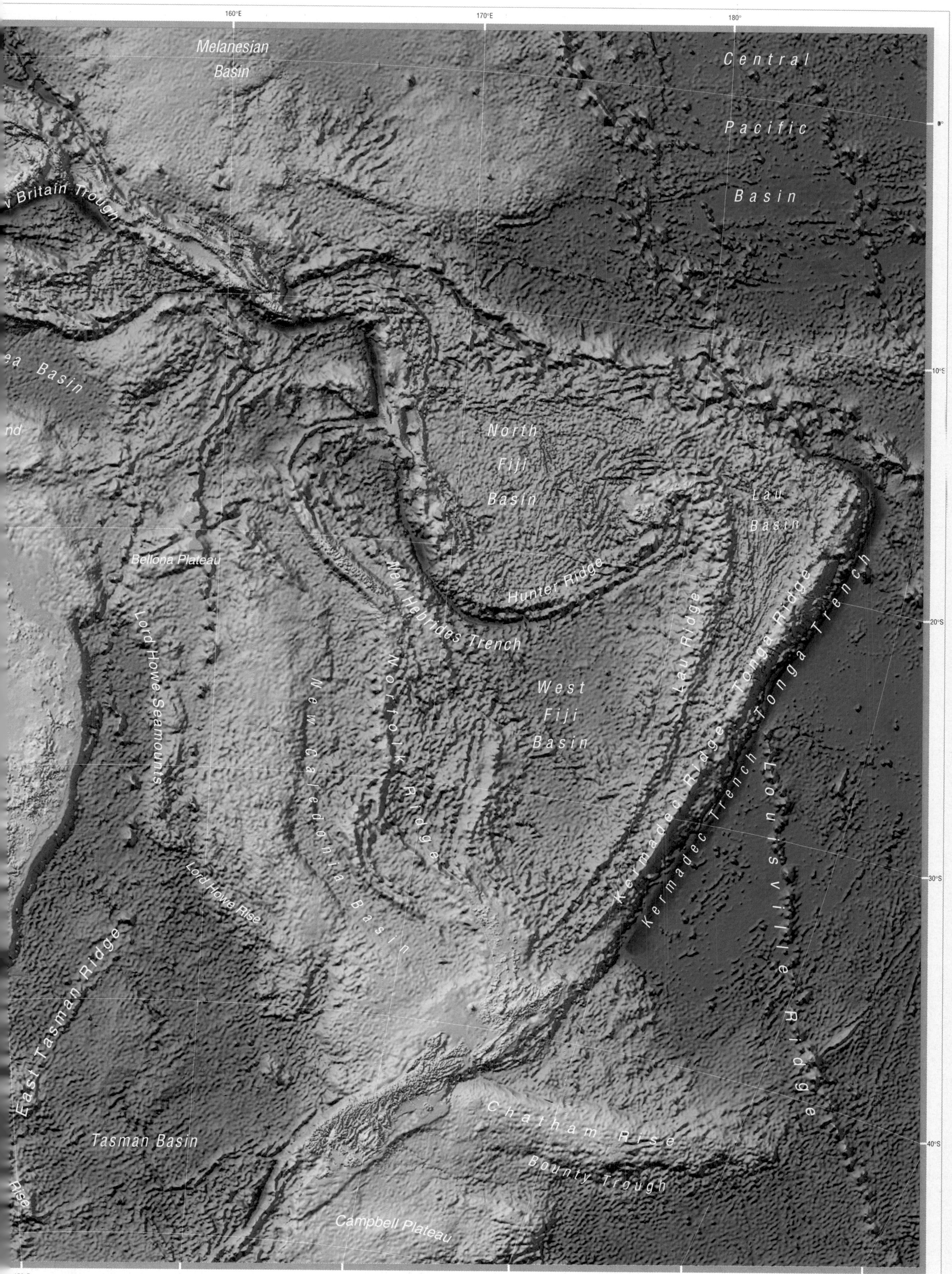
160°E
170°E
180°
Melanesian Basin
Central Pacific Basin
Britain Trough
ea Basin
nd
North Fiji Basin
Lau Basin
Bellona Plateau
Hunter Ridge
New Hebrides Trench
Lord Howe Seamounts
Norfolk Ridge
New Caledonia Basin
West Fiji Basin
Lau Ridge
Tonga Ridge
Tonga Trench
Kermadec Ridge
Kermadec Trench
Louisville Ridge
Lord Howe Rise
East Tasman Ridge
Tasman Basin
Chatham Rise
Bounty Trough
Campbell Plateau
Rise
10°S
20°S
30°S
40°S
150°E
160°E
170°E
180°
170°W
160°W

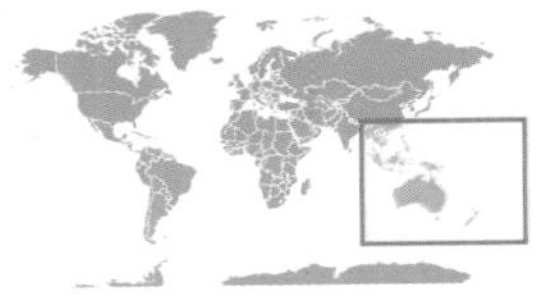

Oceania
Physical map

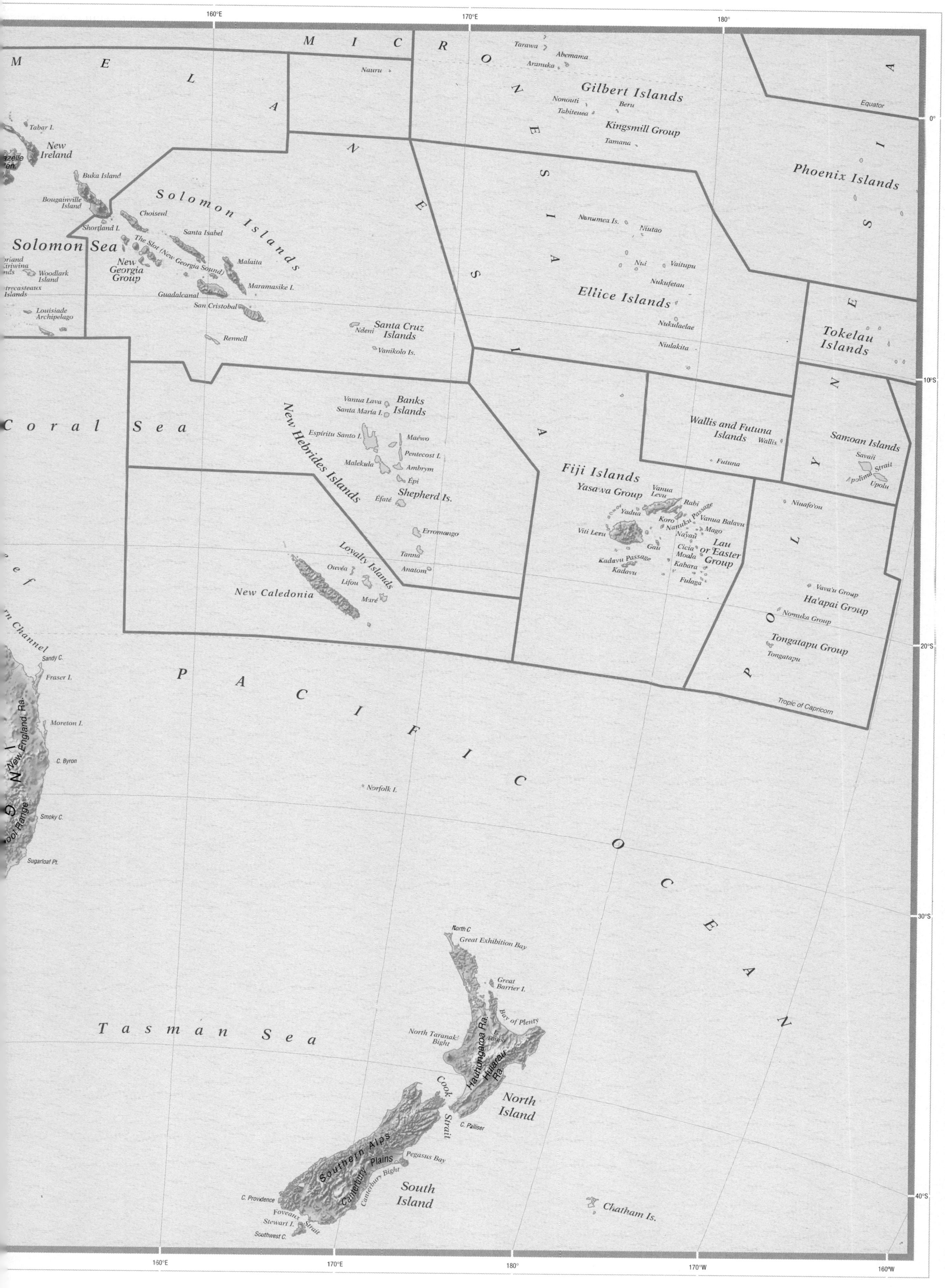
160°E
170°E
180°
M I C R O N E S I A
M E L A N E S I A
P O L Y N E S I A
Tarawa
Abemama
Aranuka
Nauru
Gilbert Islands
Nonouti
Beru
Tabiteuea
Kingsmill Group
Tamana
Equator
0°
Phoenix Islands
Tabar I.
New Ireland
Buka Island
Bougainville Island
Solomon Islands
Choiseul
Shortland I.
Santa Isabel
Solomon Sea
The Slot (New Georgia Sound)
New Georgia Group
Malaita
Woodlark Island
Maramasike I.
Guadalcanal
San Cristobal
Louisiade Archipelago
Rennell
Nanumea Is.
Niutao
Nui
Vaitupu
Nukufetau
Ellice Islands
Nukulaelae
Niulakita
Santa Cruz Islands
Ndeni
Vanikolo Is.
Tokelau Islands
10°S
Vanua Lava
Santa Maria I.
Banks Islands
New Hebrides Islands
Espiritu Santo I.
Maéwo
Pentecost I.
Malekula
Ambrym
Épi
Éfaté
Shepherd Is.
Erromango
Tanna
Anatom
Coral Sea
Wallis and Futuna Islands
Wallis
Futuna
Samoan Islands
Savaii
Apolima Strait
Upolu
Fiji Islands
Yasawa Group
Vanua Levu
Rabi
Yadua
Koro
Nanuku Passage
Vanua Balavu
Mago
Viti Levu
Nayau
Gau
Cicia
Lau or Easter Group
Moala
Kadavu Passage
Kadavu
Kabara
Fulaga
Niuafo'ou
Loyalty Islands
Ouvéa
Lifou
Maré
New Caledonia
Vava'u Group
Ha'apai Group
Nomuka Group
Tongatapu Group
Tongatapu
20°S
Tropic of Capricorn
Sandy C.
Fraser I.
Moreton I.
New England Ra.
C. Byron
Smoky C.
Sugarloaf Pt.
P A C I F I C O C E A N
Norfolk I.
30°S
North C
Great Exhibition Bay
Great Barrier I.
Bay of Plenty
North Taranaki Bight
Tasman Sea
Huiarau Ra.
Cook Strait
North Island
C. Palliser
Southern Alps
Canterbury Plains
Pegasus Bay
Canterbury Bight
South Island
C. Providence
Foveaux Strait
Stewart I.
Southwest C.
Chatham Is.
40°S
160°E
170°E
180°
170°W
160°W

Oceania
Political map

0 200 400 km
0 50 100 150 200 250 miles

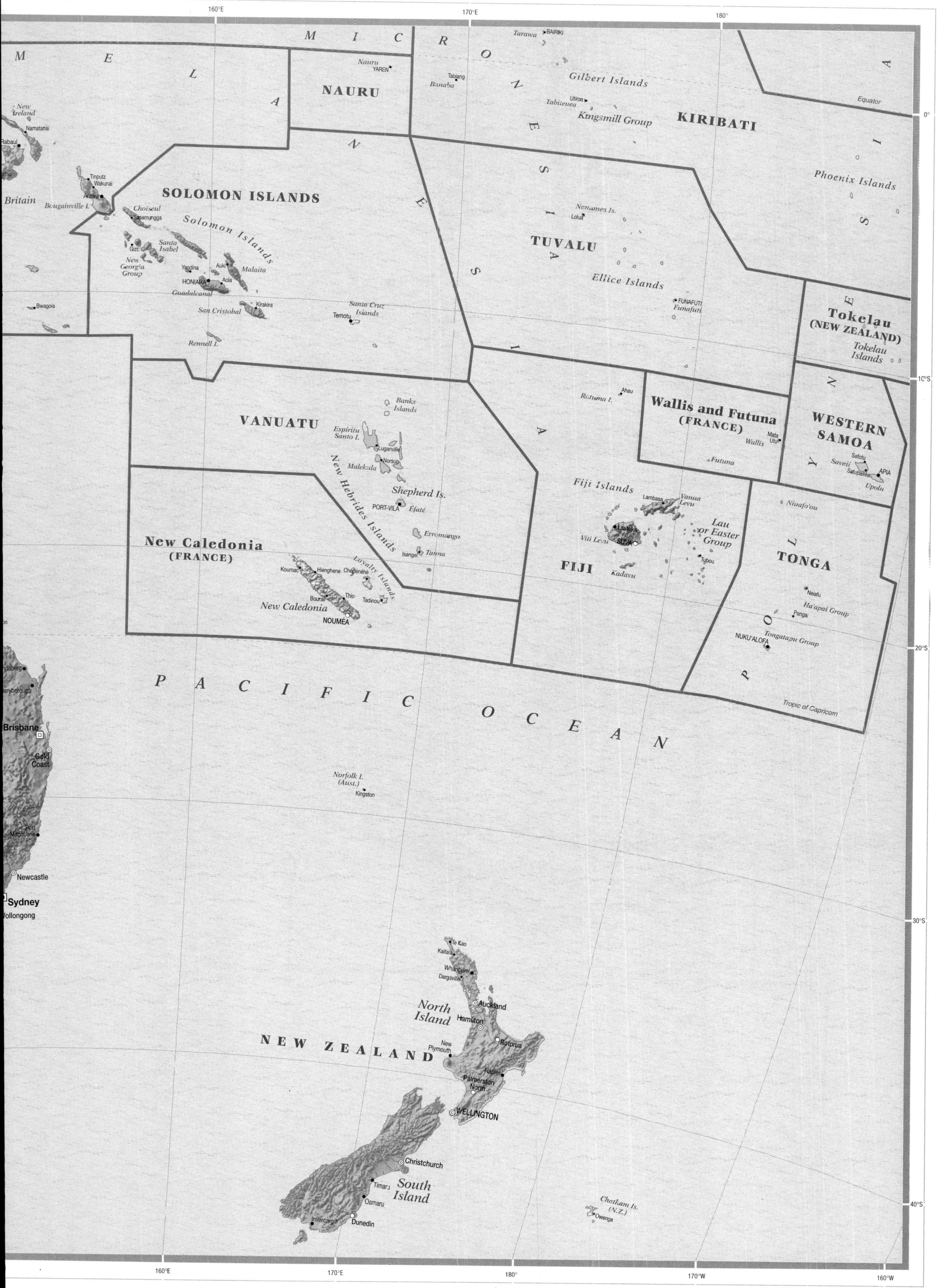
MICRONESIA
MELANESIA
POLYNESIA
NAURU
Nauru
YAREN
KIRIBATI
Tarawa
BAIRIKI
Gilbert Islands
Tabiang
Banaba
Utiroa
Tabiteuea
Kingsmill Group
Equator
Phoenix Islands
SOLOMON ISLANDS
Solomon Islands
New Ireland
Namatanai
Rabaul
Britain
Tinputz
Wakunai
Arawa
Bougainville I.
Choiseul
Sasamungga
Santa Isabel
Gizo
New Georgia Group
Yandina
Auki
Malaita
HONIARA
Aola
Guadalcanal
Kirakira
San Cristobal
Bwagoia
Rennell I.
Santa Cruz Islands
Temotu
TUVALU
Nanumea Is.
Lolua
Ellice Islands
FUNAFUTI
Funafuti
Tokelau
(NEW ZEALAND)
Tokelau Islands
VANUATU
Banks Islands
Espiritu Santo I.
Luganville
Malekula
Norsup
New Hebrides Islands
Shepherd Is.
PORT-VILA
Éfaté
Erromango
Isangel
Tanna
Rotuma I.
Ahau
Wallis and Futuna
(FRANCE)
Wallis
Mata Utu
Futuna
WESTERN SAMOA
Safotu
Savaii
Satupaitea
APIA
Upolu
New Caledonia
(FRANCE)
Koumac
Hienghene
Chépénéhé
Loyalty Islands
Thio
Bourail
Tadinou
New Caledonia
NOUMEA
FIJI
Fiji Islands
Lambasa
Vanua Levu
Lautoka
Viti Levu
SUVA
Kadavu
Lau or Eastern Group
Tubou
TONGA
Niuafo'ou
Neiafu
Ha'apai Group
Pangai
NUKU'ALOFA
Tongatapu Group
Tropic of Capricorn
PACIFIC OCEAN
Norfolk I. (Aust.)
Kingston
Brisbane
Gold Coast
Port Macquarie
Newcastle
Sydney
Wollongong
NEW ZEALAND
Te Kao
Kaitaia
Whangarei
Dargaville
North Island
Auckland
Hamilton
Rotorua
New Plymouth
Napier
Palmerston North
WELLINGTON
Christchurch
South Island
Timaru
Oamaru
Dunedin
Invercargill
Chatham Is. (N.Z.)
Owenga
160°E
170°E
180°
170°W
160°W
0°
10°S
20°S
30°S
40°S

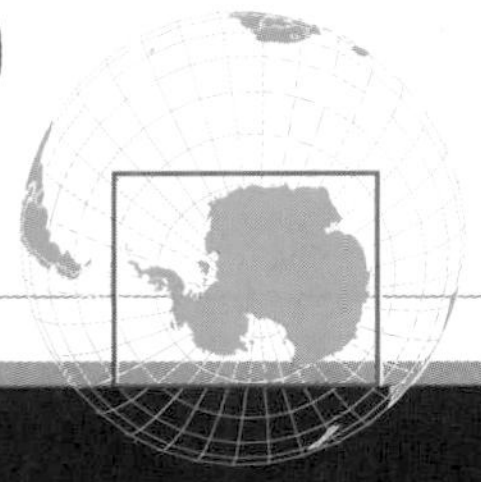

Antarctica
Satellite image

At the present time, although the Earth is in a warm interglacial climatic phase, glaciers still occupy some 15 million square kilometers, almost 10% of dry land. 95% of this surface area is concentrated in Antarctica and Greenland. In some areas of Antarctica, the

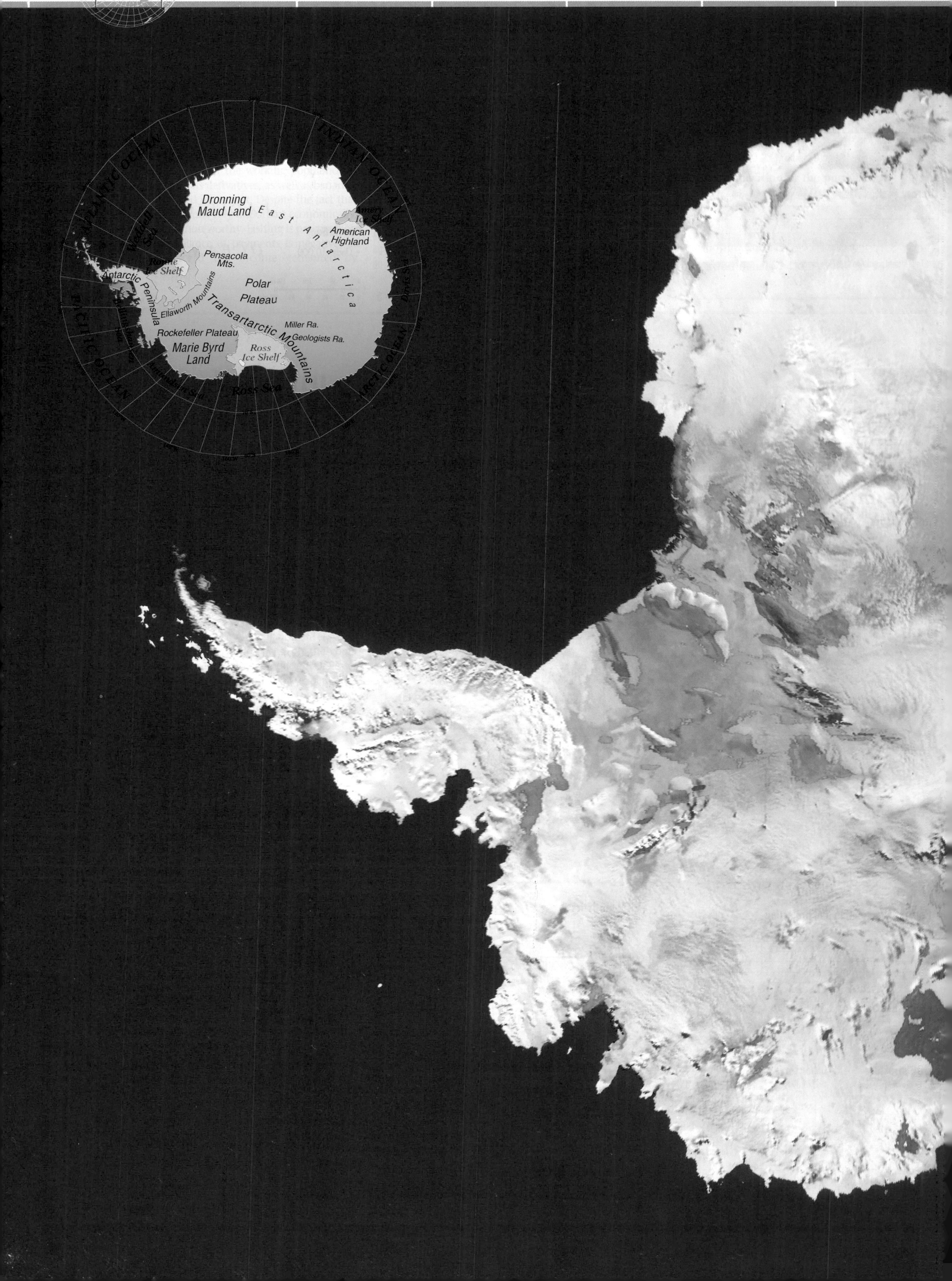

thickness of the ice sheet reaches 3,700 m, which produces an enormous pressure on the surface of the continent. Antarctica possesses scanty plant life —mosses and lichens— and a rich fauna, including fish as well as birds and mammals. The climate is characterized by having very low average temperatures, severe conditions which are accentuated by the violence of the winds, with speeds above 70 km an hour. On the coast, the average annual temperature is -30 °C, and it is even lower in the interior. The length of the night in winter —or the day in summer— increases the higher the latitude; at the South Pole, the sun remains constantly above the horizon between September and March.

Glossary

Language Abbreviations

Afr	Afrikaans
Al	Albanian
Ar	Arabic
Bul	Bulgarian
Bur	Burmese
Cam	Cambodian
Ch	Chinese
Sin	Sinhala
Cz	Czech
Dan	Danish
Dut	Dutch
Est	Estonian
Finn	Finnish
Fr	French
Gae	Gaelic
Ger	German
Gr	Greek
Heb	Hebrew
Hin	Hindi
Hung	Hungarian
Ice	Icelandic
Ind	Indonesian
It	Italian
Jap	Japanese
Kor	Korean
Lat	Latvian
Mal	Malay
Mlg	Malagasy
Mon	Mongolian
Nor	Norwegian
Per	Persian
Pol	Polish
Por	Portuguese
Rom	Romanian
Rus	Russian
S-C	Serbo-Croat
Slk	Slovak
Som	Somali
Sp	Spanish
Swe	Swedish
Tam	Tamil
Th	Thai
Tib	Tibetan
Tu	Turkish
Ur	Urdu
Vt	Vietnamese

Åkra	*Gr*	Cape
Alb	*Rom*	White
Alföld	*Hung*	Plain
Altiplanicie	*Sp*	High plain
Alto	*Sp*	Upper, peak
Alturas	*Sp*	Hills
Älv(en)	*Swe*	River
Archipiélago	*Sp*	Archipelago
Arcipelago	*It*	Archipelago
Aru	*Sin, Tam*	River
Bab	*Ar*	Strait
Badiet	*Ar*	Desert
Badiya	*Ar*	Desert
Badiyat	*Ar*	Desert
Bælt	*Dan*	Strait
Bahía *(B., Bª)*	*Ar*	Bay
Bahr	*Ar*	Channel, river, bay, lake
Baia *(B.)*	*It, Por*	Bay
Baía	*Por*	Bay
Baie	*Fr*	Bay
Baja(o)	*Sp*	Lower
Bandao	*Ch*	Peninsula
Bannaanka	*Som*	Plain
Bañado(s)	*Sp*	Marshlands
Baraji	*Tu*	Dam
Barragem	*Por*	Reservoir
Batu	*Mal*	Mountain
Belt	*Dan*	Strait
Bereg	*Rus*	Bank, shore
Berg(e)	*Ger*	Mountain(s)
Bergland	*Ger*	Upland
Besar	*Ind, Mal*	Big, great
Bílé	*Cz*	Big
Bi'r	*Ar*	Well
Blanca	*Sp*	White
Blanche	*Fr*	White
Boca	*Por, Sp*	Mouth
Bocche	*It*	Mouth, estuary
Bodden	*Ger*	Bay
Bolshoy *(Bol.)*	*Rus*	Big
Bucht	*Ger*	Bay
Bugt(en)	*Dan*	Bay
Buhairat	*Ar*	Lake
Buhayrat	*Ar*	Lake
Bukit	*Ind, Mal*	Hill, mountain
Bukten	*Nor, Swe*	Bay
Bulu	*Ind*	Mountain
Burnu	*Tu*	Point, cape
Buuraha	*Som*	Hill(s), mountain(s)
Cabo *(C.)*	*Sp*	Cape
Cadena	*Sp*	Range
Campos	*Sp*	Plain, area
Canal	*Sp*	Channel
Cao Nguyen	*Vt*	Plateau
Cap *(C.)*	*Fr*	Cape
Capo *(C.)*	*It*	Cape
Cayería	*Sp*	Islets
Cayo(s)	*Sp*	islets, rock
Cerro(s)	*Sp*	Mountain(s), hill(s), peak
Chaco	*Sp*	Plain
Chaîne	*Fr*	Range, mountain chain
Chapada	*Por*	Hills, uplands
-chedo	*Kor*	Archipelago
Chi	*Ch*	Lake
Chiao	*Ch*	Cape
Chott	*Ar*	Salt lake, marsh, intermittent lake
Chute(s)	*Fr*	Waterfalls
Ciénaga	*Sp*	Marsh
Cimpia	*Rom*	Plain
Co	*Tib*	Lake
Col	*Fr*	Pass
Colline(s)	*Fr*	Hill(s)
Cordillera *(Cord.)*	*Sp*	Range
Cordón	*Sp*	Mountain range
Costa	*Sp*	Coast
Côte	*Fr*	Coast
Coteau	*Fr*	Hills
Côtes	*Fr*	Hills
Cu Lao	*Vt*	Island
Cuchilla(s)	*Sp*	Mountain range
Da	*Ch*	Big
Daba(n)	*Mon*	Pass
Daglari *(Dag.)*	*Tu*	Mountains
Dahr	*Ar*	Region, area
Dam	*Vt*	Bay, cover
Dao	*Ch*	Island
Daryacheh-ye	*Per*	Lake
Dasht	*Per, Ur*	Desert
Depresión	*Sp*	Depression
Dépression	*Fr*	Depression
Desierto	*Sp*	Desert
Dhar	*Ar*	Hills, mountains
Djebel	*Ar*	Mountains
Dolina	*Rus*	Valley
Donau	*Ind*	Lake
Dong	*Th*	Mountain
-elv(a)	*Nor*	River
Embalse *(Emb.)*	*Sp*	Reservoir
Ensenada	*Sp*	Cove
Erg/'Erg	*Ar*	Desert with dunes
Estero(s)	*Sp*	Estuary, inlet
Estrecho	*Sp*	Strait
Ezers	*Lat*	Lake
Falaise	*Fr*	Cliff
Feng	*Ch*	Peak
Firth	*Gae*	Estuary, strait
Fjord(en)	*Dan, Nor*	Fjord, lagoon
Fjördur	*Ice*	Fjord, bay
Flói	*Ice*	Bay
Ganga	*Hin*	River
Gaoyuan	*Ch*	Plateau
-gawa *(-g.)*	*Jap*	River
Gebel	*Ar*	Mountain
-geberge	*Ger*	Mountain range
Gebergte	*Afr, Dut*	Mountain range
Gol	*Mon*	River
Golfe *(G.)*	*Fr*	Bay, gulf
Golfo *(G.)*	*It, Sp*	Bay, gulf
Gölü	*Fr*	Lake
Gora	*Rus, S-C*	Mountain
Gorje	*S-C*	Mountains, hills
Gory	*Rus*	Mountains, hills
Gran	*Sp*	Big
Grand	*Fr*	Big
Grande	*Sp, Por, Fr, It*	Big
Groot	*Afr*	Big
Grotte	*Fr*	Grotto
Grosser	*Ger*	Big
Grupo	*Sp*	Group
Guan	*Ch*	Pass
Guba	*Rus*	Bay
Gunong	*Mal*	Mountain
Gunung	*Ind, Mal*	Mountain
Hamada	*Ar*	Plateau, desert
Hamadat	*Ar*	Rocky, plateau
Hammada	*Ar*	Rock desert
Hammadat	*Ar*	Plateau
Hamun	*Per*	Marsh, salt lake
-hanto	*Jap*	Peninsula
Har	*Heb*	Mountain, hill
Hare	*Heb*	Mountain, hill
Harrar	*Ar*	Lava field
Hassi	*Ar*	Well
Hasy	*Ar*	Well
Haut(es)	*Fr*	Hill(s)
Hawr	*Ar*	Lake
He	*Ch*	River
Heide	*Ger*	Heath, moor
Hka	*Bur*	River
Hohe	*Ger*	Height
Hon	*Vt*	Islands
Hory	*Cz*	Mountains
Hu	*Ch*	Lake
Idehan	*Ar*	Sand dunes
Île(s) *(I., Is.)*	*Fr*	Island(s)
Ilha(s) *(I., Is.)*	*Por*	Island(s)
Insel(n) *(I., Is.)*	*Ger*	Island
Isla(s) *(I., Is.)*	*Sp*	Island(s)
Isle(s) *(I., Is.)*	*Fr*	Island(s)
Isola *(I.)*	*It*	Island
Isole *(Is.)*	*It*	Islands
Istmo	*Sp*	Isthmus
Jabal *(J., Jab.)*	*Ar*	Mountain(s)
Jal	*Ar*	Ridge
-järvi	*Finn*	Lake
Jazirat	*Ar*	Island
Jbel *(J.)*	*Ar*	Mountain(s)
Jebel *(J.)*	*Ar*	Mountain(s)
Jezero *(Jez.)*	*S-C*	Lake
Jezioro *(J.)*	*Pol*	Lake
Jiam	*Jap*	Island
Jiang	*Ch*	River
Jibal *(J.)*	*Ar*	Mountain(s)
-jima	*Jap*	Islands
Joki	*Finn*	River
Jökull	*Ice*	Glacier
Juzur	*Ar*	Islands
Kaap	*Afr*	Cape
Kai	*Jap*	Sea
-kaikyo	*Jap*	Strait
Kamen	*Rus*	Rock
Kanaal	*Dut*	Channel
Kanal	*Rus, Ger*	Canal, channel
Kangri	*Tib*	Mountain
Kap	*Ger*	Cape
Karoo	*Afr*	Steppe
Kas	*Cam*	Island
Kasba	*Ar*	Castle
Kavir	*Per*	Salt desert
Kediet	*Ar*	Mountain
Kep	*Al*	Cape
Kepulauan *(Kep.)*	*Ind*	Islands
Khabrat	*Ar*	Rainpool, waterhole
Khalij	*Ar*	Bay, gulf
Khao	*Th*	Peak
Khrebet *(Khr.)*	*Rus*	Mountain range
-ko	*Jap*	Lake, inlet
Ko	*Th*	Island
-kochi	*Jap*	Mountain range, highlands
Koh	*Cam*	Island
Kólpos	*Ger*	Gulf
Kong	*Ind*	Mountain
Körfezi	*Tu*	Bay, gulf
Kou	*Ch*	Pass
Kryazh	*Rus*	Ridge
Kuh(ha)	*Per*	Mountain
Kyun	*Bur*	Island
Lac *(L.)*	*Fr*	Lake
Lacul *(L.)*	*Rom*	Lake
Laem	*Th*	Point, cape, peninsula
Lago *(L.)*	*Sp*	Lake
Lagoa *(L.)*	*Por*	Lagoon
Laguna *(L.)*	*Sp*	Lagoon
Lagune *(L.)*	*Fr*	Lagoon
Laht	*Est*	Bay
Lam	*Th*	Stream
Liman	*Rus*	Bay, gulf
Ling	*Ch*	Mountain range
Llano(s)	*Sp*	Plain(s), praire(s)
Llanura	*Sp*	Plain
Loch	*Gae*	Lake, inlet
Loi	*Bur*	Mountain
Loma	*Sp*	Hill
Lough	*Gae*	Lake
Loup	*Gae*	Waterfall, cascade
Luang	*Th*	Yellow
Macizo	*Sp*	Massif
Mae	*Th*	River
Mae Nam	*Th*	River
Mal	*Al*	Mountain(s)
Mala	*S-C*	Small
Malé	*Cz*	Small
Malyy *(Mal.)*	*Rus*	Small
Man	*Kor*	Bay
Mar	*Sp*	Sea
Massif	*Fr*	Mountains, upland
Massif	*Fr*	Massif
Mesa	*Sp*	Tableland
Meseta(s)	*Sp*	Plateau
Midbar	*Heb*	Desert
-misaki	*Jap*	Point, cape
Mont(s) *(M., Mt., Mts.)*	*Fr*	Mount, mountains
Montagne(s)	*Fr*	Mountains
Montanhas	*Por*	Mountains
Montaña(s)	*Sp*	Mountains
Monte(s) *(M., Mt., Mts.)*	*Sp, Por, It*	Mountains
Monti *(M., Mt., Mts.)*	*It*	Mountains
Mörön	*Mon*	River
Motu	*Pol*	Island, rock
Moyen	*Fr*	Middle
Mui	*Vt*	Point
Mull	*Gae*	Headland
Muntii *(M., Mt., Mts.)*	*Rom*	Mountains
Mys *(M.)*	*Rus*	Cape
Na	*Bul, Rus, S-C*	On, over
-nada	*Jap*	Sea, gulf
Nafud	*Ar*	Desert, dune
Nagorye	*Rus*	Highland, uplands
Nahr	*Ar*	River
Nam	*Bur, Th, Vt*	River
Nam	*Kor,Vt,*	South(ern)
Namakzar	*Per*	Salt flat
Nan	*Ch*	South
Neem	*Est*	Cape
Nei	*Ch*	Inner
Ness	*Gae*	Promontory
Nevado	*Sp*	Peak, snowcapped
Niedere	*Ger*	Lower
Nina	*Est*	Cape
Nizina	*Rus, Pol, Cz*	Depression, lowland
Nízke	*Cz*	Small
Nizmennost	*Rus*	Lowland
Nord	*Ger*	North(ern)
Norte	*Sp*	North
Nos	*Bul, Rus*	Sprit, point
Nosy	*Mlg*	Islands
Novaya	*Rus*	New
Nur	*Mon*	Lake
Nuruu	*Mon*	Mountains
Nusa	*Ind*	Island
Nuur	*Mon*	Lake
Oka	*Jap*	Coast
Ost	*Ger*	East(ern)
Ostrov(a) *(O., Os., Ova.)*	*Rus*	Islands
Oued	*Ar*	Dry river-bed
Ouest	*Fr*	West
Ovasi	*Tu*	Plain, valley
Oya	*Sin, Tam*	River
Oya	*Nor*	Island
Ozero *(Oz.)*	*Rus*	Lake(s)
Pampa(s)	*Sp*	Plain
Paso	*Sp*	Pass
Passage	*Fr*	Pass
Passe	*Fr*	Pass
Passo	*It*	Pass
Pegunungan *(Peg.)*	*Ind*	Mountains
Pendi	*Ch*	Basin
Penisola *(Pen.)*	*It*	Peninsula
Península *(Pen.)*	*Sp*	Peninsula
Péninsule *(Pen.)*	*Fr*	Peninsula
Peniplano	*Sp*	
Peña	*Sp*	Peak
Pereval *(Per.)*	*Rus*	Pass
Peski	*Rus*	Sand desert
Phanom	*Th*	Mountain(s)
Phnom *(Phn.)*	*Cam*	Hill, mountain
Phnum *(Phn.)*	*Cam*	Hill, mountain
Pic	*Fr*	Peak
Pico	*Sp*	Peak
Pik	*Rus*	Peak
Pingyuan	*Ch*	Plain
Planalto	*Por*	Plateau
Planina *(Pla., Pl.)*	*Bul, S-C*	Mountains
Plasina	*Cz*	Tableland
Plateau	*Fr*	Plateau
Plato	*Afr, Bul, Rus*	Plateau
Platte	*Ger*	Plateau, plain
Ploskogorye	*Rus*	Plateau
Pod	*Cz*	Under, sub-
Podisul	*Rom*	Plateau
Pogorze	*Pol*	Hills
Pohorie	*Cz*	Mountain range
Pointe *(Pte.)*	*Fr*	Point
Pojezierze	*Pol*	Lake district
Polesie	*Pol*	Areas of lakes, forests and marshlands
Polje	*S-C*	Plain, basin
Poluostrov *(Pov.)*	*Rus*	Peninsula
Ponta	*Por*	Point
Pontal	*Por*	Point
Porto	*It*	Port
Presa	*Sp*	Reservoir
Proliv	*Rus*	Strait
Przedgorze	*Pol*	Mount
Pulau (-pulau) *(P., P.P.)*	*Ind, Mal*	Island(s)
Puncak	*Ind*	Mountain
Punta *(Pta.)*	*Sp,It*	Point
Qundao	*Ch*	Archipelago
Raas	*Som*	Point, cape
Ramlat	*Ar*	Sands
Rapides	*Fr*	Rapids
Ras	*Ar*	Point, cape
Ra's	*Ar*	Point, cape
Ravnina	*Rus*	Plain
Represa	*Por*	Reservoir
-retto	*Jap*	Archipelago
Ría	*Sp*	River-mouth, drowned
Rio	*Por*	River
Río	*Sp*	River
Roc	*Fr*	Rock
Roca	*Sp*	Rock
Rt.	*S-C*	Point, cape
Rud	*Per*	River
Rudohorie	*Cz*	Ore mountains
Sabkhat	*Ar*	Salt flat
Sahara	*Ar*	Desert
Sahr	*Ar*	Desert
Sahra	*Ar*	Desert
-saki	*Jap*	Point, cape
Salar	*Sp*	Salt pan
Salina(s)	*Sp*	Salt pan
Salto	*Por, Sp*	Waterfall
-sammyaku	*Jap*	Mountain range
-sanchi	*Jap*	Mountainous area, highlands
Sanmaek	*Kor*	Mountain range
Sattel	*Ger*	Pass
Se	*Cam*	River
Sebkha	*Ar*	Salt flat
Sebkhet	*Ar*	Salt flat
Sebkra	*Ar*	Salt flat
See	*Ger*	Lake
Seenplate	*Ger*	Lake district
Selat	*Ind*	Strait, channel
Selkä	*Finn*	Ridge, open water
Semenandjung *(Sem.)*	*Ind*	Peninsula
Serra *(S., Sª, Sa.)*	*Por*	Mountain range
Serranía(s) *(Serr.)*	*Sp*	Mountain range
Sever-naya, -noye, -nyy, -o	*Rus*	North(ern)
Shamo	*Ch*	Desert
Shan	*Ch*	Mountain range, mountains
Shankou	*Ch*	Pass
Shanmo	*Ch*	Mountains
Shatt	*Ar*	River, mouth
-shima	*Jap*	Islands
-shoto	*Jap*	Archipelago
Shui	*Ch*	River, creek
Shuidao	*Ch*	Strait
Sierra *(S., Sª, Sa.)*	*Sp*	Mountain range
Sistema(s)	*Sp*	Mountain range(s)
Slieve	*Gae*	Mountain
Song	*Vt*	River
Sredne	*Rus*	Middle
Step	*Rus*	Steppe
Stretto	*It*	Strait
Stung	*Cam*	River
Sud	*Fr*	South
Sund	*Swe*	Sound, strait
Tanjon'	*Mlg*	Cape
Tanjona	*Mlg*	Cape
Tanjong	*Ind, Mal*	Cape,point
Tanjon'i	*Mlg*	Cape
Tanjung	*Mal*	Cape
Tao	*Ch*	Island
Tau	*Rus*	Mountains
Taung(dan)	*Bur*	Mountain
Teluk	*Ind*	Bay
Telukan	*Ind*	Bay
Tenggara	*Ind*	Middle
Tepe	*Tu*	Hill, peak
Udde	*Swe*	Point, cape
Ujung	*Ind*	Point,cape
-ura	*Jap*	Lake, inlet
Uul	*Mon*	Mountains
Väin	*Est*	Strait
Veld	*Afr*	Plain, steppe
Velika	*S-C*	Big
Veliki	*S-C*	Big
Vel'ka	*Slk*	Big
Verkhn	*Rus*	Upper
Vinh	*Vt*	Bay
Visocina	*S-C*	Plateau
Vodokhranilische *(Vdkhr.)*	*Rus*	Reservoir
Volcán	*Sp*	Volcano
Vostochnyy	*Rus*	Eastern
Vozvyshennost *(Vozvysh.)*	*Rus*	Hills, upland
Wad *(W.)*	*Ar*	Watercourse
Wadi	*Ar*	Watercourse
Wahat	*Ar*	Oasis
Wald	*Ger*	Forest, mountains
Wan	*Ch, Jap*	Bay
Webi	*Som*	River
Wolds	*Dut*	Forest
Wschodnie	*Pol*	Western
Wyzina	*Pol*	Plateau
Xi	*Ch*	West, stream
Xiao	*Ch*	Small
Yam	*Heb*	Lake, sea
Yoma	*Bur*	Mountain range
Yuzhn-o, -yy	*Rus*	Southern
Zachodnie	*Pol*	Western
-zaki	*Jap*	Point, cape
Zalev	*Pol*	Bay, inlet, lagoon
Zaliv	*Rus*	Bay
Zapadna *(Zap.)*	*S-C*	West, western
Zapadn -aya, -o, -yy	*Rus*	Western
Západné	*Cz*	Western
Zatoka	*Pol*	Gulf
Zemlya	*Rus*	Land

Index

COUNTRY CODES

Code	Country
AC	Antigua and Barbuda
AF	Afghanistan
AG	Algeria
AJ	Azerbaijan
AL	Albania
AM	Armenia
AN	Andorra
AO	Angola
AR	Argentina
AS	Australia
AU	Austria
BA	Bahrain
BB	Barbados
BC	Botswana
BE	Belgium
BF	Bahamas, The
BG	Bangladesh
BH	Belize
BK	Bosnia and Herzegovina
BL	Bolivia
BM	Burma (Myanmar)
BN	Benin
BO	Belarus
BP	Solomon Islands
BR	Brazil
BT	Bhutan
BU	Bulgaria
BX	Brunei
BY	Burundi
CA	Canada
CB	Cambodia
CD	Chad
CE	Sri Lanka
CF	Congo
CG	Congo, Dem. Rep. of The
CH	China
CI	Chile
CM	Cameroon
CN	Comoros
CO	Colombia
CS	Costa Rica
CT	Central African Republic
CU	Cuba
CV	Cape Verde
CY	Cyprus
DA	Denmark
DJ	Djibouti
DO	Dominica
DR	Dominican Republic
EC	Ecuador
EG	Egypt
EI	Ireland
EK	Equatorial Guinea
EN	Estonia
ER	Eritrea
ES	El Salvador
ET	Ethiopia
EZ	Czech Republic
FI	Finland
FJ	Fiji
FM	Micronesia, Federated States of
FR	France
GA	Gambia, The
GB	Gabon
GG	Georgia
GH	Ghana
GJ	Grenada
GM	Germany
GR	Greece
GT	Guatemala
GV	Guinea
GY	Guyana
HA	Haiti
HO	Honduras
HR	Croatia
HU	Hungary
IC	Iceland
ID	Indonesia
IN	India
IR	Iran
IS	Israel
IT	Italy
IV	Côte d'Ivoire
IZ	Iraq
JA	Japan
JM	Jamaica
JO	Jordan
KE	Kenya
KG	Kyrgyzstan
KN	North Korea
KR	Kiribati
KS	South Korea
KU	Kuwait
KZ	Kazakhstan
LA	Laos
LE	Lebanon
LG	Latvia
LH	Lithuania
LI	Liberia
LO	Slovakia
LS	Liechtenstein
LT	Lesotho
LU	Luxembourg
LY	Libya
MA	Madagascar
MD	Moldova
MG	Mongolia
MI	Malawi
MK	Macedonia
ML	Mali
MN	Monaco
MO	Morocco
MP	Mauritius
MR	Mauritania
MT	Malta
MU	Oman
MV	Maldives
MX	Mexico
MY	Malaysia
MZ	Mozambique
NG	Niger
NH	Vanuatu
NI	Nigeria
NL	Netherlands, The
NO	Norway
NP	Nepal
NR	Nauru
NS	Suriname
NU	Nicaragua
NZ	New Zealand
PA	Paraguay
PE	Peru
PK	Pakistan
PL	Poland
PM	Panama
PO	Portugal
PP	Papua New Guinea
PU	Guinea-Bissau
PX	Palau
QA	Qatar
RM	Marshall, Islands
RO	Romania
RP	Philippines
RS	Russia
RW	Rwanda
SA	Saudi Arabia
SC	Saint Kitts and Nevis
SE	Seychelles
SF	South Africa
SG	Senegal
SI	Slovenia
SL	Sierra Leone
SM	San Marino
SN	Singapore
SO	Somalia
SP	Spain
ST	Saint Lucia
SU	Sudan, The
SW	Sweden
SY	Syria
SZ	Switzerland
TC	United Arab Emirates
TD	Trinidad and Tobago
TH	Thailand
TI	Tajikistan
TN	Tonga
TO	Togo
TP	São Tomé and Príncipe
TS	Tunisia
TU	Turkey
TV	Tuvalu
TW	Taiwan
TX	Turkmenistan
TZ	Tanzania
UG	Uganda
UK	United Kingdom
UP	Ukraine
US	United States
UV	Burkina Faso
UY	Uruguay
UZ	Uzbekistan
VC	Saint Vincent and The Grenadines
VE	Venezuela
VM	Vietnam
VT	Vatican City
WA	Namibia
WS	Western Samoa
WZ	Swaziland
YM	Yemen
YO	Yugoslavia
ZA	Zambia
ZI	Zimbabwe

A

Åno		604	67°51'N	12°52'E
Aachen	GM	584	50°45'N	6°06'E
Aalen	GM	584	48°50'N	10°06'E
Aalst	BE	570	50°56'N	4°02'E
Äänekoski	FI	578	62°36'N	25°40'E
Aarau	SZ	622	47°23'N	8°02'E
Aardenburg	NL	602	51°17'N	3°27'E
Aare	SZ	622	47°36'N	8°13'E
Aarschot	BE	570	50°59'N	4°50'E
Aba	CG	287	3°52'N	30°14'E
Aba	NI	316	5°07'N	7°22'E
Abā as Su'ūd	SA	528	17°28'N	44°06'E
Abadab, Jabal	SU	324	18°51'N	35°55'E
Ābādān	IR	502	30°20'N	48°17'E
Ābādeh	IR	502	31°10'N	52°37'E
Abadla	AG	272	31°01'N	2°44'W
Abaeté		386	19°09'S	45°27'W
Abaetetuba	BR	424	1°42'S	48°52'W
Abag Qi	CH	490	43°52'N	114°32'E
Abaiang	KR	660	2°00'N	173°00'E
Abaji	NI	316	8°28'N	6°57'E
Abak	NI	316	4°59'N	7°47'E
Abakaliki	NI	316	6°21'N	8°05'E
Abakan		466	53°43'N	91°30'E
Abakan	RS	612	53°43'N	91°26'E
Abakanskiy Khrebet		466	52°20'N	88°50'E
Abala	CF	285	1°21'S	15°30'E
Abala	NG	314	14°56'N	3°26'E
Abalak	NG	314	15°27'N	6°17'E
Aban	EK	291	1°50'N	10°52'E
Abancay	PE	436	13°35'S	72°55'W
Abanga	GB	294	0°12'N	10°11'E
Abapó	BL	422	18°50'S	63°28'W
Abari	UG	330	1°46'N	33°26'E
Abar Kūh	IR	502	31°08'N	53°17'E
Abasha	GG	495	42°12'N	42°12'E
Abashiri	JA	506	44°01'N	144°17'E
Abasolo	MX	394	24°04'N	98°23'W
Abastumani	GG	495	41°43'N	42°50'E
Abatimbo el Gumas	ET	293	10°36'N	35°13'E
Abau	PP	664	10°11'S	148°42'E
Abaújszántó	HU	590	48°17'N	21°12'E
Abay	KZ	510	49°38'N	72°53'E
Abaya	ET	293	6°20'N	37°50'E
Abaza	RS	612	52°39'N	90°06'E
Abbabis	WA	313	24°00'S	16°06'E
Abban	YM	541	16°24'N	44°05'E
Abbeville		378	29°58'N	92°08'W
Abbeville		378	34°10'N	82°22'W
Abbeville	FR	580	50°06'N	1°50'E
Abbeyfeale	EI	592	52°23'N	9°18'W
Abbeyleix	EI	592	52°54'N	7°21'W
Abbot, Mount	AS	656	20°03'S	147°45'E
Abbottābād	PK	524	34°09'N	73°13'E
'Abd al 'Aziz, Jabal	SY	531	36°25'N	40°20'E
Abd al Kuri	YM	541	12°12'N	53°13'E
Ābdānān	IR	502	32°56'N	47°28'E
Abdulyan	AJ	483	40°03'N	48°40'E
Abéché	CD	283	13°49'N	20°50'E
Abel Erasmuspass	SF	322	24°29'S	30°37'E
Ābeltī	ET	293	8°10'N	37°34'E
Abemama	KR	660	0°30'N	174°00'E
Abenab	WA	313	19°19'S	18°06'E
Abengourou	IV	288	6°44'N	3°29'W
Åbenrå	DA	576	55°02'N	9°26'E
Abensberg	GM	584	48°49'N	11°51'E
Abeokuta	NI	316	7°10'N	3°19'E
Aberchirder		558	57°33'N	2°37'W
Aberdare Range	KE	299	0°25'S	36°38'E
Aberdeen		378	33°49'N	88°32'W
Aberdeen	SF	322	32°29'S	24°05'E
Aberdeen	UK	626	57°08'N	2°06'W
Aberdeen	US	398	46°58'N	123°48'W
Aberdeen	US	398	45°27'N	98°29'W
Aberdeen L.		368	64°28'N	99°00'W
Aberfoyle	UK	626	56°11'N	4°23'W
Abergavenny	UK	626	51°50'N	3°01'W
Ābergelē	ET	293	13°06'N	38°57'E
Aberipila	UG	330	1°58'N	33°18'E
Abernathy		376	33°49'N	101°50'W
Abersoch	UK	626	52°49'N	4°30'W
Aberystwyth	UK	626	52°24'N	4°04'W
Abez'	RS	612	66°32'N	61°47'E
Abhá	SA	528	18°13'N	42°30'E
Abhar	IR	502	36°09'N	49°13'E
Abhe, Lake	DJ	289	11°10'N	41°47'E
Abibe, Serranía de	CO	430	7°50'N	76°30'W
'Ābidīn	SU	324	13°20'N	33°43'E
Abidjan	IV	288	5°19'N	4°02'W
Abiji	NI	316	6°29'N	4°24'E
Abilene		372	38°55'N	97°12'W
Abilene	US	398	32°26'N	99°43'W
Abingdon		374	36°42'N	81°58'W
Abingdon	UK	626	51°40'N	1°17'W
Abingdon Downs		648	17°36'S	143°11'E
Abiod, Jebel el	AG	272	34°45'N	7°31'E
Ab-i-Panja	AF	480	36°45'N	72°15'E
Ab-i-Safed	AF	480	36°15'N	65°50'E
Abisko	SW	621	68°19'N	18°42'E
Abitibi		370	51°04'N	80°55'W
Abitibi L.	CA	390	48°40'N	79°45'W
Abiyata	ET	293	7°37'N	38°36'E
Abja-Paluoja	EN	577	58°08'N	25°21'E
Abminga	AS	656	26°07'S	134°32'E
Abnūb	EG	290	27°16'N	31°09'E
Abo	SO	321	11°47'N	50°31'E
Åbo (Turku)	FI	578	60°27'N	22°17'E
Aboh	NI	316	5°33'N	6°32'E
Abohar	IN	496	30°09'N	74°1[illegible]'E
Aboisso	IV	288	5°28'N	3°12'W
Aboki	UG	330	2°21'N	32°41'E
Abomey	BN	276	7°11'N	1°59'E
Abomey-Calavi	BN	276	6°27'N	2°21'E
Abongabong, Gunung	ID	500	4°15'N	96°48'E
Abong-Mbang	CM	280	3°59'N	13°11'E
Abony	HU	590	47°11'N	20°00'E
Aborko	SO	321	2°54'N	43°57'E
Aborlan	RP	526	9°26'N	118°33'E
Abou Deia	CD	283	11°27'N	19°17'E
Abovyan	AM	482	40°03'N	44°32'E
Aboyne	UK	626	57°04'N	2°49'W
Abqaiq	SA	528	25°56'N	49°40'E
Abra	RP	526	17°31'N	120°23'E
Abraham's Bay	BF	402	22°21'N	72°58'W
Abrantes	PO	608	39°29'N	8°12'W
Abra Pampa	AR	419	22°43'S	65°42'W
Ábrego	CO	430	8°05'N	73°13'W
Abreojos, Punta	MX	394	26°42'N	113°35'W
Abreus	CU	406	22°17'N	80°34'W
Abrevadero	MX	394	25°23'N	102°02'W
'Abrī	SU	324	20°47'N	30°22'E
Abricots	HA	412	18°38'N	74°18'W
Abrud	RO	610	46°16'N	23°04'E
Abruka	EN	577	58°09'N	22°31'E
Absaroka Range		372	44°30'N	109°45'W
Absarokee		372	45°31'N	109°27'W
Abū aḑ Ḑuhūr	SY	531	35°44'N	37°02'E
Abual Jirab	TC	538	24°10'N	53°53'E
Abū al Khaşīb	IZ	504	30°27'N	47°59'E
Abu al Mawj, Ra's	BA	484	26°01'N	50°28'E
Abū 'Arīsh	SA	528	16°58'N	42°50'E
Abū Dawm	SU	324	16°16'N	32°36'E
Abū Dīs	SU	324	19°08'N	33°34'E
Abu Gata Hills	SU	324	6°06'N	27°44'E
Abu Ghurayb	IZ	504	33°17'N	43°59'E
Abū Ḩadrīyah	SA	528	27°20'N	48°58'E
Abū Hamad	SU	324	19°32'N	33°19'E
Abu Hashim, Bi'r	EG	290	23°42'N	34°04'E
Abū Hugar	SU	324	12°52'N	34°00'E
Abu Hulayfah	KU	514	29°08'N	48°08'E
Abuja	NI	316	9°05'N	7°20'E
Abū Jābirah	SU	324	11°04'N	26°51'E
Abu Jarjur, Ra's	BA	484	26°04'N	50°37'E
Abū Jubayhah	SU	324	11°27'N	31°14'E
Abū Kamāl	SY	531	34°27'N	40°55'E
Abū Kūk	SU	324	12°08'N	34°18'E
Abukuma-kochi	JA	506	37°30'N	140°45'E
Abulog	RP	526	18°27'N	121°27'E
Abu Madd, Ra's	SA	528	24°50'N	37°07'E
Abū Maţāriq	SU	324	10°58'N	26°17'E
Abu Mendi	ET	293	11°48'N	35°42'E
Abu Minqar, Bi'r	EG	290	26°30'N	27°35'E
Abuná (Abunã)	BL	422	9°41'S	65°23'W
Abunã	BR	424	9°42'S	65°23'W
Abunã (Abuná)	BL	422	9°41'S	65°23'W
Abu Na'im	LY	302	28°54'N	18°53'E
Abune Yosef	ET	293	12°09'N	39°11'E
Abu Rasas, Ras	MU	523	20°10'N	58°38'E
Abu Road	IN	496	24°29'N	72°47'E
Abū Rubayq	SA	528	23°44'N	39°42'E
Abu Rujmayn, Jab.	SY	531	34°52'N	38°20'E
Abū Rukbah	SU	324	12°56'N	32°00'E
Abu Shagara, Ras	SU	324	21°03'N	37°18'E
Abū Shanab	SU	324	13°57'N	27°47'E
Abuta	JA	506	42°32'N	140°44'E
Abut Head	NZ	663	43°06'S	170°17'E
Abū Tīj	EG	290	27°02'N	31°19'E
Abuyog	RP	526	10°45'N	125°01'E
Abū Zabad	SU	324	12°21'N	29°15'E
Abū Ẓaby	TC	538	24°28'N	54°22'E
Abwong	SU	324	9°07'N	32°11'E
Abyār 'Alī	SA	528	24°25'N	39°33'E
Åbybro	DA	576	57°09'N	9°45'E
Abyei	SU	324	9°36'N	28°26'E
Acacías	CO	430	3°59'N	73°46'W
Acacoyagua	MX	394	15°22'N	92°40'W
Acahay	PA	435	25°55'S	57°09'W
Açailândia		386	4°55'S	47°28'W
Acajutla	ES	409	13°35'N	89°50'W
Acámbaro	MX	394	20°02'N	100°44'W
Acandí	CO	430	8°35'N	77°22'W
Acaponeta	MX	394	22°20'N	105°37'W
Acapulco de Juárez	MX	394	16°51'N	99°54'W
Acará		384	1°55'S	48°13'W
Acarai Mountains	GY	434	1°50'N	57°30'W
Acaraú		384	2°53'S	40°07'W
Acari	BR	424	7°00'S	66°00'W
Acarí	PE	436	15°26'S	74°37'W
Acarigua	VE	440	9°33'N	69°12'W
Acatlán	MX	394	18°12'N	98°03'W
Acayucan	MX	394	17°57'N	94°55'W
Acceglio	IT	593	44°28'N	6°58'E
Accompong	JM	414	18°14'N	77°45'W
Accra	GH	296	5°34'N	0°13'W
Accra Plains	GH	296	6°00'N	0°20'E
Aceguá	UY	439	31°52'S	54°13'W
Acerra		564	40°57'N	14°22'E
Achacachi	BL	422	16°03'S	68°43'W
Achaguas	VE	440	7°46'N	68°14'W
Achalpur	IN	496	21°15'N	77°30'E
Achao	CI	428	42°28'S	73°30'W
Achar	UY	439	32°25'S	56°10'W
Achegour	NG	314	19°02'N	11°44'E
Acheng	CH	490	45°31'N	126°58'E
Achenkirch	AU	568	47°32'N	11°42'E
Achen Pass	GM	584	47°36'N	11°38'E
Achikouya Plateau	GB	294	2°00'S	14°00'E
Achill Head	EI	592	53°58'N	10°15'W
Achill Is.	EI	592	53°57'N	10°00'W
Achiltibuie	UK	626	58°00'N	5°20'W
Āchīn	AF	480	34°08'N	70°42'E
Achinsk	RS	612	56°17'N	90°30'E
Achiri	BL	422	17°10'S	69°01'W
Achit Nuur	MG	520	49°30'N	90°30'E
Achnasheen	UK	626	57°35'N	5°06'W
Achuapa	NU	415	13°03'N	86°35'W
Achupallas	EC	432	2°16'S	78°44'W
Achur'an	AM	482	41°00'N	43°30'E
Achuyevo		564	45°43'N	37°46'E
Acigöl		564	37°50'N	29°54'E
Acireale	IT	593	37°37'N	15°10'E
Ackerman		378	33°18'N	89°10'W
Acklins I.	BF	402	22°26'N	73°58'W
Acomayo		384	9°46'S	76°05'W
Aconcagua, Cerro	AR	419	32°39'S	70°00'W
Acopiara		386	6°04'S	39°23'W
Acora	PE	436	15°57'S	69°47'W
Acornhoek	SF	322	24°37'S	31°05'E
A Coruña	SP	618	43°21'N	8°24'W
Acoyapa	NU	415	11°58'N	85°10'W
Acquaviva	SM	615	43°57'N	12°25'E
Acqui Terme	IT	593	44°41'N	8°28'E
Acre		386	8°45'S	67°22'W
Acri	IT	593	39°29'N	16°23'E
Ács	HU	590	47°42'N	18°01'E
Actéon Group		654	21°30'S	136°30'W
Actopan	MX	394	20°16'N	98°58'W
Açu	BR	424	5°34'S	36°54'W
Acul-du-Nord	HA	412	19°41'N	72°19'W
Acuña	AR	419	29°55'S	57°58'W
Ada	GH	296	5°47'N	0°38'E
Ada	US	398	47°17'N	96°30'W
Ada	US	398	34°46'N	96°40'W
Ada	YO	630	45°48'N	20°08'E
Ādaba	ET	293	7°00'N	39°24'E
Adâfer el Abiod	MR	308	19°30'N	10°00'W
Adair, Bahía de	MX	394	31°30'N	113°48'W
Adair, C.	CA	390	71°30'N	71°34'W
Adairsville		378	34°22'N	84°56'W
Adak	US	398	51°27'N	177°00'W
Adam	MU	523	22°23'N	57°32'E
Adams		374	43°48'N	76°01'W
Adams		374	43°57'N	89°49'W
Adam's Bridge	IN	496	9°04'N	79°37'E
Adam's Rock		654	25°04'S	130°09'W
Adamstown		654	25°04'S	130°06'W
Adamwa Plateau	NI	316	7°08'N	10°30'E
'Adan (Aden)	YM	541	12°45'N	44°58'E
Adana	TU	535	36°59'N	35°13'E
Adanhé	GB	294	0°31'S	10°13'E
Adani	NI	316	6°44'N	7°01'E
Adapazarı	TU	535	40°46'N	30°24'E
Adarama	SU	324	17°05'N	34°54'E
Adare	EI	592	52°34'N	8°47'W
Adaut	ID	500	8°09'S	131°07'E
Adavale	AS	656	25°55'S	144°36'E
Aday	LA	517	16°18'N	107°00'E
Adda	IT	593	45°08'N	9°53'E
Ad Dabbah	SU	324	18°03'N	30°57'E
Ad Dabbūrah	SU	324	17°32'N	34°14'E
Ad Dafīnah	SA	528	23°18'N	41°58'E
Ad Dafrah	TC	538	23°25'N	53°25'E
Ad Dahna	SA	528	24°30'N	48°10'E
Ad-Dakhla		262	23°42'N	15°56'W
Ad Damazin	SU	324	11°47'N	34°20'E
Ad Damīr	SU	324	17°35'N	33°58'E
Ad Dammām	SA	528	26°06'N	50°07'E
Ad Darb	SA	528	17°44'N	42°15'E
Ad Dawḩah (Doha)	QA	527	25°16'N	51°32'E
Ad Dawhah	KU	514	29°19'N	47°49'E
Ad Dawr	IZ	504	34°27'N	43°47'E
Addayah	SY	531	36°43'N	40°50'E
Ad Dibaiyah	KU	514	28°56'N	48°10'E
Ad Dibdibah	SA	528	27°00'N	46°00'E
Ad Dilam	SA	528	23°59'N	47°10'E
Addis Ababa (Ādīs Ābeba)	ET	293	9°01'N	38°44'E
Ad Dīwānīyah	IZ	504	31°59'N	44°56'E
Addu Atoll	MV	519	0°38'S	73°10'E
Ad Du'ayn	SU	324	11°26'N	26°09'E
Ad Dujayl	IZ	504	33°51'N	44°14'E
Ad Duwādimī	SA	528	24°29'N	44°23'E
Ad Duwayd	SA	528	30°13'N	42°18'E
Ad Duwaym	SU	324	14°00'N	32°18'E
Adé	CD	283	12°39'N	21°52'E
Adeje	SP	618	28°07'N	16°43'W
Adel		378	31°08'N	83°25'W
Adelaide	AS	656	34°56'S	138°36'E
Adelaide	BF	402	65°05'S	70°01'W
Adelaide	SF	322	32°42'S	26°18'E
Adelaide Pen.	CA	390	68°05'N	97°50'W
Adelaide River	AS	656	13°15'S	131°06'E
'Adel Bagrou	MR	308	15°31'N	7°04'W
Adelbert Range	PP	664	4°30'S	145°30'E
Adelboden	SZ	622	46°29'N	7°33'E
Adele I.		648	15°10'S	123°00'E
Adelphi	JM	414	18°27'N	77°48'W
Adelphy	VC	418	13°11'N	61°08'W
Aden		372	49°02'N	111°19'W
Aden ('Adan)	YM	541	12°45'N	44°58'E
Aden, Gulf of	YM	541	12°00'N	48°00'E
Aderbissinat	NG	314	15°37'N	7°54'E
Adèrké	CD	283	21°15'N	17°26'E
Ādēt	ET	293	11°16'N	37°29'E
Adh Dhahībāt	TS	329	32°00'N	10°41'E
Adh Dhirā'	JO	510	31°15'N	35°34'E
Adhicadeeye	SO	321	8°40'N	47°09'E
Adi	CG	287	3°24'N	30°48'E
Adi	ID	500	4°18'S	133°26'E
Adiaké	IV	288	5°16'N	3°17'W
Ādī Ārk'ay	ET	293	13°27'N	38°04'E
Adica, Serra da	PO	608	38°00'N	7°30'W
Ādī Da'iro	ET	293	14°23'N	38°12'E
Adieu, C.	AS	656	32°02'S	132°13'E
Ādīgala	ET	293	10°25'N	42°14'E
Adige	IT	593	45°10'N	12°20'E
Adigeni	GG	495	41°42'N	42°42'E
Ādīgrat	ET	293	14°17'N	39°28'E
Ādī K'eyih	ER	292	14°51'N	39°22'E
Ādī Kwala	ER	292	14°38'N	38°50'E
Adilābād	IN	496	19°40'N	78°32'E
Adilang	UG	330	2°44'N	33°29'E
Adīrī	LY	302	27°30'N	13°16'E
Adirondack Mountains	US	398	44°00'N	74°30'W
Ādīs Ābeba (Addis Ababa)	ET	293	9°01'N	38°44'E
Ādīs 'Alem	ET	293	9°02'N	38°24'E
Ādīs Zemen	ET	293	12°07'N	37°47'E
Ādī Tekelezan	ER	292	15°34'N	38°47'E
Ādī Ugrī	ER	292	14°53'N	38°49'E
Adıyaman	TU	535	37°46'N	38°17'E
Adjohoun	BN	276	6°39'N	2°04'E
Adjud	RO	610	46°05'N	27°11'E
Admer, Erg d'	AG	272	24°12'N	9°10'E
Admiralty Gulf	AS	656	14°20'S	125°50'E
Admiralty Islands	PP	664	1°50'S	147°00'E
Ado Awaiye	NI	316	7°50'N	3°26'E
Ado Ekiti	NI	316	7°35'N	5°12'E
Adok	SU	324	8°11'N	30°19'E
Adolfo López Mateos	MX	394	25°12'N	112°06'W
Ādoni	IN	496	15°38'N	77°17'E
Ado Odo	NI	316	6°57'N	3°16'E
Adoru	NI	316	6°59'N	7°10'E
Adour	FR	580	43°32'N	1°32'W
Adra	SP	618	36°45'N	3°00'W
Adranga	CG	287	2°55'N	29°58'E
Adrano	IT	593	37°40'N	14°50'E
Adrar	AG	272	27°54'N	0°17'W
Adrar des Iforas	AG	272	20°00'N	2°00'E
Adrar Llassene	AG	272	21°00'N	4°00'W
Adrar Mkorn	MO	310	31°37'N	5°40'W
Adrar Souf		262	21°30'N	15°30'W
Adraskan	AF	480	33°39'N	62°16'E
Adrasman	TI	533	40°38'N	69°58'E
Adré	CD	283	13°28'N	22°12'E
Adria	IT	593	45°03'N	12°04'E
Adrian		374	38°23'N	94°21'W
Adrian		374	43°38'N	95°55'W
Adrian		374	41°53'N	84°02'W
Adriatic Sea	AL	566	43°00'N	16°00'E
Adukrom	GH	296	6°01'N	0°05'W
Aduku	UG	330	2°14'N	32°41'E
Adutiškis	LH	597	55°09'N	26°36'E
Advance		374	37°06'N	89°54'W
Adventure	GY	434	7°05'N	58°29'W
Ādwa	ET	293	14°10'N	38°54'E
Adycha	RS	612	68°13'N	134°41'E
Adzabikat I	GB	294	1°41'N	11°38'E
Adzharis Tskali	GG	495	41°40'N	42°00'E
Adzharo-Imeretinskiy Khrebet	GG	495	41°50'N	43°00'E
Adzhikend	AJ	483	40°31'N	46°20'E
Adzopé	IV	288	6°06'N	3°52'W
Aegean Sea	GR	588	39°00'N	25°00'E
Aegviidu	EN	577	59°17'N	25°37'E
Aerø	DA	576	54°48'N	10°10'E
Ærøskøbing	DA	576	54°53'N	10°25'E
A Estrada	SP	618	42°41'N	8°29'W
Äetsä	FI	578	61°18'N	22°42'E
'Af/	SA	528	23°55'N	42°56'E
'Afak	IZ	504	32°04'N	45°15'E
Āfambo	ER	292	13°33'N	41°40'E
Āfambo	ET	293	11°28'N	41°42'E
Afándou	GR	588	36°17'N	28°10'E
Afarag, Erg	AG	272	25°00'N	3°00'W
Afareaitu		654	17°38'S	147°36'W
Āfdem	ET	293	9°28'N	41°00'E
Affenrücker	WA	313	28°05'S	15°50'E
Affolle	MR	308	16°58'N	10°40'W
Afghanistan		38	33°00'N	65°00'E
Afgooye	SO	321	2°09'N	45°07'E
Afia	GB	294	1°06'N	11°43'E
'Afīf		264	23°54'N	42°55'E
Afikpo	NI	316	5°54'N	7°56'E
Åfjord	NO	604	63°58'N	10°12'E
Aflou	AG	272	34°07'N	2°06'E
Afmadow	SO	321	0°31'N	42°04'E
Afogados da Ingàzeira		386	7°45'S	37°39'W
Afognak	US	398	58°01'N	152°47'W
Afognak I.		368	58°15'N	152°30'W
A Fonsagraca	SP	618	43°08'N	7°04'W
Afore	PP	664	9°08'S	148°23'E
Afragola	IT	593	40°55'N	14°18'E
Afrânio	BR	424	8°31'S	41°00'W
Afrikanda		556	67°27'N	32°46'E
'Afrīn	SY	531	36°31'N	36°52'E
Afşin	TU	535	38°15'N	36°55'E
Afton		372	42°43'N	110°55'W
Afuá	BR	424	0°10'S	50°23'W
'Afula	IS	505	32°36'N	35°17'E
Afyon	TU	535	38°45'N	30°33'E
Agadem	NG	314	16°50'N	13°17'E
Agadez	NG	314	16°58'N	7°59'E
Agadir	MO	310	30°24'N	9°36'W
Agadyr'	KZ	510	48°15'N	72°53'E
Aga-Kauitai		654	23°10'S	134°57'W
Agalta, Montes	HO	412	15°01'N	85°48'W
Agana		654	13°28'N	144°45'E
Agarakadzor	AM	482	39°44'N	45°21'E
Āgarfa	ET	293	7°17'N	39°49'E
Āgaro	ET	293	7°51'N	36°39'E
Agartala	IN	496	23°49'N	91°16'E
Agat		654	13°25'N	145°40'E
Agata	RS	612	66°55'N	93°30'E
Agats	ID	500	5°33'S	138°08'E
Agattu	US	398	52°17'N	172°55'E
Agave	TO	328	7°14'N	0°48'E
Agawa Bay		374	47°21'N	84°37'W
Agaydar	KZ	510	50°15'N	65°17'E
Agbabu	NI	316	6°35'N	4°50'E
Agbani	NI	316	6°19'N	7°33'E
Agbaré	TO	328	7°29'N	1°24'E
Agbor Bojiboji	NI	316	6°16'N	6°13'E
Agboville	IV	288	5°56'N	4°13'W
Ağdam	AJ	483	39°59'N	46°55'E
Agdash	AJ	483	40°38'N	47°29'E
Agde	FR	580	43°19'N	3°28'E
Agdz	MO	310	30°42'N	6°26'W
Agdzhabedi	AJ	483	40°02'N	47°28'E
Agege	NI	316	6°38'N	3°19'E
Agen	FR	580	44°12'N	0°37'E
AgerbÆk	DA	576	55°36'N	8°48'E
Āgere Maryam	ET	293	5°38'N	38°14'E
Aggeneys	SF	322	29°14'S	18°51'E
Aggtelek	HU	590	48°15'N	21°15'E
Āghā Jārī	IR	502	30°42'N	49°50'E
Agiabampo		376	26°23'N	109°08'W
Agiabampo, Bahía de		376	26°30'N	109°30'W
Aginskoye	RS	612	51°08'N	114°32'E
Agjert	MR	308	16°27'N	9°18'W
Ağlasun		564	37°40'N	30°32'E
Agnew	AS	656	28°00'S	120°28'E
Agnibilékrou	IV	288	7°08'N	3°12'W
Agnita	RO	610	45°58'N	24°37'E
Ago		474	34°19'N	136°49'E
Ago Are	NI	316	8°30'N	3°25'E
Ago Iwoye	NI	316	6°57'N	3°55'E
Agona	GH	296	6°09'N	2°08'W
Agonne	FR	580	49°00'N	5°00'E
Agougadzépe	TO	328	6°51'N	0°43'E
Āgra	IN	496	27°11'N	78°01'E
Agraciada	UY	439	33°48'S	58°15'W
Agramonte	CU	406	22°41'N	81°07'W
Agri	TU	535	39°44'N	43°03'E
Agrigento	IT	593	37°19'N	13°35'E
Agrínion	GR	588	38°37'N	21°24'E
Agropoli	IT	593	40°21'N	14°59'E
Agro Pontino	IT	593	41°25'N	12°55'E
Agua Blanca		376	31°39'N	115°54'W
Àgua Boa	BR	424	14°03'S	52°10'W
Água Boa		386	17°59'S	42°24'W
Água Branca	BR	424	5°53'S	42°38'W
Agua Buena		386	24°19'S	69°54'W
Agua Buena	CS	405	8°43'N	82°55'W
Agua Caliente	BL	422	15°41'S	62°55'W
Aguacate, Cerros del	CS	405	10°02'N	84°28'W
Aguachica	CO	430	8°19'N	73°38'W
Água Clara	BR	424	20°26'S	52°52'W
Aguada	US	398	18°23'N	67°11'W
Aguada de Pasajeros	CU	406	22°23'N	80°51'W
Aguada Grande	VE	440	10°35'N	69°30'W
Aguadilla	US	398	18°26'N	67°09'W
Aguadulce	PM	417	8°15'N	80°33'W
Agua Fria		376	35°39'N	106°01'W
Agua Larga	VE	440	10°53'N	69°44'W
Agualeguas		376	26°19'N	99°31'W
Agua Linda	VE	440	5°34'N	67°07'W
Aguán	HO	412	15°55'N	85°41'W
Aguanish	CA	390	50°13'N	62°05'W
Agua Preta		386	1°41'S	63°48'W
Agua Prieta	MX	394	31°19'N	109°32'W
Aguaray	AR	419	22°16'S	63°44'W
A Guarda	SP	618	41°54'N	8°52'W
Aguarico	EC	432	0°59'S	75°11'W
Aguasay	VE	440	9°25'N	63°44'W
Aguas Blancas	AR	419	22°44'S	64°23'W
Aguas Blancas	CI	428	24°11'S	69°51'W
Aguascalientes	MX	394	21°53'N	102°18'W
Águas Formosas		386	17°05'S	40°57'W
Agua Verde	MX	394	22°54'N	105°59'W
Aguazul	CO	430	5°10'N	72°33'W
Águeda	PO	608	40°34'N	8°27'W
Aguelhok	ML	307	19°28'N	0°52'E
Agüenit		262	22°10'N	13°07'W
Aguêraktem	ML	307	23°11'N	6°20'W
Aguerguer		262	21°30'N	16°50'W
Aguidé	CT	282	6°33'N	21°57'E
Aguié	NG	314	13°31'N	7°47'E
Aguijan Island		654	14°51'N	145°34'E
Aguilâl Faï	MR	308	18°27'N	14°44'W
Aguilar de Campóo	SP	618	42°48'N	4°16'W
Águilas	SP	618	37°24'N	1°35'W
Águilas, Bahía de las	DR	408	17°50'N	71°39'W
Aguililla	MX	394	18°44'N	102°46'W
Aguja, Cabo de la	CO	430	11°20'N	74°06'W
Aguja, Punta	PE	436	5°47'S	81°06'W
Agulhas, C.	SF	322	34°49'S	20°00'E
Agung, Gunung	ID	500	8°25'N	115°28'E
Agustín Codazzi	CO	430	10°02'N	73°14'W
Agutaya	RP	526	11°08'N	120°56'E
Agwata	UG	330	1°59'N	33°00'E
Agwok	SU	324	7°52'N	28°24'E
Ahaggar	AG	272	23°10'N	5°50'E
Aha Hills	BC	276	19°47'S	21°00'E
Ahangama	CE	530	5°58'N	80°22'E
Ahar	IR	502	38°28'N	47°04'E
Ahaura	NZ	663	42°41'S	171°03'E
Ahé		654	14°30'S	146°15'W
Ahero	KE	299	0°11'S	34°54'E
Ahipara	NZ	663	35°09'S	173°11'E
Ahklun Mts.	US	398	59°15'N	160°30'W
Ahlat	TU	535	38°45'N	42°29'E
Ahlen	GM	584	51°45'N	7°55'E
Ahl Wahibah, Ramlat	MU	523	21°56'N	58°55'E

Allada	BN	276	6°39'N	2°09'E
Al Lādhiqīyah	SY	531	35°31'N	35°47'E
Al Lagowa	SU	324	11°24'N	29°08'E
Allahābād	IN	496	25°27'N	81°51'E
Allakh-Yun'	RS	612	61°08'N	138°03'E
Allanmyo	BM	487	19°22'N	95°15'E
Allanridge	SF	322	27°45'S	26°37'E
Allan Water		374	50°14'N	90°12'W
Allaq, Bi'r	LY	302	31°00'N	11°55'E
Alldays	SF	322	22°41'S	29°06'E
Alle	SZ	622	47°26'N	7°08'E
Allegan		374	42°31'N	85°51'W
Allegheny	US	398	40°27'N	80°01'W
Allegheny Mountains	US	398	38°45'N	79°33'W
Allegheny Plateau	US	398	41°30'N	78°00'W
Allen, Lough	EI	592	54°07'N	8°03'W
Allendale		378	33°00'N	81°18'W
Allende	MX	394	25°17'N	100°01'W
Allende	MX	394	28°20'N	100°53'W
Allendorf	GM	584	51°02'N	8°40'E
Allentown	US	398	40°36'N	75°28'W
Alleppey	IN	496	9°29'N	76°19'E
Aller	GM	584	52°57'N	9°11'E
Alley	JM	414	17°43'N	77°16'W
Allgäu	GM	584	47°35'N	10°10'E
Allgäuer Alpen	AU	568	47°24'N	10°15'E
Alliance	US	398	42°05'N	102°52'W
Al Lidām	SA	528	20°29'N	44°50'E
Allier	FR	580	47°18'N	8°14'E
Alligator Pond	JM	414	17°52'N	77°34'W
Allingåbro	DA	576	56°28'N	10°20'E
Allinge	DA	576	55°16'N	14°49'E
Allingham	AS	656	18°43'S	136°18'E
Al Līth	SA	528	20°09'N	40°16'E
Al Liwa (Al Jiwa)	TC	538	23°00'N	53°50'E
Liyah, Jal al	KU	514	29°45'N	47°10'E
Allonnes	FR	580	47°58'N	0°09'E
Allschwil	SZ	622	47°33'N	7°32'E
Allu		648	5°34'S	119°33'E
Al Luḩayyah	YM	541	15°42'N	42°42'E
Allumettes, Ile des		374	45°50'N	77°02'W
Alluriquín	EC	432	0°19'S	78°59'W
Alma		372	40°05'N	99°21'W
Alma		374	43°22'N	84°39'W
Alma		378	31°32'N	82°27'W
Alma	CA	390	48°30'N	71°37'W
Almacelles		562	41°44'N	0°27'E
Almaćen	VE	440	8°06'N	63°49'W
Almadén	SP	618	38°46'N	4°50'W
Al Madḩatīyah	IZ	504	32°24'N	44°40'E
Al Madīnah	SA	528	24°28'N	39°36'E
Al Madīnah al Fikrīyah	EG	290	27°56'N	30°49'E
Al Mafraq	JO	510	32°21'N	36°12'E
Al Magharah	SY	531	36°39'N	38°12'E
Al Maghārīm	YM	541	15°00'N	47°48'E
Al Maghasil	KU	514	29°45'N	48°06'E
Almagro	SP	618	38°53'N	3°43'W
Al Maḩallah al Kubrá	EG	290	30°58'N	31°10'E
Al Mahdīyah	TS	329	35°30'N	11°02'E
Al Mahdīyah	TS	329	35°30'N	11°04'E
Al Maḩmūdīyah	IZ	504	33°03'N	44°21'E
Al Mahmuri	SY	531	34°42'N	36°39'E
Al Majma'ah	SA	528	25°54'N	45°20'E
Almajului	RO	610	44°43'N	22°12'E
Al Malamm	SU	324	9°49'N	28°45'E
Al Malik, Wadi	SU	324	16°00'N	30°10'E
Al Mālikīyah	SY	531	37°10'N	42°08'E
Almalyk	UZ	539	40°50'N	69°35'E
Al Manāmah (Manama)	BA	484	26°13'N	50°35'E
Al Manaqil	SU	324	14°15'N	32°59'E
Al Manqaf	KU	514	29°06'N	48°08'E
Almansa	SP	618	38°52'N	1°05'W
Al Manshāh	EG	290	26°28'N	31°48'E
Al Mansūra	EG	290	31°03'N	31°23'E
Al Manzilah	EG	290	31°09'N	31°56'E
Almanzora	SP	618	37°14'N	1°46'W
Al Ma'qil	IZ	504	30°33'N	47°48'E
Al Maqrūn	LY	302	31°26'N	20°09'E
Al Maqwa	KU	514	29°10'N	47°59'E
Al Marfa'	TC	538	24°05'N	53°30'E
Al Marj	LY	302	32°29'N	20°47'E
Al Marsá	TS	329	36°55'N	10°18'E
Almas	BR	424	11°33'S	47°09'W
Al Masīd	SU	324	15°15'N	32°57'E
Al Matammah	SU	324	16°43'N	33°22'E
Al Maţarīyah	EG	290	31°11'N	32°02'E
Al Matnah	SU	324	13°47'N	35°03'E
Almaty	KZ	510	43°15'N	76°57'E
Al Mawşil	IZ	504	36°20'N	43°08'E
Al Mayādin	SY	531	35°01'N	40°27'E
Almazán	SP	618	41°29'N	2°32'W
Al Mazar	JO	510	31°49'N	35°39'E
Almazar	UZ	539	40°59'N	68°54'E
Almaznyy	RS	612	62°27'N	114°19'E
Al Mazraah	JO	510	31°16'N	35°31'E
Almeida	PO	608	40°43'N	6°54'W
Almeirim	BR	424	1°32'S	52°34'W
Almeirim	PO	608	39°12'N	8°38'W
Almelo	NL	602	52°21'N	6°40'E
Almenara	BR	424	16°11'S	40°42'W
Almendra, Emb. de	SP	618	41°14'N	6°13'W
Almendralejo	SP	618	38°41'N	6°24'W
Almere	NL	602	52°20'N	5°14'E
Almería	SP	618	36°46'N	2°29'W
Almería, G. de	SP	618	36°46'N	2°30'W
Al'met'yevsk	RS	612	54°53'N	52°20'E
Al'mezh		466	60°03'N	48°03'E
Älmhult	SW	621	56°33'N	14°07'E
Al Midhnab	SA	528	25°52'N	44°14'E
Al Mihrad	SA	528	23°30'N	53°00'E
Al Miknāsī	TS	329	34°37'N	9°36'E
Al Mīnā'	LE	516	34°27'N	35°48'E
Almina, Punta	SP	618	35°53'N	5°18'W
Al Mindak	SA	528	20°06'N	41°17'E
Al Minyā	EG	290	28°06'N	30°45'E
Al Miqdādiyah	IZ	504	33°59'N	44°56'E
Almirante	PM	417	9°18'N	82°24'W
Almirós	GR	588	39°11'N	22°46'E
Almiroú, Kólpos	GR	588	35°23'N	24°20'E
Al Mirza	YM	541	13°22'N	44°27'E
Almodôvar	PO	608	37°31'N	8°04'W
Almodóvar del Campo	SP	618	38°43'N	4°10'W
Almonte	SP	618	39°42'N	6°28'W
Almora		470	29°37'N	79°40'E
Al Mubarraz	SA	528	22°17'N	46°44'E
Al Mudawwarah	JO	510	29°19'N	35°59'E
Al Mudayrib	MU	523	22°37'N	58°40'E
Almudévar	SP	618	42°03'N	0°35'W
Al Mughrib	TC	538	23°10'N	52°10'E
Al Muglad	SU	324	11°02'N	27°44'E
Al Muḩarraq	BA	484	26°15'N	50°37'E
Al Mukallā	YM	541	14°31'N	49°07'E
Al Mukrīn	TS	329	35°38'N	10°54'E
Al Muladdah	MU	523	23°45'N	57°34'E
Al Munastīr	TS	329	35°46'N	10°43'E
Almuñécar	SP	618	36°44'N	3°40'W
Al Musallamīyah	SU	324	14°34'N	33°21'E
Al Musayjīd	SA	528	24°05'N	39°05'E
Al Musayyib	IZ	504	32°47'N	44°18'E
Al Muwassam	SA	528	16°25'N	42°50'E
Al Muwayh	SA	528	22°45'N	41°35'E
Al Muwayliḩ	SA	528	27°41'N	35°28'E
Alness	UK	626	57°41'N	4°15'W
Alnwick	UK	626	55°24'N	1°42'W
Alnysh	TX	537	37°16'N	62°19'E
Alofi		650	14°44'S	173°09'W
Aloi	UG	330	2°17'N	33°10'E
Aloja	LG	596	57°46'N	24°53'E
Alon	BM	487	22°12'N	95°05'E
Alon	FI	578	60°18'N	22°12'E
Along	IN	496	28°10'N	95°03'E
Alongshan	CH	490	51°36'N	122°00'E
Alor	ID	500	8°15'S	124°45'E
Alor, Kep.	ID	500	8°15'S	112°30'E
Álora	SP	618	36°47'N	4°44'W
Alor Gajah	MY	518	2°23'N	102°13'E
Alor Setar	MY	518	6°07'N	100°22'E
Alotau	PP	664	10°17'S	150°26'E
Alpen	AU	568	46°25'N	10°00'E
Alpena		370	45°03'N	83°26'W
Alpercatas, Serra das	BR	424	6°00'S	45°00'W
Alpes Cottiennes	FR	580	44°45'N	7°00'E
Alpes de Provence	FR	580	43°50'N	6°15'E
Alpes du Dauphiné	FR	580	44°40'N	6°07'E
Alpes Maritimes	FR	580	44°15'N	7°10'E
Alpha	AS	656	23°39'S	146°38'E
Alphen aan de Rijn	NL	602	52°08'N	4°40'E
Alphonse Group	SE	319	7°00'S	52°44'E
Alpi Apuane	IT	593	44°15'N	10°05'E
Alpiarça	PO	608	39°15'N	8°35'W
Alpi Bernina	SZ	622	46°15'N	9°50'E
Alpi Breónie	IT	593	46°40'N	11°10'E
Alpi Carniche	IT	593	46°40'N	13°00'E
Alpi Cozie	IT	593	44°45'N	7°00'E
Alpi Dolomitiche	IT	593	46°23'N	11°51'E
Alpi Graie	IT	593	45°30'N	7°10'E
Alpi Lepontine	SZ	622	46°25'N	8°40'E
Alpi Marittime	IT	593	44°15'N	7°10'E
Alpine	US	398	30°21'N	103°39'W
Alpi Orobie	IT	593	46°00'N	10°00'E
Alpi Pennine	IT	593	46°05'N	7°50'E
Alpi Retiche	SZ	622	46°30'N	10°00'E
Alpnach	SZ	622	46°56'N	8°15'E
Alportel	PO	608	37°11'N	7°54'W
Alps	AU	568	47°40'N	13°38'E
Alps	FR	580	46°25'N	10°00'E
Al Qābil	MU	523	23°56'N	55°49'E
Al Qaḑīmah	SA	528	22°21'N	39°09'E
Al Qaḑīrif	SU	324	14°02'N	35°24'E
Al Qadmūs	SY	531	35°05'N	36°10'E
Al Qāhirah (Cairo)	EG	290	30°03'N	31°15'E
Al Qaḩmah	SA	528	18°00'N	41°41'E
Al Qā'im	IZ	504	34°21'N	41°07'E
Al Qalībah	SA	528	28°24'N	37°42'E
Al Qāmishlī	SY	531	37°02'N	41°14'E
Al Qanāţir al Khayrīyah	EG	290	30°12'N	31°08'E
Al Qaryah al Sharqīyah	LY	302	30°25'N	13°34'E
Al Qaryāt	LY	302	30°24'N	13°36'E
Al Qaryatayn	SY	531	34°14'N	37°14'E
Al Qarẕabah	LY	302	32°07'N	23°26'E
Al Qaşabāt	LY	302	32°35'N	14°03'E
Al Qāsim	IZ	504	32°18'N	44°41'E
Al Qaşr	EG	290	25°42'N	28°53'E
Al Qaşr	JO	510	31°19'N	35°45'E
Al Qaşrayn	TS	329	35°09'N	8°48'E
Al Qaţaynah	SU	324	14°52'N	32°21'E
Al Qaţīf	SA	528	26°33'N	50°00'E
Al Qaţrūn	LY	302	24°56'N	14°38'E
Al Qayrawān	TS	329	35°40'N	10°04'E
Al Qayşūmah	SA	528	28°20'N	46°07'E
Al Qir'awn	LE	516	33°31'N	35°35'E
Alqōsh	IZ	504	36°44'N	43°06'E
Al Qu'amiyat	SA	528	19°25'N	49°00'E
Al Qubbah	LY	302	32°46'N	22°15'E
Al Quds (Jerusalem) (Yerushalayn)	IS	505	31°46'N	35°13'E
Alquízar	CU	406	22°48'N	82°35'W
Al Qunayţirah	SY	531	33°07'N	35°49'E
Al Qunfudhah	SA	528	19°08'N	41°05'E
Al Qurayn, Ra's	BA	484	25°55'N	50°35'E
Al Qurnah	IZ	504	31°00'N	47°26'E
Al Quşayr	EG	290	26°06'N	34°17'E
Al Quşayr	SY	531	34°31'N	36°35'E
Al Qūşīyah	EG	290	27°26'N	30°49'E
Al Quşūr	TS	329	35°54'N	8°53'E
Al Quţayfah	SY	531	33°45'N	36°36'E
Al Quwayid	LY	302	29°30'N	21°40'E
Al Quway'īyah	SA	528	24°03'N	45°15'E
Al Quwayrah	JO	510	29°48'N	35°19'E
Al Rabbad	TC	538	23°00'N	54°40'E
Alroy Downs	AS	656	19°18'S	136°04'E
Als	DA	576	54°59'N	10°01'E
Alsace, Plaine d'	FR	580	48°30'N	7°30'E
Alsasua (Altsasu)	SP	618	42°53'N	2°10'W
Alsfeld	GM	584	50°45'N	9°16'E
Alsózsolca	HU	590	48°04'N	20°53'E
Alston	UK	626	54°48'N	2°27'W
Alsunga	LG	596	56°59'N	21°34'E
Alta	NO	604	69°57'N	23°15'E
Altaelva	NO	604	69°58'N	23°23'E
Alta Floresta	BR	424	9°52'S	56°05'W
Alta Gracia	AR	419	31°40'S	64°26'W
Alta Gracia	NU	415	11°34'N	85°35'W
Altagracia	VE	440	10°43'N	71°32'W
Altagracia	VE	440	8°34'N	64°04'W
Altagracia de Orituco	VE	440	9°52'N	66°23'W
Altai	CH	490	48°00'N	90°00'E
Altaj	MG	520	48°18'N	89°35'E
Altamaha	US	398	31°19'N	81°17'W
Altamillos, Sa. de los	MX	394	26°30'N	103°00'W
Altamira	BR	424	3°12'S	52°12'W
Altamira	CI	428	25°47'S	69°51'W
Altamira	DR	408	19°41'N	70°50'W
Altamira	MX	394	22°24'N	97°55'W
Altamira	VE	440	8°35'N	65°34'W
Altamont	US	398	42°12'N	121°44'W
Altamonte Springs	US	398	28°40'N	81°21'W
Altamura	IT	593	40°50'N	16°33'E
Altamura	MX	394	24°50'N	108°15'W
Altan	MG	520	48°40'N	104°20'E
Altan	MG	520	48°07'N	95°45'E
Altanbulag	MG	520	47°41'N	106°22'E
Altanbulag	MG	520	49°18'N	96°20'E
Altanbulag	MG	520	50°19'N	106°30'E
Altancögo	MG	520	49°03'N	90°27'E
Altano, Capo	IT	593	39°14'N	8°21'E
Altan-Ovoo	MG	520	47°27'N	101°45'E
Altanteel	MG	520	47°08'N	92°50'E
Altar	MX	394	30°43'N	111°52'W
Altar, Desierto de	MX	394	31°50'N	114°15'W
Altavista		374	37°06'N	79°17'W
Altay	CH	490	47°51'N	88°06'E
Altay	MG	520	49°41'N	96°20'E
Altay	MG	520	46°20'N	96°18'E
Altay	RS	612	48°00'N	90°00'E
Altayskiy		466	51°58'N	85°51'E
Alt de Coma Pedrosa, Pic	AN	567	42°35'N	1°27'E
Altdorf	SZ	622	46°52'N	8°38'E
Altea	SP	618	38°35'N	0°04'W
Alteidet	NO	604	70°02'N	22°05'E
Altenburg	GM	584	50°59'N	12°27'E
Altenqoke	CH	490	36°24'N	94°35'E
Altentreptow	GM	584	53°41'N	13°15'E
Alter do Chão		384	2°32'S	54°59'W
Alter do Chão	PO	608	39°12'N	7°40'W
Alteres	MX	394	28°51'N	103°23'W
Altınekin		564	38°19'N	32°58'E
Altınhisar		564	38°00'N	34°23'E
Altınyaka		564	36°34'N	30°21'E
Altınyayla		564	36°59'N	29°33'E
Altiplano	BL	422	18°00'S	68°00'W
Altmühl	GM	584	48°54'N	11°54'E
Altmünster	AU	568	47°54'N	13°45'E
Alto		378	31°39'N	95°04'W
Alto, Pico	BR	424	4°14'S	38°54'W
Alto Alegre	BR	424	2°55'N	61°18'W
Alto Araguaia	BR	424	17°19'S	53°12'W
Alto Chicapa	AO	274	10°53'S	19°14'E
Alto Cuale	AO	274	7°34'S	16°16'E
Alto Cuilo	AO	274	10°03'S	19°31'E
Alto de la Sierra	AR	419	22°44'S	62°30'W
Alto del Carmen		388	28°46'S	70°30'W
Alto de Tamar	CO	430	7°28'N	74°23'W
Alto de Tres Morros	CO	430	7°08'N	76°11'W
Alto Douro	TP	318	0°03'N	6°32'E
Alto Garças	BR	424	16°56'S	53°32'W
Alto Molócuè	MZ	312	15°38'S	37°42'E
Alton	UK	626	51°08'N	0°59'W
Altona		372	49°06'N	97°33'W
Alton Downs	AS	656	26°07'S	138°57'E
Altônia	BR	424	23°56'S	53°54'W
Altoona		374	40°31'N	78°23'W
Alto Paraguai	BR	424	14°31'S	56°29'W
Alto Parnaíba	BR	424	9°06'S	45°57'W
Alto Purús	PE	436	9°34'S	70°36'W
Alto Río Senguer	AR	419	45°02'S	70°50'W
Alto Ritacuba	CO	430	6°30'N	72°19'W
Altos	BR	424	5°03'S	42°28'W
Alto Seco	BL	422	18°52'S	64°07'W
Alto Songo	CU	406	20°10'N	75°42'W
Alto Yuruá	PE	436	9°24'S	72°43'W
Altraga	MG	520	50°12'N	98°58'E
Altsasu (Alsasua)	SP	618	42°53'N	2°10'W
Altstätten	SZ	622	47°23'N	9°32'E
Altukhovo		560	52°41'N	34°21'E
Altun Shan	CH	490	38°36'N	89°00'E
Alturas	US	398	41°29'N	120°32'W
Altus	US	398	34°38'N	99°20'W
Altykarasu	KZ	510	49°12'N	55°52'E
Altynkul'	UZ	539	43°06'N	58°54'E
Altynovka	UP	624	51°27'N	33°11'E
Altyn-Topkan	TI	533	40°38'N	69°35'E
Altzaga (Erandio)		562	43°04'N	2°09'W
Alu (Shortland I.)	BP	666	6°55'S	155°50'E
Al 'Ubaylah	SA	528	21°59'N	50°57'E
Al Ubayyiḑ	SU	324	13°11'N	30°13'E
Alucra		564	40°20'N	38°46'E
Al Uḑayyah	SU	324	12°03'N	28°17'E
Aluk	SU	324	8°26'N	27°32'E
Alūksne	LG	596	57°25'N	27°03'E
Al 'Ulá	SA	528	26°38'N	37°55'E
Al Ulya	MU	523	22°53'N	58°13'E
Al 'Umdah	SU	324	11°47'N	28°02'E
Aluminé	AR	419	39°13'S	70°57'W
Al Uqaylah	LY	302	30°15'N	19°10'E
Al 'Uqayr	SA	528	25°39'N	50°14'E
Al Uqşur	EG	290	25°41'N	32°39'E
Ālūs	IZ	504	34°02'N	42°26'E
Alushta	UP	624	44°40'N	34°25'E
Aluta	CG	287	1°13'S	26°14'E
Al Uwaynah	QA	527	25°27'N	50°58'E
Al 'Uwaynāt	LY	302	25°48'N	10°33'E
Al 'Uyūn	SA	528	26°31'N	43°40'E
Al 'Uzayr	IZ	504	31°19'N	47°25'E
Alva	US	398	36°48'N	98°39'W
Alvalade	PO	608	37°56'N	8°24'W
Alvarado	MX	394	18°47'N	95°46'W
Alvarães	BR	424	3°14'S	64°50'W
Álvaro Obregón, Presa		376	27°52'N	109°52'W
Alvdal	NO	604	62°07'N	10°39'E
Älvdalen	SW	621	61°12'N	14°04'E
Alvear	AR	419	29°06'S	56°33'W
Alverca	PO	608	38°54'N	9°02'W
Alvesta	SW	621	56°54'N	14°33'E
Alvik	SW	621	62°24'N	17°26'E
Ålvik	NO	604	60°27'N	6°25'E
Alvito	PO	608	38°15'N	7°59'W
Älvkarleby	SW	621	60°34'N	17°27'E
Alvorada	BR	424	28°40'S	52°09'W
Alvorada	BR	424	12°28'S	49°06'W
Alvorada d'Oeste	BR	424	11°17'S	62°30'W
Alvorada do Norte	BR	424	14°25'S	46°25'W
Alvord		372	42°30'N	118°25'W
Älvros	SW	621	62°02'N	14°38'E
Älvsbyn	SW	621	65°40'N	21°00'E
Alwa	UG	330	1°51'N	33°10'E
Al Wafrah	KU	514	28°38'N	47°52'E
Al Wahat ad Dakhilah	EG	290	25°30'N	29°05'E
Al Wahat al Bahriyah	EG	290	28°15'N	28°55'E
Al Wahat al Kharijah	EG	290	25°15'N	30°35'E
Al Wajh	SA	528	26°14'N	36°28'E
Al Wakrah	QA	527	25°10'N	51°35'E
Alwar	IN	496	27°34'N	76°35'E
Al Wāsiţah	EG	290	29°20'N	31°12'E
Al Wazz	SU	324	15°01'N	30°10'E
Al Widyan	SA	528	31°30'N	42°00'E
Alxa Youqi	CH	490	39°12'N	101°39'E
Alxa Zuoqi	CH	490	38°49'N	105°31'E
Al Yamāmah	SA	528	24°11'N	47°21'E
Alyangula	AS	656	13°50'S	136°25'E
Al Yasat I.	TC	538	24°12'N	52°00'E
Alyat	AJ	483	39°57'N	49°23'E
Alybeyli Pervyye	AJ	483	39°10'N	46°48'E
Alytus	LH	597	54°24'N	24°03'E
Alzamay		468	55°33'N	98°39'E
Alzette	LU	598	49°52'N	6°07'E
Alzira	SP	618	39°09'N	0°26'W
Ama	PP	664	4°06'S	141°40'E
Amachonga, Cerros de	PE	436	6°15'S	78°45'W
Amada Gaza	CT	282	4°44'N	15°13'E
Amadeus, Lake	AS	656	24°50'S	130°45'E
Āmādi	BG	485	22°28'N	89°19'E
Amadi	SU	324	5°31'N	30°20'E
Amadjuak	CA	390	63°56'N	72°35'W
Amadjuak Lake	CA	390	64°55'N	71°00'W
Amadora	PO	608	38°45'N	9°14'W
Amager	DA	576	55°35'N	12°33'E
Amaguaña	EC	432	0°22'S	78°27'W
Amahai		478	3°20'S	128°58'E
Amajac	MX	394	21°15'N	98°46'W
Amakusa-nada	JA	506	32°35'N	130°05'E
Amakusa-shima	JA	506	32°20'N	130°05'E
Åmål	SW	621	59°03'N	12°42'E
Amala	KE	299	1°02'S	35°14'E
Amalia	SF	322	27°15'S	25°03'E
Amaliás	GR	588	37°49'N	21°23'E
Amalner	IN	496	21°03'N	75°04'E
Amaluza	EC	432	4°36'S	79°25'W
Amamapare	ID	500	4°52'S	136°50'E
Amambaí	BR	424	23°05'S	55°13'W
Amambay, Cordillera de	PA	435	23°00'S	56°00'W
Amami-shoto	JA	506	28°16'N	129°21'E
Amamula	CG	287	0°18'S	27°50'E
Amanab	PP	664	3°35'S	141°13'E
Amanavén	CO	430	4°04'N	67°44'W
Amanbayevo	KG	514	42°36'N	71°12'E
Amankaragay	KZ	510	52°25'N	64°04'E
Amankol	CH	490	40°49'N	81°54'E
Amanotkel'	KZ	510	46°06'N	61°32'E
Amanu		654	17°47'S	140°28'W
Amapá	BR	424	2°03'N	50°48'W
Amapala	HO	412	13°17'N	87°39'W
Amarante		384	6°14'S	42°49'W
Amarante	PO	608	41°46'N	8°05'W
Amarante do Marahão		384	5°36'S	46°45'W
Amaranth		372	50°36'N	98°44'W
Amarapura	BM	487	21°54'N	96°03'E
Amardalay	MG	520	46°08'N	106°23'E
Amareleja	PO	608	38°12'N	7°14'W
Amargosa Desert		376	36°36'N	116°33'W
Amargosa Ra.		376	36°30'N	116°42'W
Amarillas	CU	406	22°29'N	80°55'W
Amarillo	US	398	35°13'N	101°49'W
Amárinthos	GR	588	38°24'N	23°54'E
Amasra	TU	535	41°43'N	32°22'E
Amasya	TU	535	40°39'N	35°51'E
Amata	AS	656	26°10'S	131°10'E
Amatitlán	GT	411	14°29'N	90°37'W
Amay	BE	570	50°33'N	5°19'E
Amazar	RS	612	53°52'N	120°53'E
Amazonas	BR	424	0°10'S	49°00'W
Amazon Basin	BR	424	6°00'S	62°00'W
Amba Farit	ET	293	10°53'N	39°00'E
Āmba Gīyorgīs	ET	293	12°46'N	37°37'E
Ambahikily	MA	304	21°36'S	43°41'E
Ambāla	IN	496	30°22'N	76°48'E
Ambalajanakomby	MA	304	16°42'S	47°05'E
Ambalamanakana	MA	304	20°44'S	47°12'E
Ambalangoda	CE	530	6°16'N	80°05'E
Ambalantota	CE	530	6°07'N	81°01'E
Ambalarondra	MA	304	18°28'S	48°59'E
Ambāla Sadar		476	30°20'N	76°50'E
Ambalavao	MA	304	21°50'S	46°56'E
Ambam	CM	280	2°23'N	11°17'E
Āmba Maryam	ET	293	11°26'N	39°17'E
Ambanja	MA	304	13°41'S	48°27'E
Ambarchik	RS	612	69°39'N	162°20'E
Ambarnyy		556	65°54'N	33°43'E
Ambaro, Baie d'		268	13°23'S	48°38'E
Ambato	EC	432	1°15'S	78°37'W
Ambato Boeny	MA	304	16°28'S	46°43'E
Ambatofinandrahana	MA	304	20°33'S	46°48'E
Ambatolahy	MA	304	20°00'S	45°32'E
Ambatolampy	MA	304	19°23'S	47°25'E
Ambatomainty	MA	304	17°41'S	45°40'E
Ambatomanoina	MA	304	18°18'S	47°37'E
Ambatondrazaka	MA	304	17°50'S	48°25'E
Ambelikou	CY	494	35°07'N	32°48'E
Ámbelos, Ákra	GR	588	39°56'N	23°55'E
Amberg	GM	584	49°27'N	11°50'E
Ambergris Cay	BH	404	18°05'N	87°49'W
Amberley	NZ	663	43°09'S	172°45'E
Ambidédi	ML	307	14°35'N	11°47'W
Ambikāpur	IN	496	23°05'N	83°08'E
Ambilobe	MA	304	13°12'S	49°04'E
Ambinanindrano	MA	304	20°11'S	48°29'E
Ambinaninony	MA	304	18°35'S	49°07'E
Ambinanitelo	MA	304	15°21'S	49°35'E
Ambitle I.	PP	664	4°05'S	153°50'E
Ambla	EN	577	59°11'N	25°51'E
Amble	UK	626	55°20'N	1°35'W
Amblève	BE	570	50°28'N	5°36'E
Ambo	PE	436	10°07'S	76°10'W
Amboasary	MA	304	25°02'S	46°23'E
Amboavory	MA	304	17°18'S	48°30'E
Ambodifototra	MA	304	16°59'S	49°52'E
Ambodiharina	MA	304	20°01'S	48°46'E
Ambodiriana	MA	304	17°56'S	49°17'E
Ambohidratrimo	MA	304	18°50'S	47°26'E
Ambohijanahary	MA	304	17°24'S	48°22'E
Ambohimahasoa	MA	304	21°45'S	47°07'E
Ambohimahavelona	MA	304	23°27'S	43°53'E
Ambohimandroso	MA	304	19°31'S	47°25'E
Ambohimilanja	MA	304	19°56'S	47°59'E
Ambohinihaonana	MA	304	21°11'S	47°56'E
Ambohitralanana	MA	304	15°14'S	50°27'E
Ambohitsilaozana	MA	304	17°42'S	48°27'E
Amboin	PP	664	4°38'S	143°29'E
Amboise		562	47°25'N	0°59'E
Ambon	ID	500	3°43'S	128°12'E
Ambondro	MA	304	25°13'S	45°44'E
Amborompotsy	MA	304	20°38'S	46°16'E
Amboseli, Lake	KE	299	2°37'S	37°08'E
Ambositra	MA	304	20°31'S	47°15'E
Ambovombe	MA	304	25°11'S	46°05'E
Ambre, Ile d'	MP	309	20°02'S	57°42'E
Ambriz	AO	274	7°50'S	13°20'E
Ambrolauri	GG	495	42°31'N	43°09'E
Ambry		650	16°15'S	168°30'E
Ambrym	NH	669	16°10'S	168°10'E
Ambunti	PP	664	4°12'S	142°50'E
Amchitka	US	398	51°24'N	178°00'E
Amchitka Pass	US	398	51°35'N	180°00'
'Amd	YM	541	15°18'N	47°58'E
Am Dam	CD	283	12°46'N	20°29'E
Amdasa	ID	500	7°47'S	131°29'E
Amderma	RS	612	69°45'N	61°39'E
Am Djéména	CD	283	13°07'N	17°18'E
Amdo	CH	490	32°09'N	91°39'E
Ameca	MX	394	20°33'N	104°02'W
Amégnran	TO	328	6°28'N	1°34'E
Ameland	NL	602	53°28'N	5°43'E
Amelia		378	30°35'N	81°25'W
Amengcuingani	GB	294	0°49'S	9°51'E
Amer	NL	602	51°43'N	4°40'E
American Falls		372	42°47'N	112°51'W
American Falls Res.		372	42°47'N	112°52'W
Americus		378	32°04'N	84°13'W
Amersfoort	NL	602	52°09'N	5°23'E
Amersfoort	SF	322	27°01'S	29°51'E
Amery		374	45°18'N	92°21'W
Amery	CA	390	56°34'N	94°03'W
Ames	US	398	42°01'N	93°36'W
Amet	IN	496	25°18'N	73°56'E
Āmeya	ET	293	7°05'N	36°40'E
Amfíklia	GR	588	38°38'N	22°35'E
Amfilokhía	GR	588	38°51'N	21°10'E
Ámfissa	GR	588	38°31'N	22°24'E
Amga	RS	612	60°55'N	132°00'E
Amga	RS	612	62°38'N	134°32'E
Amgalang	CH	490	48°15'N	118°12'E
Amguid	AG	272	26°26'N	5°22'E
Amgun	RS	612	52°56'N	139°38'E
Amherst		370	47°15'N	62°26'W
Amherst		374	42°22'N	72°31'W
Amherst	BM	487	16°04'N	97°34'E
Amherst	CA	390	45°50'N	64°12'W
Amherst	US	398	42°58'N	78°47'W
Am dakan	UG	330	1°57'N	33°21'E
Amiens	FR	580	49°54'N	2°18'E
Amik Gölü	TU	535	36°22'N	36°17'E
Amilhayt, Ramlat	MU	523	18°40'N	53°50'E
Amindaion	GR	588	40°41'N	21°40'E
Aminius	WA	313	23°43'S	19°21'E
'Āmir, Ra's	LY	302	32°56'N	21°42'E
Amirante Islands	SE	319	6°00'S	53°10'E
Amistad, Presa de la	MX	394	29°26'N	101°04'W
Amlekhganj	NP	522	27°17'N	84°59'E
Åmli	NO	604	58°47'N	8°30'E
Amlia	US	398	51°55'N	173°50'W
Amlwch	UK	626	53°24'N	4°20'W
'Ammān (Amman)	JO	510	31°57'N	35°56'E
Ämmänsaari	FI	578	64°52'N	28°51'E
Ammarnäs	SW	621	65°57'N	16°07'E
Ammassalik		370	65°36'N	37°38'W
Ammersee	GM	584	48°00'N	11°07'E
Ammon		372	43°27'N	111°57'W
Amnat Charoen	TH	534	15°41'N	104°39'E
Amnok-kang (Yalu)	KN	512	39°55'N	124°22'E
Āmol	IR	502	36°28'N	52°21'E
Amorgós		564	36°50'N	25°59'E
Amorgós	GR	588	36°49'N	25°57'E
Amory		378	33°59'N	88°29'W
Amos	CA	390	48°34'N	78°07'W
Åmot	NO	604	59°33'N	7°58'E
Amotfors	SW	621	59°46'N	12°22'E
Amourj	MR	308	16°01'N	7°09'W
Amozoc	MX	394	19°02'N	98°03'W
Ampah	ID	500	1°47'S	115°08'E
Ampala, Punta	ES	409	13°09'N	87°54'W
Ampana	ID	500	0°53'S	121°32'E
Ampanavoana	MA	304	15°41'S	50°22'E
Ampanefena	MA	304	13°52'S	49°58'E
Ampang	MY	518	3°09'N	101°46'E
Ampanihy	MA	304	24°42'S	44°45'E
Amparafaravola	MA	304	17°35'S	48°13'E
Amparai	CE	530	7°17'N	81°40'E
Ampasimanjeva	MA	304	21°44'S	43°02'E
Ampasimanolotra	MA	304	18°49'S	49°04'E
Ampasinambo	MA	304	20°31'S	48°00'E
Ampato, Nevado	PE	436	15°49'S	71°53'W
Ampatuan	RP	526	6°52'N	124°28'E
Ampefy	MA	304	19°03'S	46°44'E
Amper	GM	584	48°30'N	11°57'E
Amper	NI	316	9°21'N	9°42'E
Ampisikinana	MA	304	12°57'S	49°49'E
Ampitatafika	MA	304	19°34'S	47°21'E
Ampombiantambo	MA	304	12°42'S	48°57'E
Amposta	SP	618	40°43'N	0°35'E
Amcui		374	48°20'N	67°26'W
'Amrān	YM	541	15°40'N	43°54'E
Amravati	IN	496	20°56'N	77°45'E
Amreli	IN	496	21°37'N	71°14'E
Amritsar	IN	496	31°35'N	74°53'E
Amroha		476	28°55'N	78°28'E
Amrum	GM	584	54°39'N	8°21'E
Åmsele	SW	621	64°30'N	19°17'E
Amstelveen	NL	602	52°18'N	4°52'E
Amsterdam		374	42°56'N	74°11'W
Amsterdam	NL	602	52°22'N	4°56'E
Amsterdam	SF	322	26°37'S	30°40'E
Amsterdam Rijnkanaal	NL	602	51°57'N	5°20'E
Amstetten	AU	568	48°07'N	14°52'E
Āmtali	BG	485	22°18'N	90°12'E
Am Timan	CD	283	11°02'N	20°17'E
Amtkel	GG	495	43°03'N	41°20'E
Amuay		382	11°47'N	70°15'W
Amu-Dar'ya	TX	537	37°55'N	65°14'W
Amudarya	AF	480	43°35'N	59°15'E
Amudarya	TX	537	40°00'N	62°30'E
Amudat	UG	330	1°57'N	34°57'E
Amuku Mountains	GY	434	1°49'N	58°23'W
Amund Ringnes I.	CA	390	78°20'N	96°25'W
Amundsen Gulf	CA	390	71°00'N	124°00'W
Amungen	SW	621	61°07'N	15°43'E
Amur	RS	612	51°00'N	139°00'E
'Amur, Wadi	SU	324	18°56'N	33°34'E
Amursk	RS	612	50°14'N	136°54'E
Amvrakikos Kólpos	GR	588	39°00'N	21°00'E
Amvrosiyevka	UP	624	47°47'N	38°30'E
Amyūn	LE	516	34°17'N	35°48'E
Amzabegovo	MK	599	41°49'N	22°00'E
Am Zoer	CD	283	14°13'N	21°23'E
Anaa		654	17°42'S	146°38'W
Anabar	NR	662	0°30'S	166°57'E
Anabar	RS	612	73°08'N	113°36'E
'Anabtā	IS	505	32°19'N	35°07'E
Anachucuna, Cerro	PM	417	8°36'N	77°35'W
Anaco	VE	440	9°27'N	64°28'W
Anaconda	US	398	46°07'N	112°56'W
Anadarko		376	35°04'N	98°14'W
Anadia	PO	608	40°26'N	8°26'W
Anadolu	TU	535	39°00'N	35°00'E
Anadyr	RS	612	64°54'N	176°13'E
Anadyr'	RS	612	64°44'N	177°27'E
Anadyrskaya Nizmennost		468	65°10'N	177°00'E
Anadyrskiy Khrebet		468	67°30'N	175°00'E
Anadyrskiy Zaliv	RS	612	64°00'N	178°00'W
Anadyrskoye Ploskogorye		468	67°00'N	172°00'E
Anáfi	GR	588	36°22'N	25°47'E
'Ānah	IZ	504	34°28'N	41°56'E
Anaheim	US	398	33°50'N	117°55'W
Anahidrano	MA	304	15°02'S	47°54'E
Anahola	US	398	22°08'N	159°18'W
Anahuac	MX	394	28°29'N	106°45'W
Anáhuac	MX	394	27°14'N	100°09'W
Anak	KN	512	38°30'N	125°30'E
Anakāpalle	IN	496	17°41'N	83°01'E
Analalava	MA	304	14°38'S	47°45'E
Analamaitso, Plateau d'	MA	304	16°15'S	48°15'E
Analvory	MA	304	18°58'S	46°43'E
Anamã		384	3°33'S	61°26'W
Ana María, Golfo de	CU	406	21°25'N	78°49'W
Anambas, Kep.	ID	500	3°00'N	106°00'E
Anambi	SG	319	12°50'N	16°00'W
Aname		654	20°05'S	169°55'E
Anamur	TU	535	36°06'N	32°50'E
Anan	JA	506	33°55'N	134°39'E
Ananás		384	6°22'S	48°06'W
Anand	IN	496	22°34'N	72°56'E
Anandgarh	IN	496	28°47'N	72°58'E
Anandpur		476	21°14'N	86°07'E
Ananea	PE	436	14°42'S	69°33'W
Ananindeua		384	1°22'S	48°23'W
Anantapur	IN	496	14°41'N	77°36'E
Anantnag	IN	496	33°44'N	75°09'E
Ananuri	GG	495	42°10'N	44°42'E
Anan'yev	UP	624	47°43'N	29°58'E
Anan'yevo	KG	514	42°45'N	77°40'E
Anapa		564	44°53'N	37°18'E
Anápolis	BR	424	16°20'S	48°58'W
Anapskaya		564	44°54'N	37°23'E
Anār	IR	502	30°53'N	55°18'E
Anārak	IR	502	33°19'N	53°43'E
Anarbar	IR	502	34°30'N	51°00'E
Anār Darreh	AF	480	32°46'N	61°39'E
Anarjokka	NO	604	69°00'N	25°00'E
Anascaul		558	52°09'N	10°03'W
Añasco	US	398	18°17'N	67°08'W
Anastasia		378	29°51'N	81°15'W
Anatolí	GR	588	39°38'N	20°52'E
Anatom (Kéamo)	NH	669	20°05'S	169°50'E
Añatuya	AR	419	28°28'S	62°50'W
Anbyŏn	KN	512	39°02'N	127°32'E
Anchau	NI	316	10°58'N	8°24'E
Anchorage	US	398	61°12'N	149°50'W
Anchorena	AR	419	35°41'S	65°27'W
Anchorstock Point		266	37°05'S	12°13'W
Anchovy	JM	414	18°24'N	77°56'W
Anclote Keys		378	28°11'N	82°55'W
Ancohuma, Nevado	BL	422	15°51'S	68°36'W
Ancón	PE	436	11°47'S	77°11'W
Ancona	IT	593	43°36'N	13°30'E
Ancón de Sardinas, Bahía de	EC	432	1°40'N	79°00'W
Ancud	CI	428	41°52'S	73°50'W
Ancud, Golfo de	CI	428	42°05'S	73°01'W
Anda	CH	490	46°23'N	125°18'E
Andacollo	AR	419	37°11'S	70°41'W
Andado	AS	656	25°24'S	135°27'E
Andagua	PE	436	15°30'S	72°21'W
Andahuaylas	PE	436	13°39'S	73°23'W
Andaingo Gara	MA	304	18°12'S	48°17'E
Andalgalá	AR	419	27°36'S	66°19'W
Åndalsnes	NO	604	62°34'N	7°42'E
Andalusia		378	31°18'N	86°28'W
'Andam, Wadi	MU	523	21°05'N	58°22'E
Andaman Islands		476	12°30'N	92°45'E
Andaman Sea	BM	487	10°00'N	95°00'E
Andamarca	BL	422	18°49'S	67°31'W
Andamarca	PE	436	11°46'S	74°44'W

Arismendi	VE	440	8°29'N	68°22'W
Arissa	ET	293	11°11'N	41°38'E
Aristizábal, Cabo	AR	419	45°12'S	66°32'W
Arıtaş		564	38°21'N	36°50'E
Arivechi	MX	394	28°56'N	109°11'W
Arivonimamo	MA	304	19°01'S	47°11'E
Arixang	CH	490	44°58'N	81°03'E
Ariza	SP	618	41°19'N	2°03'W
Arizaro, Salar de	AR	419	24°42'S	67°45'W
Arizgoiti	SP	618	43°13'N	2°53'W
Arizona		376	34°30'N	111°30'W
Arizona	AR	419	35°43'S	65°18'W
Arizona City		376	32°45'N	111°40'W
Arizpe	MX	394	30°20'N	110°10'W
Årjäng	SW	621	59°23'N	12°08'E
Arjasa	ID	500	6°51'S	115°16'E
Arjeplog	SW	621	66°03'N	17°54'E
Arkadak		560	51°58'N	43°30'E
Arkadelphia	US	398	34°07'N	93°03'W
Arkalokhórion	GR	588	35°09'N	25°16'E
Arkansas		374	34°45'N	92°30'W
Arkansas	US	398	33°47'N	91°04'W
Arkansas City		376	37°03'N	97°02'W
Arkanu, Jabal	LY	302	22°15'N	24°45'E
Arkhángelos	GR	588	36°12'N	28°08'E
Arkhangel'sk	RS	612	64°34'N	40°32'E
Arkhangel'skaya		564	45°40'N	40°16'E
Arkhangel'skoye		560	51°27'N	40°56'E
Arkhangel'skoye		560	55°13'N	44°07'E
Arkhara		472	49°25'N	130°07'E
Arkhipelag Nordenshelda	RS	612	76°45'N	96°00'E
Arkhipo-Osipovka		564	44°22'N	38°32'E
Arklow	EI	592	52°48'N	6°09'W
Arkonam	IN	496	13°06'N	79°40'E
Arlanza	SP	618	42°06'N	4°09'W
Arlanzón	SP	618	42°03'N	4°17'W
Arlbayev	KZ	510	49°24'N	46°50'E
Arles	FR	580	43°40'N	4°37'E
Arles-sur-Tech	FR	580	42°27'N	2°38'E
Arlington	US	398	38°53'N	77°05'W
Arlington	US	398	32°44'N	97°06'W
Arló	HU	590	48°11'N	20°16'E
Arlon	BE	570	49°41'N	5°49'E
Arltunga	AS	656	23°26'S	134°41'E
Armagh	UK	626	54°21'N	6°40'W
Armah, Wadi	YM	541	18°12'N	51°02'E
Arman'	RS	612	59°42'N	150°10'E
Armant	EG	290	25°37'N	32°32'E
Armavir	AM	482	40°09'N	44°02'E
Armavir	RS	612	45°00'N	41°08'E
Armenia		38	40°00'N	45°00'E
Armenia	CO	430	4°31'N	75°41'W
Armenia	ES	409	13°45'N	89°30'W
Armería	MX	394	18°56'N	103°57'W
Armidabán	PA	435	23°00'S	56°40'W
Armidale	AS	656	30°31'S	151°39'E
Armopa	ID	500	2°17'S	139°36'E
Armori		470	20°28'N	79°59'E
Armoricain, Massif	FR	580	48°00'N	3°00'W
Armstrong		370	50°18'N	89°02'W
Armstrong		372	50°27'N	119°12'W
Armstrong	CA	390	63°03'N	133°24'W
Armyansk	UP	624	46°06'N	33°42'E
Arnaía	GR	588	40°29'N	23°35'E
Arnarfjordur	IC	591	65°45'N	23°40'W
Arnaud	CA	390	59°50'N	69°46'W
Arnauti, C.	CY	494	35°03'N	32°16'E
Arnay-le-Duc	FR	580	47°08'N	4°29'E
Arnedo	SP	618	42°13'N	2°06'W
Årnes	NO	604	60°09'N	11°28'E
Arnhem	NL	602	12°18'S	135°59'E
Arnhem, C.	AS	656	12°20'S	136°58'E
Arnhem Land	AS	656	13°10'S	134°30'E
Arno	IT	593	31°39'N	103°38'W
Arno	RM	661	7°00'N	171°30'E
Arnold		370	46°52'N	92°05'W
Arnprior		374	45°26'N	76°21'W
Arnsberg	GM	584	51°23'N	8°05'E
Arnstadt	GM	584	50°50'N	10°57'E
Aroa	VE	440	10°26'N	68°54'W
Aroab	WA	313	26°48'S	19°39'E
Aroland	CA	390	50°14'N	86°59'W
Aroma	SU	324	15°49'N	36°08'E
Aro Mafoungui	CT	282	6°11'N	21°16'E
Arorae	KR	660	2°30'S	176°30'E
Aroroy	RP	526	12°30'N	123°23'E
Arosa	SZ	622	46°47'N	9°40'E
Årøsund	DA	576	55°15'N	9°43'E
Arousa, Ría de	SP	618	42°28'N	8°57'W
Arpaçay	TU	535	40°52'N	43°19'E
Arqalyq	KZ	510	50°13'N	66°55'E
Ar Rabaḑ	SA	528	23°11'N	39°32'E
Arraga		388	28°04'S	64°14'W
Arrah	IN	496	25°34'N	84°40'E
Arraha	ET	293	9°42'N	40°24'E
Ar Rahad	SU	324	12°43'N	30°39'E
Ar Raḩḩālīyah	IZ	504	32°44'N	43°23'E
Arraias		384	12°56'S	46°57'W
Arraiján	PM	417	8°57'N	79°39'W
Ar Ramādī	IZ	504	33°25'N	43°17'E
Ar Ramthā	JO	510	32°34'N	36°00'E
Arran		558	55°28'N	5°20'W
Arranca Barba, Cerro	NU	415	11°57'N	84°49'W
Ar Rank	SU	324	11°45'N	32°48'E
Ar Raqqah	SY	531	35°57'N	39°01'E
Arras	FR	580	50°17'N	2°47'E
Arrasate (Mondragón)		562	43°04'N	2°29'W
Ar Rass	SA	528	25°52'N	43°31'E
Ar Rastan	SY	531	34°55'N	36°44'E
Ar Rawḑah	SA	528	26°05'N	40°37'E
Ar Rawḑah	YM	541	14°27'N	47°15'E
Ar Rāwuk	YM	541	15°40'N	48°52'E
Ar Rayyān	QA	527	25°18'N	51°27'E
Arrecifal	CO	430	3°38'N	69°02'W
Arrecife	SP	618	28°58'N	13°32'W
Arrecifes	AR	419	34°03'S	60°07'W
Arrée, Monts d'	FR	580	47°41'N	4°14'W
Arriaga	MX	394	16°14'N	93°54'W
Ar Rifā'	BA	484	26°07'N	50°33'E
Ar Rifa al Gharbi	BA	484	26°08'N	50°31'E
Ar Rifa ash Sharqi	BA	484	26°07'N	50°34'E
Ar Rifā'ī	IZ	504	31°43'N	46°07'E
Ar Rimal	SA	528	21°15'N	53°30'E
Arriola	US	398	37°26'N	108°38'W
Ar Riyāḑ (Riyadh)	SA	528	24°38'N	46°43'E
Ar Riyān	YM	541	14°39'N	49°19'E
Arrochar	UK	626	56°12'N	4°44'W
Arroio Grande	BR	424	32°14'S	53°05'W
Arronches	PO	608	39°07'N	7°17'W
Arrowtown	NZ	663	44°56'S	168°50'E
Arroyo	US	398	17°58'N	66°04'W
Arroyo Blanco	CU	406	22°02'N	79°05'W
Arroyo de la Luz	SP	618	39°29'N	6°35'W
Arroyo de la Ventana	AR	419	41°40'S	66°06'W
Arroyo Grande		376	35°07'N	120°34'W
Arroyo Grande	BL	422	11°27'S	68°41'W
Arroyo Pescado	AR	419	43°00'S	70°46'W
Ar-Rub' Al-Khali	SA	528	21°00'N	51°00'E
Arrufó	AR	419	30°15'S	61°45'W
Ar Rumaylah	IZ	504	30°35'N	47°17'E
Ar Rumaythah	IZ	504	31°32'N	45°12'E
Ar Ruşayfah	JO	510	32°01'N	36°03'E
Ar Ruşayriş	SU	324	11°49'N	34°25'E
Ar Rustaq	MU	523	23°24'N	57°26'E
Ar Ruţbah	IZ	504	33°02'N	40°17'E
Ar Ruways	QA	527	26°08'N	51°13'E
Ar Ruwayshid	JO	510	32°30'N	38°12'E
Års	DA	576	56°48'N	9°32'E
Arsanjān	IR	502	29°53'N	53°19'E
Arsen'yev	RS	612	44°10'N	133°15'E
Arsk		560	56°06'N	49°54'E
Arsuk		370	61°10'N	48°27'W
Art		654	19°42'S	163°38'E
`Arta	DJ	289	11°31'N	42°50'E
Árta	GR	588	39°09'N	20°59'E
Artashat	AM	482	39°57'N	44°33'E
Arteaga	MX	394	18°20'N	102°16'W
Artem	RS	612	43°22'N	132°13'E
Artemisa	CU	406	22°49'N	82°46'W
Artëm-Ostrov	AJ	483	40°28'N	50°20'E
Artemovskiy		468	58°12'N	114°38'E
Artëmovskiy		474	43°23'N	132°19'E
Artesa de Segre	SP	618	41°54'N	1°03'E
Artesia	US	398	32°50'N	104°24'W
Arthabaska		374	46°00'N	71°56'W
Arthur Pt.	AS	656	22°08'S	150°02'E
Artibonite	HA	412	19°15'N	72°47'W
Artibonito	DR	408	19°15'N	72°47'W
Artigas	UY	439	30°24'S	56°28'W
Artik	AM	482	40°37'N	43°59'E
Artillery L.		368	63°08'N	107°45'W
Artix	FR	580	43°24'N	0°33'W
Artois, Collines de l'	FR	580	50°39'N	3°04'E
Artsyz	UP	624	45°59'N	29°25'E
Artux	CH	490	39°39'N	76°09'E
Artvin	TU	535	41°11'N	41°49'E
Artyk		468	64°12'N	145°06'E
Aru		648	6°25'S	135°08'E
Aru	CG	287	2°52'N	30°51'E
Aru, Kep.	ID	500	6°00'S	134°30'E
Arua	UG	330	3°01'N	30°55'E
A Rúa de Valdeorras	SP	618	42°24'N	7°06'W
Aruanã		384	14°54'S	51°05'W
Aruba		380	12°13'N	71°44'W
Arucas	SP	618	28°07'N	15°31'W
Arué		654	17°35'S	145°42'W
Aruliho	BP	666	9°20'S	159°47'E
Arun	NP	522	27°00'N	87°10'E
Arun Qi	CH	490	48°06'N	123°28'E
Aruppukkottai	IN	496	9°31'N	78°06'E
Arusha	TZ	327	3°22'S	36°41'E
Arusha Chine	TZ	327	3°35'S	37°20'E
Arutua		654	15°05'S	146°46'W
Aruvi Aru	CE	530	8°48'N	79°55'E
Arvada		372	39°47'N	105°05'W
Arvayheer	MG	520	46°15'N	102°48'E
Arvidsjaur	SW	621	65°35'N	19°10'E
Arvika	SW	621	59°39'N	12°36'E
Årviksand	NO	604	70°11'N	20°32'E
Arvin		376	35°12'N	118°49'W
Arxan	CH	490	47°10'N	119°57'E
Arys'	KZ	510	42°26'N	68°48'E
Arzachena	IT	593	41°04'N	9°23'E
Arzamas	RS	612	55°23'N	43°50'E
Arzew		562	35°50'N	0°19'W
Arzew, G. d'	AG	272	36°00'N	0°10'W
Arzgir		560	45°22'N	44°15'E
Arzni	AM	482	40°19'N	44°36'E
Aš	EZ	575	50°13'N	12°11'E
Ås	NO	604	59°40'N	10°48'E
Asab	WA	313	25°29'S	17°58'E
Asad, Buhayrat al	SY	531	36°00'N	38°10'E
Asadābād	AF	480	34°52'N	71°09'E
Asahan	ID	500	3°02'N	99°52'E
Asahi-dake	JA	506	44°00'N	144°00'E
Asahikawa	JA	506	43°46'N	142°22'E
Āsalē	ET	293	14°14'N	40°18'E
`Asalūyeh	IR	502	27°28'N	52°37'E
Asam	YM	541	16°08'N	49°21'E
Asamankese	GH	296	5°52'N	0°40'W
Asankrangwa	GH	296	5°48'N	2°26'W
Asansol	IN	496	23°41'N	86°59'E
Asan-wan	KS	513	37°00'N	126°45'E
Asar	CH	490	47°55'N	117°37'E
Åsarna	SW	621	62°39'N	14°21'E
Asau	WS	668	13°31'S	172°38'W
Asau Harbour	WS	668	13°10'S	172°35'W
Asawanwah	LY	302	22°15'N	18°55'E
Āsayita	ET	293	11°34'N	41°26'E
Asbesberge	SF	322	28°55'S	23°15'E
Asbest	RS	612	57°00'N	61°30'E
Asbestos		374	45°45'N	71°56'W
Ascención	BL	422	15°42'S	63°05'W
Ascension	UK	40	7°57'S	14°21'W
Ascensión	MX	394	31°06'N	107°59'W
Ascensión, Bahía de la	MX	394	19°40'N	87°30'W
Ascension Islands		266	7°50'S	14°20'W
Aschaffenburg	GM	584	49°59'N	9°09'E
Aschersleben	GM	584	51°45'N	11°28'E
Ascoli Piceno	IT	593	42°51'N	13°34'E
Ascope	PE	436	7°43'S	79°07'W
Ascot		374	45°23'N	71°44'W
Ascotán	CI	428	21°44'S	68°18'W
Ascotán, Salar de	CI	428	21°31'S	68°19'W
Āseb	ER	292	13°00'N	42°44'E
Åseda	SW	621	57°10'N	15°20'E
Asedjrad	AG	272	24°42'N	1°40'E
Aseki	PP	664	7°21'S	146°11'E
Āsela	ET	293	7°57'N	39°08'E
As Ela	DJ	289	11°01'N	42°04'E
Åsele	SW	621	64°09'N	17°23'E
Āsendabo	ET	293	7°46'N	37°14'E
Asenovgrad	BU	573	42°01'N	24°52'E
Åseral	NO	604	58°37'N	7°25'E
Aserrí	CS	405	9°50'N	84°04'W
Asha	NI	316	7°07'N	3°43'E
Ashagy Mollu	AJ	483	39°18'N	46°42'E
Ashanti Uplands	GH	296	6°45'N	1°30'W
Ashburn		378	31°42'N	83°39'W
Ashburton	AS	656	21°40'S	114°56'E
Ashburton	NZ	663	43°54'S	171°45'E
Ashburton Downs	AS	656	23°24'S	117°04'E
Ashcroft		372	50°43'N	121°17'W
Ashdod	IS	505	31°49'N	34°39'E
Ashdot Ya'aqov	IS	505	32°39'N	35°35'E
Ashdown		378	33°40'N	94°07'W
Asheboro		378	35°42'N	79°48'W
Asherton		376	28°26'N	99°45'W
Asheville	US	398	35°36'N	82°33'W
Ashford	UK	626	51°08'N	0°53'E
Ashgabat	TX	537	37°57'N	58°23'E
Ashgrove		652	23°30'S	145°00'E
Ashhurst	NZ	663	40°17'S	175°45'E
Ashibetsu	JA	506	43°31'N	142°10'E
Ashikaga		474	36°20'N	139°27'E
Ashington	UK	626	55°11'N	1°34'W
Ashish al Jahra'	KU	514	29°20'N	47°40'E
Ashizuri-misaki	JA	506	32°44'N	133°01'E
Ashkīdah	LY	302	27°33'N	14°27'E
Ashland		370	46°35'N	90°53'W
Ashland		374	38°46'N	92°15'W
Ashland		374	40°52'N	82°19'W
Ashland		376	37°11'N	99°45'W
Ashland		378	33°16'N	85°50'W
Ashland	US	398	38°28'N	82°38'W
Ashley		652	29°19'S	149°49'E
Ashley	US	398	46°01'N	99°22'W
Ashmore and Cartier Islands	AS	656	12°25'S	123°20'E
Ashmūn	EG	290	30°18'N	30°58'E
Ashoknagar		470	24°35'N	77°43'E
Ashoro	JA	506	43°16'N	143°37'E
Ashqelon	IS	505	31°40'N	34°35'E
Ash Sāda	KU	514	29°15'N	47°15'E
Ash Shabakah	IZ	504	30°49'N	40°39'E
Ash Shahaniyah	QA	527	25°23'N	51°13'E
Ash Shāmīyah	IZ	504	31°57'N	44°36'E
Ash Shamiyah (Al Badiyah al Janubiyah)	IZ	504	31°00'N	46°50'E
Ash Sharaf	YM	541	14°05'N	44°11'E
Ash Shāriqah	TC	538	25°22'N	55°23'E
Ash Sharmah	SA	528	28°01'N	35°16'E
Ash Sharqāt	IZ	504	35°27'N	43°16'E
Ash Shaţrah	IZ	504	31°25'N	46°10'E
Ash Shawal	SU	324	13°34'N	32°39'E
Ash Shawbak	JO	510	30°32'N	35°34'E
Ash Shaykh Sa`īd	YM	541	12°40'N	43°27'E
Ash Shihiyat	IZ	504	31°00'N	44°30'E
Ash Shiḩr	YM	541	14°45'N	49°36'E
Ash Shināfīyah	IZ	504	31°35'N	44°39'E
Ash Shuaybah	KU	514	29°02'N	48°08'E
Ash Shufayyah	SA	528	23°50'N	39°09'E
Ash Shumlūl	SA	528	26°31'N	47°20'E
Ash Shuqayq	KU	514	28°42'N	47°44'E
Ash Shuqayq	SA	528	17°44'N	42°01'E
Ash Shurayf	SA	528	25°43'N	39°14'E
Ashtabula	US	398	41°51'N	80°47'W
Ashtarak	AM	482	40°18'N	44°22'E
Ashti		470	18°49'N	75°11'E
Ashton		382	12°36'N	61°27'W
Ashton	SF	322	33°50'S	20°04'E
Ashton	US	398	44°04'N	111°26'W
Ashton	VC	418	12°35'N	61°26'W
Ashton Ra.	AS	656	15°15'S	127°30'E
Ashwaubenon		374	44°27'N	88°03'W
Asidonhoppo	NS	438	4°00'N	55°29'W
Asikkala	FI	578	61°10'N	25°29'E
Asilah	MO	310	35°28'N	6°02'W
Asinara, Golfo dell'	IT	593	40°56'N	8°27'E
Asinara, I.	IT	593	41°04'N	8°16'E
Asino	RS	612	57°00'N	86°09'E
Asir	SA	528	19°00'N	42°00'E
Asis, Ra's	SU	324	18°26'N	38°05'E
Aşkale	TU	535	39°55'N	40°42'E
Askaniya-Nova	UP	624	46°27'N	33°52'E
Asker	NO	604	59°50'N	10°26'E
Askham	SF	322	26°59'S	20°47'E
Askim	NO	604	59°35'N	11°10'E
Askim	SW	621	57°38'N	11°56'E
Áskion	GR	588	40°24'N	21°32'E
Askiz	RS	612	53°10'N	90°18'E
Askja	IC	591	65°03'N	16°48'W
Askvoll	NO	604	61°21'N	5°01'E
Aslanapa		564	39°13'N	29°52'E
Aşlāndūz	IR	502	39°26'N	47°23'E
Āsmār	AF	480	35°02'N	71°22'E
Āsmara (Asmera)	ER	292	15°20'N	38°56'E
Åsnen	SW	621	56°38'N	14°42'E
Āsosa	ET	293	10°04'N	34°32'E
Asoteriba, Jabal	SU	324	21°47'N	36°30'E
Aspen		372	39°11'N	106°49'W
Aspermont		376	33°08'N	100°13'W
Aspin, Col d'	FR	580	42°57'N	0°20'E
Aspindza	GG	495	41°34'N	43°15'E
Aspromonte	IT	593	38°10'N	16°00'E
Asprópirgos	GR	588	38°04'N	23°35'E
Assa	MO	310	28°37'N	9°25'W
Assa Aguiene	AG	272	23°15'N	6°04'E
Assâba	MR	308	16°40'N	11°40'W
As Sabahiyah	KU	514	29°06'N	48°06'E
Assabet el Meddahia	MR	308	22°08'N	11°53'W
As Sabkhah	SY	531	35°48'N	39°15'E
As Sabkhah al Kabirah	LY	302	29°36'N	19°25'E
Aş Şadārah	YM	541	14°30'N	48°03'E
As Sa`dīyah	IZ	504	34°11'N	45°07'E
Aş Şaff	EG	290	29°34'N	31°17'E
Aş Şāfī	JO	510	31°02'N	35°23'E
Aş Şāfiyah	SU	324	15°31'N	30°07'E
As Sahara al Janubiyah	EG	290	23°50'N	29°30'E
As Sahra an Nubiyah (Nubian Desert)	SU	324	21°08'N	32°12'E
Assal, Lake	DJ	289	11°40'N	42°26'E
Aş Şāliḩīyah	SY	531	34°44'N	40°45'E
As Sālimīyah	KU	514	29°20'N	48°04'E
As Sallūm	EG	290	31°34'N	25°09'E
As Salmān	IZ	504	30°30'N	44°35'E
As Salţ	JO	510	32°03'N	35°44'E
As Salwá	SA	528	24°45'N	50°50'E
Assam	IN	496	26°30'N	92°45'E
As Samāwah	IZ	504	31°18'N	45°17'E
Assaouas	NG	314	16°52'N	7°27'E
Aş Şarīḩ	JO	510	32°30'N	35°54'E
As Sawdā	TS	329	35°06'N	9°32'E
Aş Şawma'ah	YM	541	14°03'N	45°47'E
Asse	BE	570	50°55'N	4°12'E
Assegai	WZ	326	26°45'S	31°20'E
Assemini		562	39°17'N	9°00'E
Assen	NL	602	53°00'N	6°33'E
Assenede	BE	570	51°14'N	3°45'E
Assénoukopé	TO	328	6°31'N	1°12'E
Assens	DA	576	56°41'N	10°04'E
Assens	DA	576	55°16'N	9°55'E
Assentoft	DA	576	56°26'N	10°09'E
As Shuqqan	SA	528	23°30'N	49°00'E
As Sīb	MU	523	23°41'N	58°11'E
As Sidr	LY	302	30°36'N	18°21'E
As Sidr	SA	528	23°27'N	39°46'E
As Sinbillāwayn	EG	290	30°53'N	31°27'E
Assiniboia	CA	390	49°38'N	105°59'W
Assiniboine	CA	390	49°53'N	97°08'W
Assis	BR	424	22°40'S	50°25'W
Assling	AU	568	46°47'N	12°38'E
Assok-Ngoum	GB	294	1°45'N	11°39'E
Assok-Seng	GB	294	1°56'N	11°35'E
Assomption	SE	319	9°45'S	46°30'E
As Sudd	SU	324	7°55'N	30°38'E
As Sufāl	YM	541	14°05'N	48°42'E
Aş Şufayyah	SU	324	15°30'N	34°42'E
Aş Şukhayrah	TS	329	34°17'N	10°03'E
As Sukhnah	JO	510	32°08'N	36°04'E
As Sukhnah	SY	531	34°53'N	38°52'E
As Suki	SU	324	13°20'N	32°54'E
As Sulaymānīyah	IZ	504	35°33'N	45°26'E
As Sulaymī	SA	528	26°17'N	41°21'E
As Sulayyil	SA	528	20°27'N	45°34'E
As Sulţān	LY	302	31°05'N	17°10'E
As Sumayḩ	SU	324	9°49'N	27°39'E
As Summan	SA	528	23°00'N	49°30'E
Assumption	CA	390	58°40'N	118°36'W
Aş Şuwār	SY	531	35°30'N	40°38'E
As Suwaydā'	SY	531	32°42'N	36°34'E
As Suwayq	MU	523	23°51'N	57°26'E
Aş Şuwayrah	IZ	504	32°55'N	44°47'E
As Suways	EG	290	29°58'N	32°33'E
Astagram	BG	485	24°16'N	91°07'E
Astakós	GR	588	38°32'N	21°05'E
Astara	AJ	483	38°27'N	48°52'E
Asti	IT	593	44°54'N	8°12'E
Astillero	PE	436	13°22'S	69°37'W
Astipálaia	GR	588	36°32'N	26°20'E
Astipálaia (Stampalia)	GR	588	36°35'N	26°20'E
Astkhadzor	AM	482	40°07'N	45°21'E
Astorga	SP	618	42°27'N	6°03'W
Astoria	US	398	46°11'N	123°49'W
Åstorp	SW	621	56°08'N	12°57'E
Astove	SE	319	10°06'S	47°45'E
Astra		388	45°44'S	67°30'W
Astrakhan'	RS	612	46°21'N	48°03'E
Astrea	CO	430	9°30'N	73°59'W
Ástros	GR	588	37°24'N	22°43'E
Asuiabe	EK	291	1°13'N	9°38'E
Asuisui, Cape	WS	668	13°45'S	172°30'W
Asunción		376	30°30'N	112°15'W
Asunción	BL	422	11°46'S	67°50'W
Asunción	PA	435	25°18'S	57°38'W
Asunción, Bahía		376	27°06'N	114°11'W
Asunción Mita	GT	411	14°20'N	89°43'W
Asunción Nochixtlán	MX	394	17°28'N	97°14'W
Asunden	SW	621	58°02'N	15°36'E
Aswa	UG	330	2°58'N	32°36'E
Aswa	UG	330	2°35'N	31°27'E
Aswad, Wadi	MU	523	21°58'N	55°45'E
Aswān	EG	290	24°05'N	32°54'E
Asyūt	EG	290	27°11'N	31°11'E
Asyūti, Wadi al-	EG	290	27°10'N	31°16'E
Ata		654	21°08'S	175°05'W
Ataa	BP	666	8°32'S	161°00'E
Atabapo	VE	440	4°03'N	67°42'W
Atacama, Desierto de	CI	428	24°30'S	69°15'W
Atacama, Salar de	CI	428	23°30'S	68°15'W
Atacames	EC	432	0°52'N	79°51'W
Atafu		650	8°34'S	173°38'W
Atagay		468	55°06'N	99°23'E
Atait		654	17°41'S	145°44'W
Atakpamé	TO	328	7°34'N	1°07'E
Atalaia	BR	424	9°31'S	36°02'W
Atalaia do Norte	BR	424	4°20'S	70°12'W
Atalándi	GR	588	38°39'N	23°00'E
Atalanta	CS	405	9°43'N	82°59'W
Atalaya	PE	436	10°44'S	73°45'W
Atalaya	PM	417	8°03'N	80°56'W
Atambohobe	MA	304	22°20'S	46°47'E
Atammik		370	64°48'N	52°13'W
Atap	ID	500	3°51'N	117°02'E
Atapirire	VE	440	8°27'N	64°22'W
`Atāq	YM	541	14°33'N	46°47'E
Atar	MR	308	20°31'N	13°03'W
Atari	UG	330	1°30'N	34°26'E
Atarra	IN	496	25°17'N	80°34'E
Atascadero	US	398	35°29'N	120°40'W
Atasu	KZ	510	48°42'N	71°38'E
Atata		654	21°05'S	175°15'W
Atauro	ID	500	8°13'S	125°35'E
Ātaya	ET	293	10°21'N	39°56'E
Atbara	SU	324	17°42'N	33°59'E
Atbarah, Nahr	SU	324	17°40'N	33°58'E
Atbasar	KZ	510	51°48'N	68°20'E
At-Bashi	KG	514	41°10'N	75°47'E
Atbasi, Khrebet	KG	514	40°50'N	76°00'E
Atchafalaya B.		378	29°21'N	91°19'W
Atchison		374	39°33'N	95°07'W
Atebubu	GH	296	7°45'N	0°59'W
Ateca	SP	618	41°20'N	1°47'W
Atén	BL	422	14°55'S	68°23'W
Atenas	CS	405	9°58'N	84°23'W
Ath	BE	570	50°38'N	3°47'E
Athabasca	CA	390	58°00'N	111°00'W
Athabasca, Lake	CA	390	59°10'N	109°30'W
Āthārabāri	BG	485	24°37'N	90°44'E
Athboy	EI	592	53°37'N	6°55'W
Athenry	EI	592	53°18'N	8°45'W
Athens		374	39°19'N	82°06'W
Athens		378	32°12'N	95°51'W
Athens		378	34°48'N	86°57'W
Athens		378	35°26'N	84°35'W
Athens		378	33°57'N	83°22'W
Athens (Athínai)	GR	588	37°58'N	23°43'E
Atherton	AS	656	17°16'S	145°29'E
Athgarh	IN	496	20°32'N	85°37'E
Athi	KE	299	2°59'S	38°31'E
Athiencu	CY	494	35°04'N	33°32'E
Athínai (Athens)	GR	588	37°58'N	23°43'E
Athi River	KE	299	1°27'S	36°59'E
Athlone	EI	592	53°26'N	7°57'W
Athok	BM	487	17°12'N	95°05'E
Athol		654	46°50'S	169°00'E
Athol	NZ	663	45°31'S	168°35'E
Athol Island	BF	402	25°05'N	77°16'W
Áthos	GR	588	40°10'N	24°20'E
Athy	EI	592	52°59'N	6°59'W
Ati	CD	283	13°15'N	18°20'E
Atiak	UG	330	3°15'N	32°07'E
Ati Ardébé	CD	283	12°44'N	17°41'E
Atico	PE	436	16°11'S	73°37'W
Atikokan	CA	390	48°45'N	91°37'W
Atil		376	30°50'N	111°35'W
Atimaono		654	17°42'S	145°43'W
Atiquizaya	ES	409	13°58'N	89°45'W
Atitlán, L. de	GT	411	14°42'N	91°12'W
Atituiti		654	23°08'S	135°03'W
Ativémé	TO	328	6°25'N	1°07'E
Atka	RS	612	60°50'N	151°48'E
Atka	US	398	52°06'N	175°26'W
Atkaracalar		564	40°50'N	33°04'E
Atkarsk		560	51°52'N	45°00'E
Atkinson	US	398	42°31'N	98°58'W
Atlanta		378	33°06'N	94°09'W
Atlanta	SF	322	25°12'S	27°33'E
Atlanta	US	398	33°44'N	84°23'W
Atlantic		36	40°29'N	65°33'W
Atlantic		374	41°24'N	95°00'W
Atlantic Beach		378	30°20'N	81°23'W
Atlantic City		374	39°21'N	74°26'W
Atlantic Coastal Plain		378	33°00'N	80°00'W
Atlantic Ocean		36	40°29'N	65°33'W
Atlantis	SF	322	33°34'S	18°29'E
Atlas Bogd	MG	520	43°20'N	96°30'E
Atlas Mountains	MO	310	33°06'N	4°51'W
Atlasovo	RS	612	55°36'N	159°43'E
Atlas Saharien	AG	272	34°00'N	2°00'E
Atlas Tellien	AG	272	36°00'N	1°00'E
Atlin	CA	390	59°33'N	133°38'W
Atlin Lake	CA	390	59°30'N	133°45'W
Atlixco	MX	394	18°54'N	98°24'W
Atmore	US	398	31°01'N	87°29'W
Atocha	BL	422	20°56'S	66°14'W
Atoka		378	34°23'N	96°07'W
Atome	AO	274	11°53'S	14°34'E
Atouat	LA	517	16°01'N	107°23'E
Atouila, 'Erg	ML	307	21°01'N	4°53'W
Atoyac	MX	394	18°00'N	99°00'W
Atoyac de Álvarez	MX	394	17°12'N	100°26'W
Atqan	CH	490	37°23'N	85°19'E
Atrai	BG	485	24°07'N	89°22'E
Atrak	TX	537	37°22'N	53°54'E
Ätran	SW	621	56°53'N	12°30'E
Atrato	CO	430	8°17'N	76°58'W
Atsarat	AM	482	40°21'N	45°07'E
Aţ Ţafīlah	JO	510	30°50'N	35°36'E
Aţ Ţā'if	SA	528	21°16'N	40°25'E
At Tall	SY	531	33°36'N	36°18'E
Attalla		378	34°01'N	86°05'W
Aţ Ţallāb	LY	302	24°09'N	23°17'E
At Tamīmī	LY	302	32°19'N	23°04'E
Attapu	LA	517	14°48'N	106°50'E
Attawapiskat	CA	390	52°56'N	82°24'W
Attawapiskat	CA	390	52°57'N	82°18'W
Aţ Ţayyibah	JO	510	32°33'N	35°43'E
At Tayyibah	SY	531	32°34'N	36°15'E
Atteridgeville	SF	322	25°46'S	28°04'E
Attersee	AU	568	47°50'N	13°48'E
Attert	BE	570	49°46'N	5°47'E
Attert	LU	598	49°49'N	6°05'E
Attock	PK	524	33°54'N	72°15'E
Attu		370	67°57'N	53°38'W
Attu	US	398	52°46'N	172°08'E
At Tubayq	SA	528	29°50'N	37°30'E
Aţ Ţūr	EG	290	28°14'N	33°37'E
Aţ Ţūr	IS	505	31°47'N	35°15'E
At Turbah	YM	541	13°05'N	44°04'E
At Turrah	JO	510	32°38'N	36°00'E
Aţ Ţuwayshah	SU	324	12°21'N	26°32'E
Aţ Ţuwayyah	SA	528	27°36'N	41°13'E
Atuel	AR	419	36°17'S	66°50'W
Atuntaqui	EC	432	0°20'N	78°13'W
Atuona		654	16°30'S	167°50'E
Ātura	BG	485	24°59'N	83°50'E
Atura	UG	330	2°07'N	32°20'E
Åtvidaberg	SW	621	58°12'N	16°00'E
Atwater		376	37°20'N	120°36'W
Atwood		372	39°47'N	101°02'W
Atwood Harbour	BF	402	22°43'N	73°55'W
Atyashevo		560	54°34'N	46°06'E
Atyraū	KZ	510	47°06'N	51°54'E
Auari	BR	424	3°33'N	63°48'W
Auas	HO	412	15°29'N	84°20'W
Auasbila	HO	412	14°46'N	84°45'W
Aub	WA	313	22°56'S	17°11'E
Auba	ID	500	9°02'S	125°22'E
Aubagne	FR	580	43°17'N	5°34'E
Aubange	BE	570	49°35'N	5°48'E
Aubenas	FR	580	44°37'N	4°23'E
Auberry		376	37°04'N	119°29'W
Aubigny-sur-Nère	FR	580	47°29'N	2°26'E
Aubrac, Monts d'	FR	580	44°38'N	3°00'E
Auburn		370	42°55'N	76°33'W
Auburn		374	39°35'N	89°44'W
Auburn		374	40°23'N	95°50'W
Auburn	US	398	32°36'N	85°28'W
Auburn Range	AS	656	25°10'S	150°30'E
Aubusson	FR	580	45°57'N	2°11'E
Aucá Mahuida, Cerro	AR	419	37°45'S	68°56'W
Auce	LG	596	56°28'N	22°53'E
Auch	FR	580	43°39'N	0°35'E
Auche	BM	487	25°43'N	96°50'E
Auchenblae	UK	626	56°54'N	2°27'W
Auchi	NI	316	7°04'N	6°13'E
Auchinleck	UK	626	55°28'N	4°18'W
Auckland	NZ	663	50°40'S	163°50'E
Auckland Is.		654	51°00'S	169°00'E
Auden	CA	390	50°14'N	87°53'W
Auderghem	BE	570	50°49'N	4°26'E
Audet		374	45°39'N	70°44'W
Audierne, Baie d'	FR	580	47°57'N	4°28'W
Audincourt	FR	580	47°29'N	6°50'E
Audo Range	ET	293	6°10'N	41°45'E
Audubon		374	41°43'N	94°55'W
Aue	GM	584	50°35'N	12°42'E
Auerbach	GM	584	50°31'N	12°24'E
Augathella	AS	656	25°48'S	146°35'E
Aughrim	EI	592	52°51'N	6°20'W
Aughty Mts.	EI	592	53°00'N	9°00'W
Augier	ST	418	13°45'N	60°58'W
Augraviesvalle	SF	322	28°34'S	20°19'E
Augsburg	GM	584	48°22'N	10°53'E
Augusta		372	37°41'N	96°58'W
Augusta		378	33°28'N	81°58'W
Augusta		564	37°13'N	15°13'E
Augusta		652	34°19'S	115°09'E
Augusta	US	398	44°18'N	69°46'W
Augusta, Cabo	CO	430	11°07'N	74°51'W
Augusta, Golfo di	IT	593	37°12'N	15°13'E
Augustenborg	DA	576	54°57'N	9°53'E
Augustine	BH	404	16°57'N	88°59'W
Augustinópolis	BR	424	5°28'S	47°39'W
Augustów	PL	606	53°49'N	22°57'E
Aukam	WA	313	26°55'S	16°53'E
Au-Kéna		654	23°08'S	135°07'W
Auki	BP	666	8°45'S	160°44'E
Aulnay-sous-Bois	FR	580	48°56'N	2°30'E
Aulneau Pen.		374	49°20'N	94°30'W
Aulong	PX	664	7°16'N	134°20'E
Ault	FR	580	50°06'N	1°27'E
Aultbea		558	57°50'N	5°35'W
Auluptagel	PX	664	7°15'N	134°30'E
Auna	NI	316	10°11'N	4°43'E
Auning	DA	576	56°26'N	10°23'E
Auob	WA	313	26°26'S	20°37'E
Aur	MY	518	2°27'N	104°31'E
Aur	RM	661	8°10'N	171°00'E
Aurangābād	IN	496	24°45'N	84°22'E
Aurangābād	IN	496	19°53'N	75°19'E
Auray	FR	580	47°40'N	2°59'W
Aure	NO	604	63°16'N	8°33'E
Aureilhan	FR	580	43°15'N	0°06'E
Aurelia		374	42°42'N	95°26'W
Aurich	GM	584	53°28'N	7°29'E
Aurillac	FR	580	44°55'N	2°28'E
Aurland	NO	604	60°54'N	7°11'E
Aurora		372	40°52'N	98°00'W
Aurora		374	36°58'N	93°43'W
Aurora	GY	434	6°48'N	59°45'W
Aurora	RP	526	7°57'N	123°36'E
Aurora	US	398	39°44'N	104°50'W
Aurora	US	398	41°45'N	88°19'W
Aurora (Maéwo)	NH	669	15°10'S	168°05'E
Aus	WA	313	26°40'S	16°16'E
Au Sable		374	44°24'N	83°19'W
Ausert		262	22°34'N	14°18'W
Aussenkehr	WA	313	28°21'S	17°24'E
Ausservillgraten	AU	568	46°47'N	12°25'E
Austin		374	38°45'N	85°48'W
Austin	US	398	43°40'N	92°58'W
Austin	US	398	30°16'N	97°44'W
Australia		38	25°00'S	135°00'E
Australian Alps	AS	656	37°00'S	149°00'E
Austria		38	47°20'N	13°20'E
Austurhorn	IC	591	64°24'N	14°34'W
Autazes	BR	424	3°35'S	59°08'W
Auterive	FR	580	43°21'N	1°29'E
Autlán	MX	394	19°46'N	104°22'W
Autoua		654	16°10'S	167°50'E
Autreppe	BE	570	50°21'N	3°43'E
Autun	FR	580	46°57'N	4°17'E
Auvergne	AS	656	15°41'S	130°01'E
Aux Barques, Pt.	US	398	44°04'N	82°58'W
Auxerre	FR	580	47°48'N	3°34'E
Auzangate, Nevado	PE	436	13°47'S	71°14'W
Ava		374	36°57'N	92°39'W
Avallon	FR	580	47°29'N	3°54'E
Avalon		376	33°20'N	118°19'W
Avalon Pen.	CA	390	47°20'N	53°30'W
Avaré		386	23°05'S	48°55'W
Āvāz	IR	502	32°56'N	60°16'E
Avdzaga	MG	520	47°38'N	103°31'E
Ave	PO	608	41°20'N	8°45'W
Aveiro	BR	424	3°35'S	55°18'W
Aveiro	PO	608	40°38'N	8°39'W
Avelgem	BE	570	50°46'N	3°26'E
Avellino	IT	593	40°54'N	14°47'E
Avenal		376	36°00'N	120°07'W
Aversa	IT	593	40°58'N	14°12'E
Avesta	SW	621	60°09'N	16°12'E
Avezzano	IT	593	42°02'N	13°25'E
Aviemore	UK	626	57°12'N	3°50'W
Avigaat		370	62°14'N	49°50'W
Avignon	FR	580	43°57'N	4°49'E
Ávila	SP	618	40°41'N	4°41'W
Avilés	SP	618	43°33'N	5°55'W
Avina	GB	294	3°00'N	13°00'E
Avisio	IT	593	46°07'N	11°05'E

B

Balqash	*KZ*	**510**	46°49'N	75°00'E
Balrāmpur	*IN*	**496**	27°26'N	82°11'E
Balranald		**652**	34°38'S	143°34'E
Balş	*RO*	**610**	44°21'N	24°06'E
Balsa	*BR*	**424**	7°00'S	45°00'W
Balsapuerto	*PE*	**436**	5°50'S	76°36'W
Balsas	*BR*	**424**	7°31'S	46°02'W
Balsas	*MX*	**394**	17°55'N	102°10'W
Balsthal	*SZ*	**622**	47°19'N	7°41'E
Balta	*UP*	**624**	47°56'N	29°37'E
Baltasar Brum	*UY*	**439**	30°42'S	57°18'W
Baltasound	*UK*	**626**	60°45'N	0°50'W
Baltay		**560**	52°23'N	46°38'E
Bălţi	*MD*	**601**	47°46'N	27°56'E
Baltic Hills	*LH*	**597**	54°30'N	23°30'E
Baltic Plains	*LG*	**596**	56°30'N	25°00'E
Baltic Sea		**560**	56°00'N	18°00'E
Balţīm	*EG*	**290**	31°33'N	31°05'E
Baltimore	*US*	**398**	39°17'N	76°36'W
Baltit	*PK*	**524**	36°20'N	74°40'E
Baltiysk	*RS*	**612**	54°39'N	19°55'E
Baltoji Vokė	*LH*	**597**	54°36'N	25°12'E
Balud	*RP*	**526**	12°02'N	123°12'E
Balui	*MY*	**518**	2°10'N	114°00'E
Bālurghāt	*IN*	**496**	25°13'N	88°46'E
Balvard	*IR*	**502**	29°25'N	56°03'E
Balvi	*LG*	**596**	57°08'N	27°15'E
Balzar	*EC*	**432**	1°22'S	79°54'W
Balzers	*LS*	**597**	47°04'N	9°30'E
Bam		**468**	54°08'N	123°42'E
Bam	*IR*	**502**	29°06'N	58°21'E
Bama	*NI*	**316**	11°31'N	13°41'E
Bamaga	*AS*	**656**	10°52'S	142°25'E
Bamako	*ML*	**307**	12°39'N	8°00'W
Bamba	*ML*	**307**	17°02'N	1°24'W
Bambama	*CF*	**285**	2°32'S	13°33'E
Bambamarca	*PE*	**436**	6°41'S	78°32'W
Bambang	*RP*	**526**	16°23'N	121°06'E
Bambara	*CD*	**283**	8°56'N	18°33'E
Bambara	*NU*	**415**	13°50'N	84°10'W
Bambara Maoundé	*ML*	**307**	15°51'N	2°47'W
Bambari	*CT*	**282**	5°45'N	20°40'E
Bambera-Biyoko	*GB*	**294**	1°07'S	12°56'E
Bamberg	*GM*	**584**	49°54'N	10°52'E
Bambesa	*CG*	**287**	3°28'N	25°43'E
Bambesi	*ET*	**293**	9°45'N	34°44'E
Bambey	*SG*	**319**	14°42'N	16°28'W
Bambi	*AO*	**274**	14°03'S	15°34'E
Bambili	*CG*	**287**	3°39'N	26°07'E
Bambio	*CT*	**282**	3°54'N	16°58'E
Bamble	*NO*	**604**	59°00'N	9°37'E
Bamboo	*JM*	**414**	18°23'N	77°16'W
Bamboo Creek	*AS*	**656**	20°56'S	120°13'E
Bambouti	*CT*	**282**	5°24'N	27°12'E
Bambu	*ET*	**293**	5°52'N	35°17'E
Bamenda	*CM*	**280**	5°56'N	10°10'E
Bamenda Plateau	*CM*	**280**	6°30'N	10°40'E
Bamfield		**372**	48°50'N	125°08'W
Bāmīān	*AF*	**480**	34°50'N	67°50'E
Bamingui	*CT*	**282**	7°32'N	20°12'E
Bamingui	*CT*	**282**	8°33'N	19°05'E
Bamnet Narong	*TH*	**534**	15°30'N	101°42'E
Bampūr	*IR*	**502**	27°12'N	60°27'E
Bampur	*IR*	**502**	27°18'N	59°06'E
Bamunka	*CM*	**280**	6°00'N	10°25'E
Bamy	*TX*	**537**	38°44'N	56°48'E
Bamyili	*AS*	**656**	14°30'S	132°55'E
Baña, Punta de la	*SP*	**618**	40°34'N	0°38'E
Bana, Wadi	*YM*	**541**	13°03'N	45°24'E
Banaaney	*SO*	**321**	0°08'N	42°55'E
Banaba (Ocean I.)	*KR*	**660**	0°10'S	169°50'E
Bañado de Medina	*UY*	**439**	32°24'S	54°19'W
Bañado de Rocha	*UY*	**439**	31°36'S	55°52'W
Banagher	*EI*	**592**	53°11'N	7°59'W
Banagi	*TZ*	**327**	2°16'S	34°51'E
Banagüises	*CU*	**406**	22°46'N	80°51'W
Banalia	*CG*	**287**	1°33'N	25°20'E
Banama	*GV*	**297**	9°04'N	9°45'W
Banamba	*ML*	**307**	13°33'N	7°27'W
Banámichi		**376**	30°00'N	110°11'W
Banan, Kuh-e-	*IR*	**502**	31°00'N	56°15'E
Banana	*CG*	**287**	5°59'S	12°23'E
Banana Islands	*SL*	**320**	8°07'N	13°13'W
Bananal		**384**	12°22'S	50°23'W
Bananal, Ilha do	*BR*	**424**	12°00'S	50°15'W
Bananga		**476**	6°57'N	93°54'E
Banao	*CU*	**406**	21°49'N	79°34'W
Bānarīpāra	*BG*	**485**	22°47'N	90°10'E
Banas	*IN*	**496**	25°54'N	76°45'E
Banās, Ra's	*EG*	**290**	23°54'N	35°48'E
Banatski Karlovac	*YO*	**630**	45°04'N	21°02'E
Banatsko Novo Selo	*YO*	**630**	44°59'N	20°48'E
Ban Ay Rieng	*VM*	**540**	13°13'N	108°09'E
Banaz		**564**	38°44'N	29°47'E
Ban Bak	*LA*	**517**	15°51'N	106°47'E
Ban Ban	*LA*	**517**	19°38'N	103°34'E
Banbar	*CH*	**490**	30°49'N	95°00'E
Ban Boten	*LA*	**517**	21°11'N	101°40'E
Ban Boun Tai	*LA*	**517**	21°23'N	101°58'E
Banbridge	*UK*	**626**	54°17'N	6°12'W
Banbury	*UK*	**626**	52°03'N	1°20'W
Banchory	*UK*	**626**	57°03'N	2°31'W
Banco Chinchorro	*MX*	**394**	18°35'N	87°17'W
Bancroft		**374**	45°03'N	77°51'W
Bāndā	*IN*	**496**	25°29'N	80°20'E
Banda	*CG*	**287**	4°11'N	27°04'E
Banda	*CG*	**287**	5°22'S	19°57'E
Banda	*CT*	**282**	6°28'N	17°30'E
Banda, Kep.	*ID*	**500**	4°35'S	129°55'E
Banda, Pt.		**376**	31°50'N	116°50'W
Banda Besar	*ID*	**500**	4°34'S	129°55'E
Banda Elat	*ID*	**500**	5°40'S	132°59'E
Bandahara, Gunung	*ID*	**500**	3°46'N	97°47'E
Bandama		**266**	5°10'N	5°00'W
Bandama Blanc	*IV*	**288**	6°54'N	5°31'W
Bandama Rouge	*IV*	**288**	6°54'N	5°31'W
Bandanaira	*ID*	**500**	4°32'S	129°52'E
Ban Dang	*LA*	**517**	17°27'N	105°16'E
Ban Dan Lan Hoi	*TH*	**534**	17°00'N	99°35'E
Bandar		**470**	16°10'N	81°08'E
Bāndarban	*BG*	**485**	22°12'N	92°13'E
Bandar Beheshtī	*IR*	**502**	25°16'N	60°38'E
Bandar-e 'Abbās	*IR*	**502**	27°12'N	56°16'E
Bandar-e Anzalī	*IR*	**502**	37°28'N	49°27'E
Bandar-e Būshehr	*IR*	**502**	28°59'N	50°50'E
Bandar-e Deylam	*IR*	**502**	30°03'N	50°10'E
Bandar-e Khomeynī	*IR*	**502**	30°27'N	49°03'E
Bandar-e Kong	*IR*	**502**	26°35'N	54°56'E
Bandar-e Lengeh	*IR*	**502**	26°33'N	54°53'E
Bandar-e Māhshahr	*IR*	**502**	30°33'N	49°12'E
Bandar-e Maqām	*IR*	**502**	26°58'N	53°27'E
Bandar-e Moghūyeh	*IR*	**502**	26°36'N	54°27'E
Bandar-e Torkeman	*IR*	**502**	36°54'N	54°04'E
Bandar Seri Begawan	*BX*	**486**	4°53'N	114°56'E
Banda Sea	*ID*	**500**	5°00'S	128°00'E
Bandawe	*MI*	**306**	11°53'S	34°10'E
Bandeira, Pico da	*BR*	**424**	20°26'S	41°47'W
Bandeira, Serra do	*AO*	**274**	15°00'S	12°20'E
Bandeirantes		**386**	19°55'S	54°21'W
Bandera	*AR*	**419**	28°54'S	62°16'W
Bandera Bajada	*AR*	**419**	27°14'S	63°31'W
Banderas	*MX*	**394**	31°01'N	105°35'W
Bandholm	*DA*	**576**	54°50'N	11°29'E
Bandiagara	*ML*	**307**	14°21'N	3°37'W
Band-i-Baba	*AF*	**480**	34°37'N	62°40'E
Band-i-Baian	*AF*	**480**	34°10'N	65°30'E
Bandīpur	*NP*	**522**	27°56'N	84°25'E
Bandırma	*TU*	**535**	40°20'N	27°58'E
Band-i-Turkestan	*AF*	**480**	35°50'N	64°30'E
Bandjoun	*CM*	**280**	5°21'N	10°25'E
Bandol		**562**	43°08'N	5°45'E
Ban Don	*VM*	**540**	12°52'N	107°47'E
Bandon		**372**	43°07'N	124°24'W
Bandon	*EI*	**592**	51°45'N	8°44'W
Ban Donkhagnoung	*LA*	**517**	15°53'N	106°17'E
Ban Donkon	*LA*	**517**	20°18'N	101°39'E
Ban Douangmala	*LA*	**517**	16°23'N	105°27'E
Bandundu	*CG*	**287**	3°21'S	17°22'E
Ban Dung	*TH*	**534**	17°42'N	103°16'E
Bandung	*ID*	**500**	6°54'S	107°36'E
Bandya	*AS*	**656**	27°44'S	122°09'E
Bāneh	*IR*	**502**	35°59'N	45°53'E
Banes	*CU*	**406**	20°58'N	75°43'W
Banff		**372**	51°10'N	115°34'W
Banff	*UK*	**626**	57°40'N	2°32'W
Banfora	*UV*	**278**	10°38'N	4°46'W
Bang	*CT*	**282**	7°28'N	15°33'E
Banga	*UG*	**330**	0°09'N	32°16'E
Bangalan		**648**	3°22'N	116°14'E
Bangalore	*IN*	**496**	12°59'N	77°35'E
Bangangté	*CM*	**280**	5°08'N	10°32'E
Bangar	*BX*	**486**	4°42'N	115°03'E
Bangara	*BG*	**485**	21°50'N	89°50'E
Bangassou	*CT*	**282**	4°44'N	22°48'E
Bangau, Tanjong	*MY*	**518**	6°57'N	116°42'E
Bang Fai	*LA*	**517**	17°00'N	106°00'E
Banggai, Kep.	*ID*	**500**	1°30'S	123°15'E
Banggi	*MY*	**518**	7°17'N	117°12'E
Bang Hieng	*LA*	**517**	16°30'N	105°30'E
Bangka	*ID*	**500**	2°15'S	106°00'E
Bangka, Selat	*ID*	**500**	2°20'S	105°45'E
Bangkaru	*ID*	**500**	2°04'N	97°07'E
Bangkir	*ID*	**500**	0°48'N	120°14'E
Bangkok (Krung Thep)	*TH*	**534**	13°45'N	100°31'E
Bangkok, Bight of		**476**	13°45'N	100°31'E
Bangkok, Gulf of	*TH*	**534**	13°10'N	100°30'E
Bangladesh		**38**	24°00'N	90°00'E
Bang Mun Nak	*TH*	**534**	16°02'N	100°23'E
Bangor	*FR*	**580**	47°18'N	3°11'W
Bangor	*UK*	**626**	53°13'N	4°07'W
Bangor	*UK*	**626**	54°39'N	5°42'W
Bangor	*US*	**398**	44°48'N	68°45'W
Bangoran	*CT*	**282**	8°42'N	19°06'E
Bangouya	*GV*	**297**	10°20'N	12°57'W
Bangs		**376**	31°43'N	99°07'W
Bang Saphan	*TH*	**534**	11°12'N	99°31'E
Bangsund	*NO*	**604**	64°23'N	11°24'E
Bangu	*CG*	**287**	9°05'S	23°44'E
Bangued	*RP*	**526**	17°36'N	120°37'E
Bangui	*CT*	**282**	4°23'N	18°34'E
Bangui	*EK*	**291**	1°16'N	9°34'E
Bangui	*RP*	**526**	18°32'N	120°46'E
Bangwegne	*GB*	**294**	1°38'S	13°28'E
Bangweulu, Lake		**266**	11°05'S	29°45'E
Banhā	*EG*	**290**	30°28'N	31°11'E
Ban Ham	*LA*	**517**	20°11'N	104°15'E
Ban Hatmat	*LA*	**517**	20°03'N	102°14'E
Ban Hinkhan	*LA*	**517**	17°45'N	104°35'E
Ban Hintang	*LA*	**517**	19°18'N	103°09'E
Ban Hong	*TH*	**534**	18°18'N	98°50'E
Ban Houaphouman	*LA*	**517**	14°05'N	105°49'E
Ban Houayhai	*LA*	**517**	20°04'N	102°00'E
Ban Houaymai	*LA*	**517**	14°28'N	105°51'E
Ban Houay Pamon	*LA*	**517**	18°47'N	102°31'E
Ban Houay Sa Tip	*LA*	**517**	19°33'N	102°22'E
Ban Houayxay	*LA*	**517**	20°18'N	100°26'E
Bani	*CT*	**282**	7°06'N	22°51'E
Bani	*ML*	**307**	14°30'N	4°12'W
Baní	*DR*	**408**	18°17'N	70°20'W
Bani, Jebel	*MO*	**310**	28°30'N	9°00'W
Bania	*CT*	**282**	4°00'N	16°07'E
Baniachang	*BG*	**485**	24°31'N	91°22'E
Banian	*GV*	**297**	9°36'N	10°32'W
Baniara	*PP*	**664**	9°46'S	149°53'E
Bani-Bangou	*NG*	**314**	15°03'N	2°42'E
Bánica	*DR*	**408**	19°05'N	71°42'W
Banifing	*ML*	**307**	12°43'N	6°25'W
Bānigrām	*BG*	**485**	22°07'N	91°56'E
Banihal Pass	*IN*	**496**	33°31'N	75°13'E
Banikoara	*BN*	**276**	11°20'N	2°21'E
Bani Ma'arid	*SA*	**528**	19°50'N	46°00'E
Banī Mazār	*EG*	**290**	28°30'N	30°48'E
Banisa	*KE*	**299**	3°57'N	40°21'E
Banī Suhaylah	*IS*	**505**	31°20'N	34°20'E
Banī Suwayf	*EG*	**290**	29°05'N	31°05'E
Bāni Walīd	*LY*	**302**	31°44'N	14°01'E
Bāniyās	*SY*	**531**	35°11'N	35°57'E
Bani Yas	*TC*	**538**	23°00'N	54°00'E
Banja Koviljača	*YO*	**630**	44°30'N	19°11'E
Banja Luka	*BK*	**572**	44°46'N	17°10'E
Banjaran Besar	*MY*	**518**	5°00'N	101°30'E
Banjarmasin	*ID*	**500**	3°20'S	114°35'E
Banjul (Bathurst)	*GA*	**295**	13°27'N	16°35'W
Bank	*AJ*	**483**	39°25'N	49°15'E
Banka Banka	*AS*	**656**	18°48'S	134°01'E
Ban Kadan	*LA*	**517**	14°03'N	105°54'E
Ban Kadian	*LA*	**517**	14°26'N	105°42'E
Ban Kantang	*TH*	**534**	7°25'N	99°31'E
Ban Kapong	*TH*	**534**	8°41'N	98°27'E
Ban Kariang	*TH*	**534**	12°49'N	99°42'E
Bankas	*ML*	**307**	14°01'N	3°31'W
Bankend		**372**	51°31'N	103°51'W
Ban Keng	*LA*	**517**	20°33'N	103°50'E
Ban Kengkok	*LA*	**517**	16°26'N	105°12'E
Bankeryd	*SW*	**621**	57°51'N	14°07'E
Ban Kha	*LA*	**517**	20°01'N	103°02'E
Ban Khampho	*LA*	**517**	14°38'N	106°17'E
Ban Khlong Yai	*TH*	**534**	11°46'N	102°54'E
Ban Khok Kloi	*TH*	**534**	8°17'N	98°19'E
Ban Khon	*LA*	**517**	13°57'N	105°56'E
Ban Khuan Niang	*TH*	**534**	7°45'N	99°30'E
Bankilare	*NG*	**314**	14°35'N	0°44'E
Ban Kokpadek	*LA*	**517**	14°17'N	105°53'E
Bankouwale	*DJ*	**289**	11°49'N	42°40'E
Banks	*AS*	**656**	10°14'S	142°21'E
Banks Island		**368**	53°25'N	130°10'W
Banks Island	*CA*	**390**	73°00'N	120°00'W
Banks Islands	*NH*	**669**	13°50'S	168°00'E
Banks Peninsula	*NZ*	**663**	43°45'S	173°00'E
Banks Strait		**652**	45°30'S	148°30'E
Ban Kui Nua	*TH*	**534**	12°03'N	99°52'E
Bānkurā	*IN*	**496**	23°15'N	87°04'E
Ban Kut Bak	*TH*	**534**	17°05'N	103°49'E
Bankya	*BU*	**573**	42°42'N	23°08'E
Ban Laem	*TH*	**534**	13°13'N	99°59'E
Ban Lahanam	*LA*	**517**	16°16'N	105°16'E
Ban Len	*LA*	**517**	19°29'N	103°12'E
Ban Leum	*LA*	**517**	19°34'N	103°06'E
Ban Loboy	*LA*	**517**	17°12'N	106°09'E
Ban Mi	*TH*	**534**	15°03'N	100°52'E
Ban Mong	*VM*	**540**	19°25'N	105°15'E
Ban Muangsen	*LA*	**517**	16°56'N	105°47'E
Bann	*UK*	**626**	55°10'N	6°46'W
Ban Nadit	*LA*	**517**	19°18'N	103°09'E
Ban Nakachan	*LA*	**517**	17°19'N	105°43'E
Ban Nakala	*LA*	**517**	16°17'N	105°11'E
Ban Na Mang	*LA*	**517**	20°18'N	104°36'E
Ban Nambak	*LA*	**517**	20°38'N	102°28'E
Bannang Sata	*TH*	**534**	6°16'N	101°16'E
Ban Na Phao	*LA*	**517**	17°35'N	105°44'E
Ban Na Pho	*LA*	**517**	20°08'N	102°33'E
Ban Na San	*TH*	**534**	8°48'N	99°22'E
Ban Ngon	*TH*	**534**	17°28'N	103°26'E
Ban Nongdong	*LA*	**517**	14°54'N	105°56'E
Ban Nonnadeng	*LA*	**517**	17°00'N	104°57'E
Ban Noua Na	*LA*	**517**	20°38'N	104°25'E
Bannu	*PK*	**524**	32°59'N	70°36'E
Baños	*EC*	**432**	1°24'S	78°25'W
Ban Ou	*LA*	**517**	19°47'N	101°59'E
Bánovce nad Bebravou	*LO*	**616**	48°43'N	18°16'E
Banovići	*BK*	**572**	44°25'N	18°26'E
Banow	*AF*	**480**	35°38'N	69°15'E
Ban Pak Phanang	*TH*	**534**	8°21'N	100°12'E
Ban Paksa	*LA*	**517**	18°21'N	103°56'E
Ban Pakthoay	*LA*	**517**	18°27'N	103°26'E
Ban Pakthon	*LA*	**517**	20°09'N	102°39'E
Ban Panghai	*LA*	**517**	19°46'N	100°34'E
Ban Phaeng	*TH*	**534**	17°58'N	104°12'E
Ban Phai	*TH*	**534**	16°04'N	102°44'E
Ban Pho Chong	*LA*	**517**	19°34'N	102°20'E
Ban Phon	*LA*	**517**	15°25'N	106°42'E
Banphot Phisai	*TH*	**534**	15°56'N	99°59'E
Ban Phoumaktong	*LA*	**517**	14°07'N	105°48'E
Ban Pong	*LA*	**517**	16°56'N	104°45'E
Bānpur	*IN*	**496**	19°47'N	85°11'E
Ban Rai	*TH*	**534**	15°05'N	99°31'E
Ban Saat	*LA*	**517**	16°34'N	105°17'E
Ban Saka	*LA*	**517**	18°24'N	102°26'E
Bansalan	*RP*	**526**	6°45'N	125°14'E
Ban Senphan	*LA*	**517**	17°29'N	105°42'E
Ban Si Bun Ruang	*TH*	**534**	18°54'N	100°57'E
Ban Sieou	*LA*	**517**	19°58'N	102°17'E
Banská Bystrica	*LO*	**616**	48°44'N	19°09'E
Banská Štiavnica	*LO*	**616**	48°27'N	18°54'E
Bansko	*BU*	**573**	41°50'N	23°29'E
Bānswāra	*IN*	**496**	23°33'N	74°27'E
Ban Ta Fa	*LA*	**517**	20°26'N	100°53'E
Ban Tak	*TH*	**534**	17°02'N	99°04'E
Ban Taphan	*LA*	**517**	15°56'N	105°21'E
Bantayan	*RP*	**526**	11°04'N	123°23'E
Bantayan I.	*RP*	**526**	11°11'N	123°43'E
Banté	*BN*	**276**	8°25'N	1°52'E
Bantenan, Tanjung	*ID*	**500**	8°47'S	114°33'E
Ban Thabok	*LA*	**517**	18°22'N	103°12'E
Ban Thanaleng	*LA*	**517**	17°53'N	102°44'E
Ban Thasang	*LA*	**517**	14°28'N	105°51'E
Ban Tha Uthen	*TH*	**534**	17°34'N	104°36'E
Ban Thieng	*LA*	**517**	19°08'N	102°13'E
Bantry	*EI*	**592**	51°41'N	9°27'W
Bantry Bay	*EI*	**592**	51°38'N	9°42'W
Ban Tung	*LA*	**517**	17°09'N	104°59'E
Bantvāl		**470**	12°54'N	75°02'E
Ban Vat	*LA*	**517**	16°54'N	106°25'E
Ban Woen	*LA*	**517**	18°08'N	103°02'E
Ban Xao	*LA*	**517**	19°23'N	103°11'E
Ban Xay	*LA*	**517**	20°29'N	103°21'E
Ban Xaysoung	*LA*	**517**	17°05'N	104°50'E
Ban Xebang-Nouan	*LA*	**517**	16°00'N	105°29'E
Banyak, Kep.		**478**	2°10'N	97°15'E
Banyo	*CM*	**280**	6°45'N	11°49'E
Banyoles	*SP*	**618**	42°07'N	2°46'E
Ban Yong Sata	*TH*	**534**	7°08'N	99°41'E
Banyuwangi	*ID*	**500**	8°12'S	114°21'E
Banz	*PP*	**664**	5°48'S	144°37'E
Banza-Dounga	*CF*	**285**	4°31'S	15°02'E
Banzart, Buhayrat	*TS*	**329**	37°11'N	9°52'E
Banzyville, Collines de	*CG*	**287**	1°40'N	18°50'E
Baode	*CH*	**490**	39°00'N	111°04'E
Baoding	*CH*	**490**	38°51'N	115°23'E
Bao Ha	*VM*	**540**	22°10'N	104°20'E
Baoji	*CH*	**490**	34°22'N	107°09'E
Bao Lac	*VM*	**540**	22°56'N	105°39'E
Baolin		**474**	45°05'N	130°00'E
Baoro	*CT*	**282**	5°42'N	15°56'E
Baoshan	*CH*	**490**	25°06'N	99°09'E
Baotian		**476**	25°25'N	104°41'E
Baotou	*CH*	**490**	40°36'N	110°02'E
Baoulé	*ML*	**307**	12°36'N	6°34'W
Bapeng Godo	*ID*	**500**	1°49'S	124°46'E
Bāqa el Gharbiyya	*IS*	**505**	32°25'N	35°03'E
Baqên	*CH*	**490**	32°04'N	93°35'E
Ba'qūbah	*IZ*	**504**	33°45'N	44°38'E
Baquerizo Moreno	*EC*	**432**	1°54'S	79°33'W
Bar	*UP*	**624**	49°04'N	27°40'E
Bar	*YO*	**630**	42°05'N	19°06'E
Ba Ra	*VM*	**540**	11°49'N	106°57'E
Bara	*ID*	**500**	3°10'S	126°14'E
Bara	*NI*	**316**	10°22'N	10°44'E
Baraawe	*SO*	**321**	1°05'N	44°00'E
Barabai	*ID*	**500**	2°35'S	115°23'E
Barabinsk	*RS*	**612**	55°21'N	78°21'E
Baraboo		**370**	43°28'N	89°44'W
Baracoa	*CU*	**406**	20°21'N	74°30'W
Baracoa, Cuchillas de	*CU*	**406**	20°20'N	74°50'W
Baradères	*HA*	**412**	18°29'N	73°39'W
Baragoi	*KE*	**299**	1°47'N	36°47'E
Baragua	*VE*	**440**	10°35'N	69°56'W
Baraguá	*CU*	**406**	21°41'N	78°38'W
Bārah	*SU*	**324**	13°42'N	30°22'E
Barahona	*DR*	**408**	18°12'N	71°06'W
Barail Range	*IN*	**496**	25°09'N	93°09'E
Barajevo	*YO*	**630**	44°35'N	20°27'E
Barak	*IN*	**496**	24°52'N	92°30'E
Baraka	*CG*	**287**	4°05'S	29°04'E
Baraka	*ER*	**292**	18°13'N	37°35'E
Barakah	*SU*	**324**	10°58'N	27°59'E
Barakaldo	*SP*	**618**	43°19'N	3°00'W
Barakī Barak	*AF*	**480**	33°58'N	68°58'E
Baralaba	*AS*	**656**	24°11'S	149°49'E
Baram	*MY*	**518**	4°36'N	113°59'E
Baram, Tanjung	*MY*	**518**	4°36'N	113°58'E
Baramanni	*GY*	**434**	7°50'N	59°13'W
Bārāmati	*IN*	**496**	18°09'N	74°35'E
Baramita	*GY*	**434**	7°21'N	60°29'W
Bāran	*IN*	**496**	25°06'N	76°31'E
Baran'	*BO*	**569**	54°28'N	30°19'E
Baran, Kuh-e-	*IR*	**502**	32°02'N	60°12'E
Baranavichy	*BO*	**569**	53°08'N	26°02'E
Barang, Dasht-i-	*AF*	**480**	32°10'N	61°50'E
Baranga	*CG*	**287**	3°20'N	26°57'E
Baranikha	*RS*	**612**	68°31'N	168°15'E
Baranoa	*CO*	**430**	10°48'N	74°55'W
Baranof	*US*	**398**	56°28'N	136°23'W
Baranof I.		**368**	56°45'N	135°10'W
Baranovka	*UP*	**624**	50°18'N	27°40'E
Barão de Melgaço		**386**	16°13'S	55°58'W
Baraolt	*RO*	**610**	46°05'N	25°36'E
Baras	*RP*	**526**	13°40'N	124°22'E
Barat Daya		**648**	7°22'S	127°22'E
Barat Daya, Kep.	*ID*	**500**	7°25'S	128°00'E
Baratier	*CF*	**285**	4°09'S	14°54'E
Barauna	*BR*	**424**	5°07'S	37°38'W
Baraya	*CO*	**430**	3°10'N	75°04'W
Barbacena	*BR*	**424**	21°13'S	43°43'W
Barbacoas	*CO*	**430**	1°41'N	78°09'W
Barbacoas	*VE*	**440**	9°29'N	66°58'W
Barbados		**38**	13°10'N	59°32'W
Barbar	*SU*	**324**	18°01'N	33°59'E
Barbas, Cabo		**262**	22°17'N	16°39'W
Barbasco	*VE*	**440**	9°04'N	68°08'W
Barbastro	*SP*	**618**	42°02'N	0°08'E
Barbate	*SP*	**618**	36°12'N	5°55'W
Barberena	*GT*	**411**	14°18'N	90°22'W
Barberton	*SF*	**322**	25°47'S	31°03'E
Barbezieux-St-Hilaire	*FR*	**580**	45°28'N	0°09'W
Barbil	*IN*	**496**	22°06'N	85°20'E
Barbosa	*CO*	**430**	5°57'N	73°37'W
Barbuda	*AC*	**402**	17°41'N	61°44'W
Barcaldine	*AS*	**656**	23°34'S	145°17'E
Barcarrota	*SP*	**618**	38°31'N	6°51'W
Barcelona	*SP*	**618**	41°23'N	2°11'E
Barcelona	*VE*	**440**	10°08'N	64°42'W
Barcelos	*BR*	**424**	0°58'S	62°57'W
Barcoo	*AS*	**656**	25°30'S	142°50'E
Barcs	*HU*	**590**	45°58'N	17°28'E
Barczewo	*PL*	**606**	53°50'N	20°42'E
Barda	*AJ*	**483**	40°24'N	47°10'E
Bardagué, En.	*CD*	**283**	22°06'N	16°28'E
Bardai	*CD*	**283**	21°21'N	16°59'E
Bardas Blancas	*AR*	**419**	35°52'S	69°48'W
Bardejov	*LO*	**616**	49°17'N	21°17'E
Bardeskan	*IR*	**502**	35°12'N	57°58'E
Barcheere	*SO*	**321**	2°20'N	42°17'E
Barcidzor	*AM*	**482**	40°49'N	45°06'E
Bardīyah	*LY*	**302**	31°44'N	25°04'E
Bardonecchia	*IT*	**593**	45°05'N	6°42'E
Bareeda	*SO*	**321**	11°51'N	51°03'E
Bareilly	*IN*	**496**	28°21'N	79°25'E
Barellan		**652**	34°17'S	146°35'E
Barentin		**558**	49°33'N	0°57'E
Barents Sea		**556**	74°00'N	36°00'E
Barentu	*ER*	**292**	15°07'N	37°36'E
Barec	*MY*	**518**	3°45'N	115°27'E
Barfleur, Pointe de	*FR*	**580**	49°41'N	1°15'W
Barga	*CH*	**490**	30°51'N	81°18'E
Bargara		**652**	24°49'S	152°28'E
Bargarh	*IN*	**496**	21°20'N	83°37'E
Barg-e Matāl	*AF*	**480**	35°40'N	71°21'E
Barghanak	*AF*	**480**	33°56'N	62°26'E
Bargi		**470**	22°59'N	79°52'E
Bārguna	*BG*	**485**	22°09'N	90°07'E
Barguzin		**468**	53°27'N	109°00'E
Barguzinskiy Khrebet		**468**	55°00'N	110°30'E
Barhamjia	*NP*	**522**	26°35'N	86°54'E
Bar Harbor		**374**	44°23'N	68°13'W
Barhau	*ID*	**500**	5°19'S	102°10'E
Bāri	*IN*	**496**	26°39'N	77°36'E
Bari	*IT*	**593**	41°07'N	16°52'E
Bariadi	*TZ*	**327**	2°48'S	33°59'E
Barič	*YO*	**630**	44°38'N	20°16'E
Baricho	*KE*	**299**	3°06'S	39°47'E
Barid, Ra's	*SA*	**528**	24°17'N	37°31'E
Barī Gāv	*AF*	**480**	33°52'N	67°49'E
Barika	*AG*	**272**	35°23'N	5°22'E
Barikiwa	*TZ*	**327**	9°30'S	37°54'E
Barīkowţ	*AF*	**480**	35°18'N	71°32'E
Barillas	*GT*	**411**	15°48'N	91°18'W
Barima	*VE*	**440**	8°35'N	60°25'W
Barima, Punta	*VE*	**440**	8°36'N	60°25'W
Barinas	*VE*	**440**	8°38'N	70°12'W
Baringa	*CG*	**287**	0°58'S	21°38'E
Baringa	*CG*	**287**	0°56'N	22°07'E
Baringa-Twana	*CG*	**287**	6°17'S	16°55'E
Baringo, Lake	*KE*	**299**	0°38'N	36°05'E
Barinitas	*VE*	**440**	8°45'N	70°25'W
Baripāda	*IN*	**496**	21°56'N	86°43'E
Bārīs	*EG*	**290**	24°40'N	30°36'E
Barisah, Pegunungan		**478**	3°00'S	102°15'E
Barisakho	*GG*	**495**	42°28'N	44°55'E
Barisāl	*BG*	**485**	22°42'N	90°22'E
Barisan, Pegunungan	*ID*	**500**	3°00'S	102°15'E
Barisan Brassey	*MY*	**518**	4°54'N	117°30'E
Barisan Crocker	*BX*	**486**	5°40'N	116°20'E
Barito		**648**	1°00'S	115°00'E
Barito	*ID*	**500**	3°32'S	114°29'E
Barkava	*LG*	**596**	56°43'N	26°36'E
Barker	*AR*	**419**	37°38'S	59°24'W
Barkéwol el Abiod	*MR*	**308**	16°39'N	12°30'W
Bārkhān	*PK*	**524**	29°54'N	69°31'E
Barkley Lake		**374**	36°40'N	87°55'W
Barkly East	*SF*	**322**	30°58'S	27°36'E
Barkly Tableland	*AS*	**656**	18°00'S	136°30'E
Barkly West	*SF*	**322**	28°32'S	24°32'E
Barkol	*CH*	**490**	43°34'N	92°50'E
Bark Pt.		**374**	46°52'N	91°11'W
Barlavento, Ilhas de (Windward Islands)	*CV*	**281**	16°35'N	24°20'W
Bar-le-Duc	*FR*	**580**	48°47'N	5°10'E
Barlee, Lake	*AS*	**656**	29°10'S	119°30'E
Barlee Range	*AS*	**656**	24°00'S	115°40'E
Barletta	*IT*	**593**	41°19'N	16°17'E
Barling		**378**	35°19'N	94°18'W
Barmer	*IN*	**496**	25°45'N	71°23'E
Barmera		**652**	34°15'S	140°28'E
Barmouth		**558**	52°43'N	4°02'W
Barnaul	*RS*	**612**	53°22'N	83°45'E
Barnesville		**372**	46°39'N	96°25'W
Barnesville		**378**	33°03'N	84°09'W
Barnsdall		**376**	36°33'N	96°09'W
Barnsley	*UK*	**626**	53°33'N	1°29'W
Barnstaple	*UK*	**626**	51°06'N	4°27'W
Barnstaple Bay	*UK*	**626**	51°05'N	4°25'W
Barnwell		**378**	33°14'N	81°21'W
Baro		**268**	8°23'N	33°11'E
Baro	*GV*	**297**	10°37'N	9°42'W
Baro	*NI*	**316**	8°34'N	6°28'E
Baroda	*IN*	**496**	22°18'N	73°12'E
Barogal	*UG*	**330**	2°37'N	32°20'E
Baroghil Pass	*AF*	**480**	36°53'N	73°20'E
Barong	*CH*	**490**	31°03'N	99°19'E
Baron's Range	*AS*	**656**	23°15'S	128°00'E
Baroua	*CT*	**282**	5°35'N	24°43'E
Barqah (Cyrenaica)	*LY*	**302**	31°00'N	22°30'E
Barqin	*LY*	**302**	27°31'N	13°44'E
Barquisimeto	*VE*	**440**	10°04'N	69°19'W
Barr	*UK*	**626**	55°12'N	4°42'W
Barr, Ra's al	*BA*	**484**	25°47'N	50°34'E
Barra		**384**	11°05'S	43°10'W
Barra	*UK*	**626**	11°05'S	43°10'W
Barra, Ponta da	*MZ*	**312**	23°48'S	35°31'E
Barraca Bolanha	*PU*	**298**	12°27'N	16°14'W
Barra da Choça	*BR*	**424**	14°51'S	40°35'W
Barra de Caratasca	*HO*	**412**	15°22'N	83°44'W
Barra do Bugres	*BR*	**424**	15°04'S	57°11'W
Barra do Corda	*BR*	**424**	5°27'S	45°08'W
Barra do Cuanza	*AO*	**274**	9°18'S	13°08'E
Barra do Dande	*AO*	**274**	8°29'S	13°22'E
Barra do Garças	*BR*	**424**	15°55'S	52°15'W
Barra Falsa, Ponta da	*MZ*	**312**	22°54'S	35°36'E
Barrage de Buyo	*IV*	**288**	6°15'N	7°02'W
Barr al Hikman	*MU*	**523**	20°30'N	58°23'E
Barranca	*CS*	**405**	9°59'N	84°43'W
Barranca	*PE*	**436**	4°50'S	76°42'W
Barranca	*PE*	**436**	10°45'S	77°46'W
Barrancabermeja	*CO*	**430**	7°03'N	73°52'W
Barrancas	*AR*	**419**	36°49'S	69°55'W
Barrancas	*BL*	**422**	22°10'S	67°25'W
Barrancas	*CI*	**428**	33°27'S	70°46'W
Barrancas	*CO*	**430**	10°57'N	72°50'W
Barrancas	*VE*	**440**	8°43'N	62°11'W
Barrancas	*VE*	**440**	8°46'N	70°06'W
Barranco	*BH*	**404**	16°00'N	88°54'W
Barranco de Loba	*CO*	**430**	8°57'N	74°07'W
Barranco Minas	*CO*	**430**	3°31'N	69°49'W
Barrancos	*PO*	**608**	38°08'N	7°01'W
Barranquilla	*CO*	**430**	10°59'N	74°48'W
Barranquitas	*VE*	**440**	9°59'N	72°02'W
Barraoltului, Munții	*RO*	**610**	46°00'N	25°55'E
Barra Patuca	*HO*	**412**	15°48'N	84°17'W
Barra Punta Gorda	*NU*	**415**	11°31'N	83°47'W
Barras	*CO*	**430**	1°45'N	73°13'W
Barr. de Santa Clara	*PO*	**608**	37°30'N	8°30'W
Barre	*US*	**398**	44°11'N	72°30'W
Barreiras	*BR*	**424**	12°08'S	45°00'W
Barreirinha		**384**	2°47'S	57°03'W
Barren, Cape		**652**	40°24'S	148°29'E
Barren I., Cape	*AS*	**656**	40°25'S	148°12'E
Barretal	*MX*	**394**	24°05'N	99°07'W
Barretos	*BR*	**424**	20°33'S	48°33'W
Barrhill	*UK*	**626**	55°06'N	4°46'W
Barrie		**374**	44°24'N	79°40'W
Barrière		**372**	51°11'N	120°07'W
Barril	*CV*	**281**	16°35'N	24°30'W
Barringun	*AS*	**656**	29°01'S	145°43'E
Barron		**374**	45°24'N	91°50'W
Barros Luco	*CI*	**428**	27°39'S	70°33'W
Barrouallie	*VC*	**418**	13°14'N	61°16'W
Barrow	*AS*	**656**	20°51'S	114°46'E
Barrow	*EI*	**592**	52°14'N	6°58'W
Barrow	*US*	**398**	71°17'N	156°47'W
Barrow, Pt.	*US*	**398**	71°23'N	156°26'W
Barrow Creek	*AS*	**656**	21°33'S	133°53'E
Barrow-in-Furness	*UK*	**626**	54°07'N	3°14'W
Barrow Pt.	*AS*	**656**	14°21'S	144°37'E
Barry	*UK*	**626**	51°23'N	3°17'W
Barrydale	*SF*	**322**	33°54'S	20°43'E
Barrytown	*NZ*	**663**	42°14'S	171°19'E
Barsakelmes, Ozero	*UZ*	**539**	45°38'N	60°00'E
Barsalogho	*UV*	**278**	13°25'N	1°03'W
Bārshi	*IN*	**496**	18°14'N	75°42'E
Barsinghausen	*GM*	**584**	52°18'N	9°27'E
Barskoon	*KG*	**514**	42°10'N	77°37'E
Barstow		**376**	34°53'N	117°01'W
Bar-sur-Aube	*FR*	**580**	48°14'N	4°43'E
Bartang	*TI*	**533**	37°56'N	71°34'E
Bartaz	*AJ*	**483**	38°59'N	46°35'E
Barth	*GM*	**584**	54°22'N	12°44'E
Bartica	*GY*	**434**	6°24'N	58°37'W
Bartın	*TU*	**535**	41°38'N	32°21'E
Bartlesville	*US*	**398**	36°44'N	95°58'W
Bartolomé Masó	*CU*	**406**	20°10'N	76°57'W
Bartolomeu Dias	*MZ*	**312**	21°13'S	35°07'E
Bartoszyce	*PL*	**606**	54°12'N	20°46'E
Bartoua	*CT*	**282**	6°10'N	14°40'E
Bartow	*GM*	**584**	53°49'N	13°21'E
Barú, Volcán	*PM*	**417**	8°48'N	82°33'W
Barumun	*ID*	**500**	2°30'N	100°09'E
Barun	*CH*	**490**	36°09'N	97°19'E
Barus	*ID*	**500**	2°02'N	98°24'E
Baruunbüren	*MG*	**520**	49°16'N	104°44'E
Baruunsuu	*MG*	**520**	43°43'N	105°35'E
Baruunturuun	*MG*	**520**	49°43'N	94°25'E
Baruun-Urt	*MG*	**520**	46°42'N	113°15'E
Barwaaqo	*SO*	**321**	0°28'N	42°44'E
Barwāni	*IN*	**496**	22°02'N	74°54'E
Barwick		**374**	48°39'N	93°59'W
Barwon	*AS*	**656**	30°00'S	148°05'E
Barysaw	*BO*	**569**	54°15'N	28°30'E
Barysh		**560**	53°38'N	47°07'E
Baryshevka	*UP*	**624**	50°22'N	31°20'E
Basa	*IV*	**288**	4°38'N	6°55'W
Basankusu	*CG*	**287**	1°11'N	19°50'E
Basavilbaso	*AR*	**419**	32°22'S	58°53'W
Basawa	*IV*	**288**	8°03'N	4°06'W
Basay	*RP*	**526**	9°25'N	122°38'E
Bascharage	*LU*	**598**	49°34'N	5°55'E
Basco		**476**	20°27'N	121°58'E
Bascuñán, Cabo	*CI*	**428**	28°51'S	71°29'W
Basekpio	*CG*	**287**	4°44'N	24°40'E
Basel	*SZ*	**622**	47°33'N	7°35'E
Bashakerd, Kuhha-ye	*IR*	**502**	26°42'N	58°35'E
Bashansi		**472**	30°18'N	107°42'E
Bashi Channel	*RP*	**526**	21°25'N	121°30'E
Bashkend	*AM*	**482**	40°39'N	45°32'E
Bashmakovo		**560**	53°12'N	43°02'E
Bashtanka	*UP*	**624**	47°24'N	32°27'E
Ba'shūm	*SU*	**324**	13°26'N	31°18'E
Basilan	*RP*	**526**	6°23'N	120°08'E
Basilan Peak	*RP*	**526**	6°33'N	122°04'E
Basilan Strait	*RP*	**526**	6°49'N	122°05'E
Basildon		**558**	51°34'N	0°28'E
Basin		**372**	44°22'N	108°02'W
Basingstoke	*UK*	**626**	51°16'N	1°05'W
Basit, Ra's al	*SY*	**531**	35°51'N	35°48'E
Baška	*HR*	**574**	44°58'N	14°44'E
Başkale	*TU*	**535**	38°03'N	44°01'E
Baskatong, Rés.		**370**	46°47'N	75°50'W
Baskil	*TU*	**535**	38°34'N	38°50'E
Başmakçı		**564**	37°54'N	30°01'E
Bāsoda	*IN*	**496**	23°51'N	77°56'E
Basodesh	*TZ*	**327**	4°18'S	35°08'E
Basoko	*CG*	**287**	1°14'N	23°36'E
Bassano del Grappa	*IT*	**593**	45°46'N	11°44'E
Bassari	*TO*	**328**	9°16'N	0°46'E
Bassas da India	*FR*	**40**	21°25'S	38°52'E
Bassein	*BM*	**487**	15°56'N	94°18'E
Bassein	*BM*	**487**	16°47'N	94°44'E
Basse Terre	*TD*	**438**	10°08'N	61°18'W
Basse-Terre		**382**	16°00'N	61°43'W
Basse-Terre		**382**	16°19'N	62°25'W
Basseterre	*SC*	**417**	17°18'N	62°43'W
Bassikounou	*MR*	**308**	15°52'N	5°57'W
Basso, Plateau de	*CD*	**283**	16°10'N	22°00'E
Bass Strait	*AS*	**656**	39°20'S	145°30'E
Bassum	*GM*	**584**	52°51'N	8°44'E
Båstad	*SW*	**621**	56°26'N	12°51'E
Bastak	*IR*	**502**	27°14'N	54°22'E
Bastelicaccia	*FR*	**580**	41°55'N	8°49'E
Bastī	*IN*	**496**	26°48'N	82°43'E
Bastia		**562**	43°04'N	12°34'E
Bastia	*FR*	**580**	42°42'N	9°27'E
Bastogne	*BE*	**570**	50°00'N	5°43'E
Bastrop		**376**	30°06'N	97°19'W
Bastrop		**378**	32°46'N	91°54'W
Bastuträsk	*SW*	**621**	64°46'N	20°00'E
Basuo	*CH*	**490**	19°06'N	108°36'E
Bata	*EK*	**291**	1°50'N	9°45'E
Batabanó, Golfo de	*CU*	**406**	22°15'N	82°30'W
Batac	*RP*	**526**	18°05'N	120°35'E
Batagay	*RS*	**612**	67°38'N	134°38'E
Batagay-Alyta	*RS*	**612**	67°48'N	130°25'E
Batahirah	*MU*	**523**	18°00'N	55°30'E
Batak	*BU*	**573**	41°57'N	24°13'E
Bataka	*DO*	**407**	15°30'N	61°16'W
Batakan		**478**	4°05'S	114°38'E
Batāla	*IN*	**496**	31°48'N	75°12'E
Batama	*CG*	**287**	0°56'N	26°39'E
Batan	*RP*	**526**	20°18'N	122°14'E
Batang	*CH*	**490**	30°00'N	99°09'E
Batangafo	*CT*	**282**	7°18'N	18°18'E
Batangan, Mui	*VM*	**540**	15°15'N	108°30'E
Batangas	*RP*	**526**	13°45'N	121°03'E
Batanghari	*ID*	**500**	4°53'S	105°36'E
Batan Islands	*RP*	**526**	20°18'N	122°14'E
Batanta	*ID*	**500**	0°50'S	130°40'E
Batanta, Gunung	*ID*	**500**	0°53'S	130°36'E
Batarasa	*RP*	**526**	8°40'N	117°38'E
Bata-Siala	*CG*	**287**	4°59'S	13°14'E
Bátaszék	*HU*	**590**	46°12'N	18°43'E
Bataysk		**560**	47°08'N	39°44'E
Batchelor	*AS*	**656**	13°04'S	131°01'E
Batchwana Bay		**374**	46°53'N	84°30'W
Batdambang	*CB*	**489**	13°06'N	103°12'E
Batéké Plateau	*CF*	**285**	3°30'S	15°45'E
Batemans Bay	*AS*	**656**	35°45'S	150°11'E
Batesburg-Leesville		**378**	33°54'N	81°32'W
Batesville		**376**	28°57'N	99°37'W
Batesville		**378**	34°18'N	89°56'W
Batesville		**378**	35°46'N	91°38'W
Batetskiy		**560**	58°39'N	30°19'E

Berezina	BO	569	51°32'N	25°49'E
Berezino	BO	569	53°51'N	29°00'E
Bereznik		556	62°52'N	42°43'E
Berezniki	RS	612	59°24'N	56°46'E
Berezovka		466	56°38'N	95°37'E
Berezovka	UP	624	47°12'N	30°55'E
Berëzovka	BO	569	53°01'N	25°46'E
Berezovo	RS	612	63°56'N	65°02'E
Berezovyy	RS	612	53°04'N	133°33'E
Berg	LU	598	49°49'N	6°05'E
Berg	NO	604	69°28'N	17°13'E
Berg	SZ	622	47°35'N	9°10'E
Berga	SP	618	42°06'N	1°51'E
Bergama	TU	535	39°07'N	27°11'E
Bergamo	IT	593	45°41'N	9°40'E
Bergen	GM	584	52°49'N	9°58'E
Bergen	GM	584	54°25'N	13°26'E
Bergen	NO	604	60°23'N	5°20'E
Berg en Dal	NS	438	5°09'N	55°04'W
Bergen op Zoom	NL	602	51°30'N	4°18'E
Bergerac	FR	580	44°51'N	0°29'E
Bergisch Gladbach	GM	584	50°59'N	7°09'E
Bergsjö	SW	621	61°59'N	17°04'E
Berguent	MO	310	34°01'N	2°01'W
Bergviken	SW	621	61°09'N	16°35'E
Bergville	SF	322	28°44'S	29°22'E
Berh	MG	520	47°45'N	111°07'E
Berhala, Selat	ID	500	0°48'S	104°25'E
Berhampore	IN	496	24°06'N	88°15'E
Berhampur	IN	496	19°19'N	84°47'E
Berhida	HU	590	47°07'N	18°08'E
Beringovskiy	RS	612	63°04'N	179°18'E
Bering Sea	RS	612	60°00'N	175°00'W
Bering Strait	RS	612	66°00'N	169°00'W
Berislav	UP	624	46°51'N	33°26'E
Beritarikap, Tanjung	ID	500	3°21'S	100°28'E
Berja	SP	618	36°51'N	2°57'W
Berkåk	NO	604	62°49'N	10°03'E
Berkakit	RS	612	56°34'N	124°48'E
Berkane	MO	310	34°56'N	2°20'W
Berkel	NL	602	51°59'N	4°29'E
Berkeley	US	398	37°52'N	122°16'W
Berkovitsa	BU	573	43°14'N	23°07'E
Berlevåg	NO	604	70°51'N	29°06'E
Berlin		370	44°28'N	71°11'W
Berlin		374	39°55'N	78°57'W
Berlin		374	43°58'N	88°56'W
Berlin	GM	584	52°31'N	13°24'E
Berlín	ES	409	13°30'N	88°32'W
Bermejillo	MX	394	25°53'N	103°37'W
Bermejo	AR	419	28°24'S	69°29'W
Bermejo, Paso del	CI	428	32°50'S	70°05'W
Bermeo		562	43°26'N	2°43'W
Bermuda	UK	40	33°06'N	65°17'W
Bern	SZ	622	46°57'N	7°26'E
Bernabé Rivera	UY	439	30°18'S	56°58'W
Bernal	PE	436	5°27'S	80°45'W
Bernalda	IT	593	40°24'N	16°41'E
Bernalillo	US	398	35°18'N	106°33'W
Bernard House	CA	390	66°30'N	133°04'W
Bernay	FR	580	49°06'N	0°36'E
Bernburg	GM	584	51°43'N	11°44'E
Berner Alpen	SZ	622	46°25'N	7°45'E
Bernier	AS	656	24°53'S	112°39'E
Bernier, C.	AS	656	13°57'S	127°25'E
Bernier Bay	CA	390	71°08'N	88°00'W
Bernina Pass	SZ	622	46°25'N	10°02'E
Bernissart	BE	570	50°28'N	3°39'E
Bernolákovo	LO	616	48°12'N	17°19'E
Beronono	MA	304	20°54'S	45°04'E
Beroroha	MA	304	21°41'S	45°10'E
Beroun	EZ	575	49°57'N	14°04'E
Berounka	EZ	575	50°00'N	14°24'E
Berovo	MK	599	41°43'N	22°51'E
Berrechid	MO	310	33°16'N	7°35'W
Berriane	AG	272	32°50'N	3°46'E
Berriedale	UK	626	58°11'N	3°29'W
Berrouaghia	AG	272	36°08'N	2°55'E
Berry		378	25°37'N	78°32'W
Berryessa, L.		376	38°31'N	122°06'W
Berry Is.	BF	402	25°34'N	77°45'W
Berryville		374	36°21'N	93°34'W
Berseba	WA	313	25°59'S	17°47'E
Bershad'	UP	624	48°22'N	29°31'E
Bertam	MY	518	5°09'N	102°03'E
Bertolínia		384	7°38'S	43°57'W
Bertoua	CM	280	4°35'N	13°41'E
Bertrand, Cerro	AR	419	49°58'S	73°32'W
Bertrix		558	49°51'N	5°15'E
Beru	KR	660	1°10'S	176°00'E
Beruit	MY	518	2°30'N	111°30'E
Beruwala	CE	530	6°29'N	79°59'E
Berwick		374	41°03'N	76°14'W
Berwick-upon-Tweed	UK	626	55°47'N	2°00'W
Berzence	HU	590	46°12'N	17°09'E
Besalampy	MA	304	16°45'S	44°30'E
Besançon	FR	580	47°15'N	6°02'E
Bésao	CD	283	7°53'N	15°59'E
Besar, Gunung	ID	500	2°30'N	103°10'E
Besedino		560	51°42'N	36°28'E
Beserah	MY	518	3°52'N	103°22'E
Beshām Qala	PK	524	34°56'N	72°52'E
Beshenkovichi	BO	569	55°03'N	29°27'E
Beshkent	UZ	539	38°49'N	65°39'E
Beshlo Wenz	ET	293	11°02'N	38°29'E
Beshneh	IR	502	29°23'N	54°50'E
Beška	YO	630	45°07'N	20°04'E
Beskidy Wschodnie	PL	606	49°30'N	23°00'E
Beskidy Zachodnie	PL	606	49°40'N	21°00'E
Beskol'	KZ	510	46°13'N	81°02'E
Beslan		466	43°12'N	44°30'E
Bessarabka	MD	601	46°20'N	28°53'E
Bessarabskaya Vozvyshennost	MD	601	47°00'N	28°30'E
Bessemer		378	33°24'N	86°57'W
Bessemer	US	398	46°28'N	90°03'W
Best	NL	602	51°30'N	5°24'E
Bestamak	KZ	510	49°43'N	55°04'E
Bestobe	KZ	510	52°30'N	73°05'E
Bestuzhevo		556	61°37'N	43°58'E
Bestyakh	RS	612	61°24'N	128°50'E
Beswick	AS	656	14°35'S	133°10'E
Betafo	MA	304	19°50'S	46°51'E
Betanantanana	MA	304	18°11'S	44°09'E
Betancuría	SP	618	28°25'N	14°03'W
Betanty	MA	304	25°33'S	45°32'E
Betanzos	BL	422	19°34'S	65°27'W
Bétaré-Oya	CM	280	5°36'N	14°05'E
Bete	AO	274	11°55'S	17°42'E
Bete Hor	ET	293	11°37'N	39°02'E
Bétérou	BN	276	9°12'N	2°16'E
Beth, Oued	MO	310	34°25'N	6°26'W
Bethal	SF	322	26°26'S	29°28'E
Bethanie	WA	313	26°29'S	17°09'E
Bethany		374	40°16'N	94°01'W
Bethany		376	35°31'N	97°37'W
Bethel	US	398	60°47'N	161°45'W
Bethel Town	JM	414	18°18'N	77°57'W
Bethesda		374	38°58'N	77°06'W
Bethlehem		374	40°37'N	75°23'W
Bethlehem	SF	322	28°14'S	28°18'E
Bethulie	SF	322	30°30'S	25°58'E
Betim	BR	424	19°58'S	44°13'W
Betioky	MA	304	23°42'S	44°22'E
Betoota	AS	656	25°42'S	140°44'E
Betroka	MA	304	23°16'S	46°06'E
Bet She'an	IS	505	32°30'N	35°30'E
Betsiboka	MA	304	16°03'S	46°36'E
Betsimibaraka Escarpment	MA	304	18°00'S	49°10'E
Bettembourg	LU	598	49°31'N	6°06'E
Bettiah	IN	496	26°48'N	84°30'E
Bettyhill	UK	626	58°31'N	4°13'W
Betūl	IN	496	21°55'N	77°54'E
Betwa	IN	496	25°55'N	80°12'E
Béu	AO	274	6°14'S	15°28'E
Beulah	US	398	47°15'N	101°46'W
Beuningen	NL	602	51°51'N	5°46'E
Bevensen	GM	584	53°05'N	10°35'E
Beveridge Reef		650	20°00'S	168°00'W
Beverley	UK	626	53°50'N	0°25'W
Beverly	CS	405	9°56'N	83°02'W
Beverly Hills		378	28°54'N	82°28'W
Beverly L.		368	64°35'N	100°30'W
Bewani Mts.	PP	664	3°30'S	141°50'E
Bewār	IN	496	25°45'N	79°56'E
Bex	SZ	622	46°15'N	7°01'E
Bexon	ST	418	13°57'N	60°58'W
Bextograk	CH	490	38°30'N	86°58'E
Bey Dag.	TU	535	39°15'N	30°30'E
Bey Daglari	TU	535	36°40'N	30°15'E
Beyla	GV	297	8°41'N	8°38'W
Beylikova		564	39°42'N	31°13'E
Bēylul	ER	292	13°16'N	42°20'E
Beyneu	KZ	510	45°18'N	55°15'E
Beypazarı	TU	535	40°10'N	31°56'E
Beyra	SO	321	6°57'N	47°19'E
Beyşehir	TU	535	37°41'N	31°43'E
Beysehir Gölü	TU	535	37°40'N	31°30'E
Beytalkariim	SO	321	2°16'N	45°14'E
Bezaha	MA	304	23°30'S	44°31'E
Bezdan	YO	630	45°51'N	18°56'E
Bezhetsk	RS	612	57°47'N	36°42'E
Béziers	FR	580	43°20'N	3°12'E
Bhadrāchalam		470	17°40'N	80°53'E
Bhadrak	IN	496	21°04'N	86°30'E
Bhadrapur	NP	522	26°33'N	88°05'E
Bhadrāvati	IN	496	13°52'N	75°43'E
Bhadreswar	IN	496	22°55'N	69°54'E
Bhāg	PK	524	29°02'N	67°49'E
Bhāgalpur	IN	496	25°15'N	87°00'E
Bhāi Pheru	PK	524	31°12'N	73°57'E
Bhairab	BG	485	22°51'N	89°34'E
Bhairab Bāzār	BG	485	24°04'N	90°58'E
Bhairahawa	NP	522	27°33'N	83°27'E
Bhaironghāti		470	31°01'N	78°53'E
Bhakkar	PK	524	31°38'N	71°04'E
Bhaktapur	NP	522	27°43'N	85°27'E
Bhāluka	BG	485	24°24'N	90°24'E
Bhalwāl	PK	524	32°16'N	72°54'E
Bhamo	BM	487	24°16'N	97°14'E
Bhanrer Range	IN	496	23°48'N	80°12'E
Bhānwad	IN	496	21°56'N	69°47'E
Bhārātpur	IN	496	27°08'N	77°27'E
Bharatpur	NP	522	27°42'N	84°25'E
Bharuch	IN	496	21°42'N	72°58'E
Bhātāpāra	IN	496	21°44'N	81°56'E
Bhātiāpāra Ghāt	BG	485	23°13'N	89°42'E
Bhatinda	IN	496	30°12'N	74°57'E
Bhatkal	IN	496	13°58'N	74°34'E
Bhātpāra	IN	496	22°52'N	88°24'E
Bhavāni	IN	496	11°27'N	77°41'E
Bhavnagar	IN	496	21°46'N	72°09'E
Bhawāni Mandi		470	24°25'N	75°50'E
Bhawānipatna	IN	496	19°54'N	83°10'E
Bheramara	BG	485	24°02'N	88°58'E
Bhikna Thorī	NP	522	27°21'N	84°37'E
Bhilai	IN	496	21°13'N	81°26'E
Bhīlwāra	IN	496	25°21'N	74°38'E
Bhima	IN	496	16°25'N	77°17'E
Bhīmavaram	IN	496	16°32'N	81°32'E
Bhīmmāl	IN	496	25°00'N	72°15'E
Bhīmphedi	NP	522	27°32'N	85°07'E
Bhimunipatnam	IN	496	17°53'N	83°26'E
Bhind	IN	496	26°34'N	78°48'E
Bhiwandi	IN	496	19°18'N	73°04'E
Bhiwāni		470	28°47'N	76°08'E
Bhojpur	NP	522	27°10'N	87°03'E
Bhola	BG	485	22°04'N	89°49'E
Bhola	BG	485	22°40'N	90°33'E
Bhongweni	SF	322	30°33'S	29°26'E
Bhopāl	IN	496	23°16'N	77°24'E
Bhor	IN	496	18°10'N	73°51'E
Bhuban	IN	496	20°53'N	85°50'E
Bhubaneswar	IN	496	20°14'N	85°50'E
Bhūj	IN	496	23°16'N	69°40'E
Bhusawal	IN	496	21°03'N	75°46'E
Bhutan		38	27°30'N	90°30'E
Bia	IV	288	5°21'N	3°11'W
Bīābānak	AF	480	32°11'N	64°11'E
Biaboye	CG	287	0°22'N	28°43'E
Biafra, Baie de		266	3°20'N	9°20'E
Biafra, Bight of	EK	291	4°03'N	7°17'E
Biak	ID	500	1°00'S	136°00'E
Biak	ID	500	1°10'S	136°06'E
Biała Podlaska	PL	606	52°02'N	23°08'E
Białobrzegi	PL	606	51°39'N	20°57'E
Białogard	PL	606	54°00'N	16°00'E
Białystok	PL	606	53°08'N	23°09'E
Biami	CT	282	3°58'N	18°10'E
Bianga	CT	282	4°51'N	20°25'E
Biankouma	IV	288	7°44'N	7°37'W
Bianzhao		474	44°36'N	123°10'E
Biaro	CG	287	0°15'N	25°20'E
Biasca	SZ	622	46°21'N	8°57'E
Bibā	EG	290	28°55'N	30°59'E
Bibai	JA	506	43°19'N	141°52'E
Bibala	AO	274	14°46'S	13°21'E
Bibassé	GB	294	1°27'N	11°37'E
Bibémi	CM	280	9°19'N	13°53'E
Biberist	SZ	622	47°11'N	7°33'E
Bibiyana	BG	485	24°41'N	91°23'E
Biblián	EC	432	2°42'S	78°52'W
Bicaz	RO	610	46°55'N	26°04'E
Bicester	UK	626	51°54'N	1°09'W
Bichano	ET	293	7°53'N	35°32'E
Biche	TD	438	10°26'N	61°08'W
Bichena	ET	293	10°27'N	38°12'E
Bicheno	AS	656	41°53'S	148°18'E
Bichhia	IN	496	22°27'N	80°42'E
Bichi		468	52°10'N	139°00'E
Bichigt	MG	520	47°06'N	95°04'E
Bickerton	AS	656	13°36'S	136°06'E
Bicske	HU	590	47°29'N	18°38'E
Bida	NI	316	9°05'N	6°01'E
Bidadari, Tanjung	MY	518	5°49'N	118°21'E
Bīdar	IN	496	17°54'N	77°27'E
Bidasoa	SP	618	43°22'N	1°47'W
Biddeford	US	398	43°29'N	70°27'W
Bideford	UK	626	51°01'N	4°13'W
Bīdokht	IR	502	34°21'N	58°46'E
Bidor	MY	518	4°07'N	101°17'E
Bi Doup	VM	540	12°05'N	108°40'E
Bidrē	ET	293	5°55'N	39°38'E
Bie, Planalto do	AO	274	13°06'S	16°49'E
Biel	SZ	622	47°08'N	7°15'E
Bielawa	PL	606	50°41'N	16°37'E
Bielefeld	GM	584	52°02'N	8°32'E
Bieler See	SZ	622	47°05'N	7°09'E
Biella	IT	593	45°34'N	8°03'E
Bielsko-Biała	PL	606	49°49'N	19°02'E
Bielsk Podlaski	PL	606	52°46'N	23°12'E
Bienenbüttel	GM	584	53°08'N	10°29'E
Bien Hoa	VM	540	10°56'N	106°48'E
Bienvenue		384	3°07'N	52°42'W
Bienville, Lac	CA	390	55°05'N	72°40'W
Biescas	SP	618	42°37'N	0°18'E
Bièvre	BE	570	49°56'N	5°01'E
Bifoun	GB	294	0°20'S	10°23'E
Big		370	49°07'N	94°34'W
Biga	TU	535	40°13'N	27°14'E
Biga	TU	535	40°00'N	27°00'E
Bigadiç		564	39°23'N	28°08'E
Big Bar Creek		372	51°11'N	122°08'W
Big Bell		652	27°21'S	117°40'E
Big Belt Mts.		372	46°45'N	111°35'W
Big Bend	WZ	326	26°46'S	31°56'E
Big Black River	CA	390	53°10'N	97°25'W
Big Creek	CA	390	51°43'N	123°02'W
Big Cypress Swamp		378	26°12'N	81°36'W
Biger Nuur	MG	520	45°50'N	97°00'E
Bigfork		372	48°03'N	114°05'W
Biggar	CA	390	52°04'N	108°00'W
Bigge	AS	656	14°38'S	124°45'E
Big Hole		372	45°34'N	112°20'W
Bighorn	US	398	46°09'N	107°26'W
Big Horn Basin		372	44°15'N	108°15'W
Big Horn Mts.	US	398	43°00'N	107°00'W
Bigi	CG	287	3°02'N	22°25'E
Big Jerry Cay	BF	402	26°47'N	77°55'W
Big Lake	US	398	31°11'N	101°27'W
Big Lost		372	43°48'N	112°50'W
Bignona	SG	319	12°49'N	16°14'W
Bigosovo	BO	569	55°50'N	27°46'E
Big Pine	US	398	37°09'N	118°17'W
Big Pine Key	US	398	24°40'N	81°21'W
Big Rapids		374	43°41'N	85°29'W
Big Sable Pt.		374	44°03'N	86°31'W
Big Sandy		376	38°25'N	82°36'W
Bigsby		372	49°02'N	94°31'W
Big Sioux		372	42°29'N	96°27'W
Big Smoky Valley		376	38°40'N	117°08'W
Big Spring	US	398	32°15'N	101°28'W
Big Stone Gap		374	36°52'N	82°46'W
Big Timber	US	398	45°50'N	109°57'W
Big Trout Lake	CA	390	53°48'N	89°51'W
Biguglia	FR	580	42°37'N	9°25'E
Bigugo	BY	279	3°54'S	29°59'E
Bihać	BK	572	44°49'N	15°52'E
Bihalrwe	UG	330	0°31'S	30°43'E
Bīhar	IN	496	25°11'N	85°31'E
Biharamulo	TZ	327	2°41'S	31°04'E
Biharkeresztes	HU	590	47°08'N	21°43'E
Biharnagybajom	HU	590	47°13'N	21°14'E
Bihorel	FR	580	49°45'N	1°26'E
Bihoro	JA	506	43°46'N	144°11'E
Bijagós Archipelago	PU	298	11°15'N	16°05'W
Bij-Altay	MG	520	45°33'N	93°45'E
Bijāpur		470	18°48'N	80°48'E
Bijāpur	IN	496	16°50'N	75°42'E
Bījār	IR	502	35°52'N	47°36'E
Bijeljina	BK	572	44°45'N	19°13'E
Bijelo Polje	YO	630	43°02'N	19°45'E
Bijiang		472	26°33'N	98°56'E
Bijia Shan	CH	490	28°00'N	119°00'E
Bijie	CH	490	27°18'N	105°15'E
Bijnor	IN	496	29°25'N	78°16'E
Bīkaner	IN	496	28°01'N	73°18'E
Bikar	RM	661	12°10'N	170°05'E
Bikin	RS	612	46°48'N	134°16'E
Bikin	RS	612	46°50'N	134°02'E
Bikini	RM	661	11°50'N	165°10'E
Bikita	ZI	334	20°05'S	31°37'E
Bikori	SU	324	11°12'N	34°39'E
Bikoro	CG	287	0°45'S	18°07'E
Bilād Manaḩ	MU	523	22°47'N	57°36'E
Bilāra	IN	496	26°10'N	73°42'E
Bilāspur	IN	496	22°05'N	82°09'E
Bila Tserkva	UP	624	49°47'N	30°07'E
Bilauk Taungdan	TH	534	13°00'N	99°00'E
Bilauri	NP	522	28°40'N	80°20'E
Bilbao	SP	618	43°15'N	2°58'W
Bilbays	EG	290	30°25'N	31°34'E
Bileća	BK	572	42°53'N	18°23'E
Bilecik	TU	535	40°09'N	29°59'E
Bīleh Savār	IR	502	39°23'N	48°20'E
Bilé Karpaty	LO	616	48°50'N	17°50'E
Biłgoraj	PL	606	50°33'N	22°42'E
Bilhorod-Dnistrovs'kyy	UP	624	46°12'N	30°21'E
Bili	CG	287	4°09'N	25°10'E
Bilibino	RS	612	68°03'N	166°20'E
Bilila	MI	306	14°49'S	34°50'E
Bilin	BM	487	17°14'N	97°15'E
Bílina	EZ	575	50°32'N	13°46'E
Biliran	RP	526	11°42'N	124°08'E
Biliri	NI	316	9°52'N	11°13'E
Bilisht	AL	566	40°37'N	20°59'E
Bilis Qooqaani	SO	321	0°17'N	41°43'E
Bilit	MY	518	5°29'N	118°11'E
Biljanovce	MK	599	42°07'N	21°44'E
Billaouâr	MR	308	16°33'N	10°56'W
Billings	US	398	45°47'N	108°30'W
Billingsfors		558	58°59'N	12°15'E
Bill of Portland	UK	626	50°31'N	2°28'W
Billund	DA	576	55°44'N	9°07'E
Bilma	NG	314	18°41'N	12°56'E
Bīlo	ET	293	8°54'N	37°00'E
Bilo	GB	294	2°08'N	12°04'E
Biloela	AS	656	24°25'S	150°30'E
Bilogora	HR	574	46°06'N	16°46'E
Biloku	GY	434	1°46'N	58°33'W
Biloxi	US	398	30°23'N	88°52'W
Bilqas Qism Awwal	EG	290	31°13'N	31°21'E
Biltine	CD	283	14°32'N	20°55'E
Bilüü	MG	520	49°02'N	89°23'E
Bilwaskarma	NU	415	14°45'N	83°53'W
Bima	ID	500	8°28'S	118°43'E
Bimbo	CT	282	4°18'N	18°30'E
Bimini Is.	BF	402	25°44'N	79°15'W
Bíňa	LO	616	47°54'N	18°38'E
Bina-Etāwa		470	24°10'N	78°11'E
Binagadi	AJ	483	40°28'N	49°49'E
Binalud, Kuh-e-	IR	502	36°28'N	58°49'E
Binatang	MY	518	2°10'N	111°38'E
Binche	BE	570	50°24'N	4°10'E
Binder	CD	283	9°58'N	14°28'E
Bindu	CG	287	7°42'S	19°06'E
Bindungi	CG	287	5°31'S	17°50'E
Bindura	ZI	334	17°19'S	31°20'E
Binéfar	SP	618	41°51'N	0°18'E
Binga	ZI	334	17°38'S	27°21'E
Bingen	GM	584	49°58'N	7°54'E
Bingerville	IV	288	5°21'N	3°54'W
Binghamton	US	398	42°06'N	75°54'W
Bin Ghashīr	LY	302	32°41'N	13°11'E
Bin Ghunaymah, Jabal	LY	302	25°00'N	15°30'E
Bingley	UK	626	53°51'N	1°50'W
Bingöl	TU	535	38°53'N	40°29'E
Bingöl Dag.	TU	535	39°20'N	41°20'E
Binguibanda	CT	282	5°50'N	20°28'E
Binhai	CH	490	34°00'N	119°49'E
Binh Chau	VM	540	9°18'N	105°58'E
Binh Son	VM	540	15°18'N	108°45'E
Binjai	ID	500	3°36'N	98°30'E
Bin Jawwād	LY	302	30°48'N	18°04'E
Binkolo	SL	320	8°57'N	11°59'W
Binna, Raas	SO	321	11°09'N	51°10'E
Binongko	ID	500	5°57'S	124°02'E
Bin Qirdān	TS	329	33°09'N	11°11'E
Bintagoungou	ML	307	16°44'N	3°44'W
Bintan	ID	500	1°05'N	104°30'E
Bintang Range	MY	518	5°25'N	100°50'E
Bintimodouya	GV	297	10°39'N	14°27'W
Bint Jubayl	LE	516	33°06'N	35°25'E
Bintuhan	ID	500	4°46'S	103°22'E
Bintulu	MY	518	3°10'N	113°02'E
Bin Yauri	NI	316	10°47'N	4°47'E
Bio Bio	CI	428	37°30'S	71°30'W
Biodi	CG	287	3°19'N	28°35'E
Biograd	HR	574	43°57'N	15°27'E
Bioko	EK	291	3°30'N	8°43'E
Bickovo	HR	574	43°20'N	17°03'E
Bicugra	MO	310	30°13'N	9°22'W
Bīr	IN	496	18°59'N	75°46'E
Bir, Ras	DJ	289	11°58'N	43°21'E
Bira		472	49°00'N	132°28'E
Birag, Kuh-e-	IR	502	27°50'N	61°50'E
Birāk	LY	302	27°32'N	14°17'E
Bi'r Al Ghanam	LY	302	32°19'N	12°34'E
Bi'r 'Alī	YM	541	14°00'N	48°19'E
Bi'r 'Alī Bin Khalīfah	TS	329	34°43'N	10°04'E
Bi'r Al Mashariqah	TS	329	36°31'N	9°58'E
Birama, Punta	CU	406	20°38'N	77°16'W
Birao	CT	282	10°15'N	22°47'E
Birātnagar	NP	522	26°29'N	87°17'E
Biratori	JA	506	42°35'N	142°08'E
Birch		368	60°44'N	115°25'W
Birch		368	58°28'N	112°17'W
Birch Mountains	CA	390	57°30'N	112°30'W
Birchenough Bridge	ZI	334	19°58'S	32°20'E
Birch Grove	GJ	410	12°06'N	61°40'W
Birch Island		372	51°36'N	119°55'W
Bircot	ET	293	7°36'N	43°45'E
Birdsville	AS	656	25°54'S	139°22'E
Birdum		648	15°39'S	133°13'E
Birecik		564	37°02'N	37°58'E
Bir el Ater	AG	272	34°44'N	8°03'E
Bīr-e Olyā	IR	502	25°28'N	59°51'E
Bireuen	ID	500	5°12'N	96°41'E
Bīrganj	NP	522	27°00'N	84°52'E
Birganj	BG	485	25°51'N	88°40'E
Birigu	BR	424	21°18'S	50°19'W
Birikchul'		466	53°20'N	89°54'E
Bīrjand	IR	502	32°53'N	59°13'E
Bir Jdid	MO	310	33°23'N	8°00'W
Birkat Qarun	EG	290	29°28'N	30°40'E
Birkelane	SG	319	14°08'N	15°45'W
Birken		372	50°29'N	122°36'W
Birkenhead	UK	626	53°24'N	3°02'W
Birkirkara	MT	600	35°54'N	14°28'E
Bîrlad	RO	610	46°14'N	27°40'E
Birmay	AJ	483	39°45'N	47°57'E
Birmingham	UK	626	52°28'N	1°55'W
Birmingham	US	398	33°30'N	86°48'W
Bir Mogreïn	MR	308	25°14'N	11°35'W
Birnie I.	KR	660	3°30'S	172°00'W
Birnin Gwari	NI	316	10°39'N	6°33'E
Birnin Kebbi	NI	316	12°28'N	4°12'E
Birni Nkonni	NG	314	13°48'N	5°15'E
Birnin Kudu	NI	316	11°24'N	9°30'E
Birniwa	NI	316	12°47'N	10°14'E
Birobidzhan	RS	612	48°48'N	132°57'E
Birr	EI	592	53°06'N	7°54'W
Birrimbah	AS	656	16°26'S	132°04'E
Birrindudu	AS	656	18°22'S	129°27'E
Birsk	RS	612	55°25'N	55°32'E
Birštonas	LH	597	54°37'N	24°02'E
Bir Tamtam	MO	310	33°59'N	4°38'W
Biru	CH	490	31°33'N	93°49'E
Biruaca	VE	440	7°52'N	67°30'W
Biruni	UZ	539	41°42'N	60°44'E
Biryusa	RS	612	58°00'N	98°00'E
Biryusinsk		468	55°57'N	97°49'E
Biržai	LH	597	56°12'N	24°45'E
Birżebbuga	MT	600	35°49'N	14°31'E
Bis, L.	RO	610	43°55'N	23°50'E
Bisagana	NI	316	13°41'N	13°20'E
Bisbee	US	398	31°26'N	109°55'W
Biscarrosse	FR	580	43°22'N	0°16'E
Biscay, Bay of (Mar Cantábrico)	SP	618	44°00'N	4°00'W
Biscayne Bay		382	10°42'N	61°41'W
Bisceglie	IT	593	41°14'N	16°30'E
Bischofshofen	AU	568	47°25'N	13°13'E
Biscotasing	CA	390	47°17'N	82°06'W
Biscucuy	VE	440	9°22'N	69°59'W
Bisenge		266	0°04'N	22°16'E
Biševo	HR	574	42°59'N	16°01'E
Bishah, Wadi	SA	528	21°24'N	43°26'E
Bishkek	KG	514	42°54'N	74°36'E
Bishop		376	27°35'N	97°47'W
Bishop	US	398	37°20'N	118°23'W
Bishop's Falls	CA	390	49°01'N	55°30'W
Bishri, Jabal	SY	531	35°20'N	39°20'E
Bishti i Pallës	AL	566	41°24'N	19°24'E
Bisibanda	CT	282	5°52'N	19°54'E
Bisina, Lake	UG	330	1°38'N	33°56'E
Biskotasi L.		374	47°15'N	82°09'W
Biskra	AG	272	34°51'N	5°44'E
Biskupiec	PL	606	53°52'N	20°58'E
Bislig	RP	526	8°13'N	126°19'E
Bismarck	US	398	46°48'N	100°47'W
Bismarck Archipelago	PP	664	5°00'S	150°00'E
Bismarck Range	PP	664	5°40'S	145°40'E
Bismarck Sea	PP	664	4°00'S	148°00'E
Bismil	TU	535	37°51'N	40°40'E
Bismo	NO	604	61°54'N	8°12'E
Biso	UG	330	1°46'N	31°25'E
Bispgarden	SW	621	63°01'N	16°41'E
Biscueat Urda	IS	505	30°00'N	34°55'E
Bissau	PU	298	11°51'N	15°36'W
Bissaula	NI	316	7°01'N	10°27'E
Bissett		372	51°02'N	95°41'W
Bissora	PU	298	12°13'N	15°27'W
Bistrenci	MK	599	41°27'N	22°12'E
Bistriţa	RO	610	47°08'N	24°29'E
Bistrita	RO	610	46°30'N	26°57'E
Bitagron	NS	438	5°10'N	56°06'W
Bitale	TZ	327	4°46'S	29°41'E
Bitam	GB	294	2°05'N	11°29'E
Bitche		562	49°03'N	7°26'E
Bitkin	CD	283	11°59'N	18°13'E
Bitlis	TU	535	38°22'N	42°06'E
Bitola	MK	599	41°02'N	21°20'E
Bitonto	IT	593	41°06'N	16°41'E
Bitterfontein	SF	322	31°02'S	18°17'E
Bitteroot Range	US	398	47°06'N	115°10'W
Bitterroot		372	46°52'N	114°07'W
Bitti	IT	593	40°29'N	9°23'E
Bittou	UV	278	11°16'N	0°18'W
Bitumount	CA	390	57°23'N	111°38'W
Bitung	ID	500	1°27'N	125°11'E
Biu	NI	316	10°37'N	12°12'E
Bivolari	RO	610	47°32'N	27°26'E
Biwa-ko	JA	506	35°15'N	136°05'E
Bixby		378	35°56'N	95°52'W
Biya		466	52°30'N	86°00'E
Biyagundi	ER	292	14°28'N	37°12'E
Biysk	RS	612	52°34'N	85°15'E
Bizango-Bibéré	GB	294	0°23'N	9°33'E
Bizerte	TS	329	37°16'N	9°50'E
Bjargtangar	IC	591	65°29'N	24°32'W
Bjarkøy	NO	604	68°59'N	16°28'E
Bjästa	SW	621	63°12'N	18°30'E
Bjelasnica Visocica	BK	572	43°10'N	18°21'E
Bjelovar	HR	574	45°54'N	16°51'E
Bjerkvik	NO	604	68°32'N	17°33'E
Bjerringbro	DA	576	56°23'N	9°40'E
Bjeshkete Nemuna	AL	566	42°15'N	19°59'E
Bjørkelangen	NO	604	59°53'N	11°34'E
Björklinge		558	60°02'N	17°33'E
Björköby	FI	578	63°20'N	21°16'E
Björna	SW	621	63°33'N	18°35'E
Bjorne Pen.	CA	390	77°30'N	87°00'W
Bjugn	NO	604	63°46'N	9°44'E
Bjurholm	SW	621	63°56'N	19°13'E
Bjuv	SW	621	56°05'N	12°54'E
Bk. Klingkang	MY	518	1°30'N	111°00'E
Bk. Witti	MY	518	5°00'N	116°00'E
Blace	YO	630	43°18'N	21°18'E
Blachownia	PL	606	50°47'N	18°58'E
Black		372	51°12'N	96°32'W
Black		374	36°10'N	91°00'W
Black		378	31°30'N	91°50'W
Black	JM	414	18°05'N	77°45'W
Blackall	AS	656	24°25'S	145°28'E
Black Bay		374	45°52'N	77°21'W
Black Belt		378	33°00'N	86°00'W
Blackburn	UK	626	53°44'N	2°27'W
Black Canyon City		376	34°04'N	112°08'W
Black Cliff	WA	313	23°48'S	14°29'E
Blackdown Hills	UK	626	50°50'N	3°00'W
Blackfoot	US	398	43°11'N	112°20'W
Black Forest		372	39°00'N	104°42'W
Black Head	NZ	663	40°12'S	176°49'E
Black Head	UK	626	50°00'N	5°06'W
Black Head	UK	626	54°45'N	5°41'W
Black Hills	US	398	63°28'N	138°50'W
Black Lake		374	46°03'N	71°21'W
Black Lake	CA	390	59°07'N	105°38'W
Black Mts.		376	35°30'N	114°15'W
Black Mts.	UK	626	51°58'N	3°07'W
Blackpool	UK	626	53°49'N	3°03'W
Black Range		376	33°10'N	107°50'W
Black Reef	WA	313	24°31'S	14°35'E
Black River	JM	414	18°01'N	77°51'W
Black River Bay	JM	414	18°00'N	77°51'W
Black Rock	WA	313	24°55'S	14°46'E
Black Rock Desert		372	41°00'N	119°00'W
Blacksburg	US	398	37°13'N	80°24'W
Black Sea	GG	495	43°00'N	35°00'E
Blackshear		378	31°18'N	82°14'W
Blackstone		374	37°04'N	78°00'W
Black Tickle		370	53°27'N	55°44'W
Black Volta	GH	296	8°41'N	1°33'W
Blackwater		558	52°10'N	8°10'W
Blackwater	AS	656	23°35'S	148°53'E
Blackwater	EI	592	56°42'N	4°52'W
Blackwell		376	36°48'N	97°16'W
Blackwood	AS	656	34°00'S	115°20'E
Blackwood, C.	PP	664	7°47'S	144°30'E
Blagodarniy		560	45°06'N	43°27'E
Blagoevgrad	BU	573	42°01'N	23°06'E
Blagoveshchenka	KZ	510	43°18'N	74°12'E
Blagoveshchensk	RS	612	50°16'N	127°32'E
Blain	FR	580	47°29'N	1°45'W
Blair		372	41°32'N	96°07'W
Blair Athol		652	22°42'S	147°33'E
Blaj	RO	610	46°11'N	23°55'E
Blaka, Enneri	NG	314	20°45'N	12°43'E
Blakely		378	31°22'N	84°56'W
Blake Pt.	US	398	48°11'N	88°25'W
Blanc, Cap	FR	580	43°04'N	6°22'E
Blanc, Cap	MR	308	20°45'N	17°02'W
Blanca, Bahía	AR	419	38°55'S	62°10'W
Blanca, Cordillera	PE	436	9°10'S	77°35'W
Blanca, Punta	MX	394	29°01'N	114°35'W
Blanca Creek		376	34°50'N	102°30'W
Blanchard	ST	418	13°48'N	60°56'W
Blanche, Lake	AS	656	29°15'S	139°39'E
Blanche Channel	BP	666	8°30'S	157°45'E
Blanchisseuse	TD	438	10°47'N	61°18'W
Blanco	SF	322	33°56'S	22°25'E
Blanco, C.	US	398	42°50'N	124°33'W
Blanco, Cabo	CS	405	9°32'N	85°07'W
Blanco, Lago	CI	428	54°03'S	69°00'W
Blanda	IC	591	65°39'N	20°18'W
Blanding	US	398	37°37'N	109°28'W
Blanes	SP	618	41°41'N	2°48'E
Blangpidie	ID	500	3°45'N	96°51'E
Blankenberge	BE	570	51°19'N	3°08'E
Blanquilla, Isla	VE	440	11°51'N	64°37'W
Blanquillo	UY	439	32°52'S	55°36'W
Blansko	EZ	575	49°22'N	16°40'E
Blantyre	MI	306	15°47'S	35°00'E
Blatná	EZ	575	49°26'N	13°53'E
Blato	HR	574	42°56'N	16°48'E
Blato	MK	599	41°14'N	21°24'E
Blatten	SZ	622	46°25'N	7°49'E
Blåvands Huk	DA	576	55°32'N	8°05'E
Blavet	FR	580	47°50'N	3°30'W
Blaye-les-Mines		562	44°01'N	2°08'E
Blaze, Pt.	AS	656	12°54'S	130°11'E
Bleckede	GM	584	53°18'N	10°44'E
Bled	SI	617	46°22'N	14°08'E
Blefjell	NO	604	59°48'N	9°10'E
Blenheim		374	42°20'N	82°00'W
Blenheim	NZ	663	41°31'S	174°00'E
Blesberg	SF	322	33°26'S	22°41'E
Bleus, Monts	CG	287	1°30'N	30°30'E
Blida	AG	272	36°28'N	2°50'E
Bligh Water	FJ	660	17°00'S	178°00'E
Blind River		374	46°10'N	82°58'W
Blinman	AS	656	31°06'S	138°40'E
Blinndio	ML	307	11°37'N	6°21'W
Blitar	ID	500	8°06'S	112°09'E
Blitta	TO	328	8°20'N	0°58'E
Block		374	41°12'N	71°32'W
Bloemfontein	SF	322	29°08'S	26°10'E
Bloemhof	SF	322	27°39'S	25°36'E
Bloemspruit	SF	322	29°08'S	26°16'E
Blois	FR	580	47°35'N	1°20'E
Blomstermåla		558	56°59'N	16°20'E
Blönduós	IC	591	65°40'N	20°18'W
Bloodvein		370	51°47'N	96°43'W
Bloodvein River		372	51°46'N	96°37'W
Bloody Foreland	EI	592	55°08'N	8°17'W
Bloomfield		372	42°35'N	97°38'W
Bloomfield		374	40°45'N	92°24'W
Bloomfield		376	36°42'N	107°59'W
Bloomingdale		374	36°35'N	82°29'W
Bloomington		370	40°29'N	88°59'W
Bloomington		378	28°38'N	96°53'W
Bloomington	US	398	39°09'N	86°31'W
Bloomington	US	398	44°50'N	93°17'W
Blouberg	SF	322	23°04'S	29°00'E
Blountstown		378	30°26'N	85°02'W
Bludenz	AU	568	47°09'N	9°49'E
Blue Downs	SF	322	33°59'S	18°42'E
Bluefield		374	37°16'N	81°13'W
Bluefields	JM	414	18°10'N	78°02'W
Bluefields	NU	415	12°00'N	83°45'W
Bluefields Bay	JM	414	18°10'N	78°03'W
Blue Hill		266	15°50'S	5°35'W
Blue Hills.		374	45°50'N	91°30'W
Blue Mesa Res.		376	38°27'N	107°20'W
Blue Mount	IN	496	22°38'N	93°03'E
Blue Mountain Peak	JM	414	18°03'N	76°35'W
Blue Mountains	AS	656	33°43'S	150°20'E
Blue Mts.		374	45°00'N	70°30'W
Blue Mts.		382	6°33'N	58°49'W

Kalamare	BC	276	22°52'S	26°30'E
Kalamariá	GR	588	40°35'N	22°58'E
Kalamáta	GR	588	37°02'N	22°06'E
Kalamazoo	US	398	42°17'N	85°35'W
Kalamitskiy Zaliv	UP	624	45°05'N	33°23'E
Kalampáka	GR	588	39°42'N	21°38'E
Kalanchak	UP	624	46°15'N	33°18'E
Kalandy	MA	304	15°45'S	48°44'E
Kalangadoo		652	37°34'S	140°42'E
Kalangali	TZ	327	6°06'S	33°57'E
Kalanguy		468	51°01'N	116°31'E
Kalanshiyu, Sarir	LY	302	27°00'N	21°30'E
Kalaoa	US	398	19°43'N	155°58'W
Kalaotoa	ID	500	7°22'S	121°47'E
Kala Oya	CE	530	8°18'N	79°50'E
Kalar		468	56°00'N	119°00'E
Kālārmārchara	BG	485	21°40'N	91°55'E
Kalaroa	BG	485	22°52'N	89°02'E
Kalasin	TH	534	16°29'N	103°30'E
Kalāt	PK	524	29°02'N	66°35'E
Kalávrita	GR	588	38°01'N	22°06'E
Kalaw	BM	487	20°38'N	96°34'E
Kalbā	TC	538	25°05'N	56°20'E
Kälbäcär	AJ	483	40°07'N	46°02'E
Kalbarri	AS	656	27°39'S	114°11'E
Kaldakvísl	IC	591	64°20'N	19°00'W
Kale		564	37°23'N	28°51'E
Kale	TU	535	36°14'N	29°59'E
Kalecik		564	40°06'N	33°25'E
Kaledupa	ID	500	5°32'S	123°47'E
Kalema	CG	287	4°08'S	24°15'E
Kalemie	CG	287	5°55'S	29°10'E
Kalemyo	BM	487	23°11'N	94°04'E
Kalenda	CG	287	10°56'S	22°21'E
Kalene Hill	ZA	332	11°10'S	24°11'E
Kalevala		556	65°12'N	31°10'E
Kalewa	BM	487	23°12'N	94°18'E
Kaleya	ZA	332	15°53'S	27°41'E
Kalgoorlie-Boulder	AS	656	30°45'S	121°28'E
Kali	NP	522	27°42'N	84°25'E
Kālia	BG	485	22°23'N	90°36'E
Kāliākair	BG	485	24°05'N	90°14'E
Kaliakra, Nos	BU	573	43°23'N	28°28'E
Kalianda	ID	500	5°45'S	105°38'E
Kalibo	RP	526	11°43'N	122°22'E
Kali Gandak	NP	522	27°50'N	84°10'E
Kālīganj	BG	485	22°28'N	89°02'E
Kālikot	NP	522	29°06'N	81°41'E
Kalima	CG	287	2°34'S	26°37'E
Kalimala		470	18°04'N	81°44'E
Kalimantan (Borneo)	ID	500	1°00'N	114°00'E
Kálimnos	GR	588	36°57'N	26°59'E
Kálimnos (Calino)	GR	588	37°00'N	27°00'E
Kālimpong		472	27°04'N	88°29'E
Kalinin	TX	537	42°08'N	59°40'E
Kalininabad	TI	533	37°52'N	68°55'E
Kaliningrad		560	55°55'N	37°49'E
Kaliningrad	RS	612	54°43'N	20°30'E
Kalinino		564	45°08'N	38°59'E
Kalinino	AM	482	41°07'N	44°17'E
Kalininsk		466	51°30'N	44°28'E
Kalinkavichy	BO	569	52°08'N	29°19'E
Kalinko	GV	297	11°16'N	11°11'W
Kalinovka		560	51°54'N	34°31'E
Kalinovka	UP	624	49°28'N	28°32'E
Kaliro	UG	330	0°54'N	33°30'E
Kalis	SO	321	8°23'N	49°05'E
Kalisizo	UG	330	0°32'S	31°38'E
Kalispell	US	398	48°11'N	114°18'W
Kalisz	PL	606	51°44'N	18°04'E
Kaliua	TZ	327	5°04'S	31°48'E
Kalix	SW	621	65°51'N	23°08'E
Kalix älv	SW	621	65°47'N	23°13'E
Kalkan		564	36°15'N	29°24'E
Kalkaringi	AS	656	17°26'S	130°49'E
Kalkaska		374	44°44'N	85°10'W
Kalkfeld	WA	313	20°53'S	16°11'E
Kalkfontein	BC	276	22°13'S	20°55'E
Kalkhügel	WA	313	24°51'S	16°34'E
Kālkini	BG	485	23°06'N	90°16'E
Kalkrand	WA	313	24°04'S	17°36'E
Kallaste	EN	577	58°39'N	27°09'E
Kallavesi	FI	578	61°24'N	27°06'E
Kallinge	SW	621	56°14'N	15°17'E
Kallithéa		564	37°57'N	23°42'E
Kallsjön	SW	621	63°35'N	13°10'E
Kalmalo	NI	316	13°43'N	5°17'E
Kalmar	SW	621	56°40'N	16°22'E
Kalmarsund	SW	621	56°40'N	16°25'E
Kalmthout	BE	570	51°23'N	4°28'E
Kalmunai	CE	530	7°25'N	81°49'E
Kalmykovo	KZ	510	49°02'N	51°50'E
Kalnciems	LG	596	56°50'N	23°35'E
Kalni	BG	485	24°21'N	91°13'E
Kalnibolotskaya		564	46°01'N	40°28'E
Kalocsa	HU	590	46°32'N	19°00'E
Kalofer	BU	573	42°37'N	24°59'E
Kaloko	CG	287	6°47'S	25°48'E
Kālol	IN	496	23°15'N	72°29'E
Kalole	CG	287	3°42'S	27°22'E
Kalombo	ZA	332	13°05'S	22°48'E
Kalomo	ZA	332	17°02'S	26°30'E
Kalongan	ID	500	4°01'N	126°39'E
Kalongo	UG	330	3°03'N	33°22'E
Kaloqi	SU	324	10°52'N	30°52'E
Kālpi	IN	496	26°07'N	79°44'E
Kalpin	CH	490	40°30'N	79°02'E
Kalpitiya	CE	530	8°14'N	79°46'E
Kāl Qal'eh	AF	480	32°38'N	62°32'E
Kals	AU	568	46°59'N	12°39'E
Kaltenkirchen	GM	584	53°50'N	9°58'E
Kaltungo	NI	316	9°49'N	11°19'E
Kaluđerica	YO	630	44°45'N	20°34'E
Kaluga	RS	612	54°31'N	36°16'E
Kalu Ganga	CE	530	6°40'N	80°10'E
Kaluku	ID	500	2°31'S	119°03'E
Kalulushi	ZA	332	12°50'S	28°05'E
Kalumburu Mission	AS	656	14°15'S	126°37'E
Kalundborg	DA	576	55°41'N	11°06'E
Kalungu	UG	330	0°10'S	31°46'E
Kalungwishi	ZA	332	9°01'S	28°57'E
Kalush	UP	624	49°01'N	24°22'E
Kalutara	CE	530	6°35'N	79°58'E
Kalvarija	LH	597	54°24'N	23°14'E
Kalwelwe	ZA	332	14°41'S	28°22'E
Kalyān	IN	496	19°13'N	73°08'E
Kalyazin		560	57°14'N	37°49'E
Kama	BM	487	19°02'N	95°06'E
Kama	CG	287	3°32'S	27°07'E
Kama	RS	612	55°45'N	52°00'E
Kamachumu	TZ	327	1°35'S	31°37'E
Kamaing	BM	487	25°31'N	96°44'E
Kamaishi	JA	506	39°16'N	141°53'E
Kamajai	LH	597	55°49'N	25°30'E
Kamaka		654	23°14'S	135°03'W
Kamakura		474	35°18'N	139°32'E
Kamakusa	GY	434	5°55'N	60°37'W
Kamakwie	SL	320	9°30'N	12°14'W
Kamalampaka	TZ	327	5°37'S	30°36'E
Kamālia	PK	524	30°44'N	72°39'E
Kaman	TU	535	39°22'N	33°44'E
Kamango	CG	287	0°39'N	29°53'E
Kamanjab	WA	313	19°38'S	14°50'E
Kamanyola	CG	287	2°44'S	29°00'E
Kamaran	YM	541	15°22'N	42°10'E
Kamarang	GY	434	5°53'N	60°35'W
Kāmāreddi	IN	496	18°19'N	78°21'E
Kamar-e Zard	IR	502	33°05'N	59°10'E
Kāmārhāti	IN	496	22°40'N	88°22'E
Kamaria Falls	GY	434	6°25'N	58°48'W
Kamashi	UZ	539	38°50'N	66°28'E
Kamativi	ZI	334	18°19'S	27°04'E
Kamba	NI	316	12°02'N	4°15'E
Kambalda	AS	656	31°12'S	121°40'E
Kamba-Poko	CG	287	7°03'S	18°56'E
Kambar	PK	524	27°36'N	68°00'E
Kamberdi	CH	490	40°04'N	80°15'E
Kambia	SL	320	9°06'N	12°54'W
Kambja	EN	577	58°14'N	26°42'E
Kambove	CG	287	10°50'S	26°38'E
Kambuno, Gunung	ID	500	2°20'S	120°04'E
Kamburu Bridge	KE	299	0°46'S	37°42'E
Kamchatka	RS	612	56°15'N	162°30'E
Kamchatkskiy Poluostrov	RS	612	56°15'N	163°00'E
Kamchatskiy Proliv	RS	612	56°00'N	164°30'E
Kamchatskiy Zaliv	RS	612	55°35'N	162°21'E
Kaména Voúrla	GR	588	38°46'N	22°46'E
Kamen Dol	MK	599	41°29'N	21°54'E
Kamenets	BO	569	52°24'N	23°49'E
Kamenica	MK	599	44°51'N	15°50'E
Kameničná	LO	616	47°48'N	18°02'E
Kamenka		466	53°11'N	44°03'E
Kamenka		560	50°42'N	39°24'E
Kamenka		560	56°11'N	45°34'E
Kamenka	MD	601	48°03'N	28°42'E
Kamenka	RS	612	44°28'N	136°01'E
Kamenka	UP	624	49°02'N	32°06'E
Kamen'-na-Obi	RS	612	53°47'N	81°20'E
Kameno	BU	573	42°34'N	27°18'E
Kamenskiy		560	50°53'N	45°29'E
Kamenskoye	RS	612	62°30'N	166°12'E
Kamensk-Shakhtinskiy	RS	612	48°17'N	40°15'E
Kamensk-Ural'skiy	RS	612	56°24'N	61°55'E
Kameri		648	0°58'S	134°50'E
Kamfenda	GA	295	13°14'N	16°03'W
Kamiah		372	46°13'N	116°01'W
Kamienna Góra	PL	606	50°47'N	16°02'E
Kamień Pomorski	PL	606	53°58'N	14°47'E
Kamieskroon	SF	322	30°12'S	17°56'E
Kamiisco	JA	506	41°49'N	140°39'E
Kamiji	CG	287	6°39'S	23°17'E
Kamikawa	JA	506	43°48'N	142°49'E
Kamilukuak L.		368	62°20'N	101°40'W
Kamina	CG	287	8°44'S	25°00'E
Kaminak L.		370	62°13'N	95°00'W
Kaministiquia		370	48°32'N	89°35'W
Kamin'-Kashyrs'kyy	UP	624	51°38'N	24°58'E
Kamino-shima	JA	506	34°35'N	129°25'E
Kaminuriak L.		370	63°00'N	95°45'W
Kamiyaku	JA	506	30°25'N	130°34'E
Kamloops	CA	390	50°40'N	120°19'W
Kamloops Plateau		372	50°10'N	120°00'W
Kamlot	CB	489	11°28'N	103°42'E
Kamma		562	36°47'N	12°02'E
Kamnik	SI	617	46°14'N	14°37'E
Kamo	AM	482	40°21'N	45°08'E
Kamoa Mountains	GY	434	1°40'N	59°00'W
Kamogawa	JA	506	35°05'N	140°05'E
Kāmoke	PK	524	31°58'N	74°13'E
Kamonia	CG	287	6°52'S	20°56'E
Kamonkoli	UG	330	1°05'N	34°06'E
Kampala	UG	330	0°19'N	32°35'E
Kampalili, Mount	RP	526	7°18'N	126°18'E
Kampar		478	0°32'N	103°08'E
Kampar	MY	518	4°18'N	101°09'E
Kampen	GM	584	54°57'N	8°20'E
Kampene	CG	287	3°36'S	26°40'E
Kamphaeng Phet	TH	534	7°08'N	100°16'E
Kamp'o	KS	513	35°48'N	129°30'E
Kampong Baharu Cherating	MY	518	4°06'N	103°23'E
Kampong Batu Dua	MY	518	2°33'N	101°49'E
Kampong Batu Koyok	SN	530	1°24'N	104°03'E
Kampong Beluan	MY	518	4°08'N	102°13'E
Kampong Cham	CB	489	12°00'N	105°27'E
Kampong Chhnang	CB	489	12°15'N	104°40'E
Kampong Dingkir	MY	518	3°38'N	102°25'E
Kampong Ibal	MY	518	4°20'N	103°29'E
Kampong Jenderam	MY	518	2°52'N	101°44'E
Kampong Jereneh	MY	518	5°51'N	102°22'E
Kampong Kalamasi	BX	486	4°50'N	114°57'E
Kampong Keledik	MY	518	4°14'N	101°55'E
Kampong Kerdas	MY	518	3°14'N	101°43'E
Kampong Khleang	CB	489	13°06'N	104°08'E
Kampong Kuala Besut	MY	518	5°50'N	102°34'E
Kampong Kuala Ungar	BX	486	4°37'N	114°40'E
Kampong Lalok	MY	518	5°18'N	102°16'E
Kampong Lamunin	BX	486	4°41'N	114°43'E
Kampong Loyang	SN	530	1°23'N	103°58'E
Kampong Patong	BX	486	4°49'N	114°55'E
Kampong Penanjong	BX	486	4°51'N	114°41'E
Kampong Pokok Asam	MY	518	5°35'N	100°28'E
Kampong Saom	CB	489	10°38'N	103°30'E
Kâmpóng Sâom, B. de	CB	489	10°50'N	103°32'E
Kampong Seminei	SN	530	1°24'N	104°02'E
Kampong Spoe	CB	489	11°27'N	104°32'E
Kampong Tampasis	MY	518	5°48'N	116°34'E
Kampong Telagus	MY	518	1°03'N	110°51'E
Kampong Telupid	MY	518	5°39'N	117°07'E
Kampong Thum	CB	489	12°42'N	104°54'E
Kampong Timahu	BX	486	4°52'N	114°49'E
Kampong Timbunan	BX	486	4°57'N	114°58'E
Kampong Trabek	CB	489	11°09'N	105°28'E
Kampong Tualang	MY	518	5°58'N	100°25'E
Kampong Ukong	BX	486	4°40'N	114°38'E
Kampong Wa Baharu	MY	518	4°49'N	103°13'E
Kampot	CB	489	10°37'N	104°11'E
Kamptee		470	21°14'N	79°12'E
Kampti	UV	278	10°08'N	3°27'W
Kampung Kok Mak	MY	518	6°39'N	100°17'E
Kampyr-Ravat	KG	514	40°47'N	73°08'E
Kamrau		478	3°32'S	133°37'E
Kamsack		372	51°34'N	101°54'W
Kamsar	GV	297	10°40'N	14°36'W
Kamskoye Ust'ye		560	55°13'N	49°16'E
Kamskoye Vdkhr.		466	58°52'N	56°15'E
Kamsuuma	SO	321	0°15'N	42°47'E
Kamuela (Waimea)	US	398	20°01'N	155°40'W
Kamuk, Cerro	CS	405	9°17'N	83°04'W
Kamuli	UG	330	0°57'N	33°07'E
Kamwandu	CG	287	6°04'S	22°42'E
Kam'yanets'-Podil's'kyy	UP	624	48°40'N	26°34'E
Kāmyārān	IR	502	34°47'N	46°56'E
Kamyshevatskaya		564	46°24'N	37°56'E
Kamyshin	RS	612	50°06'N	45°24'E
Kamysh-Zarya	UP	624	47°19'N	36°41'E
Kan		466	56°00'N	95°00'E
Kanab	US	398	37°02'N	112°31'W
Kanab Plateau		376	36°26'N	112°53'W
Kanaka	ID	500	3°54'S	133°23'E
Kanana	SF	322	26°57'S	26°38'E
Kananga	CG	287	5°54'S	22°25'E
Kanash	RS	612	55°31'N	47°30'E
Kanavayén		384	5°38'N	61°48'W
Kanawha		374	38°50'N	82°09'W
Kanazawa	JA	506	36°32'N	136°39'E
Kanazi	TZ	327	2°32'S	30°37'E
Kanbalu	BM	487	23°12'N	95°31'E
Kanchanaburi	TH	534	14°01'N	99°32'E
Kanchanadit	TH	534	9°10'N	99°28'E
Kānchīpuram	IN	496	12°50'N	79°43'E
Kandalaksha	RS	612	67°09'N	32°25'E
Kandalakshskaya Bereg		556	66°30'N	35°00'E
Kandalakshskaya Guba		556	66°55'N	32°45'E
Kandale	CG	287	6°03'S	19°23'E
Kándanos	GR	588	35°20'N	23°45'E
Kandara	KE	299	0°54'S	37°00'E
Kandava	LG	596	57°02'N	22°46'E
Kandep	PP	664	5°51'S	143°29'E
Kandersteg	SZ	622	46°29'N	7°40'E
Kandhkot	PK	524	28°14'N	69°11'E
Kāndi	IN	496	23°57'N	88°02'E
Kandi	BN	276	11°08'N	2°56'E
Kandi	CG	287	3°06'N	28°16'E
Kandi, Tanjung	ID	500	1°19'N	121°28'E
Kandıra		564	41°04'N	30°09'E
Kandrāch	PK	524	25°29'N	65°29'E
Kandreho	MA	304	17°29'S	46°06'E
Kandrian	PP	664	6°13'S	149°33'E
Kandukūr	IN	496	15°13'N	79°55'E
Kandy	CE	530	7°18'N	80°38'E
Kane		374	41°39'N	78°48'W
Kaneohe	US	398	21°25'N	157°48'W
Kanëvka	RS	612	67°08'N	39°40'E
Kanevskaya		564	46°05'N	38°56'E
Kang	BC	276	23°36'S	22°45'E
Kanga	BG	485	26°47'N	98°39'E
Kanga	CG	287	1°56'N	30°01'E
Kanga	TZ	327	6°01'S	37°45'E
Kangaamiut		370	65°50'N	53°20'W
Kangaatsiaq		370	68°18'N	53°28'W
Kangaba	ML	307	11°56'N	8°25'W
Kangal	TU	535	39°15'N	37°24'E
Kangalassy	RS	612	62°23'N	129°59'E
Kangān	IR	502	27°50'N	52°03'E
Kangān	IR	502	25°48'N	57°28'E
Kangar	MY	518	6°26'N	100°12'E
Kangaré	ML	307	11°37'N	8°11'W
Kangaroo	AS	656	37°07'S	129°20'E
Kangaruma	GY	434	5°20'N	59°13'W
Kangasala	FI	578	61°28'N	24°05'E
Kangasniemi	FI	578	61°59'N	26°35'E
Kangāvar	IR	502	34°30'N	47°58'E
Kangbao		472	41°52'N	114°41'E
Kangchenjunga	NP	522	27°44'N	88°11'E
Kangding	CH	490	30°03'N	102°01'E
Kangdong	KN	512	39°08'N	126°06'E
Kangean	ID	500	6°54'S	115°20'E
Kangema	KE	299	0°40'S	36°58'E
Kangen	SU	324	6°47'N	33°09'E
Kanggye	KN	512	41°00'N	126°35'E
Kanggyŏng	KS	513	36°09'N	127°01'E
Kanghwa	KS	513	37°45'N	126°29'E
Kanghwa-do	KS	513	37°40'N	126°27'E
Kangi	SU	324	8°10'N	27°39'E
Kangiqsualujjuaq	CA	390	58°32'N	65°54'W
Kangiqsujuaq	CA	390	61°36'N	71°58'W
Kangirsuk	CA	390	60°01'N	70°01'W
Kangjin	KS	513	34°38'N	126°46'E
Kangkar Dohol	MY	518	1°54'N	103°55'E
Kangle	CH	490	35°15'N	103°39'E
Kangmar	CH	490	28°30'N	89°45'E
Kangmar	CH	490	30°45'N	85°31'E
Kangnam	KN	512	38°54'N	125°38'E
Kangnam Sanmaek	KN	512	41°00'N	126°30'E
Kangnŭng	KS	513	37°44'N	128°54'E
Kangnyŏng	KN	512	37°54'N	125°30'E
Kango	GB	294	0°09'N	10°08'E
Kangole	UG	330	1°32'N	34°09'E
Kangondi	KE	299	1°06'S	37°42'E
Kangrinboqê Feng	CH	490	31°04'N	81°18'E
Kangshan	TW	532	22°48'N	120°17'E
Kangsŏ	KN	512	38°55'N	125°30'E
Kang Xian		472	33°26'N	105°37'E
Kangxiwar	CH	490	36°15'N	78°46'E
Kangyaing	BM	487	16°00'N	94°16'E
Kanhangad		470	12°19'N	75°05'E
Kani	BM	487	22°26'N	94°51'E
Kani	IV	288	8°29'N	6°36'W
Kaniama	CG	287	7°31'S	24°11'E
Kanibadam	TI	533	40°17'N	70°25'E
Kanimekh	UZ	539	40°16'N	65°10'E
Kanim Kamen		556	68°10'N	45°00'E
Kanin, Poluostrov	RS	612	68°00'N	45°00'E
Kaningo	KE	299	0°49'S	38°32'E
Kanin Nos		556	68°38'N	43°18'E
Kanin Nos, Mys	RS	612	68°39'N	43°16'E
Kaninskiy Bereg		556	68°00'N	43°50'E
Kaniv	UP	624	49°45'N	31°28'E
Kanjiža	YO	630	46°04'N	20°03'E
Kankaanpää	FI	578	61°48'N	22°25'E
Kankakee		370	40°50'N	86°30'W
Kankakee		374	41°07'N	87°51'W
Kankan	GV	297	10°23'N	9°18'W
Kānker		470	20°17'N	81°29'E
Kankesanturai	CE	530	9°49'N	80°02'E
Kankossa	MR	308	15°56'N	11°31'W
Kankunskiy	RS	612	57°37'N	126°08'E
Kanlıavşar		564	37°13'N	38°16'E
Kannapolis	US	398	35°30'N	80°36'W
Kannauj	IN	496	27°04'N	79°55'E
Kannus	FI	578	63°53'N	23°50'E
Kano	NI	316	12°00'N	8°31'E
Kanona	ZA	332	13°04'S	30°38'E
Kanoneiland	SF	322	28°39'S	21°04'E
Kan'onji	JA	506	34°07'N	133°39'E
Kano Vlei	WA	313	19°14'S	19°20'E
Kanowit	MY	518	2°06'N	112°09'E
Kanoya	JA	506	31°23'N	130°51'E
Kānpur	IN	496	26°28'N	80°21'E
Kansas		372	38°30'N	98°30'W
Kansas	US	398	39°50'N	97°00'W
Kansas City	US	398	39°06'N	94°37'W
Kansas City	US	398	39°05'N	94°34'W
Kansenia	CG	287	10°19'S	26°05'E
Kansk	RS	612	56°13'N	95°41'E
Kansŏng	KS	513	38°22'N	128°28'E
Kansuswa	ZA	332	12°36'S	28°13'E
Kant	KG	514	42°53'N	74°51'E
Kantābānji		476	20°29'N	82°55'E
Kantchari	UV	278	12°29'N	1°31'E
Kanté	TO	328	9°57'N	1°03'E
Kantemirovka		560	49°41'N	39°51'E
Kantharalak	TH	534	14°39'N	104°39'E
Kanto-sanchi	JA	506	35°50'N	138°50'E
Kantunilkin	MX	394	21°06'N	87°29'W
Kanuku Mountains	GY	434	3°12'N	59°35'W
Kanuma	JA	506	36°33'N	139°44'E
Kanuwe	PP	664	7°00'S	143°30'E
Kanyanga	GH	296	8°27'N	0°59'W
Kanye	BC	276	24°59'S	25°21'E
Kanyilombi	ZA	332	12°32'S	24°12'E
Kanyogoga	UG	330	0°20'N	32°27'E
Kanyosha	BY	279	3°24'S	29°22'E
Kanzenze	CG	287	10°31'S	25°12'E
Kaoh Nhek	CB	489	13°05'N	107°04'E
Kaohsiung	TW	532	22°38'N	120°17'E
Kaolack	SG	319	14°09'N	16°05'W
Kaolinovo	BU	573	43°37'N	27°07'E
Kaoma	ZA	332	14°47'S	24°43'E
Kaop'ing	TW	532	22°50'N	120°30'E
Kaortchi	CD	283	18°19'N	18°50'E
Kaouadja	CT	282	7°58'N	23°31'E
Kaouar	NG	314	19°05'N	12°52'E
Kapa	BM	487	12°24'N	98°24'E
Kapaa	US	398	22°04'N	159°19'W
Kapaau	US	398	20°14'N	155°48'W
Kapalala	ZA	332	12°25'S	29°24'E
Kapalong	RP	526	7°30'N	125°41'E
Kapan	AM	482	39°12'N	46°25'E
Kapanga	CG	287	8°21'S	22°35'E
Kapaonik	YO	630	43°20'N	20°50'E
Kapāsin		470	24°54'N	74°20'E
Kapchorwa	UG	330	1°24'N	34°27'E
Kapedo	KE	299	1°10'N	36°06'E
Kapellen	BE	570	51°19'N	4°26'E
Kapenguria	KE	299	1°14'N	35°07'E
Kapengwe	ZA	332	12°33'S	31°02'E
Kapete	SL	320	8°59'N	11°59'W
Kapfenberg	AU	568	47°27'N	15°18'E
Kapingamarangi Atoll	FM	661	0°30'N	155°00'E
Kapiri Mposhi	ZA	332	13°58'S	28°41'E
Kapisillit		370	64°26'N	50°16'W
Kapit	MY	518	2°01'N	112°56'E
Kapita	UG	330	2°29'N	31°28'E
Kapka, Massif du	CD	283	15°07'N	21°45'E
Kaplice	EZ	575	48°44'N	14°29'E
Kapoe	TH	534	9°35'N	98°34'E
Kapoeta	SU	324	4°47'N	33°35'E
Kapona	CG	287	7°11'S	29°09'E
Kaporo	MI	306	9°43'S	33°50'E
Kapos	HU	590	46°44'N	18°28'E
Kaposvár	HU	590	46°22'N	17°48'E
Kappeln	GM	584	54°39'N	9°55'E
Kappl	AU	568	47°04'N	10°23'E
Kapsabet	KE	299	0°12'N	35°06'E
Kapsan	KN	512	41°10'N	128°20'E
Kaptai	BG	485	22°21'N	92°17'E
Kapuas	ID	500	0°30'S	109°00'E
Kapuas	ID	500	1°30'S	114°30'E
Kapuas Hulu, Peg.	ID	500	2°00'N	112°00'E
Kapukasing		370	48°30'N	83°30'W
Kapuskasing	CA	390	49°25'N	82°26'W
Kapustin Yar		560	48°34'N	45°45'E
Kaputa	ZA	332	8°28'S	29°40'E
Kapuvár	HU	590	47°36'N	17°02'E
Kap'yŏng	KS	513	37°50'N	127°30'E
Kara	RS	612	69°14'N	64°58'E
Kara	TO	328	10°01'N	0°25'E
Kara-Agach	KZ	510	48°00'N	80°50'E
Karaart	TI	533	39°04'N	73°35'E
Karababa Daglari	TU	535	39°30'N	36°00'E
Karabakhskiy Khr.	AJ	483	39°42'N	46°36'E
Kara-Balta	KG	514	42°50'N	73°52'E
Karabau	KZ	510	48°26'N	52°54'E
Karabekaul	TX	537	38°30'N	64°08'E
Karabelnyy, M.		556	67°00'N	49°10'E
Kara-Bogaz Gol, Zaliv	TX	537	41°00'N	54°00'E
Karabük	TU	535	41°12'N	32°37'E
Karabula	RS	612	58°02'N	97°23'E
Karabulak	KZ	510	44°54'N	78°30'E
Kara Burnu	TU	535	38°30'N	26°10'E
Karaburun		564	38°37'N	26°31'E
Karacabey	TU	535	40°13'N	28°21'E
Karacadağ	TU	535	41°57'N	27°40'E
Karacaköy		564	41°24'N	28°22'E
Karacali Dag.	TU	535	37°30'N	40°00'E
Karacal Tepe	TU	535	36°21'N	32°38'E
Karachala	AJ	483	39°50'N	48°55'E
Karachev		560	53°07'N	34°59'E
Karāchi	PK	524	24°52'N	67°03'E
Karaçoban	TU	535	39°18'N	42°09'E
Karād		470	17°17'N	74°12'E
Karadag	AJ	483	40°16'N	49°36'E
Karadarya	KG	514	40°54'N	71°45'E
Karagansay	KG	514	41°19'N	72°12'E
Karagauli	GG	495	42°01'N	43°13'E
Karagayly	KZ	510	49°22'N	75°58'E
Karaginskiy, Ozero	RS	612	58°50'N	164°00'E
Karaginskiy Zaliv		468	58°50'N	164°00'E
Karagüney Dag.	TU	535	40°05'N	34°00'E
Karaguzhikha	KZ	510	50°46'N	83°04'E
Kāraikkudi		470	10°04'N	78°47'E
Karaitivu	CE	530	8°23'N	79°47'E
Karaj	IR	502	35°48'N	50°59'E
Karaka	BP	666	7°30'S	156°40'E
Kara-Kala	TX	537	38°26'N	56°18'E
Karakelong	ID	500	4°15'N	126°48'E
Karaki		470	37°03'N	81°18'E
Karakoram Pass	CH	490	35°30'N	77°50'E
Karakoram Range	IN	496	34°00'N	78°00'E
Kara K'orē	ET	293	10°25'N	39°56'E
Karakoro	ML	307	14°43'N	12°03'W
Kara-Kul'	KG	514	41°37'N	72°39'E
Karakul'	UZ	539	39°32'N	63°50'E
Kara-Kul, Ozero	TI	533	39°00'N	74°00'E
Karakumskiy Kanal	TX	537	37°35'N	61°50'E
Karakumy, Peski	TX	537	39°00'N	60°00'E
Karakuwisa	WA	313	18°56'S	19°44'E
Karakyr, Gora	TX	537	35°40'N	62°18'E
Karama	RW	317	2°11'S	30°31'E
Karamagay	CH	490	46°16'N	87°39'E
Karaman	TU	535	37°11'N	33°14'E
Karamanlı		564	37°22'N	29°49'E
Karamar'yan	AJ	483	40°37'N	48°01'E
Karamay	CH	490	45°30'N	84°54'E
Karambewatta	CE	530	8°04'N	80°35'E
Karambi	TZ	327	2°05'S	31°31'E
Karambi	UG	330	0°03'N	29°45'E
Karamea	NZ	663	41°15'S	172°07'E
Karamea Bight	NZ	663	41°30'S	171°40'E
Karamet-Niyaz	TX	537	37°45'N	64°34'E
Karamic Gölü	TU	535	38°20'N	30°45'E
Karamiran	CH	490	37°06'N	85°15'E
Karamiran He	CH	490	38°00'N	84°30'E
Karamiran Shankou	CH	490	36°15'N	87°05'E
Karamken		468	60°12'N	151°10'E
Karamyshevo		560	57°45'N	28°42'E
Karanginskiy Zaliv	RS	612	69°55'N	165°00'E
Kāranja	IN	496	20°29'N	77°28'E
Karanlik		564	39°40'N	34°45'E
Karapelit	BU	573	43°49'N	27°34'E
Karapınar	TU	535	37°43'N	33°33'E
Karaqi	CH	490	40°45'N	77°49'E
Karari		264	15°48'N	32°30'E
Karasabai	GY	434	4°02'N	59°32'W
Karasay	CH	490	36°47'N	83°47'E
Karasburg	WA	313	28°01'S	18°45'E
Kara Sea	RS	612	76°00'N	86°00'E
Kara-Shivak	KG	514	39°31'N	72°11'E
Karasjok	NO	604	69°28'N	25°29'E
Kara-Su	KG	514	39°33'N	72°14'E
Karasu		564	41°06'N	30°41'E
Karasu	AJ	483	40°10'N	48°41'E
Karasuk	RS	612	53°44'N	78°02'E
Karāt	IR	502	34°34'N	60°34'E
Karatá, Laguna	NU	415	13°56'N	83°30'W
Karatal		466	46°43'N	75°31'E
Karataş		564	36°36'N	35°21'E
Karatash	KG	514	40°33'N	74°00'E
Karatau, Khrebet	KZ	510	43°50'N	68°30'E
Karatax Shan	CH	490	35°57'N	81°00'E
Kara-Tepe	TX	537	35°16'N	62°17'E
Karathuri	BM	487	10°55'N	98°46'E
Karatina	KE	299	0°29'S	37°08'E
Karatobe	KZ	510	49°44'N	53°30'E
Karaton	KZ	510	46°25'N	53°30'E
Karatoya	BG	485	24°13'N	89°36'E
Karatsu	JA	506	33°26'N	129°58'E
Karatugay	AJ	483	40°01'N	48°47'E
Karatünggü	CH	490	46°57'N	89°45'E
Karaturgay	KZ	510	50°00'N	65°30'E
Karaul	RS	612	70°06'N	83°10'E
Karaul-Bazar	UZ	539	39°30'N	64°48'E
Karáva	GR	588	39°18'N	21°33'E
Kara-Vakil' Pervyy	TX	537	37°53'N	60°21'E
Kara-Vakil' Vtoroy	TX	537	37°45'N	60°21'E
Karavan	KG	514	40°18'N	72°12'E
Karavelli	AJ	483	40°40'N	48°02'E
Karavostasi	CY	494	35°08'N	32°50'E
Karavukovo	YO	630	45°30'N	19°12'E
Karawang	ID	500	6°19'S	107°17'E
Karawanken	AU	568	46°25'N	14°25'E
Karayar	CH	490	37°09'N	79°04'E
Karayulgun		466	41°24'N	80°48'E
Karazhal	KZ	510	48°02'N	70°49'E
Karbaka	SU	324	18°50'N	32°24'E
Karbalā'	IZ	504	32°36'N	44°02'E
Karcag	HU	590	47°19'N	20°56'E
Kardhámila	GR	588	38°32'N	26°05'E
Kardhítsa	GR	588	39°21'N	21°55'E
Kardhitsomagoúla	GR	588	39°23'N	21°55'E
Kardiva Channel	MV	519	4°40'N	73°00'E
Kärdla	EN	577	59°00'N	22°45'E
Kareedouw	SF	322	33°57'S	24°17'E
Karema	TZ	327	6°49'S	30°26'E
Karesuando	SW	621	68°25'N	22°27'E
Karêt	MR	308	24°00'N	7°30'W
Kärevere	EN	577	58°26'N	26°29'E
Kargapazari Dag.	TU	535	40°07'N	41°35'E
Kargasok	RS	612	59°03'N	80°53'E
Kargat		466	54°39'N	78°16'E
Kargil		470	34°32'N	76°08'E
Kargopol'		556	61°30'N	38°58'E
Karhijärvi	FI	578	61°33'N	22°33'E
Karhula	FI	578	60°31'N	26°57'E
Kari	NI	316	11°14'N	10°34'E
Kariá	GR	588	38°45'N	20°39'E
Karia Ba Mohammed	MO	310	34°22'N	5°12'W
Kariaí	GR	588	40°16'N	24°15'E
Karianga	MA	304	22°22'S	47°26'E
Kariba	ZI	334	16°31'S	28°48'E
Kariba, Lake	ZA	332	17°00'S	28°00'E
Kariba Dam	ZA	332	16°32'S	28°45'E
Karibib	WA	313	21°56'S	15°50'E
Karimama	BN	276	12°04'N	3°11'E
Karimata	ID	500	1°36'S	108°55'E
Karimata, Selat	ID	500	2°05'S	108°40'E
Karimganj		472	24°50'N	92°22'E
Karīmnagar	IN	496	18°26'N	79°09'E
Karimui	PP	664	6°27'S	144°49'E
Karin	SO	321	10°51'N	45°47'E
Karin	SO	321	10°59'N	49°13'E
Karis (Karjaa)	FI	578	60°05'N	23°40'E
Karise	DA	576	55°18'N	12°13'E
Karisimbi	CG	287	1°30'S	29°27'E
Karisimbi, Volcan	RW	317	1°30'S	29°27'E
Káristos	GR	588	38°01'N	24°24'E
Karius Ra.	PP	664	6°15'S	142°50'E
Kariya	JA	506	34°58'N	136°59'E
Kārīz-e Elyās	AF	480	35°25'N	61°20'E
Karjaa (Karis)	FI	578	60°05'N	23°40'E
Karkar	PP	664	4°34'S	145°56'E
Karkar Island	PP	664	4°30'S	146°15'E
Karkinitskiy Zaliv	UP	624	45°55'N	33°00'E
Karkkila	FI	578	60°32'N	24°11'E
Kärkölä	FI	578	60°51'N	25°16'E
Karla Marksa, Pik	TI	533	37°09'N	72°26'E
Karleby (Kokkola)	FI	578	63°50'N	23°07'E
Karlik Shan	CH	490	43°00'N	94°30'E
Karlino	PL	606	54°02'N	15°52'E
Karlovac	HR	574	45°29'N	15°33'E
Karlovka	UP	624	49°27'N	35°08'E
Karlovo	BU	573	42°38'N	24°48'E
Karlovy Vary	EZ	575	50°14'N	12°52'E
Karlsborg		558	58°32'N	14°31'E
Karlshamn	SW	621	56°10'N	14°51'E
Karlskoga	SW	621	59°20'N	14°31'E
Karlskrona	SW	621	56°10'N	15°35'E
Karlsruhe	GM	584	49°00'N	8°23'E
Karlstad	SW	621	59°22'N	13°30'E
Karmah	SU	324	19°38'N	30°25'E
Karmāla	IN	496	18°25'N	75°12'E
Karmana	UZ	539	40°05'N	65°24'E
Karmi'el	IS	505	32°55'N	35°18'E
Karmøy	NO	604	59°15'N	5°15'E
Karmrashen	AM	482	40°16'N	43°53'E
Karnāl	IN	496	29°41'N	76°59'E
Karnali	NP	522	28°45'N	81°16'E
Karnaphuli Reservoir	BG	485	22°42'N	92°12'E
Karnes City		376	28°53'N	97°54'W
Karnische Alpen	AU	568	46°40'N	13°00'E
Karnobat	BU	573	42°39'N	26°59'E
Karo	CD	283	10°22'N	18°52'E
Karoi	ZI	334	16°49'S	29°41'E
Karokh	AF	480	34°28'N	62°35'E
Karomatan	RP	526	7°46'N	123°43'E
Karong		472	25°18'N	94°03'E
Karonga	MI	306	9°56'S	33°56'E
Karoonda		652	35°06'S	139°54'E
Karor	PK	524	31°13'N	70°57'E
Karora	SU	324	17°42'N	38°22'E
Káros	GR	588	36°53'N	25°39'E
Karosa	ID	500	1°48'S	119°20'E
Karoso, Tanjung	ID	500	9°50'S	118°30'E
Karpakora	AS	656	32°56'S	143°08'E
Kárpathos	GR	588	35°17'N	27°17'E
Kárpathos (Scarpanto)	GR	588	35°40'N	27°10'E
Kárpathos Strait		564	35°50'N	27°30'E
Karpaty	EZ	575	47°00'N	25°30'E
Karpaty Zachodnie	PL	606	49°40'N	20°00'E
Karpenísion	GR	588	38°55'N	21°47'E
Karpogory		556	63°59'N	44°27'E
Karranah	BA	484	26°14'N	50°31'E
Karratha	AS	656	20°46'S	116°50'E
Karre, Monts	CT	282	6°33'N	15°40'E
Kars	TU	535	40°37'N	43°05'E
Kars	TU	535	40°37'N	43°41'E
Karsakpay	KZ	510	47°50'N	66°45'E
Kärsämäki	FI	578	63°58'N	25°43'E
Karsantı		564	37°33'N	35°24'E
Kārsava	LG	596	56°47'N	27°40'E
Karshi	UZ	539	38°48'N	65°48'E
Karshinskaya Step	UZ	539	39°10'N	65°40'E
Karstula	FI	578	62°52'N	24°47'E
Kartalinskiy Khrebet	GG	495	42°15'N	45°00'E
Kartaly	RS	612	53°02'N	60°38'E
Karthala	CN	284	12°05'N	43°35'E
Kartsebi	GG	495	41°19'N	43°17'E
Kartushi	CG	287	4°27'S	26°10'E
Kartuzy	PL	606	54°20'N	18°12'E
Karuma Falls	UG	330	2°15'N	32°13'E
Karumba	AS	656	17°29'S	140°50'E
Karun	IR	502	27°08'N	56°48'E
Karungi	SW	621	66°01'N	23°53'E
Karunjie		648	16°18'S	127°12'E
Karunki	FI	578	66°01'N	24°03'E
Karup	DA	576	56°18'N	9°08'E
Karūr	IN	496	10°57'N	78°05'E
Karushe	CG	287	3°07'S	25°01'E
Kārvāndar	IR	502	27°53'N	60°44'E
Karviná		560	49°52'N	19°33'E
Karwar	IN	496	14°48'N	74°08'E
Kar'yepol'ye		556	65°32'N	43°42'E
Karymskoye	KZ	510	51°37'N	114°21'E
Kaş	TU	535	36°12'N	29°38'E
Kas	SU	324	12°30'N	24°17'E
Kasabonika	CA	390	53°31'N	88°40'W
Kasai (Casai)	CG	287	3°02'S	16°57'E
Kasaji	CG	287	10°22'S	23°27'E

Kasakalawe	ZA	332	8°47'S	31°05'E
Kasalu	ZA	332	15°08'S	27°23'E
Kasama	ZA	332	10°11'S	31°10'E
Kasan	UZ	539	39°02'N	65°32'E
Kasane	BC	276	17°49'S	25°09'E
Kasanga	TZ	327	8°28'S	31°09'E
Kasanga Falls	ZA	332	17°24'S	24°10'E
Kasangulu	CG	287	4°36'S	15°10'E
Kasansay	UZ	539	41°45'N	71°31'E
Kasar, Ras	SU	324	18°01'N	38°36'E
Kāsaragod	IN	496	12°30'N	75°00'E
Kasawo	UG	330	0°41'N	32°49'E
Kasba L.	CA	390	60°20'N	102°10'W
Kasba Tadla	MO	310	32°36'N	6°16'W
Kaseda	JA	506	31°25'N	130°19'E
Kaseke	CG	287	11°48'S	26°58'E
Kasembe	TZ	327	10°14'S	36°25'E
Kasempa	ZA	332	13°27'S	25°50'E
Kasenga	CG	287	10°22'S	28°36'E
Kasese	CG	287	1°38'S	27°07'E
Kasese	UG	330	0°10'N	30°05'E
Kaset Wisai	TH	534	15°39'N	103°35'E
Kāsganj		470	27°49'N	78°39'E
Kashabowie		374	48°39'N	90°27'W
Kashaf	IR	502	36°12'N	59°58'E
Kāshān	IR	502	33°59'N	51°29'E
Kashary		560	49°03'N	41°00'E
Kashasha	UG	330	0°46'S	30°25'E
Kashechewan	CA	390	52°18'N	81°37'W
Kashi	CH	490	39°28'N	75°57'E
Kashiba	ZA	332	10°26'S	28°39'E
Kashin		466	57°21'N	37°37'E
Kashiwa		474	35°51'N	139°57'E
Kashiwazaki	JA	506	37°22'N	138°33'E
Kāshmar	IR	502	35°14'N	58°28'E
Kashmor	PK	524	28°26'N	69°35'E
Kashofu	CG	287	2°13'S	29°02'E
Kasibu	CG	287	2°50'N	28°11'E
Kasigau	KE	299	3°50'S	38°40'E
Kasimov		466	54°56'N	41°24'E
Kasindi	CG	287	0°03'N	29°41'E
Kasinge	CG	287	6°20'S	26°59'E
Kasiruta	ID	500	0°25'S	127°12'E
Kasiui	ID	500	4°30'S	131°40'E
Kasiya	MI	306	13°46'S	33°23'E
Kaskaskia		374	37°58'N	89°57'W
Kaskattama		370	57°01'N	90°08'W
Kaskinen (Kaskö)	FI	578	62°23'N	21°13'E
Kaskö (Kaskinen)	FI	578	62°23'N	21°13'E
Kas'kovo		560	59°37'N	29°30'E
Kasnya		466	55°24'N	34°20'E
Kasompe	ZA	332	12°35'S	27°54'E
Kasonaweja	ID	500	2°15'S	138°03'E
Kasongan	ID	500	2°00'S	113°23'E
Kasongo	CG	287	4°27'S	26°40'E
Kasongo-Lunda	CG	287	6°28'S	16°49'E
Kasonguele	CG	287	5°35'S	25°36'E
Kásos	GR	588	35°16'N	26°33'E
Kásos Strait		564	35°25'N	26°40'E
Kaspi	GG	495	41°56'N	44°25'E
Kaspichan	BU	573	43°19'N	27°10'E
Kaspiysk		466	42°53'N	47°38'E
Kaspiyskiy		466	45°22'N	47°24'E
Kasr, Ra's		264	18°02'N	38°35'E
Kassala	SU	324	15°28'N	36°24'E
Kassándra	GR	588	39°51'N	23°00'E
Kassándria	GR	588	40°01'N	23°27'E
Kassar, Ra's	ER	292	18°00'N	38°30'E
Kassel	GM	584	51°19'N	9°30'E
Kastamonu	TU	535	41°22'N	33°47'E
Kastanéai	GR	588	41°38'N	26°28'E
Kastéllion	GR	588	35°12'N	25°20'E
Kastéllon, Ákra	GR	588	35°24'N	27°08'E
Kaštel Stari	HR	574	43°33'N	16°20'E
Kaštel Sućurac	HR	574	43°33'N	16°25'E
Kastoría	GR	588	40°31'N	21°15'E
Kastorías, L.	GR	588	40°31'N	21°18'E
Kastornoye		560	51°49'N	38°09'E
Kasugai	JA	506	35°14'N	136°58'E
Kasui		478	4°44'S	104°26'E
Kasukabe	JA	506	35°58'N	139°45'E
Kasulu	TZ	327	4°34'S	30°06'E
Kasumiga-ura	JA	506	36°00'N	140°25'E
Kasum-Ismailov	AJ	483	40°37'N	46°48'E
Kasungu	MI	306	13°02'S	33°29'E
Kasupe	MI	306	15°10'S	35°18'E
Kasūr	PK	524	31°07'N	74°27'E
Kasymbek	KG	514	41°18'N	74°57'E
Kaszubskie, Pojezierze	PL	606	54°15'N	18°00'E
Kataba	ZA	332	16°05'S	25°06'E
Katako-Kombe	CG	287	3°24'S	24°25'E
Katákolon	GR	588	37°40'N	21°20'E
Katale	CG	287	1°19'S	29°22'E
Katanda	CG	287	0°50'S	29°22'E
Katanda	CG	287	6°21'S	23°54'E
Katanga (Shaba Plateau)	CG	287	9°00'S	26°00'E
Katangli	RS	612	51°42'N	143°14'E
Katanning	AS	656	33°42'S	117°33'E
Katanti	CG	287	2°18'S	27°08'E
Kataragama	CE	530	6°25'N	81°20'E
Katarniān Ghāt	IN	496	28°20'N	81°09'E
Katastárion	GR	588	37°50'N	20°45'E
Katchall		476	7°57'N	93°22'E
Katea	CG	287	5°06'S	20°36'E
Katea	CG	287	5°38'S	26°14'E
Katebo	UG	330	0°02'S	32°05'E
Kateh Bāsht	IR	502	30°20'N	51°11'E
Katenga	CG	287	5°02'S	28°48'E
Kateríni	GR	588	40°16'N	22°30'E
Katesh	TZ	327	4°31'S	35°23'E
Katete	MI	306	12°16'S	33°39'E
Katete	ZA	332	14°06'S	32°05'E
Katha	BM	487	24°11'N	96°21'E
Katherine	AS	656	14°28'S	132°16'E
Katherine	AS	656	23°48'S	143°42'E
Kāthgodām	IN	496	29°16'N	79°32'E
Kathiawar	IN	496	21°58'N	70°30'E
Kāthmāndu	NP	522	27°43'N	85°19'E
Kathu	SF	322	27°41'S	23°03'E
Kathua	IN	496	32°22'N	75°31'E
Kati	ML	307	12°44'N	8°04'W
Katiéna	ML	307	13°19'N	5°38'W
Katihār	IN	496	25°32'N	87°35'E
Katiola	IV	288	8°08'N	5°06'W
Katiu		654	16°30'S	144°30'W
Katla	SU	324	11°45'N	29°19'E
Katlehong		270	26°18'S	28°08'E
Katma	CH	490	38°06'N	85°15'E
Katni	IN	496	23°51'N	80°24'E
Káto Akhaía	GR	588	38°09'N	21°32'E
Katoba	TZ	327	7°05'S	30°34'E
Katojo	UG	330	0°01'S	29°46'E
Katokhí	GR	588	38°26'N	21°15'E
Káto Nevrokópion	GR	588	41°21'N	23°51'E
Katonga	UG	330	0°03'S	32°01'E
Katoúna	GR	588	38°47'N	21°07'E
Katowice	PL	606	50°16'N	19°01'E
Katrichev		466	49°23'N	45°33'E
Katrina, Jabal	EG	290	28°31'N	33°57'E
Katrineholm	SW	621	59°00'N	16°12'E
Katsepe	MA	304	15°45'S	46°15'E
Katshi	CG	287	6°08'S	26°13'E
Katsikás	GR	588	39°37'N	20°54'E
Katsina	NI	316	13°00'N	7°36'E
Katsina	NI	316	7°48'N	8°52'E
Katsina Ala	NI	316	7°09'N	9°17'E
Katsuta	JA	506	36°23'N	140°31'E
Katsuura	JA	506	35°09'N	140°18'E
Kattakurgan	UZ	539	39°55'N	66°15'E
Kattankudi	CE	530	7°40'N	81°44'E
Kattasang Hills	AF	480	33°00'N	68°00'E
Kattegat	DA	576	57°03'N	10°51'E
Katua	GH	296	9°59'N	1°57'W
Katue	ZA	332	13°50'S	27°50'E
Katumbi	MI	306	10°49'S	33°32'E
Katun	RS	612	52°25'N	85°05'E
Katunayaka	CE	530	7°10'N	79°52'E
Katundu	ZA	332	17°25'S	24°40'E
Katuta Kampemba	ZA	332	10°47'S	28°36'E
Katwe	UG	330	0°08'S	29°52'E
Katwijk aan Zee	NL	602	52°12'N	4°25'E
Kau	ID	500	1°11'N	127°54'E
Kauai	US	398	22°19'N	159°29'W
Kauai Chanel	US	398	21°48'N	158°50'W
Kaudum	WA	313	18°37'S	21°39'E
Kauehi		654	15°50'S	145°15'W
Kaufbeuren	GM	584	47°53'N	10°37'E
Kauhajoki	FI	578	62°26'N	22°11'E
Kauhava	FI	578	63°06'N	23°05'E
Kauiki Head	US	398	20°45'N	155°59'W
Kaukauna		374	44°16'N	88°16'W
Kaukkwe Hills	BM	487	25°00'N	97°00'E
Kaukura		654	16°34'S	148°16'W
Kaulakahi Chanel	US	398	22°01'N	159°56'W
Kaulashishi	ZA	332	15°20'S	29°46'E
Kauliranta	FI	578	66°27'N	23°41'E
Kaumba	CG	287	8°24'S	24°41'E
Kaunakakai	US	398	21°05'N	157°01'W
Kauna Pt.	US	398	19°02'N	155°53'W
Kaunas	LH	597	54°54'N	23°54'E
Kauno Marios	LH	597	54°53'N	24°05'E
Kaura Namoda	NI	316	12°36'N	6°35'E
Kauro	KE	299	1°03'N	37°42'E
Kaustinen	FI	578	63°33'N	23°36'E
Kautokeino	NO	604	69°01'N	23°02'E
Kau-ye Kyun	BM	487	11°01'N	98°32'E
Kavadarci	MK	599	41°26'N	22°01'E
Kavajë	AL	566	41°11'N	19°33'E
Kavála	GR	588	40°55'N	24°37'E
Kavalerovo	RS	612	44°16'N	135°05'E
Kāvali	IN	496	14°55'N	79°59'E
Kavarna	BU	573	43°26'N	28°20'E
Kavarskas	LH	597	55°26'N	24°55'E
Kavieng	PP	664	2°33'S	150°48'E
Kavimba	BC	276	18°03'S	24°37'E
Kavir-i Namak	IR	502	34°30'N	52°40'E
Kavshiri	GG	495	41°49'N	46°14'E
Kawaaloow	SO	321	1°16'N	43°48'E
Kawachi-Nagano	JA	506	34°26'N	135°34'E
Kawagoe	JA	506	35°55'N	139°29'E
Kawaguchi	JA	506	35°49'N	139°44'E
Kawaihoa Pt.	US	398	21°46'N	160°11'W
Kawaikini		380	22°05'N	159°29'W
Kawajena	SU	324	7°30'N	28°18'E
Kawambwa	ZA	332	9°47'S	29°05'E
Kawana	ZA	332	13°05'S	25°58'E
Kawanda	UG	330	0°26'N	32°32'E
Kawanoe	JA	506	34°01'N	133°34'E
Kawardha		470	22°01'N	81°15'E
Kawasaki	JA	506	35°31'N	139°42'E
Kawazu	JA	506	34°44'N	138°59'E
Kawhia	NZ	663	38°04'S	174°49'E
Kawi, Gunung	ID	500	7°55'S	112°26'E
Kawkabān	YM	541	15°30'N	43°53'E
Kawlag, Ra's	YM	541	12°05'N	54°01'E
Kawlin	BM	487	23°47'N	95°41'E
Kawm Umbū	EG	290	24°28'N	32°57'E
Kawr 'Abd Allah	KU	514	29°55'N	48°10'E
Kawsaing	BM	487	12°41'N	98°42'E
Kawthaung	BM	487	10°01'N	98°33'E
Kax He	CH	490	43°37'N	81°48'E
Kay		466	59°57'N	52°59'E
Kaya	CT	282	7°19'N	18°17'E
Kaya	UV	278	13°05'N	1°05'W
Kaya	UV	278	12°01'N	1°51'W
Kayaapu	ID	500	5°24'S	102°22'E
Kayak I.	US	398	59°56'N	144°23'W
Kayamba Hills	ZA	332	14°10'S	26°57'E
Kayan	ID	500	2°55'N	117°35'E
Kayanga	SG	319	11°58'N	15°00'W
Kayangel Islands	PX	664	8°10'N	134°46'E
Kayangel Passage	PX	664	8°01'N	134°45'E
Kayanza	BY	279	2°55'S	29°37'E
Kayar	SG	319	14°55'N	17°07'W
Kayasa	ID	500	1°59'S	124°39'E
Kaya-san	KS	513	35°49'N	128°07'E
Kayembe-Mukulu	CG	287	9°03'S	23°57'E
Kayenta	US	398	36°43'N	110°15'W
Kayes	ML	307	14°27'N	11°26'W
Kayirma	KG	514	41°59'N	74°39'E
Kayl	LU	598	49°29'N	6°02'E
Kaynaşlı		564	40°46'N	31°19'E
Kayoa	ID	500	0°05'S	127°25'E
Kayonza	RW	317	1°54'S	30°31'E
Kayrakkum	TI	533	40°16'N	69°49'E
Kayrakkumskoye Vdkhr.	TI	533	40°20'N	70°10'E
Kaysatskoye	RS	612	49°44'N	46°51'E
Kayser Gebergte	NS	438	3°03'N	56°55'W
Kayseri	TU	535	38°43'N	35°30'E
Kayuagung	ID	500	3°24'S	104°50'E
Kazabazua		374	45°57'N	76°01'W
Kazachka		560	51°28'N	43°55'E
Kazach'ya Lopan'	UP	624	50°19'N	36°11'E
Kazach'ye	RS	612	70°44'N	136°13'E
Kazakdar'ya	UZ	539	43°27'N	59°46'E
Kazakh	AJ	483	41°05'N	45°22'E
Kazakhskiy Melkosopochnik	KZ	510	48°30'N	71°00'E
Kazakhstan		38	48°00'N	68°00'E
Kazaki		560	52°38'N	38°16'E
Kazalinsk	KZ	510	45°46'N	62°07'E
Kazan		564	40°12'N	32°41'E
Kazan'	RS	612	55°47'N	49°06'E
Kazancı		564	36°30'N	32°53'E
Kazanka	UP	624	47°50'N	32°50'E
Kazanketken	UZ	539	43°02'N	59°10'E
Kazanlŭk	BU	573	42°37'N	25°24'E
Kazanskaya		560	45°25'N	40°26'E
Kazanskaya		560	49°48'N	41°09'E
Kazantip, Mys	UP	624	45°28'N	35°51'E
Kazarman	KG	514	41°24'N	74°03'E
Kazatin	UP	624	49°43'N	28°50'E
Kazaure	NI	316	12°39'N	8°25'E
Kazbegi	GG	495	42°39'N	44°39'E
Kāzerūn	IR	502	29°37'N	51°38'E
Kazhim		466	60°21'N	51°33'E
Kazimah	KU	514	29°25'N	47°45'E
Kâzımkarabekir	TU	535	37°14'N	32°59'E
Kazincbarcika	HU	590	48°15'N	20°38'E
Kaziza	CG	287	10°42'S	23°52'E
Kazlų Rūda	LH	597	54°46'N	23°30'E
Kaztalovka	KZ	510	49°46'N	48°42'E
Kazumba	CG	287	6°25'S	22°02'E
Kazuno	JA	506	40°11'N	140°47'E
Kazy	TX	537	39°13'N	57°30'E
Kéa	GR	588	37°33'N	24°21'E
Kéa (Keos)	GR	588	37°37'N	24°20'E
Keaau	US	398	19°37'N	155°02'W
Keahole Pt.	US	398	19°44'N	156°03'W
Kealakekua	US	398	19°31'N	155°55'W
Kéamo (Anatom)	NH	669	20°05'S	169°50'E
Keanapapa Pt.	US	398	20°53'N	157°04'W
Kearney	US	398	40°41'N	99°04'W
Kearny		376	33°03'N	110°54'W
Keban		564	38°48'N	38°45'E
Keban Baraji	TU	535	38°50'N	39°20'E
Ke Bao, I. de	VM	540	21°10'N	107°50'E
Kébémer	SG	319	15°22'N	16°27'W
Kebnekaise	SW	621	67°55'N	18°40'E
K'ebri Dehar	ET	293	6°44'N	44°17'E
Kebumen	ID	500	7°40'S	109°39'E
Kecel	HU	590	46°32'N	19°16'E
Kechika		368	59°38'N	127°09'W
Keçiborlu		564	37°57'N	30°18'E
Kecskemét	HU	590	46°54'N	19°42'E
Kedabek	AJ	483	40°35'N	45°49'E
Kėdainiai	LH	597	55°17'N	23°58'E
Kedgwick River		374	47°40'N	67°29'W
Kediet Ijill	MR	308	22°38'N	12°33'W
Kediri	ID	500	7°49'S	112°01'E
Kedon		468	65°30'N	158°00'E
Kedong		472	48°04'N	126°17'E
Kédougou	SG	319	12°33'N	12°11'W
Kędzierzyn-Koźle	PL	606	50°21'N	18°12'E
Keefers		372	50°01'N	121°32'W
Keel		558	53°58'N	10°05'W
Keele	CA	390	64°24'N	124°47'W
Keele Pk.	CA	390	63°26'N	130°19'W
Keeling Islands (Cocos Islands)	AS	656	12°00'S	96°50'E
Keene		374	42°56'N	72°16'W
Keer-weer, C.	AS	656	13°53'S	141°28'E
Keetmanshoop	WA	313	26°35'S	18°08'E
Keewatin		372	49°46'N	94°34'W
Keewong	AS	656	32°15'S	145°04'E
Kefali, Kepi	AL	566	39°55'N	19°52'E
Kefallinía (Cephalonia)	GR	588	38°15'N	20°35'E
Kéfalos	GR	588	36°44'N	26°58'E
Kefamenanu		648	9°27'S	124°29'E
Kefar Ruppin	IS	505	32°27'N	35°33'E
Kefar Sava	IS	505	32°10'N	34°54'E
Keffi	NI	316	8°51'N	7°52'E
Keffin Hausa	NI	316	12°14'N	9°55'E
Keflavík	IC	591	64°01'N	22°34'W
K'eftya	ET	293	13°54'N	37°07'E
Ke Ga, Mui	VM	540	10°20'N	108°00'E
Kegalla	CE	530	7°15'N	80°21'E
Kégashka	CA	390	50°12'N	61°17'W
Kegeyli	UZ	539	42°42'N	59°36'E
Keg River	CA	390	57°48'N	117°52'W
Kehra	EN	577	59°20'N	25°20'E
Ke-hsi Mānsām	BM	487	21°56'N	97°50'E
Keighley	UK	626	53°53'N	1°55'W
Keila	EN	577	59°18'N	24°25'E
Keimoes	SF	322	28°42'S	20°58'E
Keisha	CG	287	2°37'S	27°19'E
Keiss		558	58°32'N	3°07'W
Keïta	NG	314	14°46'N	5°46'E
Keitele	FI	578	62°55'N	26°00'E
Keith		652	36°06'S	140°21'E
Keith	UK	626	57°32'N	2°56'W
Keithley Creek	CA	390	52°46'N	121°25'W
Kekaha	US	398	21°58'N	159°42'W
Kékes	HU	590	47°55'N	20°02'E
Keklau	PX	664	7°36'N	134°39'E
K'elafo	ET	293	5°37'N	44°08'E
Kelang	MY	518	3°02'N	101°27'E
Kelantan	MY	518	6°11'N	102°15'E
Këlcyrë	AL	566	40°19'N	20°11'E
Keleft	AF	480	37°21'N	66°15'E
Kelem	ET	293	4°48'N	35°58'E
Keles		564	39°55'N	29°14'E
Keles	UZ	539	41°24'N	69°12'E
Kelheim	GM	584	48°55'N	11°52'E
Kelila	ID	500	3°35'S	138°45'E
Keli Mutu	ID	500	8°47'S	121°50'E
Kelkit	TU	535	40°08'N	39°27'E
Kelkit	TU	535	40°46'N	36°31'E
Kelle	UG	330	1°39'N	33°10'E
Kellé	CF	285	0°06'S	14°33'E
Keller L.	CA	390	64°00'N	121°30'W
Kellett, C.	CA	390	71°57'N	126°02'W
Kelleys		370	41°34'N	82°40'W
Kelliher		372	51°16'N	103°44'W
Kellogg		372	47°31'N	116°07'W
Kelloselkä	FI	578	66°56'N	28°50'E
Kelly Lake	CA	390	55°15'N	120°01'W
Kelmė	LH	597	55°38'N	22°56'E
Kel'mentsi	UP	624	48°28'N	26°50'E
Kélo	CD	283	9°19'N	15°48'E
Kelowna	CA	390	49°53'N	119°29'W
Kelsey Bay		372	50°23'N	125°58'W
Kelso	UK	626	55°35'N	2°25'W
Keluang	MY	518	2°02'N	103°19'E
Keluotun		472	49°15'N	125°52'E
Kelvin		374	49°53'N	88°55'W
Kelyexeed	SO	321	8°46'N	49°12'E
Kem		556	64°57'N	34°41'E
Kem'	RS	612	64°57'N	34°36'E
Kemabong	MY	518	4°55'N	115°56'E
Ké Macina	ML	307	13°58'N	5°22'W
Kemah		564	39°36'N	39°02'E
Kemaliye	TU	535	39°16'N	38°29'E
Kemano	CA	390	53°33'N	127°57'W
Kemasik	MY	518	4°25'N	103°27'E
Kémata I	CD	283	9°13'N	18°27'E
Kembé	CT	282	4°35'N	21°54'E
Kembolcha	ET	293	11°05'N	39°44'E
Kembolcha	ET	293	9°32'N	37°30'E
Kemena	MY	518	3°30'N	113°30'E
Kemence	HU	590	48°01'N	18°52'E
Kemer	TU	535	36°36'N	30°34'E
Kemerovo	RS	612	55°20'N	86°05'E
Kemi	FI	578	65°45'N	24°33'E
Kemijärvi		556	66°42'N	27°20'E
Kemijärvi	FI	578	66°44'N	27°38'E
Kemijoki	FI	578	65°47'N	24°30'E
Keminmaa	FI	578	65°49'N	24°29'E
Kemlya		560	54°42'N	45°15'E
Kemmerer	US	398	41°47'N	110°32'W
Kemmuna	MT	600	36°01'N	14°20'E
Kemmunett	MT	600	36°01'N	14°19'E
Kemparana	ML	307	12°50'N	4°56'W
Kempele	FI	578	64°55'N	25°30'E
Kempenland	BE	570	51°19'N	4°56'E
Kempsey	AS	656	31°05'S	152°50'E
Kempston	UK	626	52°06'N	0°29'W
Kempt, L.		374	47°25'N	74°15'W
Kempten	GM	584	47°43'N	10°19'E
Kempton Park	SF	322	26°06'S	28°14'E
Kemul, Kong	ID	500	1°55'N	116°04'E
Ken	AF	480	32°08'N	61°37'E
Ken	IN	496	25°46'N	80°31'E
Kenadsa	AG	272	31°34'N	2°26'W
Kenai	US	398	60°33'N	151°15'W
Kenai Peninsula	US	398	60°00'N	150°00'W
Kenamuke Swamp	SU	324	5°55'N	33°48'E
Kenaston		372	51°30'N	106°17'W
Kendal	UK	626	54°19'N	2°45'W
Kendall	US	398	25°40'N	80°19'W
Kendallville		374	41°26'N	85°15'W
Kendari	ID	500	3°57'S	122°35'E
Kéndavros	GR	588	41°14'N	24°56'E
Kendawangan	ID	500	2°31'S	110°15'E
Kendégué	CD	283	9°59'N	18°38'E
Kendrāpāra	IN	496	20°30'N	86°25'E
Kendu Bay	KE	299	0°22'S	34°39'E
Kenedy		376	28°49'N	97°50'W
Kenema	SL	320	7°52'N	11°12'W
Këneta e Karavastasë	AL	566	40°50'N	19°28'E
Keng-Akok	GB	294	1°37'N	11°35'E
Keng Deng	LA	517	18°05'N	105°03'E
Kenge	CG	287	4°52'S	16°59'E
Keng Hkam	BM	487	21°01'N	98°29'E
Keng Tung	BM	487	21°17'N	99°36'E
Kenhardt	SF	322	29°21'S	21°09'E
Kéniéba	ML	307	12°50'N	11°14'W
Keningau	MY	518	5°20'N	116°10'E
Kénitra	MO	310	34°16'N	6°36'W
Kenmare	EI	592	51°53'N	9°35'W
Kenmare	US	398	48°40'N	102°04'W
Kenmore	AS	656	26°56'S	149°14'E
Kennebec	US	398	43°44'N	69°46'W
Kennedy		372	50°01'N	102°21'W
Kennedy Range	AS	656	24°50'S	115°10'E
Kennett		374	36°14'N	90°03'W
Kennewick	US	398	46°12'N	119°08'W
Kenogami		370	50°05'N	84°28'W
Kenogamissi		374	48°00'N	81°30'W
Keno Hill	CA	390	63°55'N	135°18'W
Kenora	CA	390	49°47'N	94°29'W
Kenosha	US	398	42°35'N	87°49'W
Kenozero, Oz.		556	62°03'N	38°14'E
Kenscoff	HA	412	18°27'N	72°17'W
Kenstséle	CF	285	1°22'S	15°05'E
Kensu	KG	514	42°45'N	78°42'E
Kent		372	49°14'N	121°47'W
Kentaū	KZ	510	43°32'N	68°36'E
Kent Group	AS	656	39°26'S	146°51'E
Kenton on Sea	SF	322	33°41'S	26°40'E
Kent Pen.	CA	390	68°30'N	107°00'W
Kentucky		374	37°30'N	85°15'W
Kentucky	US	398	38°41'N	85°11'W
Kentucky Lake	US	398	37°01'N	88°16'W
Kentwood		378	30°56'N	90°30'W
Kenya		38	1°50'N	38°00'E
Keokuk		374	40°23'N	91°23'W
Keonjhar	IN	496	21°38'N	85°35'E
Keos (Kéa)	GR	588	37°37'N	24°20'E
Kepa		556	65°10'N	32°10'E
Kepi	ID	500	6°32'S	139°19'E
Kepina		556	65°23'N	41°50'E
Kepno	PL	606	51°17'N	17°59'E
Keppel Sands		652	23°21'S	150°47'E
Kera-Kera	GB	294	0°52'S	12°39'E
Kerang		652	35°44'S	143°55'E
Kerar yu	ET	293	5°03'N	38°18'E
Keratéa	GR	588	37°48'N	23°59'E
Kerava	FI	578	60°24'N	25°07'E
Keravat	PP	664	4°21'S	152°01'E
Kerch	UP	624	45°21'N	36°28'E
Kerchenskiy Pov.	UP	624	45°23'N	36°28'E
Kerchenskiy Proliv	UP	624	45°22'N	36°28'E
Kerchenskiy Zaliv		564	45°10'N	37°00'E
Kerchevskiy	RS	612	59°57'N	56°17'E
Kerchouel	ML	307	17°10'N	0°16'E
Kerch Pen.	UP	624	45°00'N	36°00'E
Kerema	PP	664	7°58'S	145°46'E
Kerempe Burnu	TU	535	42°01'N	33°21'E
Keren	ER	292	15°47'N	38°28'E
Kerepestarcsa	HU	590	47°33'N	19°17'E
Keret		556	66°16'N	33°34'E
Kerets, Mys		556	65°20'N	39°45'E
Kerewan	GA	295	13°29'N	16°06'W
Kerguelen Islands	FR	40	49°15'S	69°10'E
Kéri	GB	294	0°46'S	10°21'E
Kericho	KE	299	0°22'S	35°17'E
Keri Kera	SU	324	12°21'N	32°45'E
Kerimäki	FI	578	61°55'N	29°17'E
Kerinci Gunung	ID	500	1°42'S	101°16'E
Keriya He	CH	490	38°30'N	82°10'E
Keriya Shankou	CH	490	35°12'N	81°44'E
Kerkebet	ER	292	16°18'N	37°24'E
Kerki	TX	537	37°50'N	65°12'E
Kerkinis, L.	GR	588	41°12'N	23°09'E
Kérkira	GR	588	39°36'N	19°54'E
Kérkira (Corfu)	GR	588	39°40'N	19°45'E
Kerkour Nourene, Massif du	CD	283	14°50'N	22°10'E
Kerkrade	NL	602	50°52'N	6°04'E
Kermān	IR	502	30°17'N	57°05'E
Kerman Desert	IR	502	28°45'N	59°45'E
Kermen	BU	573	42°30'N	26°15'E
Kermit	US	398	31°51'N	103°05'W
Kern		376	35°16'N	119°18'W
Kernersville		374	36°07'N	80°04'W
Kernville		376	35°45'N	118°25'W
Keroh	MY	518	5°43'N	101°00'E
Keros		466	60°46'N	52°51'E
Kérou	BN	276	10°50'N	2°06'E
Kérouane	GV	297	9°16'N	9°01'W
Kerowagi	PP	664	5°53'S	144°50'E
Kerrville	US	398	30°02'N	99°08'W
K'ersa	ET	293	9°27'N	41°52'E
Kertamulia	ID	500	0°23'S	109°09'E
Kerzaz	AG	272	29°27'N	1°25'W
Kesabpur	BG	485	22°55'N	89°13'E
Keşan	TU	535	40°51'N	26°37'E
Kesen'numa	JA	506	38°54'N	141°35'E
Keshan		472	48°04'N	125°54'E
Keshem	AF	480	36°48'N	70°06'E
Keshod	IN	496	21°18'N	70°15'E
Keskin	TU	535	39°41'N	33°37'E
Kesogami		370	51°06'N	80°00'W
Kessingland	UK	626	52°25'N	1°43'E
Kestell	SF	322	28°18'S	28°42'E
Kesten'ga	RS	612	65°54'N	31°50'E
Keswick	UK	626	54°36'N	3°07'W
Keszthely	HU	590	46°46'N	17°15'E
Ket	RS	612	58°55'N	81°32'E
Keta	GH	296	5°55'N	0°59'E
Keta, Ozero		468	68°44'N	90°00'E
Ketanda		468	60°30'N	142°00'E
Ketapang		478	1°52'S	109°59'E
Ketchikan	US	398	55°20'N	131°38'W
Ketchum	US	398	43°40'N	114°21'W
Kété	CM	280	4°54'N	14°33'E
Kétegyháza	HU	590	46°32'N	21°11'E
Kete Krachi	GH	296	7°46'N	0°03'W
Keterme	KG	514	40°18'N	72°22'E
Keti	AM	482	40°53'N	43°52'E
Keti Bandar	PK	524	24°08'N	67°27'E
Ketmen	KZ	510	43°20'N	81°00'E
Kétou	BN	276	7°20'N	2°35'E
Kętrzyn	PL	606	54°05'N	21°23'E
Ketta	CF	285	1°28'N	15°53'E
Kettering		374	39°41'N	84°09'W
Kettering	UK	626	52°24'N	0°43'W
Kettle Falls	US	398	48°36'N	118°03'W
Kettle River Ra.		372	48°50'N	118°25'W
Kettle Valley		372	49°03'N	118°55'W
Keudeteunom	ID	500	4°28'N	95°49'E
Keur Massène	MR	308	16°33'N	16°14'W
Keurusselkä	FI	578	62°00'N	24°30'E
Keuruu	FI	578	62°16'N	24°42'E
Kévé	TO	328	6°26'N	0°56'E
Kevron	TI	533	38°28'N	70°51'E
Kew		382	21°54'N	72°00'W
Kewanee		374	41°14'N	89°55'W
Keweenaw Bay		374	46°55'N	88°20'W
Keweenaw Pen.		374	47°15'N	88°20'W
K'ey Āfer	ET	293	5°31'N	36°44'E
Keyi	CH	490	42°12'N	82°35'E
Keyihe		468	50°40'N	122°27'E
Key Largo	US	398	25°05'N	80°26'W
Key Largo	US	398	25°16'N	80°19'W
Keynshamburg	ZI	334	19°17'S	29°37'E
Keyser		374	39°26'N	78°58'W
Keytū	IR	502	35°19'N	48°09'E
Key West		378	24°33'N	81°47'W
Kezhma	RS	612	58°59'N	101°09'E
Kezi	ZI	334	20°55'S	28°28'E
Kežmarok	LO	616	49°08'N	20°26'E
Kgalagadi Desert	BC	276	28°00'S	22°00'E
Khaanziir, Raas		268	10°55'N	45°47'E
Khabarovsk	RS	612	48°30'N	135°06'E
Khabrat Abu al Husain	JO	510	32°10'N	38°15'E
Khabur	SY	531	35°15'N	40°30'E
Khachmas	AJ	483	41°28'N	48°48'E
Khagrāchari	BG	485	23°06'N	91°58'E
Khairavat	TI	533	39°27'N	68°23'E
Khairpur	PK	524	27°32'N	68°46'E
Khairpur Nathan Shāh	PK	524	27°06'N	67°44'E
Khaishi	GG	495	42°57'N	42°12'E
Khāk-e Chūpān	AF	480	31°41'N	64°54'E
Khakhea	BC	276	24°42'S	23°27'E
Khalābat	PK	524	34°13'N	73°02'E
Khalach	TX	537	38°04'N	64°52'E
Khalándrion	GR	588	38°02'N	23°48'E
Khaldan	AJ	483	40°43'N	47°13'E
Khalkabad	UZ	539	42°41'N	59°43'E
Khalkhāl	IR	502	37°37'N	48°32'E
Khálki	GR	588	36°14'N	27°36'E
Khalkidhiki	GR	588	40°25'N	23°27'E
Khalkidhón	GR	588	40°44'N	22°36'E
Khalkís	GR	588	38°28'N	23°36'E
Khal'mer-Yu	RS	612	67°58'N	64°50'E
Khalūf	MU	523	20°29'N	58°02'E
Kham Āb	TX	537	37°30'N	65°43'E
Khamar-Daban, Khr.	RS	612	51°15'N	105°00'E
Khambhat		470	22°18'N	72°37'E
Khambhat, Gulf of	IN	496	21°00'N	72°30'E
Khāmgaon	IN	496	20°41'N	76°34'E
Khamīs Mushayṭ	SA	528	18°18'N	42°44'E
Khamkeut	LA	517	18°15'N	104°43'E
Khammam	IN	496	17°15'N	80°09'E
Khamr	YM	541	15°58'N	43°57'E
Khamza	UZ	539	40°25'N	71°30'E
Khan	WA	313	22°42'S	14°54'E
Khānābād	AF	480	36°41'N	69°07'E
Khān Abū Shāmāt	SY	531	33°40'N	36°54'E
Khānaqīn	IZ	504	34°21'N	45°22'E
Khan ash Shaykh	SY	531	33°22'N	36°06'E
Kharayzir, Jabal al		564	34°20'N	37°55'E
Kharazir, J. el	SY	531	33°55'N	37°15'E
Khāndbāri	NP	522	27°22'N	87°13'E
Khandwa	IN	496	21°50'N	76°20'E
Khandyga	RS	612	62°40'N	135°36'E
Khānewāl	PK	524	30°18'N	71°56'E
Khanh Hung	VM	540	9°35'N	105°57'E
Khaniá	GR	588	35°31'N	24°02'E
Khanka, Ozero	RS	612	56°00'N	131°00'E
Khanki	UZ	539	41°28'N	60°47'E
Khanlar	AJ	483	40°35'N	46°20'E
Khanna	IN	496	30°42'N	76°13'E
Khanna, Qa'	JO	510	32°04'N	36°26'E
Khānpur	PK	524	28°00'N	68°43'E
Khānpur	PK	524	28°39'N	70°39'E
Khān Shaykhūn	SY	531	35°26'N	36°38'E
Khantau	KZ	510	44°13'N	73°43'E
Khantayskoye, Ozero		468	68°20'N	91°00'E
Khan Tengri, Pik	KZ	510	42°13'N	80°14'E
Khanty-Mansiysk	RS	612	61°01'N	69°06'E
Khanu	TH	534	16°12'N	99°43'E
Khān Yūnus	IS	505	31°21'N	34°19'E
Khapcheranga	RS	612	49°42'N	112°24'E
Kharabali		466	47°25'N	47°15'E
Kharagpur	IN	496	22°20'N	87°20'E
Kharak	PK	524	33°07'N	71°06'E
Khārān	PK	524	28°35'N	65°25'E
Kharan	IR	502	29°00'N	57°00'E
Kharānoq	IR	502	32°20'N	54°40'E
Kharbara	IN	496	28°56'N	73°25'E
Khargon	IN	496	21°49'N	75°36'E
Khāriān	PK	524	32°49'N	73°52'E
Kharit, Wadi al	EG	290	24°26'N	33°03'E
Kharkiv	UP	624	50°00'N	36°15'E
Kharlovka	RS	612	68°47'N	37°20'E
Kharmanli	BU	573	41°56'N	25°54'E
Kharovsk	RS	612	59°59'N	40°11'E
Kharumwa	TZ	327	3°12'S	32°39'E
Khasan	RS	612	42°25'N	130°40'E
Khasavyurt	RS	612	43°15'N	46°35'E
Khāsh	AF	480	31°31'N	62°52'E
Khāsh	IR	502	28°14'N	61°12'E
Khash Desert	AF	480	31°50'N	62°30'E
Khashm al Qirbah	SU	324	14°58'N	35°55'E
Khash Rud	AF	480	31°11'N	62°05'E
Khashuri	GG	495	41°59'N	43°36'E
Khasi Hills	IN	496	25°35'N	91°38'E
Khaskovo	BU	573	41°56'N	25°33'E
Khatanga	RS	612	71°58'N	102°30'E
Khatanga	RS	612	72°55'N	106°00'E
Khatangskiy Zaliv	RS	612	73°45'N	109°00'E
Khatt Atoui	MR	308	20°04'N	15°59'W
Khātūnīyah	SY	531	36°25'N	41°13'E
Khatyrka		368	63°30'N	174°00'E
Khavast	UZ	539	40°13'N	68°50'E
Khāvda		470	23°54'N	69°43'E
Khawrah	YM	541	14°25'N	46°08'E
Khawr al Udayd	QA	527	24°36'N	51°24'E
Khawr Fakkān	TC	538	25°21'N	56°22'E
Khay'	SA	528	18°43'N	41°22'E
Khaybar	SA	528	18°47'N	42°52'E
Khaybar	SA	528	25°42'N	39°31'E
Khaybar, Harrat	SA	528	25°30'N	39°45'E
Khaydarken	KG	514	39°57'N	71°20'E
Khayelitsa	SF	322	34°03'S	18°38'E
Khazarasp	UZ	539	41°19'N	61°05'E
Khelvachauri	GG	495	41°36'N	41°40'E
Khemis Miliana	AG	272	36°15'N	2°13'E
Khémisset	MO	310	33°49'N	6°04'W
Khemmarat	TH	534	16°01'N	105°13'E
Khenchela	AG	272	35°26'N	7°08'E
Khénifra	MO	310	32°56'N	5°40'W
Khenjān	AF	480	35°36'N	68°54'E
Khersan	IR	502	31°33'N	50°22'E
Kherson	UP	624	46°39'N	32°36'E
Khersonesskiy, Mys	UP	624	44°35'N	33°23'E
Khe Sanh	VM	540	16°37'N	106°42'E
Kheta	RS	612	70°00'N	95°00'E
Khevāj	AF	480	38°13'N	70°59'E
Kheyrābād	AF	480	36°58'N	67°03'E
Kheyr Khāneh	AF	480	34°57'N	63°37'E
Khezrī	IR	502	34°01'N	58°48'E
Khilok		468	51°00'N	108°00'E
Khilok	RS	612	51°21'N	110°28'E
Khimki		560	55°54'N	37°26'E
Khíos	GR	588	38°21'N	26°09'E
Khíos (Chios)	GR	588	38°22'N	26°00'E
Khisarya	BU	573	42°30'N	24°42'E
Khishkat	TI	533	39°26'N	68°30'E
Khiv	RS	612	41°45'N	47°56'E
Khiva	UZ	539	41°21'N	60°19'E
Khizabavra	GG	495	41°31'N	43°17'E
Khlebarovo	BU	573	43°37'N	26°15'E
Khlevnoye		560	52°12'N	39°05'E
Khlung	TH	534	12°27'N	102°14'E
Khmel'nik	UP	624	49°33'N	27°58'E
Khmel'nytskyy	UP	624	49°25'N	27°00'E
Khoai, Hon	VM	540	8°26'N	104°50'E
Khobi	GG	495	42°19'N	41°53'E

Khodishar	TI	533	39°25'N	69°14'E
Khodorov	UP	624	49°24'N	24°19'E
Khodovarikha	RS	612	68°56'N	53°47'E
Khodzhakala	TX	537	38°15'N	56°48'E
Khodzheyli	UZ	539	42°25'N	59°28'E
Khokhropār	PK	524	25°42'N	70°12'E
Kholm		560	57°09'N	31°11'E
Kholm	AF	480	36°42'N	67°41'E
Kholmets		560	56°21'N	33°21'E
Kholmogorskaya		556	63°49'N	40°39'E
Kholmogory		556	64°14'N	41°39'E
Kholmsk	RS	612	47°03'N	142°04'E
Kholtoson		468	50°18'N	103°18'E
Khomas Hochland	WA	313	22°40'S	16°20'E
Khomeynīshahr	IR	502	32°41'N	51°31'E
Khomutovka		560	51°55'N	34°33'E
Khone Falls	LA	517	13°56'N	105°56'E
Khong Chiam	TH	534	15°29'N	105°16'E
Khong Sedone	LA	517	15°36'N	105°49'E
Khoni	GG	495	42°20'N	42°26'E
Khonj	IR	502	27°52'N	53°27'E
Khon Kaen	TH	534	16°26'N	102°50'E
Khonuu	RS	612	66°27'N	143°06'E
Khopër	RS	612	49°35'N	42°19'E
Khor	RS	612	47°43'N	134°41'E
Khóra	GR	588	37°04'N	21°43'E
Khor Angar	DJ	289	12°23'N	43°21'E
Khóra Sfakíon	GR	588	35°12'N	24°08'E
Khoreyver	RS	612	67°25'N	58°03'E
Khorinsk	RS	612	52°10'N	109°46'E
Khoríon	GR	588	36°[illegible]3'N	27°35'E
Khoristí	GR	588	41°08'N	24°12'E
Khorixas	WA	313	20°20'S	14°54'E
Khorof Harar	KE	299	2°14'N	40°44'E
Khorog	TI	533	37°30'N	71°36'E
Khorol	UP	624	49°47'N	33°17'E
Khorol'		474	44°25'N	132°04'E
Khorramābād	IR	502	33°30'N	48°20'E
Khorramshahr	IR	502	30°26'N	48°09'E
Kho Sawai Plateau	TH	534	16°30'N	103°50'E
Khosheutovo	RS	612	47°02'N	47°47'E
Khost	PK	524	30°13'N	67°35'E
Khotin	UP	624	48°29'N	26°30'E
Khotynets		560	53°08'N	35°24'E
Khouribga	MO	310	32°53'N	6°54'W
Khovu-Aksy	RS	612	51°08'N	93°36'E
Khowai	IN	496	24°06'N	91°38'E
Khowst	AF	480	33°19'N	69°54'E
Khowst	AF	480	35°13'N	70°51'E
Khoyniki	BO	569	51°54'N	29°58'E
Khozarek	TX	537	36°54'N	63°43'E
Khrami	GG	495	41°20'N	45°08'E
Khrenovoye		560	51°07'N	40°17'E
Khreum	BM	487	21°28'N	93°42'E
Khrisoúpolis	GR	588	40°58'N	24°42'E
Khristinovka	UP	624	48°50'N	29°58'E
Khroma		468	72°00'N	143°00'E
Khromtaū	KZ	510	50°17'N	58°27'E
Khrysokhou Bay	CY	494	35°06'N	32°25'E
Khudābād	PK	524	36°41'N	74°48'E
Khudat	AJ	483	41°38'N	48°41'E
Khudumelapye	BC	276	23°52'S	24°56'E
Khudunskiy Khrebet		468	51°40'N	110°00'E
Khudzhand	TI	533	40°17'N	69°37'E
Khuff	SA	528	24°55'N	44°43'E
Khugdyungda, Khrebet		468	66°00'N	98°00'E
Khūgīānī	AF	480	31°37'N	65°04'E
Khuis	BC	276	26°36'S	21°47'E
Khu Khan	TH	534	14°42'N	104°12'E
Khuldābād		470	20°00'N	75°11'E
Khulimsunt	RS	612	62°52'N	61°40'E
Khulna	BG	485	22°48'N	89°33'E
Khulo	GG	495	41°39'N	42°20'E
Khuma	SF	322	26°50'S	26°51'E
Khummi, Oz.	RS	612	50°22'N	137°20'E
Khunjerab Pass	PK	524	36°52'N	75°27'E
Khun Yuam	TH	534	18°49'N	97°57'E
Khurda	IN	496	20°11'N	85°37'E
Khurja		476	28°15'N	77°51'E
Khūsf	IR	502	32°46'N	58°53'E
Khushāb	PK	524	32°18'N	72°21'E
Khust	UP	624	48°10'N	23°18'E
Khutsong	SF	322	26°19'S	27°19'E
Khuwayy	SU	324	13°05'N	29°14'E
Khuyum	TI	533	38°59'N	70°19'E
Khuzdār	PK	524	27°48'N	66°37'E
Khvāf	IR	502	34°33'N	60°08'E
Khvājeh Ra'ūf	AF	480	33°19'N	64°43'E
Khvalynka		474	44°40'N	132°54'E
Khvonsār	IR	502	33°12'N	50°18'E
Khvor	IR	502	33°47'N	55°05'E
Khvormūj	IR	502	28°39'N	51°23'E
Khvorostyanka		560	52°36'N	48°59'E
Khvoshī	AF	480	34°01'N	69°14'E
Khvoy	IR	502	38°33'N	44°58'E
Khvoynaya		560	58°54'N	34°32'E
Khwaja Muhammad	AF	480	32°57'N	70°38'E
Khyrdalan	AJ	483	40°27'N	49°46'E
Kia	BP	666	7°32'S	158°26'E
Kiama	CG	287	7°15'S	17°44'E
Kiamba	RP	526	5°59'N	124°37'E
Kiambu	KE	299	1°10'S	36°50'E
Kiamichi Mts.		378	34°37'N	95°00'W
Kiangara	MA	304	17°58'S	47°02'E
Kianjavato	MA	304	21°22'S	47°52'E
Kiantajärvi	FI	578	65°03'N	29°07'E
Kiáton	GR	588	38°00'N	22°44'E
Kibæk	DA	576	56°02'N	8°51'E
Kibaha	TZ	327	6°46'S	38°55'E
Kibala	AO	274	7°23'S	13°46'E
Kibale	UG	330	0°49'N	30°42'E
Kibali	CG	287	3°37'N	28°34'E
Kibanga	CG	287	4°29'S	29°09'E
Kibangou	CF	285	3°28'S	12°17'E
Kibar		470	32°20'N	78°01'E
Kibara	TZ	327	2°09'S	33°27'E
Kibau	TZ	327	8°35'S	35°17'E
Kibawe	RP	526	7°34'N	125°00'E
Kibaya	TZ	327	5°18'S	36°34'E
Kiberege	TZ	327	7°55'S	36°50'E
Kibergneset	NO	604	70°17'N	31°04'E
Kibi	GH	296	6°10'N	0°33'W
Kibigori	KE	299	0°04'S	35°03'E
Kibindu	TZ	327	5°56'S	37°56'E
Kibinga	CG	287	4°18'S	16°55'E
Kibiti	TZ	327	7°44'S	38°57'E
Kibiya	NI	316	11°32'N	8°40'E
Kiboga	UG	330	0°55'N	31°46'E
Kiboko	KE	299	2°11'S	37°43'E
Kibombo Rive	CG	287	3°57'S	25°59'E
Kibondo	TZ	327	3°35'S	30°42'E
Kibongoto	TZ	327	3°11'S	37°06'E
Kibray	UZ	539	41°23'N	69°28'E
Kibre Mengist	ET	293	5°53'N	38°59'E
Kibungo	RW	317	2°10'S	30°32'E
Kibungo	UG	330	1°15'S	30°05'E
Kibuye	RW	317	2°03'S	29°21'E
Kibwesa	TZ	327	6°28'S	29°57'E
Kibwezi	KE	299	2°25'S	37°58'E
Kičevo	MK	599	41°31'N	20°58'E
Kichiga Pervaya	TX	537	36°33'N	61°14'E
Kichi-Uryukty	KG	514	42°43'N	77°56'E
Kidal	ML	307	18°26'N	1°24'E
Kidete	TZ	327	6°39'S	36°42'E
Kidira	SG	319	14°28'N	12°13'W
Kidnappers, C.	NZ	663	39°38'S	177°08'E
Kidodi	TZ	327	7°36'S	36°59'E
Kidsgrove	UK	626	53°05'N	2°14'W
Kidugallo	TZ	327	6°47'S	38°12'E
Kiel	GM	584	54°19'N	10°07'E
Kielce	PL	606	50°50'N	20°35'E
Kieler Bucht	DA	576	54°35'N	10°35'E
Kiémbara	UV	278	13°15'N	2°44'W
Kien Duc	VM	540	11°58'N	107°30'E
Kienge	CG	287	10°34'S	27°33'E
Kien Thanh	VM	540	9°56'N	105°06'E
Kieta	PP	664	6°13'S	155°38'E
Kietrz	PL	606	50°05'N	18°00'E
Kiev (Kyyiv)	UP	624	50°26'N	30°31'E
Kiffa	MR	308	16°37'N	11°24'W
Kifrī	IZ	504	34°42'N	44°58'E
Kifusa	CG	287	6°02'S	24°36'E
Kifwanzondo	CG	287	5°08'S	19°35'E
Kigali	RW	317	1°57'S	30°04'E
Kiganga	TZ	327	7°43'S	34°57'E
Kigoma	RW	317	2°15'S	29°50'E
Kigoma	TZ	327	4°53'S	29°37'E
Kigumba	UG	330	0°16'N	31°35'E
Kigumo	KE	299	0°48'S	36°58'E
Kigye	KS	513	36°04'N	129°13'E
Kihikihi	NZ	663	38°02'S	175°21'E
Kihnu	EN	577	58°04'N	24°00'E
Kihundo	TZ	327	9°25'S	38°59'E
Kihura	UG	330	0°35'N	30°44'E
Kii-hanto	JA	506	34°00'N	135°45'E
Kiiminki	FI	578	65°06'N	25°43'E
Kii-sanchi	JA	506	34°00'N	135°50'E
Kii-suido	JA	506	34°00'N	134°50'E
Kijang	KS	513	35°14'N	129°13'E
Kijungu	TZ	327	5°22'S	37°12'E
Kikai-shima	JA	506	28°19'N	129°59'E
Kikarara	UG	330	0°30'S	29°48'E
Kikepa Pt.	US	398	22°00'N	160°03'W
Kikinda	YO	630	45°50'N	20°29'E
Kikki	PK	524	25°42'N	62°37'E
Kikladhes (Cyclades)	GR	588	37°00'N	25°10'E
Kikoira	AS	656	33°40'S	146°40'E
Kikombo	TZ	327	6°13'S	35°59'E
Kikonai	JA	506	41°40'N	140°26'E
Kikongo-Mindanga	CG	287	4°48'S	17°24'E
Kikori	PP	664	7°25'S	144°15'E
Kikori	PP	664	7°00'S	144°00'E
Kikube	UG	330	0°53'N	32°26'E
Kikuyu	KE	299	1°15'S	36°40'E
Kikwit	CG	287	5°02'S	18°49'E
Kil		558	59°31'N	13°15'E
Kilaguni	KE	299	2°54'S	38°04'E
Kilalo	TZ	327	2°24'S	33°43'E
Kilār	IN	496	33°06'N	76°25'E
Kilauea	US	398	22°12'N	159°24'W
Kilbaha		558	52°33'N	9°52'W
Kılbasan		564	37°20'N	33°12'E
Kilbride	CA	390	47°29'N	52°58'W
Kilbuck Mts.	US	398	60°50'N	159°50'W
Kilchoan	UK	626	56°42'N	6°06'W
Kilchu	KN	512	40°58'N	129°20'E
Kilcock	EI	592	53°24'N	6°40'W
Kilcoole	EI	592	53°06'N	6°04'W
Kildare		558	53°10'N	6°55'W
Kil'den		556	69°25'N	33°54'E
Kildonan		558	58°10'N	3°51'W
Kildonan	ZI	334	17°21'S	30°34'E
Kilembe	CG	287	5°42'S	19°55'E
Kilembe	UG	330	0°12'N	30°00'E
Kilgarvan	EI	592	51°54'N	9°27'W
Kilgore	US	398	32°23'N	94°52'W
Kilgoris	KE	299	1°00'S	34°53'E
Kilifarevo	BU	573	42°59'N	25°38'E
Kilifi	KE	299	3°38'S	39°51'E
Kilimanjaro	TZ	327	3°45'S	37°45'E
Kilimatinde	TZ	327	5°51'S	34°57'E
Kilindoni	TZ	327	7°55'S	39°39'E
Kilingi-Nõmme	EN	577	58°09'N	24°58'E
Kilinochchi	CE	530	9°21'N	80°22'E
Kilis	TU	535	36°44'N	37°05'E
Kiliya	UP	624	45°27'N	29°16'E
Kilkee	EI	592	52°41'N	9°38'W
Kilkeel	UK	626	54°03'N	6°00'W
Kilkenny	EI	592	52°39'N	7°15'W
Kilkís	GR	588	41°00'N	22°53'E
Killala		558	54°12'N	9°13'W
Killala Bay	EI	592	54°15'N	9°08'W
Killarney		372	49°11'N	99°40'W
Killarney	AS	656	16°13'S	131°43'E
Killarney	EI	592	52°03'N	9°31'W
Killarney Lake	BF	402	25°03'N	77°27'W
Kill Devil Hills	US	398	36°00'N	75°39'W
Killeen	US	398	31°07'N	97°43'W
Killenaule	EI	592	52°34'N	7°40'W
Killíni	GR	588	37°56'N	22°23'E
Killough	UK	626	54°15'N	5°38'W
Killybegs	EI	592	54°38'N	8°27'W
Kilmacow	EI	592	52°18'N	7°10'W
Kilmallock	EI	592	52°24'N	8°35'W
Kilmarnock		374	37°42'N	76°22'W
Kilmarnock	UK	626	55°36'N	4°28'W
Kilmore Quay	EI	592	52°10'N	6°35'W
Kilninver	UK	626	56°20'N	5°31'W
Kilombero	TZ	327	8°31'S	37°22'E
Kilomines	CG	287	1°48'N	30°14'E
Kilosa	TZ	327	6°50'S	36°59'E
Kilpisjärvi	FI	578	69°03'N	20°47'E
Kilronan		558	53°07'N	9°40'W
Kilrush	EI	592	52°38'N	9°29'W
Kilwa	CG	287	9°17'S	28°17'E
Kilwa Kivinje	TZ	327	8°45'S	39°24'E
Kilwa Masoko	TZ	327	8°56'S	39°31'E
Kilwinning	UK	626	55°39'N	4°43'W
Kimaan	ID	500	7°58'S	138°53'E
Kimali	TZ	327	3°23'S	34°28'E
Kimamba	TZ	327	6°47'S	37°08'E
Kimasozero		556	64°23'N	31°13'E
Kimba	AS	656	33°09'S	136°26'E
Kimba	CF	285	3°24'S	14°12'E
Kimball		372	49°05'N	113°12'W
Kimball	US	398	41°14'N	103°39'W
Kimbe	PP	664	5°33'S	150°08'E
Kimberley	CA	390	49°41'N	115°59'W
Kimberley	SF	322	28°45'S	24°46'E
Kimberley, C.	AS	656	16°14'S	145°28'E
Kimberley Plateau	AS	656	17°00'S	127°00'E
Kimberling City		374	36°38'N	93°25'W
Kimberly		372	42°32'N	114°21'W
Kimch'aek	KN	512	40°38'N	129°08'E
Kimch'ŏn	KS	513	36°07'N	128°07'E
Kimhae	KS	513	35°14'N	128°53'E
Kimi	CM	280	6°05'N	11°30'E
Kími	GR	588	38°37'N	24°06'E
Kímina	GR	588	40°37'N	22°41'E
Kimito	FI	578	60°07'N	22°40'E
Kimje	KS	513	35°48'N	126°53'E
Kimméria	GR	588	41°09'N	24°57'E
Kimnyangjang-ni	KS	513	37°14'N	127°12'E
Kímolos	GR	588	36°51'N	24°20'E
Kimongo	CF	285	4°29'S	12°58'E
Kimoset	KE	299	0°13'N	35°54'E
Kimovaara		556	63°38'N	31°02'E
Kimovsk		560	53°58'N	38°32'E
Kimpanga	CG	287	7°53'S	24°23'E
Kimpese	CG	287	5°33'S	14°26'E
Kimpili Mountains	ZA	332	10°00'S	30°00'E
Kimp'o	KS	513	37°38'N	126°42'E
Kimpoko-Nsele	CG	287	4°12'S	15°34'E
Kimry		560	56°52'N	37°21'E
Kimsquit	CA	390	52°51'N	126°57'W
Kinabatangan	MY	518	5°00'N	117°30'E
Kinalung	AS	656	32°05'S	142°00'E
Kinango	KE	299	4°08'S	39°19'E
Kinbasket L.		372	51°57'N	118°02'W
Kinbrace	UK	626	58°15'N	3°56'W
Kincaid		372	49°40'N	107°00'W
Kincardine		374	44°11'N	81°38'W
Kinda	CG	287	9°18'S	25°04'E
Kindambi	CG	287	6°10'S	20°21'E
Kindat	BM	487	23°44'N	94°26'E
Kindberg	AU	568	47°30'N	15°27'E
Kindeje	AO	274	7°09'S	13°39'E
Kindembe	CG	287	5°31'S	18°49'E
Kindersley		372	51°28'N	109°08'W
Kindi	UV	278	12°26'N	2°01'W
Kindia	GV	297	10°04'N	12°51'W
Kinel'		466	53°14'N	50°39'E
Kineshma	RS	612	57°25'N	42°09'E
King		374	36°16'N	80°21'W
King		652	41°00'S	143°40'E
King	AS	656	39°44'S	144°08'E
Kingaroy		652	26°32'S	151°50'E
King City		376	36°11'N	121°06'W
Kingcome Inlet		372	50°57'N	126°12'W
Kingfield		374	44°57'N	70°09'W
Kingfisher		376	35°51'N	97°55'W
Kingfisher Lake		370	53°02'N	89°50'W
King George Is.		654	14°00'S	145°00'W
Kingisepp		560	59°22'N	28°36'E
King Leopold Ranges	AS	656	16°00'S	125°00'E
Kingman		372	37°38'N	98°06'W
Kingman	US	398	35°11'N	114°03'W
Kingman Reef	US	40	6°27'N	162°24'W
Kingoonyah	AS	656	30°54'S	135°18'E
Kingoye	CG	287	4°28'S	13°50'E
Kings		376	36°50'N	119°10'W
Kings Beach		372	39°14'N	120°01'W
Kingsburgh	SF	322	30°05'S	30°53'E
Kingscourt	EI	592	53°54'N	6°48'W
Kingsgate		372	49°00'N	116°11'W
Kingsland		376	30°39'N	98°26'W
Kingsland		378	30°47'N	81°41'W
King's Lynn	UK	626	52°45'N	0°24'E
Kingsmill Group	KR	660	4°30'S	177°00'E
Kings Mountain		378	35°14'N	81°20'W
King Sound	AS	656	17°00'S	123°30'E
Kings Peak	US	398	40°47'N	110°22'W
Kingsport	US	398	36°32'N	82°33'W
Kingston		374	39°27'N	82°54'W
Kingston		374	41°55'N	73°59'W
Kingston		376	33°59'N	96°43'W
Kingston	JM	414	18°00'N	76°48'W
Kingston	NZ	663	45°19'S	168°45'E
Kingston S.E.	AS	656	36°50'S	139°54'E
Kingston upon Hull	UK	626	53°44'N	0°20'W
Kingstown	VC	418	13°08'N	61°13'W
Kingstree		378	33°40'N	79°49'W
Kingsville	US	398	27°30'N	97°52'W
Kingushi	CG	287	5°06'S	16°30'E
King William I.	CA	390	69°00'N	97°30'W
King William's Town	SF	322	32°53'S	27°23'E
Kingwood	US	398	30°03'N	95°13'W
Kiniama	CG	287	11°26'S	28°20'E
Kınık		564	39°05'N	27°23'E
Kinkala	CF	285	4°22'S	14°46'E
Kinkosi	CG	287	5°38'S	15°40'E
Kinleith	NZ	663	38°16'S	175°54'E
Kinlochbervie		558	58°28'N	5°03'W
Kinmen		472	24°26'N	118°19'E
Kinna		558	57°30'N	12°41'E
Kinnairds Head	UK	626	57°41'N	2°00'W
Kinneret	IS	505	32°44'N	35°34'E
Kinneret-Negev Conduit	IS	505	32°52'N	35°32'E
Kinniya	CE	530	8°29'N	81°11'E
Kinoosao	CA	390	57°06'N	102°01'W
Kinosota		372	50°55'N	98°52'W
Kino Viejo	MX	394	28°50'N	111°56'W
Kinross	SF	322	26°25'S	29°05'E
Kinsale	EI	592	51°42'N	8°31'W
Kinsarvik	NO	604	60°23'N	6°42'E
Kinshasa (Léopoldville)	CG	287	4°18'S	15°17'E
Kinsley		372	37°55'N	99°24'W
Kinston		378	35°15'N	77°34'W
Kintampo	GH	296	8°03'N	1°43'W
Kintap	ID	500	3°51'S	115°13'E
Kintinku	TZ	327	5°53'S	35°14'E
Kintore	UK	626	57°13'N	2°21'W
Kintore Range	AS	656	23°00'S	129°30'E
Kintyre	UK	626	46°32'N	99°56'W
Kinvarra	EI	592	53°08'N	8°56'W
Kinyangiri	TZ	327	4°27'S	34°37'E
Kinyeti	SU	324	3°56'N	32°50'E
Kiomboi	TZ	327	4°16'S	34°22'E
Kiosk		374	46°05'N	78°53'W
Kiowa		376	37°01'N	98°29'W
Kipange	CG	287	6°08'S	24°16'E
Kiparissía	GR	588	37°14'N	21°40'E
Kiparissiakós Kólpos	GR	588	37°30'N	21°25'E
Kipawa		374	46°47'N	78°59'W
Kipawa, Lac		374	46°55'N	79°00'W
Kipengere Range	TZ	327	9°10'S	34°15'E
Kipercheny	MD	601	47°31'N	28°50'E
Kipili	TZ	327	7°26'S	30°36'E
Kipilingu	CG	287	13°14'S	29°03'E
Kipini	KE	299	2°31'S	40°31'E
Kipkarren	KE	299	0°39'N	34°51'E
Kipushi	CG	287	11°46'S	27°14'E
Kirakira	BP	666	10°30'S	161°55'E
Kirandul		470	18°45'N	81°16'E
Kiranomena	MA	304	18°17'S	46°03'E
Kirawa	NI	316	11°11'N	13°51'E
Kirbla	EN	577	58°44'N	23°57'E
Kirchbichl	AU	568	47°31'N	12°05'E
Kirchschlag	AU	568	47°30'N	16°17'E
Kirensk	RS	612	57°46'N	108°08'E
Kirghiz Steppe	KZ	510	50°00'N	55°00'E
Kirgizskiy Khrebet	KG	514	42°30'N	74°00'E
Kiri	CG	287	1°27'S	19°00'E
Kiriákion	GR	588	38°21'N	22°48'E
Kiribati		38	5°00'S	170°00'W
Kırıkhan	TU	535	36°32'N	36°19'E
Kırıkkale	TU	535	39°50'N	33°31'E
Kirikkuduk	CH	490	44°12'N	90°40'E
Kirillov		556	59°52'N	38°23'E
Kirillovka	UP	624	46°22'N	35°20'E
Kirinda	CE	530	6°13'N	81°20'E
Kirishi	RS	612	59°27'N	32°02'E
Kırka		564	39°17'N	30°33'E
Kırkağaç	TU	535	39°06'N	27°40'E
Kirkcaldy		372	50°20'N	113°14'W
Kirkcaldy	UK	626	56°06'N	3°08'W
Kirkcudbright	UK	626	54°50'N	4°02'W
Kirkee	IN	496	18°34'N	73°51'E
Kirkenær	NO	604	60°26'N	12°04'E
Kirkenes	NO	604	69°43'N	30°03'E
Kirkland		372	47°40'N	122°12'W
Kirkland Lake	CA	390	48°09'N	80°02'W
Kirklar	TU	535	40°26'N	35°10'E
Kırklareli	TU	535	41°44'N	27°12'E
Kirkman Creek	CA	390	63°00'N	139°23'W
Kirkmichael	UK	626	54°17'N	4°35'W
Kirksville	US	398	40°11'N	92°34'W
Kirkton of Glenisla	UK	626	56°44'N	3°17'W
Kirkūk	IZ	504	35°28'N	44°21'E
Kirkwall	UK	626	58°59'N	2°57'W
Kirkwood	SF	322	33°24'S	25°26'E
Kirn	GM	584	49°47'N	7°27'E
Kirongwe	TZ	327	7°48'S	39°49'E
Kiropa	TZ	327	10°51'S	34°39'E
Kirov		560	54°05'N	34°20'E
Kirov	TI	533	38°32'N	68°32'E
Kirova, Zaliv	AJ	483	39°00'N	49°00'E
Kirovakan	AM	482	40°48'N	44°30'E
Kirovgrad		466	57°26'N	60°04'E
Kirovo	UZ	539	40°26'N	70°36'E
Kirovo-Chepetsk	RS	612	58°33'N	50°01'E
Kirovohrad	UP	624	48°30'N	32°18'E
Kirovsk		556	67°37'N	33°40'E
Kirovsk	BO	569	53°16'N	29°29'E
Kirovsk	TX	537	37°42'N	60°23'E
Kirovskiy		466	44°52'N	78°12'E
Kirovskiy	RS	612	45°05'N	133°30'E
Kirovskiy	RS	612	45°51'N	48°08'E
Kirovskiy	RS	612	54°18'N	155°47'E
Kirovskoye	KG	514	42°39'N	71°35'E
Kirriemuir	UK	626	56°40'N	3°00'W
Kirsanov		466	52°38'N	42°43'E
Kırşehir	TU	535	39°09'N	34°10'E
Kirthar Range	PK	524	27°00'N	67°10'E
Kirtland		376	36°44'N	108°21'W
Kirton	UK	626	52°55'N	0°03'W
Kiru	UG	330	2°38'N	33°40'E
Kiruna	SW	621	67°51'N	20°13'E
Kirundu	CG	287	0°44'S	25°32'E
Kirya		560	55°05'N	46°51'E
Kiryanga	UG	330	1°06'N	31°04'E
Kiryū	JA	506	36°24'N	139°20'E
Kisa	SW	621	57°59'N	15°37'E
Kisakata	JA	506	39°13'N	139°54'E
Kisalama	UG	330	0°28'N	31°55'E
Kis Alföld (Little Plain)	HU	590	47°30'N	17°00'E
Kisangani	CG	287	0°30'N	25°12'E
Kisantu	CG	287	5°08'S	15°04'E
Kisar		648	7°59'S	127°07'E
Kisarawe	TZ	327	6°54'S	39°04'E
Kisarazu	JA	506	35°22'N	139°55'E
Kisbér	HU	590	47°30'N	18°02'E
Kisbey		372	49°39'N	102°40'W
Kiselevka		560	47°18'N	44°10'E
Kiselevsk	RS	612	54°00'N	86°39'E
Kisenda	CG	287	6°21'S	18°59'E
Kisenge	CG	287	10°41'S	23°10'E
Kisesa	TZ	327	3°05'S	34°09'E
Kisessa	TZ	327	2°33'S	33°02'E
Kīsh	IR	502	26°33'N	54°01'E
Kishanda	TZ	327	1°42'S	31°34'E
Kishanganj	IN	496	26°07'N	87°56'E
Kishangarh		470	27°52'N	70°34'E
Kishangarh	IN	496	26°34'N	74°55'E
Kishb, Harrat	SA	528	22°47'N	41°30'E
Kishi	NI	316	9°05'N	3°51'E
Kishiwada	JA	506	34°27'N	135°22'E
Kishoreganj	BG	485	25°54'N	89°01'E
Kishorganj	BG	485	24°26'N	90°46'E
Kishtwar		470	33°19'N	75°46'E
Kisi	CG	287	1°11'S	28°13'E
Kisiabi	UG	330	2°06'N	31°25'E
Kisigo	TZ	327	6°26'S	34°44'E
Kisii	KE	299	0°41'S	34°46'E
Kisiju	TZ	327	7°24'S	39°20'E
Kisiwani	TZ	327	4°08'S	37°57'E
Kiska	US	398	51°52'N	176°35'E
Kiskissink		374	47°56'N	72°09'W
Kiskőrös	HU	590	46°37'N	19°18'E
Kiskunfélegyháza	HU	590	46°43'N	19°51'E
Kiskunhalas	HU	590	46°26'N	19°30'E
Kiskunmajsa	HU	590	46°29'N	19°45'E
Kislovodsk	RS	612	43°55'N	42°43'E
Kismaayo	SO	321	0°21'S	42°31'E
Kiso-gawa	JA	506	35°02'N	136°45'E
Kisoro	UG	330	1°17'S	29°41'E
Kiso-sammyaku	JA	506	35°40'N	137°45'E
Kisrah	TS	329	35°49'N	9°22'E
Kíssamos	GR	588	35°30'N	23°38'E
Kissidougou	GV	297	9°11'N	10°06'W
Kissimmee		378	27°09'N	80°51'W
Kissimmee	US	398	28°18'N	81°23'W
Kissimmee, Lake		378	27°55'N	81°16'W
Kissu, Jabal	SU	324	21°35'N	25°09'E
Kissy	SL	320	8°28'N	13°12'W
Kistelek	HU	590	46°28'N	19°59'E
Kisterenye	HU	590	48°01'N	19°50'E
Kistrand	NO	604	70°27'N	25°15'E
Kisújszállás	HU	590	47°13'N	20°46'E
Kisumu	KE	299	0°06'S	34°45'E
Kisvárda	HU	590	48°13'N	22°05'E
Kiswere	TZ	327	9°26'S	39°33'E
Kita	ML	307	13°01'N	9°29'W
Kitab	UZ	539	39°07'N	66°52'E
Kita-Ibaraki	JA	506	36°48'N	140°45'E
Kitakami	JA	506	39°18'N	141°07'E
Kitakami-gawa	JA	506	38°35'N	141°19'E
Kitakami-sammyaku	JA	506	39°40'N	141°30'E
Kitakyūshū	JA	506	33°53'N	130°50'E
Kitale	KE	299	1°01'N	35°00'E
Kitami	JA	506	43°48'N	143°54'E
Kitami-sammyaku	JA	506	44°30'N	142°00'E
Kitangari	TZ	327	10°39'S	39°20'E
Kitangiri, L.	TZ	327	4°04'S	34°19'E
Kitchener	CA	390	43°27'N	80°29'W
Kitee	FI	578	62°06'N	30°09'E
Kitendwe	CG	287	7°32'S	29°47'E
Kitengo	CG	287	7°26'S	24°08'E
Kitgum	UG	330	3°19'N	32°53'E
Kitgum Matidi	UG	330	3°14'N	33°01'E
Kithimani	KE	299	1°11'S	37°27'E
Kíthira	GR	588	36°09'N	22°59'E
Kíthira (Cerigo)	GR	588	36°15'N	23°00'E
Kíthnos	GR	588	37°24'N	24°26'E
Kíthnos (Thermia)	GR	588	37°23'N	24°25'E
Kitimat	CA	390	54°03'N	128°39'W
Kitonki	SL	320	8°39'N	13°14'W
Kitozho	UG	330	0°25'S	30°07'E
Kit Stoddart's	SC	417	17°18'N	62°43'W
Kitsuki	JA	506	33°25'N	131°36'E
Kittanning		374	40°48'N	79°31'W
Kittigazuit	CA	390	69°20'N	133°42'W
Kittilä	FI	578	67°37'N	24°52'E
Kittitian Village	SC	417	17°17'N	62°41'W
Kitty Hawk		374	36°03'N	75°42'W
Kitu	CG	287	7°38'S	27°42'E
Kitui	KE	299	1°22'S	38°01'E
Kitule	CG	287	5°46'S	26°56'E
Kitumala Point	PP	664	6°20'S	147°50'E
Kitumbeine	TZ	327	2°52'S	36°13'E
Kitumbini	TZ	327	9°37'S	39°30'E
Kitunda	TZ	327	6°48'S	33°13'E
Kitunguli	TZ	327	10°30'S	40°19'E
Kitwe	ZA	332	12°49'S	28°13'E
Kitzbühel	AU	568	47°27'N	12°23'E
Kitzbühler Alpen	AU	568	47°20'N	12°20'E
Kitzingen	GM	584	49°43'N	10°09'E
Kiudang	BX	486	4°45'N	114°44'E
Kiunga		268	1°45'S	41°28'E
Kiunga	KE	299	1°45'S	41°29'E
Kiunga	PP	664	6°07'S	141°18'E
Kiuruvesi	FI	578	63°39'N	26°37'E
Kiuyu, Ras	TZ	327	4°54'S	39°51'E
Kivertsy	UP	624	50°50'N	25°28'E
Kivijarvi	FI	578	61°00'N	28°00'E
Kiviõli	EN	577	59°21'N	26°57'E
Kivi-Vigala	EN	577	58°43'N	24°22'E
Kivu, Lake	CG	287	2°00'S	29°10'E
Kiwai I.	PP	664	8°55'S	143°50'E
Kiwela	CG	287	7°56'S	27°15'E
Kiwira	TZ	327	9°10'S	33°32'E
Kiwumulo	UG	330	0°15'S	31°08'E
Kiyevka		560	46°05'N	42°57'E
Kiyevka	KZ	510	50°16'N	71°34'E
Kıyıköy		564	41°38'N	28°05'E
Kiyonga	UG	330	2°12'N	31°18'E
Kizamba	CG	287	8°00'S	17°37'E
Kizel	RS	612	59°03'N	57°40'E
Kizëma		466	61°10'N	44°49'E
Kizhaba	AJ	483	38°34'N	48°48'E
Kiziba	UG	330	0°27'S	31°40'E
Kizilawat	CH	490	38°34'N	77°37'E
Kızılcahamam		564	40°28'N	32°39'E
Kızılhisar	TU	535	37°34'N	29°18'E
Kizil Irmak	TU	535	40°30'N	34°30'E
Kizil'skoye		466	52°44'N	58°54'E
Kızıltepe	TU	535	37°12'N	40°36'E
Kizimbani	TZ	327	9°04'S	39°19'E
Kizimkazi	TZ	327	6°27'S	39°28'E
Kizlyar		466	43°51'N	46°43'E
Kızören		564	38°08'N	33°11'E
Kizukuri	JA	506	40°48'N	140°23'E
Kizyl-Atrek	TX	537	37°38'N	54°46'E
Kizyl-Kaya	TX	537	40°00'N	55°40'E
Kizyl-Murad	TX	537	35°56'N	62°53'E
Kizyl-Su	TX	537	39°46'N	52°57'E
Kjerkestinden	NO	604	68°47'N	19°06'E
Kjøllefjord	NO	604	70°56'N	27°21'E
Kjøpsvik	NO	604	68°06'N	16°21'E
Kl'ačno	LO	616	48°54'N	18°39'E
Kladanj	BK	572	44°14'N	18°42'E
Kladar		478	8°24'S	137°43'E
Kladno	EZ	575	50°09'N	14°06'E
Kladovo	YO	630	44°37'N	22°37'E
Klaeng	TH	534	12°47'N	101°39'E
Klagenfurt	AU	568	46°38'N	14°18'E
Klaipėda	LH	597	55°43'N	21°07'E
Klaksvík		558	62°14'N	6°32'W
Klamath	US	398	41°31'N	124°02'W
Klamath Falls		372	42°13'N	121°46'W
Klamath Mountains		372	42°00'N	123°20'W
Klampo	ID	500	0°07'N	116°59'E
Klarälven	SW	621	59°23'N	13°32'E
Klarup	DA	576	57°01'N	10°03'E
Klaserie	SF	322	24°33'S	31°02'E
Klášterec nad Ohří	EZ	575	50°23'N	13°10'E
Klatovy	EZ	575	49°24'N	13°18'E
Klausen Pass	SZ	622	46°52'N	8°50'E
Klawer	SF	322	31°46'S	18°37'E
Kleena Kleene	CA	390	51°57'N	124°50'W
Klein Karas	WA	313	27°34'S	18°06'E
Kleinmond	SF	322	34°19'S	19°00'E
Kleinsee	SF	322	29°40'S	17°05'E
Klein Spitzkoppe	WA	313	21°51'S	15°03'E
Klein Vaaldoorn	WA	313	28°37'S	19°06'E
Klemtu	CA	390	52°35'N	128°31'W
Kleppestø	NO	604	60°25'N	5°09'E
Klerksdorp	SF	322	26°52'S	26°40'E
Klesov	UP	624	51°20'N	26°56'E
Kletnya		560	53°23'N	33°12'E
Kletsk	BO	569	53°04'N	26°38'E
Kletskiy		560	49°19'N	43°04'E
Klichev	BO	569	53°29'N	29°21'E
Klichka	RS	612	50°26'N	118°00'E
Klimovichi	BO	569	53°37'N	31°58'E
Klimovo		560	52°23'N	32°11'E
Klimpfjäll	SW	621	65°04'N	14°50'E
Klina	YO	630	42°37'N	20°35'E
Klintehamn	SW	621	57°24'N	18°12'E
Klintsy	RS	612	52°45'N	32°14'E
Klippan	SW	621	56°07'N	13°06'E
Klipplaat	SF	322	33°02'S	24°20'E
Klisura	BU	573	42°42'N	24°27'E
Klitmøller	DA	576	57°02'N	8°31'E
Kljajićevo	YO	630	45°46'N	19°17'E
Ključ	BK	572	44°32'N	16°47'E
Kłodawa	PL	606	52°15'N	18°55'E
Kłodzko	PL	606	50°26'N	16°39'E
Klosterneuburg	AU	568	48°18'N	16°20'E
Klosters	SZ	622	46°52'N	9°52'E
Klothuhta Zayat	BM	487	18°17'N	97°21'E
Klötze	GM	584	52°37'N	11°10'E
Klougakénou	TO	328	6°18'N	1°37'E
Kluane		368	61°01'N	138°19'W
Kluane Lake		368	61°15'N	138°40'W
Kluczbork	PL	606	50°59'N	18°13'E
Klyuchevskaya Sopka	RS	612	56°04'N	160°38'E
Klyuchi	RS	612	56°18'N	160°51'E
Kmagha	BP	666	8°20'S	159°44'E
Knaresborough	UK	626	54°00'N	1°27'W
Knezha	BU	573	43°30'N	24°05'E
Knighton	UK	626	52°20'N	3°02'W
Knin	HR	574	44°02'N	16°12'E
Knittelfeld	AU	568	47°12'N	14°48'E
Knjaževac	YO	630	43°34'N	22°15'E
Knob, C.	AS	656	34°32'S	119°13'E
Knob Noster		374	38°45'N	93°33'W
Knob Peak	RP	526	30°30'N	74°00'E
Knoll Point	WA	313	25°28'S	14°51'E
Knox		374	41°17'N	86°37'W
Knox, C.	CA	390	54°09'N	133°04'W
Knox City		376	33°25'N	99°49'W
Knoxville		374	40°54'N	90°17'W
Knoxville		374	41°19'N	93°06'W
Knoxville	US	398	35°57'N	83°55'W
Knurów	PL	606	50°13'N	18°40'E
Knyazh'i Gory		560	56°05'N	35°14'E
Knysna	SF	322	34°02'S	23°01'E
Koanaka Hills	BC	276	20°08'S	21°10'E
Koani	TZ	327	6°07'S	39°18'E
Koba	ID	500	2°31'S	106°24'E
Kobar Sink	ER	292	13°35'N	40°50'E
Kobayashi	JA	506	31°59'N	130°59'E
Kobdo, Jirgalanta	MG	520	48°01'N	91°38'E
Kōbe	JA	506	34°41'N	135°11'E
Kobelyaki	UP	624	49°09'N	34°12'E
København (Copenhagen)	DA	576	55°41'N	12°34'E
Kobenni	MR	308	15°51'N	9°25'W
Kobipato, Gunung	ID	500	3°05'S	129°32'E
Koblenz	GM	584	50°21'N	7°36'E
Koblenz	SZ	622	47°36'N	8°14'E
K'obo	ET	293	12°09'N	39°38'E
Koboko	UG	330	3°26'N	30°57'E
Kobowen Swamp	SU	324	5°38'N	33°54'E
Kobozha		560	58°35'N	34°58'E
Kobra		466	60°03'N	50°47'E
Kobrin	BO	569	52°13'N	24°21'E
Kobroör	ID	500	6°12'S	134°32'E
Kobu	KS	513	35°37'N	126°46'E
Kobuk		368	66°54'N	160°38'W
Kobuleti	GG	495	41°50'N	41°45'E
Koca	TU	535	36°10'N	29°30'E
Kocaali	TU	535	41°03'N	30°52'E
Kocaaliler		564	37°19'N	30°44'E
Koçakatran Dağlari		564	39°40'N	26°40'E
Kočani	MK	599	41°55'N	22°25'E
Koçarlı		564	37°45'N	27°42'E
Kočevje	SI	617	45°38'N	14°54'E
Koch'ang	KS	513	35°41'N	127°55'E
Kochechum		468	67°00'N	98°00'E

Kochen'ga		556	60°09'N	43°33'E
Kocherinovo	BU	573	42°05'N	23°04'E
Kochetovka		560	53°02'N	40°31'E
Kōchi	JA	506	33°33'N	133°33'E
Koch I.		370	69°35'N	78°20'W
Kochkor-Ata	KG	514	41°01'N	72°29'E
Kochkorka	KG	514	42°13'N	75°46'E
Kochkurovo		560	54°02'N	45°26'E
Kochubey		466	44°24'N	46°33'E
Kochugaon	IN	496	26°34'N	90°04'E
Kodala	IN	496	19°38'N	84°57'E
Kodari	NP	522	27°56'N	85°55'E
Kodi		478	9°33'S	118°59'E
Kodiak	US	398	57°47'N	152°24'W
Kodiak	US	398	57°30'N	153°30'W
Kodino		556	63°43'N	39°41'E
Kodok	SU	324	9°51'N	32°06'E
Kodomari	JA	506	41°06'N	140°17'E
Kodori	GG	495	42°48'N	41°09'E
Kodorskiy Khr.	GG	495	43°00'N	42°00'E
Kodry	MD	601	47°30'N	27°30'E
Kodyma	UP	624	48°06'N	29°07'E
Koës	WA	313	25°57'S	19°07'E
Koesan	KS	513	36°48'N	127°48'E
Koetari	NS	438	2°05'N	56°30'W
Kofelē	ET	293	7°04'N	38°47'E
Koffiefontein	SF	322	29°24'S	25°01'E
Köflach	AU	568	47°04'N	15°06'E
Koforidua	GH	296	6°05'N	0°15'W
Kōfu	JA	506	35°38'N	138°33'E
Koga	TZ	327	6°10'S	32°20'E
Køge	DA	576	55°27'N	12°11'E
Køge Bugt	DA	576	55°30'N	12°20'E
Kogertu	KZ	510	41°06'N	68°42'E
Kogon	GV	297	11°01'N	14°42'W
Kogum-do	KS	513	34°27'N	127°11'E
Kohāt	PK	524	33°35'N	71°26'E
Kohila	EN	577	59°10'N	24°45'E
Kohīma	IN	496	25°40'N	94°07'E
Kohinggo I.	BP	666	8°05'S	157°00'E
Kohlu	PK	524	29°54'N	69°15'E
Koholana	CE	530	7°18'N	80°15'E
Kohtla-Järve	EN	577	59°24'N	27°15'E
Kohŭng	KS	513	34°37'N	127°17'E
Koidern	CA	390	61°59'N	140°30'W
Koidu	SL	320	8°38'N	10°59'W
Koigi	EN	577	58°50'N	25°45'E
Koihoa		476	8°10'N	93°28'E
Koilābās	NP	522	27°42'N	82°31'E
Koímisis	GR	588	41°13'N	23°18'E
Koindu	SL	320	8°27'N	10°20'W
Koitere	FI	578	62°58'N	30°45'E
Koito	KE	299	3°01'S	39°07'E
Koje-do	KS	513	34°52'N	128°37'E
Kojetín	EZ	575	49°21'N	17°19'E
Kojonup	AS	656	33°50'S	117°09'E
Kojsovska Hol'a	LO	616	48°47'N	20°59'E
K'ok'a Hayk'	ET	293	8°23'N	39°05'E
Kökar	FI	578	59°51'N	20°49'E
Kokas	ID	500	2°43'S	132°25'E
Kokava nad Rimavicou	LO	616	48°34'N	19°50'E
Kokcha	AF	480	37°00'N	69°50'E
Kokemäki	FI	578	61°15'N	22°21'E
Kokhanovo	BO	569	54°28'N	29°59'E
Kokhma		560	56°56'N	41°06'E
Kokkola (Karleby)	FI	578	63°50'N	23°07'E
Kokmäenjoke	FI	578	61°30'N	28°10'E
Kok-Moynok	KG	514	42°27'N	76°02'E
Koknese	LG	596	56°39'N	25°26'E
Koko	NI	316	11°26'N	4°30'E
Koko	NI	316	5°59'N	5°26'E
Kokoda	PP	664	8°54'S	147°46'E
Kokofata	ML	307	12°53'N	9°57'W
Kokola	CG	287	0°47'N	29°36'E
Kokomo		370	40°29'N	86°08'W
Kokonau	ID	500	4°42'S	136°26'E
Kokong	BC	276	24°19'S	23°04'E
Kokonselka	FI	578	61°45'N	28°50'E
Kokopo	PP	664	4°20'S	152°16'E
Kokorevka		560	52°35'N	34°16'E
Kokosi	SF	322	26°29'S	27°28'E
Kokoté	TO	328	8°01'N	1°14'E
Kokpekty	KZ	510	48°45'N	82°24'E
Koksan	KN	512	38°45'N	126°40'E
Kokshaal-Tau, Khrebet	KG	514	41°00'N	78°00'E
Kōkshetaū	KZ	510	53°15'N	69°25'E
Koksoak	CA	390	58°31'N	68°11'W
Koksŏng	KS	513	35°17'N	127°18'E
Kokstad	SF	322	30°33'S	29°25'E
Kokterek	KZ	510	42°32'N	70°16'E
Kokufu	JA	506	36°11'N	137°12'E
Kokuy		468	52°13'N	117°33'E
Koküy	CH	490	46°39'N	90°19'E
Kok-Yangak	KG	514	41°02'N	73°12'E
Kokyar	CH	490	37°22'N	77°15'E
Kol	PP	664	5°41'S	144°48'E
Kola		556	68°53'N	33°01'E
Kola	ID	500	5°30'S	134°35'E
Kolahun	LI	301	8°17'N	10°05'W
Kolaka	ID	500	4°03'S	121°38'E
Kolār	IN	496	13°08'N	78°08'E
Kolari	FI	578	67°20'N	23°47'E
Kolárovo	LO	616	47°55'N	18°00'E
Kolašin	YO	630	42°49'N	19°32'E
Kolbano	ID	500	10°02'S	124°31'E
Kolbio	KE	299	1°09'S	41°12'E
Kolbus		262	14°13'N	22°23'E
Kolbuszowa	PL	606	50°15'N	21°46'E
Kolda	SG	319	12°53'N	14°57'W
Kolding	DA	576	55°29'N	9°28'E
Kole	CG	287	2°07'N	25°21'E
Kolen	SW	621	60°49'N	16°08'E
Kölen Mountains	SW	621	65°00'N	14°00'E
Kolenté	GV	297	10°06'N	12°37'W
Kolepom		648	8°02'S	136°28'E
Kolezhma		556	64°14'N	35°53'E
Kolgaküla	EN	577	59°32'N	25°42'E
Kolga Laht	EN	577	59°32'N	25°25'E
Kolguyev, Ostrov	RS	612	69°05'N	49°15'E
Kolhāpur	IN	496	16°42'N	74°13'E
Koliba (Corubal)	PU	298	11°41'N	14°48'W
Kolín	EZ	575	50°02'N	15°12'E
Kolindrós	GR	588	40°29'N	22°29'E
Koliya	GV	297	10°25'N	14°04'W
Kolka	LG	596	57°45'N	22°35'E
Kolkasrags	LG	596	57°46'N	22°37'E
Kolkhozabad	TI	533	37°35'N	68°40'E
Kolkwitz		558	51°45'N	14°15'E
Kollidam	IN	496	11°00'N	79°45'E
Kollumúli	IC	591	65°47'N	14°22'W
Kolmanskop	WA	313	26°42'S	15°13'E
Köln	GM	584	50°56'N	6°57'E
Kolno	PL	606	53°25'N	21°56'E
Koło	PL	606	52°10'N	18°37'E
Kolo	TZ	327	4°44'S	35°50'E
Koloa	US	398	21°54'N	159°28'W
Kołobrzeg	PL	606	54°09'N	15°33'E
Kolodnya		560	54°48'N	32°09'E
Kolofata	CM	280	11°10'N	14°01'E
Kologriv		560	58°49'N	44°20'E
Kolokani	ML	307	13°35'N	8°02'W
Kololo	ET	293	7°24'N	41°55'E
Kolombangara (Nduke)	BP	666	7°50'S	157°00'E
Kolomna	RS	612	55°05'N	38°47'E
Kolomyya	UP	624	48°32'N	25°02'E
Kolondiéba	ML	307	11°05'N	6°54'W
Kolonga		654	21°09'S	175°11'W
Kolongotomo	ML	307	13°53'N	5°41'W
Kolonia	FM	661	6°57'N	158°15'E
Kolonnawa	CE	530	6°56'N	79°53'E
Kolosib	IN	496	24°14'N	92°40'E
Kolovai		654	21°09'S	175°05'W
Kolpashevo	RS	612	58°20'N	82°50'E
Kolpino	RS	612	59°45'N	30°37'E
Kolpny		560	52°13'N	37°02'E
Kolpyta	UP	624	51°23'N	30°52'E
Kolskiy Poluostrov	RS	612	67°20'N	37°00'E
Kolsva	SW	621	59°36'N	15°50'E
Kolumadulu Atoll	MV	519	2°25'N	73°10'E
Kolvereid	NO	604	64°51'N	11°33'E
Kolwezi	CG	287	10°43'S	25°28'E
Kolyma	RS	612	69°30'N	161°00'E
Kolymskaya Nizmennost	RS	612	68°30'N	154°00'E
Kolymskiy, Khrebet	RS	612	65°00'N	160°00'E
Kolyshley		560	52°40'N	44°20'E
Kolyvan'	RS	612	55°18'N	82°45'E
Kom		474	36°15'N	127°00'E
Kom	BU	573	43°10'N	23°03'E
Kom	CH	490	48°34'N	87°24'E
Kom	GB	294	2°15'N	12°00'E
Komádi	HU	590	47°00'N	21°30'E
Komadugu Gana	NI	316	13°05'N	12°24'E
Komadugu Yobe	NG	314	13°43'N	13°20'E
Komadunga Gana		262	36°05'N	12°24'E
Komagane	JA	506	35°43'N	137°55'E
Komanda	CG	287	1°23'N	29°46'E
Komandorskiye Ostrova	RS	612	55°00'N	167°00'E
Komarichi		560	52°25'N	34°47'E
Komarin	BO	569	51°26'N	30°34'E
Komárno	LO	616	47°46'N	18°08'E
Komárom	HU	590	47°43'N	18°08'E
Komati	WZ	326	25°46'S	32°43'E
Komatipoort	SF	322	25°26'S	31°56'E
Komatsu	JA	506	36°23'N	136°25'E
Komatsushima	JA	506	34°00'N	134°35'E
Komba	CG	287	2°53'N	23°59'E
Kombat	WA	313	19°43'S	17°42'E
Kombe	CG	287	4°15'S	25°06'E
Kombissiri	UV	278	12°04'N	1°20'W
Kome I.	TZ	327	2°22'S	32°28'E
Kome Island	UG	330	0°06'S	32°45'E
Komende	SL	320	7°24'N	12°07'W
Komering	ID	500	2°59'S	104°50'E
Komga	SF	322	32°34'S	27°53'E
Komjatice	LO	616	48°12'N	18°07'E
Komló	HU	590	46°12'N	18°16'E
Kommagas	SF	322	29°48'S	17°29'E
Kommunizma, Pik	TI	533	38°57'N	72°01'E
Komo	PP	664	6°05'S	142°55'E
Komodo	ID	500	8°36'S	119°30'E
Komodougou	GV	297	9°38'N	9°04'W
Komoé	IV	288	5°12'N	3°44'W
Komono	CF	285	3°15'S	13°14'E
Komonos, Monts des	IV	288	9°30'N	4°10'W
Komoran		648	8°30'S	138°39'E
Komoren	ID	500	7°00'S	139°00'E
Komotiní	GR	588	41°08'N	25°25'E
Kompasberg	SF	322	31°45'S	24°31'E
Kompiam	PP	664	5°24'S	143°54'E
Komrat	MD	601	46°18'N	28°39'E
Komsomolets, O.	RS	612	80°30'N	95°00'E
Komsomol'sk		560	57°02'N	40°23'E
Komsomol'sk	RS	612	57°25'N	86°02'E
Komsomol'sk	TX	537	39°02'N	63°36'E
Komsomol'skiy		560	45°20'N	46°02'E
Komsomol'skiy		560	54°27'N	45°49'E
Komsomol'skiy	RS	612	69°10'N	172°42'E
Komsomol'sk-na-Amure	RS	612	50°34'N	136°58'E
Komsomol'sk-na-Pechore		466	62°07'N	56°35'E
Komsomol'skoye		560	50°46'N	47°03'E
Komsomol'skoye	UP	624	47°40'N	38°05'E
Komsomol'skoye	UP	624	49°02'N	33°40'E
Komsomol'skoye	UP	624	49°36'N	36°30'E
Komukanti	WA	313	19°53'S	17°09'E
Komyshnya	UP	624	50°11'N	33°41'E
Konabonou	IV	288	7°00'N	5°30'W
Konagkend	AJ	483	41°05'N	48°36'E
Konakovo		466	56°42'N	36°46'E
Konārak	IR	502	25°21'N	60°21'E
Konar-e Khāş	AF	480	34°39'N	70°54'E
Konaweha	ID	500	3°50'S	121°30'E
Konda		466	60°00'N	67°30'E
Kondagaon		470	19°36'N	81°40'E
Kondé Sounga	CF	285	4°16'S	11°40'E
Kondinin	AS	656	32°30'S	118°16'E
Kondinskoye		466	59°37'N	67°24'E
Kondoa	TZ	327	4°54'S	35°47'E
Kondol'		560	52°49'N	45°03'E
Kondopoga		466	62°12'N	34°17'E
Kondrovo		560	54°48'N	35°56'E
Kondūz	AF	480	36°45'N	68°51'E
Koné		654	21°00'S	165°00'E
Konendu	SL	320	8°29'N	10°53'W
Konetsgor'ye		556	62°46'N	43°12'E
Konëvo		556	62°08'N	39°20'E
Kong	IV	288	9°09'N	4°37'W
Kong	LA	517	13°32'N	105°58'E
Kong, Kas	CB	489	11°20'N	103°00'E
Kongapatalabata	ID	500	6°32'S	134°26'E
Kongbo	CT	282	4°44'N	21°23'E
Kongiskiye Gory		468	65°00'N	159°00'E
Kongju	KS	513	36°27'N	127°08'E
Kong Krailat	TH	534	16°56'N	99°58'E
Kongola	WA	313	17°45'S	23°25'E
Kongolo	CG	287	5°21'S	26°59'E
Kongor	SU	324	7°10'N	31°21'E
Kongoussi	UV	278	13°19'N	1°32'W
Kongsberg	NO	604	59°40'N	9°35'E
Kongsvinger	NO	604	60°12'N	12°00'E
Kongué, Chutes de	GB	294	0°20'N	12°42'E
Kongur Shan	CH	490	38°37'N	75°20'E
Kongwa	TZ	327	6°12'S	36°25'E
Koniecpol	PL	606	50°47'N	19°41'E
Königsbrunn	GM	584	48°16'N	10°53'E
Königslutter am Elm	GM	584	52°15'N	10°49'E
Königswinter	GM	584	50°41'N	7°11'E
Königs Wusterhausen	GM	584	52°17'N	13°37'E
Konin	PL	606	52°13'N	18°16'E
Konindou	GV	297	10°42'N	10°51'W
Konispol	AL	566	39°40'N	20°09'E
Kónitsa	GR	588	40°03'N	20°44'E
Köniz	SZ	622	46°55'N	7°25'E
Konjic	BK	572	43°39'N	17°57'E
Konkiep	WA	313	26°46'S	17°13'E
Konkola	ZA	332	12°19'S	27°45'E
Konkori	GH	296	9°36'N	1°46'W
Konkouré	GV	297	9°52'N	9°45'W
Konnevesi	FI	578	62°37'N	26°17'E
Konobougou	ML	307	12°55'N	6°46'W
Konos	PP	664	3°07'S	151°42'E
Konosha		466	60°58'N	40°15'E
Konotop	UP	624	51°14'N	33°12'E
Konqi He	CH	490	40°40'N	90°10'E
Konrei	PX	664	7°44'S	134°38'E
Końskie	PL	606	51°12'N	20°25'E
Konso	ET	293	5°15'N	37°29'E
Konstantinovka		560	56°41'N	50°53'E
Konstantinovka	UP	624	49°06'N	35°41'E
Konstantinovsk		560	47°35'N	41°06'E
Konstanz	GM	584	47°40'N	9°11'E
Kontagora	NI	316	10°25'N	5°27'E
Kontcha	CM	280	7°58'N	12°14'E
Konteyevo		560	58°26'N	41°24'E
Kontich	BE	570	51°08'N	4°27'E
Kontiolahti	FI	578	62°46'N	29°51'E
Kontiomäki	FI	578	64°21'N	28°09'E
Kon Tum	VM	540	14°20'N	108°00'E
Kontum, Cao Nguyen	VM	540	13°55'N	108°05'E
Kontumdu Kontum		476	14°30'N	109°00'E
Konushin, M.		556	67°08'N	43°50'E
Kóny	HU	590	47°38'N	17°24'E
Konya	TU	535	37°52'N	32°31'E
Konya Ovasi	TU	535	37°30'N	33°20'E
Konza	KE	299	1°45'S	37°07'E
Koolpinyah		648	12°23'S	131°10'E
Koolyanobbing		652	30°50'S	119°30'E
Koonga	EN	577	58°35'N	24°09'E
Koonibba	AS	656	31°58'S	133°27'E
Koosa	EN	577	58°31'N	27°05'E
Koostatak		372	51°26'N	97°22'W
Kootenay		372	49°19'N	117°39'W
Kootenay Lake		372	49°40'N	116°50'W
Kopaigo	PP	664	5°22'S	142°31'E
Kopaonik		564	43°15'N	20°50'E
Kopargaon	IN	496	19°53'N	74°29'E
Kopargo	BN	276	9°50'N	1°33'E
Kópavogur	IC	591	64°06'N	21°55'W
Köpenick	GM	584	52°27'N	13°35'E
Koper	SI	617	45°33'N	13°44'E
Kopervik	NO	604	59°17'N	5°15'E
Kopet-Dag, Khrebet	TX	537	37°50'N	58°00'E
Kopeysk	RS	612	55°07'N	61°37'E
Kop Gecidi	TU	535	40°02'N	40°28'E
Kopia	CG	287	3°39'N	23°44'E
Köping	SW	621	59°31'N	16°00'E
Koplik	AL	566	42°13'N	19°26'E
Köpmanholmen		556	63°10'N	18°34'E
Kopondei, Tanjung	ID	500	8°03'S	122°52'E
Koppang	NO	604	61°34'N	11°04'E
Koppies	SF	322	27°14'S	27°35'E
Koprivnica	HR	574	46°10'N	16°50'E
Koprivshtitsa	BU	573	42°38'N	24°21'E
Köprü	TU	535	36°50'N	31°11'E
Köprülü		564	36°44'N	32°12'E
Kopti	UP	624	51°03'N	31°09'E
Kop'ung	KN	512	40°36'N	125°57'E
Kopyl'	BO	569	53°09'N	27°05'E
Kopys'	BO	569	54°19'N	30°18'E
Kor	IR	502	29°36'N	53°10'E
Korab	AL	566	41°44'N	20°32'E
Korablino		560	53°55'N	40°01'E
K'orahē	ET	293	6°37'N	44°18'E
Koralpe	AU	568	46°47'N	14°58'E
Koraluk	CA	390	56°12'N	61°45'W
Koramlik		470	37°32'N	85°42'E
Korangi	PK	524	24°48'N	67°07'E
Koraput	IN	496	18°49'N	82°43'E
Korba	IN	496	22°21'N	82°41'E
Korbach	GM	584	51°17'N	8°52'E
K'orbeta	ET	293	12°48'N	39°39'E
Korbu, Gunung	MY	518	4°41'N	101°18'E
Korçë	AL	566	40°37'N	20°46'E
Korčula	HR	574	42°56'N	17°07'E
Korcula	HR	574	42°57'N	16°55'E
Korculanski Kanal	HR	574	43°03'N	16°45'E
Korea, North		38	40°00'N	127°00'E
Korea, South		38	37°00'N	127°30'E
Korea Bay (Sojoson-man)	KN	512	39°20'N	124°50'E
Korea Strait	JA	506	34°00'N	129°00'E
Korem	ET	293	12°30'N	39°32'E
Korenovsk		564	45°28'N	39°27'E
Korets	UP	624	50°37'N	27°10'E
Korf	RS	612	60°20'N	165°50'E
Korgan		470	37°12'N	85°00'E
Korgas	CH	490	44°07'N	80°30'E
Korgen	NO	604	66°05'N	13°50'E
Korhogo	IV	288	9°27'N	5°38'W
Korido	ID	500	0°50'S	135°35'E
Korienzé	ML	307	15°24'N	3°47'W
Korim	ID	500	0°54'S	136°02'E
Korinós	GR	588	40°19'N	22°35'E
Korinthiakós Kólpos (Corinth, Gulf of)	GR	588	37°59'N	22°53'E
Kórinthos	GR	588	37°56'N	22°56'E
Kōriyama	JA	506	37°24'N	140°23'E
Korizo, Paso de	CD	283	22°28'N	15°27'E
Korkodon	RS	612	64°44'N	154°00'E
Korkuteli	TU	535	37°04'N	30°13'E
Korla	CH	490	41°43'N	86°09'E
Kormakiti, C.	CY	494	35°24'N	32°56'E
Körmend	HU	590	47°01'N	16°36'E
Korn	PP	664	5°50'S	144°18'E
Kornat	HR	574	43°45'N	15°06'E
Korneshty	MD	601	47°22'N	28°00'E
Kornsjø	NO	604	58°57'N	11°37'E
Koro	FJ	660	17°00'S	179°00'E
Koro	IV	288	8°35'N	7°27'W
Koro	ML	307	14°04'N	3°05'W
Koroba	PP	664	5°42'S	142°44'E
Koroglu Daglari	TU	535	40°30'N	32°30'E
Korogwe	TZ	327	5°09'S	38°29'E
Korolëvo	UP	624	48°09'N	23°08'E
Koronadal		478	6°29'N	124°48'E
Koronowo	PL	606	53°19'N	17°57'E
Koror	PX	664	7°21'N	134°22'E
Koror	PX	664	7°20'N	134°30'E
Körös	HU	590	46°43'N	20°12'E
Koro Sea	FJ	660	18°00'S	180°00'
Körösladány	HU	590	46°58'N	21°05'E
Korosten'	UP	624	50°57'N	28°39'E
Korostyshev	UP	624	50°19'N	29°04'E
Korotni		560	56°23'N	46°32'E
Koro Toro	CD	283	16°05'N	18°30'E
Korpilahti	FI	578	62°00'N	25°29'E
Korpilombolo	SW	621	66°52'N	23°02'E
Korpo (Korppoo)	FI	578	60°08'N	21°31'E
Korsakov	RS	612	46°37'N	142°47'E
Korsnäs	FI	578	62°47'N	21°12'E
Korsør	DA	576	55°19'N	11°09'E
Korsze	PL	606	54°10'N	21°09'E
Korti Linchang	CH	490	48°12'N	87°32'E
Kortrijk	BE	570	50°50'N	3°16'E
Kortsevo		560	58°52'N	42°13'E
Koryakskiy Khrebet	RS	612	57°00'N	159°25'E
Koryazhma		466	61°18'N	47°11'E
Koryŏng	KS	513	35°44'N	128°16'E
Koryukovka	UP	624	51°46'N	32°16'E
Kos (Cos)	GR	588	36°50'N	27°10'E
Kós	GR	588	36°53'N	27°18'E
Kosa	RS	612	59°56'N	55°00'E
Kosan	KN	512	38°51'N	127°25'E
Kościan	PL	606	52°01'N	16°36'E
Kościerzyna	PL	606	54°07'N	17°59'E
Kosciusko		378	33°03'N	89°35'W
Kosciusko	AS	656	36°27'S	148°16'E
Kose	EN	577	59°12'N	25°11'E
Köse	TU	535	40°13'N	39°39'E
Kosha	SU	324	20°49'N	30°32'E
Koshikijima-retto	JA	506	31°46'N	129°48'E
Koshiki-kaikyo	JA	506	31°50'N	130°05'E
Koshk	AF	480	34°56'N	62°12'E
Koshk-e Kohneh	AF	480	34°52'N	62°31'E
Koshk Sarāy	IR	502	38°28'N	45°34'E
Koshkupyr	UZ	539	41°32'N	60°21'E
Kōshoku	JA	506	36°29'N	138°05'E
Kosi	IN	496	26°00'N	86°15'E
Košice	LO	616	48°42'N	21°15'E
Koskinoú	GR	588	36°23'N	28°13'E
Koskol'	KZ	510	51°48'N	69°21'E
Koskullskulle	SW	621	67°11'N	20°45'E
Kosmynino		560	57°35'N	40°46'E
Kosoba, Gora	KZ	510	48°15'N	79°40'E
Kosŏng	KN	512	38°40'N	128°19'E
Kosŏng	KS	513	34°58'N	128°20'E
Kosov	UP	624	48°19'N	25°06'E
Kosovo Polje	YO	630	42°38'N	21°07'E
Kosovska Kamenica	YO	630	42°35'N	21°35'E
Kosovska Mitrovica	YO	630	42°53'N	20°52'E
Kosrae	FM	661	5°00'N	164°00'E
Kosrap	CH	490	38°00'N	76°12'E
Kössen	AU	568	47°40'N	12°24'E
Kossou, Lake	IV	288	7°25'N	5°30'W
Kosta	SW	621	56°49'N	15°24'E
Kostajnica	HR	574	45°14'N	16°31'E
Koster	SF	322	25°52'S	26°54'E
Kostinbrod	BU	573	42°49'N	23°13'E
Kost'kovo		556	60°02'N	33°16'E
Kostolac	YO	630	44°43'N	21°11'E
Kostomuksha		556	64°41'N	30°49'E
Kostopil'	UP	624	50°53'N	26°27'E
Kostroma	RS	612	57°46'N	40°58'E
Kostrzyn	PL	606	52°35'N	14°39'E
Kostrzyn	PL	606	52°24'N	17°15'E
Kostyantynivka	UP	624	48°32'N	37°43'E
Kostyantynivka	UP	624	46°48'N	35°26'E
Kostyukovichi	BO	569	53°20'N	32°03'E
Kostyukovka	BO	569	52°32'N	30°56'E
Koszalin	PL	606	54°12'N	16°11'E
Kőszeg	HU	590	47°23'N	16°33'E
Kota	IN	496	25°10'N	75°52'E
Kota Baharu	MY	518	6°08'N	102°15'E
Kotabaru		478	3°16'S	116°15'E
Kotabaru	ID	500	1°08'S	101°43'E
Kota Belud	MY	518	6°21'N	116°26'E
Kotabesi	ID	500	2°24'S	112°59'E
Kotabumi	ID	500	4°50'S	104°54'E
Kotadaik	ID	500	0°12'S	104°37'E
Kot Addu	PK	524	30°28'N	70°58'E
Kotajawa		478	5°37'S	104°20'E
Kotak	KG	514	41°33'N	70°15'E
Kota Kinabalu	MY	518	5°59'N	116°04'E
Kotamobagu	ID	500	0°46'N	124°19'E
Kotapād	IN	496	19°19'N	82°21'E
Kota Tinggi	MY	518	1°44'N	103°54'E
Kotel	BU	573	42°53'N	26°27'E
Kotel'nich		466	58°19'N	48°20'E
Kotel'nikovo		466	47°38'N	43°09'E
Kotelnyy, O.	RS	612	75°45'N	138°44'E
Kotel'va	UP	624	50°04'N	34°46'E
Kothagūdem	IN	496	17°33'N	80°38'E
Köthen	GM	584	51°45'N	11°58'E
Kotido	UG	330	3°00'N	34°06'E
Kotka	FI	578	60°28'N	26°55'E
Kot Kapūra	IN	496	30°35'N	74°54'E
Kotkozero		556	61°16'N	33°13'E
Kotlas	RS	612	61°16'N	46°35'E
Kotli	PK	524	33°31'N	73°55'E
Kotly		560	59°36'N	28°45'E
Kotna	PP	664	5°41'S	144°22'E
Koton Karifi	NI	316	8°06'N	6°48'E
Kotor	YO	630	42°25'N	18°46'E
Kotor Varoš	BK	572	44°37'N	17°22'E
Kotovo		466	50°18'N	44°49'E
Kotovs'k	UP	624	47°45'N	29°32'E
Kotovsk		466	52°36'N	41°32'E
Kotri	PK	524	25°22'N	68°18'E
Kot Samāba	PK	524	28°33'N	70°28'E
Kottayam	IN	496	9°35'N	76°31'E
Kotto	CT	282	4°14'N	22°02'E
Kotuy	RS	612	71°55'N	102°05'E
Kotzebue	US	398	66°53'N	162°35'W
Kotzebue Sound	US	398	68°00'N	165°00'W
Koualessis	GB	294	1°25'N	11°38'E
Kouandé	BN	276	10°20'N	1°42'E
Kouango	CT	282	5°00'N	19°59'E
Kouango, Pointe	GB	294	3°23'S	10°37'E
Kouba Olanga	CD	283	15°44'N	18°19'E
Koubia	GV	297	11°35'N	11°54'W
Koubou	CT	282	6°31'N	21°49'E
Koudougou	UV	278	12°17'N	2°22'W
Koufonisi	GR	588	34°40'N	26°10'E
Kougoulé	GB	294	0°22'N	9°55'E
Kouhu	TW	532	23°35'N	120°10'E
Kouilou	CF	285	2°47'S	11°51'E
Kouk	CT	282	7°11'N	17°18'E
Koukombou	TO	328	10°18'N	0°24'E
Koukourou	CT	282	7°10'N	20°00'E
Koula-Moutou	GB	294	1°06'S	12°30'E
Koulé	GV	297	8°02'N	9°02'W
Koulikoro	ML	307	12°53'N	7°33'W
Koulou	NG	314	12°10'N	3°06'E
Kouloun'tou	SG	319	13°15'N	13°37'W
Koum	CM	280	8°23'N	14°31'E
Koumac		654	21°30'S	164°17'E
Koumala		652	21°37'S	149°15'E
Koumameyong	GB	294	0°11'N	11°51'E
Koumandougou	GV	297	9°10'N	8°00'W
Koumantou	ML	307	11°25'N	6°49'W
Koumba	GV	297	9°07'N	10°33'W
Koumban	GV	297	10°13'N	9°28'W
Koumbia	GV	297	11°48'N	13°30'W
Koumra	CD	283	8°55'N	17°33'E
Koundara	GV	297	12°29'N	13°18'W
Kounde	CT	282	6°06'N	14°38'E
Koundian	ML	307	13°10'N	10°46'W
Koundou	GV	297	8°38'N	10°25'W
Koungheul	SG	319	13°59'N	14°48'W
Koungou, Monts	GB	294	3°20'S	11°00'E
Kouno	CD	283	9°49'N	17°38'E
Kounradskiy	KZ	510	46°59'N	75°00'E
Koupa	CT	282	7°06'N	15°44'E
Koupela	UV	278	12°11'N	0°22'W
Kouraïa Konkouré	GV	297	10°17'N	12°14'W
Kourou		384	5°10'N	52°40'W
Kourouba	ML	307	12°00'N	8°17'W
Kouroussa	GV	297	10°39'N	9°53'W
Koury	ML	307	12°08'N	4°48'W
Koutiala	ML	307	12°23'N	5°28'W
Kouto	IV	288	9°53'N	6°25'W
Koutoumo		654	22°20'S	167°40'E
Kouvola	FI	578	60°52'N	26°42'E
Kouyou	CF	285	0°45'S	16°38'E
Kovačevac	YO	630	44°26'N	20°45'E
Kovačica	YO	630	45°06'N	20°38'E
Kovda		556	66°42'N	32°52'E
Kovdor		556	67°34'N	30°24'E
Kovdozero		556	66°45'N	31°30'E
Kovdozero, Ozero		556	66°47'N	32°00'E
Kovel'	UP	624	51°13'N	24°43'E
Kovernino		560	57°07'N	43°49'E
Kovilj	YO	630	45°14'N	20°02'E
Kovilpatti	IN	496	9°10'N	77°52'E
Kovin	YO	630	44°45'N	20°59'E
Kovrov	RS	612	56°25'N	41°18'E
Kovylkino		466	54°02'N	43°56'E
Kovzha		556	58°50'N	37°30'E
Kovzhskoye, Oz.		556	61°00'N	37°15'E
Kowangge	ID	500	8°18'S	118°32'E
Kowanyama	AS	656	15°27'S	141°45'E
Kowe	CG	287	1°39'S	25°52'E
Kowloon	CH	490	22°18'N	114°09'E
Kowndalān	AF	480	32°10'N	65°55'E
Kowŏn	KN	512	39°26'N	127°15'E
Kowtal-e Zarmast	AF	480	34°35'N	62°52'E
Kowt-e 'Ashrow	AF	480	34°27'N	68°48'E
Koxlax	CH	490	38°02'N	80°27'E
Kōyama	JA	506	31°20'N	130°56'E
Koyama	GV	297	7°54'N	9°21'W
Koyda	RS	612	66°23'N	42°35'E
Koymatdag, Gory	TX	537	40°30'N	56°00'E
Koynare	BU	573	43°21'N	24°08'E
Koyukuk	US	398	64°55'N	157°32'W
Koyulhisar		564	40°18'N	37°51'E
Kozaklı		564	39°13'N	34°49'E
Kozan	TU	535	37°27'N	35°49'E
Kozáni	GR	588	40°18'N	21°47'E
Kozara	BK	572	45°00'N	17°00'E
Kozárovice	LO	616	48°18'N	18°31'E
Kozel'shchina	UP	624	49°13'N	33°51'E
Kozel'sk		560	54°02'N	35°48'E
Kozha		560	57°48'N	48°57'E
Kozhevnikovo	RS	612	73°33'N	110°18'E
Kozhikode	IN	496	11°15'N	75°46'E
Kozienice	PL	606	51°35'N	21°34'E
Kozloduy	BU	573	43°47'N	23°44'E
Kozlovo		560	56°31'N	36°16'E
Koźmin	PL	606	51°49'N	17°27'E
Koz'mino		466	61°56'N	48°24'E
Koznitsa	BU	573	42°59'N	23°33'E
Kozova	UP	624	49°26'N	25°09'E
Kożuchów	PL	606	51°45'N	15°36'E
Kozushima	JA	506	34°11'N	139°08'E
Kozyrevsk	RS	612	56°04'N	159°52'E
Kpagouda	TO	328	9°45'N	1°19'E
Kpalimé	TO	328	6°54'N	0°36'E
Kpandu	GH	296	7°00'N	0°18'E
Kpémé	TO	328	6°13'N	1°32'E
Kra	TO	328	7°11'N	1°10'E
Kraaifontein	SF	322	33°50'S	18°43'E
Krabbendijke	NL	602	51°26'N	4°07'E
Krabi	TH	534	8°04'N	98°55'E
Kra Buri	TH	534	10°24'N	98°47'E
Krach	TX	537	39°17'N	63°24'E
Kracheh	CB	489	12°29'N	106°01'E
Kragerø	NO	604	58°52'N	9°20'E
Kragujevac	YO	630	44°01'N	20°55'E
Krainka		560	54°07'N	36°21'E
Krakor	CB	489	12°32'N	104°12'E
Kraków	PL	606	50°03'N	19°58'E
Kralanh	CB	489	13°35'N	103°25'E
Kralendijk, Bonaire		382	12°10'N	68°16'W
Králiky	EZ	575	50°05'N	16°46'E
Kraljevo	YO	630	43°44'N	20°43'E
Král'ovský Chlmec	LO	616	48°25'N	21°59'E
Kramators'k	UP	624	48°43'N	37°32'E
Kramfors	SW	621	62°56'N	17°47'E
Krammer	NL	602	51°38'N	4°15'E
Kranéa Elassónos	GR	588	39°57'N	21°58'E
Kranídhion	GR	588	37°22'N	23°10'E
Kranj	SI	617	46°15'N	14°21'E
Kranskop	SF	322	28°58'S	30°52'E
Kranzberg	WA	313	21°56'S	15°40'E
Kras	SI	617	45°46'N	13°58'E
Krasilov	UP	624	49°39'N	26°58'E
Krasino	RS	612	70°45'N	54°27'E
Krāslava	LG	596	55°54'N	27°10'E
Kraslice	EZ	575	50°20'N	12°31'E
Krasnaya Gora		560	53°00'N	31°37'E
Krasnaya Gorbatka		560	55°52'N	41°46'E
Krasnaya Sloboda	BO	569	52°51'N	27°10'E
Krasnaya Zarya		560	52°47'N	37°41'E
Kraśnik	PL	606	50°55'N	22°13'E
Kraśnik Fabryczny	PL	606	50°58'N	22°12'E
Krasni Okny	UP	624	47°32'N	29°27'E
Krasnoarmeysk	RS	612	51°02'N	45°42'E
Krasnoarmeyskiy		560	47°01'N	42°12'E
Krasnoarmeyskiy	RS	612	69°35'N	172°00'E
Krasnoarmiys'k	UP	624	48°17'N	37°11'E
Krasnoborsk	RS	612	61°34'N	45°57'E
Krasnodar	RS	612	45°02'N	39°00'E
Krasnodon	UP	624	48°17'N	39°48'E
Krasnogorsk		472	48°24'N	142°06'E
Krasnogorskiy	UZ	539	41°08'N	69°45'E
Krasnogvardeysk	UZ	539	39°46'N	67°16'E
Krasnogvardeyskoye		560	45°51'N	41°31'E
Krasnogvardeyskoye	UP	624	45°30'N	34°18'E
Krasnohrad	UP	624	49°22'N	35°27'E
Krasnokamensk	RS	612	50°06'N	118°05'E
Krasnokamsk		466	58°04'N	55°48'E
Krasnokutsk	KZ	510	53°01'N	75°59'E
Krasnolesnyy		560	51°52'N	39°35'E
Krasnopavlovka	UP	624	49°09'N	36°19'E
Krasnoperekops'k	UP	624	45°58'N	33°47'E
Krasnopol'ye	UP	624	50°46'N	35°16'E
Krasnosel'kup	PS	612	65°41'N	82°29'E
Krasnoshchel'ye	PS	612	67°21'N	37°02'E
Krasnoslobodsk		560	48°39'N	44°35'E
Krasnoslobodsk		560	54°26'N	43°46'E
Krasnotur'insk	RS	612	59°46'N	60°12'E
Krasnoural'sk	RS	612	58°21'N	60°03'E
Krasnovodsk	TX	537	39°59'N	52°58'E
Krasnovodskiy Zaliv	TX	537	39°55'N	53°15'E
Krasnoyarsk	RS	612	56°01'N	92°50'E
Krasnoye		560	50°56'N	38°41'E
Krasnoye		560	52°51'N	38°47'E
Krasnoye	BO	569	54°14'N	27°05'E
Krasnoye	MD	601	46°38'N	29°50'E
Krasnozërskoye		466	53°59'N	79°14'E
Krasnystaw	PL	606	50°59'N	23°11'E
Krasnyy Bazar	AJ	483	39°41'N	46°58'E
Krasnyy Chikoy	RS	612	50°22'N	108°45'E
Krasnyy Gulyay		560	54°02'N	48°20'E
Krasnyy Kholm		560	58°03'N	37°07'E
Krasnyy Kut		466	50°58'N	47°00'E
Krasnyy Liman	UP	624	48°59'N	37°49'E
Krasnyy Luch	UP	624	48°08'N	38°56'E
Krasnyy Oktyabr'		560	56°07'N	38°53'E
Krasnyy Rog		560	53°00'N	33°45'E
Krasnyy Sulin		560	47°54'N	40°03'E
Krasnyy Yar		466	55°14'N	72°56'E
Krasnyy Yar		560	50°42'N	44°43'E
Krasnyy Yar	RS	612	46°32'N	48°21'E
Krasnyy Yar	RS	612	57°07'N	84°33'E
Kratke Range	PP	664	7°00'S	146°00'E
Kratovo	MK	599	42°05'N	22°12'E
Kravanh, Phnom (Cardamomes, Chaine des)	CB	489	12°00'N	103°50'E
Kraynovka		466	43°58'N	47°23'E
Kražiai	LH	597	55°36'N	22°42'E
Krebs		378	34°55'N	95°42'W
Krechetovo		466	60°57'N	38°31'E
Krechevitsy		560	58°37'N	31°24'E
Krefeld	GM	584	51°20'N	6°34'E
Kremastí	GR	588	36°24'N	28°08'E
Kremenchugskoye Vdkhr.	UP	624	49°30'N	32°30'E
Kremenchuk	UP	624	49°04'N	33°25'E
Kremenets'	UP	624	50°06'N	25°43'E
Kremmling		372	40°02'N	106°23'W
Kremnica	LO	616	48°42'N	18°55'E
Krems an der Donau	AU	568	48°24'N	15°36'E
Kresna	BU	573	41°44'N	23°09'E
Kresta, Zaliv	RS	612	66°00'N	179°15'W
Kréstena	GR	588	37°37'N	21°38'E
Kresttsy		560	58°15'N	32°31'E
Kretinga	LH	597	55°53'N	21°15'E
Kreuzlingen	SZ	622	47°39'N	9°11'E
Kreuztal	GM	584	50°58'N	7°59'E
Kría Vrísi	GR	588	40°41'N	22°18'E
Kribélé	CT	282	6°42'N	19°49'E
Kribi	CM	280	2°55'N	9°56'E

Krichbach	AU	568	46°39'N	13°12'E
Krichev	BO	569	53°42'N	31°43'E
Krichim	BU	573	42°03'N	24°28'E
Kriel	SF	322	26°14'S	29°16'E
Kriens	SZ	622	47°02'N	8°17'E
Kril'on		472	45°53'N	142°04'E
Krim-Krim	CD	283	8°58'N	15°48'E
Krinídhes	GR	588	41°01'N	24°18'E
Kriós, Ákra	GR	588	35°16'N	23°32'E
Krishna	IN	496	15°57'N	80°59'E
Krishna, Mouths of the	IN	496	15°45'N	81°00'E
Krishnagiri	IN	496	12°32'N	78°14'E
Krishnanagar		476	23°24'N	88°30'E
Kristiansand	NO	604	58°08'N	7°57'E
Kristianstad	SW	621	56°01'N	14°06'E
Kristiansund	NO	604	63°07'N	7°45'E
Kristiinankaupunki (Kristinestad)	FI	578	62°17'N	21°23'E
Kristineberg	SW	621	65°04'N	18°35'E
Kristinehamn	SW	621	59°20'N	14°07'E
Kristinestad (Kristiinankaupunki)	FI	578	62°17 N	21°23'E
Kriti (Crete)	GR	588	35°15 N	24°45'E
Kriva	MK	599	42°10'N	22°20'E
Kriva Palanka	MK	599	42°10'N	22°21'E
Krivichi	BO	569	54°43'N	27°17'E
Krivodol	BU	573	43°23'N	23°29'E
Krivoye Ozero	UP	624	47°56'N	30°21'E
Križevci	HR	574	46°02'N	16°32'E
Krk	HR	574	45°06'N	14°32'E
Krk	HR	574	45°02'N	14°35'E
Krka	HR	574	43°43'N	15°51'E
Krnjevo	YO	630	44°25'N	21°03'E
Krnov	EZ	575	50°06'N	17°43'E
Krocodil	SF	322	24°40'S	26°50'E
Krokom	SW	621	63°19'N	14°23'E
Krókos	GR	588	40°16'N	21°49'E
Krolovets	UP	624	51°33'N	33°23'E
Kroměříž	EZ	575	49°18'N	17°24'E
Krompachy	LO	616	48°55'N	20°52'E
Kronach	GM	584	50°14'N	11°19'E
Krong Kaoh Kong	CB	489	11°37'N	102°59'E
Krong Keb	CB	489	10°29'N	104°19'E
Kronoby (Kruunupyy)	FI	578	63°43'N	23°02'E
Kronotskiy Zaliv	RS	612	54°12'N	160°36'E
Kronprins Frederiks Bjerge		370	68°00'N	36°00'W
Kronshtadt		556	59°59'N	29°45'E
Kroonstad	SF	322	27°40'S	27°14'E
Kropotkin	RS	612	45°26'N	40°34'E
Kropotkin	RS	612	58°30'N	115°17'E
Krosno	PL	606	49°41'N	21°47'E
Krotoszyn	PL	606	51°42'N	17°27'E
Krousón	GR	588	35°13'N	24°59'E
Krrab	AL	566	19°40'N	41°10'E
Krško	SI	617	45°58'N	15°29'E
Krstaor	MK	599	40°59'N	21°21'E
Krui	ID	500	5°11'S	103°56'E
Kruin	WA	313	22°42'S	17°06'E
Kruisfontein	SF	322	34°00'S	24°44'E
Krujë	AL	566	41°30'N	19°48'E
Krulevshchina	BO	569	55°02'N	27°45'E
Krumbach	GM	584	48°15'N	10°22'E
Krumbach Markt	AU	568	47°32'N	16°11'E
Krumovgrad	BU	573	41°28'N	25°39'E
Krung Thep (Bangkok)	TH	534	13°45'N	100°31'E
Krupina	LO	616	48°21'N	19°04'E
Krupiste	MK	599	41°51'N	22°15'E
Krupka	EZ	575	50°41'N	13°52'E
Kruså	DA	576	54°51'N	9°25'E
Kruševac	YO	630	43°35'N	21°20'E
Kruševo	MK	599	41°22'N	21°15'E
Kruszwica	PL	606	52°41'N	18°18'E
Kruunupyy (Kronoby)	FI	578	63°43'N	23°02'E
Kruzof	US	398	57°09'N	136°59'W
Kryazh Polousnyy	RS	612	69°50'N	140°00'E
Kryazh Ulakhan-Sis		468	50°15'N	135°10'E
Kryazh Veteni Poyas		556	63°40'N	36°00'E
Krylovskaya		564	46°20'N	39°58'E
Krymsk		466	44°56'N	38°00'E
Krymskiye Gory	UP	624	44°45'N	34°25'E
Krymskiy Pov.	UP	624	45°35'N	34°00'E
Krynica	PL	606	49°26'N	20°58'E
Krynychky	UP	624	48°22'N	34°27'E
Kryvyy Rih	UP	624	47°55'N	33°21'E
Krzyż	PL	606	52°53'N	16°01'E
Ksar el Boukhari	AG	272	35°53'N	2°46'E
Ksar el Kebir	MO	310	35°00'N	5°59'W
Ksel, Djebel	AG	272	33°44'N	1°10'E
Ksen'yevka	RS	612	53°34'N	118°44'E
Kshenskiy		560	51°50'N	37°41'E
Kstovo		560	56°11'N	44°11'E
Ktima	CY	494	34°46'N	32°25'E
Kuah	MY	518	6°19'N	99°51'E
Kuala Belait	BX	486	4°35'N	114°11'E
Kuala Berang	MY	518	5°04'N	103°01'E
Kuala Dungun	MY	518	4°47'N	103°26'E
Kuala Kangsar	MY	518	4°46'N	100°56'E
Kuala Kerai	MY	518	5°32'N	102°12'E
Kuala Kubu Baharu	MY	518	3°34'N	101°39'E
Kuala Kurau	MY	518	5°01'N	100°26'E
Kualakurun	ID	500	1°07'S	113°53'E
Kualalangsa		476	4°32'N	98°01'E
Kuala Lipis	MY	518	4°11'N	102°03'E
Kuala Lumpur	MY	518	3°10'N	101°42'E
Kualamandah	ID	500	0°03'S	103°32'E
Kuala Pahang	MY	518	3°32'N	103°28'E
Kuala Penyu	MY	518	5°34'N	115°36'E
Kualapesaguan	ID	500	2°01'S	110°08'E
Kuala Pilah	MY	518	2°44'N	102°15'E
Kualapuu	US	398	21°09'N	157°02'W
Kuala Rompin	MY	518	2°49'N	103°29'E
Kuala Selangor	MY	518	3°21'N	101°15'E
Kualasimpang	ID	500	4°17'N	98°03'E
Kuala Terengganu	MY	518	5°20'N	103°08'E
Kualatungkal	ID	500	0°49'S	103°28'E
Kuamut	MY	518	5°13'N	117°30'E
Kuandian		474	40°47'N	124°43'E
Kuanhsi	TW	532	24°48'N	121°10'E
Kuan Shan	TW	532	23°14'N	120°54'E
Kuanshan	TW	532	23°04'N	121°10'E
Kuantan	MY	518	3°48'N	103°20'E
Kuba	AJ	483	41°21'N	48°31'E
Kubalia	PP	664	3°46'S	143°27'E
Kuban	RS	612	45°20'N	37°30'E
Kubaysah	IZ	504	33°35'N	42°37'E
Kubbum	SU	324	11°47'N	23°47'E
Kubenskoye		560	59°26'N	39°40'E
Kubenskoye, Oz.	RS	612	59°40'N	39°25'E
Küblis	SZ	622	46°54'N	9°46'E
Kubokawa	JA	506	33°12'N	133°08'E
Kubrat	BU	573	43°48'N	26°30'E
Kubumesaai	ID	500	1°31'N	115°06'E
Kučevo	YO	630	44°29'N	21°41'E
Kuchinarai	TH	534	16°32'N	104°04'E
Kuching	MY	518	1°32'N	110°21'E
Kuchl	AU	568	47°37'N	13°09'E
Kūchnay Darvīshān	AF	480	30°59'N	64°11'E
Kuçovë	AL	566	40°48'N	19°54'E
Kucura	YO	630	45°31'N	19°36'E
Kuda	ID	500	1°02'N	112°59'E
Kudan	NI	316	11°18'N	7°44'E
Kudara	TI	533	38°25'N	72°39'E
Kudat	MY	518	6°53'N	116°50'E
Kudene	ID	500	6°14'S	134°39'E
Kudirkos-Naumiestis	LH	597	54°46'N	22°53'E
Kudus	ID	500	6°48'S	110°50'E
Kudymkar		466	59°01'N	54°39'E
Kuei-shan Tao	TW	532	24°51'N	121°57'E
Kufrinjah	JO	510	32°18'N	35°42'E
Kufstein	AU	568	47°35'N	12°10'E
Kugalukn		368	68°30'N	131°00'W
Kūhak	IR	502	27°08'N	63°15'E
Kūhdasht	IR	502	33°32'N	47°36'E
Kuh Duren	IR	502	34°00'N	56°00'E
Kūhestak	IR	502	26°48'N	57°02'E
Kūhestān	AF	480	34°39'N	61°12'E
Kuh-he Bozqus	IR	502	37°50'N	47°30'E
Kuhmo	FI	578	64°08'N	29°31'E
Kuhmoinen	FI	578	61°32'N	25°06'E
Kuibul'yen	TI	533	37°55'N	69°21'E
Kuikuina	NU	415	13°28'N	84°47'W
Kuiseb		270	22°59'S	14°31'E
Kuito	AO	274	12°23'S	16°56'E
Kuiu	US	398	56°27'N	134°22'W
Kuivaniemi	FI	578	65°35'N	25°11'E
Kuivastu	EN	577	58°35'N	23°22'E
Kujang	KN	512	39°52'N	126°01'E
Kujawi	PL	606	52°30'N	18°45'E
Kuji	JA	506	40°11'N	141°46'E
Kukalaya	NU	415	13°39'N	83°37'W
Kukawa	NI	316	12°56'N	13°34'E
Kukës	AL	566	42°04'N	20°25'E
Kukhuroba	AJ	483	41°35'N	48°32'E
Kukipi	PP	664	8°11'S	146°08'E
Kukoboy		560	58°42'N	39°54'E
Kukudu	BP	666	8°02'S	157°00'E
Kukundu		648	8°01'S	156°58'E
Kul	IR	502	32°15'N	58°15'E
Kula		564	38°32'N	28°40'E
Kula	BU	573	43°53'N	22°31'E
Kula	YO	630	45°37'N	19°32'E
Kulachi	PK	524	31°56'N	70°27'E
Kulagino	KZ	510	48°24'N	51°36'E
Kulai	MY	518	1°40'N	103°36'E
Kula Kangri	BT	486	28°14'N	90°36'E
Kulākh	SA	528	21°19'N	40°48'E
Kulaly, O.	KZ	510	44°54'N	50°02'E
Kulansarik		466	41°00'N	78°43'E
Kular	RS	612	70°41'N	134°22'E
Kularua	BG	485	24°32'N	92°03'E
Kulashi	GG	495	42°12'N	42°22'E
Kulawi	ID	500	1°27'S	119°59'E
Kul'deman	TI	533	37°17'N	69°04'E
Kuldīga	LG	596	56°58'N	21°59'E
Kule	BC	276	23°02'S	20°10'E
Kulebaki		560	55°24'N	42°32'E
Kulen	CB	489	13°49'N	104°41'E
Kulen, Phnom	CB	489	13°40'N	104°00'E
Kulen Shet'	ET	293	10°00'N	43°00'E
Kulen Vakuf	BK	572	44°33'N	16°06'E
Kulgera		652	25°50'S	133°18'E
Kulikovka	UP	624	51°22'N	31°39'E
Kulim	MY	518	5°22'N	100°34'E
Kulin	AS	656	32°40'S	118°10'E
Kuliyapitiya	CE	530	7°28'N	80°02'E
Kullamaa	EN	577	58°53'N	24°05'E
Kullu		470	31°58'N	77°06'E
Kulmbach	GM	584	50°06'N	11°27'E
Kulmunda	TI	533	38°31'N	68°35'E
Kŭlob	TI	533	37°55'N	69°46'E
Kuloy		556	61°02'N	42°27'E
Kuloy	RS	612	64°58'N	43°32'E
Kul'sary	KZ	510	46°59'N	54°01'E
Kulti		476	23°44'N	86°51'E
Kulu	TU	535	39°06'N	33°05'E
Kulumadau		650	9°00'S	154°15'E
Kulunda	RS	612	52°35'N	78°57'E
Kulusuk		370	65°34'N	37°11'W
Kum	KS	513	36°20'N	126°50'E
Kumagaya	JA	506	36°08'N	139°23'E
Kumai, Telukan	ID	500	3°00'S	111°43'E
Kumaishi	JA	506	42°08'N	139°58'E
Kumajri	AM	482	40°48'N	43°50'E
Kumak	RS	612	51°10'N	60°08'E
Kumaka	GY	434	3°54'N	58°22'W
Kumamoto	JA	506	32°48'N	130°43'E
Kumane	YO	630	45°32'N	20°14'E
Kumano	JA	506	33°52'N	136°06'E
Kumanovo	MK	599	42°08'N	21°43'E
Kumar	BG	485	23°18'N	90°01'E
Kumara	NZ	663	42°37'S	171°12'E
Kumārkhāli	BG	485	23°51'N	89°15'E
Kumasi	GH	296	6°41'N	1°37'W
Kumba	CM	280	4°38'N	9°26'E
Kumba	SL	320	9°50'N	11°50'W
Kumbakonam		470	10°58'N	79°23'E
Kumbe		648	8°21'S	140°13'E
Kumbia		652	26°42'S	150°40'E
Kumbo	CM	280	6°12'N	10°40'E
Kŭmch'on	KS	513	37°46'N	126°46'E
Kumëny		560	58°07'N	49°54'E
Kumertau	RS	612	52°46'N	55°47'E
Kume-shima	JA	506	26°20'N	126°47'E
Kŭmgang	KN	512	38°37'N	127°59'E
Kŭmhwa	KS	513	38°17'N	127°28'E
Kumi	KS	513	36°08'N	128°20'E
Kumi	UG	330	1°29'N	33°56'E
Kumihama	JA	506	35°35'N	134°53'E
Kuminskiy	RS	612	58°40'N	66°34'E
Kumjawng Pass	IN	496	27°47'N	97°09'E
Kumkurgan	UZ	539	37°48'N	67°35'E
Kumla	SW	621	59°08'N	15°08'E
Kumluca	TU	535	36°22'N	30°18'E
Kummerower See	GM	584	53°49'N	12°52'E
Kumo	NI	316	10°03'N	11°13'E
Kumo-do		474	34°31'N	127°45'E
Kumon Range	BM	487	26°30'N	97°15'E
Kumragaon	NP	522	28°20'N	81°19'E
Kumru		564	40°52'N	37°16'E
Kŭmsan	KS	513	36°06'N	127°29'E
Kŭmsanp'o	KN	512	38°35'N	125°09'E
Kumsenga	TZ	327	3°47'S	30°28'E
Kumukahi, C.	US	398	19°31'N	154°48'W
Kumurkek	ID	500	7°12'S	140°05'E
Kümüx	CH	490	42°15'N	88°09'E
Kumylzhenskaya		560	49°53'N	42°35'E
Kumyskurgan	KZ	510	44°52'N	64°47'E
Kunar	AF	480	34°24'N	70°32'E
Künas	CH	490	43°08'N	84°31'E
Kunashir, Os.	JA	506	44°10'N	146°00'E
Kūnch	IN	496	25°59'N	79°09'E
Kunchha	NP	522	28°08'N	84°20'E
Kunda	EN	577	59°29'N	26°32'E
Kundelungu Mts.	CG	287	10°30'S	27°45'E
Kundiān	PK	524	32°27'N	71°28'E
Kundiawa	PP	664	6°01'S	144°56'E
Kundla	IN	496	21°20'N	71°18'E
Kunduchi	TZ	327	6°40'S	39°13'E
Kundur	ID	500	0°45'N	103°26'E
Kunduz	AF	480	37°00'N	68°30'E
Kunene (Cunene)	AO	274	16°33'S	16°20'E
Kunerma	RS	612	55°45'N	108°29'E
Kungälv	SW	621	57°52'N	11°58'E
Kungey Alatau, Khrebet	KG	514	43°00'N	77°00'E
Kungrad	UZ	539	43°02'N	58°49'E
Kungsbacka	SW	621	57°29'N	12°04'E
Kungshamn	SW	621	58°20'N	11°13'E
Kungsör		558	59°25'N	16°05'E
Kungu	CG	287	2°52'N	19°12'E
Kungu	ZA	332	10°11'S	31°13'E
Kungur	RS	612	57°25'N	56°57'E
Kungutas	TZ	327	8°28'S	33°15'E
Kunhegyes	HU	590	47°22'N	20°38'E
Kunhing	BM	487	21°18'N	98°26'E
Kunimaw Kyun	BM	487	11°50'N	97°00'E
Kuningan	ID	500	6°59'S	108°29'E
Kunlong	BM	487	23°25'N	98°39'E
Kunlun Shan	CH	490	38°15'N	85°00'E
Kunlun Shankou	CH	490	35°40'N	94°03'E
Kunmadaras	HU	590	47°26'N	20°48'E
Kunming	CH	490	25°03'N	102°40'E
Kunri	PK	524	25°11'N	69°34'E
Kunsan	KS	513	35°57'N	126°45'E
Kunshan	CH	490	31°22'N	120°57'E
Kunszentmárton	HU	590	46°50'N	20°17'E
Kuntaur	GA	295	13°40'N	14°53'W
Kuntshankoie	CG	287	3°20'S	23°34'E
Kunua	PP	664	5°46'S	154°43'E
Kununurra	AS	656	15°47'S	128°45'E
Kunwi	KS	513	36°14'N	128°33'E
Kun'ya		560	56°18'N	30°59'E
Kunya	NI	316	12°15'N	8°30'E
Kunya-Urgench	TX	537	42°19'N	59°10'E
K'unzila	ET	293	11°41'N	37°02'E
Kunzulu	CG	287	3°29'S	16°09'E
Kuocang Shan	CH	490	28°36'N	120°30'E
Kuolayarvi	RS	612	66°58'N	29°12'E
Kuopio	FI	578	62°54'N	27°41'E
Kuortane	FI	578	62°48'N	23°31'E
Kup	PP	664	5°58'S	144°48'E
Kupa	HR	574	45°28'N	16°24'E
Kupa	SI	617	41°32'N	22°01'E
Kupang	ID	500	10°12'S	123°35'E
Kupiano	PP	664	10°04'S	148°10'E
Kupino	RS	612	54°22'N	77°18'E
Kupiškis	LH	597	55°50'N	24°58'E
Kupreanof	US	398	56°53'N	133°46'W
Kupyansk	UP	624	49°42'N	37°38'E
Kupyansk-Uzlovoy	UP	624	49°39'N	37°39'E
Kuqa	CH	490	41°42'N	117°09'E
Kur	RS	612	39°24'N	49°19'E
Kura	GG	495	41°50'N	43°10'E
Kuragino	RS	612	53°53'N	92°40'E
Kurakino		560	53°43'N	44°47'E
Kuraminskiy Khrebet	TI	533	40°45'N	70°10'E
Kurashiki	JA	506	34°45'N	133°46'E
Kuraymah	SU	324	18°33'N	31°51'E
Kurayoshi	JA	506	35°26'N	133°49'E
Kurayyimah	JO	510	32°16'N	35°36'E
Kurchum	KZ	510	48°34'N	83°40'E
Kŭrdzhali	BU	573	41°37'N	25°25'E
Kurdzhinovo		466	43°59'N	40°57'E
Kure	JA	506	34°14'N	132°34'E
Küre	TU	535	41°48'N	33°43'E
Kuressaare	EN	577	58°15'N	22°28'E
Kureyka	RS	612	66°30'N	87°12'E
Kurgal'dzhinskiy	KZ	510	50°36'N	70°01'E
Kurgan	RS	612	55°27'N	65°20'E
Kurgantepa	UZ	539	40°45'N	72°45'E
Kuri	KS	513	37°36'N	127°07'E
Kuria Is.	KR	660	0°10'N	174°00'E
Kuria Muria I. (Juzur al Halaniyat)	MU	523	17°30'N	56°00'E
Kurīgrām	BG	485	25°49'N	89°39'E
Kurija	MK	599	41°32'N	22°01'E
Kurikka	FI	578	62°36'N	22°19'E
Kurilovka		466	50°44'N	48°02'E
Kuril'sk	RS	612	44°58'N	147°29'E
Kurilskiye Ostrova	RS	612	46°10'N	152°00'E
Kuring Kuru	WA	313	17°36'S	18°36'E
Kurinmas	NU	415	12°49'N	83°41'W
Kurkiyoki		556	61°18'N	29°54'E
Kurlovskiy		560	55°27'N	40°36'E
Kurmin Goro	NI	316	9°28'N	8°33'E
Kurmuk	ET	293	10°31'N	34°18'E
Kurmuk	SU	324	10°33'N	34°17'E
Kurnool	IN	496	15°45'N	78°05'E
Kuroishi	JA	506	40°38'N	140°36'E
Kuroiso	JA	506	36°58'N	140°03'E
Kuror, Jabal	SU	324	20°27'N	31°30'E
Kurort-Darasun	RS	612	51°12'N	113°40'E
Kurovskoye		560	55°34'N	38°55'E
Kurow	NZ	663	44°44'S	170°28'E
Kuršėnai	LH	597	56°00'N	22°56'E
Kurshskiy Bay	LH	597	55°05'N	21°00'E
Kursk	RS	612	51°42'N	36°07'E
Kuršumlija	YO	630	43°09'N	21°16'E
Kurşunlu	TU	535	40°51'N	33°16'E
Kurta	GG	495	42°18'N	43°56'E
Kūrtī	SU	324	18°05'N	31°33'E
Kurucaşile		564	41°50'N	32°43'E
Kuruktag	CH	490	91°30'N	90°00'E
Kuruman	SF	322	27°28'S	23°26'E
Kuruman	SF	322	26°56'S	20°39'E
Kuruman Heuwells	SF	322	27°40'S	23°25'E
Kurume	JA	506	33°19'N	130°31'E
Kurumkan	RS	612	54°18'N	110°18'E
Kurundi	AS	656	20°29'S	134°42'E
Kurunegala	CE	530	7°29'N	80°22'E
Kurungiku Mountains	GY	434	4°57'N	59°20'W
Kurupukari	GY	434	4°40'N	58°39'W
Kur'ya		466	61°42'N	57°15'E
Kurye	KS	513	35°12'N	127°28'E
Kuryongp'o-ri	KS	513	35°59'N	129°34'E
Kusadak	YO	630	44°24'N	20°49'E
Kuşadası	TU	535	37°51'N	27°15'E
Kusary	AJ	483	41°25'N	48°26'E
Kus Gölü	TU	535	40°10'N	27°57'E
Kushchevskaya		564	46°34'N	39°37'E
Kushchinskiy	AJ	483	40°33'N	46°05'E
Kusheriki	NI	316	10°32'N	6°27'E
Kushikino	JA	506	31°44'N	130°16'E
Kushimoto	JA	506	33°28'N	135°47'E
Kushiro	JA	506	42°58'N	144°23'E
Kushol	IN	496	33°41'N	76°37'E
Kushtia	BG	485	23°51'N	88°53'E
Kushva		466	59°18'N	59°45'E
Kuskokwim	US	398	60°05'N	162°25'W
Kuskokwim Bay	US	398	59°00'N	163°00'W
Kuskokwim Mountains	US	398	62°30'N	157°00'W
Kusma	NP	522	28°14'N	83°41'E
Kusŏng	KN	512	39°55'N	125°15'E
Kussharo-ko	JA	506	43°38'N	144°21'E
Kustanay	KZ	510	53°11'N	63°34'E
Kustarevka		560	54°16'N	42°16'E
Kūstī	SU	324	13°09'N	32°42'E
Kusuman	TH	534	17°20'N	104°20'E
Kut, Ko	TH	534	11°50'N	102°30'E
Kuta	NI	316	9°52'N	6°43'E
Kutacane		478	3°30'N	97°48'E
Kütahya	TU	535	39°25'N	29°59'E
Kutais		564	44°30'N	39°17'E
Kutaisi	GG	495	42°15'N	42°40'E
Kutaraja	ID	500	5°34'N	95°20'E
Kutchan	JA	506	52°53'N	140°45'E
Kutina	HR	574	45°29'N	16°47'E
Kutiwenji	NI	316	9°31'N	5°40'E
Kutkashen	AJ	483	40°58'N	47°52'E
Kutlwanong	SF	322	27°51'S	26°45'E
Kutná Hora	EZ	575	49°57'N	15°16'E
Kutno	PL	606	52°14'N	19°22'E
Kutu	CG	287	2°44'S	18°09'E
Kutu	KE	299	0°34'S	37°19'E
Kutubdia Island	BG	485	21°50'N	91°52'E
Kutubu, Lake	PP	664	6°20'S	143°00'E
Kutul, Lagh	KE	299	2°08'N	40°56'E
Kutum	SU	324	14°12'N	24°40'E
Kutu-Owanga	CG	287	2°36'S	23°12'E
Kuturga	KG	514	42°45'N	78°07'E
Kúty	LO	616	48°40'N	17°01'E
Kuujjuaq	CA	390	58°06'N	68°25'W
Kuujjuarapik	CA	390	55°17'N	77°45'W
Kuuli-Mayak	TX	537	40°14'N	52°42'E
Kuummiut		370	65°52'N	37°01'W
Kuusamo	FI	578	65°58'N	29°11'E
Kuusankoski	FI	578	60°54'N	26°38'E
Kuutse Magi	EN	577	58°02'N	26°20'E
Kuva	UZ	539	40°32'N	72°03'E
Kuvandyk		466	51°28'N	57°21'E
Kuvango	AO	274	14°28'S	16°18'E
Kuvshinovo		560	57°02'N	34°12'E
Kuwaé (Tongoa)	NH	669	17°00'S	169°00'E
Kuwait		38	29°30'N	47°45'E
Kuwait (Al Kuwayt)	KU	514	29°20'N	47°59'E
Kuwana	JA	506	35°03'N	136°40'E
Kuybyshev		560	54°57'N	49°04'E
Kuybyshevka	UP	624	47°38'N	31°42'E
Kuybyshevo	KZ	510	44°12'N	51°40'E
Kuybyshevskiy	KZ	510	53°12'N	66°48'E
Kuybyshevskoye Vdkhr.	RS	612	55°00'N	49°00'E
Kuygan	KZ	510	45°25'N	74°10'E
Kūysanjaq	IZ	504	36°05'N	44°38'E
Kuyto, Ozero	RS	612	65°08'N	31°24'E
Kuytun		468	54°21'N	101°29'E
Kuytun	CH	490	44°24'N	85°00'E
Kuyu Tingni	NU	415	14°29'N	83°55'W
Kuyuwini	GY	434	2°16'N	58°16'W
Kuzey Anadolu Daglari	TU	535	41°30'N	35°00'E
Kuzhenkino		560	57°44'N	33°59'E
Kuz'minskaya		466	62°18'N	38°21'E
Kuznetsk	RS	612	53°07'N	46°36'E
Kuznetskiy Alatau		466	54°40'N	88°20'E
Kuzomen'		556	66°17'N	36°54'E
Kuzumaki	JA	506	40°00'N	141°32'E
Kværndrup	DA	576	55°10'N	10°32'E
Kvaløy		556	69°40'N	18°30'E
Kvalsund	NO	604	70°30'N	23°59'E
Kvareli	GG	495	41°57'N	45°48'E
Kvarner	HR	574	44°48'N	14°08'E
Kvarneric	HR	574	44°42'N	14°36'E
Kvenna		558	60°01'N	7°56'E
Kvigtinden	NO	604	65°14'N	13°49'E
Kvikkjokk	SW	621	66°57'N	17°47'E
Kvinesdal	NO	604	58°19'N	6°57'E
Kvinnherad	NO	604	60°00'N	6°00'E
Kviteseid	NO	604	59°24'N	8°30'E
Kvitok	RS	612	56°03'N	98°30'E
Kwahu Plateau	GH	296	6°30'N	0°30'W
Kwail	KN	512	38°27'N	125°01'E
Kwajalein	RM	661	9°30'N	169°30'E
Kwajok	SU	324	8°19'N	28°00'E
Kwakoegron	NS	438	5°15'N	55°20'W
Kwaksan	KN	512	39°41'N	125°04'E
Kwakwani	GY	434	5°17'N	58°03'W
Kwale	KE	299	4°11'S	39°27'E
Kwale	NI	316	5°43'N	6°27'E
Kwali	NI	316	8°53'N	7°00'E
Kwaluseni	WZ	326	26°29'S	31°20'E
Kwamakuta	SF	322	30°02'S	30°51'E
KwaMashu	SF	322	29°44'S	30°55'E
Kwamen Kwesi	GH	296	8°28'N	2°11'W
Kwamouth	CG	287	3°11'S	16°14'E
Kwa Mtoro	TZ	327	5°14'S	35°26'E
Kwando (Cuando)	ZA	332	18°27'S	23°32'E
Kwangch'ŏn	KS	513	36°30'N	126°37'E
Kwangju	KS	513	35°09'N	126°55'E
Kwango-Kwilu Plateau	CG	287	9°00'S	15°50'E
Kwangwazi	TZ	327	7°47'S	38°15'E
Kwangyang	KS	513	34°58'N	127°35'E
Kwania, Lake	UG	330	1°45'N	32°45'E
Kwanmo bang	KN	512	41°42'N	129°13'E
KwaNobuhle	SF	322	33°48'S	25°23'E
Kwansan	KS	513	34°32'N	126°42'E
Kwaraha	TZ	327	4°13'S	35°48'E
Kwatarkwashi	NI	316	12°08'N	6°49'E
Kwekwe	ZI	334	18°55'S	29°49'E
Kwidzyn	PL	606	53°44'N	18°55'E
Kwīha	ET	293	13°29'N	39°33'E
Kwikila	PP	664	9°48'S	147°39'E
Kwilu (Cuilo)	CG	287	3°22'S	17°22'E
Kyabé	CD	283	9°27'N	18°57'E
Kyabram		652	36°19'S	145°03'E
Kyadet	BM	487	21°51'N	94°56'E
Kyaikto	BM	487	17°18'N	97°01'E
Kya-in Seikkyi	BM	487	16°02'N	98°08'E
Kyaka	TZ	327	1°16'S	31°25'E
Kyakhta	RS	612	50°22'N	106°30'E
Kyancutta		652	33°08'S	135°34'E
Kyangin	BM	487	18°20'N	95°14'E
Kyargozero		556	63°20'N	34°17'E
Kyaukpadaung	BM	487	20°50'N	95°08'E
Kyaukpyu	BM	487	19°25'N	93°33'E
Kyaukse	BM	487	21°36'N	96°08'E
Kybartai	LH	597	54°39'N	22°45'E
Kyeburn	NZ	663	45°09'S	170°15'E
Kyegegwa	UG	330	0°29'N	31°03'E
Kyema	UG	330	1°23'N	34°23'E
Kyenjojo	UG	330	0°37'N	30°38'E
Kyevskoye Vdkhr.	UP	624	51°00'N	29°30'E
Kyidaunggan	BM	487	19°53'N	96°12'E
Kyindwe	BM	487	20°57'N	93°51'E
Kyjov	EZ	575	49°01'N	17°07'E
Kyle		376	29°59'N	97°52'W
Kylestrome	UK	626	58°16'N	5°02'W
Kymijoki	FI	578	60°30'N	26°40'E
Kyn	RS	612	57°48'N	58°30'E
Kynuna	AS	656	21°35'S	141°54'E
Kyoga, Lake	UG	330	1°30'N	33°00'E
Kyoga-misaki	JA	506	35°46'N	135°13'E
Kyonggi-man	KN	512	37°25'N	126°00'E
Kyŏnghŭng	KN	512	42°35'N	130°30'E
Kyŏngju	KS	513	35°50'N	129°13'E
Kyŏngsan	KS	513	35°49'N	128°44'E
Kyŏngsŏng	KN	512	41°35'N	129°37'E
Kyŏngwŏn	KN	512	42°48'N	130°13'E
Kyōto	JA	506	35°00'N	135°45'E
Kyrchany		560	57°37'N	50°10'E
Kyrenia	CY	494	35°20'N	33°19'E
Kyrenia Mountains	CY	494	35°20'N	33°19'E
Kyrgyzstan		38	41°00'N	75°00'E
Kyritz	GM	584	52°56'N	12°23'E
Kyrkkazyk	KG	514	41°50'N	72°41'E
Kyrksæterøra	NO	604	63°17'N	9°06'E
Kyrönjoki	FI	578	63°14'N	21°45'E
Kyrösjärvi	FI	578	61°42'N	22°36'E
Kyrykuduk	KZ	510	49°50'N	51°53'E
Kyshlag-Zeyzit	AJ	483	41°08'N	47°14'E
Kyshtovka	RS	612	56°33'N	76°38'E
Ky Son	VM	540	19°23'N	104°07'E
Kystyk, Plato		468	71°00'N	123°00'E
Kysucké Nové Mesto	LO	616	49°18'N	18°47'E
Kysyl-Syr	RS	612	63°53'N	122°46'E
Kythrea	CY	494	35°15'N	33°29'E
Kyunhla	BM	487	23°21'N	95°19'E
Kyuquot	CA	390	50°02'N	127°23'W
Kyurdamir	AJ	483	40°21'N	48°11'E
Kyurendog, Khr.	TX	537	39°00'N	55°10'E
Kyushu	JA	506	33°00'N	131°00'E
Kyushu-sanchi	JA	506	32°35'N	131°17'E
Kyustendil	BU	573	42°17'N	22°41'E
Kyusyur	RS	612	70°39'N	127°15'E
Kywebwe	BM	487	19°21'N	94°43'E
Kyyiv (Kiev)	UP	624	50°26'N	30°31'E
Kyyjärvi	FI	578	63°02'N	24°29'E
Kyzyl	RS	612	51°42'N	94°27'E
Kyzyl-Kiya	KG	514	40°16'N	72°08'E
Kyzylkorgon	KG	514	40°11'N	73°30'E
Kyzylkum, Peski	KZ	510	39°06'N	54°25'E
Kyzyl-Mazhalyk	RS	612	51°08'N	90°36'E
Kyzyltebe	KG	514	42°12'N	75°15'E
Kyzyl-Tuu	KG	514	42°11'N	76°40'E
Kyzylzhar	KZ	510	48°17'N	69°40'E
Kzyltu	KZ	510	53°33'N	72°19'E

L

Laa an der Thaya	AU	568	48°43'N	16°23'E
La Aduana	VE	440	8°55'N	69°12'W
Laage	GM	584	53°56'N	12°21'E
Laakirchen	AU	568	47°58'N	13°49'E
La Almunia de Doña Godina	SP	618	41°29'N	1°22'W
Laas Caanood	SO	321	8°28'N	47°21'E
La Ascensión	MX	394	24°21'N	99°55'W
Laas Dawaco	SO	321	10°28'N	49°05'E
Laas Dhaareed	SO	321	10°10'N	45°59'E
Laas Qoray	SO	321	11°10'N	48°13'E
La Asturiana	AR	419	37°51'S	65°22'W
La Asunción	VE	440	11°02'N	63°53'W
La Aurora	VE	440	7°36'N	65°08'W
Laâyoune		262	27°08'N	13°11'W
La Babia	MX	394	28°34'N	102°04'W
Labaddey	SO	321	0°30'N	42°46'E
La Bañeza	SP	618	42°18'N	5°54'W
Labang	MY	518	3°15'N	113°29'E
La Barra	NU	415	12°54'N	83°32'W
La Barra	UY	439	34°55'S	54°51'W
Labason	RP	526	8°04'N	122°31'E
L'Abbaye	SZ	622	46°39'N	6°19'E
Labe (Elbe)	EZ	575	53°50'N	9°00'E
Labé	GV	297	11°19'N	12°17'W
Labelle		374	46°16'N	74°44'W
Labi	BX	486	4°23'N	114°27'E
Labian, Tanjung	MY	518	5°09'N	119°13'E
Labin	HR	574	45°05'N	14°08'E
Labinsk		466	44°39'N	40°43'E
Labis	MY	518	2°23'N	103°02'E
Labo	RP	526	14°09'N	122°51'E
La Bocana	MX	394	26°48'N	113°43'W
Laboire	ST	418	13°45'N	60°59'W
La Bonita	EC	432	0°27'N	77°30'W
La Boquilla		376	27°32'N	105°23'W
La Bostonnais		374	47°31'N	72°42'W
Labota	ID	500	2°52'S	122°10'E
Labouheyre	FR	580	44°13'N	0°55'W
Laboulaye	AR	419	34°07'S	63°24'W
Labra, Peña	SP	618	43°03'N	4°26'W
Labrador City	CA	390	52°57'N	66°55'W
Labrador Peninsula	CA	390	60°00'N	74°00'W
Labrador Sea	CA	390	57°00'N	53°00'W
La Brea	TD	438	10°14'N	61°37'W
Lábrea	BR	424	7°16'S	64°47'W
La Brea, Cerros de	PE	436	4°35'S	80°55'W
Labrieville	CA	390	49°18'N	69°34'W
Labruguière	FR	580	43°32'N	2°16'E
Labuha	ID	500	0°37'S	127°29'E
Labuhanbajo		648	8°29'S	119°54'E
Labuk	MY	518	5°54'N	117°30'E
Labuk, Telukan	MY	518	6°10'N	117°50'E
Labuništa	MK	599	41°16'N	20°36'E
Labutta	BM	487	16°09'N	94°46'E
Laç	AL	566	41°38'N	19°43'E
Lac-à-Beauce		370	47°19'N	72°46'W
La Cahouane	HA	412	18°19'N	74°15'W
Lacalahorra	SP	618	37°11'N	3°04'W
La Calera		388	32°47'S	71°12'W
La Campana		376	26°07'N	103°31'W
Lacanau-Océan	FR	580	45°00'N	1°12'W
La Candelaria	VE	440	8°41'N	67°43'W
La Canoa	VE	440	8°37'N	63°52'W
Laćarak	YO	630	45°00'N	19°34'E
La Caratica	VE	440	7°08'N	62°50'W
La Carlota	AR	419	33°26'S	63°18'W
La Carolina	SP	618	38°15'N	3°37'W
Lac-Bouchette		374	48°15'N	72°11'W
Laccadive Sea	IN	496	8°00'N	75°00'E
Lac du Bonnet	CA	390	50°15'N	96°04'W
Lac du Flambeau		374	45°58'N	89°53'W
Lac-Édouard		374	47°39'N	72°16'W
La Ceiba	CO	430	3°37'N	67°53'W
La Ceiba	HO	412	15°47'N	86°48'W
La Ceiba	VE	440	9°28'N	71°04'W
La Ceiba	VE	440	7°24'N	71°47'W
La Ceja		384	6°02'N	75°26'W
Lacepede Bay	AS	656	36°47'S	139°45'E
Lacerdónia	MZ	312	18°01'S	35°34'E
Lacha, Oz.	RS	612	61°20'N	38°48'E
La Chapelle	HA	412	18°55'N	72°19'W
La Chapelle-Saint-Luc	FR	580	48°20'N	4°03'E
La Chapelle-Saint-Mesmin		562	47°53'N	1°50'E
La Chapelle-sur-Erdre	FR	580	47°18'N	1°33'W
La Charité-sur-Loire	FR	580	47°11'N	3°01'E
La Châtre		562	46°35'N	1°59'E
La Chaux-de-Fonds	SZ	622	47°06'N	6°49'E
Lachay, Punta	PE	436	11°16'S	77°40'W
Lach Bissigh	SO	321	0°45'N	41°33'E
Lāchi	PK	524	33°23'N	71°20'E
Lachlan	AS	656	34°21'S	143°57'E
La Chorrera	CO	430	0°44'S	73°01'W
La Chorrera	PM	417	8°53'N	79°47'W
La Choux	MP	309	20°17'S	57°40'E
La Ciénaga	DR	408	18°04'N	71°06'W
Laçin	AJ	483	39°38'N	46°32'E
La Ciudad	MX	394	23°43'N	105°40'W
Lackawanna		374	42°49'N	78°49'W
Lac La Biche	CA	390	54°46'N	111°58'W
Lac La Hache		372	51°48'N	121°29'W
Lac la Martre	CA	390	63°10'N	117°16'W
Lac Le Jeune		372	50°29'N	120°30'W
Laclubar		648	8°45'S	125°55'E
Lac-Mégantic		374	45°35'N	70°53'W
La Cocha		388	27°47'S	65°34'W
Lacock	UK	626	51°24'N	2°07'W
La Coma		376	24°28'N	98°19'W
Lacombe	CA	390	52°28'N	113°44'W
La Concepción	HO	412	14°46'N	85°43'W
La Concepción	PM	417	8°31'N	82°37'W
La Conquista	NU	415	11°44'N	86°12'W
La Consulta	AR	419	33°44'S	69°07'W
La Coronilla	UY	439	33°55'S	53°31'W
la Cortinada	AN	567	42°34'N	1°31'E
La Couronne	FR	580	45°37'N	0°06'E
Lacovia	JM	414	18°04'N	77°45'W
La Crèche	FR	580	46°21'N	0°18'W
La Crescent		374	43°49'N	91°18'W
Lacret	CU	406	22°57'N	80°51'W
La Crete	CA	390	58°11'N	116°24'W
La Croche		374	47°36'N	72°44'W
La Croix Maingol	ST	418	13°57'N	61°00'W
Lacross	AS	656	14°37'S	128°04'E
La Crosse		372	38°31'N	99°18'W
La Crosse	US	398	43°48'N	91°14'W
La Cruz	AR	419	29°10'S	56°38'W
La Cruz	CO	430	1°35'N	76°58'W
La Cruz	CS	405	11°02'N	85°37'W
La Cruz	MX	394	23°55'N	106°54'W
La Cruz	UY	439	33°56'S	56°15'W
La Cruz de Río Grande	NU	415	13°06'N	84°10'W
La Cruz de Taratara	VE	440	11°03'N	69°44'W

Lac Seul	CA	390	50°20'N	92°16'W
Lac Son	VM	540	20°28'N	105°24'E
Lac Thien	VM	540	12°24'N	108°10'E
La Cuchilla	UY	439	32°35'S	53°23'W
La Cumbre, Volcán	EC	432	0°21'S	91°32'W
La Cygne		374	38°21'N	94°45'W
Ladakh Range	IN	496	34°00'N	78°00'E
L'Adamaoua, Massif de	CM	280	7°00'N	13°00'E
La Democracia	VE	440	2°28'N	67°16'W
Ladhu		654	15°30'S	167°00'E
Ladik		564	40°55'N	35°55'E
Ladismith	SF	322	33°29'S	21°16'E
Ladispoli		562	41°57'N	12°05'E
Lādīz	IR	502	28°56'N	61°19'E
Lado	SU	324	5°02'N	31°41'E
La Dorada	CO	430	5°27'N	74°40'W
Ladozhskoye Oz.	RS	612	61°00'N	31°30'E
Ladrillero, Cerro	CI	428	52°57'S	72°35'W
Ladrillo, Punta	CU	406	21°36'N	79°32'W
Ladva-Vetka		556	61°21'N	34°27'E
Lady Barron	AS	656	40°12'S	148°14'E
Ladybrand	SF	322	29°12'S	27°27'E
Lady Grey	SF	322	30°42'S	27°13'E
Lady Lake		378	28°55'N	81°55'W
Ladysmith		270	28°33'S	29°46'E
Ladysmith		374	45°27'N	91°06'W
Ladysmith	SF	322	28°33'S	29°47'E
Ladyville	BH	404	17°32'N	88°17'W
Ladyzhin	UP	624	48°40'N	29°15'E
Lae	PP	664	6°44'S	146°58'E
Lae	RM	661	8°55'N	166°05'E
Lae	TH	534	19°25'N	100°53'E
La Embocada	BL	422	15°03'S	67°00'W
La Encantada		376	28°22'N	102°34'W
La Encarnación	HO	412	14°40'N	89°05'W
Laer	GM	584	52°04'N	7°21'E
Lærdalsøyri	NO	604	61°06'N	7°29'E
La Escondida	AR	419	36°09'S	68°19'W
La Esmeralda	MX	394	27°19'N	103°38'W
La Esmeralda	PM	417	8°16'N	78°54'W
La Esmeralda	VE	440	3°12'N	65°32'W
La Esmeralda	VE	440	3°10'N	70°51'W
Laesø	DA	576	57°20'N	11°00'E
La Española (Hispaniola)	DR	408	19°00'N	71°00'W
La Esperanza	AR	419	40°26'S	68°32'W
La Esperanza	BL	422	14°01'S	64°46'W
La Esperanza	BL	422	14°34'S	62°10'W
La Esperanza	CU	406	22°46'N	83°44'W
La Esperanza	HO	412	14°18'N	88°11'W
La Esperanza	VE	440	8°55'N	60°53'W
La Esperanza, Sierra	HO	412	15°40'N	85°45'W
La Estación	SP	618	40°38'N	4°00'W
Lafaruug	SO	321	10°00'N	44°46'E
La Fayette		378	34°42'N	85°16'W
Lafayette		374	36°31'N	86°01'W
Lafayette	US	398	40°25'N	86°53'W
Lafayette	US	398	30°13'N	92°01'W
La Fe	CU	406	22°03'N	84°16'W
La Fère	FR	580	49°40'N	3°22'E
La Feria	US	398	26°09'N	97°49'W
La Ferté-Macé	FR	580	48°36'N	0°22'W
La Ferté-St-Aubin	FR	580	47°43'N	1°56'E
Lafia	NI	316	8°29'N	8°31'E
Lafiagi	NI	316	8°52'N	5°25'E
La Flèche	FR	580	47°42'N	0°05'W
La Florencia	AR	419	24°12'S	62°01'W
La Follette		374	36°22'N	84°07'W
La Fría	VE	440	8°13'N	72°15'W
Lāfūl		476	7°10'N	93°52'E
Lagamar		386	18°13'S	46°48'W
Lagan	SW	621	56°33'N	12°56'E
Lagar	IC	591	64°50'N	15°00'W
Lagarto	BR	424	10°54'S	37°41'W
Lagbo	CG	287	3°13'N	30°34'E
Lagdo, Lac de	CM	280	9°00'N	13°55'E
Lågen	NO	604	61°08'N	10°25'E
Lages	BR	424	27°51'S	50°19'W
Laggan		558	57°01'N	4°16'W
Laghouat	AG	272	33°48'N	2°53'E
Lagjit, Kepi i	AL	566	41°09'N	19°25'E
La Gloria	CU	406	21°44'N	77°39'W
Lagoa	PO	608	37°08'N	8°27'W
Lagoa Vermelha		388	28°14'S	51°32'W
Lago Blanco	AR	419	45°55'S	71°15'W
Lago Cardiel	AR	419	48°58'S	71°24'W
Lagodekhi	GG	495	41°49'N	46°16'E
La Goleta	CO	430	8°27'N	77°10'W
La Gomera	GT	411	14°05'N	91°03'W
La Gomera	SP	618	27°55'N	17°39'W
La Gonâve, Canal de (Sud, Canal du)	HA	412	18°30'N	73°00'W
La Gonâve, Golfe de	HA	412	19°00'N	73°30'W
La Gonâve, Île de	HA	412	18°51'N	73°03'W
Lago Posadas	AR	419	47°31'S	71°46'W
Lagos		266	6°27'N	3°21'E
Lagos	PO	608	37°06'N	8°41'W
Lagos de Moreno	MX	394	21°21'N	101°55'W
Lago Verde	CI	428	44°14'S	71°50'W
Lago Viedma	AR	419	49°48'S	72°07'W
La Graciosa	SP	618	29°15'N	13°30'W
La Grand-Combe	FR	580	44°13'N	4°02'E
La Grande	US	398	45°19'N	118°05'W
La Grande Rivière	CA	390	53°50'N	79°00'W
La Grange		378	29°54'N	96°52'W
La Grange	AS	656	18°41'S	121°46'E
La Grange	US	398	33°01'N	85°01'W
La Gran Sabana	VE	440	5°30'N	61°30'W
La Grita	VE	440	8°08'N	71°59'W
La Guardia	BL	422	17°54'S	63°20'W
La Guata	HO	412	15°05'N	86°23'W
Laguna Blanca	AR	419	25°08'S	58°15'W
Laguna de Duero	SP	618	41°35'N	4°43'W
Laguna de Jaco	MX	394	27°50'N	104°00'W
Laguna del Rey	MX	394	27°02'N	103°22'W
Laguna de Perlas	NU	415	12°19'N	83°40'W
Laguna Grande	AR	419	43°42'S	56°48'W
Laguna Grande	AR	419	49°33'S	70°14'W
Laguna Grande, Punta	DR	408	19°31'N	69°52'W
Laguna Mts.		376	32°48'N	116°27'W
Laguna Paiva		388	31°19'S	60°39'W
Lagunas	CI	428	20°59'S	69°41'W
Lagunas	PE	436	5°14'S	75°38'W
Laguna Salada	DR	408	19°32'N	71°05'W
Laguna Yema	AR	419	24°15'S	61°15'W
Lagundu, Tanjung	ID	500	8°47'S	118°56'E
Lagunetas	VE	440	9°34'N	71°58'W
Lagunillas	BL	422	19°38'S	63°43'W
Lagunillas	BL	422	19°14'S	65°20'W
Lagunillas	VE	440	8°31'N	71°24'W
Lagunillas	VE	440	10°08'N	71°16'W
Lagunita de Castillo	MX	394	23°28'N	100°24'W
Lagushao		474	40°29'N	125°00'E
La Habana	CU	406	23°08'N	82°22'W
Lahad Datu	MY	518	5°02'N	118°19'E
Lahad Datu, Telukan	MY	518	5°02'N	118°19'E
Laham	ID	500	0°22'N	115°24'E
Lahan Sai	TH	534	14°25'N	102°52'E
Lahat	ID	500	3°48'S	103°32'E
La Hermosa	CO	430	5°32'N	70°26'W
La Herradura	ES	409	13°21'N	88°57'W
La Higuera	CI	428	29°30'S	71°17'W
Laḥij	YM	541	13°03'N	44°52'E
Lāhījān	IR	502	37°12'N	50°01'E
Laholm	SW	621	56°28'N	13°02'E
Laholmsbukten	SW	621	56°34'N	12°26'E
Lahore	PK	524	31°35'N	74°18'E

La Hormiga	CO	430	0°30'N	76°49'W
La Horqueta	VE	440	7°51'N	60°21'W
La Horqueta	VE	440	9°14'N	62°06'W
La Horquilla	BL	422	12°34'S	64°25'W
Lahr	GM	584	48°20'N	7°52'E
Lahri	PK	524	29°11'N	68°13'E
Lahti	FI	578	60°58'N	25°40'E
La Huaca	PE	436	4°54'S	80°57'W
La Huacana	MX	394	18°58'N	101°49'W
Laï	CD	283	9°24'N	16°18'E
Laiagam	PP	664	5°31'S	143°28'E
Lai Chau	VM	540	22°03'N	103°09'E
Laie	US	398	21°39'N	157°55'W
Laifeng Tujiazu Zizhixian		472	29°30'N	109°23'E
L'Aigle	FR	580	48°46'N	0°37'E
Laignes		562	47°50'N	4°22'E
Laihia	FI	578	62°58'N	22°01'E
Lai-hka	BM	487	21°16'N	97°40'E
Laimea		648	4°25'S	122°29'E
La Inglesa	VE	440	9°13'N	63°29'W
Laingsburg	SF	322	33°12'S	20°51'E
Lainioälven	SW	621	67°22'N	22°39'E
Lairg	UK	626	58°02'N	4°24'W
Lais	ID	500	3°31'S	102°03'E
La Isabela	CU	406	22°57'N	80°01'W
Laisamis	KE	299	1°36'N	37°48'E
Laishevo		560	55°24'N	49°32'E
Laisvall	SW	621	66°08'N	17°10'E
Laitila	FI	578	60°53'N	21°41'E
Laives (Leifers)	IT	593	46°26'N	11°20'E
Laiwu	CH	490	36°12'N	117°37'E
Laiwui	ID	500	1°22'S	127°40'E
Laiyang	CH	490	36°57'N	120°40'E
Laizhou Wan	CH	490	37°36'N	119°30'E
Laja, Laguna de la	CI	428	37°21'S	71°19'W
La Jagua de Ibirico	CO	430	9°34'N	73°20'W
La Jalca	PE	436	6°29'S	77°43'W
Laje		384	10°11'S	40°58'W
Lajing La	NP	522	28°44'N	84°40'E
la Jonquera	SP	618	42°25'N	2°53'E
Lajosmizse	HU	590	47°01'N	19°33'E
La Joya		376	32°28'N	117°00'W
La Joya	MX	394	27°25'N	106°15'W
La Joya	PE	436	16°44'S	71°51'W
La Joya de los Sachas	EC	432	0°19'S	76°51'W
Lāju	IN	496	26°56'N	95°35'E
La Junta	MX	394	28°28'N	107°20'W
La Junta	US	398	37°58'N	103°32'W
Laka		556	63°00'N	11°00'E
Lakamané	ML	307	14°31'N	9°55'W
Lakato	MA	304	19°11'S	48°26'E
Lake, Point	CA	390	65°15'N	113°04'W
Lakeba	FJ	660	18°05'S	178°30'W
Lake Butler		378	30°01'N	82°20'W
Lake Cargelligo		652	33°18'S	146°23'E
Lake Charles	US	398	30°13'N	93°13'W
Lake City		374	36°13'N	84°09'W
Lake City		374	44°26'N	92°16'W
Lake City		378	30°11'N	82°38'W
Lake City		378	33°52'N	79°45'W
Lakefield		374	44°26'N	78°16'W
Lake Grace	AS	656	33°06'S	118°28'E
Lake Hamilton		378	34°25'N	93°05'W
Lake Harbour	CA	390	62°51'N	69°53'W
Lake Havasu City		376	34°28'N	114°20'W
Lakehills		376	29°34'N	98°57'W
Lake Jackson	US	398	29°02'N	95°26'W
Lake King	AS	656	33°05'S	119°40'E
Lakeland	US	398	28°02'N	81°56'W
Lake Linden		374	47°11'N	88°24'W
Lake Louise	CA	390	51°26'N	116°11'W
Lake Macleod	AS	656	24°25'S	113°28'E
Lakemba Passage		650	18°00'S	181°00'E
Lake Murray	PP	664	6°49'S	141°26'E
Lake Nash	AS	656	20°58'S	137°55'E
Lake Ngami	BC	276	20°30'S	22°40'E
Lake Oswego		372	45°25'N	122°40'W
Lake Placid		374	44°17'N	73°59'W
Lake Placid		378	27°17'N	81°21'W
Lakeport		372	39°02'N	122°54'W
Lake Providence		378	32°48'N	91°10'W
Lakeside		372	43°34'N	124°10'W
Lakeview	US	398	42°11'N	120°20'W
Lake Village		378	33°19'N	91°16'W
Lake Way	AS	656	26°58'S	120°28'E
Lakewood		374	40°05'N	74°13'W
Lakewood	US	398	39°42'N	105°04'W
Lakewood	US	398	48°09'N	122°12'W
Lake Worth		378	26°37'N	80°03'W
Lake Xau	BC	276	21°15'S	24°40'E
Lakhdenpokh'ya		556	61°31'N	30°11'E
Lakhīmpur	IN	496	27°57'N	80°46'E
Lakhpat	IN	496	23°49'N	68°47'E
Lakhva	BO	569	52°13'N	27°06'E
Laki	IC	591	64°04'N	18°11'W
Lakin		372	37°56'N	101°15'W
Lakki	PK	524	32°36'N	70°55'E
Lakkíon	GR	588	37°07'N	26°51'E
Lakonikós Kólpos	GR	588	36°35'N	22°40'E
Lakota	IV	288	5°51'N	5°41'W
Laksefjord	NO	604	70°46'N	26°53'E
Lakselv	NO	604	70°03'N	24°56'E
Lākshām	BG	485	23°14'N	91°08'E
Lakshmipur	BG	485	23°25'N	90°24'E
Lala	RP	526	7°59'N	123°46'E
Lalago	TZ	327	3°27'S	33°57'E
La Laguna	SP	618	28°29'N	16°19'W
La Laja	MX	394	21°41'N	97°43'W
Lālājīn	IR	502	34°58'N	48°29'E
Lāla Mūsa	PK	524	32°42'N	73°58'E
Lalana	MA	304	22°54'S	45°23'E
Lalang	ID	500	2°00'N	104°00'E
Lalara	GB	294	0°22'N	11°28'E
La Lata	UY	439	31°44'S	54°25'W
Lālbhitti	NP	522	26°58'N	85°55'E
l'Alcora (Alcora)	SP	618	40°04'N	0°12'W
l'Alcúdia	SP	618	39°52'N	3°07'E
La Leona	VE	440	8°58'N	63°51'W
La Leonesa	AR	419	27°03'S	58°43'W
Lalëzit, Gjiri i	AL	566	41°31'N	19°29'E
Lalībela	ET	293	12°02'N	39°02'E
La Libertad	EC	432	2°14'S	80°54'W
La Libertad	ES	409	13°29'N	89°19'W
La Libertad	GT	411	16°47'N	90°07'W
La Libertad	HO	412	14°45'N	87°37'W
La Libertad	MX	394	14°35'N	92°12'W
La Libertad	NU	415	12°13'N	85°10'W
La Ligua	CI	428	32°27'S	71°14'W
Laliki	ID	500	7°43'S	126°20'E
Lalimbue	ID	500	3°50'S	122°29'E
Lalín	SP	618	42°39'N	8°07'W
La Línea de la Concepción	SP	618	36°09'N	5°22'W
Lalin He		474	45°28'N	125°43'E
Lalitpur	IN	496	24°41'N	78°25'E
Lālmanir Hāt	BG	485	25°54'N	89°27'E
La Lobería	AR	419	41°08'S	63°05'W
La Loche		368	56°29'N	109°26'W
La Loma		376	25°28'N	103°41'W
La Loma	BL	422	14°41'S	64°51'W
Lalomanu	WS	668	14°05'S	171°30'W
La Louvière	BE	570	50°28'N	4°11'E
Lālpur	BG	485	24°11'N	88°58'E
La Luz		376	32°58'N	105°56'W
La Luz	VE	440	8°24'N	69°49'W
Lalvar	AM	482	41°14'N	44°51'E
Lalyo	SU	324	4°18'N	31°02'E

Lāma	BG	485	21°46'N	92°14'E
Lama, Ozero		468	69°30'N	90°30'E
la Maçana	AN	567	42°33'N	1°31'E
La Macarena	CO	430	2°10'N	73°48'W
La Machine		562	46°53'N	3°28'E
La Maddalena	IT	593	41°13'N	9°24'E
Lamag	MY	518	5°29'N	117°49'E
La Magdalena	CO	430	6°12'N	74°35'W
Lamaiin Hiid	MG	520	47°35'N	111°30'E
Lama-Kara	TO	328	9°33'N	1°12'E
Lamakera	ID	500	8°26'S	123°09'E
La Malbaie		374	47°39'N	70°09'W
La Maná	EC	432	0°56'S	79°13'W
Lamar		374	37°29'N	94°16'W
Lamar	US	398	38°04'N	102°36'W
La Margarita	VE	440	8°05'N	60°59'W
Lamarque	AR	419	39°24'S	65°42'W
La Martre, Lac	CA	390	63°15'N	117°55'W
Lamas	PE	436	6°25'S	76°35'W
La Masica	HO	412	15°37'N	87°07'W
Lamballe	FR	580	48°28'N	2°31'W
Lambaré	PA	435	25°21'S	57°39'W
Lambaréné	GB	294	0°42'S	10°13'E
Lambate	BL	422	16°37'S	67°36'W
Lambayeque	PE	436	6°42'S	79°55'W
Lambé Koba	ML	307	13°39'N	10°12'W
Lambert	CI	428	29°50'S	71°07'W
Lambert, C.	PP	664	4°11'S	151°32'E
Lambert's Bay	SF	322	32°06'S	18°18'E
Lambton, C.	CA	390	71°05'N	123°11'W
Lame Deer	US	398	45°37'N	106°39'W
Lamego	PO	608	41°06'N	7°49'W
Lamenu		654	16°30'S	168°10'E
Lamèque, Île		370	47°54'N	64°26'W
La Merced	BL	422	22°01'S	64°44'W
La Merced	PE	436	11°03'S	75°19'W
La Mesa	MX	394	24°14'N	99°35'W
Lamesa	US	398	32°44'N	101°57'W
La Mesa Tres Ríos		376	29°52'N	108°42'W
Lamía	GR	588	38°54'N	22°26'E
Lamin	GA	295	13°21'N	16°26'W
La Mira	MX	394	18°01'N	102°19'W
La Misa	MX	394	28°23'N	110°32'W
Lamitan	RP	526	6°39'N	122°08'E
Lammi	FI	578	61°05'N	25°01'E
Lamon Bay	RP	526	14°25'N	122°00'E
Lamoni		374	40°37'N	93°56'W
Lamont		376	35°15'N	118°54'W
Lamontville	SF	322	29°56'S	30°56'E
La Morita	MX	394	28°37'N	103°12'W
Lamotrek Atoll	FM	661	7°00'N	146°00'E
Lampa	PE	436	15°21'S	70°22'W
Lampang	TH	534	18°18'N	99°31'E
Lampasas		376	31°03'N	98°10'W
Lampazos de Naranjo	MX	394	27°02'N	100°33'W
Lampertheim	GM	584	49°36'N	8°28'E
Lampeter	UK	626	52°07'N	4°04'W
Lamphun	TH	534	18°35'N	99°01'E
Lamu	BM	487	19°14'N	94°10'E
Lamu	KE	299	2°16'S	40°53'E
Lamud	PE	436	6°09'S	77°55'W
Lamu Island	KE	299	2°17'S	40°52'E
La Mula	MX	394	29°13'N	104°26'W
La Mure	FR	580	44°54'N	5°47'E
Lam Vien, Cao Nguyen	VM	540	12°05'N	108°00'E
Lamwa	UG	330	3°38'N	32°53'E
Lana	IT	593	46°37'N	11°09'E
Lanai	US	398	20°28'N	158°13'W
Lanai City	US	398	20°49'N	156°55'W
Lanao, Lake	RP	526	7°55'N	124°20'E
Lanark	UK	626	55°39'N	3°46'W
Lanas Village	MY	518	5°20'N	116°30'E
Lanbi Kyun	BM	487	10°50'N	98°15'E
Lancang		476	22°32'N	99°56'E
Lancang Jiang (Mekong)	CH	490	30°00'N	98°00'E
Lancaster		374	39°42'N	82°35'W
Lancaster		374	40°02'N	76°18'W
Lancaster	UK	626	54°02'N	2°47'W
Lancaster	US	398	34°41'N	118°08'W
Lancaster Sound	CA	390	74°13'N	84°00'W
Lanchkhuti	GG	495	42°05'N	42°00'E
Lanciano	IT	593	42°14'N	14°23'E
Łańcut	PL	606	50°04'N	22°14'E
Lancy	SZ	622	46°11'N	6°06'E
Landau	GM	584	48°40'N	12°41'E
Landau in der Pfalz	GM	584	49°12'N	8°07'E
Landay	AF	480	30°31'N	63°47'E
Landeck	AU	568	47°08'N	10°34'E
Landen	BE	570	50°45'N	5°05'E
Lander	US	398	42°49'N	108°43'W
Landerneau	FR	580	48°27'N	4°15'W
Landes de Lanvaux	FR	580	47°48'N	2°47'W
Landrienne		374	48°33'N	77°55'W
Landri Sales		384	7°16'S	43°55'W
Landsberg	GM	584	48°03'N	10°52'E
Land's End	UK	626	50°03'N	5°42'W
Landshut	GM	584	48°32'N	12°08'E
Landskrona	SW	621	55°52'N	12°50'E
Landsmeer	NL	602	52°26'N	4°55'E
Landza	CF	285	2°40'N	18°20'E
La Negra	AR	419	39°32'S	70°20'W
La Negra	CI	428	23°46'S	70°20'W
Lanett		378	32°52'N	85°11'W
Langadhás	GR	588	40°45'N	23°04'E
Langádhia	GR	588	37°41'N	22°02'E
Langano Hayk'	ET	293	7°36'N	38°43'E
Langdon	US	398	48°45'N	98°22'W
Langebaanweg	SF	322	32°58'S	18°09'E
Langeberg	SF	322	33°34'S	18°52'E
Langeland	DA	576	55°04'N	10°53'E
Langelands Bælt	DA	576	54°50'N	10°55'E
Langelmavesi	FI	578	61°32'N	24°22'E
Langelsheim	GM	584	51°56'N	10°20'E
Langen	GM	584	53°37'N	8°36'E
Langenau	GM	584	48°30'N	10°06'E
Langenfeld	GM	584	51°06'N	6°57'E
Langenhagen	GM	584	52°27'N	9°45'E
Langenhorn	GM	584	54°40'N	8°55'E
Langenlois	AU	568	48°28'N	15°40'E
Langenthal	SZ	622	47°13'N	7°47'E
Langenwang	AU	568	47°34'N	15°37'E
Langeoog	GM	584	53°43'N	7°31'E
Langeoog	GM	584	53°45'N	7°29'E
Langepas		466	61°13'N	75°18'E
Langeskov	DA	576	55°22'N	10°36'E
Langfang	CH	490	39°30'N	116°40'E
Langgar		472	29°52'N	93°42'E
Langholm	UK	626	55°09'N	3°00'W
Langjökull	IC	591	64°39'N	20°12'W
Langkampfen	AU	568	47°32'N	12°05'E
Langkawi	MY	518	6°20'N	99°50'E
Lang Kha Tuk, Kao	TH	534	9°15'N	98°30'E
Langkon	MY	518	6°32'N	116°42'E
Langlade I.		370	46°55'N	56°20'W
Langnau im Emmental	SZ	622	46°56'N	7°47'E
Langon	FR	580	44°33'N	0°15'W
Langøya	NO	604	68°44'N	14°50'E
Langres	FR	580	47°52'N	5°19'E
Langres, Plateau de	FR	580	47°41'N	5°03'E
Langru	CH	490	36°55'N	79°33'E
Langsa	ID	500	4°28'N	97°58'E
Langsele	SW	621	63°11'N	17°04'E
Lang Shan	CH	490	41°50'N	107°50'E
Lang Son	VM	540	21°49'N	106°43'E
Langston		376	35°56'N	97°15'W
Lang Suan	TH	534	9°57'N	99°04'E

Langtang	NI	316	9°09'N	9°48'E
Langtang Lirung	NP	522	28°16'N	85°32'E
Langtou		474	40°02'N	124°19'E
Langtoutun	CH	490	46°49'N	121°50'E
Långträsk	SW	621	65°23'N	20°20'E
Langue	HO	412	13°37'N	87°39'W
Languedoc, Plaine du	FR	580	44°00'N	4°00'E
Languidic	FR	580	47°50'N	3°10'W
Langwedel	GM	584	52°58'N	9°13'E
Lan Hsü	TW	532	22°05'N	121°50'E
Länkärän	AJ	483	38°45'N	48°50'E
Lanlacuni Bajo	PE	436	13°29'S	70°25'W
Lannemezan	FR	580	43°41'N	0°24'E
Lannion	FR	580	48°44'N	3°28'W
La Nong	LA	517	16°15'N	106°40'E
La Norteña		376	29°40'N	108°27'W
Lanping	CH	490	26°27'N	99°24'E
Lansdowne House	CA	390	52°14'N	87°53'W
L'Anse	US	398	46°45'N	88°27'W
Lansing		368	63°45'N	133°28'W
Lansing		374	43°26'N	76°27'W
Lansing	US	398	42°44'N	84°34'W
Lanškroun	EZ	575	49°55'N	16°37'E
Lanslebourg-Mont-Cenis	FR	580	45°17'N	6°51'E
Lanta, Ko	TH	534	7°39'N	99°06'E
Lantouy	LA	517	22°26'N	101°43'E
Lanusei	IT	593	39°52'N	9°32'E
Lanxi		472	46°15'N	126°14'E
Lanxi	CH	490	29°12'N	119°27'E
Lanzarote	SP	618	29°05'N	13°24'W
Lanžhot	EZ	575	48°43'N	16°59'E
Lanzhou	CH	490	36°02'N	103°40'E
Laoag	RP	526	18°12'N	120°36'E
Laoang		478	12°32'N	125°00'E
Lao Cai	VM	540	22°30'N	103°57'E
Laodaodian	CH	490	51°15'N	126°42'E
Laofengkou	CH	490	46°10'N	83°37'E
Lao Fu Chai	LA	517	21°47'N	102°24'E
Laoha He	CH	490	43°24'N	120°39'E
Lao He	CH	490	32°00'N	108°30'E
Laoheishan		474	43°43'N	130°52'E
Laohekou	CH	490	32°21'N	111°39'E
Laojingou	CH	490	53°15'N	122°12'E
La Ola	CI	428	26°34'S	69°04'W
La Oliva	SP	618	28°36'N	13°56'W
Laolong	CH	490	24°06'N	115°15'E
Laon	FR	580	49°34'N	3°37'E
La Orotava	SP	618	28°23'N	16°31'W
La Oroya	PE	436	11°32'S	75°54'W
Laos		38	18°00'N	105°00'E
Laotieshan Shuidao	CH	490	38°34'N	121°00'E
Laoye Ling	CH	490	44°00'N	130°00'E
Lapa, Serra da	PO	608	40°54'N	7°30'W
La Palma	CO	430	5°22'N	74°24'W
La Palma	ES	409	14°19'N	89°10'W
La Palma	PM	417	8°23'N	78°08'W
La Palma	SP	618	28°53'N	17°48'W
La Paloma	UY	439	32°43'S	55°36'W
La Paragua	VE	440	6°50'N	63°20'W
La Pastora	VE	440	7°28'N	62°05'W
Lapataia	AR	419	54°50'S	68°34'W
La Paz	AR	419	30°45'S	59°39'W
La Paz	AR	419	33°28'S	67°33'W
La Paz	BL	422	16°30'S	68°09'W
La Paz	CO	430	10°23'N	73°10'W
La Paz	HO	412	14°19'N	87°41'W
La Paz	MX	394	24°10'N	110°18'W
La Paz	RP	526	8°19'N	125°43'E
La Paz	UY	439	34°44'S	56°15'W
La Paz Centro	NU	415	12°20'N	86°41'W
La Paz de Oriente	NU	415	11°49'N	86°08'W
La Pedrera	CO	430	1°18'S	69°43'W
La Pedrera	UY	439	34°36'S	54°07'W
Lapeer		374	43°03'N	83°19'W
La Peña	PM	417	8°07'N	81°03'W
La Perla		376	25°18'N	104°01'W
La Perla	MX	394	28°16'N	104°33'W
La Pérouse Strait (Soya-Kaikyo)	JA	506	45°45'N	142°00'E
La Pesca	MX	394	23°46'N	97°47'W
Lapia	NI	316	9°03'N	6°34'E
La Piedad Cavadas	MX	394	20°21'N	102°01'W
Lapierre House	CA	390	67°24'N	137°01'W
Lapinlahti	FI	578	63°22'N	27°24'E
La Pintada	PM	417	8°36'N	80°27'W
Lapithos	CY	494	35°20'N	33°10'E
La Place	US	398	30°03'N	90°28'W
La Placita	MX	394	18°30'N	103°33'W
La Plaine	DO	407	15°19'N	61°15'W
La Plata		374	40°01'N	92°29'W
La Plata	AR	419	34°55'S	57°57'W
La Plata	CO	430	2°23'N	75°53'W
la Pobla	SP	618	39°46'N	3°01'E
la Pobla de Lillet		562	42°15'N	1°59'E
la Pobla de Segur	SP	618	42°15'N	0°58'E
La Pocatière		374	47°22'N	70°02'W
La Porte		374	41°36'N	86°43'W
Lapovo	YO	630	44°11'N	21°06'E
La Poza	MX	394	25°48'N	112°02'W
Lappajärvi	FI	578	63°12'N	23°33'E
Lappajärvi	FI	578	63°08'N	23°40'E
Lappeenranta	FI	578	61°04'N	28°11'E
Laprida	AR	419	37°33'S	60°49'W
La Primavera	CO	430	5°30'N	70°25'W
La Pryor		376	28°56'N	99°50'W
Lâpseki		564	40°20'N	26°41'E
Laptev Sea	RS	612	76°00'N	126°00'E
Lapthal		470	30°44'N	80°08'E
Lapua	FI	578	62°57'N	23°00'E
La Puebla de Montalbán	SP	618	39°52'N	4°21'W
La Puerta	VE	440	7°29'N	70°19'W
Lapu-Lapu	RP	526	10°19'N	123°57'E
La Puntilla	EC	432	2°10'S	81°00'W
La Purísima	MX	394	26°10'N	112°04'W
Lăpuşna	MD	601	46°53'N	28°25'E
Łapy	PL	606	52°59'N	22°52'E
Laqīyat al Arbaʿīn	SU	324	20°03'N	28°02'E
La Quemada		376	28°50'N	106°59'W
La Quiaca	AR	419	22°06'S	65°37'W
L'Aquila	IT	593	42°21'N	13°23'E
La Quinta		376	33°39'N	116°18'W
Lār	IR	502	27°40'N	54°20'E
Larache	MO	310	35°12'N	6°09'W
Larak	IR	502	26°51'N	56°21'E
Laramie	US	398	41°18'N	105°35'W
Laramie Range	US	398	42°00'N	105°20'W
Larantuka	ID	500	8°21'S	122°59'E
Larat	ID	500	7°10'S	131°50'E
Larat	ID	500	7°09'S	131°45'E
La Ravoire	FR	580	45°33'N	5°57'E
La Raya	VE	440	7°20'N	65°28'W
La Raya, Ciénaga de	CO	430	8°23'N	74°31'W
Larba	AG	272	36°33'N	3°11'E
Lärbro		558	57°47'N	18°47'E
Larder Lake		374	48°05'N	79°43'W
Lardier, Cap	FR	580	43°08'N	6°36'E
Laredo	PE	436	8°06'S	78°57'W
Laredo	SP	618	43°24'N	3°25'W
Laredo	US	398	27°30'N	99°30'W
La Reforma	AR	419	37°33'S	66°14'W
La Reforma	MX	394	25°05'N	108°03'W
La Reine		374	48°52'N	79°30'W
La Réole		562	44°35'N	0°02'W
Lares	PE	436	13°04'S	72°05'W
Lares	US	398	18°18'N	66°53'W
La Resource	ST	418	13°44'N	60°57'W

La Ressource	ST	418	13°56'N	60°55'W
Lar Gerd	AF	480	35°29'N	66°40'E
Largo, Cayo	CU	406	21°32'N	81°26'W
La Rhune	FR	580	43°18'N	1°38'W
Larieu	DO	407	15°35'N	61°20'W
Larimore		372	47°54'N	97°37'W
La Rioja	AR	419	29°26'S	66°51'W
La Rioja	CU	406	20°46'N	76°36'W
Lárisa	GR	588	39°39'N	22°27'E
Lārkāna	PK	524	27°33'N	68°13'E
Larnaca	CY	494	34°55'N	33°38'E
Larnaca Bay	CY	494	34°35'N	33°45'E
Larne	UK	626	54°49'N	5°48'W
Larned		372	38°10'N	99°05'W
La Robla	SP	618	42°48'N	5°37'W
La Roche	SZ	622	46°42'N	7°08'E
La Roche-de-Rame	FR	580	44°45'N	6°35'E
La Rochelle	FR	580	46°10'N	1°09'W
La Roche-sur-Yon	FR	580	46°40'N	1°26'W
Larochette	LU	598	49°46'N	6°14'E
La Roda	SP	618	39°13'N	2°09'W
La Romana	DR	408	18°25'N	68°58'W
La Ronge	CA	390	55°06'N	105°17'W
La Ronge, Lac	CA	390	55°07'N	105°00'W
Laropi	UG	330	3°34'N	31°49'E
La Rosita	MX	394	28°24'N	101°43'W
Larouco, Serra do	PO	608	41°55'N	7°40'W
Larreynaga	NU	415	12°40'N	86°34'W
Larrey Pt.	AS	656	19°57'S	119°04'E
Larrimah		648	15°35'S	133°12'E
Larsmo	FI	578	63°43'N	22°45'E
Larsnes	NO	604	62°13'N	5°36'E
La Rumorosa		376	32°34'N	116°06'W
Laruns	FR	580	42°59'N	0°25'W
Larvik	NO	604	59°04'N	10°00'E
Lar'yak	RS	612	61°16'N	80°15'E
Lasahau	ID	500	5°01'S	122°34'E
La Salle		374	41°19'N	89°05'W
LaSalle		374	45°26'N	73°38'W
Lasan	ID	500	1°14'N	115°13'E
Las Animas		372	38°03'N	103°13'W
La Sara	AR	419	53°26'S	68°11'W
La Sarre	CA	390	48°48'N	79°12'W
Las Aves, Islas	VE	440	11°58'N	67°33'W
Las Bayas	AR	419	41°28'S	70°40'W
Las Bayas	MX	394	23°32'N	104°50'W
Lasberg	AU	568	48°28'N	14°32'E
Las Bombas	CI	428	26°02'S	70°27'W
Las Bonitas	VE	440	7°52'N	65°40'W
Las Breas	CI	428	29°06'S	70°28'W
Las Breñas	AR	419	27°05'S	61°05'W
Las Cabezas de San Juan		562	36°59'N	5°56'W
Las Cabras		376	26°58'N	100°58'W
Lascahobas	HA	412	18°50'N	71°56'W
Lascano	UY	439	33°40'S	54°12'W
Lascar, Volcán	CI	428	23°23'S	67°45'W
Las Cruces		376	29°26'N	107°24'W
Las Cruces	US	398	32°18'N	106°46'W
Las Delicias	VE	440	7°34'N	72°27'W
La Serena	CI	428	29°54'S	71°16'W
La Serena, Emb.de	SP	618	38°55'N	5°13'W
la Seu d'Urgell	SP	618	42°22'N	1°30'E
Las Eutimias	MX	394	28°17'N	102°46'W
Las Flores	AR	419	36°03'S	59°07'W
Las Flores	HO	412	14°42'N	88°36'W
Las Galletas	SP	618	28°00'N	16°39'W
Las Golondrinas		376	26°43'N	100°30'W
Lāsh-e Joveyn	AF	480	31°43'N	61°37'E
Las Heras		388	32°51'S	68°49'W
Lashio	BM	487	22°56'N	97°45'E
Lashkar Gāh	AF	480	31°35'N	64°21'E
Lasht	PK	524	36°48'N	73°01'E
Lasia	ID	500	2°10'N	96°39'E
La Sierpe	CU	406	21°45'N	79°14'W
La Sila	IT	593	39°13'N	16°23'E
L'Asile	HA	412	18°23'N	73°25'W
La Silueta, Cerro	CI	428	52°22'S	72°11'W
Las Juntas	BL	422	21°45'S	64°46'W
Las Juntas	CO	430	2°05'N	72°14'W
Łask	PL	606	51°35'N	19°08'E
Las Lajas	AR	419	38°31'S	70°22'W
Las Lajas, Cerro	AR	419	38°30'S	70°30'W
Las Lajitas	VE	440	6°55'N	65°39'W
Las Lomas	PE	436	4°40'S	80°15'W
Las Lomitas	AR	419	24°42'S	60°36'W
Las Margaritas	CO	430	6°48'N	70°26'W
Las Margaritas	MX	394	16°18'N	91°59'W
Las Martinas	CU	406	21°58'N	84°09'W
Las Matas de Farfán	DR	408	18°52'N	71°31'W
Las Mercedes	VE	440	9°07'N	66°24'W
Las Montañitas	VE	440	6°59'N	70°06'W
Las Naves	EC	432	1°17'S	79°18'W
Las Nieves	MX	394	26°24'N	105°22'W
La Solana	SP	618	38°56'N	3°14'W
Lasolo		648	3°00'S	122°00'E
La Soufrière	VC	418	13°20'N	61°11'W
La Souterraine	FR	580	46°14'N	1°29'E
Las Palmas	PM	417	8°08'N	81°27'W
Las Palmas de Gran Canaria	SP	618	28°05'N	15°24'W
Las Palomas	MX	394	31°44'N	107°37'W
Las Pampitas	BL	422	12°55'S	64°39'W
Las Pedroñeras	SP	618	39°27'N	2°40'W
Las Petas	BL	422	16°23'S	59°11'W
Las Petas	BL	422	13°53'S	66°40'W
La Spezia	IT	593	44°06'N	9°50'E
Las Piedras	BL	422	11°03'S	66°13'W
Las Piedras	PE	436	12°30'S	69°14'W
Las Piedras	UY	439	34°44'S	56°13'W
Las Piedras	VE	440	10°03'N	72°25'W
Las Piedras	VE	440	8°09'N	60°59'W
Las Plumas	AR	419	43°43'S	67°15'W
Las Rosas	MX	394	16°24'N	92°23'W
Lassul	PP	664	4°12'S	151°39'E
Las Tablas	PM	417	7°46'N	80°17'W
Las Taperas	BL	422	17°54'S	60°23'W
Last Mountain L.	CA	390	51°10'N	105°15'W
Las Toscas	AR	419	28°21'S	59°17'W
Las Toscas	UY	439	32°09'S	55°03'W
Lastoursville	GB	294	0°49'S	12°42'E
Lastovo	HR	574	42°45'N	16°53'E
Lastovo	HR	574	42°45'N	16°54'E
Lastovski Kanal	HR	574	42°50'N	16°58'E
Las Trincheras	VE	440	6°57'N	64°54'W
Lasuriashi	GG	495	42°37'N	42°46'E
Las Varas		376	29°29'N	108°01'W
Las Varas	MX	394	21°10'N	105°10'W
Las Varillas	AR	419	31°52'S	62°43'W
Las Vegas	US	398	36°10'N	115°08'W
Las Vegas	VE	440	9°35'N	68°37'W
Las Yaras	PE	436	17°53'S	70°34'W
Las Yungas	BL	422	14°30'S	67°50'W
Lata	BP	666	10°44'S	165°44'E
La Tabatière	CA	390	50°50'N	58°58'W
Latacunga	EC	432	0°56'S	78°37'W
La Tagua	CO	430	0°03'S	74°40'W
Latākhola	BG	485	23°37'N	90°07'E
La Tapona	MX	394	23°09'N	100°00'W
Latchford		374	47°20'N	79°49'W
Late	TN	667	18°50'S	175°30'W
La Tebaida	CO	430	4°28'N	75°47'W
Laterrière		374	48°18'N	71°06'W
La Teste	FR	580	44°38'N	1°08'W
Lathrop		372	37°49'N	121°16'W
Lathrop		374	39°32'N	94°19'W
La Tigra	VE	440	7°30'N	61°35'W

Masaguara	HO	412	14°22'N	87°59'W
Masai Steppe	TZ	327	4°47'S	35°36'E
Masaka	UG	330	0°20'S	31°44'E
Masaki	JA	506	33°46'N	132°42'E
Masākin	TS	329	35°44'N	10°35'E
Masalembu Besar	ID	500	5°34'S	114°26'E
Masally	AJ	483	39°03'N	48°40'E
Masamba	ID	500	2°32'S	120°20'E
Masan	KS	513	35°11'N	128°34'E
Masanga	CG	287	0°27'S	22°14'E
Masangwe	TZ	327	5°26'S	30°05'E
Masan-ni	KS	513	37°13'N	126°41'E
Masatepe	NU	415	11°55'N	86°09'W
Masavi	BL	422	19°21'S	63°19'W
Masaya	NU	415	11°58'N	86°06'W
Masbate	RP	526	12°22'N	123°36'E
Masbate	RP	526	11°51'N	122°28'E
Mascara	AG	272	35°24'N	0°08'E
Mascarene Islands (Iles Mascareignes)		270	20°00'S	57°00'E
Mascasín	AR	419	31°22'S	66°59'W
Mase	CG	287	5°49'S	25°01'E
Masereka	CG	287	0°08'S	29°20'E
Maseru	LT	301	29°19'S	27°29'E
Masfjorden	NO	604	60°48'N	5°18'E
Mashaba	ZI	334	20°03'S	30°29'E
Mashaba Mountains	ZI	334	18°53'S	30°18'E
Mash'abbe Sade	IS	505	31°00'N	34°47'E
Mashala	CG	287	5°03'S	22°51'E
Mashan		474	45°12'N	130°32'E
Mashevka	UP	624	49°26'N	34°52'E
Mashhad	IR	502	36°18'N	59°36'E
Mashike	JA	506	43°51'N	141°31'E
Mashīz	IR	502	29°55'N	56°34'E
Mashkhan	AJ	483	38°33'N	48°50'E
Mashkid	IR	502	28°02'N	63°25'E
Mashtaga	AJ	483	40°32'N	50°00'E
Mashu-ko	JA	506	43°35'N	144°32'E
Mashūray	AF	480	32°12'N	68°21'E
Masilah, Wadi al	YM	541	15°10'N	51°08'E
Masindi	UG	330	1°41'N	31°43'E
Masindi Port	UG	330	1°42'N	32°05'E
Masingnyong Sanmaek	KN	512	38°30'N	127°00'E
Masinloc	RP	526	15°32'N	119°57'E
Masirah	MU	523	20°25'N	58°50'E
Masirah, Gulf of	MU	523	20°10'N	58°10'E
Masis	AM	432	40°00'N	44°29'E
Masisea	PE	436	8°36'S	74°19'W
Masjed-e Soleymān	IR	502	31°58'N	49°18'E
Mask, Lough	EI	592	53°37'N	9°21'W
Maskall	BH	404	17°53'N	88°19'W
Maskan, Raas	SO	321	11°10'N	43°33'E
Maskanah	SY	531	35°59'N	38°03'E
Masker, Jebel	MO	310	32°23'N	5°14'W
Maskin	MU	523	23°30'N	56°50'E
Maskūtān	IR	502	26°51'N	59°49'E
Maslyanino		466	54°20'N	84°13'E
Masoala, Tanjon'i	MA	304	15°58'S	50°14'E
Masoarivo	MA	304	19°03'S	44°19'E
Masoller	UY	439	31°05'S	56°01'W
Mason		376	30°44'N	99°13'W
Masonboro		378	34°10'N	77°51'W
Mason City		374	40°12'N	89°41'W
Mason City	US	398	43°09'N	93°12'W
Masqaţ (Muscat)	MU	523	23°37'N	58°35'E
Massa	IT	593	44°02'N	10°08'E
Massachusetts		374	42°15'N	71°30'W
Massachusetts Bay		374	42°23'N	70°45'W
Massacre	DO	407	15°21'N	61°24'W
Massaguet	CD	283	12°28'N	15°26'E
Massakory	CD	283	13°00'N	15°44'E
Massangena	MZ	312	21°32'S	32°57'E
Massapê	BR	424	3°31'S	40°19'W
Massena	US	398	44°55'N	74°53'W
Massenya	CD	283	11°24'N	16°10'E
Masset		368	54°00'N	132°06'W
Massibi	AO	274	11°06'S	22°41'E
Massif Central	FR	580	45°31'N	2°35'E
Massif du Manéngouba	CM	280	5°00'N	9°50'E
Massif du Mbam	CM	280	5°54'N	10°44'E
Massif du Nkogam	CM	280	5°44'N	10°42'E
Massigui	ML	307	11°52'N	6°46'W
Massillon		374	40°47'N	81°31'W
Massinga	MZ	312	23°20'S	35°22'E
Massingir	MZ	312	23°56'S	32°06'E
Massoukou	GB	294	1°24'S	12°05'E
Mastābah	SA	528	20°52'N	39°23'E
Masterton	NZ	663	40°57'S	175°40'E
Mastgat	NL	602	51°36'N	4°00'E
Mastikho, Ákra	GR	588	38°10'N	26°00'E
Mastūj	PK	524	36°17'N	72°31'E
Mastung	PK	524	29°48'N	66°51'E
Mastūrah	SA	528	23°06'N	38°50'E
Masuda	JA	506	34°40'N	131°51'E
Masuguru	TZ	327	11°22'S	38°26'E
Masvingo	ZI	334	20°05'S	30°50'E
Maşyāf	SY	531	35°03'N	36°21'E
Mat		270	5°31'N	10°52'E
Mat	AL	566	41°39'N	19°34'E
Mata	CG	287	7°53'S	21°58'E
Matabele Plain	ZA	332	16°20'S	23°10'E
Matachel		562	38°49'N	6°16'W
Matachewan		374	47°56'N	80°39'W
Matachic		376	28°50'N	107°45'W
Mata de Guanábano	VE	440	6°13'N	68°13'W
Matadi	CG	287	5°49'S	13°27'E
Mataga	CD	283	18°18'N	19°21'E
Matagalpa	NU	415	12°55'N	85°55'W
Matagami	CA	390	49°45'N	77°38'W
Matagami	CA	390	49°50'N	77°50'W
Matagami, Lac		374	49°52'N	77°40'W
Matagorda	US	398	28°10'N	96°37'W
Matagorda Bay		378	28°35'N	96°15'W
Matagorda Pen.		378	28°35'N	96°01'W
Mataiea		654	17°42'S	145°44'W
Mataiva		654	15°00'S	148°15'W
Matak	ID	500	3°18'N	106°16'E
Matala	AO	274	14°44'S	15°02'E
Matale	CE	530	7°28'N	80°37'E
Matalom	RP	526	10°17'N	124°47'E
Matam	SG	319	15°40'N	13°16'W
Mata Mata	SF	322	25°49'S	20°01'E
Matamba	CG	287	5°57'S	22°16'E
Mataméye	NG	314	13°26'N	8°28'E
Matamoros		376	25°29'N	105°28'W
Matamoros	MX	394	26°46'N	105°36'W
Matamoros	MX	394	25°32'N	103°15'W
Matamorosa	SP	618	42°59'N	4°09'W
Matancita		376	25°09'N	111°59'W
Matanda	ZA	332	11°22'S	28°27'E
Matandu	TZ	327	8°43'S	39°22'E
Matane	CA	390	48°51'N	67°32'W
Matanga	MA	304	23°32'S	47°33'E
Matanzas	CU	406	23°03'N	81°35'W
Matanzas, Bahía de	CU	406	23°04'N	81°30'W
Mata Palacio	DR	408	18°42'N	69°19'W
Matapalo, Cabo	CS	405	8°21'N	83°17'W
Mataporquera	SP	618	42°53'N	4°10'W
Mataquescuintla	GT	411	14°32'N	90°11'W
Mataquito	CI	428	34°59'S	72°12'W
Matara	CE	530	5°57'N	80°32'E
Matara	ER	292	14°31'N	39°18'E
Mataral	BL	422	18°06'S	64°11'W
Mataram	ID	500	8°35'S	116°07'E
Mataránga	GR	588	38°31'N	21°27'E
Matarani	PE	436	17°00'S	72°06'W
Mataranka	AS	656	14°56'S	133°09'E
Mataró	SP	618	41°32'N	2°27'E
Matatiele	SF	322	30°20'S	28°48'E
Mataura	NZ	663	46°12'S	168°50'E
Mataura	NZ	663	46°34'S	168°43'E
Matautu	WS	668	13°57'S	171°55'E
Matawai	NZ	663	38°19'S	177°34'E
Maţāy	EG	290	28°25'N	30°46'E
Matay	KZ	510	45°26'N	57°11'E
Matay	KZ	510	45°55'N	78°43'E
Mateare	NU	415	12°14'N	86°26'W
Mateguá	BL	422	13°01'S	62°48'W
Matehuala	MX	394	23°39'N	100°39'W
Mateke Hills	ZI	334	21°45'S	29°32'E
Matelot	TD	438	10°49'N	61°07'W
Matera	IT	593	40°40'N	16°36'E
Matéri	BN	276	10°41'N	1°03'E
Matese	IT	593	41°25'N	14°24'E
Mátészalka	HU	590	47°57'N	22°20'E
Matetsi	ZI	334	18°16'S	25°56'E
Mathbaria	BG	485	22°18'N	89°57'E
Matheaux, Chaine des	HA	412	18°55'N	72°30'W
Mather		372	49°06'N	99°11'W
Matheson		374	48°32'N	80°28'W
Matheson Island		372	51°44'N	96°56'W
Mathew's Peak	KE	299	1°19'N	37°18'E
Mathews Range	KE	299	1°15'N	37°20'E
Mathis		376	28°05'N	97°49'W
Mathurā	IN	496	27°30'N	77°41'E
Mati	RP	526	6°57'N	126°13'E
Matías Romero	MX	394	16°53'N	95°02'W
Matíguas	NU	415	12°50'N	85°28'W
Matimbuka	TZ	327	11°10'S	35°52'E
Matina	CS	405	10°05'N	83°17'W
Matina, Boca del	CS	405	10°10'N	83°10'W
Matinicock Pt.	US	398	40°53'N	73°37'W
Mātir	TS	329	37°03'N	9°40'E
Matizi		472	33°10'N	103°27'E
Mātli	PK	524	25°02'N	68°39'E
Maţmāţah	TS	329	33°33'N	9°58'E
Mato Grosso, Planalto do	BR	424	15°30'S	56°00'W
Matoir	SL	320	8°29'N	12°24'W
Matolo-Rio	MZ	312	25°49'S	32°27'E
Matomb	CM	280	3°49'N	11°04'E
Matombo	TZ	327	7°03'S	37°46'E
Matong		650	5°15'S	152°20'E
Matopo Hills	ZI	334	20°36'S	28°28'E
Matopos	ZI	334	20°24'S	28°28'E
Matosinhos	PO	608	41°11'N	8°42'W
Mátra	HU	590	47°55'N	20°00'E
Maţraḩ	MU	523	23°37'N	58°34'E
Matrei in Osttirol	AU	568	47°00'N	12°32'E
Matsiatra	MA	304	21°25'S	45°33'E
Matsoandakana	MA	304	15°02'S	49°19'E
Matsqui		372	49°06'N	122°17'W
Matsudo	JA	506	35°47'N	139°54'E
Matsue	JA	506	35°28'N	133°04'E
Matsulu	SF	322	25°31'S	31°21'E
Matsumae	JA	506	41°26'N	140°07'E
Matsumoto	JA	506	36°12'N	137°57'E
Matsusaka	JA	506	34°34'N	136°32'E
Matsuyama	JA	506	33°50'N	132°45'E
Matsuzaki	JA	506	34°43'N	138°47'E
Matt, Hon	VM	540	18°52'N	105°58'E
Mattawa	CA	390	46°19'N	78°42'W
Matten	SZ	622	46°40'N	7°52'E
Matterhorn	SZ	622	45°59'N	7°43'E
Matthews		378	35°07'N	80°43'W
Matthews Ridge	GY	434	7°30'N	60°10'W
Matthew Town	BF	402	20°56'N	73°40'W
Matti, Sabkhat	SA	528	23°00'N	52°00'E
Mattice		374	49°37'N	83°16'W
Mattō	JA	506	36°29'N	136°34'E
Mattoon		374	39°28'N	88°22'W
Matu	VE	440	7°15'N	65°38'W
Mātua	BG	485	24°39'N	90°57'E
Matugama	CE	530	6°25'N	80°08'E
Matuku	FJ	660	19°05'S	179°50'E
Matunda, Ras	TZ	327	10°21'S	40°27'E
Matundwe Ra.	MZ	312	16°42'S	34°57'E
Matura	TD	438	10°40'N	61°04'W
Maturín	VE	440	9°45'N	63°11'W
Matveyev Kurgan		560	47°35'N	38°52'E
Matxitxaco, Cabo	SP	618	43°27'N	2°46'W
Maú	BR	424	2°40'N	60°00'W
Maúa	MZ	312	13°54'S	37°08'E
Maubeuge	FR	580	50°17'N	3°58'E
Ma-ubin	BM	487	16°44'N	95°39'E
Maud		376	35°07'N	96°46'W
Maud	UK	626	57°31'N	2°06'W
Maud, Pt.	AS	656	23°07'S	113°45'E
Maude		652	34°28'S	144°18'E
Mau-é-Ele	MZ	312	24°22'S	34°08'E
Maués	BR	424	3°24'S	57°42'W
Maués Açu	BR	424	3°22'S	57°44'W
Maughold Head	UK	626	54°17'N	4°18'W
Maui	US	398	20°37'N	155°51'W
Mauk		466	55°54'N	60°28'E
Maukkadaw	BM	487	22°58'N	94°40'E
Maule	CI	428	35°19'S	72°25'W
Mauléon	FR	580	46°55'N	0°44'W
Maullín	CI	428	41°38'S	73°37'W
Maulvi Bāzār	BG	485	24°29'N	91°47'E
Maume		374	41°50'N	84°10'W
Maumee	US	398	41°42'N	83°28'W
Maumelle		378	34°51'N	92°23'W
Maumere	ID	500	8°40'S	122°14'E
Maun	BC	276	19°59'S	23°25'E
Mauna Kea		380	19°50'N	155°58'W
Mauna Loa		380	19°29'N	155°56'W
Maunath Bhanjan	IN	496	25°57'N	83°33'E
Maunatlala	BC	276	22°36'S	27°32'E
Maungaturoto	NZ	663	36°05'S	174°23'E
Maungdaw	BM	487	20°49'N	92°22'E
Maungkan	BM	487	25°05'N	95°02'E
Maupihaa		654	16°30'S	154°00'W
Maupiti		654	16°25'S	153°51'W
Mau Rānīpur	IN	496	25°15'N	79°08'E
Maureillas-las-Illas		562	42°29'N	2°48'E
Mauren	LS	597	47°13'N	9°32'E
Maurepas, Lake		378	30°15'N	90°30'W
Maures		562	43°16'N	6°23'E
Mauriac	FR	580	45°13'N	2°20'E
Maurice, Lake	AS	656	29°28'S	130°58'E
Mauricio		270	20°18'S	57°35'E
Mauritania		38	20°00'N	12°00'W
Mauriti	BR	424	7°23'S	38°46'W
Mauritius		38	20°18'S	57°35'E
Maurs	FR	580	44°43'N	2°12'E
Maurui	TZ	327	5°07'S	38°23'E
Mau Scarpement	KE	299	0°40'S	36°02'E
Mauston		374	43°47'N	90°04'W
Mava	BP	666	7°50'S	156°20'E
Mavila	PE	436	11°56'S	69°06'W
Mavindji-Posso	GB	294	1°33'S	13°12'E
Mavinga	AO	274	15°50'S	20°21'E
Mavrovi Anovi	MK	599	41°42'N	20°45'E
Mavrovsko Jezero	MK	599	41°42'N	20°46'E
Mavuradonha Range	ZI	334	16°26'S	31°30'E
Mawa	CG	287	2°43'N	26°42'E
Mawai	MY	518	1°52'N	103°57'E
Māwand	PK	524	29°39'N	68°42'E
Mawanga	CG	287	6°21'S	17°24'E
Mawarella	CE	530	7°15'N	80°27'E
Mawasangka	ID	500	5°17'S	122°18'E
Mawer		372	50°45'N	106°24'W
Mawhun	BM	487	24°38'N	96°13'E
Māwiyah	YM	541	13°34'N	44°21'E
Mawkmai	BM	487	20°14'N	97°44'E
Mawlaik	BM	487	23°38'N	94°25'E
Mawlu	BM	487	24°28'N	96°11'E
Mawshij	YM	541	13°42'N	43°16'E
Maxcanú		380	20°35'N	89°59'W
Máximo Gómez	CU	406	22°54'N	81°02'W
Maxixe	MZ	312	23°51'S	35°21'E
Maxwelton		652	20°43'S	142°41'E
May, C.	US	398	39°01'N	74°53'W
Maya	ID	500	1°10'S	109°35'E
Maya	RS	612	59°00'N	139°00'E
Maya, Montes	GT	411	16°17'N	89°13'W
Maya Beach	BH	404	16°35'N	88°20'W
Mayaguana	BF	402	22°26'N	72°54'W
Mayaguana Passage	BF	402	22°32'N	73°15'W
Mayagüez	US	398	18°12'N	67°09'W
Mayahi	NG	314	13°58'N	7°40'E
Mayajigua	CU	406	22°14'N	79°04'W
Mayakovskogo Pik	TI	533	37°01'N	71°44'E
Mayala	CG	287	7°24'S	17°31'E
Mayama	CF	285	3°51'S	14°54'E
Mayamba	CG	287	4°46'S	16°46'E
Mayāmey	IR	502	36°25'N	55°40'E
Mayarí	CU	406	20°40'N	75°41'W
Mayarí Arriba	CU	406	20°25'N	75°32'W
Mayaro Bay	TD	438	10°15'N	60°58'W
Maych'ew	ET	293	12°47'N	39°32'E
Maydān	IZ	504	34°55'N	45°37'E
Maydh	SO	321	11°00'N	47°07'E
Maydī	YM	541	16°18'N	42°48'E
Maydolong	RP	526	11°30'N	125°30'E
Mayébout	GB	294	1°06'N	13°07'E
Mayené II	GB	294	0°00'	11°54'E
Mayenne	FR	580	48°18'N	0°37'W
Mayfa'ah	YM	541	14°15'N	47°34'E
Mayfield		374	36°44'N	88°38'W
Mayhan	MG	520	46°02'N	103°45'E
Maykain	KZ	510	51°27'N	75°52'E
Maykop	RS	612	44°35'N	40°10'E
Mayli-Say	KG	514	41°17'N	72°24'E
Maymak	KG	514	42°42'N	71°13'E
Maymyo	BM	487	22°02'N	96°28'E
Mayn		468	64°30'N	172°00'E
Mayna		466	53°00'N	91°28'E
Maynāmati	BG	485	23°29'N	91°07'E
Maynooth	EI	592	53°23'N	6°36'W
Mayo	MX	394	26°45'N	109°47'W
Mayobe	RW	317	2°13'S	29°34'E
Mayo Belwa	NI	316	9°03'N	12°03'E
Mayo Kébi	CD	283	10°00'N	15°10'E
Mayoko	CF	285	2°18'S	12°49'E
Mayo Mayo	BL	422	12°18'S	65°14'W
Mayombe, Massif du	CF	285	3°45'S	12°10'E
Mayon Volcano	RP	526	13°15'N	123°41'E
Mayo Oulo	CM	280	9°57'N	13°36'E
Mayor Buratovich	AR	419	39°15'S	62°37'W
Mayor Martínez	PA	435	27°10'S	58°16'W
Mayotte		268	12°50'S	45°10'E
May Pen	JM	414	17°58'N	77°14'W
Mayreau	VC	418	12°36'N	61°22'W
Mayrhofen	AU	568	47°10'N	11°52'E
May River	PP	664	4°17'S	141°52'E
Mayskiy	RS	612	52°17'N	129°36'E
Mayskiy, Khrebet		468	54°50'N	134°00'E
Maysville		374	39°53'N	94°21'W
Maysville		374	38°38'N	83°46'W
Maysville		376	34°49'N	97°24'W
Mayuka	ZA	332	11°28'S	30°39'E
Mayumba	GB	294	3°25'S	10°39'E
Mayupa	VE	440	6°15'N	62°46'W
Mayuram		470	11°06'N	79°40'E
Mayville	US	398	47°29'N	97°19'W
Mazabuka	ZA	332	15°51'S	27°46'E
Mazagão	BR	424	0°07'S	51°17'W
Mazambango	AO	274	7°36'S	17°13'E
Mazamet	FR	580	43°28'N	2°23'E
Mazán	PE	436	3°29'S	73°10'W
Mazapil	MX	394	24°38'N	101°34'W
Mazar	CH	490	36°27'N	77°02'E
Mazara del Vallo	IT	593	37°38'N	12°36'E
Mazār-e Sharīf	AF	480	36°42'N	67°06'E
Mazarrón	SP	618	37°36'N	1°19'W
Mazarrón, G. de	SP	618	37°30'N	1°18'W
Mazartag	CH	490	38°28'N	80°49'E
Mazashi	GG	495	42°44'N	42°45'E
Mazatán	MX	394	29°00'N	110°08'W
Mazatán	MX	394	14°52'N	92°27'W
Mazatenango	GT	411	14°32'N	91°30'W
Mazatlán	MX	394	23°13'N	106°25'W
Mažeikiai	LH	597	56°19'N	22°20'E
Mazinda	CG	287	6°59'S	18°24'E
Mazingu	CG	287	5°55'S	16°39'E
Mazirbe	LG	596	57°41'N	22°19'E
Mazocruz	PE	436	16°45'S	69°44'W
Mazoe	MZ	312	16°32'S	33°25'E
Mazoe	ZI	334	17°31'S	30°58'E
Mazomeno	CG	287	4°55'S	27°13'E
Mazong Shan	CH	490	41°30'N	97°30'E
Mazowe	ZI	334	16°32'S	33°25'E
Mazowiecka, Nizina	PL	606	52°00'N	21°00'E
Mazraat Nab	SY	531	32°50'N	35°47'E
Mazraat Zabdin	SY	531	33°17'N	35°41'E
Mazsalaca	LG	596	57°52'N	25°03'E
Mazunga	ZI	334	21°44'S	29°52'E
Mazurski, Pojezierze	PL	606	53°40'N	21°00'E
Mazyr	BO	569	52°03'N	29°16'E
Mbabala	ZA	332	16°34'S	26°57'E
Mbabala, Isla	ZA	332	11°18'S	29°44'E
Mbabane	WZ	326	26°19'S	31°08'E
Mbacké	SG	319	14°48'N	15°55'W
Mbaéré	CT	282	3°47'N	17°31'E
Mbagne	MR	308	16°10'N	13°46'W
Mbahiakro	IV	288	7°27'N	4°20'W
Mbaïki	CT	282	3°52'N	17°59'E
Mbakaou	CM	280	6°18'N	12°47'E
Mbakaou Reservoir	CM	280	6°25'N	12°45'E
Mbala	ZA	332	8°50'S	31°22'E
Mbalabala	ZI	334	20°27'S	29°03'E
Mbalam	CM	280	2°13'N	13°49'E
Mbalambala	KE	299	0°02'S	39°04'E
Mbale	UG	330	1°05'N	34°10'E
Mbali	CG	287	2°50'S	16°12'E
Mbali-Iboma	CG	287	2°23'S	17°16'E
M. Balkhan, Khr.	TX	537	39°15'N	54°30'E
Mbalmayo	CM	280	3°31'N	11°30'E
Mbalo	BP	666	9°55'S	160°37'E
Mbam	CM	280	4°24'N	11°17'E
Mbamba Bay	TZ	327	11°17'S	34°46'E
Mbam Minkoum	CM	280	3°57'N	11°24'E
Mbandaka	CG	287	0°02'N	18°18'E
Mbandjok	CM	280	4°27'N	11°55'E
Mbang	CM	280	3°57'N	14°17'E
Mbanga	CM	280	4°30'N	9°34'E
Mbang Mts.	CM	280	7°50'N	14°00'E
Mbanika	BP	666	9°10'S	159°30'E
Mbanio, Lagune	GB	294	3°35'S	11°00'E
Mbanza Congo	AO	274	6°16'S	14°15'E
Mbarangandu	TZ	327	10°12'S	36°48'E
Mbarara	UG	330	0°37'S	30°39'E
Mbari	CT	282	4°34'N	22°43'E
Mbaro	UG	330	2°28'N	31°11'E
Mbata	CT	282	3°41'N	18°18'E
Mbe	EK	291	2°07'N	10°44'E
Mbé	CM	280	7°51'N	13°36'E
Mbekweni	SF	322	33°40'S	18°59'E
Mbengwi	CM	280	6°01'N	10°00'E
Mberengwa	ZI	334	20°29'S	29°55'E
Mbereshi Mission	ZA	332	9°44'S	28°47'E
Mbeya	TZ	327	8°54'S	33°27'E
Mbeya	TZ	327	8°30'S	33°00'E
Mbeya	ZA	332	11°39'S	33°14'E
M Bigou	GB	294	1°53'S	11°56'E
Mbii	CT	282	6°27'N	22°41'E
Mbilua (Vella Lavella)	BP	666	7°35'S	156°15'E
Mbinca	CF	285	2°07'S	12°51'E
Mbingué	IV	288	10°00'N	5°54'W
Mbini	EK	291	1°33'N	9°35'E
Mbini (Woleu)	EK	291	1°36'N	9°37'E
Mbirira	TZ	327	4°21'S	30°10'E
Mbirizi	UG	330	0°23'S	31°27'E
Mbita'ama	BP	666	8°20'S	160°42'E
Mbizi	ZI	334	21°23'S	31°01'E
Mbogo	TZ	327	7°26'S	33°26'E
Mboki	CT	282	5°19'N	25°58'E
Mboko	CG	287	3°47'S	29°06'E
Mbollet Bah	GA	295	13°31'N	16°30'W
Mboloma	ZA	332	14°22'S	29°22'E
Mboma	GB	294	0°20'N	11°28'E
Mbomo	CF	285	3°15'S	13°43'E
Mbomou	CT	282	6°17'N	24°43'E
Mbomou (Bomu)	CG	287	4°08'N	22°27'E
Mboro	SG	319	15°09'N	16°54'W
Mborokua	BP	666	9°00'S	158°55'E
Mborong	ID	500	8°49'S	120°37'E
Mbouda	CM	280	5°38'N	10°15'E
Mboukou	GB	294	1°43'S	10°48'E
Mboula	CT	282	4°27'N	16°29'E
Mboumba	GB	294	0°54'S	9°37'E
Mboune, Vallée du	SG	319	14°57'N	14°16'W
Mbouomo	CF	285	0°52'S	15°04'E
M'Bour	SG	319	14°24'N	16°58'W
M'Bout	MR	308	16°02'N	12°35'W
Mbres	CT	282	6°40'N	19°46'E
M'Bridge	AO	274	7°14'S	12°52'E
Mbuji-Mayi	CG	287	6°09'S	23°37'E
Mbulo	BP	666	8°50'S	158°10'E
Mbulu	TZ	327	3°51'S	35°32'E
Mbuluzi	WZ	326	26°10'S	31°50'E
Mburucuya		388	28°03'S	58°14'W
Mbuku	KE	299	0°45'S	38°26'E
Mbuzi	ZA	332	12°18'S	32°21'E
Mbwemburu	TZ	327	9°29'S	39°39'E
Mbwikwe	TZ	327	5°24'S	34°15'E
McAlester		378	34°56'N	95°46'W
McAllen	US	398	26°12'N	98°13'W
Mc Arthur	AS	656	16°37'S	135°49'E
McCall	US	398	44°53'N	116°05'W
McCamey	US	398	31°08'N	102°13'W
McCarthy's Rust	BC	276	26°09'S	22°32'E
Mc Clintock Channel	CA	390	73°30'N	104°00'W
Mc Clintock Ra.	AS	656	18°00'S	127°00'E
McCloud		372	41°15'N	122°08'W
Mc Clure Strait		368	75°00'N	120°00'W
McComb	US	398	31°14'N	90°27'W
McCook	US	398	40°12'N	100°37'W
McCord		372	49°26'N	106°50'W
McFarland		376	35°40'N	119°13'W
McGill	US	398	39°24'N	114°46'W
McGraw Brook		374	46°49'N	66°07'W
Mc. Gregory Ra.	AS	656	26°40'S	142°45'E
Mchinga	TZ	327	9°44'S	39°42'E
Mchinji	MI	306	13°46'S	32°51'E
McIntosh		370	49°57'N	93°36'W
Mc Kay Ra.		652	23°30'S	121°40'E
McKean I.	KR	660	3°30'S	174°00'W
McKenzie		374	36°07'N	88°31'W
McKinlay	AS	656	21°16'S	141°18'E
McKinleyville		372	40°56'N	124°05'W
McKinney		376	33°11'N	96°36'W
McLeod Bay	CA	390	62°53'N	110°15'W
McLeod Lake	CA	390	54°59'N	123°02'W
M'Clintock	CA	390	57°48'N	94°12'W
Mc Millan, Lake		376	32°36'N	104°21'W
McMinnville		378	35°41'N	85°46'W
McMorran		372	51°19'N	108°45'W
McNab		372	49°21'N	112°17'W
McNamee		374	46°30'N	66°18'W
Mcocha	MI	306	12°14'S	33°21'E
McPherson	US	398	38°22'N	97°39'W
Mdabulo	TZ	327	6°59'S	33°19'E
Mdaburo	TZ	327	6°13'S	34°50'E
Mdandu	TZ	327	9°09'S	34°42'E
Mdantsane	SF	322	32°56'S	27°46'E
Meacham		372	52°06'N	105°47'W
Mead, Lake	US	398	36°01'N	114°41'W
Meade		368	70°00'N	157°00'W
Meade		376	37°17'N	100°20'W
Meadow Lake	CA	390	54°08'N	108°26'W
Meadville		374	41°38'N	80°09'W
Meaford		374	44°36'N	80°35'W
Mealhada	PO	608	40°22'N	8°27'W
Mealy Mts.		370	53°20'N	59°30'W
Meámbar	HO	412	14°47'N	87°46'W
Meander River	CA	390	59°02'N	117°42'W
Meanguera, Isla	ES	409	13°00'N	87°50'W
Meares, C.	US	398	45°29'N	123°58'W
Mearim		384	5°00'S	45°00'W
Mebane		378	36°05'N	79°16'W
Mebulu, Tanjung	ID	500	8°50'S	115°05'E
Mecapaca	BL	422	16°41'S	68°02'W
Mechanicsville		374	37°36'N	77°22'W
Mechara	ET	293	8°36'N	40°19'E
Mechelen	BE	570	51°02'N	4°28'E
Mecheria	AG	272	33°33'N	0°17'W
Méchiméré	CD	283	13°49'N	15°45'E
Mechra Benabbou	MO	310	32°39'N	7°48'W
Mecidiye		564	40°38'N	26°32'E
Mecitözü		564	40°31'N	35°19'E
Mecklenburger Bucht	GM	584	54°16'N	11°19'E
Mecklenburgische Seenplatte	GM	584	53°30'N	12°00'E
Meconta	MZ	312	14°59'S	39°50'E
Mecsek	HU	590	46°10'N	18°18'E
Mecúfi	MZ	312	13°17'S	40°33'E
Mecula	MZ	312	12°05'S	37°39'E
Medak	IN	496	18°02'N	78°16'E
Medan	ID	500	3°35'N	98°40'E
Medanitos	AR	419	27°32'S	67°36'W
Médanos	AR	419	38°50'S	62°41'W
Medanosa, Punta	AR	419	48°06'S	65°54'W
Médéa	AG	272	36°16'N	2°45'E
Medeiros Neto		386	17°20'S	40°14'W
Medellín	CO	430	6°15'N	75°35'W
Mederdra	MR	308	16°55'N	15°39'W
Mèdes, Cap des	FR	580	43°01'N	6°14'E
Medford		374	45°08'N	90°20'W
Medford		376	36°48'N	97°44'W
Medford	US	398	42°19'N	122°52'W
Medgidia	RO	610	44°15'N	28°17'E
Medi	SU	324	5°06'N	30°44'E
Media Agua	AR	419	31°59'S	68°25'W
Media Luna	CU	406	20°08'N	77°27'W
Medianeira	BR	424	25°20'S	54°05'W
Mediaş	RO	610	46°09'N	24°21'E
Medical Lake		372	47°34'N	117°40'W
Medicine Hat	CA	390	50°03'N	110°40'W
Medicine Lodge		376	37°16'N	98°34'W
Medicine Lodge		376	37°00'N	98°30'W
Medina		386	16°15'S	41°29'W
Medina Bank	BH	404	16°27'N	88°45'W
Medina del Campo	SP	618	41°18'N	4°55'W
Medina de Rioseco	SP	618	41°53'N	5°02'W
Médina Gonassé	SG	319	13°08'N	13°45'W
Medininkai	LH	597	54°32'N	25°40'E
Medinipur		476	22°26'N	87°20'E
Medio, Punta	CI	428	27°07'S	70°57'W
Mediodía	CO	430	1°49'S	72°09'W
Mediouna	MO	310	33°27'N	7°31'W
Medje	CG	287	2°25'N	27°18'E
Medjerda	TS	329	37°07'N	10°13'E
Medjerda, Djebel el	TS	329	36°30'N	8°15'E
Mednogorsk	RS	612	51°24'N	57°37'E
Medouneau	EK	291	1°01'N	10°48'E
Médouneu	GB	294	0°57'N	10°47'E
Medruriet	ER	292	16°58'N	38°23'E
Medvedevo		560	56°38'N	47°49'E
Medvedka	KZ	510	49°11'N	35°18'E
Medvënka		560	51°25'N	36°07'E
Medvezh'yegorsk	RS	612	62°55'N	34°28'E
Medvode	SI	617	46°08'N	14°26'E
Medway		374	45°36'N	68°31'W
Medyn'		560	54°58'N	35°52'E
Medzilaborce	LO	616	49°16'N	21°55'E
Meekatharra	AS	656	26°36'S	118°29'E
Meeker	US	398	40°01'N	107°53'W
Meer	BE	570	51°27'N	4°44'E
Meerane	GM	584	50°51'N	12°28'E
Meerssen	NL	602	50°53'N	5°45'E
Meerut	IN	496	28°59'N	77°42'E
Mēga	ET	293	4°03'N	38°18'E
Mega	ID	500	0°41'S	131°54'E
Megála Kalívia	GR	588	39°30'N	21°47'E
Megáli Panayía	GR	588	40°27'N	23°41'E
Megalo	ET	293	6°51'N	40°47'E
Megálon Khorion	GR	588	36°27'N	27°21'E
Megalópolis	GR	588	37°24'N	22°08'E
Meganom, Mys	UP	624	44°48'N	35°05'E
Mégara	GR	588	38°01'N	23°21'E
Megezez	ET	293	9°17'N	39°32'E
Meghna	BG	485	22°50'N	90°50'E
Megion	RS	612	61°03'N	76°06'E
Megiscane, L.		370	48°50'N	76°00'W
Megraouin, Erg	AG	272	29°00'N	3°30'W
Megrega		556	60°56'N	33°06'E
Meguzalala	MZ	312	22°28'S	31°59'E
Mehal Mēda	ET	293	10°16'N	39°40'E
Mehamn	NO	604	71°02'N	27°51'E
Mehdia	AG	272	35°25'N	1°41'E
Mehdīshahr	IR	502	35°43'N	53°19'E
Mehdiya-Plage	MO	310	34°15'N	6°41'W
Mehedintului, Muntii	RO	610	45°00'N	23°00'E
Meherpur	BG	485	23°46'N	88°38'E
Mehetia		654	17°00'S	148° 5'W
Mehikoorma	EN	577	58°13'N	27°26'E
Mehrān	IR	502	33°07'N	46°10'E
Mehran	IR	502	26°46'N	55°26'E
Mehrīz	IR	502	31°35'N	54°28'E
Mehtar Lām	AF	480	34°39'N	70°10'E
Mehun-sur-Yèvre	FR	580	47°09'N	2°13'E
Meia Meia	TZ	327	5°49'S	35°48'E
Meidougou	CM	280	6°25'N	14° 3'E
Meiganga	CM	280	6°31'N	14° 8'E
Meighen I.	CA	390	79°55'N	99°00'W
Meiktila	BM	487	20°52'N	95°52'E
Meilen	SZ	622	47°16'N	8°38'E
Meiningen	GM	584	50°33'N	10°25'E
Meiringen	SZ	622	46°44'N	8°11'E
Meissen	GM	584	51°09'N	13°29'E
Meizhou	CH	490	24°18'N	116°05'E
Mejaouda	MR	308	22°31'N	7°07'W
Mejillones	CI	428	23°06'S	70°27'W
Mejit I.	RM	661	10°15'N	171°00'E
Mekambo	GB	294	1°01'N	13°53'E
Mekane Selam	ET	293	10°38'N	38°47'E
Mek'elē	ET	293	13°30'N	39°28'E
Mékhé	SG	319	15°07'N	16°38'W
Mekhtar	PK	524	30°28'N	69°22'E
Mek'ī	ET	293	8°09'N	38°49'E
Meknès	MO	310	33°54'N	5°33'W
Meko	NI	316	7°27'N	2°51'E
Mékob	GB	294	0°41'N	12°55'E
Mekong	BM	487	21°00'N	100°30'E
Mekong (Lancang Jiang)	CH	490	30°00'N	98°00'E
Mekong, Mouths of the	VM	540	9°00'N	107°00'E
Mekong Delta	VM	540	10°20'N	106°40'E
Mekongga, Gunung	ID	500	3°38'S	121°15'E
Mékrou	BN	276	12°24'N	2°49'E
Melamo, Cabo	MZ	312	15°15'S	40°40'E
Melanesia		648	0°30'S	150°00'E
Melanje Highlands	AO	274	8°00'S	16°00'E
Melappālaiyam	IN	496	8°42'N	77°43'E
Melaque	MX	394	19°13'N	104°44'W
Melbourne		374	36°03'N	91°54'W
Melbourne	AS	656	37°50'S	145°00'E
Melbu		556	68°29'N	14°44'E
Melcher	HO	412	15°45'N	87°48'W
Melchor		388	45°05'S	74°12'W
Melchor Múzquiz	MX	394	27°53'N	101°31'W
Melchor Ocampo		376	26°03'N	99°33'W
Meldal	NO	604	63°01'N	9°41'E
Meldorf	GM	584	54°05'N	9°05'E
Mele	GG	495	42°48'N	43°04'E
Mele, Capo	IT	593	43°57'N	8°11'E
Melekeiok	PX	664	7°30'N	134°39'E
Melenci	YO	630	45°31'N	20°19'E
Melenki		560	55°20'N	41°38'E
Meleuz		466	52°58'N	55°55'E
Melfi	CD	283	11°04'N	17°56'E
Melfi	IT	593	40°59'N	15°39'E
Melfort		368	52°52'N	104°37'W
Melgaço	PO	608	42°07'N	8°16'W
Melgar de Fernamental	SP	618	42°24'N	4°15'W
Melhus	NO	604	63°17'N	10°16'E
Meligalás	GR	588	37°13'N	21°59'E
Melíki	GR	588	40°31'N	22°24'E
Melilla	SP	618	35°19'N	2°57'W
Melinca	CI	428	43°54'S	73°45'W
Melipilla		388	33°42'S	71°13'W
Melito di Porto Salvo		564	37°55'N	15°47'E
Melitopol'	UP	624	46°50'N	35°22'E
Melka Guba	ET	293	4°47'N	39°22'E
Melka Meri	ET	293	4°17'N	40°45'E
Melkbosstrand	SF	322	33°45'S	18°27'E
Mellan Fryken	SW	621	59°47'N	13°10'E
Melle	FR	580	46°13'N	0°08'W
Melle	GM	584	52°12'N	8°21'E
Melleq		562	36°00'N	8°30'E
Mellerud	SW	621	58°42'N	12°28'E
Mellie/hha	MT	600	35°57'N	14°21'E
Mellieha Bay	MT	600	35°59'N	14°22'E
Mellieha Ridge	MT	600	35°57'N	14°22'E
Mellit	SU	324	14°08'N	25°33'E
Mellor	CA	390	60°43'N	114°56'W
Melmoth	SF	322	28°35'S	31°24'E
Mělník	EZ	575	50°21'N	14°29'E
Melnik	BU	573	41°31'N	23°24'E
Mel'nitsa-Podol'skaya	UP	624	48°37'N	26°10'E
Melo	UY	439	32°22'S	54°11'W
Melolo	ID	500	9°53'S	120°38'E
Mélong	CM	280	5°07'N	9°57'E
Melrakkanes	IC	591	66°23'N	15°42'W
Melrose		374	45°40'N	94°48'W
Melrose	UK	626	55°35'N	2°43'W
Mels	SZ	622	47°02'N	9°25'E
Melton		652	37°41'S	144°35'E
Melun	FR	580	48°32'N	2°39'E

Mordovo 560 52°05'N 40°46'E
Mordves 560 54°34'N 38°13'E
Morea 652 36°44'S 141°20'E
Moreau 372 45°20'N 100°20'W
Morebattle UK 626 55°31'N 2°22'W
Morecambe Bay UK 626 54°07'N 3°00'W
Moree AS 656 29°28'S 149°51'E
Morehead 374 38°11'N 83°25'W
Morehead PP 664 8°42'S 141°37'E
Morehead City 378 34°43'N 76°43'W
Mörel SZ 622 46°21'N 8°02'E
Morelia CO 430 1°29'N 75°44'W
Morelia MX 394 19°42'N 101°10'W
Morella AS 656 22°58'S 143°52'E
Morelos 376 28°25'N 100°54'W
Morelos MX 394 19°45'N 88°43'W
Morena IN 496 26°30'N 78°04'E
Morenci 376 33°04'N 109°21'W
Morenero VE 440 8°47'N 62°56'W
Moreni RO 610 44°59'N 25°39'E
Moreno Valley 376 33°55'N 117°10'W
Moresby I. CA 390 52°45'N 131°50'W
Moreton AS 656 27°10'S 153°25'E
Morgan City 378 29°41'N 91°12'W
Morganito VE 440 5°04'N 67°44'W
Morganton 378 35°44'N 81°41'W
Morgantown US 398 39°37'N 79°57'W
Morgenzon SF 322 26°44'S 29°37'E
Morgex IT 593 45°45'N 7°02'E
Mori CH 490 43°42'N 90°19'E
Mori JA 506 42°06'N 140°35'E
Moriah TD 438 11°15'N 60°43'W
Moriarty 376 34°59'N 106°02'W
Moriarty's Range AS 656 27°40'S 145°30'E
Moribaya GV 297 9°53'N 9°33'W
Morichal CO 430 2°13'N 70°04'W
Morichal CO 430 6°38'N 71°43'W
Morija LT 301 29°38'S 27°31'E
Morin Dawa CH 490 48°28'N 124°28'E
Morioka JA 506 39°42'N 141°09'E
Moriongahela 374 40°00'N 79°55'W
Moris MX 394 28°09'N 108°31'W
Morjärv SW 621 66°04'N 22°43'E
Morki 560 56°25'N 49°01'E
Morkiny-Gory 560 57°33'N 36°18'E
Morlaix FR 580 48°34'N 3°48'W
Morley River CA 390 60°01'N 132°10'W
Mormugao 470 15°24'N 73°48'E
Morne Aux Frégates DO 407 15°21'N 61°16'W
Morne Raquette DO 407 15°27'N 61°27'W
Mornington 652 16°24'S 139°39'E
Mornington 652 38°13'S 145°04'E
Mornington, Archipiélago CI 428 49°45'S 75°20'W
Mornington Is. AS 656 16°33'S 139°24'E
Moro PE 436 9°03'S 78°12'W
Moro PK 524 26°40'N 68°00'E
Moro Almanzor SP 618 40°15'N 5°18'W
Morobe PP 664 7°47'S 147°38'E
Morocco 38 32°00'N 5°00'W
Moroceli HO 412 14°07'N 86°52'W
Morococha PE 436 11°37'S 76°09'W
Morogoro TZ 327 6°49'S 37°40'E
Moro Gulf RP 526 6°51'N 123°00'E
Morokweng SF 322 26°08'S 23°46'E
Moroleón MX 394 20°08'N 101°12'W
Morombe MA 304 21°45'S 43°22'E
Moron HA 412 18°34'N 74°15'W
Morón AR 419 34°39'S 58°37'W
Morón CU 406 22°06'N 78°38'W
Morón VE 440 10°29'N 68°11'W
Mörön MG 520 47°24'N 110°16'E
Mörön MG 520 49°38'N 100°10'E
Morona EC 432 2°52'S 77°41'W
Morona PE 436 4°45'S 77°04'W
Morondava MA 304 19°06'S 45°11'E
Morondava MA 304 20°17'S 44°17'E
Morón de la Frontera SP 618 37°08'N 5°27'W
Morondo IV 288 8°57'N 6°47'W
Moroni 372 39°31'N 111°35'W
Moroni CN 284 11°41'S 43°16'E
Moron Suma MG 520 46°53'N 104°56'E
Morosaglia FR 580 42°26'N 9°19'E
Morotai ID 500 2°20'N 128°25'E
Morotai, Selat ID 500 2°10'N 128°10'E
Moroto UG 330 2°32'N 34°39'E
Moroto UG 330 2°35'N 34°41'E
Morotuto VE 440 8°25'N 71°59'W
Morowali 648 1°52'S 121°30'E
Morozovsk 560 48°22'N 41°51'E
Morpará 384 11°34'S 43°17'W
Morpeth UK 626 55°10'N 1°38'W
Morphou CY 494 35°12'N 32°59'E
Morphou Bay CY 494 35°10'N 32°50'E
Morrilton 378 35°09'N 92°44'W
Morrinhos BR 424 17°44'S 49°07'W
Morris 374 41°21'N 88°25'W
Morris US 398 45°35'N 95°54'W
Morris 374 41°48'N 89°57'W
Morrison 374 36°20'N 92°23'W
Morristown 374 36°12'N 83°17'W
Morrisville 374 44°32'N 72°36'W
Morrito NU 415 11°37'N 85°05'W
Morro, Cabo del DR 408 19°54'N 71°39'W
Morro, Punta CI 428 27°06'S 70°55'W
Morro, Punta del MX 394 19°51'N 96°27'W
Morro Bay 376 35°22'N 120°50'W
Morrocoy VE 440 7°40'N 69°42'W
Morrocoyes VE 440 9°28'N 67°21'W
Morro de Puercos, Punta PM 417 7°14'N 80°25'W
Morro do Capão Doce BR 424 26°43'S 51°25'W
Morro do Chapéu BR 424 11°33'S 41°09'W
Morropón PE 436 5°12'S 80°00'W
Morrosquillo, Golfo de CO 430 9°35'N 75°40'W
Morrumbala MZ 312 17°20'S 35°35'E
Morrumbene MZ 312 23°39'S 35°20'E
Mors DA 576 56°44'N 8°35'E
Morse Shoe, Point SC 417 17°13'N 62°40'W
Morsetta, Cap della FR 580 42°28'N 8°38'E
Morshansk RS 612 53°26'N 41°49'E
Mortagne-au-Perche 562 48°31'N 0°33'E
Morteau FR 580 47°03'N 6°36'E
Morteros AR 419 30°42'S 62°00'W
Mortlock Islands FM 661 5°30'N 154°00'E
Morton 372 46°33'N 122°16'W
Morton 376 33°43'N 102°45'W
Mortsel BE 570 51°10'N 4°28'E
Moruga TD 438 10°05'N 61°17'W
Morvan FR 580 47°04'N 3°49'E
Morven AS 656 26°25'S 147°03'E
Morven NZ 663 44°47'S 171°06'E
Morvi IN 496 22°49'N 70°50'E
Morwell 652 43°30'S 146°00'E
Moryakovskiy Zaton RS 612 56°14'N 84°39'E
Morzhovets O. 556 66°45'N 42°30'E
Mosbach GM 584 49°21'N 9°09'E
Moscow US 398 46°43'N 116°59'W
Moscow (Moskva) RS 612 55°45'N 37°35'E
Mosel GM 584 50°22'N 7°36'E
Moselebe BC 276 25°01'S 23°12'E
Moselle FR 580 49°10'N 6°30'E
Moselle LU 598 49°35'N 6°25'E
Moses Lake US 398 47°07'N 119°16'W
Mosetse BC 276 20°42'S 26°38'E
Moseyevo 556 65°47'N 46°11'E
Mosfellsbær IC 591 64°11'N 21°38'W
Mosgiel NZ 663 45°53'S 170°20'E
Moshi TZ 327 3°21'S 37°20'E
Moshkovo RS 612 55°18'N 83°37'E
Moshupa BC 276 24°28'S 25°23'E
Mosina PL 606 52°15'N 16°51'E
Mosinee 374 44°47'N 89°42'W
Mosite CG 287 0°53'N 23°40'E
Mosjøen NO 604 65°50'N 13°12'E
Moskosel SW 621 65°51'N 19°25'E
Moskovskiy TI 533 37°36'N 69°45'E
Moskva (Moscow) RS 612 55°45'N 37°35'E
Moso 378 17°30'S 168°10'E
Mosolovo 560 54°17'N 40°32'E
Mosomane BC 276 24°03'S 26°20'E
Mosoni-Dunai HU 590 47°44'N 17°47'E
Mosonmagyaróvár HU 590 47°52'N 17°17'E
Mosouwan 466 45°00'N 86°28'E
Mosquera CO 430 2°30'N 78°29'W
Mosquito, Punta PM 417 9°05'N 77°52'W
Mosquitos, Golfo de los PM 417 9°00'N 81°15'W
Moss NO 604 59°26'N 10°42'E
Mossaka CF 285 1°13'S 16°48'E
Mossbank 372 49°56'N 105°58'W
Moss Bluff 378 30°18'N 93°11'W
Mosselbaai SF 322 34°10'S 22°06'E
Mossendjo CF 285 2°57'S 12°44'E
Mossété GB 294 1°40'S 13°20'E
Mossi Highlands UV 278 12°00'N 3°00'W
Mossman AS 656 16°28'S 145°22'E
Mossoró BR 424 5°11'S 37°20'W
Mossuril MZ 312 14°58'S 40°40'E
Most EZ 575 50°32'N 13°39'E
Mostaganem AG 272 35°56'N 0°05'E
Mostar BK 572 43°21'N 17°49'E
Mostardas BR 424 31°06'S 50°57'W
Mostiska UP 624 49°48'N 23°09'E
Mostki UP 624 49°19'N 38°30'E
Móstoles SP 618 40°19'N 3°51'W
Mosty BO 569 53°25'N 24°32'E
Mostyn MY 518 4°40'N 118°11'E
Mosvatnet NO 604 60°00'N 8°00'E
Mosvik NO 604 63°49'N 11°00'E
Mot'a 470 11°05'N 37°52'E
Mota 654 14°00'S 167°50'E
Motaba CF 285 2°03'N 18°04'E
Motacucito BL 422 17°18'S 61°17'W
Motagua GT 411 15°44'N 88°14'W
Motala SW 621 58°33'N 15°03'E
Mother Pt. BH 404 16°00'N 88°52'W
Motherwell SF 322 33°46'S 25°35'E
Motihāri IN 496 26°39'N 84°55'E
Motilla del Palancar SP 618 39°34'N 1°53'W
Motloutse 270 22°15'S 29°00'E
Motloutse BC 276 21°35'S 27°24'E
Motloutse BC 276 22°01'S 28°25'E
Moto CG 287 2°54'N 29°27'E
Motobu JA 506 26°37'N 127°55'E
Motokhovo RS 612 59°32'N 32°23'E
Motokwe BC 276 24°02'S 23°22'E
Motol' BO 569 52°19'N 25°36'E
Motovskiy Zaliv 556 69°30'N 34°00'E
Motril SP 618 36°45'N 3°31'W
Mott US 398 46°22'N 102°19'W
Motueka NZ 663 41°07'S 173°01'E
Motul MX 394 21°06'N 89°17'W
Motulalo TV 669 8°05'S 179°00'W
Motupe PE 436 6°09'S 79°44'W
Motupena Pt. PP 664 6°31'S 155°10'E
Motutunga 654 17°15'S 144°15'W
Motygino RS 612 58°11'N 94°40'E
Mou 654 21°00'S 167°10'E
Mouangko CM 280 3°39'N 9°49'E
Mouat, C. CA 390 77°36'N 77°46'W
Moúdhros GR 588 39°52'N 25°16'E
Moudjéria MR 308 17°53'N 12°20'W
Moudon SZ 622 46°40'N 6°47'E
Mougris MR 308 18°08'N 14°11'W
Mouila GB 294 1°52'S 11°01'E
Mouka CT 282 7°15'N 21°52'E
Moukandé, Monts GB 294 1°50'S 12°00'E
Moukoumbi GB 294 1°13'S 12°53'E
Moulay Idriss MO 310 34°03'N 5°31'W
Moulay Yakoub MO 310 34°05'N 5°11'W
Mould Bay CA 390 76°14'N 119°20'W
Moulins FR 580 46°33'N 3°20'E
Moulmein BM 487 16°28'N 97°39'E
Moulmeingyun BM 487 16°23'N 95°16'E
Moulouya, Oued MO 310 35°07'N 2°20'W
Moulton 378 34°28'N 87°17'W
Mound Bayou 378 33°52'N 90°43'W
Mound City 374 40°07'N 95°13'W
Moundou CD 283 8°34'N 16°05'E
Mounds 374 37°06'N 89°11'W
Moundsville 374 39°55'N 80°44'W
Moung Roessei CB 489 12°46'N 103°27'E
Mounlapamok LA 517 14°20'N 105°50'E
Mount Abu IN 496 24°36'N 72°42'E
Mountain 368 65°41'N 128°50'W
Mountain Grove 374 37°07'N 92°15'W
Mountain Home 374 36°20'N 92°23'W
Mountain Home US 398 43°07'N 115°41'W
Mountain Lake 374 43°56'N 94°55'W
Mountain View 372 41°16'N 110°20'W
Mountain View 372 42°51'N 106°23'W
Mountain View 372 49°08'N 113°36'W
Mountain View 374 36°59'N 91°42'W
Mountain View 374 35°05'N 98°44'W
Mountain View 378 35°52'N 92°07'W
Mountain View US 398 19°33'N 155°06'W
Mount Airy 374 36°29'N 80°36'W
Mount Arrowsmith AS 656 30°08'S 141°44'E
Mount Ayliff SF 322 30°48'S 29°22'E
Mount Ayr 374 40°42'N 94°14'W
Mount Barclay LI 301 6°21'N 10°39'W
Mount Barker AS 656 34°38'S 117°40'E
Mount Carmel 374 36°32'N 82°39'W
Mount Carmel 374 38°24'N 87°45'W
Mount Cavenagh 652 25°58'S 133°15'E
Mount Currie 374 50°20'N 122°44'W
Mount Darwin ZI 334 16°47'S 31°35'E
Mount Doreen AS 656 22°03'S 131°18'E
Mount Douglas AS 656 21°32'S 146°52'E
Mount Drysdale AS 656 31°10'S 145°52'E
Mount Eba AS 656 30°12'S 135°40'E
Mount Everard GY 434 7°49'N 59°28'W
Mount Fletcher SF 322 30°41'S 28°31'E
Mount Gambier AS 656 37°50'S 140°46'E
Mount Garnet AS 656 17°41'S 145°07'E
Mount Gay-Shamrock 374 37°50'N 82°00'W
Mount Hagen PP 664 5°52'S 144°13'E
Mount Hope AS 656 32°59'S 145°54'E
Mount Isa AS 656 20°44'S 139°30'E
Mount Lebanon 374 40°22'N 80°03'W
Mountlofty Ra. AS 656 15°45'S 145°15'E
Mount Magnet AS 656 28°04'S 117°49'E
Mount Margaret 378 19°52'S 138°51'E
Mount Maunganui NZ 663 37°37'S 176°12'E
Mountmellick EI 592 53°07'N 7°19'W
Mount Molloy 648 16°41'S 145°20'E
Mount Morgan AS 656 23°39'S 150°23'E
Mount Olive 378 35°11'N 78°04'W
Mount Pleasant 370 43°35'N 84°46'W
Mount Pleasant 370 40°57'N 91°33'W
Mount Pleasant 372 39°32'N 111°27'W
Mount Pleasant 378 33°09'N 94°58'W
Mount Pleasant 378 32°47'N 79°51'W
Mount Pocono 374 41°07'N 75°21'W
Mountrath EI 592 53°00'N 7°28'W
Mount Robson CA 390 53°02'N 119°14'W
Mount's Bay UK 626 50°05'N 5°29'W
Mount Selinda ZI 334 20°24'S 32°43'E
Mount Shasta US 398 41°18'N 122°18'W
Mount Standfast 384 13°12'N 59°38'W
Mount Sterling 374 39°59'N 90°45'W
Mount Surprise AS 656 18°09'S 144°19'E
Mount Union 374 40°23'N 77°52'W
Mount Vernon 374 38°19'N 88°54'W
Mount Vernon 374 40°23'N 82°29'W
Mount Vernon 374 41°55'N 91°25'W
Mount Vernon 374 37°55'N 87°53'W
Mount Vernon 378 35°11'N 95°13'W
Mount Vernon AS 656 24°09'S 118°13'E
Mount Vernon US 398 48°25'N 122°19'W
Mount Zion 374 39°46'N 88°52'W
Moura 652 24°34'S 150°01'E
Moura CD 283 13°47'N 21°13'E
Moura PO 608 38°08'N 7°27'W
Mourão PO 608 38°23'N 7°21'W
Mourdi, Dépression du CD 283 13°10'N 23°00'E
Mourdiah ML 307 14°28'N 7°28'W
Mourindi GB 294 2°32'S 10°47'E
Mourmelon-le-Grand FR 580 49°08'N 4°21'E
Mourne UK 626 54°07'N 6°07'W
Mourniai GR 588 35°28'N 24°01'E
Mousa'alli DJ 289 12°28'N 42°24'E
Mouscron BE 570 50°44'N 3°13'E
Moussayah GV 297 9°28'N 12°51'W
Mousso CD 283 17°58'N 19°50'E
Moussoro CD 283 13°39'N 16°29'E
Mouth of the Shannon EI 592 52°30'N 9°50'W
Moutier SZ 622 47°16'N 7°22'E
Moûtiers FR 580 45°29'N 6°32'E
Moutong 648 0°28'N 121°13'E
Moutrie, Lake 378 33°00'N 80°00'W
Mouydir AG 272 25°00'N 4°10'E
Mouyondzi CF 285 3°58'S 13°57'E
Mouzákion GR 588 39°26'N 21°40'E
Mouzarak CD 283 13°17'N 15°57'E
Mouzon FR 580 49°36'N 5°05'E
Moville 372 42°29'N 96°05'W
Mowanjum Mission 648 17°22'S 123°42'E
Mowbray 372 49°00'N 98°29'W
Möwe Bay WA 313 19°20'S 12°40'E
Moy EI 592 54°28'N 6°41'W
Moyalē ET 293 3°32'N 39°03'E
Moyamba SL 320 8°09'N 12°26'W
Moyen Atlas MO 310 33°30'N 4°30'W
Moyenne-Sido CT 282 8°11'N 18°44'E
Moyero 468 67°00'N 105°00'E
Moyo CG 287 3°20'S 27°37'E
Moyo UG 330 3°39'N 31°43'E
Moyobamba PE 436 6°03'S 76°58'W
Moyogalpa NU 415 11°32'N 85°42'W
Moyowosi TZ 327 3°50'S 31°00'E
Moyto CD 283 12°35'N 16°33'E
Moyu CH 490 37°16'N 79°42'E
Moyuta GT 411 14°02'N 90°05'W
Mozambique 38 18°15'S 35°00'E
Mozambique Channel CN 284 20°00'S 43°00'E
Mozambique Plain 270 20°00'S 34°30'E
Mozarlândia 384 14°47'S 50°35'W
Mozdūrān IR 502 36°09'N 60°35'E
Mozhga 560 56°27'N 52°11'E
Mpal SG 319 15°55'N 16°15'W
Mpalapata ZA 332 10°13'S 30°21'E
Mpanda TZ 327 6°22'S 31°02'E
Mpangu WA 313 17°39'S 18°15'E
Mparo UG 330 0°24'N 30°59'E
Mpese CG 287 5°14'S 15°33'E
Mpessoba ML 307 12°40'N 5°43'W
Mphoengs ZI 334 21°12'S 27°51'E
Mpigi UG 330 0°13'N 32°20'E
Mpika ZA 332 11°50'S 31°27'E
Mpo CF 285 2°24'S 15°29'E
Mpoko CG 287 3°34'S 18°03'E
Mpoko CT 282 4°19'N 18°33'E
Mpolweni SF 322 29°25'S 30°29'E
Mponela MI 306 13°31'S 33°43'E
Mpophomeni SF 322 29°33'S 30°10'E
Mporaloko GB 294 0°43'S 9°10'E
Mporokoso ZA 332 9°23'S 30°08'E
M'Pouya CF 285 2°37'S 16°13'E
Mpraeso GH 296 6°35'N 0°44'W
Mpulungu ZA 332 8°46'S 31°07'E
Mpumalanga SF 322 29°48'S 30°37'E
Mpungu WA 313 17°40'S 18°29'E
Mpwapwa TZ 327 6°21'S 36°29'E
Mrągowo PL 606 53°52'N 21°18'E
Mrkonjić Grad BK 572 44°23'N 17°05'E
Msanga TZ 327 7°21'S 38°46'E
Msida MT 600 35°54'N 14°29'E
M'Sila AG 272 35°42'N 4°33'E
Msonedi ZI 334 17°08'S 30°54'E
Msoro ZA 332 13°36'S 31°53'E
Msoun MO 310 34°16'N 3°42'W
Msoun, Oued MO 310 34°22'N 3°15'W
Msta 560 57°55'N 34°31'E
Mstislavl' BO 569 54°02'N 31°44'E
Mswega TZ 327 8°26'S 37°57'E
Mszana Dolna PL 606 49°41'N 20°05'E
Mt. Aborlan RP 526 9°31'N 118°27'E
Mtakuja TZ 327 7°22'S 30°37'E
Mtalika TZ 327 11°32'S 37°05'E
Mt. Allen NZ 663 47°05'S 167°48'E
Mt. Alta NZ 663 44°30'S 168°58'E
Mt. Anglem NZ 663 46°44'S 167°56'E
Mt. Apo RP 526 6°59'N 125°16'E
Mt. Ararat TU 535 39°40'N 44°24'E
Mt. Baco RP 526 12°49'N 121°10'E
Mt. Bajimba AS 656 29°18'S 152°07'E
Mt. Banahao RP 526 14°04'N 121°29'E
Mt. Bataan RP 526 14°31'N 120°28'E
Mt. Blik RP 526 14°31'N 120°28'E
Mt. Bona US 398 61°23'N 141°45'W
Mt. Bruce AS 656 22°26'S 118°08'E
Mt. Busa RP 526 6°08'N 124°39'E
Mt. Cagua RP 526 18°13'N 122°07'E
Mt. Calavite RP 526 13°29'N 120°24'E
Mt. Cecil Rhodes AS 656 25°14'S 121°52'E
Mt. Chamberlin US 398 69°17'N 144°54'W
Mt. Cook NZ 663 43°36'S 170°08'E
Mt. Cooke AS 656 32°26'S 116°18'E
Mt. Coricudgy AS 656 32°50'S 150°22'E
Mt. Deborah US 398 63°38'N 147°14'W
Mt. Denham JM 414 18°13'N 77°32'W
Mt. Eagle EI 592 52°10'N 9°40'W
Mt. Elbert US 398 39°07'N 106°27'W
Mt. Essendon AS 656 25°00'S 120°28'E
Mt. Etna 564 63°43'N 19°13'W
Mt. Finnigan AS 656 15°45'S 145°15'E
Mt. Fito WS 668 13°55'S 171°50'W
Mt. Gantung RP 526 8°57'N 117°48'E
Mt. Gimie ST 418 13°51'N 61°00'W
Mt. Hamiguitan RP 526 6°44'N 126°11'E
Mt. Hillaby BB 403 13°12'N 59°35'W
Mti. di Ala 562 40°35'N 9°15'E
Mti. di Ala IT 593 40°50'N 9°00'E
Mtito Andei KE 299 2°41'S 38°10'E
Mti. Volsini IT 593 42°40'N 11°55'E
Mt. Kayaganiri CT 282 6°50'N 15°00'E
Mt. Kenya KE 299 0°10'S 37°19'E
Mt. Kulal KE 299 2°43'N 36°56'E
Mt. Liamuiga SC 417 17°22'N 62°48'W
Mt. Mabu MZ 312 16°18'S 36°24'E
Mt. Magdalena MY 518 4°29'N 117°56'E
Mt. Mantalingajan RP 526 8°48'N 117°40'E
Mt. Matutum RP 526 6°22'N 125°05'E
Mt. McKinley US 398 63°04'N 151°00'W
Mt. Mecula MZ 312 13°06'S 35°42'E
Mt. Mitchell US 398 35°46'N 82°16'W
Mt. Moose 372 43°42'N 72°09'W
Mt. Morris AS 656 26°09'S 131°04'E
Mt. Murchison AS 656 43°01'S 171°22'E
Mt. Nangtud RP 526 11°17'N 122°11'E
Mt. Napier AS 656 17°33'S 129°09'E
Mt. Niénokoué IV 288 5°26'N 7°10'W
Mt. Nimba LI 301 7°34'N 8°28'W
Mt. Norfolk AS 656 40°30'S 148°00'E
Mt. Nuza ZI 334 18°43'S 32°49'E
Mtom GB 294 0°18'S 10°29'E
Mtondoni TZ 327 5°55'S 39°20'E
Mt. Ord AS 656 17°20'S 125°34'E
Mtorwi TZ 327 9°04'S 34°00'E
Mt. Ossa AS 656 41°54'S 146°01'E
Mt. Owen NZ 663 41°33'S 172°32'E
Mt. Parsons AS 656 12°30'S 137°00'E
Mt. Ragang RP 526 7°43'N 124°32'E
Mt. Ragged AS 656 33°27'S 123°27'E
Mt. Redcliffe AS 656 28°25'S 121°32'E
Mt. Ross NZ 663 41°28'S 175°21'E
Mt. Rungwe TZ 327 9°08'S 33°40'E
Mt. Ryan AS 656 15°00'S 142°30'E
Mt. Santa Isabel EK 291 3°40'N 8°50'E
Mt. Santo Tomas RP 526 16°20'N 120°34'E
Mt. Selisili WS 668 13°40'S 172°20'W
Mtsensk 466 53°17'N 36°35'E
Mt. Singleton AS 656 29°28'S 117°19'E
Mtskheta GG 495 41°51'N 44°43'E
Mt. Strangways AS 656 22°30'S 133°00'E
Mt. Toiavea WS 668 13°40'S 172°15'W
Mt. Tonkoui IV 288 7°27'N 7°39'W
Mt. Uac RP 526 12°12'N 123°40'E
Mtubatuba SF 322 28°25'S 32°11'E
Mtunzini SF 322 28°57'S 31°43'E
Mtwara TZ 327 10°16'S 40°11'E
Mt. Washington US 398 44°16'N 71°18'W
Mt. Whinham AS 656 26°08'S 130°10'E
Mt. Whitcombe NZ 663 43°13'S 170°55'E
Mt. Whitney US 398 36°35'N 118°18'W
Mt. Woodroffe AS 656 26°30'S 131°45'E
Mt. Wuteve LI 301 8°09'N 9°56'W
Mt. Yacgam RP 526 11°44'N 125°16'E
Mt. Yibir TC 538 25°40'N 56°00'E
Mt. Zeil AS 656 23°24'S 132°33'E
Mu'a 654 21°11'S 175°09'W
Muadiala CG 287 7°13'S 21°12'E
Mualama MZ 312 16°53'S 38°18'E
Muan KS 513 34°59'N 126°29'E
Muang Dakchung LA 517 15°28'N 107°16'E
Muang Gnommarat LA 517 17°36'N 105°10'E
Muang Hang LA 517 20°38'N 104°25'E
Muang Hay LA 517 21°03'N 101°49'E
Muang Hounxianghoung LA 517 21°37'N 102°18'E
Muang Kenthao LA 517 17°44'N 101°25'E
Muang Khong LA 517 14°07'N 105°51'E
Muang Khoua LA 517 21°05'N 102°31'E
Muang Lakhonpheng LA 517 15°54'N 105°34'E
Muang Liat LA 517 20°28'N 104°09'E
Muang May LA 517 14°49'N 106°56'E
Muang Mok LA 517 18°55'N 104°01'E
Muang Ou Tai LA 517 22°07'N 101°48'E
Muang Paktha LA 517 20°06'N 100°36'E
Muang Pakxan LA 517 18°23'N 103°39'E
Muang Pakxong LA 517 15°11'N 106°14'E
Muang Phang LA 517 19°15'N 103°37'E
Muang Phin LA 517 16°32'N 106°02'E
Muang Phong LA 517 16°23'N 105°26'E
Muang Sing LA 517 21°11'N 101°09'E
Muang Soukhouma LA 517 14°38'N 105°48'E
Muang Soy LA 517 20°16'N 104°32'E
Muang Tahoi LA 517 16°10'N 106°38'E
Muang Thadua LA 517 19°26'N 101°50'E
Muang Thateng LA 517 15°26'N 106°23'E
Muang Thathom LA 517 19°00'N 103°36'E
Muang Vapi LA 517 15°40'N 105°55'E
Muang Xamteu LA 517 19°59'N 104°48'E
Muang Xay LA 517 20°42'N 101°59'E
Muang Xepon LA 517 16°41'N 106°14'E
Muang Xon LA 517 20°27'N 103°19'E
Muar MY 518 2°30'N 102°35'E
Muar MY 518 2°02'N 102°34'E
Muara BX 486 5°01'N 115°04'E
Muaraancalung 648 0°27'N 116°41'E
Muarabenangin ID 500 0°58'S 115°19'E
Muarabungo ID 500 1°28'S 102°07'E
Muaradua ID 500 4°32'S 104°05'E
Muarakaman ID 500 0°09'S 116°43'E
Muarakedang 648 0°34'S 116°18'E
Muarakumpe ID 500 1°24'S 104°00'E
Muararupit ID 500 2°44'S 102°54'E
Muarasiberut ID 500 1°36'S 99°11'E
Muaratebo ID 500 1°30'S 102°26'E
Muaratewe ID 500 0°57'S 114°53'E
Muarawahau ID 500 1°02'N 116°52'E
Muari, Ras PK 524 24°49'N 66°40'E
Muatechissengue AO 274 9°10'S 20°35'E
Mubale AO 274 10°13'S 16°24'E
Mubanzi UG 330 0°57'S 31°46'E
Mubarek UZ 539 39°15'N 65°06'E
Mubayira ZI 334 18°20'S 30°36'E
Mubende UG 330 0°35'N 31°23'E
Mubi NI 316 10°16'N 13°16'E
Mubur ID 500 3°20'N 106°12'E
Mucajaí BR 424 2°27'N 60°54'W
Mucajaí 384 2°25'N 60°52'W
Muchanes BL 422 15°14'S 67°39'W
Muchinga Escarpment ZA 332 14°45'S 29°32'E
Muchinga Mountains ZA 332 12°00'S 31°45'E
Muchiri BL 422 19°04'S 63°25'W
Muchkapskiy 560 51°51'N 42°28'E
Muchuan CH 490 28°55'N 103°57'E
Muck UK 626 56°47'N 6°16'W
Mucojo MZ 312 12°04'S 40°28'E
Mucope AO 274 16°24'S 14°53'E
Mucuim 386 6°33'S 64°18'W
Mucula AO 274 6°58'S 12°50'E
Mucupina, Monte HO 412 15°08'N 86°38'W
Mucur TU 535 39°04'N 34°23'E
Mucuripe, Ponta de BR 424 3°42'S 38°28'W
Mucusso AO 274 17°59'S 21°25'E
Mucussueje AO 274 11°01'S 21°56'E
Mudan Jiang CH 490 46°18'N 129°31'E
Mudanjiang CH 490 44°34'N 129°35'E
Mudgee 652 32°36'S 149°35'E
Mud Lake 374 48°10'N 96°00'W
Mud Lake CA 390 53°15'N 60°11'W
Mudon BM 487 16°15'N 97°44'E
Mud River 368 53°46'N 123°01'W
Muecate MZ 312 14°53'S 39°38'E
Mueda MZ 312 11°39'S 39°34'E
Muela, Monte CI 428 53°22'S 72°14'W
Muelle de los Bueyes NU 415 12°04'N 84°32'W
Mueller Range AS 656 18°00'S 128°00'E
Muenster 372 52°12'N 105°00'W
Muerte, Cerro de la CS 405 9°34'N 83°45'W
Mufattam, Bi'r al LY 302 31°41'N 20°51'E
Mufulira ZA 332 12°33'S 28°14'E
Mufulwe Hills ZA 332 13°57'S 29°39'E
Mufu Shan CH 490 29°14'N 114°20'E
Mugango TZ 327 1°41'S 33°42'E
Muganskaya Step' AJ 483 39°40'N 48°30'E
Mugarripug CH 490 32°21'N 87°35'E
Mugei UG 330 3°32'N 34°15'E
Mugesera, Lake RW 317 2°07'S 30°19'E
Muggia IT 593 45°36'N 13°46'E
Mugila, Monts 268 7°00'S 29°00'E
Mugina BY 279 4°25'S 29°46'E
Muğla TU 535 37°12'N 28°22'E
Müglizh BU 573 42°36'N 25°33'E
Mugodzhary KZ 510 48°00'N 58°30'E
Mugombazi TZ 327 5°50'S 30°14'E
Muh, Sabkhat al SY 581 34°30'N 38°20'E
Muhala CG 287 5°40'S 28°43'E
Muḥammad Qawl SU 324 20°54'N 37°05'E
Muhavura RW 317 1°23'S 29°41'E
Muhehwe RW 317 2°38'S 28°58'E
Muheza TZ 327 5°10'S 38°47'E
Muhlbach (Rio di Pusteria) IT 593 46°48'N 11°39'E
Mühldorf GM 584 48°15'N 12°32'E
Muhos FI 578 64°46'N 26°00'E
Muhu EN 577 58°41'N 22°55'E
Muhulu CG 287 1°03'S 27°17'E
Muhutwe TZ 327 1°33'S 31°42'E
Mui ET 293 6°03'N 35°33'E
Muiden NL 602 52°20'N 5°04'E
Muir PP 664 5°40'S 141°35'E
Muirkirk UK 626 55°31'N 4°03'W
Muir of Ord UK 626 57°31'N 4°27'W
Muju KS 513 36°00'N 127°40'E
Mukachevo UP 624 48°27'N 22°43'E
Mukah MY 518 2°54'N 112°06'E
Mükangsar 472 29°35'N 83°37'E
Mukawwar I. SU 324 20°48'N 37°16'E
Mukdahan TH 534 16°32'N 104°43'E
Mukden BL 422 11°11'S 69°02'W
Mukeru PX 664 7°25'N 134°31'E
Muke T'uri ET 293 9°33'N 38°52'E
Mukhatgverdi GG 495 41°49'N 44°44'E
Mukhayyam al Yarmük SY 531 33°29'N 36°19'E
Mukhtadir AJ 483 41°41'N 48°46'E
Mukhtari MU 523 22°40'N 57°59'E
Mukinbudin AS 656 30°55'S 118°13'E
Mukishi CG 287 5°40'S 21°05'E
Muko UG 330 1°12'S 29°48'E
Mukono UG 330 0°22'N 32°45'E
Mukry TX 537 37°36'N 65°44'E
Muktāgācha BG 485 24°46'N 90°14'E
Muktsar IN 496 30°29'N 74°31'E
Mukuku ZA 332 12°09'S 29°50'E
Mukunsa ZA 332 9°28'S 29°37'E
Mukwakwa ZA 332 9°04'S 28°57'E
Mukwe WA 313 18°02'S 21°24'E
Mukwikile ZA 332 11°22'S 31°47'E
Mula SP 618 38°03'N 1°30'W
Mulaku Atoll MV 519 3°00'N 73°30'E
Mulaló EC 432 0°47'S 78°34'W
Mulaly KZ 510 45°27'N 78°19'E
Mulange Mts. MI 306 16°00'S 35°00'E
Mulanje MI 306 16°02'S 35°30'E
Mulas, Punta de CU 406 21°01'N 75°34'W
Mulberry 374 40°20'N 86°39'W
Mulchatna US 398 59°40'N 157°07'W
Mulchén CI 428 37°43'S 72°14'W
Mulde GM 584 51°52'N 12°15'E
Mulegé MX 394 26°54'N 111°59'W
Muleshoe 376 34°13'N 102°43'W
Mulgön KS 513 34°48'N 128°03'E
Mulgrave AS 656 10°05'S 141°40'E
Mulhacén SP 618 37°03'N 3°19'W
Mülhausen GM 584 51°13'N 10°27'E
Mulhouse FR 580 47°45'N 7°20'E
Muli CH 490 27°49'N 101°15'E
Mulia ID 500 3°44'S 137°58'E
Mulifanua WS 668 13°50'S 172°00'W
Mulilansolo Mission ZA 332 10°05'S 32°19'E
Mulima CG 287 7°19'S 28°01'E
Muling CH 490 44°55'N 130°31'E
Mulinja RW 317 2°03'S 30°07'E
Mulin'u, Cape 650 13°30'S 173°50'E
Mulinu'u, Cape WS 668 13°17'S 172°40'W
Mull UK 626 56°26'N 6°03'W
Mullaittivu CE 530 9°16'N 80°49'E
Muller, Peg. ID 500 0°40'N 113°50'E
Muller Range PP 664 6°00'S 142°30'E
Mullet Key 378 27°38'N 82°48'W
Mullewa AS 656 28°32'S 115°31'E
Müllheim GM 584 47°48'N 7°38'E
Mullingar EI 592 53°32'N 7°21'W
Mullins 378 34°12'N 79°15'W
Mullovka 560 54°12'N 49°24'E
Mulobezi ZA 332 16°47'S 25°10'E
Mulondo AO 274 15°39'S 15°12'E
Mulongo CG 287 7°50'S 27°00'E
Mulsanne FR 580 47°54'N 0°15'E
Multān PK 524 30°11'N 71°29'E
Multé MX 394 17°41'N 91°24'W
Mulu, Gunung MY 518 4°03'N 114°56'E
Mulungushi ZA 332 14°43'S 28°51'E
Mulvane 376 37°28'N 97°14'W
Mulwad SU 324 18°35'N 30°36'E
Mulyavskoye KZ 510 52°55'N 76°13'E
Mumbanza BY 279 2°46'S 29°02'E
Mumbondo AO 274 10°11'S 14°08'E
Mumbotuta Falls ZA 332 12°22'S 29°12'E
Mumbué AO 274 13°54'S 17°18'E
Mumbwa ZA 332 14°59'S 27°04'E
Mumena CG 287 11°46'S 26°31'E
Mumeng PP 664 6°59'S 146°35'E
Mumias KE 299 0°20'N 34°29'E
Mumma alah, Ra's al BA 484 25°50'N 50°30'E
Mumoni KE 299 0°31'S 38°01'E
Mumra 466 45°47'N 47°40'E
Mun, Mae Nam TH 534 15°30'N 102°50'E
Muna 500 5°00'S 122°30'E
Muna MX 394 20°28'N 89°42'W
Muná SA 528 21°25'N 39°52'E
Mu Naggava (Rennell) BP 666 11°35'S 160°10'E
Munayly KZ 510 46°47'N 54°31'E
Munbura 652 21°20'S 149°09'E
München GM 584 48°09'N 11°35'E
Münchenstein SZ 622 47°31'N 7°37'E
Muncho Lake CA 390 58°59'N 125°47'W
Munch'ŏn KN 512 39°14'N 127°22'E
Muncie 370 40°11'N 85°23'W
Munda BP 666 8°18'S 157°15'E
Mundabullangana AS 656 20°31'S 118°04'E
Munday 376 33°26'N 99°37'W
Mundemba CM 280 4°55'N 8°52'E
Mundiwindi AS 656 23°50'S 120°10'E
Mundo 364 38°19'N 1°40'W
Mundök KN 512 39°30'N 125°30'E
Mundo Novo 386 23°58'S 54°21'W
Mundo Nuevo VE 440 9°57'N 64°03'W
Mundrabilla AS 656 31°52'S 127°51'E
Mundubbera 652 25°36'S 151°18'E
Muñene ZI 334 20°37'S 30°03'E
Munenga AO 274 10°02'S 14°38'E
Munera SP 618 39°02'N 2°28'W
Mungbere CG 287 2°38'N 28°30'E
Mungeli 476 22°04'N 81°41'E
Munger IN 496 25°23'N 86°29'E
Mungia 562 43°21'N 2°50'W
Mungindi AS 656 28°59'S 149°02'E
Mungo AO 274 11°50'S 16°08'E
Mungo AO 274 7°44'S 19°56'E
Mun'gyŏng KS 513 36°44'N 128°07'E

N

Naranjos	BL	422	18°38'S	59°09'W
Narasapatnam Pt.	IN	496	16°19'N	81°43'E
Narasaraopet	IN	496	16°15'N	80°04'E
Narat	CH	490	43°21'N	84°02'E
Narathiwat	TH	534	6°26'N	101°50'E
Narat Shan	CH	490	43°08'N	83°30'E
Nārāyanganj	BG	485	23°37'N	90°30'E
Narbonne	FR	580	43°11'N	3°00'E
Narca, Ponta da		266	6°00'S	12°10'E
Narcea	SP	618	43°28'N	6°07'W
Nardaran	AJ	483	41°01'N	49°08'E
Nardò	IT	593	40°10'N	18°01'E
Narembeen	AS	656	32°04'S	118°24'E
Naréna	ML	307	12°14'N	8°38'W
Narew	PL	606	52°26'N	20°41'E
Narganá	PM	417	9°26'N	78°35'W
Narib	WA	313	24°12'S	17°44'E
Nariman	KG	514	40°34'N	72°48'E
Narin	CH	490	40°53'N	100°19'E
Narinda	MA	304	15°10'S	47°39'E
Nariz, Pico	CI	428	53°52'S	70°04'W
Narizón, Pt.		376	27°52'N	110°54'W
Narkatiāganj	IN	496	27°06'N	84°28'E
Narlı	TU	535	37°52'N	43°10'E
Narmada	IN	496	21°39'N	72°36'E
Narni		562	42°31'N	12°31'E
Naroch'	BO	569	54°54'N	26°43'E
Naro-Fominsk		560	55°23'N	36°43'E
Narok	KE	299	1°05'S	35°52'E
Naro Moru	KE	299	0°10'S	37°01'E
Narooma		652	36°13'S	150°03'E
Narovlya	BO	569	51°48'N	29°30'E
Narovorovo		654	15°10'S	168°10'E
Nārowāl	PK	524	32°06'N	74°53'E
Närpes (Närpiö)	FI	578	62°28'N	21°20'E
Narra	RP	526	9°22'N	118°31'E
Narrabri		652	30°19'S	149°47'E
Narrandera		652	34°45'S	146°33'E
Narrogin	AS	656	32°56'S	117°10'E
Narromine		652	32°09'S	148°15'E
Narsaq		370	60°55'N	46°03'W
Narsarsuaq		370	61°10'N	45°25'W
Narsimhapur	IN	496	22°57'N	79°12'E
Narsinghdi	BG	485	23°55'N	90°43'E
Narst	MG	520	47°42'N	107°50'E
Nart	CH	490	42°53'N	115°46'E
Nart	MG	520	49°09'N	105°21'E
Narubis	WA	313	26°56'S	18°36'E
Naruksovo		560	54°37'N	44°33'E
Narungombe	TZ	327	9°19'S	38°34'E
Naruto	JA	506	34°11'N	134°37'E
Narva	EN	577	59°27'N	28°02'E
Narva	EN	577	59°22'N	28°09'E
Narva Bay	EN	577	59°30'N	27°40'E
Narvacan	RP	526	17°25'N	120°28'E
Narva-Jõesuu	EN	577	59°27'N	28°03'E
Narvik	NO	604	68°24'N	17°25'E
Nar'yan-Mar	RS	612	67°39'N	53°00'E
Narymskiy Khr.	KZ	510	50°07'N	84°19'E
Naryn		466	40°54'N	71°45'E
Naryn	KG	514	41°26'N	75°58'E
Naryn Khuduk		466	45°26'N	46°33'E
Näsåker	SW	621	63°26'N	16°55'E
Nasarawa	NI	316	8°32'N	7°43'E
Năsăud	RO	610	47°17'N	24°24'E
Naseby	NZ	663	45°02'S	170°10'E
Nash Pt.	UK	626	51°23'N	3°32'W
Nashua	US	398	42°45'N	71°28'W
Nashville		374	35°58'N	77°57'W
Nashville		374	38°20'N	89°22'W
Nashville		378	31°12'N	83°15'W
Nashville		378	33°56'N	93°50'W
Nashville	US	398	36°09'N	86°47'W
Nashville Basin		378	36°00'N	86°00'W
Našice	HR	574	45°30'N	18°06'E
Nasielsk	PL	606	52°35'N	20°48'E
Nasiib	SQ	321	0°20'N	42°46'E
Näsijärvi	FI	578	61°37'N	23°42'E
Nāsik	IN	496	19°59'N	73°48'E
Nāşir	SU	324	8°37'N	33°04'E
Nasīrābād	IN	496	26°18'N	74°44'E
Nasosnyy	AJ	483	40°37'N	49°34'E
Nasrani, Jabal al		564	34°00'N	37°30'E
Nass	CA	390	55°00'N	129°50'W
Nassakini	TO	328	9°53'N	0°36'E
Nassau		650	11°56'S	165°18'W
Nassau	BF	402	25°04'N	77°21'W
Nassau, Bahía	CI	428	55°25'S	67°40'W
Nasser, Lake	EG	290	22°50'N	32°30'E
Nassian	IV	288	8°27'N	3°29'W
Nässjö	SW	621	57°39'N	14°41'E
Nassoukou	BN	276	10°46'N	1°49'E
Nastapoka Islands	CA	390	56°50'N	76°50'W
Nastola	FI	578	60°57'N	25°56'E
Nasugbu	RP	526	14°05'N	120°38'E
Nata	BC	276	20°14'S	26°10'E
Natá	PM	417	8°20'N	80°31'W
Natagaima	CO	430	3°37'N	75°06'W
Natal		478	0°33'N	99°07'E
Natal	BR	424	5°47'S	35°13'W
Naţanz	IR	502	33°31'N	51°54'E
N-Ataram, Erg	AG	272	23°54'N	1°48'E
Natashquan		370	50°09'N	61°46'W
Natashquan		370	50°06'N	61°49'W
Natchez		378	31°33'N	91°24'W
Natchitoches	US	398	31°45'N	93°05'W
Naters	SZ	622	46°20'N	7°59'E
Nāthdwāra	IN	496	24°56'N	73°49'E
Nathenje	MI	306	14°05'S	33°54'E
Nathoi, Cap (Cumberland, Cape)	NH	669	14°40'S	166°30'E
Nathorst, C.	CA	390	77°47'N	99°56'W
Natimuk		652	36°45'S	141°57'E
Natitingou	BN	276	10°19'N	1°22'E
Natividade	BR	424	11°43'S	47°47'W
Natkyizin	BM	487	14°55'N	97°57'E
Nator	BG	485	24°25'N	88°59'E
Natori	JA	506	32°12'N	140°51'E
Natron, Lake	TZ	327	2°30'S	36°10'E
Nat Taung	BM	487	23°50'N	96°30'E
Nattaung	BM	487	18°48'N	97°02'E
Nattavaara	SW	621	66°44'N	20°53'E
Natuna, Kep.	ID	500	4°00'N	108°15'E
Natuna Besar	ID	500	3°00'N	109°00'E
Naturaliste, C.	AS	656	33°31'S	114°59'E
Nau	TI	533	40°09'N	69°22'E
Naucalpan de Juárez	MX	394	19°29'N	99°14'W
Naucelle		562	44°12'N	2°21'E
Nauders	AU	568	46°53'N	10°31'E
Naudesnek	SF	322	30°44'S	28°08'E
Naujamiestis	LH	597	55°41'N	24°09'E
Naujan	RP	526	13°20'N	121°18'E
Naujoji-Akmenė	LH	597	56°19'N	22°54'E
Naumburg	GM	584	51°09'N	11°49'E
Nā'ūr	JO	510	31°53'N	35°50'E
Nauru		38	0°32'S	166°55'E
Naushki	RS	612	50°22'N	106°07'E
Naustdal	NO	604	61°30'N	5°41'E
Nauta	PE	436	4°32'S	73°33'W
Nauvo (Nagu)	FI	578	60°10'N	21°49'E
Nava	MX	394	28°25'N	100°46'W
Navabad	TI	533	37°44'N	69°59'E
Nava de la Asunción		562	41°09'N	4°29'W
Nava del Rey	SP	618	41°20'N	5°05'W
Navajo		376	36°45'N	107°36'W
Navajo Res.		376	37°00'N	107°15'W
Naval	RP	526	11°34'N	124°24'E
Navalmoral de la Mata	SP	618	39°54'N	5°32'W
Navalvillar de Pela	SP	618	39°06'N	5°28'W
Navarin, Mys	RS	612	62°15'N	179°05'E
Navarino, Isla	CI	428	55°05'S	67°40'W
Navasota		378	30°23'N	96°05'W
Navassa Island	US	40	18°25'N	75°00'W
Navatuvotu		654	17°00'S	178°00'E
Naver	UK	626	58°32'N	4°15'W
Navia	SP	618	43°32'N	6°43'W
Naviraí	BR	424	23°08'S	54°13'W
Naviti		654	17°08'S	176°48'E
Năvodari	RO	610	44°19'N	28°36'E
Navoi	UZ	539	40°09'N	65°22'E
Navojoa	MX	394	27°06'N	109°26'W
Navolato	MX	394	24°47'N	107°42'W
Návpaktos	GR	588	38°24'N	21°49'E
Návplion	GR	588	37°34'N	22°48'E
Navrongo	GH	296	10°54'N	1°06'W
Navsāri	IN	496	20°51'N	72°55'E
Nawābganj	BG	485	24°36'N	88°17'E
Nawābganj	IN	496	26°56'N	81°13'E
Nawābshāh	PK	524	26°15'N	68°25'E
Nāwah	AF	480	32°19'N	67°53'E
Nawalapitiya	CE	530	7°03'N	80°32'E
Nawān Jandānwāla	PK	524	32°04'N	71°36'E
Nāwāpur		470	19°47'N	72°41'E
Nawasif, Harrat	SA	528	20°50'N	42°00'E
Nawmah, Ra's	BA	484	25°59'N	50°27'E
Nawnghkio	BM	487	22°14'N	96°55'E
Nawngleng	BM	487	22°50'N	98°25'E
Naws, Ra's	MU	523	17°15'N	55°16'E
Naxçıvan	AJ	483	39°12'N	45°24'E
Náxos	GR	588	37°06'N	25°23'E
Naya	CO	430	3°13'N	77°22'W
Nayak	AF	480	34°44'N	66°57'E
Nayau	FJ	660	18°00'S	179°00'W
Nāy Band	IR	502	27°23'N	52°36'E
Nāy Band	IR	502	32°23'N	57°30'E
Naylors Landing	CA	390	61°49'N	121°05'W
Nayong	CH	490	26°49'N	105°16'E
Nayoro	JA	506	44°21'N	142°28'E
Nayramadlin Orgil	MG	520	49°08'N	87°49'E
Nayuci	MI	306	14°58'S	35°52'E
Nazaré		384	6°23'S	47°40'W
Nazaré	PO	608	39°36'N	9°04'W
Nazare, Baie de	GB	294	0°47'S	9°05'E
Nazareno		376	25°25'N	103°26'W
Nazarovo		466	56°01'N	90°26'E
Nazas	MX	394	25°14'N	104°08'W
Nazas	MX	394	25°35'N	105°00'W
Nazca	PE	436	14°50'S	74°57'W
Naze	JA	506	28°23'N	129°30'E
Naẕerat	IS	505	32°42'N	35°18'E
Nazilli	TU	535	37°55'N	28°21'E
Nāzir Hāt	BG	485	22°38'N	91°47'E
Nazko	CA	390	53°00'N	123°34'W
Nazrēt	ET	293	8°33'N	39°16'E
Nazyvayevsk	RS	612	55°34'N	71°21'E
Nchanga	ZA	332	12°29'S	27°55'E
Nchelenge	ZA	332	9°20'S	28°43'E
Ncheu	MI	306	14°49'S	34°38'E
Nchisi	MI	306	13°22'S	34°00'E
Ncoatom	EK	291	2°03'N	9°58'E
Ncojane	BC	276	23°10'S	20°16'E
Ndabala	ZA	332	13°28'S	29°50'E
Ndala	TZ	327	4°46'S	33°16'E
Ndalatando	AO	274	9°18'S	14°54'E
Ndali	BN	276	9°51'N	2°43'E
Ndele	CT	282	8°24'N	20°40'E
Ndélélé	CM	280	4°02'N	14°56'E
N'Dendé	GB	294	2°49'S	11°15'E
Ndengu	TZ	327	11°03'S	34°54'E
Ndeni	BP	666	10°40'S	166°00'E
Ndiago	MR	308	16°10'N	16°30'W
Ndikiniméki	CM	280	4°46'N	10°50'E
Ndim	CT	282	7°17'N	15°46'E
N'Djamena	CD	283	12°07'N	15°03'E
N'Djolé	GB	294	0°11'S	10°45'E
Ndogo, Lagune	GB	294	2°35'S	10°00'E
Ndola	ZA	332	12°58'S	28°38'E
Ndolo Corner	KE	299	1°12'S	37°55'E
Ndombi	CG	287	7°35'S	21°58'E
Ndonga		270	20°30'S	18°00'E
Ndouaniang	GB	294	0°18'N	10°03'E
Ndouci	IV	288	5°52'N	4°46'W
Ndougou	GB	294	1°39'S	9°40'E
Ndrhamcha, Sebkha	MR	308	19°00'N	16°00'W
Ndu	CG	287	4°41'N	22°49'E
Nduguti	TZ	327	4°18'S	34°42'E
Nduindui	BP	666	9°48'S	159°55'E
Nduke (Kolombangara)	BP	666	7°50'S	157°00'E
Nduli	TZ	327	7°40'S	35°46'E
Ndumbwe	TZ	327	10°14'S	39°58'E
Ndungu	TZ	327	4°22'S	38°03'E
Nea	NO	604	63°00'N	61°30'E
Néa Ankhíalos	GR	588	39°16'N	22°49'E
Néa Artáki	GR	588	38°31'N	23°39'E
Neahg, Lough	UK	626	54°38'N	6°24'W
Néa Ionía	GR	588	39°23'N	22°53'E
Néa Kallikrátia	GR	588	40°19'N	23°04'E
Néa Kíos	GR	588	37°35'N	22°44'E
Neale, Lake	AS	656	24°22'S	130°00'E
Néa Mikhanióna	GR	588	40°28'N	22°52'E
Néa Moudhaniá	GR	588	40°15'N	23°17'E
Néa Péramos		564	38°00'N	26°13'E
Neápolis	GR	588	40°19'N	21°23'E
Neápolis	GR	588	35°15'N	25°37'E
Neápolis	GR	588	36°30'N	23°04'E
Néa Potídhaia	GR	588	40°11'N	23°19'E
Near	US	398	52°11'N	172°18'E
Neath	UK	626	51°37'N	3°50'W
Néa Tríglia	GR	588	40°18'N	23°12'E
Néa Víssa	GR	588	41°35'N	26°32'E
Néa Zíkhni	GR	588	41°02'N	23°49'E
Neba		654	20°10'S	163°55'E
Nebbi	UG	330	2°29'N	31°05'E
Nebit-Dag	TX	537	39°30'N	54°22'E
Neblina, Cerro de la	VE	440	0°46'N	66°00'W
Nebo	SF	322	24°54'S	29°46'E
Nebolchi		560	59°08'N	33°21'E
Nebraska		372	41°30'N	99°30'W
Nebraska City		374	40°40'N	95°51'W
Nebrodi, Monti	IT	593	37°54'N	14°35'E
Nechayannoye	UP	624	46°57'N	31°33'E
Neches		378	29°55'N	93°52'W
Nechí	CO	430	8°07'N	74°46'W
Neckar	GM	584	49°31'N	8°26'E
Neckarsulm	GM	584	49°11'N	9°14'E
Necochea	AR	419	38°33'S	58°45'W
Necoclí	CO	430	8°26'N	76°48'W
Neded	LO	616	48°01'N	17°59'E
Nedelino	BU	573	41°27'N	25°05'E
Nedelišće	HR	574	46°23'N	16°23'E
Nederweert	NL	602	51°17'N	5°45'E
Neeb	CA	390	54°01'N	107°59'W
Neede	NL	602	52°08'N	6°37'E
Needles		372	49°52'N	118°06'W
Needles		376	34°50'N	114°36'W
Needles Pt.	NZ	663	36°04'S	175°21'E
Neepawa	CA	390	50°14'N	99°28'W
Nee Soon	SN	530	1°25'N	103°50'E
Nefasīt	ER	292	15°20'N	39°04'E
Nefas Mewch'a	ET	293	11°44'N	38°28'E
Nefţah	TS	329	33°52'N	7°53'E
Neftechala	AJ	483	39°23'N	49°16'E
Neftegorsk		564	44°22'N	39°43'E
Neftekamsk	RS	612	56°05'N	54°16'E
Neftekumsk		466	44°40'N	44°55'E
Nefteyugansk	RS	612	61°06'N	72°42'E
Nefyn		558	52°56'N	4°30'W
Négala	ML	307	12°52'N	8°27'W
Negampaha	CE	530	7°59'N	80°27'E
Nega Nega	ZA	332	15°50'S	28°02'E
Negara	ID	500	8°22'S	114°37'E
Negara	ID	500	2°37'S	115°06'E
Negaunee		374	46°30'N	87°36'W
Negēlē	ET	293	5°19'N	39°35'E
Negēlē	ET	293	7°21'N	38°42'E
Neger	IS	505	30°35'N	34°40'E
Negginan		370	53°01'N	97°18'W
Negomano	MZ	312	11°25'S	38°29'E
Negombo	CE	530	7°13'N	79°50'E
Negoreloye	BO	569	53°36'N	27°04'E
Negotin	YO	630	44°13'N	22°32'E
Negotino	MK	599	41°29'N	22°06'E
Negra, Cordillera	PE	436	9°25'S	77°40'W
Negra, Punta	BH	404	16°16'N	88°32'W
Negra, Punta	PE	436	6°06'S	81°09'W
Negra, Serr. de	BL	422	13°45'S	60°58'W
Negrais, Cape	BM	487	16°02'N	94°12'E
Negreşti	RO	610	46°50'N	27°26'E
Negril	JM	414	18°16'N	78°21'W
Negrillos	BL	422	18°47'S	68°41'W
Negrine	AG	272	34°29'N	7°31'E
Negritos	PE	436	4°38'S	81°19'W
Negro	AR	419	41°02'S	62°47'W
Negro	BR	424	3°00'S	61°00'W
Negro	UY	439	33°24'S	58°22'W
Negro	VE	440	2°00'N	67°00'W
Negros	RP	526	9°39'N	120°23'E
Nehbandān	IR	502	31°32'N	60°02'E
Nehe	CH	490	48°28'N	124°49'E
Neiba	DR	408	18°28'N	71°25'W
Neiba, Bahía de	DR	408	18°15'N	71°02'W
Neiba, Sierra de	DR	408	18°40'N	71°30'W
Neijiang	CH	490	29°34'N	105°02'E
Nei Mongol Gaoyuan	CH	490	4°00'N	103°00'E
Neineis	WA	313	21°28'S	15°04'E
Neiva	CO	430	2°56'N	75°18'W
Nejanilini L.		370	59°30'N	97°50'W
Nejd (Najd)	SA	528	25°00'N	44°30'E
Nejdek	EZ	575	50°19'N	12°43'E
Nejo	ET	293	9°30'N	35°30'E
Nek'emtē	ET	293	9°05'N	36°33'E
Nekhayevskiy		466	50°25'N	41°44'E
Nekoosa		374	44°18'N	89°54'W
Nekrasovo		560	51°10'N	45°19'E
Neksikan	RS	612	62°41'N	147°40'E
Neksø	DA	576	55°04'N	15°06'E
Nelas	PO	608	40°32'N	7°51'W
Nelidovo	RS	612	56°13'N	32°46'E
Neligh		372	42°07'N	98°01'W
Nel'kan	RS	612	57°40'N	136°10'E
Nel'kan	RS	612	63°00'N	148°21'E
Nellore	IN	496	14°26'N	79°58'E
Nelly Bay		652	19°08'S	146°48'E
Nelson	CA	390	49°29'N	117°17'W
Nelson	CA	390	57°04'N	92°30'W
Nelson	NZ	663	41°17'S	173°17'E
Nelson, C.	PP	664	9°00'S	149°30'E
Nelson, Cape		652	43°30'S	141°30'E
Nelson Forks	CA	390	59°30'N	124°01'W
Nelson House	CA	390	55°47'N	98°51'W
Nelson I.		368	60°40'N	164°45'W
Nelspruit	SF	322	25°28'S	30°58'E
Néma	MR	308	16°37'N	7°15'W
Néma, Dahr	MR	308	16°40'N	7°13'W
Neman		466	55°18'N	21°23'E
Neman		560	55°02'N	22°02'E
Neman	BO	569	53°30'N	26°30'E
Nembrala	ID	500	10°53'S	122°50'E
Ñemby	PA	435	25°22'S	57°36'W
Neméa	GR	588	37°49'N	22°40'E
Nemenčinė	LH	597	54°51'N	25°29'E
Nemetskiy, Mys	RS	612	69°58'N	31°58'E
Nemirov	UP	624	50°07'N	23°27'E
Nemours		562	48°16'N	2°42'E
Nemšová	LO	616	48°56'N	18°06'E
Nemunas	LH	597	55°18'N	21°23'E
Nemuro	JA	506	43°20'N	145°35'E
Nemuro-hanto	JA	506	43°21'N	145°46'E
Nemuro-kaikyo	JA	506	43°30'N	145°15'E
Nenagh	EI	592	52°52'N	8°12'W
Nenana		368	64°34'N	149°06'W
Nenasi	MY	518	3°08'N	103°25'E
Nendaz	SZ	622	46°11'N	7°18'E
Nendeln	LS	597	47°12'N	9°33'E
Nene	UK	626	52°48'N	0°13'E
Nengonengo		654	18°30'S	141°30'W
Nen Jiang	CH	490	45°26'N	124°39'E
Nenjiang	CH	490	49°10'N	125°12'E
Neodesha		374	37°25'N	95°40'W
Neokhorio	CY	494	35°14'N	33°28'E
Neokhórion	GR	588	38°25'N	21°17'E
Neokhórion	GR	588	39°37'N	21°59'E
Néon Karlovásion	GR	588	37°47'N	26°42'E
Néon Petrítsion	GR	588	41°16'N	23°17'E
Neosho		374	36°52'N	94°22'W
Neosho	US	398	35°48'N	95°18'W
Néos Marmarás	GR	588	40°06'N	23°47'E
Néos Skopós	GR	588	41°01'N	23°36'E
Neo-Volcánica, Cordillera	MX	394	19°30'N	100°00'W
Nepa	RS	612	59°14'N	108°14'E
Nepal		38	28°00'N	84°00'E
Nepālganj	NP	522	28°03'N	81°37'E
Nepāltār	NP	522	26°54'N	86°32'E
Nepean	CA	390	45°16'N	75°46'W
Nepeña	PE	436	9°10'S	78°23'W
Nephi		372	39°42'N	111°50'W
Nepoko	CG	287	1°40'N	27°01'E
Nera	IT	593	42°26'N	12°24'E
Nérac	FR	580	44°08'N	0°21'E
Neratovice	EZ	575	50°16'N	14°31'E
Nerchinsk		468	51°58'N	116°35'E
Nerekhta		560	57°28'N	40°34'E
Nereta	LG	596	56°10'N	25°18'E
Neretva	BK	572	43°02'N	17°27'E
Neringa	LH	597	55°19'N	21°00'E
Neris	LH	597	54°54'N	23°53'E
Néris-les-Bains	FR	580	46°17'N	2°40'E
Nerja		562	36°45'N	3°52'W
Nerokoúros	GR	588	35°27'N	24°02'E
Nerópolis	BR	424	16°25'S	49°14'W
Nerva	SP	618	37°42'N	6°32'W
Nervión, R.	SP	618	43°15'N	2°58'W
Neryungri	RS	612	56°40'N	124°40'E
Nes	NL	602	53°27'N	5°46'E
Nes	NO	604	60°33'N	9°58'E
Nesbyen	NO	604	60°34'N	9°06'E
Nesebŭr	BU	573	42°39'N	26°01'E
Neskaupstadhur	IC	591	65°10'N	13°41'W
Nesna	NO	604	66°11'N	13°03'E
Nesoddtangen	NO	604	59°51'N	10°38'E
Ness, Loch	UK	626	57°21'N	4°53'W
Ness City		372	38°27'N	99°54'W
Nesslau	SZ	622	47°13'N	9°12'E
Nesterovka		466	52°26'N	53°42'E
Nestor	TD	438	10°31'N	61°09'W
Nestor Falls		374	49°07'N	93°56'W
Nestórion	GR	588	40°25'N	21°04'E
Néstos	GR	588	40°51'N	24°44'E
Nesttun	NO	604	60°19'N	5°20'E
Nesvady	LO	616	47°56'N	18°07'E
Nesvizh	BO	569	53°13'N	26°40'E
Netanya	IS	505	32°20'N	34°51'E
Netarhāt	IN	496	23°29'N	84°16'E
Netherlands		38	52°30'N	5°45'E
Netherlands Antilles	NL	40	12°00'N	69°00'W
Netishin	UP	624	50°21'N	26°38'E
Netivot	IS	505	31°25'N	34°35'E
Neto	IT	593	39°12'N	17°09'E
Netrakona	BG	485	24°53'N	90°43'E
Nettilling Lake	CA	390	66°30'N	70°50'W
Nettleton		378	34°05'N	88°37'W
Nettuno	IT	593	41°27'N	12°40'E
Neubrandenburg	GM	584	53°34'N	13°16'E
Neuchâtel	SZ	622	46°59'N	6°55'E
Neuchâtel, Lac de	SZ	622	46°54'N	6°53'E
Neudorf		372	50°43'N	103°01'W
Neuenhagen	GM	584	52°32'N	13°41'E
Neufchâteau	BE	570	49°50'N	5°26'E
Neuhausen am Rheinfall	SZ	622	47°41'N	8°36'E
Neu Heusis	WA	313	22°37'S	16°43'E
Neukirchen	AU	568	47°15'N	12°16'E
Neukirchen	GM	584	54°52'N	8°44'E
Neum	LA	517	18°10'N	102°50'E
Neumarkt in der Oberpfalz	GM	584	49°17'N	11°28'E
Neumünster	GM	584	54°04'N	9°59'E
Neun, Nam		476	19°42'N	104°03'E
Neunkirchen	AU	568	47°43'N	16°05'E
Neunkirchen	GM	584	49°21'N	7°11'E
Neuquén	AR	419	38°57'S	68°08'W
Neuquén	AR	419	38°59'S	68°00'W
Neurara	CI	428	24°10'S	68°29'W
Neuruppin	GM	584	52°56'N	12°48'E
Neusäss	GM	584	48°24'N	10°50'E
Neusiedl am See	AU	568	47°56'N	16°50'E
Neusiedler See	AU	568	47°43'N	16°44'E
Neuss	GM	584	51°11'N	6°41'E
Neustadt am Rübenberge	GM	584	52°30'N	9°28'E
Neustadt an der Aisch	GM	584	49°35'N	10°36'E
Neustadt an der Donau	GM	584	48°48'N	11°46'E
Neustadt an der Weinstrasse	GM	584	49°21'N	8°09'E
Neustadt bei Coburg	GM	584	50°19'N	11°06'E
Neustadt in Holstein	GM	584	54°06'N	10°49'E
Neustift im Stubaital	AU	568	47°07'N	11°19'E
Neustrelitz	GM	584	53°21'N	13°03'E
Neu-Ulm	GM	584	48°24'N	10°01'E
Neuvic	FR	580	45°23'N	2°17'E
Neuwied	GM	584	50°26'N	7°28'E
Neuzelle	GM	584	52°05'N	14°38'E
Nevada		372	39°15'N	116°45'W
Nevada		374	42°01'N	93°27'W
Nevada		374	37°50'N	94°21'W
Nevada City		372	39°15'N	121°00'W
Nevada de Cocuy, Sierra	CO	430	6°30'N	72°21'W
Nevada de Santa Marta, Sierra	CO	430	11°00'N	73°00'W
Nevado, Sa. del	AR	419	35°40'S	68°30'W
Nevado Cónico, Cerro	CI	428	37°22'S	71°12'W
Nevatim	IS	505	31°13'N	34°54'E
Neve, Serra da	AO	274	13°43'S	13°10'E
Nevel'	RS	612	56°02'N	29°55'E
Nevele	BE	570	51°02'N	3°33'E
Nevel'sk	RS	612	46°40'N	141°52'E
Never		468	53°59'N	124°10'E
Nevers	FR	580	46°59'N	3°09'E
Nevesinje	BK	572	43°16'N	18°07'E
Nevinnomyssk	RS	612	44°38'N	41°57'E
Nevis		372	52°20'N	113°01'W
Nevis	SC	417	17°03'N	62°31'W
Nevis Peak	SC	417	17°09'N	62°35'W
Nevşehir	TU	535	38°38'N	34°43'E
New		378	37°00'N	81°00'W
New	GY	434	3°23'N	57°36'W
New Aiyansh	CA	390	55°12'N	129°04'W
Newala	TZ	327	10°56'S	39°18'E
New Albany		374	38°17'N	85°49'W
New Albany		378	34°29'N	89°00'W
New Amsterdam	GY	434	6°15'N	57°31'W
New Angledool	AS	656	29°07'S	147°56'E
Newark		374	39°41'N	75°45'W
Newark	US	398	40°44'N	74°10'W
Newark	US	398	40°03'N	82°24'W
Newark-on-Trent	UK	626	53°03'N	0°48'W
New Bedford	US	398	41°38'N	70°56'W
Newberg	US	398	45°18'N	122°58'W
New Bern		378	35°05'N	77°02'W
Newberry		378	34°16'N	81°37'W
Newberry	US	398	46°21'N	85°30'W
Newbiggin-by-the-Sea	UK	626	55°10'N	1°31'W
New Boston		378	33°27'N	94°24'W
New Braunfels		376	29°42'N	98°07'W
New Brigden		372	51°42'N	110°29'W
New Britain		374	41°40'N	72°47'W
New Britain	PP	664	6°04'S	148°38'E
New Brunswick		374	46°30'N	66°45'W
Newburg		374	38°09'N	85°39'W
Newburgh		374	41°29'N	74°01'W
Newburn	UK	626	54°58'N	1°44'W
Newbury	UK	626	51°24'N	1°19'W
New Bussa	NI	316	9°50'N	4°31'E
New Caledonia (Nouvelle Calédonie)		650	22°00'S	164°00'E
New Castle		374	41°00'N	80°20'W
Newcastle		372	43°51'N	104°12'W
Newcastle	AS	656	32°55'S	151°45'E
Newcastle	CA	390	47°00'N	65°34'W
Newcastle	EI	592	52°27'N	9°03'W
Newcastle	SC	417	17°12'N	62°35'W
Newcastle	SF	322	27°45'S	29°56'E
Newcastle	UK	626	54°12'N	5°53'W
Newcastle Range	AS	656	19°00'S	144°30'E
Newcastle upon Tyne	UK	626	54°58'N	1°36'W
Newcastle Waters	AS	656	17°24'S	133°24'E
New Cumnock	UK	626	55°24'N	4°11'W
Newdegate		652	33°06'S	119°01'E
New Delhi	IN	496	28°36'N	77°12'E
Newell		374	42°36'N	95°00'W
Newell	AS	656	16°24'S	145°22'E
Newellton		378	32°04'N	91°14'W
New England Ra.	AS	656	30°00'S	151°50'E
Newe Zohar	IS	505	31°09'N	35°22'E
Newfoundland	CA	390	50°07'N	55°37'W
New Galloway	UK	626	55°04'N	4°07'W
Newgate		372	49°02'N	115°12'W
New Georgia	BP	666	8°05'S	157°50'E
New Georgia Group	BP	666	8°15'S	156°30'E
New Georgia Sound (The Slot)	BP	666	7°40'S	157°00'E
New Glasgow	CA	390	45°35'N	62°39'W
New Grant	TD	438	10°17'N	61°19'W
New Guinea	ID	500	5°00'S	140°00'E
New Hampshire		374	43°30'N	71°35'W
New Hanover	PP	664	2°24'S	148°19'E
New Hanover	SF	322	29°21'S	30°32'E
New Haven		374	38°36'N	91°13'W
New Haven		374	41°04'N	85°00'W
New Haven	JM	414	18°02'N	76°52'W
New Haven	US	398	41°18'N	72°55'W
New Hazelton	CA	390	55°15'N	127°35'W
New Hebride Is.	NH	669	19°00'S	167°00'E
New Hope		378	34°32'N	86°23'W
New Iberia	US	398	30°00'N	91°49'W
New Ireland	PP	664	3°01'S	151°30'E
Newkirk		376	36°52'N	97°03'W
New Liskeard	CA	390	47°30'N	79°40'W
Newllano		378	31°06'N	93°16'W
Newman	AS	656	23°23'S	119°41'E
Newmarket		374	44°03'N	79°28'W
Newmarket	JM	414	18°10'N	77°55'W
New Martinsville		374	39°38'N	80°51'W
New Mexico		376	34°30'N	106°00'W
Newnan		378	33°21'N	84°47'W
New Norfolk	AS	656	42°47'S	147°04'E
New Orleans	US	398	29°57'N	90°04'W
New Philadelphia		374	40°29'N	81°26'W
New Plymouth	NZ	663	39°03'S	174°04'E
New Port		382	12°03'N	68°50'W
Newport		372	48°11'N	117°02'W
Newport		372	44°38'N	124°03'W
Newport		378	35°36'N	91°16'W
Newport		558	52°01'N	4°50'W
Newport	UK	626	50°42'N	1°18'W
Newport	UK	626	51°35'N	2°59'W
Newport News	US	398	36°58'N	76°25'W
New Providence	BF	402	24°47'N	77°39'W
New Quay	UK	626	52°12'N	4°21'W
Newquay	UK	626	50°24'N	5°04'W
New Roads		378	30°42'N	91°26'W
New Rockford		370	47°40'N	99°08'W
New Ross	EI	592	52°23'N	6°57'W
Newry	AS	656	16°02'S	129°16'E
Newry	UK	626	54°11'N	6°20'W
New Sandy Bay Village	VC	418	13°21'N	61°08'W
New Shagunnu	NI	316	10°20'N	4°26'E
Newton		370	41°41'N	93°02'W
Newton		374	38°59'N	88°09'W
Newton		378	30°50'N	93°45'W
Newton		378	32°19'N	89°09'W
Newton		378	35°40'N	81°13'W
Newton	UK	626	55°14'N	3°24'W
Newton	US	398	38°02'N	97°20'W
Newton Abbot	UK	626	50°32'N	3°36'W
Newton Ground	SC	417	17°23'N	62°51'W
Newtonmore	UK	626	57°04'N	4°08'W
Newton Stewart	UK	626	54°58'N	4°29'W
New Town		372	47°58'N	102°29'W
Newtown	UK	626	52°31'N	3°18'W
Newtownabbey		558	54°39'N	5°54'W
Newtownards	UK	626	54°35'N	5°40'W
New Ulm	US	398	44°18'N	94°27'W
New Waterford	CA	390	46°14'N	60°04'W
New York		374	40°44'N	73°59'W
New York	US	398	40°44'N	73°59'W
New Zealand		38	42°00'S	174°00'E
Neya		466	53°18'N	43°54'E
Neyrīz	IR	502	29°12'N	54°19'E
Neyshābūr	IR	502	36°12'N	58°50'E
Neyveli	IN	496	11°37'N	79°27'E
Neyyāttinkara	IN	496	8°24'N	77°05'E
Nezahualcóyotl	MX	394	19°26'N	99°02'W
Ngabang	ID	500	0°23'N	109°57'E
Ngabé	CF	285	3°13'S	16°09'E
Ngabordamlu, Tanjung	ID	500	6°56'S	134°11'E
Ngabu	MI	306	16°28'S	34°54'E
Ngabwe	ZA	332	13°58'S	27°19'E
Ngaga	TZ	327	10°45'S	38°45'E
Ngahere	NZ	663	42°23'S	171°29'E
Ngajangel	PX	664	8°02'N	134°44'E
Ngala	NI	316	12°21'N	14°11'E
Ngålangkang	BT	486	27°27'N	91°35'E
Ngalipaeng	ID	500	3°24'N	125°37'E
Ngaloua	NG	314	13°34'N	12°54'E
Ngalu	ID	500	10°12'S	120°40'E
Ngama	CD	283	11°47'N	17°10'E
Ngambé	CM	280	4°14'N	10°37'E
Ngambwe Rapids	ZA	332	17°19'S	24°09'E
Ngamring	CH	490	29°13'N	87°09'E
Ngangerabeli Plain	KE	299	1°30'S	40°15'E
Ngangla Ringco	CH	490	31°40'N	83°00'E
Nganglong Kangri		470	32°46'N	80°57'E
Nganglong Shan	CH	490	32°00'N	83°00'E
N'gangula	AO	274	11°00'S	13°55'E
Ngangzê Co	CH	490	31°01'N	86°56'E
Ngao	TH	534	18°46'N	99°59'E
Ngaoundal	CM	280	6°27'N	13°17'E
Ngaoundéré	CM	280	7°19'N	13°35'E
Ngaov	LA	517	30°30'N	100°10'E
Ngapara	NZ	663	44°57'S	170°45'E
Ngaputaw	BM	487	16°32'N	94°42'E
Ngara	TZ	327	2°28'S	30°39'E
Ngaras	ID	500	5°28'S	104°15'E
Ngardmau	PX	664	7°37'N	134°36'E
Ngardmau Bay	PX	664	7°35'N	134°25'E
Ngardololoc	PX	664	7°01'N	134°16'E
Ngariungs	PX	664	8°01'N	134°44'E
Ngaruawahia	NZ	663	37°40'S	175°09'E
Ngatapa	NZ	663	38°35'S	177°48'E
Ngateguil, Pt.	PX	664	7°28'N	134°35'E
Ngathainggyaung	BM	487	17°24'N	95°05'E
Ngatik	FM	661	5°30'N	156°30'E
Ngato	CM	280	3°15'N	14°58'E
Ngatpang	PX	664	7°29'N	134°31'E
Ngawa	CH	490	32°54'N	101°42'E
Ngele	CG	287	2°42'N	19°14'E
Ngerengere	TZ	327	6°45'S	38°07'E
Nggatokae	BP	666	8°55'S	158°10'E
Nggela Pile	BP	666	9°10'S	160°15'E
Nggela Sule	BP	666	8°50'S	160°15'E
Ngidinga	CG	287	5°37'S	15°17'E
Ngiryi	RW	317	1°51'S	30°05'E
Ngiva	AO	274	17°03'S	15°47'E
Ngo	CF	285	2°29'S	15°45'E
Ngobasangel	PX	664	7°15'N	134°28'E
Ngofakiaha	ID	500	0°21'N	127°25'E
Ngogwa	TZ	327	3°47'S	32°29'E
Ngoïla	CM	280	2°38'N	14°00'E
Ngoko	CF	285	1°40'N	16°03'E
Ngoko	CM	280	1°40'N	16°03'E
Ngola II	GB	294	0°53'N	11°37'E
Ngolo Falls	CT	282	5°46'N	22°04'E
Ngoma	WA	313	17°52'S	24°45'E
Ngomahuru	ZI	334	20°26'S	30°44'E
Ngombi	GB	294	1°37'S	10°54'E
Ngomedzap	CM	280	3°15'N	11°12'E
Ngom Falls	EK	291	1°42'N	10°08'E
Ngon	GB	294	2°10'N	12°04'E
Ngong	KE	299	1°22'S	36°39'E
Ngonye Falls	ZA	332	16°39'S	23°33'E
Ngoqumaima	CH	490	32°15'N	86°30'E
Ngora	UG	330	1°27'N	33°46'E
Ngoring	CH	490	35°00'N	96°47'E
Ngoring Hu	CH	490	34°52'N	97°10'E
Ngoto	CT	282	3°59'N	17°22'E
N. Goulburn	AS	656	11°28'S	133°31'E
Ngoulemakong	CM	280	3°04'N	11°26'E
Ngounié	GB	294	0°37'S	10°18'E
Ngoura	CD	283	12°52'N	16°27'E
Ngouri	CD	283	13°38'N	15°22'E
Ngourti	NG	314	15°19'N	13°12'E
Ngouyo	CT	282	5°45'N	25°19'E
Ngoywa	TZ	327	5°56'S	32°48'E
Ngozi	BY	279	2°54'S	29°50'E
Ngozi	UG	330	1°30'N	32°12'E
Ngudu	TZ	327	2°58'S	33°20'E
Nguékokh	SG	319	14°31'N	17°00'W
Nguélémendouka	CM	280	4°23'N	12°55'E
Ngui	CT	282	6°28'N	22°49'E
Nguigmi	NG	314	14°16'N	13°05'E
Nguiu	AS	656	11°45'S	130°35'E
Ngukurr	AS	656	14°44'S	134°45'E

Ngulu	FM	661	8°30'N	138°00'E
Ngum	LA	517	18°09'N	103°06'E
Ngum Res., Nam	LA	517	18°35'N	102°34'E
Nguna	NH	669	19°30'S	168°00'E
Ngundu Halt	ZI	334	20°48'S	30°48'E
Ngunga	TZ	327	3°41'S	33°34'E
Ngunza	AO	274	11°13'S	13°50'E
Nguru	NI	316	12°53'N	10°27'E
Nguru Mountains	TZ	327	6°00'S	37°30'E
Nguti	CM	280	5°17'N	9°27'E
Nguyen Binh	VM	540	22°38'N	105°55'E
Ngwedaung	BM	487	19°34'N	97°11'E
Ngwelezana	SF	322	28°46'S	31°51'E
Ngwenya	WZ	326	26°08'S	31°04'E
Ngwerere	ZA	332	15°18'S	28°19'E
Nhamundá		384	2°14'S	56°43'W
Nhandugué	MZ	312	17°50'S	33°44'E
Nhangue-ia-Pepe	AO	274	9°42'S	15°07'E
Nharêa	AO	274	11°25'S	17°03'E
Nha Trang	VM	540	12°15'N	109°12'E
Nhiep	LA	517	19°00'N	103°30'E
Nhlangano	WZ	326	27°07'S	31°12'E
Nhon Trach	VM	540	10°42'N	106°50'E
Nho Quan	VM	540	20°18'N	105°45'E
Nhulunbuy	AS	656	12°11'S	136°47'E
Niabembe	CG	287	2°14'S	27°44'E
Niabi	GG	495	41°55'N	44°22'E
Niafounké	ML	307	15°56'N	4°00'W
Niagara		374	45°46'N	87°59'W
Niagara Escarpment		374	43°50'N	80°00'W
Niagara Falls	CA	390	43°05'N	79°04'W
Niagara Falls	US	398	43°05'N	79°03'W
Niagassola	GV	297	12°19'N	9°07'W
Niah	MY	518	3°52'N	113°44'E
Niakaramandougou	IV	288	8°40'N	5°17'W
Niamanbaye	GB	294	0°26'S	11°46'E
Niamey	NI	316	13°30'N	2°06'E
Niamtougou	TO	328	9°46'N	1°06'E
Niandan	GV	297	10°39'N	9°41'W
Niangara	CG	287	3°42'N	27°53'E
Niangoloko	UV	278	10°17'N	4°55'W
Nia-Nia	CG	287	1°24'N	27°37'E
Niaqornaarsuk		370	68°14'N	52°52'W
Niari	CF	285	3°56'S	12°12'E
Nias	ID	500	1°05'N	97°35'E
Niau		654	16°30'S	146°15'W
Nibbar	TS	329	36°18'N	8°46'E
Nibong Tebal	MY	518	5°10'N	100°29'E
Nīca	LG	596	56°21'N	21°04'E
Nicaragua		38	13°00'N	85°00'W
Nicaragua, Lago de	NU	415	11°30'N	85°30'W
Nicaro	CU	406	20°42'N	75°33'W
Nicastro-Sambiase	IT	593	38°59'N	16°19'E
Nice		372	39°07'N	122°50'W
Nice	FR	580	43°42'N	7°15'E
Niceto Perez	CU	406	20°03'N	75°18'W
Niceville	US	398	30°31'N	86°29'W
Nichinan	JA	506	31°36'N	131°23'E
Nicholas Channel	CU	406	23°25'N	80°05'W
Nicholasville		374	37°52'N	84°34'W
Nicholls		378	31°31'N	82°38'W
Nicholls Town	BF	402	25°09'N	78°00'W
Nicholson	AS	656	18°02'S	128°54'E
Nickel Centre	CA	390	46°34'N	80°49'W
Nickerie	NS	438	5°59'N	57°00'W
Nickol Bay	AS	656	23°30'S	127°30'E
Nicobar Islands		476	8°00'N	93°30'E
Nicola		372	50°10'N	120°40'W
Nicolás Bravo	MX	394	18°28'N	88°57'W
Nicolás Bravo	MX	394	29°22'N	107°56'W
Nicosia		470	35°10'N	33°22'E
Nicosia	IT	593	37°45'N	14°24'E
Nicoya	CS	405	10°09'N	85°27'W
Nicoya, Golfo de	CS	405	9°47'N	84°48'W
Nicoya, Península de	CS	405	10°00'N	85°25'W
Nictau		374	47°14'N	67°09'W
Nidau	SZ	622	47°07'N	7°14'E
Nidda	GM	584	50°25'N	9°00'E
Nido, Sa. del	MX	394	29°33'N	106°48'W
Nidzica	PL	606	53°22'N	20°26'E
Nie	CT	282	6°11'N	15°13'E
Niebüll	GM	584	54°48'N	8°50'E
Niederanven	LU	598	49°39'N	6°16'E
Niederaula	GM	584	50°48'N	9°36'E
Niedere Tauern	AU	568	47°29'N	13°54'E
Niefang	EK	291	1°50'N	10°14'E
Niegocin, J.	PL	606	54°00'N	21°40'E
Niekerkshoop	SF	322	29°20'S	22°50'E
Niélé	IV	288	10°12'N	5°38'W
Niemba	CG	287	5°57'S	28°26'E
Nienburg	GM	584	52°38'N	9°13'E
Niéri Ko	SG	319	13°21'N	13°23'W
Nieuw-Amsterdam	NS	438	5°53'N	55°05'W
Nieuw-Bergen	NL	602	51°36'N	6°03'E
Nieuw-Buinen	NL	602	52°57'N	6°56'E
Nieuwegein	NL	602	52°02'N	5°05'E
Nieuwe Pekela	NL	602	53°05'N	6°59'E
Nieuweschans	NL	602	53°11'N	7°12'E
Nieuwkoop	NL	602	52°09'N	4°47'E
Nieuw Krai Ker	ID	500	6°43'S	134°24'E
Nieuwleusen	NL	602	52°35'N	6°17'E
Nieuw-Nickerie	NS	438	5°54'N	57°01'W
Nieuwouldtville	SF	322	31°22'S	19°06'E
Nieuwpoort	BE	570	51°08'N	2°45'E
Nieuwpoort-Bad	BE	570	51°09'N	2°42'E
Nieuw-Schoonebeek	NL	602	52°39'N	6°59'E
Nieve	BL	422	14°01'S	65°48'W
Nieves, Pico de las	SP	618	27°58'N	15°34'W
Niğde	TU	535	37°59'N	34°42'E
Niger		38	16°00'N	8°00'E
Niger	GV	297	5°33'N	6°33'E
Niger, Mouths of the	NI	316	4°15'N	6°00'E
Niger Basin		262	16°00'N	3°00'W
Niger Delta		266	4°50'N	6°00'E
Nigeria		38	10°00'N	8°00'E
Niger Plains	GV	297	11°00'N	10°10'W
Nightcaps	NZ	663	45°58'S	168°02'E
Night Hawk Lake		374	48°15'N	81°00'W
Nigino		466	59°39'N	45°17'E
Nigríta	GR	588	40°55'N	23°30'E
Nihiru		654	16°30'S	142°00'W
Nihonmatsu	JA	506	37°35'N	140°26'E
Niigata	JA	506	37°55'N	139°03'E
Niihama	JA	506	33°58'N	133°16'E
Niihau	US	398	21°58'N	161°34'W
Nii-jima	JA	506	34°22'N	139°16'E
Niijimahon	JA	506	34°22'N	139°16'E
Niimi	JA	506	34°59'N	133°28'E
Nijlen	BE	570	51°10'N	4°39'E
Nijmegen	NL	602	51°50'N	5°51'E
Nijverdal	NL	602	52°22'N	6°28'E
Níkaia	GR	588	39°33'N	22°27'E
Nikaria (Ikaría)	GR	588	37°35'N	26°10'E
Nikaweratiya	CE	530	7°45'N	80°07'E
Nikel'	RS	612	69°24'N	30°12'E
Nikel'tau	KZ	510	50°23'N	58°13'E
Nikiniki	ID	500	9°49'S	124°28'E
Nikishka	US	398	60°43'N	151°19'W
Nikísiani	GR	588	40°57'N	24°09'E
Nikitovka		560	50°22'N	38°25'E
Nikki	BN	276	9°56'N	3°12'E
Nikolaevo	BU	573	42°38'N	25°48'E
Nikolayevka		560	53°08'N	47°12'E
Nikolayevka	UP	624	47°32'N	30°45'E
Nikolayevka	UP	624	48°51'N	37°46'E
Nikolayevo		560	58°16'N	29°27'E
Nikolayevsk		560	50°01'N	45°26'E
Nikolayevsk-na-Amure	RS	612	53°08'N	140°44'E
Nikol'sk	RS	612	53°43'N	46°06'E
Nikol'skiy	KZ	510	47°55'N	67°30'E
Nikol'skiy Torzhok		556	59°53'N	38°46'E
Nikol'skoye		466	47°45'N	46°21'E
Nikol'skoye	RS	612	55°12'N	166°00'E
Nikonga	TZ	327	4°40'S	31°28'E
Nikonova Gora		466	60°22'N	36°07'E
Nikopol	BU	573	43°42'N	24°54'E
Nikopol'	UP	624	47°34'N	34°24'E
Niksar	TU	535	40°36'N	36°58'E
Nīkshahr	IR	502	26°13'N	60°12'E
Nikšić	YO	630	42°46'N	18°58'E
Nikumaroro (Gardner I.)	KR	660	4°30'S	174°30'W
Nikunau	KR	660	1°30'S	177°00'E
Nila		648	6°49'S	129°33'E
Niland		376	33°14'N	115°31'W
Nilande Atoll	MV	519	3°00'N	72°55'E
Nilaveli	CE	530	8°40'N	81°12'E
Nile	EG	290	15°14'S	38°26'E
Nile Delta	EG	290	31°00'N	31°00'E
Nilgiri Hills	IN	496	11°25'N	76°30'E
Nilka	CH	490	43°46'N	82°19'E
Nilphāmāri	BG	485	25°56'N	88°51'E
Nilsiä	FI	578	63°12'N	28°05'E
Nīmach	IN	496	24°28'N	74°52'E
Nīmāj		470	26°10'N	74°00'E
Nīmbahera		470	24°37'N	74°41'E
Nimba Mt.	GV	297	7°32'N	8°52'W
Nimba Mts.	GV	297	7°37'N	8°25'W
Nimebd, Mount	IV	288	7°35'N	8°30'W
Nîmes	FR	580	43°49'N	4°20'E
Nimnyrskiy	RS	612	57°48'N	125°23'E
Nimpo Lake	CA	390	52°20'N	125°08'W
Nimu		470	34°12'N	77°20'E
Nimule	SU	324	3°36'N	32°03'E
Nin	HR	574	44°14'N	15°11'E
Nindirí	NU	415	12°00'N	86°08'W
Ninety Six		378	34°10'N	82°01'W
Ninfas, Punta	AR	419	42°59'S	64°18'W
Ninga		372	49°14'N	99°53'W
Ning'an	CH	490	44°22'N	129°25'E
Ningbo	CH	490	29°52'N	121°32'E
Ningde	CH	490	26°40'N	119°31'E
Ningerum	PP	664	5°40'S	141°09'E
Ningjing Shan	CH	490	31°45'N	97°15'E
Ningming	CH	490	22°11'N	107°04'E
Ningnan		472	27°03'N	102°46'E
Ningqiang	CH	490	32°48'N	106°12'E
Ninh Hoa	VM	540	12°28'N	109°07'E
Ninigo Group	PP	664	1°10'S	144°00'E
Ninigo Is.	PP	664	1°15'S	144°15'E
Ninohe	JA	506	40°16'N	141°17'E
Ninove	BE	570	50°50'N	4°01'E
Nintavur	CE	530	7°21'N	81°51'E
Nioaque		386	21°08'S	55°48'W
Niobrara	US	398	42°45'N	98°01'W
Niokolo Koba	SG	319	13°04'N	12°43'W
Nioku	IN	496	27°56'N	94°08'E
Niono	ML	307	14°15'N	6°00'W
Nionsamoridougou	GV	297	8°43'N	8°50'W
Nioro-du-Rip	SG	319	13°45'N	15°48'W
Nioro du Sahel	ML	307	15°14'N	9°35'W
Niort	FR	580	46°19'N	0°27'W
Níos		564	36°42'N	24°25'E
Nipa	PP	664	6°09'S	143°26'E
Nipawin	CA	390	53°22'N	104°00'W
Nipe, Bahía de	CU	406	20°47'N	75°42'W
Nipe, Sa. de	CU	406	20°28'N	75°49'W
Nipigon	CA	390	49°01'N	88°16'W
Nipigon, Lake	CA	390	49°50'N	88°30'W
Nipissing, Lake	CA	390	46°15'N	79°45'W
Niquelândia	BR	424	14°23'S	48°25'W
Niquero	CU	406	20°03'N	77°35'W
Niquinohomo	NU	415	11°54'N	86°06'W
Nīr	IR	502	38°02'N	47°59'E
Nirasaki	JA	506	35°42'N	138°27'E
Ñireguao	CI	428	45°14'S	71°44'W
Nirgua	VE	440	10°09'N	68°34'W
Nirmal	IN	496	19°06'N	78°21'E
Niš	YO	630	43°19'N	21°54'E
Nişāb	SA	528	29°11'N	44°43'E
Nişāb	YM	541	14°30'N	46°30'E
Niscemi	IT	593	37°09'N	14°23'E
Nishine	JA	506	39°55'N	141°05'E
Nishino'omote	JA	506	30°44'N	131°00'E
Nishio	JA	506	34°51'N	137°03'E
Nishi-suido (Western Channel)	KS	513	34°30'N	128°00'E
Nísiros	GR	588	36°35'N	27°10'E
Nisko	PL	606	50°29'N	22°08'E
Nisporeny	MD	601	47°05'N	28°11'E
Nissan	PP	664	4°22'S	154°20'E
Nisser	NO	604	59°10'N	8°30'E
Nissum Bredning	DA	576	56°38'N	8°22'E
Nisswa		374	46°31'N	94°17'W
Nith	UK	626	55°00'N	3°36'W
Niti Pass	IN	496	30°58'N	79°53'E
Nitra	LO	616	48°19'N	18°05'E
Nittedal	NO	604	60°05'N	10°55'E
Niuafo'ou	TN	667	15°50'S	176°10'W
Niuatoputapu	TN	667	16°00'S	174°10'W
Niubiziliang	CH	490	38°43'N	92°12'E
Niue	NZ	663	19°30'S	169°51'W
Niulakita (Nurakita)	TV	669	10°10'S	179°30'W
Niumaowu		474	40°58'N	125°00'E
Niutao	TV	669	6°05'S	177°10'E
Nivala	FI	578	63°54'N	24°54'E
Nivelles	BE	570	50°36'N	4°20'E
Nivernais, Collines de	FR	580	47°00'N	3°30'E
Nivshera		466	62°22'N	52°54'E
Nixa		374	37°02'N	93°17'W
Niyut, Gunung	ID	500	1°00'N	109°59'E
Niza	PO	608	39°31'N	7°39'W
Nizāmābād	IN	496	18°40'N	78°07'E
Nizao	DR	408	18°15'N	70°12'W
Nizh. Bestyakh		468	61°55'N	129°56'E
Nizhneangarsk	RS	612	55°47'N	109°33'E
Nizhnekamsk	RS	612	55°36'N	51°47'E
Nizhneudinsk	RS	612	54°54'N	99°03'E
Nizhnevartovsk	RS	612	60°57'N	76°38'E
Nizhneyansk	RS	612	71°26'N	136°04'E
Nizhniy Baskunchak		466	48°13'N	46°50'E
Nizhniy Chir		560	48°22'N	43°05'E
Nizhniye Sergi		466	56°40'N	59°18'E
Nizhniy Kislyay		560	50°50'N	40°11'E
Nizhniy-Kuranakh		468	58°49'N	125°32'E
Nizhniy Lomov		466	53°32'N	43°40'E
Nizhniy Novgorod	RS	612	56°20'N	44°00'E
Nizhniy Odes	RS	612	63°38'N	54°54'E
Nizhniy Pyandzh	TI	533	37°12'N	68°35'E
Nizhniy Tagil	RS	612	57°55'N	59°59'E
Nizhnyaya Omra		466	62°46'N	55°44'E
Nizhnyaya Pesha		556	66°46'N	47°47'E
Nizhnyaya Poyma		468	56°11'N	97°13'E
Nizhnyaya Tunguska	RS	612	64°00'N	95°00'E
Nizhnyaya Voch'		466	61°13'N	54°12'E
Nizhyn	UP	624	51°03'N	31°53'E
Nizip	TU	535	37°01'N	37°46'E
Nízke Beskydy	LO	616	49°25'N	20°15'E
Nízké Tatry	LO	616	49°10'N	20°00'E
Nizkiy, Mys		468	61°39'N	173°47'E
Nizwá	MU	523	22°54'N	57°30'E
Nizzana	IS	505	30°52'N	34°27'E
Njardhvík	IC	591	63°58'N	22°33'W
Njaweworo	SL	320	7°54'N	10°53'W
Njazidja (Grande Comore)	CN	284	12°10'N	43°40'E
Njeru	UG	330	0°27'N	33°09'E
Njombe	TZ	327	9°20'S	34°46'E
Njombe	TZ	327	6°56'S	35°06'E
Njoro	KE	299	0°20'S	35°56'E
Njoroveto	BP	666	7°50'S	156°40'E
Njurunda	SW	621	62°16'N	17°22'E
Nkambe	CM	280	6°38'N	10°40'E
Nkandla	SF	322	28°37'S	31°05'E
Nkayi	CF	285	4°11'S	13°17'E
Nkéni	CF	285	2°01'S	16°18'E
Nkhata Bay	MI	306	11°36'S	34°18'E
Nkhotakota	MI	306	12°57'S	34°17'E
Nkimi	EK	291	1°56'N	10°21'E
Nkok	GB	294	0°23'N	9°38'E
Nkomfap	NI	316	6°12'N	8°39'E
Nkomi, Lagune	GB	294	1°35'S	9°17'E
Nkonde	TZ	327	6°20'S	30°19'E
N'Kongsamba	CM	280	4°57'N	9°56'E
Nkourala	ML	307	11°22'N	6°06'W
Nkout	CM	280	2°35'N	12°47'E
Nkubu	KE	299	0°04'S	37°40'E
Nkululu	TZ	327	6°26'S	32°49'E
Nkusi	UG	330	1°07'N	30°40'E
N. Ljusterö	SW	621	59°31'N	18°31'E
Nmai Hka	BM	487	25°42'N	97°30'E
N. Manitou	US	398	45°07'N	86°27'W
N. Maslen Nos	BU	573	42°18'N	27°47'E
Nnewi	NI	316	6°01'N	6°55'E
Noākhāli	BG	485	22°47'N	90°55'E
Noāmundi	IN	496	22°09'N	85°32'E
Noarlunga	AS	656	35°11'S	138°30'E
Noatak		368	67°00'N	162°30'W
Noayong	EK	291	1°22'N	10°42'E
Nobeoka	JA	506	32°35'N	131°40'E
Noble		376	35°08'N	97°23'W
Noblesville		374	40°02'N	86°00'W
Noboa	EC	432	1°24'S	80°23'W
Noboribetsu	JA	506	42°27'N	141°11'E
Nobres	BR	424	14°44'S	56°20'W
Noccundra	AS	656	27°50'S	142°36'E
Nocona		376	33°47'N	97°43'W
Nodashi	GG	495	43°03'N	42°24'E
Noel		374	36°32'N	94°29'W
Nogagami	CA	390	59°00'N	85°00'W
Nogales	US	398	31°20'N	110°56'W
Nogara	ET	293	13°53'N	36°32'E
Nogat	PL	606	54°17'N	19°17'E
Nogent	FR	580	48°02'N	5°21'E
Nogent-le-Rotrou	FR	580	48°19'N	0°49'E
Noginsk		560	55°51'N	38°27'E
Noginsk	RS	612	64°32'N	91°10'E
Nogliki	RS	612	51°48'N	143°10'E
Nogoonnuur	MG	520	49°33'N	90°17'E
Nogoyá	AR	419	32°24'S	59°48'W
Nogueira, Sa. de	PO	608	41°42'N	6°52'W
Noguera Pallaresa	SP	618	42°15'N	0°54'E
Noguera Ribagorzana	SP	618	41°40'N	0°43'E
Nohar	IN	496	29°11'N	74°46'E
Noh-Bec	MX	394	19°05'N	88°15'W
Noheji	JA	506	40°52'N	141°08'E
Nohkú, Punta	MX	394	19°36'N	87°26'W
Nohwa	KS	513	34°12'N	126°35'E
Noi	LA	517	17°00'N	105°00'E
Noire	MP	309	20°17'S	57°25'E
Noire (Da)	VM	540	21°30'N	104°00'E
Noirmoutier, Ile de	FR	580	46°58'N	2°12'W
Nojima-zaki	JA	506	34°56'N	139°53'E
Nokaneng	BC	276	19°41'S	22°14'E
Nokhur	TX	537	38°29'N	57°01'E
Nokia	FI	578	61°28'N	23°30'E
Nokilalaki, Gunung	ID	500	1°13'S	120°08'E
Nok Kundi	PK	524	28°46'N	62°46'E
Nokou	CD	283	14°35'N	14°47'E
Nola	CT	282	3°32'N	16°03'E
Noli, Capo di	IT	593	44°12'N	8°26'E
Nolinsk		560	57°33'N	49°57'E
Nom	CH	490	43°47'N	94°58'E
Nomad	PP	664	6°16'S	142°14'E
Nomai Bay	PX	664	7°30'N	134°35'E
Nombre de Dios, Cordillera	HO	412	15°40'N	86°40'W
Nome	US	398	64°31'N	165°24'W
Nomgon	MG	520	42°50'N	105°07'E
Nomhon	CH	490	36°23'N	96°00'E
Nomo-zaki	JA	506	32°33'N	129°44'E
Nomtsas	WA	313	24°30'S	16°45'E
Nomuka Group	TN	667	20°10'S	175°00'W
Nomwin Atoll		648	9°00'N	153°00'E
Nonacho L.		368	62°40'N	109°30'W
Nondwa	TZ	327	6°26'S	35°20'E
Nondweni	SF	322	28°11'S	30°49'E
Nong'an		474	44°26'N	125°11'E
Nong Bua	TH	534	15°52'N	100°35'E
Nong Bua Lamphu	TH	534	17°11'N	102°25'E
Nong Chang	TH	534	15°23'N	99°51'E
Nongempulu	CG	287	3°44'S	20°26'E
Nongenturi	CG	287	3°04'S	19°52'E
Nong Het	LA	517	19°29'N	103°59'E
Nong Khai	TH	534	17°52'N	102°44'E
Nongoma	SF	322	27°53'S	31°38'E
Nong Pet	LA	517	19°34'N	103°24'E
Nong Phai	TH	534	15°59'N	101°04'E
Nonidas	WA	313	22°35'S	14°37'E
Nonoai	BR	424	27°21'S	52°47'W
Nonoava	MX	394	27°28'N	106°44'W
Nonogasta	AR	419	29°18'S	67°30'W
Nonouti	KR	660	0°50'S	174°30'E
Nonsan	KS	513	36°12'N	127°05'E
Non Sung	TH	534	15°11'N	102°16'E
Nonthaburi	TH	534	13°50'N	100°29'E
Noordbeveland	NL	602	51°34'N	3°41'E
Noordoewer	WA	313	28°44'S	17°38'E
Noormarkku	FI	578	61°34'N	21°47'E
Nootka		372	49°37'N	126°37'W
Nootka		372	49°41'N	126°41'W
Nopala	MX	394	16°06'N	97°10'W
Nóqui	AO	274	5°51'S	13°25'E
Nora		558	59°31'N	15°02'E
Nor Achin	AM	482	40°18'N	44°35'E
Norala	RP	526	6°33'N	124°37'E
Noranside	AS	656	22°13'S	140°04'E
Norashen	AM	482	41°11'N	44°20'E
Norassouba	GV	297	10°55'N	9°29'W
Norberg		558	60°04'N	15°56'E
Norcia	IT	593	42°48'N	13°05'E
Nord, Massif du	HA	412	19°30'N	72°15'W
Nord-Aukra	NO	604	62°47'N	6°54'E
Nordborg	DA	576	55°03'N	9°45'E
Nordby	DA	576	55°58'N	10°34'E
Nordegg		368	52°28'N	116°05'W
Norden	GM	584	53°36'N	7°12'E
Nordenham	GM	584	53°30'N	8°29'E
Norderney	GM	584	53°44'N	7°07'E
Norderney	GM	584	53°42'N	7°09'E
Norderstedt	GM	584	53°43'N	9°59'E
Nordeste	AO	274	7°24'S	21°46'E
Nordeste de las Villas, Llanura del	CU	406	22°10'N	78°30'W
Nordfjord		558	61°54'N	5°12'E
Nordfjordeid	NO	604	61°54'N	6°00'E
Nordfriesische Inseln	GM	584	54°30'N	8°00'E
Nordhausen	GM	584	51°31'N	10°48'E
Nordholz	GM	584	53°47'N	8°36'E
Nordhorn	GM	584	52°26'N	7°05'E
Nordkapp (North Cape)	NO	604	71°11'N	25°48'E
Nordkjosbotn	NO	604	69°13'N	19°32'E
Nordli	NO	604	64°28'N	13°37'E
Nördlingen	GM	584	48°51'N	10°30'E
Nordmaling	SW	621	63°34'N	19°30'E
Nord-Ostsee-Kanal	GM	584	53°53'N	9°08'E
Nordstrand	GM	584	53°37'N	6°43'E
Nordvika	NO	604	63°25'N	8°04'E
Nore, Pic de	FR	580	43°25'N	2°27'E
Norfeo, Cabo	SP	618	42°15'N	3°16'E
Norfolk	US	398	42°01'N	97°25'W
Norfolk	US	398	36°50'N	76°16'W
Norfolk Island	AS	656	29°02'S	167°57'E
Norg	NL	602	53°04'N	6°28'E
Norheimsund	NO	604	60°22'N	6°08'E
Noril'sk	RS	612	69°20'N	88°06'E
Nor Kharberd	AM	482	40°06'N	44°29'E
Norman	US	398	35°13'N	97°26'W
Normanby		648	15°24'S	144°54'E
Normanby Island	PP	664	10°05'S	151°50'E
Normandia	BR	424	3°51'N	59°39'W
Normandie, Collines de	FR	580	48°40'N	0°30'W
Normanton	AS	656	17°40'S	141°05'E
Norman Wells	CA	390	65°18'N	126°52'W
Normétal		370	49°00'N	79°22'W
Norobanta Fula	PU	298	12°37'N	15°03'W
Norotshama	WA	313	28°22'S	17°40'E
Ñorcuinco	AR	419	41°51'S	70°54'W
Nørre Nebel	DA	576	55°47'N	8°18'E
Nørre Vorupør	DA	576	56°57'N	8°24'E
Norrköping	SW	621	58°36'N	16°11'E
Norrland	SW	621	65°00'N	19°30'E
Norrsundet	SW	621	60°56'N	17°08'E
Norrtälje	SW	621	59°46'N	18°42'E
Nors	DA	576	57°01'N	8°41'E
Norseman	AS	656	32°12'S	121°46'E
Norsjö	SW	621	64°55'N	19°29'E
Norte, Cabo do	BR	424	1°40'N	49°57'W
Norte, Punta	AR	419	42°17'S	63°45'W
Norte de Chiapas, Sa. del	MX	394	16°45'N	93°00'W
Norte de las Villas, Llanura del	CU	406	22°30'N	80°00'W
North Adams		374	42°42'N	73°06'W
Northallerton	UK	626	54°20'N	1°26'W
Northam	AS	656	31°40'S	116°40'E
Northampton	AS	656	28°21'S	114°37'E
Northampton	UK	626	52°13'N	0°53'W
North Andaman		476	13°15'N	92°55'E
North Balabac Strait	RP	526	8°10'N	117°04'E
North Battleford	CA	390	52°47'N	108°17'W
North Bay	CA	390	46°19'N	79°28'W
North Bend		372	49°51'N	121°30'W
North Bend		372	43°24'N	124°13'W
North Bengal Plains	BG	485	26°10'N	88°40'E
North Berwick	UK	626	56°03'N	2°42'W
North C.	NZ	663	34°24'S	173°05'E
North Caicos		382	21°58'N	71°54'W
North Canadian		376	36°00'N	98°15'W
North Cape		388	53°55'S	36°30'W
North Cape		654	34°30'S	173°30'E
North Cape (Nordkapp)	NO	604	71°11'N	25°48'E
North Carolina		374	35°30'N	79°15'W
North Cay	BF	402	25°05'N	77°25'W
North Channel	EI	592	46°04'N	83°21'W
North Charleston		378	32°52'N	79°58'W
North China Plain (Huabei Pingyuan)	CH	490	38°30'N	118°00'E
North Conway		374	44°03'N	71°07'W
North Crossett		378	33°09'N	91°56'W
North Dakota		372	47°30'N	100°00'W
North Dorset Downs	UK	626	51°00'N	2°30'W
North Downs	UK	626	51°17'N	0°13'W
North Eagle Butte	US	398	45°00'N	101°13'W
Northeast C.	US	398	63°16'N	168°44'W
North East Pt.	AS	656	22°27'S	150°44'E
Northeast Pt.	JM	414	18°08'N	76°20'W
North Entrance	PP	664	8°15'S	144°30'E
Northern European Plain	GM	584	53°10'N	10°00'E
Northern Mariana Is.		654	16°00'S	145°30'E
Northern Range	TD	438	10°44'N	61°15'W
Northern Sporades (Voriai Sporádhes)	GR	588	39°15'N	23°55'E
Northfield		374	44°27'N	93°09'W
Northfield		374	44°09'N	72°39'W
North Fond du Lac		374	43°48'N	88°27'W
North Fourchu	CA	390	45°43'N	60°15'W
Northgate	CA	390	49°00'N	102°16'W
North Head	NZ	663	36°25'S	174°03'E
North Horr	KE	299	3°19'N	37°04'E
North Hutchinson		378	27°33'N	80°19'W
North Huvadhu Atoll	MV	519	0°50'N	73°15'E
North Island	KE	299	4°04'N	36°03'E
North Island	NZ	663	39°00'S	176°00'E
North Kinangop	KE	299	0°36'S	36°35'E
North Knife Lake	CA	390	58°17'N	97°01'W
North Lakhimpur	IN	496	27°14'N	94°07'E
North Liberty		374	41°44'N	91°35'W
North Loup		372	41°16'N	98°24'W
North Minch	UK	626	57°54'N	5°56'W
North Myrtle Beach	US	398	33°48'N	78°41'W
North Negril Pt.	JM	414	18°22'N	78°20'W
North Ogden		372	41°17'N	111°58'W
North Pacific		36	20°32'N	159°54'E
North Platte	US	398	41°08'N	100°45'W
North Platte	US	398	41°07'N	100°42'W
North Point	BB	403	13°20'N	59°36'W
North Pole		368	64°45'N	147°20'W
North Port		378	27°03'N	82°15'W
North Pt.		374	45°00'N	83°30'W
North Richland Hills		378	32°51'N	97°13'W
North Saskatchewan	CA	390	53°14'N	105°05'W
North Sea		556	40°55'N	72°24'W
North Shields	UK	626	55°00'N	1°27'W
North Sioux City		372	42°31'N	96°29'W
North Spirit Lake	CA	390	52°26'N	92°58'W
North Star	CA	390	56°51'N	117°38'W
North Syracuse		374	43°08'N	76°07'W
North Taranaki Bight	NZ	663	38°42'S	174°15'E
North Terre Haute		374	39°31'N	87°21'W
North Tolsta	UK	626	58°20'N	6°13'W
Northton		558	57°47'N	7°04'W
North Uist	UK	626	57°35'N	8°23'W
Northumberland, C.	AS	656	38°03'S	140°39'E
Northumberland Islands	AS	656	21°40'S	150°00'E
North Union	VC	418	13°13'N	61°08'W
North Vernon		374	39°00'N	85°37'W
North Walsham	UK	626	52°49'N	1°23'E
North West C.	AS	656	21°47'S	114°07'E
Northwest Harborcreek		374	42°09'N	79°59'W
North West Highlands	UK	626	57°04'N	5°14'W
Northwest Providence Channel	BF	402	26°10'N	78°20'W
Northwest Pt.	JM	414	18°26'N	78°13'W
North West River	CA	390	53°32'N	60°08'W
North Wilkesboro		374	36°09'N	81°08'W
Northwood		372	47°44'N	97°33'W
Norton		374	36°56'N	82°36'W
Norton	US	398	39°49'N	99°53'W
Norton	ZI	334	17°53'S	30°38'E
Norton Shaw, C.	CA	390	76°27'N	78°29'W
Norton Shores		374	43°10'N	86°15'W
Norton Sound	US	398	64°00'N	164°00'W
Nortorf	GM	584	54°10'N	9°52'E
Norwalk		374	41°14'N	82°36'W
Norwalk		374	41°28'N	93°40'W
Norwalk		374	41°07'N	73°25'W
Norway		370	45°47'N	87°54'W
Norway		38	62°00'N	10°00'E
Norway House	CA	390	53°59'N	97°50'W
Norwegian Bay	CA	390	77°45'N	90°30'W
Norwegian Sea		556	70°00'N	5°00'W
Norwich		374	41°31'N	72°04'W
Norwich		374	42°32'N	75°31'W
Norwich		374	42°59'N	80°36'W
Norwich	UK	626	52°36'N	1°18'E
Norwood		374	39°09'N	84°27'W
Noshaq	AF	480	36°26'N	71°50'E
Noshiro	JA	506	40°12'N	140°02'E
Nosŏng	KS	513	35°54'N	127°33'E
Nosong, Tanjong	MY	518	5°38'N	115°36'E
Nosop (Nossob)	WA	313	26°54'S	20°41'E
Nosovaya		560	57°15'N	45°35'E
Nosovka	UP	624	50°56'N	31°35'E
Noşratābād	IR	502	29°54'N	59°59'E
Nossa Senhora da Glória		386	10°14'S	37°25'W
Nossa Senhora do Socorro		386	10°49'S	37°09'W
Noss Head	UK	626	58°28'N	3°03'W
Nossob (Nosop)	WA	313	26°54'S	20°41'E
Nossombougou	ML	307	13°06'N	7°56'W
Nossy-Bé		268	12°00'S	47°30'E
Nostheast Providence Channel	BF	402	25°40'N	77°09'W
Nosy-Varika	MA	304	20°35'S	48°32'E
Noszlop	HU	590	47°11'N	17°28'E
Notec	PL	606	52°44'N	15°25'E
Notikewin		368	56°59'N	117°38'W
Noto		472	37°48'N	137°08'E
Noto		564	36°53'N	15°04'E
Noto, Golfo di	IT	593	36°50'N	15°12'E
Notodden	NO	604	59°34'N	9°17'E
Noto-hanto	JA	506	37°20'N	137°00'E
Notoro-ko	JA	506	44°05'N	144°10'E
Notre Dame, Monts	CA	390	48°10'N	68°00'W
Notre Dame Bay	CA	390	49°50'N	55°00'W
Notre-Dame-du-Lac		374	47°36'N	68°48'W
Notre-Dame-du-Laus		374	46°05'N	75°36'W
Notre-Dame-du-Rosaire		374	48°48'N	71°23'W
Notsé	TO	328	6°57'N	1°10'E
Nottawasaga B.		374	44°40'N	80°20'W
Nottaway	CA	390	51°25'N	78°55'W
Nøtterøy	NO	604	59°14'N	10°24'E
Nottingham	UK	626	52°56'N	1°08'W
Nottingham I.	CA	390	63°20'N	77°55'W
Nouadhibou	MR	308	20°54'N	17°04'W
Nouakchott	MR	308	18°03'N	15°59'W
Noual, Sebhhet en	TS	329	34°20'N	9°45'W
Nouâmghâr	MR	308	19°22'N	16°31'W
Nouméa		650	22°16'S	166°27'E
Nouna	UV	278	12°44'N	3°52'W
Noupoort	SF	322	31°11'S	24°56'E
Nouvelle		374	48°08'N	66°19'W
Nouvelle Calédonie (New Caledonia)		650	22°00'S	164°00'E
Nouvelle France	MP	309	20°22'S	57°33'E
Nouzonville	FR	580	49°49'N	4°45'E
Nova	HU	590	46°41'N	16°41'E
Nova Andradina	BR	424	22°10'S	53°15'W
Nová Baňa	LO	616	48°26'N	18°39'E
Nova Basan'	UP	624	50°34'N	31°31'E
Nova Brasilândia	BR	424	14°58'S	54°57'W
Nová Bystrica	LO	616	49°21'N	19°01'E
Nova Caipemba	AO	274	7°26'S	14°39'E
Novaci	RO	610	45°11'N	23°40'E
Nova Cruz		386	6°28'S	35°26'W
Nová Dubnica	LO	616	48°55'N	18°09'E
Nova Friburgo	BR	424	22°16'S	42°32'W
Nova Gaia	AO	274	10°09'S	17°31'E
Nova Gorica	SI	617	45°57'N	13°39'E
Nova Gradiška	HR	574	45°16'N	17°23'E
Nova Iguaçu	BR	424	22°45'S	43°27'W
Nováky	LO	616	48°43'N	18°33'E
Nova Lamego	PU	298	12°17'N	14°13'W
Nova Londrina		386	22°45'S	53°00'W
Nova Lusitânia	MZ	312	19°53'S	34°36'E
Nova Mambone	MZ	312	21°00'S	35°00'E
Nova Olinda do Norte	BR	424	3°45'S	59°03'W
Nova Pazova	YO	630	44°56'N	20°14'E
Nova Prata	BR	424	28°47'S	51°36'W
Novara	IT	593	45°27'N	8°36'E
Nova Russas		384	4°42'S	40°34'W
Nova Sofala	MZ	312	20°10'S	34°44'E
Nova Ushytsya	UP	624	48°50'N	27°17'E
Nova Varcš	YO	630	43°28'N	19°49'E
Nova Venecia	BR	424	18°43'S	40°24'W
Nova Xavantina	BR	424	14°42'S	52°21'W
Novaya Astrakhan'	UP	624	49°07'N	38°36'E
Novaya Borovaya	UP	624	50°42'N	28°38'E
Novaya Igirma	RS	612	57°06'N	103°49'E
Novaya Ivanovka	UP	624	45°55'N	29°05'E
Novaya Kakhovka	UP	624	46°44'N	33°21'E
Novaya Kalitva		560	50°05'N	40°00'E
Novaya Kazanka	KZ	510	48°56'N	49°36'E
Novaya Ladoga		556	60°07'N	32°19'E
Novaya Mayachka	UP	624	46°36'N	33°14'E
Novaya Odessa	UP	624	47°19'N	31°47'E
Novaya Praga	UP	624	48°34'N	32°55'E
Novaya Sibir', O.	RS	612	75°00'N	149°00'E
Novaya Usman'		560	51°38'N	39°24'E
Novaya Vodolaga	UP	624	49°43'N	35°52'E
Novaya Zemlya	RS	612	74°00'N	57°00'E
Nova Zagora	BU	573	42°29'N	26°01'E
Nové Hrady	EZ	575	48°47'N	14°47'E
Nové Město nad Váhom	LO	616	48°45'N	17°50'E
Nové Město na Moravě	EZ	575	49°34'N	16°05'E
Nové Zámky	LO	616	47°59'N	18°10'E
Novgorod	RS	612	58°31'N	31°17'E
Novgorodka		560	57°03'N	28°35'E
Novgorodka	UP	624	48°22'N	32°40'E
Novgorod-Severskiy	UP	624	52°00'N	33°16'E
Novi Banovci	YO	630	44°57'N	20°17'E
Novi Bečej	YO	630	45°36'N	20°08'E
Novi Bilokorovychi	UP	624	51°07'N	28°03'E
Novi Iskŭr	BU	573	42°48'N	23°21'E
Novi Kneževac	YO	630	46°03'N	20°06'E
Novikovo		472	46°17'N	143°24'E
Novi Pazar	BU	573	43°21'N	27°12'E
Novi Pazar	YO	630	43°08'N	20°31'E
Novi Sad	YO	630	45°15'N	19°50'E
Novi Vinodolski	HR	574	45°08'N	14°48'E
Novo Airão	BR	424	1°56'S	61°25'W
Novoalekseyevka	KZ	510	50°08'N	55°39'E
Novoalekseyevka	UP	624	46°15'N	34°41'E
Novoanninskiy		560	50°32'N	42°41'E
Novo Aripuanã	BR	424	5°08'S	60°22'W
Novoazovs'k	UP	624	47°08'N	38°05'E
Novobogatinskoye	KZ	510	47°22'N	51°11'E
Novobohdanivka	UP	624	47°05'N	35°20'E
Novocheboksarsk	RS	612	56°08'N	47°30'E
Novocherkassk	RS	612	47°25'N	40°06'E
Novodevich'ye		560	53°36'N	48°50'E
Novodugino		560	55°38'N	34°18'E
Novograd-Volynskiy	UP	624	50°36'N	27°37'E
Novogrodovka	UP	624	48°12'N	37°21'E
Novogrudok	BO	569	53°36'N	25°50'E
Novo Hamburgo	BR	424	29°41'S	51°08'W
Novohradské Hory	EZ	575	48°38'N	14°40'E
Novokhopërskiy		560	51°05'N	41°34'E
Novokonstantinovka	KG	514	42°33'N	78°40'E
Novokubansk		560	45°06'N	41°03'E
Novokuybyshevsk	RS	612	53°07'N	49°58'E
Novokuznetsk	RS	612	53°45'N	87°06'E
Novolukoml'	BO	569	54°39'N	29°13'E
Novo Mesto	SI	617	45°48'N	15°10'E

Novo Miloševo	YO	630	45°43'N	20°18'E
Novomirgorod	UP	624	48°47'N	31°39'E
Novomoskovs'k	UP	624	48°37'N	35°12'E
Novomoskovsk	RS	612	54°05'N	38°13'E
Novonikolayevka	UP	624	47°59'N	35°55'E
Novonikolayevskiy		560	50°58'N	42°22'E
Novonukutskiy	RS	612	53°44'N	102°45'E
Novo-Odesskoye	KZ	510	50°25'N	72°17'E
Novo Oriente	BR	424	5°33'S	40°45'W
Novopavlovka	RS	612	51°13'N	109°14'E
Novopokrovka	UP	624	48°03'N	34°37'E
Novopokrovskaya		560	45°57'N	40°42'E
Novorontsovka	UP	624	47°30'N	33°56'E
Novorossiysk	RS	612	44°43'N	37°47'E
Novorossiyskoye	KZ	510	50°13'N	58°00'E
Novorzhev		560	57°02'N	29°20'E
Novoselitsa	UP	624	48°13'N	26°17'E
Novo Selo	MK	599	41°44'N	22°11'E
Novoselovo		466	55°04'N	90°59'E
Novosëlovskoye	UP	624	45°26'N	33°36'E
Novoshakhtinsk	RS	612	47°47'N	39°56'E
Novosibirsk	RS	612	55°02'N	82°56'E
Novosibirskiye Ostrova	RS	612	75°00'N	142°00'E
Novosil'		560	52°58'N	37°03'E
Novosokol'niki		560	56°21'N	30°10'E
Novotroitsk	RS	612	51°12'N	58°20'E
Novotroitskoye	UP	624	46°21'N	34°20'E
Novoukrainka	UP	624	48°19'N	31°32'E
Novoul'yanovsk		560	54°09'N	48°20'E
Novouzensk		466	50°28'N	48°10'E
Novovolyns'k	UP	624	50°44'N	24°10'E
Novovyatsk		466	58°29'N	49°44'E
Novovyazniki		560	56°12'N	42°10'E
Novoyamskoye		560	52°14'N	34°28'E
Novoyel'nya	BO	569	53°28'N	25°35'E
Novoye Mashezero		556	64°24'N	33°42'E
Novoyeniseysk		468	58°21'N	92°13'E
Novozybkov	RS	612	52°32'N	31°56'E
Novra		370	52°32'N	101°04'W
Novska	HR	574	45°20'N	16°59'E
Novyy Afon	GG	495	43°06'N	40°48'E
Nový Bohumín	EZ	575	49°55'N	18°20'E
Nový Bor	EZ	575	50°46'N	14°35'E
Nový Bydžov	EZ	575	50°15'N	15°30'E
Nový Jičín	EZ	575	49°36'N	18°01'E
Novyy Bug	UP	624	47°41'N	32°30'E
Novyye Sanzhary	UP	624	49°20'N	34°20'E
Novyy Oskol		560	50°45'N	37°51'E
Novyy Port	RS	612	67°40'N	72°52'E
Novyy Tap		466	57°02'N	67°45'E
Novyy Urengoy	RS	612	66°20'N	76°45'E
Nowa Dęba	PL	606	50°26'N	21°46'E
Nowa Ruda	PL	606	50°35'N	16°30'E
Nowa Sarzyna	PL	606	50°21'N	22°21'E
Nowa Sól	PL	606	51°48'N	15°43'E
Nowata		374	36°42'N	95°38'W
Nowe	PL	606	53°39'N	18°43'E
Nowe Miasto Lubawskie	PL	606	53°25'N	19°36'E
Nowgong	IN	496	26°21'N	92°40'E
Nowogard	PL	606	53°39'N	15°07'E
Nowrangapur		476	19°14'N	82°33'E
Nowshera	PK	524	34°01'N	71°59'E
Nowy Dwór Mazowiecki	PL	606	52°26'N	20°43'E
Nowy Sącz	PL	606	49°38'N	20°43'E
Nowy Targ	PL	606	49°29'N	20°02'E
Now Zād	AF	480	32°24'N	64°28'E
Noyabr'sk	RS	612	63°10'N	75°13'E
Noyon		558	49°35'N	3°00'E
N. Peron	AS	656	13°07'S	129°32'E
N. Ronaldsay	UK	626	59°21'N	2°19'W
Nsah	CF	285	2°22'S	15°19'E
Nsak	GB	294	2°17'N	12°04'E
Nsanje	MI	306	16°55'S	35°16'E
Nsawam	GH	296	5°48'N	0°21'W
Nsoc	EK	291	1°08'N	11°16'E
Nsondia	CG	287	2°16'S	16°54'E
Nsopzup	BM	487	25°51'N	97°30'E
Nsukka	NI	316	6°52'N	7°23'E
Nsuta	GH	296	5°16'N	1°59'W
Ntaja	MI	306	14°52'S	35°32'E
Ntem	CM	280	2°15'N	9°45'E
Nterguent	MR	308	19°34'N	12°59'W
Ntobwe	RW	317	1°58'S	29°38'E
Ntoroko	UG	330	1°04'N	30°30'E
Ntoum	GB	294	0°22'N	9°47'E
Ntui	CM	280	4°27'N	11°38'E
Ntulume	CG	287	7°31'S	22°36'E
Ntungamo	UG	330	0°52'S	30°16'E
Ntusi	UG	330	0°03'N	31°13'E
Ntuzuma	SF	322	29°43'S	30°56'E
Ntwetwe Pan	BC	276	20°35'S	25°30'E
Nuanetsi		270	22°40'S	31°50'E
Nuariche	MX	394	25°23'N	101°45'W
Nubian Desert (As Sahra an Nubiyah)	SU	324	21°08'N	32°12'E
Nucet	RO	610	46°28'N	22°35'E
Nüden	MG	520	43°58'N	110°37'E
Nudo de Apolobamba	BL	422	15°30'S	68°30'W
Nueces	US	393	27°50'N	97°29'W
Nueces Plains		376	28°15'N	99°55'W
Nueltin L.	CA	390	60°20'N	99°30'W
Nueva Alejandría	PE	436	5°57'S	73°27'W
Nueva Antioquia	CO	430	6°05'N	69°26'W
Nueva Arcadia	HO	412	15°00'N	88°45'W
Nueva Armenia	HO	412	13°45'N	87°10'W
Nueva Ciudad Guerrero	MX	394	26°34'N	99°13'W
Nueva Concepción	GT	411	14°10'N	91°20'W
Nueva Concepcíon	ES	409	14°08'N	89°18'W
Nueva Constitución	AR	419	35°57'S	66°10'W
Nueva Esparta	ES	409	13°47'N	87°50'W
Nueva Esperanza	AR	419	26°12'S	64°16'W
Nueva Florida	VE	440	8°57'N	69°01'W
Nueva Germania	PA	435	23°55'S	56°40'W
Nueva Gerona	CU	406	21°53'N	82°48'W
Nueva Helvecia	UY	439	34°18'S	57°14'W
Nueva Italia	MX	394	19°01'N	102°06'W
Nueva Loja	EC	432	0°06'N	76°52'W
Nueva Lubecka		388	44°32'S	70°24'W
Nueva Ocotepéque	HO	412	14°26'N	89°11'W
Nueva Palmira	UY	439	33°53'S	58°23'W
Nueva Paz	CU	406	22°46'N	81°45'W
Nueva Rosita	MX	394	27°57'N	101°13'W
Nueva San Salvador	ES	409	13°41'N	89°17'W
Nueve de Julio	AR	419	35°27'S	60°52'W
Nuevitas	CU	406	21°33'N	77°16'W
Nuevitas, Bahía de	CU	406	21°30'N	77°13'W
Nuevo, Golfo	AR	419	42°42'S	64°36'W
Nuevo Andoas	PE	436	2°41'S	76°30'W
Nuevo Berlín	UY	439	32°59'S	58°03'W
Nuevo Casas Grandes	MX	394	30°25'N	107°55'W
Nuevo Chagres	PM	417	9°13'N	80°05'W
Nuevo Delicias	MX	394	26°14'N	102°47'W
Nuevo Ideal	MX	394	24°52'N	105°04'W
Nuevo Laredo	MX	394	27°29'N	99°30'W
Nuevo León		376	25°40'N	100°00'W
Nuevo Mundo	BL	422	10°19'S	66°46'W
Nuevo Progeso	MX	394	18°38'N	92°18'W
Nuevo Progreso	MX	394	26°03'N	97°55'W
Nuevo Rocafuerte	EC	432	0°56'S	75°24'W
Nuevo Rodríguez		376	27°04'N	100°00'W
Nufenen	SZ	622	46°32'N	9°14'E
Nuga	MG	520	48°19'N	95°07'E
Nugaaleed Valley	SO	321	8°35'N	48°35'E
Nugget Pt.	NZ	663	46°28'S	169°50'E
Nuguria Islands	PP	664	3°20'S	154°55'E
Nuh, Ras	PK	524	25°06'N	62°23'E
Nui	TV	669	7°10'S	177°10'E
Nuits-Saint-Georges	FR	580	47°08'N	4°57'E
Nu Jiang (Salween)	CH	490	31°00'N	96°00'E
Nukiki	BP	666	6°45'S	156°30'E
Nuku	PP	664	3°41'S	142°28'E
Nuku'alofa	TN	667	21°08'S	175°12'W
Nukufetau	TV	669	7°55'S	179°10'E
Nuku Hiva		654	8°38'S	142°02'W
Nukulaelae	TV	669	9°30'S	179°50'E
Nukunonu		650	9°28'S	174°04'W
Nukus	UZ	539	42°29'N	59°38'E
Nules	SP	618	39°51'N	0°09'W
Nullagine	AS	656	21°53'S	120°06'E
Nullarbor	AS	656	31°26'S	130°55'E
Nullarbor Plain	AS	656	31°00'S	129°00'E
Nulu'erhu Shan	CH	490	41°42'N	119°42'E
Numan	NI	316	9°28'N	12°02'E
Numata	JA	506	36°38'N	139°03'E
Numazu		474	35°03'N	138°52'E
Numbi	CG	287	1°47'S	28°54'E
Numbulwar	AS	656	14°13'S	135°45'E
Numedalslågen	NO	604	60°00'N	9°00'E
Numfor	ID	500	1°00'N	135°00'E
Nummi	FI	578	60°24'N	23°53'E
Numto	RS	612	63°40'N	71°20'E
Numurkah		652	36°06'S	145°26'E
Nundle		652	31°28'S	151°08'E
Nungarin	AS	656	31°11'S	118°06'E
Nungnain Sum	CH	490	45°40'N	118°58'E
Nŭng-ni	KN	512	38°40'N	126°10'E
Nungo	MZ	312	13°25'S	37°46'E
Nungwe	TZ	327	2°46'S	32°01'E
Nunivak	US	398	59°51'N	168°04'W
Nuñoa	PE	436	14°28'S	70°38'W
Nunukan	ID	500	4°06'N	117°38'E
Nuon	IV	288	6°30'N	8°36'W
Nuoro	IT	593	40°19'N	9°20'E
Nupari	BP	666	10°15'S	165°50'E
Nuqūb	YM	541	14°58'N	45°47'E
Nuquí	CO	430	5°42'N	77°17'W
Nur	CH	490	36°23'N	81°07'E
Nura	KZ	510	50°30'N	69°59'E
Nūrābād	IR	502	30°07'N	51°31'E
Nurakita (Niulakita)	TV	669	10°10'S	179°30'W
Nurata	UZ	539	40°33'N	65°41'E
Nuratau, Khrebet	UZ	539	40°25'N	67°00'E
Nurek	TI	533	38°23'N	69°21'E
Nurhak		564	37°58'N	37°25'E
Nurhak Dag.	TU	535	38°04'N	37°28'E
Nuri	MX	394	28°02'N	109°22'W
Nuria, Altiplanicie de	VE	440	7°40'N	61°20'W
Nūrla		470	34°19'N	76°58'E
Nurmes	FI	578	63°32'N	29°10'E
Nurmijärvi	FI	578	60°28'N	24°48'E
Nurmo	FI	578	62°50'N	22°54'E
Nürnberg	GM	584	49°27'N	11°05'E
Nur Turu	CH	490	36°53'N	93°27'E
Nūsah	YM	541	14°00'N	46°42'E
Nusaybin	TU	535	37°04'N	41°13'E
Nusayriyah, Jabal al	SY	531	35°00'N	36°05'E
Nūshābād		470	34°05'N	51°26'E
Nu Shan	CH	490	27°00'N	99°00'E
Nushki	PK	524	29°33'N	66°01'E
Nutwood Downs	AS	656	15°49'S	134°10'E
Nuur Fanax	SO	321	4°24'N	45°24'E
Nuwākot	NP	522	28°08'N	83°53'E
Nuwara Eliya	CE	530	6°58'N	80°46'E
Nuwata	CA	390	65°08'N	77°37'W
Nuwaybi'	EG	290	28°58'N	34°39'E
Nuweveldberg	SF	322	32°19'S	22°26'E
Nwa	CM	280	6°21'N	11°04'E
Nxaunxau	BC	276	18°54'S	21°05'E
Nyaake	LI	301	4°51'N	7°36'W
Nyabing		652	33°32'S	118°09'E
Nyabisindu	RW	317	2°21'S	29°45'E
Nyabugete	BY	279	3°28'S	29°21'E
Nyagahita	RW	317	1°30'S	30°12'E
Nyagasozi	RW	317	2°10'S	29°46'E
Nya-Ghezi	CG	287	2°39'S	28°52'E
Nyagyn'		466	62°08'N	65°36'E
Nyahua	TZ	327	5°25'S	33°21'E
Nyahururu Falls	KE	299	0°02'N	36°22'E
Nyainqêntanglha Feng	CH	490	30°23'N	90°34'E
Nyainqentanglha Shan	CH	490	30°10'N	90°00'E
Nyainrong	CH	490	32°00'N	92°15'E
Nyakabindi	TZ	327	2°38'S	33°59'E
Nyakanyasi	TZ	327	1°11'S	31°13'E
Nyakishozo	UG	330	0°31'S	30°08'E
Nyakrom	GH	296	5°37'N	0°47'W
Nyaksimvol'	RS	612	62°26'N	60°52'E
Nyakulenga	ZA	332	13°03'S	23°27'E
Nyala	SU	324	12°03'N	24°53'E
Nyalam	CH	490	28°11'N	85°57'E
Nyalikungu	TZ	327	3°11'S	33°47'E
Nyamandhlovu	ZI	334	19°52'S	28°16'E
Nyamapande	ZI	334	16°58'S	32°50'E
Nyambeni Range	KE	299	0°20'N	38°00'E
Nyambiti	TZ	327	2°50'S	33°25'E
Nyamina	ML	307	13°19'N	6°59'W
Nyamlell	SU	324	9°07'N	26°58'E
Nyamtumbo	TZ	327	10°30'S	36°06'E
Nyamutera	RW	317	1°37'S	29°38'E
Nyando		270	16°15'S	34°00'E
Nyandoma		466	61°40'N	40°12'E
Nyanga		270	33°59'S	18°35'E
Nyanga	CF	285	2°58'S	10°15'E
Nyanga	GB	294	2°58'S	10°18'E
Nyanga	GB	294	1°06'S	9°03'E
Nyangui	ZI	334	17°51'S	32°46'E
Nyanyadzi	ZI	334	19°46'S	32°25'E
Nyanza-Lac	BY	279	4°20'S	29°36'E
Nyanzwa	TZ	327	7°21'S	36°17'E
Nyaruonga	TZ	327	3°01'S	30°52'E
Nyassa, Lake (Malawi)	MI	306	12°00'S	34°30'E
Nyaungu	BM	487	21°12'N	94°55'E
Nyawarungu	RW	317	2°00'S	29°40'E
Nyazura	ZI	334	18°43'S	32°10'E
Nybergsund	NO	604	61°15'N	12°20'E
Nyborg	DA	576	55°19'N	10°48'E
Nyborg	NO	604	70°10'N	28°36'E
Nybro	SW	621	56°45'N	15°54'E
Nyda	RS	612	66°36'N	72°54'E
Nyêmo	CH	490	29°24'N	90°15'E
Nyenasi	GH	296	5°36'N	1°36'W
Nyeri	KE	299	0°25'S	36°57'E
Nyerol	SU	324	8°41'N	32°02'E
Nyika Plateau	MI	306	10°40'S	33°50'E
Nyima	CH	490	31°49'N	88°07'E
Nyimba	ZA	332	14°34'S	30°48'E
Nyingchi	CH	490	29°31'N	94°24'E
Nyíradony	HU	590	47°41'N	21°55'E
Nyírbátor	HU	590	47°50'N	22°08'E
Nyíregyháza	HU	590	47°57'N	21°43'E
Nyiri Desert	KE	299	2°10'S	36°50'E
Nyivé	TO	328	6°46'N	0°35'E
Nykarleby (Uusikaarlepyy)	FI	578	63°32'N	22°32'E
Nykøbing	DA	576	54°46'N	11°53'E
Nykøbing	DA	576	55°55'N	11°41'E
Nykøbing	DA	576	56°48'N	8°52'E
Nyköping	SW	621	58°45'N	17°00'E
Nykroppa	SW	621	59°38'N	14°18'E
Nyland	SW	621	63°00'N	17°46'E
Nylstroom	SF	322	24°42'S	28°24'E
Nymagee	AS	656	32°04'S	146°20'E
Nymburk	EZ	575	50°11'N	15°03'E
Nynäshamn	SW	621	58°54'N	17°57'E
Nyngan		652	31°34'S	147°11'E
Nyoma Rap		470	33°11'N	78°38'E
Nyon	SZ	622	46°23'N	6°14'E
Nyong	CM	280	3°17'N	9°54'E
Nýřany	EZ	575	49°43'N	13°12'E
Nyrob		466	60°43'N	56°44'E
Nýrsko	EZ	575	49°18'N	13°09'E
Nyrud	NO	604	69°09'N	29°13'E
Nysa	PL	606	50°27'N	17°19'E
Nysa	PL	606	50°49'N	17°40'E
Nyssa		372	43°52'N	116°59'W
Nysted	DA	576	54°40'N	11°45'E
Nyudo-zaki	JA	506	50°30'N	69°59'E
Nyuk, Oz.	RS	612	64°27'N	31°45'E
Nyukhcha		556	63°27'N	46°32'E
Nyuksenitsa		556	60°25'N	44°15'E
Nyukzha		468	56°00'N	123°00'E
Nyúl	HU	590	47°34'N	17°40'E
Nyunzu	CG	287	5°57'S	28°01'E
Nyurba	RS	612	63°18'N	118°20'E
Nyuvchim	RS	612	61°22'N	50°42'E
Nzamata	GB	294	1°00'S	10°07'E
Nzega	TZ	327	4°13'S	33°11'E
Nzérékoré	GV	297	7°45'N	8°49'W
Nzeret	CG	287	4°17'N	22°37'E
N'zeto	AO	274	7°15'S	12°52'E
Nzi	IV	288	5°57'N	4°50'W
Nzoho	CT	282	5°20'N	20°09'E
N'zumbi	TP	318	0°04'N	6°33'E
Nzwani (Anjonan)	CN	284	12°15'S	44°25'E

O

Oa, Mull of	UK	626	55°35'N	6°19'W
Oahe, Lake	US	398	44°27'N	100°24'W
Oahu	US	398	21°19'N	158°17'W
Oakdale		378	30°48'N	92°39'W
Oakes	US	398	46°08'N	98°05'W
Oak Grove		374	36°39'N	87°26'W
Oak Grove		378	32°51'N	91°23'W
Oak Hill		374	37°58'N	81°08'W
Oakhurst		376	37°19'N	119°38'W
Oak Lake		372	49°46'N	100°38'W
Oakland		374	37°38'N	92°33'W
Oakland	US	398	37°48'N	122°16'W
Oakleigh		652	37°54'S	145°06'E
Oakley	US	398	39°07'N	100°51'W
Oakover	AS	656	21°30'S	121°00'E
Oak Ridge	US	398	36°00'N	84°16'W
Oakridge		372	43°44'N	122°27'W
Oakview		372	51°03'N	98°37'W
Oakville		374	38°28'N	90°18'W
Oamaru	NZ	663	45°05'S	170°57'E
Oarai	JA	506	36°47'N	140°32'E
Oatlands	AS	656	42°18'S	147°22'E
Oaxaca	MX	394	17°03'N	96°43'W
Ob	RS	612	61°00'N	70°00'E
Ob'		466	55°00'N	82°43'E
Oba	CA	390	49°04'N	84°06'W
Oba (Aoba)	NH	669	15°00'S	167°50'E
Obala	CM	280	4°10'N	11°32'E
Oballos	MX	394	27°27'N	101°23'W
Obama	JA	506	35°28'N	135°44'E
Oban	UK	626	56°25'N	5°28'W
Oban Hills	NI	316	5°30'N	8°35'E
O Barco	SP	618	42°25'N	6°59'W
Obaya	CG	287	1°20'S	27°46'E
Obbola	SW	621	63°41'N	20°17'E
Obeliai	LH	597	55°56'N	25°48'E
Obelisk	NZ	663	45°50'S	169°12'E
Oberá	AR	419	27°29'S	55°08'W
Oberhausen		558	51°28'N	6°51'E
Oberlin	US	398	39°47'N	100°32'W
Obernai	FR	580	48°28'N	7°29'E
Oberpfälzer Wald	GM	584	49°50'N	12°10'E
Oberpullendorf	AU	568	47°30'N	16°31'E
Oberriet	SZ	622	47°19'N	9°34'E
Oberstdorf	GM	584	47°24'N	10°17'E
Obertilliach	AU	568	46°42'N	12°38'E
Oberueckersee	GM	584	53°05'N	14°05'E
Oberursel	GM	584	50°12'N	8°35'E
Obervellach	AU	568	46°56'N	13°12'E
Oberwart	AU	568	47°18'N	16°12'E
Obi	ID	500	1°30'S	127°45'E
Obi, Kep.	ID	500	1°30'S	127°45'E
Obi, Selat	ID	500	0°52'S	127°33'E
Obiaruku	NI	316	5°51'N	6°09'E
Obidi	GB	294	0°21'S	11°45'E
Óbidos	BR	424	39°22'N	9°09'W
Óbidos	PO	608	1°55'S	55°31'W
Obigarm	TI	533	38°43'N	69°42'E
Obihiro	JA	506	42°55'N	143°12'E
Obilić	YO	630	42°41'N	21°05'E
Obira	JA	506	44°00'N	141°40'E
Obispo Bay		376	23°07'N	80°14'W
Obitochnyy Zaliv	UP	624	46°00'N	36°00'E
Oblesevo	MK	599	41°53'N	22°21'E
Obligado	PA	435	27°04'S	55°37'W
Oblivskaya		560	48°32'N	42°30'E
Obluch'ye	RS	612	49°00'N	131°05'E
Obninsk	RS	612	55°05'N	36°37'E
Obo		472	37°57'N	101°03'E
Obo	CT	282	5°24'N	26°29'E
Obock	DJ	289	11°58'N	43°17'E
Obokote	CG	287	0°52'S	26°19'E
Obo Liang	CH	490	38°49'N	92°42'E
Oborniki	PL	606	52°39'N	16°49'E
Obornyy, M.		556	67°47'N	40°45'E
Obouya	CF	285	0°56'S	15°43'E
Obozerskiy		556	63°26'N	40°19'E
Obrenovac	YO	630	44°39'N	20°12'E
Obrež	YO	630	43°46'N	21°21'E
Obsharovka		560	53°07'N	48°50'E
Obskaya Guba	RS	612	69°00'N	73°00'E
Obuasi	GH	296	6°12'N	1°40'W
Obubra	NI	316	6°05'N	8°19'E
Obudu	NI	316	6°40'N	9°10'E
Obukhov	UP	624	50°06'N	30°38'E
Obura	PP	664	6°31'S	145°57'E
Obzor	BU	573	42°49'N	27°53'E
Ocala	US	398	29°11'N	82°08'W
Ocallí	PE	436	6°09'S	78°18'W
Ocampo	MX	394	28°11'N	108°23'W
Ocampo	MX	394	27°20'N	102°21'W
Ocaña	CO	430	8°15'N	73°20'W
O Carballiño	SP	618	42°26'N	8°04'W
Occidental de Zapata, Ciénaga	CU	406	22°40'N	81°50'W
Ocean C.	US	398	59°31'N	139°47'W
Ocean City		374	38°19'N	75°05'W
Ocean Falls	CA	390	52°21'N	127°41'W
Ocean I. (Banaba)	KR	660	0°10'S	169°50'E
Ocean Park	US	398	46°29'N	124°02'W
Ocean Pines		374	38°22'N	75°10'W
Ocean Shores		372	46°57'N	124°09'W
Oceanside	US	398	33°11'N	117°22'W
Ocean View	SF	322	34°09'S	18°21'E
Ochakiv	UP	624	46°37'N	31°33'E
Ochamchira	GG	495	42°43'N	41°28'E
Ocher		466	57°52'N	54°44'E
Ochil Hills	UK	626	56°15'N	3°40'W
Ochkhamuri	GG	495	41°51'N	41°50'E
Ocho Rios	JM	414	18°23'N	77°07'W
Ochre River		370	51°03'N	99°44'W
Ochsenfurt	GM	584	49°39'N	10°05'E
Ockelbo	SW	621	60°53'N	16°43'E
Ocna Mureş	RO	610	46°23'N	23°51'E
Ocna Sibiului	RO	610	45°53'N	24°03'E
Ocnele Mari	RO	610	45°05'N	24°19'E
Ocoa	DR	408	18°16'N	70°35'W
Ocoa, Bahía de	DR	408	18°22'N	70°39'W
Ocoña	PE	436	16°24'S	73°04'W
Ocoña	PE	436	16°28'S	73°07'W
Oconee	US	398	31°58'N	82°33'W
Oconto	US	398	44°53'N	87°51'W
Oconto Falls		370	44°52'N	88°08'W
O Corgo	SP	618	42°57'N	7°25'W
Ocós	GT	411	14°29'N	92°10'W
Ocosingo	MX	394	16°54'N	92°05'W
Ocotal	NU	415	13°38'N	86°29'W
Ocotlán		380	16°48'N	96°40'W
Ocotlán	MX	394	20°21'N	102°46'W
Ocozocoautla	MX	394	16°46'N	93°22'W
Ocracoke		378	35°06'N	75°51'W
Ocros	PE	436	10°24'S	77°24'W
Octeville	FR	580	49°37'N	1°39'W
Ocú	PM	417	7°57'N	80°47'W
Ocumare del Tuy	VE	440	10°07'N	66°46'W
Ocurí	BL	422	18°50'S	65°50'W
Oda	GH	296	5°55'N	1°00'W
Oda	JA	506	35°10'N	132°27'E
Ódádhahraun	IC	591	65°09'N	17°00'W
Ŏdaejin	KN	512	41°23'N	129°43'E
Ōdate	JA	506	40°16'N	140°34'E
Odawara	JA	506	35°14'N	139°09'E
Odda	NO	604	60°04'N	6°33'E
Odder	DA	576	55°58'N	10°10'E
Odelouca	PO	608	37°11'N	8°29'W
Odem		376	27°57'N	97°34'W
Odemira	PO	608	37°36'N	8°38'W
Ödemiş	TU	535	38°13'N	27°59'E
Odendaalsrus	SF	322	27°52'S	26°41'E
Odense	DA	576	55°24'N	10°23'E
Oden Wald	GM	584	49°38'N	8°50'E
Oder	GM	584	51°40'N	10°06'E
Oder (Odra)	EZ	575	51°40'N	10°06'E
Oder-Havel-Kanal	GM	584	52°52'N	14°02'E
Odesa	UP	624	46°28'N	30°44'E
Odessa	US	398	31°50'N	102°22'W
Odiak	UG	330	1°38'N	32°56'E
Odiel	SP	618	37°11'N	6°56'W
Odienné	IV	288	9°30'N	7°34'W
Odimba	GB	294	1°08'S	10°00'E
Odintsovo		466	55°41'N	37°17'E
Odiongan	RP	526	12°24'N	121°59'E
Odivelas	PO	608	38°47'N	9°11'W
Odobeşti	RO	610	45°46'N	27°03'E
Odogbulu	NI	316	6°51'N	3°46'E
Odongk	CB	489	11°48'N	104°45'E
O'Donnell	US	398	32°57'N	101°49'W
Odoorn	NL	602	52°51'N	6°51'E
Odorheiu Secuiesc	RO	610	46°18'N	25°18'E
Odra (Oder)	EZ	575	51°40'N	10°06'E
Odravu	UG	330	3°22'N	31°16'E
Odry	EZ	575	49°40'N	17°50'E
Odžaci	YO	630	45°31'N	19°16'E
Odžak	BK	572	45°01'N	18°20'E
Odzi	ZI	334	18°58'S	32°23'E
Odzi	ZI	334	19°45'S	32°24'E
Odziba	CF	285	3°35'S	15°31'E
Oeiras	BR	424	7°01'S	42°08'W
Oelsnitz	GM	584	50°25'N	12°10'E
Oelwein		374	42°40'N	91°54'W
Oenpelli	AS	656	12°20'S	133°04'E
Oero . Nyuk		556	64°30'N	31°30'E
Oesterschelde	NL	602	51°30'N	4°00'E
Oetz	AU	568	47°12'N	10°53'E
Ofanto	IT	593	41°21'N	16°13'E
Ofaqim	IS	505	31°17'N	34°37'E
Ofenpass	SZ	622	46°39'N	10°17'E
Offenbach	GM	584	50°06'N	8°46'E
Offenburg	GM	584	48°28'N	7°56'E
Oficina María Elena	CI	428	22°21'S	69°40'W
Oficina Pedro de Valdivia	CI	428	22°36'S	69°40'W
Oftringen	SZ	622	47°19'N	7°55'E
Ōfunato	JA	506	39°04'N	141°43'E
Oga	JA	506	39°53'N	139°51'E
Ogachi	JA	506	39°01'N	140°25'E
Ōgaki		474	35°21'N	136°36'E
Ogallala	US	398	41°07'N	101°43'W
Ogawara-ko	JA	506	40°47'N	141°20'E
Ogbomosho	NI	316	8°08'N	4°14'E
Ogden		372	39°06'N	96°42'W
Ogden	US	398	41°13'N	111°58'W
Ogdensburg	US	398	44°41'N	75°29'W
Ogea Levu	FJ	660	19°00'S	178°10'W
Ogho	BP	666	6°50'S	156°50'E
Ogi	JA	506	37°49'N	138°17'E
Ogies	SF	322	26°03'S	29°04'E
Ogilvie	CA	390	65°42'N	137°54'W
Ogilvie Mountains	CA	390	64°35'N	139°30'W
Oglanly	TX	537	39°51'N	54°30'E
Oglio	IT	593	45°02'N	10°39'E
Ogmore		652	22°37'S	149°39'E
Ogoamas, Bulu	ID	500	0°40'N	120°12'E
Ogodzha	RS	612	52°45'N	132°34'E
Ogoja	NI	316	6°40'N	8°48'E
Ogoki Reservoir		370	50°50'N	87°10'W
Ogoky	CA	390	51°38'N	85°57'W
Ögöömör	MG	520	43°50'N	104°25'E
Ogooué	GB	294	0°49'S	9°00'E
Ogorelyshi		556	63°01'N	35°42'E
Ogōri	JA	506	33°23'N	130°03'E
Ogoué Maritime	GB	294	2°00'S	9°30'E
Ogr	SU	324	12°02'N	27°06'E
Ograzden Pl.	MK	599	41°30'N	22°55'E
Ogre	LG	596	56°49'N	24°36'E
Ogulin	HR	574	45°16'N	15°14'E
Ogun	NI	316	9°04'N	4°40'E
Ogurchinskiy, Os.	TX	537	38°55'N	53°02'E
Ogurugu	NI	316	6°47'N	6°56'E
Oğuz		564	39°32'N	38°51'E
Oğuzeli	TU	535	36°59'N	37°30'E
Ohafia	NI	316	5°37'N	7°50'E
Ohai	NZ	663	45°56'S	167°57'E
Ohakune	NZ	663	39°25'S	175°27'E
Ohanet	AG	272	28°40'N	8°48'E
Ōhata	JA	506	41°24'N	141°10'E
Ohau, L.	NZ	663	44°15'S	169°51'E
Ohaupo	NZ	663	37°55'S	175°18'E
Ohey	BE	570	50°26'N	5°08'E
O'Higgins	CI	428	23°39'S	70°15'W
Ohio	US	398	36°59'N	89°08'W
'Ohonua		654	21°14'S	176°10'W
Ohopoho	WA	313	18°04'S	13°51'E
Ohre	EZ	575	50°32'N	14°08'E
Ohrid	MK	599	41°08'N	20°47'E
Ohridsko Jez.	AL	566	41°02'N	20°43'E
Ohrigstad	SF	322	24°45'S	30°34'E
Ohura	NZ	663	38°51'S	174°59'E
Oiapoque	BR	424	4°00'N	52°00'W
Oiapoque	BR	424	3°52'N	51°45'W
Oiba	CO	430	6°16'N	73°19'W
Oiga	CH	490	29°22'N	92°19'E
Oil City	US	398	41°26'N	79°42'W
Oinófita	GR	588	38°18'N	23°38'E
Oinói	GR	588	38°10'N	23°25'E
Oise	FR	580	49°25'N	2°10'E
Oissel		562	49°20'N	1°05'E
Ōita	JA	506	33°14'N	131°36'E
Ojai		376	34°26'N	119°14'W
Öjebyn	SW	621	65°21'N	21°24'E
Ojinaga	MX	394	29°34'N	104°25'W
Ojiya	JA	506	37°18'N	138°48'E
Ojocaliente	MX	394	22°34'N	102°16'W
Ojo de Laguna	MX	394	29°27'N	106°23'W
Ojo de Liebre, L.	MX	394	27°45'N	114°15'W
Ojos del Salado, Cerro	CI	428	27°06'S	68°32'W
Oka	CF	285	3°34'S	15°14'E
Oka	NI	316	7°27'N	5°48'E
Oka	RS	612	54°00'N	101°00'E
Oka	RS	612	55°00'N	41°00'E
Okaba	ID	500	8°06'S	139°42'E
Okahandja	WA	313	21°59'S	16°55'E
Okaka	NI	316	9°15'N	3°12'E
Okala	CM	280	4°01'N	11°23'E
Okanagan Centre		372	50°03'N	119°27'W
Okanagan Falls		372	49°20'N	119°35'W
Okanagan L.		368	49°55'N	119°30'W
Okanagan Range		372	49°00'N	119°55'W
Okano	GB	294	0°05'S	10°57'E
Okanogan		372	48°22'N	119°34'W
Okanogan		372	48°06'N	119°43'W
Okapa	PP	664	6°31'S	145°36'E
Okaputa	WA	313	20°07'S	16°58'E
Okarem	TX	537	38°03'N	54°01'E
Okatana	WA	313	17°45'S	15°43'E
Okato	NZ	663	39°11'S	173°53'E
Okaukuejo	WA	313	19°11'S	15°56'E
Okavango	BC	276	18°53'S	22°24'E
Okavango Delta	BC	276	18°45'S	22°45'E
Okavango Swamp		270	19°30'S	23°00'E
Okaya	JA	506	36°03'N	138°03'E
Okayama	JA	506	34°39'N	133°55'E
Okazaki	JA	506	34°56'N	137°10'E
Okazize	WA	313	21°53'S	16°30'E
Okeechokee, Lake	US	398	26°56'N	80°49'W
Okeene		376	36°06'N	98°19'W
Okefenokee Swamp		378	30°45'N	82°20'W
Okeigbo	NI	316	7°10'N	4°43'E
Oke Iho	NI	316	8°02'N	3°21'E
Okemah		376	35°25'N	96°18'W
Okemos		374	42°42'N	84°26'W
Okene	NI	316	7°33'N	6°14'E
Okha	RS	612	53°34'N	142°56'E
Okhaldhunga	NP	522	27°19'N	86°30'E
Ókhi	GR	588	38°04'N	24°28'E
Okhna	KG	514	40°03'N	71°42'E
Okhotsk	RS	612	59°23'N	143°18'E
Okhotsk, Sea of	RS	612	55°00'N	150°00'E
Okiep	SF	322	29°36'S	17°52'E
Okinawa	JA	506	26°19'N	127°47'E
Okinawa-jima	JA	506	26°42'N	128°11'E
Okinawa-shoto	JA	506	26°40'N	128°00'E
Okinoerabu-shima	JA	506	27°22'N	128°35'E
Oki-shoto	JA	506	36°15'N	133°15'E
Okitipupa	NI	316	6°30'N	4°48'E
Okkan	BM	487	17°28'N	95°50'E
Oklahoma		374	35°30'N	97°30'W
Oklahoma City	US	398	35°28'N	97°30'W
Oklan		468	63°00'N	165°00'E
Okmulgee		378	35°37'N	95°57'W
Oknitsa	MD	601	48°23'N	27°26'E
Oko	NI	316	7°57'N	4°20'E
Okok	UG	330	2°06'N	33°53'E
Okondeka	WA	313	19°01'S	15°53'E
Okondja	GB	294	0°41'S	13°47'E
Okoppe	JA	506	44°26'N	143°11'E
Okotoks	CA	390	50°44'N	113°59'W
Okoyo	CF	285	1°28'S	15°04'E
Okpo	BM	487	18°07'N	95°40'E
Oksapmin	PP	664	5°16'S	142°15'E
Oksbøl	DA	576	55°38'N	8°17'E
Øksfjord	NO	604	70°14'N	22°22'E
Oksskolten	NO	604	66°01'N	14°20'E
Oktember	AM	482	40°08'N	44°01'E
Oktwin	BM	487	18°49'N	96°26'E
Oktyabr'	KZ	510	49°28'N	57°26'E
Oktyabr'sk		560	53°10'N	48°42'E
Oktyabr'skiy		466	47°59'N	43°39'E
Oktyabr'skiy		466	56°31'N	57°12'E
Oktyabr'skiy		468	56°05'N	99°26'E
Oktyabr'skiy		556	61°05'N	43°10'E
Oktyabr'skiy		560	58°19'N	44°21'E
Oktyabr'skiy	BO	569	52°38'N	28°53'E
Oktyabr'skiy	KZ	510	49°38'N	83°36'E
Oktyabr'skiy	KZ	510	49°47'N	81°16'E
Oktyabr'skiy	RS	612	54°27'N	53°24'E
Oktyabr'skiy	RS	612	52°40'N	156°14'E
Oktyabr'skiy	RS	612	53°01'N	128°37'E
Oktyabr'skiy	UZ	539	39°06'N	66°49'E
Oktyabr'skoye	RS	612	62°30'N	66°03'E
Oktyabr'skoye	UP	624	45°24'N	34°55'E
Oktyabr'skoy Revolyutsii, O.	RS	612	79°30'N	97°00'E
Ōkuchi	JA	506	32°04'N	130°37'E
Okulovka		560	58°22'N	33°18'E
Okushiri	JA	506	42°13'N	139°33'E
Okushiri-kaikyo	JA	506	42°15'N	139°40'E
Okushiri-to	JA	506	42°10'N	139°27'E
Okuta	NI	316	9°13'N	3°11'E
Okwa	BC	276	22°26'S	22°58'E
Okwa	CG	287	1°02'S	25°32'E
Ola		378	35°01'N	93°13'W
Ola		468	59°35'N	151°17'E
Olá	PM	417	8°25'N	80°39'W
Ólafsfjördhur	IC	591	66°04'N	18°39'W
Ólafsvík	IC	591	64°53'N	23°43'W
Olaine	LG	596	56°48'N	23°59'E
Olalla		372	49°16'N	119°50'W
Olanchito	HO	412	15°30'N	86°34'W
Öland	SW	621	56°44'N	16°36'E
Ölands norra udde	SW	621	57°21'N	17°02'E
Olands Sodra Udde	SW	621	56°11'N	16°24'E
Olary	AS	656	32°17'S	140°19'E
Olathe		372	38°36'N	107°58'W
Olathe	US	398	38°52'N	94°49'W
Olavarría	AR	419	36°54'S	60°17'W
Oława	PL	606	50°56'N	17°18'E
Olbia	IT	593	40°55'N	9°29'E
Ol'chan	RS	612	64°40'N	142°36'E
Old Bahama Channel	CU	406	22°30'N	78°50'W
Old Crow	CA	390	67°34'N	139°51'W
Oldeani	TZ	327	3°21'S	35°33'E
Oldeani	TZ	327	3°30'S	34°29'E
Oldebroek	NL	602	52°27'N	5°54'E
Olden	NO	604	61°50'N	6°49'E
Oldenburg	GM	584	53°09'N	8°12'E
Oldenburg	GM	584	54°18'N	10°53'E
Oldenzaal	NL	602	52°19'N	6°55'E
Olderdalen	NO	604	69°37'N	20°32'E
Old Forge		374	43°42'N	74°58'W
Old Fort Bay	BF	402	25°03'N	77°32'W
Old Fort Nelson	CA	390	58°49'N	122°33'W
Old Fort Providence	CA	390	62°16'N	114°09'W
Oldham	UK	626	53°33'N	2°07'W
Old Harbour	JM	414	17°56'N	77°07'W
Old Harbour Bay	JM	414	17°54'N	77°06'W
Oldman		372	50°00'N	114°30'W
Old Rhine	NL	602	52°10'N	4°50'E
Old Road		382	17°01'N	61°50'W
Olds	CA	390	51°47'N	114°06'W
Old Wives Lake		372	50°05'N	106°00'W
Öldziyt	MG	520	44°40'N	109°01'E
Olean		374	42°04'N	78°25'W
Olecko	PL	606	54°02'N	22°31'E
Oleiros	PO	608	39°55'N	7°55'W

Olekma	RS	612	60°22'N	120°42'E
Olëkminsk	RS	612	60°24'N	120°04'E
Olekminskiy Stanovik		468	54°55'N	120°00'E
Olekmo-Charskoye Nagorye		468	57°00'N	120°00'E
Oleksandrivka	UP	624	48°59'N	32°14'E
Olema	RS	612	64°30'N	46°10'E
Olemari	NS	438	2°30'N	54°30'W
Ølen	NO	604	59°36'N	5°48'E
Olenegorsk		556	68°09'N	33°18'E
Olenëk	RS	612	73°00'N	119°55'E
Olënek	RS	612	68°33'N	112°18'E
Olenëkskiy Zaliv	RS	612	73°20'N	121°00'E
Olenino		560	56°12'N	33°29'E
Olenitsa		556	66°29'N	35°22'E
Olenovka	UP	624	47°50'N	37°40'E
Oléron, I. d'	FR	580	45°56'N	1°18'W
Olesko	UP	624	49°58'N	24°53'E
Oleśnica	PL	606	51°12'N	17°23'E
Olet Tongo	ID	500	8°56'S	116°55'E
Olevsk	UP	624	51°13'N	27°39'E
Olevugha	BP	666	8°55'S	160°10'E
Ol'ga	RS	612	43°45'N	135°18'E
Ol'ginka		564	44°13'N	38°54'E
Ölgiy	MG	520	48°56'N	89°57'E
Ølgod	DA	576	55°49'N	8°37'E
Olhão	PO	608	37°02'N	7°50'W
Oliana	SP	618	42°04'N	1°19'E
Olib	HR	574	44°19'N	14°48'E
Oliena	IT	593	40°16'N	9°24'E
Olifants	SF	322	31°42'S	18°12'E
Olifantshoek	SF	322	25°52'S	27°18'E
Olimar	UY	439	33°10'S	54°00'W
Olimarao Atoll	FM	661	7°40'N	148°30'E
Olimbos (Olympus)	GR	588	40°05'N	22°21'E
Ólimbos	GR	588	35°44'N	27°10'E
Olímpia	BR	424	20°44'S	48°54'W
Olinalá	MX	394	17°43'N	98°46'W
Olinda, Ponta	MZ	312	18°02'S	36°58'E
Olinskiy		466	45°43'N	47°31'E
Oliva		562	38°55'N	0°07'W
Oliva de la Frontera	SP	618	38°16'N	6°55'W
Olivais	PO	608	38°46'N	9°08'W
Olive Hill		374	38°18'N	83°10'W
Olivehurst		376	39°05'N	121°33'W
Oliveira	BR	424	20°41'S	44°49'W
Olivenza	SP	618	38°41'N	7°06'W
Oliver Springs		378	36°02'N	84°20'W
Olivet	FR	580	47°52'N	1°54'E
Olivia		374	44°46'N	94°59'W
Olivone	SZ	622	46°32'N	8°57'E
Olkalou	KE	299	0°16'S	36°23'E
Ol'khovatka		560	50°17'N	39°19'E
Ol'khovka		560	49°52'N	44°34'E
Olla		378	31°54'N	92°14'W
Ollachea	PE	436	13°49'S	70°29'W
Ollagüe, Volcán	CI	428	21°18'S	68°12'W
Ollon	SZ	622	46°18'N	7°00'E
Ollūr	IN	496	10°28'N	76°14'E
Olmedo	EC	432	1°25'S	80°13'W
Olmedo	SP	618	41°17'N	4°41'W
Olmesutye	KE	299	1°54'S	35°46'E
Olmos	PE	436	5°59'S	79°46'W
Olney		374	38°43'N	88°05'W
Olney		376	33°22'N	98°45'W
Olofström	SW	621	56°16'N	14°30'E
Oloitokitok	KE	299	2°56'S	37°30'E
Olomburi	BP	666	9°03'S	161°10'E
Olomega, Laguna de	ES	409	13°19'N	88°04'W
Olomouc	EZ	575	49°35'N	17°15'E
Olonets		556	60°59'N	32°58'E
Olongapo	RP	526	14°50'N	120°16'E
Olonne-sur-Mer	FR	580	46°32'N	1°45'W
Oloron-Sainte-Marie	FR	580	43°11'N	0°36'W
Olot	SP	618	42°11'N	2°29'E
Olovyannaya	KZ	510	50°56'N	115°35'E
Oloyskiye Gory		468	66°00'N	162°00'E
Ol'sha		560	54°44'N	31°01'E
Ol'shanka	UP	624	48°14'N	30°52'E
Ol'shany	UP	624	50°03'N	35°53'E
Olst	NL	602	52°20'N	6°07'E
Olsztyn	PL	606	53°47'N	20°29'E
Olsztynek	PL	606	53°35'N	20°18'E
Olt	RO	610	43°43'N	24°51'E
Olta	AR	419	30°37'S	66°16'W
Olte, Sa. de		388	43°21'S	69°36'W
Olten	SZ	622	47°21'N	7°55'E
Olteniţa	RO	610	44°05'N	26°38'E
Oltepesi	KE	299	1°34'S	36°28'E
Olton		376	34°11'N	102°08'W
Oltu	TU	535	40°33'N	41°59'E
Oltuil	RO	610	44°55'N	24°15'E
Oluan Pi	TW	532	21°54'N	120°51'E
Oluanpi	TW	532	21°57'N	120°49'E
Oluku	NI	316	6°27'N	5°36'E
Olu Malau (Three Sisters Is.)	BP	666	10°10'S	162°00'E
Olupona	NI	316	7°36'N	4°11'E
Olutanga	RP	526	7°18'N	122°57'E
Olvega	SP	618	41°47'N	1°59'W
Olvera	SP	618	36°56'N	5°16'W
Olympia	US	398	47°02'N	122°53'W
Olympic Dam	AS	656	30°30'S	136°55'E
Olympic Mts.		372	47°52'N	123°40'W
Olympus	CY	494	34°56'N	32°52'E
Olympus (Olimbos)	GR	588	40°05'N	22°21'E
Olyutorskiy, Mys	RS	612	59°55'N	170°27'E
Olyutorskiy Zaliv	RS	612	60°15'N	168°30'E
Ōma	JA	506	41°31'N	140°55'E
Oma		556	66°36'N	46°35'E
Oma	CH	490	32°27'N	83°15'E
Ōmachi	JA	506	36°28'N	137°50'E
Ōmagari	JA	506	39°27'N	140°29'E
Omagh	UK	626	54°35'N	7°10'W
Omaguas	PE	436	4°08'S	73°15'W
Omaha	US	398	41°15'N	95°56'W
Omak	US	398	48°24'N	119°31'W
Oman		38	21°00'N	57°00'E
Oman, Gulf of	IR	502	25°00'N	58°00'E
Omaruru	WA	313	21°26'S	15°56'E
Omaruru	WA	313	22°05'S	14°14'E
Omas	PE	436	12°31'S	76°17'W
Omatako	WA	313	17°57'S	20°25'E
Omate	PE	436	16°41'S	70°59'W
Ombai, Selat	ID	500	8°30'S	125°00'E
Ombalantu	WA	313	17°32'S	14°59'E
Ombase-jima		474	34°1?'N	139°04'E
Ombellé	GB	294	1°38'S	13°24'E
Ombésa	CM	280	4°35'N	11°16'E
Ombombo	WA	313	18°03'S	14°16'E
Omboué	GB	294	1°34'S	9°15'E
Ombrone	IT	593	42°39'N	11°00'E
Ombu	CH	490	31°21'N	86°35'E
Ombúes de Lavalle	UY	439	33°55'S	57°47'W
Ombúes de Oribe	UY	439	33°18'S	56°21'W
Omchak	RS	612	61°38'N	147°55'E
Omegna	IT	593	45°52'N	8°24'E
Omeo	AS	656	37°06'S	147°36'E
'Omer	IS	505	31°17'N	34°51'E
Ometepe, Isla de	NU	415	11°30'N	85°35'W
Ometepec	MX	394	16°41'N	98°23'W
Om Hājer	ER	292	14°20'N	36°39'E
Omineca		368	56°05'N	124°05'W
Omineca Mts.		368	56°00'N	125°00'W
Omiš	HR	574	43°27'N	16°42'E
Omitara	WA	313	22°17'S	18°01'E
Omitlán	MX	394	17°06'N	99°34'W
Ōmiya		474	35°54'N	139°38'E
Om Koi	TH	534	17°48'N	98°22'E
Ommarney Bay	CA	390	73°07'N	100°11'W
Ommen	NL	602	52°31'N	6°26'E
Omoa	HO	412	15°46'N	88°02'W
Omoko	NI	316	5°21'N	6°39'E
Omolon	RS	612	68°42'N	158°36'E
Omoloy		468	65°00'N	132°00'E
Omo Wenz	ET	293	4°31'N	35°59'E
Ompah		374	45°01'N	76°50'W
Omsk	RS	612	55°00'N	73°24'E
Omsukchan	RS	612	62°32'N	155°45'E
Ōmu	JA	506	44°34'N	142°58'E
Omu Aran	NI	316	8°08'N	5°06'E
Omugo	UG	330	3°16'N	31°07'E
Omuo	NI	316	7°46'N	5°43'E
Omuranba Otjozonjou		270	19°00'S	20°00'E
Omurtag	BU	573	43°06'N	26°25'E
Ōmuta	JA	506	33°02'N	130°27'E
Omutninsk	RS	612	58°40'N	52°12'E
Onadikondo	CG	287	3°52'S	24°10'E
Onalaska		374	43°53'N	91°14'W
Onaman Lake		374	50°00'N	87°30'W
Onancock	US	398	37°42'N	75°44'W
Onangué, Lac		266	0°57'S	10°04'E
Onaping Lake		374	47°05'N	81°30'W
Oñate		376	30°10'N	107°38'W
Oñati	SP	618	43°02'N	2°24'W
Onawa		372	42°01'N	96°05'W
Onaway	US	398	45°21'N	84°13'W
Onchan		558	54°11'N	4°27'W
Oncocúa	AO	274	16°39'S	13°26'E
Onda	SP	618	39°58'N	0°15'W
Ondangua	WA	313	17°58'S	16°01'E
Ondjiva	AO	274	17°07'S	15°44'E
Ondo	NI	316	7°06'N	4°50'E
Öndörhaan	MG	520	47°19'N	110°39'E
Ondor Had	CH	490	44°57'N	120°27'E
Öndörhushuu	MG	520	47°59'N	113°55'E
Ondorkara	CH	490	46°30'N	89°27'E
Ondor Sum	CH	490	42°30'N	113°00'E
Ondorushu Falls	WA	313	17°24'S	13°55'E
Ondulada del Norte, Llanura	CU	406	22°30'N	84°00'W
One, Motu		654	15°30'S	154°55'W
One and Half Degree Channel	MV	519	1°30'N	73°20'E
Onefour		372	49°07'N	110°28'W
Onega	RS	612	63°54'N	38°08'E
Onega	RS	612	63°58'N	38°02'E
Oneida		374	36°29'N	84°30'W
Oneida	US	398	43°06'N	75°39'W
Oneida Lake		374	43°12'N	75°56'W
O'Neill	US	398	42°27'N	98°38'W
Onekotan, O.	RS	612	49°27'N	154°45'E
Oneonta		374	42°27'N	75°03'W
Onet-le-Château	FR	580	44°23'N	2°32'E
Onevai		654	21°09'S	175°09'W
Onezhskaya Guba		556	64°20'N	36°30'E
Onezhskiy, Poluostrov		556	64°35'N	38°00'E
Onezhskoye, Oz.	RS	612	61°30'N	35°45'E
Ongenga	WA	313	17°26'S	15°41'E
Ongeri	CG	287	4°37'S	25°10'E
Ongi	MG	520	46°25'N	102°17'E
Ongiyn Gol	MG	520	44°33'N	103°42'E
Ongjin	KN	512	37°55'N	125°15'E
Ongniud Qi	CH	490	42°55'N	119°03'E
Ongobit	KE	299	0°03'S	36°47'E
Ongole	IN	496	15°30'N	80°03'E
Ongon	MG	520	46°58'N	103°50'E
Onhaye	BE	570	50°15'N	4°50'E
Oni	GG	495	42°35'N	43°26'E
Oni	NI	316	6°32'N	4°14'E
Onié	GB	294	2°13'N	12°07'E
Onilahy	MA	304	23°34'S	43°45'E
Onin, Sem.		478	2°50'S	132°05'E
Onitsha	NI	316	6°07'N	6°47'E
Onjŏng	KN	512	38°35'N	125°25'E
Onjŏng	KN	512	38°42'N	125°15'E
Önjüül	MG	520	46°47'N	105°34'E
Onkivesi	FI	578	63°18'N	27°18'E
Onoda	JA	506	33°59'N	131°11'E
Ono-i-Lau	FJ	660	20°15'S	179°40'W
Onokhoy	RS	612	51°55'N	108°02'E
Onomichi	JA	506	34°25'N	133°12'E
Onon	MG	520	48°35'N	110°36'E
Onon	MG	520	49°08'N	112°38'E
Onon Gol	MG	520	51°42'N	115°50'E
Onoto	VE	440	9°36'N	65°12'W
Onotoa	KR	660	2°00'S	175°00'E
Onseepkans	SF	322	28°45'S	19°18'E
Onslow	AS	656	21°39'S	115°06'E
Onslow Bay	US	398	34°25'N	77°15'W
Onsŏng	KN	512	42°55'N	130°00'E
Ontario		372	50°00'N	86°00'W
Ontario	US	398	44°01'N	116°57'W
Ontario, Lake	CA	390	43°45'N	78°00'W
Ontinyent	SP	618	38°49'N	0°37'W
Ontojärvi	FI	578	64°08'N	29°09'E
Ontonagon	US	398	46°51'N	89°18'W
Ontong Java Atoll (Lord Howe Islands)	BP	666	5°30'S	159°30'E
Ontucht	NL	602	53°03'N	6°06'E
Onyang	KS	513	36°46'N	127°01'E
Oobagooma	AS	656	16°46'S	123°59'E
Oobale	SO	321	3°06'N	45°33'E
Oodnadatta	AS	656	27°33'S	135°28'E
Ood Weyne	SO	321	9°25'N	45°04'E
Ooldea	AS	656	30°27'S	131°50'E
Oostelijk Flevoland	NL	602	52°30'N	5°45'E
Oostende	BE	570	51°13'N	2°55'E
Oosterend	NL	602	53°24'N	5°23'E
Oosterhout	NL	602	51°39'N	4°53'E
Oosterwolde	NL	602	52°59'N	6°17'E
Oostmahorn	NL	602	53°22'N	6°09'E
Oost-Vlieland	NL	602	53°18'N	5°04'E
Ootmarsum	NL	602	52°25'N	6°54'E
Ootse	BC	276	25°00'S	25°46'E
Opaka	BU	573	43°27'N	26°10'E
Opala	CG	287	0°37'S	24°21'E
Opalaca, Cordillera	HO	412	14°00'N	87°58'W
Opalenica	PL	606	52°18'N	16°26'E
Opalton	AS	656	23°15'S	142°46'E
Opari	SU	324	3°56'N	32°03'E
Oparino		466	59°52'N	48°17'E
Opasatika	CA	390	49°32'N	82°52'W
Opatija	HR	574	45°20'N	14°16'E
Opatów	PL	606	50°48'N	21°26'E
Opava	EZ	575	49°57'N	17°55'E
Opelousas		378	30°32'N	92°04'W
Ophthalmia Range	AS	656	22°30'S	119°00'E
Opi	NI	316	6°47'N	7°26'E
Opin	ID	500	2°56'S	129°11'E
Opobo	NI	316	4°34'N	7°27'E
Opochka		560	56°43'N	28°41'E
Opoco	BL	422	19°50'S	66°42'W
Opodepe		376	29°55'N	110°39'W
Opole	PL	606	50°40'N	17°57'E
Opornyy	KZ	510	46°11'N	54°29'E
Oposhnya	UP	624	49°58'N	34°37'E
Opotiki	NZ	663	38°00'S	177°18'E
Opovo	YO	630	45°03'N	20°26'E
Opp		378	31°16'N	86°15'W
Oppdal	NO	604	62°36'N	9°40'E
Opportunity		372	47°39'N	117°14'W
Opua	NZ	663	35°19'S	174°07'E
Opunoho B.		654	17°35'S	145°25'W
Oquitoa		376	30°45'N	111°45'W
Oraba	UG	330	3°32'N	30°53'E
Oracabessa	JM	414	18°23'N	76°57'W
Oracle		376	32°37'N	110°46'W
Oradea	RO	610	47°04'N	21°56'E
Orahovac	YO	630	42°24'N	20°40'E
Orahovica	HR	574	45°32'N	17°53'E
Orai	IN	496	25°59'N	79°28'E
Oran	AG	272	35°42'N	0°38'W
Ŏrang	KN	512	41°27'N	129°40'E
Orange		374	38°14'N	78°06'W
Orange		376	33°47'N	117°51'W
Orange		378	30°05'N	93°44'W
Orange	AS	656	33°17'S	149°06'E
Orange	FR	580	44°08'N	4°48'E
Orange	WA	313	30°00'S	27°50'E
Orange, Cabo	BR	424	4°23'N	51°32'W
Orangeburg		378	33°28'N	80°52'W
Orange City		372	43°00'N	96°03'W
Orange Grove		378	27°57'N	97°56'W
Orange Hill		382	13°18'N	61°08'W
Orange Park	US	398	30°09'N	81°41'W
Orangeville		372	39°13'N	111°03'W
Orange Walk	BH	404	18°06'N	88°33'W
Orange Walk	BH	404	17°17'N	88°46'W
Orango, Ilha	PU	298	10°56'N	16°18'W
Oranienburg	GM	584	52°45'N	13°14'E
Oranje Gebergte	NS	438	3°00'N	55°05'W
Oranjemund	WA	313	28°33'S	16°26'E
Oranjestad		380	12°31'N	70°01'W
Oranmore	EI	592	53°16'N	8°56'W
Oransbari		648	1°21'S	134°16'E
Orapa	BC	276	21°18'S	25°17'E
Oras	RP	526	12°09'N	125°26'E
Orăştie	RO	610	45°50'N	23°12'E
Oraviţa	RO	610	45°02'N	21°42'E
Orbe	SZ	622	46°43'N	6°32'E
Orbetello	IT	593	42°26'N	11°12'E
Órbigo	SP	618	41°58'N	5°40'W
Orbost		652	37°42'S	148°27'E
Orcas		372	48°38'N	123°01'W
Orchard City		372	38°49'N	107°58'W
Orchard Valley		372	41°05'N	104°48'W
Orchila, Isla	VE	440	11°49'N	66°10'W
Orcopampa	PE	436	15°16'S	72°21'W
Ord	AS	656	15°30'S	128°31'E
Ord	US	398	41°36'N	98°55'W
Ordabay	KZ	510	49°50'N	48°17'E
Ordazy	KZ	510	45°30'N	63°53'E
Ordes		562	43°05'N	8°25'W
Ordino	AN	567	42°34'N	1°32'E
Ordino	AN	567	42°33'N	1°32'E
Ordos Desert (Mu Us Shamo)	CH	490	39°00'N	109°00'E
Ord River	AS	656	17°23'S	128°51'E
Ordu	TU	535	40°58'N	37°53'E
Ordubad	AJ	483	38°54'N	46°01'E
Ordway		372	38°12'N	103°44'W
Ordynskoye		466	54°22'N	81°56'E
Ordzhonikidze	AJ	483	40°51'N	47°21'E
Ordzhonikidze	UP	624	44°57'N	35°22'E
Ordzhonikidze	UP	624	47°40'N	34°03'E
Ordzhonikidzeabad	TI	533	38°34'N	69°01'E
Ore	NI	316	6°45'N	4°52'E
Orealla	GY	434	5°19'N	57°20'W
Örebro	SW	621	59°17'N	15°13'E
Oregon		372	44°00'N	120°30'W
Öregrund	SW	621	60°20'N	18°26'E
Orekhov	UP	624	47°35'N	35°47'E
Orekhovo		560	58°30'N	42°01'E
Orekhovo-Zuyevo	RS	612	55°49'N	38°59'E
Orekhovsk	BO	569	54°41'N	30°30'E
Orël	RS	612	52°57'N	36°04'E
Orellana	PE	436	6°54'S	75°04'W
Orellana, Emb. de	SP	618	39°00'N	5°24'W
Orellana la Vieja	SP	618	39°01'N	5°32'W
Orem		372	40°17'N	111°41'W
Ören		564	37°02'N	27°57'E
Orenburg	RS	612	51°45'N	55°06'E
Örenşehir		564	39°00'N	36°39'E
Orestiás	GR	588	41°30'N	26°31'E
Oresund	DA	576	55°50'N	12°40'E
Orewa	NZ	663	36°35'S	174°42'E
Orford Ness	UK	626	52°04'N	1°34'E
Orfordness		648	11°15'S	143°15'E
Órganos, Sa. de los	CU	406	22°25'N	84°00'W
Organyà	SP	618	42°13'N	1°20'E
Orgil	MG	520	48°33'N	99°20'E
Örgön	MG	520	44°44'N	100°24'E
Orgūn	AF	480	32°57'N	69°11'E
Orhaneli		564	39°54'N	29°00'E
Orhangazi		564	40°30'N	29°18'E
Orhei	MD	601	47°22'N	28°49'E
Orhon Gol	MG	520	50°14'N	105°08'E
Orhontuul	MG	520	48°58'N	104°59'E
Orhy, Pic d'	FR	580	42°59'N	1°00'W
Ori		266	11°29'N	41°49'E
Oriental de Zapata, Ciénaga	CU	406	22°10'N	80°50'W
Oriente	AR	419	38°44'S	60°37'W
Orihuela	SP	618	38°05'N	0°57'W
Orillia		374	44°37'N	79°25'W
Orimattila	FI	578	60°48'N	25°45'E
Orinoca	BL	422	18°56'S	67°15'W
Orinoco	CO	430	4°30'N	67°55'W
Orinoco, Llanos del	VE	440	8°20'N	66°00'W
Orinoco Delta	VE	440	9°00'N	61°30'W
Oriolo	IT	593	40°03'N	16°27'E
Orion	CA	390	49°27'N	110°49'W
Orissaare	EN	577	58°33'N	23°04'E
Oristano	IT	593	39°54'N	8°36'E
Oristano, Golfo di	IT	593	39°50'N	8°29'E
Orito	CO	430	0°44'N	76°51'W
Orivesi	FI	578	61°41'N	24°21'E
Orivesi	FI	578	62°16'N	29°24'E
Oriximiná	BR	424	1°45'S	55°52'W
Orizaba	MX	394	18°51'N	97°06'W
Orizona		386	17°03'S	48°18'W
Orjen	YO	630	42°30'N	18°38'E
Orka	NO	604	62°30'N	10°10'E
Orkhomenós	GR	588	38°29'N	22°59'E
Orkney		372	49°08'N	107°55'W
Orkney	SF	322	26°59'S	26°40'E
Orkney	UK	626	59°00'N	3°00'W
Orlando	US	398	28°32'N	81°22'W
Orleans		374	38°39'N	86°26'W
Orléans	FR	580	47°54'N	1°54'E
Orléans, Ile d'		374	46°58'N	71°01'W
Orlevka	KG	514	42°32'N	71°57'E
Orlov, M.		556	67°11'N	41°23'E
Orlová	EZ	575	49°51'N	18°26'E
Orlovka	KG	514	42°45'N	75°36'E
Orlovskiy		560	46°52'N	42°03'E
Orlu	NI	316	5°49'N	7°01'E
Ormāra	PK	524	25°12'N	64°38'E
Ormília	GR	588	40°17'N	23°32'E
Ormiston		372	49°44'N	105°24'W
Ormoc	RP	526	11°00'N	124°36'E
Ormond Beach		378	29°17'N	81°03'W
Ormskirk	UK	626	53°34'N	2°54'W
Ornans	FR	580	47°06'N	6°09'E
Ørnes	NO	604	66°52'N	13°42'E
Orneta	PL	606	54°07'N	20°08'E
Örnsköldsvik	SW	621	63°18'N	18°43'E
Oro		376	40°01'N	127°27'E
Oro	KN	512	40°01'N	127°27'E
Orobayaya	BL	422	13°21'S	63°45'W
Orocué	CO	430	4°48'N	71°20'W
Orodara	UV	278	10°59'N	4°55'W
Orofino	US	398	46°28'N	116°14'W
Oroluk Atoll	FM	661	7°50'N	155°30'E
Oromocto	CA	390	45°51'N	66°29'W
Oron	IS	505	30°55'N	35°01'E
Oron	NI	316	4°49'N	8°13'E
Orona (Hull I.)	KR	660	4°30'S	172°30'W
Orono		370	44°52'N	68°40'W
Orontes	SY	531	35°20'N	36°30'E
Oropoi	KE	299	3°47'N	34°19'E
Oropuche	TD	438	10°37'N	61°02'W
Oroqen Zizhiqi	CH	490	50°33'N	123°42'E
Oroquieta	RP	526	8°29'N	123°48'E
Orós	BR	424	6°14'S	38°53'W
Orosei	IT	593	40°23'N	9°42'E
Orosei, Golfo di	IT	593	40°15'N	9°44'E
Orosháza	HU	590	46°34'N	20°40'E
Orosi, Volcán	CS	405	10°59'N	85°29'W
Oroszlány	HU	590	47°29'N	18°19'E
Orotina	CS	405	9°54'N	84°31'W
Orotukan	RS	612	62°16'N	151°42'E
Oro Valley	US	398	32°23'N	110°57'W
Oroville		372	39°30'N	121°33'W
Oroville	US	398	48°56'N	119°26'W
Orovnik	MK	599	41°10'N	20°46'E
Orozco	CU	406	22°58'N	83°02'W
Orqohan	CH	490	49°30'N	121°22'E
Orro	NR	662	0°32'S	166°54'E
Orsa	SW	621	61°07'N	14°37'E
Orsha	BO	569	54°30'N	30°25'E
Orshanka		560	56°55'N	47°53'E
Orsières	SZ	622	46°02'N	7°09'E
Orsk	RS	612	51°12'N	58°34'E
Orşova	RO	610	44°43'N	22°23'E
Ørsta	NO	604	62°12'N	6°09'E
Orta		564	40°38'N	33°06'E
Ortabağ	TU	535	37°24'N	42°54'E
Ortaca	TU	535	36°49'N	28°47'E
Ortaköy		564	39°26'N	36°14'E
Ortaköy		564	38°44'N	34°03'E
Ortaköy	TU	535	40°17'N	35°16'E
Ortega	CO	430	3°56'N	75°13'W
Ortegal, Cabo	SP	618	43°45'N	7°53'W
Orthez	FR	580	43°29'N	0°46'W
Ortigosa	SP	618	42°11'N	2°42'W
Ortigueira	SP	618	43°41'N	7°51'W
Ortiz	MX	394	28°17'N	110°43'W
Ortiz	VE	440	9°37'N	67°18'W
Ortles, Monti del	IT	593	46°30'N	10°40'E
Ortoire	TD	438	10°20'N	61°00'W
Orto-Karakain	KG	514	41°02'N	75°28'E
Ortón	BL	422	10°50'S	66°04'W
Ortona	IT	593	42°21'N	14°24'E
Ortonville		372	45°18'N	96°26'W
Orto-Tokoy	KG	514	42°20'N	76°01'E
Orūmīyeh	IR	502	37°33'N	45°04'E
Orurillo	PE	436	14°44'S	70°31'W
Oruro	BL	422	17°58'S	67°07'W
Orust	SW	621	58°07'N	11°29'E
Orūzgān	AF	480	32°56'N	66°38'E
Orvieto	IT	593	42°43'N	12°07'E
Orwell		374	43°48'N	73°17'W
Orxon Gol	CH	490	48°59'N	117°38'E
Oryakhovo	BU	573	43°44'N	23°58'E
Orzhitsa	UP	624	49°48'N	32°42'E
Orzysz	PL	606	53°49'N	21°57'E
Os	NO	604	60°12'N	5°28'E
Osa		466	57°17'N	55°26'E
Osa, Península de	CS	405	8°33'N	83°30'W
Osage		370	38°36'N	91°57'W
Osage		372	49°57'N	103°35'W
Osage		374	43°17'N	92°48'W
Osage Beach		374	38°09'N	92°37'W
Osage City		374	38°38'N	95°49'W
Ōsaka	JA	506	34°40'N	135°30'E
Osakarovka	KZ	510	50°32'N	72°39'E
Osakis		372	45°52'N	95°09'W
Osan	KS	513	37°09'N	127°04'E
Osasco		386	23°31'S	46°50'W
Osawatomie		374	38°29'N	94°57'W
Osborne		372	39°26'N	98°41'W
Osborne Store	JM	414	17°52'N	77°20'W
Osby	SW	621	56°22'N	13°59'E
Oscar		384	2°50'N	52°27'W
Oscar Ra.	AS	656	18°00'S	125°00'E
Osceola		370	41°02'N	93°45'W
Osceola		378	35°42'N	89°58'W
Oschersleben	GM	584	52°02'N	11°15'E
Oscoda		374	44°25'N	83°19'W
Osen	NO	604	64°18'N	10°31'E
Osh	KG	514	40°32'N	72°48'E
Oshakati	WA	313	17°47'S	15°41'E
Oshamambe	JA	506	42°30'N	140°22'E
Oshawa	CA	390	43°54'N	78°51'W
Oshik	KS	513	36°46'N	129°07'E
Oshika-hantō	JA	506	38°20'N	141°30'E
Oshikango	WA	313	17°24'S	15°53'E
Ōshima	JA	506	34°44'N	139°22'E
O-shima	JA	506	28°00'N	129°50'E
Oshima-hantō	JA	506	42°00'N	140°30'E
Oshivelo	WA	313	18°38'S	17°08'E
Oshkosh	US	398	44°00'N	88°31'W
Oshmar'ye		466	60°03'N	63°13'E
Oshmyany	BO	569	54°25'N	25°56'E
Oshnovīyeh	IR	502	37°02'N	45°06'E
Oshogbo	NI	316	7°50'N	4°36'E
Oshu	NI	316	7°35'N	4°37'E
Oshwe	CG	287	3°24'S	19°30'E
Osicala	ES	409	13°48'N	88°09'W
Osielle	NI	316	7°11'N	3°27'E
Osijek	HR	574	45°33'N	18°42'E
Osipaonica	YO	630	44°33'N	21°04'E
Osipovichi	BO	569	53°16'N	28°37'E
Osire	WA	313	21°01'S	17°21'E
Osizweni	SF	322	27°48'S	30°09'E
Osječenica	BK	572	44°10'N	16°30'E
Oskaloosa		370	41°17'N	92°38'W
Oskarshamn	SW	621	57°16'N	16°26'E
Oskarström	SW	621	56°48'N	12°58'E
Oskélanéo	CA	390	48°07'N	75°12'W
Öskemen	KZ	510	49°58'N	82°40'E
Oskol	UP	624	49°06'N	37°24'E
Oskū	IR	502	37°55'N	46°06'E
Oslo	NO	604	59°55'N	10°45'E
Oslofjorden	NO	604	59°21'N	10°35'E
Osmānābād	IN	496	18°10'N	76°03'E
Osmancık	TU	535	40°59'N	34°49'E
Osmaniye	TU	535	37°05'N	36°14'E
Os'mino		466	59°01'N	29°06'E
Osnabrück	GM	584	52°16'N	8°03'E
Osnaburgh House	CA	390	51°07'N	90°17'W
Oso	CG	287	1°09'S	27°22'E
Osogna	SZ	622	46°19'N	8°59'E
Osogovska Pl.	MK	599	42°10'N	22°30'E
Osoj	MK	599	41°32'N	20°56'E
Osona	WA	313	22°02'S	16°56'E
Osorno	CI	428	40°34'S	73°09'W
Osoyoos	CA	390	49°01'N	119°28'W
Oss	NL	602	51°46'N	5°32'E
Óssa	GR	588	39°49'N	22°40'E
Ossa, Serra d'	PO	608	38°43'N	7°36'W
Ossabaw	US	398	31°48'N	81°02'W
Osse	NI	316	6°09'N	5°18'E
Osséja	FR	580	42°25'N	1°59'E
Ossi	IT	593	40°40'N	8°35'E
Ossineke		374	44°54'N	83°25'W
Ossora	RS	612	59°20'N	163°13'E
Ostashkov		466	57°09'N	33°06'E
Oster		560	54°01'N	32°48'E
Oster	UP	624	50°57'N	30°53'E
Osterburg	GM	584	52°47'N	11°46'E
Österbybruk		558	60°12'N	17°54'E
Österdalälven	SW	621	60°33'N	15°08'E
Østerdalen	NO	604	62°00'N	11°00'E
Osterhofen	GM	584	48°42'N	13°01'E
Osterholz-Scharmbeck	GM	584	53°14'N	8°48'E
Ostermiething	AU	568	48°03'N	12°50'E
Osterode am Harz	GM	584	51°43'N	10°14'E
Östersund	SW	621	63°11'N	14°39'E
Ostfriesische Inseln	GM	584	53°44'N	7°25'E
Östhammar	SW	621	60°16'N	18°22'E
Ostra Silen	SW	621	59°12'N	12°20'E
Ostrava	EZ	575	49°50'N	18°17'E
Ostri Rt	HR	574	42°24'N	18°32'E
Ostróda	PL	606	53°42'N	19°59'E
Ostrogozhsk		560	50°49'N	39°06'E
Ostroh	UP	624	50°20'N	26°31'E
Ostrołęka	PL	606	53°05'N	21°34'E
Ostroshitskiy Gorodok	BO	569	54°04'N	27°42'E
Ostrov	EZ	575	50°18'N	12°57'E
Ostrov	RS	612	57°20'N	28°22'E
Ostrovets	BO	569	54°37'N	25°57'E
Ostrovskaya		560	50°26'N	44°27'E
Ostrovskoye		560	57°48'N	42°15'E
Ostrowiec Świętokrzyski	PL	606	50°56'N	21°24'E
Ostrów Mazowiecka	PL	606	52°47'N	21°51'E
Ostrów Wielkopolski	PL	606	51°39'N	17°49'E
Ostryna	BO	569	53°44'N	24°32'E
Ostrzeszów	PL	606	51°25'N	17°57'E
Ostseebad Binz		558	54°23'N	13°37'E
Ostseebad Göhren	GM	584	54°20'N	13°44'E
Ostseebad Prerow	GM	584	54°26'N	12°35'E
Ostuni	IT	593	40°44'N	17°35'E
Osum	AL	566	40°48'N	19°52'E
Ōsumi-hantō	JA	506	42°00'N	140°30'E
Ōsumi-kaikyō	JA	506	31°00'N	131°00'E
Ōsumi-shotō	JA	506	30°30'N	130°00'E
Osuna	SP	618	37°14'N	5°07'W
Osupugo	KE	299	1°40'S	35°49'E
Osvaldo Cruz		386	21°47'S	50°50'W
Oswego		374	43°28'N	76°31'W
Oswego	US	398	43°27'N	76°30'W
Oswestry	UK	626	52°51'N	3°02'W
Oświęcim	PL	606	50°02'N	19°14'E
Osypenko	UP	624	46°56'N	36°48'E
Ōta		474	36°18'N	139°22'E
Ota	FR	580	42°16'N	8°45'E
Ota	JA	506	35°56'N	136°03'E
Otaki	NZ	663	40°45'S	175°08'E
Otar	KZ	510	43°32'N	75°12'E
Otaru	JA	506	43°13'N	141°00'E
Otautau	NZ	663	46°09'S	168°00'E
Otavalo	EC	432	0°14'N	78°16'W
Otavi	BL	422	19°50'S	65°24'W
Otavi	WA	313	19°39'S	17°20'E
Ōtawara	JA	506	36°52'N	140°02'E
Otchinjau	AO	274	16°30'S	13°56'E
O. T. Downs	AS	656	16°37'S	135°03'E
Oţelu Roşu	RO	610	45°32'N	22°22'E
Otematata	NZ	663	44°36'S	170°12'E
Otepää	EN	577	58°03'N	26°30'E
Oteren	NO	604	69°16'N	19°54'E
Othaya	KE	299	0°34'S	36°57'E
Othello		372	46°49'N	119°10'W
Othonoí	GR	588	39°50'N	19°08'E
Othris	GR	588	34°56'N	22°52'E
Oti	TO	328	7°48'N	0°08'E
Otinhungwa	WA	313	17°18'S	12°26'E
Otira	NZ	663	42°50'S	171°33'E
Otish, Monts	CA	390	52°20'N	70°30'W
Otjihajavara	WA	313	22°18'S	17°04'E
Otjikango	WA	313	20°12'S	16°52'E
Otjikondo	WA	313	19°55'S	15°28'E
Otjimbingue	WA	313	22°21'S	16°08'E
Otjinene	WA	313	21°05'S	18°48'E
Otjiwarongo	WA	313	20°27'S	16°39'E
Otjohorongo	WA	313	20°54'S	15°33'E
Otjokavare	WA	313	19°04'S	14°22'E
Otjosondu	WA	313	21°20'S	17°52'E
Otočac	HR	574	44°52'N	15°14'E
Otofuke	JA	506	42°59'N	143°12'E
Otog Qi	CH	490	39°04'N	107°58'E
Otog Qianqi	CH	490	38°06'N	107°47'E
Otok	HR	574	45°09'N	18°53'E
Otorohanga	NZ	663	38°11'S	175°12'E
Otra	NO	604	58°09'N	8°00'E
Otranto, Capo d'	IT	593	40°05'N	18°31'E
Otranto, Strait of	AL	566	40°00'N	19°00'E
Otrokovice	EZ	575	49°11'N	17°32'E
Ōtsu	JA	506	35°00'N	135°51'E
Ōtsuchi	JA	506	39°21'N	141°54'E
Otta		558	61°46'N	9°31'E
Otta	NI	316	6°42'N	3°14'E
Otta	NO	604	61°46'N	9°32'E
Ottappālam		470	10°46'N	76°23'E
Ottawa		374	38°36'N	95°16'W
Ottawa	CA	390	45°25'N	75°42'W
Ottawa	CA	390	45°20'N	73°58'W
Ottawa Is.	CA	390	59°30'N	80°20'W
Ottignies-Louvain-La-Neuve	BE	570	50°40'N	4°34'E
Ottobrunn	GM	584	48°04'N	11°41'E
Ottosdal	SF	322	26°49'S	26°01'E
Ottumwa	US	398	41°00'N	92°24'W
Otukpa	NI	316	7°05'N	7°40'E
Otuquis, Bañados del	BL	422	19°20'S	58°30'W
Oturkpo	NI	316	7°13'N	8°09'E
Otway, C.	AS	656	38°52'S	143°32'E
Otway, Seno	CI	428	53°00'S	71°30'W
Otwock	PL	606	52°08'N	21°19'E
Otynya	UP	624	48°44'N	24°51'E
Ötztaler Alpen	AU	568	46°45'N	10°55'E
Ou	LA	517	20°04'N	102°13'E
Ou, Nam		476	22°05'N	102°00'E
Ouachita	US	398	33°51'N	92°49'W
Ouachita, Lake		378	34°34'N	93°12'W
Ouachita Mts.	US	398	34°30'N	94°30'W
Ouaco		654	20°50'S	164°40'E
Ouadane	MR	308	20°56'N	11°37'W
Ouadda	CT	282	8°03'N	22°23'E
Ouâd Nâga	MR	308	17°56'N	15°32'W
Ouagadougou	UV	278	12°23'N	1°32'W
Ouahigouya	UV	278	13°35'N	2°25'W
Ouaka	CT	282	4°59'N	19°56'E
Oualâta	MR	308	17°18'N	7°02'W
Oualâta, Dahr	MR	308	17°48'N	7°24'W
Oualia	ML	307	13°36'N	10°23'W
Oualidia	MO	310	32°44'N	9°02'W
Ouallam	NG	314	14°19'N	2°05'E
Ouama	CT	282	4°46'N	21°22'E
Ouanaminthe	HA	412	19°33'N	71°44'W
Ouanary		384	4°13'N	51°40'W
Ouanda Djallé	CT	282	8°54'N	22°48'E
Ouandago	CT	282	7°14'N	18°52'E
Ouandja	CT	282	9°16'N	22°42'E
Ouango	CT	282	4°18'N	22°32'E
Ouaqui		384	3°27'N	54°00'W
Ouara	CT	282	5°59'N	20°14'E
Ouarane	MR	308	20°19'N	10°50'W
Ouargaye	UV	278	11°32'N	0°01'E
Ouargla	AG	272	31°58'N	5°20'E
Ouarkziz, Jebel	MO	310	28°40'N	8°35'W
Ouarra		266	5°05'N	24°26'E

Parral CI 426 36°09'S 71°50'W | *Patraikós Kólpos* GR 588 38°14'N 21°13'E | Pedro Carbo EC 432 1°50'S 80°14'W | *Penmarc'h, Pointe de* FR 580 47°48'N 4°21'W | *(P'eng-hu Lieh-tao)* TW 532 23°30'N 119°30'E

Sobhādero	PK	524	27°18'N	68°24'E
Sobinka		560	55°59'N	40°01'E
Sobolevo	RS	612	51°56'N	51°43'E
Sobradinho	BR	424	9°29'S	40°50'W
Sobradinho, Represa de	BR	424	9°40'S	42°00'W
Sobral	BR	424	3°40'S	40°18'W
Sobrália	BR	424	19°15'S	42°06'W
Sobrance	LO	616	48°45'N	22°11'E
Socabaya	PE	436	16°28'S	71°31'W
Socastee		378	33°41'N	78°59'W
Sochaczew	PL	606	52°14'N	20°15'E
Sochi	RS	612	43°35'N	39°45'E
Sŏch'ŏn	KS	513	36°07'N	127°05'E
Society Islands		654	18°00'S	154°00'W
Socorro	CO	430	6°29'N	73°16'W
Socorro	MX	394	18°48'N	110°53'W
Socorro	US	398	31°39'N	106°18'W
Socorro	US	398	34°03'N	106°53'W
Socotra (Suqutra)	YM	541	12°30'N	54°00'E
Socuéllamos	SP	618	39°17'N	2°48'W
Soda Lake		376	35°08'N	116°04'W
Sodankylä	FI	578	67°25'N	26°36'E
Soda Springs		372	42°39'N	111°36'W
Soddy-Daisy		378	35°14'N	85°11'W
Söderala		556	61°17'N	16°58'E
Söderfors	SW	621	60°21'N	17°17'E
Söderhamn	SW	621	61°18'N	17°03'E
Söderköping	SW	621	58°29'N	16°18'E
Södertälje	SW	621	59°12'N	17°37'E
Sodo	ET	293	6°54'N	37°45'E
Södra Ljusterö	SW	621	59°27'N	18°32'E
Soe	ID	500	9°52'S	124°17'E
Soekmekaar	SF	322	23°30'S	29°53'E
Soest	NL	602	52°11'N	5°18'E
Sofádhes	GR	588	39°20'N	22°06'E
Sofala, Baia de		270	20°11'S	34°45'E
Sofiya (Sofia)	BU	573	42°42'N	23°20'E
Sofiyivka	UP	624	48°03'N	33°53'E
Sofiysk	RS	612	52°15'N	133°59'E
Sofporog		556	65°48'N	31°26'E
Soga	TZ	327	6°50'S	38°52'E
Sogakofe	GH	296	6°00'N	0°36'E
Sogamoso	CO	430	5°43'N	72°56'W
Sogdiongon	RS	612	57°42'N	112°11'E
Sogeri	PP	664	7°55'S	143°28'E
Şoghād	IR	502	31°13'N	52°30'E
Sogndal	NO	604	61°14'N	7°06'E
Søgne	NO	604	58°05'N	7°49'E
Sognefjord	NO	604	61°06'N	5°10'E
Sogruma	CH	490	33°24'N	100°47'E
Söğüt		564	40°00'N	30°11'E
Sogwass	UG	330	3°37'N	34°21'E
Sŏgwip'o	KS	513	33°15'N	126°34'E
Sog Xian	CH	490	31°51'N	93°39'E
Sohano		650	5°20'S	154°50'E
Sŏhŭng	KN	512	38°27'N	126°09'E
Soignies	BE	570	50°35'N	4°04'E
Soila	CH	490	30°39'N	97°03'E
Soissons	FR	580	49°23'N	3°19'E
Sojat	IN	496	25°55'N	73°40'E
Sojoson-man (Korea Bay)	KN	512	39°20'N	124°50'E
Sokal'	UP	624	50°29'N	24°17'E
Sokch'o		474	38°10'N	128°34'E
Söke	TU	535	37°45'N	27°24'E
Sokh	UZ	539	39°57'N	71°08'E
Sokhós	GR	588	40°49'N	23°21'E
Sokhumi	GG	495	43°00'N	41°02'E
Sokna	NO	604	60°13'N	9°57'E
Soko Banja	YO	630	43°39'N	21°53'E
Sokodé	TO	328	8°59'N	1°08'E
Sokol	RS	612	59°28'N	40°10'E
Sokol	RS	612	59°53'N	150°55'E
Sokółka	PL	606	53°25'N	23°30'E
Sokolo	ML	307	14°44'N	6°08'W
Sokolov	EZ	575	50°11'N	12°38'E
Sokołów Podlaski	PL	606	52°24'N	22°15'E
Sokoto	NI	316	13°02'N	5°13'E
Sokoto	NI	316	11°24'N	4°07'E
Sokoto Plains	NI	316	12°45'N	5°00'E
Sokyryany	UP	624	48°27'N	27°25'E
Sola		382	21°40'N	77°41'W
Sola	NO	604	58°53'N	5°36'E
Solana	RP	526	17°39'N	121°41'E
Solânea	BR	424	6°45'S	35°39'W
Solano	CO	430	0°41'N	75°14'W
Solano	RP	526	16°31'N	121°11'E
Solano	VE	440	2°00'N	66°57'W
Solano, Bahía	CO	430	6°20'N	77°26'W
Solano, Punta		380	6°17'N	77°28'W
Solberg	SW	621	63°46'N	17°37'E
Solca	RO	610	47°42'N	25°51'E
Sol de Julio	AR	419	29°33'S	63°27'W
Soldeu	AN	567	42°35'N	1°40'E
Soldotna	US	398	60°29'N	151°03'W
Soledad		376	36°25'N	121°19'W
Soledad		380	10°55'N	74°46'W
Soledad	HO	412	13°35'N	87°07'W
Soledad (East Falkland)		388	51°55'S	59°00'W
Soledad de Doblado	MX	394	19°03'N	96°25'W
Soledad de Graciano Sánchez	MX	394	22°12'N	100°56'W
Solenzo	UV	278	12°11'N	4°05'W
Solhan	TU	535	38°58'N	41°03'E
Soligalich		466	59°05'N	42°17'E
Soligorsk	BO	569	52°48'N	27°32'E
Solihull	UK	626	52°25'N	1°47'W
Solikamsk	RS	612	59°39'N	56°47'E
Sol'-Iletsk	RS	612	51°10'N	54°56'E
Solimões	BR	424	0°10'S	49°00'W
Solingen	GM	584	51°10'N	7°03'E
Solís	UY	439	34°22'S	55°27'W
Solís de Mataojo	UY	439	34°36'S	55°29'W
Solita	CO	430	0°52'N	75°35'W
Solitaire	WA	313	23°55'S	16°01'E
Sollefteå	SW	621	63°10'N	17°16'E
Sollentuna	SW	621	59°28'N	17°54'E
Sóller	SP	618	39°46'N	2°42'E
Solling	GM	584	51°44'N	9°28'E
Solna	SW	621	59°22'N	18°01'E
Solntsevo		466	51°24'N	36°45'E
Solo	ID	500	6°47'S	112°33'E
Solok	ID	500	0°48'S	100°39'E
Solokh-Aul		466	43°48'N	39°41'E
Sololá	GT	411	14°46'N	91°11'W
Soloma	GT	411	15°43'N	91°27'W
Solomon		372	10°52'S	144°41'E
Solomon		376	39°30'N	98°00'W
Solomon Islands		38	8°00'S	159°00'E
Solomon Islands	BP	666	9°00'S	158°15'E
Solomon Sea	BP	666	11°00'S	160°15'E
Solor, Kep.	ID	500	8°50'S	123°50'E
Solotcha		560	54°48'N	39°51'E
Solothurn	SZ	622	47°12'N	7°32'E
Solotvina	UP	624	47°57'N	23°52'E
Solovetskiy O.		556	65°07'N	35°53'E
Solov'yevsk		468	54°14'N	124°26'E
Solsgirth		372	50°29'N	100°55'W
Solsona	SP	618	41°59'N	1°31'E
Solt	HU	590	46°48'N	19°00'E
Solta	HR	574	43°23'N	16°17'E
Solţānābād	IR	502	36°23'N	58°02'E
Soltau	GM	584	52°59'N	9°50'E
Sol'tsy		560	58°08'N	30°20'E
Solund	NO	604	61°05'N	4°49'E
Sölvesborg		558	56°04'N	14°33'E
Solway Firth	UK	626	54°38'N	3°48'W
Solwezi	ZA	332	12°11'S	26°24'E
Sōma	JA	506	37°48'N	140°57'E
Soma	TU	535	39°10'N	27°36'E
Somabhula	ZI	334	19°42'S	29°40'E
Somain	FR	580	50°22'N	3°17'E
Somalia		38	6°00'N	48°00'E
Sombor		564	45°46'N	19°07'E
Som Det	TH	534	16°35'N	103°45'E
Someren	NL	602	51°23'N	5°43'E
Somero	FI	578	60°37'N	23°32'E
Somerset		374	40°00'N	79°04'W
Somerset	US	398	37°04'N	84°36'W
Somerset East	SF	322	32°43'S	25°35'E
Somerset Island	CA	390	73°15'N	93°30'W
Somerton		376	32°35'N	114°42'W
Somerville		374	46°18'N	67°32'W
Somes	HU	590	48°07'N	22°20'E
Somesul Cald	RO	610	46°44'N	23°22'E
Somesul Mare	RO	610	47°09'N	23°55'E
Somme	FR	580	50°13'N	1°08'E
Somme, Baie de	FR	580	50°14'N	1°33'E
Sommeiller, Pointe	FR	580	45°08'N	6°51'E
Sommen	SW	621	57°52'N	15°05'E
Sömmerda	GM	584	51°08'N	11°06'E
Somosomo Str.		654	16°30'S	180°00'
Somotillo	NU	415	13°02'N	86°55'W
Somoto	NU	415	13°28'N	86°35'W
Somovo		560	51°44'N	39°22'E
Somuncurá, Meseta de	AR	419	41°30'S	67°15'W
Somvix	SZ	622	46°44'N	8°57'E
Son	IN	496	25°42'N	84°52'E
Soná	PM	417	8°01'N	81°19'W
Sona-Bata	CG	287	4°54'S	15°09'E
Sonaguera	HO	412	15°38'N	86°20'W
Sonāmukhi	BG	485	24°39'N	89°34'E
Sonātala	BG	485	25°03'N	89°30'E
Sŏnch'ŏn	KN	512	39°48'N	124°55'E
Sondera	DA	576	54°50'N	9°30'E
Sønderborg	DA	576	54°55'N	9°47'E
Sønderho	DA	576	55°21'N	8°26'E
Sønder Nissum	DA	576	56°18'N	8°12'E
Sondershausen	GM	584	51°22'N	10°52'E
Søndre Strømfjord		370	67°00'N	50°42'W
Sondrio	IT	593	46°10'N	9°51'E
Sonepur	IN	496	20°50'N	83°55'E
Song	MY	518	2°01'N	112°33'E
Song Cau	VM	540	13°26'N	109°12'E
Sŏngch'ŏn	KN	512	39°16'N	126°12'E
Songea	TZ	327	10°41'S	35°39'E
Songhua Jiang	CH	490	47°42'N	132°30'E
Songhwa	KN	512	38°21'N	125°08'E
Sŏnghwan	KS	513	36°55'N	127°08'E
Songino	MG	520	48°54'N	95°54'E
Songjiang	CH	490	42°30'N	128°16'E
Songjŏng	KS	513	35°08'N	126°48'E
Sŏngju	KS	513	35°55'N	128°17'E
Song-Kel, Ozero	KG	514	41°50'N	75°12'E
Songkhla	TH	534	7°12'N	100°36'E
Song Khram, Mae Nam	TH	534	17°50'N	103°50'E
Songling	CH	490	48°01'N	121°09'E
Song Ma	VM	540	21°03'N	103°43'E
Sŏngman	KS	513	37°24'N	127°07'E
Songnim	KN	512	38°45'N	125°40'E
Songo	AO	274	7°22'S	14°51'E
Songo	MZ	312	15°35'S	32°46'E
Songololo	CG	287	5°42'S	14°02'E
Songpan	CH	490	32°36'N	103°35'E
Songsak	IN	496	25°39'N	90°36'E
Sŏngsan	KS	513	33°25'N	126°55'E
Songshanpu		474	42°24'N	124°09'E
Songt'an	KS	513	37°02'N	127°04'E
Songwŏn	KN	512	40°22'N	125°53'E
Songxi		472	26°16'N	116°55'E
Sonid Youqi	CH	490	42°43'N	112°39'E
Sonid Zuoqi	CH	490	43°57'N	113°58'E
Sonīpat		476	28°59'N	77°01'E
Sonkajärvi	FI	578	63°40'N	27°31'E
Sonkovo		560	57°47'N	37°09'E
Son La	VM	540	21°18'N	103°54'E
Sonmiāni	PK	524	25°26'N	66°36'E
Sonmiani Bay	PK	524	25°15'N	66°30'E
Sonneberg	GM	584	50°21'N	11°10'E
Sonningdale		372	52°23'N	107°41'W
Sonntagberg	AU	568	47°59'N	14°46'E
Sono		384	10°00'S	47°30'W
Sonora		372	37°59'N	120°22'W
Sonora	MX	394	28°48'N	111°49'W
Sonora	US	398	30°34'N	100°38'W
Sonora Desert	US	398	30°00'N	113°00'W
Sonoyta	MX	394	31°53'N	112°53'W
Sonoyta	MX	394	31°15'N	113°10'W
Sonqor	IR	502	34°47'N	47°36'E
Sŏnsan	KS	513	36°14'N	128°18'E
Sonseca	SP	618	39°42'N	3°57'W
Sonsón	CO	430	5°42'N	75°18'W
Sonsonate	ES	409	13°43'N	89°44'W
Sonsorol		648	4°57'N	132°26'E
Sonta	YO	630	45°36'N	19°06'E
Son Tay	VM	540	21°07'N	105°30'E
Sonthofen	GM	584	47°31'N	10°17'E
Sonvico	SZ	622	46°03'N	8°59'E
Sook	MY	518	5°09'N	116°20'E
Sooyaac	SO	321	0°03'N	42°17'E
Soperton		378	32°22'N	82°35'W
Sop Hao	LA	517	20°33'N	104°27'E
Sophie		384	3°58'N	53°29'W
Sopka	LA	517	20°29'N	103°41'E
Sop Kai	LA	517	21°03'N	102°27'E
Sop Nhom	LA	517	21°32'N	102°47'E
Sopo	SU	324	8°01'N	26°04'E
Sopoo	CS	405	11°10'N	85°40'W
Sopor		470	34°18'N	74°18'E
Sopot	BU	573	42°39'N	24°45'E
Sopot	MK	599	42°14'N	21°44'E
Sopot	PL	606	54°27'N	18°34'E
Sop Prap	TH	534	17°53'N	99°20'E
Sopron	HU	590	47°41'N	16°36'E
Sopronkőhida	HU	590	47°43'N	16°37'E
Sopxai	LA	517	20°45'N	104°19'E
Sôr	PO	608	43°42'N	7°41'W
Sora	IT	593	41°44'N	13°37'E
Sorak-san	KS	513	38°07'N	128°28'E
Sorata	BL	422	15°47'S	68°40'W
Sorel	CA	390	46°03'N	73°07'W
Sorell, C.	AS	656	42°12'S	145°11'E
Sorell-Midway Point		652	42°47'S	147°33'E
Soreq	IS	505	31°56'N	34°42'E
Sorfta	ET	293	6°43'N	39°10'E
Sorgues	FR	580	44°00'N	4°52'E
Sorgun	TU	535	39°49'N	35°11'E
Soria	SP	618	41°30'N	2°30'W
Soriano	UY	439	33°24'S	58°19'W
Sorikmerapi, Gunung	ID	500	0°41'N	99°33'E
Soritor	PE	436	6°06'S	77°04'W
Sorkh, Kuh-e	IR	502	33°00'N	55°00'E
Sorkh Āb	AF	480	32°33'N	62°56'E
Sornac	FR	580	45°40'N	2°12'E
Sorø	DA	576	55°26'N	11°34'E
Sorocaba	BR	424	23°29'S	47°27'W
Sorochinsk		466	52°26'N	53°10'E
Soroki	MD	601	48°09'N	28°18'E
Soroksan-Dunai	HU	590	47°10'N	19°00'E
Sorol	FM	661	8°30'N	140°15'E
Sorong	ID	500	0°53'S	131°15'E
Soropalca	BL	422	20°16'S	65°44'W
Soroti	UG	330	1°43'N	33°37'E
Sørøya	NO	604	70°48'N	21°45'E
Soroysundet	NO	604	70°37'N	23°15'E
Sorraia		562	38°56'N	8°53'W
Sørreisa	NO	604	69°09'N	18°10'E
Sorriso	BR	424	12°33'S	55°41'W
Sorris-Sorris	WA	313	20°59'S	14°47'E
Sorsele	SW	621	65°32'N	17°30'E
Sorsk		466	54°01'N	90°12'E
Sorso	IT	593	40°48'N	8°34'E
Sorsogon	RP	526	12°58'N	124°00'E
Sort	SP	618	42°24'N	1°08'E
Sört	MG	520	49°19'N	104°24'E
Sortavala	RS	612	61°42'N	30°41'E
Sortland	NO	604	68°41'N	15°22'E
Sorūbī	AF	480	34°36'N	69°43'E
Sosa	KS	513	37°29'N	126°47'E
Sŏsan	KS	513	36°47'N	126°27'E
Soshanguve	SF	322	25°30'S	28°06'E
Soskovo		560	52°45'N	35°23'E
Sosneado, Cerro	AR	419	34°45'S	69°59'W
Sosnitsa	UP	624	51°32'N	32°30'E
Sosnivka	UP	624	50°17'N	24°15'E
Sosnovets		556	64°26'N	34°27'E
Sosnovka		560	53°14'N	41°22'E
Sosnovka		560	57°48'N	51°43'E
Sosnovka	RS	612	66°30'N	40°35'E
Sosnovo		556	60°33'N	30°17'E
Sosnovo-Ozerskoye	RS	612	52°31'N	111°34'E
Sosnovskoye		560	55°48'N	43°10'E
Sosnovyy Bor		556	59°54'N	29°07'E
Sosnowiec	PL	606	50°14'N	19°07'E
Soso	CT	282	3°55'N	15°30'E
Sosok	ID	500	0°17'N	110°14'E
Sosúa	DR	408	19°45'N	70°31'W
Sos'va	RS	612	59°10'N	61°50'E
Sota	BN	276	11°52'N	3°24'E
Sotavento, Ilhas de (Leeward Islands)	CV	281	15°00'N	23°35'W
Sotik	KE	299	0°41'S	35°07'E
Sotkamo	FI	578	64°08'N	28°25'E
Soto la Marina	MX	394	23°46'N	98°13'W
Sotouboua	TO	328	8°34'N	0°59'E
Sotra		558	60°20'N	5°03'E
Sotta	FR	580	41°32'N	9°12'E
Sotuta	MX	394	20°36'N	89°01'W
Souanké	CF	285	2°03'N	14°07'E
Soubre	IV	288	5°47'N	6°36'W
Soudan		652	20°03'S	137°01'E
Soúdha	GR	588	35°29'N	24°04'E
Souflíon	GR	588	41°12'N	26°18'E
Soufrière		382	15°13'N	61°22'W
Soufrière	DO	407	15°14'N	61°22'W
Soufrière	ST	413	13°51'N	61°03'W
Sougéta	GV	297	10°09'N	12°32'W
Souillac		270	20°30'S	57°30'E
Souillac	FR	580	44°53'N	1°28'E
Souk Ahras	AG	272	36°17'N	7°56'E
Souk el Arba du Rharb	MO	310	34°40'N	6°00'W
Sŏul (Seoul)	KS	513	37°34'N	127°00'E
Soumman		562	36°30'N	4°30'E
Sound of Jura	UK	626	55°39'N	5°52'W
Sourdough Inn	CA	390	62°30'N	140°50'W
Soure	BR	424	0°42'S	48°30'W
Soure	PO	608	40°03'N	8°38'W
Sour El Ghozlane	AG	272	36°09'N	3°41'E
Souris		372	49°37'N	100°15'W
Souris		372	49°30'N	101°00'W
Souris Plain		372	48°10'N	100°00'W
Sous, Oued	MO	310	30°22'N	9°37'W
Sousa	BR	424	6°44'S	38°10'W
Soustons	FR	580	43°45'N	1°19'W
Sous Vent, Îles		654	16°00'S	152°00'W
South Africa		38	30°00'S	26°00'E
South Allan		372	51°46'N	106°04'W
Southampton	UK	626	50°54'N	1°24'W
Southampton, C.	CA	390	62°08'N	83°38'W
Southampton I.	CA	390	64°30'N	84°30'W
South Andaman		476	11°45'N	92°45'E
South Augusta	US	398	33°25'N	82°01'W
South Bass		370	41°38'N	82°59'W
South Baymouth		374	45°33'N	82°02'W
South Bend		372	46°39'N	123°47'W
South Bend	US	398	41°40'N	86°15'W
South Boston		374	36°41'N	78°54'W
South Branch	CA	390	47°55'N	59°02'W
Southbridge	NZ	663	43°47'S	172°14'E
South Caicos		382	21°30'N	71°51'W
South Cape (Ka Lae)	US	398	18°55'N	155°41'W
South Carolina		378	34°00'N	81°00'W
South China Sea	BX	486	15°00'N	115°00'E
South Dakota		372	44°30'N	100°15'W
South Dorset Downs	UK	626	50°50'N	2°30'W
South Downs	UK	626	50°59'N	0°49'W
South Dum Dum		472	22°36'N	88°25'E
South East C.	AS	656	43°38'S	146°52'E
Southeast C.	US	398	62°57'N	169°40'W
South East Cape		652	48°00'S	147°30'E
South East Point		652	44°00'S	145°40'E
Southeast Point	BF	402	22°15'N	72°40'W
South East Pt.	AS	656	39°09'S	146°22'E
Southeast Pt.	JM	414	17°53'N	76°11'W
Southend-on-Sea	UK	626	51°32'N	0°42'E
South Entrance	PP	664	8°30'S	144°30'E
Southern Alps	NZ	663	43°30'S	170°30'E
Southern Cross	AS	656	31°13'S	119°20'E
Southern Indian L.	CA	390	57°10'N	98°40'W
Southern Pine Hills		378	31°00'N	89°00'W
Southern Pines		378	35°10'N	79°23'W
Southern Sporades		564	36°50'N	20°40'E
Southern Uplands		558	55°30'N	3°30'W
South Esk Tableland	AS	656	20°30'S	127°00'E
Southey	CA	390	50°56'N	104°30'W
Southfield	JM	414	17°53'N	77°41'W
South Fork		372	49°36'N	108°43'W
South Fork Republican		372	40°03'N	101°31'W
South Fulton		374	36°29'N	88°52'W
South Georgia		388	54°15'S	36°45'W
South Harbour		370	46°52'N	60°28'W
South Hatia Island	BG	485	22°19'N	91°07'E
South Haven		374	42°24'N	86°16'W
South Henik L.		370	61°30'N	97°25'W
South Hill		374	36°43'N	78°07'W
South Horr	KE	299	2°06'N	36°55'E
South Hutchinson		372	38°01'N	97°56'W
South Huvadhu Atoll	MV	519	0°30'N	73°00'E
South Indian Lake	CA	390	56°49'N	98°59'W
South Island	KE	299	2°38'N	36°36'E
South Island	NZ	663	43°00'S	171°00'E
South Kinangop	KE	299	0°43'S	36°39'E
South Knife Lake	CA	390	58°13'N	96°23'W
South Lake		370	46°25'N	62°03'W
South Lake Tahoe		372	38°56'N	119°57'W
South Loup		372	41°04'N	98°39'W
South Molton	UK	626	51°01'N	3°50'W
South Nahami	CA	390	61°50'N	121°19'W
South Nahanni	CA	390	61°03'N	123°22'W
South Negril Pt.	JM	414	18°14'N	78°22'W
South Pacific		36	49°13'S	143°50'W
South Platte	US	398	39°24'N	105°10'W
South Point		266	7°57'S	14°17'W
Southport		378	33°55'N	78°01'W
Southport		652	27°59'S	153°25'E
Southport	UK	626	53°38'N	3°01'W
South Pt.		378	29°05'N	89°15'W
South Sandwich Islands	UK	40	57°45'S	26°30'W
South Saskatchewan	CA	390	53°14'N	105°05'W
South Seal		370	58°28'N	98°08'W
South Shields		558	54°59'N	1°25'W
South Sumter		378	33°52'N	80°19'W
South Taranaki Bight	NZ	663	39°40'S	174°10'E
South Ubian	RP	526	5°11'N	120°30'E
South Uist	UK	626	57°13'N	8°20'W
South Weldon		374	36°24'N	77°36'W
South Wellesley Islands		648	16°30'S	140°00'E
South West Bay	BF	402	25°00'N	77°32'W
South West C.	AS	656	43°33'S	146°03'E
Southwest C.	NZ	663	47°17'S	167°28'E
South West Cape		652	47°40'S	146°00'E
Southwest Point	BF	402	22°16'N	72°47'W
Southwest Pt.		378	29°00'N	89°30'W
Southwest Pt.	PP	664	2°14'S	146°34'E
Southwold	UK	626	52°20'N	1°41'E
South Yarmouth		374	41°40'N	70°11'W
Soutpansberg	SF	322	23°02'S	29°18'E
Souvigny	FR	580	46°32'N	3°11'E
Souzel	PO	608	38°57'N	7°40'W
Sovata	RO	610	46°35'N	25°04'E
Soverato Marina	IT	593	38°41'N	16°33'E
Sovetsk		466	57°37'N	48°58'E
Sovetsk	RS	612	55°05'N	21°53'E
Sovetskaya Gavan'	RS	612	48°58'N	140°18'E
Sovetskiy		560	56°45'N	48°30'E
Sovetskoye		466	42°52'N	45°41'E
Sovetskoye		466	47°18'N	44°31'E
Sovets'kyy	UP	624	45°20'N	34°56'E
Sovsin'torg	KG	514	42°22'N	77°54'E
Sowa	CH	490	29°11'N	99°54'E
Soweto	SF	322	26°16'S	27°50'E
Soya-Kaikyo (La Pérouse Strait)	JA	506	45°45'N	142°00'E
Soya-misaki	JA	506	45°31'N	141°58'E
Soyang L.	KS	513	38°00'N	127°56'E
Soyaux	FR	580	45°39'N	0°12'E
Sozh	BO	569	51°57'N	30°48'E
Sozopol	BU	573	42°25'N	27°42'E
Spa	BE	570	50°30'N	5°52'E
Spadillo, Punta	IT	593	36°49'N	12°00'E
Spain		38	40°00'N	4°00'W
Spalding		652	33°30'S	138°37'E
Spallumcheen		372	50°23'N	119°13'W
Spanish Fork	US	398	40°06'N	111°39'W
Spanish Point	AC	402	17°33'N	61°44'W
Spanish Point	EI	592	52°51'N	9°27'W
Spanish Town		382	18°27'N	64°25'W
Spanish Town	JM	414	17°59'N	76°57'W
Spanish Wells	BF	402	25°32'N	76°45'W
Sparta		374	38°07'N	89°42'W
Sparta		374	43°56'N	90°48'W
Sparta		378	33°16'N	82°58'W
Sparta		378	35°55'N	85°27'W
Spartanburg	US	398	34°56'N	81°55'W
Spartel, C.	MO	310	35°46'N	5°55'W
Spárti	GR	588	37°04'N	22°26'E
Spartivento, Capo	IT	593	37°55'N	16°03'E
Spartivento, Capo	IT	593	38°52'N	8°50'E
Sparwood	CA	390	49°43'N	114°54'W
Spas-Demensk		560	54°25'N	34°01'E
Spas-Klepiki		560	55°08'N	40°10'E
Spasskaya Guba		556	62°13'N	33°48'E
Spassk-Dal'niy	RS	612	44°37'N	132°48'E
Spasskoye		560	55°52'N	45°42'E
Spátha, Ákra	GR	588	35°40'N	23°44'E
Spean Bridge	UK	626	56°53'N	4°54'W
Spearfish	US	398	44°29'N	103°51'W
Spearman		376	36°11'N	101°11'W
Spedden		368	54°08'N	111°43'W
Speke Gulf	TZ	327	2°10'S	33°50'E
Spence Bay	CA	390	69°32'N	93°31'W
Spencer		374	38°48'N	81°21'W
Spencer		374	39°17'N	86°46'W
Spencer	US	398	43°08'N	95°08'W
Spencer, Cape		652	40°30'S	136°30'E
Spencer, Cape	AS	656	35°18'S	136°56'E
Spencer Gulf	AS	656	34°00'S	137°00'E
Spenser Mts.	NZ	663	42°15'S	172°30'E
Spentrup	DA	576	56°33'N	10°02'E
Sperkhiás	GR	588	38°54'N	22°07'E
Sperrin Mts.	UK	626	54°48'N	7°05'W
Spessart	GM	584	49°55'N	9°25'E
Spétsai	GR	588	37°15'N	23°08'E
Spey	UK	626	57°43'N	3°06'W
Speyer	GM	584	49°19'N	8°26'E
Spezand	PK	524	29°59'N	67°00'E
Spezzano Albanese	IT	593	39°40'N	16°19'E
Spicer		374	45°13'N	94°56'W
Spicer Is.	CA	390	68°10'N	79°00'W
Spiddle		558	53°14'N	9°19'W
Spiekeroog	GM	584	53°44'N	7°41'E
Spiez	SZ	622	46°41'N	7°40'E
Spijkenisse	NL	602	51°51'N	4°20'E
Spílion	GR	588	35°13'N	24°32'E
Spillimacheen		368	50°54'N	116°22'W
Spīn Būldak	AF	480	31°01'N	66°24'E
Spindale		378	35°21'N	81°55'W
Spiro		378	35°14'N	94°37'W
Spišská Belá	LO	616	49°11'N	20°28'E
Spišská Nová Ves	LO	616	48°57'N	20°34'E
Spitak	AM	482	40°49'N	44°16'E
Spital am Pyhrn	AU	568	47°39'N	14°20'E
Spittal an der Drau	AU	568	46°48'N	13°30'E
Split	HR	574	43°31'N	16°26'E
Split Lake	CA	390	56°15'N	96°05'W
Splügen	SZ	622	46°33'N	9°19'E
Špoģi	LG	596	56°05'N	26°44'E
Spokane	US	398	47°39'N	117°25'W
Spokane	US	398	47°54'N	118°20'W
Spoleto	IT	593	42°44'N	12°44'E
Spooner		374	45°49'N	91°53'W
Sporades		564	36°30'N	27°00'E
Spornoye	RS	612	62°20'N	151°03'E
Spotsylvania Courthouse		374	38°12'N	77°35'W
Sprague		372	49°02'N	95°38'W
Sprague		372	42°34'N	121°52'W
Spree	GM	584	52°32'N	13°13'E
Spremberg	GM	584	51°33'N	14°22'E
Spring	US	398	30°04'N	95°25'W
Spring Bay		374	45°44'N	82°19'W
Springbok	SF	322	29°40'S	17°53'E
Spring City		378	35°41'N	84°51'W
Springdale		378	34°40'N	80°47'W
Springdale	CA	390	49°30'N	56°04'W
Springdale	US	398	36°11'N	94°07'W
Springer	US	398	36°21'N	104°35'W
Springerville		376	34°08'N	109°17'W
Springfield		370	41°50'N	76°44'W
Springfield		372	44°02'N	123°01'W
Springfield		374	36°30'N	86°53'W
Springfield		374	44°14'N	94°58'W
Springfield		374	39°55'N	83°48'W
Springfield		378	30°09'N	85°36'W
Springfield	US	398	37°24'N	102°36'W
Springfield	US	398	37°12'N	93°17'W
Springfield	US	398	39°48'N	89°38'W
Springfield	US	398	42°06'N	72°35'W
Springfield10		374	43°17'N	72°28'W
Springfontein	SF	322	30°16'S	25°42'E
Spring Hill		378	28°26'N	82°37'W
Springhill		378	33°00'N	93°28'W
Spring Lake		378	35°10'N	78°58'W
Spring Mts.		376	36°10'N	115°38'W
Springs		374	41°00'N	72°09'W
Springsure	AS	656	24°07'S	148°05'E
Spring Valley		372	49°56'N	105°24'W
Spring Valley		372	39°15'N	114°25'W
Spring Valley		374	41°19'N	89°11'W
Spring Valley		376	32°44'N	116°59'W
Springville		372	40°09'N	111°36'W
Springville		374	42°30'N	78°40'W
Sprucedale		374	45°29'N	79°28'W
Spruce Grove	CA	390	53°32'N	113°55'W
Spruce View		372	52°05'N	114°19'W
Spulico, Capo	IT	593	39°57'N	16°38'E
Spur		376	33°28'N	100°51'W
Spurn Head	UK	626	53°34'N	0°07'E
Spur Tree	JM	414	18°00'N	77°34'W
Sputnik	KZ	510	51°10'N	78°00'E
Spuzzum		372	49°37'N	121°26'W
Spy Hill	CA	390	50°36'N	101°41'W
Squamish		372	49°42'N	123°10'W
Squatec		374	47°53'N	68°43'W
Squillace, Golfo di	IT	593	38°45'N	16°50'E
Sragen	ID	500	2°27'S	138°57'E
Srbjani	MK	599	41°29'N	20°57'E
Srbobran	YO	630	45°33'N	19°48'E
Sre Ambel	CB	489	11°07'N	103°46'E
Srebrenica	BK	572	44°06'N	19°18'E
Sredinnyy Khrebet	RS	612	56°00'N	158°00'E
Sredna Gora	BU	573	42°30'N	25°00'E
Srednebelaya	RS	612	50°41'N	128°04'E
Srednekolymsk	RS	612	67°27'N	153°40'E
Sredne Russkaya Vozvyshennos	RS	612	52°00'N	35°00'E
Sredne-Sibirskoye Ploskogorye	RS	612	65°00'N	105°00'E
Sredniy Ikorets		560	51°04'N	39°44'E
Srednogorie	BU	573	42°43'N	24°10'E
Srednyaya Akhtuba		560	48°42'N	44°52'E
Sre Khtum	CB	489	12°10'N	106°52'E
Śrem	PL	606	52°05'N	17°01'E
Sremčica	YO	630	44°41'N	20°24'E
Sremska Mitrovica	YO	630	44°59'N	19°37'E
Sremski Karlovci	YO	630	45°12'N	19°56'E
Srêng	CB	489	13°21'N	103°27'E
Sre Noy	CB	489	13°49'N	104°01'E
Srêpôk	CB	489	13°33'N	106°16'E
Sretensk	RS	612	52°15'N	117°43'E
Sri Gangānagar	IN	496	29°55'N	73°53'E
Sri Jayawardanapura	CE	530	6°54'N	79°54'E
Srikākulam	IN	496	18°18'N	83°54'E
Sri Kālahasti	IN	496	13°45'N	79°43'E
Sri Lanka		38	7°00'N	81°00'E
Srimangal	BG	485	24°19'N	91°44'E
Srīnagar	IN	496	34°05'N	74°49'E
Srīvardhan	IN	496	18°05'N	73°00'E
Środa Wielkopolska	PL	606	52°14'N	17°17'E
Srpska Crnja	YO	630	45°43'N	20°42'E
Staberhuk	GM	584	54°24'N	11°18'E
Stade	GM	584	53°36'N	9°29'E
Staden	BE	570	50°59'N	3°01'E
Stadskanaal	NL	602	53°00'N	6°55'E
Stadtbergen	GM	584	48°22'N	10°51'E
Staffanstorp	SW	621	55°38'N	13°13'E
Stafford		372	37°57'N	98°36'W
Stafford	UK	626	52°47'N	2°05'W
Staicele	LG	596	57°50'N	24°45'E
Stakhanov	UP	624	48°34'N	38°40'E
Stalden	SZ	622	46°14'N	7°52'E
Stalham	UK	626	52°46'N	1°31'E
Stalheim	NO	604	60°50'N	6°40'E
Stalina Kanal		556	64°00'N	34°50'E
Stallworthy, C.	CA	390	81°22'N	93°29'W
Stalowa Wola	PL	606	50°34'N	22°03'E
Sta Luzia, Barragem de	PO	608	40°00'N	8°00'W
Stamboliyski	BU	573	42°08'N	24°32'E
Stamford		374	41°03'N	73°32'W
Stamford		376	32°56'N	99°48'W
Stamford	AS	656	21°16'S	143°49'E
Stampa	SZ	622	46°20'N	9°34'E
Stampalia (Astipálaia)	GR	588	36°35'N	26°20'E
Stampriet	WA	313	24°21'S	18°27'E
Stamps		378	33°21'N	93°29'W
Stamsund	NO	604	68°06'N	13°48'E
Stanaford		374	37°48'N	81°09'W
Stanberry		374	40°13'N	94°32'W
Standard		372	51°07'N	112°59'W
Standerton	SF	322	26°57'S	29°15'E
Standish		374	43°59'N	83°57'W
Stanford		374	37°31'N	84°39'W
Stanford	SF	322	34°26'S	19°27'E
Stange	NO	604	60°43'N	11°11'E
Stanger	SF	322	29°20'S	31°18'E
Stanhope		374	45°01'N	71°47'W
Stanichno-Luganskoye	UP	624	48°39'N	39°30'E
Stanišić	YO	630	45°56'N	19°10'E
Stanislaus		372	37°40'N	121°14'W
Stanke Dimitrov	BU	573	42°16'N	23°07'E
Stanley		388	51°42'S	57°51'W
Stanley	UK	626	54°52'N	1°42'W
Stanley	US	398	48°19'N	102°23'W
Stanley Res.	IN	496	11°54'N	77°50'E
Stanovo	YO	630	44°00'N	20°52'E
Stanovoye Nagorye		468	56°00'N	114°00'E
Stanovoy Khrebet	RS	612	56°20'N	126°00'E
Stanovoy Kolodez'		560	52°49'N	36°16'E
Stans	SZ	622	46°57'N	8°21'E
Stansmore Ra.	AS	656	21°00'S	128°30'E
Stanthorpe		652	28°40'S	151°57'E
Stanton		372	41°57'N	97°13'W
Stanton		374	37°50'N	83°51'W
Stanton		376	32°07'N	101°47'W
Stanton	CA	390	69°45'N	128°53'W
Staples		374	46°21'N	94°47'W
Star'		560	53°37'N	34°09'E
Starachowice	PL	606	51°04'N	21°04'E
Stará L'ubovňa	LO	616	49°18'N	20°42'E
Stara Moravica	YO	630	45°52'N	19°28'E
Stara Pazova	YO	630	44°59'N	20°10'E
Stara Planina	BU	573	43°15'N	25°00'E
Stará Turá	LO	616	48°46'N	17°41'E
Staraya Mayna		466	54°36'N	48°57'E
Staraya Racheyka		560	53°22'N	48°01'E
Staraya Russa	RS	612	58°00'N	31°23'E
Staraya Vyzhevka	UP	624	51°26'N	24°26'E
Stara Zagora	BU	573	42°26'N	25°38'E
Starbuck		372	45°36'N	95°31'W
Starbuck		372	49°46'N	97°37'W
Starbuck I.	KR	660	6°00'S	156°00'W
Starčevo	YO	630	44°48'N	20°42'E
Star City		378	33°56'N	91°50'W
Stargard Szczeciński	PL	606	53°20'N	15°03'E
Stari Grad	HR	574	43°10'N	16°36'E
Staritsa		560	56°30'N	34°56'E
Starke		378	29°56'N	82°06'W
Starkville	US	398	33°27'N	88°48'W
Star Lake		374	44°09'N	75°01'W
Star Mountains	PP	664	5°10'S	141°50'E
Starnberger See	GM	584	47°55'N	11°19'E
Starobil's'k	UP	624	49°16'N	38°56'E
Starobin	BO	569	52°44'N	27°28'E
Staroderevyankovskaya		564	46°08'N	38°56'E
Starodub		560	52°35'N	32°46'E
Starogard Gdański	PL	606	53°58'N	18°33'E
Starokostyantyniv	UP	624	49°45'N	27°13'E
Starominskaya		564	46°32'N	39°05'E
Staro Selo	YO	630	44°18'N	21°06'E
Staroshcherbinovskaya		564	46°38'N	38°40'E
Starovelichkovskaya		564	45°26'N	38°44'E
Start Pt.	UK	626	50°13'N	3°38'W

Start Pt.	UK	626	59°16'N	2°21'W
Stary Sącz	PL	606	49°34'N	20°39'E
Staryye Dorogi	BO	569	53°02'N	28°16'E
Staryy Krym	UP	624	45°02'N	35°06'E
Staryy Oskol'	RS	612	51°17'N	37°51'E
Stassfurt	GM	584	51°52'N	11°35'E
Staszów	PL	606	50°33'N	21°10'E
State College	US	398	40°47'N	77°51'W
Staten		374	40°35'N	74°11'W
Statesboro	US	398	32°26'N	81°47'W
Statesville		378	35°46'N	80°53'W
Staunton		374	39°00'N	89°47'W
Staunton	US	398	38°08'N	79°04'W
Stavanger	NO	604	58°58'N	5°41'E
Staveley	UK	626	53°16'N	1°21'W
Stavely		372	50°10'N	113°38'W
Stavishche	UP	624	49°23'N	30°12'E
Stavropol'	RS	612	45°03'N	41°58'E
Stavrós	GR	588	40°40'N	23°42'E
Stawell		652	37°03'S	142°46'E
Stayner		374	44°25'N	80°05'W
Stayton		372	44°48'N	122°47'W
Stead		372	50°26'N	96°27'W
Steamboat Springs	US	398	40°29'N	106°49'W
Steckborn	SZ	622	47°40'N	8°59'E
Steelman		372	49°18'N	102°36'W
Steelville		374	37°58'N	91°21'W
Steenbergen	NL	602	51°35'N	4°19'E
Steenburg Lake		374	44°50'N	77°42'W
Steenkool	ID	500	2°07'S	133°32'E
Steen River	CA	390	59°35'N	117°10'W
Steens Mts.		372	42°35'N	118°35'W
Steenwijk	NL	602	52°47'N	6°07'E
Steep Point		652	26°00'S	113°30'E
Ştefăneşti	RO	610	47°48'N	27°12'E
Stefanov	LO	616	48°40'N	17°11'E
Stefansson I.	CA	390	73°30'N	105°30'W
Steffen, Cerro	AR	419	44°23'S	71°41'W
Steffen Strait	PP	664	2°30'S	150°50'E
Steffisburg	SZ	622	46°47'N	7°38'E
Stege	DA	576	54°59'N	12°18'E
Stegersbach	AU	568	47°10'N	16°10'E
Steilloopbrug	SF	322	23°26'S	28°37'E
Steinach	AU	568	47°05'N	11°28'E
Steinakirchen am Forst	AU	568	48°04'N	15°02'E
Stein am Rhein	SZ	622	47°40'N	8°51'E
Steinbach	CA	390	49°32'N	96°41'W
Steinfort	LU	598	49°40'N	5°55'E
Steinhausen	WA	313	21°49'S	18°14'E
Steinkjer	NO	604	64°01'N	11°30'E
Steinkopf	SF	322	29°15'S	17°14'E
Steinshamn	NO	604	62°46'N	6°28'E
Steinsland	NO	604	60°12'N	5°06'E
Stekene	BE	570	51°12'N	4°02'E
Steklyanka		560	59°08'N	41°37'E
Stella	SF	322	26°33'S	24°53'E
Stellenbosch		270	33°55'S	18°51'E
Stello, Monte	FR	580	42°47'N	9°25'E
Stenay	FR	580	49°29'N	5°12'E
Stendal	GM	584	52°36'N	11°51'E
Stende	LG	596	57°11'N	22°33'E
Stenungsund	SW	621	58°05'N	11°49'E
Stepanakert	AJ	483	39°50'N	46°46'E
Stepanavan	AM	482	41°01'N	44°23'E
Stepantsevo		560	56°08'N	41°42'E
Stephan Strait	PP	664	4°00'S	145°10'E
Stephens, C.	NZ	663	40°42'S	173°57'E
Stephens Creek	AS	656	31°50'S	141°30'E
Stephenville	CA	390	48°33'N	58°35'W
Stephenville	US	398	32°13'N	98°12'W
Stephenville Crossing		370	48°30'N	58°20'W
Stepnoy		466	54°04'N	60°26'E
Stepnoye		560	51°24'N	46°52'E
Stepnoye	KG	514	43°11'N	73°57'E
Stepnyak	KZ	510	52°50'N	70°50'E
Steptoe Valley		372	39°40'N	114°45'W
Sterkspruit	SF	322	30°32'S	27°21'E
Sterkstroom	SF	322	31°34'S	26°33'E
Sterling		370	41°47'N	89°41'W
Sterling		378	38°12'N	98°12'W
Sterling	US	398	40°37'N	103°12'W
Sterling	US	398	60°31'N	150°48'W
Sterling City		376	31°50'N	100°58'W
Sterling Heights		370	42°35'N	83°03'W
Sterlington		378	32°41'N	92°05'W
Sterlitamak	RS	612	53°37'N	55°58'E
Šternberk	EZ	575	49°44'N	17°18'E
Sterzing (Vipiteno)	IT	593	46°53'N	11°25'E
Štětí	EZ	575	50°27'N	14°23'E
St-Étienne		270	21°10'S	55°30'E
Stettler	CA	390	52°19'N	112°43'W
Steuben		374	44°30'N	67°57'W
Steubenville		374	40°21'N	80°37'W
Stevenage	UK	626	51°55'N	0°13'W
Stevens Point		370	44°31'N	89°34'W
Stevensville		372	46°30'N	114°05'W
Stewart	CA	390	55°56'N	129°59'W
Stewart Crossing	CA	390	63°23'N	136°40'W
Stewart I.	NZ	663	47°00'S	167°50'E
Stewart Is.	BP	666	8°10'S	162°15'E
Stewart Town	JM	414	18°23'N	77°27'W
Stewartville		374	43°51'N	92°29'W
Steynrus	SF	322	27°57'S	27°34'E
Steynsburg	SF	322	31°18'S	25°49'E
Steyr	AU	568	48°03'N	14°25'E
Steytlerville	SF	322	33°20'S	24°21'E
Stiavnické Pohorie	LO	616	48°40'N	18°45'E
Stiens	NL	602	53°16'N	5°46'E
Stigler		378	35°15'N	95°07'W
Stikine	CA	390	56°42'N	131°48'W
Stikine	CA	390	56°37'N	132°21'W
Stikine Range		368	58°45'N	130°00'W
Stilbaai	SF	322	34°22'S	21°24'E
Stilís	GR	588	38°55'N	22°36'E
Stilling	DA	576	56°04'N	10°00'E
Stillwater	US	398	36°06'N	97°03'W
Stillwater Range		372	39°48'N	118°10'W
Stilo, Punta	IT	593	38°26'N	16°35'E
Stilwell		374	35°48'N	94°37'W
Štimlje	YO	630	42°27'N	21°02'E
Stinnett		376	35°49'N	101°26'W
Štip	MK	599	41°44'N	22°12'E
Stirling		652	31°57'S	115°48'E
Stirling	AS	656	21°44'S	133°45'E
Stirling	UK	626	56°07'N	3°57'W
Stjørdal	NO	604	63°28'N	10°56'E
St Joseph	DO	407	15°24'N	61°26'W
Stockdale		376	29°14'N	97°57'W
Stockerau	AU	568	48°23'N	16°13'E
Stockholm	SW	621	59°20'N	18°04'E
Stockpoort	SF	322	23°24'S	27°20'E
Stockport	UK	626	53°24'N	2°09'W
Stockton		372	39°25'N	99°16'W
Stockton		374	37°41'N	93°47'W
Stockton	US	398	37°57'N	121°17'W
Stockton-on-Tees	UK	626	54°34'N	1°19'W
Stockton Plateau		376	30°30'N	102°30'W
Stod	EZ	575	49°38'N	13°10'E
Stodolishche		560	54°11'N	32°39'E
Stoeng Treng	CB	489	13°31'N	105°58'E
Stoer, Pt. of	UK	626	58°15'N	5°21'W
Stoffberg	SF	322	25°25'S	29°50'E
Stoke-on-Trent	UK	626	53°00'N	2°09'W
Stokes Bay	CA	390	45°00'N	81°22'W
Stokes Range	AS	656	17°00'S	130°30'E
Stokksnes	IC	591	64°13'N	15°00'W

Stokmarknes	NO	604	68°33'N	14°53'E
Stolac	BK	572	43°05'N	17°58'E
Stolberg	GM	584	50°46'N	6°13'E
Stolbovoi, Mys		468	56°42'N	163°19'E
Stolbovoy, O.	RS	612	74°05'N	136°00'E
Stolbtsy	BO	569	53°29'N	26°44'E
Stolin	BO	569	51°53'N	26°51'E
Stöllet	SW	621	60°25'N	13°15'E
Stompneuspunt	SF	322	32°41'S	17°58'E
Ston	HR	574	42°50'N	17°42'E
Stonehaven	UK	626	56°57'N	2°12'W
Stonehenge	AS	656	24°22'S	143°17'E
Stoner	CA	390	53°38'N	122°39'W
Stonewall		372	50°08'N	97°19'W
Stonewall		378	32°07'N	88°46'W
Stoney Creek		374	43°13'N	79°46'W
Stony Creek Camp	CA	390	30°48'N	136°00'W
Stony Hill	JM	414	18°05'N	76°48'W
Stonyhill Point		266	37°08'S	12°14'W
Stony Rapids	CA	390	59°16'N	105°50'W
Stora Le	SW	621	59°05'N	11°55'E
Stora Lulevatten	SW	621	67°08'N	19°20'E
Storavan		556	65°42'N	18°12'E
Storby		558	60°11'N	19°31'E
Stord		558	59°50'N	5°14'E
Store Bælt	DA	576	55°35'N	10°52'E
Storebø	NO	604	60°05'N	5°11'E
Stor-Elvdal	NO	604	61°29'N	10°59'E
Støren	NO	604	63°02'N	10°18'E
Storeytown		374	46°34'N	66°09'W
Stor I.	CA	390	78°52'N	86°30'W
Storlien	SW	621	63°19'N	12°03'E
Storm Lake	US	398	42°38'N	95°12'W
Stornoway		372	51°17'N	102°02'W
Stornoway	UK	626	58°12'N	6°23'W
Storozhevsk		466	61°57'N	52°20'E
Storozhinets	UP	624	48°10'N	25°43'E
Storsjön	SW	621	60°29'N	16°39'E
Storslett	NO	604	69°46'N	21°01'E
Storsteinnes	NO	604	69°14'N	19°15'E
Storsteinsfjellet	NO	604	68°14'N	17°52'E
Storthoaks		372	49°23'N	101°36'W
Storuman	SW	621	65°06'N	17°06'E
Storuman	SW	621	65°14'N	16°54'E
Storvreta	SW	621	59°58'N	17°42'E
Stosch, Isla	CI	428	49°09'S	75°26'W
Stoung	CB	489	12°50'N	104°19'E
Stour	UK	626	52°00'N	0°30'E
Stovring		558	56°53'N	9°51'E
Stowmarket	UK	626	52°11'N	0°59'E
Stoyba	RS	612	52°48'N	131°42'E
Strabane	UK	626	54°43'N	7°27'W
Strachan	UK	626	57°01'N	2°32'W
Strachur	UK	626	56°10'N	5°04'W
Stracin	MK	599	42°09'N	22°01'E
Straffan	EI	592	53°18'N	6°37'W
Strahan		652	42°09'S	145°20'E
Strakonice	EZ	575	49°15'N	13°54'E
Straldzha	BU	573	42°36'N	26°41'E
Strallegg	AU	568	47°24'N	15°43'E
Stralsund	GM	584	54°18'N	13°03'E
Stranda	NO	604	62°19'N	6°54'E
Strandby	DA	576	57°29'N	10°28'E
Strandhill		558	54°16'N	8°35'W
Strängnäs	SW	621	59°22'N	17°00'E
Stranraer	UK	626	54°54'N	5°02'W
Strasbourg	FR	580	48°35'N	7°44'E
Strasburg		372	46°04'N	100°19'W
Strasburg		374	38°59'N	78°21'W
Strasheny	MD	601	47°08'N	28°36'E
Strassen	LU	598	49°37'N	6°04'E
Stratford		374	43°20'N	81°00'W
Stratford		376	36°20'N	102°04'W
Stratford	NZ	663	39°20'S	174°17'E
Stratford-upon-Avon	UK	626	52°11'N	1°42'W
Strathaven	UK	626	55°40'N	4°04'W
Strathgorden	AS	656	42°46'S	146°02'E
Strathmore		372	51°03'N	113°23'W
Strathnaver	CA	390	53°17'N	122°30'W
Strathy Pt.	UK	626	58°35'N	4°01'W
Stratton	CA	390	48°41'N	94°10'W
Straubing	GM	584	48°53'N	12°34'E
Straumnes	IC	591	66°25'N	23°08'W
Straumsjøen	NO	604	68°40'N	14°26'E
Strausberg	GM	584	52°35'N	13°53'E
Strawberry		372	38°11'N	120°00'W
Strawberry		372	40°10'N	110°00'W
Strazhitsa	BU	573	43°14'N	25°58'E
Streaky Bay	AS	656	32°49'S	134°13'E
Streator		374	41°07'N	38°50'W
Strehaia	RO	610	44°37'N	23°12'E
Strekov	LO	616	47°53'N	18°24'E
Strelcha	BU	573	42°30'N	24°19'E
Strenči	LG	596	57°37'N	25°41'E
Streshin	BO	569	52°43'N	30°07'E
Stretto di Messina	IT	593	38°15'N	15°35'E
Streymoy		558	62°08'N	7°00'W
Strezhevoy	RS	612	60°43'N	77°34'E
Strib	DA	576	55°32'N	9°47'E
Stříbro	EZ	575	49°45'N	13°00'E
Strickland	PP	664	6°30'S	142°00'E
Strimasund	SW	621	66°04'N	14°56'E
Strimón	GR	588	40°37'N	24°03'E
Strimonikós, Kólpos	GR	588	40°30'N	24°10'E
Strobel, Lago	AR	419	48°22'S	71°12'W
Strobl	AU	568	47°43'N	13°29'E
Strøby Egede		558	55°25'N	12°12'E
Stroeder	AR	419	40°11'S	62°37'W
Str. of Singapore	ID	500	1°15'N	104°00'E
Stroitel'		560	50°47'N	36°29'E
Strokestown		558	53°47'N	8°06'W
Stromboli, I.	IT	593	38°47'N	15°13'E
Strome	CA	390	52°48'N	112°04'W
Stromeferry	UK	626	57°20'N	5°34'W
Strømmen		558	59°57'N	11°00'E
Strømmes		388	54°01'S	36°12'W
Stromness	UK	626	58°57'N	3°18'W
Stroms	SW	621	63°30'N	16°00'E
Strömsbruk	SW	621	61°49'N	17°18'E
Strömsburg		372	41°06'N	97°35'W
Strömstad	SW	621	58°56'N	11°10'E
Strömsund	SW	621	63°51'N	15°35'E
Strong		374	44°48'N	70°13'W
Stronsay	UK	626	59°09'N	2°35'W
Strontian	UK	626	56°42'N	5°35'W
Stropkov	LO	616	49°12'N	21°39'E
Stroud		376	35°44'N	96°39'W
Stroud	UK	626	51°45'N	2°12'W
Struan	UK	626	57°23'N	6°24'W
Struer	DA	576	56°29'N	8°34'E
Struga	MK	599	41°11'N	20°41'E
Strugi-Krasnyye		466	58°17'N	29°06'E
Struisbaai	SF	322	34°48'S	20°03'E
Struma	BU	573	40°47'N	23°51'E
Strumble Head	UK	626	52°01'N	5°04'W
Strumica	MK	599	41°26'N	22°39'E
Strumica	MK	599	41°30'N	22°25'E
Strunino		560	56°23'N	38°34'E
Strydenburg	SF	322	29°57'S	23°41'E
Stryn	NO	604	61°55'N	6°47'E
Strzelce Krajeńskie	PL	606	52°52'N	15°32'E
Strzelce Opolskie	PL	606	50°31'N	18°18'E
Strzyżów	PL	606	49°52'N	21°48'E
Stuart		378	27°11'N	80°14'W
Stuartburn		372	49°08'N	96°43'W
Stuart Island		372	50°22'N	125°08'W

Stuart Lake		368	54°32'N	124°35'W
Stuart Plain		648	16°30'S	133°30'E
Stuarts Draft		374	38°01'N	79°02'W
Stubbekøbing	DA	576	54°53'N	12°03'E
Stučka	LG	596	56°35'N	25°12'E
Studénka	EZ	575	49°43'N	18°05'E
Stuie	CA	390	52°23'N	126°05'W
Stun Seng		476	14°00'N	105°00'E
Stupava	LO	616	48°16'N	17°01'E
Stupinc		560	54°53'N	38°05'E
Stupnički Botinec	HR	574	45°45'N	15°57'E
Sturgeon	CA	390	45°24'N	84°38'W
Sturgeon Bay		374	44°50'N	87°22'W
Sturgeon Lake		374	44°28'N	78°42'W
Sturgeon Weir	CA	390	54°17'N	101°51'W
Sturgis		372	51°56'N	102°32'W
Sturgis		374	41°48'N	85°25'W
Sturgis		374	37°32'N	87°59'W
Sturgis	US	398	44°24'N	103°30'W
Štúrovo	LO	616	47°48'N	18°44'E
Sturt Creek	AS	656	19°30'S	128°00'E
Sturt Desert	AS	656	28°00'S	140°30'E
Stutterheim	SF	322	32°34'S	27°25'E
Stuttgart		378	34°30'N	91°33'W
Stuttgart	GM	584	48°47'N	9°12'E
Štvrtok	LO	616	48°04'N	17°20'E
Stykkishólmur	IC	591	65°03'N	22°43'W
Suai	ID	500	9°21'S	125°17'E
Suai	MY	518	3°48'N	113°33'E
Suan		382	10°20'N	74°53'W
Suan	KN	512	38°46'N	126°21'E
Suana	CG	287	6°36'S	20°05'E
Suao	TW	532	24°37'N	121°48'E
Suapi		386	15°32'S	67°31'W
Suaqui Grande	MX	394	28°24'N	109°54'W
Suardi	AR	419	30°32'S	61°58'W
Suárez		380	1°00'N	74°00'W
Suárez	CO	430	6°46'N	73°16'W
Suárez	CO	430	2°57'N	76°42'W
Suau	PP	664	10°36'S	150°02'E
Suavanao	BP	666	7°36'S	158°42'E
Subačius	LH	597	55°44'N	24°47'E
Subarnarekha	IN	496	21°34'N	87°24'E
Subata	LG	596	56°01'N	25°54'E
Subaytiah	TS	329	35°14'N	9°08'E
Subbética, Cordillera	SP	618	37°45'N	3°15'W
Subcarpatii Moldovei	RO	610	46°54'N	26°05'E
Subi	ID	500	2°55'N	108°50'E
Sublette		376	37°28'N	100°50'W
Submeseta Norte	SP	618	41°30'N	5°00'W
Submeseta Sur	SP	618	39°00'N	5°00'W
Subotica	YO	630	46°06'N	19°41'E
Subulussalam	ID	500	2°39'N	97°52'E
Sučany	LO	616	49°05'N	19°00'E
Success		372	50°27'N	108°05'W
Suceava	RO	610	47°40'N	26°16'E
Suches	BL	422	14°47'S	69°19'W
Suchilapan	MX	394	17°23'N	94°59'W
Suchitoto	ES	409	13°56'N	89°02'W
Sucila	MX	394	21°11'N	88°19'W
Suckling, C.	PP	664	9°01'S	146°37'E
Suckling, Mount	PP	664	9°49'S	148°53'E
Sucre	BL	422	19°02'S	65°17'W
Sucre	CO	430	8°49'N	74°44'W
Sucre	EC	432	1°16'S	80°26'W
Sucre	VE	440	10°25'N	63°30'W
Sucúa	EC	432	2°28'S	78°10'W
Sucuriju		384	1°39'N	49°57'W
Sucuriú	BR	424	20°47'S	51°38'W
Sud, Canal du	HA	412	18°40'N	73°05'W
Sud, Canal du				
(La Gonâve, Canal de)	HA	412	18°30'N	73°00'W
Sud, Massif du	HA	412	18°20'N	72°50'W
Suda	RS	612	59°11'N	37°30'E
Sudak	UP	624	44°51'N	34°58'E
Sudan		38	15°00'N	30°00'E
Sudbury	CA	390	46°30'N	81°00'W
Sudbury	UK	626	52°02'N	0°44'E
Suddie	GY	434	7°07'N	58°29'W
Süderbrarup	GM	584	54°38'N	9°47'E
Sud-Est, Passe		654	23°11'S	135°03'W
Sudety	EZ	575	50°30'N	16°00'E
Sudi	TZ	327	10°06'S	39°55'E
Sudirman, Peg.		648	4°30'S	137°00'E
Sudislavl'		560	57°53'N	41°43'E
Sudogda		560	55°57'N	40°50'E
Sud-Ouest, Passe		654	23°11'S	134°58'W
Sudzha		560	51°12'N	35°15'E
Sue	SU	324	7°41'N	28°03'E
Sueca	SP	618	39°12'N	0°19'W
Suedinenie	BU	573	42°16'N	24°33'E
Suez, Gulf of	EG	290	30°30'N	32°15'E
Suez Canal	EG	290	29°57'N	32°34'E
Süf	JO	510	32°19'N	35°50'E
Şufaynah	SA	528	23°09'N	40°32'E
Sufers	SZ	622	46°34'N	9°21'E
Suffield		372	50°12'N	111°10'W
Suffolk		374	36°44'N	76°35'W
Şūfiān	IR	502	38°17'N	45°59'E
Sugar City		372	43°52'N	111°44'W
Sugar Land		378	29°37'N	95°38'W
Sugarloaf Key		378	24°34'N	81°34'W
Sugarloaf Pt.	AS	656	32°26'S	152°32'E
Sugbai Passage	RP	526	5°22'N	120°27'E
Süget	CH	490	41°16'N	87°15'E
Sugoy		468	64°00'N	155°30'E
Sugun	CH	490	39°52'N	76°46'E
Sugut	MY	518	6°10'N	117°30'E
Sugut, Tanjong	MY	518	6°27'N	117°43'E
Suha Gora	MK	599	41°50'N	21°05'E
Suhaia, L.	RO	610	43°43'N	25°15'E
Suhait	CH	490	39°36'N	105°04'E
Şuḩār	MU	523	24°21'N	56°42'E
Suhaylah	MU	523	24°48'N	56°12'E
Suhl	GM	584	50°36'N	10°42'E
Suhr	SZ	622	47°22'N	8°04'E
Şuḩut		564	38°32'N	30°33'E
Süï	PK	524	28°37'N	69°19'E
Sui, Laem	TH	534	9°23'N	99°19'E
Suibin	CH	490	47°18'N	131°48'E
Suide		472	37°30'N	110°14'E
Suifen He		474	43°20'N	131°46'E
Suifenhe	CH	490	44°23'N	131°09'E
Suihua	CH	490	46°38'N	126°58'E
Suijiang	CH	490	28°39'N	103°57'E
Suileng	CH	490	47°15'N	127°04'E
Suining	CH	490	33°53'N	117°55'E
Suining	CH	490	30°31'N	105°31'E
Suipacha	BL	422	21°35'S	65°36'W
Suir	EI	592	52°17'N	7°00'W
Suis, Hasy	LY	302	26°20'N	10°32'E
Sui Xian	CH	490	31°42'N	113°21'E
Suiyang	CH	490	27°56'N	107°10'E
Suizhong		472	40°21'N	120°21'E
Suj	CH	490	42°04'N	107°54'E
Sujangarh	IN	496	27°42'N	74°28'E
Sujawal	PK	524	24°36'N	68°05'E
Sukabumi	ID	500	6°55'S	106°56'E
Sukadana	ID	500	1°15'S	109°59'E
Sukadana, Telukan	ID	500	1°24'S	109°50'E
Sukagawa	JA	506	37°17'N	140°23'E
Sukaraja	ID	500	2°21'S	110°37'E
Sukau	MY	518	5°32'N	118°17'E
Sukch'ŏn	KN	512	39°24'N	125°38'E
Sukhana	RS	612	68°45'N	118°00'E
Sukhcharer Hät	BG	485	22°23'N	91°05'E

Sukhe Bator	MG	520	46°54'N	113°25'E
Sukhindol	BU	573	43°11'N	25°10'E
Sukhinichi		560	54°06'N	35°20'E
Sukhobezvodnoye		560	57°03'N	44°55'E
Sukhona	RS	612	60°46'N	46°24'E
Sukhothai	TH	534	17°01'N	99°49'E
Sukkertoppen		370	65°25'N	52°40'W
Sukkur	PK	524	27°42'N	68°52'E
Sukleya	MD	601	46°49'N	29°43'E
Sükösd	HU	590	46°17'N	19°00'E
Sukumo	JA	506	32°56'N	132°44'E
Sula	NO	604	61°08'N	4°55'E
Sula, Kep. (Celebes)	ID	500	1°52'S	125°22'E
Sulaco	HO	412	14°55'N	87°16'W
Sulaco	HO	412	15°01'N	87°44'W
Sulaiman Range	PK	524	30°30'N	70°10'E
Sulakyurt		564	40°10'N	33°44'E
Sulanheer	MG	520	42°41'N	109°20'E
Sula Obootoyn Suma	MG	520	48°02'N	111°22'E
Sulawesi (Celebes)	ID	500	2°00'S	121°00'E
Sulaymān	TS	329	36°42'N	10°30'E
Sulechów	PL	606	52°05'N	15°37'E
Sulęcin	PL	606	52°26'N	15°06'E
Suleja	NI	316	9°10'N	7°11'E
Sulejów	PL	606	51°20'N	19°51'E
Šulekovo	LO	616	48°26'N	17°46'E
Sulina	RO	610	45°09'N	29°38'E
Sulingen	GM	584	52°41'N	8°48'E
Sulitjelma	NO	604	67°08'N	16°02'E
Sullana	PE	436	4°53'S	80°41'W
Sullivan		374	38°12'N	91°09'W
Sullivan		374	39°05'N	87°24'W
Sullivan		374	39°35'N	88°36'W
Sullivan Bay		372	50°52'N	126°49'W
Sulphur		376	34°30'N	96°58'W
Sulphur		378	30°14'N	93°22'W
Sultan	CA	390	47°36'N	82°45'W
Sultan Dag.	TU	535	38°20'N	31°20'E
Sultan Hamud	KE	299	2°01'S	37°22'E
Sultanhanı		564	38°15'N	33°33'E
Sultan Kucarat	RP	526	7°16'N	124°18'E
Sultānpur	IN	496	26°16'N	82°04'E
Sulu Archipelago	RP	526	6°00'N	121°00'E
Sülüklü		564	38°53'N	32°21'E
Sülüktü	KG	514	39°56'N	69°34'E
Suluova	TU	535	40°50'N	35°39'E
Sulūq	LY	302	31°40'N	20°15'E
Sulusaray		564	40°00'N	36°06'E
Sulu Sea	RP	526	9°00'N	120°00'E
Sulu Sea Is.		476	9°00'N	119°00'E
Sulzbach-Rosenberg	GM	584	49°30'N	11°45'E
Sumalata	ID	500	0°59'N	122°30'E
Sumampa	AR	419	29°22'S	63°28'W
Sumangat, Tanjong	MY	518	6°38'N	117°31'E
Sumartin	HR	574	43°17'N	16°51'E
Sumatera (Sumatra)	ID	500	0°00'	102°00'E
Sumaúma	BR	424	7°50'S	60°02'W
Sumba	ID	500	10°00'S	120°00'E
Sumba, Île	CG	287	1°42'N	19°30'E
Sumba, Selat	ID	500	9°05'S	120°00'E
Sumbawa	ID	500	8°40'S	118°00'E
Sumbawanga	TZ	327	7°58'S	31°37'E
Sumbay	PE	436	15°58'S	71°23'W
Sumbe	AO	274	11°12'S	13°50'E
Sumbi	CG	287	4°58'S	13°21'E
Sumbundu	GA	295	13°23'N	15°32'W
Sumburgh Head	UK	626	59°50'N	1°16'W
Sumbuya	SL	320	7°39'N	11°58'W
Sumdo	CH	490	29°11'N	100°07'E
Sümeg	HU	590	46°59'N	17°17'E
Sumène	FR	580	43°59'N	3°43'E
Sumenep	ID	500	7°01'S	113°52'E
Sumesar Range	NP	522	27°30'N	84°30'E
Sumidero	CU	406	22°27'N	83°55'W
Sümiyn Bulag	MG	520	49°08'N	114°53'E
Sumki		466	55°03'N	65°44'E
Summerdown	WA	313	21°24'S	18°29'E
Summerland	CA	390	49°36'N	119°41'W
Summerside	CA	390	46°24'N	63°47'W
Summersville		374	38°16'N	80°51'W
Summerville	US	398	33°01'N	80°10'W
Summit		378	31°17'N	90°28'W
Summit City		372	40°41'N	122°24'W
Summit Lake	CA	390	54°17'N	122°38'W
Summit Roadhouse	CA	390	63°05'N	136°26'W
Sumpangbinangae	ID	500	4°23'S	119°39'E
Sumpango	GT	411	14°39'N	90°44'W
Šumperk	EZ	575	49°58'N	16°58'E
Sumprabum	BM	487	26°33'N	97°34'E
Sumqayıt	AJ	483	40°36'N	49°38'E
Sumskiy Posad		556	64°15'N	35°25'E
Sumter		378	33°55'N	80°20'W
Sumurup	ID	500	2°00'S	101°22'E
Sumuştā al Waqf	EG	290	28°55'N	30°51'E
Sumy	UP	624	50°54'N	34°48'E
Suna		560	57°51'N	50°05'E
Sunamganj	BG	485	25°04'N	91°24'E
Sunan	KN	512	39°12'N	125°42'E
Sunan Yugurzu Zizhixian	CH	490	38°58'N	99°24'E
Sunbury		374	40°51'N	76°47'W
Sunchales	AR	419	30°56'S	61°34'W
Sunch'ang	KS	513	35°22'N	127°09'E
Suncho Corral	AR	419	27°56'S	63°27'W
Sunch'ŏn	KN	512	39°25'N	125°56'E
Sunch'ŏn	KS	513	34°57'N	127°29'E
Sun City	SF	322	25°21'S	27°00'E
Sun City West		376	33°39'N	112°20'W
Sunda, Selat	ID	500	6°00'S	105°45'E
Sundalbayshing	MG	520	46°11'N	95°08'E
Sundance		372	44°24'N	104°22'W
Sundarbans	BG	485	22°00'N	89°00'E
Sundargarh	IN	496	22°07'N	84°02'E
Sundargarh		470	31°32'N	76°53'E
Sundbyberg		558	59°22'N	17°54'E
Sunderland	UK	626	54°54'N	1°22'W
Sündiken Dağları		564	39°57'N	31°14'E
Sundown		378	49°06'N	96°16'W
Sundridge		374	45°46'N	79°24'W
Sunds	DA	576	56°12'N	9°01'E
Sundsvall	SW	621	62°23'N	17°20'E
Sundumbili	SF	322	29°04'S	31°12'E
Sungaiapit	ID	500	0°44'N	102°13'E
Sungaibali	ID	500	3°25'S	116°24'E
Sungaiguntung	ID	500	0°18'N	103°37'E
Sungaikakap	ID	500	0°04'S	109°12'E
Sungai Kolok	TH	534	6°02'N	101°57'E
Sungaikupang		648	3°03'S	115°58'E
Sungai Lembing	MY	518	3°55'N	103°02'E
Sungailiat	ID	500	1°51'S	106°08'E
Sungaipakning	ID	500	1°20'N	102°06'E
Sungaipenuh	ID	500	2°05'S	101°23'E
Sungai Petani	MY	518	5°39'N	100°30'E
Sungaipinang	ID	500	0°48'S	114°04'E
Sungairalak	ID	500	0°27'S	102°59'E
Sungaiselan	ID	500	2°24'S	105°59'E
Sungai Simpang	SN	530	1°26'N	103°50'E
Sungai Siput	MY	518	4°49'N	101°04'E
Sungaitiram	ID	500	0°47'S	117°12'E
Sŭngho	KN	512	38°59'N	125°58'E
Sungiema	ID	500	8°14'N	10°37'W
Sŭngju	KS	513	35°00'N	127°20'E
Sungsang		478	2°22'S	104°56'E
Sŭngt'ong-ni	KN	512	39°58'N	126°31'E
Sungurlare	BU	573	42°46'N	26°47'E
Sungurlu	TU	535	40°10'N	34°23'E
Sunjiapuzi		474	42°02'N	126°34'E

Sun Kosi	NP	522	26°55'N	87°09'E
Sunland Park		376	31°47'N	106°35'W
Sunndalsøra	NO	604	62°40'N	8°33'E
Sunne	SW	621	59°50'N	13°09'E
Sunnynook		372	51°17'N	111°40'W
Sunnyside		372	48°43'N	122°18'W
Sunnyvale	US	398	37°22'N	122°02'W
Sun Prairie		374	43°11'N	89°12'W
Sunray		376	36°01'N	101°49'W
Sunrise		376	26°08'N	80°15'W
Suntar	RS	612	62°10'N	117°40'E
Suntar Khayata, Khrebet	RS	612	62°00'N	143°00'E
Suntu	ET	293	8°06'N	36°57'E
Sunwu	CH	490	49°24'N	127°21'E
Sunyani	GH	296	7°20'N	2°20'W
Sunyati		270	21°30'S	29°15'E
Sunzu	ZA	332	9°01'S	31°30'E
Suoi Rut	VM	540	20°45'N	105°04'E
Suolahti	FI	578	62°34'N	25°52'E
Suomenselkä		556	63°45'N	26°00'E
Suomussalmi	FI	578	64°54'N	29°00'E
Suo-nada	JA	506	33°50'N	131°30'E
Suonenjoki	FI	578	62°37'N	27°08'E
Suong	CB	489	11°55'N	105°39'E
Suonne	FI	578	61°40'N	26°30'E
Suouroy		558	61°30'N	6°15'W
Suoyarvi		556	62°05'N	32°21'E
Supachuy	BL	422	13°29'S	64°31'W
Supe	PE	436	10°48'S	77°44'W
Superb		368	51°53'N	109°27'W
Superfosfatnyy	UZ	539	39°41'N	66°52'E
Superior		372	40°01'N	98°04'W
Superior		374	46°43'N	92°06'W
Superior		376	33°17'N	111°05'W
Superior, Lake	CA	390	48°00'N	80°00'W
Superior Upland	US	398	45°00'N	89°30'W
Supetar	HR	574	43°25'N	16°32'E
Suphan Buri	TH	534	14°28'N	100°07'E
Supía	CO	430	5°27'N	75°39'W
Supiori		478	0°45'S	135°30'E
Supra		466	60°51'N	64°49'E
Sup'ung Res.	KN	512	40°27'N	124°58'E
Şūq 'Abs	YM	541	16°30'N	43°12'E
Sūq ash Shuyūkh	IZ	504	30°53'N	46°28'E
Şuqaylabiyah	SY	531	35°22'N	36°23'E
Suqian	CH	490	33°57'N	118°16'E
Suqutra (Socotra)	YM	541	12°00'N	54°00'E
Şūr	LE	516	33°15'N	35°10'E
Şūr	MU	523	22°54'N	59°32'E
Sur, Pt.	US	398	36°18'N	121°52'W
Sur, Punta	AR	419	36°53'S	56°39'W
Sura	RS	612	56°06'N	46°00'E
Sūrāb	PK	524	28°29'N	66°16'E
Surabaya	ID	500	7°13'S	112°45'E
Surada	IN	496	19°45'N	84°26'E
Surakarta	ID	500	7°32'S	110°50'E
Surakhany		466	40°25'N	50°01'E
Surallah	RP	526	6°23'N	124°41'E
Surami	GG	495	42°01'N	43°35'E
Suramskiy Khrebet	GG	495	42°15'N	43°30'E
Suran	SY	531	35°17'N	36°45'E
Šurany	LO	616	48°05'N	18°11'E
Surat	AS	656	27°10'S	149°04'E
Surat	IN	496	21°10'N	72°50'E
Suratgarh	IN	496	29°19'N	73°54'E
Surat Thani	TH	534	9°08'N	99°20'E
Surazh		466	53°01'N	32°24'E
Surazh	BO	569	55°25'N	30°44'E
Surčin	YO	630	44°47'N	20°17'E
Surdulica	YO	630	42°41'N	22°10'E
Surendranagar	IN	496	22°40'N	71°43'E
Suretka	CS	405	9°34'N	82°56'W
Surfer's Paradise		652	28°03'S	153°25'E
Surgères	FR	580	46°06'N	0°45'W
Surgidero de Batabano	CU	406	22°41'N	82°18'W
Surgut	RS	612	61°15'N	73°20'E
Süri	IN	496	23°55'N	87°32'E
Súria	SP	618	41°50'N	1°45'E
Surigao	RP	526	9°45'N	125°30'E
Surin	TH	534	14°53'N	103°29'E
Suriname	NS	438	5°55'N	55°10'W
Suripa	VE	440	7°49'N	69°54'W
Surkhandar'ya	UZ	539	37°30'N	67°30'E
Surkhet	NP	522	28°36'N	81°36'E
Surkhob	TI	533	39°30'N	71°00'E
Surma	BG	485	25°00'N	91°50'E
Sur Masirah	MU	523	20°25'N	58°44'E
Sürmene	TU	535	40°55'N	40°07'E
Surnadal	NO	604	62°59'N	8°42'E
Surovikino		560	48°36'N	42°51'E
Surrey	CA	390	49°07'N	122°51'W
Sursee	SZ	622	47°10'N	8°06'E
Sursk		560	53°04'N	45°42'E
Surskoye		560	54°28'N	46°44'E
Surt	LY	302	31°13'N	16°35'E
Sürüç	TU	535	36°58'N	38°24'E
Surud, Raas	SO	321	11°10'N	47°30'E
Suruga-wan	JA	506	34°51'N	138°33'E
Surulangun	ID	500	2°37'S	102°45'E
Surumu	BR	424	3°22'N	60°19'W
Surup	RP	526	6°17'N	126°10'E
Surwakwima Falls	GY	434	6°06'N	60°40'W
Susac	HR	574	42°46'N	16°31'E
Süsah	LY	302	32°54'N	21°58'E
Süsah	TS	329	35°49'N	10°36'E
Susaki	JA	506	33°22'N	133°17'E
Susamyrtau, Khr.	KG	514	42°08'N	73°15'E
Susana	PU	298	12°18'N	16°28'W
Susanville	US	398	40°24'N	120°39'W
Suşehri	TU	535	40°11'N	38°06'E
Sušice	EZ	575	49°14'N	13°31'E
Susna	US	398	62°00'N	150°00'W
Suslonger		560	56°18'N	48°13'E
Susquehanna	US	398	39°32'N	76°04'W
Susques	AR	419	23°25'S	66°29'W
Sussex	CA	390	45°43'N	65°31'W
Susten Pass	SZ	622	46°44'N	8°27'E
Susua	ID	500	3°30'S	120°54'E
Susubona	BP	666	8°17'S	159°29'E
Susuka	BP	666	6°30'S	157°00'E
Susuman	RS	612	62°47'N	148°10'E
Susurluk		564	39°54'N	28°10'E
Susuz	TU	535	40°47'N	43°07'E
Susville	FR	580	44°22'N	6°58'E
Susz	PL	606	53°43'N	19°21'E
Sutherland		270	32°23'S	20°39'E
Sutherland		372	41°09'N	101°07'W
Sutherland	SF	322	32°24'S	20°40'E
Sutherland Falls	NZ	663	44°48'S	167°44'E
Sutherlin		372	43°23'N	123°18'W
Sutlej	IN	496	29°23'N	71°02'E
Sutterton		558	52°54'N	0°05'W
Sutton		372	40°36'N	97°51'W
Suttsu	JA	506	42°48'N	140°14'E
Sutwik I.		368	56°34'N	157°12'W
Su'u	BP	666	9°05'S	161°00'E
Suugant	MG	520	45°32'N	107°00'E
Su'uholo	BP	666	9°45'S	161°58'E
Süüj	MG	520	47°51'N	104°03'E
Suunui	KS	513	36°32'N	128°02'E
Suurberge	SF	322	33°00'S	24°58'E
Suurbraak	SF	322	34°01'S	20°39'E
Suure-Jaani	EN	577	58°33'N	25°28'E
Suur Väin	EN	577	58°40'N	23°25'E
Suva	FJ	660	18°08'S	178°25'E
Suvainiškis	LH	597	56°10'N	25°17'E

T

Tangali	GV	297	11°21'N	11°56'W
Tangalla	CE	530	6°03'N	80°48'E
Tanganyika, Lake	CG	287	6°00'S	29°30'E
Tangará da Serra	BR	424	14°37'S	57°29'W
Tangarare	BP	666	9°29'S	159°35'E
Tanger	MO	310	35°45'N	5°49'W
Tangerhütte	GM	584	52°26'N	11°48'E
Tangermünde	GM	584	52°33'N	11°57'E
Tanggo		472	31°37'N	93°18'E
Tanggula Shan	CH	490	33°00'N	92°00'E
Tanggula Shankou	CH	490	32°42'N	92°27'E
Tanggulashanqu	CH	490	34°13'N	92°24'E
Tangi	PK	524	34°18'N	71°40'E
Tangjin	KS	513	36°54'N	126°38'E
Tangkak	MY	518	2°16'N	102°33'E
Tangki Ayer	BX	486	4°55'N	114°56'E
Tangkit Tebak	ID	500	5°01'S	104°34'E
Tanglag	CH	490	34°00'N	99°27'E
Tangmai		472	30°08'N	95°08'E
Tango	AO	274	8°06'S	15°38'E
Tangra Yumco	CH	490	31°00'N	86°38'E
Tangshan	CH	490	39°37'N	118°10'E
Tangub	RP	526	8°03'N	123°44'E
Tanguiéta	BN	276	10°37'N	1°16'E
Tangwanghe		472	48°26'N	129°34'E
Tangyuan		472	46°42'N	129°55'E
Tanhaçu		384	14°01'S	41°17'W
Taniantaweng Shan	CH	490	31°20'N	98°00'E
Tanicuchí	EC	432	0°47'S	78°38'W
Tanimbar, Kep.	ID	500	7°30'S	131°30'E
Taniwel	ID	500	2°53'S	128°27'E
Tanjay	RP	526	9°31'N	123°09'E
Tanjon' Androntany	MA	304	12°24'S	48°45'E
Tanjong Malim	MY	518	3°41'N	101°31'E
Tanjung	ID	500	2°11'S	115°23'E
Tanjungbalai	ID	500	2°58'N	99°48'E
Tanjungbatu	ID	500	0°41'N	103°26'E
Tanjungbatu	ID	500	3°00'S	116°15'E
Tanjungkarang-Telukbetung	ID	500	5°26'S	105°16'E
Tanjungpandan	ID	500	2°45'S	107°39'E
Tanjungpinang	ID	500	0°55'N	104°30'E
Tanjungpriok		478	6°06'S	106°53'E
Tanjungredeb	ID	500	2°09'N	117°29'E
Tanjungselor	ID	500	2°51'N	117°22'E
Tanjungwira	ID	500	0°05'S	117°26'E
Tānk	PK	524	32°13'N	70°23'E
Tanlay		562	47°50'N	4°05'E
Tann	GM	584	50°55'N	9°42'E
Tanna (Tana)	NH	669	19°30'S	169°30'E
Tannan	YM	541	35°01'N	135°09'E
Tannay		562	47°21'N	3°36'E
Tannheim	AU	568	47°29'N	10°30'E
Tannis Bugt	DA	576	57°40'N	10°15'E
Tannum Sands		652	23°57'S	151°22'E
Tannu Ola, Khrebet	RS	612	51°00'N	94°00'E
Tano	GH	296	5°07'N	2°56'W
Tanoriki		654	15°00'S	168°10'E
Tânout	NG	314	14°58'N	8°53'E
Tanques de Guadalupe		376	24°46'N	102°08'W
Tanquián	MX	394	21°37'N	98°38'W
Tanshui	TW	532	25°11'N	121°25'E
Tānsing	NP	522	27°52'N	83°33'E
Tantā	EG	290	30°47'N	31°00'E
Tantabin	BM	487	18°50'N	96°29'E
Tan-Tan	MO	310	28°26'N	11°06'W
Tantoyuca	MX	394	21°21'N	98°14'W
Tanuku	IN	496	16°45'N	81°48'E
Tanumshede	SW	621	58°44'N	11°19'E
Tanyang	KS	513	36°56'N	128°19'E
Tanyurer		468	66°00'N	175°00'E
Tanzania		38	6°00'S	35°00'E
Tao He	CH	490	34°30'N	102°10'E
Taole	CH	490	38°49'N	106°39'E
Taongi	RM	661	13°50'N	169°30'E
Taormina	IT	593	37°51'N	15°17'E
Taos	US	398	36°24'N	105°34'W
Taos Pueblo		376	36°26'N	105°32'W
Taoudenni	ML	307	22°40'N	4°00'W
Taounate	MO	310	34°33'N	4°39'W
Taourirt	AG	272	26°41'N	0°13'E
Taourirt	MO	310	34°25'N	2°54'W
Taoyuan		472	28°54'N	111°27'E
Taoyuan	TW	532	25°00'N	121°18'E
Tapa	EN	577	59°16'N	25°58'E
Tapachula	MX	394	14°54'N	92°17'W
Tapaga Pt.	WS	668	14°05'S	171°10'W
Tapah	MY	518	4°11'N	101°16'E
Tapajós	BR	424	2°24'S	54°41'W
Tapaktuan	ID	500	3°16'N	97°11'E
Tapalqué	AR	419	36°21'S	60°01'W
Tapan	ID	500	2°10'S	101°04'E
Tapanahoni	NS	438	4°22'N	54°27'W
Tapanlieh	TW	532	21°58'N	120°46'E
Tapanui	NZ	663	45°57'S	169°16'E
Tapará, Sa. do	BR	424	2°45'S	52°15'W
Taparo	TD	438	10°25'N	61°15'W
Tapauá	BR	424	5°40'S	64°21'W
Tapauá	BR	424	5°45'S	64°23'W
Tapaz	RP	526	11°16'N	122°32'E
Tapes	BR	424	30°40'S	51°24'W
Tapeta	LI	301	6°30'N	8°52'W
Taphan Hin	TH	534	16°13'N	100°26'E
Ta Phraya	TH	534	14°00'N	102°49'E
Tapi Aike	AR	419	51°03'S	71°46'W
Tapiche	PE	436	4°59'S	73°51'W
Tapili	CG	287	3°25'N	27°40'E
Tapini	PP	664	8°22'S	146°57'E
Tapirapecó, Sierra	VE	440	2°00'N	64°30'W
Taplejung	NP	522	27°21'N	87°40'E
Tapolca	HU	590	46°53'N	17°26'E
Tappahannock		374	37°55'N	76°51'W
Tappalang	ID	500	2°51'S	118°54'E
Tapti	IN	496	21°00'N	73°00'E
Tapu, Motu		654	21°09'S	175°09'W
Tapul Group	RP	526	5°31'N	120°57'E
Tapun	IN	496	27°35'N	96°22'E
Tapung		478	0°30'N	101°00'E
Tapurah	BR	424	12°53'S	56°29'W
Taqab	SU	324	19°50'N	30°16'E
Taqātu' Hayyā	SU	324	18°20'N	36°22'E
Taquari	BR	424	18°40'S	57°30'W
Taquarituba	BR	424	23°31'S	49°15'W
Taquil	EC	432	3°54'S	79°18'W
Tara		652	27°17'S	150°28'E
Tara	RS	612	56°54'N	74°22'E
Tara	YO	630	43°21'N	18°51'E
Tara	ZA	332	16°57'S	26°47'E
Taraba	NI	316	7°52'N	10°58'E
Tarabo		266	8°30'N	10°15'E
Tarabuco	BL	422	19°10'S	64°57'W
Ţarābulus	LE	516	34°25'N	35°51'E
Ţarābulus (Tripoli)	LY	302	32°52'N	13°10'E
Tarabulus (Tripolitania)	LY	302	31°00'N	15°00'E
Taraco	BL	422	16°27'S	68°52'W
Taradale	NZ	663	39°32'S	176°51'E
Tarahumara, Sierra		376	27°00'N	107°15'W
Tarai	NP	522	27°30'N	87°00'E
Tarairí	BL	422	21°05'S	63°28'W
Tarakan	ID	500	3°21'N	117°36'E
Tarakan	ID	500	3°18'N	117°38'E
Tarakit	KE	299	2°00'N	35°08'E
Tarakliya	MD	601	45°54'N	28°40'E
Tārākot	NP	522	28°53'N	82°59'E
Taramana	ID	500	8°12'S	124°51'E
Tarancón	SP	618	40°01'N	3°00'W
Taranto	IT	593	40°28'N	17°14'E
Taranto, Golfo di	IT	593	40°08'N	17°20'E
Tarapacá	CI	428	19°55'S	69°31'W
Tarapacá	CO	430	2°52'S	69°44'W
Tarapaina	BP	666	9°24'S	161°21'E
Tarapoa	EC	432	0°08'S	76°25'W
Tarapoto	PE	436	6°30'S	76°25'W
Tarare	FR	580	45°54'N	4°26'E
Tarariras	UY	439	34°17'S	57°37'W
Tarascon	FR	580	43°47'N	4°39'E
Tarascon-sur-Ariège	FR	580	42°51'N	1°36'E
Tarashcha	UP	624	49°34'N	30°30'E
Tarasp	SZ	622	46°47'N	10°15'E
Tarata	BL	422	17°37'S	66°01'W
Tarata	PE	436	17°28'S	70°02'W
Tarauacá	BR	424	8°10'S	70°42'W
Tarauru-roa		654	23°07'S	135°11'W
Tara-Vai		654	23°08'S	134°55'W
Taravao B.		654	17°41'S	145°37'W
Tarawa	KR	660	1°30'N	173°00'E
Tarawera, L.	NZ	663	38°12'S	176°27'E
Tarazá	CO	430	7°35'N	75°21'W
Tarazona	SP	618	41°54'N	1°44'W
Tarazona de la Mancha	SP	618	39°15'N	1°55'W
Tarbagatay, Khrebet	KZ	510	49°11'N	86°15'E
Tarbaj	KE	299	2°13'N	40°07'E
Tarbat Ness	UK	626	57°51'N	3°46'W
Tarbela Dam	PK	524	34°12'N	72°49'E
Tarbert	UK	626	57°54'N	6°48'W
Tarbes	FR	580	43°13'N	0°04'E
Tarboro		378	35°54'N	77°31'W
Tárcoles	CS	405	9°45'N	84°37'W
Tarcoola	AS	656	30°41'S	134°33'E
Tardienta	SP	618	41°59'N	0°32'W
Taree	AS	656	31°54'S	152°28'E
Tärendö	SW	621	67°10'N	22°39'E
Tarfawi, Bi'r	EG	290	22°57'N	29°55'E
Tarfawi, Bi'r at	LY	302	29°34'N	24°03'E
Tarfaya	MO	310	27°55'N	12°54'W
Targalak	CH	490	39°19'N	74°49'E
Targuist	MO	310	34°57'N	4°18'W
Tarhūnah	LY	302	32°26'N	13°38'E
Tari	AO	274	8°09'S	14°23'E
Tari	PP	664	5°51'S	142°55'E
Tarialan	MG	520	49°38'N	101°59'E
Tariana	CO	430	0°53'N	69°11'W
Táriba	VE	440	7°49'N	72°13'W
Tarīf	TC	538	24°03'N	53°46'E
Tarifa	EC	432	2°01'S	79°46'W
Tarifa	SP	618	36°01'N	5°36'W
Tarifa, Punta de	SP	618	36°01'N	5°36'W
Tarija	BL	422	21°31'S	64°45'W
Tariku		478	3°04'S	138°09'E
Tarīm	YM	541	16°03'N	49°00'E
Tarim	CH	490	39°06'N	77°01'E
Tarime	TZ	327	1°21'S	34°22'E
Tarim He	CH	490	41°05'N	86°40'E
Tarim Liuchang	CH	490	40°47'N	87°12'E
Tarim Pendi	CH	490	41°00'N	84°00'E
Tarin	AF	480	33°00'N	66°30'E
Taring	ID	500	3°50'N	97°33'E
Tarīn Kowt	AF	480	32°37'N	65°51'E
Taripe	BT	486	27°39'N	91°27'E
Tar Island	CA	390	57°00'N	111°29'W
Taritatu	ID	500	2°54'S	138°27'E
Tarkastad	SF	322	32°01'S	26°16'E
Tarkhankut, Mys	UP	624	45°21'N	32°30'E
Tarkio		374	40°26'N	95°23'W
Tarko-Sale	RS	612	64°55'N	77°49'E
Tarkwa	GH	296	5°18'N	1°59'W
Tarlac	RP	526	15°29'N	120°35'E
Tarlak	CH	490	41°51'N	84°12'E
Tarlton Downs	AS	656	22°37'S	136°47'E
Tarma	PE	436	11°25'S	75°42'W
Tarn	FR	580	44°06'N	1°02'E
Tärnaby	SW	621	65°43'N	15°16'E
Tarnak	AF	480	31°25'N	65°30'E
Tarnica	PL	606	49°30'N	23°00'E
Tarnobrzeg	PL	606	50°35'N	21°41'E
Tarnogskiy Gorodok	RS	612	60°30'N	43°33'E
Tarnos	FR	580	43°32'N	1°28'W
Tarnów	PL	606	50°01'N	20°59'E
Tarō	JA	506	39°45'N	141°59'E
Taro	IT	593	31°00'N	84°16'E
Tarok Tso	CH	490	31°10'N	84°00'E
Ţārom	IR	502	28°11'N	55°46'E
Taron		650	4°30'S	153°30'E
Taroom	AS	656	25°39'S	149°48'E
Tarouca	PO	608	41°01'N	7°47'W
Taroudannt	MO	310	30°29'N	8°52'W
Tarp	GM	584	54°40'N	9°24'E
Tarpa	HU	590	48°06'N	22°32'E
Tarqui	CO	430	2°06'N	75°50'W
Tarqui	PE	436	1°35'S	75°15'W
Tarquinia	IT	593	42°15'N	11°46'E
Tarrafal	CV	281	15°17'N	23°46'W
Tarragona	SP	618	41°00'N	0°45'W
Tàrrega	SP	618	41°39'N	1°09'E
Tarri	SO	321	0°42'N	41°38'E
Tarso Ahon	CD	283	20°23'N	18°18'E
Tarso Emissi	CD	283	21°13'N	18°32'E
Tarso Tieroko	CD	283	20°45'N	17°52'E
Tarsumdo	CH	490	33°54'N	99°19'E
Tarsus	TU	535	36°55'N	34°53'E
Tart	CH	490	37°04'N	92°52'E
Tartagal	AR	419	22°32'S	63°49'W
Tartu	EN	577	58°23'N	26°43'E
Ţarţūs	SY	531	34°53'N	35°53'E
Tarutyne	UP	624	46°12'N	29°09'E
Tarvagatay Nuur	MG	520	48°30'N	99°00'E
Tarvisio	IT	593	46°30'N	13°35'E
Tasajera, Sierra de la	MX	394	29°36'N	105°26'W
Tasawāh	LY	302	25°59'N	13°29'E
Tasbuget	KZ	510	44°46'N	65°33'E
Taşburun	TU	535	39°59'N	44°14'E
Täsch	SZ	622	46°03'N	7°47'E
Ta Seng	CB	489	13°24'N	104°47'E
Tashanta	RS	612	49°43'N	89°11'E
Tashauz	TX	537	41°50'N	59°58'E
Tāsh Gozar	AF	480	37°14'N	67°10'E
Tashi	CH	490	40°15'N	96°04'E
Tashi Gang	BT	486	27°19'N	91°34'E
Tashi Yång-tsi Dzong	BT	486	27°35'N	91°28'E
Tashkent (Toshkent)	UZ	539	41°18'N	69°18'E
Tashkepri	TX	537	36°18'N	62°38'E
Tash-Kumyr	KG	514	41°21'N	72°14'E
Tashla	RS	612	51°46'N	52°45'E
Tashtagol	RS	612	52°47'N	87°53'E
Tasikmalaya	ID	500	7°20'S	108°12'E
Tasil	SY	531	32°50'N	35°58'E
Tasiusaq		370	60°11'N	44°47'W
Tasjon	SW	621	64°15'N	15°47'E
Taşkent		564	36°55'N	32°31'E
Tasker	NG	314	15°04'N	10°42'E
Taşköprü	TU	535	41°30'N	34°14'E
Taskul	PP	664	2°33'S	150°27'E
Tas-Kystabys		468	63°00'N	145°00'E
Tasman Bay	NZ	663	41°00'S	173°20'E
Tasmania	AS	656	39°18'S	147°03'E
Tasman Mts.	NZ	663	41°07'S	172°33'E
Tasman Sea	AS	656	40°00'S	163°00'E
Tăşnad	RO	610	47°29'N	22°35'E
Tasotkel'	KZ	510	51°21'N	66°33'E
Taşova		564	40°46'N	36°20'E
Tassara	NG	314	16°48'N	5°39'E
Tassialouc, L.		370	59°03'N	74°00'W
Tassili-n-Ajjer	AG	272	26°05'N	6°00'E
Tassilioua-n-Ahaggar	AG	272	20°30'N	5°00'E
Tasso Fragoso	BR	424	8°30'S	45°45'W
Tasu	CA	390	52°46'N	132°02'W
Taşucu	TU	535	36°19'N	33°53'E
Tasudi	BM	487	18°34'N	97°10'E
Tata	CG	287	2°35'N	30°33'E
Tata	HU	590	47°39'N	18°19'E
Tata	MO	310	29°45'N	7°59'W
Tataba	ID	500	1°18'S	122°51'E
Tatabánya	HU	590	47°34'N	18°25'E
Tatakoto		654	17°19'S	138°10'W
Tata Mailau	ID	500	8°55'S	125°30'E
Tatamba	BP	666	8°23'S	159°48'E
Tatarbunary	UP	624	45°51'N	29°37'E
Tatarsk	RS	612	55°13'N	75°58'E
Tatarskiy Proliv	RS	612	51°00'N	141°00'E
Tatau	MY	518	2°53'N	112°51'E
Tataurovo		466	57°48'N	49°34'E
Tatāwīn	TS	329	32°57'N	10°27'E
Tate		372	51°27'N	104°50'W
Tatema	GV	297	9°57'N	13°54'W
Tatevges	AM	482	39°25'N	46°23'E
Tateyama	JA	506	34°59'N	139°52'E
Tathlith	SA	528	19°32'N	43°30'E
Tatilt	MR	308	18°34'N	14°59'W
Tatishchevo		560	51°40'N	45°35'E
Tatkon	BM	487	20°07'N	96°13'E
Tatlayoko Lake	CA	390	51°40'N	124°23'W
Tatnam, C.	CA	390	57°15'N	91°02'W
Tatrang	CH	490	38°27'N	85°37'E
Tatry	PL	606	49°35'N	20°00'E
Tatsinskiy		560	48°11'N	41°17'E
Tatsuno	JA	506	34°52'N	134°33'E
Tatuí	BR	424	23°21'S	47°51'W
Tatus Dağ.	TU	535	41°00'N	40°30'E
Tatvan	TU	535	38°30'N	42°16'E
Tauá	BR	424	5°59'S	40°16'W
Taubaté	BR	424	23°02'S	45°33'W
Tauberbischofsheim	GM	584	49°37'N	9°40'E
Tauca	PE	436	8°29'S	78°03'W
Tauchik	KZ	510	44°21'N	51°19'E
Tauere		654	17°00'S	141°00'W
Taufkirchen	GM	584	48°08'N	12°26'E
Taufstein	GM	584	50°31'N	9°14'E
Taukum, Peski	KZ	510	44°50'N	75°30'E
Taulihawa	NP	522	27°32'N	83°03'E
Taumarunui	NZ	663	38°51'S	175°13'E
Taung	SF	322	27°32'S	24°43'E
Taungdwingyi	BM	487	20°01'N	95°33'E
Taunggyi	BM	487	20°47'N	97°02'E
Taungthonlon	BM	487	25°00'N	95°55'E
Taungup	BM	487	18°51'N	94°14'E
Taungup Pass	BM	487	18°40'N	94°45'E
Taungzun	BM	487	15°38'N	98°05'E
Taunsa	PK	524	30°42'N	70°39'E
Taunton		374	41°54'N	71°05'W
Taunton	UK	626	51°01'N	3°06'W
Taunus	GM	584	50°15'N	8°15'E
Taupo	NZ	663	38°41'S	176°05'E
Taupo, L.	NZ	663	38°39'S	175°55'E
Tauragė	LH	597	55°15'N	22°17'E
Tauranga	NZ	663	37°41'S	176°10'E
Taureau, L.		374	46°50'N	73°50'W
Taurianova	IT	593	38°21'N	16°01'E
Taurion	FR	580	45°53'N	1°24'E
Taurisano	IT	593	39°57'N	18°13'E
Tauroa Pt.	NZ	663	35°11'S	173°06'E
Tauste	SP	618	41°55'N	1°15'W
Tauta	PP	664	5°50'S	145°58'E
Tautama		654	25°07'S	130°06'W
Tautira		654	17°42'S	145°46'W
Tauu	PP	664	4°35'S	156°57'E
Tavaí	PA	435	26°07'S	55°32'W
Tavanbulag	MG	520	47°23'N	101°55'E
Tavani	CA	390	62°04'N	93°06'W
Tavas	TU	535	37°34'N	29°04'E
Tavaux	FR	580	47°02'N	5°24'E
Tavda		466	59°30'N	66°00'E
Tavda	RS	612	58°03'N	65°15'E
Tavernes de la Valldigna		562	39°04'N	0°16'W
Tavernier		378	25°00'N	80°30'W
Taveta	KE	299	3°24'S	37°41'E
Taveuni	FJ	660	16°50'S	179°50'E
Tavignano		562	42°06'N	9°33'E
Tavin	MG	520	46°23'N	105°48'E
Tavin	MG	520	49°45'N	106°40'E
Tavira	PO	608	37°07'N	7°39'W
Tavoliere della Puglia	IT	593	41°35'N	15°25'E
Tavoy	BM	487	14°05'N	98°12'E
Tavoy Point	BM	487	13°32'N	98°10'E
Tavrichanka		472	43°20'N	131°52'E
Tavşanlı	TU	535	39°33'N	29°30'E
Taw	UK	626	51°05'N	4°13'W
Tawaeli	ID	500	0°43'S	119°53'E
Tawas City		374	44°16'N	83°31'W
Tawau	MY	518	4°15'N	117°54'E
Tawi	TZ	327	8°17'S	38°52'E
Tawi Sulaym	MU	523	22°33'N	58°40'E
Tawitawi	RP	526	5°10'N	120°10'E
Tawitawi Group	RP	526	5°10'N	120°15'E
Tawiyah	MU	523	23°24'N	57°46'E
Ţawkar	SU	324	18°26'N	37°44'E
Tawu	TW	532	22°24'N	120°53'E
Ţāwūq	IZ	504	35°08'N	44°27'E
Tāwurghā'	LY	302	32°02'N	15°06'E
Tawurghā', Sabkhat	LY	302	31°10'N	15°15'E
Tawzar	TS	329	33°55'N	8°08'E
Taxenbach	AU	568	47°17'N	12°57'E
Taxila	PK	524	33°45'N	72°50'E
Taxis River		374	46°27'N	66°28'W
Taxkorgan	CH	490	37°46'N	75°13'E
Tay	UK	626	56°35'N	4°18'W
Tay, Loch	UK	626	56°31'N	4°10'W
Tayabamba	PE	436	8°17'S	77°18'W
Taybola		556	68°26'N	33°22'E
Tayeegle	SO	321	4°02'N	44°31'E
Tayezhnyy		466	61°12'N	62°40'E
Taygan	MG	520	46°21'N	97°17'E
Taygonos, Poluostrov	RS	612	61°20'N	161°00'E
Taylor		376	30°34'N	97°24'W
Taylor		376	34°27'N	110°05'W
Taylor Ridge		378	34°38'N	85°13'W
Taylors		378	34°55'N	82°17'W
Taylorville		374	39°32'N	89°17'W
Taymā'	SA	528	27°38'N	38°29'E
Taymouth		374	46°11'N	66°37'W
Taymura		468	63°46'N	98°01'E
Taymyr, Ozero		468	74°30'N	102°30'E
Taymyr, Poluostrov	RS	612	76°00'N	104°00'E
Tay Ninh	VM	540	11°18'N	106°04'E
Tayoltita	MX	394	24°05'N	105°56'W
Tayshet	RS	612	55°57'N	98°00'E
Taytay	RP	526	10°49'N	119°31'E
Ţayyebāt	IR	502	34°44'N	60°45'E
Taz	RS	612	67°32'N	78°40'E
Taza	MO	310	34°10'N	4°00'W
Tazacorte	SP	618	28°38'N	17°56'W
Tazawako	JA	506	39°41'N	140°43'E
Tazekka, Jebel	MO	310	34°05'N	4°12'W
Tazenakht	MO	310	30°35'N	7°12'W
Tazewell		374	37°06'N	81°31'W
Tazicheng		472	46°37'N	123°08'E
Tazin L.		368	59°48'N	109°05'W
Tazirbu	LY	302	25°45'N	21°00'E
Tazovskiy	RS	612	67°28'N	78°42'E
Tazrouk	AG	272	23°27'N	6°14'E
Tāzughrān	TS	329	36°54'N	10°52'E
Tbilisi	GG	495	41°42'N	44°45'E
Tbilisskaya		564	45°21'N	40°12'E
Tchabal Gangdaba	CM	280	7°44'N	12°45'E
Tchamba	CM	280	8°37'N	12°48'E
Tchamba	TO	328	9°02'N	1°25'E
Tchacurou	BN	276	8°53'N	2°36'E
Tchetti	BN	276	7°50'N	1°40'E
Tchibanga	GB	294	2°51'S	11°02'E
Tchikala-Tcholohanga	AO	274	12°38'S	16°03'E
Tchindjenje	AO	274	12°49'S	14°56'E
Tchin Tabaradene	NG	314	15°58'N	5°50'E
Tchitondi	CF	285	4°33'S	12°08'E
Tchollirè	CM	280	8°24'N	14°10'E
Tchula		378	33°10'N	90°13'W
Tczew	PL	606	54°06'N	18°48'E
Teague		378	31°37'N	96°17'W
Teahupoo		654	17°44'S	145°45'W
Te Anau	NZ	663	45°24'S	167°46'E
Te Anaud, Lake	NZ	663	45°12'S	167°48'E
Teano Ra.	AS	656	23°00'S	119°00'E
Teapa	MX	394	17°34'N	92°57'W
Te Araroa	NZ	663	37°38'S	178°20'E
Tearce	MK	599	42°05'N	21°04'E
Te Aroha	NZ	663	37°30'S	175°43'E
Tea Tree Gully		652	26°30'S	138°50'E
Tea Tree Well	AS	656	22°09'S	133°24'E
Teavaro		654	17°36'S	145°37'W
Te Awamutu	NZ	663	38°00'S	175°19'E
Tebaga, Djebel	TS	329	33°30'N	9°30'W
Tebedu	MY	518	1°01'N	110°22'E
Teberda		466	43°27'N	41°44'E
Tébessa	AG	272	35°24'N	8°07'E
Tébessa, Djebel	TS	329	35°20'N	8°20'E
Tebessetamane	ML	307	16°10'N	2°09'E
Tebicuary	PA	435	26°36'S	58°16'W
Tebingtinggi	ID	500	3°20'N	99°09'E
Tebykty	KG	514	41°25'N	74°03'E
Tecalitlán	MX	394	19°27'N	103°17'W
Tecate	MX	394	32°34'N	116°38'W
Tecer Daglari	TU	535	39°40'N	37°55'E
Techirghiol	RO	610	44°03'N	28°34'E
Tecka	AR	419	43°29'S	70°48'W
Tecolote	MX	394	32°34'N	114°59'W
Tecoluca	ES	409	13°32'N	88°47'W
Tecomán	MX	394	18°55'N	103°52'W
Tecoripa	MX	394	28°37'N	109°57'W
Tecpan	MX	394	17°15'N	100°41'W
Tecpán Guatemala	GT	411	14°46'N	91°00'W
Tecuala	MX	394	22°23'N	105°27'W
Tecuci	RO	610	45°50'N	27°25'E
Tecumseh		374	40°22'N	96°11'W
Tecumseh		374	42°00'N	83°56'W
Tecumseh		376	35°15'N	96°56'W
Ted Ceidaar Dabole	SO	321	4°24'N	43°55'E
Tedjert	AG	272	19°43'N	5°59'E
Tedodita Sakan	BM	487	18°12'N	97°12'E
Tedzhen	TX	537	37°24'N	60°38'E
Tedzhenstroy	TX	537	36°55'N	60°53'E
Teel	MG	520	48°03'N	100°30'E
Teepee Creek	CA	390	55°22'N	118°24'W
Tees	UK	626	52°28'N	113°19'W
Tefé		384	3°22'S	64°42'W
Tefé	BR	424	3°22'S	64°42'W
Tefenni		564	37°18'N	29°47'E
Teferič	YO	630	43°59'N	20°59'E
Tegal	ID	500	6°52'S	109°08'E
Tegelen	NL	602	51°20'N	6°08'E
Tegermensay	KG	514	41°42'N	70°38'E
Tegernsee	GM	584	47°43'N	11°44'E
Tegheri, Bi'r	LY	302	26°47'N	10°18'E
Tegina	NI	316	10°04'N	6°13'E
Tégouma	NG	314	15°54'N	11°06'E
Tegsh	MG	520	48°40'N	95°58'E
Tégua		654	13°10'S	166°30'E
Tegucigalpa	HO	412	14°06'N	87°13'W
Teguise	SP	618	29°03'N	13°33'W
Tehachapi Mts.		376	34°55'N	118°40'W
Tehamiyam	SU	324	18°20'N	36°32'E
Tehek L.	CA	390	64°55'N	95°30'W
Tehiga'i, Plateau de	NG	314	21°30'N	14°55'E
Tehkummah		374	45°39'N	82°01'W
Tehoru	ID	500	3°23'S	129°30'E
Tehrān	IR	502	35°40'N	51°26'E
Tehuacán	MX	394	18°24'N	97°25'W
Tehuantepec	MX	394	16°20'N	95°14'W
Tehuantepec, Golfo de	MX	394	16°00'N	94°50'W
Teide	SP	618	28°16'N	16°38'W
Teifi	UK	626	52°07'N	4°42'W
Teiga, Jabal	SU	324	15°18'N	25°40'E
Teignmouth	UK	626	50°33'N	3°29'W
Teixeira de Freitas	BR	424	17°31'S	39°44'W
Teixeira Pinto	PU	298	12°04'N	16°02'W
Teixeiro	SP	618	43°07'N	8°03'W
Tejen	TX	537	37°23'N	60°31'E
Tejina	SP	618	28°32'N	16°21'W
Tejn	DA	576	55°15'N	14°51'E
Tejo (Tajo)	SP	618	38°40'N	9°24'W
Tejo Inlet	PO	608	38°40'N	9°24'W
Tejutla	ES	409	14°10'N	89°06'W
Tejutla	GT	411	15°07'N	91°48'W
Tekamah		372	41°46'N	96°13'W
Tékane	MR	308	16°35'N	15°24'W
Te Kao	NZ	663	34°38'S	173°00'E
Tekapo, L.	NZ	663	43°53'S	170°31'E
Te Karaka	NZ	663	38°29'S	177°52'E
Te Kauwhata	NZ	663	37°22'S	175°07'E
Tekax	MX	394	20°12'N	89°17'W
Tekeli	KZ	510	44°48'N	78°57'E
Tekes	CH	490	43°09'N	81°42'E
Tekes He	CH	490	43°35'N	82°30'E
Tekeze (Satit)	ET	293	14°20'N	35°50'E
Tekirdağ	TU	535	40°59'N	27°31'E
Tekkeköy		564	41°14'N	36°29'E
Teknāf	BG	485	20°52'N	92°15'E
Te Kopuru	NZ	663	36°02'S	173°55'E
Teku		478	0°46'S	123°26'E
Te Kuiti	NZ	663	38°20'S	175°10'E
Tel	IN	496	20°50'N	83°54'E
Tela	HO	412	15°47'N	87°27'W
Télagh	AG	272	34°47'N	0°34'W
Télataï	ML	307	16°31'N	1°30'E
Telavi	GG	495	41°55'N	45°28'E
Tel Aviv-Yafo	IS	505	32°04'N	34°46'E
Telč	EZ	575	49°11'N	15°28'E
Telde	SP	618	28°00'N	15°25'W
Telefomin	PP	664	5°07'S	141°37'E
Telegraph Creek	CA	390	57°54'N	131°10'W
Telekhany	BO	569	52°31'N	25°51'E
Telêmaco Borba	BR	424	24°20'S	50°36'W
Telen		478	0°26'N	116°42'E
Telertheba, Djebel	AG	272	24°10'N	6°51'E
Teles Pires		384	9°00'S	55°10'W
Telfs	AU	568	47°18'N	11°04'E
Telica	NU	415	12°31'N	86°52'W
Télig	ML	307	22°37'N	3°43'W
Télimélé	GV	297	10°54'N	13°02'W
Telipok	MY	518	6°05'N	116°11'E
Telire	CS	405	9°34'N	82°53'W
Teljo, Jabal	SU	324	14°37'N	25°52'E
Tel. Kamrau	ID	500	3°32'S	133°37'E
Tell City		374	37°57'N	86°46'W
Tellicherry	IN	496	11°45'N	75°32'E
Tellier	AR	419	47°39'S	66°03'W
Tello	CO	430	3°04'N	75°08'W
Telluride		376	37°56'N	107°48'W
Telmen Nuur	MG	520	48°50'N	97°18'E
Telok Anson	MY	518	4°02'N	101°01'E
Teloloapan	MX	394	18°21'N	99°51'W
Telpaneca	NU	415	13°32'N	86°17'W
Telsen	AR	419	42°24'S	66°57'W
Telšiai	LH	597	55°59'N	22°15'E
Telukdalem	ID	500	0°35'N	97°49'E
Telukmelano	ID	500	1°06'S	109°58'E
Telukmerbau	ID	500	2°04'N	100°38'E
Tema	GH	296	5°37'N	0°01'W
Temacine	AG	272	33°01'N	6°01'E
Temagami	CA	390	47°04'N	79°47'W
Temanggung		478	7°18'S	110°10'E
Témara	MO	310	33°55'N	6°55'W
Tematangi		654	22°00'S	140°30'W
Temax	MX	394	21°09'N	88°56'W
Temba	SF	322	25°23'S	28°16'E
Tembagapura	ID	500	4°20'S	137°00'E
Tembenchi		468	66°00'N	96°00'E
Tembesi	ID	500	1°43'S	103°06'E
Tembisa	SF	322	26°02'S	28°14'E
Temblador	VE	440	8°59'N	62°44'W
Temblor Mts.		376	35°20'N	119°55'W
Tembo	CG	287	7°41'S	17°23'E
Tembo Aluma	AO	274	7°42'S	17°17'E
Tembue	MZ	312	14°49'S	32°50'E
Temburong	BX	486	4°40'N	115°05'E
Teme	CH	490	37°31'N	101°19'E
Temecula		376	33°29'N	117°08'W
Temelkovo	BU	573	42°36'N	22°56'E
Temelli		564	39°44'N	32°22'E
Temerin	YO	630	45°25'N	19°53'E
Temerloh	MY	518	3°27'N	102°25'E
Teminabuan	ID	500	1°26'S	132°01'E
Temir	KZ	510	49°08'N	57°06'E
Temirtaū	KZ	510	50°05'N	72°56'E
Témiscaming		370	46°42'N	79°03'W
Temixco	MX	394	18°50'N	99°13'W
Temma	AS	656	41°14'S	144°42'E
Temoe		654	23°28'S	134°15'W
Temora		652	34°26'S	147°32'E
Temores	MX	394	27°16'N	108°17'W
Temósachic	MX	394	28°57'N	107°51'W
Tempe	US	398	33°25'N	111°56'W
Tempe Downs	AS	656	24°22'S	132°24'E
Tempio Pausania	IT	593	40°54'N	9°06'E
Tempisque	CS	405	10°12'N	85°14'W
Temple		376	34°16'N	98°14'W
Temple	US	398	31°05'N	97°20'W
Templemore	EI	592	52°47'N	7°50'W
Templin	GM	584	53°07'N	13°29'E
Tempo		558	54°23'N	7°28'W
Tempoal	MX	394	21°31'N	98°23'W
Tempué	AO	274	13°26'S	18°52'E
Têmpung	CH	490	37°12'N	99°15'E
Temryuk		564	45°17'N	37°24'E
Temryukskiy Proliv		564	45°24'N	37°20'E
Temuco	CI	428	38°44'S	72°36'W
Temuka	NZ	663	44°15'S	171°16'E
Ten		382	25°49'N	81°41'W
Ten	CO	430	25°49'N	81°41'W
Tena	EC	432	0°59'S	77°49'W
Ténado	UV	278	12°12'N	2°36'W
Tenāli	IN	496	16°15'N	80°35'E
Tenares	DR	408	19°22'N	70°21'W
Tenasserim	BM	487	12°05'N	99°01'E
Tenasserim	BM	487	13°00'N	98°45'E
Tenasserim, Great	BM	487	12°24'N	98°37'E
Ten Boer	NL	602	53°17'N	6°41'E
Tenby	UK	626	51°40'N	4°42'W
Tendaho	ET	293	11°42'N	40°57'E
Tende	FR	580	44°05'N	7°36'E
Tendō	JA	506	38°21'N	140°22'E
Tendrara	MO	310	33°03'N	2°00'W
Tendrovskaya Kosa	UP	624	46°12'N	31°50'E
Ténenkou	ML	307	14°28'N	4°55'W
Ténéré, Erg du	NG	314	17°35'N	10°55'E
Ténéré du Tafassasset	NG	314	21°00'N	11°00'E
Tenerife	SP	618	28°39'N	16°48'W
Ténès	AG	272	36°31'N	1°18'E
Teng, Nam	BM	487	20°10'N	98°00'E
Te Nggano	BP	666	11°50'S	162°20'E
Tenggara, Nusa	ID	500	9°00'S	120°00'E
Tenggara Barat, Nusa		648	9°50'S	117°30'E
Tenggara Timur, Nusa		648	9°30'S	122°00'E
Tenggarong	ID	500	0°24'S	116°58'E
Tengger Shamo	CH	490	38°00'N	104°10'E
Tengiz, Ozero	KZ	510	51°44'N	73°26'E
Tenguel	EC	432	3°00'S	79°46'W
Teng Xian		476	23°21'N	110°54'E
Tenhult	SW	621	57°43'N	14°19'E
Tenigerbad	SZ	622	46°41'N	8°58'E
Tenja	HR	574	45°30'N	18°45'E
Tenke	CG	287	10°35'S	26°07'E
Tenkodogo	UV	278	11°47'N	0°22'W
Tennant Creek	AS	656	19°39'S	134°12'E
Tennessee		374	35°45'N	86°15'W
Tennessee	US	398	40°24'N	90°50'W
Tennessee Res.		378	34°50'N	87°30'W
Teno	CI	428	34°52'S	71°11'W
Ténoko		654	23°08'S	135°00'W
Tenom	MY	518	5°08'N	115°57'E
Tenorio, Volcán	CS	405	10°40'N	85°01'W
Tenosique	MX	394	17°29'N	91°26'W
Tenryu-gawa	JA	506	34°39'N	137°48'E
Tensif, Oued	MO	310	32°02'N	9°22'W
Tensift		262	32°02'N	9°22'W
Tenta	ET	293	10°47'N	38°24'E
Tente	ID	500	8°35'S	118°42'E
Tentena	ID	500	1°47'S	120°39'E
Tenterden	UK	626	51°03'N	0°42'E
Tenterfield		652	29°03'S	152°01'E
Tenth Mile	MY	518	1°26'N	110°19'E
Ten Thousand Islands		378	25°52'N	81°29'W
Tentolomatinan, Gunung	ID	500	0°56'N	121°48'E
Tenus	KE	299	2°09'N	35°07'E
Teo	SP	618	42°45'N	8°30'W
Teocaltiche	MX	394	21°27'N	102°35'W
Teófilo Otoni	BR	424	17°51'S	41°30'W
Te'Okutu	UG	330	2°21'N	31°36'E
Téonta		654	20°10'S	166°15'E
Teotônio Vilela		386	9°56'S	36°22'W
Tepa	ID	500	7°52'S	129°31'E
Tepache	MX	394	29°31'N	109°31'W
Tepalcatepec	MX	394	19°11'N	102°51'W
Tepatitlán	MX	394	20°49'N	102°44'W
Tepechitlán	MX	394	21°40'N	103°20'W
Tepeciköran		564	37°22'N	35°37'E
Tepehuaje	MX	394	23°29'N	97°48'W
Tepehuanes	MX	394	25°21'N	105°44'W
Tepehuanes, Sierra de	MX	394	25°30'N	105°30'W
Tepelenë	AL	566	40°18'N	20°01'E
Tepelska Plasina	EZ	575	50°00'N	13°00'E
Tēpī	ET	293	7°12'N	35°27'E
Tepic	MX	394	21°30'N	104°54'W
Teplice	EZ	575	50°38'N	13°50'E
Tepoca, Cabo	MX	394	29°22'N	112°29'W
Tepoca, Cabo	MX	394	30°16'N	112°51'W
Tepoto		654	14°21'S	142°51'W
Tequila	MX	394	20°53'N	103°48'W
Ter	SP	618	42°01'N	3°12'E
Tera		562	41°54'N	5°44'W
Téra	NG	314	14°01'N	0°45'E
Terakeka	SU	324	5°26'N	31°45'E
Teramo	IT	593	42°39'N	13°42'E
Ter Apel	NL	602	52°52'N	7°04'E

Tercan	TU	535	39°47'N	40°24'E
Tercero		388	32°55'S	69°19'W
Terchová	LO	616	49°16'N	19°02'E
Terebovlya	UP	624	49°18'N	25°43'E
Terek	KG	514	40°01'N	73°33'E
Terekhovka	BO	569	52°13'N	31°27'E
Terekli-Mekteb		466	44°10'N	45°52'E
Terek-Say	KG	514	41°30'N	71°11'E
Teren'ga		560	53°42'N	48°24'E
Terengganu	MY	518	5°17'N	103°05'E
Terenos		386	20°27'S	54°52'W
Teresina	BR	424	5°04'S	42°45'W
Teresópolis	BR	424	22°26'S	42°59'W
Terespol	PL	606	52°03'N	23°37'E
Terevinto	BL	422	17°43'S	63°23'W
Tergnier	FR	580	49°39'N	3°18'E
Tergun Daba Shan	CH	490	38°23'N	95°35'E
Terhathum	NP	522	27°07'N	87°32'E
Teriberka		556	69°10'N	35°10'E
Teriberskiy, Mys		556	69°15'N	35°09'E
Terkos Gölü	TU	535	41°30'N	28°40'E
Termas del Arapey	UY	439	30°58'S	57°35'W
Termas de Río Hondo	AR	419	27°29'S	64°52'W
Terme		564	41°12'N	36°59'E
Termez	UZ	539	37°14'N	67°16'E
Terminal		376	24°45'N	101°31'W
Termini Imerese	IT	593	37°59'N	13°42'E
Términos, L. de	MX	394	18°37'N	91°33'W
Termit-Kaoboul	NG	314	15°38'N	11°25'E
Termoli	IT	593	42°00'N	14°58'E
Termunten	NL	602	53°18'N	7°03'E
Ternate	ID	500	0°48'N	127°20'E
Ternberg	AU	568	47°56'N	14°21'E
Terneuzen	NL	602	51°20'N	3°50'E
Terney	RS	612	45°03'N	136°37'E
Terni	IT	593	42°33'N	12°38'E
Ternitz	AU	568	47°43'N	16°02'E
Ternopil'	UP	624	49°33'N	25°35'E
Ternovka		560	51°40'N	41°38'E
Ternovka	UP	624	48°31'N	36°06'E
Terpeniya, Mys	RS	612	48°39'N	143°30'E
Terpeniya, Zaliv	RS	612	49°00'N	143°30'E
Terpní	GR	588	40°56'N	23°27'E
Terrabona	NU	415	12°44'N	85°58'W
Terrace	CA	390	54°31'N	128°36'W
Terrace Bay	CA	390	48°47'N	87°06'W
Terrace Heights		372	46°36'N	120°26'W
Terracina	IT	593	41°17'N	13°14'E
Terråk	NO	604	65°05'N	12°25'E
Terralba	IT	593	39°42'N	8°38'E
Terrassa	SP	618	41°34'N	2°01'E
Terrasson-la-Villedieu	FR	580	45°07'N	1°18'E
Terre Haute	US	398	39°28'N	87°24'W
Terre Neuve	HA	412	19°36'N	72°47'W
Terrier-Rouge	HA	412	19°38'N	71°57'W
Tersakan	TX	537	38°24'N	55°57'E
Tersakkan	KZ	510	50°30'N	68°30'E
Terschelling	NL	602	53°25'N	5°12'E
Terskey Alatau, Khrebet	KG	514	42°00'N	77°00'E
Terskiy Bereg		556	66°00'N	39°00'E
Tertenia		562	39°41'N	9°34'E
Teruel	SP	618	40°21'N	1°06'W
Tervel	BU	573	43°45'N	27°24'E
Tervola	FI	578	66°04'N	24°49'E
Tešanj	BK	572	44°37'N	18°00'E
Teseney	ER	292	15°08'N	36°40'E
Teshi	GH	296	5°35'N	0°06'W
Teshig	MG	520	49°56'N	102°34'E
Teshikaga	JA	506	43°28'N	144°30'E
Teshio	JA	506	44°53'N	141°44'E
Teshio-dake	JA	506	43°58'N	142°54'E
Teshio gawa	JA	506	44°53'N	141°45'E
Tesiyn Gol	MG	520	50°50'N	96°00'E
Teslić	BK	572	44°37'N	17°52'E
Teslin	CA	390	60°10'N	132°43'W
Teslin	CA	390	61°34'N	134°54'W
Teslin Crossing	CA	390	61°15'N	134°36'W
Teslin Lake		368	60°00'N	132°30'W
Teslin River	CA	390	60°28'N	133°26'W
Tësovo-Netyl'skiy		560	58°47'N	31°04'E
Tessalit	ML	307	20°12'N	1°00'E
Tessaoua	NG	314	13°46'N	7°59'E
Tessenderlo	BE	570	51°04'N	5°05'E
Tessier		372	51°48'N	107°26'W
Testa, Capo	IT	593	41°14'N	9°08'E
Testa del Gargano	IT	593	41°49'N	16°11'E
Tét	HU	590	47°31'N	17°31'E
Tetas, Punta	CI	428	23°30'S	70°37'W
Tete	MZ	312	16°12'S	33°34'E
Tête-à-la-Baleine	CA	390	50°41'N	59°20'W
Tétégégié		654	23°06'S	135°11'W
Tetepare	BP	666	8°40'S	157°35'E
Teterow		558	53°47'N	12°34'E
Teteven	BU	573	42°55'N	24°16'E
Tetiaroa		654	17°00'S	149°25'W
Tetiyev	UP	624	49°23'N	29°40'E
Tëtkino	RS	612	51°17'N	34°17'E
Tétouan	MO	310	35°34'N	5°22'W
Tetovo	MK	599	42°01'N	20°59'E
Tetri-Tskaro	GG	495	41°33'N	44°28'E
Tetulia	BG	485	22°15'N	90°37'E
Tetulia	BG	485	26°30'N	88°21'E
Teuco	AR	419	25°38'S	60°12'W
Teúl	MX	394	21°28'N	103°29'W
Teulada	IT	593	38°58'N	8°46'E
Teulada, Capo	IT	593	38°51'N	8°38'E
Teulon		372	50°23'N	97°16'W
Teupasenti	HO	412	14°13'N	86°42'W
Teustepe	NU	415	12°25'N	85°48'W
Teutoburger Wald	GM	584	52°05'N	8°20'E
Teuva	FI	578	62°29'N	21°44'E
Tevere	IT	593	41°44'N	12°14'E
Teverya	IS	505	32°47'N	35°32'E
Tevli	BO	569	52°20'N	24°15'E
Tevriz	RS	612	57°30'N	72°23'E
Tewantin-Noosa	AS	656	26°23'S	153°02'E
Tewo	DJ	289	11°26'N	42°03'E
Texada		372	49°40'N	124°26'W
Texarkana	US	398	33°26'N	94°03'W
Texas		376	31°15'N	99°15'W
Texel	NL	602	53°07'N	4°32'E
Texistepeque	ES	409	14°08'N	89°30'W
Texoma, Lake	US	398	33°50'N	96°34'W
Teya	RS	612	60°24'N	92°38'E
Teyateyaneng	LT	301	29°09'S	27°44'E
Teykovo		466	56°52'N	40°34'E
Teylān	AF	480	35°32'N	64°47'E
Teyvareh	AF	480	33°21'N	64°25'E
Tezhler	AM	482	40°42'N	44°31'E
Teziutlán	MX	394	19°49'N	97°21'W
Tezpur		472	26°38'N	92°48'E
Tezu	IN	496	27°55'N	96°10'E
Tha	LA	517	20°07'N	100°36'E
Thaba Nchu	SF	322	29°13'S	26°50'E
Thaba Putsoa	LT	301	29°35'S	28°04'E
Thabaung	BM	487	17°02'N	94°48'E
Thabazimbi	SF	322	24°36'S	27°24'E
Thabeikkyin	BM	487	22°53'N	95°59'E
Tha Bo	TH	534	17°51'N	102°35'E
Thādiq	SA	528	25°18'N	45°52'E
Thagaya	BM	487	19°19'N	96°18'E
Thai Binh	VM	540	20°26'N	106°19'E
Thailand		38	15°00'N	100°00'E
Thailand, Gulf of	CB	489	10°00'N	102°00'E
Thai Nguyen	VM	540	21°36'N	105°49'E
Thakhek	LA	517	17°24'N	104°50'E
Thākurgaon	BG	485	26°02'N	88°28'E
Thākurmunda	IN	496	21°32'N	86°09'E
Thal	PK	524	33°22'N	70°33'E
Thalang	TH	534	8°01'N	98°19'E
Thalberg		372	50°22'N	96°30'W
Thale	GM	584	51°45'N	11°03'E
Thale Luang	TH	534	7°50'N	100°30'E
Thalgau	AU	568	47°50'N	13°14'E
Thalheim bei Wels	AU	568	48°08'N	14°02'E
Tha Mai	TH	534	12°37'N	102°01'E
Thamarit	MU	523	17°39'N	54°02'E
Thames	CA	390	42°19'N	82°27'W
Thames	NZ	663	37°07'S	175°34'E
Thames	UK	626	37°07'S	175°34'E
Thāna	IN	496	19°12'N	72°58'E
Thāneswar	BG	485	24°33'N	90°59'E
Thang Duc	VM	540	13°45'N	107°34'E
Thanggu		472	27°54'N	88°31'E
Thangool		652	24°29'S	150°35'E
Thanh Hoa	VM	540	19°48'N	105°45'E
Thanh Lang Xa	VM	540	17°58'N	105°50'E
Thanjavur	IN	496	10°48'N	79°09'E
Thaon-les-Vosges	FR	580	48°15'N	6°25'E
Thap Put		476	8°31'N	98°38'E
Thap Sakae	TH	534	11°30'N	99°37'E
Tharād	IN	496	24°24'N	71°38'E
Thargomindah	AS	656	28°00'S	143°49'E
Thar or Great Indian Desert	PK	524	27°00'N	71°00'E
Tharrawaddy	BM	487	17°39'N	95°48'E
Tharthar, Wadi ath	IZ	504	33°59'N	43°12'E
Tha Sala	TH	534	8°40'N	99°56'E
Thásos	GR	588	40°30'N	24°28'E
Thatcher		376	32°50'N	109°45'W
That Khe	VM	540	22°15'N	106°27'E
Thaton	BM	487	16°55'N	97°22'E
That Phanom	TH	534	16°57'N	104°42'E
Tha Tum	TH	534	15°19'N	103°41'E
Thaungdut	BM	487	24°26'N	94°42'E
Tha Wang Pha	TH	534	19°06'N	100°49'E
Thaya	AU	568	48°37'N	16°56'E
Thayawthadangyi Kyun	BM	487	12°20'N	98°00'E
Thayer		374	36°31'N	91°32'W
Thayetmyo	BM	487	19°19'N	95°10'E
Thazi	BM	487	20°51'N	96°05'E
Thebaide	GJ	410	12°03'N	61°40'W
The Bight	BF	402	24°18'N	75°28'W
The Bottom		382	17°36'N	63°15'W
The Calvados Chain	PP	664	11°00'S	152°30'E
The Dalles	US	398	45°35'N	121°10'W
Thedford		374	43°09'N	81°51'W
The English Companys	AS	656	11°50'S	136°32'E
The Gap	AS	656	31°07'S	141°42'E
The Grampians	AS	656	37°20'S	142°30'E
The Granites	AS	656	20°35'S	130°21'E
The Grenadines		382	12°40'N	61°15'W
The Hague ('s-Gravenhage)	NL	602	52°04'N	4°20'E
The Heads		372	42°44'N	124°30'W
the Hebrides, Sea of	UK	626	57°07'N	6°55'W
The Hermitage	NZ	663	43°44'S	170°06'E
Thelepte	TS	329	35°00'N	8°37'E
Thelon	CA	390	64°16'N	96°05'W
Thema, Lake	RW	317	1°50'S	30°50'E
The Narrows	SC	417	17°12'N	62°38'W
Theodore		372	51°26'N	102°55'W
Theodore		378	30°32'N	88°10'W
Theodore	AS	656	24°57'S	150°05'E
Theodore Roosevelt Lake		376	33°40'N	111°10'W
The Pas	CA	390	53°50'N	101°15'W
The Peak		266	7°55'S	14°20'W
The Range	ZI	334	19°00'S	31°02'E
Thermaïkós Kólpos	GR	588	40°23'N	22°47'E
Thermia (Kíthnos)	GR	588	37°23'N	24°25'E
Thermopolis	US	398	43°38'N	108°12'W
The Rope		654	25°06'S	130°08'W
The Slot (New Georgia Sound)	BP	666	7°40'S	157°00'E
Thesprotikón	GR	588	39°15'N	20°47'E
Thessalon		374	46°15'N	83°34'W
Thessaloníki	GR	588	40°38'N	22°56'E
Thetford	UK	626	52°25'N	0°45'E
Thetford Mines		374	46°05'N	71°18'W
Thetkala	BM	487	17°01'N	96°36'E
Theun	LA	517	105°30'N	18°00'E
Theunissen	SF	322	28°24'S	26°43'E
The Valley		382	18°13'N	63°04'W
The Wash	UK	626	52°59'N	0°11'E
Thibaud	DO	407	15°36'N	61°24'W
Thibodaux		378	29°47'N	90°49'W
Thicket Portage	CA	390	55°19'N	97°42'W
Thief		372	48°10'N	96°10'W
Thief Lake		374	48°29'N	95°53'W
Thief River Falls	US	398	48°07'N	96°10'W
Thien Ngon	VM	540	11°34'N	106°00'E
Thiers	FR	580	45°51'N	3°34'E
Thiès	SG	319	14°48'N	16°56'W
Thiet Tra	VM	540	20°18'N	105°09'E
Thika	KE	299	1°03'S	37°05'E
Thiladunmathi Atoll	MV	519	6°30'N	72°50'E
Thimad al Khuwaymah	LY	302	29°19'N	17°08'E
Thimianá	GR	588	38°18'N	26°08'E
Thimphu	BT	486	27°29'N	89°37'E
Thio		654	21°20'S	166°10'E
Thionville	FR	580	49°22'N	6°10'E
Thiotte	HA	412	18°15'N	71°51'W
Thiou	UV	278	13°48'N	2°40'W
Thira		262	36°28'N	25°25'E
Thíra	GR	588	36°28'N	25°25'E
Thirsty, Mount	AS	656	32°05'S	121°38'E
Thisted	DA	576	56°57'N	8°42'E
Thistilfjördur	IC	591	66°20'N	15°25'W
Thistle	AS	656	35°01'S	136°13'E
Thívai	GR	588	38°19'N	23°18'E
Thjórsá	IC	591	63°47'N	20°48'W
Thlanship	IN	496	24°09'N	93°14'E
Thlewiaza		368	60°28'N	94°42'W
Thoa		368	60°31'N	109°45'W
Thoen	TH	534	17°36'N	99°12'E
Thoeng	TH	534	19°41'N	100°12'E
Thohoyandou	SF	322	22°57'S	30°28'E
Thoi Binh	VM	540	9°24'N	105°03'E
Tholen	NL	602	51°30'N	4°05'E
Thomas		376	35°44'N	98°44'W
Thomas, Lake		376	32°40'N	101°00'W
Thomassique	HA	412	19°05'N	71°50'W
Thomaston		378	32°53'N	84°19'W
Thomasville		378	31°54'N	87°44'W
Thomasville	US	398	30°50'N	83°58'W
Thomazeau	HA	412	18°39'N	72°05'W
Thom Bay	CA	390	70°09'N	92°24'W
Thomonde	HA	412	19°01'N	71°58'W
Thompson		372	30°46'N	93°37'W
Thompson	CA	390	55°45'N	97°52'W
Thompson Falls		372	47°35'N	115°21'W
Thompson Landing	CA	390	62°57'N	110°43'W
Thomson	AS	656	25°11'S	142°53'E
Thon Buri	TH	534	13°43'N	100°29'E
Thon Cam Lo	VM	540	16°48'N	107°00'E
Thônex	SZ	622	46°11'N	6°11'E
Thongwa	BM	487	16°46'N	96°32'E
Thon Lac Nghiep	VM	540	11°19'N	108°54'E
Thonon-les-Bains	FR	580	46°22'N	6°28'E
Thon Song Pha	VM	540	11°49'N	108°42'E
Thoreau		376	35°24'N	108°13'W
Thorigné-Fouillard		562	48°09'N	1°35'E
Thorlákshöfn	IC	591	63°50'N	21°23'W
Thornaby-on-Tees	UK	626	54°32'N	1°18'W
Thorne		374	46°39'N	79°05'W
Thornloe	CA	390	47°40'N	79°46'W
Thornton Dale		558	54°14'N	0°43'W
Thorp		370	44°57'N	90°47'W
Thorsby		378	32°54'N	86°42'W
Thórshöfn	IC	591	66°11'N	15°18'W
Thoubāl		472	24°38'N	94°01'E
Thouin, C.	AS	656	20°20'S	118°10'E
Thousand		370	44°17'N	76°30'W
Thousand	US	398	25°46'N	81°41'W
Thousand Oaks		376	34°10'N	118°50'W
Thowa	KE	299	1°33'S	40°03'E
Thrakikón Pélagos	GR	588	40°15'N	24°25'E
Thredbo Village		652	41°30'S	148°00'E
Three Forks		372	45°53'N	111°33'W
Three Hills		372	51°42'N	113°16'W
Three Hummock	AS	656	40°21'S	144°55'E
Three Kings I.	NZ	663	34°10'S	172°05'E
Three Kings Is.		654	34°00'S	171°00'E
Three Pagodas Pass	TH	534	15°18'N	98°23'E
Three Points		376	32°04'N	111°18'W
Three Points, Cape	GH	296	4°43'N	2°05'W
Three Rivers		376	28°27'N	98°10'W
Three Rivers	AS	656	25°07'S	119°09'E
Three Sisters Is. (Olu Malau)	BP	666	10°10'S	132°00'E
Three Springs	AS	656	29°32'S	115°45'E
Throckmorton		376	33°10'N	99°10'W
Throne		372	52°03'N	111°17'W
Throssel Ra.	AS	656	21°15'S	121°30'E
Thrumster		558	58°23'N	3°08'W
Thud Pt.	AS	656	12°58'S	141°35'E
Thuin	BE	570	50°20'N	4°17'E
Thuir	FR	580	42°38'N	2°45'E
Thumayd	MU	523	23°26'N	58°07'E
Thun	SZ	622	46°45'N	7°37'E
Thunder Bay	CA	390	48°24'N	89°15'W
Thuner See	SZ	622	46°42'N	7°44'E
Thung Song	TH	534	8°09'N	99°41'E
Thunkar	BT	486	27°53'N	91°03'E
Thuré	FR	580	46°50'N	0°27'E
Thüringer Wald	GM	584	47°52'N	8°49'E
Thurles	EI	592	52°41'N	7°48'W
Thurloo Downs	AS	656	29°17'S	143°29'E
Thurnwald Range	PP	664	4°50'S	142°00'E
Thurø By	DA	576	55°03'N	10°40'E
Thursday Island	AS	656	10°38'S	142°12'E
Thurso	UK	626	58°35'N	3°31'W
Thurso	UK	626	58°36'N	3°30'W
Thusis	SZ	622	46°41'N	9°25'E
Thyolo	MI	306	16°04'S	35°09'E
Tia		652	31°12'S	151°50'E
Tía Juana	VE	440	10°16'N	71°22'W
Tianbaoshan		474	42°57'N	128°57'E
Tiancang	CH	490	40°27'N	99°35'E
Tiandong		476	23°36'N	107°08'E
Tian'e	CH	490	25°00'N	107°09'E
Tianeti	GG	495	42°07'N	44°58'E
Tiangang		474	43°53'N	126°57'E
Tiangbi	CT	282	6°00'N	21°08'E
Tianguá	BR	424	3°44'S	40°59'W
Tianjin	CH	490	39°07'N	117°12'E
Tianjun	CH	490	37°15'N	99°01'E
Tianlin	CH	490	24°18'N	106°12'E
Tianmen	CH	490	30°38'N	113°10'E
Tianqiaoling		474	43°35'N	129°38'E
Tianshan	CH	490	43°51'N	120°04'E
Tianshifu		474	41°17'N	124°22'E
Tianshui	CH	490	34°34'N	105°42'E
Tianshui	CH	490	37°09'N	106°45'E
Tianshuihai	CH	490	35°19'N	79°33'E
Tiantaiyong	CH	490	42°47'N	117°12'E
Tianyang	CH	490	23°45'N	106°54'E
Tiarel		654	17°36'N	145°44'W
Tiaret	AG	272	35°22'N	1°19'E
Tías	SP	618	28°57'N	13°39'W
Tiassalé	IV	288	5°54'N	4°50'W
Tiatucurá	UY	439	32°21'S	56°33'W
Tib, Ra's at		562	37°10'N	11°00'E
Tibati	CM	280	6°26'N	12°36'E
Tibé, Pic de	GV	297	8°52'N	8°54'W
Tiber		562	41°44'N	12°14'E
Tiberias	IS	505	32°46'N	35°30'E
Tiberias, L.		564	32°48'N	35°35'E
Tibesti, Sarir	LY	302	21°30'N	17°30'E
Tibesti Ennedi	CD	283	21°30'N	17°30'E
Tibet, Plateau of (Xizang Gaoyuan)	CH	490	33°00'N	92°00'E
Tibiri	NG	314	13°34'N	7°04'E
Tiblesului, Muntii	RO	610	47°33'N	24°05'E
Tibnīn	LE	516	33°12'N	35°24'E
Tibooburra	AS	656	29°26'S	142°01'E
Tibrikot	NP	522	29°02'N	82°47'E
Tibro	SW	621	58°26'N	14°10'E
Tibú	CO	430	8°39'N	72°42'W
Tibugá, Golfo de		384	5°45'N	77°20'W
Tiburon	HA	412	18°20'N	74°24'W
Tiburón	MX	394	29°08'N	112°57'W
Tiburón, Cabo	PM	417	8°40'N	77°23'W
Tiburon, Cap	HA	412	18°18'N	74°24'W
Ticatica	BL	422	20°11'S	66°21'W
Tîchît	MR	308	18°28'N	9°30'W
Tîchît, Dahr	MR	308	18°30'N	9°25'W
Tichla		262	21°36'N	14°57'W
T'īcho	ET	293	7°48'N	39°26'E
Ticino	SZ	622	45°09'N	9°14'E
Ţicleni	RO	610	44°53'N	23°24'E
Ticllos	PE	436	10°16'S	77°16'W
Ticucha	BL	422	19°37'S	63°52'W
Ticul	MX	394	20°24'N	89°32'W
Tidaholm	SW	621	58°11'N	13°57'E
Tiddas	MO	310	33°35'N	6°18'W
Tiddim	BM	487	23°22'N	93°40'E
Tidikelt	AG	272	27°00'N	1°30'E
Tidjikdja	MR	308	18°33'N	11°25'W
Tidore	ID	500	0°41'N	127°24'E
Tidra, Ile	MR	308	19°45'N	16°49'W
Tiébélé Corabie	UV	278	11°06'N	0°59'W
Tiébissou	IV	288	7°10'N	5°13'W
Tiéboro	CD	283	21°20'N	17°07'E
Tiechang		474	41°40'N	126°12'E
Tiéfinzo	IV	288	10°25'N	7°29'W
Tiel	NL	602	51°53'N	5°26'E
Tieli		472	46°57'N	128°03'E
Tieling	CH	490	42°17'N	123°48'E
Tielongtan	CH	490	34°43'N	79°19'E
Tielt	BE	570	51°00'N	3°19'E
Tiemba	IV	288	9°00'N	7°40'W
Tienen	BE	570	50°48'N	4°57'E
Tiénigbe	IV	288	8°09'N	5°44'W
Tien Shan (Tyan-Shan)	KG	514	42°00'N	80°00'E
Tien Yen	VM	540	19°07'N	105°39'E
Tien Yen	VM	540	21°19'N	107°24'E
Tieri		652	23°02'S	148°22'E
Tierp	SW	621	60°20'N	17°30'E
Tierra Amarilla	CI	428	27°29'S	70°17'W
Tierra Blanca	MX	394	18°27'N	96°21'W
Tierra Colorada	MX	394	17°10'N	99°31'W
Tierra del Fuego	CI	428	53°52'S	66°57'W
Tierralta	CO	430	8°11'N	76°04'W
Tiétar	SP	618	39°50'N	6°01'W
Tietè		386	20°40'S	51°35'W
Tieyon	AS	656	26°12'S	133°52'E
Tifariti		262	26°08'N	10°33'W
Tiffin		374	41°06'N	83°10'W
Tiflet	MO	310	33°54'N	6°20'W
Tifton	US	398	31°27'N	83°30'W
Tifton Upland		378	32°00'N	82°10'W
Tifu		478	3°42'S	126°23'E
Tiga		654	21°11'S	167°51'E
Tigane	SF	322	26°44'S	26°25'E
Tiger Falls	GY	434	4°00'N	58°00'W
Tighina	MD	601	46°49'N	29°29'E
Tigil'	RS	612	57°48'N	158°40'E
Tignère	CM	280	7°22'N	12°39'E
Tignes	FR	580	45°30'N	6°55'E
Tigre	AR	419	34°25'S	58°34'W
Tigre	PE	436	4°26'S	74°05'W
Tigres, Baia dos	AO	274	16°40'S	11°50'E
Tigris	IZ	504	31°00'N	47°25'E
Tiguent	MR	308	17°15'N	16°00'W
Tiguesmat	MR	308	24°54'N	8°14'W
Tigui	CD	283	18°38'N	18°47'E
Tigzirt	AG	272	36°53'N	4°09'E
Tihamah		264	20°00'N	41°00'E
Tihamat	YM	541	15°00'N	45°55'E
Tihamat Asir	SA	528	18°00'N	42°10'E
Tihosuco	MX	394	20°11'N	88°18'W
Tihuatlán	MX	394	20°44'N	97°32'W
Tījī	LY	302	32°01'N	11°22'E
Tijuana	MX	394	32°31'N	117°02'W
Tijucas	BR	424	27°14'S	48°38'W
Tikal	GT	411	17°13'N	89°35'W
Tikamgarh		470	24°44'N	78°50'E
Tikanlik	CH	490	40°42'N	87°37'E
Tikaré	UV	278	13°17'N	1°43'W
Tikehau		654	14°53'S	148°19'W
Tikéi		654	15°00'S	144°30'E
Tikhoretsk	RS	612	45°51'N	40°07'E
Tikhvin	RS	612	59°39'N	33°31'E
Tiko	CM	280	4°05'N	9°22'E
Tikota		470	16°51'N	75°31'E
Tikrīt	IZ	504	34°36'N	43°42'E
Tiksha		556	64°09'N	32°23'E
Tiksi		468	71°36'N	128°48'E
Tila	MX	394	17°24'N	92°29'W
Tilamuta	ID	500	0°30'N	122°20'E
Tilarán, Cordillera de	CS	405	10°20'N	84°45'W
Tilburg	NL	602	51°34'N	5°06'E
Tilcha	AS	656	29°36'S	140°54'E
Tilemsi, Vallée du	ML	307	16°15'N	0°02'E
Tilghman		378	38°42'N	76°27'W
Tilin	BM	487	21°41'N	94°06'E
Tilisarao	AR	419	32°44'S	65°18'W
Tillabéry	NG	314	14°13'N	1°27'E
Tillamook		372	45°27'N	123°50'W
Tillamook Head		372	45°56'N	123°58'W
Tilley	CA	390	50°27'N	111°39'W
Tillmans Corner		378	30°35'N	88°10'W
Tillsonburg		374	42°51'N	80°44'W
Tilney		372	50°14'N	105°24'W
Tilomar	ID	500	9°21'S	125°08'E
Tilomonte	CI	428	23°47'S	68°07'W
Tilopozo	CI	428	23°47'S	68°15'W
Tilos	GR	588	36°25'N	27°25'E
Tilpa	AS	656	30°57'S	144°24'E
Tilst	DA	576	56°12'N	10°07'E
Tiltagara	AS	656	31°51'S	144°53'E
Tilting	CA	390	49°42'N	54°04'W
Tim		466	51°37'N	37°07'E
Tim	DA	576	56°12'N	8°19'E
Ţimā	EG	290	26°54'N	31°26'E
Timagami, Lake		374	46°57'N	80°05'W
Timaná	CO	430	1°58'N	75°56'W
Timanskiy Kryazh	RS	612	65°00'N	51°00'E
Timaru	NZ	663	44°24'S	171°15'E
Timashevsk		466	45°37'N	38°57'E
Timbákion	GR	588	35°04'N	24°46'E
Timbaúba	BR	424	7°31'S	35°19'W
Timbédra	MR	308	16°15'N	8°10'W
Timber Bay	CA	390	54°07'N	105°42'W
Timberlake		374	37°20'N	79°14'W
Timberville		374	38°38'N	78°46'W
Timbío	CO	430	2°20'N	76°40'W
Timbiquí	CO	430	2°46'N	77°42'W
Timbo	GV	297	10°38'N	11°50'W
Timbué, Ponta	MZ	312	18°49'S	36°22'E
Timenocalin, Hasy	LY	302	27°09'N	11°48'E
Timetrine	ML	307	19°27'N	0°26'W
Timétrine, Djebel	ML	307	19°20'N	0°42'W
Timetrout, Jebel	MO	310	31°54'N	4°46'W
Timfristós	GR	588	38°57'N	21°49'E
Timi	CY	494	34°44'N	32°31'E
Tìmia	NG	314	18°04'N	8°40'E
Timimoun	AG	272	29°15'N	0°15'E
Timis	RO	610	45°48'N	25°39'E
Timiskaming, Lake		374	47°20'N	79°30'W
Timişoara	RO	610	45°45'N	21°13'E
Timkapaul'	RS	612	61°30'N	62°20'E
Tim Merhsoi	NG	314	19°00'N	6°00'E
Timmiarmiut		370	62°32'N	42°13'W
Timmins	CA	390	48°28'N	81°20'W
Timon		384	5°05'S	42°51'W
Timor	ID	500	8°50'S	126°00'E
Timor Sea	ID	500	10°30'S	126°00'E
Timotes	VE	440	8°59'N	70°44'W
Timpton	RS	612	58°43'N	127°12'E
Timrå	SW	621	62°29'N	17°18'E
Timsher	RS	612	60°41'N	54°48'E
Timsher	RS	612	62°06'N	54°45'E
Tin, Ra's at	LY	302	32°37'N	23°08'E
Tinaca Pt.	RP	526	5°34'N	125°18'E
Tinaco	VE	440	9°42'N	68°26'W
Tinajo	SP	618	29°03'N	13°40'W
Tinambung		478	3°31'S	119°01'E
Tinaquillo	VE	440	9°55'N	68°18'W
Tinca	RO	610	46°46'N	21°57'E
Tin Can Bay		652	25°55'S	153°00'E
Tindivanam	IN	496	12°15'N	79°39'E
Tindouf	AG	272	27°41'N	8°09'W
Tindouf, Hammada		262	27°45'N	8°25'W
Tineo	SP	618	43°20'N	6°25'W
Ti-n-Essako	ML	307	18°14'N	2°50'E
Tinga	CT	282	9°21'N	23°38'E
Ting Dowuli	LI	301	6°54'N	10°23'W
Tingi Mountains	SL	320	8°55'N	10°47'W
Tingjegaon	NP	522	29°14'N	83°19'E
Tingo María	PE	436	9°09'S	75°56'W
Tingréla	IV	288	10°29'N	6°24'W
Tingri	CH	490	28°30'N	86°33'E
Tingsryd	SW	621	56°32'N	14°59'E
Tinguéré Mbi	CT	282	5°45'N	20°04'E
Tinguipaya	BL	422	19°11'S	65°51'W
Tinguiririca, Volcán	CI	428	34°49'S	70°21'W
Tingvoll	NO	604	62°54'N	8°12'E
Tinharé	BR	424	13°30'S	38°52'W
Tinh Gia	VM	540	19°27'N	105°42'E
Tinian		654	14°58'N	145°31'E
Tinian Island		654	15°05'N	145°33'E
Tiniteqilaaq		370	65°53'N	37°47'W
Tinkisso	GV	297	11°21'N	9°10'W
Tin Merzouga		262	23°00'N	11°00'E
Tinogasta	AR	419	28°04'S	67°34'W
Tinombo		478	0°23'S	120°16'E
Tínos	GR	588	37°39'N	25°07'E
Tinputz	PP	664	5°33'S	155°00'E
Tinrhert, Hamada	AG	272	29°00'N	9°00'E
Tinrhir	MO	310	31°31'N	5°32'W
Tinsukia	IN	496	27°30'N	95°22'E
Tinta	PE	436	14°09'S	71°25'W
Tintagel Head	UK	626	50°39'N	4°45'W
Tîntâne	MR	308	16°25'N	10°10'W
Tintigny	BE	570	49°41'N	5°31'E
Tintina	AR	419	27°02'S	62°43'W
Tintinara		652	35°54'S	140°03'E
Tinto		562	37°12'N	6°56'W
Tinui	NZ	663	40°52'S	176°04'E
Tinyahuarco	PE	436	10°45'S	76°18'W
Ti-n-Zaouâten	AG	272	19°58'N	3°01'E
Ti-n-Zaouâtene	ML	307	19°56'N	2°58'E
T'i'o	ER	292	14°39'N	40°54'E
Tioga	US	398	48°23'N	102°56'W
Tiom	ID	500	3°52'S	138°22'E
Tioman	MY	518	2°48'N	104°11'E
Tipac, Monte	BR	424	3°34'N	51°20'W
Tipitapa	NU	415	12°10'N	86°06'W
Tipo-Tipo		478	6°31'N	122°08'E
Tipperary	EI	592	52°28'N	8°10'W
Tipton		374	38°39'N	92°46'W
Tipton		374	41°46'N	91°07'W
Tipton		376	34°30'N	99°08'W
Tiptūr	IN	496	13°16'N	76°29'E
Tiracambu, Serra do	BR	424	3°15'S	46°30'W
Tiran	SA	528	27°56'N	34°34'E
Tiranë	AL	566	41°20'N	19°50'E
Tirano	IT	593	46°13'N	10°10'E
Tiran Sinafir	EG	290	27°55'N	34°44'E
Tirāp	IN	496	27°10'N	95°48'E
Tirari Desert	AS	656	28°00'S	138°20'E
Tiraspol	MD	601	46°50'N	29°37'E
Tirat Karmel	IS	505	32°46'N	34°58'E
Tire	TU	535	38°04'N	27°45'E
Tiree	UK	626	56°25'N	6°52'W
Tirest	ML	307	20°23'N	1°07'E
Tirgol	ET	293	7°49'N	33°02'E
Tîrgovişte	RO	610	44°56'N	25°27'E
Tîrgu Bujor	RO	610	45°53'N	27°55'E
Tîrgu Cărbuneşti	RO	610	44°57'N	23°31'E
Tîrgu Frumos	RO	610	47°12'N	27°00'E
Tîrgu Jiu	RO	610	45°03'N	23°17'E
Tîrgu Lăpuş	RO	610	47°27'N	23°52'E
Tîrgu Mureş	RO	610	46°32'N	24°34'E
Tîrgu Neamţ	RO	610	47°12'N	26°22'E
Tîrgu Ocna	RO	610	46°16'N	26°37'E
Tîrgu Secuiesc	RO	610	46°00'N	26°08'E
Tirich Mir	PK	524	36°15'N	71°50'E
Tiriri	UG	330	1°53'N	33°27'E
Tiris		262	24°00'N	14°00'W
Tirlyanskiy		466	54°14'N	58°35'E
Tîrnăveni	RO	610	46°20'N	24°17'E
Tírnavos	GR	588	39°45'N	22°17'E
Tiro	GV	297	9°45'N	10°39'W
Tīr Pol	AF	480	34°36'N	61°15'E
Tirso		562	40°10'N	9°00'E
Tiruchchirāppalli	IN	496	10°49'N	78°41'E
Tiruchendūr	IN	496	8°29'N	78°07'E
Tirunelveli	IN	496	8°44'N	77°42'E
Tiruntán	PE	436	7°55'S	74°54'W
Tirupati	IN	496	13°39'N	79°25'E
Tiruppattūr	IN	496	12°30'N	78°34'E
Tiruppūr	IN	496	11°06'N	77°21'E
Tiruvannāmalai	IN	496	12°13'N	79°04'E
Tisbury	UK	626	51°04'N	2°05'W
Tisdale	CA	390	52°50'N	104°02'W
Tisei, Cimpia	RO	610	45°15'N	20°17'E
Tishkovka	UP	624	48°30'N	30°56'E
Tishkovo	RS	612	46°02'N	48°36'E
Tishomingo		376	34°14'N	96°40'W
Tišnov	EZ	575	49°21'N	16°16'E
Tisovec	LO	616	48°41'N	19°57'E
Tissa	MO	310	34°18'N	4°40'W
Tissemsilt	AG	272	35°36'N	1°49'E
Tisul'		466	55°45'N	88°19'E
Tisza	HU	590	47°50'N	21°00'E
Tiszaföldvár	HU	590	46°59'N	20°15'E
Tiszafüred	HU	590	47°37'N	20°46'E
Tiszakécske	HU	590	46°56'N	20°06'E
Tiszalök	HU	590	48°01'N	21°23'E
Tiszavasvári	HU	590	47°58'N	21°21'E
Tit	AG	272	26°57'N	1°29'E
Titano	SM	615	43°55'N	12°27'E
Titao	UV	278	13°46'N	2°04'W
Titay	RP	526	7°49'N	122°32'E
Titel	YO	630	45°13'N	20°18'E
Titi	CF	285	3°14'S	12°40'E
Titicaca, Lago	BL	422	16°01'S	64°14'W
Titlagarh		476	20°18'N	83°09'E
Tit Mellil	MO	310	33°34'N	7°29'W
Titograd	YO	630	42°27'N	19°15'E
Titova Mitrovica	YO	630	42°53'N	20°51'E
Titovo Užice	YO	630	43°52'N	19°51'E
Titov Veles	MK	599	41°41'N	21°46'E
Titu	RO	610	44°39'N	25°32'E
Titule	CG	287	3°17'N	25°32'E
Titusville		374	41°37'N	79°40'W
Titusville		378	28°36'N	80°48'W
Tiva	KE	299	2°20'S	38°48'E
Tivaouane	SG	319	14°57'N	16°49'W
Tivat	YO	630	42°25'N	18°41'E
Tiverton	UK	626	50°54'N	3°29'W
Tivoli	IT	593	41°58'N	12°48'E
Ţīwī	MU	523	22°49'N	59°16'E
Tixán	EC	432	2°08'S	78°48'W
Tixkokob	MX	394	21°00'N	89°24'W
Tixtla	MX	394	17°34'N	99°26'W
Tizimín		380	21°09'N	88°09'W
Tizi Ouzou	AG	272	36°42'N	4°03'E
Tiznit	MO	310	29°43'N	9°43'W
Tjæreborg	DA	576	55°28'N	8°35'E
Tjeldstø	NO	604	60°35'N	4°46'E
Tjeukermeer	NL	602	52°50'N	6°00'E
Tjilatjap	ID	500	7°44'S	109°00'E
Tjirebon	ID	500	6°44'S	108°34'E
Tjorn	SW	621	57°56'N	11°14'E
Tjøtta	NO	604	65°52'N	12°26'E
Tkhab, Gora	RS	612	44°36'N	38°27'E
Tkibuli	GG	495	42°22'N	42°59'E
Tkvarcheli	GG	495	42°51'N	41°41'E
Tlacotepec	MX	394	17°46'N	99°59'W
Tlahualilo	MX	394	26°07'N	103°27'W
Tlalnepantla	MX	394	19°00'N	99°00'W
Tlalnepantla de Galeana		380	19°33'N	99°12'W
Tláloc, Cerro	MX	394	19°25'N	98°42'W
Tlaltenango	MX	394	21°47'N	103°19'W
Tlapa	MX	394	17°33'N	98°33'W
Tlapehuala	MX	394	18°13'N	100°31'W
Tlaquepaque		380	20°39'N	103°19'W
Tlaxiaco	MX	394	17°16'N	97°41'W
Tlell	CA	390	53°33'N	131°56'W
Tlemcen	AG	272	34°54'N	1°19'W
Tleta Sidi Mbarek Bou Guedra	MO	310	32°16'N	8°59'W
Tlhabane	SF	322	25°38'S	27°12'E
Tlinshe	KZ	510	50°08'N	47°52'E
Tlokweng	BC	276	24°40'S	25°58'E
Tłuszcz	PL	606	52°25'N	21°27'E
Tmassah	LY	302	26°22'N	15°48'E
To	UV	278	12°45'N	2°59'W
Toa	CU	406	20°24'N	74°32'W
Toa, Cuchillas de	CU	406	20°10'N	85°00'W
Toabré	PM	417	8°40'N	80°19'W
Toamasina	MA	304	18°10'S	49°23'E
Toasi	GH	296	6°39'N	1°49'W
Toau		654	16°39'S	147°14'W
Toay	AR	419	36°40'S	64°21'W
Toba	CH	490	31°18'N	97°42'E
Toba	JA	506	34°28'N	136°50'E
Toba, Lake	ID	500	2°35'N	98°50'E
Tobago	TD	438	11°15'N	62°18'W

U

Ukwatutu	CG	287	4°44'N	27°33'E
Ulaanbaatar	MG	520	47°55'N	106°53'E
Ulaan Dabaa	MG	520	48°01'N	107°40'E
Ulaandel	MG	520	46°24'N	113°34'E
Ulaan-Ereg	MG	520	46°54'N	109°45'E
Ulaangom	MG	520	49°58'N	92°02'E
Ulaanhudag	MG	520	47°30'N	104°22'E
Ulaanjirem	MG	520	45°04'N	105°35'E
Ulaantolgoy	MG	520	46°40'N	92°48'E
Ulaan-Uul	MG	520	44°15'N	111°14'E
Ulaan-Uul	MG	520	46°05'N	100°50'E
Ulan	CH	490	36°54'N	98°30'E
Ulan Buh Shamo	CH	490	40°24'N	106°30'E
Ulan-Burgasy, Khrebet	RS	612	52°45'N	109°00'E
Ulan Erge		466	46°19'N	44°53'E
Ulangati	CG	287	3°01'S	25°32'E
Ulan-Kholl		466	45°26'N	46°51'E
Ulan Mod	CH	490	39°52'N	104°49'E
Ulansuhai Nur	CH	490	40°56'N	108°49'E
Ulan Tohoi	CH	490	40°53'N	101°25'E
Ulan-Ude	RS	612	51°50'N	107°36'E
Ulan Ul Hu	CH	490	34°48'N	90°22'E
Ulapes	AR	419	31°35'S	66°15'W
Ulaş		564	39°27'N	37°03'E
Ulassai	IT	593	39°49'N	9°30'E
Ulastay		472	42°55'N	86°45'E
Ulawa I.	BP	666	9°50'S	161°59'E
Ulaya	TZ	327	7°04'S	36°54'E
Ul'ba	KZ	510	50°16'N	83°22'E
Ulchin	KS	513	36°59'N	129°24'E
Ulcinj	YO	630	41°56'N	19°13'E
Ulco	SF	322	28°19'S	24°12'E
Ulcumayo	PE	436	11°01'S	75°55'W
Uldz	MG	520	48°40'N	112°00'E
Ulefoss	NO	604	59°17'N	9°16'E
Ulgain Gol		472	45°43'N	118°11'E
Ulhāsnagar	IN	496	19°11'N	73°09'E
Ulindi	CG	287	1°40'S	25°52'E
Ulithi Atoll	FM	661	10°00'N	139°55'E
Uljma	YO	630	45°03'N	21°10'E
Ul'kan	RS	612	55°54'N	107°47'E
Ulla	BO	569	55°14'N	29°15'E
Ulladulla		652	35°21'S	150°28'E
Ullāpāra	BG	485	24°19'N	89°34'E
Ullapool	UK	626	57°54'N	5°10'W
Ulla Ulla	BL	422	15°03'S	69°16'W
Ulldecona	SP	618	40°36'N	0°27'E
Ullensvang	NO	604	60°18'N	6°38'E
Ulloma	BL	422	17°30'S	68°32'W
Ullsfjorden	NO	604	70°10'N	20°00'E
Ullung do		474	37°30'N	130°52'E
Ŭllyul	KN	512	38°30'N	125°12'E
Ulm	GM	584	48°23'N	9°58'E
Ulonguè	MZ	312	14°43'S	34°21'E
Ulricehamn	SW	621	57°48'N	13°25'E
Ulrichen	SZ	622	46°30'N	8°18'E
Ulrichsberg	AU	568	48°41'N	13°54'E
Ulrum	NL	602	53°22'N	6°20'E
Ulsan	KS	513	35°33'N	129°19'E
Ulsteinvik	NO	604	62°20'N	5°53'E
Ulu	ID	500	2°45'N	125°24'E
Ulu	SU	324	10°43'N	33°29'E
Ulúa	HO	412	15°53'N	87°44'W
Ulubāria		476	22°28'N	88°06'E
Ulubat Gölü	TU	535	40°10'N	28°35'E
Ulubey		564	40°51'N	37°46'E
Ulubey		564	38°25'N	29°18'E
Uluborlu	TU	535	38°05'N	30°28'E
Uludere	TU	535	37°27'N	42°51'E
Uludoruk Tepe	TU	535	37°29'N	44°00'E
Ulugqat	CH	490	39°47'N	74°15'E
Uluguru	TZ	327	7°04'S	37°16'E
Ulukışla		564	37°33'N	34°40'E
Ulul		648	8°00'N	150°30'E
Ulundi	SF	322	28°18'S	31°25'E
Ulungur He	CH	490	46°58'N	87°28'E
Ulungur Hu	CH	490	47°20'N	87°10'E
Uluru (Ayers Rock)	AS	656	25°23'S	131°05'E
Ulus		564	41°35'N	32°39'E
Ulutau, Gora	KZ	510	49°00'N	67°10'E
Ulutau, Gory	KZ	510	49°00'N	67°00'E
Ulu Tiram	MY	518	1°36'N	103°49'E
Ulverston	UK	626	54°12'N	3°06'W
Ulverstone		652	41°09'S	146°10'E
Ulvik	NO	604	60°34'N	6°54'E
Ulvila	FI	578	61°26'N	21°53'E
Ul'yanovka		560	59°38'N	30°46'E
Ul'yanovka	UP	624	48°20'N	30°13'E
Ul'yanovo		560	53°43'N	35°32'E
Ul'yanovo	UZ	539	40°07'N	68°30'E
Ulysses	US	398	37°34'N	101°21'W
Ulyzhilanshik		466	49°30'N	65°00'E
Ulze, L.	AL	566	41°41'N	19°55'E
Uma	CH	490	52°36'N	120°39'E
Umag	HR	574	45°25'N	13°32'E
Umala	BL	422	17°24'S	67°58'W
Uman'	UP	624	48°45'N	30°17'E
Umán	MX	394	20°53'N	89°45'W
Umarkot	IN	496	19°40'N	82°13'E
Umarkot	PK	524	25°22'N	69°44'E
Um as Samin	SA	528	22°00'N	55°30'E
Umatac		654	13°20'N	145°40'E
Umatilla		372	45°54'N	119°20'W
Umba	RS	612	66°41'N	34°21'E
Umbakumba		648	13°53'S	136°47'E
Umbeara		652	25°56'S	133°46'E
Umboi		648	5°21'S	147°30'E
Umboi Island	PP	664	7°50'S	147°50'E
Um Dafuq	SU	324	10°31'N	23°18'E
Umeå	SW	621	63°50'N	20°17'E
Ume älv	SW	621	63°47'N	20°16'E
Umedpur	BG	485	22°31'N	89°59'E
Umët		466	54°08'N	42°42'E
Umhali Beach	SF	322	29°30'S	31°14'E
Umhausen	AU	568	47°08'N	10°56'E
Umi	UG	330	3°32'N	31°49'E
Umingmaktok	CA	390	67°41'N	107°53'W
Umka	YO	630	44°41'N	20°19'E
Umkomaas	SF	322	30°12'S	30°45'E
Umlazi	SF	322	29°57'S	30°52'E
Umm al Abīd	LY	302	27°31'N	15°02'E
Umm al Amad	QA	527	25°29'N	51°24'E
Umm al Arānib	LY	302	26°08'N	14°44'E
Umm al Birak	SA	528	23°26'N	39°13'E
Umm al Ghirbāl, Bi'r	LY	302	31°00'N	15°10'E
Umm al Khashab	SA	528	17°23'N	42°32'E
Umm al Qaywayn	TC	538	25°35'N	55°34'E
Umm al Quhab	QA	527	25°29'N	50°58'E
Umm ash Shubrum	QA	527	25°10'N	51°13'E
Umm as Samim	MU	523	21°25'N	55°40'E
Umm as Suwayyah	QA	527	25°39'N	51°27'E
Umm Bab	QA	527	25°13'N	50°48'E
Umm Buru	SU	324	15°03'N	23°43'E
Umm Dam	SU	324	13°45'N	30°59'E
Umm Dhibbān	SU	324	14°14'N	29°37'E
Umm Dhibbān	SU	324	15°26'N	32°51'E
Umm Durmān	SU	324	15°38'N	32°28'E
Umm el Faḥm	IS	505	32°31'N	35°09'E
Umm Hibal, Bi'r	EG	290	23°29'N	33°19'E
Umm Inderaba	SU	324	15°12'N	31°54'E
Umm Kaddādah	SU	324	13°36'N	26°42'E
Umm Lajj	SA	528	25°02'N	37°16'E
Umm Na'Sam	BA	484	26°05'N	50°25'E
Umm Qasbah	KU	514	29°00'N	48°10'E
Umm Qaşr	IZ	504	30°02'N	47°56'E
Umm Qawzayn	SU	324	14°17'N	27°13'E

Umm Qays	JO	510	32°39'N	35°41'E
Umm Ruwābah	SU	324	12°54'N	31°13'E
Umm Salal Muhammad	QA	527	25°25'N	51°24'E
Umm Sayyālah	SU	324	14°25'N	31°10'E
Umnak I.	US	398	53°17'N	169°03'W
Umniati	ZI	334	18°39'S	29°47'E
Umniati	ZI	334	17°30'S	29°23'E
Umphang	TH	534	16°01'N	98°52'E
Umpqua		372	43°40'N	124°12'W
Umpulo	AO	274	12°42'S	17°42'E
Ŭmsŏng	KS	513	36°53'N	127°41'E
Umtata	SF	322	31°35'S	28°47'E
Umtentweni	SF	322	30°42'S	30°28'E
Umuahia	NI	316	5°32'N	7°29'E
Umuarama	BR	424	23°49'S	53°19'W
Umuda I.	PP	664	8°15'S	144°50'E
Umu Duru	NI	316	5°41'N	7°15'E
Umunede	NI	316	6°16'N	6°18'E
Umurlce		564	37°50'N	27°58'E
Umzingwani	ZI	334	20°16'S	28°48'E
Umzinto	SF	322	30°19'S	30°38'E
Umzinto North	SF	322	30°18'S	30°40'E
Una		470	20°49'N	71°02'E
Una	BK	572	45°16'N	16°55'E
Unaí	BR	424	16°23'S	46°53'W
Unalaska	US	398	53°19'N	167°05'W
Unalaska I.	US	398	54°00'N	167°30'W
'Unayzah	SA	528	26°06'N	43°59'E
Unayzah, Jabal	IZ	504	30°30'N	35°47'E
Unchahra		470	24°23'N	80°47'E
Uncía	BL	422	18°27'S	66°37'W
Uncompahgre Plateau		376	38°30'N	108°30'W
Undaunda	ZA	332	15°15'S	28°59'E
Unden	SW	621	58°52'N	14°24'E
Underberg	SF	322	29°47'S	29°30'E
Underbool		652	35°10'S	141°49'E
Underwood		374	44°18'N	81°29'W
Undu		470	26°21'N	71°41'E
Undu Cape	FJ	660	16°05'S	179°55'W
Undzhi	TI	533	40°18'N	69°42'E
Unecha	RS	612	52°50'N	32°40'E
Unga I.	US	398	55°10'N	160°30'W
Ungama Bay	KE	299	2°45'S	40°20'E
Ungava Bay	CA	390	59°00'N	67°30'W
Unggi	KN	512	42°20'N	130°24'E
Ungheni	MD	601	47°12'N	27°48'E
Unguía	CO	430	8°01'N	77°04'W
Unhŭng	KN	512	41°18'N	128°30'E
Uni		560	57°46'N	51°30'E
União	BR	424	4°35'S	42°52'W
União dos Palmares		386	9°10'S	36°02'W
Uničov	EZ	575	49°46'N	17°08'E
Unije	HR	574	44°39'N	14°15'E
Unimak I.	US	398	55°01'N	164°52'W
Unini	PE	436	10°40'S	73°54'W
Union		378	32°34'N	89°07'W
Union		378	34°42'N	81°37'W
Union	GJ	410	12°12'N	61°40'W
Union	US	398	45°12'N	117°51'W
Unión	AR	419	35°09'S	65°57'W
Unión	CS	405	8°36'N	83°03'W
Unión	PA	435	24°48'S	56°33'W
Union City		374	41°53'N	79°50'W
Union City	US	398	36°25'N	89°03'W
Uniondale	SF	322	33°40'S	23°08'E
Unión de Reyes	CU	406	22°48'N	81°32'W
Unión de Tula	MX	394	19°58'N	104°16'W
Unión Hidalgo	MX	394	16°28'N	94°50'W
Union I.	VC	418	12°36'N	61°26'W
Union Springs		378	32°08'N	85°42'W
Uniontown		374	39°53'N	79°43'W
Uniontown		378	32°26'N	87°30'W
Unionville		374	40°28'N	93°00'W
United Arab Emirates		38	24°00'N	54°00'E
United Kingdom		38	54°00'N	4°00'W
United States		38	44°57'N	103°55'W
United States Ra.	CA	390	82°00'N	73°00'W
Unitsa		556	62°36'N	34°28'E
Unity	CA	390	52°27'N	109°10'W
Universal City	US	398	29°32'N	98°17'W
Universales, Mts.	SP	618	40°18'N	1°33'W
University City		374	38°40'N	90°18'W
Unjha	IN	496	23°48'N	72°24'E
Unjŏn	KN	512	39°39'N	125°31'E
Unnão	IN	496	26°33'N	80°30'E
Uno, Ilha	PU	298	11°15'N	16°13'W
Ŭnp'a	KN	512	38°25'N	125°46'E
Unquillo		388	31°14'S	64°19'W
Unsan	KN	512	40°06'N	125°54'E
Ŭnsan-ŭp	KN	512	39°24'N	126°01'E
Unst	UK	626	60°47'N	0°43'W
Unstrut	GM	584	51°10'N	11°48'E
Unsu-nodongjagu	KN	512	40°40'N	127°04'E
Unterseen	SZ	622	46°41'N	7°50'E
Unteruecker See	GM	584	53°00'N	14°00'E
Unterweissenbach	AU	568	48°26'N	14°46'E
Unuli Horog	CH	490	35°07'N	91°49'E
Ünye	TU	535	41°08'N	37°17'E
Unzha		466	57°20'N	43°08'E
Unzimkulu	SF	322	30°16'S	29°56'E
Uonquén	VE	440	5°07'N	61°46'W
Uozu	JA	506	36°48'N	137°24'E
Upala	CS	405	10°54'N	85°02'W
Upano	EC	432	2°43'S	78°15'W
Upata	VE	440	8°01'N	62°24'W
Upemba, Lake	CG	287	8°36'S	26°26'E
Upi	RP	526	6°57'N	124°09'E
Úpice	EZ	575	50°31'N	16°01'E
Upington	SF	322	28°27'S	21°15'E
Upiriwombe	ZA	332	10°07'S	33°21'E
Upleta	IN	496	21°44'N	70°17'E
Upolu	WS	668	13°50'S	171°50'W
Upolu Pt.	US	398	20°16'N	155°51'W
Upper Arlington		374	40°00'N	83°03'W
Upper Arrow L.		368	50°25'N	117°56'W
Upper Conaree	SC	417	17°19'N	62°42'W
Upper Darby		374	39°57'N	75°16'W
Upper Horton		652	30°08'S	150°26'E
Upper Hutt	NZ	663	41°07'S	175°04'E
Upper Klamath Lake		372	42°24'N	121°53'W
Upper Laberge	CA	390	60°57'N	135°06'W
Upper Lake		372	41°45'N	120°09'W
Upper Liard	CA	390	60°03'N	128°54'W
Upper Lough Erie	UK	626	54°15'N	7°50'W
Upper Manzanilla	TD	438	10°31'N	61°04'W
Upper Red Lake		370	48°08'N	94°45'W
Upper Vaughan		370	44°49'N	64°14'W
Upplands-Väsby	SW	621	59°31'N	17°54'E
Uppsala	SW	621	59°52'N	17°38'E
Upsala	CA	390	49°03'N	90°28'W
Upshi		470	33°50'N	77°49'E
Upstart, C.	AS	656	19°41'S	147°45'E
Upstart Bay	AS	656	19°30'S	148°00'E
Ura	BT	486	27°25'N	90°55'E
Uracoa	VE	440	9°00'N	62°21'W
Urad Qianqi	CH	490	40°40'N	108°45'E
Urahoro		474	42°42'N	143°42'E
Urakawa	JA	506	42°09'N	142°47'E
Ural	RS	612	47°00'N	51°48'E
Uralla		652	30°39'S	151°30'E
Ural'sk	KZ	510	51°12'N	51°22'E
Ural'skiy		466	51°37'N	51°39'E
Uralskiy Khrebet	RS	612	60°00'N	60°00'E
Urambo	TZ	327	5°04'S	32°03'E
Urana		652	35°20'S	146°16'E
Uranium City		368	59°34'N	108°37'W

Urapunga	AS	656	14°42'S	134°33'E
Uraras	WA	313	23°14'S	14°44'E
Uraricoera	BR	424	3°02'N	60°30'W
Uraricoera	BR	424	3°27'N	60°59'W
Urasoe	JA	506	26°15'N	127°43'E
Urawa		472	35°51'N	139°39'E
Uray	RS	612	60°08'N	64°48'E
Urayfijan	KU	514	28°54'N	43°11'E
Urazaly	TX	537	35°58'N	62°52'E
Urazovka		560	55°24'N	45°38'E
Urazovo		560	50°04'N	38°04'E
Urbana		374	40°06'N	88°45'W
Urbandale		374	41°37'N	93°42'W
Urbano Noris	CU	406	20°36'N	76°08'W
Urcos	PE	436	13°42'S	71°38'W
Urda	KZ	510	48°46'N	47°26'E
Urdaneta	RP	526	15°59'N	120°34'E
Urdgol	MG	520	47°50'N	92°39'E
Urdinskiy Khrebet		468	54°00'N	98°00'E
Urdzhar	KZ	510	47°05'N	81°38'E
Ure	UK	626	54°05'N	1°20'W
Ureki	GG	495	41°59'N	41°47'E
Uren		372	50°29'N	103°46'W
Uren	CS	405	9°33'N	82°55'W
Uren'		560	57°28'N	45°49'E
Ureña	VE	440	7°55'N	72°28'W
Urengoy	RS	612	65°58'N	78°25'E
Uréparapara		654	13°40'S	167°30'E
Ures	MX	394	29°26'N	110°24'W
Urgal		468	51°12'N	132°58'E
Urgench	UZ	539	41°33'N	60°38'E
Ürgüp	TU	535	38°38'N	34°56'E
Urgut	UZ	539	39°23'N	67°15'E
Urho	CH	490	46°06'N	85°07'E
Uribante	VE	440	7°18'N	70°44'W
Uribe	CO	430	3°13'N	74°24'W
Uribia	CO	430	11°43'N	72°16'W
Urica	VE	440	9°43'N	64°01'W
Uricani	RO	610	45°20'N	23°09'E
Urim	IS	505	31°18'N	34°31'E
Urimán	VE	440	5°21'N	62°39'W
Urique	MX	394	26°55'N	107°56'W
Uriranteriña	VE	440	4°19'N	63°49'W
Uritskiy	KZ	510	53°19'N	65°34'E
Urjala	FI	578	61°05'N	23°32'E
Urk	NL	602	52°40'N	5°36'E
Urla	TU	535	38°18'N	26°46'E
Urlaţi	RO	610	44°59'N	26°14'E
Urlyutyub	KZ	510	53°44'N	75°02'E
Urma as Sughra	SY	531	36°08'N	36°54'E
Urman		466	54°52'N	56°52'E
Urmi	RS	612	48°44'N	134°16'E
Urmia, L.	IR	502	37°40'N	45°30'E
Urner Alpen	SZ	622	46°40'N	8°40'E
Urom	NI	316	6°42'N	6°20'E
Uroševac	YO	630	42°22'N	21°10'E
Ŭroteppa	TI	533	39°55'N	69°01'E
Ur-Otkel'	KZ	510	49°14'N	62°50'E
Urrao		380	6°20'N	76°11'W
Urru Co	CH	490	31°40'N	98°00'E
Urshel'skiy		560	55°41'N	40°13'E
Urt	MG	520	43°26'N	101°36'E
Urta-Kyzyl	KG	514	40°18'N	72°39'E
Urt Moron	CH	490	36°53'N	93°01'E
Uruáchic	MX	394	27°52'N	108°14'W
Uruaçu	BR	424	14°30'S	49°10'W
Uruana		386	15°30'S	49°41'W
Uruapan	MX	394	31°37'N	116°12'W
Uruapan	MX	394	19°24'N	102°04'W
Urubamba	PE	436	13°18'S	72°07'W
Urubamba	PE	436	10°44'S	73°45'W
Urubichá	BL	422	15°23'S	62°57'W
Urubuquara, Serra	BR	424	3°30'S	52°21'W
Urucará	BR	424	2°32'S	57°45'W
Uruçuí	BR	424	7°12'S	44°31'W
Uruçuí, Serra do	BR	424	9°00'S	44°45'W
Uruçuí Prêto	BR	424	7°20'S	44°38'W
Urucur	ET	293	13°20'N	41°01'E
Urucurituba	BR	424	2°41'S	57°40'W
Uruguaiana	BR	424	29°46'S	57°03'W
Uruguay		38	33°00'S	56°00'W
Uruguay	AR	419	28°00'S	55°00'W
Uruhe	CH	490	51°49'N	124°30'E
Urukthapel	PX	664	7°12'N	134°27'E
Urumaco	VE	440	11°12'N	70°16'W
Urumita	CO	430	10°34'N	73°01'W
Urumpirai	CE	530	9°43'N	80°02'E
Ürümqi	CH	490	43°47'N	87°34'E
Urup, O.	RS	612	46°00'N	150°00'E
Urusha	RS	612	54°03'N	122°54'E
Uru Uru, Lago	BL	422	18°06'S	67°08'W
Uruwira	TZ	327	6°27'S	31°21'E
Uruyén	VE	440	5°41'N	62°25'W
Urville I. D'	NZ	663	40°50'S	173°52'E
Uryupinsk		466	50°47'N	42°00'E
Urzhum		466	57°08'N	50°00'E
Urziceni	RO	610	44°43'N	26°38'E
Usa	JA	506	33°26'N	131°16'E
Usagara	TZ	327	2°41'S	33°00'E
Uşak	TU	535	38°41'N	29°25'E
Usakos	WA	313	22°00'S	15°36'E
Usambara Mts	TZ	327	8°23'S	35°42'E
Usango Flats	TZ	327	8°30'S	34°15'E
Usedom	GM	584	53°52'N	13°55'E
Useldange	LU	598	49°46'N	5°59'E
Useless Loop	AS	656	26°14'S	113°22'E
Usevia	TZ	327	7°06'S	31°14'E
'Usfān	SA	528	21°55'N	39°22'E
Ushachi	BO	569	55°11'N	28°37'E
Ushaki		560	59°29'N	30°59'E
Ushakovskoye	RS	612	71°00'N	178°31'W
Ushashi	TZ	327	2°00'S	33°57'E
'Ushayrah	SA	528	21°46'N	40°38'E
Ushaysh al Jahra'	KU	514	29°19'N	47°40'E
Ushetu	TZ	327	4°10'S	32°16'E
Ushibuka	JA	506	32°11'N	130°01'E
Ushirombo	TZ	327	3°29'S	31°58'E
Ushtobe	KZ	510	45°16'N	78°00'E
Ushuaia	AR	419	54°47'S	68°18'W
Ushumun	RS	612	52°47'N	126°32'E
Ushurekchen Gory		468	65°15'N	161°00'E
Usi	KN	512	40°41'N	125°40'E
Usicayos	PE	436	14°10'S	69°52'W
Usinge	TZ	327	5°05'S	31°18'E
Usino	PP	664	5°32'S	145°22'E
Usinsk		560	53°20'N	48°42'E
Usk	CA	390	54°38'N	128°25'W
Usman'		466	52°02'N	39°44'E
Usmas Ezers	LG	596	57°11'N	22°10'E
Usoke	TZ	327	5°06'S	32°20'E
Usol'ye-Sibirskoye	RS	612	52°45'N	103°41'E
Uson	RP	526	12°13'N	123°50'E
Uspallata	AR	419	32°35'S	69°20'W
Uspantán	GT	411	15°23'N	90°50'W
Usquil	PE	436	7°49'S	78°25'W
Ussel	FR	580	45°33'N	2°19'E
Ussoque	AO	274	12°21'S	15°06'E
Ussure	TZ	327	4°39'S	34°23'E
Ussuri	RS	612	48°27'N	135°04'E
Ussuriysk	RS	612	43°48'N	131°59'E
Usta Muhammad	PK	524	28°11'N	68°03'E
Ust'-Bagaryak		466	56°08'N	61°52'E
Ust'-Barguzin	RS	612	53°27'N	108°59'E
Uster	SZ	622	47°20'N	8°42'E
Ustica	IT	593	38°39'N	12°34'E
Ustica, I. di	IT	593	38°42'N	13°11'E

Ust'-Ilimsk	RS	612	58°03'N	102°39'E
Ust'-Ilimskiy Vdkhr.		468	57°00'N	102°21'E
Ust'-Ilych	RS	612	62°32'N	56°44'E
Ústí nad Labem	EZ	575	50°39'N	14°02'E
Ústí nad Orlicí	EZ	575	49°59'N	16°24'E
Ust'-Ishim	RS	612	57°42'N	71°10'E
Ustka	PL	606	54°32'N	13°50'E
Ust'-Kamchatsk	RS	612	56°15'N	162°30'E
Ust'-Karsk	RS	612	52°43'N	118°48'E
Ust-Khmelëvka		466	58°54'N	61°47'E
Ust'-Kulom	RS	612	61°42'N	53°40'E
Ust'-Kut	RS	612	56°46'N	105°40'E
Ust'-Kuyga	RS	612	70°01'N	135°36'E
Ust'-Labinsk		564	45°13'N	39°42'E
Ust'-Luga		560	59°40'N	28°19'E
Ust'-Man'ya	RS	612	62°11'N	60°20'E
Ust'-Maya	RS	612	60°26'N	134°30'E
Ust'-Nera	RS	612	64°34'N	143°12'E
Ust'-Nyukzha	RS	612	56°34'N	121°37'E
Ust'-Ocheya		466	62°23'N	48°36'E
Ust'-Olenëk	RS	612	73°00'N	119°48'E
Ust'-Omchug	RS	612	61°09'N	149°38'E
Ust'-Onolva		466	59°37'N	54°51'E
Ust'-Ordynskiy		468	52°48'N	104°45'E
Ust'-Pinega		556	64°09'N	41°55'E
Ust'-Port	RS	612	69°40'N	84°26'E
Ustrzyki Dolne	PL	606	49°26'N	22°35'E
Ust'-Tsil'ma	RS	612	65°27'N	52°12'E
Ust'-Tym	RS	612	59°27'N	80°01'E
Ust'-Uda	RS	612	54°04'N	103°14'E
Ust'-Uls	RS	612	60°33'N	58°32'E
Ust'-Uyskoye		466	54°16'N	63°54'E
Ustyurt, Plato	KZ	510	43°00'N	56°00'E
Ustyuzhna		560	58°51'N	36°23'E
Usu	CH	490	44°27'N	84°36'E
Usuki	JA	506	33°08'N	131°49'E
Usulután	ES	409	13°21'N	88°27'W
Usuma	CG	287	4°24'N	26°35'E
Usumacinta	GT	411	17°10'N	91°10'W
Usun Apau Plateau	MY	518	3°00'N	115°00'E
Usutu	WZ	326	26°35'S	31°11'E
Uta	ID	500	4°33'S	136°01'E
Utagiin Huryee	MG	520	49°59'N	101°15'E
Utah		372	39°15'N	111°45'W
Utajärvi	FI	578	64°45'N	26°23'E
Utale	MI	306	15°13'S	34°59'E
Utan	ID	500	8°24'S	117°07'E
Utaofai		654	17°39'S	145°44'W
'Uta Vava'u	TN	667	18°30'S	174°00'W
Utebo		562	41°43'N	1°00'W
Utembo	AO	274	17°05'S	21°57'E
Utena	LH	597	55°30'N	25°36'E
Utengule	TZ	327	8°53'S	35°45'E
Utete	TZ	327	7°59'S	38°47'E
Uthai Thani	TH	534	15°22'N	100°03'E
Uthal	PK	524	25°48'N	66°37'E
Uthman	SY	531	32°40'N	36°07'E
Utica	US	398	43°06'N	75°13'W
Utiel	SP	618	39°34'N	1°13'W
Utila	HO	412	16°05'N	86°54'W
Utila, Isla de	HO	412	16°06'N	86°56'W
Utinga	BR	424	12°06'S	41°05'W
Utirik	RM	661	11°20'N	170°00'E
Utl'ukskiy Liman	UP	624	46°15'N	35°12'E
Uto	JA	506	32°40'N	130°39'E
Utopia	AS	656	22°14'S	134°33'E
Utorgosh		560	58°17'N	30°15'E
Utrecht	NL	602	52°05'N	5°07'E
Utrera	SP	618	37°11'N	5°47'W
Utrillas	SP	618	40°49'N	0°51'W
Utsjoki	FI	578	69°53'N	27°00'E
Utsunomiya	JA	506	36°33'N	139°52'E
Utta		466	46°23'N	46°01'E
Uttaradit	TH	534	17°38'N	100°06'E
Uttarkashi		470	30°44'N	78°27'E
Uttar Patiata	BG	485	24°19'N	89°21'E
Utuado	US	398	18°16'N	66°42'W
Utubulak		466	46°54'N	86°23'E
Utumbari	UG	330	3°16'N	31°09'E
Utupua	BP	666	11°20'S	166°25'E
Uubulan	MG	520	48°35'N	101°56'E
Uujim	MG	520	48°54'N	89°37'E
Uulu	EN	577	58°17'N	24°35'E
Üüreg Nuur	MG	520	45°30'N	91°00'E
Uusikaarlepyy (Nykarleby)	FI	578	63°32'N	22°32'E
Uusikaupunki	FI	578	60°48'N	21°25'E
Uus Nuur		472	50°00'N	93°00'E
Uva		466	56°59'N	52°13'E
Uvalde	US	398	29°12'N	99°47'W
Uvarovo		466	51°59'N	42°15'E
Uvat	RS	612	59°09'N	68°51'E
Uvel'skiy		466	54°26'N	61°22'E
Uverito	VE	440	8°07'N	64°43'W
Uverito	VE	440	8°42'N	62°35'W
Uvinza	TZ	327	5°06'S	30°22'E
Uvira	CG	287	3°24'S	29°08'E
Uvita, Punta	CS	405	9°08'N	83°45'W
Uvongo	SF	322	30°50'S	30°23'E
Uvs Nuur	MG	520	50°20'N	92°45'E
Uwa	JA	506	33°21'N	132°31'E
Uwajima	JA	506	33°13'N	132°34'E
Uwaragala	CE	530	6°16'N	80°31'E
Uwayl	SU	324	8°46'N	27°24'E
Uwayrid, Harrat al		264	27°00'N	37°30'E
Uwekuli	ID	500	1°25'S	121°06'E
Uxin Ju	CH	490	39°04'N	109°01'E
Uxin Qi	CH	490	38°16'N	108°40'E
Uyaly	KZ	510	44°36'N	60°55'E
Uyaly	TI	533	37°58'N	68°42'E
Uyandina		468	69°00'N	140°00'E
Uyar		466	55°48'N	94°20'E
Uychi	UZ	539	41°01'N	71°51'E
Üydzin	MG	520	44°07'N	106°50'E
Uyo	NI	316	5°03'N	7°56'E
Uyönch	MG	520	46°03'N	92°01'E
Uyuni	BL	422	20°28'S	66°50'W
Uyuni, Salar de	BL	422	20°20'S	67°42'W
Uzak	KG	514	40°24'N	72°45'E
Uzbekistan		38	41°00'N	64°00'E
Uzcudún	AR	419	44°13'S	66°09'W
Uzen'	KZ	510	43°27'N	53°10'E
Uzerche		562	45°25'N	1°34'E
Uzès	FR	580	44°01'N	4°25'E
Uzgen	KG	514	40°46'N	73°18'E
Uzhhorod	UP	624	48°37'N	22°18'E
Uzhok, Pereval	UP	624	49°00'N	22°54'E
Uzhur	RS	612	55°18'N	89°50'E
Uzin	UP	624	49°50'N	30°24'E
Uznach	SZ	622	47°13'N	8°59'E
Üzümlü	TU	535	37°32'N	31°37'E
Uzunbulak	CH	490	45°13'N	84°12'E
Uzunköprü	TU	535	41°16'N	26°41'E
Uzunlar	AM	482	41°03'N	44°37'E
Užventis	LH	597	55°47'N	22°39'E
Uzwil	SZ	622	47°26'N	9°08'E
Uzyntokay	TX	537	38°25'N	56°37'E

V

Vaal	SF	322	29°04'S	23°38'E
Vaala	FI	578	64°33'N	26°50'E
Vaals	NL	602	50°46'N	6°00'E
Vaalserberg	NL	602	50°46'N	5°59'E
Vaalwater	SF	322	24°10'S	28°06'E
Vaasa (Vasa)	FI	578	63°06'N	21°36'E
Vabalninkas	LH	597	55°58'N	24°45'E
Vabkent	UZ	539	40°02'N	64°30'E
Vác	HU	590	47°47'N	19°08'E
Vacaria	BR	424	28°30'S	50°56'W
Vacaville		372	38°21'N	121°59'W
Vache		382	17°58'N	73°34'W
Vache, Île à	HA	412	18°04'N	73°38'W
Vachi		466	42°04'N	47°14'E
Vacov	EZ	575	49°08'N	13°44'E
Vad		560	55°32'N	44°12'E
Vadheim	NO	604	61°13'N	5°47'E
Vadodara		470	22°18'N	73°12'E
Vadsø	NO	604	70°05'N	29°46'E
Vadstena	SW	621	58°27'N	14°54'E
Vadul-Luy-Vode	MD	601	47°05'N	29°05'E
Vaduz	LS	597	47°08'N	9°31'E
Værøy	NO	604	67°40'N	12°39'E
Vågåmo	NO	604	61°53'N	9°06'E
Vagar		558	62°05'N	7°15'W
Vaggeryd	SW	621	57°30'N	14°07'E
Vaghena	BP	666	7°40'S	157°50'E
Vagos	PO	608	40°33'N	8°41'W
Váh	LO	616	47°55'N	18°01'E
Vahitahi		654	19°00'S	138°41'W
Vahsel, Cape		388	54°15'S	36°05'W
Vaiau, Pt.		654	17°43'S	145°46'W
Vaich, Mui da	VM	540	11°50'N	108°40'E
Väike-Maarja	EN	577	59°08'N	26°15'E
Vail		372	39°38'N	106°22'W
Vailoa	WS	668	14°00'S	171°24'W
Vaina		654	21°11'S	175°10'W
Vaiņode	LG	596	56°26'N	21°52'E
Vairaatea		654	19°30'S	139°30'W
Vairao		654	17°43'S	145°45'W
Vaitahu		654	9°55'S	140°09'W
Vaitupu	TV	669	7°15'S	178°15'E
Vaiusu	WS	668	13°47'S	171°47'W
Vaivre-et-Montoille	FR	580	47°37'N	6°05'E
Vakfıkebir	TU	535	41°03'N	39°17'E
Vakh	RS	612	60°45'N	76°45'E
Vakhan	AF	480	37°01'N	72°40'E
Vakhanskiy Khr.	TI	533	38°30'N	71°00'E
Vakhrushev		472	48°59'N	142°58'E
Vakhsh	TI	533	37°43'N	68°50'E
Vakhsh	TI	533	37°06'N	68°18'E
Vakhtan		466	57°58'N	46°42'E
Valachchenai	CE	530	7°42'N	81°36'E
Valamaz		466	57°28'N	52°06'E
Valaská Belá	LO	616	48°52'N	18°23'E
Valašské Meziříčí	EZ	575	49°28'N	17°58'E
Val-Bélair		370	46°50'N	71°25'W
Valbo	SW	621	60°40'N	17°00'E
Valcheta	AR	419	40°42'S	66°09'W
Valdagno		562	45°38'N	11°18'E
Val d'Amour		374	47°57'N	66°41'W
Valday		560	57°57'N	33°15'E
Valdayskaya Vozvyshennost		466	57°00'N	33°30'E
Val de Loire	FR	580	47°40'N	1°35'E
Valdemarpils	LG	596	57°22'N	22°35'E
Valdemarsvik	SW	621	58°12'N	16°36'E
Valdense	UY	439	34°20'S	57°14'W
Valdepeñas	SP	618	38°46'N	3°23'W
Valderaduey		562	41°32'N	5°42'W
Valderas	SP	618	42°05'N	5°27'W
Val-de-Reuil	FR	580	49°15'N	1°12'E
Valderrobres	SP	618	40°53'N	0°09'E
Valdés, Península	AR	419	42°30'S	64°00'W
Val-des-Bois		374	45°54'N	75°35'W
Valdez	EC	432	1°13'N	79°00'W
Valdez	US	398	61°07'N	146°20'W
Valdivia	CI	428	39°48'S	73°14'W
Valdivia	CO	430	7°11'N	75°27'W
Val-d'Or		374	48°06'N	77°47'W
Valdosta	US	398	30°49'N	83°16'W
Valdragone	SM	615	43°56'N	12°27'E
Valdres	NO	604	61°00'N	9°00'E
Vale		372	43°58'N	117°15'W
Vale	GG	495	41°37'N	42°52'E
Valea lui Mihai	RO	610	47°31'N	22°08'E
Valemount		368	52°50'N	119°15'W
Valença	BR	424	13°22'S	39°05'W
Valença	PO	608	42°02'N	8°38'W
Valença do Piauí	BR	424	6°24'S	41°45'W
Valence	FR	580	44°56'N	4°54'E
Valencia		376	34°47'N	106°41'W
Valencia	CO	430	8°15'N	76°09'W
Valencia	EC	432	0°56'S	79°21'W
Valencia	HO	412	14°44'N	85°14'W
Valencia	RP	526	9°37'N	124°14'E
Valencia	RP	526	7°57'N	125°03'E
Valencia	TD	438	10°39'N	61°12'W
Valencia	UK	626	51°57'N	10°38'W
Valencia	VE	440	10°11'N	68°00'W
Valencia (València)	SP	618	39°27'N	0°23'W
Valencia, Golfo de	SP	618	39°30'N	0°00'
Valencia de Alcántara	SP	618	39°25'N	7°14'W
Valencia de Don Juan	SP	618	42°18'N	5°31'W
Valencia I.	EI	592	51°54'N	10°22'W
Valenciennes	FR	580	50°21'N	3°31'E
Valendas	SZ	622	46°47'N	9°16'E
Vălenii de Munte	RO	610	45°11'N	26°02'E
Valentigney	FR	580	47°28'N	6°50'E
Valentin	RS	612	43°07'N	134°19'E
Valentine	US	398	42°52'N	100°33'W
Valentines	UY	439	33°16'S	55°06'W
Valenza	IT	593	45°01'N	8°38'E
Våler	NO	604	60°40'N	11°50'E
Valera	VE	440	9°19'N	70°37'W
Valga	EN	577	57°47'N	26°02'E
Valiente, Punta	PM	417	9°10'N	81°54'W
Valinco, Golfe de	FR	580	41°40'N	8°49'E
Valira	AN	567	42°31'N	1°32'E
Valjean		372	50°28'N	106°33'W
Valjevo	YO	630	44°17'N	19°53'E
Valka	LG	596	57°46'N	26°00'E
Valkeakoski	FI	578	61°15'N	23°58'E
Valkeala	FI	578	60°57'N	26°48'E
Valki	UP	624	49°50'N	35°37'E
Valkininkai	LH	597	54°21'N	24°50'E
Val'kumey		468	69°37'N	170°13'E
Valladolid	MX	394	20°41'N	88°12'W
Valladolid	SP	618	41°39'N	4°43'W
Vallata del Darror	SO	321	11°00'N	50°00'E
Valldal	NO	604	62°18'N	7°10'E
Valle	EC	432	2°56'S	78°57'W
Valle	NO	604	59°12'N	7°32'E
Valle Central	CI	428	35°00'S	71°50'W
Valle Central	CS	405	10°00'N	84°15'W
Vallecillo		376	26°40'N	99°58'W
Valle de Allende	MX	394	26°56'N	105°24'W
Valle de Banderas	MX	394	20°50'N	105°13'W
Valle de Jinámar	SP	618	28°02'N	15°25'W
Valle de La Pascua	VE	440	9°13'N	66°00'W
Valle de Santo Domingo	MX	394	25°29'N	111°56'W
Valle de Zaragoza	MX	394	27°28'N	105°49'W
Valledupar	CO	430	10°29'N	73°15'W
Valle Fértil, Sa. del		388	30°25'S	67°51'W
Vallegrande	BL	422	18°29'S	64°06'W
Valle Hermoso	MX	394	19°10'N	88°32'W
Valle Hermoso	MX	394	25°40'N	97°48'W
Vallehermoso	SP	618	28°09'N	17°15'W
Vallejo		372	38°06'N	122°15'W
Vallenar	CI	428	28°35'S	70°46'W
Valleraugue	FR	580	44°05'N	3°38'E
Valle San Telmo	MX	394	30°58'N	116°06'W

Valletta	MT	600	35°54'N	14°31'E
Valley		378	32°48'N	85°10'W
Valley Center		372	37°50'N	97°22'W
Valley Centre		372	51°47'N	107°50'W
Valley City	US	398	46°55'N	98°00'W
Valley East	CA	390	46°41'N	81°02'W
Valley Falls		374	39°19'N	95°27'W
Valley Head	RP	526	17°55'N	122°10'E
Valley River		372	51°15'N	100°08'W
Valley Spring		376	30°51'N	98°49'W
Valley Station	US	398	38°06'N	85°52'W
Valli di Comacchio	IT	593	44°37'N	11°57'E
Vallières	HA	412	19°26'N	71°55'W
Vallo della Lucania	IT	593	40°14'N	15°16'E
Vallorbe	SZ	622	46°43'N	6°23'E
Valls	SP	618	41°17'N	1°15'E
Valluga	AU	568	47°09'N	10°13'E
Val Marie	CA	390	49°14'N	107°44'W
Valmiera	LG	596	57°33'N	25°24'E
Valognes	FR	580	49°31'N	1°28'W
Valpaços	PO	608	41°36'N	7°19'W
Vālpārai	IN	496	10°22'N	76°58'E
Valparaíso	CI	428	33°02'S	71°38'W
Valparaíso	CO	430	1°11'N	75°42'W
Valparaíso	MX	394	22°46'N	103°34'W
Valpovo	HR	574	45°39'N	18°25'E
Valréas	FR	580	44°23'N	4°59'E
Vals	SF	322	27°23'S	26°30'E
Vals, Tanjung	ID	500	8°26'S	137°38'E
Valsād	IN	496	20°38'N	72°56'E
Val-Senneville	CA	390	48°10'N	77°43'W
Valspan	SF	322	27°54'S	24°49'E
Vals Platz	SZ	622	46°37'N	9°11'E
Valtellina	IT	593	46°11'N	9°55'E
Valuyki	RS	612	50°14'N	38°08'E
Valvedditturai	CE	530	9°49'N	80°10'E
Valverde	SP	618	27°47'N	17°56'W
Valverde de Júcar	SP	618	39°43'N	2°12'W
Valverde del Camino	SP	618	37°34'N	6°45'W
Valverde del Fresno	SP	618	40°13'N	6°52'W
Våmhus		558	61°06'N	14°27'E
Vamizi, Ilha	MZ	312	11°02'S	40°40'E
Vammala	FI	578	61°20'N	22°54'E
Vámos	GR	588	35°24'N	24°12'E
Vámosmikola	HU	590	47°58'N	18°47 E
Vámospércs	HU	590	47°32'N	21°54'E
Van	TU	535	38°30'N	43°23'E
Van Alstyne		376	33°25'N	96°34'W
Vanard	ST	418	13°56'N	60°59'W
Vanavana		654	20°30'S	139°00'W
Vanavara	RS	612	60°22'N	102°16'E
Van Buren		378	35°26'N	94°20'W
Van Chan	VM	540	21°36'N	104°30'E
Vanchskiy Khr.	TI	533	38°35'N	71°55'E
Vancouver	CA	390	49°15'N	123°07'W
Vancouver, Cape		652	35°00'S	118°00'E
Vancouver Island	CA	390	49°40'N	125°50'W
Vancouver Island Ranges		372	49°30'N	125°30'W
Vandalia		374	39°18'N	91°29'W
Vandalia		374	38°57'N	89°05'W
Vandans	AU	568	47°05'N	9°52'E
Vandenberg Village		376	34°41'N	120°28'W
Vanderbijlpark	SF	322	26°42'S	27°49'E
Vanderhoof	CA	390	54°01'N	124°01'W
Vanderlin I.		648	15°40'S	136°30'E
Van Diemen, C.	AS	656	11°09'S	130°23'E
Van Diemen Gulf		648	11°15'S	131°00'E
Vändra	EN	577	58°39'N	25°02'E
Vandysh		466	61°20'N	40°15'E
Vandžiogala	LH	597	55°07'N	23°58'E
Vanegas	MX	394	23°51'N	100°52'W
Vänern	SW	621	58°49'N	12°45'E
Vänersborg	SW	621	58°22'N	12°19'E
Van Fong, Vinh	VM	540	12°15'N	108°35'E
Vanga	KE	299	4°39'S	39°13'E
Vangaindrano	MA	304	23°21'S	47°36'E
Van Gölü	TU	535	38°33'N	42°46'E
Vangsvik	NO	604	69°11'N	17°43'E
Vanguard		372	49°55'N	107°18'W
Vangunu I.	BP	666	9°00'S	158°00'E
Vang Vieng	LA	517	18°56'N	102°27'E
Van Harinxmakanaal	NL	602	53°15'N	7°00'E
Van Hoa	VM	540	21°12'N	107°33'E
Van Horn	US	398	31°02'N	104°49'W
Van Horn Mts.		376	30°42'N	104°50'W
Vani	GG	495	42°04'N	42°31'E
Vanikolo Is.	BP	666	11°40'S	166°40'E
Vanimo	PP	664	2°42'S	141°18'E
Vanino		472	49°05'N	140°18'E
Van Lear		374	37°46'N	82°43'W
Vännäs	SW	621	63°55'N	19°45'E
Vannes	FR	580	47°39'N	2°45'W
Van Ninh	VM	540	12°41'N	109°12'E
Vanoise, Massif de la	FR	580	45°20'N	6°40'E
Van Rees, Pegunungan	ID	500	2°35'S	138°15'E
Vanrhynsdorp	SF	322	31°37'S	18°44'E
Vanrook	AS	656	16°57'S	141°57'E
Vansbro	SW	621	60°31'N	14°13'E
Vanscoy		372	52°00'N	106°59'W
Vansittart Bay	AS	656	15°15'S	127°00'E
Vantaa	FI	578	60°15'N	24°59'E
Vantage		372	49°50'N	106°02'W
Vanua Balavu	FJ	660	17°00'S	179°00'W
Vanua Lava	NH	669	13°55'S	167°30'E
Vanua Levu	FJ	660	16°05'S	179°00'E
Vanuatu		38	16°00'S	167°00'E
Van Wert		374	40°52'N	84°35'W
Vanwyksvlei	SF	322	30°21'S	21°49'E
Van Yen	VM	540	21°03'N	104°42'E
Vanzylsrus	SF	322	26°52'S	22°04'E
Vao		654	22°17'S	167°35'E
Vapnyarka	UP	624	48°32'N	28°46'E
Vara	SW	621	58°16'N	12°57'E
Varadero	CU	406	23°09'N	81°16'W
Varakļāni	LG	596	56°37'N	26°44'E
Varalé	IV	288	9°40'N	3°17'W
Varāmīn	IR	502	35°20'N	51°39'E
Vārānāsi	IN	496	25°19'N	83°01'E
Varandey	RS	612	68°49'N	57°59'E
Varangerfjorden	NO	604	70°00'N	30°00'E
Varangerhalvøya	NO	604	70°25'N	29°30'E
Varano, L. di	IT	593	41°53'N	15°45'E
Varaždin	HR	574	46°18'N	16°20'E
Varazze	IT	593	44°21'N	8°34'E
Varberg	SW	621	57°06'N	12°15'E
Vardar	MK	599	40°35'N	22°50'E
Varde	DA	576	55°38'N	8°29'E
Varde	DA	576	55°40 N	8°50'E
Vardenis	AM	482	40°11'N	45°43'E
Vardenisskiy Khr.	AM	482	39°58'N	45°25'E
Várdha	GR	588	38°01'N	21°22'E
Vardhoúsia Ori	GR	588	38°40'N	22°10'E
Vardø	NO	604	70°22'N	31°06'E
Varel	GM	584	53°24'N	8°08'E
Varella, Mui	VM	540	12°53'N	109°28'E
Varen	FR	580	44°09'N	1°53'E
Varėna	LH	597	54°13'N	24°34'E
Varennes-Vauzelles	FR	580	47°03'N	3°08'E
Vareš	BK	572	44°10'N	18°20'E
Varese	IT	593	45°49'N	8°49'E
Vargashi		466	55°21'N	65°51'E
Vargem Grande	BR	424	3°32'S	43°54'W
Varginha	BR	424	21°33'S	45°26'W
Varhaug	NO	604	58°37'N	5°39'E
Vári	GR	588	37°50'N	23°48'E
Varilhes		562	43°02'N	1°37'E
Varillas		386	24°14'S	69°05'W
Varkaus	FI	578	62°19'N	27°55'E
Varkhani	GG	495	41°41'N	42°50'E
Värmdolandet	SW	621	59°20'N	18°33'E
Varmeln	SW	621	59°32'N	12°54'E
Varna		466	53°24'N	60°58'E
Varna	BU	573	43°13'N	27°55'E
Värnamo	SW	621	57°11'N	14°02'E
Varnavino		560	57°24'N	45°04'E
Varnek	RS	612	69°44'N	60°05'E
Varniai	LH	597	55°45'N	22°22'E
Varnsdorf	EZ	575	50°55'N	14°37'E
Varos	MK	599	41°21'N	21°32'E
Varoška Rijeka	BK	572	45°06'N	16°01'E
Várpalota	HU	590	47°12'N	18°08'E
Värska	EN	577	57°58'N	27°38'E
Vartashen	AJ	483	41°06'N	47°28'E
Vartholomión	GR	588	37°52'N	21°13'E
Varto	TU	535	39°10'N	41°28'E
Varva	UP	624	50°30'N	32°44'E
Varzaneh	IR	502	32°25'N	52°39'E
Várzea Alegre	BR	424	6°47'S	39°17'W
Várzea da Palma	BR	424	17°36'S	44°44'W
Várzea Grande		386	15°39'S	56°08'W
Varzobkala	TI	533	38°45'N	68°49'E
Varzuga	RS	612	66°24'N	36°37'E
Vasa (Vaasa)	FI	578	63°06'N	21°36'E
Vásárosnamény	HU	590	48°08'N	22°19'E
Vaşcău	RO	610	46°28'N	22°28'E
Vascos, Montes	SP	618	42°51'N	2°28'W
Vashka	RS	612	64°53'N	45°47'E
Vasile Roaită	RO	610	44°03'N	28°38'E
Vasilevichi	BO	569	52°15'N	29°50'E
Vasilevo	MK	599	41°29'N	22°39'E
Vasilikón	GR	588	38°26'N	23°40'E
Vasil'kov	UP	624	50°11'N	30°19'E
Vasil'kovka	UP	624	48°12'N	36°02'E
Vasil'yevka	UP	624	47°26'N	35°16'E
Vaslui	RO	610	46°38'N	27°44'E
Vassan		374	48°13'N	77°55'W
Vassar		372	49°06'N	95°50'W
Västerås	SW	621	59°37'N	16°33'E
Västerdalälven	SW	621	60°33'N	15°08'E
Västervik	SW	621	57°45'N	16°38'E
Vasto		564	42°07'N	14°42'E
Vastra Silen	SW	621	59°14'N	12°09'E
Vasvár	HU	590	47°03'N	16°48'E
Vasyugan		466	59°07'N	80°46'E
Vasyurinskaya		564	45°07'N	39°25'E
Vaté (Éfaté)	NH	669	17°50'S	168°00'E
Vaterstetten	GM	584	48°07'N	11°47'E
Vathí	GR	588	37°45'N	26°59'E
Vatican City		38	41°54'N	12°27'E
Vaticano, Capo	IT	593	38°37'N	15°50'E
Vatilau	BP	666	8°50'S	160°00'E
Vatnajökull	IC	591	64°34'N	17°25'W
Vatne	NO	604	62°33'N	6°36'E
Vatneyri	IC	591	65°35'N	23°58'W
Vatoa	FJ	660	19°40'S	178°00'W
Vatomandry	MA	304	19°20'S	48°59'E
Vatra Dornei	RO	610	47°21'N	25°22'E
Vättern	SW	621	58°05'N	14°24'E
Vatulele	FJ	660	18°30'S	177°50'E
Vatutino	UP	624	49°01'N	31°03'E
Vaughn	US	398	47°33'N	111°34'W
Vaupés	CO	430	0°02'N	67°16'W
Vauvilliers		654	22°10'S	167°35'E
Vauxhall		372	50°04'N	112°07'W
Vaux-sur-Mer	FR	580	45°39'N	1°02'W
Vavatenina	MA	304	17°28'S	49°12'E
Vava'u Group	TN	667	18°45'S	174°00'W
Vavenby		372	51°35'N	119°44'W
Vavoua	IV	288	7°23'N	6°29'W
Vavuniya	CE	530	8°45'N	80°30'E
Växjö	SW	621	56°53'N	14°49'E
Vaygach, Os.	RS	612	70°00'N	59°30'E
Váyia	GR	588	38°19'N	23°11'E
Vazante		386	18°00'S	46°54'W
Vazashen	AM	482	41°01'N	45°17'E
Važec	LO	616	49°04'N	19°59'E
Vazhgort		556	64°01'N	47°02'E
Vázquez	CU	406	21°08'N	76°44'W
Vecht	NL	602	52°35'N	6°05'E
Vechta	GM	584	52°43'N	8°17'E
Vecpiebalga	LG	596	57°01'N	25°50'E
Vecsés	HU	590	47°24'N	19°17'E
Vecumnieki	LG	596	56°36'N	24°31'E
Vedi	AM	482	39°55'N	44°43'E
Veedersburg		374	40°06'N	87°15'W
Veenendaal	NL	602	52°02'N	5°33'E
Vefsna	NO	604	65°50'N	13°12'E
Vega	NO	604	65°39'N	11°50'E
Vega Baja		382	18°27'N	66°23'W
Vega del Guadiana	SP	618	38°40'N	6°00'W
Vegafjorden	NO	604	65°32'N	11°54'E
Vegårshei	NO	604	58°43'N	8°49'E
Veghel	NL	602	51°37'N	5°33'E
Vegorritis, L.	GR	588	40°45'N	21°48'E
Veguellina de Órbigo	SP	618	42°27'N	5°53'W
Végueta	FE	436	11°02'S	77°39'W
Vehkalahti	FI	578	60°33'N	27°09'E
Veimandu Channel	MV	519	2°00'N	73°00'E
Veinticinco de Diciembre	PA	435	24°47'S	56°42'W
Veinticinco de Mayo		388	34°35'S	68°33'W
Veinticinco de Mayo	AR	419	35°26'S	60°10'W
Veinticinco de Mayo	AR	419	37°48'S	67°41'W
Veintiocho de Mayo	EC	432	3°38'S	78°54'W
Veintiocho de Noviembre	AR	419	51°39'S	72°18'W
Veintisiete de Abril	CS	405	10°15'N	85°45'W
Veisiejai	LH	597	54°06'N	23°42'E
Vejen	DA	576	55°29'N	9°09'E
Vejer de la Frontera	SP	618	36°15'N	5°58'W
Vejle	DA	576	55°42'N	9°32'E
Vela, Cabo de la	CO	430	12°13'N	72°10'W
Vela Luka	HR	574	42°58'N	16°44'E
Velardeña	MX	394	25°05'N	103°43'W
Velas, Cabo	CS	405	10°21'N	85°52'W
Velasco	CU	406	21°55'N	78°19'W
Velasco, Sa. de		388	29°45'S	64°30'W
Velasco Ibarra	EC	432	1°03'S	79°37'W
Velaviuro	BP	666	7°20'S	157°30'E
Velázquez	UY	439	34°02'S	54°17'W
Velddrif	SF	322	32°47'S	18°10'E
Velden	AU	568	46°37'N	14°03'E
Velden	NL	602	51°25'N	6°10'E
Veldhoven	NL	602	51°25'N	5°25'E
Velebit Planina	HR	574	44°32'N	15°14'E
Velebitski Kanal	HR	574	44°47'N	14°51'E
Velence	HU	590	47°14'N	18°39'E
Velenje	SI	617	46°22'N	15°07'E
Velešta	MK	599	41°14'N	20°39'E
Velestínon	GR	588	39°23'N	22°45'E
Veleta	SP	618	37°04'N	3°22'W
Vélez	CO	430	6°01'N	73°41'W
Vélez-Málaga	SP	618	36°47'N	4°06'W
Vélez Rubio	SP	618	37°39'N	2°04'W
Velika Gorica	HR	574	45°44'N	16°04'E
Velika Kapela	HR	574	45°14'N	15°00'E
Velika Kladuša	BK	572	45°11'N	15°49'E
Velika Morava	YO	630	44°43'N	21°03'E
Velika Plana	YO	630	44°20'N	21°05'E
Velikaya		468	64°00'N	175°00'E
Velikaya		560	57°48'N	28°20'E
Velikaya Guba		466	62°15'N	35°05'E
Velikaya Lepetikha	UP	624	47°11'N	33°57'E
Velikaya Novosilka	UP	624	47°50'N	36°50'E
Veliki	YO	630	45°50'N	19°10'E
Veliki Crljeni	YO	630	44°28'N	20°18'E
Veliki Javornik	SI	617	46°05'N	15°25'E
Veliki Trnovac	YO	630	42°29'N	21°45'E
Velikiy Berëznyy	UP	624	48°54'N	22°28'E
Velikiy Burluk	UP	624	50°04'N	37°23'E
Velikiye Borki	UP	624	49°31'N	25°45'E
Velikiye Luki	RS	612	56°20'N	30°32'E
Velikiy Lyuben'	UP	624	49°44'N	23°44'E
Velikiy Ustyug	RS	612	60°48'N	46°18'E
Velikodolinskoye	UP	624	46°20'N	30°35'E
Velikodvorskiy		560	55°15'N	40°41'E
Veliko Tŭrnovo	BU	573	43°04'N	25°39'E
Velikovisochnoye	RS	612	67°16'N	52°01'E
Velikoye		560	57°21'N	39°47'E
Velikoye	RS	612	59°32'N	37°01'E
Velille	PE	436	14°31'S	71°53'W
Vélingara	SG	319	13°10'N	14°06'W
Vélingara	SG	319	15°00'N	14°41'W
Velingrad	BU	573	42°01'N	24°00'E
Velizh	RS	612	55°36'N	31°12'E
Vel'ká Bytča	LO	616	49°13'N	18°34'E
Vel'ka Fatra	LO	616	48°50'N	19°05'E
Vel'ké Kapušany	LO	616	48°33'N	22°05'E
Vel'ké Kostol'any	LO	616	48°31'N	17°44'E
Vel'ke Leváre	LO	616	48°30'N	17°00'E
Velké Meziříčí	EZ	575	49°21'N	16°01'E
Vel'ké Rovné	LO	616	49°18'N	18°35'E
Vel'ké Zálužie	LO	616	48°18'N	17°56'E
Vel'ký ďur	LO	616	48°13'N	18°27'E
Vel'ký Krtíš	LO	616	48°11'N	19°20'E
Vella Lavella (Mbilua)	BP	666	7°35'S	156°15'E
Velletri	IT	593	41°41'N	12°47'E
Velle Vue Maurel	MP	309	20°04'S	57°35'E
Vellore	IN	496	12°56'N	79°08'E
Vélon	GR	588	37°58'N	22°46'E
Vel'sk	RS	612	61°05'N	42°08'E
Veluwemer	NL	602	52°22'N	5°38'E
Velvendós	GR	588	40°15'N	22°04'E
Vemb	DA	576	56°21'N	8°21'E
Vembanad Lake	IN	496	9°35'N	76°25'E
Vemdalen	SW	621	62°26'N	13°51'E
Véménd	HU	590	46°09'N	18°37'E
Venado, I.	CS	405	9°59'N	85°04'W
Venado Tuerto	AR	419	33°45'S	61°58'W
Venafro	IT	593	41°29'N	14°02'E
Venamo, Cerro	VE	440	5°57'N	61°23'W
Venamu		384	2°26'S	59°37'W
Venamu	GY	434	6°00'N	61°55'W
Vena Park	AS	656	18°34'S	141°17'E
Vence	FR	580	43°43'N	7°07'E
Vendas Novas	PO	608	38°41'N	8°27'W
Vendenga	RS	612	63°27'N	47°56'E
Vendeuvre-sur-Barse		562	48°14'N	4°28'E
Vendôme	FR	580	47°48'N	1°04'E
Veneta		372	44°02'N	123°20'W
Veneta, Laguna	IT	593	45°25'N	12°19'E
Venëv		560	54°21'N	38°16'E
Venezia	IT	593	45°26'N	12°19'E
Venezia, Golfo di	IT	593	43°08'N	12°00'E
Venezuela		38	8°00'N	66°00'W
Venezuela, Golfo de	VE	440	11°30'N	71°00'W
Vengan, Mys	RS	612	70°40'N	68°00'E
Vengurla	IN	496	15°52'N	73°38'E
Venice		378	27°05'N	82°26'W
Vénissieux	FR	580	45°41'N	4°53'E
Venjan	SW	621	60°56'N	13°54'E
Venjansjon	SW	621	60°54'N	14°00'E
Venlo	NL	602	51°22'N	6°10'E
Venn		372	51°37'N	105°18'W
Vennesla	NO	604	58°17'N	7°59'E
Venray	NL	602	51°32'N	5°59'E
Vent, Iles du		654	18°30'S	150°00'W
Venta de Baños	SP	618	41°55'N	4°30'W
Ventanas	EC	432	1°27'S	79°28'W
Ventersburg	SF	322	28°05'S	27°08'E
Venterstad	SF	322	30°47 S	25°48'E
Ventimiglia	IT	593	43°47 N	7°36'E
Ventiseri	FR	580	41°56 N	9°20'E
Ventnor	UK	626	50°36'N	1°11'W
Ventoux, Mont	FR	580	44°09'N	5°17'E
Ventspils	LG	596	57°23'N	21°32'E
Ventuari	VE	440	3°58'N	67°02'W
Ventura (San Buenaventura)	US	398	34°16'N	119°17'W
Venturina	IT	593	43°02'N	10°36'E
Vénus, Pt.		654	17°35'S	145°42'W
Venustiano Carranza	MX	394	16°21'N	92°33'W
Venustiano Carranza, Presa		376	27°29'N	100°40'W
Vép	HU	590	47°13'N	16°41'E
Ver		654	14°10'S	167°40'E
Vera	AR	419	29°28'S	60°13'W
Vera	BR	424	12°22'S	55°19'W
Vera	SP	618	37°15'N	1°52'W
Vera, C.	CA	390	76°13'N	89°10'W
Vera Cruz	PM	417	8°53'N	79°38'W
Veracruz	MX	394	19°12'N	96°08'W
Veradale		372	47°39'N	117°11'W
Veragua Abajo	DR	408	19°39'N	70°20'W
Verāval	IN	496	20°55'N	70°23'E
Verbania	IT	593	45°56'N	8°33'E
Verbicaro		564	39°45'N	15°55'E
Vercelli	IT	593	45°19'N	8°24'E
Verda		374	36°50'N	83°13'W
Verdal	NO	604	63°47'N	11°30'E
Verde	BL	422	14°30'S	60°30'W
Verde	MX	394	21°30'N	99°00'W
Verde	MX	394	26°15'N	107°00'W
Verde	PA	435	23°09'S	57°37'W
Verde, Bahía	AR	419	39°15'S	62°10'W
Verde, Cape		38	16°00'N	24°00'W
Verde Island Passage	RP	526	13°34'N	120°51'E
Verden	GM	584	52°55'N	9°14'E
Verdhikoússa	GR	588	39°47'N	21°58'E
Verdon	FR	580	43°43'N	5°46'E
Verdun	FR	580	49°10'N	5°23'E
Vereb'yë		560	53°41'N	32°42'E
Vereeniging	SF	322	26°40'S	27°56'E
Vereshagino	RS	612	64°14'N	83°37'E
Vereshchagino		466	58°05'N	54°40'E
Veretskiy, Pereval	UP	624	48°45'N	23°19'E
Vergara	UY	439	32°56'S	53°57'W
Vergeletto	SZ	622	46°13'N	8°35'E
Verhknyaya Toyma	RS	612	62°14'N	45°03'E
Verín	SP	618	41°56'N	7°26'W
Verin Dzhrapi	AM	482	40°35'N	43°41'E
Verin-Getashen	AM	482	40°08'N	45°15'E
Veriora	EN	577	57°58'N	27°22'E
Verkh. Angara		468	56°06'N	111°30'E
Verkhazovka	RS	612	50°54'N	48°45'E
Verkhnebakanskiy		564	44°51'N	37°39'E
Verkhnedneprovskiy		560	54°59'N	33°20'E
Verkhnedvinsk	BO	569	55°47'N	27°56'E
Verkhnetulomskiy	RS	612	68°37'N	31°46'E
Verkhnevilyuysk	RS	612	63°27'N	120°18'E
Verkhniy At Uryakh		468	62°39'N	150°07'E
Verkhniy Baskunchak		560	48°14'N	46°44'E
Verkhniye Kigi		466	55°25'N	58°37'E
Verkhniy Mamon		560	50°10'N	40°23'E
Verkhniy Rogachik	UP	624	47°15'N	34°21'E
Verkhnyaya Inta	RS	612	66°05'N	60°31'E
Verkhnyaya Zolotitsa	RS	612	65°41'N	40°22'E
Verkhoshizhem'ye		560	58°01'N	49°07'E
Verkhotur'ye		466	58°52'N	60°48'E
Verkhov'ye		560	52°49'N	37°14'E
Verkhoyansk	RS	612	67°35'N	133°27'E
Verkhoyanskiy Khrebet	RS	612	67°00'N	129°00'E
Verkh. Taymyra	RS	612	74°00'N	98°00'E
Verlo	CA	390	50°19'N	108°36'W
Vermilion	CA	390	53°22'N	110°51'W
Vermilion Bay		374	49°51'N	93°24'W
Vermilion Bay		378	29°43'N	91°59'W
Vermillion		372	42°46'N	96°55'W
Vermillion Ra.		374	47°50'N	92°00'W
Vérmion	GR	588	40°30'N	22°00'E
Vermont		374	44°00'N	72°45'W
Vernāg	IN	496	33°33'N	75°15'E
Vernal	US	398	40°27'N	109°31'W
Verneuil-sur-Avre	FR	580	48°44'N	0°56'E
Vernier	SZ	622	46°13'N	6°05'E
Vernon		378	33°45'N	88°06'W
Vernon	CA	390	50°15'N	119°18'W
Vernon	FR	580	49°04'N	1°29'E
Vernon	US	398	34°09'N	99°17'W
Vero Beach		378	27°38'N	80°23'W
Véroia	GR	588	40°31'N	22°12'E
Verona		374	38°12'N	79°00'W
Verona		378	34°11'N	88°43'W
Verona	IT	593	45°26'N	10°59'E
Verpelét	HU	590	47°51'N	20°14'E
Verrès	IT	593	45°40'N	7°42'E
Verrettes	HA	412	19°03'N	72°28'W
Verron Ra.	PP	664	4°15'S	155°40'E
Versailles		374	38°03'N	84°43'W
Versailles	FR	580	48°48'N	2°07'E
Versalles	BL	422	12°44'S	63°18'W
Vershino-Darasunskiy		468	52°20'N	115°32'E
Vershino-Shakhtaminskiy		468	51°18'N	117°54'E
Versoix	SZ	622	46°17'N	6°10'E
Vert, C.	SG	319	14°45'N	17°32'W
Vertes hegys	HU	590	47°25'N	18°20'E
Verteyevka	UP	624	51°10'N	31°52'E
Vertientes	CU	406	21°16'N	78°09'W
Vertou		562	47°10'N	1°28'W
Vertus	FR	580	48°54'N	4°00'E
Verviers	BE	570	50°35'N	5°52'E
Verwoerdburg	SF	322	25°48'S	28°13'E
Vescovato	FR	580	42°29'N	9°26'E
Vesdre	BE	570	50°37'N	5°37'E
Veselí nad Lužnicí	EZ	575	49°11'N	14°42'E
Veselí nad Moravou	EZ	575	48°57'N	17°24'E
Veselovskoye Vodokhranilische		466	47°00'N	41°18'E
Vesëloye	UP	624	47°01'N	34°55'E
Veselynove	UP	624	47°21'N	31°14'E
Veshenskaya		560	49°38'N	41°43'E
Veshkayma		560	54°03'N	47°08'E
Vesijärvi	FI	578	61°06'N	25°28'E
Vesoul	FR	580	47°37'N	6°10'E
Vesta	CS	405	9°43'N	83°03'W
Vestbjerg	DA	576	57°08'N	9°59'E
Vestby	NO	604	59°36'N	10°45'E
Vestbygd	NO	604	58°06'N	6°32'E
Vesterålen	NO	604	68°45'N	14°56'E
Vesterø Havn	DA	576	57°18'N	10°56'E
Vestervig		558	56°46'N	8°20'E
Vestfjord	NO	604	68°08'N	15°00'E
Vestmannaeyjar	IC	591	63°25'N	20°16'W
Vestnes	NO	604	62°38'N	7°02'E
Vesuvio	IT	593	40°49'N	14°26'E
Ves'yegonsk		466	58°40'N	37°16'E
Veszprém	HU	590	47°06'N	17°55'E
Vészto	HU	590	46°55'N	21°16'E
Vet	SF	322	28°30'S	26°10'E
Veteli	FI	578	63°28'N	23°45'E
Veteran	CA	390	52°00'N	111°07'W
Veternik	YO	630	45°16'N	19°45'E
Vetka	BO	569	52°33'N	31°10'E
Vetlanda	SW	621	57°26'N	15°04'E
Vetluga		466	57°51'N	45°47'E
Vetluga		560	57°51'N	45°47'E
Vetluzhskiy		560	57°11'N	45°07'E
Vetluzhskiy		560	58°23'N	45°26'E
Vetovo	BU	573	43°42'N	26°16'E
Vetralla	IT	593	42°19'N	12°03'E
Vetrino	BO	569	55°25'N	28°28'E
Veurne	BE	570	51°04'N	2°39'E
Vevey	SZ	622	46°27'N	6°50'E
Veynes	FR	580	44°32'N	5°49'E
Veys	IR	502	31°29'N	48°52'E
Vezirköprü	TU	535	41°09'N	35°28'E
Viacha	BL	422	16°39'S	68°18'W
Viamão		388	30°05'S	51°02'W
Vian		378	35°29'N	94°58'W
Viana	AO	274	8°54'S	13°22'E
Viana	BR	424	3°13'S	44°55'W
Viana	BR	424	20°23'S	40°30'W
Viana do Alentejo	PO	608	38°20'N	8°00'W
Viana do Bolo	SP	618	42°11'N	7°06'W
Viana do Castelo	PO	608	41°42'N	8°50'W
Vianden	LU	598	49°56'N	6°11'E
Viangchan (Vientiane)	LA	517	17°59'N	102°37'E
Viangphoukha	LA	517	20°41'N	101°04'E
Viar		562	37°36'N	5°50'W
Viareggio	IT	593	43°52'N	10°14'E
Viatskiy Uval		560	57°00'N	49°50'E
Vibble	SW	621	57°36'N	18°15'E
Viborg	DA	576	56°26'N	9°24'E
Vibo Valentia	IT	593	38°41'N	16°06'E
Vic	SP	618	41°56'N	2°15'E
Vicam	MX	394	27°35'N	110°20'W
Vic-en-Bigorre	FR	580	43°23'N	0°03'E
Vicente Guerrero	MX	394	23°44'N	103°58'W
Vicente Guerrero	MX	394	19°36'N	89°39'W
Vicente Guerrero	MX	394	30°45'N	116°00'W
Vicenza	IT	593	45°33'N	11°33'E
Vic-Fezensac	FR	580	43°46'N	0°18'E
Vichacla	BL	422	20°38'S	65°38'W
Vichada	CO	430	4°55'N	67°50'W
Vichadero	UY	439	31°44'S	54°39'W
Viche	EC	432	0°38'N	79°33'W
Vichuga		466	57°13'N	41°56'E
Vichy	FR	580	46°07'N	3°25'E
Vicksburg		378	32°21'N	90°52'W
Vico	FR	580	42°20'N	12°10'E
Viçosa		386	20°45'S	42°53'W
Vic-sur-Cère	FR	580	44°59'N	2°37'E
Victor Harbor		652	35°34'S	138°37'E
Victoria	AR	419	32°37'S	60°10'W
Victoria	AS	656	15°12'S	129°43'E
Victoria	CI	428	38°13'S	72°20'W
Victoria	ES	409	13°57'N	88°38'W
Victoria	GJ	410	12°11'N	61°42'W
Victoria	GV	297	10°50'N	14°33'W
Victoria	HO	412	14°56'N	87°23'W
Victoria	MY	518	5°18'N	115°14'E
Victoria	RO	610	45°44'N	24°41'E
Victoria	RP	526	13°11'N	121°16'E
Victoria	SE	319	4°37'S	55°27'E
Victoria	US	398	38°51'N	99°08'W
Victoria	US	398	28°48'N	97°00'W
Victoria (Rabat)	MT	600	36°02'N	14°14'E
Victoria, Lac		374	48°50'N	77°30'W
Victoria, Lake	KE	299	1°00'S	33°00'E
Victoria Beach	CA	390	50°42'N	96°34'W
Victoria de las Tunas	CU	406	20°58'N	76°57'W
Victoria Falls	ZI	334	17°56'S	25°50'E
Victoria Falls	ZI	334	17°35'S	25°51'E
Victoria Island	CA	390	70°00'N	110°00'W
Victoria Nile	UG	330	2°14'N	31°26'E
Victoria River Downs	AS	656	16°24'S	131°00'E
Victorias	RP	526	10°54'N	123°05'E
Victoria Strait	CA	390	69°30'N	100°00'W
Victoriaville	CA	390	46°03'N	71°57'W
Victoria West	SF	322	31°24'S	23°07'E
Victorica	AR	419	36°13'S	65°27'W
Victorino	VE	440	2°48'N	67°50'W
Victorville		376	34°32'N	117°17'W
Vicuña	CI	428	30°02'S	70°44'W
Vicuña Mackenna	AR	419	33°54'S	64°23'W
Vidalia	US	398	32°13'N	82°24'W
Videira		386	27°00'S	51°08'W
Videle	RO	610	44°17'N	25°31'E
Vidim	RS	612	56°25'N	103°12'E
Vidin	BU	573	43°59'N	22°52'E
Vidisha	IN	496	23°32'N	77°49'E
Vidlitsa		556	61°12'N	32°24'E
Vidor		378	30°07'N	94°00'W
Vidora	CA	390	49°20'N	109°25'W
Vidostern	SW	621	57°04'N	14°01'E
Vidsel	SW	621	65°50'N	20°31'E
Viedma	AR	419	40°48'S	63°00'W
Vieille Case		382	15°36'N	61°25'W
Vieja Isabel, Punta	PM	417	9°02'N	81°46'W
Vieja Palestina	MX	394	29°07'N	100°59'W
Viejo, Cerro	PE	436	4°49'S	79°27'W
Viekšniai	LH	597	56°14'N	22°31'E
Vielha	SP	618	42°42'N	0°48'E
Vielle Case	DO	407	15°37'N	61°24'W
Vienenburg	GM	584	51°57 N	10°34'E
Vienna		374	37°24 N	88°53'W
Vienna		374	39°19'N	81°32'W
Vienna		378	32°05'N	83°47'W
Vienna (Wien)		560	48°12'N	16°22'E
Vienne	FR	580	46°35'N	0°20'E
Vienne	FR	580	47°13'N	0°05'E
Vientiane (Viangchan)	LA	517	17°59'N	102°37'E
Vieques		382	17°59'N	65°24'W
Vieques, Isla de	US	398	18°08'N	65°25'W
Vierwald-stätter See	SZ	622	51°15'N	6°23'E
Vierzon	FR	580	47°13'N	2°05'E
Viesca	MX	394	25°21'N	102°48'W
Viesīte	LG	596	56°21'N	25°33'E
Vietnam		38	16°00'N	106°00'E
Viet Tri	VM	540	21°18'N	105°25'E
Vieux Fort	ST	418	13°44'N	60°58'W
Vievis	LH	597	54°46'N	24°48'E
Viga	RP	526	13°52'N	124°18'E
Vigan	RP	526	17°34'N	120°23'E
Vigevano	IT	593	45°19'N	8°51'E
Vigia	BR	424	0°51'S	48°06'W
Vigía del Fuerte	CO	430	6°35'N	76°54'W
Vignemale	FR	580	42°46'N	0°08'W
Vigo	SP	618	42°14'N	8°43'W
Vigo, Ría de	SP	618	42°15'N	8°45'W
Vigrestad	NO	604	58°34'N	5°42'E
Vihanti	FI	578	64°28'N	24°57'E
Vihāri	PK	524	30°02'N	72°21'E
Vihorlát	LO	616	48°50'N	22°05'E
Vihti	FI	578	60°25'N	24°20'E
Viitasaari	FI	578	63°05'N	25°48'E
Viivikonna	EN	577	59°19'N	27°42'E
Vijayanagar		472	27°22'N	96°50'E
Vijayawada	IN	496	16°31'N	80°37'E
Vijosë (Aóös)	AL	566	40°37'N	19°20'E
Vik	NO	604	61°05'N	6°33'E
Vík	IC	591	63°25'N	18°57'W
Vikajärvi	FI	578	66°37'N	26°08'E
Vikedal	NO	604	59°29'N	5°52'E
Vikeke	ID	500	8°52'S	126°22'E
Vikersund	NO	604	59°59'N	9°57'E
Vikeså	NO	604	58°38'N	6°06'E
Vikhorevka	RS	612	56°05'N	101°15'E
Vikna	NO	604	64°52'N	10°54'E
Vila Bela da Santíssima Trindade	BR	424	15°01'S	59°57'W
Vila Bittencourt	BR	424	1°24'S	69°25'W
Vilacollo	BL	422	20°37'S	68°04'W
Vila Conceição	TP	318	0°03'N	6°34'E
Vila da Maganja	MZ	312	17°18'S	37°31'E
Vila de Sena	MZ	312	17°26'S	35°02'E
Vila do Bispo	PO	608	37°05'N	8°55'W
Vila do Conde	PO	608	41°21'N	8°45'W
Vila Fontes	MZ	312	17°49'S	35°23'E
Vila Franca de Xira	PO	608	38°57'N	9°00'W
Vilaine	FR	580	47°30'N	2°27'W
Viļaka	LG	596	57°11'N	27°41'E
Vilanandro, Tanjona	MA	304	16°11'S	44°27'E
Vilanculos	MZ	312	22°00'S	35°18'E
Viļāni	LG	596	56°33'N	26°57'E
Vilano Beach		378	29°55'N	81°17'W
Vila Nova de Fozcoa	PO	608	41°05'N	7°12'W
Vila Nova de Gaia	PO	608	41°08'N	8°37'W
Vila Nova de Milfontes	PO	608	37°43'N	8°47'W
Vila Nova do Seles	AO	274	11°24'S	14°15'E
Vilanova i la Geltrù	SP	618	41°13'N	1°44'E
Vila Pouca de Aguiar	PO	608	41°30'N	7°39'W
Vila Real	PO	608	41°18'N	7°45'W
Vila Real de Santo António	PO	608	37°12'N	7°27'W
Vilar Formoso	PO	608	40°37'N	6°50'W
Vila Rica	BR	424	10°00'S	51°04'W
Vila-seca de Soldiana	SP	618	41°07'N	1°09'E
Vila Velha	BR	424	3°13'N	51°13'W
Vila Velha Argolas	BR	424	20°20'S	40°17'W
Vila Velha de Ródão	PO	608	39°40'N	7°42'W
Vila Verde	PO	608	41°39'N	8°26'W
Vila Viçosa	PO	608	38°47'N	7°25'W
Vila-Vila	CI	428	19°17'S	69°23'W
Vilcabamba, Cordillera	PE	436	13°00'S	73°00'W
Vilcanota, Cord. de	PE	436	13°46'S	71°18'W
Vil'cha	UP	624	51°22'N	29°27'E
Vileyka	BO	569	54°30'N	26°55'E
Vilhelmina	SW	621	64°37'N	16°39'E
Vilhena	BR	424	12°43'S	60°07'W
Viliya	BO	569	54°54'N	23°53'E
Viljandi	EN	577	58°24'N	25°36'E
Viljoenskroon	SF	322	27°13'S	26°57'E
Vilkaviškis	LH	597	54°39'N	23°02'E
Vilkija	LH	597	55°03'N	23°35'E
Vil'kitskogo, Proliv	RS	612	77°55'N	103°00'E
Villa	SZ	622	46°43'N	9°10'E
Villa Abecia	BL	422	21°00'S	65°23'W
Villa Alemana	CI	428	33°03'S	71°23'W
Villa Alota	BL	422	21°24'S	67°34'W
Villa Altagracia	DR	408	18°40'N	70°10'W
Villa Ángela	AR	419	27°35'S	60°43'W
Villa Angel Flores	MX	394	24°50'N	107°39'W
Villa Aroma	BL	422	17°22'S	67°45'W
Villa Atamisqui	AR	419	28°29'S	63°48'W
Villa Atuel	AR	419	34°50'S	67°54'W
Villaba	RP	526	11°12'N	124°24'E
Villabate	IT	593	38°04'N	13°26'E
Villa Bella	BL	422	10°23'S	65°24'W
Villablino	SP	618	42°56'N	6°19'W
Villa Bruzual	VE	440	9°20'N	69°06'W
Villa Bustos	AR	419	29°17'S	67°02'W
Villa Cañás	AR	419	34°00'S	61°36'W
Villacañas	SP	618	39°38'N	3°20'W
Villa Carlos Paz	AR	419	31°24'S	64°31'W
Villacarrillo	SP	618	38°07'N	3°05'W
Villach	AU	568	46°36'N	13°50'E
Villa Comaltitlán	MX	394	15°11'N	92°34'W
Villa Constitución	AR	419	33°14'S	60°20'W
Villa Corzo	MX	394	16°10'N	93°15'W
Villa de Cos	MX	394	23°17'N	102°21'W
Villa de Costa Rica	MX	394	24°34'N	107°23'W
Villa de Cura	VE	440	10°02'N	67°29'W
Villa del Carmen	UY	439	33°15'S	56°01'W
Villa del Rosario	AR	419	31°35'S	63°32'W

Villa de María	AR	419	29°54'S	63°43'W
Villa de San Antonio	HO	412	14°19'N	87°37'W
Villa Dolores	AR	419	31°58'S	65°11'W
Villadossola	IT	593	46°04'N	8°16'E
Villa El Carmen	NU	415	11°59'N	86°31'W
Villa Federal	AR	419	30°58'S	58°46'W
Villa Flores	MX	394	16°14'N	93°14'W
Villa Florida	PA	435	26°25'S	57°02'W
Villa Franca	PA	435	26°16'S	58°09'W
Villafranca de los Barros	SP	618	38°34'N	6°20'W
Villafranca di Verona		562	45°21'N	10°50'E
Villafranca Tirrena	IT	593	38°14'N	15°26'E
Villagarcia	SP	618	42°36'N	8°45'W
Villagarzón	CO	430	1°02'N	76°37'W
Villa General San Martin	AR	419	31°24'S	68°30'W
Villa Gesell	AR	419	37°13'S	56°57'W
Villa Gonzalez	DR	408	19°32'N	70°47'W
Villagrán		376	24°27'N	99°29'W
Villagrande Strisaili	IT	593	39°58'N	9°30'E
Villaguay	AR	419	31°51'S	59°01'W
Villa Guillermina	AR	419	28°14'S	59°28'W
Villa Hayes	PA	435	25°06'S	57°34'W
Villahermosa	MX	394	17°59'N	92°55'W
Villa Hidalgo	MX	394	26°16'N	104°54'W
Villa Hidalgo	MX	394	30°09'N	109°20'W
Villa Hidalgo	MX	394	21°45'N	105°13'W
Villa Huidobro	AR	419	34°50'S	64°35'W
Villa Industrial	CI	428	17°47'S	69°43'W
Villaines-la-Juhel	FR	580	48°21'N	0°17'W
Villa Ingavi	BL	422	21°49'S	63°34'W
Villa Iris	AR	419	38°10'S	63°15'W
Villa Isabela	DR	408	19°49'N	71°03'W
Villa Jaragua	DR	408	18°29'N	71°30'W
Villajoyosa (la Vila Joiosa)		562	38°31'N	0°14'W
Villa Juárez	MX	394	27°09'N	109°52'W
Villa La Angostura	AR	419	40°47'S	71°40'W
Villa Lázaro Cárdenas	MX	394	20°29'N	97°40'W
Villalba	SP	618	43°18'N	7°41'W
Villalbin	PA	435	27°10'S	57°57'W
Villaldama	MX	394	26°30'N	100°26'W
Villalón de Campos	SP	618	42°06'N	5°02'W
Villalonga	AR	419	39°53'S	62°35'W
Villa López	MX	394	27°00'N	105°02'W
Villa Mainero		376	24°34'N	99°37'W
Villa María	AR	419	32°25'S	63°15'W
Villa Marín	BL	422	20°46'S	67°47'W
Villamartín	SP	618	36°52'N	5°38'W
Villa Minetti	AR	419	28°37'S	61°39'W
Villa Montes	BL	422	21°15'S	63°30'W
Villa Nueva	GT	411	14°31'N	90°35'W
Villa Nueva	NU	415	12°58'N	86°49'W
Villanueva	CO	430	10°37'N	72°59'W
Villanueva	CO	430	5°16'N	71°18'W
Villanueva	HO	412	15°19'N	88°00'W
Villanueva	MX	394	22°21'N	102°53'W
Villanueva de Córdoba	SP	618	38°20'N	4°37'W
Villanueva del Arzobispo		562	38°10'N	3°00'W
Villanueva de la Serena	SP	618	38°58'N	5°48'W
Villanueva de los Castillejos	SP	618	37°30'N	7°16'W
Villanueva de los Infantes	SP	618	38°44'N	3°01'W
Villány	HU	590	45°52'N	18°27'E
Villa Ocampo	AR	419	28°28'S	59°22'W
Villa Ocampo	MX	394	26°27'N	105°31'W
Villa Ojo de Agua	AR	419	29°31'S	63°42'W
Villa Oliva	PA	435	26°01'S	57°53'W
Villa Orestes Pereyra		376	26°30'N	105°41'W
Villapinzón	CO	430	5°13'N	73°36'W
Villaputzu	IT	593	39°26'N	9°34'E
Villar	BL	422	19°37'S	64°21'W
Villarcayo	SP	618	42°56'N	3°34'W
Villardevos	SP	618	41°55'N	7°18'W
Villa Regina		388	39°06'S	67°04'W
Villa Rica	PE	436	10°43'S	75°17'W
Villa Riva	DR	408	19°11'N	69°55'W
Villa Rosario	CO	430	7°50'N	72°28'W
Villarrica	CI	428	39°16'S	72°13'W
Villarrica	PA	435	25°45'S	56°26'W
Villarrica, Lago	CI	428	39°15'S	72°06'W
Villarrica, Volcán	CI	428	39°25'S	71°57'W
Villarrobledo	SP	618	39°16'N	2°36'W
Villarrubia de los Ojos	SP	618	39°13'N	3°36'W
Villars-sur-Glâne	SZ	622	46°47'N	7°07'E
Villas		374	39°01'N	74°56'W
Villa Sandino	NU	415	12°03'N	84°59'W
Villa Santa Rosa	AR	419	31°44'S	68°19'W
Villaseca de Laciana	SP	618	42°56'N	6°15'W
Villa Serrano	BL	422	19°06'S	64°22'W
Villasimius	IT	593	39°08'N	9°31'E
Villa Tapia	DR	408	19°18'N	70°25'W
Villa Tunari	BL	422	16°57'S	65°23'W
Villa Unión		376	28°13'N	100°42'W
Villa Unión		388	29°18'S	68°12'W
Villa Unión	MX	394	18°07'N	92°51'W
Villa Unión	MX	394	23°10'N	106°12'W
Villa Unión	MX	394	23°58'N	104°02'W
Villaurbana	IT	593	39°53'N	8°46'E
Villa Valeria	AR	419	34°20'S	64°55'W
Villa Vázquez	DR	408	19°45'N	71°27'W
Villavicencio	CO	430	4°09'N	73°37'W
Villa Viscarra	BL	422	17°59'S	65°36'W
Villazón	BL	422	22°06'S	65°36'W
Ville Bonheur	HA	412	18°49'N	72°12'W
Villedieu-les-Poêles	FR	580	48°50'N	1°13'W
Ville-di-Pietrabugno	FR	580	42°43'N	9°25'E
Villefagnan	FR	580	46°01'N	0°05'E
Villefranche-de-Rouergue	FR	580	44°21'N	2°03'E
Ville-Marie	CA	390	47°19'N	79°26'W
Villemur-sur-Tarn	FR	580	43°51'N	1°30'E
Villena	SP	618	38°38'N	0°51'W
Villenave-d'Ornon		562	44°46'N	0°33'W
Villeneuve	SZ	622	46°23'N	6°55'E
Villeneuve-sur-Lot	FR	580	44°24'N	0°43'E
Villeneuve-sur-Yonne	FR	580	48°05'N	3°18'E
Ville Platte		378	30°41'N	92°16'W
Villers-Cotterêts	FR	580	49°15'N	3°05'E
Villers-le-Lac	FR	580	47°04'N	6°40'E
Villerupt	FR	580	49°28'N	5°56'E
Villeurbanne	FR	580	45°46'N	4°53'E
Villiers	SF	322	27°02'S	28°36'E
Villingen-Schwenningen	GM	584	48°04'N	8°28'E
Villupuram		470	11°56'N	79°29'E
Vilnius	LH	597	54°41'N	25°19'E
Vilppula	FI	578	62°01'N	24°28'E
Vils	AU	568	47°33'N	10°38'E
Vilsbiburg	GM	584	48°27'N	12°21'E
Vilshofen	GM	584	48°38'N	13°11'E
Vilvoorde	BE	570	50°56'N	4°26'E
Vilyuy	RS	612	64°00'N	125°00'E
Vilyuysk	RS	612	63°45'N	121°35'E
Vilyuyskoye Plato	RS	612	66°45'N	114°00'E
Vilyuyskoye Vodokhranilische	RS	612	62°48'N	111°00'E
Vimianzo	SP	618	42°53'N	8°00'W
Vimioso	PO	608	41°35'N	6°32'W
Vimmerby	SW	621	57°40'N	15°51'E
Vimoutiers	FR	580	48°55'N	0°12'E
Vimperk	EZ	575	49°03'N	13°47'E
Vina	CM	280	6°38'N	13°24'E
Viña del Mar	CI	428	33°02'S	71°34'W
Vinadio	IT	593	44°18'N	7°10'E
Viñales	CU	406	22°37'N	83°43'W
Vinanivao	MA	304	15°53'S	50°16'E
Vinaròs	SP	618	40°29'N	0°30'E
Vincennes		374	38°40'N	87°31'W
Vinces	EC	432	1°33'S	79°44'W
Vinces	EC	432	0°30'S	79°30'W
Vinchina	AR	419	28°46'S	68°10'W
Vinchina	AR	419	29°55'S	68°00'W
Vinchos	PE	436	13°16'S	74°21'W
Vindeby	DA	576	55°02'N	10°37'E
Vindelälven	SW	621	63°54'N	19°52'E
Vindeln	SW	621	64°12'N	19°44'E
Vindhya Range	IN	496	24°37'N	82°00'E
Vine Grove		374	37°48'N	85°58'W
Vineland		374	39°29'N	75°01'W
Vineta	WA	313	22°35'S	14°32'E
Vinh	VM	540	18°39'N	105°39'E
Vinhais	PO	608	41°50'N	7°00'W
Vinh Long	VM	540	10°15'N	105°57'E
Vinh Quoi	VM	540	9°33'N	105°35'E
Vinh Thanh	VM	540	14°03'N	108°47'E
Vinica	MK	599	41°53'N	22°30'E
Vinita		374	36°38'N	95°09'W
Vinjeøra	NO	604	63°12'N	8°56'E
Vînju Mare	RO	610	44°25'N	22°52'E
Vinkovci	HR	574	45°18'N	18°49'E
Vinniki	UP	624	49°49'N	24°08'E
Vinnytsya	UP	624	49°14'N	28°29'E
Vinon-sur-Verdon	FR	580	43°44'N	5°48'E
Vinstra	NO	604	61°36'N	9°45'E
Vinsulla		372	50°55'N	120°14'W
Vintar	RP	526	18°14'N	120°39'E
Vinton		374	42°10'N	92°01'W
Viny		560	58°22'N	32°13'E
Vinzili	RS	612	56°58'N	65°46'E
Violette Brook		374	47°21'N	67°40'W
Vipiteno (Sterzing)	IT	593	46°53'N	11°25'E
Vipya Mts.	MI	306	11°50'S	33°46'E
Vir	HR	574	44°18'N	15°03'E
Virac	RP	526	13°36'N	124°14'E
Virandozero		556	64°02'N	36°00'E
Viranşehir	TU	535	37°13'N	39°45'E
Virār	IN	496	19°28'N	72°48'E
Virbalis	LH	597	54°38'N	22°49'E
Virden		372	49°51'N	100°56'W
Virden		374	39°30'N	89°46'W
Vire	FR	580	49°20'N	1°07'W
Virei	AO	274	15°43'S	12°57'E
Viren	SW	621	58°53'N	15°44'E
Virgen	AU	568	47°00'N	12°27'E
Virgin		376	18°49'N	64°48'W
Virgin Gorda		382	18°32'N	64°20'W
Virginia		374	37°30'N	78°30'W
Virginia	SF	322	28°07'S	26°54'E
Virginia	US	398	47°31'N	92°32'W
Virginia Beach	US	398	36°51'N	75°58'W
Virgin Islands	US	40	18°00'N	65°00'W
Virgin Passage	US	398	25°00'N	86°00'W
Viriat	FR	580	46°15'N	5°13'E
Virochey	CB	489	13°59'N	106°49'E
Viroin	BE	570	50°05'N	4°43'E
Viroqua		374	43°33'N	90°53'W
Viro Viro	BL	422	17°39'S	63°08'W
Virovitica	HR	574	45°50'N	17°24'E
Virrat	FI	578	62°13'N	23°41'E
Virserum		558	57°19'N	15°35'E
Virton	BE	570	49°34'N	5°32'E
Virtsu	EN	577	58°34'N	23°31'E
Virú	PE	436	8°25'S	78°45'W
Virudunagar	IN	496	9°36'N	77°58'E
Viru-Jaagupi	EN	577	59°27'N	26°41'E
Virunga		268	1°00'S	29°50'E
Virunga Mts.	CG	287	1°23'S	29°38'E
Viry-Châtillon	FR	580	48°40'N	2°22'E
Vis	HR	574	43°05'N	15°59'E
Vis	HR	574	43°03'N	16°12'E
Visākhapatnam	IN	496	17°42'N	83°18'E
Visalia	US	398	36°19'N	119°17'W
Visayan Sea	RP	526	11°35'N	123°51'E
Visby	SW	621	57°38'N	18°18'E
Viscount Melville Sound	CA	390	74°00'N	108°00'W
Visé	BE	570	50°44'N	5°42'E
Višegrad	BK	572	43°47'N	19°19'E
Visegrád	HU	590	47°47'N	18°58'E
Viseu		384	1°12'S	46°07'W
Viseu	PO	608	40°39'N	7°55'W
Vişeu de Sus	RO	610	47°43'N	24°26'E
Vishera	RS	612	60°30'N	68°00'E
Vishnevets	UP	624	49°54'N	25°45'E
Vishnevka	KZ	510	50°49'N	72°12'E
Vishnëvka	MD	601	46°20'N	28°27'E
Vishnëvoye	UP	624	50°23'N	30°22'E
Vishoek	SF	322	34°08'S	18°26'E
Vislanda		558	56°47'N	14°27'E
Visnagar	IN	496	23°42'N	72°33'E
Višnjevac	HR	574	45°33'N	18°38'E
Viso, M.	IT	593	44°40'N	7°07'E
Visoko	BK	572	43°59'N	18°11'E
Visp	SZ	622	46°17'N	7°53'E
Vista Hermosa	CO	430	3°01'N	73°44'W
Vistonís, L.	GR	588	41°03'N	25°07'E
Vistula (Wisla)	PL	606	54°21'N	18°57'E
Visviri	CI	428	17°35'S	69°30'W
Vita		372	49°08'N	96°34'W
Viterbo	CO	430	5°03'N	75°53'W
Viterbo	IT	593	42°25'N	12°06'E
Vitez	BK	572	44°10'N	17°48'E
Vitiaz Strait	PP	664	5°50'S	147°00'E
Vitichi	BL	422	20°13'S	65°29'W
Vitigudino	SP	618	41°01'N	6°26'W
Viti Levu	FJ	660	18°00'S	177°30'E
Vitim	RS	612	59°28'N	112°34'E
Vitim	RS	612	59°26'N	112°34'E
Vitimskiy	RS	612	58°14'N	113°18'E
Vitimskoye Ploskogorye	RS	612	54°00'N	113°30'E
Vitis	AU	568	48°45'N	15°10'E
Vitomirica	YO	630	42°42'N	20°21'E
Vitor	PE	436	16°26'S	71°49'W
Vitoria	BR	424	2°54'S	52°01'W
Vitória	BR	424	20°19'S	40°21'W
Vitória da Conquista	BR	424	14°51'S	40°51'W
Vitória de Santo Antão	BR	424	8°07'S	35°18'W
Vitória do Mearim		384	3°28'S	44°53'W
Vitoria-Gasteiz	SP	618	42°51'N	2°40'W
Vitorino Freire	BR	424	4°03'S	45°14'W
Vitorog	BK	572	44°08'N	17°04'E
Vitré	FR	580	48°08'N	1°12'W
Vitrolles	FR	580	43°28'N	5°15'E
Vitry-le-François	FR	580	48°44'N	4°35'E
Vitry-sur-Seine	FR	580	48°47'N	2°23'E
Vitshumbi	CG	287	0°41'S	29°23'E
Vitsyebsk	BO	569	55°12'N	30°11'E
Vittangi	SW	621	67°41'N	21°39'E
Vittel	FR	580	48°12'N	5°57'E
Vittoria	IT	593	36°57'N	14°32'E
Vittorio Veneto	IT	593	45°59'N	12°18'E
Vivarais, Monts du	FR	580	44°55'N	4°15'E
Vivero	SP	618	43°40'N	7°35'W
Vivi		468	65°00'N	97°00'E
Vivian		378	32°52'N	93°59'W
Vizbegovo	MK	599	42°02'N	21°25'E
Vizcachilla	BL	422	21°22'S	66°28'W
Vizcaíno, Desierto de		376	27°40'N	113°40'W
Vizcaíno, Sierra	MX	394	27°20'N	114°30'W
Vize		564	41°34'N	27°45'E
Vizhas	RS	612	66°39'N	45°57'E
Vizhnitsa	UP	624	48°15'N	25°11'E
Vizianagaram	IN	496	18°07'N	83°25'E
Vizinga		466	61°05'N	50°04'E
Viziru	RO	610	45°01'N	27°42'E
Vjose	AL	566	40°37'N	19°20'E
Vlaardingen	NL	602	51°55'N	4°21'E
Vladikavkaz	RS	612	43°00'N	44°40'E
Vladimir	RS	612	56°10'N	40°25'E
Vladimirovac	YO	630	45°03'N	20°52'E
Vladimirovka	KG	514	42°32'N	71°54'E
Vladimirovka	KZ	510	53°28'N	64°02'E
Vladimir-Volynskiy	UP	624	50°51'N	24°20'E
Vladivostok	RS	612	43°08'N	131°54'E
Vlagtwedde	NL	602	53°01'N	7°06'E
Vlăhiţa	RO	610	46°21'N	25°31'E
Vlajna	YO	630	42°47'N	21°57'E
Vlasenica	BK	572	44°11'N	18°57'E
Vlašim	EZ	575	49°42'N	14°54'E
Vlasotince	YO	630	42°58'N	22°08'E
Vlieland	NL	602	53°12'N	4°34'E
Vliestroom	NL	602	53°15'N	5°05'E
Vlijmen	NL	602	51°42'N	5°14'E
Vlissingen	NL	602	51°27'N	3°35'E
Vlorë	AL	566	40°27'N	19°30'E
Vltava	EZ	575	50°20'N	14°29'E
Vöcklamarkt	AU	568	48°00'N	13°29'E
Vodice	HR	574	45°29'N	14°03'E
Vodlozero, Oz.		556	62°20'N	36°55'E
Vodňany	EZ	575	49°09'N	14°11'E
Vodno	MK	599	41°59'N	21°25'E
Vodskov	DA	576	57°06'N	10°02'E
Vogan	TO	328	6°20'N	1°32'E
Vogar	CA	390	50°57'N	98°39'W
Vogel, C.	PP	664	9°41'S	150°03'E
Voghera	IT	593	44°59'N	9°00'E
Vognema		466	59°59'N	38°10'E
Vogošća	BK	572	43°54'N	18°24'E
Voh		654	20°55'S	164°55'E
Vohilava	MA	304	21°46'S	47°55'E
Vohilava	MA	304	21°04'S	48°00'E
Vohimena	MA	304	17°20'S	48°38'E
Vohimena, Tanjon'i		270	25°36'S	45°09'E
Vohipeno	MA	304	22°22'S	47°51'E
Vohiposa	MA	304	20°59'S	47°09'E
Vohitrambo	MA	304	23°16'S	47°32'E
Võhma	EN	577	58°38'N	25°33'E
Voi	KE	299	3°23'S	38°34'E
Voinjama	LI	301	8°25'N	9°45'W
Voiron	FR	580	45°22'N	5°35'E
Voitsberg	AU	568	47°03'N	15°09'E
Vojens	DA	576	55°15'N	9°19'E
Vojka	YO	630	44°56'N	20°10'E
Vojnice	LO	616	47°50'N	18°25'E
Vojvodina	YO	630	45°30'N	20°00'E
Voka	CF	285	4°40'S	14°40'E
Vokea I.	PP	664	3°30'S	144°00'E
Vokhma	RS	612	58°56'N	46°46'E
Vokhtoga		466	58°47'N	41°03'E
Völklingen	GM	584	49°15'N	6°51'E
Voknavolok		556	64°57'N	30°30'E
Volary	EZ	575	48°55'N	13°53'E
Volcán	PM	417	8°46'N	82°38'W
Volcano	US	398	19°25'N	155°14'W
Volchansk	UP	624	50°18'N	36°57'E
Volchikha	RS	612	52°02'N	80°23'E
Volda	NO	604	62°10'N	6°02'E
Volendam		558	52°30'N	5°04'E
Volga		372	44°19'N	96°55'W
Volga		560	57°57'N	38°24'E
Volga	RS	612	45°51'N	47°58'E
Volgodonsk		560	47°32'N	42°09'E
Volgograd	RS	612	48°45'N	44°25'E
Volgogradskoye Vdkhr.		466	50°00'N	45°25'E
Volgorechensk		560	57°30'N	41°02'E
Volinskaya Vozvysn.	UP	624	50°45'N	25°30'E
Völkermarkt	AU	568	46°39'N	14°37'E
Volkhov		466	60°08'N	32°20'E
Volkhov	RS	612	59°55'N	32°20'E
Volkovysk	BO	569	53°10'N	24°28'E
Volksrust	SF	322	27°21'S	29°50'E
Vol'nogorsk	UP	624	48°31'N	34°02'E
Volnovakha	UP	624	47°36'N	37°30'E
Volochanka	RS	612	71°00'N	94°28'E
Volochayevka	RS	612	48°34'N	134°31'E
Volochisk	UP	624	49°32'N	26°10'E
Volodarsk		560	56°13'N	43°10'E
Volodarskiy		466	46°24'N	48°32'E
Volodarskoye	KZ	510	53°18'N	68°08'E
Volodarskoye	UP	624	47°12'N	37°20'E
Vologda	RS	612	59°13'N	39°54'E
Volokonovka		466	50°29'N	37°51'E
Vólos	GR	588	39°21'N	22°57'E
Volosnka		466	61°20'N	40°06'E
Volosovo		560	59°26'N	29°29'E
Volot		560	57°56'N	30°42'E
Volovets	UP	624	48°43'N	23°11'E
Volovo		560	53°33'N	38°02'E
Voloye		560	54°09'N	34°35'E
Volozhin	BO	569	54°05'N	26°32'E
Vol'sk	RS	612	52°02'N	47°23'E
Volta	GH	296	5°46'N	0°41'E
Volta, Lake	GH	296	7°30'N	0°15'E
Volta Basin	GH	296	8°30'N	1°30'W
Volta Blanche	UV	278	10°05'N	2°05'W
Voltaire, C.	AS	656	14°14'S	125°35'E
Volta Noire	IV	288	8°41'N	1°33'W
Volta Noire	UV	278	8°41'N	1°33'W
Volta Redonda	BR	424	22°32'S	44°07'W
Volta Rouge	UV	278	10°34'N	0°30'W
Volturno	IT	593	41°01'N	13°55'E
Vólvi, L.	GR	588	40°41'N	23°28'E
Volzhsk		466	55°53'N	48°20'E
Volzhskiy	RS	612	48°49'N	44°44'E
Vom	NI	316	9°44'N	8°47'E
Vonavono	BP	666	8°10'S	157°00'E
Vondanka		466	59°07'N	47°52'E
Vondrozo	MA	304	22°49'S	47°20'E
Vonguda		556	63°51'N	38°31'E
Vónitsa	GR	588	38°55'N	20°53'E
Vonna		556	59°55'N	9°55'E
Võnnu	EN	577	58°17'N	27°03'E
Voorne	NL	602	51°51'N	4°04'E
Vopnafjördhur	IC	591	65°44'N	14°52'W
Vopnafjördur	IC	591	65°50'N	14°40'W
Voras Oros	MK	599	40°59'N	21°50'E
Vorder Grauspitz	LS	597	47°03'N	9°35'E
Vorderrhein	SZ	622	46°50'N	9°24'E
Vordingborg		558	55°01'N	11°55'E
Vorë	AL	566	41°23'N	19°40'E
Vóriai Sporádhes (Northern Sporades)	GR	588	39°15'N	23°55'E
Vorkuta	RS	612	67°30'N	64°00'E
Vorma		558	60°10'N	11°00'E
Vormsi	EN	577	59°03'N	22°47'E
Vóroi	GR	588	35°04'N	24°49'E
Vorokhta		560	48°17'N	24°34'E
Voronezh	RS	612	51°38'N	39°12'E
Voronezh	RS	612	51°31'N	39°05'E
Voronov, Mys		556	60°15'N	32°05'E
Voronovo	BO	569	54°09'N	25°19'E
Voronovytsya	UP	624	49°06'N	28°41'E
Vorontsovka		560	50°37'N	40°21'E
Voronya		556	69°10'N	35°50'E
Voron'ye		560	58°00'N	42°01'E
Voropayevo	BO	569	55°09'N	27°13'E
Vorotynets		560	56°04'N	45°52'E
Vorozhba	UP	624	51°12'N	34°13'E
Vorsma		560	55°59'N	43°16'E
Vorst	BE	570	51°04'N	5°00'E
Vorstershoop	SF	322	25°50'S	23°03'E
Vörts, Lake	EN	577	58°16'N	26°03'E
Võru	EN	577	57°50'N	27°03'E
Vorzel'	UP	624	50°33'N	30°09'E
Vosburg		270	30°34'S	22°52'E
Vosburg	SF	322	30°35'S	22°53'E
Vosges	FR	580	47°54'N	7°00'E
Vosketap'	AM	482	39°48'N	44°39'E
Voskresenka		560	50°59'N	46°28'E
Voskresenskoye		560	56°51'N	45°26'E
Voskresenskoye		560	59°26'N	37°56'E
Voss	NO	604	60°38'N	6°24'E
Vostochnyy		472	42°45'N	133°04'E
Vostochnyy Sayan	RS	612	53°00'N	97°00'E
Vostok I.	KR	660	10°00'S	152°00'W
Votice	EZ	575	49°39'N	14°39'E
Votkinsk	RS	612	57°03'N	53°59'E
Votofo	CT	282	6°23'N	17°27'E
Vot Tandé		654	13°30'S	167°50'E
Votuporanga	BR	424	20°24'S	49°59'W
Vouga	PO	608	40°41'N	8°40'W
Vougba	CT	282	5°05'N	23°00'E
Voúxa, Ákra	GR	588	35°36'N	23°36'E
Vouziers	FR	580	49°24'N	4°42'E
Voyenno-Antonovka	KG	514	42°52'N	74°24'E
Voynitsa		556	65°08'N	30°16'E
Voy-Vozh	RS	612	62°54'N	54°58'E
Voza	BP	666	6°55'S	156°40'E
Vozdvizhenskoye		560	56°58'N	45°37'E
Vozhe, Oz.	RS	612	60°40'N	39°00'E
Vozhega		466	60°29'N	40°12'E
Vozherovo		466	58°39'N	44°05'E
Vozhgora	RS	612	64°32'N	48°27'E
Voznesensk	UP	624	47°33'N	31°20'E
Voznesenskoye		560	54°54'N	42°46'E
Voznesen'ye		466	61°01'N	35°30'E
Vozvyshennost Karabil	TX	537	36°30'N	63°00'E
Vpadina Assake-Audan	UZ	539	42°05'N	56°30'E
Vráble	LO	616	48°15'N	18°19'E
Vradiyivka	UP	624	47°52'N	30°36'E
Vrang	TI	533	37°00'N	72°22'E
Vrangelya, O.	RS	612	71°00'N	179°30'E
Vranica	BK	572	43°57'N	17°44'E
Vranje	YO	630	42°33'N	21°54'E
Vranjska Banja	YO	630	42°33'N	22°00'E
Vranov nad Teplou	LO	616	48°54'N	21°41'E
Vrapčište	MK	599	41°50'N	20°53'E
Vratsa	BU	573	43°13'N	23°33'E
Vrav		558	59°40'N	8°00'E
Vrbas	BK	572	45°07'N	17°31'E
Vrbas	YO	630	45°34'N	19°39'E
Vrbové	LO	616	48°38'N	17°44'E
Vrchlabí	EZ	575	50°38'N	15°36'E
Vrede	SF	322	27°25'S	29°10'E
Vredefort	SF	322	27°01'S	27°23'E
Vredenburg-Saldanha	SF	322	32°54'S	17°59'E
Vredendal	SF	322	31°40'S	18°30'E
Vrhnika	SI	617	45°58'N	14°18'E
Vrigstad	SW	621	57°21'N	14°26'E
Vrnjačka Banja	YO	630	43°37'N	20°54'E
Vrondádhos	GR	588	38°24'N	26°08'E
Vršac	YO	630	45°07'N	21°18'E
Vrútky	LO	616	49°07'N	18°55'E
Vrutok	MK	599	41°46'N	20°50'E
Vryburg	SF	322	26°57'S	24°44'E
Vryheid	SF	322	27°46'S	30°48'E
Vsetín	EZ	575	49°20'N	18°00'E
Vstrechnyy		468	68°08'N	166°30'E
Vtácnik	LO	616	48°40'N	18°40'E
Vuadil'	UZ	539	40°11'N	71°43'E
Vuca	ET	293	7°33'N	35°50'E
Vučitrn	YO	630	42°49'N	20°58'E
Vught	NL	602	51°39'N	5°18'E
Vukovar	HR	574	45°21'N	19°00'E
Vuktyl	RS	612	63°45'N	57°19'E
Vulavu	BP	666	8°15'S	159°50'E
Vulcan	RO	610	45°23'N	23°16'E
Vulcăneşti	MD	601	45°41'N	28°24'E
Vulcano, I.	IT	593	38°24'N	14°58'E
Vŭlchedrŭm	BU	573	43°42'N	23°27'E
Vŭlchi Dol	BU	573	43°24'N	27°33'E
Vu Liet	VM	540	18°42'N	105°22'E
Vung Da Nang	VM	540	16°08'N	108°11'E
Vung Tau	VM	540	10°20'N	107°03'E
Vunmarama		654	15°30'S	168°10'E
Vuoggatjålme	SW	621	66°33'N	16°22'E
Vuohijärvi	FI	578	61°00'N	27°50'E
Vuoksa	FI	578	60°40'N	29°50'E
Vuollerim	SW	621	66°25'N	20°36'E
Vuotso	FI	578	68°07'N	27°06'E
Vuranimala	BP	666	9°00'S	160°30'E
Vŭrbitsa	BU	573	43°00'N	26°38'E
Vuria	KE	299	3°25'S	38°18'E
Vurnary		560	55°29'N	46°58'E
Vŭrshets	BU	573	43°12'N	23°17'E
Vwawa	TZ	327	9°07'S	32°55'E
Vyāra	IN	496	21°07'N	73°24'E
Vyatka	RS	612	58°35'N	49°39'E
Vyatka	RS	612	55°00'N	50°10'E
Vyatskiye Polyany		466	56°14'N	51°04'E
Vyatskoye		560	57°52'N	40°16'E
Vyazemskiy	RS	612	47°32'N	134°45'E
Vyaz'ma		560	55°13'N	34°18'E
Vyazniki		560	56°15'N	42°10'E
Vyazovaya		466	54°55'N	58°22'E
Vyazovka		466	52°50'N	48°23'E
Vyazovka	RS	612	48°19'N	45°36'E
Vyborg	RS	612	60°42'N	28°45'E
Vychegda	RS	612	61°18'N	46°36'E
Vygonichi		560	53°08'N	34°05'E
Vygozero, Ozero		556	63°30'N	35°00'E
Vyksa		466	55°18'N	42°11'E
Vylkove	UP	624	45°24'N	29°35'E
Vym'	RS	612	62°13'N	50°25'E
Vynohradiv	UP	624	48°09'N	23°02'E
Vypolzovo		466	57°53'N	33°42'E
Vyritsa		560	59°25'N	30°21'E
Vyselki		564	45°35'N	39°39'E
Vyshgorod	UP	624	50°35'N	30°30'E
Vyshgorodok	RS	612	57°02'N	28°01'E
Vyshniy Volochek	RS	612	57°35'N	34°34'E
Vyškov	EZ	575	49°17'N	17°00'E
Vyškovce nad Ipl'om	LO	616	48°03'N	18°51'E
Vysokaya Gora		560	55°54'N	49°19'E
Vysoké Mýto	EZ	575	49°57'N	16°10'E
Vysoké Tatry	LO	616	49°08'N	20°13'E
Vysokogornyy	RS	612	50°07'N	139°09'E
Vysokopol'ye	UP	624	47°29'N	33°32'E
Vysokovsk		560	56°19'N	36°33'E
Vysokoye		560	56°43'N	34°55'E
Vysokoye	BO	569	52°22'N	23°22'E
Vysotsk		556	60°38'N	28°34'E
Vyšší Brod	EZ	575	48°37'N	14°19'E
Vytegra	RS	612	61°00'N	36°27'E
Vzmor'ye		472	47°51'N	142°31'E

W

Wa	GH	296	10°03'N	2°29'W
Waajid	SO	321	3°48'N	43°15'E
Waal	NL	602	48°00'N	10°47'E
Waalre	NL	602	51°23'N	5°27'E
Waalwijk	NL	602	51°41'N	5°04'E
Wabag	PP	664	5°29'S	143°42'E
Wabasca		368	55°58'N	113°50'W
Wabash		374	40°47'N	85°49'W
Wabash	US	398	37°48'N	88°02'W
Wabasha		374	44°23'N	92°01'W
Wabe Gestro	ET	293	4°17'N	42°02'E
Wabigoon	CA	390	49°43'N	92°35'W
Wabi Shebele		268	0°12'S	42°45'E
Wabowden	CA	390	54°55'N	98°38'W
Wąbrzeźno	PL	606	53°17'N	18°57'E
Wabu	KS	513	37°36'N	127°13'E
Wabuda I.	PP	664	8°10'S	144°50'E
Waccasassa B.		378	29°08'N	82°50'W
Wach'īlē	ET	293	4°33'N	39°04'E
Waco	US	398	31°33'N	97°08'W
Wad	PK	524	27°21'N	66°22'E
Wad al Ḥaddād	SU	324	13°49'N	33°32'E
Wad an Nail	SU	324	12°31'N	34°09'E
Wad Bandah	SU	324	13°06'N	27°57'E
Waddān	LY	302	29°10'N	16°08'E
Waddan, Jabal	LY	302	29°30'N	16°45'E
Waddenzee	NL	602	53°00'N	4°59'E
Wadduwa	CE	530	6°40'N	79°56'E
Wadena		372	51°57'N	103°48'W
Wadena	US	398	46°26'N	95°08'W
Wädenswil	SZ	622	47°14'N	8°40'E
Wadern	GM	584	49°32'N	6°53'E
Wad Ḥāmid	SU	324	16°34'N	32°47'E
Wādī an Naṭrūn	EG	290	30°25'N	30°13'E
Wādī As Sīr	JO	510	31°57'N	35°49'E
Wādī Az Zarqā'	TS	329	36°41'N	9°25'E
Wādī Ḥalfā'	SU	324	21°54'N	31°24'E
Wādī Mūsá	JO	510	30°19'N	35°29'E
Wad Jabjabah	SU	324	22°37'N	33°17'E
Wadley		378	32°51'N	82°24'W
Wad Medanī	SU	324	14°24'N	33°32'E
Waegwan	KS	513	35°59'N	128°23'E
Wafangdian	CH	490	39°37'N	122°00'E
Wafania	CG	287	1°21'S	20°20'E
Wagagai	UG	330	1°07'N	34°31'E
Wagenfeld-Hasslingen	GM	584	52°33'N	8°35'E
Wageningen	NL	602	51°58'N	5°40'E
Wageningen	NS	438	5°45'N	56°40'W
Wagga Wagga	AS	656	35°07'S	147°22'E
Wagin		652	33°18'S	117°21'E
Waginger See	GM	584	47°56'N	12°47'E
Wagna	AU	568	46°45'N	15°33'E
Wagner	US	398	43°04'N	98°17'W
Wagoner		374	35°57'N	95°22'W
Wągrowiec	PL	606	52°48'N	17°12'E
Wāh	PK	524	33°48'N	72°42'E
Wahai	ID	500	2°48'S	129°30'E
Wahiawa	US	398	21°30'N	158°01'W
Wahoo		372	41°12'N	96°37'W
Wahpeton	US	398	46°15'N	96°36'W
Wahrenholz	GM	584	52°37'N	10°36'E
Waiau	NZ	663	42°39'S	173°03'E
Waiau	NZ	663	45°50'S	159°50'E
Waibakul	ID	500	9°36'S	119°35'E
Waidhofen an der Thaya	AU	568	48°49'N	15°17'E
Waidhofen an der Ybbs	AU	568	47°58'N	14°46'E
Waigala	UG	330	0°20'N	33°24'E
Waigama	ID	500	1°52'S	129°49'E
Waigeo	ID	500	0°14'S	130°45'E
Waika	CG	287	2°21'S	25°43'E
Waikabubak	ID	500	9°38'S	119°25'E
Waikanae	NZ	663	40°52'S	175°04'E
Waikari	NZ	663	42°58'S	172°41'E
Waikawa	NZ	663	46°38'S	169°08'E
Waikerie		652	34°11'S	139°59'E
Waikoloa Village	US	398	19°54'N	155°48'W
Waikouaiti	NZ	663	45°36'S	170°41'E
Wailua	US	398	22°03'N	159°20'W
Wailuku	US	398	20°53'N	156°30'W
Wailuo	CH	490	20°33'N	110°27'E
Waima	SL	320	7°56'N	11°27'W
Waimangaroa	NZ	663	41°41'S	171°48'E
Waimate	NZ	663	44°45'S	171°03'E
Waimea (Kamuela)	US	398	20°01'N	155°40'W
Wainfleet All Saints	UK	626	53°06'N	0°15'E
Wainganga	IN	496	19°36'N	79°48'E
Waingapu	ID	500	9°41'S	120°16'E
Waini	GY	434	8°24'N	59°51'W
Waipahu	US	398	21°23'N	158°00'W
Waipapa Pt.	NZ	663	46°40'S	168°52'E
Waipara	NZ	663	43°03'S	172°45'E
Waipawa	NZ	663	39°56'S	176°35'E
Waipio	US	398	20°06'N	155°35'W
Waipiro	NZ	663	38°01'S	178°20'E
Waipukurau	NZ	663	40°00'S	176°33'E
Wairoa	NZ	663	39°02'S	177°26'E
Waitaki	NZ	663	44°57'S	171°09'E
Waitara	NZ	663	39°00'S	174°14'E
Waitato	NZ	663	37°15'S	175°10'E
Waitemata	NZ	663	36°50'S	174°37'E
Waite Park		374	45°33'N	94°13'W
Waitotara	NZ	663	39°47'S	174°43'E
Waiuku	NZ	663	37°15'S	174°44'E
Wajabula	ID	500	2°17'N	128°14'E
Wajima	JA	506	37°24'N	136°54'E
Wajir	KE	299	1°45'N	40°04'E
Waka	CG	287	0°48'S	20°10'E
Waka	CG	287	1°01'N	20°13'E
Waka	ET	293	7°04'N	37°10'E
Waka, Tanjung	ID	500	2°29'S	126°03'E
Wakasa-wan	JA	506	35°45'N	135°40'E
Wakatipu, Lake	NZ	663	45°05'S	168°34'E
Wakayama	JA	506	34°13'N	135°11'E
Wakeeney		372	39°01'N	99°52'W
Wakefield		372	42°16'N	96°51'W
Wakefield	JM	414	18°25'N	77°43'W
Wakefield	UK	626	53°42'N	1°29'W
Wakefield	US	398	46°28'N	89°55'W
Wake Forest		378	35°58'N	78°30'W
Wake Island	US	40	19°00'N	169°00'E
Wakema	BM	487	16°36'N	95°11'E
Wake Village		378	33°25'N	94°06'W
Wakhan	AF	480	37°00'N	73°00'E
Wakkanai	JA	506	45°25'N	141°40'E
Wakkerstroom	SF	322	27°21'S	30°08'E
Wakopa		372	49°05'N	99°50'W
Waku Kungo	AO	274	11°21'S	15°07'E
Wakunai	PP	664	5°52'S	155°13'E
Wakuya	JA	506	38°32'N	141°08'E
Wala	TZ	327	5°46'S	32°04'E
Walade	BP	666	9°38'S	161°30'E
Walagan		468	52°35'N	124°34'E
Walamba	ZA	332	13°29'S	28°45'E
Wal Athiang	SU	324	7°42'N	29°40'E
Walawe Ganga	CE	530	6°06'N	81°01'E
Wałbrzych	PL	606	50°46'N	16°17'E
Walchensee	GM	584	47°35'N	11°21'E
Walcheren	NL	602	51°30'N	3°29'E
Walcourt	BE	570	50°14'N	4°25'E
Wałcz	PL	606	53°16'N	16°28'E
Waldbillig	LU	598	49°48'N	6°17'E
Walden		374	46°20'N	81°23'W
Waldersee		372	50°34'N	99°03'W
Waldkirch	GM	584	48°06'N	7°58'E
Waldo		372	49°12'N	115°13'W
Waldport		372	44°25'N	124°04'W
Waldron		372	50°51'N	102°31'W
Waldron		378	34°53'N	94°05'W
Waldshut-Tiengen		562	47°37'N	8°15'E
Walea, Selat	ID	500	0°30'S	122°30'E
Waleabahi	ID	500	0°15'S	122°20'E
Walensee	SZ	622	47°07'N	9°12'E
Walenstadt	SZ	622	47°07'N	9°18'E
Walewale	GH	296	10°21'N	0°48'W
Walferdange	LU	598	49°39'N	6°08'E
Walgett		652	30°01'S	148°07'E

Walhachin	CA	390	50°45'N	120°59'W
Walhalla	US	398	48°54'N	97°55'W
Walikale	CG	287	1°25'S	28°03'E
Walker		372	38°49'N	118°45'W
Walker Lake		372	38°44'N	118°43'W
Walkers Ferry	MI	306	15°31'S	34°52'E
Walkerston		652	21°10'S	149°04'E
Wallace		372	47°28'N	115°55'W
Wallace Lake	CA	390	51°02'N	95°20'W
Wallal Downs	AS	656	19°47'S	120°40'E
Wallaroo		652	33°56'S	137°38'E
Walla Walla	US	398	46°03'N	118°20'W
Wallenhorst	GM	584	52°21'N	8°01'E
Wallibu		382	13°18'N	61°13'W
Wallis		378	29°37'N	96°03'W
Wallis, Îles		650	13°50'S	176°00'W
Wallis and Futuna Islands		40	11°00'S	179°00'E
Wallowa Mts.		372	45°12'N	117°19'W
Walls	UK	626	60°13'N	1°33'W
Wallumbilla	AS	656	26°36'S	149°11'E
Walnut Ridge		374	36°04'N	90°57'W
Walpole		652	34°57'S	116°44'E
Walsall	UK	626	52°36'N	2°00'W
Walsenburg		376	37°36'N	104°46'W
Walsh		372	49°57'N	110°03'W
Walsh		648	16°39'S	143°54'E
Walsrode	GM	584	52°52'N	9°35'E
Walterboro		378	32°54'N	80°40'W
Walter F. George Res.		378	31°49'N	85°08'W
Walters		376	34°21'N	98°18'W
Waltershausen	GM	584	50°54'N	10°34'E
Walthourville		378	31°45'N	81°38'W
Walungchung Gola	NP	522	27°41'N	87°48'E
Walvisbaai	SF	313	22°57'S	14°30'E
Walvis Bay	SF	322	22°57'S	14°30'E
Wama	AO	274	12°14'S	15°33'E
Wamaza	CG	287	4°13'S	27°07'E
Wamba	CG	287	2°07'N	27°49'E
Wamba	KE	299	0°59'N	37°19'E
Wamba	NI	316	8°56'N	8°37'E
Wamego		374	39°12'N	96°18'W
Wamena	ID	500	4°05'S	138°51'E
Wami	TZ	327	6°08'S	38°49'E
Wamlana	ID	500	3°07'S	126°31'E
Wampum		372	49°03'N	95°50'W
Wampusirpi	HO	412	15°11'N	84°37'W
Wāna	PK	524	32°17'N	69°35'E
Wanaaring	AS	656	29°42'S	144°09'E
Wanaka	NZ	663	44°42'S	169°10'E
Wanaka Lake	NZ	663	44°30'S	169°08'E
Wanapitei Lake		374	46°45'N	80°45'W
Wanchese		374	35°50'N	75°38'W
Wanda	AR	419	25°58'S	54°35'W
Wandalongo	CT	282	6°25'N	19°53'E
Wanda Shan	CH	490	46°00'N	132°00'E
Wandering River	CA	390	55°12'N	112°26'W
Wandi	UG	330	3°06'N	30°59'E
Wanding	CH	490	24°04'N	98°03'E
Wando	KS	513	34°18'N	126°45'E
Wandoan	AS	656	26°08'S	149°57'E
Wanfried	GM	584	51°11'N	10°10'E
Wanganella		652	35°13'S	144°49'E
Wanganui	NZ	663	39°54'S	175°01'E
Wangaratta	AS	656	36°22'S	146°20'E
Wangasi Turu	GH	296	8°53'N	0°28'W
Wangdü Phodrang	BT	486	27°29'N	89°54'E
Wangen	GM	584	47°41'N	9°50'E
Wangerooge	GM	584	53°47'N	7°55'E
Wanggamet, Gunung	ID	500	10°07'S	120°14'E
Wang Gaxun	CH	490	36°42'N	98°47'E
Wang Hip, Kao	TH	534	8°18'N	99°43'E
Wangiwangi	ID	500	5°20'S	123°35'E
Wangjiang		472	30°07'N	116°41'E
Wangmo	CH	490	25°11'N	106°03'E
Wangolodougou	IV	288	9°58'N	5°09'W
Wangou		474	42°04'N	126°57'E
Wangqing		474	43°18'N	129°47'E
Wang Saphung	TH	534	17°18'N	101°46'E
Wang Thong	TH	534	16°50'N	100°26'E
Wang'uru	KE	299	0°41'S	37°22'E
Wangziguan		472	33°30'N	105°13'E
Wān Hsa-la	BM	487	20°26'N	98°40'E
Wān Hwè-ün	BM	487	19°10'N	97°44'E
Wani, Gunung	ID	500	4°29'S	123°01'E
Wanie-Rukula	CG	287	0°14'N	25°34'E
Wanilla		652	34°30'S	135°41'E
Wanless	CA	390	54°10'N	101°22'W
Wanle Weyne	SO	321	2°37'N	44°54'E
Wanon Niwat	TH	534	17°38'N	103°46'E
Wānow	AF	480	32°38'N	65°54'E
Wansra	ID	500	1°07'S	134°57'E
Wanuma	PP	664	4°50'S	145°19'E
Wanwei	CH	490	21°31'N	108°09'E
Wanxian	CH	490	30°48'N	108°21'E
Wanyuan		472	32°04'N	108°02'E
Wanzai		472	28°06'N	114°27'E
Wapakoneta		374	40°34'N	84°11'W
Wapato		372	46°26'N	120°25'W
Wapenamanda	PP	664	5°39'S	143°51'E
Wapinda	CG	287	3°41'N	22°48'E
Waqên	CH	490	33°02'N	102°36'E
Waqqāş	JO	510	32°33'N	35°36'E
War		374	37°18'N	81°41'W
Warangal	IN	496	18°08'N	79°35'E
Warbah	KU	514	30°00'N	48°15'E
Warburg	GM	584	51°29'N	9°09'E
Warburton	AS	656	26°08'S	126°33'E
Warburton	AS	656	27°55'S	137°28'E
Warburton Bay		368	63°50'N	111°30'W
Warburton Range	AS	656	26°00'S	126°00'E
Ward	NZ	663	41°50'S	174°08'E
Warden		372	46°58'N	119°02'W
Warden	SF	322	27°51'S	28°58'E
Wardha	IN	496	20°45'N	78°37'E
Ward Hunt, C.	PP	664	8°02'S	148°08'E
Ward Hunt Strait	PP	664	9°30'S	150°00'E
Wardija Ridge	MT	600	35°56'N	14°22'E
Wardlow		372	50°54'N	111°33'W
Wardner		372	49°24'N	115°26'W
Wardo		648	1°02'S	135°50'E
Ware	CA	390	57°25'N	125°38'W
Wareegto	SO	321	1°27'N	42°25'E
Waregem	BE	570	50°53'N	3°25'E
Wareham	UK	626	50°41'N	2°06'W
Waremme	BE	570	50°41'N	5°15'E
Waren	GM	584	53°31'N	12°41'E
Waren	ID	500	2°18'S	136°22'E
Warffum	NL	602	53°24'N	6°34'E
War Galoh	SO	321	6°17'N	47°31'E
Warin Chamrap	TH	534	15°12'N	104°53'E
Warka	PL	606	51°47'N	21°12'E
Warkworth		654	36°15'S	175°00'E
Warkworth	NZ	663	36°24'S	174°43'E
Warley		558	52°29'N	2°00'W
Warli		472	28°07'N	101°33'E
Warman	CA	390	52°19'N	106°34'W
Warmbad	SF	322	24°53'S	28°17'E
Warmbad	WA	313	28°27'S	18°44'E
Warminster	UK	626	51°12'N	2°11'W
Warm Springs	US	398	44°45'N	121°15'W
Warnemünde	GM	584	54°10'N	12°05'E
Warner		378	35°29'N	95°18'W
Warner	CA	390	49°17'N	112°12'W
Warner Mts.		372	41°38'N	121°18'W
Warner Robins	US	398	32°36'N	83°35'W
Warnes	BL	422	17°30'S	63°10'W
Warnow	GM	584	54°06'N	12°09'E
Warooka		652	35°00'S	137°24'E
Waropko		648	5°35'S	140°47'E
Warrabri	AS	656	21°00'S	134°24'E
Warracknabeal		652	36°15'S	142°25'E
Warrakunta Pt.	AS	656	14°38'S	135°32'E
Warrego	AS	656	30°24'S	145°21'E
Warrego Range	AS	656	25°00'S	146°30'E
Warren		370	41°50'N	79°09'W
Warren		372	48°11'N	96°46'W
Warren		374	42°29'N	89°59'W
Warren		374	46°27'N	80°18'W
Warren		378	33°36'N	92°03'W
Warren		652	31°42'S	147°49'E
Warren	US	398	42°32'N	83°02'W
Warren	US	398	41°14'N	80°49'W
Warren Landing		370	53°42'N	97°54'W
Warrenpoint	UK	626	54°09'N	6°16'W
Warrensburg		374	38°45'N	93°44'W
Warrenton		270	28°06'S	24°51'E
Warrenton		372	46°09'N	123°55'W
Warrenton		374	38°42'N	77°47'W
Warrenton		378	33°24'N	82°39'W
Warrenton	SF	322	28°07'S	24°51'E
Warri	NI	316	5°32'N	5°44'E
Warrina	AS	656	28°12'S	135°50'E
Warringah		652	33°46'S	151°16'E
Warrington	UK	626	53°23'N	2°36'W
Warrnambool	AS	656	38°23'S	142°29'E
Warroad	US	398	48°54'N	95°18'W
Warsa	ID	500	0°47'S	135°55'E
Warsaw		370	41°14'N	85°51'W
Warsaw		374	38°14'N	93°22'W
Warsaw		378	34°59'N	78°05'W
Warsaw (Warszawa)	PL	606	52°13'N	20°59'E
Warshiikh	SO	321	2°17'N	45°47'E
Warstein		558	51°27'N	8°22'E
Warszawa		466	52°13'N	20°59'E
Warszawa (Warsaw)	PL	606	52°13'N	20°59'E
Warta	PL	606	52°36'N	14°37'E
Waru	ID	500	3°25'S	130°39'E
Warwick		374	41°41'N	71°22'W
Warwick	AS	656	28°14'S	152°01'E
Warwick	UK	626	52°17'N	1°35'W
Warzhong		472	28°10'N	100°52'E
Wasagaming		372	50°39'N	99°58'W
Wasagu	NI	316	11°22'N	5°48'E
Wasatch Range	US	398	40°45'N	111°45'W
Wasbank	SF	322	28°19'S	30°06'E
Wasco		376	35°35'N	119°20'W
Waseca		374	44°04'N	93°30'W
Washāp	PK	524	27°08'N	63°26'E
Washburn		370	46°40'N	90°53'W
Washburn	US	398	47°17'N	101°01'W
Washdyke	NZ	663	44°21'S	171°15'E
Washington		372	45°28'N	87°13'W
Washington		372	39°49'N	97°03'W
Washington		374	38°39'N	87°10'W
Washington		374	40°42'N	89°24'W
Washington		374	41°17'N	91°41'W
Washington		376	37°07'N	113°30'W
Washington		378	33°44'N	82°44'W
Washington		378	35°32'N	77°03'W
Washington	US	398	38°53'N	77°00'W
Washington	US	398	45°28'N	87°13'W
Washington (Washington Court House)		374	39°32'N	83°26'W
Washington I.	KR	660	4°55'N	160°10'W
Washita		378	35°00'N	98°00'W
Wasilków	PL	606	53°12'N	23°13'E
Wasilla	US	398	61°34'N	149°26'W
Wasimni	NI	316	7°45'N	3°25'E
Wasior	ID	500	2°43'S	134°30'E
Wasiri	ID	500	7°35'S	126°36'E
Waskada		372	49°06'N	100°48'W
Waskaganish (Rupert House)	CA	390	51°30'N	78°45'W
Waskesiu Lake	CA	390	53°54'N	106°01'W
Wasletan	ID	500	7°55'S	131°08'E
Waspam	NU	415	14°44'N	83°58'W
Wassen	SZ	622	46°42'N	8°35'E
Wassenaar	NL	602	52°09'N	4°24'E
Wasser	WA	313	26°05'S	18°08'E
Wasserbillig	LU	598	49°43'N	6°31'E
Wassou	GV	297	10°02'N	13°39'W
Wassy	FR	580	48°30'N	4°57'E
Wasu	PP	664	5°58'S	147°12'E
Waswanipi, L.		374	49°33'N	76°26'W
Watampone	ID	500	4°32'S	120°20'E
Watansopeng	ID	500	4°21'S	119°53'E
Wat Bot	TH	534	17°00'N	100°19'E
Waterberg	WA	313	20°31'S	17°14'E
Waterberge	SF	322	24°31'S	27°29'E
Waterbury	US	398	41°32'N	73°02'W
Water Cay	BF	402	26°42'N	78°22'W
Waterford	EI	592	52°14'N	7°06'W
Waterhen L.	CA	390	52°06'N	99°34'W
Waterloo	AS	656	16°38'S	129°18'E
Waterloo	BE	570	50°43'N	4°23'E
Waterloo	NS	438	5°56'N	56°59'W
Waterloo	SL	320	8°17'N	12°15'W
Waterloo	TD	438	10°28'N	61°28'W
Waterloo	US	398	42°29'N	92°20'W
Waterproof		378	31°48'N	91°23'W
Waterton Park		372	49°03'N	113°55'W
Watertown	US	398	44°53'N	97°06'W
Watertown	US	398	43°58'N	75°54'W
Waterval-Boven	SF	322	25°39'S	30°20'E
Waterville		374	46°16'N	67°35'W
Waterville		374	44°33'N	69°37'W
Waterville	EI	592	51°50'N	10°10'W
Watford	UK	626	51°40'N	0°24'W
Watford City		372	47°48'N	103°16'W
Wa'th	SU	324	8°10'N	32°07'E
Watheroo		652	30°17'S	116°04'E
Watkins Glen		374	42°22'N	76°52'W
Watmuri	ID	500	7°25'S	131°40'E
Watonga		376	35°50'N	98°24'W
Watowato, Bukit	ID	500	1°01'N	128°07'E
Watsa	CG	287	3°03'N	29°32'E
Watseka		374	40°46'N	87°44'W
Watson Lake	CA	390	60°04'N	128°42'W
Watsonville		376	36°54'N	121°45'W
Wattsview		372	50°22'N	101°13'W
Wattwil	SZ	622	47°18'N	9°05'E
Watubela, Kep.	ID	500	4°35'S	131°40'E
Watugedara	CE	530	6°15'N	80°03'E
Wau	PP	664	7°20'S	146°43'E
Wauchope		652	31°27'S	152°44'E
Waukesha		370	43°00'N	88°13'W
Waukomis		376	36°16'N	97°53'W
Waukon		370	43°16'N	91°28'W
Waurika		376	34°10'N	97°59'W
Wausau		370	44°57'N	89°37'W
Wautoma		374	44°04'N	89°17'W
Wave Hill		648	17°29'S	130°57'E
Waveney	UK	626	52°35'N	1°39'E
Waverley		652	33°54'S	151°16'E
Waverley	AS	656	38°10'S	147°11'E
Waverley	NZ	663	39°46'S	174°38'E
Waverley Downs	AS	656	29°03'S	143°54'E
Waverly		370	42°43'N	92°28'W
Waverly		374	36°05'N	87°47'W
Waverly		374	37°02'N	77°05'W
Waverly		374	39°07'N	82°59'W
Wavre	BE	570	50°43'N	4°37'E
Wāw	SU	324	7°42'N	27°59'E
Waw	BM	487	17°28'N	96°41'E
Wawa	CA	390	47°59'N	84°47'W
Wawa	NI	316	9°55'N	4°23'E
Wawa	NU	415	13°53'N	83°28'W
Wāw al Kabīr	LY	302	25°20'N	16°43'E
Wawanesa		372	49°36'N	99°41'W
Wawo	ID	500	3°41'S	121°04'E
Wawoi	PP	664	7°00'S	143°00'E
Wawota		372	49°54'N	102°02'W
Wawotobi	ID	500	3°51'S	122°06'E
Waxahachie		376	32°24'N	96°51'W
Waxxari	CH	490	38°36'N	87°21'E
Way, Ko	CB	489	10°00'N	103°00'E
Wayakuba	ID	500	0°50'S	127°50'E
Wayamli	ID	500	1°00'N	128°31'E
Waycross	US	398	31°12'N	82°21'W
Waygay		478	2°23'S	125°59'E
Wayhaya		478	1°48'S	124°22'E
Wayne		372	42°13'N	97°01'W
Waynesboro		374	39°45'N	77°34'W
Waynesboro		378	31°40'N	88°38'W
Waynesburg		374	39°53'N	80°10'W
Waynesville		374	37°49'N	92°12'W
Waynesville		378	35°29'N	82°59'W
Waza	CM	280	11°25'N	14°34'E
Wazay	AF	480	33°22'N	69°26'E
Wazīrābād	PK	524	32°27'N	74°07'E
W. Caicos		382	21°35'N	72°25'W
Wea	DJ	289	11°30'N	42°51'E
Weagamow Lake	CA	390	52°57'N	91°20'W
Weam	PP	664	8°36'S	141°08'E
Weatherford		376	32°45'N	97°47'W
Weatherford		376	35°31'N	98°42'W
Weaverville	US	398	40°43'N	122°56'W
Webb City		374	37°08'N	94°27'W
Webbwood		374	46°16'N	81°53'W
Webequie	CA	390	52°59'N	87°21'W
Webi Jubba	SO	321	0°50'N	42°50'E
Webster	US	398	45°19'N	97°31'W
Webster City		374	42°28'N	93°48'W
Webuye	KE	299	0°37'N	34°36'E
Weda		648	0°21'N	127°52'E
Wedau	PP	664	10°05'S	150°02'E
Weddell		388	51°57'S	61°48'W
Wedel	GM	584	53°35'N	9°43'E
Weduar, Tanjung	ID	500	6°00'S	132°50'E
Wedweil	SU	324	9°00'N	27°12'E
Wedza	ZI	334	18°37'S	31°34'E
Weed	US	398	41°25'N	122°23'W
Weenen	SF	322	28°51'S	30°05'E
Weeping Water		374	40°52'N	96°08'W
Weert	NL	602	51°15'N	5°43'E
Weesp	NL	602	52°19'N	5°02'E
Weethalle	AS	656	33°53'S	146°38'E
Wee Waa		652	30°14'S	149°26'E
Węgorzewo	PL	606	54°13'N	21°44'E
Węgrów	PL	606	52°24'N	22°01'E
Wehnī	ET	293	12°40'N	36°39'E
Weichang	CH	490	41°55'N	117°42'E
Weida	GM	584	50°46'N	12°04'E
Weiden	GM	584	49°41'N	12°10'E
Weifang	CH	490	36°42'N	119°05'E
Weihai	CH	490	37°30'N	122°05'E
Wei He	CH	490	37°00'N	114°30'E
Weihuling		474	43°35'N	127°48'E
Weilburg	GM	584	50°29'N	8°16'E
Weilheim	GM	584	47°50'N	11°09'E
Weïma Plateau	DJ	289	12°20'N	42°50'E
Weimar		378	29°42'N	96°46'W
Weimar	GM	584	50°59'N	11°19'E
Weinan	CH	490	34°30'N	109°30'E
Weinfelden	SZ	622	47°34'N	9°06'E
Weingarten	GM	584	47°48'N	9°38'E
Weinheim	GM	584	49°33'N	8°40'E
Weining		472	26°51'N	104°14'E
Weipa		648	12°38'S	141°55'E
Weir River	CA	390	56°50'N	94°05'W
Weirton		374	40°24'N	80°35'W
Weiser	US	398	44°15'N	116°58'W
Weishan	CH	490	25°15'N	100°20'E
Weishan Hu	CH	490	34°36'N	117°15'E
Weissenbach	AU	568	47°26'N	10°38'E
Weissenburg im Bayern	GM	584	49°02'N	10°59'E
Weissenfels	GM	584	51°12'N	11°58'E
Weissmies	SZ	622	46°07'N	8°00'E
Weisswasser	GM	584	51°31'N	14°38'E
Weitra	AU	568	48°42'N	14°53'E
Weixi	CH	490	27°12'N	99°15'E
Weixin	CH	490	27°48'N	105°04'E
Weiya	CH	490	41°49'N	94°24'E
Weiyuanpu		474	42°42'N	124°18'E
Weiz	AU	568	47°14'N	15°35'E
Weizhou Dao	CH	490	21°03'N	109°02'E
Weizhouxu	CH	490	21°00'N	109°02'E
Weiziyu		474	41°40'N	124°30'E
Wejherowo	PL	606	54°36'N	18°14'E
Wekame	BM	487	15°46'N	97°48'E
Welātām	BM	487	26°37'N	98°22'E
Welbekend	SF	322	24°40'S	28°58'E
Weldiya	ET	293	11°50'N	39°41'E
Welford	AS	656	25°07'S	143°43'E
Weligama	CE	530	5°58'N	80°25'E
Welk'īt'ē	ET	293	8°17'N	37°47'E
Welkom	SF	322	28°00'S	26°44'E
Welland	UK	626	52°52'N	0°03'W
Wellawaya	CE	530	6°44'N	81°06'E
Wellesley	AS	656	16°46'S	139°24'E
Wellesley Islands		648	15°30'S	139°00'E
Wellfleet		374	41°56'N	70°02'W
Wellington		372	39°32'N	110°44'W
Wellington		372	40°42'N	105°00'W
Wellington		376	34°51'N	100°12'W
Wellington		376	37°15'N	97°22'W
Wellington		652	32°33'S	148°57'E
Wellington	NZ	663	41°17'S	174°47'E
Wellington	SF	322	33°38'S	19°00'E
Wellington	UK	626	50°59'N	3°14'W
Wellington, Isla	CI	428	49°20'S	74°40'W
Wells		374	43°44'N	93°43'W
Wells	CA	390	53°04'N	121°41'W
Wells	US	398	41°06'N	114°57'W
Wells, Lake	AS	656	26°43'S	123°10'E
Wellsboro		374	41°44'N	77°18'W
Wellsford		654	36°10'S	174°10'E
Wellsford	NZ	663	36°17'S	174°33'E
Wells-next-the-Sea	UK	626	52°57'N	0°51'E
Wellston		374	39°06'N	82°32'W
Wellsville		374	39°04'N	91°34'W
Wellsville		374	42°07'N	77°56'W
Wellton		376	32°40'N	114°08'W
Wels	AU	568	48°10'N	14°02'E
Welshpool		374	44°53'N	66°57'W
Welshpool	UK	626	52°39'N	3°07'W
Welwel	ET	293	7°03'N	45°24'E
Wembere	TZ	327	4°19'S	34°17'E
Wembesi	SF	322	29°01'S	29°47'E
Wemindji	CA	390	53°00'N	78°49'W
Wenago	ET	293	6°19'N	38°16'E
Wenatchee	US	398	47°25'N	120°18'W
Wenchang	CH	490	19°36'N	110°42'E
Wencheng	CH	490	27°48'N	120°04'E
Wenchi	GH	296	7°44'N	2°06'W
Wendell		372	42°46'N	114°42'W
Wendeng	CH	490	37°12'N	122°01'E
Wendji	CG	287	0°04'S	18°10'E
Wendou Borou	GV	297	11°26'N	13°53'W
Wendover	US	398	40°44'N	114°02'W
Wengshui	CH	490	28°27'N	99°52'E
Wengyuan	CH	490	24°21'N	114°06'E
Wenquan	CH	490	44°58'N	81°03'E
Wenquan	CH	490	33°12'N	91°49'E
Wenshan	CH	490	23°21'N	104°13'E
Wenshui	CH	490	37°24'N	112°00'E
Wen Xian		472	32°52'N	104°40'E
Wenzhou	CH	490	27°58'N	120°39'E
Wepener	SF	322	29°44'S	27°02'E
Werda	BC	276	25°13'S	23°14'E
Werdēr	ET	293	6°58'N	45°20'E
Were Īlu	ET	293	10°36'N	39°26'E
Werinama	ID	500	3°33'S	130°10'E
Werkendam	NL	602	51°49'N	4°54'E
Wernecke Mountains		368	64°40'N	130°00'W
Werner Lake		372	50°28'N	94°55'W
Wernigerode	GM	584	51°50'N	10°47'E
Werota	ET	293	11°54'N	37°42'E
Werra	GM	584	51°26'N	9°39'E
Werrimull		652	34°25'S	141°37'E
Wertheim	GM	584	49°45'N	9°31'E
Wervershoof	NL	602	52°44'N	5°10'E
Wervik	BE	570	50°47'N	3°02'E
Wesel	GM	584	51°39'N	6°36'E
Weser	GM	584	53°32'N	8°34'E
Weslaco		376	26°09'N	97°59'W
Weslemkoon		374	44°59'N	77°25'W
Wesley	DO	407	15°34'N	61°19'W
Wesleyville		370	49°09'N	53°34'W
Wessel	AS	656	11°30'S	136°18'E
Wessel, C.	AS	656	11°01'S	136°46'E
Wesselburen	GM	584	54°13'N	8°55'E
Wessington Springs	US	398	44°04'N	98°34'W
Wesson		378	31°42'N	90°23'W
West		376	31°48'N	97°05'W
Westall, Pt.	AS	656	32°55'S	134°03'E
West Allis		374	43°00'N	88°00'W
West Bend		372	51°29'N	103°41'W
West Bend		374	43°25'N	88°11'W
Westbourne		372	50°08'N	98°35'W
West Branch Susquehanna		374	40°53'N	76°48'W
West Bromwich	UK	626	52°31'N	2°00'W
Westbury	UK	626	51°15'N	2°11'W
West Crossett		378	33°08'N	91°59'W
West Dawson	CA	390	64°06'N	139°39'W
West Des Moines		374	41°34'N	93°42'W
West End		372	50°33'N	102°24'W
West End		382	18°23'N	64°41'W
West End	BF	402	26°40'N	78°58'W
West End	BF	402	26°41'N	78°58'W
Westerland	GM	584	54°54'N	8°18'E
Westerlo	BE	570	51°05'N	4°55'E
Western Channel (Nishi-suido)	KS	513	34°30'N	128°00'E
Western Desert		264	30°12'N	30°10'E
Western Dvina (Daugava)	LG	596	57°00'N	24°00'E
Western Ghats	IN	496	14°00'N	75°00'E
Western Head	CA	390	43°59'N	64°40'W
Western I.	PP	664	2°05'S	146°05'E
Western Samoa		38	13°35'S	172°20'W
Western Sierra Madre	US	398	33°00'N	112°00'W
Westerschelde	NL	602	51°20'N	3°50'E
Westerville		374	40°06'N	82°55'W
Westerwald	GM	584	50°38'N	7°45'E
West Falkland (Gran Malvina)		388	51°45'S	59°00'W
West Fargo		372	46°52'N	96°54'W
Westfield		374	40°02'N	86°07'W
West Fork		374	35°55'N	94°11'W
West Frankfort		374	37°53'N	88°55'W
West Friesische Inseln	NL	602	53°40'N	5°30'E
Westgate	CA	390	52°50'N	101°39'W
West Hawk Lake		372	49°46'N	95°11'W
West Helena		378	34°33'N	90°38'W
Westhill	UK	626	57°09'N	2°15'W
West I.		648	15°15'S	136°15'E
West Liberty		374	37°55'N	83°15'W
West Lorne		374	42°36'N	81°36'W
West Melbourne		378	28°04'N	80°39'W
West Memphis		378	35°08'N	90°11'W
West Mifflin		374	40°23'N	79°52'W
Westminster		372	39°50'N	105°02'W
Westmoreland	AS	656	17°20'S	138°14'E
West Nicholson	ZI	334	21°04'S	29°22'E
Weston		370	44°48'N	92°04'W
Weston		374	39°02'N	80°27'W
Weston	MY	518	5°13'N	115°36'E
Weston-super-Mare	UK	626	51°20'N	2°58'W
West Palm Beach	US	398	26°42'N	80°03'W
West Plains	US	398	36°43'N	91°51'W
West Plains (Plains)		376	37°15'N	100°35'W
West Point		372	41°50'N	96°42'W
West Point		378	33°36'N	88°39'W
West Poplar		372	49°00'N	106°22'W
Westport		372	46°53'N	124°06'W
Westport		374	44°41'N	76°24'W
Westport		654	41°30'S	171°30'E
Westport	EI	592	53°48'N	9°31'W
Westport	NZ	663	41°45'S	171°38'E
West Pt.	AS	656	40°56'S	144°37'E
Westpunt		382	12°22'N	69°09'W
Westray	UK	626	59°14'N	3°45'W
Westside		378	34°17'N	83°46'W
West-Terschelling	NL	602	53°22'N	5°13'E
West Union		374	38°47'N	83°32'W
West Union		374	42°57'N	91°48'W
West Valley City	US	398	40°41'N	111°57'W
West Vancouver		372	49°20'N	123°11'W
Westville		374	40°02'N	87°38'W
West Virginia		374	38°30'N	80°30'W
Westward Ho		372	51°47'N	114°31'W
Westwold		372	50°28'N	119°45'W
Westwood		372	40°18'N	121°00'W
Westwood	ZA	332	15°23'S	28°00'E
West Wyalong		652	33°55'S	147°13'E
Wetar, I.	ID	500	7°48'S	126°18'E
Wetar, Selat	ID	500	8°20'S	126°30'E
Wetaskiwin	CA	390	52°58'N	113°22'W
Wete	CG	287	4°35'S	24°31'E
Wete	TZ	327	5°01'S	39°43'E
Wetheral		558	54°52'N	2°49'W
Wetlet	BM	487	22°22'N	95°47'E
Wetteren	BE	570	51°00'N	3°53'E
Wettingen	SZ	622	47°28'N	8°19'E
Wetzlar	GM	584	50°33'N	8°29'E
Wevelgem	BE	570	50°48'N	3°10'E
Wewak	PP	664	3°34'S	143°38'E
Wexford	EI	592	52°20'N	6°28'W
Wexford Harbour	EI	592	52°20'N	6°24'W
Weyburn	CA	390	49°40'N	103°51'W
Weymouth	UK	626	50°36'N	2°27'W
Weymouth, C.	AS	656	12°36'S	143°24'E
Whakatane	NZ	663	37°56'S	176°58'E
Whale Cay	BF	402	26°40'N	78°25'W
Whale Cove	CA	390	62°10'N	92°36'W
Whaletown		372	50°07'N	125°03'W
Whalsay	UK	626	60°20'N	0°59'W
Whangamata	NZ	663	37°12'S	175°53'E
Whangarei	NZ	663	35°43'S	174°20'E
Wharfe	UK	626	53°51'N	1°08'W
Wharton		378	29°18'N	96°06'W
Wharton L.		368	64°00'N	99°55'W
Whataroa	NZ	663	43°16'S	170°23'E
Whatatutu	NZ	663	38°23'S	177°51'E
Wheatland	US	398	42°03'N	104°57'W
Wheaton		370	45°48'N	96°29'W
Wheaton-Glenmont		374	39°02'N	77°03'W
Wheeler		376	35°26'N	100°16'W
Wheeler Peak	US	398	35°00'N	105°00'W
Wheelersburg		374	38°43'N	82°51'W
Wheeling		374	40°03'N	80°43'W
Whidbey	US	398	47°59'N	122°38'W
Whidbey, Pt.	AS	656	34°36'S	135°08'E
Whistler	CA	390	50°07'N	122°58'W
Whitby	UK	626	54°28'N	0°36'W
White		378	35°00'N	91°25'W
White	JM	414	66°32'S	49°00'E
White Bay	CA	390	50°00'N	56°30'W
White Bear	CA	390	50°53'N	108°13'W
Whitebeech	CA	390	52°03'N	101°42'W
White City		372	50°26'N	104°22'W
White Cliffs	AS	656	30°51'S	143°05'E
White Cloud		374	43°32'N	85°46'W
Whitecourt	CA	390	54°09'N	115°41'W
White Deer		376	35°26'N	101°10'W
Whitefish	US	398	48°24'N	114°20'W
Whitefish B.		370	46°40'N	84°45'W
Whitefish Station		368	69°23'N	133°37'W
Whitefish Station	CA	390	68°52'N	136°52'W
White Hall		374	39°26'N	90°24'W
White Hall		378	34°16'N	92°05'W
Whitehall		372	45°51'N	112°06'W
Whitehall		374	44°22'N	91°18'W
Whitehall		374	43°32'N	73°24'W
Whitehall		374	39°56'N	82°53'W
Whitehall	UK	626	59°08'N	2°36'W
Whitehaven	UK	626	54°32'N	3°35'W
White Head		370	44°38'N	66°43'W
Whitehorse	CA	390	60°43'N	135°03'W
White Horse Hills	UK	626	51°15'N	1°50'W
White Lake		374	45°18'N	76°31'W
White Lake		378	29°45'N	92°30'W
Whiteman Range	PP	664	5°50'S	150°00'E
Whitemark	AS	656	40°07'S	148°01'E
Whitemouth		372	49°57'N	95°58'W
Whitemouth		372	49°30'N	95°55'W
Whitemouth Lake		374	49°14'N	95°40'W
White Mts.		374	44°10'N	71°35'W
White Mts.		376	37°30'N	118°15'W
White Mts.	US	398	65°00'N	145°00'W
Whiten Head	UK	626	58°34'N	4°33'W
White Nile	SU	324	15°38'N	32°31'E
White Otter L.		374	49°05'N	91°52'W
White River	CA	390	48°36'N	85°17'W
Whiteriver		376	33°50'N	109°57'W
White Rock		652	16°59'S	145°45'E
White Sands		376	32°22'N	106°28'W
Whitesands		654	19°30'S	169°35'E
Whitesboro		376	33°39'N	96°54'W
White Sea	RS	612	65°30'N	38°00'E
Whitestone Village	CA	390	66°25'N	138°25'W
White Sulphur Springs		374	37°47'N	80°17'W
Whiteville		378	34°20'N	78°42'W
White Volta	GH	296	10°05'N	2°05'W
Whitewater		374	42°50'N	88°43'W
Whitewater	CA	390	49°12'N	100°17'W
Whitewood	CA	390	50°20'N	102°16'W
Whithorn	UK	626	54°44'N	4°25'W
Whitianga	NZ	663	36°50'S	175°42'E
Whitley City		374	36°43'N	84°28'W
Whitney		378	31°57'N	97°19'W
Whitney	CA	390	45°30'N	78°14'W
Whitney Point		374	42°19'N	75°58'W
Wholdaia L.	CA	390	60°45'N	104°10'W
Whyalla	AS	656	33°02'S	137°35'E
Whyjonta	AS	656	29°41'S	142°28'E
Wiawer	UG	330	2°42'N	33°39'E
Wiawso	GH	296	6°12'N	2°29'W
Wichabai	GY	434	2°54'N	59°32'W
Wich'alē	ET	293	11°30'N	39°36'E
Wichian Buri	TH	534	15°39'N	101°07'E
Wichita		378	33°55'N	98°20'W
Wichita	US	398	37°41'N	97°20'W
Wichita Falls	US	398	33°54'N	98°30'W
Wichita Mts.		376	34°45'N	98°40'W
Wick	UK	626	58°26'N	3°05'W
Wickenburg		376	33°58'N	112°43'W
Wickepin		652	32°46'S	117°30'E
Wickham		652	20°42'S	117°08'E
Wicklow	EI	592	52°59'N	6°03'W
Wicklow Head	EI	592	52°57'N	6°00'W
Wicklow Mts.	EI	592	53°05'N	6°20'W
Widewater	CA	390	55°22'N	115°02'W
Widgiemooltha	AS	656	31°30'S	121°34'E
Widnau	SZ	622	47°24'N	9°37'E
Wiek		558	54°36'N	13°17'E
Wielkopolska	PL	606	52°30'N	17°00'E
Wielkopolsko-Kujawskie, Pojezierze	PL	606	52°50'N	17°00'E
Wieluń	PL	606	51°10'N	18°33'E
Wien (Vienna)		560	48°12'N	16°22'E
Wien Basin	AU	568	48°10'N	16°40'E
Wiener Neustadt	AU	568	47°48'N	16°13'E
Wierden	NL	602	52°22'N	6°36'E
Wieringerwerf	NL	602	52°51'N	5°02'E
Wies	AU	568	46°43'N	15°15'E
Wiesbaden	GM	584	50°04'N	8°14'E
Wiesen	AU	568	47°44'N	16°20'E
Wiesmoor	GM	584	53°25'N	7°44'E
Wigan	UK	626	53°32'N	2°37'W
Wiggins		378	30°51'N	89°08'W
Wight, Isle of	UK	626	52°38'N	1°17'W
Wigry, J.	PL	606	54°00'N	23°50'E
Wijchen	NL	602	51°49'N	5°44'E
Wijhe	NL	602	52°23'N	6°08'E
Wijk en Aalburg	NL	602	51°45'N	5°07'E
Wik'ro	ET	293	13°47'N	39°36'E
Wikwemikong		370	45°48'N	81°43'W
Wil	SZ	622	47°28'N	9°03'E
Wilber		372	40°28'N	96°57'W
Wilberforce		374	45°02'N	78°13'W
Wilburton		378	34°55'N	95°18'W
Wilcannia	AS	656	31°34'S	143°23'E
Wilcox		372	50°07'N	104°41'W
Wild Cove	CA	390	50°41'N	56°10'W
Wildendr̈nbach	AU	568	48°45'N	16°28'E
Wildeshausen	GM	584	52°54'N	8°26'E
Wild Goose	CA	390	48°30'N	89°07'W
Wildhaus	SZ	622	47°12'N	9°21'E
Wildspitze	AU	568	46°53'N	10°52'E
Wildwood		374	38°59'N	74°49'W
Wilge	SF	322	27°03'S	28°20'E
Wilhelm, Mount	PP	664	5°45'S	145°05'E
Wilhelmina Gebergte	NS	438	3°45'N	56°30'W
Wilhelminakanaal	NL	602	51°47'N	4°51'E
Wilhelmshaven	GM	584	53°31'N	8°08'E
Wilhelmstal	WA	313	21°54'S	16°20'E
Wilkes-Barre	US	398	41°14'N	75°52'W
Wilkinsburg		374	40°26'N	79°52'W
Willamette		372	45°39'N	122°46'W
Willard		372	41°24'N	112°02'W
Willard		374	37°18'N	93°25'W
Willcox	US	398	32°15'N	109°49'W
Willebroek	BE	570	51°04'N	4°22'E
Willemstad		380	12°06'N	68°56'W
Willen		372	50°10'N	101°13'W
Willeroo	AS	656	15°17'S	131°35'E
William Creek	AS	656	28°55'S	136°21'E
Williams		372	39°09'N	122°08'W
Williams		376	35°14'N	112°11'W
Williamsburg		374	37°16'N	76°42'W
Williamsburg		374	36°44'N	84°09'W

Yalpuk, Ozero	UP	624	45°25'N	28°37'E
Yalpunga	AS	656	29°02'S	142°03'E
Yalta	UP	624	44°30'N	34°10'E
Yalu	CH	490	39°55'N	124°20'E
Yalu (Amnok-kang)	KN	512	39°55'N	124°22'E
Yalutorovsk	RS	612	56°40'N	66°18'E
Yaluwe	CG	287	0°07'S	24°12'E
Yalvaç	TU	535	38°17'N	31°11'E
Yam, Ramlat		264	17°00'N	46°00'E
Yamada	JA	506	39°28'N	141°57'E
Yamagata	JA	506	38°15'N	140°15'E
Yamaguchi	JA	506	34°10'N	131°29'E
Yamal, Poluostrov	RS	612	70°00'N	70°00'E
Yamansu	CH	490	41°54'N	93°54'E
Yamasá	DR	408	18°46'N	70°01'W
Yamato	JA	506	37°38'N	139°46'E
Yambah	AS	656	23°07'S	133°48'E
Yambata	CG	287	2°26'N	21°58'E
Yambéring	GV	297	11°49'N	12°21'W
Yambio	SU	324	4°34'N	28°23'E
Yambol	BU	573	42°29'N	26°30'E
Yambrasbamba	PE	436	5°45'S	77°54'W
Yamdena	ID	500	7°36'S	131°25'E
Yamethin	BM	487	20°26'N	96°09'E
Yamin, Puncak	ID	500	4°39'S	140°06'E
Yam Kinneret (L. Tiberias) (Sea of Galilee)	IS	505	32°47'N	35°32'E
Yamm		466	58°26'N	28°03'E
Yamolota	CG	287	2°12'N	23°11'E
Yamoussoukro	IV	288	6°49'N	5°17'W
Yampol'	UP	624	48°15'N	28°17'E
Yampol'	UP	624	49°58'N	26°15'E
Yamsk	RS	612	59°35'N	154°10'E
Yamuna	IN	496	25°30'N	81°53'E
Yamunānagar	IN	496	30°07'N	77°20'E
Yan	NI	316	10°04'N	12°12'E
Yana	RS	612	70°00'N	135°00'E
Yanac		652	36°08'S	141°26'E
Yanagawa	JA	506	33°10'N	130°24'E
Yanahuanca	PE	436	10°30'S	76°30'W
Yan'an	CH	490	36°36'N	109°27'E
Yanaoca	PE	436	14°13'S	71°26'W
Yanaul		466	56°15'N	54°49'E
Yanbu` al Baḩr	SA	528	24°05'N	38°03'E
Yancannia	AS	656	30°15'S	142°46'E
Yancheng	CH	490	33°22'N	120°07'E
Yanchi	CH	490	43°23'N	94°24'E
Yanchiwan	CH	490	39°12'N	95°45'E
Yandaxkak	CH	490	39°01'N	88°33'E
Yandé		654	20°07'S	163°23'E
Yandev	NI	316	7°22'N	9°03'E
Yandina	BP	666	9°05'S	159°15'E
Yandongi	CG	287	2°51'N	22°16'E
Yandoon	BM	487	17°02'N	95°39'E
Yandun	CH	490	42°21'N	94°06'E
Yanfolila	ML	307	11°09'N	8°09'W
Yangalia	CT	282	6°56'N	21°01'E
Yangambi	CG	287	0°47'N	24°28'E
Ya'ngamdo		472	31°50'N	94°28'E
Ya'ngamdo	CH	490	31°12'N	94°13'E
Yangamo	CM	280	4°58'N	14°03'E
Yangbajain		472	30°13'N	90°25'E
Yangchun	CH	490	22°09'N	111°46'E
Yangdachengzi		474	43°57'N	124°26'E
Yangdŏk	KN	512	39°13'N	126°39'E
Yanggao	CH	490	40°18'N	113°43'E
Yanggu	KS	513	38°06'N	127°59'E
Yangiabad	UZ	539	41°08'N	70°06'E
Yangī Qal`eh	AF	480	37°28'N	69°36'E
Yangiyer	UZ	539	40°17'N	68°48'E
Yangiyul'	UZ	539	41°06'N	69°03'E
Yangjiang	CH	490	21°51'N	111°57'E
Yangkang		472	37°41'N	98°45'E
Yangmei	TW	532	24°55'N	121°08'E
Yangming Shan	CH	490	26°07'N	111°55'E
Yangon (Rangoon)	BM	487	16°47'N	96°10'E
Yangor	NR	662	0°31'S	166°54'E
Yangoru	PP	664	3°39'S	143°18'E
Yangquan	CH	490	37°53'N	113°35'E
Yangsan	KS	513	35°20'N	129°02'E
Yangshuo	CH	490	24°46'N	110°30'E
Yang Talat	TH	534	16°24'N	103°23'E
Yangtze (Chang Jiang)	CH	490	28°46'N	104°38'E
Yangtze (Fuchun Jiang)	CH	490	30°15'N	120°15'E
Yangtze (Jinsha Jiang)	CH	490	28°50'N	104°36'E
Yangtze (Tuotuo He)	CH	490	34°03'N	93°06'E
Yangyang	KS	513	38°04'N	128°38'E
Yangyuan	CH	490	40°04'N	114°12'E
Yangzhou	CH	490	32°23'N	119°25'E
Yangzishao		474	42°26'N	126°09'E
Yanhe	CH	490	28°34'N	108°27'E
Yanhu		472	43°24'N	88°12'E
Yanhuqu	CH	490	32°31'N	82°30'E
Yanisyarvi, Oz.		556	62°00'N	30°50'E
Yanja	CG	287	1°40'S	17°42'E
Yanji	CH	490	42°52'N	129°30'E
Yanjin	CH	490	28°03'N	104°13'E
Yanjing	CH	490	29°06'N	98°32'E
Yankara	NI	316	11°47'N	7°05'E
Yankok	PP	664	3°32'S	142°13'E
Yankton	US	398	42°52'N	97°23'W
Yano-Indigirskaya Nizmennost	RS	612	71°00'N	140°00'E
Yanonge	CG	287	0°38'N	24°40'E
Yan Oya	CE	530	8°55'N	81°01'E
Yanqi	CH	490	42°03'N	86°33'E
Yanrey	AS	656	22°31'S	114°48'E
Yanshan	CH	490	23°36'N	104°19'E
Yanshiping	CH	490	33°34'N	92°00'E
Yanshou	CH	490	45°27'N	128°18'E
Yanskiy Zaliv	RS	612	71°50'N	136°00'E
Yantabulla	AS	656	29°21'S	145°00'E
Yantai	CH	490	37°31'N	121°24'E
Yantara	AS	656	29°52'S	142°17'E
Yantarnyy		560	54°52'N	19°57'E
Yantongshan		474	43°17'N	125°59'E
Yantra	BU	573	43°38'N	25°34'E
Yanwa	CH	490	27°36'N	99°00'E
Yany Kurgan	KZ	510	43°55'N	67°15'E
Yanyuan	CH	490	27°24'N	101°32'E
Yao	CD	283	12°50'N	17°32'E
Yao'an		472	25°32'N	101°12'E
Yaoundé	CM	280	3°52'N	11°32'E
Yaoxiaoling		472	48°03'N	127°42'E
Yapacani	BL	422	16°00'S	64°25'W
Yapei	GH	296	9°10'N	1°10'W
Yapen		648	1°41'S	136°00'E
Yapen, Selat	ID	500	1°00'S	135°00'E
Yapeyú	AR	419	29°27'S	56°49'W
Yapirga	BL	422	19°36'S	62°32'W
Yap Islands	FM	661	9°30'N	138°00'E
Yaque del Sur	DR	408	18°17'N	71°06'W
Yaqui	MX	394	27°19'N	110°01'W
Yaqui	MX	394	27°37'N	110°39'W
Yaqui, Boca de		376	27°50'N	111°00'W
Yaquina Head	US	398	44°40'N	124°04'W
Yara	CU	406	20°16'N	76°57'W
Yaraguanal	CU	406	21°38'N	78°02'W
Yaraia	SL	320	8°56'N	11°08'W
Yaraka	AS	656	24°53'S	144°05'E
Yaramaniapuka, Gunung	ID	500	4°06'S	135°44'E
Yaransk		466	57°19'N	47°54'E
Yaraoua	CT	282	6°00'N	20°44'E
Yardimci Burnu	TU	535	36°13'N	30°25'E
Yardymly	AJ	483	38°54'N	48°15'E
Yarega		466	63°24'N	53°25'E
Yaremcha	UP	624	48°27'N	24°33'E
Yaren	NR	662	0°33'S	166°55'E
Yargora	MD	601	46°26'N	28°27'E
Yarí	CO	430	0°23'S	72°16'W
Yarīm	YM	541	14°19'N	44°21'E
Yaritagua	VE	440	10°05'N	69°08'W
Yarkant He	CH	490	40°28'N	80°52'E
Yarker		374	44°23'N	76°46'W
Yarkovo		466	57°24'N	67°05'E
Yarloop		652	32°58'S	115°54'E
Yarlung Zangbo Jiang	CH	490	24°02'N	90°59'E
Yarma		564	37°49'N	32°54'E
Yarmolintsy	UP	624	49°12'N	26°50'E
Yarmouth		374	41°42'N	70°13'W
Yarnema		556	62°58'N	39°22'E
Yarobawal	GA	295	13°26'N	14°13'W
Yaroslavl'	RS	612	57°37'N	39°52'E
Yaroslavskiy	RS	612	44°11'N	132°14'E
Yarrawonga		652	36°01'S	146°00'E
Yar-Sale	RS	612	66°50'N	70°50'E
Yartsevo		560	55°04'N	32°40'E
Yartsevo	RS	612	60°14'N	90°12'E
Yarumal	CO	430	6°58'N	75°24'W
Yarwa		472	30°12'N	99°14'E
Yary	RS	612	68°54'N	66°30'E
Yasa	CG	287	3°42'S	21°24'E
Yasachnaya		468	65°00'N	152°00'E
Yasawa		654	16°42'S	177°37'E
Yasawa Group	FJ	660	17°00'S	177°40'E
Yasenskaya		564	46°21'N	38°16'E
Yashalta		560	46°20'N	42°17'E
Yashbum	YM	541	14°18'N	46°55'E
Yashi	NI	316	12°22'N	7°55'E
Yashikera	NI	316	9°46'N	3°24'E
Yashima	JA	506	39°13'N	140°00'E
Yashkino		466	52°41'N	53°26'E
Yashkul'	RS	612	46°11'N	45°21'E
Yashma	AJ	483	40°43'N	49°28'E
Yásica Abajo	DR	408	19°38'N	70°35'W
Yāsīn	PK	524	36°21'N	73°19'E
Yasinya	UP	624	48°16'N	24°21'E
Yasnogorsk		560	54°29'N	37°42'E
Yasothon	TH	534	15°45'N	104°08'E
Yass		652	34°50'S	148°55'E
Yasugi	JA	506	35°26'N	133°15'E
Yāsūj	IR	502	30°40'N	51°36'E
Yasun Burnu	TU	535	41°08'N	37°41'E
Yat	NG	314	20°31'N	13°30'E
Yata	BL	422	10°29'S	65°26'W
Yata	BL	422	13°20'S	66°35'W
Yatağan		564	37°20'N	28°09'E
Yaté		654	22°05'S	167°00'E
Yates Center		374	37°52'N	95°43'W
Yathkyed L.	CA	390	62°40'N	98°00'W
Yatina	BL	422	20°44'S	64°44'W
Yatolema	CG	287	0°16'N	24°31'E
Yatsushiro	JA	506	32°30'N	130°36'E
Yaţţah	IS	505	31°27'N	35°05'E
Yatta Plateau	KE	299	2°00'S	38°00'E
Yatton	UK	626	51°23'N	2°49'W
Yauca	PE	436	15°40'S	74°32'W
Yauca	PE	436	15°51'S	74°31'W
Yauco	US	398	18°02'N	66°51'W
Yauli	PE	436	11°42'S	75°26'W
Yaúna Moloca	CO	430	0°52'S	70°08'W
Yaupi	EC	432	2°50'S	77°55'W
Yaután	PE	436	9°31'S	78°00'W
Yauyos	PE	436	12°24'S	75°57'W
Yavaraté	CO	430	0°37'N	69°13'W
Yavari	PE	436	4°21'S	70°02'W
Yavatmāl	IN	496	20°24'N	78°08'E
Yavay, Pov.	RS	612	72°30'N	75°15'E
Yaveo	MX	394	17°19'N	95°42'W
Yavita	VE	440	2°55'N	67°26'W
Yaviza	PM	417	8°11'N	77°41'W
Yavorov	UP	624	49°56'N	23°23'E
Yavuzeli		564	37°20'N	37°33'E
Yawatahama	JA	506	33°27'N	132°24'E
Yawatongguzlangar	CH	490	37°01'N	83°09'E
Yawe	SL	320	7°24'N	11°42'W
Yaya		466	56°12'N	86°26'E
Yaypan	UZ	539	40°23'N	70°48'E
Yaysan	KZ	510	50°51'N	56°14'E
Yayuan		474	41°44'N	126°12'E
Yazd	IR	502	31°53'N	54°22'E
Yazdān	IR	502	33°31'N	60°53'E
Yazgulemskiy Khr.	TI	533	38°00'N	71°00'E
Yazhma	RS	612	66°54'N	44°34'E
Yazmān	PK	524	29°08'N	71°45'E
Yazoo		378	32°22'N	91°00'W
Yazoo City		378	32°50'N	90°24'W
Yazovir Iskur	BU	573	42°30'N	23°30'E
Yazykovo		466	54°18'N	47°24'E
Yazyurdu		564	38°48'N	36°56'E
Ybbs an der Donau	AU	568	48°10'N	15°05'E
Ybycuí	PA	435	26°01'S	57°03'W
Yding Skovhøj	DA	576	56°00'N	9°47'E
Ye	BM	487	15°15'N	97°51'E
Yean	KS	513	35°42'N	128°49'E
Yeay Sen, Chrouy	CB	489	11°12'N	103°03'E
Yebawmi	BM	487	25°15'N	95°45'E
Yebbi-Bou	CD	283	20°58'N	18°04'E
Yébiqué, Enneri	CD	283	22°04'N	17°49'E
Yebyu	BM	487	14°15'N	98°12'E
Yecheng	CH	490	37°53'N	77°25'E
Yech'ŏn	KS	513	36°39'N	128°27'E
Yecla	SP	618	38°37'N	1°07'W
Yécora	MX	394	28°20'N	108°58'W
Yedashe	BM	487	19°09'N	96°21'E
Yedintsy	MD	601	48°10'N	27°19'E
Yeditepe		564	35°58'N	36°01'E
Yeed	SO	321	4°33'N	43°02'E
Yeeda River	AS	656	17°36'S	123°39'E
Yeelirrie	AS	656	27°17'S	120°06'E
Yefimovskiy		560	59°30'N	34°40'E
Yefremov		560	53°09'N	38°07'E
Yegorlykskaya		466	46°34'N	40°39'E
Yegor'yevsk		560	55°23'N	39°02'E
Yehuda, Midbar	IS	505	31°30'N	32°25'E
Yei	SU	324	4°05'N	30°40'E
Yekaterinoslavka		468	50°23'N	129°07'E
Yekaterinovka		560	52°03'N	44°21'E
Yekepa	LI	301	7°35'N	8°32'W
Yekhegnadzor	AM	482	39°45'N	45°20'E
Yekimovichi		466	54°07'N	33°18'E
Yelabuga		466	55°45'N	52°04'E
Yelan'		466	50°57'N	43°44'E
Yelarbon		652	28°34'S	150°45'E
Yelets	RS	612	52°37'N	38°30'E
Yeletskiy	RS	612	67°04'N	64°00'E
Yelgu	SU	324	10°01'N	33°31'E
Yélimané	ML	307	15°08'N	10°34'W
Yelizavetinka		466	51°46'N	59°45'E
Yelizavetino		560	59°29'N	29°46'E
Yelizavetopol'skoye	RS	612	52°51'N	60°36'E
Yelizavety, Mys	RS	612	54°26'N	142°42'E
Yelizovo	RS	612	53°11'N	158°23'E
Yell	UK	626	60°40'N	1°28'W
Yellel	AG	272	35°43'N	0°29'E
Yellow Grass		372	49°48'N	104°10'W
Yellowknife		368	62°31'N	114°13'W
Yellowknife	CA	390	62°27'N	114°22'W
Yellow River (Huang He)	CH	490	37°32'N	118°19'E
Yellow Sea	KS	513	36°00'N	124°00'E
Yellowstone	US	398	48°00'N	103°59'W
Yellowstone Lake		372	44°27'N	110°22'W
Yellville		374	36°13'N	92°41'W
Yel'nya		466	54°35'N	33°11'E
Yelshanka		560	51°49'N	46°23'E
Yel'sk	BO	569	51°48'N	29°09'E
Yel'tsy		466	56°40'N	33°51'E
Yelwa	NI	316	10°50'N	4°44'E
Yelwa	NI	316	8°49'N	9°40'E
Yema	CG	287	5°45'S	12°17'E
Yemaotai		474	42°20'N	122°53'E
Yema Shan	CH	490	39°10'N	96°25'E
Yematan	CH	490	34°42'N	98°00'E
Yematan	CH	490	37°18'N	98°22'E
Yemel'yanovo		466	56°11'N	92°40'E
Yemen		38	15°30'N	47°30'E
Yemetsk	RS	612	63°28'N	41°45'E
Yemil'chino	UP	624	50°52'N	27°48'E
Yemmiganur		470	15°44'N	77°29'E
Yen, Mui	VM	540	13°55'N	108°40'E
Yenagoa	NI	316	4°55'N	6°16'E
Yenakiyeve	UP	624	48°14'N	38°13'E
Yenangyaung	BM	487	20°28'N	94°53'E
Yenanma	BM	487	19°46'N	94°48'E
Yen Bai	VM	540	21°41'N	104°51'E
Yenda		652	34°15'S	146°11'E
Yende	CF	285	3°06'N	18°31'E
Yende Millimou	GV	297	8°53'N	10°11'W
Yendi	GH	296	9°26'N	0°01'W
Ye-ngan	BM	487	21°09'N	96°27'E
Yenge	CG	287	0°49'S	22°32'E
Yengisar	CH	490	38°55'N	76°09'E
Yengo	CF	285	0°22'N	15°29'E
Yengué	GB	294	2°14'S	11°16'E
Yenice		564	39°55'N	27°18'E
Yenice		564	41°12'N	32°20'E
Yenice	TU	535	41°35'N	32°03'E
Yeniceoba		564	38°53'N	32°48'E
Yenihisar		564	37°23'N	27°15'E
Yeniköy		564	41°18'N	28°43'E
Yenimehmetli	TU	535	39°26'N	32°10'E
Yenişehir		564	40°16'N	29°39'E
Yenisey	RS	612	62°00'N	98°00'E
Yenisey Ridge		468	59°00'N	93°00'E
Yeniseysk	RS	612	58°27'N	92°10'E
Yeniseyskiy Zaliv	RS	612	72°30'N	80°00'E
Yeniugou	CH	490	34°24'N	97°55'E
Yen Minh	VM	540	23°07'N	105°06'E
Yeno	GB	294	1°42'S	11°33'E
Yenotayevka	RS	612	47°16'N	47°03'E
Yenshui	TW	532	23°18'N	120°14'E
Yeovil	UK	626	50°57'N	2°38'W
Yepes	SP	618	39°54'N	3°38'W
Yeppoon	AS	656	23°08'S	150°44'E
Yerakhtur		560	54°43'N	41°09'E
Yerakovoúni	GR	588	39°01'N	22°39'E
Yeraliyev	KZ	510	43°12'N	51°39'E
Yeranos	AM	482	40°12'N	45°11'E
Yerbanís		376	24°45'N	103°50'W
Yerbent	TX	537	39°19'N	58°36'E
Yerevan	AM	482	40°11'N	44°30'E
Yerichaña	VE	440	4°17'N	64°19'W
Yerington		372	38°59'N	119°09'W
Yerköy	TU	535	39°38'N	34°29'E
Yermak	KZ	510	52°02'N	76°55'E
Yermish'		560	54°46'N	42°16'E
Yermitsa	RS	612	66°56'N	52°18'E
Yermo		376	34°53'N	116°49'W
Yerofey Pavlovich	RS	612	53°58'N	121°58'E
Yeroḩam	IS	505	31°00'N	34°55'E
Yerolimín	GR	588	36°29'N	22°23'E
Yershov		466	51°20'N	48°17'E
Yershovka	KZ	510	54°07'N	64°59'E
Yertoma	RS	612	63°32'N	47°48'E
Yertsevo	RS	612	60°48'N	40°05'E
Yerupaja, Cerro	PE	436	10°16'S	76°54'W
Yerushalayim (Al Quds) (Jerusalem)	IS	505	31°46'N	35°13'E
Yesa	BL	422	19°32'S	62°29'W
Yesa, Emb. de	SP	618	42°36'N	1°09'W
Yesagyo	BM	487	21°38'N	95°14'E
Yesan	KS	513	36°41'N	126°51'E
Yesil	TU	535	37°20'N	33°13'E
Yesil'	KZ	510	51°58'N	66°24'E
Yeşildere		564	37°09'N	33°31'E
Yeşilgölcük		564	38°14'N	34°47'E
Yeşilhisar	TU	535	38°21'N	35°05'E
Yeşilova		564	37°30'N	29°43'E
Yesodot	IS	505	31°49'N	34°52'E
Yessentuki	RS	612	44°03'N	42°51'E
Yessey	RS	612	68°29'N	102°10'E
Yesud HaMa`ala	IS	505	33°03'N	35°35'E
Yete I	CG	287	1°02'S	20°15'E
Yetman		652	28°37'S	114°42'E
Yetti	MR	308	26°10'N	7°50'W
Ye-u	BM	487	22°46'N	95°26'E
Yeu, I. d'	FR	580	46°43'N	2°20'W
Yevla	IN	496	20°02'N	74°29'E
Yevlashëvo		560	53°07'N	46°50'E
Yevlax	AJ	483	40°37'N	47°09'E
Yevpatoriya	UP	624	45°12'N	33°22'E
Yevsug	UP	624	49°13'N	39°18'E
Ye Xian		472	33°37'N	113°20'E
Yeyik	CH	490	36°45'N	83°34'E
Yeysk	RS	612	46°42'N	38°17'E
Yeyungou	CH	490	42°00'N	85°03'E
Yezhikha		560	58°06'N	47°46'E
Ygatimí	PA	435	24°05'S	55°30'W
Yhú	PA	435	25°01'S	55°56'W
Yí	UY	439	33°07'S	57°08'W
Yialousa	CY	494	35°32'N	34°11'E
Yi'an	CH	490	47°52'N	125°17'E
Yianamassok	GB	294	0°49'N	11°24'E
Yiannitsá	GR	588	40°48'N	22°25'E
Yiánnouli	GR	588	39°40'N	22°23'E
Yibin	CH	490	28°45'N	104°33'E
Yichang	CH	490	30°41'N	111°16'E
Yichun	CH	490	47°42'N	128°54'E
Yichun	CH	490	27°45'N	114°24'E
Yidu		472	30°24'N	111°32'E
Yidu	CH	490	36°40'N	118°27'E
Yiftaḥ	IS	505	33°07'N	35°33'E
Yigo		654	13°31'N	145°53'E
Yihe Suuji	MG	520	48°15'N	106°18'E
Yilan	CH	490	46°18'N	129°33'E
Yildiz Dag.	TU	535	41°50'N	27°30'E
Yıldızeli	TU	535	39°52'N	36°38'E
Yilehuli Shan	CH	490	51°20'N	124°20'E
Yiliang	CH	490	27°34'N	104°00'E
Yiliping	CH	490	37°54'N	93°19'E
Yilong		472	31°34'N	106°24'E
Yima	CH	490	34°45'N	111°51'E
Yimbi	CT	282	4°27'N	18°32'E
Yimen	CH	490	24°39'N	102°09'E
Yimianpo		474	45°04'N	128°03'E
Yinan	CH	490	35°32'N	118°27'E
Yinchuan	CH	490	38°27'N	106°12'E
Yingcheng		472	30°57'N	113°36'E
Yingcheng		474	44°08'N	125°54'E
Yingchengzi		474	43°12'N	125°30'E
Yingde	CH	490	24°09'N	113°24'E
Ying'emen		474	42°10'N	125°05'E
Yinggehai	CH	490	18°30'N	108°39'E
Yinggen	CH	490	19°01'N	109°48'E
Ying He		472	32°30'N	116°30'E
Yinghua		472	45°58'N	123°13'E
Yingjiang	CH	490	24°48'N	98°04'E
Yingkou	CH	490	40°39'N	122°16'E
Yingshan		472	31°06'N	106°35'E
Yingshan		472	31°37'N	113°50'E
Yingtan	CH	490	28°13'N	117°00'E
Yingui	CM	280	4°32'N	10°20'E
Yining	CH	490	43°53'N	81°20'E
Yining	CH	490	44°00'N	81°39'E
Yinmabin	BM	487	22°05'N	94°54'E
Yin Shan	CH	490	41°30'N	109°00'E
Yioúra	GR	588	39°24'N	24°10'E
Yirga `Alem	ET	293	6°45'N	38°25'E
Yirga Ch'efē	ET	293	6°10'N	38°12'E
Yirkā	IS	505	32°57'N	35°13'E
Yirol	SU	324	6°33'N	30°30'E
Yirrkala		648	12°15'S	136°50'E
Yirshi	CH	490	47°17'N	119°48'E
Yishui		472	35°48'N	118°37'E
Yíthion	GR	588	36°45'N	22°34'E
Yitulihe		468	50°38'N	121°34'E
Yitung		474	43°20'N	125°17'E
Yiwanquan	CH	490	43°21'N	92°05'E
Yiwu	CH	490	43°15'N	94°34'E
Yixing	CH	490	31°21'N	119°49'E
Yiyang		472	34°30'N	112°10'E
Yiyang	CH	490	28°22'N	117°24'E
Yiyang	CH	490	28°36'N	112°19'E
Yiyu	IN	496	28°33'N	94°38'E
Yiyuankou		472	40°10'N	119°35'E
Yizhang	CH	490	25°23'N	112°57'E
Yizheng	CH	490	32°15'N	119°12'E
Ylakiai	LH	597	56°17'N	21°51'E
Ylig Bay		654	13°26'N	145°47'E
Yliharmä	FI	578	63°08'N	22°45'E
Yli-Ii	FI	578	65°22'N	25°47'E
Ylikiiminki	FI	578	65°00'N	26°07'E
Yli-Kitka	FI	578	66°08'N	28°30'E
Ylistaro	FI	578	62°57'N	22°31'E
Ylitornio	FI	578	66°19'N	23°41'E
Ylivieska	FI	578	64°03'N	24°29'E
Ylöjärvi	FI	578	61°31'N	23°32'E
Ymir		372	49°17'N	117°13'W
Yngaren	SW	621	58°49'N	16°08'E
Ynykchanskiy	RS	612	60°15'N	137°43'E
Yoakum		376	29°17'N	97°08'W
Yoboki	DJ	289	11°30'N	42°06'E
Yocalla	BL	422	19°24'S	65°56'W
Yŏch'ŏn	KS	513	34°45'N	127°40'E
Yoco	VE	440	10°36'N	62°24'W
Yocón	HO	412	15°01'N	86°42'W
Yodŏk		472	39°39'N	126°51'E
Yog Pt.	RP	526	14°04'N	124°12'E
Yogyakarta	ID	500	7°48'S	110°22'E
Yoichi	JA	506	43°12'N	140°41'E
Yojoa, Lago de	HO	412	14°52'N	87°59'W
Yŏju	KS	513	37°18'N	127°38'E
Yōka	JA	506	35°23'N	134°45'E
Yokadouma	CM	280	3°31'N	15°03'E
Yokana	CG	287	0°48'N	22°52'E
Yokkaichi	JA	506	34°57'N	136°37'E
Yoko	CM	280	5°32'N	12°19'E
Yoko	GB	294	0°32'N	12°55'E
Yokohama	JA	506	35°28'N	139°37'E
Yokolo	CG	287	0°38'S	22°57'E
Yokosuka	JA	506	35°16'N	139°40'E
Yokote	JA	506	39°18'N	140°34'E
Yola	NI	316	9°12'N	12°29'E
Yolaina, Serranías de	NU	415	11°45'N	84°05'W
Yolombo	CG	287	1°36'S	23°12'E
Yom, Mae Nam	TH	534	15°52'N	100°16'E
Yombi	GB	294	1°26'S	10°37'E
Yŏmju	KN	512	39°54'N	124°36'E
Yomou	GV	297	7°34'N	9°16'W
Yona		654	13°28'N	145°47'E
Yonago	JA	506	35°26'N	133°20'E
Yonaguni-jima	JA	506	24°27'N	123°00'E
Yonaha-dake	JA	506	26°43'N	128°13'E
Yŏnan	KN	512	37°54'N	126°10'E
Yonezawa	JA	506	37°55'N	140°07'E
Yŏngam	KS	513	34°45'N	126°42'E
Yongamp'o	KN	512	39°56'N	124°23'E
Yong'an	CH	490	25°57'N	117°21'E
Yong'an Guan	CH	490	25°41'N	111°18'E
Yŏngbyŏn		474	39°49'N	125°48'E
Yongchang	CH	490	38°16'N	102°06'E
Yŏngch'ŏn	KS	513	35°58'N	128°56'E
Yongde	CH	490	24°03'N	99°17'E
Yongding	CH	490	24°48'N	116°45'E
Yŏngdŏk	KS	513	36°24'N	129°22'E
Yŏngdong	KS	513	36°10'N	127°47'E
Yongfu		472	24°59'N	109°59'E
Yonggang	KN	512	38°51'N	125°25'E
Yŏnggwang	KS	513	35°16'N	126°31'E
Yŏnghae	KS	513	36°32'N	129°24'E
Yonghe	CH	490	36°43'N	110°39'E
Yŏnghŭng	KN	512	39°33'N	127°14'E
Yongji		474	43°40'N	126°28'E
Yongjing	CH	490	36°00'N	103°16'E
Yŏngju	KS	513	36°49'N	128°37'E
Yongmun-san	KS	513	37°34'N	127°33'E
Yongning	CH	490	38°17'N	106°17'E
Yongo	CG	287	1°31'S	21°49'E
Yong Peng	MY	518	2°01'N	103°04'E
Yongping		472	25°24'N	99°36'E
Yongren	CH	490	26°03'N	101°39'E
Yongshan	CH	490	28°10'N	103°34'E
Yongsheng	CH	490	26°41'N	100°45'E
Yongshou		472	34°40'N	108°10'E
Yongshun	CH	490	29°00'N	109°48'E
Yongtai		472	25°52'N	118°55'E
Yŏngwŏl	KS	513	37°11'N	128°28'E
Yŏngwŏn	KN	512	39°49'N	126°32'E
Yongxin	CH	490	26°56'N	114°12'E
Yongxing		472	26°08'N	113°06'E
Yŏng-yang	KS	513	36°40'N	129°07'E
Yonibana	SL	320	8°26'N	12°14'W
Yonkers	US	398	40°56'N	73°53'W
Yonne	FR	580	48°23'N	2°58'E
Yonsa	KN	512	41°54'N	129°00'E
Yŏnsan	KN	512	38°52'N	126°15'E
Yoontoy	SO	321	0°08'S	42°34'E
Yopal	CO	430	5°21'N	72°23'W
Yopurga	CH	490	39°15'N	76°45'E
Yorito	HO	412	15°04'N	87°17'W
York		372	40°52'N	97°35'W
York		374	39°57'N	76°43'W
York		378	32°29'N	88°17'W
York	UK	626	53°56'N	1°05'W
Yorke Peninsula	AS	656	35°00'S	137°30'E
York Factory		370	57°02'N	92°17'W
York Landing	CA	390	56°06'N	96°05'W
York Sd.	AS	656	14°50'S	125°05'E
Yorkshire Moors	UK	626	54°15'N	1°00'W
Yorkshire Wolds	UK	626	54°00'N	0°30'W
Yorkton	CA	390	51°13'N	102°28'W
Yorktown		376	28°58'N	97°30'W
Yoro	HO	412	15°08'N	87°08'W
Yoro Beri Kunda	GA	295	13°30'N	14°45'W
Yorosso	ML	307	12°22'N	4°47'W
Yorubaland, Plateau of	NI	316	8°00'N	4°30'E
Yoshida	JA	506	33°16'N	132°33'E
Yoshkar-Ola	RS	612	56°40'N	47°55'E
Yos Sudarso Island	ID	500	7°50'S	138°30'E
Yŏsu	KS	513	34°44'N	127°44'E
Yotaú	BL	422	16°03'S	63°03'W
Yotei-zan	JA	506	42°49'N	140°49'E
Yotvata	IS	505	29°53'N	35°03'E
Youanmi	AS	656	28°37'S	118°49'E
Youdunzi	CH	490	37°54'N	91°36'E
Youghal	EI	592	51°55'N	7°51'W
Youghal Bay	EI	592	51°52'N	7°50'W
Youhamba	CT	282	6°55'N	20°51'E
Youhao	CH	490	47°52'N	128°48'E
You Jiang	CH	490	22°50'N	108°06'E
Youlou	GB	294	0°54'S	12°36'E
Young		372	51°47'N	105°45'W
Young		652	34°19'S	148°18'E
Young	UY	439	32°41'S	57°38'W
Young Nick's Head	NZ	663	38°44'S	177°57'E
Young's Rock		654	25°00'S	130°10'W
Youngstown	CA	390	51°32'N	111°13'W
Youngstown	US	398	41°05'N	80°38'W
Youshashan	CH	490	38°21'N	90°55'E
Youssoufia	MO	310	32°15'N	8°32'W
Youyang		472	28°52'N	108°45'E
Youyi	CH	490	46°47'N	131°46'E
Yowela	ZA	332	11°49'S	27°09'E
Yozgat	TU	535	39°50'N	34°48'E
Ypané	PA	435	25°27'S	57°32'W
Ypé Jhú	PA	435	23°57'S	55°26'W
Yreka	US	398	41°44'N	122°38'W
Ysabel Channel	PP	664	2°00'S	150°00'E
Yssingeaux	FR	580	45°07'N	4°06'E
Ystad	SW	621	55°25'N	13°46'E
Ytrac	FR	580	44°55'N	2°22'E
Ytre Arna	NO	604	69°23'N	25°49'E
Ytterbyn		556	65°48'N	23°11'E
Ytterhogdal	SW	621	62°11'N	14°56'E
Yuan'an		472	31°03'N	111°34'E
Yuan Jiang	CH	490	29°00'N	110°00'E
Yuanjiang	CH	490	28°49'N	112°22'E
Yuanli	TW	532	24°27'N	120°39'E
Yuanlin	CH	490	49°57'N	121°30'E
Yuanlin	TW	532	23°58'N	120°34'E
Yuanling	CH	490	28°28'N	110°22'E
Yuanmou	CH	490	25°41'N	101°51'E
Yuanping	CH	490	38°42'N	112°42'E
Yuanshanzi		472	39°14'N	99°25'E
Yuanyang	CH	490	23°12'N	102°40'E
Yuba City	US	398	39°08'N	121°36'W
Yūbari	JA	506	43°04'N	141°59'E
Yūbetsu	JA	506	44°14'N	143°37'E
Yucatán, Península del	MX	394	19°30'N	89°00'W
Yucheng		472	36°56'N	116°39'E
Yuci	CH	490	37°42'N	112°43'E
Yudoma		468	59°00'N	137°00'E
Yudu	CH	490	25°58'N	115°24'E
Yuechi	CH	490	30°30'N	106°28'E
Yuendumu	AS	656	22°16'S	131°49'E
Yuexi	CH	490	30°53'N	116°21'E
Yuexi	CH	490	28°36'N	102°30'E
Yueyang	CH	490	29°22'N	113°05'E
Yugan	CH	490	28°40'N	116°40'E
Yugoslavia		38	44°00'N	21°00'E
Yugo-Vostochnyye Karakumy	TX	537	37°40'N	64°00'E
Yuhuan	CH	490	28°07'N	121°13'E
Yuil'sk	RS	612	63°41'N	69°39'E
Yu Jiang	CH	490	23°24'N	110°05'E
Yukarıgöklü		564	37°20'N	37°59'E
Yukhary Lyaki	AJ	483	40°32'N	47°26'E
Yuki Kengundu	CG	287	3°57'S	19°34'E
Yukon	CA	390	62°32'N	163°54'W
Yukon Crossing	CA	390	62°21'N	136°29'W
Yukon Delta	US	398	62°45'N	164°00'W
Yüksekova	TU	535	37°34'N	44°17'E
Yukseyevo		466	59°52'N	54°19'E
Yulara	AS	656	25°16'S	130°58'E
Yuleba	AS	656	26°37'S	149°23'E
Yulee		378	30°37'N	81°36'W
Yuli	CH	490	41°47'N	86°45'E
Yuli	NI	316	9°42'N	10°16'E
Yuli	TW	532	23°20'N	121°18'E
Yulin	CH	490	38°17'N	109°45'E
Yulin	CH	490	22°37'N	110°09'E
Yul'yevka	KZ	510	52°07'N	64°16'E
Yuma	RS	612	65°04'N	33°20'E
Yuma	US	398	40°07'N	102°43'W
Yuma	US	398	32°42'N	114°37'W
Yuma, Bahía de	DR	408	18°21'N	68°35'W
Yumbe	UG	330	3°28'N	31°15'E
Yumbel	CI	428	37°08'S	72°32'W
Yumbi	CG	287	1°14'S	26°14'E
Yumbi	CG	287	1°53'S	16°32'E
Yumbi	CG	287	3°13'N	18°39'E
Yumbo	CO	430	3°35'N	76°28'W
Yumen	CH	490	39°49'N	97°30'E
Yumenzhen	CH	490	40°16'N	97°12'E
Yumiin Jisa	MG	520	46°12'N	99°02'E
Yumin	CH	490	45°58'N	82°27'E
Yuna	DR	408	19°12'N	69°37'W
Yunak	TU	535	38°49'N	31°45'E
Yunan		476	23°14'N	111°30'E
Yuncharà	BL	422	21°47'S	65°11'W
Yundum	GA	295	13°21'N	16°41'W
Yungay	CI	428	37°07'S	72°01'W
Yunguyo	PE	436	16°15'S	69°05'W
Yunjinghong	CH	490	21°58'N	100°48'E
Yunkai Dashan	CH	490	22°30'N	111°00'E
Yunlong	CH	490	25°49'N	99°27'E
Yunnan Plateau		476	26°00'N	103°00'E
Yunta	AS	656	32°35'S	139°33'E
Yunxi	CH	490	33°00'N	110°24'E
Yun Xian		472	24°25'N	100°06'E
Yun Xian		472	32°49'N	110°49'E
Yunyang		472	30°59'N	108°51'E
Yupukarri	GY	434	3°40'N	59°21'W
Yuqing	CH	490	27°11'N	107°55'E
Yura		386	20°07'S	66°07'W
Yuracyacu	PE	436	5°52'S	77°15'W
Yuratishki	BO	569	54°02'N	25°56'E
Yurga	RS	612	55°42'N	84°51'E
Yurgamysh		466	55°21'N	64°28'E
Yurimaguas	PE	436	5°54'S	76°05'W
Yuriria	MX	394	20°12'N	101°09'W
Yuroma		556	65°10'N	45°35'E
Yürük		564	40°56'N	27°04'E
Yur'ya		466	59°03'N	49°17'E
Yur'yevets		560	57°17'N	43°04'E
Yur'yevets		560	56°06'N	40°16'E
Yur'yevka	UP	624	48°44'N	36°02'E
Yur'yev-Pol'skiy		560	56°30'N	39°41'E
Yuryuzan'	RS	612	54°52'N	58°26'E
Yuscarán	HO	412	13°56'N	86°51'W
Yushala		466	57°04'N	64°17'E
Yushan	CH	490	28°39'N	118°15'E
Yü Shan	TW	532	23°28'N	120°57'E
Yushe	CH	490	37°03'N	112°57'E
Yushkozero	RS	612	64°45'N	32°07'E
Yushu		472	33°01'N	96°44'E
Yushu		474	41°39'N	124°50'E
Yushu	CH	490	44°47'N	126°31'E
Yushugou		474	44°08'N	127°05'E
Yusŏng	KS	513	36°21'N	127°20'E
Yustozero		556	62°47'N	33°33'E
Yusufeli	TU	535	40°49'N	41°33'E
Yutian	CH	490	36°51'N	81°42'E
Yutiangao		472	42°50'N	119°42'E
Yuto		386	23°38'S	64°28'W
Yuty	PA	435	26°32'S	56°18'W
Yü-weng Tao Tao	TW	532	23°36'N	119°30'E
Yuxi		472	24°23'N	102°34'E
Yuxia		472	24°28'N	104°20'E
Yu Xian	CH	490	39°47'N	114°33'E
Yuyao	CH	490	30°03'N	121°09'E

Yuza	JA	506	39°01'N	139°54'E
Yuzawa	JA	506	39°10'N	140°30'E
Yuzha		560	56°35'N	42°01'E
Yuzhno-Kuril'sk	RS	612	43°59'N	145°52'E
Yuzhno Muyskiy Khrebet		468	56°00'N	113°00'E
Yuzhno-Sakhalinsk	RS	612	46°57'N	142°44'E
Yuzhno-Sukhokumsk		560	44°42'N	45°27'E
Yuzhno-Surkhanskoye, Ozero	UZ	539	37°53'N	67°42'E
Yuzhnoural'sk		466	54°26'N	61°15'E
Yuzhno-Yeniseyskiy	RS	612	58°48'N	94°39'E
Yuzhnyy		560	47°20'N	41°51'E
Yuzhnyy	KZ	510	49°23'N	72°57'E
Yuzhnyy, Mys	RS	612	58°00'N	156°00'E
Yuzhnyy Alichurskiy, Khr.	TI	533	37°30'N	73°30'E
Yuzhnyy Anynyskiy Khrebet		468	67°30'N	165°00'E
Yuzhnyy Bug	UP	624	49°00'N	29°00'E
Yuzhnyy Ural	RS	612	52°00'N	59°00'E
Yuzhong	CH	490	35°51'N	104°01'E
Yverdon	SZ	622	46°47'N	6°39'E
Yvetot	FR	580	49°37'N	0°46'E
Ywamun	BM	487	20°31'N	95°25'E
Ywathit	BM	487	19°10'N	97°30'E

Z

Za, Oued	MO	310	34°33'N	3°02'W
Zaachila	MX	394	16°57'N	96°45'W
Zaalayskiy Khr.	KG	514	39°30'N	73°00'E
Zaanstad	NL	602	52°26'N	4°50'E
Žabalj	YO	630	45°23'N	20°04'E
Zabaykal'sk	RS	612	49°38'N	117°19'E
Żabbar	MT	600	35°52'N	14°32'E
Zabīd	YM	541	14°11'N	43°18'E
Zabid, Wadi	YM	541	14°07'N	43°06'E
Zabjani	MK	599	41°27'N	21°24'E
Žabljak	YO	630	43°09'N	19°08'E
Zābol	IR	502	31°02'N	61°30'E
Zābolī	IR	502	27°07'N	61°40'E
Zabqung	CH	490	31°27'N	87°18'E
Zabré	UV	278	11°10'N	0°38'W
Zábřeh	EZ	575	49°53'N	16°52'E
Zabrze	PL	606	50°19'N	18°47'E
Zaburun'ye	KZ	510	46°50'N	50°12'E
Zabzuga	GH	296	9°17'N	0°22'E
Zacapa	GT	411	14°58'N	89°32'W
Zacapu	MX	394	19°50'N	101°43'W
Zacate, Boca	CS	405	8°54'N	83°37'W
Zacatecas	MX	394	22°47'N	102°35'W
Zacatecoluca	ES	409	13°30'N	88°52'W
Zacatepec	MX	394	18°38'N	99°11'W
Zacatlán	MX	394	19°56'N	97°58'W
Zachary		378	30°38'N	91°09'W
Zachodniopomorskie, Pojezierze	PL	606	53°10'N	15°40'E
Zacoalco	MX	394	20°14'N	103°35'W
Zadar	HR	574	44°07'N	15°15'E
Zadetkyi Kyun	BM	487	9°58'N	98°13'E
Zadi	AO	274	6°08'S	14°48'E
Zadi	BM	487	14°31'N	97°59'E
Zadi (Inkisi)	CG	287	4°46'S	14°52'E
Zadoi	CH	490	33°09'N	95°04'E
Zadonsk		560	52°23'N	38°55'E
Zafra	SP	618	38°25'N	6°25'W
Żagań	PL	606	51°37'N	15°19'E
Žagarė	LH	597	56°21'N	23°15'E
Zāgheh-ye Pā'īn	IR	502	33°30'N	48°42'E
Zaghwān	TS	329	36°24'N	10°09'E
Zagnanado	BN	276	7°16'N	2°21'E
Zagnanado Plateau	BN	276	7°18'N	2°28'E
Zagora	MO	310	30°18'N	5°52'W
Zagorá	GR	588	39°26'N	23°07'E
Zagorje	SI	617	46°08'N	15°00'E
Zagreb	HR	574	45°48'N	16°00'E
Zagros Mountains (Zagros, Kuhha-ye)	IR	502	33°40'N	47°00'E
Zaharat al Batn	IZ	504	31°30'N	43°00'E
Zāhedān	IR	502	29°30'N	60°52'E
Zahirābād	IN	496	17°41'N	77°37'E
Zaḩlah	LE	516	33°51'N	35°52'E
Záhony	HU	590	48°23'N	22°10'E
Ẓahrān	SA	528	17°40'N	43°30'E
Zaïo	MO	310	34°57'N	2°44'W
Zaire		38	0°00'	25°00'E
Zaječar	YO	630	43°54'N	22°17'E
Zaka	ZI	334	20°21'S	31°27'E
Zakamensk	RS	612	50°23'N	103°17'E
Zakháro	GR	538	37°30'N	21°39'E
Zakharovo		560	54°22'N	39°17'E
Zakhmet	TX	537	37°46'N	62°33'E
Zākhū	IZ	504	37°08'N	42°41'E
Zaki Biam	NI	316	7°31'N	9°37'E
Zákinthos	GR	538	37°40'N	20°25'E
Zákinthos (Zante)	GR	538	37°47'N	20°47'E
Zakopane	PL	606	49°18'N	19°58'E
Zakouma	CD	283	10°51'N	19°49'E
Zala	AO	274	7°50'S	14°03'E
Zala	ET	293	6°28'N	37°13'E
Zala	HU	590	46°42'N	17°16'E
Zalaapáti	HU	590	46°43'N	17°07'E
Zalaegerszeg	HU	590	46°50'N	16°51'E
Zalalövő	HU	590	46°51'N	16°36'E
Zalamea de la Serena	SP	618	38°39'N	5°39'W
Zalanga	NI	316	10°37'N	10°10'E
Zalari		468	53°34'N	102°32'E
Zalaszentgrót	HU	590	46°57'N	17°05'E
Zalău	RO	610	47°12'N	23°03'E
Žalec	SI	617	46°15'N	15°10'E
Zaleshchiki	UP	624	48°38'N	25°44'E
Zalev Szczecinski	PL	606	53°46'N	14°14'E
Zalew Wislany	PL	606	54°20'N	19°30'E
Ẓalim	SA	528	22°43'N	42°10'E
Zalingei	SU	324	12°53'N	23°26'E
Zalṭan	LY	302	28°56'N	19°45'E
Zalṭan	LY	302	32°53'N	11°49'E
Zaltan, Bi'r	LY	302	28°27'N	19°46'E
Zaltan, Jabal	LY	302	28°37'N	19°43'E
Zalun	BM	487	17°29'N	95°34'E
Zalut	BM	487	13°41'N	98°10'E
Zamafora	NI	316	12°10'N	5°00'E
Zamālat As Sawāsī	TS	329	35°21'N	10°33'E
Zamárdi	HU	590	46°53'N	17°57'E
Zambeze (Zambezi)	AO	274	18°50'S	36°17'E
Zambezi	ZA	332	13°30'S	23°03'E
Zambezi (Zambeze)	AO	274	18°50'S	36°17'E
Zambezi Escarpment	ZA	332	17°02'S	27°19'E
Zambia		38	14°15'S	28°00'E
Zamboanga	RP	526	7°04'N	122°06'E
Zamboanga Peninsula		478	7°32'N	122°16'E
Zambrano	CO	430	9°45'N	74°49'W
Zambrów	PL	606	52°59'N	22°15'E
Zambujal de Cima	PO	608	38°26'N	9°08'W
Zamoi	CG	287	3°57'N	24°22'E
Zamoi	CG	287	4°53'N	27°26'E
Zamora	EC	432	4°04'S	78°58'W
Zamora	EC	432	2°59'N	78°13'W
Zamora	MX	394	19°59'N	102°16'W
Zamora	SP	618	41°31'N	5°45'W
Zamora Pico de Oro	MX	394	16°20'N	90°45'W
Zamość	PL	606	50°43'N	23°15'E
Zamtang	CH	490	32°25'N	101°05'E
Zamurro, Sierra de	VE	440	4°40'N	63°30'W
Zamus, Bi'r	LY	302	24°20'N	14°59'E
Zam'yany		466	46°48'N	47°37'E
Zamzam, Wadi	LY	302	31°24'N	15°17'E
Zamzfora		262	12°50'N	5°30'E
Zanaga	CF	285	2°51'S	13°50'E
Zanatepec	MX	394	16°29'N	94°21'W
Záncara		562	39°18'N	3°17'W
Zanda	CH	490	31°31'N	79°49'E
Zanderij	NS	438	5°27'N	55°12'W
Zandu-Kansabala	CG	287	5°10'S	18°16'E
Zandvoort	NL	602	52°22'N	4°32'E
Zanesville		374	39°56'N	82°00'W
Zangezurskiy Khrebet	AM	482	39°30'N	45°54'E
Zango	NI	316	13°03'N	8°29'E
Zanja de Lira	VE	440	8°39'N	68°06'W
Zanjān	IR	502	36°40'N	48°29'E
Zanjón		388	27°55'S	64°15'W
Zante (Zákinthos)	GR	588	37°47'N	20°47'E
Zanthus	AS	656	31°02'S	123°34'E
Zanul'ye	RS	612	60°38'N	49°24'E
Zanzibar	TZ	327	6°10'S	39°11'E
Zanzibar I.	TZ	327	6°05'S	39°37'E
Zanzuzi	TZ	327	2°55'S	33°49'E
Zaouiet Kounta	AG	272	27°13'N	0°12'W
Zaoyang	CH	490	32°07'N	112°42'E
Zaozernyy	RS	612	55°58'N	94°42'E
Zaozer'ye		560	57°12'N	38°15'E
Zaozhuang	CH	490	34°52'N	117°33'E
Zap	TU	535	37°30'N	44°00'E
Zapadna Morava	YO	630	43°42'N	21°23'E
Zapadnaya	BO	569	55°29'N	28°47'E
Zapadnaya Dvina		560	56°16'N	32°04'E
Zapadnaya Dvina		560	55°40'N	29°00'E
Západné Karpaty	LO	616	49°15'N	20°00'E
Zapadno Sibirskaya Ravnina	RS	612	60°00'N	75°00'E
Zapadnyy Sayan	RS	612	53°00'N	94°00'E
Zapai	CG	287	4°55'N	25°16'E
Zapala	AR	419	38°54'S	70°04'W
Zapaleri, Cerro	BL	422	22°49'S	67°11'W
Zapata	US	398	26°54'N	99°16'W
Zapata, Llanura de	CU	406	22°30'N	81°00'W
Zapata, Península de	CU	406	22°20'N	81°35'W
Zapatosa, Ciénaga de	CO	430	9°06'N	73°50'W
Zapicán	UY	439	33°31'S	54°55'W
Zapiga	CI	428	19°38'S	69°53'W
Zapolyarnyy	RS	612	69°26'N	30°51'E
Zapopan	MX	394	20°44'N	103°25'W
Zaporizhzhya	UP	624	47°49'N	35°11'E
Zapotal	EC	432	1°21'S	79°23'W
Zapotal, Punta	CS	405	10°31'N	85°49'W
Zapotillo	EC	432	4°23'S	80°15'W
Zapotiltic	MX	394	19°37'N	103°25'W
Zaprešić	HR	574	45°51'N	15°48'E
Zaprudnya		560	56°34'N	37°26'E
Zapucay	UY	439	31°44'S	55°13'W
Zapug	CH	490	33°15'N	80°47'E
Zaqatala	AJ	483	41°38'N	46°39'E
Zaqên	CH	490	33°21'N	94°30'E
Zara	TU	535	39°55'N	37°46'E
Zarafshon	UZ	539	41°31'N	64°15'E
Zaragoza	CO	430	7°30'N	74°52'W
Zaragoza	MX	394	31°39'N	106°20'W
Zaragoza	MX	394	22°02'N	100°44'W
Zaragoza	MX	394	28°30'N	100°57'W
Zaragoza	SP	618	41°38'N	0°52'W
Zarand	IR	502	30°49'N	56°34'E
Zaranda Hill	NI	316	9°57'N	9°32'E
Zarandului, Muntii	RO	610	46°10'N	22°15'E
Zaranj	AF	480	31°06'N	61°53'E
Zarasai	LH	597	55°44'N	26°15'E
Zárate	AR	419	34°06'S	59°02'W
Zarautz	SP	618	43°17'N	2°10'W
Zaraysk		560	54°46'N	38°53'E
Zaraza	VE	440	9°21'N	65°19'W
Zarca, Meseta de la		376	25°55'N	105°00'W
Zārch	IR	502	32°00'N	54°14'E
Zard Dangeh, Kuh-e	IR	502	33°19'N	52°13'E
Zard Halqeh, Kuh-e	IR	502	31°40'N	49°58'E
Zard Kuh	IR	502	32°22'N	50°04'E
Zardob	AJ	483	40°13'N	47°43'E
Zard Shehneh, Kuh-e	IR	502	30°20'N	51°34'E
Zarechensk		556	66°40'N	31°23'E
Zarechnoye	UP	624	51°49'N	26°08'E
Zareh Sharan	AF	480	33°08'N	68°47'E
Zargān	IR	502	29°46'N	52°43'E
Zarghūn Shahr	AF	480	32°51'N	68°25'E
Zaria	NI	316	11°06'N	7°44'E
Zarinsk		466	53°43'N	84°56'E
Zărneşti	RO	610	45°33'N	25°18'E
Žarnovica	LO	616	48°29'N	18°43'E
Zarós	GR	588	35°08'N	24°54'E
Zarqa	JO	510	32°07'N	35°33'E
Zarrineh	IR	502	37°05'N	45°54'E
Zarrīn Shahr	IR	502	32°23'N	51°23'E
Zaruma	EC	432	3°41'S	79°37'W
Zarumilla	PE	436	3°30'S	80°16'W
Żary	PL	606	51°38'N	15°09'E
Zarzaïtine	AG	272	28°06'N	9°47'E
Zarzal	CO	430	4°24'N	76°04'W
Zas	SP	618	43°06'N	8°54'W
Zasa	LG	596	56°17'N	25°58'E
Zaskar Mts.	IN	496	33°15'N	77°40'E
Zaslavl'	BO	569	54°00'N	27°17'E
Zastron	SF	322	30°18'S	27°05'E
Zasul'ye	RS	612	64°41'N	47°48'E
Žatec	EZ	575	50°20'N	13°33'E
Zaterechnyy		466	44°48'N	45°11'E
Zatoka	UP	624	46°04'N	30°28'E
Zaunguzskiye Karakumy	TX	537	40°30'N	60°00'E
Zavāreh	IR	502	33°27'N	52°30'E
Zavdi'el	IS	505	31°40'N	34°45'E
Zavet	BU	573	43°46'N	26°40'E
Zavidovići	BK	572	44°27'N	18°09'E
Zavitinsk	RS	612	50°07'N	129°27'E
Zavodoukovsk		466	56°30'N	66°32'E
Zavolzhsk		560	57°28'N	42°10'E
Zavolzh'ye		560	56°39'N	43°24'E
Závora, Ponta	MZ	312	24°31'S	35°10'E
Zawadzkie	PL	606	50°37'N	18°28'E
Zawi	ZI	334	17°13'S	30°02'E
Zawiercie	PL	606	50°30'N	19°26'E
Zawīlah	LY	302	26°10'N	15°07'E
Zāwiyat al Mukhaylá	LY	302	32°10'N	22°15'E
Zāwiyat Masūs	LY	302	31°27'N	21°02'E
Zawr, Jal az	KU	514	29°35'N	47°10'E
Zaydābād	AF	480	34°17'N	69°07'E
Zayetkon	BM	487	20°47'N	95°32'E
Zaysan	KZ	510	47°28'N	84°52'E
Zaysan, Ozero	KZ	510	48°00'N	84°00'E
Zayü	CH	490	28°39'N	97°30'E
Zaza	CU	406	21°37'N	79°32'W
Zazafotsy	MA	304	22°13'S	46°22'E
Zazárida	VE	440	11°13'N	70°29'W
Zázrivá	LO	616	49°17'N	19°10'E
Zborov	LO	616	49°22'N	21°18'E
Zborov	UP	624	49°40'N	25°09'E
Žd'ár nad Sázavou	EZ	575	49°34'N	15°57'E
Zdolbunov	UP	624	50°31'N	26°15'E
Zdunje	MK	599	41°48'N	20°53'E
Zduńska Wola	PL	606	51°36'N	18°56'E
Zdvinsk	RS	612	54°42'N	78°40'E
Zé	BN	276	6°47'N	2°18'E
Zeballos	CA	390	49°59'N	126°51'W
Zeballos, Monte	AR	419	47°01'S	71°42'W
Żebbuġ	MT	600	35°52'N	14°26'E
Zebediela	SF	322	24°18'S	29°15'E
Zé Doca	BR	424	3°17'S	45°39'W
Zeebrugge	BE	570	51°20'N	3°12'E
Zeehan	AS	656	41°53'S	145°20'E
Ze'elim	IS	505	31°12'N	34°32'E
Zeerust	SF	322	25°32'S	26°05'E
Zefat	IS	505	32°58'N	35°30'E
Zegher, Hamada	LY	302	27°18'N	11°30'E
Zehdenick	GM	584	52°59'N	13°20'E
Zeist	NL	602	52°06'N	5°14'E
Zeitz	GM	584	51°03'N	12°09'E
Żejtun	MT	600	35°51'N	14°32'E
Zêkog	CH	490	35°00'N	101°34'E
Zele	BE	570	51°04'N	4°02'E
Zelenoborsk	RS	612	61°33'N	64°15'E
Zelenoborskiy		556	66°49'N	32°20'E
Zelenodol's'k	UP	624	47°36'N	33°41'E
Zelenodol'sk	RS	612	55°51'N	48°33'E
Zelenogorsk		466	60°12'N	29°42'E
Zelenograd	RS	612	56°00'N	37°12'E
Zelenogradsk	RS	612	54°58'N	20°29'E
Zelentsovo	RS	612	59°52'N	45°00'E
Zelhem	NL	602	52°00'N	6°21'E
Želiezovce	LO	616	48°03'N	18°40'E
Zelimai	LI	301	7°53'N	9°31'W
Zelinggou	CH	490	37°21'N	97°48'E
Zell am See	AU	568	47°19'N	12°47'E
Zelma	CA	390	51°50'N	105°55'W
Zelouane	MO	310	35°04'N	2°57'W
Zelów	PL	606	51°28'N	19°14'E
Zeltweg		562	47°11'N	14°45'E
Želva	LH	597	55°13'N	25°06'E
Zel'va	BO	569	53°09'N	24°49'E
Zelzate	BE	570	51°12'N	3°49'E
Žemaičiu Naumiestis	LH	597	55°22'N	21°42'E
Zemaicu Hills	LH	597	55°50'N	22°30'E
Zembra		262	37°08'N	10°49'E
Zêmdasam		472	33°03'N	101°31'E
Zemen	BU	573	42°28'N	22°45'E
Zemetchino		560	53°30'N	42°38'E
Zemio	CT	282	5°02'N	25°09'E
Zemlet Tdefal	MR	308	21°50'N	10°50'W
Zemlya Frantsa-Iosifa	RS	612	81°00'N	55°00'E
Zemmora	AG	272	35°42'N	0°44'E
Zemo-Rene	GG	495	42°00'N	44°21'E
Zemst	BE	570	50°59'N	4°28'E
Zemtsy		560	56°15'N	32°23'E
Zênda	CH	490	32°47'N	97°30'E
Zendeh Jān	AF	480	34°21'N	61°45'E
Zenica	BK	572	44°12'N	17°53'E
Zen'kov	UP	624	50°12'N	34°22'E
Zenza do Itombe	AO	274	9°17'S	14°13'E
Žepče	BK	572	44°26'N	18°03'E
Zepu	CH	490	38°12'N	77°17'E
Zeravshan	TI	533	39°10'N	68°39'E
Zeravshan	UZ	539	39°22'N	63°45'E
Zeravshanskiy Khrebet	TI	533	39°15'N	69°00'E
Zergamouchi, Enneri	NG	314	21°56'N	13°34'E
Zermatt	SZ	622	46°01'N	7°44'E
Zernograd		560	46°51'N	40°18'E
Zeroud	TS	329	35°50'N	10°13'W
Zerqan	AL	566	41°30'N	20°21'E
Zestafoni	GG	495	42°07'N	43°03'E
Zetel	GM	584	53°25'N	7°59'E
Zevenbergen	NL	602	51°39'N	4°36'E
Zevgolatíon	GR	588	37°56'N	22°47'E
Zeya	RS	612	53°45'N	127°16'E
Zeya	RS	612	50°15'N	127°35'E
Zeysko Bureinskaya Ravnina	RS	612	51°00'N	129°00'E
Zeyskoye Vdkhr.	RS	612	54°30'N	127°45'E
Zêzere	PO	608	39°28'N	8°20'W
Zgara, Vallée de	ML	307	17°30'N	2°30'E
Zghartā	LE	516	34°23'N	35°53'E
Zgierz	PL	606	51°51'N	19°25'E
Zgorzelec	PL	606	51°09'N	15°01'E
Zhabasak	KZ	510	50°22'N	61°41'E
Zhabinka	BO	569	52°12'N	24°01'E
Zhag'yab	CH	490	30°38'N	97°40'E
Zhailma	KZ	510	51°32'N	61°37'E
Zhaksy	KZ	510	51°56'N	67°22'E
Zhalanash	KZ	510	51°11'N	65°03'E
Zhaldama	KZ	510	50°27'N	65°39'E
Zhaltyr	KZ	510	51°36'N	69°50'E
Zhanatas	KZ	510	43°34'N	69°45'E
Zhanatilsu	KZ	510	46°20'N	78°17'E
Zhangaözen	KZ	510	43°21'N	52°50'E
Zhangaqazaly	KZ	510	45°50'N	62°10'E
Zhangguangcai Ling	CH	490	43°53'N	127°51'E
Zhanghei	CH	490	41°09'N	114°45'E
Zhanghua	TW	532	24°05'N	120°32'E
Zhangiztobe	KZ	510	49°09'N	81°05'E
Zhangjiachuan Huizu Zizhixian	CH	490	34°57'N	106°01'E
Zhangjiakou	CH	490	40°45'N	114°51'E
Zhangling	CH	490	52°39'N	123°32'E
Zhangping	CH	490	25°18'N	117°24'E
Zhangpu	CH	490	24°06'N	117°36'E
Zhangshu	CH	490	28°03'N	115°30'E
Zhangye	CH	490	38°55'N	100°27'E
Zhangzhou	CH	490	24°30'N	117°39'E
Zhanhe	CH	490	48°39'N	127°37'E
Zhanjiang	CH	490	21°11'N	110°22'E
Zhanterek	KZ	510	47°54'N	54°16'E
Zhanyu		472	44°31'N	122°40'E
Zhao'an	CH	490	23°41'N	117°09'E
Zhaodong	CH	490	46°04'N	125°58'E
Zhaojue	CH	490	28°01'N	102°46'E
Zhaoqing	CH	490	23°04'N	112°27'E
Zhaotong	CH	490	27°18'N	103°42'E
Zhaoyuan	CH	490	37°21'N	120°24'E
Zharigayev	KZ	510	49°24'N	46°50'E
Zhari Namco	CH	490	31°06'N	85°36'E
Zharkamys	KZ	510	48°01'N	56°26'E
Zharkovskiy		560	55°52'N	32°17'E
Zharma	KZ	510	48°48'N	80°50'E
Zharmysh	KZ	510	44°11'N	52°28'E
Zharyk	KZ	510	48°52'N	72°51'E
Zhashkov	UP	624	49°15'N	30°06'E
Zhaskayrat	KZ	510	45°05'N	64°45'E
Zhatay	RS	612	62°10'N	129°49'E
Zhaxigang		466	32°32'N	79°41'E
Zhaxizê	CH	490	30°01'N	96°45'E
Zhaylaukol'	KZ	510	44°50'N	70°27'E
Zhdanovsk	AJ	483	39°48'N	47°36'E
Zheduo Shankou	CH	490	30°06'N	101°48'E
Zhêhor	CH	490	31°38'N	100°16'E
Zhelang	CH	490	22°39'N	115°32'E
Zhelaniya, Mys	RS	612	76°57'N	68°35'E
Zheleznodorozhnyy		560	54°22'N	21°19'E
Zheleznodorozhnyy	RS	612	62°35'N	50°55'E
Zheleznogorsk	RS	612	52°19'N	35°21'E
Zheleznogorsk-Ilimskiy	RS	612	56°34'N	104°08'E
Zhelou	CH	490	24°57'N	105°48'E
Zhëltoye	RS	612	51°38'N	56°36'E
Zheltyye Vody	UP	624	48°21'N	33°32'E
Zhen'an	CH	490	33°28'N	109°07'E
Zhenba	CH	490	32°33'N	107°57'E
Zheng'an	CH	490	28°33'N	107°24'E
Zhenghe		472	27°23'N	118°51'E
Zhengning	CH	490	35°27'N	108°24'E
Zhengxiangbai Qi	CH	490	42°18'N	115°00'E
Zhengyang	CH	490	32°36'N	114°22'E
Zhengzhou	CH	490	34°45'N	113°39'E
Zhenjiang	CH	490	32°12'N	119°25'E
Zhenjiangguan		472	32°17'N	103°45'E
Zhenkang	CH	490	23°53'N	99°01'E
Zhenlai	CH	490	45°49'N	123°12'E
Zhenping		472	33°02'N	112°14'E
Zhenping	CH	490	31°55'N	109°30'E
Zhenxiong	CH	490	27°26'N	104°49'E
Zhenyuan	CH	490	23°51'N	100°50'E
Zhenyuan	CH	490	27°03'N	108°27'E
Zherdevka		560	51°51'N	41°28'E
Zherong	CH	490	27°12'N	119°51'E
Zhestyanka		466	51°36'N	49°24'E
Zhetybay	KZ	510	43°36'N	52°06'E
Zhetybay	KZ	510	48°51'N	48°06'E
Zhezqazghan	KZ	510	47°47'N	67°46'E
Zhicheng	CH	490	30°18'N	111°30'E
Zhidachov	UP	624	49°23'N	24°08'E
Zhidan		472	36°50'N	108°46'E
Zhidoi	CH	490	34°04'N	95°03'E
Zhigalovo	RS	612	54°48'N	105°08'E
Zhigansk	RS	612	66°45'N	123°20'E
Zhijiang		472	27°27'N	109°41'E
Zhijin		472	26°42'N	105°45'E
Zhilinda	RS	612	70°08'N	114°00'E
Zhilino		560	54°54'N	21°56'E
Zhiloy	AJ	483	40°40'N	50°35'E
Zhiren'kupa	KZ	510	50°51'N	54°50'E
Zhirnovsk		560	50°59'N	44°46'E
Zhitkovichi	BO	569	52°14'N	27°52'E
Zhitkovo	RS	612	60°42'N	29°20'E
Zhizhgin Os.		556	65°11'N	36°50'E
Zhlobin	BO	569	52°54'N	30°03'E
Zhmerinka	UP	624	49°02'N	28°06'E
Zhob	PK	524	32°04'N	69°50'E
Zhob	PK	524	31°20'N	69°27'E
Zhodino	BO	569	54°06'N	28°21'E
Zholymbet	KZ	510	51°45'N	71°44'E
Zhongba	CH	490	29°39'N	84°05'E
Zhongdian	CH	490	27°48'N	99°40'E
Zhongdu	CH	490	24°40'N	109°42'E
Zhongjiang		472	31°04'N	104°41'E
Zhongli	TW	532	24°57'N	121°13'E
Zhongning	CH	490	37°27'N	105°40'E
Zhongshan	CH	490	22°30'N	113°21'E
Zhongwei	CH	490	37°30'N	105°09'E
Zhongyang		472	37°24'N	111°10'E
Zhoujiajing		472	38°53'N	102°24'E
Zhoukou	CH	490	33°37'N	114°37'E
Zhoushan Qundao	CH	490	30°00'N	122°00'E
Zhouzhi	CH	490	34°07'N	108°13'E
Zhovkva	UP	624	50°04'N	23°58'E
Zhovtnevoye	UP	624	46°52'N	32°02'E
Zhovtnevoye	UP	624	50°56'N	34°23'E
Zhuanghe	CH	490	39°40'N	123°01'E
Zhuanglang	CH	490	35°07'N	106°01'E
Zhubgyügoin	CH	490	33°27'N	97°00'E
Zhucheng	CH	490	36°00'N	119°24'E
Zhudong	TW	532	24°44'N	121°03'E
Zhugqu	CH	490	33°45'N	104°17'E
Zhuhai	CH	490	22°16'N	113°33'E
Zhuji	CH	490	29°42'N	120°13'E
Zhukovka		560	53°32'N	33°44'E
Zhukovskiy	RS	612	55°35'N	38°08'E
Zhumadian	CH	490	32°57'N	114°02'E
Zhunan	TW	532	24°41'N	120°52'E
Zhuokeji	CH	490	31°46'N	102°12'E
Zhuolu	CH	490	40°21'N	115°12'E
Zhuoxian	CH	490	39°30'N	115°57'E
Zhuozi	CH	490	40°51'N	112°32'E
Zhushan	CH	490	32°13'N	110°13'E
Zhuxi		472	32°21'N	109°40'E
Zhuzhou	CH	490	27°49'N	113°09'E
Zhylandy	KZ	510	48°00'N	69°07'E
Zhytomyr	UP	624	50°15'N	28°40'E
Ziārat-e Shāh Maqşūd	AF	480	31°59'N	65°30'E
Žiar nad Hronom	LO	616	48°35'N	18°52'E
Zia Town	LI	301	5°46'N	7°51'W
Zībāk	AF	480	36°34'N	71°22'E
Zibo	CH	490	36°47'N	118°02'E
Zichang	CH	490	37°06'N	109°37'E
Židlochovice	EZ	575	49°02'N	16°37'E
Zielona Góra	PL	606	51°56'N	15°30'E
Zienzu	LI	301	6°53'N	9°45'W
Zierikzee	NL	602	51°39'N	3°55'E
Ziersdorf	AU	568	48°31'N	15°55'E
Zigaing	BM	487	20°02'N	93°32'E
Zigey	CD	283	14°43'N	15°47'E
Zigong	CH	490	29°23'N	104°46'E
Zigui	CH	490	31°00'N	110°42'E
Ziguinchor	SG	319	12°34'N	16°16'W
Zihuatanejo	MX	394	17°38'N	101°33'W
Zijing Shan	CH	490	36°47'N	111°09'E
Zilair		466	52°14'N	57°26'E
Zile	TU	535	40°18'N	35°54'E
Žilina	LO	616	49°13'N	18°44'E
Zillah	LY	302	28°33'N	17°35'E
Zillertaler Alpen	AU	568	47°00'N	11°55'E
Zillis	SZ	622	46°37'N	9°27'E
Zilme	YM	541	16°24'N	43°48'E
Zilupe	LG	596	56°23'N	28°07'E
Zima	RS	612	53°55'N	102°04'E
Zimapán	MX	394	20°45'N	99°21'W
Zimatlán	MX	394	16°52'N	96°47'W
Zimba	TZ	327	7°52'S	31°49'E
Zimba	ZA	332	17°19'S	26°12'E
Zimbabwe		38	19°00'S	29°00'E
Zimnicea	RO	610	43°40'N	25°22'E
Zimnitsa	BU	573	42°35'N	26°36'E
Zimniy Bereg		556	67°30'N	44°00'E
Zimnyatskiy		560	49°43'N	42°53'E
Zimovniki		466	47°08'N	42°28'E
Zinacatepec	MX	394	18°20'N	97°13'W
Zina	SZ	622	46°08'N	7°38'E
Zinder	NG	314	13°49'N	8°59'E
Zinga	CT	282	3°43'N	18°35'E
Zingst		558	54°26'N	12°48'E
Zingyaik	BM	487	16°42'N	97°26'E
Ziniaré	UV	278	12°35'N	1°18'W
Zinihu	CH	490	39°03'N	105°24'E
Zinjibār	YM	541	13°07'N	45°22'E
Zinnowitz	GM	584	54°04'N	13°54'E
Zion		374	42°26'N	87°49'W
Zion	SC	417	17°08'N	62°33'W
Zion Hill		382	17°09'N	62°32'W
Zipaquirá	CO	430	5°02'N	74°00'W
Ziqudukou	CH	490	33°01'N	95°51'E
Zirbiti	GG	495	41°39'N	44°21'E
Zirc	HU	590	47°16'N	17°52'E
Zirje	HR	574	43°39'N	15°40'E
Zirl	AU	568	47°17'N	11°14'E
Ziro	IN	496	27°35'N	93°49'E
Zi Shui	CH	490	28°48'N	112°38'E
Zistersdorf	AU	568	48°32'N	16°45'E
Zittau	GM	584	50°54'N	14°50'E
Živinice	BK	572	44°27'N	18°39'E
Ziway	ET	293	7°56'N	38°43'E
Ziway Hayk'	ET	293	8°00'N	38°50'E
Zixing	CH	490	25°57'N	113°24'E
Ziya He	CH	490	39°09'N	117°10'E
Ziyang	CH	490	30°06'N	104°39'E
Ziyang	CH	490	32°30'N	108°31'E
Ziyuan	CH	490	26°06'N	110°39'E
Zizhong	CH	490	29°48'N	104°50'E
Zizhou	CH	490	37°37'N	110°02'E
Zizur Mayor (Zizur Nagusia)	SP	618	42°47'N	1°41'W
Zlataritsa	BU	573	43°02'N	25°53'E
Zlaté Hory	EZ	575	50°16'N	17°24'E
Zlaté Moravce	LO	616	48°23'N	18°24'E
Zlatibor	YO	630	42°40'N	19°50'E
Zlatna	RO	610	46°07'N	23°13'E
Zlatograd	BU	573	41°23'N	25°06'E
Zlatoust	RS	612	55°10'N	59°40'E
Zlatoustovsk	RS	612	52°58'N	133°38'E
Zlin	EZ	575	49°13'N	17°40'E
Zlīţan	LY	302	32°28'N	14°34'E
Złocieniec	PL	606	53°32'N	16°00'E
Zlot	YO	630	44°01'N	21°59'E
Złotoryja	PL	606	51°07'N	15°55'E
Złotów	PL	606	53°21'N	17°03'E
Zmajevo	YO	630	45°27'N	19°42'E
Znamenka		560	52°54'N	35°59'E
Znamenka	UP	624	48°43'N	32°33'E
Znamensk	RS	612	54°37'N	21°13'E
Znamenskoye		466	53°17'N	35°41'E
Żnin	PL	606	52°48'N	17°40'E
Znojmo	EZ	575	48°51'N	16°03'E
Zoar	SF	322	33°29'S	21°58'E
Zobia	CG	287	2°53'N	26°02'E
Zoco	CH	490	32°19'N	80°57'E
Zod	AM	482	40°12'N	45°52'E
Zoétélé	CM	280	3°15'N	11°53'E
Zoetermeer	NL	602	52°03'N	4°30'E
Zofu	CG	287	6°09'S	26°56'E
Zogang	CH	490	29°43'N	97°51'E
Zogqên	CH	490	32°15'N	98°52'E
Zográfos		564	37°59'N	23°48'E
Zohreh	IR	502	30°04'N	49°31'E
Zoigê	CH	490	33°37'N	102°57'E
Zoissa	TZ	327	5°41'S	36°23'E
Zola		270	32°00'S	26°13'E
Zola	SF	322	32°01'S	26°14'E
Zollikofen	SZ	622	47°00'N	7°27'E
Zolochëv	UP	624	50°17'N	35°59'E
Zolochiv	UP	624	49°48'N	24°54'E
Zolotinka	RS	612	56°15'N	124°49'E
Zolotkovo		560	55°32'N	41°06'E
Zolotonosha	UP	624	49°40'N	32°02'E
Zolotoye		560	50°49'N	45°53'E
Zolotukhino		560	52°05'N	36°23'E
Zomba	MI	306	15°23'S	35°20'E
Zonda	AR	419	31°33'S	68°44'W
Zongia	CG	287	2°15'N	25°07'E
Zongjiafangzi	CH	490	36°17'N	97°02'E
Zongo	BL	422	16°07'S	68°02'W
Zongo	CG	287	4°21'N	18°36'E
Zongo	CG	287	4°46'S	14°55'E
Zonguldak	TU	535	41°27'N	31°49'E
Zongyang	CH	490	30°41'N	117°12'E
Zonhoven	BE	570	50°59'N	5°21'E
Zonza	FR	580	41°44'N	9°09'E
Zoo Baba	NG	314	18°14'N	13°03'E
Zoolende	GB	294	0°46'N	13°06'E
Zorārganj	BG	485	22°51'N	91°32'E
Zorgo	UV	278	12°15'N	0°36'W
Zorinsk	UP	624	48°25'N	38°34'E
Zorita	SP	618	39°17'N	5°42'W
Zorritos	PE	436	3°40'S	80°40'W
Żory	PL	606	50°03'N	18°42'E
Zorzor	LI	301	7°47'N	9°26'W
Zotoua-Bombo	CT	282	5°43'N	15°37'E
Zottegem	BE	570	50°52'N	3°48'E
Zouar	CD	283	20°27'N	16°32'E
Zouîrât	MR	308	22°42'N	12°30'W
Zousfana, Oued	AG	272	30°30'N	2°18'W
Zq'qya Zangbo		472	31°15'N	90°00'E
Zrenjanin	YO	630	45°23'N	20°23'E
Zuarungu	GH	296	10°47'N	0°48'W
Zuata	VE	440	8°22'N	65°12'W
Zubova Polyana		560	54°04'N	42°51'E
Zubtsov		466	56°10'N	34°36'E
Zuchwil	SZ	622	47°12'N	7°34'E
Zuckerhütl	AU	568	46°58'N	11°09'E
Zudáñez	BL	422	19°06'S	64°44'W
Zuénola	IV	288	7°26'N	6°03'W
Zuera	SP	618	41°52'N	0°47'W
Zufar (Dhofar)	MU	523	17°00'N	54°10'E
Zug		262	21°36'N	14°09'W
Zug	SZ	622	47°10'N	8°31'E
Zugdidi	GG	495	42°30'N	41°53'E
Zuger See	SZ	622	47°07'N	8°29'E
Zughrar, Bi'r	LY	302	30°14'N	10°17'E
Zugspitze	GM	584	47°25'N	10°59'E
Zuidbeveland	NL	602	51°27'N	3°40'E
Zuidelijk Flevoland	NL	602	52°22'N	5°20'E
Zuidhorn	NL	602	53°14'N	6°23'E
Zuidlaardermeer	NL	602	53°06'N	6°28'E
Zuienkerke	BE	570	51°16'N	3°10'E
Zújar	SP	618	37°33'N	2°50'W
Zújar, Emb. de	SP	618	38°56'N	5°27'W
Zula	ER	292	15°15'N	39°40'E
Zulia	VE	440	9°04'N	72°18'W
Zulueta	CU	406	22°22'N	79°34'W
Zumba	EC	432	4°52'S	79°09'W
Zumbagua	EC	432	0°58'S	78°54'W
Zumbo	MZ	312	15°35'S	30°25'E
Zumpango	MX	394	17°39'N	99°30'W
Zundert	NL	602	51°28'N	4°40'E
Zungue	AO	274	9°20'S	17°10'E
Zunhua	CH	490	40°09'N	117°57'E
Zuni	US	398	35°04'N	108°50'W
Zuni Mts.		376	35°09'N	108°18'W
Zunyi	CH	490	27°41'N	106°54'E
Zuoz	SZ	622	46°36'N	9°57'E
Županja	HR	574	45°04'N	18°42'E
Zuqar, Jabal		264	14°04'N	42°22'E
Žur	YO	630	42°10'N	20°38'E
Zura		466	57°36'N	53°24'E
Zūrābād	IR	502	35°43'N	61°04'E
Zurayghiţ	SA	528	26°29'N	40°33'E
Zurbāţīyah	IZ	504	33°09'N	46°03'E
Zurich		374	43°26'N	81°37'W
Zürich	SZ	622	47°22'N	8°32'E
Zürichsee	SZ	622	47°13'N	8°45'E
Żuromin	PL	606	53°04'N	19°55'E
Żurrieq	MT	600	35°50'N	14°28'E
Zuru	NI	316	11°26'N	5°14'E
Zurzach	SZ	622	47°35'N	8°17'E
Zutphen	NL	602	52°08'N	6°12'E
Zuwārah	LY	302	32°54'N	12°04'E
Zuyevka	RS	612	58°25'N	51°07'E
Zvečka	YO	630	44°38'N	20°10'E
Zvenigorodka	UP	624	49°05'N	30°58'E
Zvenigovo		560	55°58'N	48°02'E
Zverevo		560	48°01'N	40°07'E
Zverinogolovskoye	RS	612	54°28'N	64°50'E
Zvijezda	BK	572	44°10'N	18°20'E
Zvishavane	ZI	334	20°20'S	30°02'E
Zvolen	LO	616	48°35'N	19°08'E
Zvornik	BK	572	44°23'N	19°05'E
Zwaagwesteinde	NL	602	53°16'N	6°03'E
Zwedru	LI	301	6°04'N	8°08'W
Zweibrücken	GM	584	49°15'N	7°22'E
Zweisimmen	SZ	622	46°33'N	7°22'E
Zweletemba	SF	322	33°38'S	19°29'E
Zwelitsha	SF	322	32°54'S	27°20'E
Zwickau	GM	584	50°43'N	12°30'E
Zwoleń	PL	606	51°21'N	21°36'E
Zwolle		378	31°37'N	93°38'W
Zwolle	NL	602	52°30'N	6°05'E
Żychlin	PL	606	52°15'N	19°37'E
Żyrardów	PL	606	52°04'N	20°26'E
Zyryan	KZ	510	49°43'N	84°20'E
Zyryanka	RS	612	65°50'N	150°51'E
Żywiec	PL	606	49°41'N	19°13'E
Zyyi	CY	494	34°43'N	33°20'E